S0-COO-279

Principles of Accounting

Third Edition

To our esteemed colleague
Albert Slavin
who has retired from active participation in this edition.

Principles of Accounting

Third Edition

Isaac N. Reynolds *University of North Carolina at Chapel Hill*

Allen B. Sanders *Elon College*

A. Douglas Hillman *Drake University*

The Dryden Press

Chicago New York Philadelphia San Francisco Montreal Toronto
London Sydney Tokyo Mexico City Rio de Janeiro Madrid

Acquisitions Editor: John Bragg
Project Editor: Nancy Shanahan
Managing Editor: Jane Perkins
Design Director: Alan Wendt
Production Manager: Mary Jarvis

Text and Cover designer: Harry Voigt
Copyeditor: Michele Heinz
Indexer: Lois Oster
Compositor: The Clarinda Company
Text Type: 10/12 Garamond

Library of Congress Cataloging in Publication Data

Reynolds, Isaac N.
Principles of accounting.

Rev. ed. of: Elementary accounting, 2nd ed. c1981.
Includes index.
1. Accounting. I. Sanders, Allen B. II. Hillman, A. Douglas. III. Reynolds, Isaac N. Elementary accounting. IV. Title.
HF5635.R43 1983 657 83-14013
ISBN 0-03-063313-3

Printed in the United States of America
456–032–987654321

Copyright 1984 CBS College Publishing
Copyright 1981, 1978 The Dryden Press
All rights reserved

Address orders:
383 Madison Avenue
New York, NY 10017

Address editorial correspondence:
One Salt Creek Lane
Hinsdale, IL 60521

CBS College Publishing
The Dryden Press
Holt, Rinehart and Winston
Saunders College Publishing

Preface

In the first and second editions of this book, our primary aim was to develop a text that students could read, understand, and apply. We retain that focus in *Principles of Accounting,* third edition. The authors continue to find that the majority of students in first-year accounting courses have very limited experience in and knowledge about the world of business. When they face some of the more complex issues in accounting, their difficulties can be reduced by a textbook that makes liberal use of illustrations and explanations in simple language. We do this in a logical sequence, emphasizing in every chapter the teaching of accounting fundamentals.

Principles of Accounting, third edition, is a book written with the student in mind. Many changes have come about as a result of students' questions and suggestions that arose while using the second edition. Many other changes have come from the suggestions and recommendations of the largest team of reviewers we have ever used. This dedicated group from two-year and four-year colleges and universities in all sections of the country brought a wealth of teaching experience and a variety of viewpoints. The result is an enhancement of this book's greatest strength—teachability. The book is also more authoritative, accurate, and up-to-date. A practicing managerial accountant, A. Douglas Hillman of Drake University joined the team of authors for this edition.

Primarily designed for the two-semester or three-quarter course, this book is also suitable for a one-semester course when chapters are used selectively.

Highlights of Changes in the Third Edition

In addition to its simplified explanations and writing style, the third edition has been strengthened in the following ways:

1. A new introduction has been written for each chapter. A deliberate effort has been made to relate the material to modern commercial problems to show the student how each topic fits into the business world and the overall framework of accounting.

2. The end-of-chapter material continues to contain about 12 to 14 single-concept exercises that cover each important new concept introduced in the chapter. There are also 12 to 14 problems, divided equally into A and B sections, each of which integrates several accounting concepts. Newly included in the integrative problems are two *thought-provoking problems* for each chapter. Some of these are taken from real-life situations, in which national and regional United States firms are identified.

3. Illustrations in Chapter 9, "Internal Control of Cash: the Voucher System," have been replaced with a set of real-life forms using the same companies. Greater emphasis is placed on the voucher system as an internal control tool

4. A new Chapter 14 covers authoritative bodies and describes sources of GAAP. It has been thoroughly rewritten to include a better description of the FASB's concept statements and the new plans for a governmental accounting standards-setting body (the GASB). It also covers price-level accounting concepts and *FASB Statement No. 33.*

5. The chapters on partnerships (15) and corporate capital structure (16 and 17) have been completely overhauled to present a much more thorough and updated picture.

6. Chapter 20 uses the work sheet to develop the statement of changes in financial position. New illustrations have been tested in two first-year classes and found to improve the students' understanding of these concepts.

7. Chapter 21 contains a new section with guidelines for income and retained earnings disclosure. It is made easy for the student to understand by the use of diagrams showing a conceptual overview. Each illustration is keyed by boxed numbers to explanations that follow.

8. Chapter 22, "Branch Accounting and Consolidated Statements," is new. The common theme among the topics in this chapter is the concept of reciprocal accounts and their use. A brief appendix to Chapter 22 covers the basic concepts of international accounting.

9. The entire managerial section has been expanded and strengthened. Typical is the addition of an appendix to Chapter 26 which explains direct (variable) costing. Because direct costing and the contribution margin approach lead directly to cost-volume-profit analysis, this material has been moved forward from Chapter 28 to Appendix 26.1.

10. Compound interest techniques are discussed in the appendix to Part Three. These are used in Chapters 18, 19, and 28. Instructors who prefer not to teach this subject may omit it without losing continuity of material.

11. Income tax issues are discussed in Appendix A to the book. Actual tax returns are used in the expanded illustration.

Organization of the Book

The book is divided into five parts:

1. The Accounting Model
2. Accounting Systems
3. Income Measurement
4. Organizational Forms and Reporting Issues
5. Cost Accumulation and Control

Part One (Chapters 1–6)

Part One develops the elementary accounting model step by step. Each chapter uses the simplest organizational form, the single proprietorship, to accomplish this objective. The first five chapters explain and illustrate the concepts and techniques of the steps in the accounting cycle. An optional appendix to Chapter 4 (Appendix 4.1) covers reversing entries. Chapter 6 discusses accounting for a merchandising firm.

Part Two (Chapters 7–9)

Part Two continues to emphasize single proprietorships in introducing various accounting systems or subsystems. Chapter 7 uses special journals to illustrate overall accounting systems. Chapter 8 discusses a payroll system, and Chapter 9 explains the control of cash and the voucher system as an internal control device.

Part Three (Chapters 10–13)

Part Three deals with income measurement and valuation issues relating to various assets. These chapters also use the single proprietorship to illustrate and explain basic concepts in more depth. The appendix to this part thoroughly covers the compound interest techniques that are used in several areas of the book.

Part Four (Chapters 14–22)

This part opens with a new chapter (Chapter 14) that describes the source of accounting guidelines, the major accounting principles, and price-level issues. Chapter 15 contains a discussion of the various business organizational forms. Chapters 15, 16, and 17 develop the accounting ideas related to partnerships and corporations. Then the accounting for issuance of bonds and for investments in bonds and stocks (Chapters 18 and 19) is discussed. Both the straight line and interest methods of amortizing premium and discount elements are included in the bond discussions. Chapter 20 illustrates the statement of changes in financial position, using the work sheet method. This chapter gives students a basic understanding of the content of this fourth major financial statement. Chapter 21 extensively covers financial statement analysis and interpretation. A new chapter (Chapter 22) has been added to describe and illustrate branch accounting and consolidated statements; an appendix to this chapter covers international accounting.

Part Five (Chapters 23–28)

Part Five describes the accounting for general manufacturing operations and for job order and process cost systems. Job order and process cost systems are covered separately in Chapters 24 and 25, followed by chapters on budgeting (Chapter 26), standard cost accounting (Chapter 27), and the use of cost information in management decisions (Chapter 28). Appendix 26.1 covers direct costing and cost-volume-profit analysis.

End-of-Book Appendixes

Three appendixes are included at the end of the book. Appendix A includes a discussion of the basic income tax formula. Flow diagrams are used to present an overview of income taxes. Appendix B contains consolidated financial statements of a *Fortune* 500 company, Dennison Manufacturing Company. Appendix C presents compound interest tables for the four basic compound interest techniques.

Special Teaching Features of the Book

Principles of Accounting, third edition, contains many features that will enhance the teaching of accounting to students who have had no business experience.

1. Learning goals are listed after each chapter introduction. The student is told what major concepts he or she is expected to understand.

2. As key terms are introduced and defined in the book they are shown in blue. A glossary at the end of each chapter defines each key term for that chapter as well as other terms used there.

3. The debit-credit-balance form of ledger account is emphasized throughout the book, starting with Chapter 2.

4. The totality of accounting is emphasized in the early chapters. This should enable the student to see its broad influence and the scope of the accounting sequence while learning specific techniques and relationships.

5. Many of the key concepts are highlighted in red for easy recognition.

6. The book's first 14 chapters emphasize the single proprietorship form. The second 14 chapters use and expand on the more complex corporate entity.

7. The book contains many teaching diagrams and flow charts.

8. Some optional topics are discussed in appendixes to chapters. Any or all of the appendixes may be omitted with no loss of continuity, or they all may be taught along with the chapters. Examples of such topics are reversing entries (Appendix 4.1) and international accounting (Appendix 22.1). This organizational feature gives the instructor much flexibility.

9. Each chapter contains 12 to 14 single-concept exercises. They may be used in classroom laboratory situations or as homework. These enable the instructor to illustrate an application of each major chapter concept.

10. Other end-of-chapter material includes questions and problems for in-class or out-of-class assignments. The problems are mostly integrative, that is, they integrate in one problem several concepts discussed in the chapter. The problems are broken down into two sections: A and B problems. The A problems may be assigned in one semester, then the B problems assigned in a later semester. Each A problem has a corresponding B problem which covers the same concepts, except for the final A and B problems in each chapter, which are intended to be especially thought provoking.

11. Each exercise and problem has a red side head that describes its aim or content.

12. There is a sizable and expanded section on cost accumulation and control—of which all students should have some knowledge. It opens with a simple chapter on financial accounting for a manufacturing firm. Some instructors may want to use only this chapter, while others may find it desirable to continue with the material in Chapters 24–28.

13. Chapter 26 describes and illustrates a complete budgeting structure for a manufacturing concern. In this comprehensive illustration, the ultimate emphasis is on profit planning. A natural follow-up to this theme is a consideration of standard cost accounting (Chapter 27) and the use of accounting data for management decisions (Chapter 28).

14. Appendix A gives a diagrammatic overview of the basic tax formula for the individual income tax and the corporate income tax.

15. The type is set in a ragged-right format that is easier for the eye to follow from one line to the next.

The Teaching Package

In addition to the text, this package includes the instructor's manual, solutions manual, two test banks, transparency acetates, three practice sets, a study guide, and working papers.

For the Instructor

Instructor's Manual This manual is unlike any other manual that accompanies a principles accounting textbook. Separate from the *Solutions Manual,* it contains seven sections, as follows:

I. Guide to the Use of the *Instructor's Manual*
II. List and Description of Elements in the Learning Package
III. Suggested Assignments
IV. Chapter Organizers for Each Chapter
  a. Summary of Major Concepts
  b. Behavioral Objectives
  c. Lecture Notes
  d. Content Analysis of Exercises and Problems
V. Suggested Uses for the Teaching Transparencies
VI. References to Authoritative Sources (including a brief summary of each FASB pronouncement up to October 1983)
VII. Solutions to the Practice Sets

Solutions Manual This manual contains answers to all end-of-chapter questions, solutions to exercises, and solutions to A and B problems.

Transparency Acetates Two sets of transparencies are included: (1) solutions to exercises and to problems, and (2) multicolor teaching transparencies which use color to reinforce important figures and concepts found in the text.

Test Banks A and B Bound in one volume, each of the test banks contains two parts: (1) a set of 30 true–false and multiple choice questions for each chapter (these are suitable for computer scoring), and (2) a set of achievement tests for each semester, consisting of (a) periodic tests for logical chapter groupings, (b) a midterm examination, and (c) a comprehensive final examination. Test banks A and B have the same depth of coverage and level of difficulty. Solutions are included with the test banks. Achievement tests are readily reproducible on any copying machine.

For the Student

Study Guide by A. Douglas Hillman, Drake University This learning aid differs from the usual workbook of exercises found with most accounting texts. In programmed format, the *Study Guide* is keyed directly to this textbook; it literally leads the student through some of the more difficult concepts in the book. Each chapter also contains a self-test of learning goal achievement with answers.

Working Papers (Two Volumes) There is a working paper designed for each exercise and for each pair of A and B problems. The first volume includes those for the first half of the text; the second volume, those for the second half. Some of the working papers for earlier chapters are partially completed; in later chapters, the working papers contain less help for the student.

Practice Sets by Donald R. Davis, St. Louis Community College This learning package includes three practice sets in manual and computerized versions. The anticipated solution time for the manual version of each set is 10 to 15 hours.

1. *Frances and Daughter* is a single proprietorship practice set with documents. Designed to be used when the student has completed Chapter 6, most of the transaction data are contained in business documents rather than in narrative form. This set uses only a general journal, a general ledger, and subsidiary ledgers.

2. *MEE-High Furniture Store* features a wholesale furniture business (a single proprietorship) using special journals, the general journal, the general ledger, and subsidiary ledgers. It is designed to be used after the student has completed Chapter 7, but it would be an excellent review instrument with which to introduce the second quarter or semester course.

3. *Catalina Island Corporation* is a corporate practice set. It is designed to be used after the student has completed Chapter 17. Although a few operational transactions are included, the main focus is on analyzing and recording

transactions that directly affect the capital structure. Thus the ideas and concepts in Chapters 16 and 17 are reinforced.

Acknowledgments and Thanks

Many individuals have a hand in producing a book like this one—the authors, many thoughtful reviewers, editors, production people, typists, and other professionals. We sincerely thank all those who helped. We are especially indebted to those who reviewed the manuscript and provided suggestions for improvements that have been significant. We take complete responsibility, however, for any errors which may still be present in the book. Some of the dedicated teachers, practicing accountants, students, and various professionals whose suggestions have made this work possible are listed below.

Jack Armitage *University of Wyoming–Laramie*
Alvin Bryan *Central State University*
Andrew J. Butula *Middlesex County College*
Craig Christopherson *Richland College*
Elsie Coker *University of South Carolina–Columbia*
Carolyn Elfland *University of North Carolina–Chapel Hill*
Kenneth O. Elvik *Iowa State University*
Donald F. Geren *Northeastern Illinois University*
Louis Gilles *University of South Carolina–Conway*
Maxwell P. Godwin *Southwest Texas State University*
Sharron M. Graves *Steven F. Austin State University*
Roy Gross *Dutchess Community College*
Hazel D. Hicks *Jacksonville State University*
Arthur S. Hirschfield *Bronx Community College of the City University of New York*
George C. Holdren *University of Nebraska–Lincoln*
Mel Holthus *Iowa State University*
John E. Klett *Indian River Community College*
Sam K. Kniffen *University of South Dakota–Vermillion*
Frank Korman *Mountain View College*
Jerry Lancio *Florida Keys Community College*
Larry Larson *Triton College*
H. Nelson Lunn *Middle Tennessee State University*
J. Michael Marr *Elon College*
John D. Minch *Cabrillo College*
M. E. Moustafa *California State University–Long Beach*
G. Kenneth Nelson *Pennsylvania State University*
Victoria K. Passikoff *Dutchess Community College*
Charles J. Pineno *Clarion State College*
Glenda Ried *University of Toledo*
Ed Rinetti *Los Angeles City College*
John Savchak *Drexel University*
F. W. Schaeberle *Western Michigan University*
Martin Shotzberger *Elon College*
Dale Simon *Kirkwood Community College*
S. Murray Simons *Northeastern University*
David L. Thompson *College of Lake County*
DuWayne Wacker *University of North Dakota–Grand Forks*
Dieter H. Weiss *Ferris State College*
Susan M. Wiley *Defiance College*
Elizabeth G. Williams *Auburn University*
Ray Wilson *St. Petersburg Junior College*

Also, we would like to thank the staff of Dryden Press—John Bragg, Nancy Shanahan, Alan Wendt, Jane Perkins—as well as Michele Heinz, copyeditor, Nancy Maybloom, proofreader, and Harry Voigt, designer, for their help in turning the manuscript into a bound book after Stevie Glass Champion of Chapel Hill, North Carolina, and Gail Alston of Burlington, North Carolina, spent many hours typing the original manuscript. Finally, we are especially indebted to Mark D. Stephens, CPA, of North Carolina Central University, who solved every exercise and problem in this book to check the original solutions of the authors.

Isaac N. Reynolds *Chapel Hill, North Carolina*
Allen B. Sanders *Elon College, North Carolina*
A. Douglas Hillman *Des Moines, Iowa*

January 1984

Contents

Part One

The Accounting Model

1 The Environment and Basic Structure of Accounting

Introduction

This chapter explains what accounting is and briefly traces the history of accounting from 5000 B.C. to the present. It explains who uses accounting information and describes some ways in which this information serves as the basis for decision making. It discusses the accounting profession and the types of work that accountants perform. With knowledge of uses and users of accounting, the methods and techniques in this book take on more meaning. Next, the development of the basic structure of accounting is started. The most basic concept in accounting—the entity concept—is explained. Then the accounting equation and the balance sheet are introduced, and their elements explained.

To obtain the data needed to prepare a balance sheet and other financial statements, a rational accounting system must be developed. After noting the evidence by which the accountant learns that a business event has occurred, some accounting systems or ways to record these events (transactions) accurately are discussed. Next, the double-entry system—in general use in modern business—is introduced. *Using only transactions affecting the balance sheet,* the basic concepts and tools of accounting are developed. These form the basis for an extended illustration that describes journalizing and posting techniques in Chapter 2.

The early parts of this book deal mainly with accounting for single proprietorships. Two other forms of business, partnerships and corporations, are discussed in detail in Chapters 15, 16, and 17.

Learning Goals

To be able to define accounting and to appreciate the reasons for the study of accounting and its history.

To identify the various users of accounting information and to compare some ways users make decisions with accounting information.

To form an idea of the nature of accounting as a profession.

To describe the entity concept.

To recognize assets, liabilities, and owner's equity and their relationship.

To be able to read a balance sheet and know its classifications.

To understand the transactions approach to recording of accounting information.

To know the function of the accounts and the ledger.

Nature of Accounting

Accounting information is used in making decisions about how wealth is to be distributed all over the world. How many loaves of bread to put on a supermarket shelf in New York or in Paris is decided by looking at records that show how many are usually sold in that store each day. The price of a loaf of bread in Los Angeles depends in part upon the costs of making the dough, baking it, wrapping it, and transporting it to the shelf of a store. To know these costs every group in the chain from the farmer to the merchant needs accounting information. What people buy depends upon the amount of income they have. Salaries and wages, unemployment benefits, social security payments, interest on savings, and many other sources of income are all based on accounting records. The same is true of large companies; management decides to build new buildings or purchase new equipment if accounting information indicates money can be made available and that these actions will be profitable. The term **profit** (net income) is used to describe the reward to an organization for bringing together people and resources to render services, to make and sell products, or to accomplish another objective. Because accounting is so important to society, this book is intended to provide a basic understanding of how accounting information is developed and used. Decision making will be shown to be the primary reason for accounting records and reports.

Definition of Accounting

Accounting consists of the gathering of financial and other economic data. In the metric system the basic physical unit of measure is the meter. In accounting in the United States and Canada the basic financial unit of measure is the dollar. Just as physical measurements are provided by the metric system, economic measurements are provided by the accounting system and are stated in financial terms. These economic measurements are put together in reports that carry the information essential for planning activities, for control of operations, and for decision making by managers of business units.

Accounting also provides financial reports that are needed by outside persons who invest in business units, lend money to them, or extend credit to them. Accounting also furnishes reports to be used by government agencies which regulate business and by tax authorities such as the Internal Revenue Service which must determine that the correct amount of tax is collected. When the unit accounted for is a *not-for-profit organization* (such as a

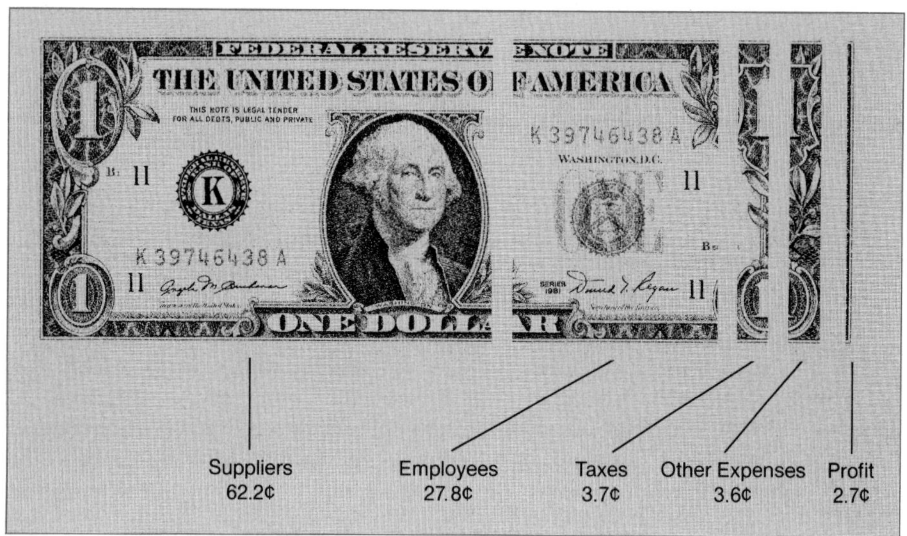

Figure 1–1 **Where a Typical Sales Dollar Goes**

school, hospital, church, or other charitable group), its members and those who contribute to it need to know for what purposes and in what proportions their money is being used. Accounting reports tell them.

Accounting

In summary,* accounting *is the set of rules and methods by which financial and economic data are collected, processed, and summarized into reports that can be used in making decisions.

Informative financial reports and the accounting records from which they are prepared are developed and extensively illustrated in Chapters 1 through 6. Often these reports are accompanied by graphics, such as Figure 1–1, that shows how one company divides each dollar of sales.

The next sections of this part provide a brief history of accounting, present a discussion of the uses of accounting in decision making, and describe the types of work that accountants do.

History of Accounting

Some of the world's first documents date from 5000 B.C.; even then the need to account for holdings of wealth prompted the development of a form of writing referred to as script.[1] The temple priests of Sumer operated a tax system that brought under their control vast stocks of grain, animals, and estates. It was necessary for these priests to develop accounting methods to (1) main-

[1]Claude S. George, *The History of Management Thought,* 2d ed. (Englewood Cliffs, N.J.: Prentice-Hall, 1972), p. 4.

tain managerial control of collections, loans, repayments, and other transactions and (2) give an account of their management over these holdings.

The Egyptian civilization, covering a broad span from about 5000 B.C. to 525 B.C., is described as one in which great construction projects were completed involving the labor of thousands of people, the operation of large stone quarries, and the large-scale transportation of building materials. Out of these operations arose a need for an information system to keep details of transactions in both business and government affairs. In Babylonian textile mills in existence about 600 B.C., production control records were kept, and workers were paid based upon the amount of their production. In 1494, an Italian monk named Luca Pacioli included a section on bookkeeping in a mathematics textbook. This was the first known printed description of double-entry bookkeeping, described later.

In early America, accounting generally served to maintain a firm's records of business dealings with its customers. As the United States moved toward an industrial economy, the appearance of large companies created requirements for more accounting information. New inventions brought forth new products, and rapid population growth helped create a demand for them. Accounting methods and techniques had to be developed to meet these changes. Today almost every large commercial firm prepares an annual report. Annual reports in booklet form contain financial information useful to a great variety of readers. (See Appendix B for extracts from an *Annual Report* of Dennison Manufacturing Company.)

Why Study Accounting?

A group of accounting educators joined together in 1971 to study the approach to teaching the introductory college course in accounting. This group was sponsored by a national accounting firm, Price Waterhouse and Company. Its report said: "The purpose of accounting is to provide information that is useful in decision making affecting resource allocation . . . at all levels in society. . . ."[2] Each of us must make financial decisions daily. Those decisions will be much better if the person who makes them understands how the information upon which he or she relies was developed. In business and in personal transactions, the person with a knowledge of accounting will have a distinct advantage.

Another reason to study accounting is that many persons work directly in the field of accounting. They may record purchases and sales, compute payrolls, or obtain cost and expense information in business firms. Others may work in not-for-profit organizations or in government. Some work as accountants; others in tasks involving sales, production management, personnel, and many other functions. They all need record systems to show how money of

---

[2] ***A New Introduction to Accounting: Report of the Study Group on Introductory Accounting*** **(New York: Price Waterhouse and Company, 1971), p. 11.**

the organization was used, and they need to be able to read and understand financial reports.

Many persons work in public accounting. Some keep records for organizations that are too small to afford their own accounting departments. Others perform a function known as **auditing**—the independent review of the financial records of an organization. Public accountants also perform management services such as the design of accounting systems, or help businesses prepare their tax returns. No matter what job a person holds in the accounting field, he or she will benefit from a complete understanding of accounting.

Perhaps the most important reason of all to study accounting is that most people must use accounting information in their personal and business lives. The next section gives examples of people not in accounting jobs who depend upon accounting information. These persons need to know how to interpret the information available to them. If they understand accounting, their interpretations will more likely lead to sound choices among the many possible courses of action that may be open to them.

Who Uses Accounting Information?

External Users

External users are persons or groups outside an organization who need and use accounting information about that organization. Following are some examples of external users.

Investors seek information that will allow them to study and compare the financial health and earning ability of business firms. Sometimes they lend money to a business firm, thus becoming **creditors.** Individuals or institutions (for example, large insurance companies) with excess funds on hand may lend those funds to large corporations. In such a case, the lenders (or creditors) receive interest in payment for the use of their money.

Sometimes investors would rather invest as owners than as creditors in order to receive a portion of the profits. Owner investors may be individuals, insurance companies, large universities, or other organizations that have accumulated more cash than they need for day-to-day expenditures.

As a basis for their investment decisions, all investors depend upon accounting information included in financial reports. In deciding whether or not to invest in a particular company, investors ask questions such as: Does this company have a history of profitable operations? How does its rate of profit compare with that of other companies?

Contributors to not-for-profit organizations, such as community funds, churches, colleges, service clubs, and similar organizations, need accounting reports. They want to know how their funds are being used so they can determine whether or not the organization deserves continued support and what the amount of such support should be. They ask questions such as: What percentage of each contributed dollar actually serves the purpose of the organization? What percentage is used for administrative expenses? They look to accounting reports for the answers.

Taxing authorities, regulatory agencies, and other governmental institutions use accounting information. Income tax returns are prepared with information taken directly from accounting records of individuals and businesses. The reports accompanying payment of taxes to fund federal social security programs or to fund unemployment compensation payments are based upon payroll records.

Important to consumers is the use of accounting reports by governmental regulatory commissions. Some of these commissions have the legal authority to set the rates that may be charged for services to the public. Rates that public utilities such as gas or electric producers are allowed to charge usually are based on the concept of allowing those companies to earn a fair, but not excessive, profit. Thus, decisions involving setting of rates are based on accounting information.

Internal Users

Internal users of accounting are those users in an organization who must make managerial decisions regarding operations.

Planning is the management function that defines the goals and objectives of the operation. Budget preparation is an important part of the planning function. A **budget** is simply a financial plan for a future period. The starting point in preparing a budget is the accounting records of the current and prior years.

Controlling is the management function of checking on operations of an enterprise and acting when necessary to redirect them. The accounting system provides special reports to each responsible manager. An example is a report to the sales manager, showing planned sales of merchandise to date compared with actual sales to date.

Cost determination is another management function. Many internal decisions require information about costs of operation. A firm may have to bid competitively against others for a specific job; if the price it bids exceeds cost plus a reasonable profit, it probably will not be awarded the contract. On the other hand, if the firm bids less than its cost to perform the job, it may be awarded the contract but will also incur a loss.

What Accountants Do

About 150,000 accountants in the United States have passed a uniform national examination and are designated by state laws as **certified public accountants** (CPAs). One of the major jobs of a CPA is auditing. After reviewing the organization's records, the CPA issues an audit report, which contains an opinion as to the fairness with which the organization's accounting reports reflect its financial condition and operating results. This professional role is referred to as the *attest function* of accounting. CPAs perform other types of work besides auditing. They do tax work for clients, help design accounting systems, and render other managerial services.

In addition to the CPAs, accountants work in every type of institution in society. They work at various levels in business, government, government-related, and not-for-profit organizations. Some hold certificates attesting to their professional competence. The **Certificate in Management Accounting** (CMA) is granted to persons who demonstrate ability in management accounting by passing a national examination. Other accountants are **Certified Internal Auditors** (CIA). These internal auditors perform a review function but work solely on the records of the firm by which they are employed.

Although much of accounting work is highly specialized and is performed in many types of organizations, the greatest number of accountants work at keeping the records of commercial enterprises. For this reason, illustrations and problems in this book focus mostly upon private business.

The Entity Concept

To understand accounting, one must clearly understand the meaning of an **accounting entity.**

Accounting entity

An* accounting entity *is any organizational unit for which financial and economic data are gathered and processed.

Suppose that Lucy Genova owns, in addition to personal items, a realty company, a motorcycle repair shop, a trucking company, and two sales companies. These are shown in graphic form as follows:

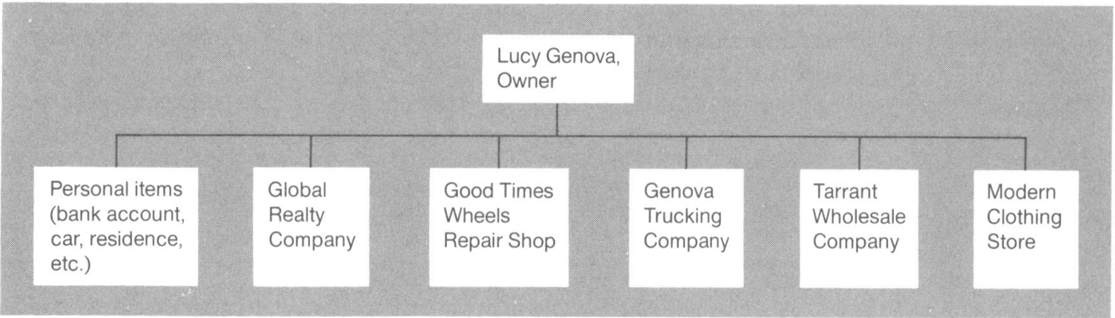

If total attention is focused on Lucy Genova, the accountant may lose sight of the individual business and economic units. The accounting information for all of Genova's activities lumped together is useless in making decisions for any single unit. A set of records must be provided for *each* of the individual business and economic units so that planning and controlling decisions can be made. The focal point of attention must be the individual unit rather than the owner. Each such unit is an accounting entity.

To clarify the entity concept and reinforce its importance, each of the businesses owned by Lucy Genova is illustrated as the basic accounting model developed in Chapters 1 through 6. In each case, the reader is urged to note how important it is for the owner to have information about the specific accounting entity to make decisions about operation and control of that entity. Other concepts necessary to understanding accounting are now presented in the following sections.

Assets

The **assets** of a business are everything of value held by the business. The word value as used here means future usefulness to a continuing business enterprise. Cash, notes and accounts receivable (amounts owed to the business by customers), land, buildings, and high-grade, readily marketable stocks or bonds of other companies are examples of assets in a business.[3] An asset is recorded on the books of the acquiring entity as its actual full cost (historical cost), even though it has not been fully paid for in cash (referred to as the *cost principle*). The amount of any debt or claim against the asset is included in the liabilities.

Equities: Liabilities and Owner's Equity

Equities are claims against the total assets of a business. The two major classifications of individuals who have equities in a business are **creditors** (liability holders) and **owners.**

A business's liabilities are owed to creditors. **Liabilities** (debts) are claims of creditors against the assets of the business unit. Accounts payable, notes payable, and wages owed to employees are examples of liabilities.

Owner's equity involves ownership claims against a business's assets. **Owner's equity** (net worth) is the excess of total assets over total liabilities. Because creditor claims (debts) have priority over claims of the owner or owners, owner's equity claims are secondary (or residual).

The Accounting Equation

Because equities represent the total claims against assets, *assets must equal equities.* This relationship is shown as follows:

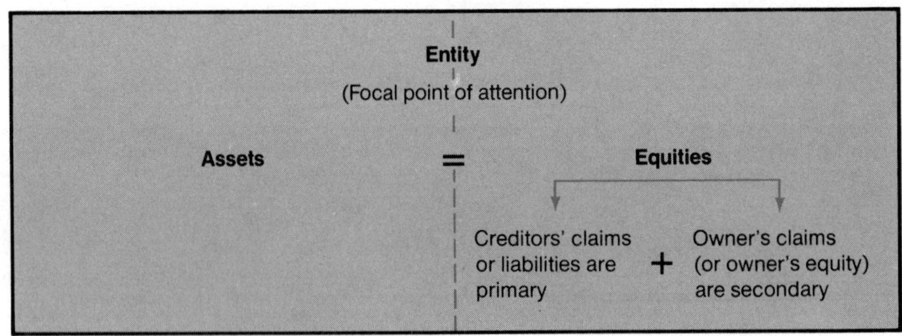

[3]Some items—for example, the loyalty of a work force—cannot be stated in dollar terms. Such items are not currently listed in the accounting records. Much research in this area is underway now; it is usually referred to as *human resources accounting.*

As illustrated, the equities of the unit are broken down into primary claims—those of the creditors—and secondary claims—those of the owner(s).[4] Since assets are derived from these two sources, the following is true:

Assets = Liabilities + Owner's equity.

This is the *basic accounting equation,* which expresses the financial position of any business entity at all times. **Net assets,** a term often used in business, may be found as follows:

Assets − Liabilities = Net assets (equal to owner's equity).

The Balance Sheet

The **balance sheet** is an expanded expression of the accounting equation. It summarizes the assets, liabilities, and owner's equity of a business entity as of a specific point in time. This statement is also called a statement of financial position. A common form of balance sheet, the *account form,* for the Modern Clothing Store (owned by Lucy Genova) with the accounting equation superimposed is shown in Figure 1–2.[5] Another form of the same statement, the

Assets = Liabilities + Owner's Equity

MODERN CLOTHING STORE
Balance Sheet
December 31, 1985

Assets			Liabilities and Owner's Equity		
Current assets:			Current liabilities:		
Cash	$ 325		Accounts payable	$12,060	
Temporary investments	1,900		Notes payable	2,060	
Accounts receivable	11,025		Accrued wages payable	970	
Notes receivable	2,520		Total current liabilities		$15,090
Merchandise inventory	14,750		Long-term liabilities:		
Prepaid insurance	275		Bank loan payable (due		
Office supplies	26		June 1, 1990)	$ 4,000	
Store supplies	89		Mortgage payable	10,000	
Total current assets		$30,910	Total long-term liabilities		14,000
Property, plant, and equipment:			Total liabilities		$29,090
Land	$ 3,000		Owner's equity:		
Building	10,000		Lucy Genova, capital		20,570
Store equipment	2,500				
Delivery equipment	3,250				
Total property, plant, and equipment		18,750			
Total assets		$49,660	Total liabilities and owner's equity		$49,660

Figure 1–2 Balance Sheet—Account Form

[4]Note that owners may be singular or plural. There may be a single owner, two owners, or several owners of an individual business entity.

[5]The form of the statement resembles an account described later in Figure 1–10.

MODERN CLOTHING STORE
Balance Sheet
December 31, 1985

Assets		
Current assets:		
Cash	$ 325	
Temporary investments	1,900	
Accounts receivable	11,025	
Notes receivable	2,520	
Merchandise inventory	14,750	
Prepaid insurance	275	
Office supplies	26	
Store supplies	89	
Total current assets		$30,910
Property, plant, and equipment:		
Land	$ 3,000	
Building	10,000	
Store equipment	2,500	
Delivery equipment	3,250	
Total property, plant, and equipment		18,750
Total assets		$49,660
Liabilities and Owner's Equity		
Current liabilities:		
Accounts payable	$12,060	
Notes payable	2,060	
Accrued wages payable	970	
Total current liabilities		$15,090
Long-term liabilities:		
Bank loan payable (due June 1, 1990)	$ 4,000	
Mortgage payable	10,000	
Total long-term liabilities		14,000
Total liabilities		$29,090
Owner's equity:		
Lucy Genova, capital		20,570
Total liabilities and owner's equity		$49,660

Figure 1–3
Balance Sheet—Report Form[6]

report form, is shown in Figure 1–3. Both are acceptable. They express the basic accounting equation in detail by showing amounts of specific asset, liability, and owner's equity items. The balance sheet is a snapshot of the status of assets, liabilities, and owner's equity at any moment. Operations that take place later will make changes, but the basic equation is always true.

The heading of *any* financial statement usually contains three lines of information:

1. Name of the business.
2. Name of the statement.
3. Date of the statement or period of time covered.

[6]This version is called the *report form* because it is in the form of a typical one-page report.

The date given in the balance sheets illustrated here shows that they present the financial position of the firm as of the close of business on December 31, 1985.

Dollar signs are used on formal statements at the top of each column of figures. A new column is created whenever a line is drawn for addition, subtraction, or other reasons. A double line is drawn under any amount that is the final result of a series of calculations. Each specific element of the balance sheet is explained in the next section.

Need for Classification in a Financial Statement

To be of maximum value to an analyst, banker, creditor, employee, or other interested person, a financial statement should be classified. The kind of classification and the order of arrangement to be shown in the statement depend on tradition, the nature of the business activity, and the expected use of the statement. These classifications aid in the communication of information to readers. In the example, assets and liabilities of the Modern Clothing Store are classified as to their nature.

Statement classification

Classification *is the arrangement of financial statement items into groupings that have some common basis or similarity.*

Classification of Assets—Current Assets

Current assets consist of cash and other assets that are expected to be converted into cash or to be used in the operation of the business within one year.[7] Current assets are usually listed in descending order of their expected conversion into cash (liquidity). The current assets of the Modern Clothing Store in order of liquidity are the following:

Cash Any item that a bank will accept as a deposit and that is immediately available and acceptable as a means of payment is **cash.** It includes coins, currency, traveler's checks, checks, money orders, and the amount on deposit in the entity's checking account.

Temporary Investments Businesses that have a temporary excess of cash on hand and want to earn interest on it may buy promises to pay issued by other companies (usually referred to as commercial paper) or by governmental agencies or institutions (notes or bonds).

Accounts Receivable Amounts due from customers for services rendered, for merchandise, or for any asset sold on credit are **accounts receivable.** Figure 1–4 shows a simple sales ticket for merchandise sold on credit, describing a source of accounts receivable. Such credit arrangements are called *open accounts.*

---

[7]If the period required to convert noncash short-life assets into cash (the operating cycle) is longer than one year, this longer operating cycle is the period used to determine whether an asset is current.

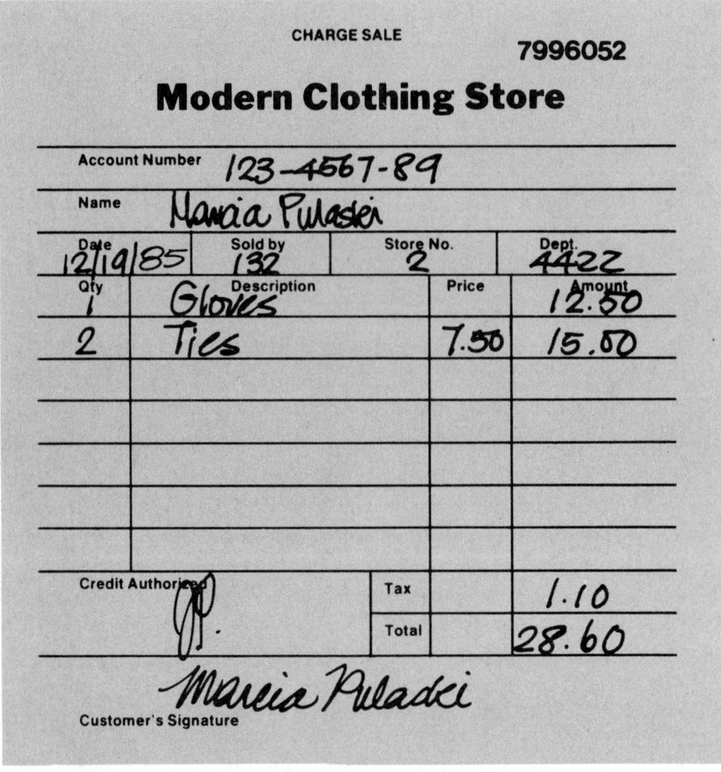

CHARGE SALE

7996052

Modern Clothing Store

Account Number	123-4567-89		
Name	Marcia Pulaski		
Date 12/19/85	Sold by 132	Store No. 2	Dept. 4422

Qty	Description	Price	Amount
1	Gloves		12.50
2	Ties	7.50	15.00
Credit Authorized		Tax	1.10
		Total	28.60

Marcia Pulaski

Customer's Signature

Figure 1–4
Sales Ticket

Notes Receivable Notes receivable are formal written promises to pay a fixed amount of money at a future date. Most notes can usually be exchanged for cash at a bank.

Merchandise Inventory Businesses that offer products for sale must have them readily available. All the merchandise on hand at any given time is called **merchandise inventory.** Merchandise inventory items are found on retail store shelves and in stockrooms or warehouses.

Prepaid Items Services and supplies acquired to be consumed during the next 12 months are **prepaid items.** They are assets because they are items of value that have future usefulness in business operations. Some examples of prepaid items are:

Prepaid Insurance Every business must protect itself against hazards. Consequently, businesses take out insurance policies for protection. The cost of this type of protection, an insurance premium, is paid in advance. Insurance policies commonly are issued against such hazards as fire, burglary, personal injury, business interruption, and injury to employees (workmen's compensation). The unexpired portion is an asset.

Office Supplies Supplies such as stamps, stationery, and business forms required in an office are grouped under the title office supplies and are current assets of the business.

Store Supplies Store supplies include wrapping paper, twine, paper bags, and similar items used in a store. They are also classified as current assets. Office supplies and store supplies to be used in the general operation of the business should not be included in merchandise inventory.

Classification of Assets–Property, Plant, and Equipment

Property, plant, and equipment comprises assets used over a long period in the operation of a business. They are customarily listed on the balance sheet according to their degree of permanence; the most permanent item is listed first. Some typical property, plant, and equipment assets are:

Land Land is shown separately. Although land and the buildings on the land are usually sold together, they are classified separately because the buildings will deteriorate through usage, whereas the land will not. Land is considered the most permanent asset.

Buildings Buildings owned by the business appear on the balance sheet. Rented buildings are not owned and are, therefore, not assets.

Store Equipment Showcases, counters, and shelves are typical permanent items of store equipment used in selling the merchandise inventory.

Delivery Equipment Delivery equipment consists of trucks, cars, and other types of equipment owned and used for the delivery of products to customers.

Classification of Liabilities–Current Liabilities

The term **current liabilities** designates obligations whose liquidation (payment or settlement) is reasonably expected to require the use of current assets or the creation (substitution) of other current liabilities. All liabilities to be paid within a one-year period are classified as current. In general, they are listed in their probable order of liquidation; those that are expected to be paid first are shown first, those to be paid next follow, and so on. Some typical current liabilities are:

Accounts Payable Purchases on credit result in **accounts payable** to the buyer. They are the unpaid amounts owed to creditors from purchases on an account arrangement. They are usually due to be paid within 30 days and are also called open accounts.

Notes Payable The opposite of notes receivable, **notes payable** are formal written promises by the entity to pay money to creditors. Trade notes payable arise from the purchases of merchandise or services used in the course of business. Notes payable to a bank arise when a company borrows money for business use. Notes payable are classified as current liabilities unless the date for payment is more than one year in the future.

Accrued Liabilities **Accrue** means to increase by growth or to accumulate in a uniform manner. Accrued wages payable and accrued interest payable are typical accrued liabilities. These are debts that have accumulated because of the passage of time and that are not yet due for payment. These items are customarily placed last among the current liabilities.

Classification of Liabilities—Long-Term Liabilities

Debts that are not due for at least a year are called **long-term liabilities.** They may appear on the balance sheet in any sequence.

Mortgage Payable A **mortgage payable** is a debt owed by the business for which specific assets are pledged as security. The borrower issues a legal document that is secured by a pledge of specific assets and is called a **mortgage.**

Bonds Payable As a means of raising funds, some businesses borrow money by issuing bonds. *Bonds* are long-term promises to repay funds that are borrowed; they usually extend over a period of 10 to 30 years.

Classification of Ownership Claims–Owner's Equity

The form of a business organization determines the manner of reporting the owner's equity on the balance sheet. A business owned by an individual is referred to as a **single proprietorship.** The Modern Clothing Store is a single proprietorship owned by Lucy Genova. Her equity is shown on the balance sheet as follows (see Figure 1–2):

Owner's equity:	
Lucy Genova, capital	$20,570

The owner's equity for the single proprietorship is listed with the name of the proprietor, followed by the word "capital." The total owner's equity is shown as one item because there are no legal restrictions on withdrawals by a single proprietor. In the *partnership* form, two or more persons voluntarily join in a business venture to earn and share profits. If the Modern Clothing Store were a partnership owned by Lucy Genova and Dale Page, the owner's equity of each would be shown on the balance sheets in Figures 1–2 and 1–3 as follows:

Partners' equity:		
Lucy Genova, capital	$10,570	
Dale Page, capital	10,000	
Total partners' equity		$20,570

Another form of business organization, the *corporation,* is a legal entity that has been issued a charter by the state in which it is established. Most corporations have multiple owners, who are issued stock certificates that indicate how much of a business each *stockholder* or *shareholder* owns. The owner's equity of each stockholder is not disclosed separately on the balance sheet but is shown collectively classified by source. For example, the *common stock* caption is used to describe initial investments in common stock by owners. A caption entitled *retained earnings* is used to describe corporate profits not yet paid out to stockholders. If the Modern Clothing Store is a corporation, the owners' equity could be shown on the balance sheet in Figures 1–2 and 1–3 as follows:

Stockholders' equity:		
Common stock	$15,000	
Retained earnings	5,570	
Total stockholders' equity		$20,570

Other sources of stockholders' equity are discussed in Chapters 16 and 17.

Overview of Financial Reports

In this chapter, the focus has been on the balance sheet because it is the financial statement that portrays the basic accounting equation. The accounting model, however, produces other statements, as diagrammed in Figure 1–5. At the beginning of any time period, a mix of the elements in the basic accounting equation is shown on the balance sheet in detail. During the period, the elements change as the business conducts operations to earn a profit. A description of the inflows of resources from operations is called a *revenue;* a description of the outflows of resources is called an *expense.* When the revenues of a period are greater than the expenses of a period, the business has earned a profit. The details of such operations are shown in a financial statement called the *income statement.* Because a profit increases total assets without an offsetting increase in total liabilities, it causes the owner's equity to increase. For the same reason, any portion of those profits taken out of the business will result in a decrease in owner's equity. To show

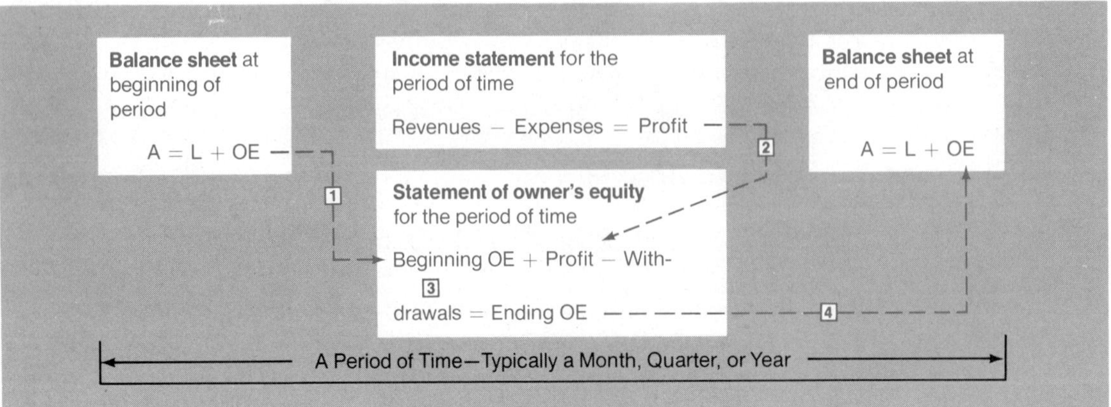

Figure 1–5 **How Financial Statements Fit Together**

these changes, a *statement of owner's equity* is prepared. Note in Figure 1–5 that both an income statement and a statement of owner's equity span a period of time, while the balance sheet does not.

The period of time covered between two balance sheets may be any period that is useful to readers of the statements. Typical periods covered are a month, a quarter, or a year. A balance sheet at the end of one period becomes the balance sheet at the beginning of the next period. As Figure 1–5 illustrates, they are linked together by the income statement and the statement of owner's equity as follows:

1 A beginning owner's equity amount is shown on the beginning balance sheet. It is picked up on the statement of owner's equity.

2 The profit for the period is shown on the income statement. It is also picked up on the statement of owner's equity.

3 Withdrawals—usually cash—by the owner during the period are recorded in the accounting records. This figure is also recorded on the statement of owner's equity.

4 The new amount of owner's equity is then computed and shown on the end-of-period balance sheet.

This process repeated period after period provides to statement readers a constant flow of useful information. Methods and procedures for recording transactions to produce the financial statements are explained in the following section and in the next chapters.

Developing the Accounting System

Objective Evidence—The Business Document

Business firms are initially created by investments by owners. These firms buy and sell assets, collect receivables, pay debts, and engage in other operating activities. In accounting, these activities are referred to as **transactions.** Before an accountant can record or process a transaction, he or she must be made aware that the transaction has taken place. In other words, there must be some objective evidence of the transaction—usually in the form of a *business document.* For example, an accountant can learn that cash has been paid out of the firm by viewing either a copy of a check, the check stub of a checkbook, or a receipt for payment of cash. A copy of the supplier's invoice (the description of the item shipped in terms of quantity and price) could be used to indicate that supplies or merchandise had been purchased. Other appropriate accounting forms will indicate that transactions have occurred.

These business documents flow across the accountant's desk. They are first used in developing accounting information as described in this chapter. These documents are then filed for future reference and for review by the independent certified public accountant. In this section, the effect of some transactions on the financial position of one of the businesses owned by Lucy Genova is illustrated.

Transactions of the Global Realty Company

All businesses go through an initial cycle in which the owner makes an investment and acquires various assets prior to opening the doors to start regular operations. The transactions involved in the organization of the Global Realty Company, a single proprietorship owned and operated by Lucy Genova, illustrate this cycle.[8]

1985		
Jul.	1	Global Realty Company was organized by Lucy Genova. She opened a bank account under the name of Global Realty Company and made a deposit, taken from her personal savings account, of $50,000 to start the new business.
	5	Purchased land and building for $30,000 in cash. The land was valued at $5,000; the building at $25,000. Issued check no. 1.
	11	Received furniture purchased on open charge account from the Jones Company for $8,000; supplier's invoice dated July 8, 1985.
	20	Paid the Jones Company $5,000 on amount owed to it. Issued check no. 2.
	25	The company found that some of the furniture was not what it wanted, so it sold the furniture, which had cost $1,800, to James Hill for $1,800 on account. Hill promised to pay this amount in 30 days; issued invoice no. 1.
	29	Collected $1,000 from James Hill on amount he owed to Global Realty Company for the furniture sold to him on July 25.

[8]Although Lucy Genova owns other businesses, each is treated as a separate *accounting entity* so that she can have information to make better decisions about any one of them.

The following discussion is based on these transactions.

Analysis of Transactions—Effect on Accounting Equation

Since the balance sheet is an expanded variation of the accounting equation, it stands to reason that the total of the two sides should always be equal. A possible solution to the problem of accumulating data is the preparation of a balance sheet immediately after each transaction. Obviously, this is not feasible since even the smallest business has hundreds if not thousands of transactions each day. However, each transaction does change the amounts in the elements of the basic accounting equation; therefore, balance sheets prepared after each transaction would each be different. To illustrate this effect on balance sheet elements, consider the 6 transactions of Global Realty Company.

Transaction 1 *Initial investment of $50,000 by owner on July 1.*

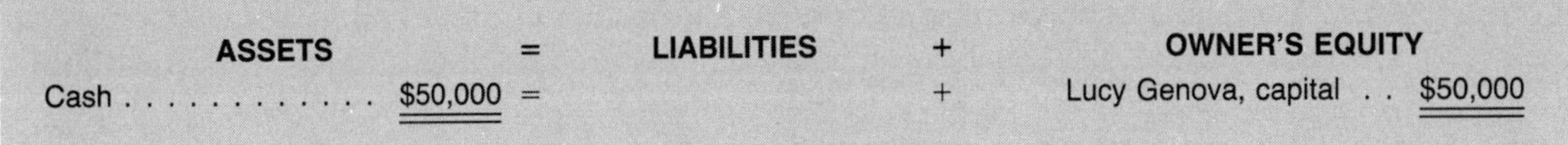

ASSETS		=	LIABILITIES	+	OWNER'S EQUITY	
Cash	$50,000	=		+	Lucy Genova, capital . .	$50,000

The asset cash has increased from zero to $50,000. The investment also creates owner's equity of $50,000; Lucy Genova, capital, has increased from zero to that amount. The equation is in balance.

Transaction 2 *Purchase of land and building for $30,000.*
After this transaction on July 5, the elements of the equation appear as follows:

ASSETS		=	LIABILITIES	+	OWNER'S EQUITY	
Cash	$20,000					
Land	5,000					
Building	25,000				Lucy Genova, capital . .	$50,000
Totals	$50,000	=		+		$50,000

The asset cash has decreased from $50,000 to $20,000 because $30,000 of it was exchanged for two new assets, land and building, at a cost of $5,000 and $25,000, respectively. Total assets remain at $50,000. Since no equities are changed, the equation remains in balance.

Transaction 3 *Purchase of furniture on account for $8,000.*
The July 11 purchase on credit has created a debt to the Jones Company of $8,000. This liability increase is accompanied by an increase in total assets because the new asset, furniture, was added at a cost of $8,000. The elements now are:

ASSETS		=	LIABILITIES		+	OWNER'S EQUITY	
Cash	$20,000						
Land	5,000						
Building	25,000						
Furniture	8,000		Accounts payable	$8,000		Lucy Genova, capital	$50,000
Totals	$58,000	=		$8,000	+		$50,000

This transaction has caused an increase in total assets, but the corresponding increase in total liabilities keeps the equation in balance at $58,000 = $8,000 + $50,000.

Transaction 4 *Payment of accounts payable of $5,000.*
On July 20, a check for $5,000 was sent to the Jones Company in partial payment of the debt created by the purchase of furniture. Since the entire debt was not paid, a balance of $3,000 is still owed to the Jones Company. The equation elements now are:

ASSETS		=	LIABILITIES		+	OWNER'S EQUITY	
Cash	$15,000						
Land	5,000						
Building	25,000						
Furniture	8,000		Accounts payable	$3,000		Lucy Genova, capital	$50,000
Totals	$53,000	=		$3,000	+		$50,000

Here the cash reduction is accompanied by a reduction in liabilities in the same amount. The equation remains in balance at $53,000 = $3,000 + $50,000.

Transaction 5 *Sale of furniture on account for $1,800.*
On July 25, part of the furniture was found to be unsuitable and was sold to James Hill at its cost price of $1,800. Hill did not pay the Global Realty Company at the time of this transaction but promised to complete payment in 30 days. The elements of the equation now appear as follows:

ASSETS		=	LIABILITIES		+	OWNER'S EQUITY	
Cash	$15,000						
Accounts receivable	1,800						
Land	5,000						
Building	25,000						
Furniture	6,200		Accounts payable	$3,000		Lucy Genova, capital	$50,000
Totals	$53,000	=		$3,000	+		$50,000

Total assets have not changed because this transaction is simply an exchange of one asset for another. Furniture with a cost of $1,800 has been given up, and a new asset, accounts receivable, has been created for the same amount. The sale has no effect on liabilities or owner's equity. Global Realty Company

GLOBAL REALTY COMPANY
Summarized Accounting Equation Revealing Financial Position
For Month Ended July 31, 1985

Date		Business Transaction	Cash	Assets + Accounts Receivable	+ Land	+ Building	+ Furniture	= Liabilities: Accounts Payable	+ Owner's Equity: Lucy Genova, Capital
1985 Jul.	1	Investment of $50,000 cash to start business	+$50,000					=	+$50,000
	5	Purchased land and building for $30,000 in cash. Land is appraised at $5,000; building at $25,000	−30,000		+$5,000	+$25,000			
		Balances . .	$20,000 +		$5,000 +	$25,000		=	$50,000
	11	Purchased furniture on account from the Jones Company for $8,000					+$8,000	+$8,000	
		Balances . .	$20,000 +		$5,000 +	$25,000 +	$8,000 =	$8,000 +	$50,000
	20	Paid the Jones Company $5,000 on account	−5,000					− 5,000	
		Balances . .	$15,000 +		$5,000 +	$25,000 +	$8,000 =	$3,000 +	$50,000
	25	Sold furniture at cost to James Hill for $1,800 on account		+$1,800			− 1,800		
		Balances . .	$15,000 +	$1,800 +	$5,000 +	$25,000 +	$6,200 =	$3,000 +	$50,000
	29	Collected $1,000 from James Hill on account	+1,000	−1,000					
		Balances. . .	$16,000 +	$ 800 +	$5,000 +	$25,000 +	$6,200 =	$3,000 +	$50,000

Figure 1–6 **Summarized Accounting Equation**

continues to owe $3,000 to Jones Company. The equation remains in balance at $53,000 = $3,000 + $50,000.

Transaction 6 *Collection of accounts receivable of $1,000.*
After James Hill made a payment of $1,000 on the amount owed for the furniture, the elements of the equation on July 29, 1985, became:

ASSETS		=	LIABILITIES		+	OWNER'S EQUITY	
Cash	$16,000						
Accounts receivable	800						
Land	5,000						
Building	25,000						
Furniture	6,200		Accounts payable	$3,000		Lucy Genova, capital	$50,000
Totals	$53,000	=		$3,000	+		$50,000

As in Transaction 5, the July 29 transaction is an exchange of one asset for another. Cash is increased by $1,000 and the asset accounts receivable decreased by $1,000. All totals remain the same, with the equation in balance at $53,000 = $3,000 + $50,000. No more transactions occurred during July.

Figure 1–6 shows in summary form the effect of each of these six transactions with a breakdown of the accounting equation across the top into individual elements. The balances show the status of each element at the end of each transaction.

A balance sheet showing the status of the basic accounting equation for Global Realty Company at the end of business on July 31, 1985, appears in Figure 1–7. Note that the individual elements of the expanded accounting equation have been properly classified.

GLOBAL REALTY COMPANY
Balance Sheet
July 31, 1985

Assets			Liabilities and Owner's Equity	
Current assets:			Current liabilities:	
Cash	$16,000		Accounts payable	$ 3,000
Accounts receivable	800		Owner's equity:	
Total current assets		$16,800	Lucy Genova, capital	50,000
Property, plant, and equipment:				
Land	$ 5,000			
Building	25,000			
Furniture	6,200			
Total property, plant, and equipment		36,200		
Total assets		$53,000	Total liabilities and owner's equity	$53,000

Figure 1–7 **Balance Sheet as of July 31, 1985**

Accumulation of Transaction Data

Since it is not feasible to prepare a balance sheet after each transaction and the form used in Figure 1–6 would be very large and complex, it is necessary to use some other method to accumulate transaction data. The next sections deal with this problem and begin the development of the double-entry accounting system.

A Separate Page for Each Item

A possible solution to the problem of data accumulation for an expanded number of assets and liabilities is to designate a separate page for each asset, liability, and owner's equity item, and to record the increases and decreases in the accounting equation elements directly into these separate pages. Using the transactions of Global Realty Company, this method may be illustrated:

ASSET PAGES

		Cash	Page 101
1985			
Jul.	1	Investment by owner	+$50,000
	5	Purchase of land and building	− 30,000
	20	Payment to Jones Company on account	− 5,000
	29	Collection from James Hill	+ 1,000
		(Cash on hand $16,000)	

		Accounts Receivable	Page 111
1985			
Jul.	25	Sale of furniture on account	+$1,800
	29	Collection on account	− 1,000
		(Balance receivable $800)	

		Land	Page 151
1985			
Jul.	5	Purchase of land	+$5,000

		Building	Page 152
1985			
Jul.	5	Purchase of building	+$25,000

		Furniture	Page 157
1985			
Jul.	11	Purchase of furniture on account	+$8,000
	25	Sale of furniture at cost	− 1,800
		(Furniture on hand $6,200)	

LIABILITY PAGES

	Accounts Payable	Page 201
1985		
Jul. 11	Purchase of furniture on account	+$8,000
20	Payment on account	− 5,000
	(Balance payable $3,000)	

OWNER'S EQUITY PAGES

	Lucy Genova, Capital	Page 301
1985		
Jul. 1	Investment by owner	+$50,000

A comment should be made about the page numbering system. The pages could be numbered 1, 2, 3, 4, 5, 6, 7. It would be better if the numbers used have a specific meaning—for example, 100–199 for assets, 200–299 for liabilities, and 300–399 for owner's equity items—especially if there are unassigned numbers left for expansion.

At the end of a designated period, the **balance,** or final amount, of each page may be obtained by adding the plus and minus items and subtracting the total of the minus items from the total of the plus items. These balances can then be arranged as a classified balance sheet as was shown in Figure 1–7.

Although this procedure permits unlimited expansion, it is still inadequate. Use of the plus and minus signs contributes to arithmetic errors, and there is no economical way to run a mathematical check on the accuracy of the items contained in the accounting equation. Something else needs to be done to the system.

Division of Each Accounting Page into Columns—Creation of Accounts

A possible solution is to divide each page, referred to in accounting as an **account,** into two sections by drawing a line down the middle of the page and using both sides to record financial information. The accounting equation

$$\text{Assets} = \text{Liabilities} + \text{Owner's equity}$$

suggests the following possible arrangement: Assets appear on the left side of the equation; therefore, the left side of the account is used to record increases of assets, and the opposite side, the right side, is used to record decreases. Similarly, since liabilities and owner's equity appear on the right side of the accounting equation, the right side of the account is used to record increases in liability and owner's equity accounts, and the opposite side, the left side, is used to record decreases. An account number replaces the page number. An example of this kind of account is shown here.

		Account Title			Account Number
Date	Explanation	Amount	Date	Explanation	Amount
	Use this side to record increases in assets and decreases in liability and owner's equity items.			Use this side to record decreases in assets and increases in liability and owner's equity items	

Again using the same six transactions of Global Realty Company, the "account" feature of the accounting system is demonstrated. Before information is recorded in the accounts (see Figure 1–8), each transaction is analyzed in the light of the procedure just described for recording the information.

1985

Jul. 1 Global Realty Company was organized and the proprietor, Lucy Genova, invested cash of $50,000 to start the business. Cash, an asset, is increased by $50,000, and Lucy Genova, Capital, an owner's equity item, is likewise increased. The $50,000 is placed on the left side of the asset account Cash because an asset is increased by an amount on the left side. The same amount is placed on the right side of the owner's equity account Lucy Genova, Capital to increase that account.

5 Purchased land and building for $30,000 in cash. The cost of the land was determined to be $5,000; the building, $25,000. Both land and building are assets and are increased; thus, the $5,000 and the $25,000 are placed on the left sides of the Land and Building accounts, respectively. The Cash account is decreased by $30,000; thus, this amount is placed on the right side of the Cash account.

11 Purchased furniture on account from the Jones Company for $8,000. The asset furniture is increased by $8,000; this amount is placed on the left side of the Furniture account. A liability account Accounts Payable is increased by the amount due the Jones Company; $8,000 is placed on the right side of the Accounts Payable account to indicate that it has been increased.

20 Paid the Jones Company $5,000 on account. The liability accounts payable is decreased and the asset cash is also decreased. The $5,000 is placed on the left side of the Accounts Payable account to record the decrease; the same figure is placed on the right side of the asset account Cash to reflect the decrease.

25 Sold furniture that cost $1,800 to James Hill for $1,800 on account. The asset accounts receivable is increased by $1,800 and the asset furniture is decreased by $1,800. The increase in the asset accounts receivable is shown by placing the amount on the left side of the Accounts Receivable account; and the decrease in the asset furniture is shown by placing the amount on the right side of the Furniture account.

29 Collected $1,000 from James Hill on account. The asset cash is increased by $1,000; the asset accounts receivable is decreased by $1,000. The increase of the asset cash is shown by placing the $1,000 on the left side of the Cash account; the decrease of the asset accounts receivable is shown by placing the $1,000 on the right side of the Accounts Receivable account.

These transactions would appear in the accounts as shown in Figure 1–8.

Figure 1–8 **Accounts of Global Realty Company on July 31, 1985**

Cash — Acct. No. 101

Date		Explanation	Amount	Date		Explanation	Amount
1985				1985			
Jul.	1	Investment by owner[a]	50,000	Jul.	5	Purchased land and building	30,000
	29	Collection from Hill	1,000		20	Payment to Jones Co.	5,000
		16,000	51,000				35,000

Accounts Receivable — Acct. No. 111

Date		Explanation	Amount	Date		Explanation	Amount
1985				1985			
Jul.	25	Sold furniture on account	1,800	Jul.	29	Collection from Hill	1,000
		800					

Land — Acct. No. 151

Date		Explanation	Amount	Date		Explanation	Amount
1985							
Jul.	5	Purchased land	5,000				

Building — Acct. No. 152

Date		Explanation	Amount	Date		Explanation	Amount
1985							
Jul.	5	Purchased building	25,000				

Furniture — Acct. No. 157

Date		Explanation	Amount	Date		Explanation	Amount
1985				1985			
Jul.	11	Purchased furniture on account	8,000	Jul.	25	Sold furniture on account	1,800
		6,200					

Accounts Payable — Acct. No. 201

Date		Explanation	Amount	Date		Explanation	Amount
1985				1985			
Jul.	20	Payment to Jones Co.	5,000	Jul.	11	Purchased furniture on account	8,000
						3,000	

Lucy Genova, Capital — Acct. No. 301

Date		Explanation	Amount	Date		Explanation	Amount
				1985			
				Jul.	1	Investment by owner	50,000

[a]After the journal is introduced, it will be evident that explanations in the accounts are rarely needed; also, at that time two more columns will be added to provide a cross-reference to the journal.

GLOBAL REALTY COMPANY
Trial Balance
July 31, 1985

Account Number	Account Title	Left-Side Balances	Right-Side Balances
101	Cash	$16,000	
111	Accounts Receivable	800	
151	Land	5,000	
152	Building	25,000	
157	Furniture	6,200	
201	Accounts Payable		$ 3,000
301	Lucy Genova, Capital		50,000
	Totals	$53,000	$53,000

Figure 1–9
Trial Balance

After all transactions are recorded, the accounts are **footed;** that is, each amount column containing more than one entry is totaled in small figures (in practice this is usually done in pencil) under the last amount on each side (see the Cash account, for example). Then the balance of each account is determined by subtracting the smaller amount from the larger. The balance is placed in the Explanation column of the side with the larger amount. As a check on the accuracy of the work, a listing of the account balances is made. The total of the balances on the left side of the accounts is compared to the total of the balances on the right side. Since the left-hand balances represent the left side and the right-hand balances the right side of the accounting equation items, their totals should be equal. As this is a test or a trial of the equality of the balances, it is called a **trial balance** (see Figure 1–9).

If the totals agree, it is presumed that the accounting is accurate up to this point. This presumption may not be correct, for the equality shows only that the sum of the left-hand balances equals the sum of the right-hand balances. Yet the accountant, acting as if it is correct, proceeds to complete the remaining steps in the accounting process. After the trial balance is prepared, a classified balance sheet similar to Figure 1–7 can be prepared from it.

Tools of Accounting

Before the remainder of the basic accounting model is discussed in Chapter 2, the following accounting tools are considered: (a) the T account, (b) debits and credits, and (c) the formal account.

The T Account

A T account is so named because of its shape. Owing to its simplicity, this form makes it easy to understand the effects of transactions on a given account. Each **T account** consists of a left side and a right side, with the title of the account written across the top.

Account Title	
Left side (the debit side)	Right side (the credit side)

Debits and Credits

Although originally the terms debit and credit had a specific meaning related to debtor and creditor accounts, today they are used as nouns, verbs, or adjectives depending on whether one is talking about an amount on the left side (a **debit**) or the right side (a **credit**), or the process of placing an amount on the left side *(to debit)* or the right side *(to credit),* or the characteristics of information on the left side (a *debit entry*) or the right side (a *credit entry*).

Debit and credit ***The left side of the T form of an account is called the* debit *side, and the right side is called the* credit *side.***

Substituting the terms debit and credit for the words left side and right side, the following rules may be stated:

Debit an account to record:	Credit an account to record:
An increase of an asset	A decrease of an asset
A decrease of a liability	An increase of a liability
A decrease in the owner's equity	An increase in the owner's equity

The relationship of the rules of debit and credit to the balance sheet and to the accounting equation may be illustrated as follows:

Assets (Property Owned by a Business)		=	Liabilities (Creditors' Claims to Assets)		+	Owner's Equity (Owner's Claims to Assets)	
Debit increase	Credit decrease		Debit decrease	Credit increase		Debit decrease	Credit increase

The abbreviation for debit is **Dr.;** for credit is **Cr.** For any account in the above illustration, the side marked "increase" is the *normal balance* side, since increases will normally exceed decreases.

The Formal Account

In actual business practice, the T account is expanded to a formal account. An **account** is a recording device used for sorting accounting information into similar groupings. It often consists of two sides with four columns on each side: the date, an explanation, the page number of the source from which the amount was transferred (called the *folio column*), and the debit or credit amount.[9] Transferring transaction information to an account is called **posting.** A standard form for the account for Cash is shown in Figure 1–10.[10] Note that the folio column is indicated by an F.

---

[9] The folio column is also called a posting reference (P.R.).

[10] A variation of the T form is the three-amount-column form of account. That form is introduced in Chapter 2.

Cash — Acct. No. 101

Date	Explanation	F	Debit	Date	Explanation	F	Credit

Figure 1–10
T Form of Account

The collection of all the accounts is called a **ledger.** It may be a book or other storage medium. Larger businesses that have electronic data processing use magnetic disks or some other form of record for an account. In all cases, the basic concepts are the same as in the handwritten model.

The accounting process is next adapted to include information about revenues and expenses in Chapter 2.

Glossary

Account A recording device used for sorting accounting information into similar groupings.

Accounting The set of rules and methods by which financial and economic data are collected and transformed into useful reports for decision making.

Accounts payable Unpaid amounts or debts which a business owes to creditors from purchases on open account.

Accounts receivable Amounts due from customers for services rendered or for sales made to them.

Accrued Accumulated or grown over a period of time.

Asset A thing of value owned by an economic enterprise.

Auditing Independent review of an entity's accounting reports usually made by a certified public accountant.

Balance The difference between the total of the debit amounts and the total of the credit amounts in an account.

Balance sheet The statement that summarizes the assets, liabilities, and owner's (or owners') equity of a business unit as of a specific date.

Budget A financial plan for a future period developed in organizational detail.

Cash Currency, coins, traveler's checks, checks, and any other items that a bank will accept for deposit.

CIA A certified internal auditor.

CMA Holder of the Certificate in Management Accounting.

Controlling The management function which consists of monitoring actual versus planned activity and taking corrective action where appropriate.

CPA A certified public accountant.

Credit The right-hand side of the T form of an account, the amount shown on the right side of an account, or the process of placing an amount on the right side of an account.

Creditors Persons or groups to whom debts are owed.

Current assets Cash and other assets that will be consumed or converted into cash within one year.

Current liabilities Liabilities to be paid within one year.

Debit The left-hand side of the T form of an account, the amount shown on the left side of an account, or the process of placing an amount on the left side of an account.

Entity The focal point of attention of accounting records; an organization such as a business.

Equities Claims against the total assets of a business.

External users Individuals, groups, or organizations outside the enterprise who make use of its accounting information.

Footing The totaling of a column of figures and showing of the total in small pencil figures under the last amount in the column, or the total derived from this procedure.

Internal users Individuals within a firm who need accounting information.

Ledger The book that contains all the ledger accounts; or a collection of ledger accounts in any form.

Liability An obligation of a business, or a creditor's claim against the assets of a business.

Long-term liabilities Debts of a business that are not due for at least one year.

Merchandise inventory The stock of products held by a business for resale to its customers.

Mortgage payable A debt—usually long-term—for which specific assets are pledged as securities.

Net assets Total assets minus total liabilities.

Notes payable A balance sheet caption most commonly used for short-term notes to creditors.

Owner's equity The owner's or owners' claims against assets of a business. As used in this text, owner's equity implies that the business is a single proprietorship and, therefore, represents the proprietor's claims against assets of the single proprietorship.

Planning Setting the goals and objectives for a future period.

Posting Transferring transaction information to an account.

Prepaid items Unconsumed amounts of current assets that will normally be used in the coming year.

Profit The reward to an organization for rendering services or providing products.

Property, plant, and equipment The long-lived assets of a firm that are used in the operations of the firm and are not held for resale.

Single proprietorship A business owned by a single individual.

Statement classification Grouping of similar elements of the accounting equation in a financial statement.

T account A simple form of ledger account in the shape of a T, used for analyzing transactions and for teaching purposes.

Temporary investments Stocks or bonds that can be readily resold, purchased when an excess of cash is on hand for a short period.

Transaction A business activity or event which has taken place.

Trial balance A statement that shows the name and balance of all ledger accounts arranged according to whether they are debits or credits. The total of the debits must equal the total of the credits in this statement.

Questions

Q1–1 What are two examples of internal users of accounting information? External users? Explain how each would use information from accounting reports.

Q1–2 What are some of the types of organizations in which accountants work?

Q1–3 What is a CPA? How does one become a CPA? Give some examples of tasks that CPAs perform.

Q1–4 In 1982, an aerospace company, Allegheny International, advertised in *Business Week* that it had acquired Sunbeam Corporation with its line of kitchen appliances. Should the accounting records of the two corporations be merged into a single accounting entity? Why or why not?

Q1–5 What are the characteristics of an asset? A liability? An owner's equity item?

Q1–6 What are the classifications of assets? Of liabilities? Explain how to determine when an item falls into each classification.

Q1–7 What is the basic accounting equation? Explain how a balance sheet is a representation of the basic accounting equation.

Q1–8 At the end of a recent fiscal year, Dan River Inc. had total assets of $407 million and total stockholders' equity of $205 million. How much was the corporation's total liabilities?

Q1–9 What is a business transaction? Can there be a business transaction that does not change two or more elements of the accounting equation? Explain.

Q1–10 Why do accountants use debits and credits to record business transactions?

Q1–11 Does a debit to an asset account reflect an increase in that asset or a decrease? Use the accounting equation to explain how the rules for debit and credit are developed.

Q1–12 Is a trial balance with equal debit and credit totals always correct? Discuss.

Q1–13 A purchase of furniture for cash was correctly debited to the Furniture account but erroneously credited to Accounts Receivable. What is the effect on the trial balance totals? On total current assets? On total assets? What accounts have incorrect balances?

Q1–14 At the end of a recent fiscal year, Denny's Inc. paid more than $15 million to rent some of its Denny's Restaurants and Winchell's Donut House sites for varying short-term periods. Are these buildings and land sites assets on Denny's balance sheet? Why or why not?

Exercises

E1–1

Users of financial reports

In March 1982, news releases reported that Biomedical Reference Laboratories, Inc. had 1981 profits of $5.1 million after taxes on $51.7 million sales of its services to more than 14,000 clients. Comment on this news as follows:

1. With supporting computations, show how these profits compare with those in Figure 1–1.

2. From the following list of possible users of this information, show whether each is an internal user or an external user and explain why this news would be of interest to each.

a. The company president.
b. A prospective investor in Biomedical common stock.
c. The Internal Revenue Service.
d. Biomedical's budget director.
e. A large commercial bank in that area.
f. Biomedical's present shareholders.
g. The 1,700 employees in the Biomedical system.

E1–2

Entity concept

Irvin Stein owns a checking account, a savings account, a residence with personal property, Stein's Camera Repair Center, and Capital City Audio Sales. How many accounting entities are involved? Name them.

E1–3 *The accounting equation*

On lines 1, 2, and 3 below are amounts (in millions) from annual reports of U. S. corporations. Fill in the missing amounts.

Total Assets	Total Liabilities	Owners' Equity
$383.2	$118.7	$?
?	263.3	195.4
$544.5	?	178.4

E1–4 *The accounting equation*

Provide the missing amounts below:

Current Assets	Property, Plant, and Equipment	Current Liabilities	Long-Term Liabilities	Owner's Equity
$12,000	$38,000	$10,000	$20,000	$?
34,000	46,000	?	36,000	24,000
?	60,000	16,000	50,000	20,000
12,000	?	6,000	40,000	10,000
20,000	36,000	10,000	?	21,000

E1–5 *Balance sheet classification*

Identify each of the following as (1) a current asset, (2) a property, plant, and equipment item, (3) a current liability, (4) a long-term liability, or (5) an owner's equity item:

a. Accounts payable
b. Accounts receivable
c. Bonds payable
d. Buildings
e. Cash
f. Delivery equipment
g. Rich Helmke, capital
h. Land
i. Notes payable (due June 17, 1990)
j. Notes receivable (due 60 days from date)
k. Office supplies
l. Prepaid insurance
m. Store equipment

E1–6 *Computation of current assets and current liabilities*

On December 31, 1985, the following captions and amounts appeared on the balance sheet of Lei Beck, Electronics Consultant:

Accounts payable	$14,250
Accounts receivable	58,800
Accrued wages payable	3,180
Bank loan payable (due June 1, 1986)	15,000
Bank loan payable (due June 1, 1993)	7,500
Office supplies	2,250
Prepaid insurance	6,300
Shop equipment	8,400
Testing supplies	5,625

1. Compute the amount of current assets.

2. Compute the amount of current liabilities.

E1–7 *Preparation of account form of balance sheet*

The following alphabetical list of accounts is taken from the records of the North State Store for December 31, 1985:

Accounts Payable	$125,000
Accounts Receivable	138,000
Building	400,000
Cash	250,000
Delivery Equipment	140,000
Edith Conklin, Capital	614,000
Land	115,000
Merchandise Inventory	70,000
Mortgage Payable (due July 1, 1996)	280,000
Notes Payable (due April 1, 1986)	110,000
Notes Receivable	18,000
Prepaid Insurance	12,000
Wages Payable	14,000

Prepare a balance sheet in account form.

E1–8 *Account balances, trial balance, and balance sheet*

The following T accounts were taken from the ledger of Will Mahone Company on October 31, 1985:

Cash

Debit	Credit
65,000	53,200
12,000	1,500
	450
	1,050
	300
	125

Land

Debit	Credit
10,000	

Office Supplies

Debit	Credit
100	
450	

Accounts Payable

Debit	Credit
125	435
110	110

Maintenance Supplies

Debit	Credit
500	
435	

Mortgage Payable

Debit	Credit
10,000	50,000

Prepaid Insurance

Debit	Credit
1,500	

Will Mahone, Capital

Debit	Credit
	86,700

Machine

Debit	Credit
20,000	

Delivery Equipment

Debit	Credit
1,050	

Building

Debit	Credit
72,000	

Office Equipment

Debit	Credit
600	

1. Determine the account balances, and prepare a trial balance as of October 31, 1985 in the proper order.

2. Prepare a report form balance sheet.

E1–9 *Errors in balance sheet classifications*

The following balance sheet is presented:

ATWATER APPLIANCE COMPANY
Balance Sheet
For the Year Ended December 31, 1985

Assets

Current assets:		
Cash	$ 4,000	
Accounts receivable	12,000	
Building	24,000	
Merchandise inventory	6,000	
Total current assets		$46,000
Property, plant, and equipment:		
Temporary investments	$ 6,000	
Store equipment	3,000	
Office supplies	200	
Delivery equipment	2,700	
Total property, plant, and equipment		11,900
Total assets		$57,900

Liabilities and Owner's Equity

Current liabilities:		
Accounts payable	$13,200	
Notes payable (due June 1, 1986)	4,000	
Notes payable (due July 1, 2000)	2,000	
Total current liabilities		$19,200
Long-term liabilities:		
Mortgage payable (due May 1, 1999)	$16,000	
Accrued wages and salaries payable	500	
Total long-term liabilities		16,500
Total liabilities		$35,700
Owner's equity:		
Maria Atwater, capital		22,200
Total liabilities and owner's equity		$57,900

List the errors in this statement.

E1–10 *Determining account balances*

On May 20, 1985, Val Zumbro withdrew $80,000 from his savings account and deposited it in a business bank account to create Zumbro's Computer Service. On the same date, he used $10,000 of the business cash to purchase computer repair and testing equipment. He also purchased repair parts for cash at a cost of $2,730. Compute the balance in the Cash account at the end of the day.

E1–11 *Recording transactions in the accounts*

On July 2, 1985, Melinda Moon, Attorney, paid office rent for three months in advance at the rate of $450 per month. On the same date, she purchased an item of office equipment for $900 in cash. Determine the account titles to be used and record these transactions directly in the accounts. Do not provide explanations.

E1–12 *Identifying debits and credits*

Following is a set of three T accounts; each represents one of the terms in the basic accounting equation.

Any Asset		Any Liability		All Owner's Equity	
1	2	3	4	5	6

For each of the numbers 1 through 6 shown therein, indicate whether an entry on that side would be an increase or a decrease.

E1–13 *Trial balance*

Following are the balances from the general ledger accounts of Royal Music Supplies on July 31, 1985:

Acct. No.	Account Title	Amount
101	Cash	$ 2,100
110	Accounts Receivable	4,350
113	Notes Receivable	5,270
120	Prepaid Insurance	800
130	Merchandise Inventory	21,780
151	Land	11,500
154	Building	48,270
160	Store Equipment	12,310
201	Accounts Payable	1,875
203	Notes Payable	3,750
235	Mortgage Payable	26,800
301	Nora Policastro, Capital	?

Prepare a trial balance.

A Problems

P1–1A *Computing missing amount, total assets, and total liabilities*

The loan officer of a bank is considering a request from the Oshkosh Company for a loan. She obtained the following balance sheet figures by telephone:

Cash	$ 9,600
Accounts receivable	124,800
Merchandise inventory	156,000
Store equipment	220,800
Accounts payable	36,000
Notes payable	?
Equipment mortgage payable	96,000
Caroline Gallimore, capital	278,400

After hanging up the phone, she realized that she had failed to write down the amount of notes payable.

Required:

1. Compute the amount of total assets.
2. Compute the amount of total liabilities.
3. Supply the missing figure for notes payable.

P1–2A *Preparing an account form balance sheet with capital balance not given*

The following information is available for Eller's Drug Store as of December 31, 1985:

Temporary investments	$ 5,000
Accounts receivable	15,000
Wages payable	6,250
Building	50,000
Prepaid insurance	600
Inventories	28,750
Jeff Eller, capital	?
Accounts payable	11,250
Cash on hand	500
Cash in bank	5,000
Land	10,000
Mortgage payable	40,000

Required: Prepare a balance sheet for Eller's Drug Store in account form.

P1–3A *Correcting a trial balance*

The Dobbins Garage was started on March 21, 1985. During the first several days of operations, its part-time bookkeeper (a high school student who had a few months' instruction in bookkeeping) recorded the transactions and rendered the following unbalanced trial balance as of March 31, 1985:

DOBBINS GARAGE
Trial Balance
March 31, 1985

Account Title	Debits	Credits
Accounts Payable	$ 8,550	
Accounts Receivable		$10,000
Building	50,000	
Ken Dobbins, Capital	75,000	
Cash	15,500	
Furniture	6,000	
Land		12,000
Mortgage Payable		20,000
Notes Payable	10,350	
Notes Receivable		8,000
Service Supplies	2,800	
Temporary Investments		9,600
Totals	$168,200	$59,600

Required: Assuming that the amounts are correct but that the inexperienced bookkeeper did not understand the proper debit-credit position of some accounts, prepare a corrected trial balance showing the accounts in correct balance sheet order.

P1–4A *Entering transactions in accounts; trial balance*

The following transactions were engaged in by Marr Framing Service owned by Mike Marr during June 1985:

1985		
Jun.	3	Mike Marr invested $100,000 in cash to create Marr Framing Service.
	7	Purchased framing supplies for $4,000 on account.
	10	Purchased equipment for $10,000 in cash.

Required:

1. Enter these transactions directly into the accounts without explanations (provide account titles and account numbers).

2. Prepare a trial balance as of June 10, 1985.

P1–5A *Posting to formal accounts*

The following account numbers and titles were designed for Pike's Peak Car Rental, a single proprietorship:

101	Cash	150	Office Equipment
111	Accounts Receivable	201	Accounts Payable
120	Land	210	Notes Payable
130	Building	301	Lisa Lamar, Capital
140	Automobiles		

During the first month of operation the following transactions occurred:

1985	
Apr. 4	Lamar deposited $105,000 in cash in a bank account in the name of the business, Pike's Peak Car Rental.
5	Purchased land for $10,000 and a building on the lot for $30,000. A cash payment of $15,000 was made, and a promissory note was issued for the balance.
8	Purchased 15 new automobiles at $5,200 each from the Allied Motor Company. A down payment of $20,000 in cash was made; the balance was promised in 30 days.
12	Sold one automobile to a company employee at cost. The employee paid $1,000 in cash and agreed to pay the balance within 30 days.
15	One automobile proved defective and was returned to the Allied Motor Company. The amount due was reduced by $5,200.
16	Purchased a cash register and office desks for $1,850 in cash.
26	Paid $12,800 in cash to the Allied Motor Company on account and gave a 60-day note payable for the balance.

Required:

1. Using the account numbers and account titles provided, post the April transactions directly into formal accounts. Do not write explanations in the accounts.

2. Determine the account balances as of April 30, 1985.

3. Prepare a trial balance as of April 30, 1985.

P1–6A *Thought-provoking problem: using accounting information*

In early 1982, Western Electric Company, Incorporated included the following data in a "Five-Year Highlights" section of its 1981 *Annual Report:*

(Dollars in millions)	1981	1980	1979	1978	1977
Sales	$13,008	$12,032	$10,964	$9,522	$8,135
Net income	711	693	636	561	490
Property, plant, and equipment	2,868	2,654	2,402	2,269	2,133
Invested capital:					
Debt	1,482	1,798	1,275	1,131	960
Owners' equity	4,991	4,449	4,022	3,513	3,363

Required:

1. Compute the net income (net profit) as a percent of sales for each year.

2. Compute the owners' equity as a percent of total invested capital for each year.

3. Compute the property, plant, and equipment as a percent of debt for each year.

4. Based on these computations, what is your opinion of (a) stability and consistency of profits, (b) protection for owners as evidenced by their share of total invested capital, and (c) protection for creditors as evidenced by the property, plant, and equipment to cover their equity?

5. Comment on any trends that you note over the five-year period.

B Problems

P1–1B *Computing missing amount, total assets, and total liabilities*

Lisa Ray is considering the purchase of a business from Bruce Ring. Ray copied the balance sheet figures and went home to consider how much to offer. Later she noted that she had failed to include the amount of notes payable. She does have the following data:

Cash	$ 1,600
Accounts receivable	20,800
Delivery supplies	26,000
Delivery equipment	36,800
Accounts payable	6,000
Notes payable	?
Equipment mortgage payable	16,000
Bruce Ring, capital	46,400

Required:

1. Compute the amount of total assets.

2. Compute the amount of total liabilities.

3. Supply the missing figure for notes payable.

P1–2B *Preparing an account form balance sheet with capital balance not given*

The following information is available for Feinberg's Hardware as of August 31, 1985:

Temporary investments	$ 6,000
Accounts receivable	18,000
Wages payable	7,500
Building	60,000
Prepaid insurance	720
Inventories	34,500
Dan Feinberg, capital	?
Accounts payable	13,500
Cash on hand	600
Cash in bank	6,000
Land	12,000
Mortgage payable	48,000

Required: Prepare a balance sheet for Feinberg's Hardware in account form.

P1–3B *Correcting a trial balance*

Oglala Repair Shop was opened for business on February 14, 1985. During the first two weeks of operations, its part-time bookkeeper recorded the transactions and prepared the following unbalanced trial balance as of February 28, 1985:

OGLALA REPAIR SHOP
Trial Balance
February 28, 1985

Account Title	Debits	Credits
Accounts Payable	$ 10,260	
Accounts Receivable		$12,000
Building	60,000	
Marla Oglala, Capital	90,000	
Cash	18,600	
Furniture	7,200	
Land		14,400
Mortgage Payable		24,000
Notes Payable (due in 30 days)	12,420	
Notes Receivable (due in 60 days)		9,600
Repair Supplies	3,360	
Temporary Investments		11,520
Totals	$201,840	$71,520

Required: Assuming that the amounts are correct but that the inexperienced bookkeeper did not understand the proper debit-credit position of some accounts, prepare a trial balance showing the accounts in correct balance sheet order.

P1–4B *Entering transactions in accounts: trial balance*

The Elite Photo Service, owned by Sandra Beach, engaged in the following transactions during September 1985:

1985		
Sep.	2	Sandra Beach invested $120,000 in cash to create the Elite Photo Service.
	5	Purchased photo supplies for $6,000 on account.
	9	Purchased equipment for $18,500 in cash.

Required:

1. Enter these transactions directly into the accounts without explanations (provide account titles and account numbers).

2. Prepare a trial balance as of September 9, 1985.

P1–5B *Posting to formal accounts*

The following account numbers and titles were designed for Terry's Rentals, a single proprietorship:

101 Cash
111 Accounts Receivable
120 Land
130 Building
140 Rental Equipment
150 Office Equipment
201 Accounts Payable
210 Notes Payable
301 Terry Lea, Capital

During the first month of operations, the following transactions occurred:

1985		
Jul.	1	Lea deposited $43,000 in cash in a bank account in the name of the business, Terry's Rentals.
	4	Purchased land for $4,000 and a building on the lot for $12,000. A cash payment of $6,000 was made, and a promissory note was issued for the balance.

7 Purchased rental equipment for $31,200 from the Church Street Company. A down payment of $8,000 was made; the balance was promised to be paid in 30 days.
8 Sold a lawn mower to an employee at its cost of $250. The employee paid $50 in cash and agreed to pay the balance in 30 days.
9 A chain saw proved to be defective and was returned to the Church Street Company. The amount due was reduced by $300.
11 Purchased a typewriter and an office desk for $740 in cash.
29 Paid $2,900 in cash to the Church Street Company and gave a 90-day note payable for the balance.

Required:

1. Using the account numbers and account titles provided, post the July transactions directly into formal accounts. Do not write explanations in the accounts.

2. Determine the account balances as of July 31, 1985.

3. Prepare a trial balance as of July 31, 1985.

P1–6B
Thought-provoking problem: where would you invest?

The March 15, 1982 issue of *Business Week* presented a "Corporate Scoreboard" that reported 1981 sales and profits for 1,200 companies. The following are selected from that report:

	Washington Post	**Playboy Enterprises**
1981 total sales	$753.4 million	$312.8 million
1981 profits	32.7 million	2.0 million

Required:

1. Based on this information alone, which company appears to present the better investment opportunity? Show computations to support your answer.

2. Realizing that sales and profit information for a single year are not enough data on which to base an investment decision, indicate what additional information you would seek and why.

2 Income Statement Accounts: Fundamentals and Journalizing

Introduction

In the preceding chapter, transactions of the Global Realty Company were analyzed in terms of their effect on asset, liability, and owner's equity accounts, and the information was entered directly into the accounts. Records can be kept in this manner. However, most businesses need more detailed information as well as a means of ensuring a properly functioning and systematic procedure for the recording of transactions. This chapter starts with a look at a simple accounting system that will accomplish this purpose for Global Realty Company.

The chapter introduces and illustrates new steps in the accounting sequence. Emphasized in the chapter are the operational changes in owner's equity—revenues, gains, expenses, losses, and withdrawals by the owner.

Introduced also are controlling and subsidiary accounts (to be defined later). These are discussed at this point to permit the reader to see the totality of the accounting process. These fundamentals will be illustrated in the Good Times Wheels Repair Shop, an extended example, that is started in this chapter and completed in Chapter 3.

Learning Goals

To understand the components of a simple accounting system, particularly the journalizing of simple transactions and posting to ledger accounts.

To prepare an end-of-period trial balance and balance sheet.

To use the three-amount-column form of ledger account.

To understand the nature and use of temporary owner's equity accounts—nominal accounts (revenues, gains, expenses, losses, and proprietor's drawings)—to collect changes in owner's equity.

To know the rules for use of debit and credit for both permanent and temporary accounts.

To recognize the need for and the method of using subsidiary ledgers and their relationship to controlling accounts.

To describe the preparation of and use of a chart of accounts.

To journalize the normal recurring transactions of service organizations.

A Simple Accounting System

Before returning to the Global Realty Company illustration, it is important to see a simple overall accounting system. The steps in a simple accounting system are presented in pictorial form as shown in Figure 2–1.

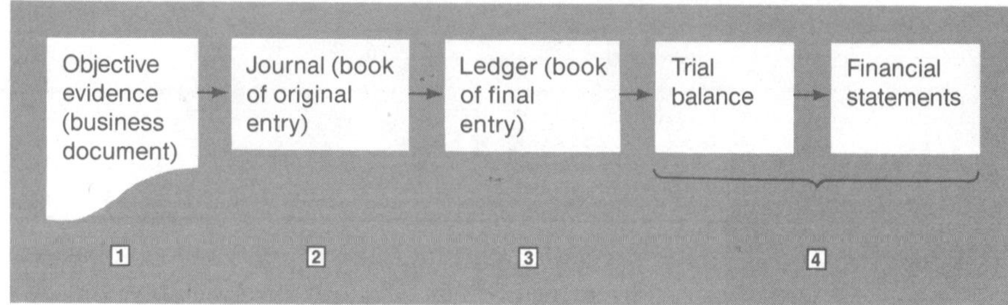

Figure 2–1
A Simple Accounting System

[1] Every entry made in an accounting system must have objective evidence, usually a business document, to justify the entry.

[2] Every business needs a chronological record of transactions and a complete history of all transactions recorded in the order they occurred and in one place. It is often necessary to view a transaction in its entirety in terms of the specific business unit. Since every transaction consists of at least one debit and one credit, the entry is necessarily recorded on different ledger pages. If the ledger contains many accounts, it may be difficult to reconstruct the debit and credit for any single transaction. Therefore, all entries must be first recorded in the **general journal** (or journal), a book of original entry.

[3] To have information available for later summarization and classification, it is necessary to sort it into homogeneous groups. To do so, it is necessary to transfer the information—a process called posting—from the journal to the ledger accounts. All journal entries, therefore, must be *posted* to the ledger. Absolutely no entries are made in a ledger except those posted from a journal. There is no other source for ledger entries.

[4] A test check is made of the accounting system in the form of a trial balance. Financial statements are then prepared from the information presented in the trial balance.

Illustration of Journalizing and Posting

As a means of introducing the basic accounting sequence, two of the steps introduced in Figure 2–1—that of journalizing and posting are reviewed and expanded.

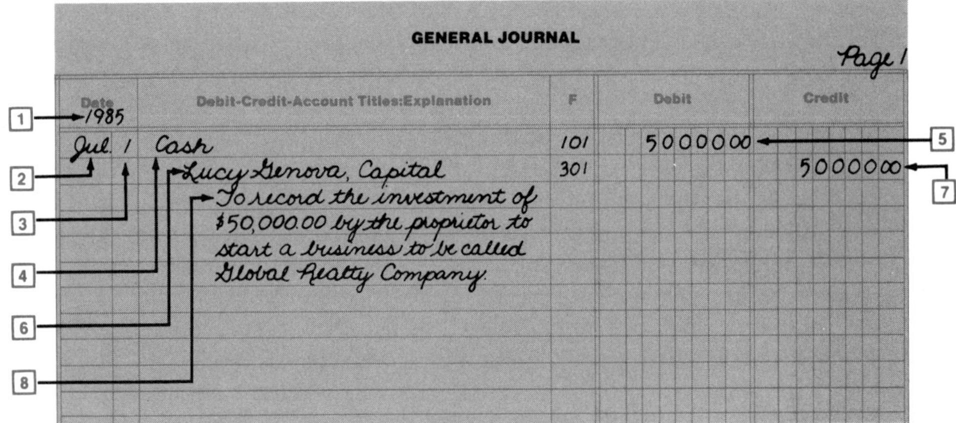

Figure 2–2 **The Journalizing Process in the General Journal**

1. Journalizing
2. Posting

1.* Journalizing *is recording transactions in a book called a* journal, *a book of original entry. The record of a transaction in the journal is called a journal entry.
2.* Posting *is transferring amounts in the journal to the correct accounts in the* ledger, *a book of final entry.

The foregoing process is illustrated by the July 1 transaction of Global Realty Company in which Lucy Genova invested $50,000 to start the Global Realty Company. This transaction is first recorded in the journal as shown in Figure 2–2. The form of the journal in this figure is referred to as the *general journal.*

[1] The year is written in small figures at the top of the Date column. It should be written in that position on every page of the journal.

[2] The month of the first transaction recorded on this page is entered. It is not necessary to write the month again on this page unless it changes.

[3] The date of each transaction is entered.

[4] The title of the account debited is placed in the Debit-Credit-Account Titles: Explanation column against the date line. In order to eliminate confusion, it is important that *the account title written in the journal entry should be the exact title of the account as it appears in the ledger.*

[5] The amount of the debit is entered in the Debit amount column.

[6] The title of the account credited should be indented approximately one inch from the Date column.

[7] The amount of the credit is entered in the Credit column.

[8] The explanation is entered on the next line, indented an additional one inch. It should contain all the essential information as well as a reference to the relevant source document from which the information was obtained—check number, cash receipt date or number, and so on.

In journals, ledger accounts, and trial balances, the use of two zeros or a dash in the cents column to indicate that the cents are zero is a matter of choice. Thus, an amount may be written 2,375.00 or 2,375.—. In a balance sheet and other statements containing a mixture of items with and without cents, it is preferable, for the sake of appearance, to use zeros for those items having no cents. In this book, most examples contain whole dollar amounts; thus the cents column is often omitted in statements, journals, and ledgers. Dollar signs should *not* be written in journals and ledger accounts. They should be used in the balance sheet and all other formal statements.

Notice that the journal does not *replace* the ledger account. The journal is called a book of *original entry.* It is necessary first to journalize the transaction and then to post to the proper accounts in the ledger. **Posting** is the term used to describe the transfer of a transaction from the journal to the ledger.

Figure 2–3 illustrates the posting of the July 1 entry from the general journal to the ledger. Posting normally should be done daily. Explanations of numbered items in Figure 2–3 follow:

[1] The debit amount ($50,000), the journal page (1), and the date (Jul. 1) are entered on the debit side of the Cash account in the ledger. The year (1985) is written at the top of the Date column. Remember that dollar signs are not used in journals or ledgers.

[2] The ledger account number for the debit entry (101) is entered in the folio (F) column of the journal to cross-reference the journal and the ledger. *The presence of the account number here indicates that the item has been posted; so it must not be inserted until after the posting has been made.*

[3] The credit amount ($50,000), the journal page (1), and the date (Jul. 1) are entered on the credit side of the Lucy Genova, Capital account in the ledger. The year (1985) is written at the top of the Date column.

[4] The ledger account number for the credit entry (301) is entered in the folio column of the journal to complete the cross-referencing. It follows again that the cross-reference in the journal indicates that the posting to the ledger has been completed.

Explanations are not usually given in the Explanation columns of the ledger accounts. The cross-reference to the journal page from which the information was recorded permits any interested person to find quickly a complete story of the transaction in the journal. Short explanations are used in the ledger accounts only when deemed especially useful in particular transactions. The total journalizing and posting sequence for the Global Realty Company is described and illustrated next.

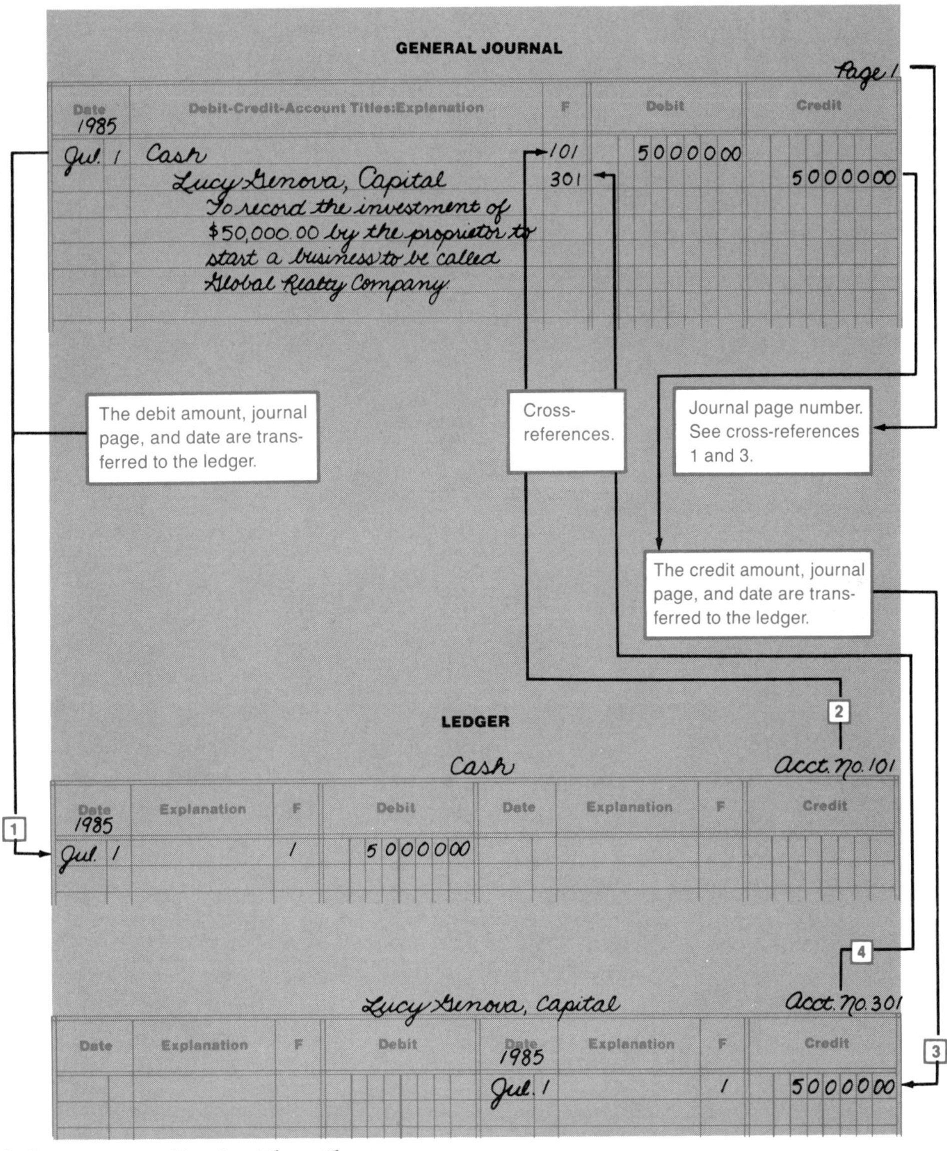

Figure 2–3 **Posting Flow Chart**

The Accounting Sequence for Global Realty Company

Now the foregoing steps in the accounting system are illustrated for all the Global Realty Company transactions stated in Chapter 1. Assuming that objective evidence indicates that the transactions have taken place, the six transactions are first journalized, including the repeating of the July 1 transaction; then the amounts are posted to traditional T form ledger accounts; and last a trial balance and financial statements are prepared.

GENERAL JOURNAL

Page 1

Date 1985		Debit-Credit-Account Titles:Explanation	F	Debit	Credit
Jul.	1	Cash	101	5000000	
		Lucy Genova, Capital	301		5000000
		To record the investment of $50,000.00 by the proprietor to start a business to be called Global Realty Company.			
	5	Land	151	500000	
		Building	152	2500000	
		Cash	101		3000000
		To record purchase of land and building for cash; issued check no. 1.			
	11	Furniture	157	800000	
		Accounts Payable	201		800000
		To record purchase of furniture on account; supplier's invoice is dated July 8, 1985: Jones Company $8,000			
	20	Accounts Payable	201	500000	
		Cash	101		500000
		To record payment on account; issued check no. 2: Jones Company $5,000			
	25	Accounts Receivable	111	180000	
		Furniture	157		180000
		To record credit sale of furniture at cost; invoice no. 1: James Hill $1,800			
	29	Cash	101	100000	
		Accounts Receivable	111		100000
		To record collection on account: James Hill $1,000			

Figure 2–4 General Journal of Global Realty Company

Journalizing and Posting

As a starting point, the six transactions of Global Realty Company discussed in Chapter 1 are repeated below.

1985	
Jul. 1	The Global Realty Company was organized by Lucy Genova. She opened a bank account under the name of Global Realty Company and made a deposit, taken from her personal savings account, of $50,000 to start the new business.
5	Purchased land and building for $30,000 in cash. The land was valued at $5,000; the building at $25,000. Issued check no. 1.
11	Received furniture purchased on open charge account from the Jones Company for $8,000; supplier's invoice dated July 8, 1985.
20	Paid the Jones Company $5,000 on amount owed to it. Issued check no. 2.
25	The company found that some of the furniture was not what it wanted, so it sold the furniture, which had cost $1,800, to James Hill for $1,800 on account. Hill promised to pay this amount in 30 days; issued invoice no. 1.
29	Collected $1,000 from James Hill on amount he owed to Global Realty Company for the furniture sold to him on July 25.

These transactions are first journalized as shown in Figure 2–4. Although cross-reference figures are shown in the folio column, they would *not* be entered until after posting to the ledger. *Note also that a blank line is left to separate each journal entry.*

The transactions are posted from page 1 of the general journal to the ledger accounts shown in Figure 2–5. The cross-references are entered in both the journal and the accounts.

LEDGER

Cash — Acct. No. 101

Date	Explanation	F	Debit	Date	Explanation	F	Credit
1985				1985			
Jul. 1		1	50,000.00	Jul. 5		1	30,000.00
29	16,000.00	1	1,000.00	20		1	5,000.00
			51,000.00				35,000.00

Accounts Receivable — Acct. No. 111

Date	Explanation	F	Debit	Date	Explanation	F	Credit
1985				1985			
Jul. 25	800.00	1	1,800.00	Jul. 29		1	1,000.00

Land — Acct. No. 151

Date	Explanation	F	Debit	Date	Explanation	F	Credit
1985							
Jul. 5		1	5,000.00				

Figure 2–5 General Ledger of Global Realty Company

Building Acct. No. 152

Date	Explanation	F	Debit	Date	Explanation	F	Credit
1985							
Jul. 5		1	2500000				

Furniture Acct. No. 157

Date	Explanation	F	Debit	Date	Explanation	F	Credit
1985				1985			
Jul. 11	6,200.00	1	800000	Jul. 25		1	180000

Accounts Payable Acct. No. 201

Date	Explanation	F	Debit	Date	Explanation	F	Credit
1985							
Jul. 20		1	500000	Jul. 11	3,000.00	1	800000

Lucy Genova, Capital Acct. No. 301

Date	Explanation	F	Debit	Date	Explanation	F	Credit
				1985			
				Jul. 1		1	5000000

Figure 2–5 (Continued)

After all journal entries are posted, the accountant foots each account as shown in the ledger that follows the journal.

This accounting system is called **double-entry accounting** because it requires that each record of a transaction have debits and credits with total debits equal to total credits. Every transaction does not necessarily have a single debit and a single credit. For example, the July 5 entry of the business involves two debits totaling $30,000 and one credit of $30,000. A journal entry that has more than one debit or credit is called a **compound entry.** Regardless of the number of accounts debited and credited in a single transaction, the total amount of all debits must equal the total amount of all credits in each transaction. It follows that the total of the debit balances and the total of the credit balances in the ledger of all the accounts must also be equal.

Trial Balance

As stated in Chapter 1, it is customary to prepare a trial balance to test the equality of the debit and credit balances in the ledger before a formal balance sheet is prepared. The accountant could prepare a balance sheet directly from the accounts, but the trial balance furnishes a convenient summary of

GLOBAL REALTY COMPANY
Trial Balance
July 31, 1985

Acct. No.	Account Title	Debits	Credits
101	Cash	$16,000	
111	Accounts Receivable	800	
151	Land	5,000	
152	Building	25,000	
157	Furniture	6,200	
201	Accounts Payable		$ 3,000
301	Lucy Genova, Capital		50,000
	Totals	$53,000	$53,000

Figure 2–6 Trial Balance of Global Realty Company

the information for the preparation of the balance sheet. The July 31, 1985, trial balance of Global Realty Company is shown in Figure 2–6. The trial balance proves the equality of debits and credits but not the accuracy of the accounts. For example, an entire transaction could be omitted, the debit and credit amounts of an entry could be identically incorrect, a wrong account could be debited or credited, or both the debit and credit amounts for a given transaction could be posted twice. If the trial balance is in balance, however, the accountant considers this reasonable evidence of accuracy and proceeds from that point.

Balance Sheet

The next step in the illustrated accounting sequence is the preparation of the formal balance sheet for Global Realty Company (Figure 2–7). Note that Figure 2–7 is the same as Figure 1–7. Also keep in mind that this form of the balance sheet is referred to as the **account form** because information is placed on the left and right sides of the statement as accounting information is placed in the traditional account (the T form).[1]

As indicated previously, dollar signs are used on formal statements. They should be placed at the beginning of each column of figures. Note, however, that a new column of figures is started whenever a line is drawn for addition or subtraction, as can be seen in Figure 2–7.

In the preceding illustration, the transactions of Global Realty Company were journalized. The information in the journal was posted to appropriate accounts. Account balances were determined, and a trial balance was prepared. A balance sheet was prepared from the information summarized in the trial balance. Only balance sheet accounts, referred to as real accounts, were used in these illustrations.

[1]The alternative form of the balance sheet described in Chapter 1 is called the **report form** since it is prepared in the same manner as a typical report.

GLOBAL REALTY COMPANY
Balance Sheet
July 31, 1985

Assets			Liabilities and Owner's Equity	
Current assets:			Current liabilities:	
Cash	$16,000		Accounts payable	$ 3,000
Accounts receivable	800		Owner's equity:	
Total current assets		$16,800	Lucy Genova, capital	50,000
Property, plant, and equipment:				
Land	$ 5,000			
Building	25,000			
Furniture	6,200			
Total property, plant, and equipment		36,200		
Total assets		$53,000	Total liabilities and owner's equity	$53,000

Figure 2–7 The Account Form of the Balance Sheet

The Three-Amount-Column Ledger Account

Before additional changes in owner's equity are discussed, consider one more basic tool of accounting, the use of a popular variation of the ledger account—the three-amount-column account.

The T form of ledger account that was used in the preceding illustration is an excellent device for teaching certain concepts and will be used for that purpose throughout the book. The three-amount-column form of ledger account has good theoretical and practical reasons for its use. It is widely used in practice.

Sometimes referred to as the debit-credit-balance form of *ledger account,* the three-amount-column account is easy to prepare and is extremely useful when frequent reference has to be made to the balance of an account. Its use also aids the preparation of the trial balance, since the balance of each individual account is already determined. Because the form is used for illustration later in this chapter and in most of the illustrations throughout the remainder of the book, its use is illustrated here.[2]

The Cash account of Global Realty Company (see Figure 2–5) is illustrated in Figure 2–8 in the debit-credit-balance ledger account.

Note that the preparer must know the type of balance (debit or credit) of each account. The Cash account, for instance, normally has a debit balance, as stated in the illustration. In this chapter and in a few illustrations in the next three chapters, the debit-credit status of the account balances will be indicated by a notation similar to that indicated in Figure 2–8.

[2]Another variation adds a fourth column so that the Balance column can be divided into debits and credits. The authors have intentionally avoided this form to encourage the readers to conceptualize the meaning of debit and credit.

Cash — Acct. No. 101

Date 1985		Explanation	F	Debit	Credit	Balance
Jul.	1		1	50000 00		50000 00
	5		1		30000 00	20000 00
	20		1		5000 00	15000 00
	29		1	1000 00		16000 00[a]

Balance is a debit.

[a]If an account contains a negative (opposite-from-normal) balance, it should be circled.

Figure 2–8 Three-Amount-Column Ledger Account

Recording Changes in Owner's Equity

The expansion of the accounting system beyond the simple illustration involving the six transactions creating the Global Realty Company requires that the transactions other than investment that change owner's equity be examined. These are: revenues, gains, expenses, losses, and withdrawal by proprietor.

Revenues

The term **revenue** describes the source of the inflows of assets; it involves a process that generates new assets in exchange for (1) services rendered, (2) sales of merchandise, (3) earnings from investments in stocks and bonds, and (4) advantageous settlement of liabilities at less than the amount of the debt.[3] Since revenue involves an earnings process, the term does not include increases in assets arising from owner's investments or from borrowed funds. For revenue to be earned, it does not have to be collected immediately in cash; it is sufficient that claims for cash on customers or clients exist. Although revenue items are first recorded in separate accounts, they ultimately increase the owner's capital account balance because this account reflects the total investment of the owner and the retention of the accumulation of all past net earnings (past revenues less expenses). The method of accounting for revenue is discussed later in the chapter.

A distinction must be made between revenues and assets. As learned in Chapter 1, *assets* are things of value (resources) held in a firm. *Revenues* represent one *source* of the inflow of assets. In other words, in the double entry process both the assets flowing in and the source (often revenues) of the assets must be accounted for.

[3]In its *Statement of Financial Accounting Concepts No. 3,* the Financial Accounting Standards Board (FASB) defined revenue as ". . . inflows or other enhancements of assets of an entity or settlement of its liabilities (or a combination of both) during a period from delivering or producing goods, rendering services, or other activities that constitute the entity's ongoing major or central operations."

Revenue accounts are created to accumulate the amounts earned during a specified period—usually one year; for teaching purposes, however, a shorter period of one month will often be used. The title of a revenue account should indicate the nature of the source of revenue; examples are Commissions Earned, Sales, Interest Earned, Dividends Earned, Accounting Fees Earned, and Shop Repair Revenue.

Since revenues ultimately act to increase the owner's capital account, the rules for increasing and decreasing owner's equity apply. Revenue accounts, therefore, are *credited when they are increased;* the particular asset that is increased is *debited.* Revenue accounts are debited to reflect decreases. The normal balance of a revenue account is therefore a credit balance. To illustrate the journalizing of revenue transactions, several companies that earned different kinds of revenue are considered. At the end of a period, these revenue accounts are closed out, and the excess of revenues over expenses is transferred to the owner's capital account. (This process is illustrated in the next chapter.)

First, suppose that on August 3, 1985, the Global Realty Company sells a house and lot and receives a commission of $500 in cash; this can be recorded in its journal as follows:

GENERAL JOURNAL Page 29

Date	Debit-Credit-Account Titles:Explanation	F	Debit	Credit
1985				
Aug. 3	Cash		500 00	
	Commissions Earned			500 00
	To record receipt of			
	commission earned on			
	sale of house and lot.			

Note that the account representing the cash received was increased, and the account representing the source of the cash—the revenue—was also increased. Next, assume that on July 30, 1985, Marjory Sanger, CPA, bills the Baker Company for $1,000 for an annual audit that she has made; her journal entry might look like this:

GENERAL JOURNAL Page 42

Date	Debit-Credit-Account Titles:Explanation	F	Debit	Credit
1985				
Jul. 30	Accounts Receivable		1000 00	
	Accounting Fees Earned			1000 00
	To record billing			
	of following client for audit:			
	Baker Company $1,000.00			

The recording of revenue in the period that it is earned prior to its being collected is adhering to a concept referred to as the accrual basis of accounting (discussed more fully in Chapter 4).

Gains

Gains are similar to revenues in that they represent an inflow of assets from incidental transactions of an entity, and they have the same debit and credit rules as revenues for increasing and decreasing their accounts.[4] The most common source of gains is the sale or trade-in of assets other than merchandise inventory. As a usual rule, the gain element is only the excess of the selling price over the cost of the item sold or exchanged. In the introductory chapters of this book, gains are *not* emphasized; only revenues are considered.

Expenses

The next cause of change in owner's equity is **expenses,** the expired cost of the *assets consumed* and *services received* during a specified period and used in the production of revenue during that same period. Expense accounts are created to accumulate the amounts incurred during a specific period. The title of the account should indicate the cause of the expense. Since expenses ultimately act to decrease the owner's capital account, the rules for increases and decreases to owner's equity apply. Therefore, an expense account is debited when it is increased because it ultimately will decrease owner's equity. It is credited when it is decreased; the normal balance is a debit. When an expense is recorded by a debit, the offsetting credit is to Cash, to a liability account, or to some other asset account. The recording process for expenses is illustrated by the following five transactions, which took place at Global Realty Company:

1985		
Aug.	2	Paid $900 in rent for the month of August.
	10	Purchased an advertisement in the local newspaper for $75 in cash.
	15	Paid semimonthly salaries of $2,000.
	20	Had some office equipment repaired by Able Company at a cost of $45 to be paid in September.
	31	Determined that $185 of office supplies had been consumed in August. The amount of the office supplies originally purchased was debited to an asset account, Office Supplies.[6]

[4]The FASB, in its *Statement of Financial Accounting Concepts No. 3,* "Elements of Financial Statements of Business Enterprises," defines gains as ". . . increases in equity (net assets) from peripheral or incidental transactions of an entity and from all other transactions and other events and circumstances affecting the entity during a period except those that result from revenues or investments by owners."

[5]In its *Statement of Financial Accounting Concepts No. 3,* the FASB defined expenses as ". . . outflows or other using up of assets or incurrences of liabilities (or a combination of both) during a period from delivering or producing goods, rendering services, or carrying out other activities that constitute the entity's ongoing major or central operations."

[6]This transaction is illustrated at this point to demonstrate that expenses consist of assets consumed as well as cost of services received. It is normally treated as an end-of-period adjusting entry, discussed in Chapter 4.

These transactions are recorded in the general journal as follows:

GENERAL JOURNAL

Page 29

Date 1985		Debit-Credit-Account Titles:Explanation	F	Debit	Credit
Aug.	2	Rent Expense[a]		900 00	
		Cash			900 00
		To record payment of rent for month of August 1985			
	10	Advertising Expense		75 00	
		Cash			75 00
		To record payment for advertising.			
	15	Salaries Expense[b]		2000 00	
		Cash			2000 00
		To record payment of semimonthly salaries.			
	20	Repairs Expense - Office Equipment		45 00	
		Accounts Payable			45 00
		To record repairs to office equipment on account from: Able Company $45.00			
	31	Office Supplies Expense		185 00	
		Office Supplies			185 00
		To record consumption of office supplies for month.			

[a]For a more complete explanation of why expenses are recorded as debits, see Figure 2–10.

[b]As discussed in Chapter 8, both state and federal income taxes and social security taxes will have to be withheld from salaries paid to employees; thus, pending payment of those items to the appropriate governmental units, liability accounts would be credited. In the interest of simplicity and teachability, these are ignored at this time.

In the foregoing journal entries recording expenses, note that the first three involve immediate payments for expenses where credits to Cash are made. The fourth one involves the creation of an accounts payable liability. The fifth records the use of supplies during a period: in this case, the credit is to the asset account, Office Supplies. Note that for each expense account the normal balance is a debit balance.

Losses

Losses are similar to expenses in that they represent an expiration of costs—the using up of assets. They differ from expenses, however, since losses do not usually help to produce revenues.[7] Neither gains nor losses are emphasized in the introductory chapters of this book. Revenues and expenses are the primary components involved in measuring the results from operations.

Before the remaining cause of change in owner's equity (withdrawals by the owner) is discussed, the relationship of revenues to expenses in the determination of net income or net earnings—the measuring of the results of operations for a period of time—is considered. Broadly speaking, the excess of revenues over expenses is called *net income;* it is defined more specifically later.

Operational Terms

To determine the results of operations, it is important to understand the meaning of certain operational terms.

Cost and expense

Cost, *the amount to purchase an asset, becomes an* expense *when the purchased item is no longer an asset; that is, when it can no longer produce future revenue.*

It is necessary to distinguish between an expense and a cost. A *cost* is the amount paid or payable in either cash or the equivalent for goods, services, or other assets purchased. Thus a cost of a resource that benefits the future is recorded as an asset. When a cost no longer has asset status—that is, when its potential to produce future revenue is lost—it is said to be expired and thus to have become typically an *expense.* From this statement the following conclusions are warranted:

Expenses = Expired costs (used up in *producing* this period's revenue).
Assets = Unexpired costs (to be used to produce future revenue).

For example, rent paid in advance for three months is an asset, prepaid rent. As time passes, this becomes rent expense.

A **disbursement** is a payment in cash or by check. Hence, a machine may be acquired at a cost of $10,000; the transaction is completed by a disbursement in the form of a check for $10,000. As the machine is used in operations, it loses part of its service value, or depreciates. The original purchase is not an expense. However, the expiration of service potential is a depreciation expense. The required adjusting process to record these changes is discussed in detail in Chapter 4.

---

[7]The FASB, in its *Statement of Financial Accounting Concepts No. 3,* "Elements of Financial Statements of Business Enterprises," defines losses as ". . . decreases in equity (net assets) from peripheral or incidental transactions of an entity and from all other transactions and other events and circumstances affecting the entity during a period except those that result from expenses or distributions to owners."

Operating Results

Most businesses cannot keep the detailed records necessary to indicate the expense of each service rendered and therefore cannot determine the net income or net loss from each transaction. Even when it is possible, the clerical costs involved in getting the information would not justify the end result. For example, a lawyer bills his client $1,000 for services performed. How much did it cost the lawyer to perform the service and how much net income did he make on this one transaction? The lawyer might total the number of hours he devoted to the case and arrive at an expense in terms of time spent. But how about the rent for his office? The secretary's salary? The telephone bill? The electricity bill? Since the determination of the exact expense involved in rendering service for a particular client would require a considerable amount of record keeping, accounting has evolved another and easier method for accomplishing an acceptable result. Attempts are seldom made to determine the cost of each service; instead, records of revenue and expense are kept for a period, perhaps a year or a shorter period of time.

Matching concept

At the end of the period, the period's expenses are* matched *against the period's revenue to determine the net income or net loss for that period. This information is contained in a financial statement called an* income statement, *discussed and illustrated later in Chapter 3.

In measuring the results of operations for a period of time, the accountant compares revenues and expenses to determine operating results. Depending upon whether the expenses or the revenues are greater, a business may have a net income or a net loss for the period. **Net income** (also called comprehensive income,[8] net earnings, or profit) for any period is measured by deducting total expenses from total revenues for that period.[9] It shows the change in owner's equity resulting from business operations. The operations information shown on the income statement that results in an increase in owner's equity may be generally expressed in equation form as

$$\text{Total revenues} - \text{Total expenses} = \text{Net income.}$$

If revenues exceed expenses, the right-hand figure is *net income.* If the total expenses for a period exceed the revenues for that period, however, a **net loss** results, and the owner's equity is decreased. The equation now becomes

$$\text{Total expenses} - \text{Total revenues} = \text{Net loss.}$$

Net loss

The term* net loss *should not be confused with the term* losses. *Net loss is equivalent to a negative net income; whereas losses are gross expirations of costs that do not make a contribution to the production of revenue.

---

[8]The FASB in *Statement of Financial Accounting Concepts No. 3* defines comprehensive income as ". . . the change in equity (net assets) of an entity during a period from transactions and other events and circumstances from non-owner sources. It includes all changes in equity during a period except those resulting from investments by owners and distributions to owners."

[9]Even though gains and losses are ignored initially, it should be understood that net income = (total revenues + total gains) − (total expenses + total losses).

Withdrawals by Proprietor

The third cause of change in owner's equity is withdrawals by the owner. Although there are no restrictions on withdrawals by a proprietor in a single proprietorship, most withdrawals are made in anticipation that net income has been or will be earned. For a single proprietorship, this kind of withdrawal is debited to a special proprietor's or owner's drawing account. The reasons for this accounting are: (1) the earnings of a single proprietorship belong to the owner, (2) it is beneficial for the owner to have a record of periodic withdrawals, and (3) there are no legal restrictions on the withdrawal of earnings by a proprietor. Therefore, the owner of a single proprietorship may withdraw cash or any other asset in expectation of income. Suppose, for example, Lucy Genova, owner of Global Realty Company, withdrew cash of $500 on September 2, 1985. This transaction would be recorded in the general journal of the company as follows:

GENERAL JOURNAL

Page 30

Date	Debit-Credit-Account Titles:Explanation	F	Debit	Credit
1985				
Sep. 2	Lucy Genova, Drawing		500 00	
	Cash			500 00
	To record withdrawal by			
	owner in expectation of income.			

The amount of the owner's drawing decreases owner's equity and is shown on the statement of owner's equity (illustrated later in Chapter 3). Unlike expenses, however, withdrawals by owners do not affect the calculation of net income. For this reason, they are not included in the income statement.

Expanding Rules for Debits and Credits

Since new types of accounts have been introduced, the rules for debiting and crediting accounts can now be expanded and restated as follows:

Debit to record:

1. An increase of an asset account
2. An increase of an expense account
3. An increase of owner's drawing account
4. A decrease of a liability account
5. A decrease in an owner's equity account
6. A decrease in a revenue account

Credit to record:

1. A decrease of an asset account
2. A decrease of an expense account
3. A decrease of owner's drawing account
4. An increase of a liability account
5. An increase in an owner's equity account
6. An increase in a revenue account

The relationship of the rules of debits and credits to the accounting equation is diagramed in T account form in Figure 2–9.

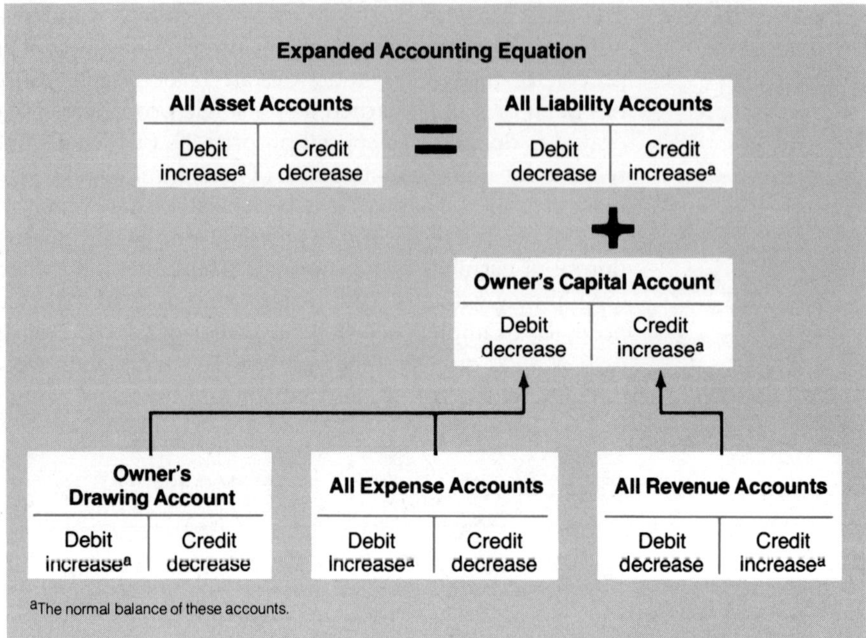

Figure 2–9 Expanded Accounting Equation

Although the debit-credit processing rules for expenses and the owner's drawing are the same, it should be emphasized again that the owner's drawing account is not an expense account. *The payment made to the owner in the form of a withdrawal does not produce revenue.* Another important basic accounting concept shown in Figure 2–9 is the normal balance of the accounts. Note that asset, owner's drawing, and expense accounts normally have a debit balance; whereas liability, owner's capital, and revenue accounts normally have a credit balance.

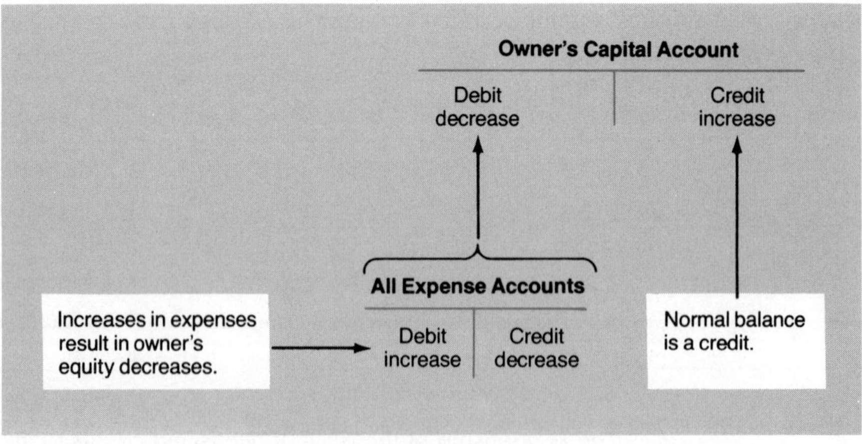

Figure 2–10 Relationship of Expenses to Capital

It is evident from the expanded accounting equation that a *decrease* in owner's equity results in a debit entry. Note that when the decrease in owner's equity is temporarily entered in an expense account, the expense account is *increased* (debited). All expense accounts are designed to *accumulate* expired costs, which are later transferred as reductions to the owner's capital account. The specific relationship between the expense accounts and the owner's capital account is further illustrated in Figure 2–10.

It naturally follows that withdrawals by the proprietor reduce owner's equity. As they occur (increase), they are also recorded as debits.

The General Ledger and Subsidiary Ledgers

Asset, liability, owner's capital, revenue, expense, and owner's drawing accounts have now been introduced. These accounts that are incorporated in the regular end-of-period financial statements are kept in a separate book or collection, called the **general ledger.** Other ledgers that are supplementary, subordinate, or supporting to the general ledger are referred to as **subsidiary ledgers.** The general ledger may actually be a loose-leaf binder, a bound book, cards in open trays, punched cards, or one of several types of computer data storage devices. General ledger accounts are usually arranged in the sequence in which they will appear in the financial statements—that is, assets, liabilities, owner's equity, revenues, and expenses.

Accounts Receivable Subsidiary Ledger

Many businesses have a large number of customers, and detailed information must be kept of transactions with each one. A separate account thus is required for each. If the general ledger were to include each customer's account, it would become too large and unwieldy. Consequently, a summary account, Accounts Receivable, is maintained in the general ledger showing the combined increases and decreases in the amounts due from all customers. The individual customer accounts are kept in a separate, or subsidiary, ledger called the **accounts receivable subsidiary ledger.** The Accounts Receivable account in the general ledger, referred to as a controlling account, summarizes those individual customers' accounts that are assigned to the subsidiary ledger. After all transactions for the period have been entered, the balance of the Accounts Receivable account in the general ledger should be equal to the sum of the individual account balances in the subsidiary ledger.

Accounts Payable Subsidiary Ledger

Many businesses have a large number of individual creditors. Consequently, individual creditors' accounts are kept in a subsidiary ledger called the **accounts payable subsidiary ledger;** Accounts Payable, another controlling or summary account, is kept in the general ledger showing total increases and decreases in amounts due to creditors. After all transactions for the period have been entered, the balance of the Accounts Payable account in the general ledger should be equal to the sum of the individual account balances in the subsidiary ledger.

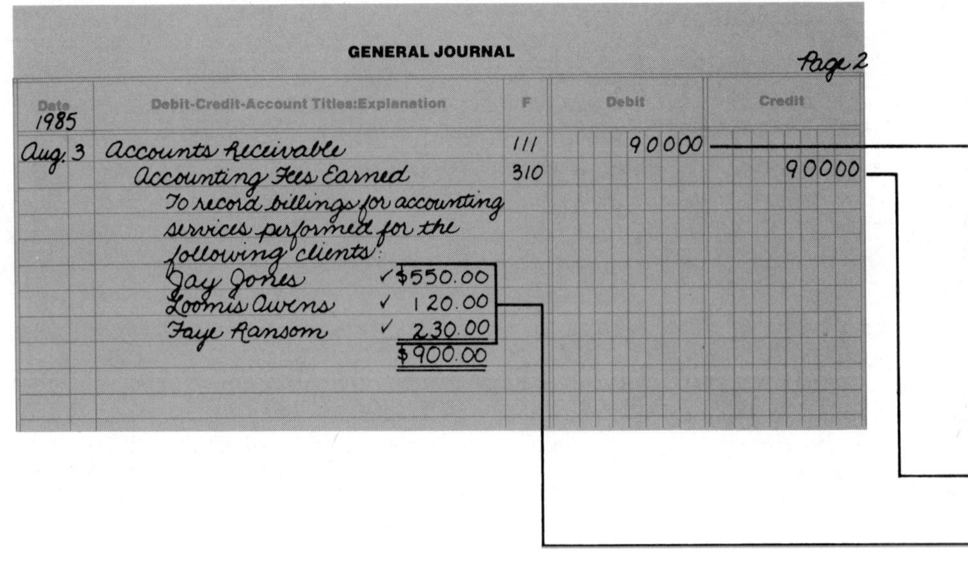

Figure 2–11
Posting to Control and Subsidiary Accounts

Controlling Accounts

As mentioned above, the Accounts Receivable and Accounts Payable accounts appearing in the general ledger are referred to as **controlling accounts.** They contain summary totals of many transactions, the details of which appear in subsidiary ledgers. The accounts receivable subsidiary ledger is sometimes referred to as the **customers ledger;** the accounts payable subsidiary ledger, as the **creditors ledger.**

Controlling account

***A controlling account** is any account in the general ledger that controls or is supported by a number of other accounts in a separate ledger.*

Other controlling accounts and their appropriate subsidiary ledgers may be established when subcategories exist in enough quantities to make it more efficient to assign these accounts to a separate ledger—for example, in the case of inventory or property, plant, and equipment items.

Posting to the General Ledger and Subsidiary Ledgers

To illustrate the method of posting from the general journal to the general and subsidiary ledgers, the following transaction is considered. On August 3, 1985, Ace Small Business Services billed the following clients for professional accounting services performed:

Jay Jones	$550
Loomis Owens	120
Faye Ransom	230

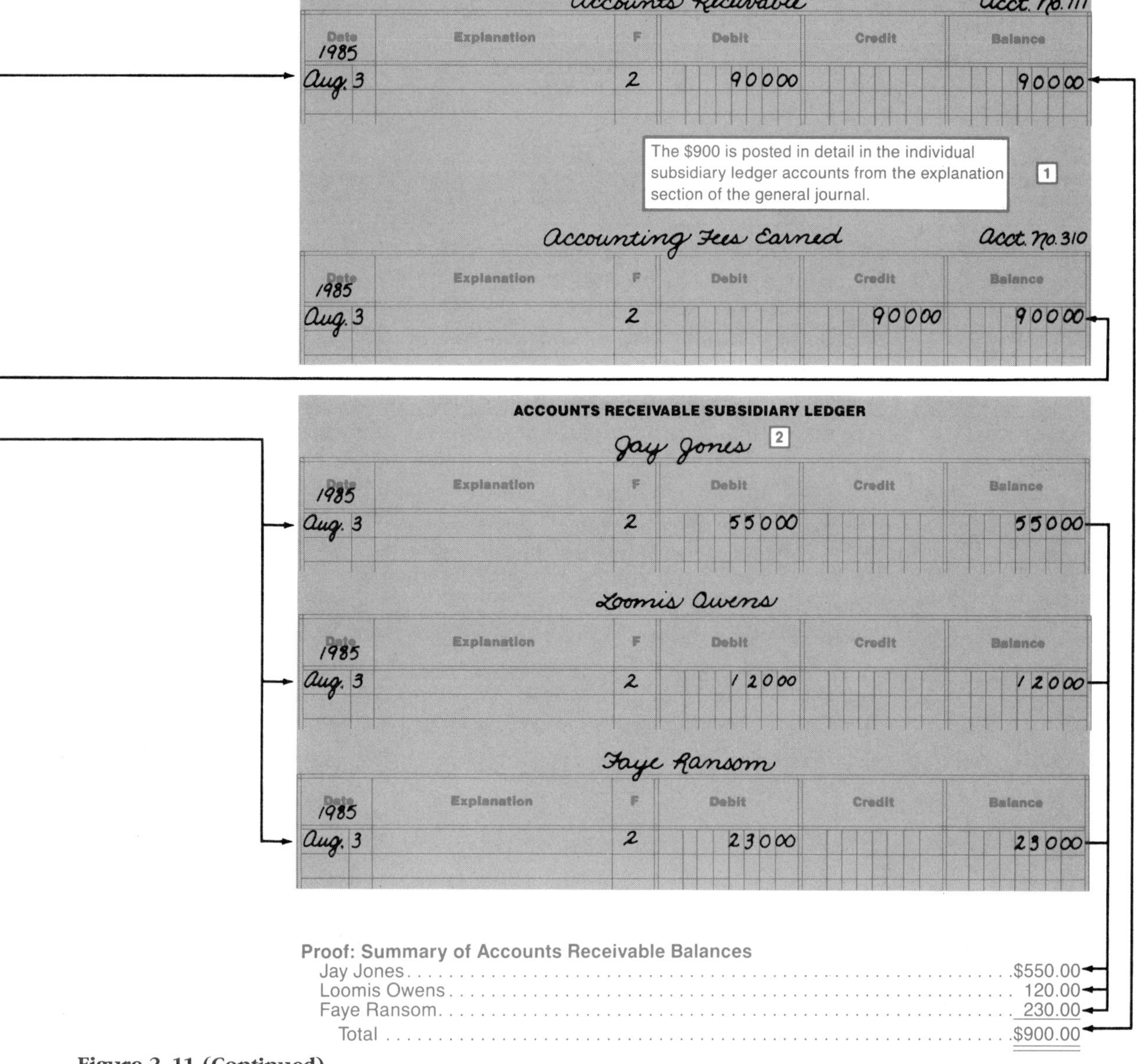

Figure 2–11 (Continued)

This information is recorded and posted as indicated in Figure 2–11.

An explanation of the figures in Figure 2–11 follows:

[1] Figure 2–11 shows the total posting of the $900 debit to the Accounts Receivable account in the general ledger and detailed posting to the subsidiary ledger accounts. Each customer is debited for the amount shown in the ex-

planation of the general journal entry; the balance is extended to the Balance column; the journal page number is entered in the folio (F) column; and the date is entered. After each posting has been completed, a check mark (√) is entered to the left of each amount in the Explanation column of the general journal to indicate that the amount has been posted to the proper subsidiary ledger account. A check mark is used rather than a page number because subsidiary accounts in the illustration may not be numbered but may be kept in alphabetical order.

2 The three-amount-column form of ledger account is also used for the accounts receivable subsidiary ledger. This form is used in subsidiary ledgers for two reasons: (1) the balances have to be referred to quite often, and (2) the form is adaptable to machine accounting, which is frequently employed for subsidiary ledger accounting.

Obviously, a business such as a department store that makes hundreds of credit sales daily does not list each one in the journal entry explanation; instead, postings to the subsidiary ledger accounts are made from the copies of the sales tickets. The principle, however, is the same as illustrated in Figure 2–11.

At first it may seem that this dual accounting for accounts receivable would result in double debits that would be incorrectly reflected in the trial balance. Note carefully, however, that only one debit goes into the Accounts Receivable controlling account for later use in the trial balance. The amounts entered in the accounts receivable subsidiary ledger will *not* go in the trial balance, but the total of the uncollected balances at the end of a period will be compared with the single balance of the Accounts Receivable controlling account as a check on the accuracy of both the accounts receivable subsidiary ledger and the Accounts Receivable controlling account in the general ledger. Entries to the Accounts Payable controlling account and the accounts payable subsidiary ledger are handled similarly.

The Accounting Sequence Illustrated

In the remaining part of this chapter and in Chapter 3, the accounting sequence is expanded into nine steps and is illustrated through the example of the Good Times Wheels Repair Shop, one of the newly formed proprietorship enterprises organized and owned by Lucy Genova. At the very outset, note that even though Lucy Genova owns several business enterprises, a separate set of books is maintained for the motorcycle repair shop because the owner will need to know specific information about the repair shop to make sound decisions about operating it. These steps are: (1) selecting a chart of accounts, (2) analyzing and journalizing the transactions, (3) posting to the general and subsidiary ledgers, (4) preparing a trial balance, (5) preparing a schedule of accounts receivable, (6) preparing a schedule of accounts payable, (7) preparing the financial statements, (8) closing the revenue, expense, and owner's drawing accounts, and (9) taking a postclosing trial balance. An explanation of each step in the sequence is presented along with the accounting procedure for that step.

Selecting a Chart of Accounts

The first step in establishing an efficient accounting system that will satisfy the needs of management, government agencies, and other interested groups is the construction of a **chart of accounts.**

Chart of accounts

A separate account should be set up for each item that appears in the financial statements to make the statements easier to prepare. The* chart of accounts *is the complete listing of account titles to be used by the entity.

The classification and the order of the items in the chart of accounts correspond to those in the statements. A chart of accounts for the Good Times Wheels Repair Shop is shown in Figure 2–12.

Account titles should be carefully selected to suit the needs of the business and should indicate clearly and precisely the nature of the accounts to ensure

GOOD TIMES WHEELS REPAIR SHOP
Chart of Accounts

Asset Accounts (100–199)

Current Assets (100 –150)
- 101 Cash
- 121 Accounts Receivable
- 131 Motorcycle Parts and Supplies
- 141 Prepaid Insurance

Property, Plant, and Equipment (151 –199)
- 151 Land
- 161 Automotive Tools and Equipment.

Liability and Owner's Equity Accounts (200–399)

Current Liabilities (200 – 250)
- 201 Accounts Payable
- 202 Notes Payable

Long-Term Liabilities (251 – 299)

Owner's Equity (300 – 399)
- 301 Lucy Genova, Capital
- 311 Lucy Genova, Drawing

Income Statement Accounts (400–599)

Revenue (400 – 499)
- 401 Motorcycle Repair Revenue

Expenses (500 – 599)
- 501 Rent Expense—Shop Building
- 502 Rent Expense—Automotive Tools and Equipment
- 504 Salaries Expense
- 508 Electricity and Water Expense
- 509 Motorcycle Parts and Supplies Expense

Clearing and Summary Accounts (600–699)[a]
- 601 Income Summary

[a]The use of the Income Summary account is explained in Chapter 3.

Figure 2–12 Chart of Accounts—Good Times Wheels Repair Shop

proper recording of transactions. However, titles are not standardized; for example, one business may use Unexpired Insurance and another Prepaid Insurance to describe the same asset.

In Figure 2–12, a three-digit system is used to number the accounts. A larger business with a number of departments or branches may use four or more digits. Notice that in this illustration accounts 100–199 represent assets; accounts 200–399 represent liabilities and owner's equity; and accounts 400–599 represent *income statement* accounts (revenue and expense accounts that are incorporated in the income statement). The more detailed breakdown for current assets, property, plant, and equipment, and current liabilities, for example, can be seen in the chart. The gaps between the assigned account numbers allow for addition of accounts as they are needed by the business.

Analyzing and Journalizing Transactions

The transactions of the Good Times Wheels Repair Shop that occurred during January 1985 are given below. Before making entries in the journal, the accountant must analyze each transaction in terms of increases and decreases in the expanded accounting equation and must apply the basic system of debits and credits that has already been outlined. For the first four transactions listed, the analytical thinking that must precede journalizing is described. These analyses may be studied as a guide to future action.

1985

Jan. 3 Lucy Genova opened a bank account under the name of her new business, Good Times Wheels Repair Shop. She deposited $30,000 in cash to start the new business. An asset, cash, is received by the Good Times Wheels Repair Shop. To record an increase of an asset, it must be debited; therefore, the Cash account is debited for $30,000. The increase in the owner's equity account, Lucy Genova, Capital, is shown by a credit to that account.

4 Rented a temporary shop and paid $300 for the January rent; issued check no. 1. Since all the rent will have expired by the time the financial statements are prepared, it is considered an expense of the month of January. An increase of an expense account is recorded by a debit; therefore, the Rent Expense—Shop Building account is debited. The decrease of the asset, cash, is recorded by a credit to Cash. A single rent account may be sufficient for all rented buildings and equipment. In this case, the accountant felt that managerial analyses required a separate rent expense account for the shop building.

5 Rented automotive tools and equipment until the firm could purchase its own. Rent in the amount of $80 was paid for January; issued check no. 2. As in the preceding transaction, all this rent will have expired before the financial statements are prepared; therefore, it is considered an expense of January. An increase of an expense account is recorded by a debit—in this case to Rent Expense—Automotive Tools and Equipment. The decrease of the asset, cash, is recorded by a credit to Cash. Again, a single rent expense account may have been sufficient.

5 Purchased motorcycle parts and supplies described on invoice no. 306 from the Southern Supply Company for $400 on account. The Motorcycle Parts and Supplies account is an asset and is increased by the transaction; the increase in the asset is shown by a debit to Motorcycle Parts and Supplies. Since the purchase was on credit, a liability is created. To record the increase in the liability, the Accounts Payable account is credited. The amount

payable to the particular creditor, the Southern Supply Company, must be shown in the books. A note should be made in the Explanation column of the journal to the effect that the creditor is the Southern Supply Company, so that the amount can be posted to the accounts payable subsidiary ledger.

10 Purchased land as a prospective building site for $10,000. Paid $4,000 in cash (check no. 3) and issued a one-year note payable for the balance.

12 Made repairs on George Shipman's motorcycle for $40. Shipman asked that a charge account be opened in his name; he promises to settle the account within 30 days. This arrangement was authorized by the service manager.

26 Made repairs on Jay Munson's motorcycle for $180. A charge account was opened in his name.

29 Purchased motorcycle parts and supplies from the Delco Supply House for $250 on account (invoice no. 1004).

29 Paid the Southern Supply Company $300 on account (check no. 4).

31 Paid electricity and water bills of $80 for January (check no. 5).

31 Made motorcycle repairs for various cash customers for $4,800.

31 Paid $1,700 in salaries for the month (check no. 6 issued to obtain payroll cash).

31 Lucy Genova withdrew $300 in cash in anticipation that at least that much income had been earned (check no. 7).

31 Purchased automotive tools and equipment for cash, $4,000 (check no. 8). The list price was $5,000.

31 Paid a premium of $600 (check no. 9) on a 12-month comprehensive insurance policy; the policy becomes effective on February 1, 1985.

31 Received a check for $10 from George Shipman as part payment of his account.

31 Took a physical inventory of motorcycle parts and supplies; it showed that parts and supplies costing $375 were on hand, thus indicating that $275 (January 5 purchase of $400, plus January 29 purchase of $250, minus inventory of $375) worth of motorcycle parts and supplies had been used, becoming an expense. Originally, as motorcycle parts and supplies were purchased, they were debited to an asset account. Now, as the amount used becomes known, an entry is made debiting an expense account, Motorcycle Parts and Supplies Expense, to show that the expense account has been increased, and crediting an asset account, Motorcycle Parts and Supplies, to show that the asset account has been decreased. (This type of apportionment transaction is normally recorded in an adjusting entry, explained in Chapter 4. It is presented here to broaden the scope of this illustration.)

The results of this analytical reasoning are presented in Figure 2–13. Note that space is left between entries to ensure that they are separate and distinct.

Figure 2–13 General Journal Entries for January

GENERAL JOURNAL

Page 1

Date	Debit-Credit-Account Titles:Explanation	F	Debit	Credit
1985				
Jan. 3	Cash		30000 00	
	Lucy Genova, Capital			30000 00
	To record investment by			
	proprietor to start a business			
	to be called Good Times			
	Wheels Repair Shop.			

Page 1 (continued)

Date	Debit-Credit-Account Titles:Explanation	F	Debit	Credit
4	Rent Expense—Shop Building		300 00	
	Cash			300 00
	To record payment of rent on shop building for month of January 1985; issued check no. 1.			
5	Rent Expense—Automotive Tools and Equipment		80 00	
	Cash			80 00
	To record payment of rent for automotive tools and equipment for month of January 1985; issued check no. 2.			
5	Motorcycle Parts and Supplies		400 00	
	Accounts Payable			400 00
	To record purchase of parts and supplies on account on invoice no. 306: Southern Supply Company $400.00			
10	Land		10000 00	
	Cash			4000 00
	Notes Payable			6000 00
	To record purchase of land; issued check no. 3 and gave a one-year note for the balance.			
12	Accounts Receivable		40 00	
	Motorcycle Repair Revenue			40 00
	To record billings for repairs rendered to: George Shipman $40.00			

GENERAL JOURNAL

Page 2

Date	Debit-Credit-Account Titles:Explanation	F	Debit	Credit
1985				
Jan. 26	Accounts Receivable		180 00	
	Motorcycle Repair Revenue			180 00
	To record billings for repairs rendered to: Jay Munson $180.00			

Figure 2–13 (Continued)

GENERAL JOURNAL

Page 2 (continued)

Date	Debit-Credit-Account Titles:Explanation	F	Debit	Credit
29	Motorcycle Parts and Supplies		25000	
	Accounts Payable			25000
	To record purchase of parts and supplies on account on invoice no. 1004: Delco Supply House $250.00			
29	Accounts Payable		30000	
	Cash			30000
	To record payment; issued check no. 4 to: Southern Supply Company $300.00			
31	Electricity and Water Expense		8000	
	Cash			8000
	To record payment of electricity and water bills for month of January; issued check no. 5.			
31	Cash		480000	
	Motorcycle Repair Revenue			480000
	To record the rendering of repair services to cash customers.			
31	Salaries Expense		170000	
	Cash[a]			170000
	To record payment of salaries for January; issued check no. 6 to obtain payroll cash.			
31	Lucy Genova, Drawing		30000	
	Cash			30000
	To record withdrawal by owner in anticipation of income earned; issued check no. 7.			

[a]As indicated previously, the company would have to withhold certain payroll taxes (discussed in Chapter 8).

Figure 2–13 (Continued)

GENERAL JOURNAL

Page 3

Date		Debit-Credit-Account Titles:Explanation	F	Debit	Credit
1985					
Jan.	31	Automotive Tools and Equipment		4 000 00	
		Cash			4 000 00
		To record purchase of tools			
		and equipment at a cost of			
		$4,000.00 (list price, $5,000.00);			
		issued check no. 8.			
	31	Prepaid Insurance		600 00	
		Cash			600 00
		To record payment of insurance			
		premium for 12 months;			
		insurance is effective February 1,			
		1985; issued check no. 9.			
	31	Cash		10 00	
		Accounts Receivable			10 00
		To record collection to			
		apply on account of			
		George Shipman $10.00			
	31	Motorcycle Parts and Supplies Expense		275 00	
		Motorcycle Parts and Supplies			275 00
		To record cost of parts and supplies			
		used during month of January.			

Figure 2–13 (Continued)

Glossary

Account form of balance sheet A form of the balance sheet that shows the assets on the left side of the statement and the liabilities and owner's equity on the right side.

Accounts payable subsidiary ledger The group of individual creditors' accounts in a separate ledger that are controlled by the general ledger account Accounts Payable.

Accounts receivable subsidiary ledger The group of individual customers' accounts in a separate ledger that are controlled by the general ledger account Accounts Receivable.

Chart of accounts A list of all accounts in the general ledger which the entity anticipates using. Their numbering system indicates the types of accounts by subgroups.

Compound entry A journal entry with more than one debit or credit.

Controlling account One account in the general ledger that controls and is supported by a group of accounts in a separate subsidiary ledger.

Cost The amount paid or payable in either cash or its equivalent for goods, services, or other assets purchased.

Creditors ledger See *Accounts payable subsidiary ledger.*

Customers ledger See *Accounts receivable subsidiary ledger.*

Disbursement An actual payment by cash or check.

Double-entry accounting A system of recording both the debit and credit aspect of each transaction.

Expense Expired cost; the material used and service utilized in the production of revenue during a specific period.

Gain Increase in net assets from incidental transactions of an entity, except those that result from revenues or investment by owners.

General journal The accounting record in which a transaction is first recorded. It is called a book of original entry.

General ledger The main group of ledger accounts that are incorporated in the trial balance. It does not include the separate accounts that are in the subsidiary ledgers.

Income statement The statement for a period showing revenues and expenses for that period with the determination of net income.

Journalizing The process of recording a transaction, analyzed in terms of its debits and credits, in a record of original entry referred to as a journal.

Loss Expired cost; the materials used and services utilized that did not produce any revenue and that results from incidental transactions of an entity.

Matching concept The matching of incurred expenses and earned revenue for a given time period in order to determine net income for that period.

Net income Excess of revenue over expenses for a given period.

Net loss Excess of expenses over revenue for a given period.

Posting The process of transferring an amount recorded in the journal to the indicated account in the ledger.

Report form of balance sheet A form of the balance sheet that shows the assets at the top of the statement with the liabilities and owner's equity appearing immediately below the assets.

Revenue A term describing the source of inflows of assets received in exchange for services rendered, sales of products or merchandise, earnings from interest and dividends on investments, and advantageous settlement of liabilities at less than the amount of the debt.

Subsidiary ledger A group of accounts in a separate ledger that provides information in detail about one controlling account in the general ledger.

Questions

Q2–1 Student A argued that the journal is useless since all the data are repeated in the ledger. Student B disagreed and said that the journal was the most important document. With whom do you agree? Discuss.

Q2–2 Define *revenue.* Does the receipt of cash by a business indicate that revenue has been earned? Explain.

Q2–3 The sales of all assets are not revenue. Give examples of a type of sale that is revenue and a type that is not revenue. Discuss the reasons why in each case.

Q2–4 Define *expense.* Does the payment of cash by a business indicate that an expense has been incurred? Explain. Distinguish between a cost, an expense, and a disbursement.

Q2–5 What are the benefits of using subsidiary ledgers?

Q2–6 Define the *matching concept.* Why is it important in income determination?

Q2–7 State the rules of debits and credits for revenues and expenses.

Q2–8 What is the normal balance of each of the following accounts (debit or credit): (a) Cash, (b) Rent Expense, (c) Accounts Payable, (d) Owner's Capital, (e) Service Revenue, (f) Owner's Drawing, (g) Accounts Receivable?

Q2–9 Would it be possible to have a set of books in balance if the rules for debits and credits were reversed? Is there any reason for the specific rules now in existence as compared to rules of a direct reverse nature?

Q2–10 Define *owner's drawing.* Is drawing an expense? Explain.

Q2–11 Is the excess of cash received by a business over the cash paid out net income? Discuss.

Q2–12 When an account is debited, does the balance of the account always increase? Explain.

Q2–13 Would the sale of a cash register by a clothing dry cleaner usually be recorded as follows?

Cash	XX	
Dry Cleaning Revenue		XX

Explain.

Q2–14 What is a ledger account? Indicate two forms of the account. State the reasons and circumstances for using each form.

Exercises

E2–1

Use of three-amount-column account

The Cash account of the Zoom Corporation for a one-week period showed the following entries:

Cash — Acct. No. 101

Date		Explanation	F	Debit	Date		Explanation	F	Credit
1985					1985				
Dec.	2	Balance	√	85,400	Dec.	3		49	9,000
	4		50	40,000		5		51	38,000
	5		55	20,400		6		55	27,000
	9		60	36,200		10		61	10,450

Using a three-amount-column account, recast the foregoing transactions in that account.

E2–2

Effect of transactions on elements of accounting equation

Some of the possible effects of a transaction are listed:

1. An asset increase accompanied by an asset decrease.
2. An asset increase accompanied by an owner's equity increase.
3. An asset increase accompanied by a liability increase.
4. An asset increase accompanied by a revenue increase.
5. An asset decrease accompanied by a liability decrease.
6. An asset decrease accompanied by an owner's equity decrease.
7. An asset decrease accompanied by an expense increase.
8. An expense increase accompanied by a liability increase.

Using the identifying numbers to the left of the listed combinations, indicate the effect of each of the following transactions.

Example: Invested cash in the business. *Answer:* (2)

(a) Collected a commission on the sale of real estate not previously billed.
(b) Paid an account payable.
(c) Borrowed money from a bank and issued a note.
(d) Collected an account receivable.
(e) Performed a service and received payment in cash.
(f) Paid for an ad in a newspaper.

E2–3
Effect of errors on trial balance

A new accountant began work on January 2, 1985. Unfortunately, he made several errors that were discovered by the auditor (the outside independent accountant who is hired to review the company's books) during the year-end review. For each error described below, indicate the effect of the error (by filling out a solution form like that illustrated below). Treat each error separately; do not attempt to relate the errors to one another.

Suggested Solution Form:

Error	Would the December 31, 1985, trial balance be out of balance?		If yes, by how much?	Which would be larger?	
	Yes	No		Debit total	Credit total
a b etc.					

Errors:

a. A cash register was purchased for $2,200 and cash was paid and credited. The debit was entered twice in the asset account.
b. A debit to the Cash account of $3,121 was posted as $3,211.
c. Cash collections of $4,475 from customers in settlement of their accounts were not posted to the Accounts Receivable account but were posted correctly to the Cash account and to accounts in the accounts receivable subsidiary ledger.
d. A purchase of office supplies of $450 was recorded as a credit to Cash and also as a credit to Office Supplies.

E2–4
Journalizing and posting transactions

The following transactions were engaged in by Foister's Framing Service owned by James Foister during June 1985:

1985		
Jun.	3	James Foister invested $60,000 in cash to create Foister's Framing Service.
	6	Purchased land and building for $20,000 in cash and a 20-year mortgage payable for $50,000. The land was appraised at $9,000 and the building at $61,000.
	7	Purchased framing supplies from Kleb Company for $4,000 on account.
	30	Sold one-third of the lot purchased on June 6 for $3,000. The buyer, Gulf Sands Company, paid $1,200 in cash and issued a 90-day note for $1,800.

1. Journalize the transactions. (Assign numbers to journal pages.)

2. Post to T form of formal ledger accounts. (Assign appropriate numbers to accounts.)

E2–5
Journalizing cash transactions

The following cash receipts and cash payment transactions involving different companies occurred during a period:

a. A realty company received a commission of $5,000 on the sale of land for a client. This commission had not previously been recorded.
b. A corporation received semiannual interest of $70,500 on its temporary investments.
c. Landard Corporation received monthly rentals of $50,000; the entire amount was for property rented during the current month.
d. A company paid salaries for the month of $10,200.
e. A company purchased an advertisement in the local newspaper for $250.

Record the foregoing transactions in a general journal using a–e instead of dates.

E2–6 *Recording revenue transactions*

The following cash receipt transactions occurred at the Delores Realty Company during the month of August 1985:

1985		
Aug.	1	Jane Delores, the owner, invested additional cash of $60,000 in the business.
	7	Received a commission of $4,500 from the sale of a house and lot.
	8	Received $8,100 in cash from the issuance of a note payable to a bank.
	31	Received $400 in interest from U.S. government bonds.
	31	Received $600 in cash for August rent of part of the company's building.

Journalize the *revenue* transactions only. State why the others are not revenue items.

E2–7 *Recording expense transactions*

The following were among the cash payment transactions at the Houston Garage during the month of May 1985:

1985		
May	3	Paid $12,000 for a truck.
	7	Paid $4,000 in salaries for the month.
	9	Paid $9,300 in settlement of an open account.
	12	Paid $700 for a typewriter.
	16	Withdrew $3,600 in cash in anticipation of profits.
	22	Paid $580 for rent of the office for May.

Journalize the *expense* transactions only. State why the others are not expense items.

E2–8 *Analysis of transactions*

The August 1985 transactions of Continental Travel Service owned by James Pendergrass are given below:

1985		
Aug.	1	Paid $450 for an advertisement in the travel section of the *Durham Tribune.*
	2	Arranged a round-the-world trip for Mr. and Mrs. Franklin Pepard. Collected a commission of $380 in cash from the steamship company.
	3	Arranged fly-now, pay-later Asian trips for several clients. The Triangle Airway System agreed to a commission of $980 for services rendered; this account is collected by the end of the month.
	4	Another advertisement was placed in the *Durham Tribune* for $370; this account is payable in ten days.
	16	Pendergrass withdrew $3,500 in anticipation that profits had been earned.
	19	Collected $980 from Triangle Airway System.

Following the example given below for the August 1 transaction, analyze each transaction and prepare the necessary journal entry.

Example:

Aug. 1
a. Advertising is an operating expense. Increases in expenses are recorded by debits. Debit Advertising Expense for $450.
b. The asset Cash was decreased. Decreases of assets are recorded by credits. Credit Cash for $450.
c. Journal entry:

	Debit	Credit
Advertising Expense	450	
Cash		450

E2–9
Accounts Receivable controlling and subsidiary accounting

The following transactions occurred at the Dutens Dog Grooming Clinic:

1985			
Nov.	1	Billed the following customers for $280 for dog grooming:	
		Timothy Amal	$ 60
		John Carson	80
		Thomas Queens	140
		Total	$280
	30	Received $210 on account from the following customers:	
		Timothy Amal	$ 50
		John Carson	60
		Thomas Queens	100
		Total	$210

1. Prepare general journal entries to record the transactions. (Assign numbers to journal pages.)

2. Post to general ledger and accounts receivable subsidiary ledger accounts. (Assign appropriate numbers to general ledger accounts.)

3. Prepare a schedule of accounts receivable.

E2–10
Analyzing the Cash account

The Cash account in the general ledger of Tulley's Auto Repair is given in T account form:

Cash		Acct. No. 101	
(1)	3,000	(3)	850
(2)	650	(5)	625
(4)	1,200	(6)	750

Item 1 is Tulley's original investment on April 1. Items 2 and 4 are cash receipts, and Items 3, 5, and 6 are cash payments made during April.

1. What is the balance of the account to be shown in the trial balance as of the end of April?

2. Will Tulley's income statement for the month of April reflect a net loss of $375 —the excess of cash payments ($2,225) over cash receipts ($1,850) other than the original investment? Explain.

E2–11
Calculation of net income or net loss

Shown below are selected, simplified T accounts for Electronic Repairs for the month ended June 30, 1985:

Cash	
10,000	100
200	65
820	600
	300

Supplies Expense	
500	
625	
417	

Salaries Expense	
50	
38	
89	

Accounts Payable	
160	800
120	250
	650

Service Revenue

	200
	460
	480
	822
	282
	418

Samuel Evans, Drawing

75	
25	

Rent Expense

80	

Based on the above information, calculate the amount of the net income (or net loss) for Electronic Repairs. Show your work.

E2–12 *Journalizing transactions with the owner*

Shown below are *selected* transactions for the single proprietorship of Ubuy Company:

1985

Jan. 1	John Ubuy started a single proprietorship by making a cash investment of $20,000.
Mar. 16	Ubuy withdrew $980 from the business for his personal use.
Apr. 4	Ubuy invested an additional $5,000 in the business.
Sep. 23	Ubuy made an additional withdrawal of $2,500 in anticipation of income earned.

Prepare general journal entries to record the transactions.

A Problems

P2–1A *Journalizing and posting transactions; preparing a trial balance*

The following account numbers and titles were designed for the Herman Car Rental System, a single proprietorship:

101	Cash	150	Office Equipment
111	Accounts Receivable	201	Accounts Payable
120	Land	205	Notes Payable
130	Building	301	John Herman, Capital
140	Automobiles		

During the first month of operation the following transactions occurred:

1985

Apr. 4	Herman deposited $150,000 in cash in a bank account in the name of the business, Herman Car Rental System.
5	Purchased land for $20,000 and a building on the lot for $50,000. A cash payment of $25,000 was made, and a promissory note was issued for the balance.
6	Purchased 12 new automobiles at $6,200 each from the Ames Motor Company. A down payment of $24,000 in cash was made; the balance of this open account is due in 30 days.
12	Sold one automobile to a company employee at cost. The employee paid $1,000 in cash and agreed to pay the balance of this open account within 30 days.
14	One automobile proved defective and was returned to Ames Motor Company. The amount due was reduced by $6,200.
15	Purchased a cash register and office desks for $2,850 in cash.
28	Paid $12,800 in cash to Ames Motor Company on account and gave a 60-day note payable for the balance.

Required:

1. Journalize the transactions, beginning with page number 1 in the journal.

2. Post to T form ledger accounts, showing cross-references.

3. Prepare a trial balance.

4. Prepare a balance sheet from the trial balance.

P2–2A
Accounts Payable controlling and subsidiary accounting

On July 1, 1985, the Supro Electronics Repair Company purchased electronic supplies on account as follows:

Baker Company	$ 4,050
Goodson Company	6,710
Lawson Corporation	2,040
Total	$12,800

On July 14, 1985, the Supro Electronics Repair Company paid its creditors on account as follows:

Baker Company	$2,000
Goodson Company	3,000
Lawson Corporation	1,000
Total	$6,000

Required:

1. Prepare general journal entries to record the transactions, assigning numbers to journal pages.

2. Since the Cash account has a debit balance of $12,500, enter this amount as a debit balance and post to general ledger and accounts payable subsidiary ledger accounts. Assign appropriate numbers to general ledger accounts, and use the three-amount-column form of account.

3. Prepare a schedule of accounts payable.

P2–3A
Preparing a chart of accounts and journalizing transactions

James Goodheart, M.D., decided to start his own medical clinic. Transactions for the month of April 1985 follow:

1985		
Apr.	1	Deposited $60,000 in a checking account under the business name, The Goodheart Clinic.
	4	Paid $1,200 for the first month's building rent.
	7	Purchased office equipment for $4,500. Paid $1,000 in cash and issued a note payable for the balance.
	10	Paid $385 for a one-year insurance policy on the office equipment, effective April 1, 1985.
	14	Paid $450 in cash for office supplies.
	15	Billed the following patients for services rendered: James Farquar . . . . $700 Freeman Hodgson . . . . 625 Tony Lawson 580
	21	Received cash from the following patients: James Farquar . . . . $485 Freeman Hodgson 525
	24	Received $2,235 in cash for medical services rendered not previously billed.
	29	Withdrew $1,000 for personal use.
	30	Paid $622 for miscellaneous general expenses for April.

Required:

1. Prepare journal entries to record the transactions, beginning with page number 1 in the journal.

2. Suggest a chart of accounts for the clinic, and explain why the particular numbers are used in the chart.

P2–4A

Journalizing transactions; calculating net income

Below is a list of accounts used by VIP Assurance Agency, a building security company, followed by a series of transactions for the month of February 1985:

Chart of Accounts

Acct. No.	Title	Acct. No.	Title
101	Cash	301	Timothy Furlough, Capital
121	Accounts Receivable	310	Timothy Furlough, Drawing
131	Office Supplies	401	Security Service Revenue
141	Prepaid Insurance	402	Special Events Revenue
151	Building	501	Salary Expense
160	Patrol Cars	510	Insurance Expense
165	Weapons	520	Supplies Expense
201	Accounts Payable	601	Income Summary
205	Notes Payable		

1985		
Feb.	4	Acquired a patrol car. Paid a $2,500 cash down payment and signed a $5,000 note for the remaining cost of the car.
	7	Purchased $1,500 of office supplies on account from Carolina Supply.
	8	Paid the $900 premium on a 3-year insurance policy on employees.
	14	Performed security services at a special rock concert event. Billed promoters of Rooney Tooney Band $4,000 for these services.
	15	Paid employees' salaries of $3,500.
	20	Paid $500 to Carolina Supply on the purchase of February 7.
	28	Total office supplies used during the month of February were $500.
	28	Billed regular security clients $40,000 for February security services.
	28	Furlough withdrew $1,000 in anticipation of income earned.

Required:

1. Journalize the transactions. Assign numbers to journal pages.

2. Considering the February 15 and 28 transactions as the only expenses, what is VIP's net income for February 1985? Show your calculations. What other expenses do you think should be considered?

P2–5A

Journalizing and posting transactions

Listed below is a partial chart of accounts for Front Street Parking, a single proprietorship owned by Steven Marks. Marks started the business on September 8, 1985. The transactions for September are listed following the partial chart of accounts.

Partial Chart of Accounts

Acct. No.	Title	Acct. No.	Title
101	Cash	302	Steven Marks, Drawing
151	Parking Decks	401	Parking Fees Revenue
201	Accounts Payable	501	Repairs Expense
202	Notes Payable	502	Security Expense
301	Steven Marks, Capital	503	Salaries Expense

1985		
Sep.	8	Deposited $200,000 in a checking account under the business name, Front Street Parking.
	9	Purchased an existing downtown parking deck for $125,000. Paid $60,000 in cash and issued a note payable for the balance.
	15	Parking fees received for the first week amounted to $2,550.
	17	Several potholes were repaired at a cost of $635, paid in cash.
	19	Marks signed a contract with the city for parking of city-owned vehicles. The charge for September was $950. The charge was collected.
	22	Parking fees received for the second week (excluding the city fee) were $2,950.
	25	Because of frequent vandalism, a security firm—Allied Security—was hired. The fee for the remainder of September was $105, payable on October 5.
	30	Parking fees received for the remainder of the month amounted to $6,200.
	30	The parking attendant was paid the monthly salary of $960.
	30	Marks withdrew $2,500 from the business for personal use.

Required:

1. Prepare journal entries to record the transactions. Assign numbers to journal pages beginning with number 1.

2. Open accounts and post from the journal to the appropriate ledgers. Use the three-amount-column accounts.

3. Prepare a trial balance.

P2–6A *Journalizing transactions; posting to control and subsidiary accounts*

Pipken Hoffman decided to open his own business. Knowing that more and more people were burning wood because of the high cost of fuel oil, Hoffman became a chimney sweep. During the month of February 1985, the following transactions occurred:

1985		
Feb.		Deposited $8,000 in a checking account under the business name, Pip the Sweep.
	3	Paid a $400 premium on a one-year health insurance policy.
	4	Purchased a 1978 pickup truck for $1,500 cash.
	5	Purchased cleaning supplies (brushes, old sheets, and so on) from John's Surplus for $105 on account.
	10	Billed the following clients for services rendered: Gary Anderson . . . . $75 Tony Hooker . . . . 40 Doug S. Melson 60
	11	Cleaned two chimneys and received $210 in cash.
	14	Hoffman withdrew $100 for personal use.
	19	Received bill from Snell's Service Station for truck repairs in the amount of $103.

20 Received cash from the following customers as payment on account:

Gary Anderson	$60
Tony Hooker	25
Doug S. Melson	40

25 Paid $50 for an advertisement in the *Village Newspaper.*
26 Paid $50 for miscellaneous general expenses.
28 Cleaned three chimneys and received $402 in cash.
28 Paid John's Surplus in full for the purchase of February 5.
28 Determined that $50 worth of the cleaning supplies were used during February.

Required:

1. Journalize all the transactions. Assign numbers to journal pages beginning with number 1.

2. Open accounts for Accounts Receivable and Accounts Payable, along with their subsidiary ledgers. Post *only* the parts of the journal entries that affect either Accounts Receivable or Accounts Payable. Use the three-amount-column accounts.

3. Sum the accounts receivable and accounts payable subsidiary ledger balances and check the totals against the control account balances.

P2–7A *Thought-provoking problem: effect of recording error*

David Stowe purchased plumbing supplies on account from Davis Supplies, Inc., for $600 and from Parker Distributors for $250. Stowe debited Plumbing Supplies for $850 and mistakenly credited Accounts Receivable for $850 in the general ledger. The credit postings to the accounts payable subsidiary ledger were correctly made.

Required:

1. What effect would the error have on the debit and credit totals of the trial balance taken at the end of the month?

2. What accounts in the trial balance would be incorrectly stated?

3. Could the error be discovered? How?

4. What effect does this error have on owner's equity?

B Problems

P2–1B *Journalizing and posting transactions; preparing a trial balance*

The following account numbers and titles were designed for Rea's Rentals, a single proprietorship:

101	Cash	150	Office Equipment
111	Accounts Receivable	201	Accounts Payable
120	Land	205	Notes Payable
130	Building	301	Rea Deal, Capital
140	Rental Equipment		

During the first month of operations, the following transactions occurred:

1985

Jul. 1 Deal deposited $42,500 in cash in a bank account in the name of the business, Rea's Rentals.
5 Purchased land for $5,000 and a building on the lot for $11,500. A cash payment of $7,000 was made, and a promissory note was issued for the balance.
6 Purchased rental equipment for $41,200 from Front Street Company. A down payment of $6,000 was made; the balance of the open account is due in 30 days.
7 Sold a lawn mower to an employee at its cost of $275. The employee paid $75 in cash and agreed to pay the balance of this open account in 30 days.
8 A chain saw proved to be defective and was returned to Front Street Company. The amount due was reduced by $450.

11 Purchased a typewriter and an office desk for $940 in cash.
29 Paid $3,900 in cash to Front Street Company and gave a 90-day note payable for the balance.

Required:

1. Journalize the transactions, beginning with page number 1 in the journal.

2. Post to T form ledger accounts, showing cross-references.

3. Prepare a trial balance.

4. Prepare a balance sheet from the trial balance.

P2–2B *Accounts Receivable controlling and subsidiary accounting*

The following transactions occurred at the Adden Rug Cleaning Company:

1985

Sep.	1	Billed customers for $285 for rug cleaning work, as follows:	
		Charles Abbott	$ 75
		Morgan Hooley	120
		Arthur Rogers	90
		Total	$285
	30	Received $135 on account from the following customers:	
		Charles Abbott	$ 25
		Morgan Hooley	60
		Arthur Rogers	50
		Total	$135

Required:

1. Prepare general journal entries to record the transactions, assigning numbers to journal pages.

2. Post to general ledger and accounts receivable subsidiary ledger accounts. Assign appropriate numbers to general ledger accounts and use the three-amount-column form of account.

3. Prepare a schedule of accounts receivable.

P2–3B *Preparing a chart of accounts and journalizing transactions*

Grace Hillhaven, M.D., decided to start her own medical clinic. Transactions for the month of March 1985 follow:

1985

Mar.	1	Deposited $75,000 in a checking account under the business name, Hillhaven Day Hospital.	
	3	Paid $1,500 for the first month's building rent.	
	8	Purchased office equipment for $4,000. Paid $2,000 in cash and issued a note payable for the balance.	
	11	Paid $450 for a one-year insurance policy on the office equipment, effective March 1, 1985.	
	15	Paid $365 in cash for office supplies.	
	17	Billed the following patients for services rendered:	
		Rachael Carson	$600
		Thomas Dawson	720
		Jim Emerson	490
	20	Received cash from the following patients:	
		Rachael Carson	$350
		Thomas Dawson	400
	26	Received $2,430 in cash for medical services rendered not previously billed.	
	30	Withdrew $950 for personal use.	
	30	Paid $910 for miscellaneous general expenses for March.	

Required:

1. Prepare journal entries to record the transactions, beginning with page number 1 in the journal.

2. Suggest a chart of accounts for the clinic, and explain why the particular numbers are used in the chart.

P2–4B *Journalizing transactions; calculating net income*

Below is a list of accounts used by Rest Secured, a building security company, followed by a series of transactions for the month of April 1985:

Chart of Accounts

Acct. No.	Title	Acct. No.	Title
101	Cash	301	James Anderson, Capital
121	Accounts Receivable	310	James Anderson, Drawing
131	Office Supplies	401	Security Service Revenue
141	Prepaid Insurance	402	Special Events Revenue
151	Building	501	Salary Expense
160	Patrol Cars	510	Insurance Expense
165	Weapons	520	Supplies Expense
201	Accounts Payable	601	Income Summary
205	Notes Payable		

1985		
Apr.	4	Acquired a patrol car. Paid a $4,000 cash down payment and signed a $5,000 note for the remaining cost of the car.
	7	Purchased $1,250 of office supplies on account from Carolyn & Tricia's Supply.
	8	Paid the $780 premium on a three-year insurance policy on employees.
	14	Performed security services at a special rock concert event. Billed promoters of Groovey Tuney Band $3,500 for these services.
	15	Paid employees' salaries of $4,200.
	20	Paid $950 to Carolyn & Tricia's Supply.
	28	Total office supplies used during the month of April were $410.
	28	Billed regular security clients $45,000 for April security services.
	28	Anderson withdrew $750 in anticipation of income earned.

Required:

1. Journalize the transactions. Assign numbers to journal pages.

2. Considering the April 15 and 28 transactions as the only expenses, what is Rest Secured's net income for April 1985? Show your calculations. What other expenses do you think should be considered?

P2–5B *Journalizing and posting transactions*

Listed below is a partial chart of accounts for Parking Decks of the United States, a single proprietorship owned by Thomas Dort. Dort started the business on October 7, 1985. The transactions for October are listed below the partial chart of accounts.

Partial Chart of Accounts

Acct. No.	Title	Acct. No.	Title
101	Cash	302	Thomas Dort, Drawing
151	Parking Decks	401	Parking Fees Revenue
201	Accounts Payable	501	Repairs Expense
202	Notes Payable	502	Security Expense
301	Thomas Dort, Capital	503	Salaries Expense

1985

Oct. 7 Deposited $192,500 in a checking account under the business name, Parking Decks of the United States.
10 Purchased an existing downtown parking deck for $105,000. Paid $70,000 in cash and issued a note payable for the balance.
12 Parking fees received for the first week amounted to $2,200.
15 Several potholes were repaired at a cost of $550, paid in cash.
17 Dort signed a contract with the city for parking of city-owned vehicles. The charge for October was $450. The charge was collected.
20 Parking fees received for the second week (excluding the city fee) were $2,550.
27 Because of frequent vandalism, a security firm—Timothy's Firm—was hired. The fee for the remainder of October was $95, payable on November 5.
30 Parking fees received for the remainder of the month amounted to $5,900.
30 The parking attendant was paid a monthly salary of $1,050.
30 Dort withdrew $2,000 from the business for personal use.

Required:

1. Prepare journal entries to record the transactions. Assign numbers to journal pages beginning with number 1.

2. Open accounts and post from the journal to the appropriate ledgers. Use the three-amount-column accounts.

3. Prepare a trial balance.

P2–6B

Journalizing transactions: posting to control and subsidiary accounts

Tired of working for someone else, Scotty McAdams decided to open his own business. Knowing that more and more people were burning wood because of the high cost of fuel oil, McAdams became a chimney sweep. During the month of January 1985, the following transactions occurred:

1985

Jan. 1 Deposited $3,800 in a checking account under the business name, Scotty the Sweep.
2 Paid a $280 premium on a one-year health insurance policy.
7 Purchased a 1976 pickup truck for $1,200 cash.
8 Purchased cleaning supplies (brushes, old sheets, and so on) from Sam's Warehouse Supplies for $80 on account.
11 Billed the following clients for services rendered:

Paul Janee	$105
Tom Nelson	120
Jane Thomas	85

12 Cleaned two chimneys and received $250 in cash.
16 McAdams withdrew $80 for personal use.

17 Received bill from Walker's Service Station for truck repairs in the amount of $65.
18 Received cash from the following customers as payment on account:

Paul Janee	$ 75
Tom Nelson	100
Jane Thomas	50

24 Paid $65 for an advertisement in the *Donham Register.*
30 Paid $58 for miscellaneous general expenses.
31 Cleaned three chimneys and received $435 in cash.
31 Paid Sam's Warehouse Supplies in full for the purchase of January 8.
31 Determined that $60 worth of the cleaning supplies were used during January.

Required:

1. Journalize all the transactions. Assign numbers to journal pages beginning with number 1.

2. Open accounts for Accounts Receivable and Accounts Payable, along with their subsidiary ledgers. Post *only* the parts of the journal entries that affect either Accounts Receivable or Accounts Payable. Use the three-amount-column accounts.

3. Sum the accounts receivable and accounts payable subsidiary ledger balances, and check the totals against the control account balances.

P2–7B

Thought-provoking problem: determining liquidity and credit decision

Following, in alphabetical order, are some of the items found in the balance sheet of Tampa Bay Corporation as of December 31, 1985:

Accounts payable	$40,000
Accounts receivable	16,000
Building	80,000
Cash	4,200
Delivery equipment	35,000
Land	20,000
Notes payable (due March 1, 1986)	12,000
Notes receivable (due April 15, 1990)	20,000

Required:

1. Compute total current assets.

2. Compute total current liabilities.

3. Tampa Bay Corporation, being short of cash, has asked the First National Bank for a 60-day loan of $10,000. As a bank loan officer, would you approve the loan? What factors would influence your decision?

3 Income Statement Accounts and Completion of the Basic Accounting Sequence

Introduction

Before the Good Times Wheels Repair Shop illustration is completed, this chapter reviews the expanded overall accounting system. A specific objective of the early chapters of this book is to keep the broad picture—the total forest—in the minds of the reader as the authors plant each individual tree. As each step is added to the overall picture, the reader must know exactly how that step fits into the total accounting structure. The major new phases in this chapter are additions to the end-of-period process: the new statements (the income statement and the statement of owner's equity) and closing entries.

Learning Goals

To explain the nature of an extended simple accounting system.

To prepare an income statement, statement of owner's equity, balance sheet, closing entries, and postclosing trial balance.

To prepare a statement of owner's equity when there is a beginning balance in the proprietor's capital account.

To state the interrelationship of financial statements of a single proprietorship.

Review of the Overall Accounting System

Recall that nine steps in the accounting sequence have been defined. The first two steps (selecting a chart of accounts and analyzing and journalizing the transactions) were completed in Chapter 2. In this chapter the journal entries recorded in Chapter 2 are posted (step 3), and a trial balance is prepared (step 4). Schedules of accounts receivable and accounts payable are prepared (steps 5 and 6); the financial statements including income statement, statement of owner's equity, and the balance sheet are prepared (step 7); and rev-

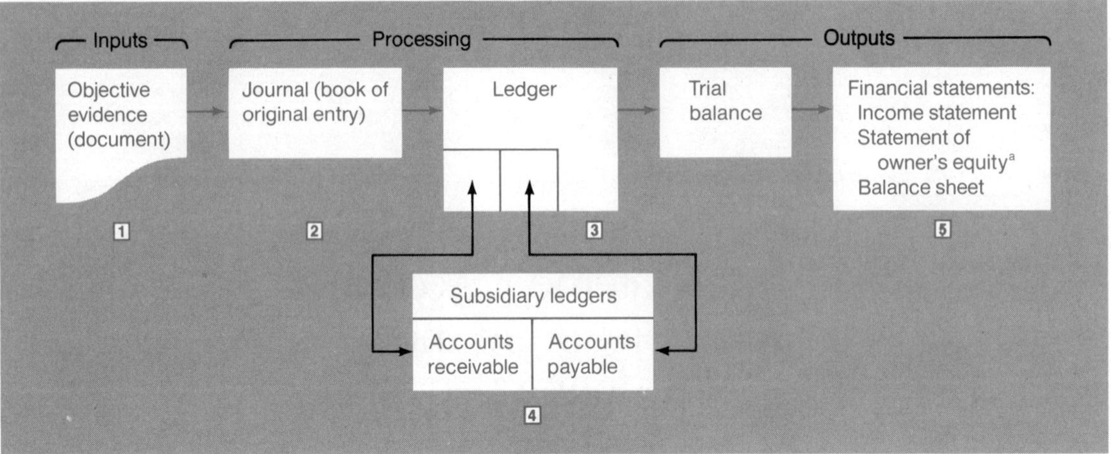

[a]For a corporation, the equivalent statement is a statement of retained earnings.

Figure 3–1 **The Accounting System**

enue, expense, and owner's drawing accounts are closed (step 8). Finally, a postclosing trial balance is prepared (step 9).

Before this illustration proceeds, the flow of information through an accounting system is graphically presented in Figure 3–1. Note that this system is designed to show how the parts relate to each other; it does not show all of the individual steps listed above.

Explanation to numbered items follows:

1 Every entry in an accounting system must have objective evidence, usually a document such as an invoice or bill, to justify the entry. These business documents, referred to as **inputs** into the accounting system, are the method by which data are introduced into the accounting system.

2 All transactions are analyzed and recorded first in a journal, a book of original entry.

3 All journal entries must be posted to the ledger. Absolutely no transaction entries can be made in a ledger except those posted from a journal. There is no other source for ledger entires. The journalizing and posting part is referred to as **processing.**

4 Various subsidiary ledgers—represented here by accounts receivable and accounts payable—present in each a detailed breakdown of a larger account in the general ledger, referred to as a **controlling account.**

5 As a test check of the equality of debits and credits, a trial balance is prepared. The final **outputs** of the system are the financial statements. These are prepared from the information taken from the ledgers.

An Illustration—The Good Times Wheels Repair Shop

The illustration of the Good Times Wheels Repair Shop, a single proprietorship owned and operated by Lucy Genova, is continued here. Remember that accounting records for the Good Times Wheels Repair Shop are maintained separately from Genova's personal records or the records of any of her other business enterprises. The books of Good Times will provide necessary information for decision making in that business only.

Journalizing

The transactions of the Good Times Wheels Repair Shop for January 1985 were analyzed and journalized (step 2 in the accounting sequence) in Chapter 2. The journal entries are shown on pages 67 to 70. The folio cross reference should be entered in the journal and account(s) only *after the posting has been completed.* As stated previously, this sequence is important (1) to show that the posting has been done, and (2) to provide the journal source of the account data.

Posting to the Ledgers (Step 3)

The timing of the posting process is a matter of personal preference, expediency, and whether or not records are maintained by a computer, but all postings must be completed before financial statements can be prepared. Accounts with customers and creditors should be kept up-to-date so that the account balances are readily available. Because of this, it is best to post from the journal to the subsidiary ledgers on a daily basis. (If you are unsure about posting procedure, see Figure 2–3 for a review.)

As the transactions are posted to the ledger, the appropriate journal page number is entered in the folio (F) column of the ledger account. Immediately afterwards, the account numbers are entered in the general journal folio (F) column.

The posting of the transactions of the Good Times Wheels Repair Shop to three-amount-column ledger accounts for January 1985 is shown in the general ledger below:

GENERAL LEDGER

Cash — Acct. No. 101

Date 1985		Explanation	F	Debit	Credit	Balance
Jan.	3		1	30000 00		30000 00
	4		1		300 00	29700 00
	5		1		80 00	29620 00
	10		1		4000 00	25620 00
	29		2		300 00	25320 00
	31		2		80 00	25240 00
	31		2	4800 00		30040 00
	31		2		1700 00	28340 00
	31		2		300 00	28040 00
	31		3		4000 00	24040 00
	31		3		600 00	23440 00
	31		3	10 00		23450 00

Balance is a debit

Accounts Receivable — Acct. No. 121

Date 1985		Explanation	F	Debit	Credit	Balance
Jan.	12		1	40 00		40 00
	26		2	180 00		220 00
	31		3		10 00	210 00

Balance is a debit

Motorcycle Parts and Supplies — Acct. No. 131

Date 1985		Explanation	F	Debit	Credit	Balance
Jan.	5		1	400 00		400 00
	29		2	250 00		650 00
	31		3		275 00	375 00

Balance is a debit

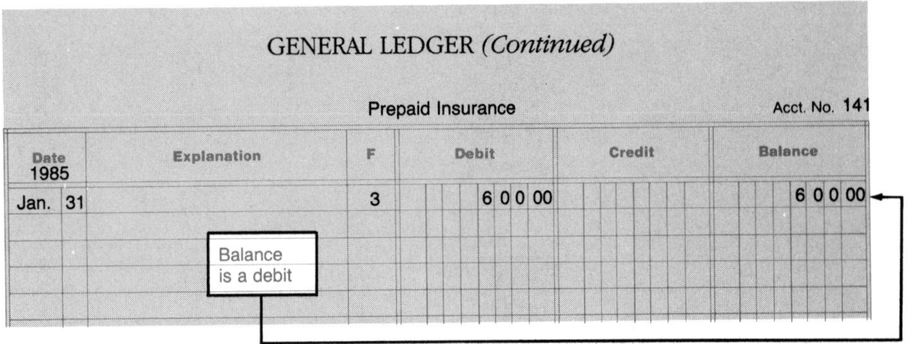

GENERAL LEDGER *(Continued)*

Prepaid Insurance — Acct. No. 141

Date 1985		Explanation	F	Debit	Credit	Balance
Jan.	31		3	600 00		600 00

Land — Acct. No. 151

Date 1985		Explanation	F	Debit	Credit	Balance
Jan.	10		1	1000 00		1000 00

Balance
is a debit

Automotive Tools and Equipment — Acct. No. 161

Date 1985		Explanation	F	Debit	Credit	Balance
Jan.	31		3	400 00		400 00

Balance
is a debit

Accounts Payable — Acct. No. 201

Date 1985		Explanation	F	Debit	Credit	Balance
Jan.	5		1		400 00	400 00
	29		2		250 00	650 00
	29		2	300 00		350 00

Balance
is a credit

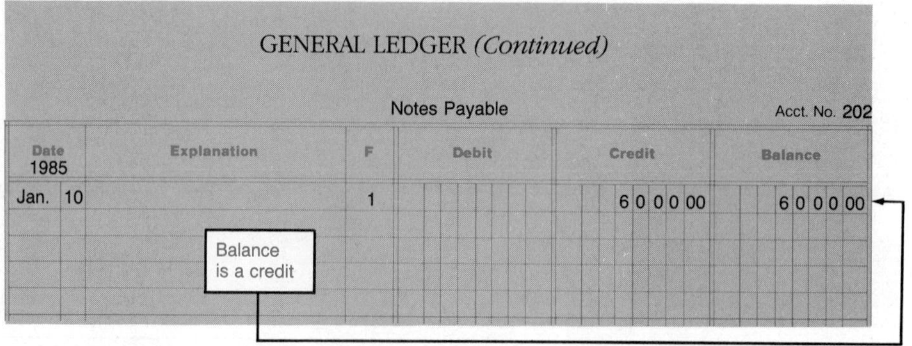

GENERAL LEDGER *(Continued)*

Notes Payable — Acct. No. 202

Date 1985		Explanation	F	Debit	Credit	Balance
Jan.	10		1		6000 00	6000 00

Lucy Genova, Capital — Acct. No. 301

Date 1985		Explanation	F	Debit	Credit	Balance
Jan.	3		1		30000 00	30000 00

Balance is a credit

Lucy Genova, Drawing — Acct. No. 311

Date 1985		Explanation	F	Debit	Credit	Balance
Jan.	31		2	300 00		300 00

Balance is a debit

Motorcycle Repair Revenue — Acct. No. 401

Date 1985		Explanation	F	Debit	Credit	Balance
Jan.	12		1		40 00	40 00
	26		2		180 00	220 00
	31		2		4800 00	5020 00

Balance is a credit

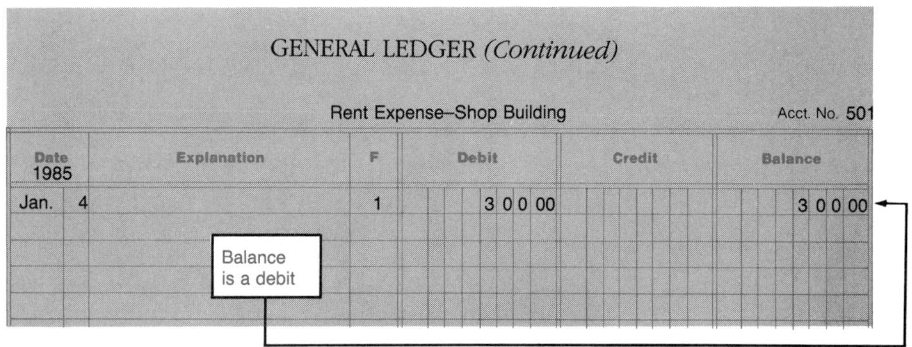

GENERAL LEDGER *(Continued)*

Rent Expense–Shop Building — Acct. No. 501

Date 1985		Explanation	F	Debit	Credit	Balance
Jan.	4		1	300 00		300 00

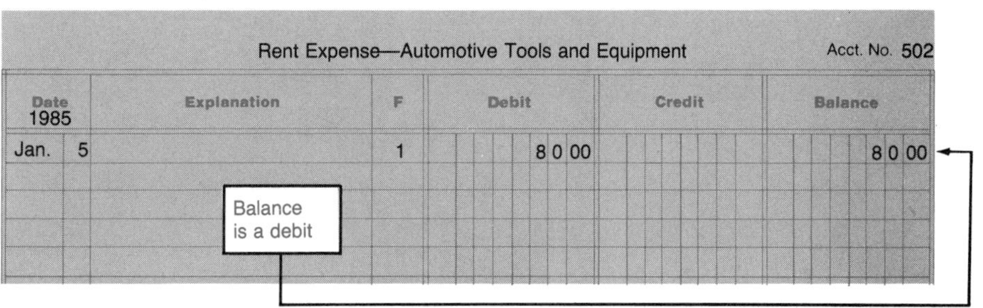

Rent Expense—Automotive Tools and Equipment — Acct. No. 502

Date 1985		Explanation	F	Debit	Credit	Balance
Jan.	5		1	80 00		80 00

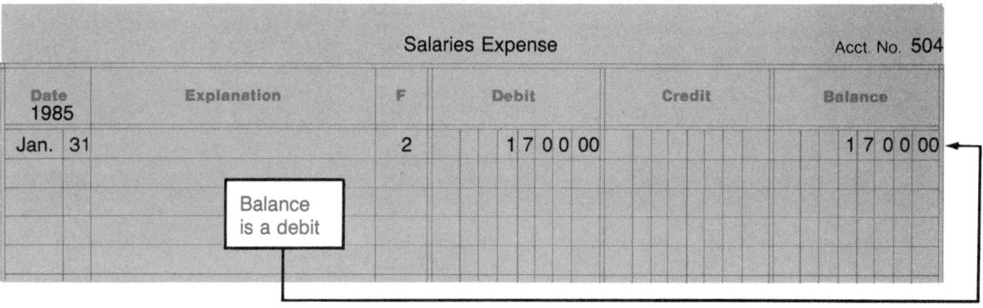

Salaries Expense — Acct. No. 504

Date 1985		Explanation	F	Debit	Credit	Balance
Jan.	31		2	1700 00		1700 00

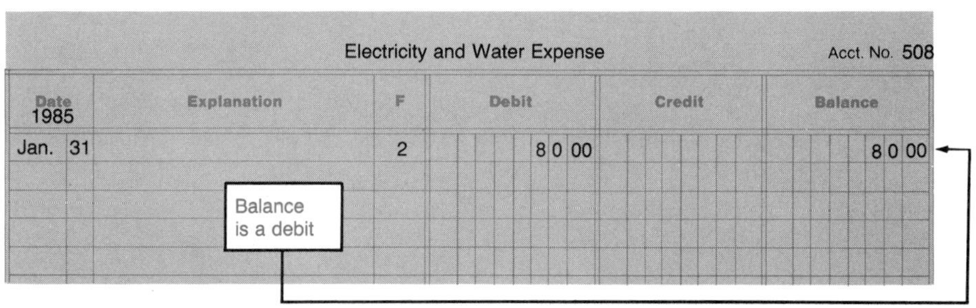

Electricity and Water Expense — Acct. No. 508

Date 1985		Explanation	F	Debit	Credit	Balance
Jan.	31		2	80 00		80 00

GENERAL LEDGER *(Continued)*

Motorcycle Parts and Supplies Expense — Acct. No. 509

Date 1985		Explanation	F	Debit	Credit	Balance
Jan.	31		3	275 00		275 00

Balance is a debit

Income Summary[a] — Acct. No. 601

Date		Explanation	F	Debit	Credit	Balance

[a]This account has no entries until the closing entries (explained later in this chapter) are posted.

ACCOUNTS RECEIVABLE SUBSIDIARY LEDGER

Jay Munson

Date 1985		Explanation	F	Debit	Credit	Balance
Jan.	26		2	180 00		180 00

Balance is a debit

George Shipman

Date 1985		Explanation	F	Debit	Credit	Balance
Jan.	12		1	40 00		40 00
	31		3		10 00	30 00

Balance is a debit

ACCOUNTS PAYABLE SUBSIDIARY LEDGER

Delco Supply House

Date 1985		Explanation	F	Debit	Credit	Balance
Jan.	29		2		250 00	250 00

Balance is a credit

Southern Supply Company

Date 1985		Explanation	F	Debit	Credit	Balance
Jan.	5		1		400 00	400 00
	29		2	300 00		100 00

Balance is a credit

Preparing a Trial Balance (Step 4)

After the accounts posted in the general ledger are up-to-date and the January 31 balances are obtained, they are listed in the trial balance as follows:

GOOD TIMES WHEEL REPAIR SHOP
Trial Balance
January 31, 1985

Acct. No.	Account Title	Debits	Credits
101	Cash	$23,450	
121	Accounts Receivable	210	
131	Motorcycle Parts and Supplies	375	
141	Prepaid Insurance	600	
151	Land	10,000	
161	Automotive Tools and Equipment	4,000	
201	Accounts Payable		$ 350
202	Notes Payable		6,000
301	Lucy Genova, Capital		30,000
311	Lucy Genova, Drawing	300	
401	Motorcycle Repair Revenue		5,020
501	Rent Expense—Shop Building	300	
502	Rent Expense—Automotive Tools and Equipment	80	
504	Salaries Expense	1,700	
508	Electricity and Water Expense	80	
509	Motorcycle Parts and Supplies Expense	275	
	Totals	$41,370	$41,370

Preparing a Schedule of Accounts Receivable (Step 5)

The fact that the trial balance is in balance is one bit of evidence of the accuracy of the accounting up to this point; the accountant, therefore, takes the next step, and prepares a **schedule of accounts receivable.**

At the end of a designated accounting period (one month in this example), the total of all the balances of customers' accounts should agree with the balance of the Accounts Receivable controlling account in the general ledger. A schedule of accounts receivable usually is prepared to check this agreement. The schedule of accounts receivable taken from the Good Times Wheels Repair Shop accounts receivable subsidiary ledger shows that the total of all customer accounts is $210, which agrees with the balance of Accounts Receivable that is also $210.

GOOD TIMES WHEELS REPAIR SHOP
Schedule of Accounts Receivable
January 31, 1985

Jay Munson	$180
George Shipman	30
Total accounts receivable	$210

Preparing a Schedule of Accounts Payable (Step 6)

The next step, similar to the one before, involves the preparation of a **schedule of accounts payable.** At the end of the accounting period, the total of the balances of individual creditors' accounts payable should equal the balance of the Accounts Payable controlling account. The schedule of accounts payable taken from the shop accounts payable subsidiary ledger shows that the total of the creditor accounts is $350, which agrees with the balance of Accounts Payable, which is also $350.

GOOD TIMES WHEELS REPAIR SHOP
Schedule of Accounts Payable
January 31, 1985

Delco Supply House	$250
Southern Supply Company	100
Total accounts payable	$350

Preparing the Financial Statements from the Trial Balance (Step 7)

The income statement, the statement of owner's equity, and the balance sheet are usually prepared at the end of the accounting period. They are marked with an exhibit letter or number that can be used for cross-referencing remarks. In this book, they are marked as follows:

- ☐ **Income Statement: Exhibit A.**
- ☐ **Statement of Owner's Equity: Exhibit B.**
- ☐ **Balance Sheet: Exhibit C.**

These statements for the Good Times Wheels Repair Shop follow in the order indicated above. Since the first two have not yet been illustrated, they are discussed more fully than the balance sheet.

The Income Statement

An **income statement** shows the results of operations for a given period of time. The income statement shown in Figure 3–2 was prepared from the trial balance of the Good Times Wheels Repair Shop. Its heading shows the following:

1. Name of the business.
2. Name of the statement.
3. Period covered by the statement.

It is important that the period covered be specified clearly. The date, January 31, 1985, is not sufficient; it alone does not indicate whether the net income of $2,585 was earned in one day, one month, or one year ended January 31, 1985. In order to interpret meaningfully the statement, the reader must know how long a period it took for the firm to earn the $2,585.

For a simple, service-type firm, there is no standard order for listing accounts in the income statement. Size of each revenue and expense item may be one criterion; but the sequence of the accounts in the chart of accounts is probably a better basis for establishing the sequence in the statement. The latter criterion is followed in Figure 3–2 because it is less likely to lead to errors. Note that although the Good Times Wheels Repair Shop is owned by Lucy Genova, the income and other statements are prepared for the business entity—for the Good Times Wheels Repair Shop.

GOOD TIMES WHEELS REPAIR SHOP
Income Statement
For the Month Ended January 31, 1985
Exhibit A

Revenue:		
Motorcycle repair revenue		$5,020
Expenses:		
Rent expense—shop building	$ 300	
Rent expense—automotive tools and equipment	80	
Salaries expense	1,700	
Electricity and water expense	80	
Motorcycle parts and supplies expense	275	
Total expenses		2,435
Net income		$2,585

Figure 3–2
Income Statement

GOOD TIMES WHEELS REPAIR SHOP — **Exhibit B**
Statement of Owner's Equity
For the Month Ended January 31, 1985

Original investment, January 3, 1985	$30,000
Add: Net income for January 1985	2,585
Subtotal	$32,585
Deduct: Withdrawals	300
Lucy Genova, capital, January 31, 1985	$32,285

Figure 3–3 Statement of Owner's Equity for New Business

Statement of Owner's Equity

The **statement of owner's equity** shows the changes that take place in the proprietor's (or owner's) capital over a given period of time; it should cover the same period as the income statement. Net income, withdrawals by the owner, and additional investments by the owner are reflected in the statement. The statement of owner's equity of the Good Times Wheels Repair Shop for the first month of its operation is shown in Figure 3–3. Its heading is similar to that of the income statement.

The Balance Sheet

Since the January 31, 1985, capital balance of the Good Times Wheels Repair Shop has now been determined (see Figure 3–3), it is possible to prepare the classified balance sheet, as shown in Figure 3–4. The figure shows the account form of balance sheet.

Note that the heading of the balance sheet contains the *single date* January 31, 1985. This statement is like a still photograph revealing the financial posi-

GOOD TIMES WHEELS REPAIR SHOP — **Exhibit C**
Balance Sheet
January 31, 1985

Assets			Liabilities and Owner's Equity		
Current assets:			Current liabilities:		
Cash	$23,450		Accounts payable	$ 350	
Accounts receivable	210		Notes payable	6,000	
Motorcycle parts and supplies	375		Total current liabilities		$ 6,350
Prepaid insurance	600		Owner's equity:		
Total current assets		$24,635	Lucy Genova, capital		32,285
Property, plant, and equipment:					
Land	$10,000				
Automotive tools and equipment	4,000				
Total property, plant, and equipment		14,000			
Total assets		$38,635	Total liabilities and owner's equity		$38,635

Figure 3–4 **Account Form of Balance Sheet**

tion as of the close of business on that day. The income statement and statement of owner's equity, on the other hand, are like moving pictures—they show certain changes that have taken place during a specific period.

Closing the Revenue, Expense, and Owner's Drawing Accounts (Step 8)

Revenue, expense, and owner's drawing accounts are used to measure part of the changes that take place in the owner's capital account. At the end of an accounting period, these temporary or **nominal accounts** are closed (balances are reduced to zero) so that they may be used to accumulate changes in owner's equity for the next period. Therefore, closing entries are made to transfer the final effects of the temporary owner's equity accounts to the owner's capital account—a permanent or **real account.**

Temporary or nominal accounts

***The revenue, expense, and owner's drawing accounts are closed at the end of a specified period. For this reason, these accounts are often called temporary owner's equity accounts, or* nominal accounts.**

Permanent or real accounts

The term* real *is applied to the accounts that appear in the balance sheet; these accounts are not closed at the end of a period. They carry amounts forward from one period to the next.

The Closing Procedure

The revenue and expense account balances are closed to an end-of-period summary account, Income Summary. The balance of the Income Summary account (a credit balance represents net income and a debit balance, net loss) is closed to the owner's capital account. This action is required because net income or net loss changes the owner's capital account balance. Since the owner's drawing account is *not an expense account,* it is not closed to Income Summary; rather, it is closed directly to the owner's capital account. After the revenue and expense accounts are closed, they have zero balances and are now available to accumulate information for measuring operating changes in the owner's capital account in the next accounting period. The drawing account also has a zero balance after closing.

Using the T form of the ledger accounts, the closing procedure is illustrated in Figure 3–5. The caption *Closing Entries* is written in the middle of the first unused line in the general journal under the transactions of the period, and the closing entries are begun directly under that.[1] They are posted immediately to the general ledger. As indicated in Figure 3–5, the closing entries are made in the following sequence:

[1]Later, a group of entries called *adjusting entries* will be introduced; they will be entered between the transactions and closing entries.

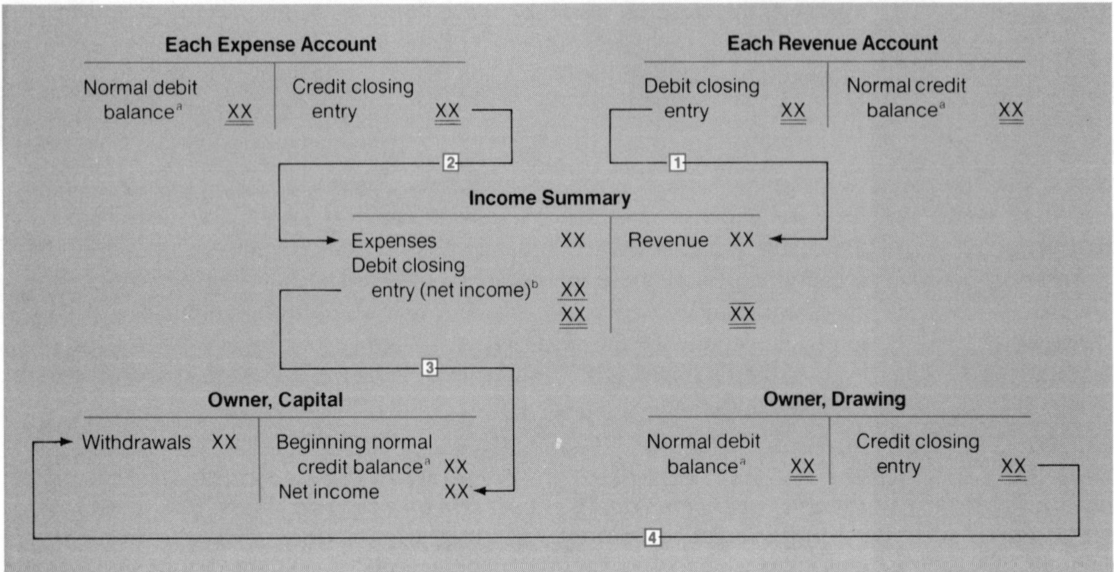

[a]While it is true that these accounts have a normal balance as indicated, they may on certain occasions have an opposite from normal or negative balance.

[b]It is assumed that the company has a net income. A net loss would require a credit to close this account.

Figure 3–5 **The Closing Procedure Flow**

1 In one compound entry, each revenue account (with a credit balance) is debited, and the *sum* of the revenue items is credited to the Income Summary account.

2 In a second compound entry, each expense account (with a debit balance) is credited, and the sum of the expense items is debited to the Income Summary account.

3 After entries 1 and 2 are posted, a credit balance in the Income Summary account represents net income; a debit balance, net loss. The balance of the account is transferred to the owner's capital account.

4 The owner's drawing account is closed directly to the capital account by a debit to the capital account and a credit to the drawing account.

Unlike regular transaction entries, which require analysis and judgment, the closing process is purely mechanical and involves only the shifting and summarizing of previously determined amounts. The closing journal entries of the Good Times Wheels Repair Shop on January 31, 1985, are shown in Figure 3–6.

The presence of account numbers in the folio column of the journal indicates that the closing journal entries have been posted to the ledger accounts indicated in the journal (see Figure 3–6). Closing may be indicated by the words *Closing entry* in the Explanation columns of the nominal accounts, as shown in Figure 3–7.

GENERAL JOURNAL — Page 4

Date 1985		Debit-Credit-Account Titles:Explanation	F	Debit	Credit
		Closing Entries			
Jan.	31	Motorcycle Repair Revenue	401	5 0 2 0 00	
		Income Summary	601		5 0 2 0 00
		To close revenue to			
		summary account.			
	31	Income Summary	601	2 4 3 5 00	
		Rent Expense—Shop Building	501		3 0 0 00
		Rent Expense—Automotive Tools			
		and Equipment	502		8 0 00
		Salaries Expense	504		1 7 0 0 00
		Electricity and Water Expense	508		8 0 00
		Motorcycle Parts and Supplies Expense	509		2 7 5 00
		To close expenses to			
		summary account.			
	31	Income Summary	601	2 5 8 5 00	
		Lucy Genova, Capital	301		2 5 8 5 00
		To transfer net income to			
		the capital account.			
	31	Lucy Genova, Capital	301	3 0 0 00	
		Lucy Genova, Drawing	311		3 0 0 00
		To close the amount withdrawn			
		by the proprietor to the			
		capital account.			

Figure 3–6
Closing Entries

The Condition of the Closed Nominal Accounts

After the closing entries have been posted, the temporary owner's equity, or nominal, accounts have zero balances, as shown in Figure 3–7. As stated before, they can now be used to accumulate relevant information about revenues, expenses, and drawing for February 1985 in the case of the Good Times Wheels Repair Shop.

GENERAL LEDGER *(Nominal Accounts Only)*

Lucy Genova, Drawing — Acct. No. 311

Date 1985		Explanation	F	Debit	Credit	Balance
Jan.	31		2	3 0 0 00		3 0 0 00
	31	Closing entry	4		3 0 0 00	—0—

Figure 3–7
The Nominal Accounts after Closing

GENERAL LEDGER *(Continued)*

Motorcycle Repair Revenue — Acct. No. 401

Date 1985		Explanation	F	Debit	Credit	Balance
Jan.	12		1		40 00	40 00
	26		2		180 00	220 00
	31		2		4800 00	5020 00
	31	Closing entry	4	5020 00		—0—

Rent Expense—Shop Building — Acct. No. 501

Date 1985		Explanation	F	Debit	Credit	Balance
Jan.	4		1	300 00		300 00
	31	Closing entry	4		300 00	—0—

Rent Expense—Automotive Tools and Equipment — Acct. No. 502

Date 1985		Explanation	F	Debit	Credit	Balance
Jan.	5		1	80 00		80 00
	31	Closing entry	4		80 00	—0—

Salaries Expense — Acct. No. 504

Date 1985		Explanation	F	Debit	Credit	Balance
Jan.	31		2	1700 00		1700 00
	31	Closing entry	4		1700 00	—0—

Figure 3–7 (Continued)

GENERAL LEDGER *(Continued)*

Electricity and Water Expense — Acct. No. 508

Date 1985		Explanation	F	Debit	Credit	Balance
Jan.	31		2	80 00		80 00
	31	Closing entry	4		80 00	—0—

Motorcycle Parts and Supplies Expense — Acct. No. 509

Date 1985		Explanation	F	Debit	Credit	Balance
Jan.	31		3	275 00		275 00
	31	Closing entry	4		275 00	—0—

Income Summary — Acct No. 601

Date 1985		Explanation	F	Debit	Credit	Balance
Jan.	31	Revenue	4		5020 00	5020 00
	31	Expenses	4	2435 00		2585 00
	31	Closing to capital	4	2585 00		—0—

Figure 3–7 (Continued)

How the Lucy Genova, Capital Account Looks after Closing

Figure 3–8 shows how the Lucy Genova, Capital account will look after the closing entries have been posted. Notice that the balance is $32,285, the amount that was shown on the balance sheet in Figure 3–4. The other real accounts are not affected by the closing entries. Their account balances will remain the same as shown in these accounts on pages 88–90.

GENERAL LEDGER

Lucy Genova, Capital — Acct. No. 301

Date 1985		Explanation	F	Debit	Credit	Balance
Jan.	3		1		3 0 0 0 0 00[a]	3 0 0 0 0 00
	31		4		2 5 8 5 00[b]	3 2 5 8 5 00
	31		4	3 0 0 00[c]		3 2 2 8 5 00

Figure 3–8
The Proprietor's Capital Account after Closing to It

[a]Original investment by Lucy Genova.
[b]Result of closing net income from Income Summary.
[c]Result of closing the drawing account to the capital account.

Taking a Postclosing Trial Balance (Step 9)

After the closing entries have been posted, a **postclosing trial balance** is taken from the general ledger. Since only real accounts have open balances, *the accounts and account balances in the postclosing trial balance are the same as those in the balance sheet.* The postclosing trial balance tests the debit and credit equality of the general ledger before the accounts receive postings of the next accounting period. Its formal preparation, however, is optional, and a comparison of the general ledger account balances with the balance sheet will serve the same purpose.

In any case, it is essential to start a new period with the accounts in proper balance. To show why: Suppose an error were made in the closing process for January 1985. The capital account would reflect the error. If no postclosing trial balance were taken, no accounting procedure would reveal the error until the end of the next accounting period when the trial balance was prepared. The accountant may not think to first look back at the preced-

GOOD TIMES WHEELS REPAIR SHOP
Postclosing Trial Balance
January 31, 1985

Acct. No.	Account Title	Debits	Credits
101	Cash	$23,450	
121	Accounts Receivable	210	
131	Motorcycle Parts and Supplies	375	
141	Prepaid Insurance	600	
151	Land	10,000	
161	Automotive Tools and Equipment	4,000	
201	Accounts Payable		$ 350
202	Notes Payable		6,000
301	Lucy Genova, Capital		32,285
	Totals	$38,635	$38,635

Figure 3–9
The Postclosing Trial Balance

ing closing process for the error. He or she could spend precious time looking for errors in the current period data before examining the previous accounting period. The postclosing trial balance of the Good Times Wheels Repair Shop is shown in Figure 3–9.

Statement of Owner's Equity Where There Is a Beginning Balance in the Owner's Capital Account

Since the Good Times Wheels Repair Shop was organized on January 3, 1985, there was a zero balance in the account, Lucy Genova, Capital, until the initial investment was made. In the first statement of owner's equity shown in Figure 3–3, the original investment is shown as the beginning item. In periods following the initial period, the opening item for the statement of owner's equity will be the capital balance at the end of the preceding period. To illustrate, suppose this shop had the following for February 1985:

Net income	$5,000
Owner's withdrawals	1,000

Then its statement of owner's equity for February 1985 would appear as presented in Figure 3–10.

The illustration of the simple accounting system will be completed with consideration of how the financial statements are interrelated using information for the Good Times Wheels Repair Shop.

Interrelationships of the Financial Statements for a Single Proprietorship

To demonstrate a meaningful interrelationship between the January and February statements for the Good Times Wheels Repair Shop, abbreviated end-of-February statements are required. In addition to the statement of owner's equity in Figure 3–10, assume the condensed data as presented in Figure 3–11.

GOOD TIMES WHEELS REPAIR SHOP
Statement of Owner's Equity
For the Month Ended February 28, 1985

Lucy Genova, capital, January 31, 1985	$32,285[a]
Add: Net income for February 1985	5,000
Subtotal	$37,285
Deduct: Withdrawals	1,000
Lucy Genova, capital, February 28, 1985	$36,285

[a]The ending capital balance is taken from the information shown in Figure 3–3.

Figure 3–10
Statement of Owner's Equity for Second Month of Operation

GOOD TIMES WHEELS REPAIR SHOP
Balance Sheet Data[a]
February 28, 1985

Total assets	$48,635
Total liabilities	$12,350
Owner's equity:	
Lucy Genova, capital (from Figure 3–10)	36,285
Total liabilities and owner's equity	$48,635

GOOD TIMES WHEELS REPAIR SHOP
Income Statement Data[a]
For the Month Ended February 28, 1985

Revenues (totals)	$9,420
Expenses (totals)	4,420
Net income	$5,000

[a]Summary totals are given. This procedure is not acceptable for solving end-of-chapter material.

Figure 3–11 Assumed February Summary Statements for Good Times Wheels Repair Shop

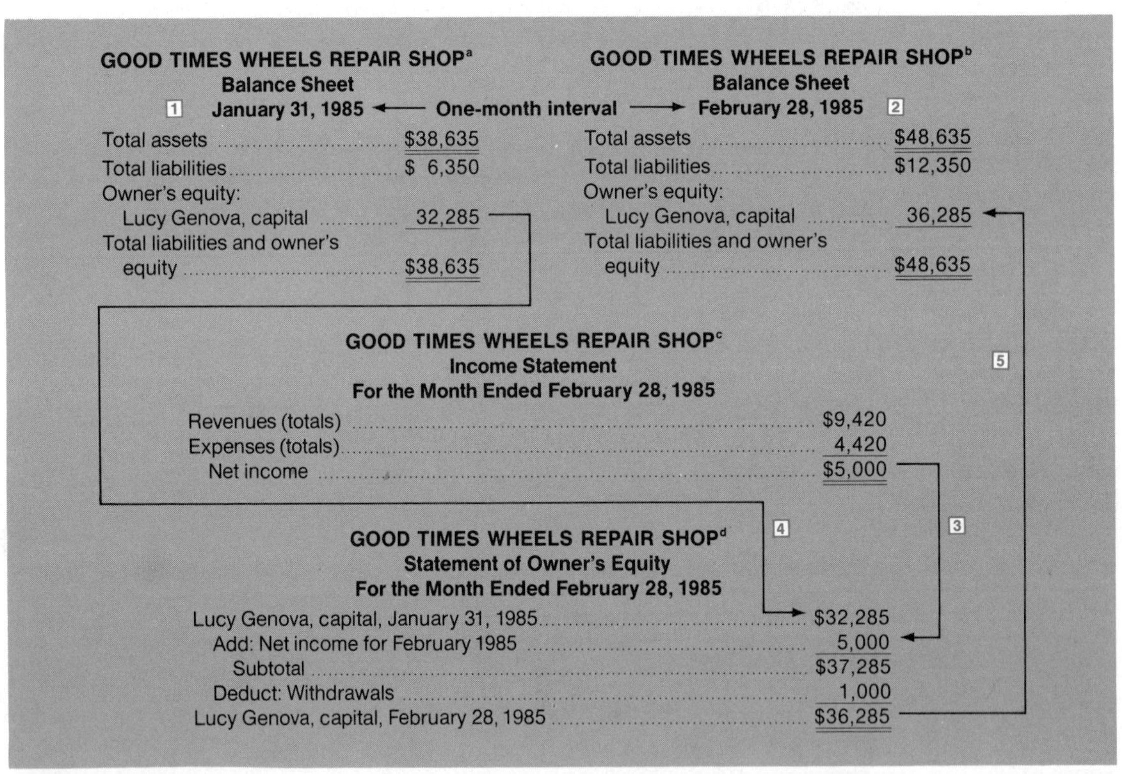

GOOD TIMES WHEELS REPAIR SHOP[a]
Balance Sheet
1 **January 31, 1985** ← **One-month interval** →

Total assets	$38,635
Total liabilities	$ 6,350
Owner's equity:	
Lucy Genova, capital	32,285
Total liabilities and owner's equity	$38,635

GOOD TIMES WHEELS REPAIR SHOP[b]
Balance Sheet
February 28, 1985 2

Total assets	$48,635
Total liabilities	$12,350
Owner's equity:	
Lucy Genova, capital	36,285
Total liabilities and owner's equity	$48,635

5

GOOD TIMES WHEELS REPAIR SHOP[c]
Income Statement
For the Month Ended February 28, 1985

Revenues (totals)	$9,420
Expenses (totals)	4,420
Net income	$5,000

4 3

GOOD TIMES WHEELS REPAIR SHOP[d]
Statement of Owner's Equity
For the Month Ended February 28, 1985

Lucy Genova, capital, January 31, 1985	$32,285
Add: Net income for February 1985	5,000
Subtotal	$37,285
Deduct: Withdrawals	1,000
Lucy Genova, capital, February 28, 1985	$36,285

[a]Data from Figure 3–4.
[b]Data from Figure 3–11.
[c]Data from Figure 3–11.
[d]Data from Figure 3–10.

Figure 3–12 **The Interrelationship of Financial Statements**

1 The information on the January 31, 1985, balance sheet in effect becomes the beginning amount for February. Therefore, the date of the first balance sheet is also the beginning date of the statement of owner's equity and the income statement. (*For the Month Ended February 28, 1985* means the period beginning immediately after January 31.)

2 The date of the second balance sheet (February 28, 1985) is also the ending date of the statement of owner's equity and the income statement.

3 The net income for February ($5,000) is transferred from the income statement to the statement of owner's equity.

4 The capital balance in the first balance sheet ($32,285) is the same as the beginning amount in the statement of owner's equity.

5 The end-of-period capital balance ($36,285) is transferred from the statement of owner's equity to the balance sheet dated February 28, 1985.

There is a significant interrelationship among the balance sheet, the income statement, and the statement of owner's equity, as illustrated in Figure 3–12. This figure shows a comparison of statements prepared at the end of January with those for February for the Good Times Wheels Repair Shop. The income statement shows the net amount remaining after revenues have been matched with expenses for a given period. This amount, the net income, shows the changes that have taken place in owner's equity as a result of the operations for the period. It is transferred to the statement of owner's equity. The statement of owner's equity shows additional changes that have taken place in owner's equity—in this particular case, the withdrawals by the owner. The end-of-period balance of capital is transferred to the end-of-period balance sheet, which presents information as of a moment of time—that is, at the end of the accounting period. The income statement and the statement of owner's equity help to explain the changes in the owner's equity during the interval between balance sheets. Though it is not absolutely necessary, it is helpful if the statements are prepared in this sequence: (1) income statement, (2) statement of owner's equity, and (3) balance sheet.

Again, note that summary totals are used in the figure so that the statements can be presented on one page. As indicated previously, this procedure is not acceptable for solving the end-of-chapter materials; details should be given on all statements shown in Figure 3–12.

Glossary

Closing the books The process of clearing the temporary or nominal accounts at the end of a period; this requires preparation of closing journal entries and posting of these entries to the nominal accounts that are closed.

Controlling account A general ledger account supported by a subsidiary ledger.

Income statement A statement showing all revenue and expense items for a given period, arranged so that total expenses are subtracted from total revenues, revealing the net income earned during that period.

Inputs Data introduced into the accounting system through objective evidence such as business documents.

Nominal accounts Temporary accounts that collect and measure part of the change that takes place in applicable owner's equity account(s). They are closed out at the end of each accounting period.

Outputs The various statements, schedules, and reports produced by an accounting system.

Postclosing trial balance A trial balance of the ledger accounts that have balances—the real accounts—taken after closing entries have been recorded and posted.

Processing A method of sorting and analyzing data in terms of their effect on accounts; processing is done through a journal and various ledgers.

Real accounts The accounts that are not closed and that are incorporated in the balance sheet.

Schedule of accounts payable A listing of a business's individual creditors with the amount owed to each and the total owed to all creditors at a given moment in time.

Schedule of accounts receivable A listing of a business's individual customers (debtors) with the amount owed by each and the total amount receivable from all customers.

Statement of owner's equity A statement showing the changes that occurred in a proprietor's capital during a given period.

Questions

Q3–1 Why are journal entries posted to accounts when each journal entry already contains details of a complete transaction?

Q3–2 Discuss the nature and purpose of the income statement.

Q3–3 What items are different on a statement of owner's equity prepared for the first period of the life of a single proprietorship versus that for the second period?

Q3–4 What is the purpose of closing the books? Using T accounts for Revenues, Expenses, Income Summary, Owner's Capital, and Drawing, diagram the closing process.

Q3–5 Draw a diagram showing the interrelationship of the balance sheet, income statement, and statement of owner's equity.

Q3–6 What item is common to each of the following pairs of statements: (a) The income statement and the statement of owner's equity? (b) The statement of owner's equity and the balance sheet as of the beginning of an accounting period? (c) The statement of owner's equity and the balance sheet as of the end of an accounting period?

Q3–7 List and explain the reasons for the various steps in the accounting sequence presented in Chapters 2 and 3.

Q3–8 Why are expense and revenue accounts called temporary accounts when some of them receive entries daily?

Q3–9 Which accounts are closed by a debit to Income Summary? Which accounts are closed by a credit to Income Summary?

Q3–10 What is the function of the Income Summary account?

Q3–11 When should the temporary owner's equity accounts be closed?

Q3–12 What is the purpose of a postclosing trial balance?

Q3–13 Assuming both revenue and expense accounts have been closed, what does (a) a credit balance in the Income Summary account indicate? (b) A debit balance in the Income Summary account indicate?

Q3–14 What is the purpose of (a) the schedule of accounts receivable? (b) The schedule of accounts payable?

Q3–15 How can you know whether a trial balance is a preclosing trial balance or a postclosing trial balance?

Exercises

E3 – 1 *Reconstructing entries and preparing a statement of owner's equity*

The following three accounts are from the general ledger of Davido Company for the year ended December 31, 1985:

Jackson Davido, Capital — Acct. No. 301

Date		Explanation	F	Debit	Credit	Balance
1985						
Jan.	1	Credit balance	√			50,000
Sep.	4		50		10,000	60,000
Dec.	31	Closing entry	60		20,000	80,000
	31	Closing entry	60	19,000		61,000

Jackson Davido, Drawing — Acct. No. 302

Date		Explanation	F	Debit	Credit	Balance
1985						
Mar.	10		38	5,000		5,000
Jul.	6		40	7,000		12,000
Dec.	20		52	7,000		19,000
	31	Closing entry	60		19,000	0

Income Summary — Acct. No. 601

Date		Explanation	F	Debit	Credit	Balance
1985						
Dec.	31	Closing entry	60		100,000	100,000
	31	Closing entry	60	80,000		20,000
	31	Closing entry	60	20,000		0

1. Reconstruct the journal entries giving rise to the foregoing information with the exception of the January 1, 1985, balance in Jackson Davido's capital account. The $50,000 beginning balance of Jackson Davido, Capital account balance is the cumulative result of many transactions occurring prior to January 1, 1985. Use summary accounts for revenues and expenses entitled *Revenues* and *Expenses.*

2. Prepare a statement of owner's equity for 1985.

E3 – 2 *Journalizing accounts receivable transactions; using controlling and subsidiary accounts*

The following transactions occurred at the Village Solarheat Company:

1985

Jan. 1 Billed customers for $350 for repair work to solar panels, as follows:

Barlow Ainsley	$ 50
José Bonita	100
Ramez Carmino	75
Peter Owens	125
Total	$350

31 Received $265 on account from the following customers:

Barlow Ainsley	$ 40
José Bonita	75
Ramez Carmino	50
Peter Owens	100
Total	$265

1. Prepare general journal entries to record the transactions.

2. Post to general ledger and accounts receivable subsidiary ledger accounts. (Assign appropriate numbers to the journal page and general ledger accounts.)

3. Prepare a schedule of accounts receivable.

E3 – 3 *Journalizing accounts payable transactions; using controlling and subsidiary accounts*

On April 15, 1985, the Silento Television Repair Company purchased television replacement parts on account, as follows:

Benton Television Supply	$195
Gardo Company	110
Mount Tirzah TV Repair Parts, Inc.	90
Timberland, Inc.	385
Total	$780

On April 30, 1985, the Silento Television Repair Company paid its creditors, as follows:

Benton Television Supply	$100
Gardo Company	60
Mount Tirzah TV Repair Parts, Inc.	80
Timberland, Inc.	300
Total	$540

1. Prepare general journal entries to record the transactions.

2. Post to general ledger and accounts payable subsidiary ledger accounts. (Assign appropriate numbers to the journal page and general ledger accounts and place a $1,200 beginning balance in the Cash account.)

3. Prepare a schedule of accounts payable.

E3 – 4 *Preparing financial statements from a trial balance*

The trial balance of Brooks Copying Company as of December 31, 1985, the end of the current accounting period, is presented below:

BROOKS COPYING COMPANY
Trial Balance
December 31, 1985

Acct. No.	Account Title	Debits	Credits
101	Cash	$ 4,594	
121	Duplicating Supplies	5,895	
131	Prepaid Insurance	1,722	
141	Printing Equipment	70,100	
201	Accounts Payable		$ 945
211	Notes Payable		16,800
301	Harold Brooks, Capital		41,018
311	Harold Brooks, Drawing	18,360	
401	Copying Revenue		74,460
501	Salaries and Wages Expense	24,005	
502	Rent Expense	3,960	
503	Utilities Expense	3,075	
504	Duplicating Supplies Expense	1,512	
		$133,223	$133,223

Prepare an income statement, a statement of owner's equity, and a balance sheet for Brooks Copying Company.

E3–5 *Correcting a statement of owner's equity*

Shown below is a statement of owner's equity that was prepared incorrectly:

Statement of Owner's Equity
JOHNSTON COMPANY
December 31, 1985

Withdrawals	$–3,000
Plus: Net income	10,500
Subtotal	$ 7,500
Plus: Additional investment	2,000
Subtotal	$ 9,500
Plus: John Johnston, capital, January 1, 1985	15,000
Total equity	$ 24,500

Prepare a correct statement of owner's equity for Johnston Company.

E3–6 *Journalizing closing entries*

As of December 31, 1985, the ledger of the Sylvan Company contained the following account balances, among others: Cash, $96,000; Notes Receivable, $25,500; Joseph Sylvan, Capital, $56,500; Commissions Earned, $110,000; Rent Earned, $9,000; Salaries Expense, $56,000; Office Supplies Expense, $8,200; Miscellaneous Expense, $15,500; Joseph Sylvan, Drawing, $8,000. (All the nominal accounts that are to be closed are included.) Journalize the closing entries.

E3–7 *Computing missing figures for single proprietorships*

Financial information for three different single proprietorships follows:

	(a)	(b)	(c)
Net income (loss) for 1985	$160,000	$?	$(23,400)
Owner's equity at beginning of year	?	215,000	100,000
Owner's equity at end of year	290,000	204,000	60,400
Withdrawals by owner during 1985	30,500	20,600	?

Supply the missing figures. (Assume no additional investments were made during 1985.)

E3–8 *Working backwards to determine net income and preparing income statement*

The following information is taken from the books of the Samuels Company:

SAMUELS COMPANY **Exhibit B**
Statement of Owner's Equity
For the Year Ended December 31, 1985

Sam Samuels, capital, January 1, 1985	$ 34,500
Add: Net income for 1985	68,500
Subtotal	$103,000
Deduct: Withdrawals	23,000
Sam Samuels, capital, December 31, 1985	$ 80,000

The expenses for 1985 were: salaries and wages, $34,640; advertising expense, $6,900; rent expense, $5,540; and miscellaneous expense, $12,340. The revenue came from only one source—commissions earned. Prepare a formal income statement for the Samuels Company. Show your computations of the amounts that are not given.

E3–9 *Closing entries*

The following statement has been prepared for the Daye Storage Company:

DAYE STORAGE COMPANY
Income Statement
For the Month Ended April 30, 1985

Exhibit A

Revenue:		
Storage fees		$29,880
Expenses:		
Office rent expense	$2,500	
Salaries expense	8,800	
Miscellaneous expense	2,780	
Total expenses		14,080
Net income		$15,800

During the year, Richard Daye withdrew $1,800. What closing entries were necessary for Daye Storage Company?

A Problems

P3–1A *Performing accounting sequence steps*

Jeraldine Kennedy, M.D., opened an office for the practice of medicine. During the month of May 1985, the following transactions occurred:

1985			
May	1	Invested $60,000 in cash and opened an account in the name of The Hill Health Haven.	
	4	Purchased medical supplies on account:	
		Eason Medical Supply	$2,050
		Thompson Supply Company	1,200
	5	Paid $1,500 for May rent of building.	
	6	Rented medical equipment from Scott Rentals, Inc., and paid $3,000 for May rent.	
	8	Paid $900 for miscellaneous general expenses.	
	9	Received $8,000 in cash for professional services rendered but not previously billed.	
	14	Paid on account $1,050 to Eason Medical Supply and $600 to Thompson Supply Company.	
	24	Mailed statements to the following patients for services rendered:	
		Stanley Sapp	$ 400
		William Thompson	1,300
	30	Received on account in cash $350 from William Thompson and $200 from Stanley Sapp.	
	31	Determined that $800 of medical supplies had been consumed.	

Required:

1. Journalize the transactions.

2. Post to the general ledger, accounts receivable subsidiary ledger, and accounts payable subsidiary ledger. (Assign numbers to the journal pages and general ledger accounts.)

3. Take a trial balance.

4. Prepare schedules of accounts receivable and accounts payable as of May 31, 1985.

5. Prepare an income statement, a statement of owner's equity, and a balance sheet.

6. Journalize the closing entries and post them.

7. Prepare a postclosing trial balance.

P3 – 2A
Performing accounting sequence steps

The following transactions occurred during July 1985 at the Werley Roof Repair Company:

1985		
Jul.	1	Turin Werley invested $25,600 in cash and opened an account in the name of the business, Werley Roof Repair Company.
	4	Paid $360 for two days' rental of a derrick and pulley assembly used on a repair job.
	10	Purchased United States Government bonds for $7,500 in cash.
	15	Collected $6,030 in cash on completion of roofing repair work not previously billed.
	19	Signed an agreement with Roxboro College to repair dormitory roofs for $4,900. The work is to be completed during August and September.
	23	Werley withdrew $500 to spend on his vacation at Myrtle Beach.
	27	Paid $785 for repair materials used on jobs during the month.
	29	Paid $2,540 in salaries and wages.
	31	Completed roofing repair work for Horace Spencer in the amount of $2,580. Spencer promised to pay for the work on August 15.

Use the following account titles and numbers:

101	Cash	401	Repair Service Revenue
115	Temporary Investments	501	Salaries and Wages Expense
118	Accounts Receivable	503	Repair Materials Expense
301	Turin Werley, Capital	505	Rental Expense
302	Turin Werley, Drawing	601	Income Summary

Required:

1. Journalize the transactions (assigning numbers to journal pages).

2. Post to general ledger accounts.

3. Take a trial balance.

4. Prepare an income statement, a statement of owner's equity, and a balance sheet.

5. Journalize and post the closing entries.

6. Take a postclosing trial balance.

P3–3A *Preparing closing entries and postclosing trial balance*

The trial balance of the Cutchin Company on December 31, 1985, follows:

THE CUTCHIN COMPANY
Trial Balance
December 31, 1985

Acct. No.	Account Title	Debits	Credits
101	Cash	$ 85,000	
111	Accounts Receivable	6,640	
121	Supplies	2,988	
131	Equipment	35,200	
201	Accounts Payable		$ 6,640
301	Sarah Cutchin, Capital, January 1, 1985		109,651
311	Sarah Cutchin, Drawing	3,320	
401	Commissions Earned		26,900
411	Rent Earned		9,300
501	Salaries Expense	12,122	
502	Advertising Expense	1,660	
503	Supplies Expense	2,656	
504	Miscellaneous Expense	2,905	
	Totals	$152,491	$152,491

Required:

1. Set up three-amount-column accounts for Sarah Cutchin, Capital and Sarah Cutchin, Drawing, for each revenue and expense account listed in the trial balance, and the Income Summary account (Acct. No. 601). Enter the account balances.

2. Journalize the closing entries and post to the accounts (assign page numbers to the journal).

3. Prepare a postclosing trial balance.

P3–4A *Performing accounting sequence steps*

Puree Waters, a plumber, opened his own shop. During the month of February 1985, he completed the following transactions:

1985			
Feb.	1	Invested $12,500 in cash in the name of the business, Waters Plumbing.	
	3	Paid $510 rent for shop space for the month of February.	
	5	Purchased plumbing supplies on account from:	
		Dawson Industries	$380
		Plummer Supplies, Inc.	590
		The Queens Plumbing Supply Company	940
	8	Rented a used truck from the Stewart Motor Company and paid $600 for February rent.	
	10	Paid $400 in cash for rent of shop equipment.	
	15	Paid $300 in cash for rent of plumbing equipment.	
	19	Received $930 in cash for a completed plumbing job.	
	23	Paid creditors on account:	
		Dawson Industries	$140
		Plummer Supplies, Inc.	70
		The Queens Plumbing Supply Company	280
	28	Waters withdrew $520 for his personal use.	

28 Purchased the following, paying cash of $3,000 and signing a 6-month note for the balance:

Truck	$19,000
Shop equipment	3,000
Plumbing equipment	2,000

Use the following account numbers and titles:

101	Cash	302	Puree Waters, Drawing
121	Plumbing Supplies	401	Plumbing Revenue
161	Truck	501	Rent Expense—Shop Space
171	Shop Equipment	502	Rent Expense—Truck
181	Plumbing Equipment	503	Rent Expense—Shop Equipment
201	Accounts Payable	504	Rent Expense—Plumbing Equipment
211	Notes Payable	601	Income Summary
301	Puree Waters, Capital		

Required:

1. Journalize the transactions (assigning numbers to the journal pages).

2. Post to the general ledger and accounts payable subsidiary ledger.

3. Take a trial balance.

4. Prepare a schedule of accounts payable as of February 28, 1985.

5. Prepare an income statement, a statement of owner's equity, and a balance sheet. Assume that no plumbing supplies were used during February.

6. Journalize the closing entries and post them.

7. Prepare a postclosing trial balance.

P3–5A *Preparing end-of-period statements and thought-provoking question*

On May 1, 1985, Wayne Watchers opened the Zenith Health Spa. Watchers decided to invest $10,000 in cash in the business. He opened an account at the First National Bank in the name of the business and deposited the cash. The monthly rates at the health spa are as follows:

Weight reduction program	$29
Deluxe exercise routine	46

Supplies acquired for the business cost $2,260. Expenses incurred and paid during the first month were:

Rent expense	$ 6,280
Wages—reduction program	14,300
Wages—exercise routine	16,100
Heat, light, and water	1,480
Maintenance expense	900

The following advertising expenses were incurred but are not payable until the following month:

Local newspaper	$1,360
Local radio station	1,520
Local magazine	1,900

All the supplies were used during the first month. Revenues for the first month were from the following customers:

1,000 customers for the weight reduction program
310 customers for the deluxe exercise routine

Required:

1. Prepare an income statement for May.

2. Prepare a statement of owner's equity for May.

3. Compute the amount of the cash balance as of May 31. How can the business incur a loss when there is so much cash in the bank?

P3–6A
Thought-provoking problem: management steps related to accounting information

Katherine Kudson invested $50,000 to open a business. She hired a manager and various service personnel to do all the work for her. During the first year, the business earned only $1,200. Kudson called the manager to her home and told him that she expected a greater return on her money. "I can get 9.4 percent if I invest in any money market plan," she told the manager. "You must make sure that the business earns more than this rate. From an accounting point of view, what do you recommend?"

Required: Assume that you are the manager. Frame a reply to Kudson. In your reply, discuss revenues, expenses, and a possibility of a normal long-run operational pattern. Be creative in your reply; relate the management steps to accounting, however.

B Problems

P3–1B
Performing accounting sequence steps

Timothy James, M.D., opened an office for the practice of medicine. During the month of March 1985, the following transactions occurred:

1985			
Mar.	1	Invested $40,000 in cash and opened an account in the name of The Health Clinic.	
	4	Purchased medical supplies on account:	
		Burton Medical Supply	$1,620
		Gurton Supply	980
	5	Rented medical equipment from Scutter Rentals, Inc.; paid $2,150.	
	6	Paid $900 for March rent of a building.	
	8	Paid $750 for miscellaneous general expenses.	
	10	Received $4,200 in cash for professional services rendered but not previously billed.	
	14	Paid on account $620 to Burton Medical Supply and $380 to Gurton Supply.	
	23	Mailed statements to the following patients for services rendered:	
		Dunston Elkins	$650
		Mellisa Tooms	175
	31	Received on account in cash $250 from Dunston Elkins and $75 from Mellisa Tooms.	
	31	Determined that $400 of medical supplies had been consumed.	

Required:

1. Journalize the transactions.

2. Post to the general ledger, accounts receivable subsidiary ledger, and accounts payable subsidiary ledger. (Assign numbers to the journal pages and general ledger accounts.)

3. Take a trial balance.

4. Prepare schedules of accounts receivable and accounts payable as of March 31, 1985.

5. Prepare an income statement, a statement of owner's equity, and a balance sheet.

6. Journalize the closing entries and post them.

7. Prepare a postclosing trial balance.

P3–2B
Performing accounting sequence steps

The following transactions occurred during October 1985 at Bobbie's Roof Repair Company:

1985		
Oct.	1	Bobbie Barrow invested $35,000 in cash and opened an account in the name of the business, Bobbie's Roof Repair Company.
	4	Paid $620 for two days' rental of a derrick and pulley assembly used on a repair job.
	9	Purchased United States Government bonds for $15,000 in cash.
	15	Collected $9,060 in cash on completion of roofing repair work not previously billed.
	20	Signed an agreement with Mid-Western College to repair dormitory roofs for $8,800. The work is to be completed during November and December.
	25	Barrow withdrew $850 to spend on her vacation in the Ozarks.
	27	Paid $1,270 for repair materials used on jobs during the month.
	29	Paid $5,680 in salaries and wages.
	30	Completed roofing work for Elston Howard in the amount of $5,160. Howard promised to pay for the work on November 12.

Use the following account titles and numbers:

101	Cash	401	Repair Service Revenue
115	Temporary Investments	501	Salaries and Wages Expense
118	Accounts Receivable	503	Repair Materials Expense
301	Bobbie Barrow, Capital	505	Rental Expense
302	Bobbie Barrow, Drawing	601	Income Summary

Required:

1. Journalize the transactions (assigning numbers to journal pages).

2. Post to general ledger accounts.

3. Take a trial balance.

4. Prepare an income statement, a statement of owner's equity, and a balance sheet.

5. Journalize and post the closing entries.

6. Take a postclosing trial balance.

P3–3B *Preparing closing entries and postclosing trial balance*

The trial balance of the Yount Company on December 31, 1985, follows:

THE YOUNT COMPANY
Trial Balance
December 31, 1985

Acct. No.	Account Title	Debits	Credits
101	Cash	$127,800	
111	Accounts Receivable	11,280	
121	Supplies	5,976	
131	Equipment	56,400	
201	Accounts Payable		$ 13,380
301	Judith Yount, Capital, January 1, 1985		159,902
311	Judith Yount, Drawing	6,640	
401	Commissions Earned		52,800
411	Rent Earned		16,700
501	Salaries Expense	20,244	
502	Advertising Expense	3,320	
503	Supplies Expense	5,312	
504	Miscellaneous Expense	5,810	
	Totals	$242,782	$242,782

Required:

1. Set up three-amount-column accounts for Judith Yount, Capital and Judith Yount, Drawing, for each revenue and expense account listed in the trial balance, and the Income Summary account (Acct. No. 601). Enter the account balances.

2. Journalize the closing entries and post to the accounts (assign page numbers to the journal).

3. Prepare a postclosing trial balance.

P3–4B *Performing accounting sequence steps*

Martin Sink, a plumber, opened his own shop. During the month of September 1985, he completed the following transactions:

1985			
Sep.	1	Invested $16,500 in cash in the name of the business, Sink Plumbing.	
	3	Paid $620 rent for shop space for the month of September.	
	5	Purchased plumbing supplies on account from:	
		Edison Industries	$ 775
		Fussell Plumbing Company	1,650
		Nelson Supply House	1,010
	7	Rented a used truck from the Poper Motor Company and paid $675 for September rent.	
	10	Paid $425 in cash for rent of shop equipment.	
	18	Paid $350 in cash for rent of plumbing equipment.	
	19	Received $1,860 in cash for a completed plumbing job.	
	25	Paid creditors on account:	
		Edison Industries	$375
		Fussell Plumbing Company	650
		Nelson Supply House	510
	30	Sink withdrew $950 for his personal use.	
	30	Purchased the following, paying cash of $4,500 and signing a 6-month note for the balance:	
		Truck	$18,400
		Shop equipment	2,800
		Plumbing equipment	1,600

Use the following account numbers and titles:

101	Cash	302	Martin Sink, Drawing
121	Plumbing Supplies	401	Plumbing Revenue
161	Truck	501	Rent Expense—Shop Space
171	Shop Equipment	502	Rent Expense—Truck
181	Plumbing Equipment	503	Rent Expense—Shop Equipment
201	Accounts Payable	504	Rent Expense—Plumbing Equipment
211	Notes Payable	601	Income Summary
301	Martin Sink, Capital		

Required:

1. Journalize the transactions (assigning numbers to journal pages).

2. Post to the general ledger and accounts payable subsidiary ledger.

3. Take a trial balance.

4. Prepare a schedule of accounts payable as of September 30, 1985.

5. Prepare an income statement, a statement of owner's equity, and a balance sheet.

6. Journalize the closing entries and post them.

7. Prepare a postclosing trial balance.

P3–5B
Preparing end-of-period statements and thought-provoking questions

On July 1, 1985, Harvey Tunney opened the Earth Child Health Spa. Tunney decided to invest $19,500 in cash in the business. He opened an account at the Third National Bank in the name of the business and deposited the cash. The monthly rates at the health spa are as follows:

Weight reduction program	$51
Deluxe exercise routine	86

Supplies acquired for the business cost $3,850. Expenses incurred and paid during the first month were:

Rent expense	$11,960
Wages—reduction program	29,800
Wages—exercise routine	31,400
Heat, light, and water	3,510
Maintenance expense	1,200

The following advertising expenses were incurred but are not payable until the following month:

Local newspaper	$1,850
Local radio station	1,950
Local magazine	1,780

All the supplies were used during the first month. Revenues for the first month were from the following customers:

950 customers for the weight reduction program
345 customers for the deluxe exercise routine

Required:

1. Prepare an income statement for July.

2. Prepare a statement of owner's equity for July.

3. Compute the amount of the cash balance as of July 31. How can the business incur a loss when there is so much cash in the bank?

P3–6B
Thought-provoking problem: impact of decision on net income

During the first year that the Roberts Garage was in business, it earned only 5 percent on John Roberts's investment of $60,000. Roberts considered what he might do to increase net income to at least the 15 percent level. He thought about these alternatives:

1. Reducing the number of mechanics by one.

2. Decreasing advertising.

3. Charging more for the repair jobs.

Required: Assume that you are the accountant for the Roberts Garage. Consider what influence each of the foregoing alternatives might have on net income and prepare a report for Roberts advising him of the possible consequences.

4 End-of-Period Adjusting Entries

Introduction

Chapters 2 and 3 presented a complete but simple service company illustration with the transactions of the Good Times Wheels Repair Shop. Now it is time to fine-tune the accounting model to obtain a means of determining a more accurate income or loss figure. A similar but more complex illustration is used in Chapters 4 and 5 to introduce five of the types of adjustments that are recorded at the end of the period to complete the accounting process. First, in Chapter 4, the adjustment process is discussed in detail through an illustration using the Genova Trucking Company, another enterprise owned and operated by Lucy Genova. The remaining steps in the end-of-period process for the Genova Trucking Company are completed in Chapter 5. Two accounting methods are compared in this chapter: the cash basis and the accrual basis.

Learning Goals

To be able to describe the accrual basis of accounting.

To be able to describe the cash basis of accounting.

To understand the need for adjusting entries and the specific point in the accounting cycle at which adjusting entries are made.

To be able to explain the reasons for the different types of adjusting entries.

To be able to classify adjustments into two broad groups—accruals and deferrals.

To prepare and journalize five types of adjusting entries for a single proprietorship.

An Overview of the Adjustment Process

The Accounting Bases

Two accounting bases are used in practice: (1) the accrual basis and (2) the cash basis. Generally accepted accounting principles typically require the use of the accrual basis; it is the only basis that is emphasized in this book. A concept, however, often can be better understood when it is compared with its opposite. Therefore, a beginning look at the cash basis should provide a means of better grasping the meaning of the accrual basis.

Cash Basis of Accounting

Under the **cash basis of accounting,** revenue is recognized and recorded only when the cash is received. Expenses are recognized in the period when payment is made. Recording of revenues and expenses during an accounting period is based on an inflow and outflow of cash. A matching of cash receipts and cash disbursements is done to determine operating results during the period. This method is simple in application but in most cases does not produce information that permits an acceptable measurement of net income. For example, it does not recognize revenues earned but uncollected as being earned and does not recognize expenses incurred but unpaid. Hence, it matches only some revenues and expenses for a given period. Recall that, from a theoretical viewpoint, an *expense is incurred* when the effort is expended (the asset status is lost) in attempting to create revenue. *Revenue is said to be earned* in a given period when the service has been performed or the product delivered (the necessary efforts, except cash collection, are made to bring the revenue into being).

There are instances, particularly in small businesses, in which the cash basis of accounting is used with acceptable results. For example, if a firm has no receivables and no payables, it can use the cash basis of accounting and still get an adequate matching of expired costs (expenses) against earned revenue of a given period. Mixed systems—combinations of the cash basis and the accrual basis (often referred to as the modified cash basis)—are found in practice, but in many of these cases an independent accountant is engaged to convert the end-of-year financial reports to an accrual basis.

Accrual Basis of Accounting

The **accrual basis of accounting** is based on the principle that all revenue earned during a period and all the related incurred expenses of earning that revenue assignable to the period must be determined. These then are matched against each other to determine net income or net loss. Revenues are recognized at the time of sale of the services or merchandise, and expenses are usually recognized at the time the services are received and used in the production of revenue. This is the concept, discussed earlier, of matching revenue and expenses for a given period.

Matching revenues and expenses

The central goal of the accrual basis of accounting is to achieve a better matching of the earned revenue of a period with the incurred expenses of that period, regardless of when, whether, or how much cash has been received or paid.

Comparison of Cash and Accrual Bases of Accounting

The cash and accrual bases may produce different net income figures, as the following example will show. The Carolyn Elfland Company, which does landscape gardening, performed work during August for which it charged $1,000. It received $600 on August 15 and $400 on September 11. Wages of $550 (the only expense) were paid on August 31. No work was performed during September.

	Cash Basis		Accrual Basis	
	August	September	August	September
Revenue	$600	$400	$1,000	$0
Expense	550	0	550	0
Net income	$ 50	$400	$ 450	$0

The accrual basis of accounting presents a more useful picture of operating results because revenue is reflected in the period to which it properly belongs—the period in which it was earned. Net income is the difference between revenue earned and expenses incurred during the accounting period. The accrual method, by matching expenses incurred with revenue earned for the period, presents the better measurement of net income. Since it results in more useful financial statements, most businesses keep their books on the accrual basis.

During the accounting period, regular business transactions are recorded as they occur. At the end of a period, the accountant will find the ledger accounts incomplete; some new accounts must be brought onto the books, and others must be brought up to date. This is called the adjustment process, and the journal entries necessary to accomplish it are referred to as adjusting entries. This process is required if the financial statements are to reflect the company's position realistically—its assets and equities—as of the end of the period and the results of its operations—revenue earned and expenses incurred—during the period.

Adjusting Entries

At the end of each period, the accountant must make **adjusting entries** to bring the accounts up to date. This process reveals revenues which have been earned and expenses which have been incurred; income for the period can then be measured accurately. At the same time, this process updates assets, liabilities, and owner's equity (through the updating of revenues and expenses) so that financial position at a given point in time is more accurately stated.

An Overview of Adjustments

It is impractical and sometimes impossible to record the day-to-day changes in certain accounts. For example, when the premium payment is made on an insurance policy, the asset, Prepaid Insurance, is usually debited. At the end of the accounting period, however, only part of the balance of the Prepaid

Insurance account represents an asset. The amount that has expired with the passage of time is an expense representing the cost of insurance protection received. At the end of the accounting period, therefore, Prepaid Insurance contains both an asset and an expense element. A **short-term cost apportionment adjustment** is necessary to record the correct amount of Insurance Expense and to reduce Prepaid Insurance. A similar situation exists with revenue received in advance; for example, rent may be collected a year in advance. As used here as well as in other adjustments, **apportionment** simply means dividing among two or more periods a cost or revenue that has already been paid or received (and recorded). Both of these apportionments are called **deferrals** because the recognition of expense or revenue has been postponed. Such apportionment could be either short-term or long-term.

Another type of adjusting entry may be required to record an **accrual**—for both expenses and revenue—(previously unrecorded data). Assume, for example, that a company paid wages on March 28 for the two-week period that ended on that date. However, the employees worked on March 29, 30, and 31. If March 31 is the end of the accounting period, recognition must be given to this unrecorded but incurred wages expense as well as to the corresponding increase in the liability. An **accrued expense adjustment** is needed so that the financial statements may show the liability and the proper assignment of the expense to the period. In a similar manner, an **accrued revenue** adjustment is needed to record such items as unrecorded interest that has been earned but is not yet due to be collected. Note that in this context the term **accrued** simply means accumulated, built up, or grown.

Adjusting entries have a different goal than entries that record regular business transactions. Regular business transactions start and complete their cycles within an accounting period. Adjusting entries deal with continuous transactions. The adjusting entry for wages, for example, records a change that has been occurring daily—the increase in a liability incurred—but is unrecorded. The adjusting entry for insurance expense, on the other hand, recognizes the amount of day-to-day expiration of an item that was recorded in an asset account at the time of acquisition. Both items, whether originally recorded or not, undergo continuous change. Accounts must be updated to reflect that change any time financial statements are to be prepared.[1] Adjustments are illustrated next in the Genova Trucking Company illustration.

An Accounting Illustration—The Genova Trucking Company as a Single Proprietorship

The adjusting process is illustrated here through an example. Assume that the Genova Trucking Company started business on June 1, 1985. As a convenience in the illustration of the end-of-period procedures, also assume that

[1]An adjustment not discussed here is *bad debts expense*. It is covered in Chapter 11.

GENOVA TRUCKING COMPANY
Trial Balance
June 30, 1985

Acct. No.	Account Title	Debits	Credits
101	Cash	$ 5,250	
111	Accounts Receivable	550	
112	Notes Receivable	1,440	
131	Office Supplies	230	
141	Prepaid Insurance	2,160	
142	Prepaid Rent	1,500	
201	Office Equipment	1,400	
211	Trucks	26,000	
301	Accounts Payable		$ 200
302	Notes Payable		8,000
321	Unearned Rent		600
401*	Lucy Genova, Capital		25,000
404*	Lucy Genova, Drawing	500	
501	Trucking Revenue		7,465
601	Heat and Light Expense	40	
602	Maintenance and Repairs Expense	375	
603	Telephone and Telegraph Expense	95	
604	Gas and Oil Expense	525	
605	Wages Expense	1,200	
	Totals	$41,265	$41,265

Other information required for adjustments:

a. Rent in the amount of $1,500 was prepaid for three months on June 1.
b. Insurance premium of $2,160 for a comprehensive three-year insurance policy was prepaid on June 1.
c. The June 30, 1985, inventory of office supplies amounted to $60.
d. The company rented out one of its trucks on a part-time basis and collected rent of $600 in advance for six months starting June 1.
e. The office equipment purchased on June 1, 1985, has an estimated life of 10 years and a salvage value of $200 at the end of that period; this is to be depreciated by the straight line method.
f. The trucks purchased on June 1, 1985, have an estimated life of five years and a salvage value of $1,000 each ($2,000 in total) at the end of that period; they are to be depreciated by the straight line method.
g. The company received a $1,440, fifteen percent, 30-day note on June 10.
h. Wages of $150 for June 28, 29, and 30 have not been paid or recorded.
i. The company borrowed money from a bank on June 12 and issued a 45-day, 16 percent note for $8,000.

*Note that the capital and drawing accounts of the Genova Trucking Company are numbered 401 and 404. This is acceptable, particularly if a number of different types of liabilities are expected.

Figure 4–1 Trial Balance and Supplementary Information

the books are closed on June 30 (books are customarily closed annually). The trial balance taken from the Genova Trucking Company's general ledger and other information related to the adjustment process are shown in Figure 4–1.

The adjusting entries must be journalized and posted to ledger accounts. The end-of-period financial statements—income statement, balance sheet, and statement of owner's equity—must reflect both regular transactions data and adjustment data for the period.

Short-Term Cost Apportionments—A Type of Deferral

At the *end of the period,* certain accounts contain mixtures of asset and expense elements. In the Genova Trucking Company example, there are three such accounts that require short-term cost apportionment adjustments. The accountant follows three steps in adjusting the accounts involving a short-term cost apportionment between asset and expense elements:[2]

1. Determine the balance of each account to be adjusted.
2. Determine the amount of the asset and expense elements in each account.
3. Record the adjusting entries to bring the accounts into agreement with the amounts determined in step 2.

Adjustment of Prepaid Rent

On June 1, the Genova Trucking Company paid $1,500 in cash for three months' rent.

Step 1. The general ledger shows the following balance in the account:

Asset as of June 1

Prepaid Rent Acct. No. 142

Date		Explanation	F	Debit	Credit	Balance
1985 Jun.	1		1	1,500		1,500

The information in the foregoing ledger account (and other similar illustrations in this chapter) is reproduced from the original ledger and includes folio references for the original data. Note that the Prepaid Rent account is definitely an asset as of June 1.

Step 2. The amount of expense applicable to June is $500 = ($1,500 ÷ 3 months). By June 30, therefore, Prepaid Rent before adjustment has become a mixed account consisting of an expense element of $500 and an asset element of $1,000. The $500 expense element relates to the rent cost which has expired in June. The $1,000 asset element relates to the rent cost that will benefit July and August. (Since the nature of accounts used in short-term apportionments adjustment changes, the time when it has the specific characteristic is indicated in the appropriate box.)

[2] Each of the three costs to be illustrated was originally recorded as an asset. If originally recorded as an expense, the adjustment would be different (see "Alternative Adjustment Methods for Deferrals" later in this chapter).

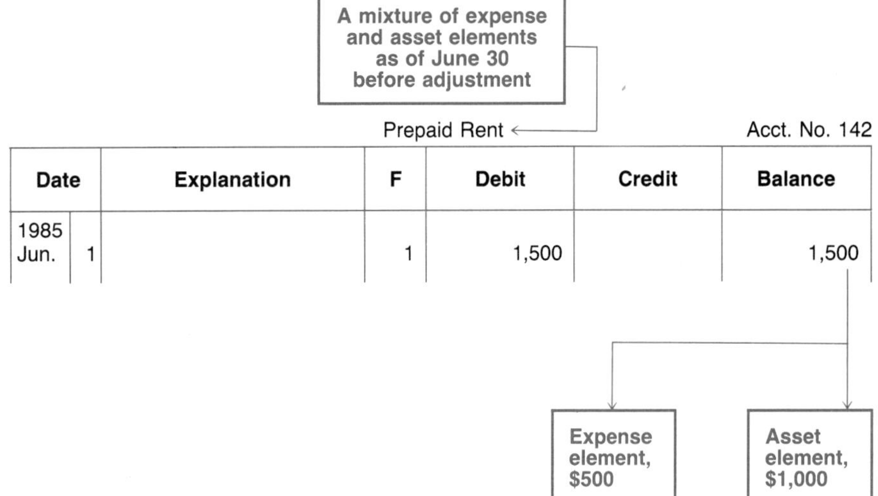

Prepaid Rent — Acct. No. 142

Date		Explanation	F	Debit	Credit	Balance
1985 Jun.	1		1	1,500		1,500

Step 3. For teaching purposes the adjusting entries for the Genova Trucking Company are made and posted as each adjustment is explained. The timing of journalizing the adjustments is optional; it may be delayed until the formal financial statements have been prepared from a work sheet (discussed in Chapter 5).

The required adjusting entry is shown below with the folio references indicating that posting has been done:

GENERAL JOURNAL — Page 4

Date		Debit-Credit-Account Titles: Explanation	F	Debit	Credit
1985 Jun.	30	Rent Expense	606	500	
		Prepaid Rent	142		500
		To record rent expense for June.			

By crediting the asset account for $500, the expense element is removed from the asset account; debiting the expense account inserts the $500 into Rent Expense. This is shown by the following posting in the ledger accounts:

Asset after adjustment

Prepaid Rent — Acct. No. 142

Date		Explanation	F	Debit	Credit	Balance
1985 Jun.	1		1	1,500		1,500
	30	Adjustment	4		500	1,000

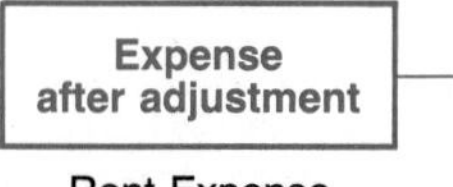

Rent Expense — Acct. No. 606

Date		Explanation	F	Debit	Credit	Balance
1985						
Jun.	30	Adjustment	4	500		500

Prepaid rent ($1,000) is classified in the balance sheet as a current asset, and rent expense ($500) appears in the income statement as an expense.

Adjustment of Prepaid Insurance

The Genova Trucking Company paid a premium of $2,160 for a comprehensive three-year insurance policy, effective June 1, 1985.

Step 1. Prepaid Insurance, before adjustment, shows a balance of $2,160. The title Prepaid Insurance classifies it as an asset account, but on June 30, 1985, it is in fact a mixture of an asset and an expense element.

Step 2. By computation we can determine that the expense element for the month of June is $60 = ($2,160 ÷ 36 months) and that the unused portion of $2,100 is the asset prepayment benefiting future periods.

Step 3. The following adjusting entry is made:

GENERAL JOURNAL — Page 4

Date		Debit-Credit-Account Titles: Explanation	F	Debit	Credit
1985					
Jun.	30	Insurance Expense	607	60	
		Prepaid Insurance	141		60
		To record insurance expense for June.			

The information is shown in the following ledger accounts after posting:

Asset
after adjustment

Prepaid Insurance — Acct. No. 141

Date		Explanation	F	Debit	Credit	Balance
1985						
Jun.	1		1	2,160		2,160
	30	Adjustment	4		60	2,100

Expense after adjustment

Insurance Expense — Acct. No. 607

Date		Explanation	F	Debit	Credit	Balance
1985 Jun.	30	Adjustment	4	60		60

Prepaid insurance ($2,100) is typically classified in the balance sheet as a current asset, although in this case part of it technically could be disclosed in some noncurrent asset caption of the balance sheet since the remaining life of the policy is two years and eleven months. The classification of the item as a current asset is justified on the basis that the average life of the several business insurance policies a business would normally own would be one year or less. Insurance expense ($60) appears in the income statement as an expense.

Adjustment of Office Supplies

Step 1. On the trial balance (Figure 4–1), Office Supplies has a debit balance of $230, representing a purchase made on June 6. Again, the title, Office Supplies, indicates that the account is an asset; but on June 30, 1985, it contains a mixture of asset and expense elements because some of the supplies have been used.

Step 2. The inventory (a physical count) taken on June 30 showed $60 worth of unused supplies; therefore, the expense element is $170 = ($230 − $60) of supplies used.

Step 3. The expense of $170 is removed from the mixed account by the following adjusting entry, and the adjustment information is posted to the accounts shown below the journal entry:

GENERAL JOURNAL — Page 4

Date		Debit-Credit-Account Titles: Explanation	F	Debit	Credit
1985 Jun.	30	Office Supplies Expense	608	170	
		Office Supplies	131		170
		To record supplies used during June.			

Asset after adjustment

Office Supplies — Acct. No. 131

Date		Explanation	F	Debit	Credit	Balance
1985 Jun.	6		1	230		230
	30	Adjustment	4		170	60

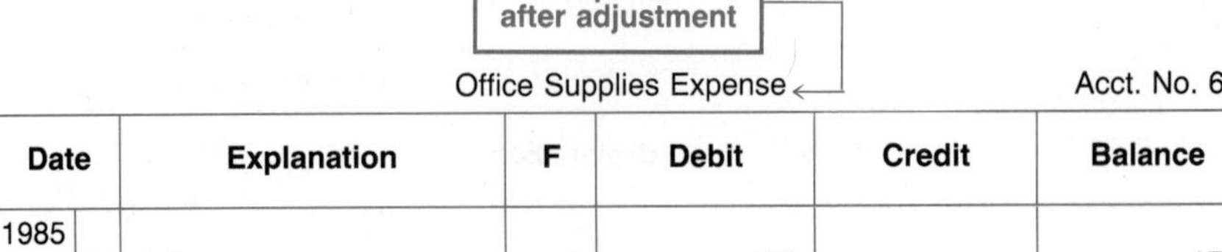

Office Supplies Expense — Acct. No. 608

Date		Explanation	F	Debit	Credit	Balance
1985 Jun.	30	Adjustment	4	170		170

Office supplies ($60) is classified in the balance sheet as a current asset, and office supplies expense ($170) appears in the income statement as an expense.

Short-Term Revenue Apportionment—A Second Type of Deferral

Adjustment of Unearned Rent

At the end of the period, some accounts contain mixtures of liability and revenue elements. The same three steps are followed in making short-term revenue apportionments of amounts originally recorded in liability accounts.[3] The Genova Trucking Company had only one such adjustment. On June 1, the company signed a contract for the use of one of its trucks on a part-time basis and received an advance payment of $600 for six months' rent. At that time, Cash was debited and a liability account, Unearned Rent, was credited for $600. By June 30, 1985, the Unearned Rent account represents a mixture of liability and revenue elements. Therefore, on June 30, the portion earned in the month of June must be transferred from the liability account, Unearned Rent, to the revenue account, Rent Earned. The unearned portion must remain in Unearned Rent as a liability because the Genova Trucking Company must provide the use of its truck on a part-time basis for another five months.

Step 1. The amount of the unearned rent liability as of June 1, 1985, in the ledger account is shown below:

Liability
as of June 1

Unearned Rent — Acct. No. 321

Date		Explanation	F	Debit	Credit	Balance
1985 Jun.	1		1		600	600

[3]Again, the reader is referred to the section found later in this chapter, "Alternative Adjustment Methods for Deferrals." The way a deferral adjustment is made depends on how the original entry was recorded.

Note that the Unearned Rent is definitely a liability as of June 1.

Step 2. The rent actually earned in June is \$100 = (\$600 ÷ 6 months); therefore by June 30 the Unearned Rent account consists of revenue and liability elements.

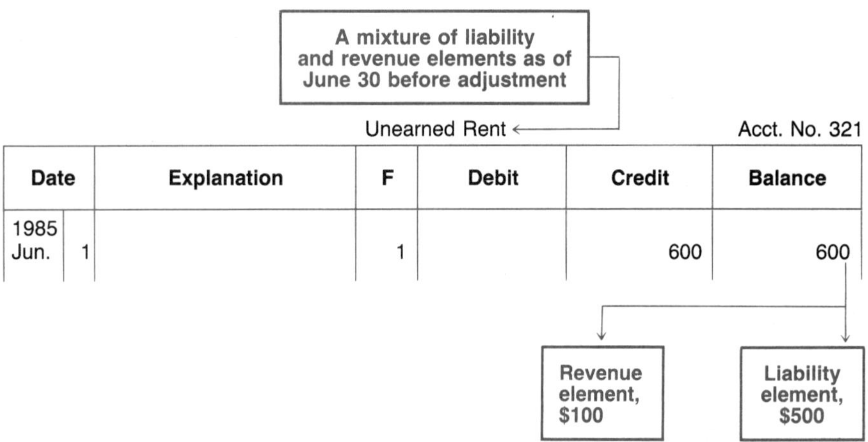

Unearned Rent — Acct. No. 321

Date		Explanation	F	Debit	Credit	Balance
1985 Jun.	1		1		600	600

Step 3. The following adjusting entry is made:

GENERAL JOURNAL — Page 4

Date		Debit-Credit-Account Titles: Explanation	F	Debit	Credit
1985 Jun.	30	Unearned Rent	321	100	
		Rent Earned	511		100
		To record revenue earned from rental of trucks during June.			

The revenue element is removed from the liability account, Unearned Rent, and recorded in a revenue account as shown below:

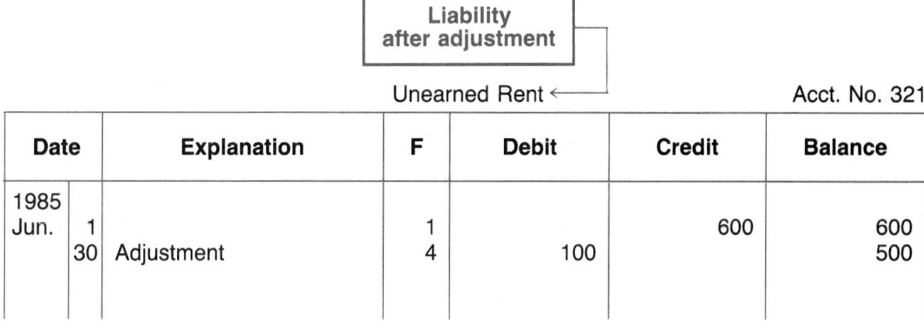

Unearned Rent — Acct. No. 321

Date		Explanation	F	Debit	Credit	Balance
1985 Jun.	1		1		600	600
	30	Adjustment	4	100		500

Revenue after adjustment

Rent Earned — Acct. No. 511

Date		Explanation	F	Debit	Credit	Balance
1985 Jun.	30	Adjustment	4		100	100

Rent earned ($100) appears in the income statement as a revenue item, and unearned rent ($500) appears in the balance sheet as a current liability.

Long-Term Cost Apportionments—A Third Type of Deferral

Two of Genova Trucking Company's adjusting entries involve the recording of long-term asset cost expiration. Three steps similar to the short-term cost apportionments are followed.

Adjustment for Depreciation of Office Equipment

Step 1. The trial balance, Figure 4–1, shows a balance of $1,400 in the Office Equipment account.
Step 2. The equipment, acquired on June 1 for $1,400, is estimated to have a useful life of 10 years, or 120 months, and a salvage value of $200 at the end of that period. **Salvage** or **residual value** is the estimated price for which an asset may be sold when it is no longer serviceable to the business. In effect, the use of office equipment for 10 years has a net cost of $1,200 = ($1,400 − $200). A portion of this cost expires in each accounting period during the useful life of the equipment. This periodic expired cost, called **depreciation expense,** requires no periodic cash outlay, but nevertheless is a continuous expense of operating the business.

Depreciation expense

***The portion of the cost of a property, plant, and equipment asset assigned to the accounting period is called* depreciation expense.**

A number of methods may be used in calculating the periodic depreciation expense. Depreciation for the month of June is computed in this case by using the **straight line method,** in which a uniform portion of the cost is assigned to each period. Other depreciation methods used in practice are discussed in Chapter 13. The straight line method is a popular method mainly because of its simplicity of calculation:

$$\frac{\text{Cost} - \text{Salvage value}}{\text{Estimated months of useful life}} = \text{Depreciation per month.}$$

The depreciation expense for the office equipment in June is computed as $10.

$$\frac{\$1{,}400 - \$200}{120} = \$10.$$

Step 3. The following adjusting entry is made:

GENERAL JOURNAL — Page 4

Date		Debit-Credit-Account Titles: Explanation	F	Debit	Credit
1985					
Jun.	30	Depreciation Expense—Office Equipment	609	10	
		Accumulated Depreciation—Office Equipment	201A		10
		To record depreciation for June.			

Both of the foregoing accounts are new. The account credited, Accumulated Depreciation—Office Equipment, is called a **contra asset account,** because its balance is deducted from Office Equipment to show the book value, or carrying value, of the asset. Other contra, or negative-type accounts are established to measure separately specific deductions from parent-type accounts whose amounts need to be preserved. For instance, contra liability, contra revenue, or even contra expense accounts are used; but none of these is used as frequently as the contra asset accounts described here. Office Equipment is not credited directly because depreciation is an estimate, and it is informative to keep asset cost separate from the estimated expiration of cost. When separate accounts are used, the original cost and the accumulated depreciation can be determined readily. The June 30 adjusting information is shown in the following ledger accounts:

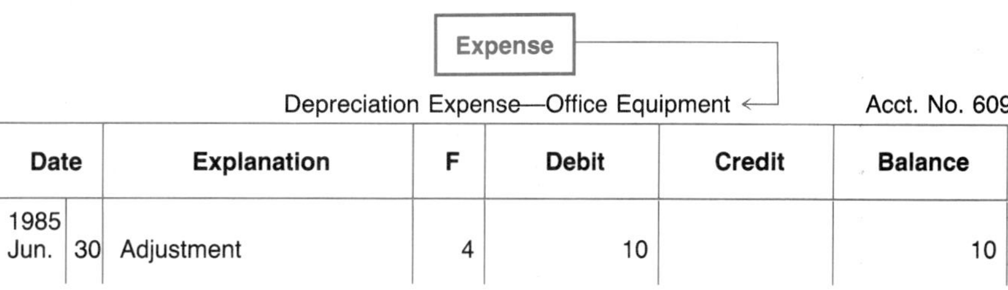

Depreciation Expense—Office Equipment — Acct. No. 609

Date		Explanation	F	Debit	Credit	Balance
1985						
Jun.	30	Adjustment	4	10		10

Contra asset account

Accumulated Depreciation—Office Equipment — Acct. No. 201A

Date		Explanation	F	Debit	Credit	Balance
1985						
Jun.	30	Adjustment	4		10	10

In the balance sheet (see Figure 5–9), the contra asset account, Accumulated Depreciation—Office Equipment, is deducted from Office Equipment; the remainder is the **undepreciated cost,** that is, the portion of the cost of the asset that is not yet charged to expense. Depreciation expense—office equipment ($10) is shown in the income statement as an expense.

Adjustment for Depreciation of Trucks

Step 1. On June 1, the Genova Trucking Company purchased two trucks for business use, each costing $13,000. Because the useful life of trucks is limited, a portion of the cost is allocable to each month (June in this case) the trucks are used. It is estimated that their useful life is five years, or 60 months, at the end of which time each truck will have a salvage value of $1,000.

Step 2. The computation and recording of the depreciation expense for the trucks is similar to that for the office equipment. The depreciation expense for June for the two trucks is calculated by the straight line method as follows:

$$\frac{\text{Cost of \$13,000} - \text{Salvage value of \$1,000}}{\text{60 months}} = \text{\$200 depreciation per month for } \textit{each} \text{ truck, or \$400 for two trucks}$$

Step 3. The following adjusting entry is made on June 30 and posted to the accounts shown after the journal entry:

GENERAL JOURNAL — Page 4

Date		Debit-Credit-Account Titles: Explanation	F	Debit	Credit
1985 Jun.	30	Depreciation Expense—Trucks	610	400	
		Accumulated Depreciation—Trucks	211A		400
		To record depreciation for June.			

Expense

Depreciation Expense—Trucks — Acct. No. 610

Date		Explanation	F	Debit	Credit	Balance
1985 Jun.	30	Adjustment	4	400		400

Contra asset account

Accumulated Depreciation—Trucks — Acct. No. 211A

Date		Explanation	F	Debit	Credit	Balance
1985 Jun.	30	Adjustment	4		400	400

Depreciation expense—trucks and accumulated depreciation—trucks are classified in the financial statements in the same manner as was depreciation expense—office equipment and accumulated depreciation—office equipment. Depreciation expense—trucks is shown on the income statement as an expense and accumulated depreciation—trucks is deducted from the trucks amount on the balance sheet (see Figures 5–7 and 5–9).

Accumulated Depreciation accounts are used to accumulate the current and all the past periodic charges made to expense and to set up in one account the amount of the deduction for asset valuation. Depreciation Expense shows the expired cost for the accounting period and is closed along with the other expense accounts in an entry that transfers the total expense to Income Summary. Assume that the same adjusting entry for trucks is made on July 31. After it is posted, the general ledger accounts for Trucks, Depreciation Expense—Trucks, and Accumulated Depreciation—Trucks appear as follows:

Trucks — Acct. No. 211

Date		Explanation	F	Debit	Credit	Balance
1985						
Jun.	1		1	26,000		26,000

Accumulated Depreciation—Trucks — Acct. No. 211A

Date		Explanation	F	Debit	Credit	Balance
1985						
Jun.	30	Adjustment	4		400	400
Jul.	31	Adjustment	8		400	800

Depreciation Expense—Trucks — Acct. No. 610

Date		Explanation	F	Debit	Credit	Balance
1985						
Jun.	30	Adjusting entry	4	400		400
	30	Closing entry	5		400	0
Jul.	31	Adjusting entry	8	400		400

Balance before the July closing is a debit.

The cost of the trucks and the accumulated depreciation are shown on the balance sheet on July 31 as follows:

Property, plant, and equipment:		
Trucks	$26,000	
Deduct: Accumulated depreciation—trucks	800	$25,200

The $25,200 figure is referred to as the **book value** of the trucks.

In the next sections, adjustments for accruals are illustrated. Both revenues and expenses accrue and must be recorded.

Accrued Revenues—The First of Two Types of Accruals

Accrued revenues include items that have been accumulated and earned in a given period but not recorded in the accounts and for which cash collections have not yet been received or recorded. At the end of the accounting period, the accountant records the revenue in the period in which it is earned and also records the accompanying receivable, an asset. The accrued revenue adjustment described is that of unrecorded interest.

Adjustment for Unrecorded Interest Revenue

Step 1. The Genova Trucking Company made a loan of $1,440 to one of its suppliers, who signed a 30-day, 15 percent, interest-bearing note dated June 10. An entry was made on June 10 debiting Notes Receivable and crediting Cash for $1,440.

Step 2. The company earned interest on the loan for 20 days in June (note that in counting days for accrual of interest, the date of the note is not counted; hence the time in this case is calculated for June 11–June 30 inclusive). The interest will be received on the maturity date, July 10, when the amount due (principal plus total interest) is paid by the supplier. Interest earned accrues with the passage of time. The 20 days' interest earned by June 30 means that Interest Earned (a revenue account) should be $12, and Genova has an asset (interest receivable) of $12.

The formula for computing simple interest (interest on the original principal only) is shown in Figure 4–2.[4]

$$\text{Interest} = \text{Principal} \times \text{Interest rate} \times \frac{\text{Elapsed time in days}}{360}$$

Figure 4–2
Interest Formula

[4]A more detailed presentation of the calculation of interest is found in Chapter 10.

The uncollected interest accrued through June 30 is computed as follows:

$$\text{Interest} = \$1{,}440 \times 0.15 \times \frac{20}{360} = \$12.$$

In the calculation we can see that when the principal is multiplied by the interest rate, the interest for one year, $216 = ($1,440 × 0.15), is determined. Thus the interest for one year ($216) must be multiplied by the elapsed fraction of a year (20/360 or 1/18) to determine the interest for 20 days, which is $12. The use of 360 days in the formula is consistent with commercial practice. The primary reason for its use is the simplicity of calculation.

Step 3. In order to reflect this unrecorded information in the accounts, the formal adjusting entry debiting Accrued Interest Receivable and crediting Interest Earned is made on June 30 and posted to the accounts indicated below:

GENERAL JOURNAL Page 4

Date		Debit-Credit-Account Titles: Explanation	F	Debit	Credit
1985					
Jun.	30	Accrued Interest Receivable	113	12	
		Interest Earned	521		12
		To record interest revenue accrued during June 11–30, 1985.			

Asset

Accrued Interest Receivable Acct. No. 113

Date		Explanation	F	Debit	Credit	Balance
1985						
Jun.	30	Adjustment	4	12		12

Revenue

Interest Earned Acct. No. 521

Date		Explanation	F	Debit	Credit	Balance
1985						
Jun.	30	Adjustment	4		12	12

Accrued interest receivable ($12) is a current asset in the balance sheet. Interest earned is a revenue in the income statement. In all accrual adjustments, accrued revenues will be found to cause assets to increase.

Accrued Expenses—The Second Type of Accrual

Accrued expenses are expenses that have been incurred or accumulated in a given period but have not yet been paid. (Recall that an expense is said to be incurred in the period when the effort to produce revenue is made.) At the end of the accounting period the accountant must record the expense in the proper period of incurrence and must record the accompanying liability. The first accrued expense adjustment described here involves unrecorded wages expense.

Adjustment for Unrecorded Wages Expense

Step 1. Wages Expense contains two debits of $600 each, representing gross wages earned every two weeks by employees through June 27.
Step 2. The employees earned wages of $150 for work on June 28, 29, and 30, the last three days of the accounting period. Although the company will not pay the employees again until July 11, it has nevertheless incurred $150 of wages expense for these three days, and a $150 liability exists as of June 30.
Step 3. An adjusting entry is made to record the $150 in wages expense incurred for the last three days of June and to reflect the liability. It is then posted to the accounts shown after the journal entry:

GENERAL JOURNAL Page 4

Date		Debit-Credit-Account Titles: Explanation	F	Debit	Credit
1985					
Jun.	30	Wages Expense	605	150	
		Accrued Wages Payable	311		150
		To record wages expense accrued during June 28–30, 1985.			

Expense

Wages Expense Acct. No. 605

Date		Explanation	F	Debit	Credit	Balance
1985						
Jun.	13		2	600		600
	27		3	600		1,200
	30	Adjustment	4	150		1,350

Liability

Accrued Wages Payable Acct. No. 311

Date		Explanation	F	Debit	Credit	Balance
1985						
Jun.	30	Adjustment	4		150	150

Wages expense ($1,350) is shown in the income statement as an expense; accrued wages payable ($150) is shown in the balance sheet as a current liability (see Figures 5–7 and 5–9). Just the opposite of an accrual of a revenue, all accruals of expenses cause increases in liabilities instead of assets.

Adjustment for Unrecorded Interest Expense

Step 1. On June 12, the Genova Trucking Company borrowed $8,000 from the bank and signed a 45-day, 16 percent interest-bearing note payable. This transaction was recorded in the general journal by debiting Cash and crediting Notes Payable for $8,000.

Step 2. The cost of the use of the $8,000—interest expense—continues throughout the 45 days because interest expense accumulates with the passage of time. The total interest expense plus the $8,000 principal amount will be paid to the bank on July 27, the maturity, or due, date. However, unpaid interest expense on an interest-bearing note payable for the period from the day after June 12 through June 30 inclusive (18 days—the date of the note is not counted, but June 30 is) must be recognized by an adjusting entry reflecting Interest Expense and Accrued Interest Payable.

Using the formula shown in Figure 4–2, the unpaid interest expense accrued on June 30 is computed as follows:

$$\text{Interest} = \$8{,}000 \times 0.16 \times \frac{18}{360} = \$64.$$

Step 3. The formal adjusting entry is made on June 30 and posted to the accounts indicated below:

GENERAL JOURNAL — Page 5

Date		Debit-Credit-Account Titles: Explanation	F	Debit	Credit
1985					
Jun.	30	Interest Expense	611	64	
		Accrued Interest Payable	303		64
		To record interest expense accrued during June 13–30, 1985.			

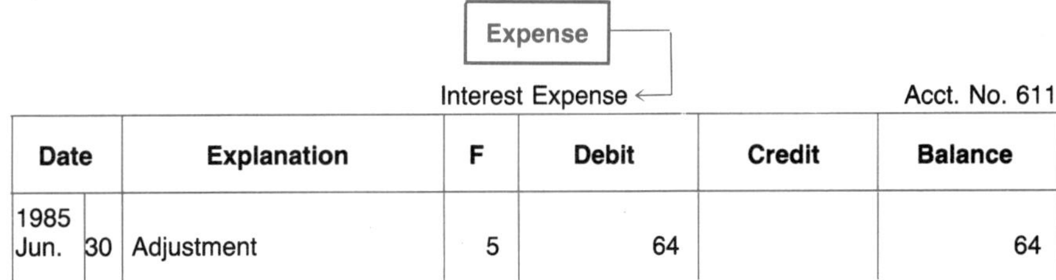

Interest Expense — Acct. No. 611

Date		Explanation	F	Debit	Credit	Balance
1985						
Jun.	30	Adjustment	5	64		64

Liability

Accrued Interest Payable — Acct. No. 303

Date		Explanation	F	Debit	Credit	Balance
1985						
Jun.	30	Adjustment	5		64	64

Interest expense ($64) is reported as an expense in the income statement. Accrued interest payable ($64) appears as a current liability in the balance sheet; it is actually an **accrued liability** (liability for an expense accumulated and incurred during one accounting period but not payable until a future accounting period). Expenses incurred for which invoices have not yet been received—telephone, heat, light, water, and so on—are also in this category. These may be estimated and recorded by debits to appropriate expense accounts and a credit to Accrued Utilities Payable or a similarly named account.

Summary of Adjustments

As stated previously, the adjustments are classified into two broad groups, deferrals and accruals. Figure 4–3 summarizes five types of adjustments into these classifications and gives brief summary entries for each type of adjustment.

As noted previously, the way a deferral adjustment is made depends on how the original entry was recorded. Because the reader will encounter deferrals that have been debited to expense or credited to a revenue, this idea is expanded in the next section.

Broad Classification	No.	Kind of Adjustment	Brief Definition	Pro Forma Adjusting Entry[a]
Deferrals	1	Short-term cost apportionment. Assumption: The original debit is made to an asset account.	A prepaid item that benefits two or more periods; if the original amount is debited to an asset, it is necessary to apportion expense to appropriate periods.	Dr. Appropriate Expense (E) Cr. Prepaid Asset (A)
	2	Short-term revenue apportionment. Assumption: The original credit is made to a liability account.	A revenue item that is collected in advance of the period(s) earned; if the amount is credited to a liability account, it is necessary to apportion the revenue to the appropriate period in which it is earned.	Dr. Unearned ______ (L) Cr. Appropriate Revenue (R)
	3	Long-term cost apportionment. (Note: this is always originally debited to an asset.)	A prepaid item that benefits the present and several future periods; the amount must be apportioned to the periods benefited by the prepayment.	For a depreciable property, plant, and equipment item: Dr. Depreciation Expense (E) Cr. Accumulated Depreciation (Contra A)
Accruals	4	Accrued revenue.	Revenue earned in a given period but not yet collected or recorded.	Dr. Accrued ______ Receivable (A) Cr. Appropriate Revenue (R)
	5	Accrued expense.	Expense incurred in a given period but not yet paid or recorded.	Dr. Appropriate Expense (E) Cr. Accrued ______ Payable (L)

[a]Codes used: A, asset; R, revenue; E, expense; L, liability; Contra A, contra asset or valuation account.

Figure 4–3 **Summary of Deferrals and Accruals**

Alternative Adjustment Methods for Deferrals

Accountants do record deferrals in at least two different ways. For instance, prepaid insurance (or other short-term costs) may be initially recorded as an asset and then adjusted as shown on page 126. Alternatively, the accountant might originally record the prepaid amount in an Insurance Expense account (that is, debit Insurance Expense and credit Cash). At the end of the period, the accountant would then remove from the expense account the amount still unexpired or prepaid for the future. Had the Genova Trucking Company originally recorded the insurance premium in the Insurance Expense account, the adjusting entry as of June 30, 1985, would be a debit to Prepaid Insurance, $2,100, and a credit to Insurance Expense, $2,100.

Similarly, unearned rent revenue (or other short-term revenues) may be initially recorded as a liability and then adjusted as shown on page 129. The accountant alternatively might record the unearned amount upon receipt in a Rent Earned account (debit Cash and credit Rent Earned). At the end of the period, the accountant then would have to remove from the revenue account the amount still unearned at that time. Had the Genova Trucking Company originally recorded the advance receipt of rent in the Rent Earned account, the adjusting entry as of June 30, 1985, would be a debit to Rent Earned, $500, and a credit to Unearned Rent, $500, to record the correct amount of the liability element.

Application of the Materiality Concept to Adjustments

The preceding adjustments were made to update the assets, liabilities, expenses, and revenues of the Genova Trucking Company. After they are made, a correctly stated income statement and balance sheet can be prepared. No exceptions were mentioned to the general rule that all adjustments should be made.

One exception (usually referred to as the **materiality concept**) generally accepted in practice is that adjustments do not have to be made for insignificant, immaterial, or trivial items. For example, the box of paper clips in the bookkeeper's desk as of the balance sheet date is an asset of the company, although its cost has been debited to expense. It is possible but not practical to make an adjusting entry for the asset value of the unused clips. Because of the item's small cost, failure to make the adjustment will have no material effect on the financial statements and cannot mislead the user of such statements. A similar situation exists with respect to other minor items of supply or services.

Materiality concept

The need for adjustment and the need for full disclosure do not apply to insignificant, immaterial, or trivial matters.

The accountant is faced with the problem of determining what is material and what is immaterial. For instance, an item costing $100 may be material in a small business, whereas an item costing $1,000 may be insignificant in a multimillion-dollar business. The decision hinges on whether the failure to disclose a given item separately will affect the decision of an informed statement user. For example, it may not be misleading to combine several insignificant items of expense or revenue into one account. It may be very misleading to combine a significant loss from a lawsuit with a regular expense account. Regardless of the amount, it may be necessary to disclose an item separately because it may be an essential component in a business decision or because of its very nature. For example, even a small bribe to an official of a foreign government may have far-reaching implications.

Appendix 4.1
Reversing Entries

Introduction

In some situations, it is possible to save time and to reduce the cost of performing the accounting function by the use of a specially designed procedure. One such procedure involves the use of reversing entries. **Reversing entries** are made at the beginning of the next accounting period and are the reverse of certain previous year adjusting entries. The preparation of these entries is not a required step in the accounting process, and they should be prepared only when they are beneficial to the accountant. This appendix contains an explanation of reversing procedures.

Learning Goals

To explain the relationship of the reversing entries to the adjustments and to the accounting cycle.

To be able to make reversing entries for accruals and deferrals.

To identify adjusting entries that are never reversed.

To identify adjusting entries that are reversed.

Illustrations

Assume a small company with a five-day work week pays its employees each Friday. The payroll is $500 a day, or $2,500 for a five-day work week. Throughout the period, year 1, the company's accountant makes a journal entry each Friday as follows:

		Salaries and Wages Expense		2,500	
		Cash			2,500
		To record payment of salaries for the week.			

Next, assume that the last day of the period is December 31 and that it falls on a Wednesday. All expenses of this year must be recorded before the expense accounts are closed and financial statements as of December 31 are prepared. An adjusting entry, therefore, must be made to record the salaries expense and the related liability to the employees for Monday, Tuesday, and Wednesday of year 1, the days that they have worked since the preceding payday on Friday. The adjusting entry for the $1,500 = (3 × $500) is journalized as follows:

Year	1				
Dec.	31	Salaries and Wages Expense		1,500	
		Accrued Salaries Payable			1,500
		To record the accrued salaries for the last three days of December.			

When closing entries are made, the Salaries and Wages Expense account is reduced to zero. The liability account, Accrued Salaries Payable, remains open with its $1,500 balance at the beginning of the new period, year 2. On the next regular payday, Friday, January 2, the company's accountant may elect not to follow the reversing procedure and to record the $2,500 weekly payroll by a debit of $1,500 to Accrued Salaries Payable, a debit of $1,000 to Salaries and Wages Expense (for Thursday and Friday), and a credit of $2,500 to Cash. However, analyzing the payment into the amount applicable to a liability ($1,500) and to an expense ($1,000) requires more knowledge and accounting experience than if the entry were identical to the other weekly payroll entries made during the year.

Making a reversing entry on the first day of the new accounting period simplifies the recording of routine transactions and removes the need for reference back to previous adjustments. The reversing entry for the $1,500 year-end accrual of salaries should be dated January 1, year 2 and is:

Year	2				
Jan.	1	Accrued Salaries Payable		1,500	
		Salaries and Wages Expense			1,500
		To reverse the accrual of salaries made on December 31, year 1.			

The reversing entry reduces the Accrued Salaries Payable account to zero by transferring the $1,500 liability to the credit column of the Salaries and Wages Expense account. Thus, this expense account will have a credit balance of $1,500 before the first payroll is paid. This credit (negative) balance is circled to indicate that it is opposite from a normal credit balance. On Friday, January 2, year 2, the normal payroll entry for $2,500 is made in the same way as on every other Friday during the year, as follows:

Year	2				
Jan.	2	Salaries and Wages Expense		2,500	
		Cash			2,500
		To record the salaries for the week ended January 2, year 2.			

After this January 2 entry has been posted, the expense account shows a debit balance of only $1,000, the result of the January 1 reversing entry and the January 2 payroll entry. The end results are exactly the same as if no reversing entry had been used and the company's accountant had split the debit side of the January 2 payroll entry between Accrued Salaries Payable and Salaries and Wages Expense.

The two accounts are shown below to illustrate the effect of posting the adjusting entry on December 31, year 1, and the reversing entry on January 1, year 2.

Salaries and Wages Expense

Date		Explanation	F	Debit	Credit	Balance
Year	1					
Various		Balance—51 entries of 2,500				127,500
Dec.	31	Adjusting		1,500		129,000
	31	Closing			129,000	0
Year	2					
Jan.	1	Reversing			1,500	(1,500)
	2	Weekly Payroll		2,500		1,000

Accrued Salaries Payable

Date		Explanation	F	Debit	Credit	Balance
Year	1					
Dec.	31	Adjusting			1,500	1,500
Year	2					
Jan.	1	Reversing		1,500		0

Which Adjusting Entries May be Reversed

Any accrual adjustment may be reversed; the reversal is optional. Examples are accrued interest expense, accrued interest revenue, and accrued salaries expense. Accrued adjustments bring expenses and revenues and the accompanying liability or asset into the records and are followed by payment or receipt of cash in the next period.

Adjusting entries for both short-term and long-term cost apportionments originally recorded as assets are not reversed. If deferrals originally are recorded in an expense account or revenue account (see Alternative Adjustment Methods for Deferrals section earlier in Chapter 4), the subsequent adjusting entries are reversed. Figure A4–1 shows a summary of accruals and deferrals and the last column of this figure indicates whether an adjusting entry should be reversed.

Guideline for Reversal

Again, reversing entries are devices which can be helpful under some circumstances. They should be used *only* when they are beneficial to the accountant. If a particular optional adjustment procedure requiring reversing

Broad Classification	No.	Kind of Adjustment	Brief Definition	Pro Forma Adjusting Entry[a]	Do you reverse?
Accruals	1	Accrued revenue	Revenue earned in a given period but not yet collected or recorded.	Dr. Accrued ______ Receivable (A) Cr. Appropriate Revenue (R)	Reversing is optional.
	2	Accrued expense	Expense incurred in a given period but not yet paid or recorded.	Dr. Appropriate Expense (E) Cr. Accrued ______ Payable (L)	Reversing is optional.
Deferrals	3.1	Short-term cost apportionment. Assumption: The original debit entry is made to an asset account.	A prepaid item that benefits two or more periods; if the original amount is debited to an asset, it is necessary to apportion expense to appropriate periods.	Dr. Appropriate Expense (E) Cr. Prepaid Asset (A)	No, reversing is never done.
	3.2	Short-term cost apportionment. Assumption: The original debit entry is made to an expense account.	A prepaid item that benefits two or more periods; if for convenience the original amount is debited to an expense account, the unexpired portion at the adjustment date must be removed from the expense account and set up as an asset.	Dr. Prepaid Asset (A) Cr. Appropriate Expense (E)	Yes, it is necessary to reverse this kind of adjusting entry.
	4.1	Short-term revenue apportionment. Assumption: The original credit entry is made to a liability account.	A revenue item that is collected in advance of the period(s) earned; if the amount is credited to a liability account, it is necessary to apportion the revenue to the appropriate period in which it is earned.	Dr. Unearned ______ (L) Cr. Appropriate Revenue (R)	No, reversing is never done.
	4.2	Short-term revenue apportionment. Assumption: The original credit entry is made to a revenue account.	A revenue item collected in advance of the period(s) earned; if for convenience the original amount is credited to a revenue account, the unearned portion at the adjustment date must be removed from the revenue account and set up as a liability.	Dr. Appropriate Revenue (R) Cr. Unearned ______ (L)	Yes, it is necessary to reverse this kind of adjusting entry.
	5	Long-term cost apportionment. (Note: this is always originally debited to an asset.)	A prepaid item that benefits the present and several future periods; the amount must be apportioned to the periods benefited by the prepayment.	For a depreciable property, plant, and equipment item: Dr. Depreciation Expense (E) Cr. Accumulated Depreciation (Contra A)	No, reversing is never done.

[a]Codes used: A, asset; R, revenue; E, expense; L, liability; Contra A, contra asset or valuation account.

Figure A4–1 **Summary of Accruals and Deferrals**

entries is helpful in some way to a firm, it should be used. If some beneficial results—ease of recording or saving in time and effort—are not achieved, it should not be used. Adjustments for deferrals originally set up as assets and liabilities are never reversed. Adjustments for long-term cost apportionments are never reversed.

Glossary

Accounting depreciation The system of allocation of a part of the cost of a property, plant, and equipment item (that has a limited useful life) over its estimated useful life in a systematic and rational manner.

Accrual basis of accounting The basis that assumes that revenue is realized at the time of the sale of goods or services, regardless of when the cash is received; expenses are recognized at the time the services are received and utilized or an asset is consumed in the production of revenue, regardless of when payment for these services or assets is made.

Accruals A classification of adjustments that is required to update unrecorded accumulated revenues and expenses.

Accrued Accumulated or built onto.

Accrued expenses Expenses that have been incurred in a given period—for example, services received and used—but that have not yet been paid or recorded.

Accrued liability The liability for an expense that has been accumulated but not yet paid or recorded.

Accrued revenues Revenues that have been earned in a given period but that have not yet been collected or recorded.

Accumulated Depreciation An account which reveals all past depreciation that has been recorded on a depreciable property, plant, and equipment item and charged against revenue; it is in essence a postponed credit to the applicable property, plant, and equipment account.

Adjusting entries Entries for regular continuous transactions whose recording has been postponed to the end of an accounting period for the convenience of the accountant; they are made to update revenue, expense, asset, liability, and owner's equity accounts as required by the accrual basis of accounting.

Apportionment The dividing of a cost or revenue among two or more periods.

Book value The difference between the original cost of a depreciable property, plant, and equipment item and its related accumulated depreciation.

Cash basis of accounting The basis that reflects the recognition of revenue at the time that cash is received for the sale of goods and services and the recognition of expenses in the period of the payment for the expense.

Contra account A negative element of (offset to) a related account that is shown in a separate account; the contra account should always be shown in the ledger immediately following the account of which it is a reduction. Both assets and liabilities may have contra accounts.

Deferrals A classification of adjustments that includes short-term revenue apportionments, short-term cost apportionments, and long-term cost apportionments. They are called deferrals because the recognition of expense or revenue is deferred until adjusting entries are made.

Depreciation See *Accounting depreciation.*

Depreciation expense The amount of property, plant, and equipment cost that is assigned to a given period.

Earned revenue Revenue is said to be earned when substantially all efforts to bring it into existence have been expended except the collection of the revenue in the form of cash.

Long-term cost apportionment adjustment An adjustment requiring the apportioning of the cost of a long-lived asset between the current period and a future time span of two or more years.

Materiality concept An accounting concept that requires an item that is large enough and significant enough to influence decisions by statement users to be separately identified in accounting statements.

Reversing entries Entries made on the first day of a new fiscal period that are reversals of adjusting entries.

Salvage value The estimated scrap value or resale value that a property, plant, and equipment item should have at the end of its estimated useful life. Also called residual value.

Short-term cost apportionment adjustment An adjustment that requires that a previously recorded prepaid item be apportioned between the current period and a future short period (usually a year). The prepayment may be originally debited to an asset or to an expense account.

Short-term revenue apportionment adjustment An adjustment that requires that a previously recorded advance collection of a revenue be apportioned between the current period and a future short period (usually one year). The advance collection may be originally credited to a liability or a revenue account.

Straight line method of depreciation A method that allocates the cost of a depreciable asset over the estimated useful life of the asset in equal amounts for each time period.

Undepreciated cost The remaining property, plant, and equipment cost to be charged as depreciation in the future; mathematically, it is the original cost of a property, plant, and equipment item less the sum of the accumulated depreciation and any salvage value.

Unearned revenues Revenue payments received in advance of the earning process.

Questions

Q4–1 The adjustment process is really a question of measuring net income first and balance sheet items second. From an income measurement point of view, why is it important to match all incurred expenses against all earned revenue to determine net income?

Q4–2 (a) What are the essential differences between the cash basis of accounting and the accrual basis of accounting? (b) Since the accrual basis is the only one that satisfies the basic accounting needs, how can a firm justify the use of the cash basis? Discuss.

Q4–3 (a) What purpose is served by adjusting entries? (b) What types of events make adjusting entries necessary?

Q4–4 Most adjustments are grouped into two categories—deferrals and accruals. Discuss these terms and indicate what kinds of adjustments would fall in each group.

Q4–5 There are two methods of recording and adjusting for deferrals. Discuss these methods. Do you see any problems with alternative methods?

Q4–6 Does the need to make adjusting entries at the end of a period mean that errors were made in the accounts during the period? Discuss.

Q4–7 Define the following terms: (a) accrued revenues, (b) accrued expenses, (c) short-term cost apportionments, (d) long-term cost apportionments, (e) short-term revenue apportionments.

Q4–8 (a) What is a contra account? (b) Name one contra account involved in adjusting entries. (c) What is the specific purpose served by the contra account you just named?

Q4–9 On the balance sheet, where do you classify the following: (a) prepaid insurance, (b) unearned rent, (c) accrued interest receivable, (d) accrued wages payable.

Q4–10 During 1985, the Elfland Company made prepayments of premiums on 1-year, 2-year, and 3-year property insurance policies. The company recorded the premium payments in an account that it calls Prepaid Property Insurance.

a. At the close of 1985, will the necessary adjusting entry be a deferral or an accrual?
b. Which of the following types of accounts will be affected by the related adjusting entry required at the end of the year: (1) asset, (2) liability, (3) revenue, (4) expense?

Q4–11 At the end of the fiscal year, a company has a 150-day interest-bearing note payable that had been issued to a supplier 90 days earlier.

a. Will the interest on the note as of the end of the current year represent a deferral or an accrual?
b. Which of the following types of accounts will be affected by the related adjusting entry at the end of the current year: (1) asset, (2) liability, (3) revenue, (4) expense?
c. Assuming that the note is not paid until maturity, what fraction of the total interest should be allocated to the year in which the note is paid?

Q4–12 (a) Do you agree with the statement that "items of little or no consequence may be dealt with as expediency may suggest"? (b) Do you agree with the statement that "problems of materiality are easily resolved and, in any case, are not very important"?

Q4–13 (Appendix) When earned but uncollected revenue is not recorded until the end of the year—for example, interest earned—the reversing entry on January 1 of the next year is optional. Explain what account is affected when the revenue is collected, depending on whether or not a reversing entry is made.

Q4–14 (Appendix) (a) Define long-term cost apportionment and give an example of a transaction that would require such an apportionment. (b) Would the adjustment for long-term cost apportionment ever be reversed?

Q4–15 (Appendix) (a) List two kinds of adjustments in which the reversing entry is optional. (b) Give an example of the reversing entry for each type of adjustment.

Q4–16 (Appendix) (a) What is the purpose of reversing entries? (b) Under what conditions would the reversing procedure be advantageous?

Exercises

E4–1 *Calculating information from adjustment data*

a. The balance sheets of the Stonehinge Company as of December 31, 1985 and 1986, showed office supplies totaling $3,040 and $3,420, respectively. During 1986, office supplies totaling $4,300 were purchased. What was the amount of office supplies expense for the year 1986?

b. The balances of the Prepaid Insurance account of the Jobello Company were as follows:

December 31, 1985	$1,465
December 31, 1986	960

The income statement for 1986 showed insurance expense of $1,820. What was the total cash expenditure for insurance premiums during 1986?

E4–2 *Depreciation adjustment and related contra*

The O'Neal Company purchased a new van on January 1, 1985, for $12,800. The van had an estimated useful life of five years and a trade-in value at the end of that time of $800.

a. What is the amount of depreciation expense for 1985?
b. What is the balance in the Accumulated Depreciation—Vans account at the end of 1985? 1987?
c. What will be the book value of the vans on the balance sheet of December 31, 1985? December 31, 1987?
d. Why is the depreciation amount credited to Accumulated Depreciation—Vans rather than directly to Vans?

E4–3 *Accrued expense adjustment*

The Amity Company employs 8 sales clerks at a weekly salary of $320 each. The clerks are paid on Friday, the last day of a five-day work week. Make the adjusting journal entry, assuming that the accounting period ended on a Monday. On a Wednesday.

E4–4 *Cost apportionment adjustments*

The trial balance of the Atchison Company on December 31, 1985, included the following account balances before adjustments:

Prepaid Insurance	$ 1,980
Prepaid Advertising Supplies	2,640
Prepaid Rent	3,960
Office Supplies	4,950
Office Equipment	10,890

Data for adjustments on December 31, 1985, follow:

a. On November 1, 1985, the company purchased a two-year comprehensive insurance policy for $1,980.
b. Advertising supplies on hand totaled $990.
c. On September 1, 1985, the company paid one year's rent in advance.
d. The office supplies inventory was $2,376.
e. The office equipment was purchased on July 1, 1985, and has an estimated useful life of 10 years and a salvage value of $990.

Journalize the adjusting entries.

E4–5 *Various adjustments*

Make the end-of-month adjusting journal entries for the Mangus Company for the following items:

a. The debit balance of the Prepaid Insurance account is $3,450. Of this amount, $2,100 is expired.
b. Accrued salaries and wages payable total $680.
c. The Office Supplies account has a debit balance of $1,620; $178 is on hand.
d. Depreciation on store equipment is $890; on office equipment, $715.
e. Accrued interest receivable is $342.
f. Accrued interest payable is $287.

E4–6 *Alternative adjustment for unearned subscription revenue*

The Scoop Magazine Company credited Subscription Revenue for $45,000 received from subscribers to its new monthly magazine. All subscriptions were for 12 issues. The initial issue was mailed during September 1985.

1. Make the adjusting journal entry on December 31, 1985.

2. Suppose the initial issue was mailed during January 1985 and the last issue in December. Is an adjusting journal entry needed on December 31, 1985? If so, what is the journal entry?

E4–7 *Various adjustments*

Prepare adjusting journal entries from the following information pertaining to the accounts of Fast Action Company at the end of September 1985:

a. Accrued rent receivable, $1,022.
b. Accrued interest payable, $418.
c. Accrued taxes payable, $619.
d. Accrued wages payable, $2,425.
e. A trenching machine was rented during September from the Quality Equipment Rent Company at the rate of $30 per hour. The machine was used for a total of 272 hours during the month. The corporation had made an initial payment of $2,550 to Quality Equipment Rent Company for the rental of the machine that was debited to Prepaid Equipment Rent.
f. Accrued interest on municipal bonds owned, $867.
g. As of September 30, the unbilled service fees for completed work amounted to $2,958.
h. The company signed an order form on September 30, 1985, to purchase a trenching machine for $48,560.

E4–8 *Accrued interest adjustments*

On April 15, the Chope Company received a 30-day, 16 percent note for $2,400 from a customer. On April 20, the company borrowed $6,800 from the bank on its own 30-day, 16 percent note. Make journal entries to adjust the Chope Company books on April 30.

E4–9
Various adjustments

Because of an impending damage suit, the accountant for Good Times Service Company unexpectedly disappeared just before the close of the company's accounting year. In his haste to leave, he did not have a chance to discuss what adjusting entries would be necessary at the end of the year, December 31, 1985. Fortunately, however, he did jot down a few notes that provided some leads. The following are his notes:

a. Depreciation on furniture and equipment for the year is $8,675.
b. Charge off $1,800 of expired insurance from prepaid account for the year.
c. Accrued interest at end of year on note payable to bank is $3,410.
d. No bill received yet from car rental agency for salesmen's cars—should be about $14,600 for the year.
e. Two days' salaries will be unpaid at year-end; total weekly (five days) salary is $7,200.

1. On the basis of the information available, prepare adjusting journal entries with brief explanations.

2. What other normal or usual adjustments may have to be recorded in addition to the foregoing? Briefly explain each one.

E4–10
Alternative methods of accounting for deferrals

(Appendix) Jennifer Kennedy, D.D.S, has just graduated from dental school. She is in the process of starting her own practice and has ordered subscriptions to some popular magazines to put in her waiting room. She must pay for the 12-month subscriptions in advance. On May 1, 1985, she sends checks totaling $156 to the various publishers. The part-time bookkeeper she has hired to manage her billings has the option of making the entry on May 1, 1985, as indicated in Case I or as indicated in Case II.

Case I:

GENERAL JOURNAL

Date		Debit-Credit-Account Titles: Explanation	F	Debit	Credit
1985					
May	1	Prepaid Magazine Subscriptions		156	
		Cash			156
		To record payment for 12-month magazine subscriptions.			

Case II:

GENERAL JOURNAL

Date		Debit-Credit-Account Titles: Explanation	F	Debit	Credit
1985					
May	1	Magazine Subscription Expense		156	
		Cash			156
		To record payment for 12-month magazine subscriptions.			

Make the adjusting journal entry and closing journal entry as of December 31, 1985, and December 31, 1986, and any reversing journal entries needed on January 1, 1986, assuming (a) the bookkeeper used the Case I method; and (b) the bookkeeper used the Case II method.

E4–11 *When to use reversing entries*

(Appendix) List which adjusting journal entries below would have a reversing entry. (If optional, specify.)

GENERAL JOURNAL

Date		Debit-Credit-Account Titles: Explanation	F	Debit	Credit
	a	Salaries Expense		20,525	
		Accrued Salaries Payable			20,525
	b	Depreciation Expense—Vans		1,250	
		Accumulated Depreciation—Vans			1,250
	c	Accrued Interest Receivable		820	
		Interest Earned			820
	d	Life Insurance Expense		1,050	
		Prepaid Life Insurance			1,050
	e	Subscriptions Earned		18,400	
		Unearned Subscriptions			18,400
	f	Prepaid Rent		2,280	
		Rent Expense			2,280
	g	Unearned Rent		960	
		Rent Earned			960

E4–12 *Accounting for unearned rent*

(Appendix) Susan Barnes received rent of $3,600 for one year beginning May 1, 1985. She recorded the transaction as follows:

GENERAL JOURNAL

Date		Debit-Credit-Account Titles: Explanation	F	Debit	Credit
1985 May	1	Cash		3,600	
		Unearned Rent			3,600

1. What adjusting journal entry is required on December 31, 1985?
2. What reversing journal entry, if any, would you make?
3. What nominal account could have been credited instead of Unearned Rent?
4. What adjusting journal entry would then be necessary?
5. What reversing journal entry, if any, would you make?

A Problems

P4–1A *Cash and accrual basis*

Selected transactions of the Eason Sales Company for 1985 are given:

1985		
Jan.	1	Purchased a four-year insurance policy for $3,600 cash.
Jul.	1	Bought two trucks and paid $41,500 in cash. The trucks are expected to last five years, at the end of which time their salvage value will be $2,000 each.
Dec.	31	Paid $900 rent for the three-month period ending March 31, 1986.
	31	Purchased office supplies for $350 cash.

Required:

1. Prepare journal entries to record the transactions using the accrual basis.

2. Prepare the adjusting journal entries as of December 31, 1985, using the accrual basis. The company closes its books annually on December 31.

3. Prepare the journal entries to record the transactions using the cash basis.

4. What adjusting journal entries would be made if the Eason Sales Company were on the cash basis?

P4–2A *Adjustments and effect on statements*

Certain unadjusted account balances from the trial balance of Darrell Noblitt's Consulting Firm for the year ended December 31, 1985, are given below:

DARRELL NOBLITT'S CONSULTING FIRM
Partial Trial Balance
December 31, 1985

Account Title	Debits	Credits
Accounts Receivable	$50,000	
Notes Receivable	21,000	
Prepaid Insurance	4,320	
Office Supplies	3,480	
Automobiles	30,000	
Accumulated Depreciation—Automobiles		$ 6,000
Notes Payable		9,000
Revenue—Consulting Fees		490,000
Interest Earned		1,000
Rent Earned		2,400
Advertising Expense	2,200	
Rent Expense	50,000	
Salaries Expense	51,000	
Property Taxes Expense	3,450	
Heat and Light Expense	2,600	

Adjustment data on December 31 are as follows:

a. Office supplies on hand totaled $750.
b. Depreciation for the year was $3,000.
c. Estimated heat and light expense not recorded was $410.
d. Of the amount shown for Interest Earned, $300 was unearned as of December 31, 1985.
e. The balance of the Prepaid Insurance account consists of $1,440 for the premium on a three-year policy dated July 1, 1985, and $2,880 for premiums on a three-year policy dated January 1, 1985.
f. Advertising supplies on hand were $280.
g. The balance of the Notes Payable account represents an 18 percent interest-bearing note dated January 1, 1985, due July 1, 1986.
h. The rent expense is $5,000 a month.
i. Salaries earned by employees but not paid were $2,500.
j. Property taxes accrued were $280.
k. On January 1, 1985, the Noblitt Firm subleased a section of its rented space. The lease with the tenant specifies the minimum yearly rental fee to be the greater of $2,400, payable at the beginning of each month, or 5 percent of gross sales. The amount of the adjustment in rent, if there is any adjustment, is due on January 15, 1986. The tenant reported sales of $53,000 for 1985.

l. Included in the Revenue—Consulting Fees account are advance payments of $15,500 by clients for services to be rendered early in 1986.

Required: Using the format shown below

1. Record adjusting journal entries.
2. Indicate the financial statement classification of each account in each entry.
3. Show the amount reported on the financial statements.

Example: Item a.

Item	Adjusting Journal Entries December 31, 1985	Dr.	Cr.	Financial Statement Classification	Amount Reported on Financial Statement
a	Office Supplies Expense	2,730		Expense	2,730
	Office Supplies		2,730	Current asset	750

P4–3A
Adjusting entries for deferrals and accruals

After an analysis of the accounts and the other records of Rumpkin Company, a single proprietorship, the following information is made available for the year ended December 31, 1985:

a. The Office Supplies account has a debit balance of $2,500. Office supplies on hand at December 31 total $810.
b. The Prepaid Rent account has a debit balance of $16,400. Included in this amount is $1,500 paid in December for the succeeding January; $14,900 has expired.
c. The Prepaid Insurance account has a debit balance of $5,760. It consists of the following policies purchased during 1985:

Policy No.	Date of Policy	Life of Policy	Premium
XY-462	January 1	3 years	$3,600
C3PX	April 1	2 years	1,440
Y206	October 1	1 year	720

d. The Prepaid Advertising account has a debit balance of $5,400. Included in this amount is $900 paid to a local monthly magazine for advertising space in its January and February 1986 issues.
e. At the close of the year, three notes receivable were on hand:

Date	Face Value	Total Time of Note in Days	Interest Rate (%)
November 1	$15,000	90	16
December 1	18,000	60	18
December 16	9,000	30	20

f. At the close of the year, two notes payable were outstanding:

Date	Face Value	Total Time of Note in Days	Interest Rate (%)
September 2	$18,000	180	15
November 1	21,000	90	18

g. Salaries and wages accrued totaled $4,800.
h. The Rent Earned account has a credit balance of $28,800 representing receipt of payment on a one-year lease effective May 1, 1985.
i. The Store Equipment account has a debit balance of $40,500. The equipment has an estimated useful life of 10 years and a salvage value of $4,500. All store equipment was acquired prior to January 1, 1985, and has a remaining life of five years.
j. The Vans account has a debit balance of $13,000. The van was purchased on June 1, 1984, and has an estimated life of five years and a salvage value of $1,500.
k. Property taxes accrued were $3,100.

Required: Prepare the adjusting journal entries required at December 31, 1985.

P4–4A
Adjusting and closing entries from a trial balance and added data

The unadjusted trial balance of the Wise Company contained the following accounts as of December 31, 1985:

WISE COMPANY
Partial Trial Balance
December 31, 1985

Acct. No.	Account Title	Debits	Credits
121	Accrued Interest Receivable	$ 0	
131	Office Supplies	950	
132	Prepaid Insurance	3,920	
133	Prepaid Advertising	0	
205	Accrued Wages Payable		$ 0
212	Unearned Rent		0
406	Rent Earned		222,000
410	Interest Earned		1,950
503	Wages Expense	51,000	
504	Advertising Expense	9,000	
505	Insurance Expense	0	
506	Office Supplies Expense	0	
601	Income Summary		0

Additional information includes the following:
a. Interest that had accrued on notes receivable at December 31, 1985, amounted to $420.
b. The inventory of office supplies at December 31, 1985, was $620.
c. The insurance records show that $2,000 of insurance has expired during 1985.
d. Included in Advertising Expense is a prepayment of a $1,500 contract for advertising space in a regional magazine; 60 percent of this contract has been used, and the remainder will be used in the following year.
e. Wages due to employees of $1,800 had accrued as of December 31, 1985.
f. Rent collected in advance that will not be earned until 1986 amounted to $9,500.

Required:

1. Open the accounts listed in the trial balance and record the balance in the appropriate column as of December 31, 1985.

2. Journalize the adjusting entries and post to the appropriate accounts. In the accounts, identify the postings by writing "Adjusting" in the explanation columns.

3. Prepare journal entries to close the revenue and expense accounts. Do *not* transfer net income to the capital account.

4. Post the closing entries. In the accounts, identify the postings by writing "Closing" in the explanation columns.

P4–5A *The accounting cycle assuming monthly closing*

On March 1, 1985, Davido Company was created by Gomez Davido and completed the following transactions during the month of March:

1985			
Mar.	1	Gomez Davido transferred $8,000 from his savings account to an account under the name, Davido Company.	
	1	Paid $300 for office supplies.	
	1	Purchased second-hand office equipment for $900 in cash.	
	4	Issued a check for $300 for March rent.	
	5	Paid a premium of $192 for an insurance policy on the equipment, effective March 1.	
	9	Purchased supplies on account to be used in repair work, as follows:	
		Fisher, Inc.	$ 240
		Harrison Supply Company	280
		Isaacs Company	160
		Rex Supplies Unlimited	480
		Total	$1,160
	15	Received $5,200 for repair work completed but not previously billed.	
	19	Additional repair work was completed, and bills were sent out, as follows:	
		Baker and Sons	$ 840
		Able Jacobs	480
		Harvey Walters	280
		Yonton Younts	224
		Total	$1,824
	21	Paid $170 for the telephone service for the month.	
	24	Paid the following creditors:	
		Fisher, Inc.	$ 80
		Harrison Supply Company	160
		Isaacs Company	80
		Rex Supplies Unlimited	240
		Total	$560
	28	Received cash from customers to apply on account, as follows:	
		Baker and Sons	$200
		Able Jacobs	80
		Harvey Walters	40
		Yonton Younts	40
		Total	$360
	30	Gomez Davido withdrew $1,200.	

Supplementary data as of March 31, 1985, were as follows:

a. The insurance premium paid on March 5 is for one year.

b. A physical count shows that office supplies on hand total $150, and repair supplies on hand total $270.

c. The office equipment has an estimated useful life of six years with no salvage value.

Required:

1. Open the following accounts in the general ledger: Cash, 101; Accounts Receivable, 111; Office Supplies, 136; Repair Supplies, 137; Prepaid Insurance, 140; Office Equipment, 163; Accumulated Depreciation—Office Equipment, 163A; Accounts Payable, 201; Gomez Davido, Capital, 301; Gomez Davido, Drawing, 302; Repair Revenue, 401; Insurance Expense, 502; Rent Expense, 503; Office Supplies Expense, 508; Telephone and Telegraph Expense, 509; Repair Supplies Expense, 512; Depreciation Expense—Office Equipment, 517; Income Summary, 601.

2. Open accounts in the accounts receivable subsidiary ledger for Baker and Sons, Able Jacobs, Harvey Walters, and Yonton Younts.

3. Open accounts in the accounts payable subsidiary ledger for Fisher, Inc., Harrison Supply Company, Isaacs Company, and Rex Supplies Unlimited.

4. Record all the transactions in the general journal, post to the appropriate ledgers, and prepare a trial balance.

5. Journalize and post the adjusting entries.

6. Prepare a trial balance after the adjustments have been posted.

7. Prepare an income statement, a balance sheet, and a statement of owner's equity.

8. Prepare a schedule of accounts receivable.

9. Prepare a schedule of accounts payable.

10. Prepare closing entries in the general journal and post to the general ledger.

11. Prepare a postclosing trial balance.

P4–6A
Thought-provoking problem: cash or accrual basis?

A new accountant for the Deborah Rich Company prepared the following condensed income statement for the year ended December 31, 1985, and the condensed balance sheet as of the same date:

DEBORAH RICH COMPANY **Exhibit A**
Income Statement
For the Year Ended December 31, 1985

Revenue from services		$142,850
Operating expenses:		
Insurance expense	$ 4,095	
Miscellaneous expense	14,820	
Office supplies expense	1,365	
Wages expense	46,800	67,080
Net income		$ 75,770

DEBORAH RICH COMPANY **Exhibit B**
Balance Sheet
December 31, 1985

Assets

Cash	$ 33,650
Accounts receivable	32,760
Equipment	118,950
Total assets	$185,360

Liabilities and Owner's Equity

Accounts payable	$ 32,760
Deborah Rich, capital	152,600
Total liabilities and owner's equity	$185,360

The new accountant urged that net income would better approximate reality if the modified cash basis (modified by the omission of the items described below) were used; hence he had not recorded any of the following:

a. Depreciation of equipment (acquired January 1, 1985): usually with an estimated life of 10 years, with no salvage value.
b. Wages earned by employees that have not been paid, $2,550.
c. Office supplies on hand, $525 (purchases during 1985 were debited to Office Supplies Expense).
d. Unexpired insurance premiums, $1,650; all premiums were debited to Insurance Expense.

Required:

1. Do you agree with the new accountant? Why? If not, how would you reply to his argument?

2. If you do not agree with the accountant, what adjusting entries would you make? Prepare these in general journal form.

3. Prepare revised *classified* statements giving effect to the adjustments prepared in requirement 2.

B Problems

P4–1B
Cash and accrual basis

Selected transactions of the Raison Consulting Service for 1985 are given:

1985	
Jan. 1	Purchased a three-year insurance policy for $2,700 cash.
Jul. 1	Bought two vans and paid cash of $19,000. The vans are expected to last five years, at the end of which time their salvage value will be $1,000 each.
Dec. 31	Paid $1,200 rent for the four-month period ending April 30, 1986.
31	Purchased office supplies for $710 cash.

Required:

1. Prepare journal entries to record the transactions using the accrual basis.

2. Prepare the adjusting journal entries as of December 31, 1985, using the accrual basis. The company closes its books annually on December 31.

3. Prepare the journal entries to record the transactions using the cash basis.

4. What adjusting journal entries would be made if the Raison Consulting Service were on the cash basis?

P4–2B
Adjustments and effect on statements

Certain unadjusted account balances from the trial balance of Rex Davidson's Accounting Service for the year ended December 31, 1985, are given:

REX DAVIDSON'S ACCOUNTING SERVICE
Partial Trial Balance
December 31, 1985

Account Title	Debits	Credits
Accounts Receivable	$74,000	
Notes Receivable	38,800	
Prepaid Insurance	5,184	
Office Supplies	2,084	
Vans	34,000	
Accumulated Depreciation—Vans		$ 7,200
Notes Payable		10,600
Revenue—Accounting Fees		768,000
Interest Earned		1,960
Rent Earned		3,840
Advertising Expense	3,880	
Rent Expense	64,000	
Salaries Expense	78,400	
Property Taxes Expense	5,360	
Heat and Light Expense	3,840	

Adjustment data on December 31 are as follows:

a. Office supplies on hand totaled $250.
b. Depreciation for the year was $3,600.
c. Estimated heat and light expense not recorded was $510.
d. Of the amount shown for Interest Earned, $500 was unearned as of December 31, 1985.
e. The balance of the Prepaid Insurance account consists of $1,728 for the premium on a three-year policy dated July 1, 1985, and $3,456 for premiums on a three-year policy dated January 1, 1985.
f. Advertising supplies on hand were $280.
g. The balance of the Notes Payable account represents an 18 percent interest-bearing note dated January 1, 1985, due July 1, 1986.
h. The rent expense is $6,400 a month.
i. Salaries earned by employees but not paid were $2,300.
j. Property taxes accrued were $325.
k. On January 1, 1985, the Davidson Accounting Service subleased a section of its rented space. The lease with the tenant specifies the minimum yearly fee to be the greater of $3,840, payable at the beginning of each month, or five percent of gross sales. The amount of the adjustment in rent, if there is any adjustment, is due on January 15, 1986. The tenant reported sales of $84,800 for 1985.
l. Included in the Revenue—Accounting Fees account are advance payments of $24,000 by clients for services to be rendered early in 1986.

Required: Using the format shown below

1. Record adjusting journal entries.

2. Indicate the financial statement classification of each account in each entry.

3. Show the amount reported on the financial statements.

Example: Item a.

Item	Adjusting Journal Entries December 31, 1985	Dr.	Cr.	Financial Statement Classification	Amount Reported on Financial Statement
a	Office Supplies Expense	1,834		Expense	1,834
	Office Supplies		1,834	Current asset	250

P4–3B *Adjusting entries for deferrals and accruals*

After an analysis of the accounts and the other records of Dunbar Company, a single proprietorship, the following information is made available for the year ended December 31, 1985:

a. The Office Supplies account has a debit balance of $3,595. Office supplies on hand at December 31 total $950.

b. The Prepaid Rent account has a debit balance of $27,920. Included in this amount is $2,460 paid in December for the succeeding January; $25,460 has expired.

c. The Prepaid Insurance account has a debit balance of $9,058. It consists of the following policies purchased during 1985:

Policy No.	Date of Policy	Life of Policy	Premium
NCC-1702	January 1	3 years	$5,184
2004	April 1	2 years	2,074
DV-19	October 1	1 year	1,800

d. The Prepaid Advertising account has a debit balance of $9,750. Included in this amount is $1,560 paid to a local monthly magazine for advertising space in its January and February 1986 issues.

e. At the close of the year, three notes receivable were on hand:

Date	Face Value	Total Time of Note in Days	Interest Rate (%)
November 1	$22,600	90	16
December 1	24,920	60	18
December 16	15,440	30	20

f. At the close of the year, two notes payable were outstanding:

Date	Face Value	Total Time of Note in Days	Interest Rate (%)
September 2	$24,760	180	16
November 1	38,000	90	18

g. Salaries and wages accrued totaled $8,500.

h. The Rent Earned account has a credit balance of $41,472 representing receipt of payment on a one-year lease effective May 1, 1985.

i. The Store Equipment account has a debit balance of $60,750. The equipment has an estimated useful life of 10 years and a salvage value of $5,750. All store equipment was acquired prior to January 1, 1985.

j. The Vans account has a debit balance of $22,700. The vans were purchased on June 1, 1984, and have an estimated life of five years and a salvage value of $3,700.
k. Property taxes accrued were $5,500.

Required: Prepare the adjusting journal entries required at December 31, 1985.

P4–4B *Adjusting and closing entries from a trial balance and added data*

The unadjusted trial balance of the Hight Company contained the following accounts as of December 31, 1985:

HIGHT COMPANY
Partial Trial Balance
December 31, 1985

Acct. No.	Account Title	Debits	Credits
121	Accrued Interest Receivable	$ 0	
131	Office Supplies	2,800	
132	Prepaid Insurance	6,940	
133	Prepaid Advertising	0	
205	Accrued Wages Payable		$ 0
212	Unearned Rent		0
406	Rent Earned		136,000
410	Interest Earned		2,800
503	Wages Expense	110,000	
504	Advertising Expense	18,000	
505	Insurance Expense	0	
506	Office Supplies Expense	0	
601	Income Summary		0

Additional information is given below:
a. Interest that had accrued on notes receivable at December 31, 1985, amounted to $970.
b. The inventory of office supplies at December 31, 1985, was $785.
c. The insurance records show that $4,000 of insurance has expired during 1985.
d. Included in Advertising Expense is a prepayment of a $3,400 contract for advertising space in a regional magazine; 30 percent of this contract has been used, and the remainder will be used in the following year.
e. Wages due to employees of $3,800 had accrued as of December 31, 1985.
f. Rent collected in advance that will not be earned until 1986 amounted to $18,000.

Required:

1. Open the accounts listed in the trial balance, and record the balance in the appropriate column as of December 31, 1985.

2. Journalize the adjusting entries and post to the appropriate account. In the accounts, identify the postings by writing "Adjusting" in the explanation columns.

3. Prepare journal entries to close the revenue and expense accounts. Do *not* transfer the net income (or net loss) to the capital account.

4. Post the closing entries. In the accounts, identify the postings by writing "Closing" in the explanation columns.

P4–5B *The accounting cycle assuming monthly closing*

On July 1, 1985, Janie Company, a single proprietorship, was created to operate a repair shop. During July the following transactions were completed:

1985		
Jul.	1	Janie Aspin transferred $16,500 from her money market savings account to an account at First City Bank under the name of Janie Company.
	1	Paid $500 for office supplies.

1 Purchased second-hand office equipment for $2,500 in cash.
4 Issued a check for $600 for July rent.
7 Paid a premium of $384 for an insurance policy on the equipment, effective July 1.
10 Purchased supplies on account to be used in repair work, as follows:

Ames Manufacturers	$ 960
Elmer and Associates	480
Patrick Company	560
Thomas's Supply Company	320
Total	$2,320

14 Received $10,400 for repair work completed but not previously billed.

18 Additional repair work was completed, and bills were sent out as follows:

James Baker	$ 960
Melissa Lawson	1,680
Roger Sutton	560
Thomas Tutterow	448
Total	$3,648

22 Paid $320 for telephone service for the month.
26 Paid the following creditors:

Ames Manufacturers	$ 480
Elmer and Associates	160
Patrick Company	320
Thomas's Supply Company	160
Total	$1,120

29 Received cash from customers to apply on account, as follows:

James Baker	$160
Melissa Lawson	400
Roger Sutton	80
Thomas Tutterow	80
Total	$720

31 Janie Aspin withdrew $2,400 in cash from the business.

Supplementary data as of July 31, 1985, were as follows:

a. The insurance premium paid on July 7 is for one year.
b. A physical count shows that office supplies on hand total $250, and repair supplies on hand total $450.
c. The office equipment has an estimated useful life of six years with no salvage value.

Required:

1. Open the following accounts in the general ledger: Cash, 101; Accounts Receivable, 111; Office Supplies, 136; Repair Supplies, 137; Prepaid Insurance, 140; Office Equipment, 163; Accumulated Depreciation—Office Equipment, 163A; Accounts Payable, 201; Janie Aspin, Capital, 301; Janie Aspin, Drawing, 302; Repair Revenue, 401; Insurance Expense, 502; Rent Expense, 503; Office Supplies Expense, 508; Telephone and Telegraph Expense, 509; Repair Supplies Expense, 512; Depreciation Expense—Office Equipment, 517; Income Summary, 601.

2. Open accounts in the accounts receivable subsidiary ledger for James Baker, Melissa Lawson, Roger Sutton, and Thomas Tutterow.

3. Open accounts in the accounts payable subsidiary ledger for the Ames Manufacturers, Elmer and Associates, Patrick Company, and Thomas's Supply Company.

4. Record all the transactions in the general journal, post to the appropriate ledgers, and prepare a trial balance.

5. Journalize and post the adjusting entries.
6. Prepare a trial balance after the adjustments have been posted.
7. Prepare an income statement, a balance sheet, and a statement of owner's equity.
8. Prepare a schedule of accounts receivable.
9. Prepare a schedule of accounts payable.
10. Prepare closing entries in the general journal and post to the general ledger.
11. Prepare a postclosing trial balance.

P4–6B *Thought-provoking problem: interpreting adjusting entry*

The closing entries and postclosing trial balance of the Fulton Consulting Company, as of December 31, 1985, are given below. A yearly accounting period is used. Tyson Fulton, the proprietor, had an equity of $18,050 on January 1, 1985.

GENERAL JOURNAL Page 12

Date		Debit-Credit-Account Titles: Explanation	F	Debit	Credit
		Closing Entries			
1985					
Dec.	31	Rental Revenue		5,500	
		Consulting Revenue		21,600	
		Income Summary			27,100
	31	Income Summary		20,050	
		Rent Expense			1,800
		Insurance Expense			400
		Supplies Expense			150
		Commission Expense			16,500
		Depreciation Expense—Office Equipment			1,000
		Miscellaneous Expense			200
	31	Income Summary		7,050	
		Tyson Fulton, Capital			7,050
	31	Tyson Fulton, Capital		2,050	
		Tyson Fulton, Drawing			2,050

FULTON CONSULTING COMPANY
Postclosing Trial Balance
December 31, 1985

Account Title	Debits	Credits
Cash	$ 8,300	
Office Supplies	150	
Prepaid Insurance	1,600	
Office Equipment	16,000	
Accumulated Depreciation—Office Equipment		$ 2,000
Notes Payable to Banks		1,000
Tyson Fulton, Capital		23,050
Total	$26,050	$26,050

Required:

1. An income statement for 1985.

2. A statement of owner's equity.

3. Fulton believes that the income statement should show a deduction of an interest expense based on the average prime bank rate multiplied by his capital balance at the beginning of the year. Assuming that you are the accountant for Fulton, should you make this entry as an adjusting entry? Why? Why not?

5 Completion of the Accounting Cycle

Introduction

In the preceding chapter, the end-of-period adjustment process was illustrated through the use of the Genova Trucking Company example. This chapter first presents a broad overview of the complete accounting process so that the reader can see both the individual components and the panoramic sweep of the process. Then this chapter illustrates the additional end-of-period steps in the accounting cycle other than those discussed in Chapter 4. The major new concept in these steps is the work sheet.

Learning Goals

To explain the steps in the accounting cycle.

To be able to prepare a work sheet.

To prepare from the work sheet an income statement, a statement of owner's equity, and a balance sheet.

To journalize adjusting and closing entries in the general journal using data from the work sheet and to post those entries.

To be capable of preparing a postclosing trial balance.

To journalize, in the period following adjustments, transactions that are related to those adjustments.

Review of the Accounting Process

Before the illustration of the Genova Trucking Company as a single proprietorship is resumed, the overall picture of the accounting process is reviewed: (1) to see what has been covered and (2) to see what the example now must cover. Figure 5–1 shows the individual phases of the accounting process. In Chapters 1 to 3, there were illustrated the various steps that must be taken during the accounting period: (1) selecting a proper chart of accounts; (2) collecting business information through the use of business documents, analyzing transactions, and journalizing; and (3) posting the journal entries to the appropriate ledgers.

In this chapter, certain steps illustrated in Chapters 1 through 4 are reinforced, and some new dimensions are added to the accounting process

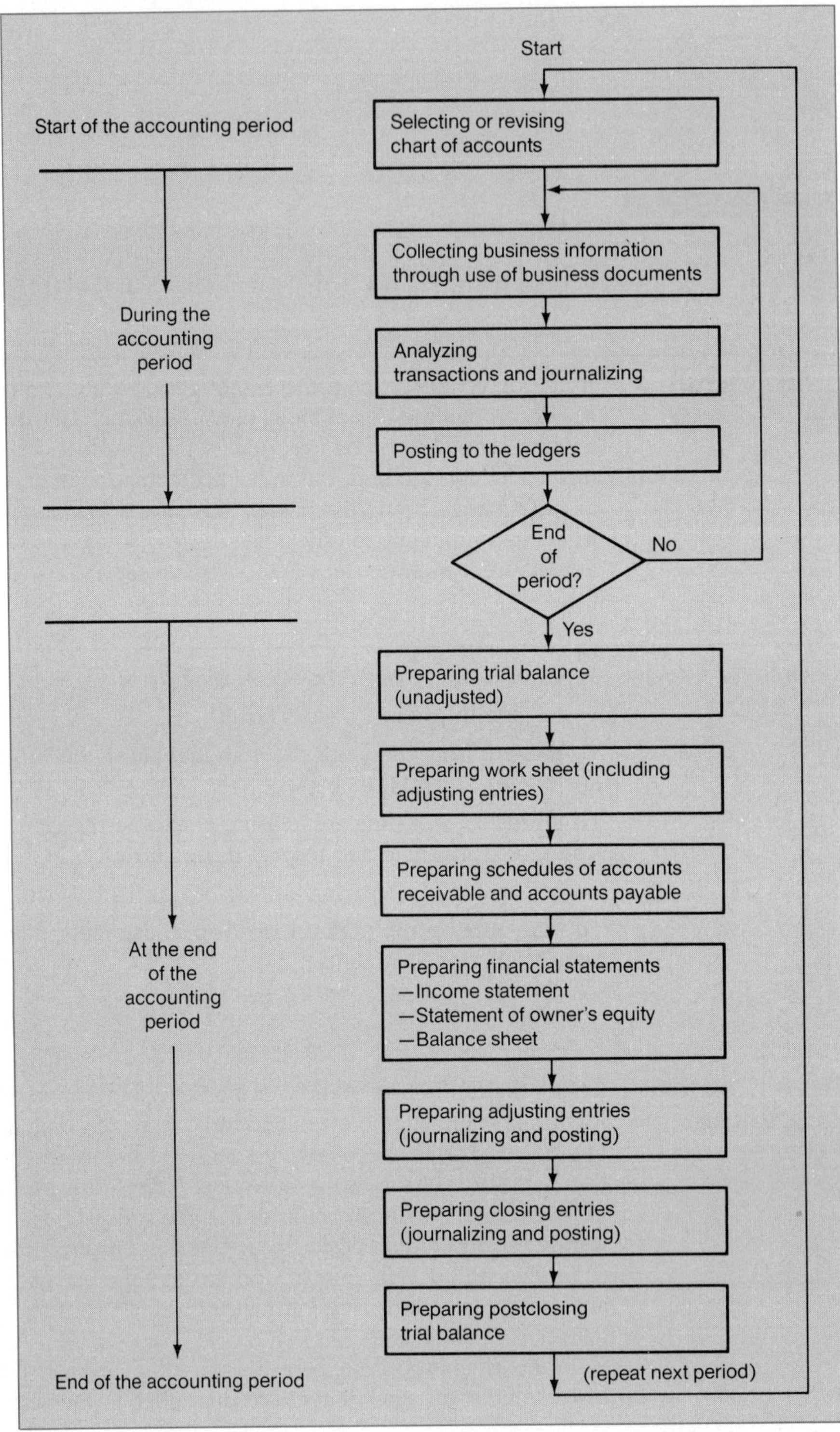

Figure 5–1 Diagram of the Accounting Process

through the Genova Trucking Company example. As can be seen from Figure 5–1, the accounting phases that must be accomplished at the end of the accounting period are: (1) preparing the unadjusted trial balance; (2) collecting the adjustment information, placing the adjustment data on the work sheet, and completing the work sheet; (3) preparing the schedules of accounts receivable and accounts payable; (4) preparing the financial statements; (5) journalizing and posting the adjustments; (6) journalizing and posting the closing entries; and (7) preparing a postclosing trial balance.

An Accounting Illustration— The Genova Trucking Company as a Single Proprietorship (Continued)

Resuming the illustration of the Genova Trucking Company as a single proprietorship, the next phase of the accounting process—that of preparing a work sheet—is discussed. (The reader should turn back to Figure 4–1 in Chapter 4 to review the initial information needed for adjustments presented in reference to this example.)

The Work Sheet

The end-of-period **work sheet** is a tool used by the accountant to bring together information necessary in the preparation of the formal financial statements. It is not a substitute for the financial statements but is the document from which they are prepared. Although the work sheet is not absolutely essential, it would be difficult in most instances to prepare the statements directly from the journals and ledgers since that approach would often require consolidating material from books, cards, and other documents. The work sheet bridges the gap between the accounting records and the formal statements and permits the calculation of the effect of the adjustments and determination of net income or net loss before the adjustments are formally journalized and posted to the ledger. It does not, however, eliminate the necessity for journalizing and posting these adjusting entries and the closing entries at the end of the accounting period.[1]

Overview of the Work Sheet

Before a step-by-step preparation of the work sheet for the Genova Trucking Company is illustrated, the basic format of a work sheet is presented (see Figure 5–2). The heading is entered first; it shows the name of the company, the term *work sheet,* and the period covered. Then the trial balance before

[1]While the work sheet does not eliminate journalizing adjusting and closing entries *at the end of the accounting period* (usually a year), it does provide a means for preparation of financial statements for shorter periods without going through the formal journalizing process.

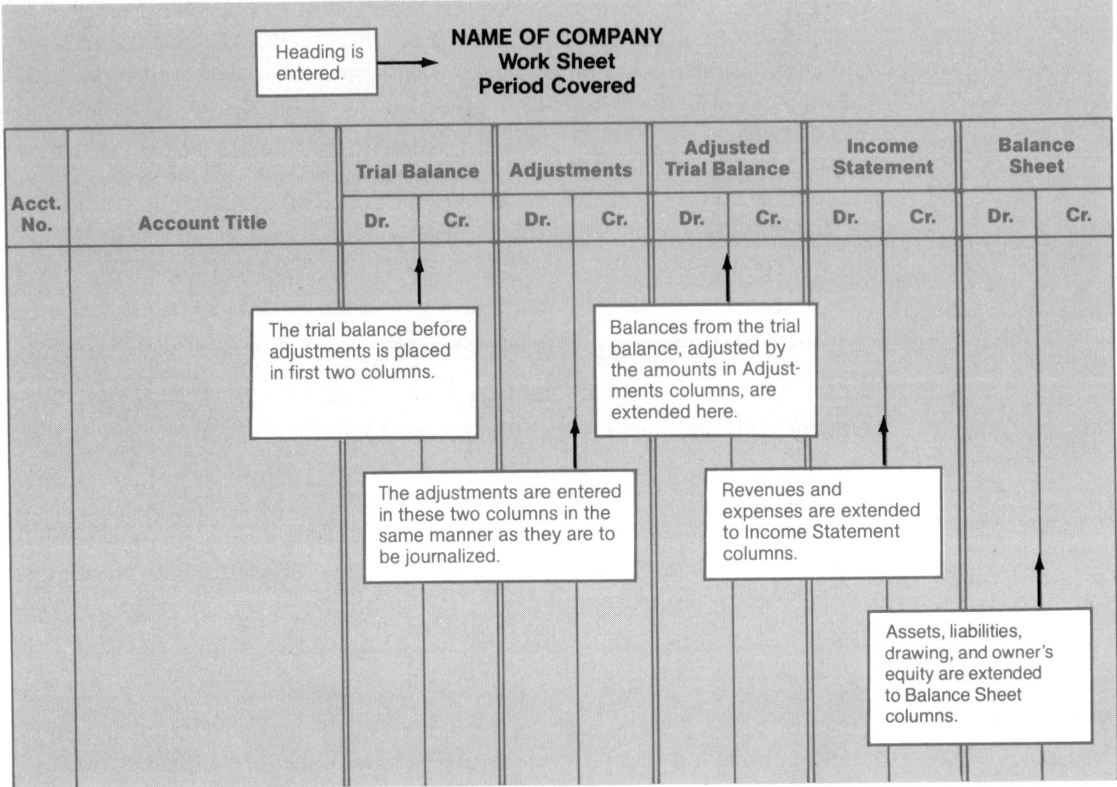

Figure 5–2 **Pictorial View of a Work Sheet**

adjustments and closing is entered in the first two columns (instead of as a separate statement). The adjustments are then recorded in the Adjustments columns in the same manner as they will be journalized. If an account to be debited or credited is not listed in the trial balance before closing, its title is added below the trial balance totals. Next, the information in the first four columns for each account is combined or netted to determine the adjusted trial balance figures; these are extended to the Adjusted Trial Balance columns. These figures are then extended to either the Income Statement columns (revenues and expenses) or the Balance Sheet columns (assets, liabilities, owner's drawing, and owner's capital). The net income or net loss is the difference between the two Income Statement subtotals. When it is entered to balance these columns and in the appropriate debit or credit Balance Sheet column, it should cause the two Balance Sheet columns to balance.

Four Steps in Preparing the Work Sheet of the Genova Trucking Company

Preparing the work sheet for the Genova Trucking Company breaks down into four steps. The first step, as indicated above, is the entering of the heading and trial balance.

Step 1. The heading for our illustrative company as shown in Figure 5–3 is:

GENOVA TRUCKING COMPANY
Work Sheet
For the Month Ended June 30, 1985

The trial balance is next entered; the trial balance account numbers, titles, and amounts are entered either directly from the general ledger or from a prepared listing, if available. The account titles are entered in the space provided, and the amounts are entered in the first pair of money columns. The work sheet of the Genova Trucking Company after completion of Step 1 appears in Figure 5–3.

Step 2. The adjustments are generally entered on the work sheet before they are formally journalized. This procedure helps speed up preparation of the formal financial statements—income statement, statement of owner's equity, and balance sheet. Nine adjustments for the Genova Trucking Company were discussed in detail in Chapter 4. Now they are given an identification key letter (a, b, c, and so on) and are entered on the work sheet:

- ☐ Adjustment (a): To adjust for expired rent.
- ☐ Adjustment (b): To adjust for expired insurance.
- ☐ Adjustment (c): To adjust for office supplies used.
- ☐ Adjustment (d): To adjust for the rent that is earned.
- ☐ Adjustment (e): To adjust for depreciation of the office equipment.
- ☐ Adjustment (f): To adjust for depreciation of the trucks.
- ☐ Adjustment (g): To adjust for the accrued interest revenue.
- ☐ Adjustment (h): To adjust for the accrued wages expense.
- ☐ Adjustment (i): To adjust for the accrued interest expense.

The identification key letter is used to cross-reference and to identify the debit adjustment title with the credit adjustment title as they are entered in the Adjustments columns. Any additional accounts required by the adjusting entries could be written below the trial balance with their assigned account numbers. (Another way lists all the accounts in the Trial Balance columns, even those with zero balances.) In Entry (a), for example, Rent Expense is debited for $500. Since this account does not appear in the trial balance, the account number and title are written on the line immediately below the trial balance totals, and the amount is entered directly in the Adjustments Debit column on the same line. The $500 is also entered in the Adjustments Credit column opposite Prepaid Rent. In this adjustment, only one of the accounts involved had to be written in below the trial balance. In Entry (e), however, both the debited and the credited accounts had to be written in. After all the adjustments are entered, the Adjustments columns are added as a proof of

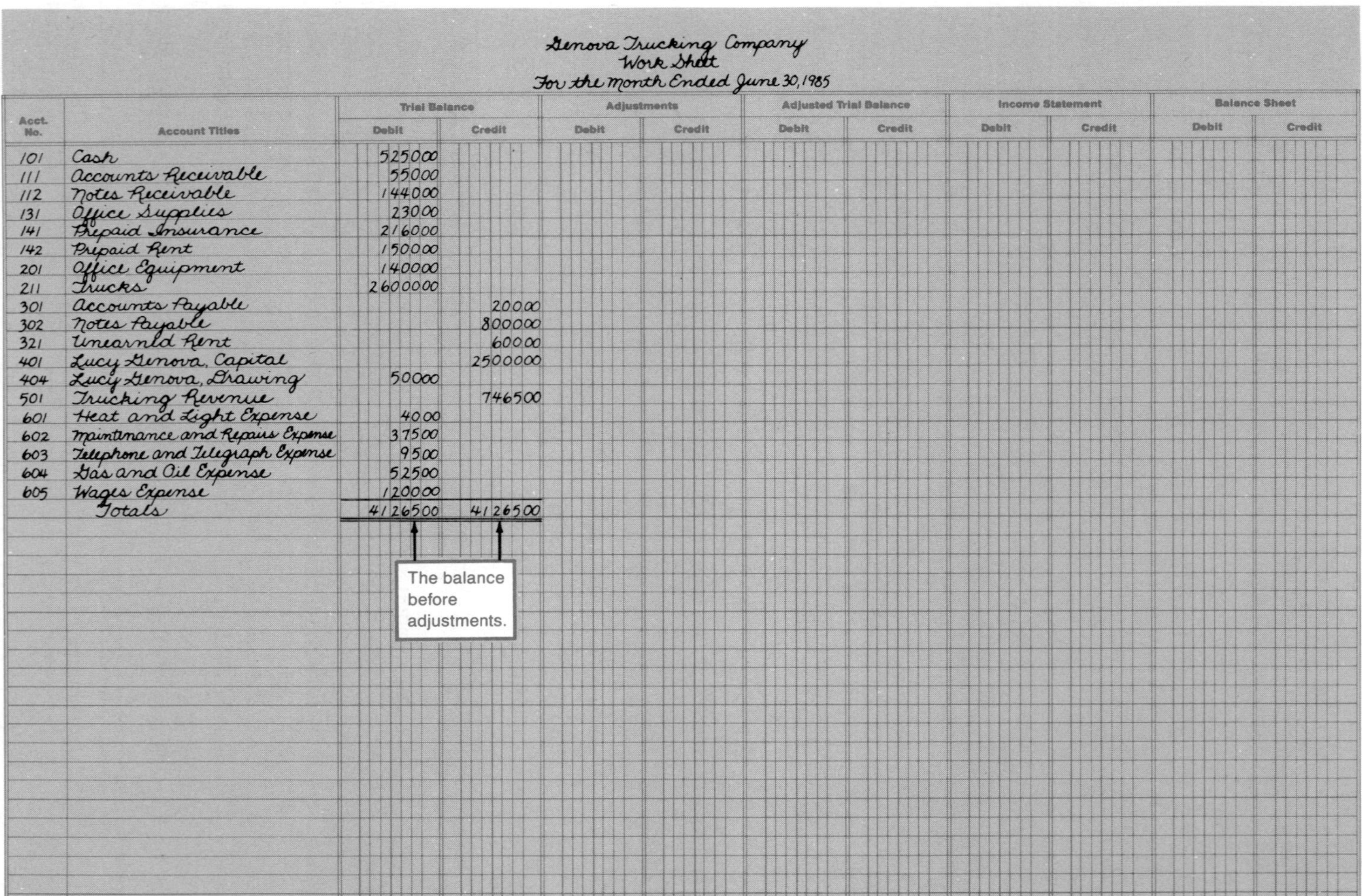

Genova Trucking Company
Work Sheet
For the Month Ended June 30, 1985

Acct. No.	Account Titles	Trial Balance		Adjustments		Adjusted Trial Balance		Income Statement		Balance Sheet	
		Debit	Credit	Debit	Credit	Debit	Credit	Debit	Credit	Debit	Credit
101	Cash	5250 00									
111	Accounts Receivable	550 00									
112	Notes Receivable	1440 00									
131	Office Supplies	230 00									
141	Prepaid Insurance	2160 00									
142	Prepaid Rent	1500 00									
201	Office Equipment	1400 00									
211	Trucks	26000 00									
301	Accounts Payable		200 00								
302	Notes Payable		8000 00								
321	Unearned Rent		600 00								
401	Lucy Genova, Capital		25000 00								
404	Lucy Genova, Drawing	500 00									
501	Trucking Revenue		7465 00								
601	Heat and Light Expense	40 00									
602	Maintenance and Repairs Expense	375 00									
603	Telephone and Telegraph Expense	95 00									
604	Gas and Oil Expense	525 00									
605	Wages Expense	1200 00									
	Totals	41265 00	41265 00								

Figure 5–3 **Work Sheet, Step 1: Trial Balance Entered**

their equality. The work sheet following the completion of Step 2 is shown in Figure 5–4.

Step 3. Computations in this step result in the **adjusted trial balance** figure. The amounts extended to the Adjusted Trial Balance columns result from combining the amounts in the Trial Balance columns with the amounts in the Adjustments columns as follows:

- ☐ If there are no adjustments to an account, extend a debit trial balance amount to the debit column of the Adjusted Trial Balance, and extend a credit trial balance amount to the credit column of the Adjusted Trial Balance.
- ☐ If the account in the trial balance has a debit balance, add its debit adjustments and subtract its credit adjustments. The result, if a debit, is extended to the Adjusted Trial Balance Debit column; if a credit, it is extended to the Credit column.
- ☐ If the account in the trial balance has a credit balance, add its credit adjustments, and subtract its debit adjustments. The adjusted balance is extended to the proper Adjusted Trial Balance column.
- ☐ For the accounts listed below the trial balance totals, extend the adjustment amounts directly to the appropriate Adjusted Trial Balance column.

The amounts in the Adjusted Trial Balance columns will be the same as the balances in the general ledger accounts after adjusting entries have been journalized and posted. Each line on the work sheet essentially represents a general ledger account and functions in the same manner as to the debit and credit position. For example, after the adjusting entries are journalized and posted, the Prepaid Rent account appears in the general ledger as shown below:

Prepaid Rent Acct. No. 142

Date		Explanation	F	Debit	Credit	Balance
1985 Jun.	1		1	1,500		1,500
	30	Adjustment	4		500	1,000

The new balance is a debit of $1,000, which is the amount shown opposite Prepaid Rent in the Adjusted Trial Balance Debit column of the work sheet. The work sheet following the completion of Step 3 is shown in Figure 5–5.

Step 4. The amounts in the Adjusted Trial Balance columns are extended either to the Income Statement columns or to the Balance Sheet columns, depending on their statement classification. Each amount must be extended to only one column; *no figure is ever extended to more than one place.* Expense and revenue accounts are entered in the Income Statement columns; asset, liability, and owner's capital and drawing accounts are entered in the Balance Sheet columns. The four columns are then subtotaled.

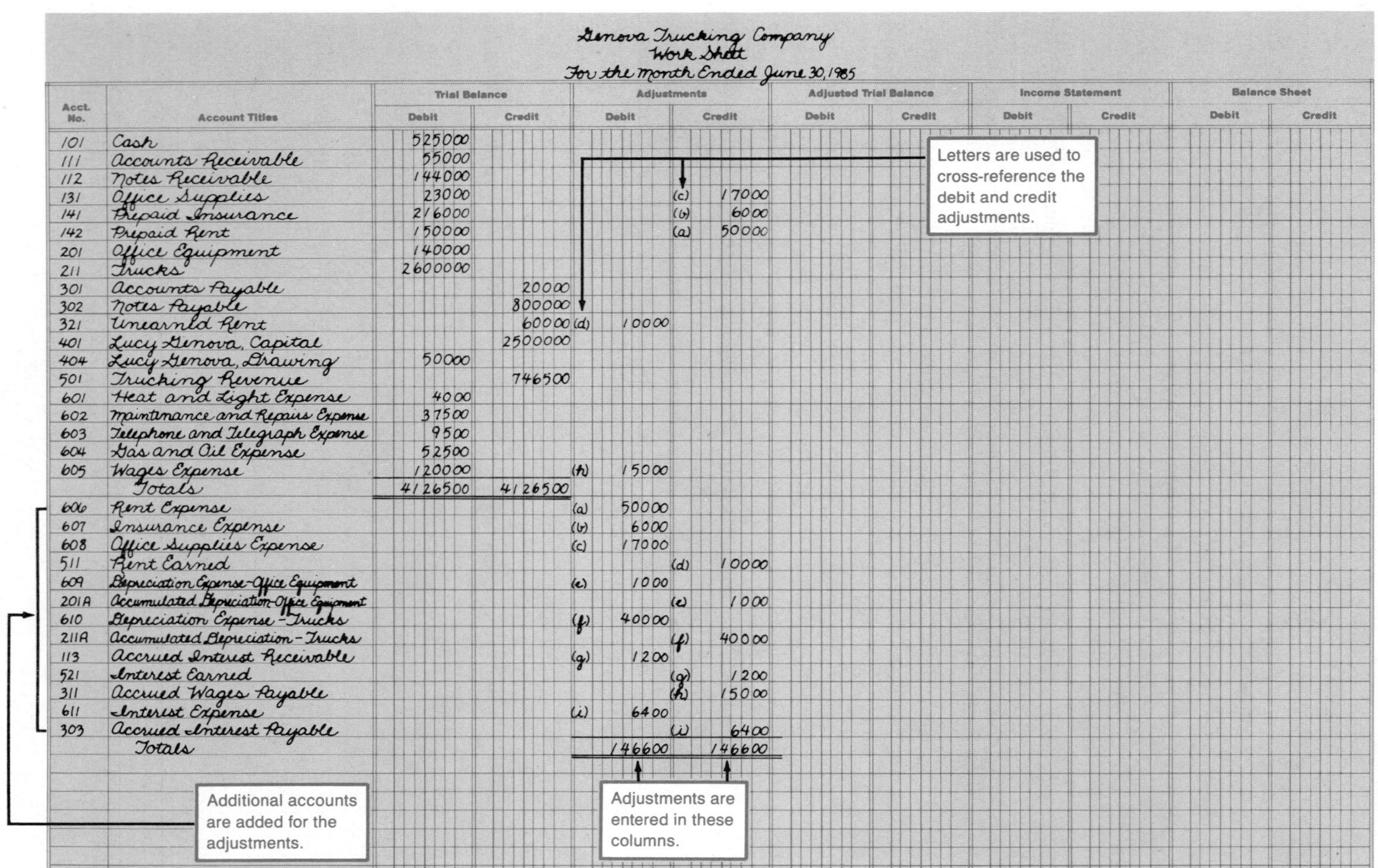

Genova Trucking Company
Work Sheet
For the Month Ended June 30, 1985

Acct. No.	Account Titles	Trial Balance Debit	Trial Balance Credit	Adjustments Debit	Adjustments Credit	Adjusted Trial Balance Debit	Adjusted Trial Balance Credit	Income Statement Debit	Income Statement Credit	Balance Sheet Debit	Balance Sheet Credit
101	Cash	5250 00									
111	Accounts Receivable	550 00									
112	Notes Receivable	1440 00									
131	Office Supplies	230 00			(c) 170 00						
141	Prepaid Insurance	2160 00			(b) 60 00						
142	Prepaid Rent	1500 00			(a) 500 00						
201	Office Equipment	1400 00									
211	Trucks	26000 00									
301	Accounts Payable		200 00								
302	Notes Payable		8000 00								
321	Unearned Rent		600 00	(d) 100 00							
401	Lucy Genova, Capital		25000 00								
404	Lucy Genova, Drawing	500 00									
501	Trucking Revenue		7465 00								
601	Heat and Light Expense	40 00									
602	Maintenance and Repairs Expense	375 00									
603	Telephone and Telegraph Expense	95 00									
604	Gas and Oil Expense	525 00									
605	Wages Expense	1200 00		(h) 150 00							
	Totals	41265 00	41265 00								
606	Rent Expense			(a) 500 00							
607	Insurance Expense			(b) 60 00							
608	Office Supplies Expense			(c) 170 00							
511	Rent Earned				(d) 100 00						
609	Depreciation Expense-Office Equipment			(e) 10 00							
201A	Accumulated Depreciation-Office Equipment				(e) 10 00						
610	Depreciation Expense-Trucks			(f) 400 00							
211A	Accumulated Depreciation-Trucks				(f) 400 00						
113	Accrued Interest Receivable			(g) 12 00							
521	Interest Earned				(g) 12 00						
311	Accrued Wages Payable				(h) 150 00						
611	Interest Expense			(i) 64 00							
303	Accrued Interest Payable				(i) 64 00						
	Totals			1466 00	1466 00						

Figure 5–4 **Work Sheet, Step 2: Adjustments Entered**

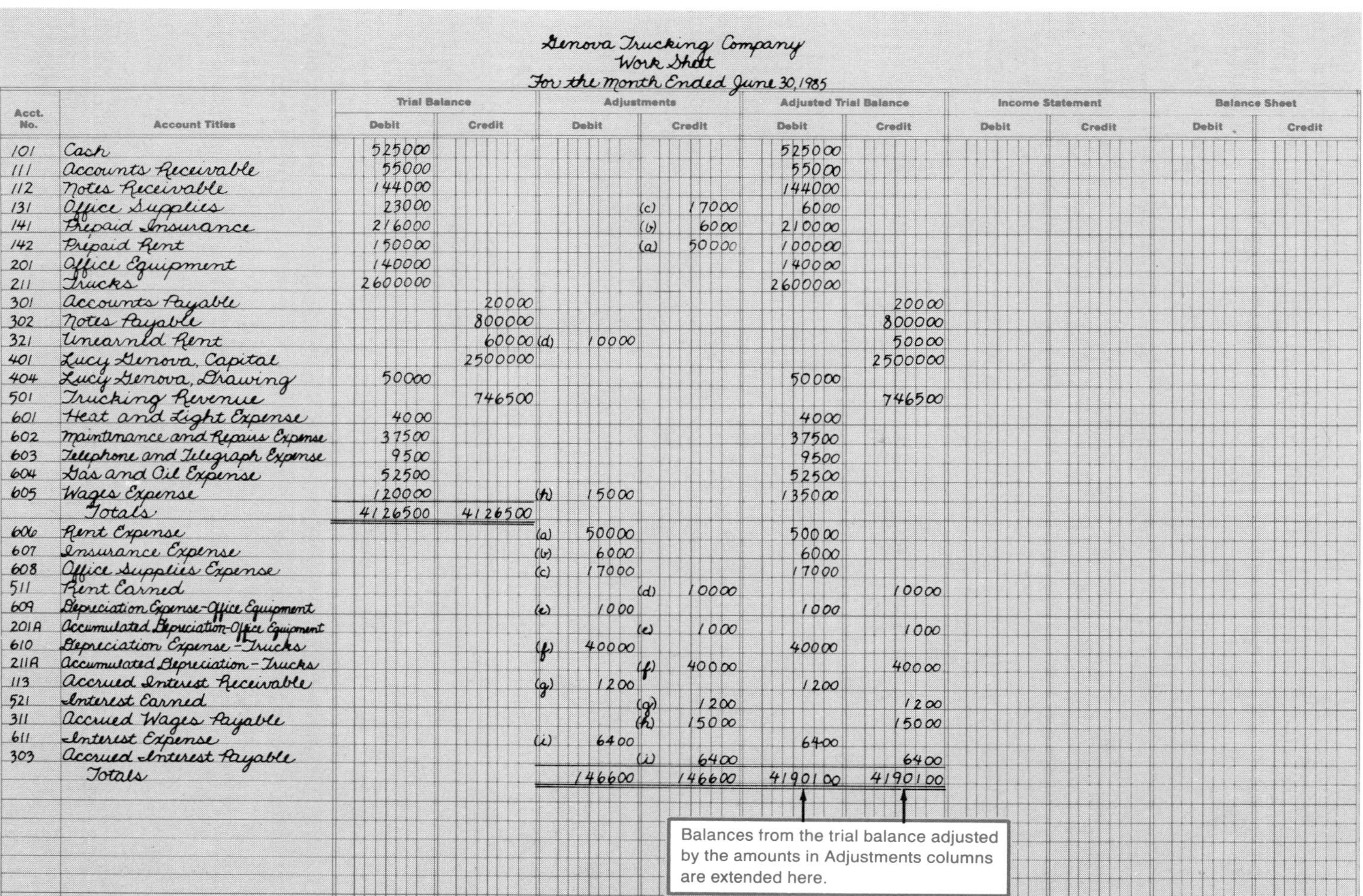

Genova Trucking Company
Work Sheet
For the Month Ended June 30, 1985

Acct. No.	Account Titles	Trial Balance		Adjustments		Adjusted Trial Balance		Income Statement		Balance Sheet	
		Debit	Credit	Debit	Credit	Debit	Credit	Debit	Credit	Debit	Credit
101	Cash	5250 00				5250 00					
111	Accounts Receivable	550 00				550 00					
112	Notes Receivable	1440 00				1440 00					
131	Office Supplies	230 00			(c) 170 00	60 00					
141	Prepaid Insurance	2160 00			(b) 60 00	2100 00					
142	Prepaid Rent	1500 00			(a) 500 00	1000 00					
201	Office Equipment	1400 00				1400 00					
211	Trucks	26000 00				26000 00					
301	Accounts Payable		200 00				200 00				
302	Notes Payable		8000 00				8000 00				
321	Unearned Rent		600 00	(d) 100 00			500 00				
401	Lucy Genova, Capital		25000 00				25000 00				
404	Lucy Genova, Drawing	500 00				500 00					
501	Trucking Revenue		7465 00				7465 00				
601	Heat and Light Expense	40 00				40 00					
602	Maintenance and Repairs Expense	375 00				375 00					
603	Telephone and Telegraph Expense	95 00				95 00					
604	Gas and Oil Expense	525 00				525 00					
605	Wages Expense	1200 00		(h) 150 00		1350 00					
	Totals	41265 00	41265 00								
606	Rent Expense			(a) 500 00		500 00					
607	Insurance Expense			(b) 60 00		60 00					
608	Office Supplies Expense			(c) 170 00		170 00					
511	Rent Earned				(d) 100 00		100 00				
609	Depreciation Expense—Office Equipment			(e) 10 00		10 00					
201A	Accumulated Depreciation—Office Equipment				(e) 10 00		10 00				
610	Depreciation Expense—Trucks			(f) 400 00		400 00					
211A	Accumulated Depreciation—Trucks				(f) 400 00		400 00				
113	Accrued Interest Receivable			(g) 12 00		12 00					
521	Interest Earned				(g) 12 00		12 00				
311	Accrued Wages Payable				(h) 150 00		150 00				
611	Interest Expense			(i) 64 00		64 00					
303	Accrued Interest Payable				(i) 64 00		64 00				
	Totals			1466 00	1466 00	41901 00	41901 00				

Figure 5–5 Work Sheet, Step 3: Adjusted Trial Balance Entered

The difference between the subtotals of the Income Statement columns is the net income or net loss for the period. A net income is indicated if the subtotal of the credit column exceeds the subtotal of the debit column. The excess is entered in the Income Statement Debit column and in the Balance Sheet Credit column just below the column subtotals. This procedure records on the work sheet the increase in the owner's equity resulting from an excess of revenue over expenses during the period. A net loss is indicated if the subtotal of the Income Statement Debit column exceeds that of the Income Statement Credit column. A loss is shown on the work sheet in the Income Statement Credit column and the Balance Sheet Debit column just below the column subtotals. The designation "Net income (or loss) for the month," whichever is pertinent, is entered in the Account Title column on the same line. Note, however, that net income or net loss is the result of a calculation and is not an account title.

The work sheet following the completion of Step 4 is illustrated in Figure 5–6. In this figure, note particularly the method of subtotaling the columns. After the net income is extended to the Balance Sheet Credit column, the final debit and credit totals should be equal.

If the differences between the Income Statement Debit and Credit columns (net income) and the Balance Sheet Debit and Credit columns are not the same, an error has definitely been made. The totaling and ruling of the last four columns of the work sheet (Step 4) is illustrated in Figure 5–6. Note that balancing the last four columns provides only a limited proof of the accuracy of the work sheet—proof that the equality of debits and credits has been maintained throughout its preparation. The extension of the Cash account debit into the Income Statement Debit column, for example, would not destroy the debit-credit relationship of the work sheet, although statements prepared from that work sheet would be inaccurate. Note also that the total of the Balance Sheet Debit column need not correspond with the total assets reported in the statement. Accumulated Depreciation—Trucks, for example, is extended to the Balance Sheet Credit column because it represents a balance sheet account with a credit balance. It is neither an asset nor a liability but rather a deduction from Trucks, and is referred to as a contra asset account.

The work sheet may vary in form—particularly with respect to the number of columns—to meet specific needs of the user. Two examples are: (1) the Adjusted Trial Balance columns may be omitted, and (2) an extra pair of columns could be created for statement of owner's equity data. If both of the foregoing alternatives are present, it would be necessary to combine the initial trial balance amounts with any adjustment amounts as the extensions are made to the appropriate statement pair of columns.

Preparation of Financial Statements from the Work Sheet

With the work sheet prepared as indicated in Figure 5–6, (1) the income statement is prepared from the amounts in the Income Statement columns of the work sheet, and (2) the statement of owner's equity and the balance sheet are prepared from the amounts in the Balance Sheet columns. In the preparation of financial statements, care should be taken to use each amount

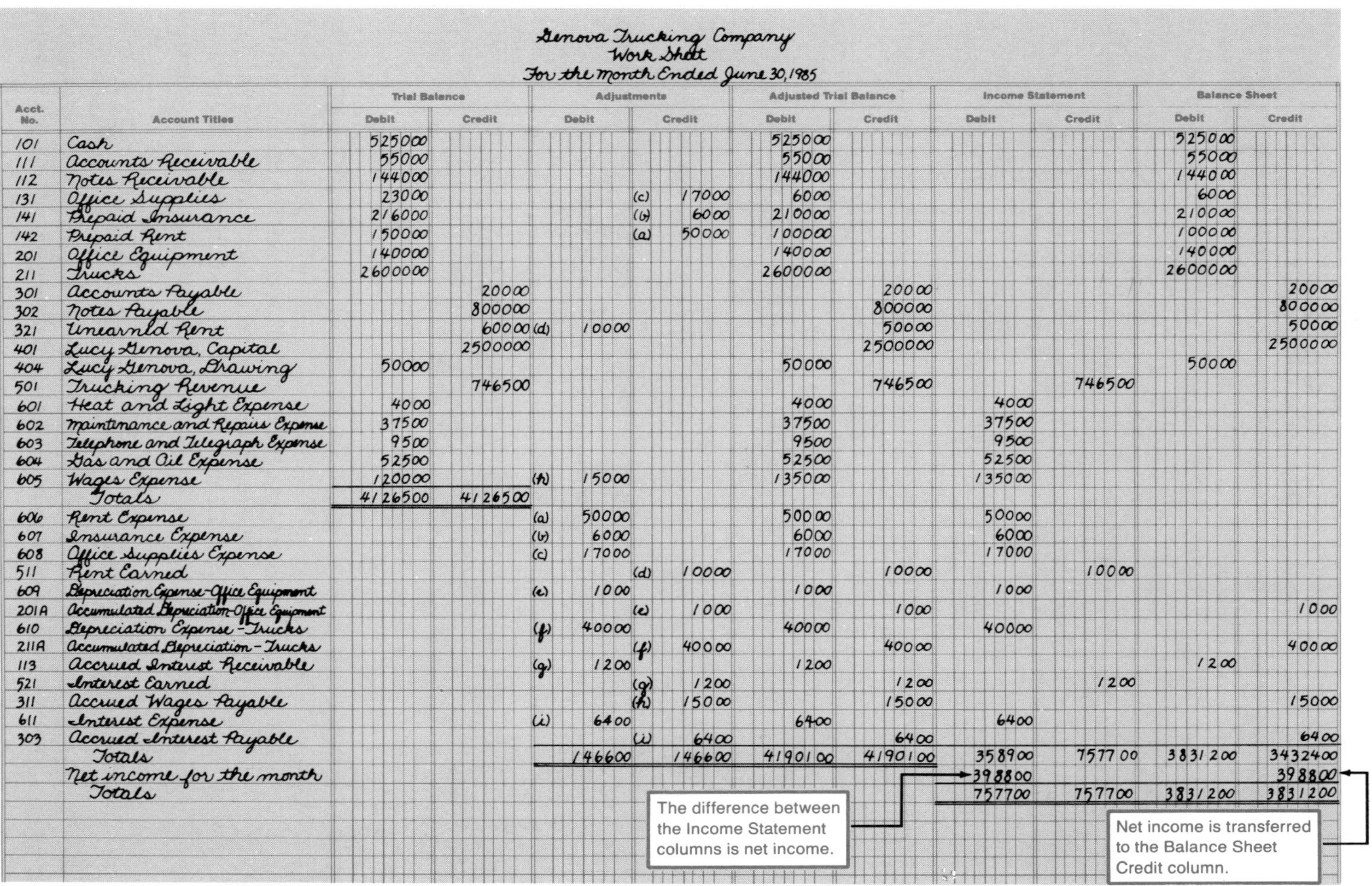

Genova Trucking Company
Work Sheet
For the Month Ended June 30, 1985

Acct. No.	Account Titles	Trial Balance		Adjustments		Adjusted Trial Balance		Income Statement		Balance Sheet	
		Debit	Credit	Debit	Credit	Debit	Credit	Debit	Credit	Debit	Credit
101	Cash	5250 00				5250 00				5250 00	
111	Accounts Receivable	550 00				550 00				550 00	
112	Notes Receivable	1440 00				1440 00				1440 00	
131	Office Supplies	230 00			(c) 170 00	60 00				60 00	
141	Prepaid Insurance	2160 00			(b) 60 00	2100 00				2100 00	
142	Prepaid Rent	1500 00			(a) 500 00	1000 00				1000 00	
201	Office Equipment	1400 00				1400 00				1400 00	
211	Trucks	26000 00				26000 00				26000 00	
301	Accounts Payable		200 00				200 00				200 00
302	Notes Payable		8000 00				8000 00				8000 00
321	Unearned Rent		600 00	(d) 100 00			500 00				500 00
401	Lucy Genova, Capital		25000 00				25000 00				25000 00
404	Lucy Genova, Drawing	500 00				500 00				500 00	
501	Trucking Revenue		7465 00				7465 00		7465 00		
601	Heat and Light Expense	40 00				40 00		40 00			
602	Maintenance and Repairs Expense	375 00				375 00		375 00			
603	Telephone and Telegraph Expense	95 00				95 00		95 00			
604	Gas and Oil Expense	525 00				525 00		525 00			
605	Wages Expense	1200 00		(h) 150 00		1350 00		1350 00			
	Totals	41265 00	41265 00								
606	Rent Expense			(a) 500 00		500 00		500 00			
607	Insurance Expense			(b) 60 00		60 00		60 00			
608	Office Supplies Expense			(c) 170 00		170 00		170 00			
511	Rent Earned				(d) 100 00		100 00		100 00		
609	Depreciation Expense—Office Equipment			(e) 10 00		10 00		10 00			
201A	Accumulated Depreciation—Office Equipment				(e) 10 00		10 00				10 00
610	Depreciation Expense—Trucks			(f) 400 00		400 00		400 00			
211A	Accumulated Depreciation—Trucks				(f) 400 00		400 00				400 00
113	Accrued Interest Receivable			(g) 12 00		12 00				12 00	
521	Interest Earned				(g) 12 00		12 00		12 00		
311	Accrued Wages Payable				(h) 150 00		150 00				150 00
611	Interest Expense			(i) 64 00		64 00		64 00			
303	Accrued Interest Payable				(i) 64 00		64 00				64 00
	Totals			1466 00	1466 00	41901 00	41901 00	3589 00	7577 00	38312 00	34324 00
	Net income for the month							3988 00			3988 00
	Totals							7577 00	7577 00	38312 00	38312 00

Figure 5–6 Work Sheet, Step 4: Complete

GENOVA TRUCKING COMPANY
Income Statement
For the Month Ended June 30, 1985

Exhibit A

Revenues:		
Trucking revenue		$7,465
Interest earned[a]		12
Rent earned[a]		100
Total revenues		$7,577
Expenses:		
Heat and light expense	$ 40	
Maintenance and repairs expense	375	
Telephone and telegraph expense	95	
Gas and oil expense	525	
Wages expense	1,350	
Rent expense	500	
Insurance expense	60	
Office supplies expense	170	
Depreciation expense—office equipment	10	
Depreciation expense—trucks	400	
Interest expense[a]	64	
Total expenses		3,589
Net income (to Exhibit B)		$3,988

[a]For a merchandising business, these items are usually shown in other revenue and other expenses sections of the income statement (see Figure 6–2).

Figure 5–7
Income Statement

GENOVA TRUCKING COMPANY
Statement of Owner's Equity
For the Month Ended June 30, 1985

Exhibit B

Lucy Genova, original investment June 1, 1985	$25,000
Add: Net income for month of June—(Exhibit A)	3,988
Subtotal	$28,988
Deduct: Withdrawals	500
Lucy Genova, capital, June 30, 1985 (to Exhibit C)	$28,488

Figure 5–8
Statement of Owner's Equity

just once and in its proper debit and credit relation. The debit-credit relationship is not shown in the statements, but it is present. In the balance sheet, for example, Accumulated Depreciation—Trucks, with a credit balance of $400, is deducted from Trucks, which has a debit balance. Net income (or loss) appears in both the income statement and the statement of owner's equity.

The financial statements of the Genova Trucking Company for June are shown in Figures 5–7, 5–8, and 5–9. Since the company was organized on June 1, 1985, it had no beginning capital balance; the first amount shown in the statement of owner's equity is the initial investment of $25,000 by the

GENOVA TRUCKING COMPANY Balance Sheet June 30, 1985			Exhibit C
Assets			
Current assets:			
Cash		$ 5,250	
Accounts receivable		550	
Notes receivable		1,440	
Accrued interest receivable		12	
Office supplies		60	
Prepaid insurance		2,100	
Prepaid rent		1,000	
Total current assets			$10,412
Property, plant, and equipment:			
Office equipment	$ 1,400		
Deduct: Accumulated depreciation	10	$ 1,390	
Trucks	$26,000		
Deduct: Accumulated depreciation	400	25,600	
Total property, plant, and equipment			26,990
Total assets			$37,402
Liabilities and Owner's Equity			
Current liabilities:			
Accounts payable		$ 200	
Notes payable		8,000	
Accrued interest payable		64	
Accrued wages payable		150	
Unearned rent		500	
Total current liabilities			$ 8,914
Owner's equity:			
Lucy Genova, capital (Exhibit B)			28,488
Total liabilities and owner's equity			$37,402

Figure 5–9
Balance Sheet

owner, Lucy Genova. The remaining items on this statement are the usual ones—net income earned and withdrawals made by the owner.

Updating of Accounts after Preparation of the Work Sheet

Recording Adjustments in the General Journal

As a practical matter, formal adjusting entries are usually not journalized until after the financial statements have been prepared. The adjusting entries then may be taken directly from the Adjustments columns of the work sheet and dated as of the last day of the accounting period. The caption "Adjusting Entries" is written in the general journal on the line following the last regular general journal entry. After the adjusting entries have been posted, the general ledger account balances will correspond witih the amounts in the Adjusted Trial Balance columns of the work sheet. Although the adjusting journal entries for the Genova Trucking Company have already been made as they were introduced (see Chapter 4), to add realism to the accounting job

GENERAL JOURNAL — Page 4

Date		Debit-Credit-Account Titles: Explanation	F	Debit	Credit
1985		Adjusting Entries			
Jun.	30	Rent Expense	606	500	
		Prepaid Rent	142		500
		To record rent expense for June.			
	30	Insurance Expense	607	60	
		Prepaid Insurance	141		60
		To record insurance expense for June.			
	30	Office Supplies Expense	608	170	
		Office Supplies	131		170
		To record office supplies used during June.			
	30	Unearned Rent	321	100	
		Rent Earned	511		100
		To record revenue earned from rental of trucks during June.			
	30	Depreciation Expense—Office Equipment	609	10	
		Accumulated Depreciation—Office Equipment	201A		10
		To record depreciation for June.			
	30	Depreciation Expense—Trucks	610	400	
		Accumulated Depreciation—Trucks	211A		400
		To record the depreciation for June.			
	30	Accrued Interest Receivable	113	12	
		Interest Earned	521		12
		To record interest revenue accrued during June 11–30, 1985.			
	30	Wages Expense	605	150	
		Accrued Wages Payable	311		150
		To record wages expense accrued during June 28–30, 1985.			
	30	Interest Expense	611	64	
		Accrued Interest Payable	303		64
		To record interest expense accrued during June 13–30, 1985.			

Figure 5–10 **Adjusting Entries**

they are collected and repeated in Figure 5–10 in order to emphasize the recommended timing of the recording process. The account numbers in the folio column indicate that they have been posted.

The Result of Adjusting Entries

When all the adjusting entries are recorded in the journal and posted to the general ledger, the accounts are updated, eliminating the mixed elements in the accounts. Accounts consisting of asset and expense elements and accounts containing liability and revenue elements now have been apportioned so that each element is recorded in a separate account. Advance payments for goods and services to be consumed in the future are shown in the appropriate asset accounts; advance receipts for future revenue are shown in liability accounts;

and all other supplementary data not previously recorded but necessary for the preparation of financial statements are available in the ledger. The general ledger should contain all the accounts and amounts—expense, revenue, asset, liability, and owner's equity—necessary for the presentation of the financial position of the company as of the end of the accounting period and the results of its operations for the period then ended. Failure to adjust any mixed asset or liability account or failure to record an accrual results in incorrect financial statements. However, the materiality concept applies to adjusting entries. It is not necessary to adjust for items too insignificant to influence a decision made by a user of the financial statements.

Recording Closing Entries Directly from the Work Sheet

The caption "Closing Entries" is written in the middle of the first unused line on the journal page under the adjusting entries. The closing entries are recorded (Figure 5–11) and then posted to the general ledger. The reader should recall (see Chapter 3) that **closing entries** are made to empty (close, reduce balance to zero) those temporary accounts that are set up to measure some of the changes in the owner's capital account during a given period of

GENERAL JOURNAL — Page 5

Date		Debit-Credit-Account Titles: Explanation	F	Debit	Credit
1985		Closing Entries			
Jun.	30	Trucking Revenue	501	7,465	
		Rent Earned	511	100	
		Interest Earned	521	12	
		Income Summary	902		7,577
		To close revenue accounts.			
	30	Income Summary	902	3,589	
		Heat and Light Expense	601		40
		Maintenance and Repairs Expense	602		375
		Telephone and Telegraph Expense	603		95
		Gas and Oil Expense	604		525
		Wages Expense	605		1,350
		Rent Expense	606		500
		Insurance Expense	607		60
		Office Supplies Expense	608		170
		Depreciation Expense—Office Equipment	609		10
		Depreciation Expense—Trucks	610		400
		Interest Expense	611		64
		To close expense accounts.			
	30	Income Summary	902	3,988	
		Lucy Genova, capital	401		3,988
		To transfer net income to the owner's capital account.			
	30	Lucy Genova, Capital	401	500	
		Lucy Genova, Drawing	404		500
		To close the drawing account to the owner's capital account.			

Figure 5–11 **Closing Entries**

time. In the closing process, the net effect reflected in these temporary accounts is transferred to the owner's capital account. The closing entries can be made directly from the work sheet in the following sequence:

Entry 1. Each account in the Income Statement Credit column is debited, and their sum (the subtotal in the Credit column) is credited to the Income Summary account.

Entry 2. Each account in the Income Statement Debit column is credited, and their sum (the subtotal in the Debit column) is debited to the Income Summary account.

Entry 3. The balance of Income Summary, which, after posting Entries 1 and 2, represents the net income or the net loss as shown on the work sheet, is transferred to Lucy Genova, Capital.

Entry 4. The balance of Lucy Genova, Drawing is closed into Lucy Genova, Capital. The amount of this entry is the amount on the Lucy Genova, Drawing account line in the Balance Sheet Debit column of the work sheet. It should be emphasized that Lucy Genova, Drawing is *never* closed to the Income Summary. The amount in the drawing account represents a withdrawal in anticipation of income. It is not an expense and has nothing to do with income determination.

The General Ledger after Closing

The general ledger of the Genova Trucking Company is reproduced after the adjusting and closing entries have been posted. In reproducing the general ledger, exact dates are used when the information is given in the previous discussion. Otherwise, the date of June 30 and the balance of the account as taken from the trial balance in Figure 4–1 are inserted because the detailed transactions were omitted from this example. It should be noted that, when a balance is brought forward from another ledger page or ledger, the information is recorded in only the Balance column of the ledger account. A check mark is placed in the folio column to indicate that the particular amount was not posted at this time from a journal. The original amounts represented by the balance, however, were posted from journals and such procedure was reflected in the preceding ledgers and journals. The notations "Debit balance" or "Credit balance," "Adjustment," and "Closing entry" are shown in the Explanation column as an aid in tracing the amounts to their sources. As a means of reinforcing the debit-credit nature of each account balance, this characteristic is again shown (as it was in Chapters 2 and 3). It should be noted, however, that the use of the boxed debit/credit characteristic is a teaching aid and would not be shown in the ledger of any company.

GENERAL LEDGER

Balance is a debit.

Cash — Acct. No. 101

Date		Explanation	F	Debit	Credit	Balance
1985 Jun.	30	Debit balance	√			5,250

Balance is a debit.

Accounts Receivable — Acct. No. 111

Date		Explanation	F	Debit	Credit	Balance
1985 Jun.	30	Debit balance	√			550

Balance is a debit.

Notes Receivable — Acct. No. 112

Date		Explanation	F	Debit	Credit	Balance
1985 Jun.	10		2	1,440		1,440

Balance is a debit.

Accrued Interest Receivable — Acct. No. 113

Date		Explanation	F	Debit	Credit	Balance
1985 Jun.	30	Adjustment	4	12		12

Balance is a debit.

Office Supplies — Acct. No. 131

Date		Explanation	F	Debit	Credit	Balance
1985 Jun.	6		1	230		230
	30	Adjustment	4		170	60

Balance is a debit.

Prepaid Insurance — Acct. No. 141

Date		Explanation	F	Debit	Credit	Balance
1985						
Jun.	1		1	2,160		2,160
	30	Adjustment	4		60	2,100

Balance is a debit.

Prepaid Rent — Acct. No. 142

Date		Explanation	F	Debit	Credit	Balance
1985						
Jun.	1		1	1,500		1,500
	30	Adjustment	4		500	1,000

Balance is a debit.

Office Equipment — Acct. No. 201

Date		Explanation	F	Debit	Credit	Balance
1985						
Jun.	1		1	1,400		1,400

Balance is a credit.

Accumulated Depreciation—Office Equipment — Acct. No. 201A

Date		Explanation	F	Debit	Credit	Balance
1985						
Jun.	30	Adjustment	4		10	10

Balance is a debit.

Trucks — Acct. No. 211

Date		Explanation	F	Debit	Credit	Balance
1985						
Jun.	1		1	26,000		26,000

Balance is a credit.

Accumulated Depreciation—Trucks Acct. No. 211A

Date		Explanation	F	Debit	Credit	Balance
1985 Jun.	30	Adjustment	4		400	400

Balance is a credit.

Accounts Payable Acct. No. 301

Date		Explanation	F	Debit	Credit	Balance
1985 Jun.	30	Credit balance	√			200

Balance is a credit.

Notes Payable Acct. No. 302

Date		Explanation	F	Debit	Credit	Balance
1985 Jun.	12		2		8,000	8,000

Balance is a credit.

Accrued Interest Payable Acct. No. 303

Date		Explanation	F	Debit	Credit	Balance
1985 Jun.	30	Adjustment	4		64	64

Balance is a credit.

Accrued Wages Payable Acct. No. 311

Date		Explanation	F	Debit	Credit	Balance
1985 Jun.	30	Adjustment	4		150	150

Balance is a credit.

Unearned Rent — Acct. No. 321

Date		Explanation	F	Debit	Credit	Balance
1985						
Jun.	1		1		600	600
	30	Adjustment	4	100		500

Balance is a credit.

Lucy Genova, Capital — Acct. No. 401

Date		Explanation	F	Debit	Credit	Balance
1985						
Jun.	1		1		25,000	25,000
	30	Net Income, closing entry	5		3,988	28,988
	30	Drawing, closing entry	5	500		28,488

Balance *before closing* is a debit.

Lucy Genova, Drawing — Acct. No. 404

Date		Explanation	F	Debit	Credit	Balance
1985						
Jun.	30	Debit balance	√			500
	30	Closing entry	5		500	0

Balance *before closing* is a credit.

Trucking Revenue — Acct. No. 501

Date		Explanation	F	Debit	Credit	Balance
1985						
Jun.	30	Credit balance	√			7,465
	30	Closing entry	5	7,465		0

Balance *before closing* is a credit.

Rent Earned — Acct. No. 511

Date		Explanation	F	Debit	Credit	Balance
1985						
Jun.	30	Adjustment	4		100	100
	30	Closing entry	5	100		0

Balance *before closing* is a credit.

Interest Earned — Acct. No. 521

Date		Explanation	F	Debit	Credit	Balance
1985						
Jun.	30	Adjustment	4		12	12
	30	Closing entry	5	12		0

Balance *before closing* is a debit.

Heat and Light Expense — Acct. No. 601

Date		Explanation	F	Debit	Credit	Balance
1985						
Jun.	30	Debit balance	√			40
	30	Closing entry	5		40	0

Balance *before closing* is a debit.

Maintenance and Repairs Expense — Acct. No. 602

Date		Explanation	F	Debit	Credit	Balance
1985						
Jun.	30	Debit balance	√			375
	30	Closing entry	5		375	0

Balance *before closing* is a debit.

Telephone and Telegraph Expense — Acct. No. 603

Date		Explanation	F	Debit	Credit	Balance
1985						
Jun.	30	Debit balance	√			95
	30	Closing entry	5		95	0

Balance *before closing* is a debit.

Gas and Oil Expense — Acct. No. 604

Date		Explanation	F	Debit	Credit	Balance
1985						
Jun.	30	Debit balance	√			525
	30	Closing entry	5		525	0

Balance *before closing* is a debit.

Wages Expense — Acct. No. 605

Date		Explanation	F	Debit	Credit	Balance
1985						
Jun.	13		2	600		600
	27		3	600		1,200
	30	Adjustment	4	150		1,350
	30	Closing entry	5		1,350	0

Balance *before closing* is a debit.

Rent Expense — Acct. No. 606

Date		Explanation	F	Debit	Credit	Balance
1985						
Jun.	30	Adjustment	4	500		500
	30	Closing entry	5		500	0

Balance *before closing* is a debit.

Insurance Expense — Acct. No. 607

Date		Explanation	F	Debit	Credit	Balance
1985						
Jun.	30	Adjustment	4	60		60
	30	Closing entry	5		60	0

Balance *before closing* is a debit.

Office Supplies Expense — Acct. No. 608

Date		Explanation	F	Debit	Credit	Balance
1985						
Jun.	30	Adjustment	4	170		170
	30	Closing entry	5		170	0

Balance *before closing* is a debit.

Depreciation Expense—Office Equipment — Acct. No. 609

Date		Explanation	F	Debit	Credit	Balance
1985						
Jun.	30	Adjustment	4	10		10
	30	Closing entry	5		10	0

Balance *before closing* is a debit.

Depreciation Expense—Trucks — Acct. No. 610

Date		Explanation	F	Debit	Credit	Balance
1985						
Jun.	30	Adjustment	4	400		400
	30	Closing entry	5		400	0

Balance *before closing* is a debit.

Interest Expense Acct. No. 611

Date		Explanation	F	Debit	Credit	Balance
1985						
Jun.	30	Adjustment	4	64		64
	30	Closing entry	5		64	0

Balance *before closing* is a credit.

Income Summary Acct. No. 902

Date		Explanation	F	Debit	Credit	Balance
1985						
Jun.	30	Closing—for revenue items	5		7,577	7,577
	30	Closing—for expense items	5	3,589		3,988
	30	Closing—transfer of net income to capital	5	3,988		0

GENOVA TRUCKING COMPANY
Postclosing Trial Balance
June 30, 1985

Acct. No.	Account Title	Debits	Credits
101	Cash	$ 5,250	
111	Accounts Receivable	550	
112	Notes Receivable	1,440	
113	Accrued Interest Receivable	12	
131	Office Supplies	60	
141	Prepaid Insurance	2,100	
142	Prepaid Rent	1,000	
201	Office Equipment	1,400	
201A	Accumulated Depreciation—Office Equipment		$ 10
211	Trucks	26,000	
211A	Accumulated Depreciation—Trucks		400
301	Accounts Payable		200
302	Notes Payable		8,000
303	Accrued Interest Payable		64
311	Accrued Wages Payable		150
321	Unearned Rent		500
401	Lucy Genova, Capital		28,488
	Totals	$37,812	$37,812

Figure 5–12
Postclosing Trial Balance

The Postclosing Trial Balance

The postclosing trial balance of the Genova Trucking Company, taken from the general ledger, is shown in Figure 5–12.

Subsequent Period Entries Related to Accruals

The adjusting entries are recorded in the general journal and posted to the general ledger. Three of the adjusting entries—(g), (h), and (i) (see Figure 5–4)—are **accruals;** they involve accrual of previously unrecorded revenue or expense items assignable to June. Thus the receipt or payment of cash in July must be analyzed to determine the respective effect of the transaction on June and on July accounts. As an example, consider the next regular payment of the payroll on July 11, 1985.

Paying the Accrued Wages Payable

The next regular pay day at the Genova Trucking Company is July 11. On July 1, Wages Expense had a zero balance as a result of the closing entries on June 30, but the Accrued Wages Payable account had a credit balance of $150 as a result of the adjusting entries. Assuming that the biweekly wages again amounted to $600, the entry on July 11 to record this payment is:

GENERAL JOURNAL — Page 7

Date		Debit-Credit-Account Titles: Explanation	F	Debit	Credit
1985					
Jul.	11	Accrued Wages Payable	311	150	
		Wages Expense	605	450	
		Cash	101		600
		To record the payment of biweekly wages.			

Observe that in the Accrued Wages Payable and Wages Expense accounts, reproduced below, these results have been achieved: the biweekly wages of $600 are divided so that $150 that had been recognized as a June expense is debited to Accrued Wages Payable and $450 is recorded as an expense in July. Accrued Wages Payable now has a zero balance.

GENERAL LEDGER

Accrued Wages Payable — Acct. No. 311

Date		Explanation	F	Debit	Credit	Balance
1985						
Jun.	30	Adjustment	4		150	150
Jul.	11		7	150		0

Wages Expense Acct. No. 605

Date		Explanation	F	Debit	Credit	Balance
1985						
Jun.	13		2	600		600
	27		3	600		1,200
	30	Adjustment	4	150		1,350
	30	Closing entry	5		1,350	0
Jul.	11		7	450		450

The Accounting Cycle—Review

In this chapter and the preceding ones, the complete **accounting cycle** of a service business has been presented. The cycle—the total picture—consists of 11 steps, which are reviewed below:

1. *Selecting an appropriate chart of accounts,* which consists of selecting the accounts that are likely to be needed for financial statements and designating a numerical index system for them. Once this is done, in subsequent periods the accountant merely uses the correct accounts contained in the original chart of accounts or adds any new accounts that may be created by expansion or shifts of business for a given firm.

2. *Collecting business information through the use of business documents, analyzing the transactions, and journalizing,* which consists of capturing the information, analyzing, and recording transactions in chronological order in the journal.

3. *Posting,* which consists of transferring debits and credits to the appropriate ledgers and to the proper accounts in the ledgers.

4. *Preparing a trial balance,* or summarizing the general ledger accounts to test the equality of debits and credits; this can be prepared as a part of the work sheet.

5. *Preparing a schedule of accounts receivable,* which is summarizing the accounts receivable ledger accounts and reconciling the total with the balance of the Accounts Receivable controlling account in the general ledger.

6. *Preparing a schedule of accounts payable,* which is summarizing the accounts payable ledger accounts and reconciling the total with the balance of the Accounts Payable controlling account in the general ledger.

7. *Preparing the work sheet,* or assembling and classifying information in columnar form to facilitate the preparation of financial statements.

8. *Preparing the financial statements* from the work sheet; these are the income statement, statement of owner's equity, and balance sheet.

9. *Adjusting the books,* or recording and posting the adjusting entries from the work sheet.

10. *Closing the books,* which consists of recording and posting the closing entries from the Income Statement columns of the work sheet.

11. *Taking a postclosing trial balance,* or totaling the open-account balances to prove the equality of the debits and credits in the general ledger.

To keep the Genova Trucking Company illustration simple, steps 9, 10, and 11 were illustrated for a period of only one month. Most businesses use a yearly accounting period; the adjusting and closing entries are actually recorded in the journals and ledgers at the end of this period. However, those businesses *do* prepare monthly work sheets and monthly financial statements—called **interim statements**—for the management's use.

Glossary

Accounting cycle The steps that must be followed to process and record information, summarize and classify this information, and prepare the books to accomplish these steps during the next period.

Accruals A classification of adjustments that includes accrued revenues and accrued expenses.

Adjusted trial balance A trial balance prepared after the adjusting entries are made.

Closing entries Those journal entries that close the nominal accounts at the end of a period—that is, reduce these accounts to a zero balance. In the closing process, the net effect of this closing is transferred to the owner's capital account.

Deferrals A classification of adjustments which includes short-term revenue apportionments and long-term cost apportionments.

Interim statements Any statements that are made during the period but not including those statements made at the end of the period.

Keying of adjustments The method of cross-referencing the debit amount(s) of an adjustment to the credit amount(s); letters a, b, c, and so on are often used for the keying of adjustments.

Work sheet An orderly and systematic method of collecting information needed for the preparation of financial statements.

Questions

Q5–1 Identify the steps an accountant would take at the end of an accounting period. Why is each step taken?

Q5–2 (a) What is the purpose of the work sheet? (b) Can the work of the accountant be completed without the use of the work sheet?

Q5–3 (a) Why are the parts of each entry in the adjustment columns cross-referenced with either letters or numbers? (b) How is the amount to be extended into another column determined?

Q5–4 (a) What determines the column into which an amount is to be extended? (b) Is the work sheet foolproof?

Q5–5 Student A argues that since the work sheet has columns headed Income Statement and Balance Sheet, there is no need to prepare any end-of-period statement except the statement of owner's equity. Student B counters that formal statements for balance sheet, income statement, and statement of owner's equity should be prepared. With which student do you agree? Why?

Q5–6 Since adjustments are entered on the work sheet, does this step eliminate the need for journalizing the adjustments and posting them to the ledger accounts? Why or why not?

Q5–7 Is it possible to prepare the formal financial statements from a four-column work sheet consisting of the trial balance amounts and all the necessary adjustments?

Q5–8 (a) When would the amounts for Depreciation Expense and for Accumulated Depreciation be the same in the adjusted trial balance column of the work sheet? (b) When would these amounts be different?

Exercises

E5–1 *Effect of errors in adjustments on statements*

The inexperienced accountant for the San Diego Company prepared the following condensed income statement for the year ended December 31, 1985, and the condensed balance sheet as of the same date:

SAN DIEGO COMPANY **Exhibit A**
Income Statement
For the Year Ended December 31, 1985

Revenue from services		$73,575
Operating expenses:		
Insurance expense	$ 2,048	
Miscellaneous expense	7,410	
Office supplies expense	682	
Wages expense	23,400	33,540
Net income		$40,035

SAN DIEGO COMPANY **Exhibit C**
Balance Sheet
December 31, 1985

Assets

Cash	$ 6,825
Accounts receivable	16,380
Equipment	59,475
Total assets	$82,680

Liabilities and Owner's Equity

Accounts payable	$16,380
Deborah Diego, capital	66,300
Total liabilities and owner's equity	$82,680

The following items were overlooked by the accountant in the preparation of the statements:

a. Depreciation of equipment (acquired January 1, 1985); estimated life, 10 years; no salvage value.
b. Wages earned by employees that have not been paid, $1,170.
c. Office supplies on hand, $275 (purchases during 1985 were debited to Office Supplies Expense).
d. Unexpired insurance premiums, $710.

1. Journalize all necessary adjusting entries.

2. Prepare revised *classified* financial statements after all adjustments have been made.

E5–2
Simple work sheet

The Ringo Company's adjusted trial balance, taken from the work sheet for the year ended December 31, 1985, was as follows:

RINGO COMPANY
Adjusted Trial Balance
December 31, 1985

Account Title	Debits	Credits
Cash	$ 33,450	
Accounts Receivable	27,100	
Equipment	59,350	
Accumulated Depreciation		$ 20,000
Accounts Payable		11,560
Notes Payable		16,400
John Ringo, Capital		64,440
John Ringo, Drawing	12,500	
Service Revenue		95,000
Heat and Light Expense	4,500	
Wages Expense	62,500	
Depreciation Expense	8,000	
Totals	$207,400	$207,400

1. Enter the adjusted trial balance on a work sheet.

2. Complete the work sheet.

3. Prepare an income statement, a statement of owner's equity, a balance sheet, and the closing journal entries.

E5–3
Adjusting, closing, and future-year entries for accruals

The Saint John Company incurred the following transactions during 1985:

1985		
Nov.	1	Received 16 percent, 90-day note receivable in the amount of $8,000 in exchange for an account receivable.
Dec.	1	Issued a 15 percent, 60-day note payable in the amount of $2,500 to eliminate an account payable.
	31	The year ended on Wednesday. Weekly wages are $1,500, and Saint John has a five-day work week that ends on Friday.

1. Journalize the transactions, adjusting entries, and closing of the nominal accounts created.

2. Prepare journal entries to record collection of the note receivable, payment of the note payable, and payment of the weekly wages. (Wages are paid each Friday.)

E5–4
Analyzing adjusting entries and determining statement effect

The following information is taken from Raymond Company's books as of December 31, 1985:

Unadjusted Trial Balance Amount		Adjustment Data	
1. Prepaid Insurance	$ 3,600	Expired insurance	$1,800
2. Rent Expense	12,000	Rent paid in advance as of end of year	3,000
3. Wages Expense	18,000	Accrued wages	950
4. Interest Expense	900	Accrued interest	180
5. Unearned Rent	7,200	Rent earned	2,400
6. Interest Earned	3,150	Interest unearned at end of year	1,120

For each account: (a) prepare the adjusting journal entry; (b) state the amount to be shown in the income statement; (c) state the amount to be shown in the balance sheet.

E5–5 *Work sheet, accrual basis income statement, and determining cash basis income*

Following is the trial balance of Roxboro Lawn Mower Service for the month of July, the first month of operations:

ROXBORO LAWN MOWER SERVICE
Trial Balance
July 31, 1985

Account Title	Debits	Credits
Cash	$ 8,000	
Accounts Receivable	2,600	
Service Supplies	900	
Prepaid Insurance	650	
Accounts Payable		$ 900
Benjamin Lacy, Capital		10,470
Benjamin Lacy, Drawing	900	
Service Revenue		3,200
Advertising Expense	350	
Miscellaneous Expense	560	
Telephone and Telegraph Expense	250	
Wages Expense	360	
Totals	$14,570	$14,570

Supplementary data on July 31 were as follows:
a. Service supplies on hand were $720.
b. Expired insurance was $610.
c. Wages earned by employees but not paid were $208.

1. Enter the trial balance on a work sheet.

2. Complete the work sheet for the month of July.

3. Prepare an income statement for the month.

4. How much would net income be if the cash basis of accounting were used?

E5–6 *Partial work sheet*

Column totals for the partially completed work sheet of the Lyle Corporation are shown below:

	Income Statement		Balance Sheet	
	Dr.	Cr.	Dr.	Cr.
Totals	46,950	60,600	129,300	115,650

Complete the work sheet.

A Problems

P5–1A
Work sheet and end-of-period statements

Addie's Bake Shop's adjusted trial balance, taken from the work sheet for the month ended July 31, 1985, was as follows:

ADDIE'S BAKE SHOP
Adjusted Trial Balance
July 31, 1985

Account Title	Debits	Credits
Cash	$12,195	
Accounts Receivable	3,340	
Baking Supplies	6,200	
Prepaid Insurance	4,120	
Building	36,000	
Accumulated Depreciation—Building		$14,820
Land	8,800	
Accounts Payable		5,200
Notes Payable		3,120
Notes Payable to Banks, due July 31, 1989		9,360
Addie Spencer, Capital		29,129
Addie Spencer, Drawing	2,235	
Baking Revenue		25,670
Heat and Light Expense	412	
Telephone and Telegraph Expense	204	
Wages Expense	3,180	
Baking Supplies Expense	9,420	
Insurance Expense	516	
Depreciation Expense—Building	724	
Property Tax Expense	2,050	
Accrued Wages Payable		182
Interest Expense	165	
Accrued Interest Payable		130
Property Taxes Payable		1,950
Totals	$89,561	$89,561

Required:

1. Enter the adjusted trial balance on a work sheet using the appropriate two columns.

2. Complete the work sheet.

3. Prepare an income statement, a statement of owner's equity, and a balance sheet.

P5–2A *Completion of a work sheet*

The general ledger of Nicholas's Golfing Green showed the following balances at December 31, 1985. The books are closed annually on December 31. The company obtains revenue from its driving ranges and from a concession stand.

Account Title	Debits	Credits
Cash	$ 35,200	
Golfing Supplies	12,960	
Prepaid Insurance	10,800	
Prepaid Rent	11,700	
Golfing Equipment	85,000	
Accumulated Depreciation—Golfing Equipment		$ 22,050
Mortgage Payable		50,400
Denise Nicholas, Capital		36,796
Denise Nicholas, Drawing	12,960	
Golf Driving Revenue		76,080
Concession Revenue		10,350
Wages Expense	18,400	
Maintenance Expense	3,725	
Utilities Expense	2,780	
Telephone and Telegraph Expense	495	
Miscellaneous Expense	1,656	
Totals	$195,676	$195,676

Supplementary data include the following:

a. Golfing supplies on hand, based on a physical count, totaled $850.

b. The balance of the Prepaid Insurance account represents the premium on a four-year insurance policy, effective January 1, 1985.

c. Rent expense for the year was $8,100.

d. The golfing equipment has an expected life of 10 years and a salvage value of $1,500. No equipment was acquired during the year.

e. Salaries earned by employees but unpaid on December 31 were $205.

Required:

1. Enter the trial balance on a work sheet.

2. Complete the work sheet.

3. Why is the difference between the totals of the Income Statement columns and the totals of the Balance Sheet columns the same amount?

P5–3A *The complete accounting cycle*

On January 1, 1985, Daniel Isaacs opened a repair shop. During January the following transactions were completed:

1985		
Jan.	1	Transferred $12,000 from his personal savings account to a checking account under the name of Isaacs Repair Service.
	2	Paid $300 for office supplies.
	3	Purchased second-hand office equipment for $800 in cash.
	4	Issued a check for $400 for January rent.
	5	Paid a premium of $144 for an insurance policy on the equipment, effective January 1.

9 Purchased supplies on account to be used in repair work, as follows:

Fulton and Sams, Inc.	$ 310
Hinton Supply Company	340
James Company	220
Lampoon Supplies	460
Total	$1,330

15 Received $5,250 for repair work completed but not previously billed.

19 Additional repair work was completed, and bills were sent out, as follows:

Easley Eason	$ 940
Grady Lawson	580
Hilton Milton	290
Nelson Peters	320
Total	$2,130

21 Paid $180 for the telephone service for the month.

24 Paid the following creditors:

Fulton and Sams, Inc.	$110
Hinton Supply Company	120
James Company	120
Lampoon Supplies	160
Total	$510

28 Received cash from customers to apply on account, as follows:

Easley Eason	$540
Grady Lawson	180
Hilton Milton	90
Nelson Peters	120
Total	$930

30 Isaacs withdrew $1,500 in cash for his personal use.

Supplementary data as of January 31, 1985, were as follows:

a. The insurance premium paid on January 5 is for one year.

b. A physical count shows that office supplies on hand total $120 and repair supplies on hand total $360.

c. The office equipment has an estimated useful life of six years with no salvage value.

Required:

1. Open the following accounts in the general ledger: Cash, 101; Accounts Receivable, 111; Office Supplies, 136; Repair Supplies, 137; Prepaid Insurance, 140; Office Equipment, 163; Accumulated Depreciation—Office Equipment, 163A; Accounts Payable, 201; Daniel Isaacs, Capital, 301; Daniel Isaacs, Drawing, 302; Repair Revenue, 401; Insurance Expense, 502; Rent Expense, 503; Office Supplies Expense, 508; Telephone and Telegraph Expense, 509; Repair Supplies Expense, 512; Depreciation Expense—Office Equipment, 517; Income Summary, 601.

2. Open accounts in the accounts receivable subsidiary ledger for Easley Eason, Grady Lawson, Hilton Milton, and Nelson Peters.

3. Open accounts in the accounts payable subsidiary ledger for Fulton and Sams, Inc., Hinton Supply Company, James Company, and Lampoon Supplies.

4. Record all the transactions in the general journal, post to the appropriate ledgers, and enter the general ledger account balances directly in the Trial Balance columns of the work sheet.

5. Enter the adjustment data in the Adjustments columns of the work sheet.

6. Complete the work sheet.

7. Prepare an income statement, a balance sheet, and a statement of owner's equity.
8. Prepare a schedule of accounts receivable.
9. Prepare a schedule of accounts payable.
10. Prepare adjusting journal entries in the general journal.
11. Post the adjusting journal entries from the general journal to the general ledger.
12. Prepare closing entries in the general journal and post to the general ledger.
13. Prepare a postclosing trial balance.

P5–4A
End-of-period process

The *Hill Weekly,* a small-town weekly newspaper, was founded by Roger Wilcoxen and began operations on August 1, 1984. The date is now July 31, 1985, and the company bookkeeper wishes to adjust and close the books in order to prepare end-of-year statements. As a local certified public accountant, you have been asked to offer recommendations as to what adjusting and closing entries are necessary.

After talking with Wilcoxen about your very limited responsibilities, you ask the bookkeeper to let you see the company balance sheet as of the close of business on August 1, 1984 (the opening day) and the unadjusted trial balance as of today (July 31, 1985, the end of the first year's operations). He shows you the balance sheet given below and the trial balance given on page 197.

THE HILL WEEKLY
Balance Sheet
August 1, 1984
(After one day's operation)

Exhibit C

Assets			**Liabilities and Owner's Equity**		
Current assets:			Current liabilities:		
Cash	$ 15,000		Accounts payable	$4,000	
Accounts receivable—advertisers	2,400		Notes payable	4,800	
Accounts receivable—subscribers	1,600		Unearned advertising	2,400	
Supplies inventory	5,000		Unearned subscriptions	1,600	
Total current assets		$ 24,000	Total current liabilities		$ 12,800
Land and depreciable assets:			Long-term liabilities:		
Land	$ 35,000		Mortgage payable		100,000
Building	120,000				
Printing equipment	40,000		Owner's equity:		
Office equipment	6,000		Roger Wilcoxen, Capital		112,200
Total land and depreciable assets		201,000			
Total assets		$225,000	Total liabilities and owner's equity		$225,000

Assume that you had been asked when the company started operations to suggest what general ledger account titles were needed. You now notice that the bookkeeper has placed all these titles on the trial balance, including the accounts with a zero balance. During a talk with Wilcoxen and his bookkeeper, you make the following notes:

a. The supplies inventory consists of items that cost $5,700. You note that some items had been debited to Supplies Inventory and some to Supplies Expenses.
b. The building has an estimated useful life of 50 years and no salvage value.
c. The printing equipment has an estimated useful life of 11 years and an estimated salvage value of $4,800.
d. The office equipment has an estimated useful life of 10 years and an estimated salvage value of $600.

e. Interest of $36 for the month of July 1985 on the note payable will be paid on August 1, 1985, when the regular $200 installment payment will be made.
f. Unearned advertising as of July 31 is determined to be $900.
g. Unearned subscriptions as of July 31 are determined to be $5,600.
h. Salaries and wages that have been earned by employees but that are not due to be paid until the next payday (in August) amount to $675.
i. Interest of $792 on the mortgage payable for the month of July will be paid on August 1, 1985, when the regular $800 principal payment is made.
j. The company's insurance coverage is provided by a single comprehensive 24-month policy that began on August 1, 1984.
k. The trial balance prepared as of July 31, 1985, is given as follows:

THE HILL WEEKLY
Trial Balance
July 31, 1985

Account Title	Debits	Credits
Cash	$ 32,000	
Accounts Receivable—Advertisers	5,000	
Accounts Receivable—Subscribers	2,200	
Unexpired Insurance	0	
Supplies Inventory	5,000	
Land	30,000	
Building	120,000	
Accumulated Depreciation—Building		$ 0
Printing Equipment	40,000	
Accumulated Depreciation—Printing Equipment		0
Office Equipment	6,000	
Accumulated Depreciation—Office Equipment		0
Accounts Payable		5,200
Notes Payable		3,600
Unearned Advertising		2,400
Unearned Subscriptions		1,600
Accrued Salaries and Wages Payable		0
Accrued Interest Payable		0
Mortgage Payable		95,200
Roger Wilcoxen, Capital		112,200
Roger Wilcoxen, Drawing	0	
Advertising Revenue		75,800
Subscriptions Revenue		65,400
Depreciation Expense—Building	0	
Depreciation Expense—Printing Equipment	0	
Depreciation Expense—Office Equipment	0	
Interest Expense	4,730	
Insurance Expense	3,600	
Promotional Expense	8,600	
Salaries and Wages Expense	66,950	
Supplies Expense	31,600	
Utilities Expense	5,720	
Totals	$361,400	$361,400

Required:

1. Enter the trial balance on a work sheet.
2. Complete the work sheet.
3. Prepare an income statement, a statement of owner's equity, and a balance sheet.
4. Journalize all needed adjusting entries.
5. Journalize the closing entries.

P5–5A *Alternative adjustment methods and reversing entries*

The unadjusted trial balance of the Nittny Company contained the following accounts as of December 31, 1985:

NITTNY COMPANY
Partial Trial Balance
December 31, 1985

Acct. No.	Account Title	Debits	Credits
121	Accrued Interest Receivable	$ 0	
131	Office Supplies	2,550	
132	Prepaid Insurance	8,760	
133	Prepaid Advertising	0	
205	Accrued Wages Payable		$ 0
212	Unearned Rent		0
406	Rent Earned		663,000
410	Interest Earned		2,850
503	Wages Expense	150,000	
504	Advertising Expense	24,000	
505	Insurance Expense	0	
506	Office Supplies Expense	0	
601	Income Summary		0

Additional information includes the following:

a. Interest that had accrued on notes receivable at December 31, 1985, amounted to $660.
b. The inventory of office supplies at December 31, 1985, was $900.
c. The insurance records show that $3,000 of insurance has expired during 1985.
d. Included in Advertising Expense is a prepayment of a $3,600 contract for advertising space in a regional magazine; 70 percent of this contract has been used, and the remainder will be used in the following year.
e. Wages due to employees of $4,800 had accrued as of December 31, 1985.
f. Rent collected in advance that will not be earned until 1986 amounted to $24,000.

Required:

1. Open the accounts listed in the trial balance and record the balance in the Balance column as of December 31, 1985.
2. Journalize the adjusting entries and post to the appropriate accounts. In the accounts, identify the postings by writing "Adjusting" in the explanation columns.
3. Prepare journal entries to close the revenue and expense accounts. Do not transfer net income to the capital account.
4. Post the closing journal entries. In the accounts, identify the postings by writing "Closing" in the explanation columns.
5. On January 1, 1986, journalize the necessary reversing entries (including the optional ones). Post to the appropriate accounts. In the accounts, identify the postings by writing "Reversing" in the explanation columns.

P5–6A *Thought-provoking problem: interpreting adjusting and reversing entries*

The unadjusted and adjusted trial balance of the James Fulton Realty Company along with a portion of the general journal is given below. Fulton did not make any additional investment in his business during 1985.

JAMES FULTON REALTY COMPANY
Trial Balances
December 31, 1985

Account Title	Unadjusted Debits	Unadjusted Credits	Adjusted Debits	Adjusted Credits
Cash	$ 50,000		$ 50,000	
Notes Receivable	10,500		10,500	
Accrued Interest Receivable	0		420	
Office Supplies	4,250		3,750	
Prepaid Insurance	1,270		960	
Office Equipment	25,200		25,200	
Accumulated Depreciation—Office Equipment		$ 7,560		$ 10,080
Notes Payable to Banks		20,000		20,000
Accrued Interest Payable		0		126
James Fulton, Capital		51,970		51,970
James Fulton, Drawing	7,000		7,000	
Commissions Earned		62,000		62,000
Salaries Expense	33,000		33,000	
Other Expenses	8,000		11,330	
Interest Expense	3,150		3,276	
Interest Earned		840		1,260
Totals	$142,370	$142,370	$145,436	$145,436

GENERAL JOURNAL

Date		Debit-Credit-Account Titles: Explanation	F	Debit	Credit
1986 Jan.	1	Interest Earned		420	
		Accrued Interest Receivable			420
		To reverse.			
	1	Accrued Interest Payable		126	
		Interest Expense			126
		To reverse.			

Required:

1. Prepare an income statement for 1985.

2. Prepare a statement of owner's equity.

3. Did the accountant make only two adjusting entries: (1) for accrued interest receivable and (2) for accrued interest payable? If others were made, indicate what entries were made and the amounts of the adjustments—you do not need to make the adjusting entries.

4. Why would the accountant choose to make reversing entries for the two accrued interest adjustments?

B Problems

P5–1B *Work sheet and end-of-period statements*

Mama's Cake Shop's adjusted trial balance, taken from the work sheet for the month ended July 31, 1985, was as follows:

MAMA'S CAKE SHOP
Adjusted Trial Balance
July 31, 1985

Account Title	Debits	Credits
Cash	$ 4,150	
Accounts Receivable	5,210	
Baking Supplies	11,500	
Prepaid Insurance	7,340	
Building	54,000	
Accumulated Depreciation—Building		$ 29,940
Land	16,800	
Accounts Payable		10,900
Notes Payable		6,340
Notes Payable to Banks (due December 31, 1989)		18,820
Jane Douglas, Capital		18,748
Jane Douglas, Drawing	2,580	
Baking Revenue		43,340
Heat and Light Expense	715	
Telephone and Telegraph Expense	260	
Wages Expense	5,210	
Baking Supplies Expense	18,650	
Insurance Expense	838	
Depreciation Expense—Building	1,350	
Property Tax Expense	3,950	
Accrued Wages Payable		385
Interest Expense	180	
Accrued Interest Payable		310
Property Taxes Payable		3,950
Totals	$132,733	$132,733

Required:

1. Enter the adjusted trial balance on a work sheet using the appropriate columns.

2. Complete the work sheet.

3. Prepare an income statement, a statement of owner's equity, and a balance sheet.

P5–2B *Completion of a work sheet*

The general ledger of Putt-A-Rama, showed the following balances at December 31, 1985. The books are closed annually on December 31. Putt-A-Rama obtains revenue from its putting courses and from a concession stand.

Account Title	Debits	Credits
Cash	$ 18,500	
Putting Supplies	6,780	
Prepaid Insurance	5,750	
Prepaid Rent	5,950	
Putting Equipment	46,000	
Accumulated Depreciation—Putting Equipment		$ 11,050
Mortgage Payable		25,500
Mike Mazur, Capital		22,270
Mike Mazur, Drawing	6,550	
Putting Revenue		42,040
Concession Revenue		6,150
Wages Expense	11,900	
Maintenance Expense	2,365	
Utilities Expense	2,010	
Telephone and Telegraph Expense	265	
Miscellaneous Expense	940	
Totals	$107,010	$107,010

Supplementary data include the following:

a. Putting supplies on hand based on a physical count totaled $475.

b. The balance of the Prepaid Insurance account represents the premium on a three-year insurance policy, effective January 1, 1985.

c. Rent expense for the year was $2,975.

d. The putting equipment has an expected life of 10 years and a salvage value of $1,000. No equipment was acquired during the year.

e. Salaries earned by employees, but unpaid on December 31, were $115.

Required:

1. Enter the trial balance on a work sheet.

2. Complete the work sheet.

3. Why is the difference between the totals of the Income Statement columns and the totals of the Balance Sheet columns the same amount?

P5–3B *The complete accounting cycle*

On May 1, 1985, Jensen Jolly opened a repair shop. During March the following transactions were completed:

1985		
May	1	Transferred $18,000 from his personal savings account to a checking account under the name of Jolly's Fixum Shop.
	2	Paid $600 for office supplies.
	3	Purchased second-hand office equipment for $1,410 in cash.
	4	Issued a check for $700 for May rent.
	7	Paid a premium of $210 for an insurance policy on the equipment, effective May 1.
	10	Purchased repair supplies on account to be used in repair work, as follows:

Elmers Brothers	$1,080
Fussell Manufacturers	690
Land Company	740
Queens Supply Company	410
Total	$2,920

14 Received $12,450 for repair work completed and not previously billed.

18 Additional repair work was completed, and bills were sent out as follows:

James Cadwaller	$1,050
Betsy Floyd	1,790
Nelson Tilson	860
Thomas Wagner	658
Total	$4,358

22 Paid $435 for telephone service for the month.

26 Paid the following creditors:

Elmers Brothers	$ 580
Fussell Manufacturers	390
Land Company	240
Queens Supply Company	210
Total	$1,420

31 Received cash from customers to apply on account, as follows:

James Cadwaller	$ 450
Betsy Floyd	790
Nelson Tilson	160
Thomas Wagner	158
Total	$1,558

31 Jolly withdrew $2,600 in cash for his personal use.

Supplementary data as of May 31, 1985, were as follows:

a. The insurance premium paid on May 7 is for one year.

b. A physical count shows that office supplies on hand total $290 and repair supplies on hand total $980.

c. The office equipment has an estimated useful life of six years with no salvage value.

Required:

1. Open the following accounts in the general ledger: Cash, 101; Accounts Receivable, 111; Office Supplies, 136; Repair Supplies, 137; Prepaid Insurance, 140; Office Equipment, 163; Accumulated Depreciation—Office Equipment, 163A; Accounts Payable, 201; Jensen Jolly, Capital, 301; Jensen Jolly, Drawing, 302; Repair Revenue, 401; Insurance Expense, 502; Rent Expense, 503; Office Supplies Expense, 508; Telephone and Telegraph Expense, 509; Repair Supplies Expense, 512; Depreciation Expense—Office Equipment, 517; Income Summary, 601.

2. Open accounts in the accounts receivable subsidiary ledger for James Cadwaller, Betsy Floyd, Nelson Tilson, and Thomas Wagner.

3. Open accounts in the accounts payable subsidiary ledger for Elmers Brothers, Fussell Manufacturers, Land Company, and Queens Supply Company.

4. Record all the transactions in the general journal, post to the appropriate ledgers, and enter the general ledger account balances directly in the Trial Balance columns of the work sheet.

5. Enter the adjustment data in the Adjustments columns of the work sheet.

6. Complete the work sheet.

7. Prepare an income statement, a balance sheet, and a statement of owner's equity.

8. Prepare a schedule of accounts receivable.

9. Prepare a schedule of accounts payable.

10. Prepare adjusting journal entries in the general journal.

11. Post the adjusting journal entries from the general journal to the general ledger.

12. Prepare closing journal entries in the general journal and post to the general ledger.

13. Prepare a postclosing trial balance.

P5–4B *End-of-period process*

The *Chapel Ledger,* a small-town biweekly newspaper, was founded by Samuel Pipkin and began operations on May 1, 1984. The date is now April 30, 1985, and the company bookkeeper wishes to adjust and close the books in order to prepare end-of-year statements. As a local certified public accountant, you have been asked to offer recommendations as to what adjusting and closing entries are necessary.

After talking with Pipkin about your very limited responsibilities, you ask the bookkeeper to let you see the company balance sheets as of the close of business on May 1, 1984 (the opening day), and the unadjusted trial balance as of today (April 30, 1985, the end of the first year's operations). He shows you the balance sheet given below and the trial balance given on page 204.

THE CHAPEL LEDGER
Balance Sheet
May 1, 1984
(After one day's operations)

Exhibit C

Assets			**Liabilities and Owner's Equity**		
Current assets:			Current liabilities:		
Cash	$ 15,400		Accounts payable	$4,800	
Accounts receivable—advertisers	3,880		Notes payable	5,760	
Accounts receivable—subscribers	2,920		Unearned advertising	3,880	
Supplies inventory	6,000		Unearned subscriptions	2,920	
Total current assets		$ 28,200	Total current liabilities		$ 17,360
			Long-term liabilities:		
Land and depreciable assets:			Mortgage payable		120,000
Land	$ 36,000		Owner's equity:		
Building	144,000		Samuel Pipkin, capital		126,040
Printing equipment	48,000				
Office equipment	7,200				
Total land and depreciable assets		235,200			
Total assets		$263,400	Total liabilities and owner's equity		$263,400

Assume that you had been asked when the company started operations to suggest what general ledger account titles were needed. Now you notice that the bookkeeper has placed all these titles on the trial balance, including the accounts with a zero balance. During a talk with Pipkin and his bookkeeper, you make the following notes:

a. The April 30, 1985, supplies inventory consists of items that cost $6,840. You note that some items had been debited to Supplies Inventory and some to Supplies Expense.

b. The building has an estimated useful life of 50 years and no salvage value.

c. The printing equipment has an estimated useful life of 11 years and an estimated salvage value of $5,760.

d. The office equipment has an estimated useful life of 10 years and an estimated salvage value of $720.

e. Interest of $43 for the month of April 1985 on the note payable will be paid on May 1, 1985, when the regular $240 installment payment will be made.

f. Unearned advertising as of April 30 is determined to be $1,100.
g. Unearned subscriptions as of April 30 are determined to be $6,820.
h. Salaries and wages that have been earned by employees but that are not due to be paid until the next payday (in May) amount to $790.
i. Interest of $597 on the mortgage payable for the month of April will be paid on May 1, when the regular $600 principal payment is made.
j. The company's insurance coverage is provided by a single comprehensive 24-month policy that began on May 1, 1984.
k. The trial balance prepared as of April 30, 1985, is given as follows:

THE CHAPEL LEDGER
Trial Balance
April 30, 1985

Account Title	Debits	Credits
Cash	$ 35,600	
Accounts Receivable—Advertisers	6,000	
Accounts Receivable—Subscribers	2,640	
Unexpired Insurance	0	
Supplies Inventory	6,000	
Land	38,000	
Building	144,000	
Accumulated Depreciation—Building		$ 0
Printing Equipment	48,000	
Accumulated Depreciation—Printing Equipment		0
Office Equipment	7,200	
Accumulated Depreciation—Office Equipment		0
Accounts Payable		6,240
Notes Payable		4,320
Unearned Advertising		2,880
Unearned Subscriptions		1,920
Accrued Salaries and Wages Payable		0
Accrued Interest Payable		0
Mortgage Payable		114,240
Samuel Pipkin, Capital		133,840
Samuel Pipkin, Drawing	0	
Advertising Revenue		90,960
Subscriptions Revenue		78,480
Depreciation Expense—Building	0	
Depreciation Expense—Printing Equipment	0	
Depreciation Expense—Office Equipment	0	
Interest Expense	5,676	
Insurance Expense	4,320	
Promotional Expense	10,320	
Salaries and Wages Expense	80,340	
Supplies Expense	37,920	
Utilities Expense	6,864	
Totals	$432,880	$432,880

Required:

1. Enter the trial balance on a work sheet.

2. Complete the work sheet.

3. Prepare an income statement, a statement of owner's equity, and a balance sheet.

4. Journalize all needed adjusting entries.

5. Journalize the closing entries.

P5–5B
Alternative adjustment methods and reversing entries

The unadjusted trial balance of the Moffie Company contained the following accounts as of December 31, 1985:

MOFFIE COMPANY
Partial Trial Balance
December 31, 1985

Acct. No.	Account Title	Debits	Credits
121	Accrued Interest Receivable	$ 0	
131	Office Supplies	2,700	
132	Prepaid Insurance	6,840	
133	Prepaid Advertising	0	
205	Accrued Wages Payable		$ 0
212	Unearned Rent		0
406	Rent Earned		140,000
410	Interest Earned		2,900
503	Wages Expense	120,000	
504	Advertising Expense	18,000	
505	Insurance Expense	0	
506	Office Supplies Expense	0	
601	Income Summary		0

Additional information is given below:

a. Interest that had accrued on notes receivable at December 31, 1985, amounted to $595.
b. The inventory of office supplies at December 31, 1985, was $725.
c. The insurance records show that $2,500 of insurance has expired during 1985.
d. Included in Advertising Expense is a prepayment of a $2,500 contract for advertising space in a regional magazine; 65 percent of this contract has been used, and the remainder will be used in the following year.
e. Wages due to employees of $3,400 had accrued as of December 31, 1985.
f. Rent collected in advance that will not be earned until 1986 amounted to $16,800.

Required:

1. Open the accounts listed in the trial balance, and record the balance in the Balance column as of December 31, 1985.

2. Journalize the adjusting entries and post to the appropriate account. In the accounts, identify the postings by writing "Adjusting" in the explanation columns.

3. Prepare journal entries to close the revenue and expense accounts. Do not transfer the net income or net loss to the capital account.

4. Post the closing entries. In the accounts, identify the postings by writing "Closing" in the explanation columns.

5. On January 1, 1986, journalize the necessary reversing entries (including the optional ones). Post to the appropriate accounts. In the accounts, identify the postings by writing "Reversing" in the explanation columns.

P5–6B
Thought-provoking problem: issue of salary of proprietor

The closing entries of the Thomas Realty Company as of December 31, 1985, are given below. A yearly accounting period is used. Tyson Thomas, the proprietor, had a capital balance of $15,000 on January 1, 1985; he made one additional investment of $5,000 during the year.

GENERAL JOURNAL

Date		Debit-Credit-Account Titles: Explanation	F	Debit	Credit
1985		Closing Entries			
Dec.	31	Rental Revenue		5,500	
		Commission Revenue		21,600	
		Income Summary			27,100
	31	Income Summary		20,050	
		Rent Expense			1,800
		Insurance Expense			400
		Supplies Expense			150
		Commission Expense			16,500
		Depreciation Expense—Office Equipment			1,000
		Miscellaneous Expense			200
	31	Income Summary		7,050	
		Tyson Thomas, Capital			7,050
	31	Tyson Thomas, Capital		2,050	
		Tyson Thomas, Drawing			2,050

Required:

1. Prepare an income statement for 1985.

2. Prepare a statement of owner's equity for 1985.

3. Thomas argues that since he works full time in his business the income statement for the single proprietorship should show a deduction of a reasonable amount for his service to the business. Do you agree or disagree? Comment.

6 Accounting for a Merchandising Firm

Note: At this point, it is assumed that the reader has learned the headings for the general journal and for ledger accounts. In some illustrations, the headings are omitted to concentrate on ideas and not on form.

Introduction

In all previous chapters, the businesses for which records are maintained have earned revenue from providing a service. Their income statements—limited to revenues and operating expenses—have been relatively easy to prepare. However, a great number of businesses earn revenue from selling merchandise to customers. Examples are Sears, Roebuck and Company, K mart, and J C Penney. In these merchandising businesses, there is an additional cost—the cost of merchandise sold. Since a merchandising business is involved in the purchase of goods, their handling, and their sale, additional accounts are needed to record these transactions. Also, the income statements are more complex.

This chapter examines the functions and the financial statement classifications of the accounts needed for a merchandising business and shows how to complete the work sheet and financial statements for this type of business. The chapter closes with a discussion of the "management by exception" principle, especially as it relates to the managerial control of cash discounts.

Learning Goals

To understand the concept of cost of goods sold.

To identify the functions and financial statement classifications of merchandising accounts.

To compute the cost of goods sold.

To prepare and complete a work sheet for a merchandising business.

To be able to explain the difference between the income statements for nonmerchandising and merchandising businesses.

To journalize and post to the merchandising accounts in the closing process.

To journalize transactions involving cash discounts using both the net and gross price methods.

To be able to distinguish between cash discounts and trade discounts and to compute both.

Merchandising: An Overview

The principal difference between a merchandising firm and a service firm is the need to include the cost of merchandise that was sold during the period in computing net income. In general terms, the cost of goods sold is the cost, to the merchandising firm, of the merchandise that was sold to customers during the accounting period. There are alternative approaches to determining cost of goods sold. One of these, the **periodic inventory method,** determines inventory and cost of goods sold only at the end of each accounting period. (This is the method used in this chapter.) The other, the **perpetual inventory method,** produces a continuous record of goods on hand and cost of goods sold.

Under the periodic inventory method, cost of goods sold can be calculated only after a cost is determined for the merchandise remaining on hand at the end of the period (usually done by physical count and tracing to cost records). To simplify the discussion and to focus on the important merchandising concepts in this chapter, it will be assumed that the end-of-period inventory valuations have already been determined. In Chapter 12, the determination of the periodic inventory valuation is discussed, and the perpetual inventory method is explained.

In broad terms, the income statement of a merchandising firm takes on the following form:[1]

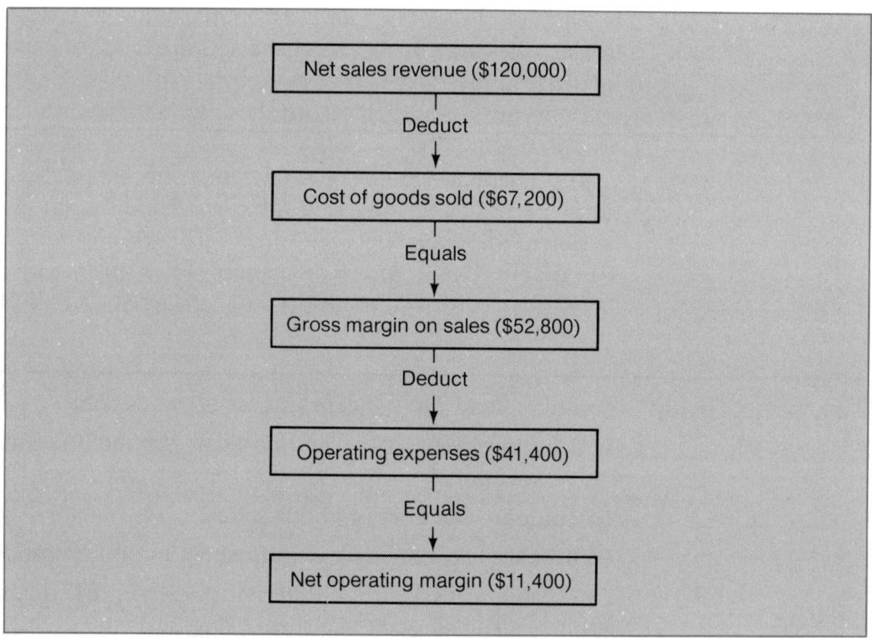

The next several sections contain discussions of the various accounts needed to develop *net sales revenue* and *cost of goods sold.*

---

[1]The amounts used in this illustration come from the example used later in the chapter—Tarrant Wholesale Company.

Sales Revenue Accounts

The Sales Account

Sales are transactions involving the transfer of goods or services in exchange for cash or a promise to pay at a later date. A sale of merchandise is recorded by a credit to the revenue account, Sales. Suppose, for example, that the Tarrant Wholesale Company sold merchandise on credit to John Roundtree. This transaction would be recorded as shown below:

1985 Dec.	6	Accounts Receivable		200	
		Sales			200
		Sold merchandise on account to: John Roundtree $200			

The debit to Accounts Receivable (or to Cash if the sale is for cash) records an increase in an asset. The credit to Sales, a revenue account, records the gross increase in the owner's equity. This credit constitutes a recovery of the cost of the merchandise sold as well as a profit. However, many businesses would find it next to impossible to divide each sale into a return of cost and a profit. Therefore, the entire sale price of the goods is recorded as revenue. The total cost of goods sold for the year becomes a deduction from the year's total revenue in the income statement. The calculation of the cost of goods sold is explained later in the chapter.

A copy of the invoice showing the sale to John Roundtree appears in Figure 6–1.

TARRANT WHOLESALE COMPANY
Sherbourne, Mass. 02666

DATE SOLD: 12/6/85	No. X00137	SALESMAN JB	OUR INVOICE No. 10032
TERMS: F.O.B. Destination 2/10, n/30	SOLD TO John Roundtree		CUSTOMER ORDER No. A232
	TOWN AND STATE Cambridge, Ma. 12115		LEDGER FOLIO S10006
	SHIP BY Allen Motor Freight	WHEN TO SHIP 12/6/85	

ITEM No.	SHIPPER'S CHECK	QUANTITY	DESCRIPTION	UNIT	PRICE	AMOUNT
67181	✓	84	Relzohn, Semi-cut	Lb.	$1.00	$ 84 00
4979	✓	10	Keg, 10 gal. Hearthstone	Ea.	8.50	85 00
347	✓	2	Jar, 1 qt. Acrolyx	Ea.	15.50	31 00
			Total			$200 00

Figure 6–1 **Sales Invoice**

The Sales Returns and Allowances Account

A customer may return merchandise because it is not exactly as ordered, or the customer may be entitled to an allowance, or a reduction of the amount owed, for defective or broken goods not worth returning. The effect of the entry to record a return or allowance is the opposite of a sale. However, when Cash or the customer's account is credited, an account entitled **Sales Returns and Allowances,** a contra account to Sales, is debited. This contra account is used, rather than Sales, so that a record may be available of the amount of returns and allowances. If John Roundtree returned 10 pounds of relzohn, item number 67181, as defective, the journal entry would be:

1985					
Dec.	9	Sales Returns and Allowances		10	
		Accounts Receivable			10
		Defective merchandise was returned by:			
		John Roundtree $10			

A business form called a **credit memorandum** is issued to Roundtree to advise that his account has been credited for the return. It is not necessary to change the inventory amount. The loss of defective units is automatically included in the cost of the goods sold computation (discussed later).

The Sales Discounts Account

The customer who pays within a stated discount period may be allowed a **cash discount,** or reduction in price. If the buyer pays within the discount period, the seller has the cash available during the interval between the end of the discount period and the end of the credit period for reinvestment in the business. The balance in the uncollected accounts receivable for that interval has also been reduced.

Sales discounts are computed on the invoice price; the conditions of payment are stated on the invoice. Two examples of cash discount terms are 2/10, n/30, and 1/10, n/60. The first of these terms, *2/10, n/30* (read two ten, net thirty), means that if the buyer pays within 10 days from the date shown on the invoice, two percent may be deducted from the invoice price, or the buyer may take 30 days before paying the total invoice price.

It is important to recognize the magnitude of the discount offered. This can be done best if the discount is converted into its equivalent annual interest rate. Assuming terms of 2/10, n/30, the cost of the additional 20 days is high, because the loss of the two percent discount amounts to one-tenth of one percent per day = (2 percent ÷ 20), or 36 percent per 360-day year = (0.1 percent × 360). The prudent manager should compare carefully the cost of the failure to take a cash discount with current interest rates.

Since the effect of a discount is to reduce the amount actually received from the sale, Sales Discounts is debited for the amount of the discount. **Sales Discounts** is a contra account to Sales and is also used to supply management with valuable information about the business. When discounts are offered, the customer is in fact being offered the choice of paying (1) the full amount of the invoice or (2) the full amount reduced by the amount of the discount. The seller does not know at the time of the sale whether the customer is going to take the discount, so the customer is charged the full amount of the sale. If the sale was recorded under the **gross price method** (that is, journalized initially at the full invoice amount) and payment is received within the discount period, the collection is recorded as follows:

					Debit	Credit
1985						
Dec.	16	Cash			186.20	
		Sales Discounts			3.80	
		Accounts Receivable				190.00
		Received payment from John Roundtree for the sale of December 6 less the 2% cash discount:				
		Gross sale price	$200.00			
		Merchandise returned	10.00			
		Accounts receivable balance	$190.00			
		2% discount[a]	3.80			
		Cash received	$186.20			
		John Roundtree	$190.00			

[a]Discount is allowed only on the $190 of merchandise actually retained.

It is not necessary to place the details of returns and discount computations in the journal entry explanations. In this chapter, it is done only so the reader can see the source of debits and credits.

An alternative procedure to the gross price method is discussed later in this chapter.

The following partial income statement of Tarrant Wholesale Company, whose accounts are used for illustrative purposes throughout this chapter, shows the classification of the Sales and its contra accounts to derive net sales revenue.

TARRANT WHOLESALE COMPANY **Exhibit A**
Income Statement
For the Year Ended December 31, 1985

Gross sales revenue		$124,200
Deduct: Sales returns and allowances	$2,400	
Sales discounts	1,800	4,200
Net sales revenue		$120,000

Cost of Goods Sold Accounts

Net Cost of Purchases

The Purchases Account It is common in merchandising businesses to use a separate **Purchases** account for all merchandise bought for resale. The account is not used for the purchase of operating supplies, for example, or for store equipment. It is debited for the cost of the goods bought for resale as shown on the seller's invoice. It therefore provides a record of the cost of the goods purchased during the period—not a record of the goods on hand.

During the year, the Purchases account is debited with each receipt of merchandise. This account is increased as each purchase is recorded. Credits to the account are made to close the account or to correct errors. A typical entry to record a purchase of merchandise of $800 from Jay Stores is:

1985 Dec.	5	Purchases		800	
		Accounts Payable			800
		Purchased merchandise on account, terms 1/10, n/30: Jay Stores $800			

The Transportation In Account The invoice price of goods may include the cost of transporting the goods from the seller's place of business to that of the buyer. If so, no separation is made, and the entire purchase price is debited to Purchases. If the cost of transportation is not included, the freight cost may be borne by the buyer, who debits the amount to **Transportation In** or Freight In. This account is added to Purchases in the income statement to determine the delivered cost of merchandise. The buyer makes an entry as follows:

1985 Dec.	7	Transportation In		50	
		Cash			50
		Paid for freight charges on merchandise purchased F.O.B. shipping point.			

The following terms are used in connection with the transportation of merchandise:

Transportation terms

1. The term* F.O.B. *(free on board)* shipping point *indicates that title (ownership of the goods) passes to the buyer when the seller turns the shipment over to a common carrier. The owner of the merchandise while it is in transit (the buyer) bears the freight cost from the point of shipment to the destination.
2. The term* F.O.B. destination *indicates that title passes to the buyer at the destination. The owner of the merchandise while it is in transit (the seller) bears the freight cost to the buyer's location. (Sometimes the buyer pays the cost and deducts the amount from the payment to the seller.)

The Purchases Returns and Allowances Account

Goods bought for resale may be defective, broken, or not of the quality or quantity ordered. Either they may be returned for credit, or the seller may make an adjustment by reducing the original price. The buyer makes an entry as follows:

1985 Dec.	8	Accounts Payable		100	
		Purchases Returns and Allowances . .			100
		Returned defective merchandise to vendor:			
		Jay Stores $100			

Purchases Returns and Allowances is a contra account to Purchases. The same result could be accomplished by crediting Purchases, but it is useful to management to have the books show total purchases as well as total purchases returns and allowances. Analysis of the Purchases Returns and Allowances account may indicate the need for changes in the procedures for ordering and handling merchandise.

The Purchases Discounts Account

The **Purchases Discounts** account, a contra account to Purchases, is used to record cash discounts on the purchase price of goods for payments that are made within the discount period specified by the seller. A typical payment entry within the discount period is:

1985 Dec.	13	Accounts Payable		700	
		Cash			693
		Purchases Discounts			7
		Paid for merchandise purchased on December 5 less discount:			
		Gross purchase $800			
		Merchandise returned 100			
		Accounts payable balance $700			
		1% discount 7			
		Cash paid $693			
		Jay Stores $700			

The Net Cost of Purchases Disclosed

The net cost of purchases, then, is the total cost of purchases plus transportation in, minus purchases returns and allowances and purchases discounts. The amounts for Tarrant Wholesale Company are as follows:

Purchases		$63,580
Transportation in		4,800
Gross delivered cost of purchases		$68,380
Deduct: Purchases returns and allowances	$1,500	
Purchases discounts	3,600	5,100
Net cost of purchases		$63,280

The Merchandise Inventory Account

Illustrated in this chapter is the periodic inventory method. Under the periodic inventory method, merchandise purchased is recorded at *cost* in the Purchases account; merchandise sold is recorded at *selling price* in the Sales account. Therefore, an account called **Merchandise Inventory** is needed to show the cost of merchandise actually on hand at the end of each accounting period. The amount is determined by making a list of the goods on hand, with an actual count of each showing physical quantities and cost. This *ending inventory* is entered in the books and becomes the *beginning inventory* of the next period. The amount in the ledger account will not be changed until the end of the next accounting period because the Merchandise Inventory account is not used during the period. Since the account remains open, its balance—the beginning inventory—appears in the trial balance at the end of the period and is charged against income by a debit to Income Summary and a credit to Merchandise Inventory when the books are closed. Concurrently, in the closing entries, the new ending merchandise inventory is entered as a debit to Merchandise Inventory and a credit to Income Summary. Thus the amount of the beginning inventory has been eliminated and replaced by the amount of the ending inventory. After the closing entries are posted, the Merchandise Inventory account in the general ledger of the Tarrant Wholesale Company appears as shown below:[2]

Merchandise Inventory — Acct. No. 121

Date		Explanation	F	Debit	Credit	Balance
1984						
Dec.	31	1	12	15,400		15,400
1985						
Dec.	31	2	20		15,400	0
	31	3	20	11,480		11,480

1 The debit amount of $15,400 is the cost of the merchandise inventory on hand as of December 31, 1984 (the beginning inventory).

2 The credit posting of $15,400 closes the account temporarily and transfers the balance to Income Summary.

3 The debit posting of $11,480 is the cost of the merchandise inventory on hand as of December 31, 1985 (the ending inventory); this amount will remain unchanged in the account until the books are closed again on December 31, 1986.

Cost of Goods Sold

The cost of goods sold section of the Tarrant Wholesale Company income statement can now be presented in full. The net cost of purchases, illustrated earlier, is repeated here to show that when using the periodic inventory system it is necessary to add the beginning inventory to the net cost of pur-

[2]Although some accountants prefer to use an adjusting entry to record the change in inventory valuation, the authors prefer that adjustment from beginning to ending inventory be accomplished in closing entries.

chases to arrive at the cost of merchandise available for sale, and then to deduct the ending inventory to arrive at the **cost of goods sold.** (Note how major amounts are kept in the right-hand column with computations of subtotals moved left as necessary.)

Cost of goods sold:				
Merchandise inventory, January 1, 1985			$15,400	
Purchases		$63,580		
Transportation in		4,800		
Gross delivered cost of purchases		$68,380		
Deduct: Purchases returns and allowances	$1,500			
Purchases discounts	3,600	5,100		
Net cost of purchases			63,280	
Cost of merchandise available for sale			$78,680	
Deduct: Merchandise inventory, December 31, 1985			11,480	
Cost of goods sold				$67,200

This type of computation to determine the cost of goods sold is necessary because sales are recorded only at selling price under the periodic method. A continuous record of the *cost* of each individual sale is not recorded under the periodic method.

Gross Margin on Sales

The **gross margin on sales** is the difference between net sales revenue and cost of goods sold. The term *gross* indicates that the expenses necessary to operate the business must still be deducted to arrive at the net operating margin. If the gross margin on sales is less than the operating expenses, the difference is a net operating loss for the period. The amounts for Tarrant are as follows (the detailed computations of net sales revenue and cost of goods sold have already been illustrated and are not repeated here):

Net sales revenue	$120,000
Cost of goods sold	67,200
Gross margin on sales	$ 52,800

Functions of the Merchandise Accounts

The following T accounts summarize the functions of the merchandise accounts described in this chapter and their locations in the financial statements. The description *Balance* in each account refers to the balance before the closing entries have been posted. After the closing entries are posted, all the merchandise accounts except Merchandise Inventory have zero balances.

Sales

Debited	Credited
At the end of the accounting period to close the account.	During the accounting period for the sales price of goods sold. *Balance before closing* A credit representing cumulative sales for the period to date. *Statement classification* In the income statement as the first item on the statement.

Sales Returns and Allowances

Debited	Credited
During the accounting period for unwanted merchandise returned by customers and allowances granted for defective or broken goods. *Balance before closing* A debit representing cumulative sales returns and allowances for the period to date. *Statement classification* In the income statement, a deduction from sales revenue.	At the end of the accounting period to close the account.

Sales Discounts

Debited	Credited
During the accounting period for the amounts that the customers deduct from the gross sales price when payment is made within the period established by the seller. *Balance before closing* A debit representing cumulative sales discounts taken by customers for the period to date. *Statement classification* In the income statement, a deduction from sales revenue.	At the end of the accounting period to close the account.

Purchases

Debited	Credited
During the accounting period for the purchase price of goods bought for resale. *Balance before closing* A debit representing cumulative purchases for the period to date. *Statement classification* In the income statement, added to the beginning inventory under cost of goods sold.	At the end of the accounting period to close the account.

Transportation In

Debited	Credited
Debited During the accounting period for delivery costs—freight or cartage—on merchandise purchases. *Balance before closing* A debit representing cumulative costs for the period to date incurred by the buyer for the delivery of merchandise. *Statement classification* In the income statement, in the cost of goods sold section, added to purchases.	*Credited* At the end of the accounting period to close the account.

Purchases Returns and Allowances

Debited	Credited
Debited At the end of the accounting period to close the account.	*Credited* During the accounting period for unwanted merchandise returned to the vendor or allowances received for defective or broken merchandise. *Balance before closing* A credit representing cumulative purchases returns and allowances for the period to date. *Statement classification* In the income statement, in the cost of goods sold section, as a deduction from the gross cost of merchandise purchased.

Purchases Discounts

Debited	Credited
Debited At the end of the accounting period to close the account.	*Credited* During the accounting period for the amounts of discount from the gross purchase price of merchandise when payment was made within the period established by the seller. *Balance before closing* A credit representing cumulative purchases discounts taken for the period to date. *Statement classification* In the income statement, in the cost of goods sold section, as a deduction from the gross cost of merchandise purchased.

Merchandise Inventory

Debit side	Credited
Beginning balance A debit representing the cost of goods on hand at the beginning of the period. This was the ending inventory of the previous period. *Debited* At the end of each accounting period for the merchandise actually on hand (the *ending balance* of the account). *Statement classification* 1. In the balance sheet the ending inventory under current assets. 2. In the income statement, in the cost of goods sold section, the beginning inventory is added to purchases and the ending inventory is deducted from the cost of merchandise available for sale.	*Credited* At the end of each accounting period to remove the beginning inventory from the account.

TARRANT WHOLESALE COMPANY
Income Statement
For the Year Ended December 31, 1985

Exhibit A

Gross sales revenue				$124,200
Deduct: Sales returns and allowances			$ 2,400	
Sales discounts			1,800	4,200
Net sales revenue				$120,000
Cost of goods sold:				
Merchandise inventory, January 1, 1985			$15,400	
Purchases		$63,580		
Transportation in		4,800		
Gross delivered cost of purchases		$68,380		
Deduct: Purchases returns and allowances	$1,500			
Purchases discounts	3,600	5,100		
Net cost of purchases			63,280	
Cost of merchandise available for sale			$78,680	
Deduct: Merchandise inventory, December 31, 1985			11,480	
Cost of goods sold				67,200
Gross margin on sales				$ 52,800
Deduct: Operating expenses:				
Selling expenses:				
Sales salaries expense		$12,000		
Transportation out expense		2,400		
Advertising expense		3,000		
Total selling expenses			$17,400	
General and administrative expenses:				
Rent expense		$ 6,000		
Property tax expense		7,800		
Heat and light expense		2,160		
Miscellaneous general expense		480		
Insurance expense		1,920		
Supplies expense		2,040		
Depreciation expense—machinery and equipment		3,600		
Total general and administrative expenses			24,000	
Total operating expenses				41,400
Net operating margin				$ 11,400
Other revenue:				
Interest earned		$ 125		
Rent earned		300	$ 425	
Other expenses:				
Interest expense		$ 75		
Loss on sale of equipment		100	175	250
Net income				$ 11,650

Figure 6–2 **Income Statement**

The Operating Expense Accounts

Operating expenses include salaries, postage, telephone and telegraph, computer services, heat and light, insurance, advertising, and any other expired costs incurred for goods or services used in operating the business. The breakdown of operating expenses into a detailed account for each type facilitates analyses and comparisons that aid in cost control. The amount of detail shown depends on the size and type of the business and on the needs and wishes of management.

The operating expenses are often classified into selling or general and administrative. Those incurred in packaging, advertising, selling, and delivering the product are classified as **selling expenses.** Sales salaries, commissions, and supplies used in the sales department are examples of expenses incurred in making the sale. Expenses of delivering the product include freight paid by the seller (transportation out expense—not to be confused with transportation in) and the expense of operating delivery vehicles. Expenses such as rent, taxes, and insurance, to the extent that they are incurred in selling the product, are also classified as selling expenses. Other operating expenses are classified as **general and administrative expenses,** including office expenses, computer services, executive salaries, and the portion of rent, taxes, and insurance applicable to the administrative function of the business.

Expenses that are common to both selling and administrative functions may be apportioned on some equitable basis. If an apportionment is not practicable, the account should be classified under the function it serves most. In Figure 6–2, the operating expense accounts that are entirely related to selling are classified as such; all the others are classified as general and administrative.

If the operating expense accounts in the general ledger are too numerous, it is advisable to remove them to subsidiary selling expense and general and administrative expense ledgers. Two controlling accounts are substituted in the general ledger—Selling Expense Control and General and Administrative Expense Control—in place of the accounts that have been removed. (The function of controlling accounts was explained in Chapter 2.)

Net Operating Margin

Net operating margin measures the net revenue from the major operating function of the business. In Figure 6–2, the total operating expenses of $41,400 are deducted from the gross margin on sales of $52,800 to arrive at the net operating margin of $11,400.[3]

Other Revenue and Other Expenses

Revenue and expenses that are generated by transactions not related to the principal activity of the business are classified as **other revenue** and **other expenses.** These sections of the income statement serve a valuable function; they permit calculation of the net operating margin without its being distorted by nonoperating items and link the net operating margin for the period with the net income for that period.

[3]Some accountants prefer to list the expenses in decreasing order of size of these amounts. However, the relative sizes of amounts change over the years. Once an account number has been assigned, there is less possibility of error if expenses are listed in account number order from the work sheet.

Other Revenue

In Figure 6–2, Tarrant Wholesale Company shows $125 in interest earned and $300 in rent earned under other revenue. These additional examples are included under other revenue because they arose from a source other than the sale of merchandise, the basic business purpose of Tarrant. Other examples of items classified as other revenue are gains from the sale of temporary investments, dividends on shares of stock owned, and gains from the sale of property, plant, and equipment.

Other Expenses

Nonoperating expenses, such as interest on money borrowed from the bank or on notes given to creditors for the purchase of merchandise or losses from the sale of property, plant, and equipment, are shown under other expenses. In Figure 6–2, there are $75 in interest expense and $100 from a loss on a sale of equipment under this heading. The loss is the excess of the undepreciated cost of the equipment over the sales price.

The accountant added $250, the excess of other revenue over other expenses, to the net operating margin. If other expenses exceed other revenue, the expenses are listed first and the excess is deducted from the net operating margin. In the absence of other revenue or other expenses, net operating margin becomes net income and net operating loss becomes net loss.

The complete income statement for the Tarrant Wholesale Company for the year ended December 31, 1985, is shown in Figure 6–2. It was prepared from the work sheet shown later (Figure 6–5).

Work Sheet for a Merchandising Business

The procedure for completing the work sheet of a merchandising business is similar to that of a service business, with the exception of the account for merchandise inventory. At the end of the period, the balance of the Merchandise Inventory account, the beginning inventory of $15,400, is extended to the Income Statement Debit column of the work sheet because it is part of the cost of merchandise available for sale. The ending inventory, $11,480, is entered in the Income Statement Credit column because it is an offset or deduction from the accounts comprising the total cost of goods available for sale that will have been extended into the income statement debit column.[4] The ending inventory amount is also entered in the Balance Sheet Debit column because it is a balance sheet asset. Note that the ending inventory amounts are always entered on the same horizontal line as the beginning inventory. Entering an income statement credit and a balance sheet debit maintains the essential debit/credit equality of the work sheet as illustrated in Figure 6–3. The complete work sheet is shown in Figure 6–5.

[4]Some accountants prefer to handle the end-of-period inventory change as an adjustment on the worksheet and in the adjusting entries. When this is done, the end result remains the same.

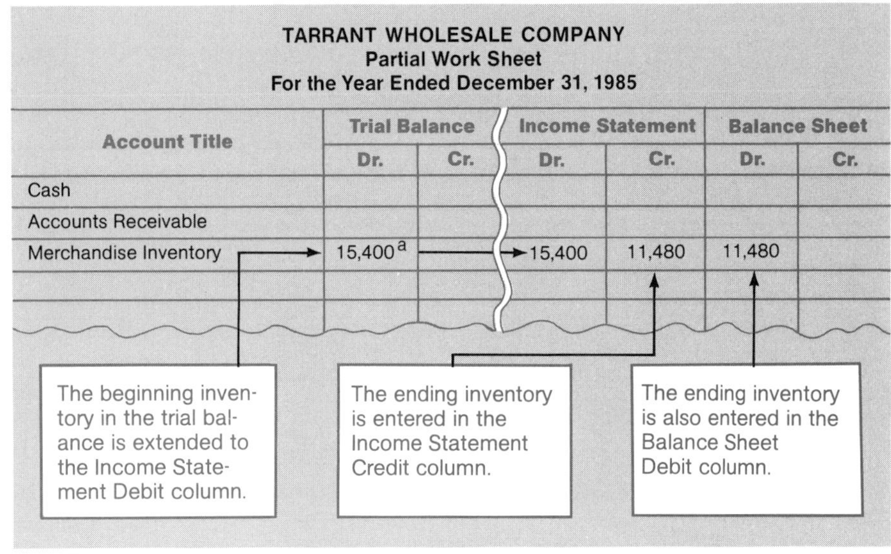

Figure 6–3
Partial Work Sheet

[a]This amount also appears in the Adjusted Trial Balance Debit column.

Trial Balance Columns

The account balances in the trial balance are taken from the general ledger of the Tarrant Wholesale Company as of December 31, 1985.

Adjustments Columns

The adjustments are entered in the Adjustments columns of the work sheet in the same manner as illustrated in Chapter 5. No entry is made in these columns for the change in the Merchandise Inventory account. That change is accomplished directly through the Income Statement and the Balance Sheet columns, as shown in Figure 6–3.

Adjusted Trial Balance Columns

The combined Trial Balance and Adjustments column amounts are extended to the Adjusted Trial Balance columns.

Income Statement Columns

All the account balances that enter into the measurement of net income are extended to the Income Statement columns. The income statement accounts that enter into the determination of gross margin on sales are shown in Figure 6–4.

The difference between the column totals in Figure 6–4 is $52,800 = ($140,780 − $87,980). It is the same as the gross margin on sales in the formal income statement (Figure 6–2) because all the accounts that enter into

Acct. No.	Account Title	Income Statement	
		Dr.	Cr.
121	Merchandise Inventory	15,400	11,480
401	Sales		124,200
402	Sales Returns and Allowances	2,400	
403	Sales Discounts	1,800	
501	Purchases	63,580	
502	Transportation In	4,800	
503	Purchases Returns and Allowances		1,500
504	Purchases Discounts		3,600
	(Totals of the foregoing items)	87,980	140,780

Figure 6–4 Abstract from the Work Sheet

the determination of the gross margin are present. Similar examples could be shown using all the other sections of the income statement and balance sheet.

Balance Sheet Columns

All the amounts used to prepare the balance sheet and statement of owner's equity are extended to the Balance Sheet columns.

Statements Prepared from the Work Sheet

The income statement illustrated in Figure 6–2, the statement of owner's equity illustrated in Figure 6–6, and the classified balance sheet shown in Figure 6–7 are prepared directly from the work sheet (Figure 6–5), not from the ledger accounts or other sources. Information for all sections except the owner's equity amount is taken directly from the work sheet. The new owner's equity amount, however, must be taken from the statement of owner's equity or computed as the work sheet beginning-of-year capital amount plus net income minus the drawing amount.

Closing Entries

The procedure for recording the closing entries in a merchandising business is essentially the same as that in a service business (illustrated in Chapter 3).[5] The only difference involves the accounts introduced in this chapter. The

[5]Adjusting entries are journalized from the work sheet as explained in Chapter 5, and are not illustrated again here.

TARRANT WHOLESALE COMPANY
Work Sheet
For the Year Ended December 31, 1985

Acct. No.	Account Title	Trial Balance		Adjustments		Adjusted Trial Balance		Income Statement		Balance Sheet	
		Dr.	Cr.	Dr.	Cr.	Dr.	Cr.	Dr.	Cr.	Dr.	Cr.
101	Cash	7,200				7,200				7,200	
111	Accounts Receivable	39,800				39,800				39,800	
121	Merchandise Inventory	15,400				15,400		15,400	11,480	11,480	
131	Office Supplies	3,240			(b) 2,040	1,200				1,200	
141	Prepaid Insurance	3,740			(a) 1,920	1,820				1,820	
151	Machinery and Equipment	70,100				70,100				70,100	
151A	Accumulated Depreciation—Machinery and Equipment		7,200		(c) 3,600		10,800				10,800
201	Accounts Payable		17,700				17,700				17,700
202	Notes Payable		7,300				7,300				7,300
221	Mortgage Payable		20,000				20,000				20,000
301	Lucy Genova, Capital		65,150				65,150				65,150
302	Lucy Genova, Drawing	1,000				1,000				1,000	
401	Sales		124,200				124,200		124,200		
402	Sales Returns and Allowances	2,400				2,400		2,400			
403	Sales Discounts	1,800				1,800		1,800			
501	Purchases	63,580				63,580		63,580			
502	Transportation In	4,800				4,800		4,800			
503	Purchases Returns and Allowances		1,500				1,500		1,500		
504	Purchases Discounts		3,600				3,600		3,600		
601	Sales Salaries Expense	12,000				12,000		12,000			
602	Transportation Out Expense	2,400				2,400		2,400			
603	Advertising Expense	3,000				3,000		3,000			
701	Rent Expense	6,000				6,000		6,000			
702	Property Tax Expense	7,800				7,800		7,800			
703	Heat and Light Expense	2,160				2,160		2,160			
704	Miscellaneous General Expense	480				480		480			
801	Interest Earned		125				125		125		
802	Rent Earned		300				300		300		
821	Interest Expense	75				75		75			
822	Loss on Sale of Equipment	100				100		100			
	Totals	247,075	247,075								
705	Insurance Expense			(a) 1,920		1,920		1,920			
706	Office Supplies Expense			(b) 2,040		2,040		2,040			
707	Depreciation Expense—Machinery and Equipment			(c) 3,600		3,600		3,600			
	Totals			7,560	7,560	250,675	250,675	129,555	141,205	132,600	120,950
	Net income for the year							11,650			11,650
	Totals							141,205	141,205	132,600	132,600

Figure 6–5 Work Sheet

TARRANT WHOLESALE COMPANY — **Exhibit B**
Statement of Owner's Equity
For the Year Ended December 31, 1985

Lucy Genova, capital, January 1, 1985	$65,150
Add: Net income for the year (Exhibit A)	11,650
Subtotal	$76,800
Deduct: Withdrawals	1,000
Lucy Genova, capital, December 31, 1985	$75,800

Figure 6–6
Statement of Owner's Equity

closing entries, including the closing of the beginning merchandise inventory and the recording of the ending inventory, are also prepared from the work sheet. They are shown in Figure 6–8. The accounts that enter into the determination of the cost of goods sold under the periodic system are in boldface type. After the closing entries are posted, all the revenue and expense accounts have zero balances. The remaining accounts—the open balance sheet accounts—are used to prepare a postclosing trial balance.

TARRANT WHOLESALE COMPANY — **Exhibit C**
Balance Sheet
December 31, 1985

Assets

Current assets:		
Cash	$ 7,200	
Accounts receivable	39,800	
Merchandise inventory	11,480	
Office supplies	1,200	
Prepaid insurance	1,820	
Total current assets		$ 61,500
Property, plant, and equipment:		
Machinery and equipment	$70,100	
Deduct: Accumulated depreciation	10,800	
Total property, plant, and equipment		59,300
Total assets		$120,800

Liabilities and Owner's Equity

Current liabilities:		
Accounts payable	$17,700	
Notes payable	7,300	
Total current liabilities		$ 25,000
Long-term liabilities:		
Mortgage payable		20,000
Total liabilities		$ 45,000
Owner's equity:		
Lucy Genova, capital (Exhibit B)		75,800
Total liabilities and owner's equity		$120,800

Figure 6–7
Balance Sheet

GENERAL JOURNAL					Page 20
		Closing Entries			
1985					
Dec.	31	**Merchandise Inventory**	121	**11,480**	
		Sales	401	124,200	
		Purchases Returns and Allowances	503	**1,500**	
		Purchases Discounts	504	**3,600**	
		Interest Earned	801	125	
		Rent Earned	802	300	
		Income Summary	901		141,205
		To record the ending inventory and to close the revenue and the credit balance merchandising accounts.			
	31	Income Summary	901	129,555	
		Merchandise Inventory	121		**15,400**
		Sales Returns and Allowances	402		2,400
		Sales Discounts	403		1,800
		Purchases	501		**63,580**
		Transportation In	502		**4,800**
		Sales Salaries Expense	601		12,000
		Transportation Out Expense	602		2,400
		Advertising Expense	603		3,000
		Rent Expense	701		6,000
		Property Tax Expense	702		7,800
		Heat and Light Expense	703		2,160
		Miscellaneous General Expense	704		480
		Interest Expense	821		75
		Loss on Sale of Equipment	822		100
		Insurance Expense	705		1,920
		Office Supplies Expense	706		2,040
		Depreciation Expense—Machinery and Equipment	707		3,600
		To close the beginning inventory, the expense, and the debit balance merchandising accounts.			
	31	Income Summary	901	11,650	
		Lucy Genova, Capital	301		11,650
		To transfer net income to capital.			
	31	Lucy Genova, Capital	301	1,000	
		Lucy Genova, Drawing	302		1,000
		To close drawing to capital.			

Figure 6–8
Closing Entries

Management Control—The Exception Principle

The control principle of **management by exception** involves isolating those amounts or accounts which indicate operating inefficiencies and focusing attention on the areas that might require corrective action. Since only exceptions from the norm require such corrective action, management's task is simplified and expedited by separating from the mass of data the exceptional items for further study. The alternative method for recording cash discounts, the discounts lost method, is an application of the principle of management by exception.

Purchases Discounts Lost Method

Under the **gross price method,** the volume of discounts granted or taken is accumulated in the Sales Discounts and Purchases Discounts accounts. Management is interested primarily, however, not in the amount of discounts taken, but rather in the exceptions—that is, the *discounts not taken.*

The alternative procedure for recording purchase discounts is called the **purchases discounts lost method** or the **net price method.** Purchases are recorded at net—invoice price minus discount—and discounts lost are entered in a special account. The Purchases Discounts account would not then be required.

To illustrate the accounting for discounts lost, assume that a purchase of $5,000 in merchandise is received on July 5, with terms of 2/10, n/30, and that the invoice is paid July 15. The entries for the purchase and payment are:

1985					
Jul.	5	Purchases		4,900	
		Accounts Payable			4,900
		Purchased merchandise on account ($5,000 less 2%):			
		Ace Company $4,900			
	15	Accounts Payable		4,900	
		Cash			4,900
		Paid for merchandise purchased on July 5:			
		Ace Company $4,900			

If the invoice were not paid until July 30, the entries would be:

1985					
Jul.	5	Purchases		4,900	
		Accounts Payable			4,900
		Purchased merchandise on account:			
		Ace Company $4,900			
	30	Accounts Payable		4,900	
		Purchases Discounts Lost		100	
		Cash			5,000
		Paid for merchandise purchased on July 5:			
		Ace Company $4,900			

Under the discounts lost procedure, the debit to Purchases is $4,900 whether or not the discount is lost, and the lost discount of $100 appears in a separate account, isolating the amount for the detection of possible laxities in procedures. The loss of available discounts may indicate a weakness in the organization, such as lack of bank credit or slowness in processing invoices for payment. The Purchases Discounts Lost account is classified under other expenses.

There are some disadvantages to recording purchases at the net price: (1) the amount of discounts taken is not reported separately in the income statement; (2) statements from creditors do not agree with net of discount amounts recorded in the accounts payable ledger; (3) the additional information may not justify the increased clerical costs and inconveniences; and (4) an adjusting entry is needed at the end of the period to record lapsed discounts by debiting Purchases Discounts Lost and crediting Accounts Payable. However, for many firms, the strengthened internal control gained from using the net price method outweighs these disadvantages. If there is a need for management to monitor sales discounts, the net price method could also be used to record sales. Under the net price method, sales discounts lost would be credited to the Sales Discounts Not Taken account. They would be reported as other revenue in the income statement.

Trade Discounts

Another class of discount is the trade discount, which, unlike the cash discount, is not related to the prompt payment of the invoice. A **trade discount** is a percentage reduction from a list price; the list price is not recorded in the accounts. The seller prints a catalog in which the prices of the various articles are shown. The actual price charged may differ from the list price because of the class of buyer (wholesalers, retailers, and so on), the quantity ordered, or changes in the catalog. The granting of trade discounts eliminates the need for frequent reprinting of catalogs or printing different lists for different classes of buyers.

If more than one discount is given—a so-called **chain discount**—each discount is applied successively to the declining balance to arrive at the invoice price. Thus, the invoice price of an item listed at $300 less trade discounts of 20 percent, 10 percent, and 5 percent is $205.20, computed as follows:

List price	$300.00
Less 20% discount	60.00
Remainder	$240.00
Less 10% discount	24.00
Remainder	$216.00
Less 5% discount	10.80
Invoice price	$205.20

Another way to compute the actual price is to multiply the list price by the complements of the discounts: for example, $300 × 0.80 × 0.90 × 0.95 = $205.20. The journal entry on the buyer's books is:

1985					
Nov.	4	Purchases		205.20	
		Accounts Payable			205.20
		To record merchandise purchased.			

Note that the purchase is recorded at the billing price. There is no need, therefore, for an accountant to record trade discounts.

Sales Taxes Payable

Most states have a law which levies a sales tax on the purchase of certain types of merchandise by customers. The typical law levies a tax on the customer buying the merchandise but requires the seller to collect the tax and to remit it to the appropriate governmental unit. To illustrate, assume that a retail sales tax of 4 percent is levied on all sales in a given state. If Saleo Company sells merchandise for cash with a retail sales price of $10,000, it would have to collect $10,400. This transaction is recorded as follows:

1985					
Jun.	30	Cash		10,400	
		Sales			10,000
		Sales Taxes Payable			400
		To record cash sales with a 4 percent sales tax.			

Although Saleo Company collects the sales taxes, the amount belongs to the state government; hence a liability must be created for the amount payable to the state government. It is a current liability. The company must file a sales tax return—usually each month. At the time the return is filed, the sales tax is paid. Then an entry is made debiting Sales Taxes Payable and crediting Cash.

Glossary

Cash discount A reduction in price offered by terms of sale to encourage payment within a shorter period.

Chain discount A multiple percentage reduction from a list price with each discount in the chain applied successively to the declining balance to arrive at the billing price.

Cost of goods sold A computation that appears on the income statement in a separate section. It is calculated by adding net purchases to the beginning inventory to derive the cost of goods available for sale and then deducting from this sum the ending inventory.

Credit memorandum A business form issued to a customer to advise that his or her account has been credited for a return of merchandise or an allowance for defective merchandise.

F.O.B. destination A term indicating the point at which the title to merchandise passes to the buyer; here the title would pass when the goods arrive at their destination. The owner (the seller) of the goods while they are in transit should bear the cost of freight.

F.O.B. destination A term indicating the point at which the title to merchandise passes to the buyer; here the title would pass when the goods arrived at their destination. The owner (the seller) of the goods while they are in transit should bear the cost of freight.

F.O.B. shipping point A term indicating the point at which the title to merchandise passes to the buyer; here the title would pass when the seller placed the goods on the common carrier (railroad or truck). The owner (the buyer) of the goods while they are in transit should bear the cost of the freight.

General and administrative expenses Expired cost of goods or services generally reflecting the cost of operating expenses other than the direct marketing cost.

Gross margin The excess of net sales revenue over the cost of goods sold.

Gross price method Accounting for cash discounts by accumulating the amount of the discount in Sales Discounts and in Purchases Discounts accounts.

Merchandise Inventory An account which shows merchandise on hand (at cost price) at the end of the accounting period. The ending inventory of one period becomes the beginning inventory of the next period.

Net cost of purchases The cost of all merchandise bought for sale, including transportation in but reduced by purchases returns and allowances and purchases discounts.

Net price method Procedures that apply the principle of management by exception by requiring that purchases be recorded at net of discount prices in anticipation of qualifying for the discount (purchases discounts lost method).

Operating expenses The cost of goods or services expired or used in operating the business, excluding cost of goods sold.

Other revenue and other expenses Items of ordinary revenue and expense that arise from a source other than the basic business purpose of the company.

Periodic inventory method Means of determining the amount of merchandise actually on hand at the end of each accounting period by making a list of the goods on hand, with an actual count of each, showing physical quantities and cost.

Perpetual inventory method A method in which a continuous record of merchandise on hand is maintained.

Purchases An account debited for the cost of merchandise bought for resale.

Purchases Discounts An account credited with amounts of deductions from invoice price that are allowed for payment within the stated discount period.

Purchases Returns and Allowances An account credited for cost of merchandise returned to a vendor or for allowances for defective merchandise purchases received.

Sales An account credited for the selling price of merchandise sold.

Sales Discounts An account debited for the amounts that customers deduct from the invoice price when payment is made within the stated discount period.

Sales Returns and Allowances An account debited for selling price of merchandise returned by customers or allowances for defective merchandise returned to them.

Selling expenses Direct expenses incurred in marketing a product.

Trade discount A percentage reduction in a list price that results in the net price or billing price. Unlike the cash discounts, it is not recorded in the accounts.

Transportation In An account debited for various delivery costs of merchandise purchases.

Questions

Q6–1 Why is the income statement for a merchandising business more complicated than for a service business?

Q6–2 Student A says that because cost of goods sold is an item that can't be controlled by management, there is little need to be concerned with it. Do you agree? Give examples to support your answer.

Q6–3 Sales discounts cause a business to collect less cash from sales. Why, then, would a company offer them to its customers? Does management really want customers to take advantage of sales discounts? Why or why not?

Q6–4 Why not debit the Purchases account for all purchases, including store supplies, advertising supplies, and postage stamps, for example?

Q6–5 How does the use of contra accounts for purchases returns and allowances and for purchases discounts strengthen internal control in a business?

Q6–6 How can the use of management by exception be applied to strengthen internal control over purchases discounts?

Q6–7 It has been estimated that billions of dollars are lost in the United States each year because of shoplifting. How does this loss affect the cost of goods sold in businesses that use the periodic inventory system?

Q6–8 If a seller in Pittsburgh, Pennsylvania sells to a buyer in Williamsport, Pennsylvania would you expect the invoice price to be higher if terms were F.O.B. destination or F.O.B. shipping point? Why?

Q6–9 Does a work sheet for a merchandising business need a column for adjustments? Why or why not?

Q6–10 In what columns of the work sheet are the elements that make up cost of goods sold found? How is cost of goods sold treated in the closing entries when a periodic inventory system is used?

Q6–11 What is the difference between selling expenses and general and administrative expenses? Between operating expenses and other expenses?

Q6–12 How does a trade discount differ from a cash discount?

Q6–13 Could interim financial statements be made from the work sheet without journalizing adjusting and closing entries? Do you think this is done frequently? Why or why not?

Exercises

E6–1 *Calculation of total merchandise available and cost of goods sold*

During the year, the Towson Company purchased merchandise costing $45,000. In each of the following cases, calculate (a) the total merchandise available for sale and (b) the cost of goods sold for the year.

Case	Beginning Inventory	Ending Inventory
1	$ 0	$ 0
2	9,000	0
3	12,000	15,000
4	0	3,000

E6–2
Computation of net sales, net purchases, cost of goods sold, and gross margin on sales

The following information is taken from the books of Galax Company:

Merchandise inventory, January 1, 1985	$ 1,800
Merchandise inventory, January 31, 1985	1,300
Sales	12,900
Transportation in	400
Purchases discounts	330
Sales returns and allowances	210
Purchases	5,600
Sales discounts	120
Purchases returns and allowances	100

Compute for the month of January: (a) net sales, (b) net purchases, (c) cost of goods sold, (d) gross margin on sales.

E6–3
Calculation of gross sales

The following information was taken from the books of the Dominion Company:

Merchandise inventory, beginning	$ 6,500
Net cost of purchases	31,200
Total operating expenses	15,600
Other expenses	650
Merchandise inventory, ending	5,200
Net income	3,250

Calculate the gross sales for the period.

E6–4
Normal balances of merchandising accounts

For each of the following merchandising accounts, indicate whether the balance before closing is a debit or a credit:

Sales	Transportation In
Sales Returns and Allowances	Purchases Returns and Allowances
Sales Discounts	Purchases Discounts
Purchases	Merchandise Inventory

E6–5
Inventories in the work sheet

A section of the work sheet of the Saki Company is presented below. Enter the beginning and the ending inventory amounts in the appropriate columns.

	Trial Balance		Income Statement		Balance Sheet	
Account Title	**Dr.**	**Cr.**	**Dr.**	**Cr.**	**Dr.**	**Cr.**
Cash	4,000				4,000	
Accounts Receivable	11,000				11,000	
Merchandise Inventory						

Beginning inventory	$19,500
Ending inventory	23,100

E6–6 *Income statement from work sheet*

The following account balances were taken from the Income Statement columns of Sawyer Company work sheet for the year ended December 31, 1985:

Account Title	Income Statement Dr.	Income Statement Cr.
Merchandise Inventory	23,760	25,650
Sales		62,370
Sales Returns and Allowances	745	
Sales Discounts	1,215	
Purchases	19,210	
Transportation In	1,015	
Purchases Returns and Allowances		610
Purchases Discounts		1,730
Selling Expenses	4,590	
General and Administrative Expenses	9,720	
Totals	60,255	90,360
Net Income	30,105	
Totals	90,360	90,360

The Balance Sheet Debit column showed a balance of $3,500 for Colby Sawyer, Drawing. Prepare an income statement.

E6–7 *Determination of missing income statement amounts*

The following financial data pertain to Osaka, Kobe, and Hilo companies. Fill in the missing amounts for each company:

	Osaka Company	Kobe Company	Hilo Company
Sales	$?	$31,640	$?
Merchandise inventory, beginning	?	4,620	6,930
Purchases	31,790	?	28,611
Transportation in	2,400	1,440	?
Gross delivered cost of purchases	34,190	20,514	?
Purchases returns and allowances	750	450	450
Purchases discounts	1,800	?	1,620
Net cost of purchases	?	18,984	?
Cost of merchandise available for sale	39,340	23,604	?
Merchandise inventory, ending	11,480	?	10,557
Cost of goods sold	?	16,716	25,074
Gross margin on sales	22,240	?	24,676
Total operating expenses	?	7,650	14,625
Net operating margin	10,090	?	?
Other revenue	?	0	650
Other expenses	50	300	?
Net income	10,190	?	9,951

E6–8 *Sales and purchases discounts—gross price method*

Using the gross price procedures, prepare general journal entries to record the following transactions: (a) on the books of the Welch Company, (b) on the books of the Raven Company, and (c) on the books of each company, assuming that the terms were F.O.B. shipping point.

1985		
Oct.	4	Welch Company sold merchandise to the Raven Company for $9,600, terms 2/10, n/30; F.O.B. destination.
	7	The Raven Company paid $275 freight on receipt of the shipment.
	8	The Raven Company returned some unsatisfactory merchandise and received credit for $300.
	14	The Raven Company mailed a check to the Welch Company for the net amount due.

E6–9 *Recording a purchase—net price method*

On June 5, 1985, VTS Company, which uses the net price procedure, purchased merchandise for $7,000, terms 2/10, n/30. The invoice was paid on July 1, 1985.

1. Journalize the purchase and the payment of the invoice.

2. Is the net cost of purchases the same under both the gross and the net procedures? Show your computations.

3. Assume that VTS desires to take advantage of all purchases discounts. Is there any advantage in using the gross price method of recording the purchase of merchandise?

E6–10 *Closing entries*

The following amounts are found in the Income Statement columns of the work sheet of the Newberry Company for the year ended June 30, 1985:

Account Title	Debit	Credit
Merchandise Inventory	$ 47,520	$ 51,300
Sales		124,740
Sales Returns and Allowances	1,490	
Sales Discounts	2,430	
Purchases	38,420	
Transportation In	2,030	
Purchases Returns and Allowances		1,220
Purchases Discounts		3,460
Selling Expenses Control	9,180	
General and Administrative:		
Expenses Control	19,440	
Totals	$120,510	$180,720
Net Income	60,210	
Totals	$180,720	$180,720

The Phyllis Newberry, Drawing account has a debit balance of $18,700. Journalize the closing entries.

E6–11 *Thought-provoking discount exercise: (partial payment)*

Juan's, Inc. grants customer discounts on partial payments made within the discount period. On June 10, 1985, the company sold merchandise to Jean Glick for $20,000, terms 2/10, n/30. On June 20, 1985, the company received a check in the amount of $10,000. On July 8, 1985, it received a check for the balance due. Journalize the sale and both collection entries using the gross price method on Juan's books. Then journalize the transactions using the net price method on Jean Glick's books.

E6–12 *Trade discounts*

Mesa Company purchased merchandise from Grant Stores with a list price of $12,000 and a trade discount of 20, 10, and 5 percent. Cash discount terms were 2/10, n/30. The invoice date was April 8, 1985. Journalize the purchase and payment on April 17, 1985.

E6–13 *Sales taxes*

Nielk Company records cash sales in a daily summary entry. On July 5, 1985, total cash sales were $18,200. The state sales tax rate is 4%. Record the July 5 sales in a general journal entry.

A Problems

P6–1A *Use of merchandising accounts*

Itasca Company had the following transactions:

1985		
Feb.	4	Purchased merchandise from St. Paul Company at an invoice price of $8,000; terms n/30, F.O.B. shipping point.
	6	Paid Overnight Express $20 for delivery cost of the purchase of February 4.
	6	Upon inspection, noted that merchandise invoiced at $1,200 in the St. Paul shipment was the wrong model. Returned the incorrect merchandise by Overnight Express collect as authorized by St. Paul Company.
	8	Sold merchandise to Susan Sexton in amount of $1,620; terms 2/10, n/30, F.O.B. shipping point.
	18	Received a check from Susan Sexton in total payment of her purchase of February 8.
	19	Sold merchandise to Dale Page in amount of $1,500; terms 2/10, n/30, F.O.B. destination.
	19	Paid $225 to Overnight Express for delivery of merchandise to Page.
	20	Page reported that an item in the shipment was defective; it was agreed that Page would retain the item and receive a credit of $100.
	28	Received a check from Dale Page for amount due.
Mar.	4	Paid the St. Paul Company the amount due on the purchase of February 4.

Required:

1. Journalize the above transactions using the gross price method. Assign journal page numbers.

2. Open general ledger accounts and post the journal entries. Assign account numbers to all accounts and place a beginning balance of $12,200 in the Cash account as of February 4.

P6–2A *Computation of cost of goods sold*

The Kirkwood Company had the following balances in its general ledger accounts at September 30, 1985, the end of its fiscal year:

Account Title	Debits	Credits
Merchandise Inventory	$ 27,200	
Sales		$600,000
Sales Discounts	2,400	
Purchases	316,300	
Transportation In	8,200	
Purchases Returns and Allowances		3,670
Purchases Discounts		31,630
Transportation Out Expense	7,260	

The merchandise inventory determined by physical count on September 30, 1985, was $32,480.

Required: Show the cost of goods sold section of the income statement for 1985.

P6–3A *Income statement from data given*

The adjusted trial balance of the Buckeye Company on December 31, 1985 included the following accounts:

Account Title	Debits	Credits
Merchandise Inventory	$ 27,100	
Sales		$652,800
Sales Returns and Allowances	6,250	
Sales Discounts	6,500	
Purchases	398,000	
Transportation In	6,250	
Purchases Returns and Allowances		7,020
Transportation Out Expense	2,210	
Advertising Expense	12,400	
Sales Salaries Expense	160,000	
Administrative Salaries Expense	32,000	
Office Supplies Expense	4,800	
Depreciation Expense—Office Equipment	1,200	
Interest Expense	8,600	

The merchandise inventory on December 31, 1985 was determined to be $24,600.

Required: Prepare an income statement for 1985.

P6–4A *Completion of a work sheet, preparation of statements, adjusting and closing entries*

Following is the trial balance of Zumbro Company on December 31, 1985 (the end of the fiscal year):

Account Title	Debits	Credits
Cash	$ 55,200	
Temporary Investments	145,200	
Accounts Receivable	319,800	
Notes Receivable	54,600	
Accrued Interest Receivable	0	
Merchandise Inventory	390,000	
Store Supplies	60,900	
Advertising Supplies	38,100	
Prepaid Insurance	19,500	
Store Equipment	315,900	
Accumulated Depreciation—Store Equipment		$ 78,000
Accounts Payable		171,600
Notes Payable (due 1986)		180,000
Accrued Interest Payable		0
Accrued Wages Payable		0
Unearned Rent		2,400
Val Zumbro, Capital		624,000
Val Zumbro, Drawing	42,900	
Sales		1,950,000

Purchases	1,103,700	
Transportation In	19,500	
Advertising Expense	0	
Store Supplies Expense	0	
Depreciation Expense—Store Equipment	0	
Heat, Light, and Power Expense[a]	39,000	
Miscellaneous General Expense	66,300	
Rent Expense[a]	37,500	
Sales Salaries Expense	199,700	
Office Salaries Expense	96,700	
Interest Expense	11,700	
Interest Earned		3,000
Rent Earned		7,200
Totals	$3,016,200	$3,016,200

[a]Classified as general and administrative expense.

The merchandise inventory at December 31, 1985 has been determined to be $293,000.

Data for adjustments are as follows:

a. Accrued interest receivable is $546.
b. Store supplies on hand are determined to have a valuation of $2,400.
c. Advertising supplies on hand are determined to have a valuation of $9,300.
d. Depreciation of store equipment for 1985 is $22,425.
e. Interest of $3,420 is accrued on notes payable.
f. Wages earned as of December 31 but not due to be paid until January are $3,000; they are equally divided between sales salaries and office salaries.
g. The last quarterly rent collection for October, November, and December was credited to Unearned Rent when collected on October 1, 1985.
h. The insurance policy is new; none expired in 1985.

Required:

1. Enter the above balances in a work sheet and complete the work sheet.

2. Prepare (a) an income statement, (b) a statement of owner's equity, and (c) a balance sheet.

3. Journalize the adjusting and the closing entries.

P6–5A *Recording purchases net of discount*

The following transactions were completed by the Iowa Company during July 1985:

1985		
Jul.	2	Purchased merchandise from the Cornell Company for $500, terms 3/10, n/30, F.O.B. destination.
	3	Purchased merchandise on account from the Kirkwood Company for $425, terms 1/10, n/30, F.O.B. shipping point.
	4	Paid freight charges of $10 on the merchandise purchased from the Kirkwood Company.
	5	Received a $50 credit (gross amount) for defective merchandise returned to the Kirkwood Company.
	11	Paid the Cornell Company.
	31	Paid the Kirkwood Company.

Required:

1a. Journalize the transactions using the gross price method.

1b. Prepare the cost of goods sold section of the income statement. Assume the following inventories: July 1, $250; July 31, $425.

2a. Journalize the transactions using the net price procedure.

2b. Prepare the cost of goods sold section of the income statement. Assume inventories are identical to those in Part 1b.

3. Under the net price procedure, how are purchases discounts lost classified in the income statement?

P6–6A
Thought-provoking problem: Borrow to take advantage of cash discounts?

Perry Drug Stores, Inc. is described in its 1981 *Annual Report* as a ". . . rapidly growing Midwestern drugstore chain, with proven expertise for blending new areas of retailing into basic drugstore operations." From 1977 to 1981, cost of goods sold has been about 70 percent of net sales. The company has a financing agreement with a bank that provides for unsecured loans of up to five million dollars at prime rate of interest. (The prime rate is the rate a bank charges its most creditworthy customers.) In 1981, the approximate average annual interest rate for loans under this agreement was 18.7 percent. Would the company have benefitted by borrowing under this agreement in 1981 to take advantage of cash discounts on merchandise purchases of 1/10, n/30? Of 2/10, n/30? Provide computations and discussion to explain your answer.

B Problems

P6–1B
Use of merchandising accounts

Lander Company had the following transactions:

1985		
Apr.	1	Purchased merchandise from Winthrop Company at an invoice price of $11,200; terms n/30, F.O.B. shipping point.
	2	Paid Fastair Express $728 for delivery cost of the purchase of April 1.
	2	Upon inspection, noted that merchandise invoiced at $1,680 in the Winthrop shipment was the wrong size. Returned the incorrect merchandise by Fastair Express collect as authorized by Winthrop Company.
	5	Sold merchandise to Lester Raines in amount of $2,260; terms 2/10, n/30, F.O.B. shipping point.
	15	Received a check from Lester Raines in total payment of the purchase of April 5.
	19	Sold merchandise to Susan Wilhelm in amount of $2,100; terms 2/10, n/30, F.O.B. destination.
	19	Paid $315 to Fastair Express for delivery of merchandise to Wilhelm.
	22	Wilhelm reported that an item in the shipment was defective; it was agreed that Wilhelm would retain the item and receive a credit of $140.
	29	Received a check from Susan Wilhelm for the amount due.
May	4	Paid the Winthrop Company the amount due on the purchase of April 4.

Required:

1. Journalize the above transactions using the gross price method. Assign journal page numbers.

2. Open general ledger accounts and post from the journal entries. Assign account numbers to all accounts, and place a beginning balance of $17,080 in the Cash account as of April 1.

P6–2B *Computation of cost of goods sold*

The Bellvue Company had the following balances in its general ledger accounts at June 30, 1985, the end of the fiscal year:

Account Title	Debits	Credits
Merchandise Inventory	$ 43,520	
Sales		$960,000
Sales Discounts	3,840	
Purchases	506,080	
Transportation In	13,120	
Purchases Returns and Allowances		5,872
Purchases Discounts		50,608
Transportation Out Expense	11,616	

The merchandise inventory determined by physical count on June 30, 1985, was $51,968.

Required: Show the cost of goods sold section of the income statement for 1985.

P6–3B *Income statement from data given*

The adjusted trial balance of the Keystone Company on December 31, 1985, included the following accounts:

Account Title	Debits	Credits
Merchandise Inventory	$ 24,390	
Sales		$587,520
Sales Returns and Allowances	5,625	
Sales Discounts	5,850	
Purchases	358,200	
Transportation In	5,625	
Purchases Returns and Allowances		6,318
Purchases Discounts		5,373
Transportation Out Expense	1,989	
Advertising Expense	11,160	
Sales Salaries Expense	144,000	
Administrative Salaries Expense	25,600	
Office Supplies Expense	4,320	
Depreciation Expense—Office Equipment	1,080	
Interest Expense	7,740	

The merchandise inventory on December 31, 1985 was determined to be $22,140.

Required: Prepare an income statement for 1985.

P6-4B *Completion of a work sheet, preparation of statements, adjusting and closing entries*

Following is the trial balance of Walbusser Company on December 31, 1985 (the end of the fiscal year):

Account Title	Debits	Credits
Cash	$ 49,680	
Temporary Investments	130,680	
Accounts Receivable	287,820	
Notes Receivable	49,140	
Accrued Interest Receivable	0	
Merchandise Inventory	351,000	
Store Supplies	54,810	
Advertising Supplies	34,290	
Prepaid Insurance	17,549	
Store Equipment	284,310	
Accumulated Depreciation—Store Equipment		$ 70,201
Accounts Payable		154,440
Notes Payable (due 1986)		162,000
Accrued Interest Payable		0
Accrued Wages Payable		0
Unearned Rent		2,160
Lynn Walbusser, Capital		561,598
Lynn Walbusser, Drawing	38,610	
Sales		1,755,000
Purchases	993,330	
Transportation In	17,550	
Advertising Expense	0	
Store Supplies Expense	0	
Depreciation Expense—Store Equipment	0	
Heat, Light, and Power Expense[a]	35,100	
Miscellaneous General Expense	59,670	
Rent Expense[a]	33,750	
Sales Salaries Expense	179,730	
Office Salaries Expense	87,030	
Interest Expense	10,530	
Interest Earned		2,700
Rent Earned		6,480
Totals	$2,714,579	$2,714,579

[a]Classified as general and administrative expense.

The merchandise inventory at December 31, 1985 has been determined to be $283,700. Data for adjustments are as follows:

a. Accrued interest receivable is $492.
b. Store supplies on hand are determined to have a valuation of $2,160.
c. Advertising supplies on hand are determined to have a valuation of $8,370.
d. Depreciation of store equipment for 1985 is $20,182.
e. Interest of $3,078 is accrued on notes payable.
f. Wages earned as of December 31 but not due to be paid until January are $2,700; they are equally divided between sales salaries and office salaries.
g. The last quarterly rent collection for October, November, and December was credited to Unearned Rent when collected on October 1, 1985.
h. The insurance policy is new; none expired in 1985.

Required:

1. Enter the above balances in a work sheet and complete the work sheet.

2. Prepare (a) an income statement, (b) a statement of owner's equity, and (c) a balance sheet.

3. Journalize the adjusting and the closing entries.

P6–5B
Recording purchases net of discount

The following transactions were completed by the Massasoit Company during November 1985:

1985		
Nov.	6	Purchased merchandise from the Bay Path Company for $1,000, terms 3/10, n/30, F.O.B. destination.
	8	Purchased merchandise on account from the Stonehill Company for $950, terms 1/10, n/30, F.O.B. shipping point.
	11	Paid freight charges of $10 on the merchandise purchased from the Stonehill Company.
	13	Received a $50 credit (gross amount) for defective merchandise returned to the Stonehill Company.
	15	Paid the Bay Path Company.
	26	Paid the Stonehill Company.

Required:

1a. Journalize the transactions using the gross price method.

1b. Prepare the cost of goods sold section of the income statement. Assume the following inventories: November 1, $500; November 30, $950.

2a. Journalize the transactions using the net price procedure.

2b. Prepare the cost of goods sold section of the income statement. Assume inventories are identical to those in Part 1b.

3. Under the net price procedure, how are purchases discounts lost classified in the income statement?

P6–6B
Thought-provoking problem: When is a drugstore really a drug store?

Perry Drug Stores, Inc. has provided the following data in its 1981 *Annual Report:*

(Dollars in millions)	1981	1980	1979	1978	1977
Net sales	$192.066	$136.425	$109.275	$89.155	$69.75
Prescription sales	30.429	22.024	17.426	13.204	10.910

Perry further states that it recognizes ". . . senior citizens as the most prolific of all purchasers of prescribed medicines." It also notes that persons 65-years-of-age or older will make up 20 percent of the population of 1990. How much do you think Perry is relying on the "graying of America" for its future? Support your answer with computations.

Part Two

Accounting Systems

7 An Introduction to Accounting Systems: Special Journals

Introduction

At this point, the reader should understand the fundamentals of recording transactions in the accounting records and reporting results in financial statements. These fundamental methods and concepts can now be put together into an accounting system (a set of interrelated documents, records, rules, and procedures). In each type of business, certain unique features may present a need to adapt documents or procedures. However, the basic goal is an effective and efficient flow of information to produce accurate and useful accounting records. This chapter describes briefly how an accounting system is designed for a business. After a discussion of record systems design, a simple manual system is illustrated, using the New Generation Shop, a store owned and operated by June Cox. The concepts used in manual accounting systems are the same as those used in mechanized and computerized systems. A brief discussion of the use of automated data processing in accounting concludes the chapter.

Learning Goals

To understand how financial statements and accounting reports depend upon a transaction based record system.

To trace the flow of data from source documents into the system and the flow of useful information out.

To make journal entries in a manual system with four specialized journals and a general journal.

To know when to post column totals when posting from specialized journals into the ledger.

To understand that posting column totals from specialized journals to the ledger produces the same result as posting individual entries.

Design of a Record System

The transaction is the basic source of accounting information; it is central to the data collection process. Before data processing by any system can begin, some evidence must exist that a transaction has occurred. A set of procedures and standard forms must require employees to make a record each time a transaction occurs. A general name for these business papers is **source documents.** Source document forms are often purchased in sets of multicopy, one-time carbon sheets. An example of a source document called a sales **invoice** is shown in Figure 7–1. Figure 7–1 is evidence that chemicals have been sold and shipped to a customer. The original copy will be mailed to the customer as a request for payment. Other copies will go to the accounting department to be used to record the accounts receivable increase in a journal and in the customer's account in the subsidiary ledger. Another source document, a **receiving report** (shown in Figure 7–2), evidences receipt of three items of supplies and equipment by the receiving department. The signature of Billie High verifies receipt on October 20, 1985.

In the user department, where the order originated, Julius Rich has indicated its receipt. Accordingly, this document is evidence that an account payable exists. A copy of it must be sent to the accounting department for recording in a journal and the ledgers.

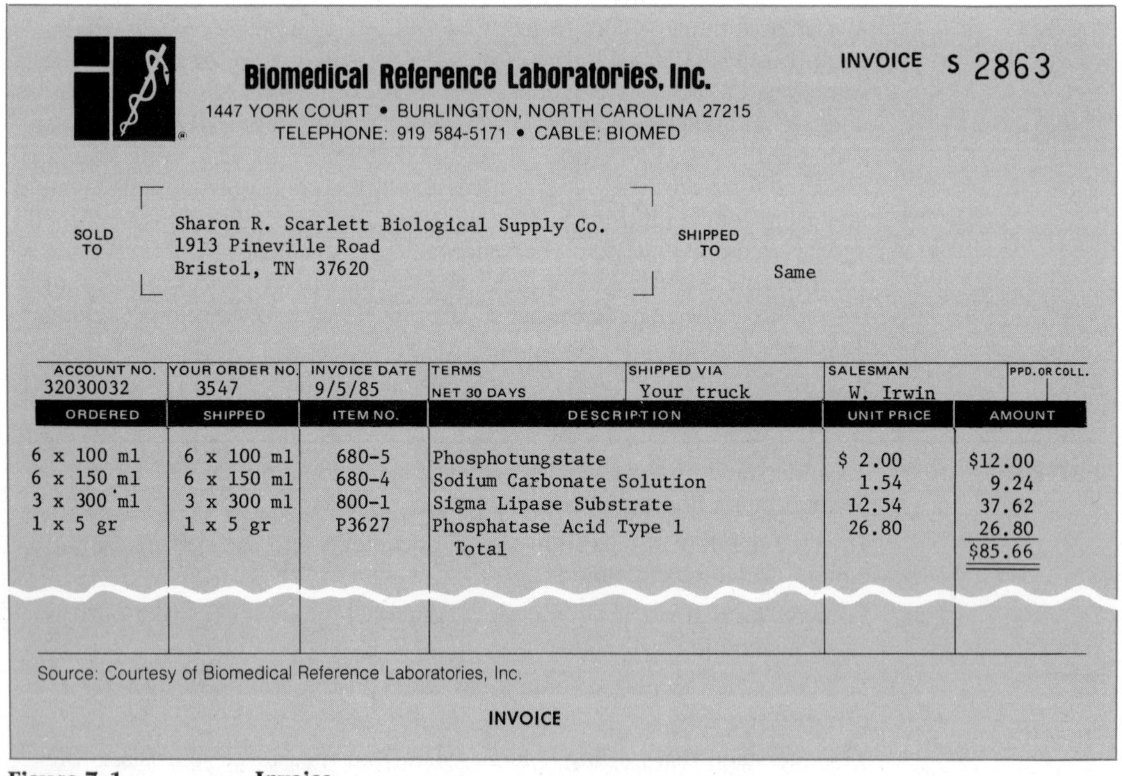
Biomedical Reference Laboratories, Inc.
1447 YORK COURT • BURLINGTON, NORTH CAROLINA 27215
TELEPHONE: 919 584-5171 • CABLE: BIOMED

INVOICE S 2863

SOLD TO
Sharon R. Scarlett Biological Supply Co.
1913 Pineville Road
Bristol, TN 37620

SHIPPED TO
Same

ACCOUNT NO.	YOUR ORDER NO.	INVOICE DATE	TERMS	SHIPPED VIA	SALESMAN	PPD. OR COLL.
32030032	3547	9/5/85	NET 30 DAYS	Your truck	W. Irwin	

ORDERED	SHIPPED	ITEM NO.	DESCRIPTION	UNIT PRICE	AMOUNT
6 x 100 ml	6 x 100 ml	680-5	Phosphotungstate	$ 2.00	$12.00
6 x 150 ml	6 x 150 ml	680-4	Sodium Carbonate Solution	1.54	9.24
3 x 300 ml	3 x 300 ml	800-1	Sigma Lipase Substrate	12.54	37.62
1 x 5 gr	1 x 5 gr	P3627	Phosphatase Acid Type 1	26.80	26.80
			Total		$85.66

Source: Courtesy of Biomedical Reference Laboratories, Inc.

INVOICE

Figure 7–1 **Invoice**

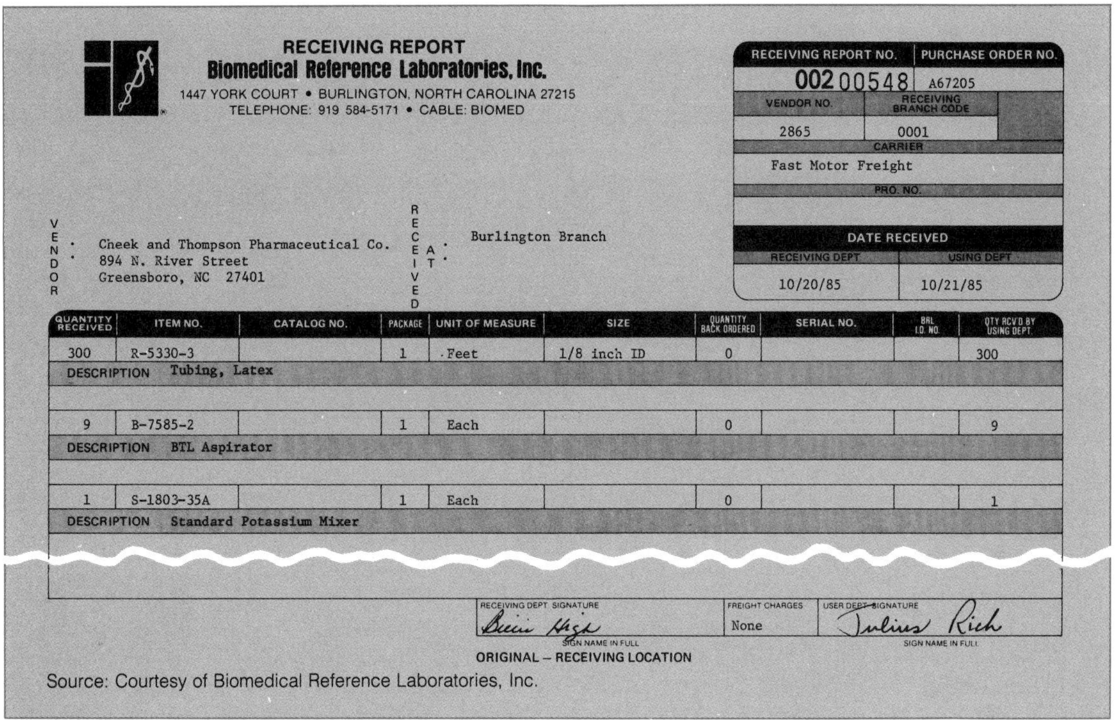
RECEIVING REPORT
Biomedical Reference Laboratories, Inc.
1447 YORK COURT • BURLINGTON, NORTH CAROLINA 27215
TELEPHONE: 919 584-5171 • CABLE: BIOMED

RECEIVING REPORT NO.	PURCHASE ORDER NO.
00200548	A67205

VENDOR NO.	RECEIVING BRANCH CODE
2865	0001

CARRIER: Fast Motor Freight

PRO. NO.:

VENDOR: Cheek and Thompson Pharmaceutical Co.
894 N. River Street
Greensboro, NC 27401

RECEIVED AT: Burlington Branch

DATE RECEIVED

RECEIVING DEPT	USING DEPT
10/20/85	10/21/85

QUANTITY RECEIVED	ITEM NO.	CATALOG NO.	PACKAGE	UNIT OF MEASURE	SIZE	QUANTITY BACK ORDERED	SERIAL NO.	BRL I.D. NO.	QTY RCV'D BY USING DEPT.
300	R-5330-3		1	Feet	1/8 inch ID	0			300
DESCRIPTION Tubing, Latex									
9	B-7585-2		1	Each		0			9
DESCRIPTION BTL Aspirator									
1	S-1803-35A		1	Each		0			1
DESCRIPTION Standard Potassium Mixer									

RECEIVING DEPT SIGNATURE: Bruce Hage — SIGN NAME IN FULL
FREIGHT CHARGES: None
USER DEPT SIGNATURE: Julius Rich — SIGN NAME IN FULL

ORIGINAL – RECEIVING LOCATION

Source: Courtesy of Biomedical Reference Laboratories, Inc.

Figure 7–2 **Receiving Report**

These are but two examples of the many source documents on which details of each transaction are recorded. Now the data must be introduced into the system. Data can be processed from these documents by handwritten procedures, accounting machines, electronic equipment, or a combination of these. As volume and variety of information become larger, the accounting system must become more sophisticated. Figure 7–3 shows that these means of data collection all lead to the same results. The information flow is from input to output. Source documents provide input data describing and measuring in dollars each transaction. **Processing** consists of a series of steps, such as classifying or summarizing, which will change the original data to a useful form. The output is in the form of reports.

Development of the system is generally in four stages: (1) study and design, (2) implementation, (3) operation, and (4) audit as to efficiency. The company's work is studied and a method of data collection is proposed for adoption. Once adopted, it is put into operation for verification, for review for improvements and redesign, and for testing for effectiveness of the controls. The flow of information from the source of input to the disposition of the output is examined with the following considerations:

- ☐ Where will the information be found and stored?
- ☐ Who will use the information?

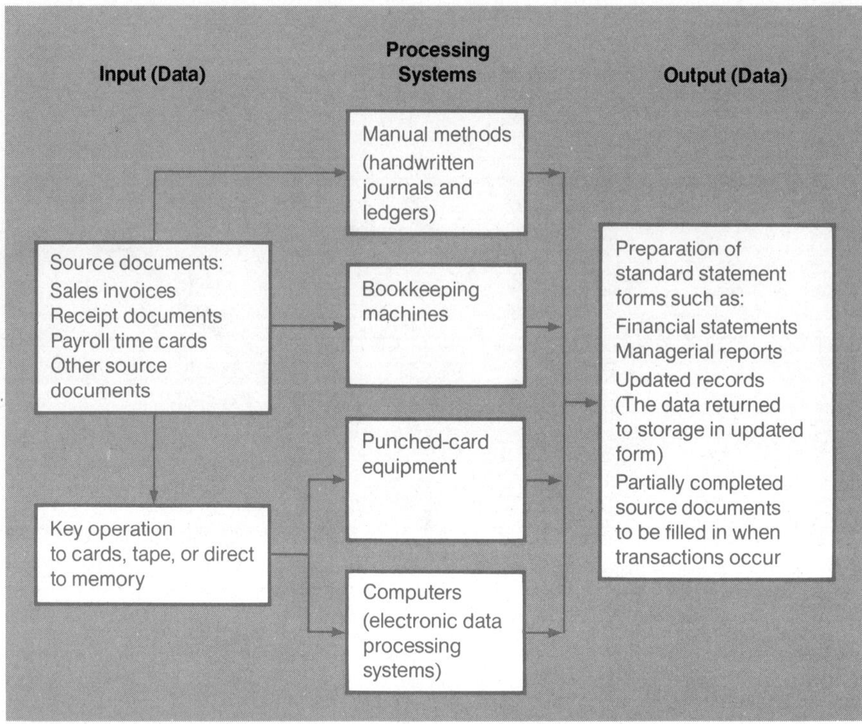

Figure 7–3 Information Flow Chart

- ☐ How will the information be used?
- ☐ When will the information be needed?

Thus, setting up a system for collecting and processing data in a business requires a total examination of the business and its environment. In view of all this, the evolution of a simple manual system is now illustrated by expanding the journal with no change to the ledgers.

Expansion of the General Journal: Evolution of a Simple Manual System

As the frequency of similar transactions increases, a means of processing data that is more efficient than the two-column general journal must be devised. Time and effort must be saved. With use of the two-column journal, each entry must be posted individually to its general ledger accounts, and in subsidiary ledger accounts each entry must be posted a second time. In essence, the data in the journal are repeated in detail in the ledgers. In a large business, thousands of transactions occur each day.

Accounting records and procedures should meet the needs of the individual business firm. For example, for a small firm where one accountant records all the transactions, additional columns (each representing an account that receives repeated entries) may be added to the general journal. As the number of transactions increases and the processing becomes too much for one accountant, similar transactions can be grouped into classes, with a special journal used to record each class of transactions. The combination of accounting records and procedures designed for an entity is known as its **accounting system.** An important feature of any accounting system is its ability to strengthen internal control.

Internal Control

Internal control ***is the plan of organization, procedures, and equipment used in a business to protect its assets from improper use and to promote efficiency in operations.***

Special Journals

The manual system illustrated in the following pages saves time in recording the transactions and in posting. It also enables a business to divide the work among several employees. Modifying some of the journals and subsidiary ledgers for use with computers makes it even more useful.

The procedures in the preceding chapters can be modified by creating several **special journals,** each of which carries a special class of transactions. The number and kinds of journals used are influenced by the type of business and the information desired. The model used in this text is shown in the following chart:

Journal	Class of Transaction	Symbol
Sales Journal	Sale of *merchandise* on account	S
Purchases Journal	Purchase of *merchandise* on account	P
Cash Receipts Journal	Receipt of cash from *all* sources	CR
Cash Payments Journal	Payment of cash for *all* purposes	CP
General Journal	All other transactions that are not grouped in the four classes above—for example, closing or adjusting entries or purchase of equipment or supplies on credit	J

Special journals bring two primary advantages to an accounting system: (1) they increase efficiency of processing, and (2) they strengthen internal control. Examples of increased efficiency of processing include:

- ☐ Similar transactions are grouped in chronological sequence in one place. All credit sales of merchandise, for example, are entered in the sales journal.
- ☐ The repeated writing of many account titles—Sales, Purchases, Cash, and so on—is eliminated.
- ☐ Postings to the general ledger are made from column totals rather than item by item, thereby reducing the volume of work.
- ☐ The responsibility of recording transactions can be divided among several individuals to speed up the work of journalizing.

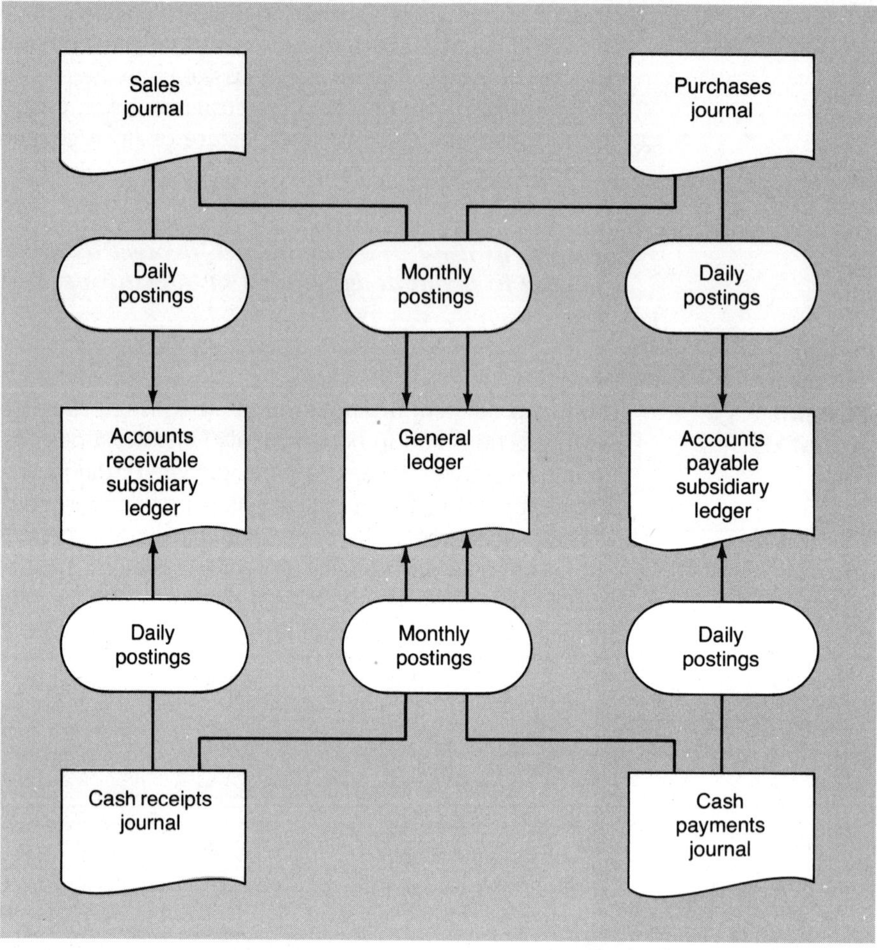

Figure 7–4 Special Journals Information Flow

Examples of strengthened internal control are:

☐ The general ledger has fewer entries and is therefore more compact and less likely to contain errors.

☐ The division of duties separates recording of credit sales from recording of collections for them and the recording of purchases from the recording of payment for them.

☐ The cash receipts and payments journals provide daily and monthly information that can be compared to bank deposit slips and to checkbook stubs as a further control over cash.

This chapter emphasizes the sales/cash receipts cycle and the purchases/cash payments cycle. The information in these two cycles flows from source documents through the special journals into both the general ledger and the subsidiary ledger accounts. Figure 7–4 diagrams this flow. The individual journals for the New Generation Shop are illustrated throughout this chapter. They should be studied in the context of the overall information flow shown in Figure 7–4.

Sales Journal

All sales of merchandise on account are recorded in the **sales journal.** The following transactions at the New Generation Shop, which began to use special journals in June 1985 illustrate the use of the sales journal.

1985		
Jun.	7	Sold merchandise to Shirley Lloyd, $400, terms 2/10, n/30, invoice no. 1.
	8	Sold merchandise to Frank P. Allen, $600, terms 2/10, n/30, invoice no. 2.
	8	Sold merchandise to Linda Weavil, $300, terms 2/10, n/30, invoice no. 3.
	30	Sold merchandise to Earl Menova, $800, terms 2/10, n/30, invoice no. 4.

When merchandise is sold on account, the transaction is recorded in the sales journal as follows:

1. The date of the transaction is entered in the Date column.
2. Sales invoices (see Figure 7–1) are numbered in sequence; the numbers are entered in chronological order in the Sales Invoice No. column.
3. The name of the customer to whom the sale was made is entered in the Account Debited column.
4. The terms of the sale are listed in the Terms column.
5. If the subsidiary ledger account has a customer number, it is entered in the folio (F) column when posting is complete; otherwise, a check mark is entered.
6. The amount of the sale is entered in the Amount column.

The sales journal illustrated in Figure 7–5 shows the entries for sales of merchandise on account. Each will result in a debit to the Accounts Receivable account and to the customer's account in the accounts receivable subsidiary ledger and a credit to the Sales account. The effect is the same as if they were entered in a two-column general journal. These transactions are *not* recorded in the general journal.

As indicated in Figure 7–4, postings are made as described in the following sections.

Daily Postings The daily posting in the subsidiary ledger is usually done in the following sequence:

1. The amount of the sale is posted to the Debit column of the customer's account and is added to the balance, if any, in the Balance column.
2. The journal symbol and page number (in this case, S1, "S" for sales journal and "1" for page number) are written in the folio (F) column.
3. The date of the sale is recorded in the Date column.

SALES JOURNAL Page 1

Date		Sales Invoice No.	Account Debited	Terms	F	Amount
1985						
Jun.	7	1	Shirley Lloyd	2/10,n/30	✓	400
	8	2	Frank P. Allen	2/10,n/30	✓	600
	8	3	Linda Weavil	2/10,n/30	✓	300
	30	4	Earl Menova	2/10,n/30	✓	800
			Total			2,100

Accounts Receivable debit and Sales credit

Figure 7–5
Sales Journal

4. A check mark (or the customer account number) is placed in the folio (F) column of the sales journal to indicate that the entry has been posted.

Monthly Postings At the end of the month, the Amount column of the sales journal is totaled. The total, the date of the posting, and the sales journal page number are then posted as a debit in the Accounts Receivable controlling account and as a credit in the Sales account in the general ledger. The general ledger account numbers are recorded in the sales journal immediately below the footing. To minimize errors, a systematic procedure should be followed in posting. The following sequence is suggested:

Debit posting:

1. The amount is posted to the Debit money column of the Accounts Receivable account in the general ledger.
2. The journal symbol (S1) is written in the folio (F) column of the account.
3. The end-of-month date is recorded in the Date column; in this case it is June 30, 1985.
4. The Accounts Receivable account number is written in parentheses below and to the left of the double rule in the Amount column of the sales journal.

Credit posting:

5. The same amount as the debit posting is posted to the Credit money column of the Sales account in the general ledger.
6. The journal symbol (S1) is written in the folio (F) column of the account.

7. The date is recorded in the Date column.

8. The Sales account number is written in parentheses below the double rule in the Amount column of the journal, to the right of the debit posting reference number.

Postings from the sales journal of the New Generation Shop for June 1985 are shown in Figure 7–6.

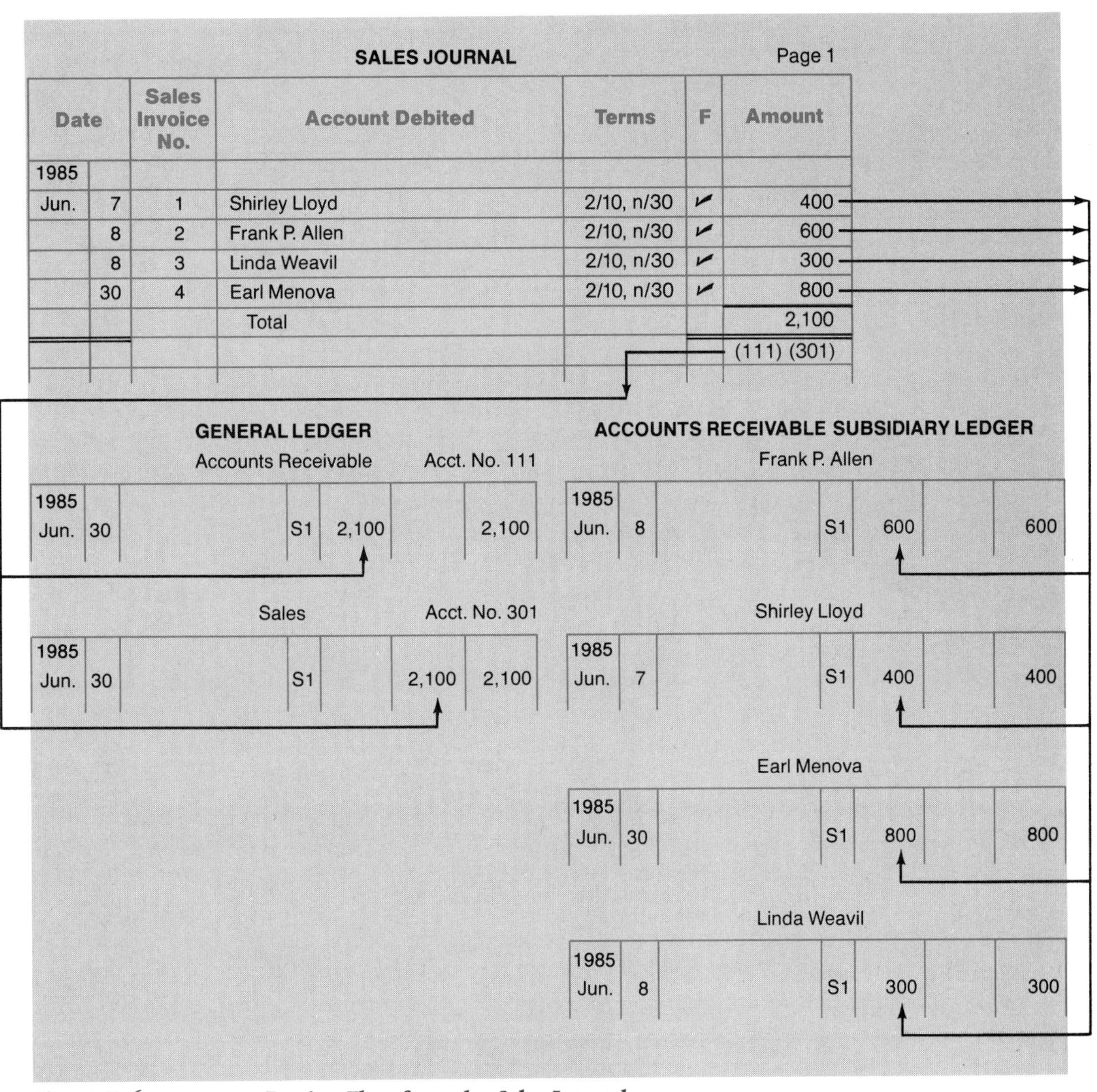

SALES JOURNAL Page 1

Date		Sales Invoice No.	Account Debited	Terms	F	Amount
1985						
Jun.	7	1	Shirley Lloyd	2/10, n/30	✓	400
	8	2	Frank P. Allen	2/10, n/30	✓	600
	8	3	Linda Weavil	2/10, n/30	✓	300
	30	4	Earl Menova	2/10, n/30	✓	800
			Total			2,100
						(111) (301)

GENERAL LEDGER

Accounts Receivable Acct. No. 111

1985						
Jun.	30		S1	2,100		2,100

Sales Acct. No. 301

1985						
Jun.	30		S1		2,100	2,100

ACCOUNTS RECEIVABLE SUBSIDIARY LEDGER

Frank P. Allen

1985						
Jun.	8		S1	600		600

Shirley Lloyd

1985						
Jun.	7		S1	400		400

Earl Menova

1985						
Jun.	30		S1	800		800

Linda Weavil

1985						
Jun.	8		S1	300		300

Figure 7–6 **Posting Flow from the Sales Journal**

Purchases Journal

All purchases of merchandise on account are recorded in the **purchases journal.** The relationship of the purchases journal and the accounts payable subsidiary ledger is similar to that of the sales journal and the accounts receivable subsidiary ledger. The transactions of the New Generation Shop during June 1985 illustrate the use of this journal.

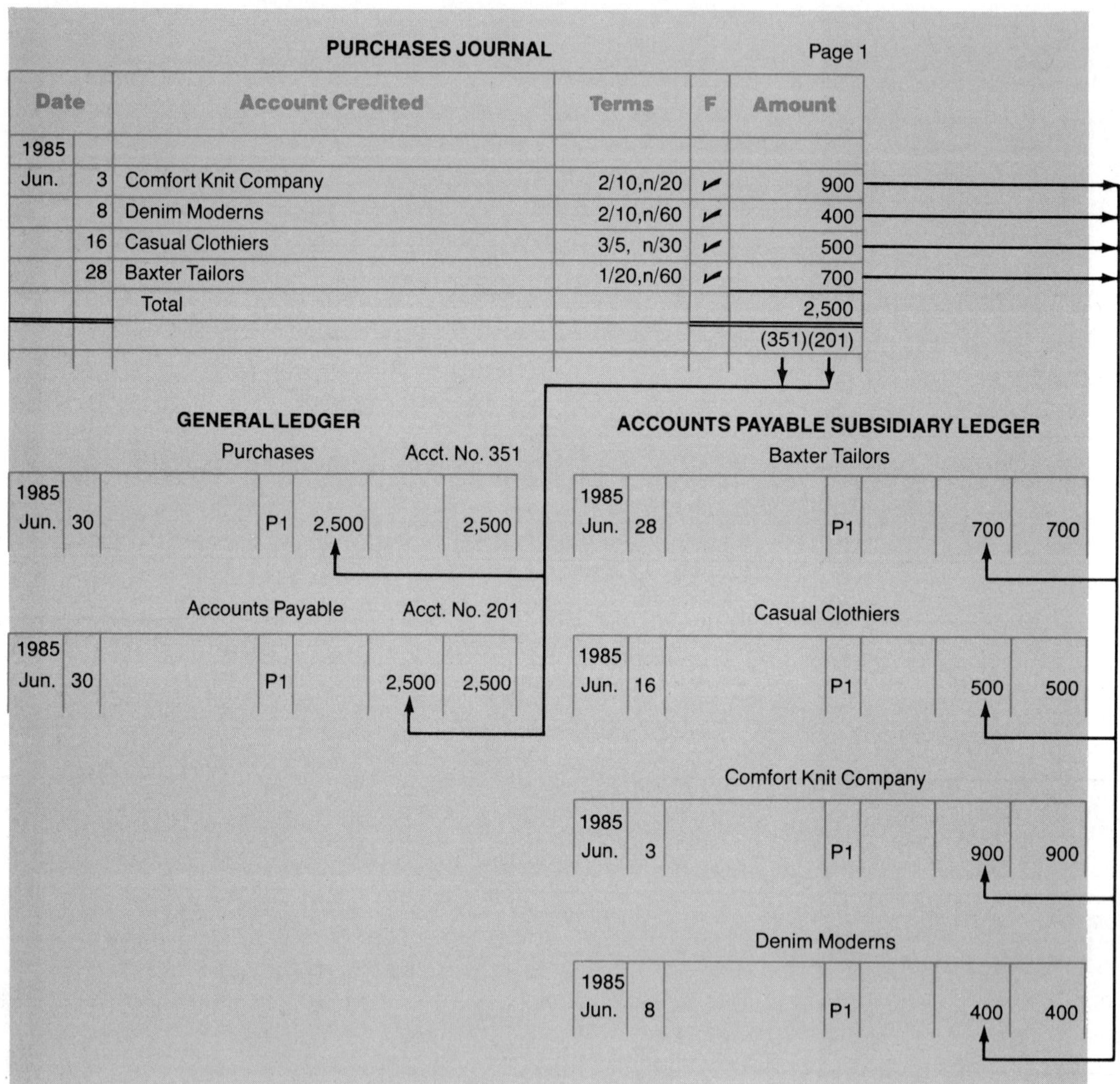

PURCHASES JOURNAL Page 1

Date		Account Credited	Terms	F	Amount
1985					
Jun.	3	Comfort Knit Company	2/10,n/20	✓	900
	8	Denim Moderns	2/10,n/60	✓	400
	16	Casual Clothiers	3/5, n/30	✓	500
	28	Baxter Tailors	1/20,n/60	✓	700
		Total			2,500
					(351)(201)

GENERAL LEDGER

Purchases Acct. No. 351

Date			Ref.	Debit	Credit	Balance
1985						
Jun.	30		P1	2,500		2,500

Accounts Payable Acct. No. 201

Date			Ref.	Debit	Credit	Balance
1985						
Jun.	30		P1		2,500	2,500

ACCOUNTS PAYABLE SUBSIDIARY LEDGER

Baxter Tailors

Date			Ref.	Debit	Credit	Balance
1985						
Jun.	28		P1		700	700

Casual Clothiers

Date			Ref.	Debit	Credit	Balance
1985						
Jun.	16		P1		500	500

Comfort Knit Company

Date			Ref.	Debit	Credit	Balance
1985						
Jun.	3		P1		900	900

Denim Moderns

Date			Ref.	Debit	Credit	Balance
1985						
Jun.	8		P1		400	400

Figure 7–7 **Posting Flow from the Purchases Journal**

1985

Jun.	3	Purchased merchandise on account from Comfort Knit Company, \$900, terms 2/10, n/20.
	8	Purchased merchandise on account from Denim Moderns, \$400, terms 2/10, n/60.
	16	Purchased merchandise on account from Casual Clothiers, \$500, terms 3/5, n/30.
	28	Purchased merchandise on account from the Baxter Tailors, \$700, terms 1/20, n/60.

Figure 7–7 shows how these transactions are recorded in the purchases journal and posted to the general and subsidiary ledger accounts. Each transaction is posted separately as a credit to the accounts payable subsidiary ledger to support the credit posted at the end of the month to the Accounts Payable controlling account in the general ledger. Transactions are usually posted to the subsidiary ledger daily. The date of the entry in the subsidiary ledger account is the invoice date. At the end of the month, the Amount column of the purchases journal is footed. This total is posted to the Purchases account in the general ledger as a debit. The same total is posted to the Accounts Payable controlling account in the general ledger as a credit.

Cash Receipts Journal

All transactions involving the receipt of cash are entered in the **cash receipts journal.** The column headings typically provide the flexibility necessary to record cash receipts from customers or any other source and to record sales discounts. The form may be varied, particularly in the number and headings of the columns, to meet the needs of the individual business. Using the cash receipts of the New Generation Shop, an explanation of the various columns in the cash receipts journal (illustrated in Figure 7–8) follows:

CASH RECEIPTS JOURNAL — PAGE 1

Date		Explanation	Debits					Credits					
			Cash	Sales Discounts	Other Accounts			Account Credited	Accounts Receivable		Sales	Other Accounts	
					Account Title	F	Amt.		✓	Amt.		F	Amt.
1985													
Jun.	1	Invested in business	2,500					J. Cox, Capital					2,500
	10	Payment in full	588	12				F.P. Allen	✓	600			
	15	Cash sales	1,000					Sales			1,000		
	17	Payment in full	392	8				S. Lloyd	✓	400			
	22	Borrowed from bank	600					Notes Payable					600
	30	Cash sales	950					Sales			950		
	30	Payment on account	100		Notes Receivable		200	Linda Weavil	✓	300			
		Totals	6,130	20			200			1,300	1,950		3,100

Figure 7–8 Cash Receipts Journal

1. The date of the transaction is entered in the Date column.

2. The explanation of the transaction is written in the Explanation column.

3. There are three Debit columns. Cash debits are entered in the first Debit column. Every transaction entered in this journal includes a debit to Cash.

4. The Sales Discounts Debit column is used for recording discounts granted to customers for paying within the discount period. (Throughout this chapter, the gross price method is used.)

5. The Other Accounts Debit column is for debits to general ledger accounts for which no special columns have been provided.

6. The name of the general ledger or subsidiary ledger account to be credited is written in the Account Credited column.

7. When a charge customer makes a payment on account, an entry is made in the Accounts Receivable Credit column, the first of three Credit columns. The amount entered is the actual amount of credit to Accounts Receivable despite discounts properly taken by the customer.

8. Sales of *merchandise* for cash are entered in the Sales Credit column.

9. The Other Accounts Credit column is for credits to general ledger accounts for which no special columns have been provided.

10. There are three folio columns—two labeled (F) and one labeled (✓); a posting symbol indicating that the amount has been posted to the general ledger or to the accounts receivable subsidiary ledger is placed in the folio columns.

In previous chapters, transactions involving the receipt of cash were recorded in a simple two-column general journal. Similar transactions are recorded in the cash receipts journal in Figure 7–8. Although transactions may be entered on a single line, the equality of debits and credits is still maintained through the use of multiple columns. The cash receipts transactions of the New Generation Shop are presented below; immediately following each transaction is an analysis of the debit-credit relationship of the entries in Figure 7–8 to indicate their effect on the accounts. These transactions, however, are actually recorded *only* in the cash receipts journal, not in the general journal.

Transaction:

Jun. 1 June Cox, the owner, invested $2,500 in the New Generation Shop.

In the cash receipts journal, Cash is debited by entering the amount in the Cash Debit column. Since there is no special column for J. Cox, Capital, the account title is written in and the amount is entered in the Other Accounts Credit column.

Transaction:

Jun. 10 Received payment in full from Frank P. Allen.

The sales journal shows that on June 8, merchandise with an invoice price of $600 was sold to Frank P. Allen, terms 2/10, n/30. Since payment was made within 10 days, Allen deducted $12 from the invoice price and paid $588. Entering the three amounts in the special columns as shown has the same effect on the general ledger as entering them in a general journal entry. The customer's name is entered in the Account Credited column for posting to the accounts receivable subsidiary ledger. If cash receipts from charge customers are numerous, a daily total may be entered from an adding machine tape; in that event, posting to the subsidiary ledger is done from supporting documents.

Transaction:

Jun. 15 Cash sales for the first half of the month were $1,000.

The word *Sales* is written in the Account Credited column to fill the space. However, it could be omitted since both the debit and credit amounts are entered in the special columns. Although a one-half month summary amount is used to simplify the illustration, cash sales should be recorded during each business day.

Transaction:

Jun. 17 Received full payment from Shirley Lloyd.

The sales journal shows that on June 7 merchandise with an invoice price of $400 was sold to Shirley Lloyd, terms 2/10, n/30. Since payment was made within 10 days, she deducted $8 from the invoice amount and paid $392.

Transaction:

Jun. 22 Borrowed $600 from the bank on a note payable.

Since there is no special column for the Notes Payable account, the amount is entered in the Other Accounts Credit column, and the name of the account is written in the Account Credited column.

Transaction:

Jun. 30 Cash sales for the last half of the month were $950.

This transaction is recorded in the same manner as the June 15 cash sales.

Transaction:

Jun. 30 Received $100 from Linda Weavil on account and a promissory note payable in 30 days for the balance in her account.

The sales journal shows that on June 8 merchandise with an invoice price of $300 was sold to Linda Weavil, terms 2/10, n/30. The Sales Discounts account is not involved in this partial payment because the discount period has expired.

At the end of the month, the columns in the cash receipts journal are footed. Since each entry contains equal debits and credits, it follows that the total of the Debit column footings should equal the total of the Credit column footings. This equality should be proved for each special journal before the column totals are posted to the general ledger. Otherwise, errors in the special journals may not be detected, the ledger will not have equal total debit and credit balances, and the trial balance will not balance. Moreover, the controlling accounts may not agree with their corresponding subsidiary ledgers. The cash receipts journal of the New Generation Shop is proved by cross-footing it. This procedure involves a comparison of the sum of the debit totals with the sum of the credit totals. For this cash receipts journal, the debit totals are ($6,130 + $20 + $200) = $6,350; the credit totals are ($1,300 + $1,950 + $3,100) = $6,350. Postings from the cash receipts journal are shown in Figure 7–9. Individual credit postings made to the accounts receivable subsidiary ledger support the $1,300 credit posting to the Accounts Receivable controlling account in the general ledger. A check mark is entered in the folio (√) column on the line of the entry to indicate that the item has been posted to the customer's account in the subsidiary ledger. Any positive balance in a customer's account would normally be a debit. Transactions have already been posted to these accounts from the sales journal.[1]

The totals of the Cash Debit column ($6,130) and the Sales Discounts Debit column ($20) are posted to the respective general ledger accounts. The regular sequence for transferring an amount from a journal to a ledger is followed. The general ledger account number entered in parentheses below the double rule in each column shows that the total has been posted to that account.

The (X) below the Other Accounts Debit column means that the column total has not been posted to the general ledger. The $200 debit to Notes Receivable was posted individually during the month. The account number of Notes Receivable (112) was entered in the folio (F) column of the journal at the time the posting was done.

The Accounts Receivable account is credited for $1,300, and the Sales account is credited for $1,950. These postings are also dated June 30. No posting symbol is used in the folio (F) column on the line of the entry for a cash sale because the item does not require individual posting.

The (X) below the double rule in the Other Accounts Credit column indicates that the column total is not to be posted to the general ledger. The total is not posted because the $2,500 credit to J. Cox, Capital and the $600 credit to Notes Payable were posted separately during the month. The ledger page numbers of these accounts were entered in the folio (F) column of the jour-

---

[1]Earl Menova's account is shown out of sequence in Figure 7–9 to simplify illustration of the posting flow. His unpaid balance of $800 is a debit and is equal to the balance in the Accounts Receivable account in the general ledger.

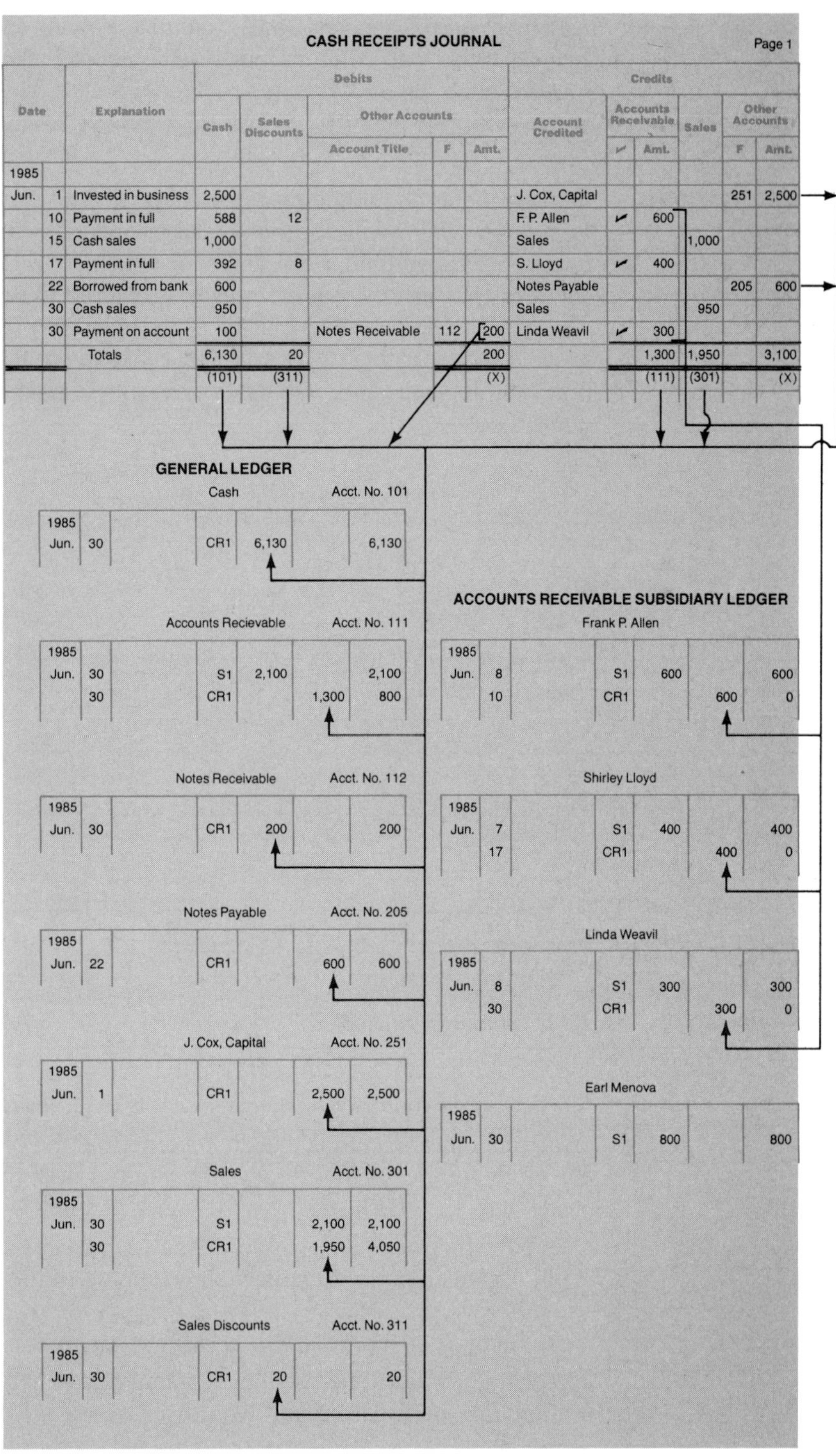

CASH RECEIPTS JOURNAL Page 1

Date		Explanation	Debits: Cash	Debits: Sales Discounts	Debits: Other Accounts: Account Title	F	Amt.	Account Credited	Credits: Accounts Receivable ✓	Amt.	Credits: Sales	Credits: Other Accounts F	Amt.
1985													
Jun.	1	Invested in business	2,500					J. Cox, Capital				251	2,500
	10	Payment in full	588	12				F. P. Allen	✓	600			
	15	Cash sales	1,000					Sales			1,000		
	17	Payment in full	392	8				S. Lloyd	✓	400			
	22	Borrowed from bank	600					Notes Payable				205	600
	30	Cash sales	950					Sales			950		
	30	Payment on account	100		Notes Receivable	112	200	Linda Weavil	✓	300			
		Totals	6,130	20			200			1,300	1,950		3,100
			(101)	(311)			(X)			(111)	(301)		(X)

GENERAL LEDGER

Cash Acct. No. 101

1985						
Jun.	30		CR1	6,130		6,130

Accounts Recievable Acct. No. 111

1985						
Jun.	30		S1	2,100		2,100
	30		CR1		1,300	800

Notes Receivable Acct. No. 112

1985						
Jun.	30		CR1	200		200

Notes Payable Acct. No. 205

1985						
Jun.	22		CR1		600	600

J. Cox, Capital Acct. No. 251

1985						
Jun.	1		CR1		2,500	2,500

Sales Acct. No. 301

1985						
Jun.	30		S1		2,100	2,100
	30		CR1		1,950	4,050

Sales Discounts Acct. No. 311

1985						
Jun.	30		CR1	20		20

ACCOUNTS RECEIVABLE SUBSIDIARY LEDGER

Frank P. Allen

1985						
Jun.	8		S1	600		600
	10		CR1		600	0

Shirley Lloyd

1985						
Jun.	7		S1	400		400
	17		CR1		400	0

Linda Weavil

1985						
Jun.	8		S1	300		300
	30		CR1		300	0

Earl Menova

1985						
Jun.	30		S1	800		800

Figure 7–9 Posting Flow from the Cash Receipts Journal

nal when the posting was done. Note that account numbers 251 and 205 are written in the folio column of the cash receipts journal in Figure 7–9. Postings from the Other Accounts Credit column are dated as of the date of the entry.

Cash Payments Journal

Cash payments should be made by check, and all check payments are entered in the **cash payments journal.** Small payments in currency may be made from a petty cash fund, procedures for which are discussed in Chapter 9. The check to establish the fund, however, is entered in the cash payments journal.

A typical cash payments journal is illustrated in Figure 7–10. The columns provide for recording cash payments, either to creditors or for any other purpose, and for recording purchases discounts. Explanation of the various columns follows:

CASH PAYMENTS JOURNAL — Page 1

Date		Check No.	Explanation	Credits: Cash	Credits: Purchases Discounts	Credits: Other Accounts: Account Title	F	Amt.	Debits: Account Debited	Accounts Payable ✓	Accounts Payable Amt.	Purchases	Other Accounts F	Other Accounts Amt.
1985														
Jun.	1	1	Scuba Realty	150					Rent Expense					150
	10	2	Payment in full	882	18				Comfort Knit Co.	✓	900			
	14	3	Payment in full	392	8				Denim Moderns	✓	400			
	15	4	Cash purchases	200					Purchases			200		
	30	5	Partial payment	300		Notes Payable		200	Casual Clothiers	✓	500			
	30	6	Withdrawal of cash	400					J. Cox, Drawing					400
	30	7	Various items	100					Misc. General Exp.					100
			Totals	2,424	26			200			1,800	200		650

Figure 7–10 **Cash Payments Journal**

1. The date of the disbursement of cash is entered in the Date column.

2. Detailed information is initially recorded on the check stub, which bears the same number as the check. Entries in the cash payments journal are then made from the check stub, and the check number is listed in the Check No. column.

3. An explanation of the transaction is entered in the Explanation column.

4. There are three Credit columns located to the left of the Debit columns. In a special journal, the sequence of columns need not follow the traditional placement. Cash will be used in each transaction entered in this journal and is therefore the first column.

5. The Purchases Discounts Credit column is used for recording discounts taken on invoices paid within the discount period.

6. Credits to general ledger accounts other than those for which a special column has been provided, such as Cash and Purchases Discounts, are recorded in the Other Accounts Credit column.

7. The name of the general ledger or subsidiary ledger account to be debited is written in the Account Debited column.

8. When a creditor is paid, the amount is entered in the Accounts Payable Debit column. The amount entered is the actual amount of the check plus any purchases discounts taken.

9. The purchase of merchandise for cash is entered in the Purchases Debit column.

10. The Other Accounts Debit column is used for entries to general ledger accounts that have no special column.

11. There are three folio columns, two labeled (F) and one labeled (✔); a posting symbol indicating that the amount has been posted to the general ledger or to the accounts payable subsidiary ledger is placed in the appropriate folio column.

Although most transactions may be entered on a single line, some may require more than one line. Each *new* transaction entry should begin on a vacant line. The equality of debits and credits is maintained through the use of multiple columns.

The cash payments of the New Generation Shop (see Figure 7–10) are presented on this and the next few pages. Each is analyzed in terms of debits and credits to indicate their effect on the accounts. They represent cash payments made by the New Generation Shop in June 1985.

Transaction:

Jun. 1 Issued check no. 1 in the amount of $150 for the June rent.

The $150 decrease in cash is entered in the Cash column on the same line as the explanation. Since there is not a special debit column for Rent Expense, the account title is written in the Account Debited column, and the $150 debit amount to Rent Expense is shown in the Other Accounts column. Note that this entire transaction appears on a single line.

Transaction:

Jun. 10 Paid Comfort Knit Co. in full; check no. 2.

The purchases journal shows that on June 3, merchandise with an invoice price of $900 was purchased from Comfort Knit Company, terms 2/10, n/20. Since payment was made within 10 days, a two percent discount of $18 is taken and a check for $882 is issued. Entering the three amounts in the special columns has the same effect on the general ledger as recording them in a general journal entry. The creditor's name is entered in the Account Debited column for posting to the accounts payable subsidiary ledger.

Transaction:

Jun. 14 Paid Denim Moderns in full; check no. 3.

The explanation for this entry is similar to that for the entry of June 10.

Transaction:

Jun. 15 Purchased merchandise and issued a check for the full amount of the invoice; check no. 4.

Purchases of merchandise on account are entered in the purchases journal. A company may occasionally purchase merchandise for cash, probably from another company with which no credit relationship exists. These cash purchases are recorded directly in the cash payments journal. If cash purchases of merchandise occur frequently, a special Purchases Debit column may be provided in the cash payments journal.

Transaction:

Jun. 30 Paid Casual Clothiers $300 on account (check no. 5) and issued a promissory note for the balance, to be paid in 30 additional days.

Reference to the purchases journal shows that on June 16 merchandise with an invoice price of $500 was purchased from the Casual Clothiers, terms 3/5, n/30. Since the discount period has expired, no discount is taken.

Transaction:

Jun. 30 J. Cox, the owner, withdrew $400 (check no. 6) for her personal use in anticipation of earned income.

Since there is no special column for personal withdrawals, the cash withdrawal is entered in the Other Accounts Debit column. If such withdrawals are numerous, a special debit column with the heading J. Cox, Drawing could be provided.

Transaction:

Jun. 30 Issued check no. 7 in the amount of $100 for miscellaneous general expenses.

The expense account is debited for various items purchased and consumed during the month.

Before the end-of-the-month postings are made, the columns of the cash payments journal should be cross-footed. For this cash payments journal, the debit totals are ($1,800 + $200 + $650) = $2,650; the credit totals are ($2,424 + $26 + $200) = $2,650. The total debit and total credit postings from this journal to the general ledger are equal. Posting from the cash payments journal of the New Generation Shop is shown in Figure 7–11.

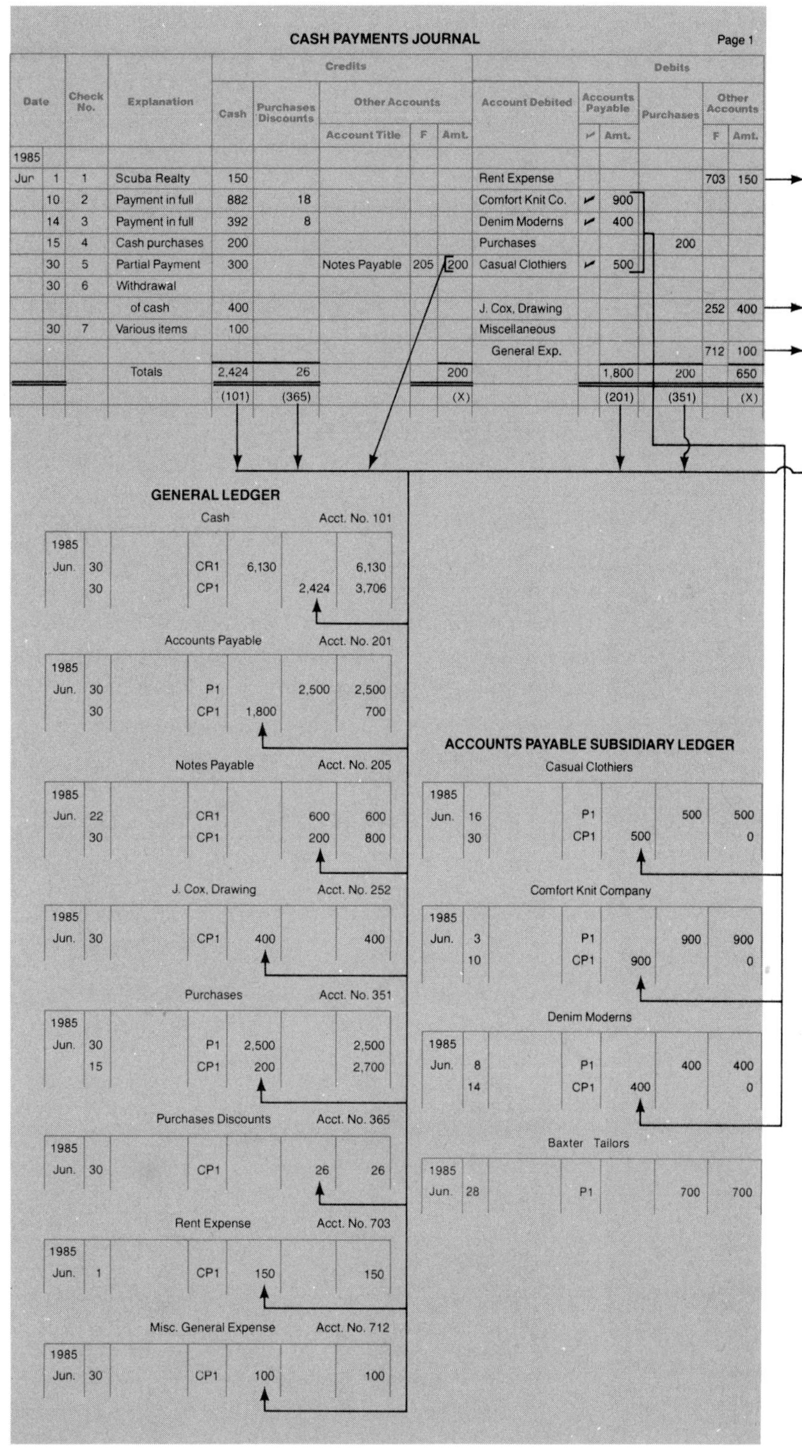

CASH PAYMENTS JOURNAL — Page 1

Date		Check No.	Explanation	Credits: Cash	Credits: Purchases Discounts	Other Accounts: Account Title	F	Amt.	Account Debited	Accounts Payable ✓	Accounts Payable Amt.	Debits: Purchases	Other Accounts F	Other Accounts Amt.
1985														
Jun	1	1	Scuba Realty	150					Rent Expense				703	150
	10	2	Payment in full	882	18				Comfort Knit Co.	✓	900			
	14	3	Payment in full	392	8				Denim Moderns	✓	400			
	15	4	Cash purchases	200					Purchases			200		
	30	5	Partial Payment	300		Notes Payable	205	200	Casual Clothiers	✓	500			
	30	6	Withdrawal of cash	400					J. Cox, Drawing				252	400
	30	7	Various items	100					Miscellaneous General Exp.				712	100
			Totals	2,424	26			200			1,800	200		650
				(101)	(365)			(X)			(201)	(351)		(X)

GENERAL LEDGER

Cash — Acct. No. 101

Date		Explanation	F	Debit	Credit	Balance
1985						
Jun.	30		CR1	6,130		6,130
	30		CP1		2,424	3,706

Accounts Payable — Acct. No. 201

Date		Explanation	F	Debit	Credit	Balance
1985						
Jun.	30		P1		2,500	2,500
	30		CP1	1,800		700

Notes Payable — Acct. No. 205

Date		Explanation	F	Debit	Credit	Balance
1985						
Jun.	22		CR1		600	600
	30		CP1		200	800

J. Cox, Drawing — Acct. No. 252

Date		Explanation	F	Debit	Credit	Balance
1985						
Jun.	30		CP1	400		400

Purchases — Acct. No. 351

Date		Explanation	F	Debit	Credit	Balance
1985						
Jun.	30		P1	2,500		2,500
	15		CP1	200		2,700

Purchases Discounts — Acct. No. 365

Date		Explanation	F	Debit	Credit	Balance
1985						
Jun.	30		CP1		26	26

Rent Expense — Acct. No. 703

Date		Explanation	F	Debit	Credit	Balance
1985						
Jun.	1		CP1	150		150

Misc. General Expense — Acct. No. 712

Date		Explanation	F	Debit	Credit	Balance
1985						
Jun.	30		CP1	100		100

ACCOUNTS PAYABLE SUBSIDIARY LEDGER

Casual Clothiers

Date		Explanation	F	Debit	Credit	Balance
1985						
Jun.	16		P1		500	500
	30		CP1	500		0

Comfort Knit Company

Date		Explanation	F	Debit	Credit	Balance
1985						
Jun.	3		P1		900	900
	10		CP1	900		0

Denim Moderns

Date		Explanation	F	Debit	Credit	Balance
1985						
Jun.	8		P1		400	400
	14		CP1	400		0

Baxter Tailors

Date		Explanation	F	Debit	Credit	Balance
1985						
Jun.	28		P1		700	700

Figure 7–11 **Posting Flow from the Cash Payments Journal**

The individual debit postings to the accounts payable subsidiary ledger support the $1,800 debit posting to the Accounts Payable controlling account in the general ledger. Each check mark in the folio (✔) column of the cash payments journal indicates that a posting has been made to the supplier's account in the subsidiary ledger. Note that the balance of each account is either a credit or zero.

The Accounts Payable account is debited for $1,800 as of June 30. The total of the Purchases Debit column, $200, is posted to the Purchases account in the general ledger.

The total of the Other Accounts Debit column is not posted because each amount must be posted separately. The numbers of these accounts—703, 252, and 712—are entered in the folio (F) column. The (X) below the double rule in the Other Accounts Debit column indicates that the column total is not posted to the general ledger.

The totals of the Cash Credit column ($2,424) and the Purchases Discounts Credit column ($26) are posted to the general ledger. The basic posting steps are followed. The general ledger account numbers are placed in parentheses below the double rules in the columns to indicate that the postings have been done.

The total of the Other Accounts Credit column is not posted since each entry in the column has been individually posted at the time the entry was made in the journal. The folio (F) column indicates the account to which the entry was posted.

Result of Posting

When all posting from the four special journals in the New Generation Shop illustration is complete, a trial balance can be prepared as follows:

NEW GENERATION SHOP
Trial Balance
June 30, 1985

Acct. No.	Account Title	Debits	Credits
101	Cash	$3,706	
111	Accounts Receivable	800	
112	Notes Receivable	200	
201	Accounts Payable		$ 700
205	Notes Payable		800
251	June Cox, Capital		2,500
252	June Cox, Drawing	400	
301	Sales		4,050
311	Sales Discounts	20	
351	Purchases	2,700	
365	Purchases Discounts		26
703	Rent Expense	150	
712	Miscellaneous General Expense	100	
	Totals	$8,076	$8,076

To enhance understanding of the posting procedures from special journals, the reader is encouraged to draw T accounts, post from the journals in this chapter, and verify this trial balance.

Combined Cash Receipts and Payments Journal

Many small businesses use a combined cash receipts and cash payments journal, sometimes called a **cashbook.** This journal is simply a combination of the cash receipts journal and the cash payments journal described earlier. The specialized debit and credit columns (except for cash) are unique to the needs of the particular entity using it. Such a journal is appropriate not only to small commercial enterprises but to many not-for-profit organizations such as fraternities and sororities, civic clubs, and professional service organizations.

Other Special Journals

Other special journals may be adopted as the need for them becomes apparent. Such a need is indicated if labor may be saved or if the special journal provides an element of flexibility in the accounting system. Examples of other special journals are sales returns and allowances journal, purchases returns and allowances journal, notes receivable register, notes payable register, and voucher register.

Entries in the General Journal

Although special journals provide for recording frequently recurring transactions, a need remains for recording (1) unusual current transactions, (2) correcting entries, and (3) adjusting and closing entries. For these purposes, a two-column general journal is used in conjunction with the special journals.

Unusual Current Transactions All the transactions that cannot be entered in the special journals are recorded in the general journal. Sales returns and allowances and purchases returns and allowances, for example, are entered in the general journal if special journals for these transactions are not maintained. Other typical current transactions recorded in the general journal include credit purchases of assets other than merchandise inventory, the incurrence of liabilities for services, notes received from customers to apply toward accounts receivable, and notes issued to creditors to apply toward accounts payable.

Correcting Entries If it is discovered that an error has been made in the process of journalizing and posting, it can be corrected by a general journal entry. Erasures should be avoided because they may create doubt about the reason for the erasures in the minds of persons who examine the records. This becomes particularly important when the records are audited and when they are offered as evidence in cases of litigation.

Assume that a $15 entry, recording the payment of an invoice for repairs to machinery, has been journalized in the cash payments journal with a debit to the Machinery account. The debit should have been to an expense account; the error may be corrected by the following entry in the general journal:

1985					
Jul.	26	Maintenance and Repairs Expense . . .		15	
		Machinery			15
		To correct entry of July 19 in cash payments journal.			

If an error in a journal entry is discovered before it is posted, it may be corrected by drawing a line through the incorrect account or amount and entering the correction immediately above it.

Adjusting and Closing Entries Adjusting and closing entries are always recorded in the general journal.

Direct Posting from Business Documents to Subsidiary Ledgers

In many business firms, data can be processed more efficiently and rapidly by posting from the original documents—sales invoices, sales slips, purchase invoices, and so on—directly to the *subsidiary ledgers* instead of first copying the information in special journals and then posting to the accounts. For example, if sales slips are serially numbered, a binder file of duplicate slips arranged in numerical order can take the place of a more formal sales journal. Amounts from the individual slips are posted daily to the accounts receivable subsidiary ledger; at the end of a designated period—a week or a month—the sales slips in the binder file are totaled and the following general journal entry is made:

1985					
Aug.	31	Accounts Receivable		120,000	
		Sales			120,000
		To record charge sales for the month of August.			

A similar procedure may be used to record purchases on account.

If postings are made from sales slips to the accounts receivable subsidiary ledger, and if for any reason a special sales journal is still desired, a streamlined journal can be constructed by simply eliminating the Account Debited, Terms, and folio (F) columns, as shown below. Entries to such a sales journal may be made in batches; for example, a single line may read:

SALES JOURNAL

Date	Sales Invoice Numbers	Amount
1985 Aug. 12	13,500 –13,599	18,329.21

A batch could represent a day's credit sales, or simply a predetermined quantity of invoices or sales slips. The use of *batch totals* is one means of checking the accuracy of posting to subsidiary ledgers.

These changes in procedure and the increasing use of direct posting from original documents are discussed here to add emphasis to a statement made earlier in the chapter. Accounting records and procedures should be designed to meet the needs of the particular business firm.

Automated Processing

Many companies use manual accounting systems similar to the model described in this chapter. Such systems are flexible enough to meet the unique needs of a single proprietorship or a small corporation. By the 1940s and 1950s, posting machines and similar electromechanical equipment were in common use. These machines had internal registers into which could be keyed a beginning balance and current transaction data to produce a record of transactions and a new balance. In the 1950s companies began to use punched-card data processing equipment—especially in subsidiary ledger maintenance—and the larger companies began to acquire computers.

Today the state of the small minicomputer and personal computer technology is such that almost any business can process many of its accounting records by computer. Costs to purchase a small computer system adequate for the records of an average single proprietorship are only a few thousand dollars. There still remains the problem of **programming** (instructing the computer how to manipulate data), but even that has been lessened with wide usage of a programming language called BASIC. The equipment for all automated systems will do only what it is instructed. Accordingly, the ideas, concepts, and procedures for a manual system are as important as ever to today's accountant who may work in or design computerized systems.

Glossary

Accounting system The various processing steps, equipment, personnel, and procedures that change original data to useful form.

Cashbook A simplified combination of the cash receipts journal and the cash payments journal.

Cash payments journal A special journal in which *all* cash payments are recorded.

Cash receipts journal A special journal in which *all* cash receipts are recorded.

General journal The book of original entry in which all transactions that do not fit into special journals are recorded.

Internal control The plan of organization, procedures, and equipment used in a business to protect its assets from improper use and to promote efficiency in operations.

Invoice A form that provides evidence of sale and delivery of merchandise; it indicates that an account receivable exists.

Processing A series of activities that make data useful. Classifying and summarizing are examples.

Programming Instructing a computer how to manipulate data.

Purchases journal A special journal in which credit purchases of merchandise are recorded.

Receiving report A form that provides information on materials received; it indicates that an account payable exists.

Sales journal A special journal in which credit sales of merchandise are recorded.

Source documents Business papers on which each individual transaction is recorded. They provide objective evidence of transactions.

Special journals Books of original entry that have been designed so that each receives the initial recording of specialized classifications of transactions.

Questions

Q7–1 What are the basic purposes of business documents? Is a receiving report really useful when a shipment received is already described by the supplier's invoice?

Q7–2 Do you agree that the structure of an accounting system depends on when, by whom, and how the data will be used? Give some specific examples in your answer.

Q7–3 What is internal control? Can you cite some specific examples of things that would strengthen internal control in a merchandising business?

Q7–4 How do special journals strengthen internal control? Promote efficiency?

Q7–5 Do special journals eliminate the need for a general journal? Explain.

Q7–6 How do special journals reduce postings to the general ledger? Do you feel that this is an advantage of special journals? Why or why not?

Q7–7 When are postings from special journals made to the subsidiary ledgers? To the general ledgers? Why is such timing of postings desirable?

Q7–8 When is a special column for an account provided in the cash receipts and cash payments journal?

Q7–9 The following questions relate to the cash receipts journal illustrated in this chapter:

a. What are the special columns?

b. Why is the journal cross-footed at the end of each month?

c. Explain the postings from this journal (1) to the general ledger and (2) to the accounts receivable subsidiary ledger.

Q7–10 The column headings listed below might appear in one or more special journals.

a. Other Accounts—Debit
b. Purchases—Debit
c. Accounts Payable—Debit
d. Accounts Receivable—Credit
e. Office Supplies—Debit
f. Other Accounts—Credit
g. Accounts Payable—Credit
h. Cash—Credit
i. Accounts Receivable—Debit
j. Cash—Debit

The company maintains subsidiary ledgers for accounts receivable and accounts payable. For each of the headings, state the special journal or journals in which it would be found and whether or not the amounts entered in the column would be posted as a total, separately, or both as a total and separately.

Q7–11 What changes in the relationships shown in Figure 7–4 would be required:

a. If bookkeeping machines were used?

b. If EDP equipment were installed?

Q7–12 What are at least three types of entries that would always be made in the general journal?

Exercises

E7–1 *Use of sales journal*

Alabama Merchandisers uses an accounting system with the special journals described in this chapter. From the following list of selected transactions, journalize *only* those that belong in the sales journal:

1985		
Sep.	2	Sold merchandise to Tom Hamilton on account, $500, terms 2/10, n/30.
	5	Sold merchandise to Susan Sexton for cash, $825.
	9	Sold land to Jay Garbarino in amount of $20,000; accepted 30-day, 15 percent note receivable from Garbarino.
	12	Sold a piece of excess furniture to June Mesta on account, $980.

E7–2 *Use of purchases journal*

Scottish Woolen Goods Company uses the special journals described in this chapter. From the following list of selected transactions, journalize *only* those that belong in the purchases journal:

1985		
Jul.	5	Purchased merchandise from the Glasgow Sales Company for $1,875. Issued check no. 586 in payment.
	11	Purchased merchandise from Edinburgh Company for $2,275 on account. Terms were 2/10, n/30; Scottish Woolen Goods Company expects to pay in 10 days.
	15	Purchased merchandise from Dumfries Wholesalers on account for $9,345. Terms are 1/10, n/30; it is doubtful that this discount can be taken.
	19	Purchased store supplies from Moffat Company for $320 on account. Terms are 2/10, n/30.
	26	Purchased office supplies from Dundee Company for $250. Issued check no. 658 in payment.

E7–3 *Use of cash receipts journal*

Tampa Company uses a cash receipts journal. Journalize the following transactions:

1985		
Apr.	4	Received a check from Tarpon Springs Corporation in amount of $2,352 in payment of a $2,400 account receivable less discount.
	5	Borrowed $10,000 from Bank of Mullet Key on a 90-day, 18 percent note.
	8	Made total cash sales of merchandise for the day in amount of $3,720.

9 Sold for cash to Largo Used Furniture Company a piece of excess office equipment for $800. (The equipment was sold at book value, so there was no gain or loss on the sale.)
11 Collected a total of $3,090 in payment of a $3,000 note plus interest by Bellaire Company.
12 Received a check for $500 from George Ozoha plus a 90-day, 16 percent note for $500 in settlement of an overdue $1,000 account receivable.

E7–4 *Use of cash payments journal*

The Houston Corporation uses a cash payments journal. Journalize the following selected transactions:

1985

Jan. 3 Paid with check no. 832 to Crosby Company an account payable of $4,000 less two percent discount.
4 Purchased merchandise for cash from Alvino Sales, issuing check no. 841 for $6,240.
7 Purchased a tract of land from Sugar Land Realty for $20,000. Issued check no. 855 for $5,000 and a mortgage note payable for the balance.
8 Paid to the Bank of Needville a $6,000 note plus $210 interest, using check no. 862.
10 Paid the Newgulf Sales Company for a $5,000 merchandise purchase made on January 3, terms 2/10, n/30. Issued check no. 890 for the proper amount.

E7–5 *Indentification of journal sources*

Cedar Crest Company uses sales, purchases, cash receipts, cash payments, and general journals. On December 31, 1985, it had the following amounts in its general ledger after journals had been posted:

Cash

F	Debit	Credit	Balance
1	58,000		58,000
2		38,000	20,000

Accounts Receivable

F	Debit	Credit	Balance
3	60,000		60,000
4		20,000	40,000

Accounts Payable

F	Debit	Credit	Balance
5		19,500	19,500
6	8,000		11,500

Sales

F	Debit	Credit	Balance
7		60,000	60,000
8		18,000	78,000
9	78,000		0

Purchases

F	Debit	Credit	Balance
10	19,500		19,500
11	6,000		25,500
12		25,500	0

Purchases Returns and Allowances

F	Debit	Credit	Balance
13		1,800	1,800
14	1,800		0

On a sheet of paper, opposite numbers 1 through 14 corresponding to the numbers that appear in the folio columns of the accounts, indicate the most probable journal source for each posting. Use the journal symbols illustrated in this chapter.

E7–6 *Posting from sales journal*

The sales journal of Romney Wholesalers shows the following sales of merchandise during November 1985:

SALES JOURNAL Page 42

Date		Sales Invoice No.	Account Debited	Terms	F	Amount
1985						
Nov.	1	381	Slanesville Stores, Inc.	2/10,n/30		2,610
	1	382	Jersey Mountain Company	2/10,n/30		940
	1	383	Hampshire's, Inc.	2/10,n/30		1,027
	30	784	Augusta Orchard Supply	2/10,n/30		2,100
	30	785	Springfield Company	2/10,n/30		726
	30	786	Slanesville Stores, Inc.	2/10,n/30		1,187
	30	787	Hampshire's, Inc.	2/10,n/30		2,120
			Total			10,710

Post the appropriate amounts to the accounts receivable subsidiary ledger and to the general ledger.

E7–7 *Posting from cash receipts journal*

The cash receipts journal of GT Stores is shown below. Create account numbers, post to the general ledger and to any subsidiary ledger(s) involved, and show all posting references. Disregard account balances.

CASH RECEIPTS JOURNAL Page 1

Date		Explanation	Debits: Cash	Debits: Sales Disc.	Debits: Other Accounts: Account Title	F	Amount	Credits: Account Credited	Accounts Receivable: ✓	Accounts Receivable: Amount	Sales	Other Accounts: F	Other Accounts: Amount
1985													
Jun.	3	Invested in business	2,500					W. Ray, Capital					2,500
	10	Payment in full	588	12				William Ramey		600			
	15	Cash sales	1,000					Sales			1,000		
	18	Payment in full	396	4				Ella Gray		400			
	21	Borrowed from bank	600					Notes Payable					600
	28	Cash sales	950					Sales			950		
	28	Payment on account	100		Notes Receivable		200	Arthur James		300			
		Totals	6,134	16			200			1,300	1,950		3,100

E7–8 *Sales journal with batch numbers*

The Muhlenberg Company uses a sales journal but posts to customer accounts in the accounts receivable subsidiary ledger from copies of sales invoices. Sales are entered daily by batch totals. The following sales were made during the first week of June 1985:

Date	Invoice Numbers	Total Amount
Jun. 3	2,851–2,972	$6,820
4	2,973–3,113	7,256
5	3,114–3,243	5,082
6	3,244–3,366	6,117
7	3,367–3,518	8,546

Journalize the sales for the week in a sales journal.

E7–9 *Posting from cash journals*

The Cash account of Erie Company had a balance of $19,870 on April 30, 1985, before posting from the special journals. The Cash column of the cash receipts journal showed a total of $75,200 for April; the Cash column of the cash payments journal showed a total of $63,100. Enter the beginning balance in a three-column cash account and post the indicated amounts from page 54 of the cash receipts journal and page 38 of the cash payments journal.

E7–10 *Journalizing return of merchandise*

The Gaston Company received information from Vanessa Mize that merchandise shipped to her arrived with one item damaged beyond repair. She did not wish a replacement item, so the company credited her account for $392 on May 6, 1985. Design the appropriate journal and journalize this transaction.

E7–11 *Cashbook entries*

Sigma Alpha Chi fraternity at State University uses a combined cash receipts and payments journal with headings as follows:

		Debits		Credits			Other Accounts			
				Cash Paid						
Date	Explanation	Cash Rec.	Accounts Payable	Check No.	Amount	Dues Revenue	Title	F	Debit	Credit

Enter the following selected transactions for the month of September:

1985

Sep. 2 Collected dues for the month of September, $1,440
9 Paid an account payable by issuing check no. 152 for $96.
16 Collected additional dues, $160.
30 Paid chapter house rent by issuing check no. 153 for $600.

A Problems

P7–1A *Sales and collection transactions*

University City Sales had the following selected transactions in April 1985:

1985

Apr. 1 Sold merchandise to Clayton Company on account; invoice price $2,000; terms 2/10, n/30; invoice no. 0117.
3 Sold merchandise to Wellston Company on account; invoice price $3,600; terms 2/10, n/30; invoice no. 0118.

4 Received a check from Maplewood, Inc., in payment of a sale made March 27; invoice price $1,400; terms 2/10, n/30.
5 Authorized an allowance of $200 to be credited to the account of Clayton Company, who reported that merchandise in the sale of April 1 was defective.
5 Sold merchandise to Richmond Heights Company on account; invoice price $1,800; terms 2/10, n/30; invoice no. 0119.
8 Recorded cash sales for the day amounting to $6,200.
10 Sold excess store supplies to Kirkwood Company on account; invoice price $195; terms n/15.
12 Received a check from Wellston Company for the amount due.
15 Received a check from Richmond Heights Company for the amount due.
15 Recorded cash sales for the day amounting to $6,560.
19 Sold merchandise to Maplewood, Inc., on account; invoice price $1,500; terms 2/10, n/30; invoice no. 0120.
25 Received a check from Kirkwood Company for the amount due.
29 Sold merchandise to Wellston Company on account; invoice price $2,600; terms 2/10, n/30; invoice no. 0121.
29 Received a check from Maplewood, Inc., for the amount due.
30 Received a check from Clayton Company for the amount due.

Required:

1. Journalize the April transactions in the appropriate journals using the gross price method.

2. Open the necessary accounts in the general ledger and accounts receivable ledger; enter a debit balance in the account of Maplewood, Inc., and in the Accounts Receivable account of $1,400 representing a sale recorded on March 27, 1985. Also enter a $500 debit balance in the Store Supplies account.

3. Post the April transactions to both ledgers (provide account numbers for the general ledger accounts).

P7–2A *Purchases and payment transactions*

The Auburn Company had the following selected transactions in October 1985:

1985

Oct. 2 Purchased merchandise from Lee Company on account; invoice price $3,700; terms 1/10, n/30.
3 Purchased office supplies from Beulah Company on account; invoice price $300; terms n/15.
4 Purchased merchandise from Opelika, Inc., on account; invoice price $1,850; terms 2/10, n/30.
7 Paid Gold Hill Company for a purchase made on September 28; invoice price $3,200, terms 2/10, n/30; check no. 870.
12 Purchased merchandise for cash from the Pepperell Company; invoice price $825; check no. 871.
14 Paid Opelika, Inc., the amount due; check no. 872.
15 Purchased merchandise from Gold Hill Company on account; invoice price $3,600; terms 2/10, n/30.
18 Paid Beulah Company the amount due; check no. 873.
18 Returned merchandise that was the wrong size to Gold Hill Company; invoice price $600.
24 Paid Gold Hill Company the amount due; check no. 874.
28 Purchased merchandise from Opelika, Inc., on account; invoice price $2,750; terms 2/10, n/30.
30 Paid Lee Company the amount due; check no. 875.

Required:

1. Journalize the October transactions in the appropriate journals using the gross price method.

2. Open the necessary accounts in the general ledger and the acccounts payable subsidiary ledger; enter a credit balance in the account of Gold Hill Company and in the Accounts Payable account in the amount of $3,200 representing a purchase made on September 28, 1985. Also enter a debit of $25,600 in the Cash account.

3. Post the October transactions to both ledgers (provide account numbers for the general ledger accounts).

P7–3A *Journalizing to all journals*

The Outlet Sales Company started operations on August 1, 1985. During August, the company used the following accounts:

Cash 101	R. McGhee, Capital 301
Accounts Receivable 111	Sales 401
Notes Receivable 115	Sales Discounts 402
Prepaid Insurance 117	Sales Returns and Allowances 403
Office Supplies 118	Purchases 501
Land 151	Purchases Discounts 502
Store Building 154	Purchases Returns and Allowances 503
Store Fixtures 156	Transportation In 504
Office Equipment 158	Salaries Expense 601
Accounts Payable 201	Delivery Expense 611
Notes Payable 202	Office Expense 621
Mortgage Payable 251	Utilities Expense 631

The following transactions occurred during August:

1985		
Aug.	1	Renee McGhee invested $50,000 cash in her new business.
	1	Purchased store building and site for $60,000, of which $15,000 is considered land cost. Paid $10,000 in cash and issued a mortgage note for the balance.
	1	Purchased store fixtures on account from the Chelsea Company for $6,800, terms n/60.
	5	Purchased merchandise on account from Templeton Company, $4,000; invoice date August 6, terms 2/10, n/60.
	6	Purchased a three-year fire insurance policy for $720 cash.
	8	Purchased merchandise for $5,000 cash.
	9	Returned unsatisfactory merchandise to Templeton Company and received credit for $800.
	13	Sold merchandise to Bailey Myers on account, $8,200; invoice no. 1, terms 1/10, n/30.
	15	Paid Templeton Company the amount due.
	15	Cash sales for August 1 through 15 were recorded today, $3,400.
	16	Sold merchandise to Marie Owens on account, $4,700; invoice no. 2, terms 1/10, n/30.
	16	Paid salaries for August 1 through 15 totaling $2,650 (ignore payroll taxes).
	20	Purchased merchandise on account from Rockland Company, $4,900; invoice date August 20, terms 1/10, n/30.
	21	Received bill for $130 from the Masson Supply Company for items chargeable to Office Expense, terms n/30.
	23	Received merchandise returned by Marie Owens; issued credit memo no. 1 for $2,000.
	23	Received check from Bailey Myers for invoice no. 1, less discount.

26 Received check from Marie Owens for balance due on invoice no. 2, less discount.
29 Sold merchandise on account to Walter Rockingham, $4,000; invoice no. 3, terms 1/10, n/30.
29 Paid $215 cash for electricity.
29 Paid the Rockland Company for the invoice of August 20, less discount.
31 Cash sales from August 16 through 31 were $1,950.
31 Paid salaries for August 16 through 31 totaling $2,850 (ignore payroll taxes).
31 Received a bill for $96 from the Delivu Company for delivery service for the month.
31 Purchased two filing cabinets and a typewriter at a cost of $750 and various office supplies at a cost of $300; paid $350 by check and issued a $700 note payable for the balance.

Required:

1. Record the transactions in a general journal, a cash receipts journal, a cash payments journal, a sales journal, and a purchases journal.

2. Indicate how the posting would be made from the journals by entering the appropriate posting references.

P7–4A *Complex examples of cash receipts and payments*

The following cash receipts and cash payments requiring multiple debits and credits occurred at the Concordia Company during May 1985:

1985

May 1 Purchased the assets and assumed the liabilities of a competing business for $79,500 in cash. Following are additional details of the transaction:

Assets Received		Liabilities Assumed	
Accounts receivable	$ 9,500	Accounts payable	$ 5,000
Merchandise inventory	25,000	Mortgage payable	10,000
Land	20,000		
Building	40,000		

2 Purchased office equipment for $5,000 and office supplies for $800; paid $2,800 in cash and issued a 90-day note payable for the balance.
3 Sold one-half the land purchased on May 1 for $10,000; received $5,000 in cash and a 60-day note receivable for the balance.
6 Accepted $3,000 in cash and a 60-day note receivable for $6,500 for the accounts receivable acquired in the May 1 transaction.

Required: Record the transactions in a cash receipts journal and a cash payments journal.

P7–5A *Reconstruction of controlling account from subsidiary postings*

The accounts receivable subsidiary ledger of North Iowa Company is reproduced below.

Cedar Falls Company

1985						
Jan.	1	Debit balance	√			900
	10		S6	400		1,300
	18		CR4		900	400
	25		J9		100	300
	28		S6	500		800

Dewar Company

1985						
Jan.	1	Debit balance	√			395
	14		J8		45	350
	15		S6	670		1,020
	31		CR4		250	770

Waterloo Company

1985						
Jan.	1	Debit balance	√			350
	4		CR4		350	0
	11		S6	410		410
	21		S6	380		790
	28		CR4		150	640
	30		J10		50	590

Required:

1. Reconstruct the Accounts Receivable controlling account exactly as it appears in the general ledger of North Iowa Company after all postings from the journals have been completed. Include dates and posting references.

2. Verify the ending balance by preparing a schedule of accounts receivable.

P7–6A
Thought-provoking problem: opinion on an accounting system

Dempster Distributors is a petroleum products dealer. It operates several trucks that are constantly filling fuel tanks for customers who use fuel oil for home heating. For each such delivery a sales ticket is prepared. A meter on the truck stamps the number of gallons delivered at each stop. These sales tickets are returned to the accounting department at the end of each day, where they are priced so that invoices can be mailed to customers. Customers are allowed a discount of one cent per gallon if they pay within 10 days of the billing date.

Fuel oil is stored in a large tank that is refilled about twice a week by tankers from the area distributor. Each time the distributor's tanker delivers a load, a receiver's report is prepared and sent to the accounting department. The distributor requires payment monthly and does not offer a discount.

The business has 32 employees. They are paid on the 15th and the last day of each month. Supplies and other expenses are billed to Dempster Distributors; almost all suppliers offer terms of 2/10, n/30.

You have been asked for your opinion on an accounting system for Dempster Distributors. The president, Mildred Dempster, has posed these questions:

1. Should she use a sales journal? Why or why not? If she should, what procedure should be used to record entries to it and get invoices mailed to customers as soon as possible after deliveries?

2. Does she need a purchases journal, or could all purchases be recorded in the general journal? Explain.

3. Would a cash receipts journal be a good idea (about 75 to 100 checks are received by mail per day)? If so, what special columns should be included?

4. Is there any advantage to the use of a cash payments journal? Explain.

B Problems

P7–1B *Sales and collection transactions*

Tarrant Sales had the following selected transactions in July 1985:

1985	
Jul. 1	Sold merchandise to Saginaw Company on account; invoice price $3,400; terms 2/10, n/30; invoice no. 0205.
3	Sold merchandise to Watauga, Inc., on account; invoice price $6,120; terms 2/10, n/30; invoice no. 0206.
4	Received a check from Carswell Company in payment of a sale made June 27; invoice price $2,380; terms 2/10, n/30.
5	Authorized an allowance of $340 to be credited to the account of Saginaw Company.
5	Sold merchandise to Arlington Company on account; invoice price $3,060; terms 2/10, n/30; invoice no. 0207.
8	Recorded cash sales for the day amounting to $10,540.
10	Sold excess office supplies to Fort Worth Company on account; invoice price $332; terms n/15.
12	Received a check from Watauga, Inc., for the amount due.
15	Received a check from Arlington Company for the amount due.
19	Sold merchandise to Carswell Company on account; invoice price $2,550; terms 2/10, n/30; invoice no. 0208.
25	Received a check from Fort Worth Company for the amount due.
29	Sold merchandise to Watauga, Inc., on account; invoice price $4,420; terms 2/10, n/30; invoice no. 0209.
29	Received a check from Carswell Company for the amount due.
30	Received a check from Saginaw Company for the amount due.

Required:

1. Journalize the July transactions in the appropriate journal using the gross price method.

2. Open the necessary accounts in the general ledger and the accounts receivable subsidiary ledger; enter a debit balance in the account of Carswell Company and in the Accounts Receivable account in the amount of $2,380 representing a sale recorded on June 27, 1985. Also enter a debit balance of $950 in the Office Supplies account.

3. Post the July transactions to both ledgers (provide account numbers for the general ledger accounts).

P7–2B *Purchases and payment transactions*

The Pensacola Company had the following selected transactions in January 1985:

1985	
Jan. 2	Purchased merchandise from Warrington Company on account; invoice price $5,920; terms 1/10, n/30.
3	Purchased office supplies from Gull Point Company on account; invoice price $480; terms n/15.
4	Purchased merchandise from Santa Rosa Company on account; invoice price $2,960; terms 2/10, n/30.
7	Paid Milton Company for a purchase made on December 30, 1984; invoice price $5,120; terms 2/10, n/30; check no. 970.
12	Purchased merchandise for cash from Yellow River Sales; invoice price $1,320; check no. 971.
14	Paid Santa Rosa Company the amount due; check no. 972.
15	Purchased merchandise from Milton Company on account; invoice price $5,760; terms 2/10, n/30.
18	Paid Gull Point Company the amount due; check no. 973.

18 Returned merchandise that was the wrong model to Milton Company; invoice price $360.
24 Paid Milton Company the amount due; check no. 974.
28 Purchased merchandise from Santa Rosa Company on account; invoice price $4,400; terms 2/10, n/30.
30 Paid Warrington Company the amount due; check no. 975.

Required:

1. Journalize the January transactions in the appropriate journals using the gross price method.

2. Open the necessary accounts in the general ledger and the accounts payable subsidiary ledger; enter a credit balance in the account of Milton Company and the Accounts Payable account in the amount of $5,120 representing a purchase made on December 30, 1984. Also enter a debit balance of $42,120 in the Cash account.

3. Post the January transactions to both ledgers (provide account numbers for general ledger accounts).

P7–3B *Journalizing to all journals*

The Yuma Company started operations on May 2, 1985. During May, the company used the following accounts:

Cash 101	S. Yuma, Capital 301
Accounts Receivable 111	Sales 401
Notes Receivable 115	Sales Discounts 402
Prepaid Insurance 117	Sales Returns and Allowances 403
Office Supplies 118	Purchases 501
Land 151	Purchases Discounts 502
Store Building 154	Purchases Returns and Allowances 503
Store Fixtures 156	Transportation In 504
Office Equipment 158	Salaries Expense 601
Accounts Payable 201	Delivery Expense 611
Notes Payable 202	Office Expense 621
Mortgage Payable 251	Utilities Expense 631

The following transactions occurred during May:

1985

May 2 Sara Yuma invested $75,000 in her new business.
2 Purchased a store building and site for $150,000, of which $37,500 is considered land cost. Paid $25,000 in cash and issued a mortgage note for the balance.
2 Purchased store fixtures on account from Gila Mountain Company for $17,000, terms n/60.
6 Purchased merchandise on account from the Laguna Company, $10,000; invoice date May 6, terms 2/10, n/60.
6 Purchased a three-year fire insurance policy for $1,800 cash.
9 Purchased merchandise for $12,500 cash.
10 Returned unsatisfactory merchandise to Laguna Company and received credit for $2,000.
13 Sold merchandise on account to David Tacana, $20,500; invoice no. 1, terms 1/10, n/30.
16 Paid Laguna Company the amount due.
16 Cash sales for May 2 through 14 were recorded today, $9,500.
16 Sold merchandise on account to San Luis Company, $11,750; invoice no. 2, terms 1/10, n/30.
16 Paid salaries for May 2 through 14 totaling $6,625 (ignore payroll taxes).
20 Received bill for $325 from Jane Perkins for items chargeable to Office Expense, terms n/30.

21 Purchased merchandise on account from Gadsden Company, $12,250; invoice date May 20, terms 1/10, n/30.
21 Received merchandise returned by San Luis Company; issued credit memo no. 1 for $5,000.
23 Received check from David Tacana for invoice no. 1, less discount.
26 Received check from San Luis Company for balance owed on invoice no. 2, less discount.
28 Sold merchandise on account to Dome, Inc., $10,000; invoice no. 3, terms 1/10, n/30.
28 Paid $535 for electricity for the month
28 Paid the Gadsden Company for the invoice of May 20, less discount.
31 Cash sales for May 16 through 31 were $4,875.
31 Paid salaries for May 16 through 31 totaling $7,125 (ignore payroll taxes).
31 Received a bill from the Imperial Company for delivery service for May, $240.
31 Purchased office equipment for $1,875 and office supplies for $750; paid $875 by check and issued a $1,750 note payable for the balance.

Required:

1. Record the transactions in a general journal, a cash receipts journal, a cash payments journal, a sales journal, and a purchases journal.

2. Indicate how the posting would be made from the journals by inserting the appropriate posting references.

P7–4B *Complex examples of cash receipts and payments*

The following receipts and cash payments requiring multiple debits and credits occurred at the Oshkosh Company during September 1985:

1985

Sep. 2 Purchased the assets and assumed the liabilities of a competing business for $127,200 in cash. Following are additional details of the transaction:

Assets Received		Liabilities Assumed	
Accounts receivable	$15,200	Accounts payable	$ 8,000
Merchandise inventory	40,000	Mortgage payable	16,000
Land	32,000		
Building	64,000		

2 Purchased office equipment for $8,000 and office supplies for $1,280. Paid $4,280 in cash and gave a 90-day note payable for the balance.
3 Sold one-half the land purchased on September 2 for $16,000; received $8,000 in cash and a 60-day note receivable for the balance.
6 Accepted $5,200 in cash and a 60-day note receivable for $10,000 for the accounts receivable acquired on September 2.

Required: Record the transactions in a cash receipts journal and a cash payments journal.

P7–5B *Reconstruction of controlling account from subsidiary postings*

The accounts receivable ledger for the Massachusetts Company is reproduced below:

Bridgewater Company

1985						
Feb.	1	Debit balance	√			1,440
	11		S6	640		2,080
	18		CR4		1,440	640
	25		J9		160	480
	28		S6	800		1,280

Framingham Company

1985						
Feb.	1	Debit balance	√			632
	14		J8		72	560
	15		S6	1,072		1,632
	28		CR4		400	1,232

Springfield Company

1985						
Feb.	1	Debit balance	√			560
	4		CR4		560	0
	11		S6	656		656
	21		S6	608		1,264
	28		CR4		240	1,024
	28		J10		80	944

Required:

1. Reconstruct the Accounts Receivable controlling account exactly as it appears in the general ledger of the Massachusetts Company after all postings from the journals have been completed. Include dates and posting references.

2. Verify the ending balance by preparing a schedule of accounts receivable.

P7–6B *Thought-provoking problem: design an accounting system*

Penny Cleaners specializes in 24-hour service for all types of cleaning, including dry cleaning of clothing, draperies, and small rugs that are brought to their location. Such work is done on a cash basis only; customers pay when they pick up their articles. Penny also has several portable cleaning outfits that are taken to homes and businesses in specially equipped vans to clean rugs on the customers' premises. About 60–80 such jobs are performed per week, and billed on the day of service to the customer with terms of 2/10, n/30. Some cleaning supplies are purchased for cash; about 75 percent of them are purchased on credit. Most suppliers offer some type of cash discount for early payment. The company has 18 employees who are paid by check on the 15th and the last day of each month.

Jim Penny, the owner, is not satisfied with his present accounting system, which consists of a general journal, a general ledger, and copies of bills sent to customers and received from suppliers. He never seems to be able to get an accurate figure for accounts payable. Customers have been complaining that they have been billed twice for rug cleaning work. One good customer came in last week and paid for a home cleaning job done months ago that had never been billed to her. Penny also wonders if the correct amount of cash is being deposited in the bank daily.

Required: Recommend changes to Mr. Penny's accounting system to help overcome these problems. Be specific as to documents you would use and details of any additional accounting records.

8 Payroll System

Introduction

In its 1981 *Annual Report,* Ingersoll-Rand Company reported that 33.1 percent of its total sales revenue was used to pay employees. This is typical of today's large enterprises; costs of having the services of a group of employees are second only to payments to suppliers. Payroll taxes are a major source of revenue to both the federal and state governments. Accordingly, it is important for the accountant to understand the many aspects of payroll computation and to record payroll information accurately. This chapter describes the accounting for payrolls. It covers computation of gross pay, payroll deductions, and net pay (take-home pay). The recording and reporting of income taxes, Social Security taxes, and other deductions withheld from employees' gross pay are explained. Also discussed are the calculation, recording, and reporting of employers' Social Security tax and unemployment compensation taxes.

Learning Goals

To be able to identify and calculate the various payroll deductions and payroll taxes that apply to business.

To list major parts of the Social Security program.

To compute net pay due.

To record a periodic payroll and the employer's payroll taxes.

To understand the requirements for reporting and remittance of payroll taxes.

To understand accrual of vacation pay liability.

To describe effective control of payroll.

Gross Pay

The total earnings of an employee before any deductions are applied is known as **gross pay.** It is computed in several ways. For some employees, periodic gross pay is a fractional amount of an annual salary. For example, a person with an annual salary of $36,000 would have a gross pay of $3,000 per monthly pay period. Another popular method of determining an employee's gross pay is to use an hourly wage rate—sometimes coupled with an incentive bonus for good production—for weekly or semimonthly pay periods. If Cynthia Winters worked at the rate of $12 per hour for a 40-hour week, her gross pay would be $480 = ($12 × 40).

A federal law, the **Fair Labor Standards Act,** popularly known as the Federal Wage and Hour Law, establishes federal minimum wages, requires overtime pay, and regulates child labor. The law relates to those employed in interstate commerce and in the production of goods for interstate commerce. It currently requires that workers not specifically exempted be paid a minimum hourly rate and an overtime wage of *time and one-half,* or one and one-half times the hourly rate, for time worked over 40 hours a week. If no more than 40 hours are worked in a week, no overtime compensation need be paid regardless of the number of hours worked in any one day. Employers and employees may, of course, agree to more favorable terms, such as time and one-half for all work over eight hours in any day and double time for Sunday or holiday work. The act does not place a limitation on total working time; it fixes the 40-hour work week as the basis for overtime pay. Thus, if Cynthia Winters worked a total of 45 hours in one week her gross pay would be:

Regular pay for 40 hours ($12 × 40)	$480
Regular pay for overtime hours ($12 × 5)	60
Premium pay for overtime hours ($12 × 1/2 × 5)	30
Gross pay earned	$570

Payroll Deductions

The periodic total wage or salary earned by an employee is not the amount the employee will take home. From the total or gross pay, a number of **payroll deductions** may be withheld for many purposes. The amount remaining after deductions is **net pay.** The source and nature of these deductions will be discussed before the discussion and illustrations of payroll accounting.

The deductions may be grouped into two broad classes:

1. Payroll taxes
   a. Social Security program taxes
   b. Federal income tax withholdings
   c. State and local income tax withholdings
2. Voluntary deductions
   a. Pension and retirement plans

b. Group health and life insurance
c. Charitable contributions
d. Union dues
e. Other miscellaneous deductions

Social Security Program: Federal Insurance Contributions Act (FICA)

The **Social Security program** dates back to 1935. A part of this national program is the Federal Insurance Contributions Act (FICA) that imposes a tax on both employees and employers. Those taxes are used to provide benefits to retired workers, their families, and their survivors.

Under the **Federal Insurance Contributions Act (FICA),** both employers and employees contribute equal amounts based on a stated percentage of taxable wages paid. The employee portion must be withheld by the employer from each payment of taxable wages until the currently designated base amount of taxable wages has been reached. After the **taxable wage base** has been earned, no further amounts are withheld during the remainder of that calendar year (see the Mary Bunting example on page 285). An employee who works for more than one employer during the year may, as a result, have more than the annual maximum withheld. The excess tax on the employee may be recovered or offset against the income tax when the employee files the annual federal income tax return (Form 1040). The employers involved have no corresponding right to recover their matching share of the excess deductions.

The FICA was expanded in 1965 to include a federal medicare program. Medicare provides hospital and other medical insurance for those age 65 and older. The medical insurance cost is included in the FICA deduction and the matching employer's tax.

Federal Income Tax Withholding[1]

Employers must withhold from each employee's taxable earnings an amount required by law and by regulation of the Internal Revenue Service (IRS). The amount that is withheld depends on the amount of earnings, the number of allowances claimed, and the frequency of the withholding period. Certain classes of wage payments are exempt. Each employee fills out an **Employee's Withholding Allowance Certificate, Form W–4** (shown in Figure 8–1) indicating the number of allowances claimed at the start of his or her employment and when the number of allowances changes. The employee may claim allowances for himself or herself, for his or her spouse (unless the spouse is employed and claims his or her own allowance), and for each qualified dependent. Additional exemptions may be claimed for old age (65 years

[1]A nonpayroll type of federal income tax withholding was included in the Tax Equity and Fiscal Responsibility Act (TEFRA) of 1982. It required banks and other companies to withhold at a stated rate of 10 percent from interest and dividends paid or credited to individuals. Withholding is scheduled to begin on July 1, 1983; however, intensive efforts are being made at the time this is written to cause the repeal of this part of the Act. Due to the uncertain implementation of this withholding requirement, it is not illustrated in this text.

Form **W-4** (Rev. January 1983)

Department of the Treasury—Internal Revenue Service

Employee's Withholding Allowance Certificate

OMB No. 1545-0010 Expires 8-31-85

1 Type or print your full name: William S. Ford

2 Your social security number: 123-45-6789

Home address (number and street or rural route): 50 Joy Street

City or town, State, and ZIP code: Boston, MA 02115

3 Marital Status: ☐ Single ☒ Married ☐ Married, but withhold at higher Single rate

Note: If married, but legally separated, or spouse is a nonresident alien, check the Single box.

4 Total number of allowances you are claiming (from line F of the worksheet on page 2) 3

5 Additional amount, if any, you want deducted from each pay . . . . $

6 I claim exemption from withholding because (see instructions and check boxes below that apply):

a ☐ Last year I did not owe any Federal income tax and had a right to a full refund of **ALL** income tax withheld, **AND**

b ☐ This year I do not expect to owe any Federal income tax and expect to have a right to a full refund of **ALL** income tax withheld. If both a and b apply, enter the year effective and "EXEMPT" here . . ▶ Year

c If you entered "EXEMPT" on line 6b, are you a full-time student? . . . . ☐ **Yes** ☐ **No**

Under the penalties of perjury, I certify that I am entitled to the number of withholding allowances claimed on this certificate, or if claiming exemption from withholding, that I am entitled to claim the exempt status.

Employee's signature ▶ William S. Ford Date ▶ January 2, 1985

7 Employer's name and address **(Employer: Complete 7, 8, and 9 only if sending to IRS)**: Needham Company, 123 Constitution Ave., Boston MA 02115

8 Office code: 0

9 Employer identification number: SF 56-0868005

Detach along this line. Give the top part of this form to employer; keep the lower part for your records.

Figure 8–1 **Employee's Withholding Allowance Certificate (Form W–4)**

or older) and blindness of the claimant or spouse. Tax rates are subject to change; persons responsible for payrolls should be acquainted with the latest tax rates and regulations—federal, state, and, in some cases, municipal. The Internal Revenue Service furnishes withholding tables for different payroll periods in its *Circular E, Employer's Tax Guide.* Figure 8–2 illustrates a **wage bracket withholding table** for weekly payrolls. Assume that William S. Ford, whose withholding allowances are shown in Figure 8–1, earns gross pay of $621.50 in the week ended February 11. The employer would find the amount of tax to be withheld on the line for wages at least $620 but less than $630. Under the column for three withholding allowances, the indicated amount of tax to be withheld is $105.20.

Other Tax Deductions

A number of states and some cities levy income taxes on the gross earnings of the employee subject to withholding. In some states, employees as well as employers are taxed under the state unemployment insurance programs. In some states, employees are also taxed to provide funds for the cost of disability benefits. Such additional tax assessments are generally deducted from gross earnings by the employer and remitted to the designated agencies.

Voluntary Deductions

Voluntary deductions include amounts withheld for such purposes as pension and retirement benefits, group health insurance, life insurance, charitable contributions, union dues, and others covered in the illustrations and prob-

MARRIED Persons—WEEKLY Payroll Period

(For Wages Paid After June 1982 and Before July 1983)

And the wages are—		And the number of withholding allowances claimed is—										
At least	But less than	0	1	2	3	4	5	6	7	8	9	10 or more
		The amount of income tax to be withheld shall be—										
$310	$320	$42.70	$39.10	$35.40	$31.80	$28.10	$24.80	$21.70	$18.70	$15.60	$12.50	$9.40
560	570	104.50	98.80	93.60	88.40	83.20	78.00	73.00	68.40	63.70	59.10	54.50
570	580	107.70	101.50	96.30	91.10	85.90	80.70	75.50	70.80	66.10	61.50	56.90
580	590	110.90	104.70	99.00	93.80	88.60	83.40	78.20	73.20	68.50	63.90	59.30
590	600	114.10	107.90	101.70	96.50	91.30	86.10	80.90	75.70	70.90	66.30	61.70
600	610	117.30	111.10	104.90	99.20	94.00	88.80	83.60	78.40	73.30	68.70	64.10
610	620	120.50	114.30	108.10	102.00	96.70	91.50	86.30	81.10	76.00	71.10	66.50
620	630	123.70	117.50	111.30	105.20	99.40	94.20	89.00	83.80	78.70	73.50	68.90
630	640	126.90	120.70	114.50	108.40	102.20	96.90	91.70	86.50	81.40	76.20	71.30
640	650	130.10	123.90	117.70	111.60	105.40	99.60	94.40	89.20	84.10	78.90	73.70
650	660	133.30	127.10	120.90	114.80	108.60	102.50	97.10	91.90	86.80	81.60	76.40
660	670	136.80	130.30	124.10	118.00	111.80	105.70	99.80	94.60	89.50	84.30	79.10
670	680	140.50	133.50	127.30	121.20	115.00	108.90	102.70	97.30	92.20	87.00	81.80
680	690	144.20	137.10	130.50	124.40	118.20	112.10	105.90	100.00	94.90	89.70	84.50
690	700	147.90	140.80	133.70	127.60	121.40	115.30	109.10	103.00	97.60	92.40	87.20
700	710	151.60	144.50	137.40	130.80	124.60	118.50	112.30	106.20	100.30	95.10	89.90
710	720	155.30	148.20	141.10	134.00	127.80	121.70	115.50	109.40	103.20	97.80	92.60
720	730	159.00	151.90	144.80	137.70	131.00	124.90	118.70	112.60	106.40	100.50	95.30
730	740	162.70	155.60	148.50	141.40	134.30	128.10	121.90	115.80	109.60	103.50	98.00
740	750	166.40	159.30	152.20	145.10	138.00	131.30	125.10	119.00	112.80	106.70	100.70
750	760	170.10	163.00	155.90	148.80	141.70	134.50	128.30	122.20	116.00	109.90	103.70
760	770	173.80	166.70	159.60	152.50	145.40	138.20	131.50	125.40	119.20	113.10	106.90
770	780	177.50	170.40	163.30	156.20	149.10	141.90	134.80	128.60	122.40	116.30	110.10
780	790	181.20	174.10	167.00	159.90	152.80	145.60	138.50	131.80	125.60	119,50	113.30
790	800	184.90	177.80	170.70	163.60	156.50	149.30	142.20	135.10	128.80	122.70	116.50
800	810	188.60	181.50	174.40	167.30	160.20	153.00	145.90	138.80	132.00	125.90	119.70
810	820	192.30	185.20	178.10	171.00	163.90	156.70	149.60	142.50	135.40	129.10	122.90
820	830	196.00	188.90	181.80	174.70	167.60	160.40	153.30	146.20	139.10	132.30	126.10
830	840	199.70	192.60	185.50	178.40	171.30	164.10	157.00	149.90	142.80	135.70	129.30
840	850	203.40	196.30	189.20	182.10	175.00	167.80	160.70	153.60	146.50	139.40	132.50
850	860	207.10	200.00	192.90	185.80	178.70	171.50	164.40	157.30	150.20	143.10	136.00
		37 percent of the excess over $860 plus—										
$860 and over		209.00	201.90	194.70	187.60	180.50	173.40	166.30	159.20	152.00	144.90	137.80

Page 11

Figure 8–2 **Wage Bracket Withholding Table**

lems.[2] Some require the employee's written authorization specifying the terms and amounts for withholding (for example, charitable contributions and life insurance). Some withholdings are made automatically because of contractual terms to which the employee is subject (for example, union dues withheld and paid to the union in total by the employer). Other deductions result from individual arrangements between employer and employee (for example, repayment of a loan or an advance and savings plans). Amounts

[2]The number of voluntary deductions has increased in recent years as employees have taken advantage of plans such as Individual Retirement Arrangements (IRAs) to defer payment of income tax to later years.

withheld are remitted to the agency involved—the union treasurer, the insurance company, the treasurer of the charitable fund, and so on.

Employer Payroll Taxes

Certain payroll taxes are levied on the employer in addition to those deducted from employees' wages. They are discussed in the following sections.

Federal Insurance Contributions Act (FICA)

As mentioned earlier, the FICA tax is levied in equal amounts on employees and employers. Thus, an employer must pay a matching sum for all FICA deductions from employee pay.

Federal Unemployment Tax Act

The **Federal Unemployment Tax Act (FUTA)** establishes a program administered locally by the states for payments to persons who become unemployed. Under it, a tax is levied on employers only. There is no withholding for this purpose. The current tax rate is applied to taxable wages until the wages reach the current **taxable wage base.** There is no further tax liability on the employer for wages paid beyond the maximum taxable base during the remainder of that calendar year.

State Unemployment Compensation Tax

All the states have laws requiring the payment of unemployment compensation taxes. The state unemployment compensation systems are tied in to the federal unemployment system, which pays part of the administration costs of the state systems. Funds are provided by a payroll tax levy on the employer and, in three states (Alabama, Alaska, and New Jersey), on both employer and employees. Unemployed persons who qualify for benefits are paid by a state agency from funds acquired through the tax.

State unemployment tax laws vary in their detail and application. There are maximum rates which may be reduced on a merit basis if the employer's annual contributions are sufficiently in excess of withdrawals for unemployment payments made to discharged employees. The merit-rating plan provides an incentive to employers to maintain steady employment. Employers who maintain a stable work force and whose employees experience relatively little unemployment will pay a lower rate than employers with a less favorable unemployment experience and unemployment expenditures. A recent range in one state was from a low of 2.6 percent to a high of 6.4 percent levied on employers only. The typical rate before merit rating is approximately 2.7 percent in most states. Unemployed persons who meet the eligibility requirements receive compensation for periods specified by state law. As an example, weekly benefits in one state range from a minimum of $15 to a maximum amount equal to two-thirds of the statewide average weekly wage rate. The number of weeks payable ranges from 13 to 26. Both the amount of unemployment benefits and the number of weeks payable depend on wages earned and amount of time worked during a base period.

Wage Bases and Tax Rates

The FICA and the FUTA wage bases and tax rates may be changed by Congress at any time. They have been increased steadily over the years. *To simplify the computations in all illustrations and problems in this textbook (except for illustrations of some actual forms), the following assumed wage bases and tax rates are used* (the accounting principles and recording procedures are the same regardless of the bases and the rates used):

1. For FICA computations—an assumed tax rate of 14 percent; 7 percent each on employer and on employee, limited to a taxable wage base of $36,000 during a calendar year.

2. For FUTA computations—an assumed tax rate only on employers of 5 percent, limited to a taxable wage base of $10,000 with a maximum of 4 percent payable to the state and 1 percent payable to the federal government.

The taxable wage base is the same for all employees and applies to each employee. The amount of wages in any year subject to FICA or FUTA payroll taxes is limited to a taxable wage base. Therefore, earnings of those employees who have reached the taxable wage base in the current year will be excluded when calculating the employee and employer payroll tax liabilities.

In the payroll period during which an employee's cumulative earnings exceed the taxable wage base, the portion up to the wage base is taxable. For example, assume that Mary Bunting earns $3,400 a month. By October 31, 1985, her accumulated earnings will be $34,000 = ($3,400 × 10 months). The portion of her November gross earnings subject to FICA taxes is $2,000, computed as follows:

Taxable wage base	$36,000
Year-to-date earnings through October	34,000
Remaining taxable amount	$ 2,000

The FICA tax deduction from Mary Bunting's gross pay will be based on the amount that brings her accumulated earnings for 1985 up to $36,000. The $1,400 earned in excess of the base in November is not subject to FICA taxes, nor will her December gross pay be subject to FICA withholding. Similarly, the employer will pay a matching amount for November and none in December on her earnings.

Recording the Payroll

Accurate payroll records are necessary to determine operating expenses and to report earnings information to employees and to federal, state, and other agencies. A payroll register must show the names, earnings, and payroll deductions of all employees for each pay period. A **yearly individual compensation record** for each employee showing his or her earnings and deductions must also be kept. In most large businesses these records are maintained by computer; some smaller organizations keep manual records.

					PAYROLL	
					Earnings	
Dept[a]	Name of Employee	Rate or Salary	Total Hours Worked	Overtime Hours	Regular and Overtime	Overtime Premium
S	James B. Skinner	$ 12.00	44.0	4.0	$ 528.00	$24.00
S	Mary Burke	12.50	42.0	2.0	525.00	12.50
S	John T. Howard	11.00	40.0		440.00	
E	Richard E. Aldrich	750.00	40.0		750.00	
O	William S. Ford	15.00	42.0	2.0	630.00	15.00
			208.0	8.0	$2,873.00	$51.50

[a]S = Salesperson; E = Executive; O = Office.
[b]Income tax amounts are assumed.

Figure 8–3 **Payroll Register for Orbit Company**

Whether maintained by computer or by hand, the content generally is as shown in Figures 8–3 and 8–4. The payroll register shown in Figure 8–3 is for the Orbit Company and covers a period of one week that ended on May 31, 1985. As previously indicated, a typical payroll register also would show other voluntary deductions such as union dues or retirement plans.

The total gross pay of $2,924.50 is assigned to the three expense classifications shown in the Department column of the payroll register. Then, a journal entry is made to record the payroll for each pay period. The entry to record the amounts in the Orbit Company's payroll register for the week ended May 31, 1985, is as follows:[3]

1985					
May	31	Sales Salaries Expense		1,529.50	
		Executive Salaries Expense		750.00	
		Office Salaries Expense		645.00	
		FICA Taxes Payable			204.72
		Federal Income Tax Withholding Payable			630.40
		State Income Tax Withholding Payable			49.74
		Group Health Insurance Premiums Payable			150.00
		Salaries and Wages Payable			1,889.64
		Payroll for the week ended May 31, 1985, with assumed FICA rate of 7.0 percent.			

The individual earnings record for William S. Ford is shown in Figure 8–4. The entries in his record for May 31 (like the entries for the other employees) are taken directly from and match the amounts in the payroll register.

[3]The entries in this chapter are all made in general journal form to emphasize the accounts debited and credited. If special journals or a voucher system is in use (see Chapters 7 and 9), different journals would be used for some entries.

REGISTER							Week Ended 5/31/85
	Deductions						
Total	FICA	Federal Income Tax[b]	Group Health	Sate Income Tax[b]	Total	Net Pay	Check Number
$ 552.00	$ 38.64	$117.60	$ 18.75	$ 9.29	$ 184.28	$ 367.72	141
537.50	37.63	121.30	18.75	9.05	186.73	350.77	142
440.00	30.80	95.50	18.75	7.41	152.46	287.54	143
750.00	52.50	162.20	56.25	12.63	283.58	466.42	144
645.00	45.15	133.80	37.50	11.36	227.81	417.19	145
$2,924.50	$204.72	$630.40	$150.00	$49.74	$1,034.86	$1,889.64	

Figure 8–3 (Continued)

The payroll register facilitates the preparation of each weekly payroll for the Orbit Company. The individual earnings record enables the company to prepare the annual tax reports (Form W–2, for example) for each employee and to report on deductions. In effect, it serves as a subsidiary record of the company's payroll transactions for the accounting period.

YEARLY INDIVIDUAL COMPENSATION RECORD

Employee No. 141

FOR YEAR ENDING DECEMBER 19 85

Soc. Sec. No. 123–45–6789

NAME William S. Ford

HOURS FULL WEEK 40

ADDRESS 50 Joy St., Boston, Mass. 02115

EARNINGS FULL WEEK $600.00

	TIME			EARNINGS RECORD					DEDUCTIONS				
					Other Compensation								
Period Ending	Days	Hrs	Rate	Salary or Wages	Detail	Amount	Total	Total To Date	Federal Old Age	Federal Income Tax	State Income Tax	Health Plan	Net Paid
FW'D		720	15.00	10,800 00			10,800 00	10,800.00	756.00	1,983.60	181.80	675.00	7,203.60
5/3		40.0	15.00	600 00			600 00		42.00	110.20	10.10	37.50	400.20
5/10		40.0	15.00	600 00			600 00		42.00	110.20	10.10	37.50	400.20
5/17		40.0	15.00	600 00			600 00		42.00	110.20	10.10	37.50	400.20
5/24		40.0	15.00	600 00			600 00		42.00	110.20	10.10	37.50	400.20
5/31		42.0	15.00	645 00			645 00		45.15	133.80	11.36	37.50	417.19
Period Total		202.0		3,045 00			3,045 00		213.15	574.60	51.76	187.50	2,017.99

Figure 8–4 Individual Earnings Record

In the journal entry to record the payroll, the debits are to a selling expense account for $1,529.50 and to two general and administrative expense accounts for $1,395.00, or a total payroll of $2,924.50, of which the employees' take-home pay is $1,889.64 (Figure 8–3). If a departmental breakdown of expenses is not considered necessary by management, the single gross pay total of $2,924.50 could be debited to Salaries and Wages Expense. The credits are to liability accounts for various amounts withheld by the employer and to a liability account for net pay due to employees. The liability for net pay is usually paid at about the same time the payroll is recorded and requires a journal entry as follows:

1985					
May	31	Salaries and Wages Payable		1,889.64	
		Cash			1,889.64
		Payment of May 31 payroll.			

To strengthen internal control over payroll, many companies have a special payroll account at the bank to be used only for individual salary and wage payments. When the liability for net pay is due to be paid, a single check is written to transfer the exact amount needed to the payroll checking account. The journal entry just shown would record such a transfer for Orbit Company. The other liabilities are paid at various dates as discussed in later sections of this chapter. The important concept is that total gross pay must be paid to someone and is an expense of the period.

Recording the Employer's Payroll Tax Expense

The employer's payroll tax expense may be recorded at the end of each payroll period or at the end of each month. Assume that the Orbit Company records the payroll tax expense for each payroll and that, because of its merit-rating record, it is subject to a state unemployment tax rate of only 2 percent (reduced for merit from assumed 4 percent maximum). For a week in early January where no employee has reached the $10,000 wage base for unemployment compensation tax, the payroll tax entry on a gross payroll of $2,924.50 would be:

1985					
Jan.	11	Payroll Tax Expense		292.47	
		FICA Taxes Payable			204.72
		State Unemployment Taxes Payable			58.50
		Federal Unemployment Taxes Payable			29.25
		To record payroll taxes for week ended January 11, computed as follows: FICA tax ($2,924.50 × 0.07); State unemployment compensation tax ($2,924.50 × 0.02); and Federal unemployment compensation tax ($2,924.50 × 0.01).			

The debit is to the Payroll Tax Expense account; the three credits are the liabilities to the federal and state agencies. The liability for FICA taxes ($204.72) matches the amount deducted from the employee's wages.

Later in the year, some employees begin to reach wage bases for payroll taxes. From Figure 8–4, it can be seen that William S. Ford had earned $10,800 in the year-to-date (YTD) prior to the pay period ending May 3, 1985. He has passed the $10,000 base, and Orbit Company is no longer subject to unemployment compensation tax on his earnings. Assume further that year-to-date (YTD) earnings of other employees at the pay period ended May 24, 1985, were:

James B. Skinner	$ 9,200
Mary Burke	9,825
John T. Howard	9,200
Richard E. Aldrich	16,500

There would be no change in FICA taxes; all five employees are below the $36,000 wage base. However, the amounts subject to unemployment compensation tax on May 31 are:

Employee	Remaining Base ($10,000 − Taxed to Date)	Remaining Taxable in 1985 On May 31	Remaining Taxable in 1985 After May 31
Skinner	($10,000 − $ 9,200) = $800	$ 552	$248
Burke	(10,000 − 9,825) = 175	175	0
Howard	(10,000 − 9,200) = 800	440	360
Aldrich	(10,000 − 10,000) = 0	0	0
Ford	(10,000 − 10,000) = 0	0	0
Pay subject to unemployment compensation tax		$1,167	$608

Under these circumstances, the employer's payroll tax entry on May 31, 1985 is:

Date		Account		Debit	Credit
1985 May	31	Payroll Tax Expense		239.73	
		FICA Taxes Payable			204.72
		State Unemployment Taxes Payable			23.34
		Federal Unemployment Taxes Payable			11.67
		To record payroll taxes for week ended May 31, computed as follows: FICA tax ($2,924.50 × 0.07); State unemployment tax ($1,167 × 0.02); and Federal unemployment tax ($1,167 × 0.01).			

Reaching FICA Tax Base

When the wage base for FICA tax is reached, all Social Security (FICA) withholding and matching employer's FICA tax ceases until the following January. At a salary of $750 per week, Richard E. Aldrich of Orbit Company will reach the assumed base of $36,000 at the end of 48 weeks—November 30, 1985. At this point, all FICA taxes on Aldrich's pay will cease. Assume that with some overtime, William S. Ford will have gross earnings of $35,740 by the week ended December 6, 1985. In the next week, only $260 = ($36,000 − $35,740) will be taxable for FICA purposes. Orbit Company will withhold $18.20 = ($260 × 0.07) from Ford's pay for FICA taxes in that week and will

Form **941** (Rev. October 1982) Department of the Treasury Internal Revenue Service

Employer's Quarterly Federal Tax Return

▶ For Paperwork Reduction Act Notice, see page 2.

OMB No. 1545-0029 Expires 2-28-83

T | FF | FD | FP | I | T

Your name, address, employer identification number, and calendar quarter of return. (If not correct, please change.) ▶

Name (as distinguished from trade name)

Date quarter ended: March 31,1985

Trade name, if any: Orbit Company

Employer identification number: SF 56-0868005

Address and ZIP code: 123 Constitution Avenue, Boston, MA 02115

If address is different from prior return, check here ▶ ☐

Record of Federal Tax Liability and Deposits (Complete if line 13 is $500 or more)

If you made eighth-monthly deposits using the 95% rule, check here . ▶ ☐

If you are a first-time 3-banking-day depositor, check here . . . . . ▶ ☐

See the instructions under Rule (4) on page 4 for details .

a. Date wages paid (Day)	b. Tax liability	c. Date of deposit (Optional)	d. Amount deposited (Optional)
	Overpayment from previous quarter . . ▶		
First month of quarter 1st–3rd A			
4th–7th B	990.50		
8th–11th C	1,002.00		
12th–15th D			
16th–19th E	1,095.60	1/21/85	3,088.10
20th–22nd F			
23rd–25th G	1,002.48		
26th–last H			
I Total . . ▶	4,090.58		3,088.10
Second month of quarter 1st–3rd I	1,025.42		
4th–7th J			
8th–11th K	999.80	2/14/85	3,027.70
12th–15th L	962.40		
16th–19th M			
20th–22nd N	1,008.22		
23rd–25th O			
26th–last P			
II Total . . ▶	3,995.84		3,027.70
Third month of quarter 1st–3rd Q	1,202.65	3/1/85	3,173.27
4th–7th R			
8th–11th S	1,015.28		
12th–15th T	1,003.17		
16th–19th U			
20th–22nd V	998.60	3/25/85	3,017.05
23rd–25th W			
26th–last X	1,035.82		
III Total . . ▶	5,255.52		6,190.32
IV Total for quarter (add lines I, II, and III) . .	13,341.94	Column b total must equal line 13	12,306.12
V Final deposit made for quarter. (Enter 0 if included in line IV.)		4/15/85	1,035.82

If you are not liable for returns in the future, write "FINAL" . . . . . ▶

Date final wages paid . . ▶

Line	Amount
1 Number of employees (except household) employed in the pay period that includes March 12th (complete first quarter only) . . . . ▶	5
2 Total wages and tips subject to withholding, plus other compensation . . . . ▶	38,408 50
3 Total income tax withheld from wages, tips, annuities, sick pay, gambling, etc . ▶	8,195 20
4 Adjustment of withheld income tax for preceding quarters of calendar year . . ▶	None
5 Adjusted total of income tax withheld	8,195 20
6 Taxable FICA wages paid: $ 38,408 50 times 13.4% equals tax .	5,146 74
7 a Taxable tips reported: $ None times 6.7% equals tax .	None
b Tips deemed to be wages (see instructions): $ None times 6.7% equals tax .	None
8 Total FICA taxes (add lines 6, 7a, and 7b)	5,146 74
9 Adjustment of FICA taxes (see instructions) . . . ▶	None
10 Adjusted total of FICA taxes .	5,146 74
11 Total taxes (add lines 5 and 10) . . . . ▶	13,341 94
12 Advance earned income credit (EIC) payments, if any . ▶	None
13 Net taxes (subtract line 12 from line 11)	13,341 94
14 Total deposits for quarter from your records or from column d . . . . ▶	13,341 94
15 Undeposited taxes due (subtract line 14 from line 13). Enter here and pay to Internal Revenue Service . ▶	None

16 If line 14 is more than line 13, enter overpayment here ▶ $ and check if to be: ☐ Applied to next return, or ☐ Refunded.

Under penalties of perjury, I declare that I have examined this return, including accompanying schedules and statements, and to the best of my knowledge and belief it is true, correct, and complete.

Signature ▶ John F. Orbit Title ▶ Owner Date ▶ April 30,1985

Please file this form with your Internal Revenue Service Center (see instructions on "Where to File"). Form **941** (Rev. 10-82)

Figure 8–5 Employer's Quarterly Federal Tax Return

include only $260 of Ford's pay in the computation of employer's matching FICA payroll tax for that week. Neither Ford nor the company will pay any further FICA tax on Ford's wages in 1985. In January 1986 a new cycle of taxation starts again for all employees.

Reporting and Payment of Payroll Taxes

The report forms and payment schedules for the amounts withheld from employees' earnings and the employer's payroll taxes are explained in *Circular E, Employer's Tax Guide,* published by the Internal Revenue Service. In almost every major city in the United States, a bank is designated as an authorized depository to receive deposits of these funds from employers.

On or before the last day of the month following the close of each quarter, the employer files an **Employer's Quarterly Federal Tax Return** (see Figure 8–5) reporting the federal income taxes withheld and the amount of total FICA tax.[4] Note in Figure 8–5 that tips received are subject to both federal income and FICA taxes. Employees are required by law to report to their employers the amount of tips received. All these amounts must be deposited during the quarter on the prescribed time schedule in an approved federal depository bank.

Annually, the employer must furnish a **Wage and Tax Statement** (form W–2) to each employee (see Figure 8–6). The form shows the amount of

1 Control number	22222	OMB No. 1545–0008	
2 Employer's name, address, and ZIP code Orbit Company 123 Constitution Avenue Boston, MA 02115		3 Employer's identification number SF 56-0868005	4 Employer's State number 04-987654321
		5 Stat. employee ☐ Deceased ☐ Pension plan ☐ Legal rep. ☐ 942 emp. ☐ Subtotal ☐ Correction ☐ Void ☐	
		6	7 Advance EIC payment
8 Employee's social security number 123-45-6789	9 Federal income tax withheld 6,073.60	10 Wages, tips, other compensation 32,318.00	11 FICA tax withheld 2,262.26
12 Employee's name, address, and ZIP code William S. Ford 50 Joy Street Boston, MA 02115		13 FICA wages 32,318.00	14 FICA tips None
		16 Employer's use	

17 State income tax	18 State wages, tips, etc.	19 Name of State
580.00	32,318.00	MA
20 Local income tax	**21 Local wages, tips, etc.**	**22 Name of locality**
None	None	Boston

Form **W-2 Wage and Tax Statement 1982** Copy B To be filed with employee's FEDERAL tax return. This information is being furnished to the Internal Revenue Service. Department of the Treasury Internal Revenue Service

Figure 8–6 Wage and Tax Statement (Form W–2)

[4]The rates used in Figure 8–5 are those in effect at the time the form was applicable.

taxable wages paid the employee during the year, federal income taxes withheld, FICA taxes withheld, and state income taxes withheld (if applicable). The original of each Form W–2 is provided by the employer to the Social Security Administration to provide information about Social Security payments into each person's account (Employers are urged to send magnetic tapes or disks instead of the individual forms when possible). Copies of the form are given to applicable governmental agencies and to the employee to attach to federal, state, and local income tax returns.

Deposits of federal unemployment taxes are required on or before the last day of the month following the close of the calendar quarter if the liability for the current quarter (and prior quarters during the year) is greater than $100. Otherwise, the amount due is sent directly to the IRS with the annual FUTA return on Form 940 due on or before January 31 of the following year.

Accrual of Salaries and Wages

If the end of the payroll period does not coincide with the end of the accounting period, an adjusting entry is made for salaries and wages earned but not paid. The several salary and expense accounts are debited and Accrued Salaries and Wages Payable is credited. The employer's payroll tax expense on the accrued payroll for the partial pay period should be recognized, although there is no legal liability for the tax until the wages are actually paid. The reason for this recognition is that under the accrual basis all expense items applicable to the salaries and wages of the period should be measured and recorded. An employer is liable for payroll taxes in the calendar year in which the payment for services was made. The time of payment rather than the time the services were performed establishes the legal existence of the liability. The accrued liability, however, is the amount that should be matched with the revenues of a period for proper determination of income. For better matching of expenses with revenues, the FASB specifies another accrual of payroll expense—pay for compensated absences.

Liabilities for Compensated Absences

The FASB has concluded that an employee's right to receive compensation for future absences should be accrued during the time the employee renders services leading to that benefit.[5] The board has indicated that such accruals should be made only if the future right to receive pay is attributable to services already rendered, the payment of such compensation is probable, and the amount can be reasonably estimated.[6] While such conditions may not always be present for sick leave, they usually do exist in the case of vacation pay. Such absences for which employees are paid are called **compensated**

[5]*Statement of Financial Accounting Standards No. 43,* "Accounting for Compensated Absences" (Stamford, Conn.: FASB, November 1980), paragraph 1.

[6]Ibid., paragraph 6.

absences. To illustrate, assume that the LeBlanc Company has 50 employees who are paid an average of $500 per week and has a policy of allowing each employee a two-week paid vacation per year. The total cost of the paid vacations (a form of compensated absence) is $50,000 = (50 employees × $500 × 2 weeks). Since this cost is actually earned as employees work, it should be accrued during their 50 working weeks; it will be paid during the time they are on vacation. Further, assume that one-half the employees are in the sales force; the remainder are employed in various administrative departments. The entry to accrue the liability for the week ended February 8, 1985 is:

1985					
Feb.	8	Vacation Pay Expense—Selling		500	
		Vacation Pay Expense—General and Administrative		500	
		Liability for Vacation Pay			1,000
		Accrual of liability for 1/50 of annual vacation pay.			

If 15 employees take a week of vacation during the week ended July 12, the entry to record payment of their compensated absence is:[7]

1985					
Jul.	12	Liability for Vacation Pay		7,500	
		FICA Taxes Payable			525
		Federal Income Tax Withholdings Payable			1,278
		State Income Tax Withholdings Payable			175
		Cash			5,522
		Payment to 15 employees for one week's vacation.			

The liability account balance should be shown as a current liability on the balance sheet. Conceivably, if a large number of employees take paid vacations early in the year—for example, during slack periods of business—the liability account could have a debit balance due to payments made faster than the liability is accrued. Such a debit balance should be shown as a current asset with a caption such as "prepaid vacation pay." A debit balance would be a temporary situation as the account should clear to a zero balance at year end if all employees have taken their two-week vacations.

Similar accruals should be made for sick pay and other forms of compensated absences if the conditions of *FASB Statement No. 43* are met. A primary purpose of such accruals is to adhere more closely to the matching standard. Expenses to be matched with revenues are recorded in the period in which the act that causes the expense occurs—in this case, use of employee ser-

[7]No employee has reached the $36,000 FICA base; income tax amounts are assumed.

vices. A similar situation exists with company costs of pension plans and other post-retirement benefits. These are complex issues and are left for a later course in accounting.

Managerial Control of Payroll

The payroll of a firm is a significant part of total expense, making continuous management control essential. The availability of machines and high-speed electronic equipment has facilitated the processing of payroll data and the establishment of effective controls at a reasonable cost. But the use of an electronic data processing system for the payroll does not lessen the need for built-in self-policing control devices and procedures as part of the payroll system. Computer programs and data processing systems can be manipulated to defraud the firm.

Effective managerial control of payroll requires that:

☐ Management has properly authorized the payroll payment.

☐ Wages paid be correct and have been received by authorized employees; that is, for example, that no fictitious names or names of persons no longer employed have been listed on the payroll.

☐ The numerous reports based on payroll information that are made to governmental agencies, union organizations, and employees be reliable.

☐ Adequate security systems are in effect to prevent unauthorized access to computer programs for the payroll.

Glossary

Compensated absences Absences such as vacations or sick leave for which employees are paid.

Employee's Withholding Allowance Certificate The form (W–4) prepared by each employee showing the number of withholding allowances currently claimed for establishing the amount of federal income taxes to be withheld by the employer from the employee's earnings.

Employer's Quarterly Federal Tax Return The form (941) on which employers must report the amount of federal income taxes and FICA taxes withheld and the dates and amounts deposited on the taxable wages paid during each quarterly period.

Fair Labor Standards Act The federal law (also called the Federal Wage and Hour Law) that fixes minimum hourly and overtime rates for workers in industries engaged directly in the production of goods for interstate commerce.

Federal income tax withholding An amount deducted from gross pay by the employer and remitted to the Internal Revenue Service.

Federal Insurance Contributions Act (FICA) A federal law requiring both employers and employees to contribute equal amounts based on a stated percentage of taxable wages paid; it provides funds to the Social Security program.

Federal Unemployment Tax Act (FUTA) A federal law that levies a tax on the employer at a specified rate up to a limited amount of wages paid; it provides funds to the Social Security program.

FICA tax See *Federal Insurance Contributions Act (FICA).*

FUTA tax See *Federal Unemployment Tax Act (FUTA).*

Gross pay Total wages before any deductions; this amount is the salaries and wages expense.

Net pay Wages after all deductions; this is referred to as take-home pay.

Payroll deductions Amounts withheld from gross pay by the employer; these include federal and state taxes, union dues, and medical insurance.

Social Security program Federal laws that include programs to provide benefits to retired workers, their families, and their survivors, financed by taxes on wages at rates and base levels revised from time to time by Congress.

Taxable wage base The amount of employee earnings that are subject to FICA and FUTA taxes.

Wage and Tax Statement The form (W–2) that each employer must furnish to each employee annually showing the amount of taxable wages paid the employee during the year, the amount of federal and state income taxes withheld, and the amount of FICA taxes withheld.

Wage bracket withholding table A table furnished by the Internal Revenue Service for reference by the employer in determining the amount of federal income taxes to be withheld from employee earnings.

Yearly individual compensation record The individual record of each employee showing his or her earnings, deductions, and net pay.

Questions

Q8–1 What is gross pay? Net pay? Why should total gross pay be debited to expense when it is not all paid to employees?

Q8–2 (a) What are three common payroll taxes levied on an employer? (b) When and in what manner does the employer pay the tax?

Q8–3 (a) What is a state unemployment merit-rating plan? (b) Do you believe that the use of merit-rating plans is justified? Why or why not?

Q8–4 (a) What two types of federal taxes are most employers required to withhold from their employees' wages? (b) When do taxes withheld become liabilities to the employer? (c) In what manner is the employer required to pay the amounts withheld to the responsible federal agency?

Q8–5 What are some requirements of effective internal control of payroll?

Q8–6 What deductions are required by law? What are some other deductions that may be withheld by the employer?

Q8–7 What portion of an employee's earnings are subject to FICA taxes during a payroll period when total earnings for the year exceed the taxable wage base? Illustrate.

Q8–8 What is the purpose of the Fair Labor Standards Act?

Q8–9 What is the purpose and function of the payroll register? The individual earnings record?

Q8–10 Explain the nature and classification of the accounts debited and the accounts credited in a journal entry to record (a) the payroll and (b) the employer's payroll taxes.

Q8–11 Why should an employer begin to recognize the expense of vacation pay before the vacations are taken? Does such recognition provide a cash fund to pay for vacations?

Note: Unless indicated otherwise, the following rates and amounts are to be used in solving the payroll exercises and problems in this chapter.

a. *FICA tax:* 7 percent each on employer and employee, applicable to the first $36,000 paid to an employee during a calendar year.

b. *Federal unemployment compensation tax:* A maximum of 5 percent on the first $10,000 paid to each covered employee during each calendar year, with 4 percent payable to the state and 1 percent to the federal government.

Exercises

E8–1
Computing gross pay

Joan McDonald is paid at the rate of $12.00 per hour. During the week ended March 14, 1985, she worked 46 hours because of a need to catch up on filling orders. Compute her gross pay for the week.

E8–2
Using income tax withholding table

Using Figure 8–2, compute the federal income taxes withheld from each of the following Porter Company employees' earnings for the week ended December 6, 1985:

Employee	Gross Earnings	No. of Withholding Allowances	Year-to-Date Earnings to November 29, 1985
Jay Learned	$725	4	$ 9,800
Oscar LeHand	743	1	35,500
Betty Wolfe	792	5	38,000

E8–3
Computing FICA tax withheld

Refer to E8–2. What amount of FICA tax will the employer withhold from each employee's earnings for the week ended December 6, 1985?

E8–4
Computing FICA tax expense

Refer to E8–2. Compute the employer's FICA tax expense (a) for the week and (b) for the year through December 6, 1985.

E8–5
Computing FUTA tax expense

Refer to E8–2. Compute the employer's FUTA tax expense (a) for the week ended December 6, 1985 and (b) for the year ended December 31, 1985.

E8–6
Recording a payroll, payment, and employer's tax expense

The payroll records of the Toni Company for the week ended February 8, 1985, showed the following:

Total wages earned		$5,500
Deductions:		
FICA tax	$385	
Federal income tax	825	
United Fund	100	1,310
Net amount paid		$4,190

Record in general journal form: (a) total payroll, (b) payment of the payroll, (c) employer's payroll tax expense. No employee has earned $10,000 in the year to date.

E8–7
Computing payroll tax expense

The following payroll data for the year 1985 were taken from the records of the Geneva Company:

Total wages expense	$950,000
Amount of employee wages in excess of $10,000	650,000
Amount of employee wages in excess of $36,000	200,000

Calculate the employer's payroll tax expense for the year.

E8–8 *Total cost of an employee*

The York Company had 15 employees who worked during an entire calendar year. One of them, Patricia Collins, earned $37,000. What was the total expenditure for her services for the year?

E8–9 *FICA and FUTA taxes when base wage limit is reached*

Payroll data for three selected employees of Tuskegee Corporation are as follows:

Employee	Earnings through October 18, 1985	Earnings for Week of October 25, 1985
George Abraham	$ 9,645.00	$760.00
Mary Jackson	35,810.50	800.00
Earnest Walters	37,215.75	820.00

Compute for this payroll (1) FICA deductions for each employee and (2) total employer's payroll tax expense.

E8–10 *Recognizing expense and payment of vacation pay*

Auburn Corporation has 100 employees who earn an average of $700 per week and receive a two-week paid vacation each year. Expenses of the paid vacations are recognized evenly over the first 50 weeks of the year. Prepare general journal entries for the following:

a. Recording of vacation pay expense in the week ended January 11, 1985.
b. Recording of the payment of vacation pay on January 11 to six employees who went on a cruise to Bermuda during the second week in January. Federal and state taxes withheld were $947.40 and $127.00 respectively.

E8–11 *Internal control over payroll and other uses of data*

As a product of its payroll system, the Germaine Company receives a weekly report of year-to-date hours worked and year-to-date total labor cost subdivided by department. Describe some possible uses of this report (including other reports to be used at the same time) (a) by the plant superintendent, (b) by the supervisors of production departments, and (c) by the accounting department.

A Problems

P8–1A *Computing gross and net pay with deductions given*

Livingston Company has four employees. Payroll data for the week ended April 26, 1985 are as follows:

	Hours	Hourly	Deductions		
Employee	Worked	Rate	Income Tax	FICA	Other
Sue Modesto	44	$14.00	$154.90	$45.08	$27.18
Al Schwab	40	13.50	132.20	37.80	16.10
Julie Sullivan	42	13.50	139.80	40.64	20.15
Mike Williams	45	14.00	162.30	46.55	21.75

Required: Compute gross and net pay for each employee and for the Livingston Company.

P8–2A *Completing a payroll register and recording the payroll*

The following information is available for the Rho Company for the week ended December 6, 1985:

Employee	Pay Rates	Hours Worked	YTD Earnings through Nov. 29	No. of Allowances	Union Dues	Med. Ins.	Pen. Fund	State Income Taxes
Jay Elgar	$15/hr.	43	$29,720	2	$7	$15	$20	$ 8
Brenda Fields	740/wk.	40	35,520	1	0	20	30	12
Gail Klaus	15/hr.	40	10,200	2	5	10	25	9
Eugene Little	16/hr.	44	36,220	4	8	15	30	10
Boris Sisk	15/hr.	42	28,600	3	8	15	28	9

Time-and-a-half is paid for overtime. All employees are married. Fields is the manager; all others are in the sales force.

Required:

1. Prepare the payroll register.
2. Record the payroll in a general journal entry.

P8–3A *Preparing a payroll register and entries to record the payroll, its payment, and employer taxes*

The following information is available for the Norfolk Office of National Company for the week ended June 21, 1985:

Employee	Gross Pay	YTD Earnings through June 14	No. of Allowances	Health Plan Deduction
Joyce Breeze	$750	$18,000	2	$32.60
Robert Hill	620	7,800	3	19.20
Marie Ray	625	9,650	1	18.60

All employees are in the sales force and each is married. Joyce Breeze has worked at a second job in 1985 and has earned $14,200 from that employer in the year to date. There are no state income taxes.

Required:

1. Complete a payroll register for the week ended June 21, 1985.
2. Prepare a general journal entry to record the payroll.
3. Prepare a general journal entry to record payment of the payroll.
4. Prepare a general journal entry to record the employer's payroll taxes.

P8–4A *Computing payroll and taxes at various wage bases*

Valencia Company has five employees for whom the following data are available for the week ended October 25, 1985:

Employee	Gross Pay	YTD Earnings through October 18	Income Tax Federal	Income Tax State
Charles Addison	$800	$36,000	$187.80	$88.40
Kathy Durado	750	9,700	162.20	55.10
Sue Georgia	730	10,000	154.80	52.40
Booker Hargrove	840	35,820	188.40	76.00
Julie Seibert	740	8,600	158.50	51.70

Required:

1. Prepare a general journal entry to record the payroll (use a single expense account to record employee pay).

2. Prepare a general journal entry to record payment of the payroll.

3. Prepare a general journal entry to record the employer's payroll taxes.

P8–5A
Liability for vacation pay

Gallaudet Corporation has 1,000 employees who earn an average of $650 per week. Each employee is entitled to two weeks of paid vacation per year; the company recognizes the expense during the first 50 weeks of the year.

Required:

1. A general journal entry to recognize the vacation pay expense for the week ended January 11, 1985.

2. A general journal entry to record the payment of vacation pay on January 18, 1985 to 25 employees who took a two-week cruise to Nassau. Federal and state income taxes withheld were $3,175.00 and $396.50, respectively.

3. By the end of March, the liability account for vacation pay had a debit balance. Is this an error? Explain.

P8–6A
Thought-provoking problem: remittance of taxes

In January 1985, the Nottingham Corporation expects to have the following tax experience:

	FICA		
Week Ending	**Employee Deductions**	**Employer Tax**	**Federal Income Tax Withheld**
Jan. 4	$400	$400	$2,000
11	380	380	1,900
18	450	450	2,000
25	425	425	1,800

Interest rates are relatively high, and the treasurer wants to retain cash until the last possible day. Cash held is temporarily invested at 18 percent per year. Assume the penalty for late remittance of taxes is 1½ percent of any undeposited taxes in excess of $3,000 that are on hand at the end of any month. She has proposed that the January taxes be held until January 31 and remitted in a single lump sum along with the penalty.

Required: Compare the interest earnings on undeposited tax money in January with the penalties and make an appropriate recommendation to the treasurer.

B Problems

P8–1B
Computing gross and net pay with deductions given

Pikes Peak Company has four employees. Payroll data for the week ended July 12, 1985 are as follows:

			Deductions		
Employee	**Hours Worked**	**Hourly Rate**	**Income Tax**	**FICA**	**Other**
Marge Burnett	40	$15.00	$140.10	$42.00	$26.70
Bill Gravelli	46	14.00	170.12	48.02	18.65
Lisa Holder	44	14.50	162.30	46.69	22.40
Millis Waller	42	14.50	147.50	43.65	20.18

Required: Compute gross and net pay for each employee and for Pikes Peak Company.

P8–2B *Completing a payroll register and recording the payroll*

The following information is available for the Jacoby Company for the week ended December 13, 1985:

Employee	Pay Rates	Hours Worked	YTD Earnings through Dec. 6	No. of Allow-ances	Union Dues	Med. Ins.	Pen. Fund	State Income Taxes
A. Long	$13.50/hr.	44	$25,380	2	$10	$20	$25	$10
L. Salvo	750/wk.	40	35,950	4	0	15	30	12
J. Romero	14.50/hr.	40	29,600	3	8	15	28	9
P. Glennon	15.50/hr.	42	29,950	1	7	10	30	14
T. Plummer	16.50/hr.	43	36,400	2	8	15	26	12

Time-and-a-half is paid for overtime. All employees are married. Salvo is the manager; all others are in the sales force.

Required:

1. Prepare the payroll register.

2. Record the payroll in a general journal entry.

P8–3B *Preparing a payroll register and entries to record the payroll, its payment, and employer taxes*

The following information is available for Radio Station WSOE for the week ended October 25, 1985:

Employee	Gross Pay	YTD Earnings through Oct. 18	No. of Allowances	Health Plan Deductions
Marie Bailey	$650	$27,300	2	$28.70
Rick Gorke	620	9,750	1	22.60
Bruce Ring	640	9,360	2	24.70

Marie Bailey is the station manager. She also works for another company, where she has earned $9,250 in the year to date. Gorke is in programming and Ring in sales; they have earned $20,000 and $16,250, respectively, at another company before coming to work at WSOE. There are no state income taxes.

Required:

1. Complete a payroll register for the week ended October 25, 1985.

2. Prepare a general journal entry to record the payroll.

3. Prepare a general journal entry to record payment of the payroll.

4. Prepare a general journal entry to record the employer's payroll taxes.

P8–4B
Computing payroll and taxes at various wage bases

Averett Company has five employees for whom the following data are available for the week ended November 15, 1985:

Employee	Gross Pay	YTD Earnings through Nov. 8	Income Tax Federal	Income Tax State
Jan Avery	$820	$36,800	$198.60	$82.00
Jacob Bernstein	750	9,250	162.20	75.00
Bea Feinberg	775	10,000	183.80	82.50
Lisa Ray	740	9,680	165.60	68.70
Justin Seibert	875	39,375	206.55	95.10

Required:

1. Prepare a general journal entry to record the payroll (use a single expense account for employee pay).

2. Prepare a general journal entry to record the payment of the payroll.

3. Prepare a general journal entry to record the employer's payroll taxes.

P8–5B
Liability for vacation pay

Grand View Corporation has 600 employees who earn an average of $750 per week. Each employee is entitled to two weeks of paid vacation per year; the company recognizes the expense during the first 50 weeks of the year.

Required:

1. A general journal entry to recognize the vacation pay expense for the week ended January 18, 1985.

2. A general journal entry to recognize payment of vacation pay on January 25, 1985, to 20 employees who took a two-week tour of the west coast. Federal and state income taxes withheld were $3,250.60 and $380.65, respectively.

3. By the end of March, the liability account for vacation pay had a debit balance. Is this an error? Explain.

P8–6B
Thought-provoking problem: total cost of an employee

Engleman Company employed Agnes Price for the entire year of 1985 at an hourly rate of $16.00. Price worked 2,000 regular hours and 300 overtime hours during the year. Engleman Company has an employee group health plan toward which it contributes $21.50 per month for each employee and a supplemental retirement plan toward which it contributes 8 percent of total employee earnings. The supervisor of Price's department is shocked to find that the accountant has allocated more than $45,000 in cost to his department for Ms. Price's services. He argues that with 2,300 hours worked, Price has earned less than $40,000 even with overtime premium and demands a correction of the cost allocation.

Required: Show by computations the exact total cost of Agnes Price's services to Engleman Company in 1985.

9 Internal Control of Cash: The Voucher System

Introduction

Cash includes any item that a bank customarily accepts for deposit—coins, currency, savings accounts, bank drafts, cashier's checks, money orders, bank credit card sales invoices, traveler's checks, and foreign and domestic checking account balances. Effective management and control of cash are very important to a firm because cash represents instantly available purchasing power and nearly every transaction ultimately involves the exchange of cash. In its 1981 *Annual Report,* General Motors Corporation indicated that the interest cost of one source of cash—borrowing—had increased in total from $368.4 million in 1979 to $995.2 million in 1981. Other corporations are reporting similar experiences to such a degree that cash management is of primary importance to all institutions today. Good cash management requires (1) that an adequate cash balance be maintained at all times, and (2) that sufficient safeguards be established to prevent theft or misappropriation.

This chapter examines internal control concepts, petty cash fund operation, the use of a checking account, and monthly bank reconciliation procedures. It then describes a system of internal control—the voucher system. The design and use of the voucher, the voucher register, and the check register to control cash payments are discussed. Although these records are somewhat mechanical, the aspect of a voucher system as an aid to the internal control of cash payments is stressed.

Learning Goals

To know the concepts of internal control of cash.

To record entries using an imprest petty cash system.

To read and interpret monthly bank statements and to prepare a bank reconciliation.

To make the journal entries required after the bank reconciliation.

To understand the use of vouchers to achieve internal control of disbursements.

To record transactions in the voucher register and the check register.

To know whether to post individual transaction entries or column totals from the voucher register to ledger accounts.

To describe the relationship between the voucher files and the voucher register.

Control of Cash

Internal Control

One of the primary functions of management is to protect the assets of a business against avoidable loss. It is important to organize the supervision of the accounting records in a way that will (1) control the receipt of cash, (2) minimize or prevent the unauthorized payment of cash, and (3) eliminate errors.

Employees must be carefully selected and trained and their duties, responsibilities, and authority clearly defined. Adequate organization also requires separation of duties, so that no one person is in complete charge of any business transaction. An error—whether intentional or not—is more likely to be discovered if a cash transaction is handled by two or more persons. It is customary business practice, for example, for one person to make the sale and prepare a sales slip and for another to receive the cash or record the charge to the customer's account. One person may prepare the payroll and another the payroll checks. One employee may prepare a check for payment to a creditor, another employee or an officer may sign the check, and a third employee may post the debit to the creditor's account.

Adequate organization also provides for periodic inspections to see how well the accounting work is being done. The reliability of the financial statements is directly related to the adequacy of the system of self-policing referred to as *internal control.* Consequently, the independent auditor whose task is to render an opinion on the fairness of the statements must first evaluate the adequacy of the internal control system. Based on this evaluation, the auditor determines the nature and extent of the audit procedures. If internal control is judged to be strong, the auditor may follow procedures requiring fewer tests or less detailed examination than if internal control is weak. It is common practice for annual reports to have a *Report of Management* statement that accompanies the auditor's opinion statement. In it, management accepts full responsibility for the financial statements and states that it has an adequate internal control system.

Cash Control

Cash is naturally vulnerable to theft or misuse. If it is handled and controlled properly, both the employer and the employee benefit—the employer safeguards the asset and the employee avoids suspicion of inaccuracy or dishonesty. Safeguards must be designed to prevent the following:

- ☐ Theft of cash receipts covered by failure to record the transaction in the cash receipts journal. For example, scrap and waste material may be sold by an employee for cash and not reported.
- ☐ Delay in recording the receipt of cash (the cash being withheld during the interval) or recording false entries. For example, cash may be pocketed on receipt of a payment from a customer and his or her accounts receivable subsidiary ledger account credited. The general ledger debit, however, may be made to an account such as Sales Returns and Allowances.
- ☐ The recording of false debits to expense accounts or other accounts to cover fraudulent cash withdrawals. For example, a branch supervisor may carry a terminated employee's name on the payroll for several additional pay periods, forging the endorsement of the former employee on payroll checks that continue to be issued.
- ☐ Theft of cash by computer. For example, cash may be transferred to an unauthorized account by changing the computer program.

Certain basic controls must be instituted to prevent the misuse of funds. Individual responsibility for each step in the flow of cash must be clearly established. On receipt, all checks should be endorsed and rubber-stamped *For deposit only* to prevent their misuse. Total cash receipts should be deposited intact daily; payments should be made by company check and not out of cash receipts. Automated accounting control devices should be used wherever possible.

The protection of cash against losses through fraud, error, and carelessness requires certain fundamental steps, including:

- ☐ Clear separation of duties and responsibilities.
- ☐ Provision of the necessary facilities, such as cash registers.
- ☐ Definite written instructions that control authorization for payment of cash.
- ☐ Organization of the flow and recording of documents so that, whenever possible, the work of one employee is subject to automatic verification by another. The handling of cash should be separated from the record keeping, so that no one person both receives or disburses cash and also records it in the cash journals.
- ☐ Periodic testing to see if internal controls are operating effectively. For example, at unannounced times, recorded cash receipts should be compared with cash on hand and deposits that have been made.
- ☐ Establishing controls over access to computers and computer programs.

Petty Cash

For adequate internal control, total cash receipts should be *deposited intact daily* and disbursements normally should be made by check. There are occasions, however, when payment by check is impractical, such as for postage, small contributions, express charges, taxi fares, and minor supplies. A special **petty cash fund** should be set up for these purposes. The fund is placed in

PETTY CASH VOUCHER

[X] PAY IN CASH NO. 324

All expenditures paid in cash must be explained and receipted for on this voucher.

VERIFIED

CASHIER January 14 19 85

PAY Jim Brady

Thirty-five and 75/100 -------------------- DOLLARS

CHARGE Postage Expense ACCOUNT NO. 603

DESCRIPTION Special Mailings

APPROVED FOR PAYMENT RECEIVED PAYMENT

Jim Brady

Figure 9–1
Petty Cash Voucher

custody of one person. Each payment should be supported by a receipt signed by the person receiving the cash (a **petty cash voucher**) that shows the purpose of the expenditure, the date, and the amount (see Figure 9–1).

To establish the petty cash fund, a check for the amount to be placed in the fund is drawn to the order of the fund custodian and cashed. The journal entry to record the establishment of a petty cash fund of $500 by the High Company is:

1985					
Aug.	3	Petty Cash		500	
		Cash			500
		Established petty cash fund.			

Safekeeping of the money and the signed vouchers is the responsibility of the custodian, who should be provided with a secure petty cash box or cash register.

When the cash in the fund approaches a stated minimum, or at the end of each accounting period, the fund is replenished; the signed petty cash vouchers serve as evidence of the disbursements. Assume that on August 31, 1985, the High Company petty cash fund consisted of cash and signed receipts for expenditures as shown:

Cash	$ 47.00
Postage stamps and parcel post	112.00
Telegrams and outside telephone calls	54.00
Supplies for exhibition booth at regional sales meeting	114.50
Blank form pads	12.75
Truck delivery expenses on purchases	158.25
Total	$498.50
Shortage	1.50
Total to be accounted for	$500.00

The custodian is issued a check for $453 = ($500 − $47) to replenish the fund to its original cash balance of $500. The entry to record this check is:

1985					
Aug.	31	Postage Expense		112.00	
		Telephone and Telegraph Expense		54.00	
		Sales Promotion Expense		114.50	
		Office Supplies Expense		12.75	
		Transportation In		158.25	
		Cash Over and Short[a]		1.50	
		Cash			453.00
		Replenished petty cash fund.			

[a]See next section.

The Petty Cash account in the general ledger remains at its original balance of $500. The method described here is called the **imprest petty cash system** because a fixed amount of money has been advanced in trust to a custodian. There are no further debits or credits to Petty Cash unless the amount of the fund itself is either increased or decreased. Thus, the $500 balance is imprest upon the account. The entry to increase the amount of the fund is a debit to Petty Cash and a credit to Cash. The fund should be replenished at the end of each accounting period, even when it is above its stated minimum cash balance, to record all the expenses incurred during the period and to bring the amount of currency and coins on hand in the fund up to the balance of the Petty Cash account in the general ledger. Unannounced inspections should be held at intervals to determine that the amount of cash plus receipted vouchers is equal to the fund balance.

Cash Over and Short

In the foregoing illustration, a cash shortage of $1.50 was found when the petty cash fund was replenished. It is also true that the daily count of cash in the cash registers may differ from the cash register readings. If the records do not disclose a clerical error, it may be assumed that the overage or shortage was caused by an error in making change. The discrepancy should be entered in the books as a debit or a credit to the Cash Over and Short account. To illustrate, assume that a cash register tape shows cash sales for the day of $1,000, but the count shows the cash on hand to be $1,003.13. The journal entry to record the cash sales based on the cash register tape total, the cash based on the actual count, and the cash overage is:

1985					
Nov.	30	Cash		1,003.13	
		Sales			1,000.00
		Cash Over and Short			3.13
		To record cash sales and cash overage.			

If the cash count showed $996.87, the Cash Over and Short account would be debited instead of credited.

Cash over and short is classified on the income statement as general and administrative expense if a debit or other revenue if a credit. Overages and shortages considered unreasonable should be investigated.

The Bank Statement

Most transactions ultimately involve the receipt or payment of cash, often in the form of a **check**—a written order directing a bank to pay a specified amount of money to the order of a payee (see Figure 9–2). When opening an account with a bank, the person or persons who will sign checks must fill out signature card forms (see Figure 9–3 for a typical signature card form). New cards must be completed whenever there is a change in authority to sign checks. Figure 9–4 is a typical form used for listing the cash and checks that make up a deposit to be credited to the depositor's account.

A carbon copy of the check is one way of communicating the payment information to the accounting department for recording. Banks customarily send depositors a monthly statement together with the cancelled checks and

No. ________ $ ________

________ 19 ____

To ________

For ________

	DOLLARS	CENTS
Bal. Bro't. For'd.		
Am't. Deposited		
" " "		
" " "		
Total		
Am't. This Check		
Bal. Car'd. For'd.		

FOR PRACTICE ONLY
NOT NEGOTIABLE

NO. ________

00-000
000

________ 19 ____

PAY TO THE ORDER OF ________ $ ________

________ DOLLARS

Wachovia
Wachovia Bank & Trust Company, N.A.

FOR ________

⑆0000⑈0000⑆ 1239 876543⑈

NOT NEGOTIABLE

Source: Courtesy Wachovia Bank and Trust Company, N.A.

Figure 9–2 **Check and Check Stub**

notices of bank charges and credits. The bank statement shows the activities for the month; it should list, at a minimum:

- ☐ Beginning balance.
- ☐ Deposits received.
- ☐ Checks paid.
- ☐ Other charges and credits to the account.
- ☐ Ending balance.

Account(s) Number 1239-876-543 | ☒ Checking ☐ Passbook Savings ☐ Statement Savings

☐ Joint with right of survivorship ☐ Joint without right of survivorship ☒ Individual or other

Account(s) to be set up in the following name(s):

Customer No. 1 Clearwater Company

Customer No. 2 None

Sign John C. Clearwater

Sign None

Initials | Date Jan. 2, 1981 | Branch North

Each account checked above is accepted by Wachovia Bank & Trust Company, N.A., also subject to the provisions stated on the reverse side of this card. Above are the duly authorized signatures which the Bank will recognize in the payment of funds or the transaction of other business.

222 Rev. 12-78

Source: Courtesy Wachovia Bank and Trust Company, N.A.

Figure 9–3
Signature Card

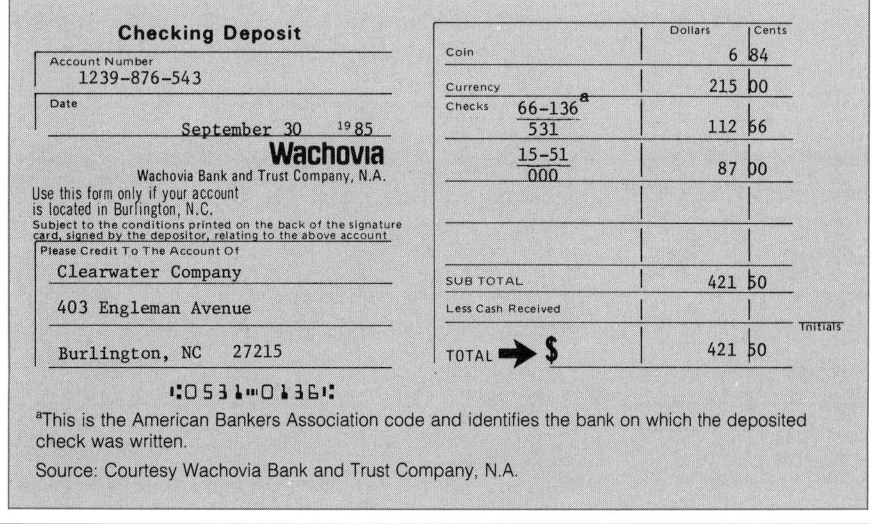

Checking Deposit

Account Number 1239-876-543

Date September 30 19 85

Wachovia
Wachovia Bank and Trust Company, N.A.

Use this form only if your account is located in Burlington, N.C.

Subject to the conditions printed on the back of the signature card, signed by the depositor, relating to the above account

Please Credit To The Account Of
Clearwater Company
403 Engleman Avenue
Burlington, NC 27215

		Dollars	Cents
Coin		6	84
Currency		215	00
Checks	66-136[a] / 531	112	66
	15-51 / 000	87	00
SUB TOTAL		421	50
Less Cash Received			
TOTAL ➡ $		421	50

Initials

⑆0531⑉0136⑆

[a]This is the American Bankers Association code and identifies the bank on which the deposited check was written.

Source: Courtesy Wachovia Bank and Trust Company, N.A.

Figure 9–4
Deposit Ticket

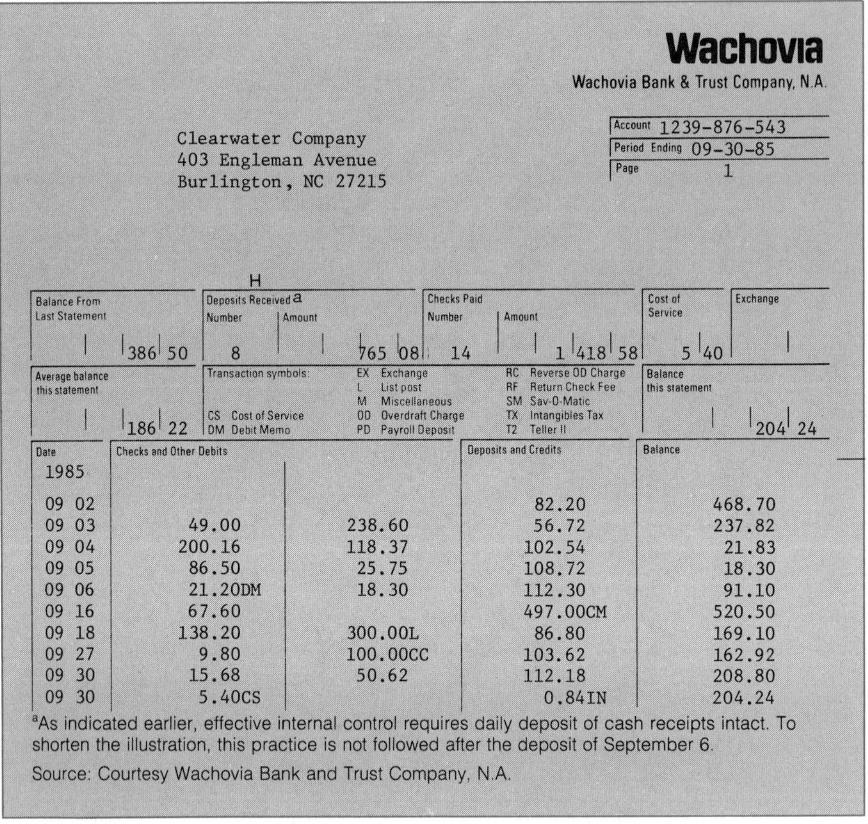

Wachovia
Wachovia Bank & Trust Company, N.A.

Clearwater Company
403 Engleman Avenue
Burlington, NC 27215

Account 1239-876-543
Period Ending 09-30-85
Page 1

Balance From Last Statement	Deposits Received[a] Number	Deposits Received Amount	Checks Paid Number	Checks Paid Amount	Cost of Service	Exchange
386.50	8	765.08	14	1,418.58	5.40	

Average balance this statement: 186.22

Transaction symbols: CS Cost of Service; DM Debit Memo; EX Exchange; L List post; M Miscellaneous; OD Overdraft Charge; PD Payroll Deposit; RC Reverse OD Charge; RF Return Check Fee; SM Sav-O-Matic; TX Intangibles Tax; T2 Teller II

Balance this statement: 204.24

Date 1985	Checks and Other Debits		Deposits and Credits	Balance
09 02			82.20	468.70
09 03	49.00	238.60	56.72	237.82
09 04	200.16	118.37	102.54	21.83
09 05	86.50	25.75	108.72	18.30
09 06	21.20DM	18.30	112.30	91.10
09 16	67.60		497.00CM	520.50
09 18	138.20	300.00L	86.80	169.10
09 27	9.80	100.00CC	103.62	162.92
09 30	15.68	50.62	112.18	208.80
09 30	5.40CS		0.84IN	204.24

[a]As indicated earlier, effective internal control requires daily deposit of cash receipts intact. To shorten the illustration, this practice is not followed after the deposit of September 6.

Source: Courtesy Wachovia Bank and Trust Company, N.A.

Figure 9–5
Bank Statement

The September 1985 bank statement of Clearwater Company is shown in Figure 9–5. The letter codes in its upper section identify entries on the statement other than checks paid by the bank and deposits credited. Certain letter codes commonly used by banks are explained below.[1]

(CS) Cost of Service (Service Charge) Unless depositors keep a specified minimum balance in the bank, a *service charge* is imposed by the bank for its costs of handling the account.

(DM) Debit Memo This memo is a deduction from the depositor's account. Typical is a customer's check previously deposited but uncollectible (NSF) reported in a debit memo. It is a debit memo to the bank because the bank's liability to the depositor for the amount on deposit is reduced. From

[1]The item **(EX) Exchange** is used only in international transactions.

the depositor's point of view, it is a reduction in the bank balance and a credit—*not* a debit—to the Cash account in the ledger.

(CM) Credit Memo This memo is a credit, usually shown in the Deposits column, for items collected; for example, the collection of a note receivable left at the bank by a depositor. It is a credit memo to the bank because the bank's liability to the depositor is increased. From the depositor point of view, it is an increase in the bank balance and a debit—*not* a credit—to the Cash account in the ledger.

(CC) Certified Check When the depositor requests a certified check, the bank immediately deducts the amount of the check from the depositor's balance. This procedure assures the payee that the check will be paid upon presentation.

(IN) Interest Some banks pay interest based on daily balances in checking accounts.

(LS or L) List A list is a tape enclosed with the bank statement listing two or more amounts to support the coded entry on the bank statement.

(OD) Overdraft Charge An overdraft is the amount by which withdrawals exceed the depositor's available balance. The overdraft, if permitted, is usually entered as a negative amount in the Balance column. A charge is made for this service because the overdraft is a temporary loan made by the bank.

(PD) Payroll Deposit A payroll deposit is a type of electronic fund credit, handled by a computerized system for transferring funds between depositors' accounts without using checks or cash. The accounts and amounts are charged or credited from entries on magnetic tapes furnished by the employer.

(RF) Return Check Fee If the amount of a check exceeds a bank balance without prior arrangements for an overdraft, the bank will return the check to the person who included it in a deposit. Such returned checks are accompanied by a debit memo citing **"not sufficient funds" (NSF)** as the reason for failure to accept it. A return check fee is charged against the writer of the check.

(SM) Sav-O-Matic Many banks feature a plan to help customers build up savings, here called "Sav-O-Matic." With customer authorization, a specified amount is transferred at regular intervals from the checking to the savings account.

(TX) Intangibles Tax Some states levy a property tax against bank account balances. In some cases, it is collected for the state by the bank with a charge against the customer's account.

(T2) Teller II Many banks have automatic banking machines that allow a customer to withdraw, deposit, or transfer funds 24 hours a day. Teller II is the name used by Wachovia Bank and Trust Company for its system.

Reconciliation Procedure

The use of a business checking account is essential to control of cash. Total receipts should be deposited intact daily and all payments should be made by check, as emphasized earlier. For each entry in the depositor's books, there should be a counterpart in the bank's books. Each total daily debit to Cash in the depositor's books should be matched by a credit entry to the depositor's account in the bank's books. All credit entries to Cash in the depositor's books should be matched by debit entries at the bank to the depositor's account. For instance, daily cash received from customers is recorded in the company's books by debiting Cash and crediting Accounts Receivable or Sales; the bank, on receiving the daily deposit, increases the depositor's account. The company records a check written in payment to a creditor by debiting Accounts Payable and crediting Cash; the bank decreases the depositor's account when the check arrives at the bank.

The records of the depositor and of the bank normally will not agree at the end of the month. Items will appear on one record but not on the other because of the time lag in recording deposits and checks, special charges and credits of which the depositor is unaware, or errors or irregularities. The two balances must be reconciled and the true or **adjusted cash balance** determined. The **bank reconciliation** is a statement that shows the items that account for the difference between the Cash account balance and the bank statement balance. One of its primary purposes is to strengthen internal control over cash. It is prepared as follows:

1. Deposits shown on the bank statement are compared with daily entries in the cash receipts journal. Deposits made too late in the month to be credited by the bank on the current statement are referred to as **deposits in transit.** The bank reconciliation for the previous month should be inspected for any deposits in transit at the end of that period; they should appear as the early deposits of the current period. Any such items not on the statement should be investigated.

2. Checks paid and returned by the bank (cancelled checks) should be arranged in numerical order and compared with the entries in the cash payments journal. Checks that have not yet been presented by the payees to the bank for payment are called **outstanding checks.** The previous bank reconciliation should be inspected to see that outstanding checks from that reconciliation have now cleared through the bank on this statement.

3. Special debits and credits made by the bank—usually reported in debit or credit memos—are compared with the depositor's books to see if they have already been recorded.

4. Any errors in the bank's or the depositor's records that become apparent during completion of the prior steps are listed. The chance of bank errors is small unless there is an error in coding a document.

A format for bank reconciliation is given in Figure 9–6. Errors and adjustments in the *Per Books* section require entries in the general journal or special cash journals to correct the books. Adjustments in the *Per Bank* section do not require entries in the depositor's books, but action may be necessary to see that they are recorded in the bank's books.

NAME
Bank Reconciliation
Date

Per Books			Per Bank		
Cash balance per ledger, date		$XXX	Cash balance per bank statement, date .		$XXX
Add:			Add:		
(1) Any proper increases in cash already recorded by the bank that have not been recorded as yet by the firm *Example:* Collection of note by bank	$XX		(1) Any proper increases in cash already recorded by the firm that have not been recorded as yet by the bank *Example:* Deposits in transit . . .	$XX	
(2) Any error in the firm's books that failed to reveal a proper increase in cash or that improperly decreased cash *Example:* Check from customer for $90 entered as $70	XX	XX	(2) Any error by the bank that failed to reveal a proper increase in cash or that improperly decreased cash *Example:* Another depositor's check incorrectly charged to this depositor's account . .	XX	XX
Subtotal		$XXX	Subtotal		$XXX
Deduct:			Deduct:		
(1) Any proper decreases in cash already recorded by the bank that have not been recorded as yet by the firm *Example:* Bank service charges	$XX		(1) Any proper decreases in cash already recorded by the firm that have not been recorded as yet by the bank *Example:* Outstanding checks .	$XX	
(2) Any error in the firm's books that failed to reveal a proper decrease in cash or that improperly increased cash *Example:* Check issued in payment to a creditor for $462 entered as $426	XX	XX	(2) Any error by the bank that failed to reveal a proper decrease in cash or that improperly increased cash *Example:* Firm's deposit of $679 entered by bank as $697	XX	XX
Adjusted cash balance, date		$XXX	Adjusted cash balance, date		$XXX

Figure 9–6 **Format for a Bank Reconciliation**

Preparation of a bank reconciliation is illustrated here using the Clearwater Company's bank statement for September, shown in Figure 9–5. In the Clearwater Company's August 1985 bank reconciliation, a deposit of $82.20 made on August 30 was listed as a *deposit in transit.* Outstanding checks on August 31 were:

Check No.	Amount	Check No.	Amount
637	$ 49.00	641	$ 86.50
638	238.60	642	25.75
639	15.00	643	5.00
640	201.06	644	118.37

The Cash account of Clearwater Company showed activity in September as follows:

Deposits[a]		Checks	
Date	Amount	Check No.	Amount
Sep. 2	$ 56.72	645	$ 18.30
3	102.54	646	110.00
4	108.72	647	10.00
5	112.30	648	180.00
17	86.80	649	138.20
26	103.62	650	67.60
27	112.18	651	100.00
30	421.50	652	30.20
		653	9.80
		654	21.50
		655	15.68
		656	50.62
		657	9.85
		658	3.72
		659	13.80
		660	12.95

[a]As indicated earlier, effective internal control requires daily deposit of cash receipts intact. To shorten the illustration, this practice is not followed after the deposit of September 5 (recorded September 6 on the bank statement).

The balance in the Cash account on September 30, 1985, is $41.58. The balance for September 30 shown on the bank statement (Figure 9–5) is $204.24. The following are noted by Clearwater's accountant in studying the bank statement:

1. The debit memorandum dated September 6 for $21.20 represented a customer's check included in an earlier deposit and returned marked "NSF." This check has not yet been charged back to the customer's account on Clearwater's books.

2. The credit memorandum for $497.00 dated September 16 represented a $500.00 credit and a $3.00 collection fee for a note receivable collected by the bank for Clearwater. There was no interest on the face value of this note.

3. The $300.00 debit marked L (List) on September 18 was a list that recorded the charging of check nos. 646, 647, and 648. This information is needed to determine the checks that are outstanding.

4. The $100.00 debit marked CC (Certified Check) on September 27 was for check no. 651 certified for Clearwater Company on that date. It was among the checks returned as paid by the bank; even if it were not, it would *not* be included as an outstanding check on September 30 because it was deducted from Clearwater's balance on the date of certification—not on the date it was paid by the bank.

Noting these facts, Clearwater's accountant then verifies that the deposit in transit on August 31 is credited on the September bank statement. The next task is to trace the August 31 outstanding checks and checks written in September to the bank statement. All that are not debited thereon are listed as outstanding checks. Then a bank reconciliation, as shown in Figure 9–7, is prepared.

CLEARWATER COMPANY
Bank Reconciliation
September 30, 1985

Cash balance per ledger, September 30				$ 41.58
Add: Customer note collected by bank	[1]	$500.00		
Less: Collection charge		3.00	$497.00	
Interest earned on account	[2]		0.84	
Error in check no. 640	[3]		0.90	498.74
Subtotal				$540.32
Deduct: Customer's NSF check	[4]		$ 21.20	
Bank service charge	[5]		5.40	26.60
Adjusted cash balance, September 30				$513.72

Cash balance per bank statement, September 30			$204.24
Add: Deposit in transit	[6]		421.50
Subtotal			$625.74
Deduct: Outstanding checks:[a]	[7]		
No. 639		$15.00	
643		5.00	
652		30.20	
654		21.50	
657		9.85	
658		3.72	
659		13.80	
660		12.95	112.02
Adjusted cash balance, September 30			$513.72

[a]A lengthy list of outstanding checks is usually shown on the reverse, with only the total shown here.

Figure 9–7 **Bank Reconciliation**

The following comments are made about the numbered items on the reconciliation in Figure 9–7:

[1] Clearwater Company had a note receivable from a customer made out for its maturity value due on September 16. Since the customer had an account at the same bank, the note was delivered to the bank with a request that it be

collected. The bank, after securing permission from the customer, debited his account on September 16 for $500.00 and credited Clearwater's. There was a $3.00 service charge for this service. Neither the $500.00 credit nor the $3.00 charge has been recorded in Clearwater's books, so the note proceeds is added to the balance per books and the service charge is deducted in the reconciliation.

2 The interest earned on this checking account has been credited by the bank but is not on the company's records. It is added to the balance per books.

3 When the checks were traced to the bank statement, it was discovered that check no. 640 in payment for equipment repairs had been recorded in error as $201.06. The correct amount, as shown on the bank statement and the cancelled check, is $200.16. Since the credit to the Cash account was $0.90 greater than it should have been, this amount is added to the balance per books.

4 As indicated earlier, a customer's check for $21.20 had been returned marked "NSF." Since it was rejected for deposit by the bank, it must be deducted from the balance per books.

5 The monthly bank service charge has not been entered in the company's books and must be deducted from the balance per books.

6 The deposit of September 30 in amount of $421.50 (see Figure 9–4) was received at the bank too late to be included in this bank statement. It is added to the balance per bank statement and should appear as the first deposit on the October statement.

7 A comparison of the checks previously outstanding and those paid in September with the debits on the statement shows that two checks listed on the bank reconciliation had not yet reached the bank. Check nos. 639 and 643 were outstanding on August 31 and still did not clear through the bank in September. It is not unusual (although not a sound financial practice) for some recipients of checks to be negligent in depositing them. If these two checks continue to be outstanding, there is a possibility that they have been lost; correspondence to verify their receipt may be in order.

Recording the Adjustments

The adjustments made to the cash balance per ledger (often called the *Per Books* section) in the bank reconciliation require journal entries to update Clearwater Company's accounts so that the Cash account balance will be in agreement with the adjusted balance in the reconciliation. Other ledger account balances are also affected; the entries could be made in the cash receipts journal and cash payments journal because they are in effect receipts and payments of cash. If those journals have been balanced and posted as of September 30, the adjustments can be recorded in the general journal. All adjustments can be made in one compound entry or in separate entries as follows:

1985					
Sep.	30	Cash		497.00	
		Collection Fees Expense		3.00	
		Notes Receivable			500.00
		Collection of customer note made out for face value.			
	30	Cash		0.84	
		Interest Earned			0.84
		Credit of interest on checking account from September bank statement.			
	30	Cash		0.90	
		Repairs Expense			0.90
		Error in check no. 604 written for $200.16 but recorded at $201.06.			
	30	Accounts Receivable		21.20	
		Cash			21.20
		Customer's NSF check deducted on September bank statement: Ann Lanier $21.20			
	30	Bank Service Charge Expense		5.40	
		Cash			5.40
		Cost of checking account service in September.			

After the entries are posted, the Cash account will have a new balance of $513.72 and will be up to date with unrecorded bank transactions as of the date of the bank statement. The other affected accounts are also updated.

Only the items from the reconciliation that either increase or decrease the balance per books need to be entered in the journal. The items that increase or decrease the balance per bank already have been recorded on the depositor's books and therefore require *no adjusting entry*. Any errors made by the bank should be brought to the bank's attention. If a running cash balance is maintained in the checkbook, the necessary adjustments must be made there also. Other forms of bank reconciliation, that reconcile from a bank statement balance to a balance per checkbook, are often found in blank on the reverse side of the monthly bank statement. However, the form used in Figures 9–6 and 9–7 strengthens internal control over cash by highlighting all differences between the accounts and the bank's records. It also shows that the balances for both the bank and the Cash account are reconciled to the adjusted cash figure at the end of each month.

Another important cash management technique is the cash forecast. It is discussed with budgets in Chapter 26.

To this point, the emphasis in this chapter has been on internal control in cash management practices. A second important emphasis is cash *expenditure* control. An essential ingredient in a system that strengthens control over cash expenditures is the voucher system, discussed in the following sections.

The Voucher System

The accounting system must be designed not only to record transactions and prepare financial statements but also to achieve other managerial objectives. An important objective of management is to strengthen internal control to protect the assets of the business against loss through errors or fraud. The achievement of this objective goes hand in hand with the achievement of maximum operating efficiency and maximum earnings. A properly functioning voucher system plays a key role in establishing and maintaining effective internal control.

The **voucher system** is a method of verifying the accuracy of creditor claims and authorizing payment. The system covers any transaction that will require the payment of cash (except for payments out of petty cash). These include the payment of expenses or the purchase of merchandise, services, supplies, and plant items. Expenditures are verified, classified, and recorded; when authorized, they are paid by check. The duties of reporting the receipt of goods or services, authorizing expenditures, and signing checks are distributed. This helps prevent cash from being disbursed from the business without proper approval by permitting disbursement only after verifications have been made by several members of the organization.

The voucher system is strengthened when a firm uses a set of carefully designed business documents; an important one is a written purchase order, as illustrated in Figure 9–8. A **purchase order** is a formal authorization for a vendor to provide the goods or services described therein and to bill the buyer for them at the specified price. The records of the Tennessee Aircraft Supply Company are used here to illustrate the workings of a voucher system.

The Voucher

The **voucher** is a serially numbered form giving written authorization for recognizing an obligation and later authorizing the payment. It is prepared from the seller's invoice or group of invoices and from other documents that serve as evidence of the liability. It is sometimes called a *check request* or a *request for check.*

The voucher, not the invoice, is the basis for the accounting entry. A typical voucher is shown in Figure 9–9. The invoice (Figure 9–10), the purchase order, and other supporting documents are the evidence for the voucher. The voucher form, tailored to meet the needs of a particular business, should provide space for such things as:

☐ Summary of the invoice data.

☐ Account number(s) and amounts to be debited.

☐ Details of payment.

☐ Initials of persons who have checked accuracy of quantities, unit prices, extensions, and discount terms.

☐ Signature of the person who authorizes the payment.

☐ Signature of the person who records the voucher.

PURCHASE ORDER

09055

THIS ORDER NUMBER MUST APPEAR ON ALL PACKAGES, INVOICES AND SHIPPING PAPERS.

TENNESSEE AIRCRAFT SUPPLY
1234 Tenth Street
Gatlinburg, TN 37738

DATE December 2, 1984

SHIP TO (SAME AS ABOVE UNLESS OTHERWISE NOTED.)
Same as above

ORDERED FROM
Wheaton Company
1213 River Street
Romney, WV 26757

PLEASE ENTER OUR ORDER IN ACCORDANCE WITH PRICES, DELIVERY AND SPECIFICATIONS GIVEN.

DATE REQUIRED	SHIP VIA (CHEAPEST WAY UNLESS OTHERWISE SPECIFIED)	F.O.B.	PPD.	COLL.	TERMS
12-29-84	Truck	Destination	X		2/10,n/30

QUANTITY ORDERED	QUANTITY RECEIVED	DESCRIPTION	UNIT PRICE	AMOUNT
125		LX323 Seat belt assemblies	21.00	2,625.00
125		LX820 Seat belt assembly mounts	7.00	875.00
		Total		3,500.00

ACKNOWLEDGE ORDER IMMEDIATELY AND IF ANY ITEM CANNOT BE SHIPPED PROMPTLY, NOTIFY US.

BY J. W. Moore
AUTHORIZED SIGNATURE

ORIGINAL PURCHASE ORDER

Source: Courtesy Gate City Printing, Inc., Greensboro, N.C.

Figure 9–8
Purchase Order

VOUCHER
TENNESSEE AIRCRAFT SUPPLY
1234 Tenth Street
Gatlinburg, TN 37738

No. 314

Make Check Payable to:
Wheaton Company
1213 River Street
Romney, WV 26757

Date Check Needed: Jan. 8, 1985

Purchase Order No.: 09055

Invoice No.: A2160
Invoice Date: 12/29/84
Terms: 2/10, n/30

Account Numbers:		Amounts:
Credit:	201	$3,500.00
Debit:	501	$3,500.00

Inspected by: RQP

Prices, Extensions, and Terms Checked: LN

Approved for Payment: D R Jones

Figure 9–9
Voucher

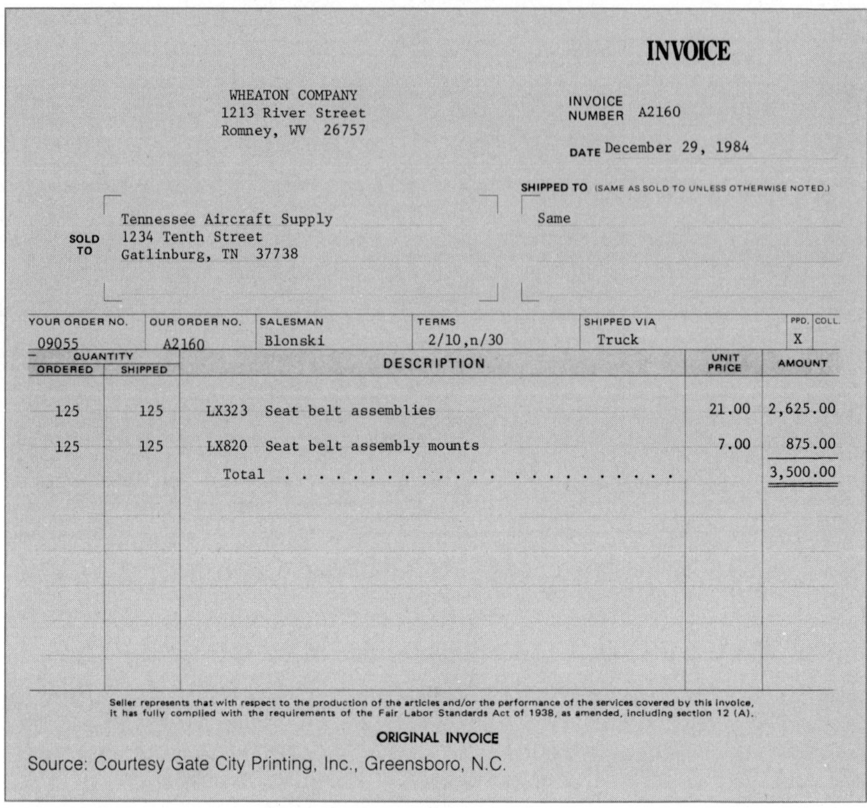

INVOICE

WHEATON COMPANY
1213 River Street
Romney, WV 26757

INVOICE NUMBER A2160

DATE December 29, 1984

SOLD TO Tennessee Aircraft Supply
1234 Tenth Street
Gatlinburg, TN 37738

SHIPPED TO (SAME AS SOLD TO UNLESS OTHERWISE NOTED.) Same

YOUR ORDER NO.	OUR ORDER NO.	SALESMAN	TERMS	SHIPPED VIA	PPD.	COLL.
09055	A2160	Blonski	2/10,n/30	Truck	X	

QUANTITY ORDERED	QUANTITY SHIPPED	DESCRIPTION	UNIT PRICE	AMOUNT
125	125	LX323 Seat belt assemblies	21.00	2,625.00
125	125	LX820 Seat belt assembly mounts	7.00	875.00
		Total		3,500.00

Seller represents that with respect to the production of the articles and/or the performance of the services covered by this invoice, it has fully complied with the requirements of the Fair Labor Standards Act of 1938, as amended, including section 12 (A).

ORIGINAL INVOICE

Source: Courtesy Gate City Printing, Inc., Greensboro, N.C.

Figure 9–10
Invoice

In Figure 9–9, voucher 314 has been prepared to authorize payment to Wheaton Company for a shipment of merchandise. The voucher shows that the Purchases account (501) will be debited for $3,500. Vouchers Payable (201) will be credited.[2] Payment has been authorized by the manager, D. R. Jones, whose signature appears in the approval block. Initials of persons who verified count, price, and so on are also on the voucher.

The invoice for this merchandise, shown in Figure 9–10, carries cash discount terms of 2/10, n/30. In this example, it will be recorded using the gross price procedure. However, the net price procedure can be used with a voucher system.

The Voucher Register

The **voucher register,** a special journal for recording all liabilities approved for payment, is ruled in Debit and Credit columns for frequently used accounts. It must be tailored to meet the needs of a particular enterprise. The register provides columns for each general class of expenditure and Other

[2]The Vouchers Payable account is a recognition that a liability is ready for payment. The liability may have existed—for example, as a note payable—before it is approved for payment with a voucher.

General Ledger Accounts column with space for the number of the specific account to be debited. It combines almost unlimited flexibility with economy of space. The voucher register for Tennessee Aircraft Supply is shown in Figure 9–11. The voucher register is used for recording all authorized payments except petty cash. Each transaction is entered in the voucher register first, followed by an entry in the check register *when payment is made.*

Vouchers are entered in the voucher register in numerical order. An entry is made in the Credit Vouchers Payable column for the amount due on each voucher. The account or accounts to be debited are indicated on the voucher, and entries are made in one of the special debit columns. If no special column applies, the Other General Ledger Accounts column provides space for the name of the account to be debited, a ledger folio (F) column, and an Amount Debit column. Entries in this column may be posted to the ledger daily; *all the other columns are posted in total only at the end of the month* to the general ledger account indicated in the column heading. Ledger folio references are shown beneath the double ruling for the items. The posting procedure is the same as for other special journals. Some of the entries in Figure 9–11 are explained in a later section.

Transactions involving liabilities that are not initially credited to Vouchers Payable—notes payable and accrued expenses, for example—are usually not entered in the voucher register until liability for payment is recognized. Vouchers are not prepared for accrued expenses because the amounts as accrued do not represent the amounts for which a check will be written. When payment is authorized and vouchers are prepared, any accrued liabilities are debited and the Vouchers Payable credit is entered (see vouchers 335, 336, and 337 in Figure 9–11).

The function of the Vouchers Payable account is the same as that of the Accounts Payable account. It is a controlling account—its balance represents the total of the unpaid vouchers recorded in the voucher register. Unpaid vouchers may, therefore, be readily determined to be those without entries on the corresponding line of the Paid column or those in the unpaid voucher file. At the end of the period, a list of the unpaid vouchers in the file should be prepared for reconciliation with the balance of the Vouchers Payable account in the general ledger.

The Check Register

All check payments must be recorded in the book of original entry called the **check register.** No payment is made until a specific voucher has been prepared, recorded, and approved. Hence, each entry is a debit to Vouchers Payable, a credit to Cash, and a credit to Purchases Discounts, if any. No other debit and credit columns are needed because the transaction already has been classified under an appropriate heading in the voucher register. Checks are entered in the check register in numerical sequence, one line to each check. At the time the check is entered, a notation must also be made in the Paid column of the voucher register showing the date of payment and the check number.

VOUCHER

				Paid		Credit
Date		Voucher Number	Name	Date	Check No.	Vouchers Payable
1985				1985		
Jan.	3	314	Wheaton Company	1/8	709	3,500
	3	315	Dover Furniture Company	1/5	708	800
	6	316	L. Kett			90
	10	317	Palmer Company	1/24	731	1,212
	10	318[a]	Payroll	1/10	711	1,575
	10	319	Petty Cash	1/10	712	80
	10	320	Helene Ellis Company	Canc.	333 – 334	4,000
	31	333	Helene Ellis Company			2,000
	31	334	Helene Ellis Company			2,000
	31	335	Internal Revenue Service	1/31	732	850
	31	336	State Division of Employment Security	1/31	733	297
	31	337	Internal Revenue Service	1/31	734	315
			Totals			22,324
						(201)

[a]Note that each new voucher is entered on the next totally vacant line.

Figure 9–11 **Voucher Register**

The check register will include a Purchases Discounts column only if the vouchers are recorded in the voucher register at gross invoice amounts. Also, this register shows the serial number of the check and the number of the voucher being paid.

Companies that use the net price method (discussed in Chapter 6) prepare each voucher for the net amount due. This means that if payment is not made within the discount period, an additional voucher will be required, underscoring the expense for lost discounts. The entry in the voucher register for the additional voucher is a debit to Purchases Discounts Lost and a credit to Vouchers Payable. One check is made out for the full amount due, as shown by the two vouchers. The check register for Tennessee Aircraft Supply is illustrated in Figure 9–12 and discussed below.

REGISTER Page 8

Debit			Other General Ledger Accounts		
Purchases	Miscellaneous Selling Expense	Miscellaneous General Expense	Other Accounts Debit	F	Amount Debit
3,500					
			Office Equipment	163	800
		90			
			{Notes Payable	203	1,200
			{Interest Expense	851	12
			Salaries and Wages Payable	211	1,575
30	25	25			
4,000					
			Vouchers Payable	201	4,000
			{FICA Taxes Payable	212	280
			{Income Tax Withholding Payable	215	570
			State Unemployment Taxes Payable	213	297
			Federal Unemployment Taxes Payable	214	315
9,780	475	243			11,826
(351)	(600)	(700)			(X)

Figure 9–11 (Continued)

Control of Unpaid Vouchers

A schedule of unpaid vouchers—the ones that have not been marked either "Paid" or "Cancelled" in the Paid column—is prepared at the end of the month. Its total should correspond to the balance of the Vouchers Payable account in the general ledger. Thus the unpaid vouchers file is a subsidiary record supporting the Vouchers Payable account. It is often maintained by payment due date to gain better control of discounts.

Recording and Paying Vouchers

The first entry in the voucher register is for approved voucher 314, payable to the Wheaton Company for $3,500 worth of merchandise received, terms 2/10, n/30. On January 8, check 709 is issued to the Wheaton Company for $3,430. An entry is made in the check register, dated that day, debiting

CHECK REGISTER Page 6

Date		Voucher No.	Name	Check No.	Vouchers Payable Dr.	Purchases Discounts Cr.	Cash Cr.
1985 Jan.	5	315	Dover Furniture Company	708	800		800
	8	314	Wheaton Company	709	3,500	70	3,430
	9	302	Johnson and Son	710	305		305
	10	318	Payroll	711	1,575		1,575
	10	319	Petty Cash	712	80		80
	24	317	Palmer Company	731	1,212		1,212
	31	335	Internal Revenue Service	732	850		850
	31	336	State Div. of Employ. Sec.	733	297		297
	31	337	Internal Revenue Service	734	315		315
			Totals		13,154	113	13,041
					(201)	(365)	(101)

Figure 9–12
Check Register

Vouchers Payable for $3,500 and crediting Purchases Discounts and Cash for $70 and $3,430, respectively. The number 314 entered in the Voucher Number column cross-references the check with the paid voucher. After this entry is made, the date of the entry and the check number are entered in the Paid column of the voucher register on the line for voucher 314. The voucher with its supporting documents is removed from the unpaid voucher file and filed in the vendor's file, a file of paid copies of all vouchers arranged in chronological order.

When a note payable becomes due, a voucher is prepared for the maturity value of the note and entered in the voucher register. In Figure 9–11, voucher 317 was issued to authorize payment of a 30-day, 12 percent note to Palmer Company. Two lines are required for the amounts debited in the Other Accounts column: Notes Payable ($1,200) and Interest Expense ($12). The payment of the voucher then is recorded in the check register in the usual manner.

Under the voucher system, the payroll for the period is recorded as usual in the payroll records. The liability is entered in the general journal by debiting the payroll expense accounts and crediting Salaries and Wages Payable and the accounts for the deductions. A voucher is prepared for the amount of the net payroll, and a check is issued to transfer cash to the payroll account. In Figure 9–11, the payroll of January 10 is covered by voucher 318; check 711 was issued.

At the end of the month, payment of the tax liabilities is recorded in the voucher register. Voucher 335 and check 732 are made payable to the Internal Revenue Service.

January 31 is also the last day for filing the state unemployment tax form for the last quarter (October through December). Voucher 336 and check 733 were made payable to the State Division of Employment Security.

Assuming that the total payroll subject to the federal unemployment compensation tax was $31,500 in 1985, voucher 337 records the liability for $315 = ($31,500 × 0.01).

Cancelling and Replacing Vouchers

Certain transactions do not fall into the routine pattern of the voucher system. For effective internal control, the voucher system requires that the amount of the voucher be exactly the same as the amount of the check to be issued when payment is due, except for purchases subject to discount. Provision must be made, however, for cancelling and replacing vouchers. In Figure 9–11, voucher 320 was prepared on January 10 with the assumption that it will be paid in full when due, but it is later paid in two installments. The original voucher is cancelled and a new voucher is issued for *each installment* (vouchers 333 and 334). The entry in the voucher register contains a debit to Vouchers Payable in the Other General Ledger Accounts Debit column for the amount of the original voucher. The credits to Vouchers Payable are entered on two lines and numbered consecutively. A notation is made in the Paid column opposite the entry for the original voucher indicating its cancellation and referring to the new voucher numbers.

Posting from the Voucher Register and the Check Register

All voucher register money columns are totaled at the end of the month. The totals of the debit columns and of the credit columns should be equal. The totals of all the special columns are posted to the proper accounts in the general ledger; the amounts in the Other General Ledger Accounts Debit column have been posted individually. A posting symbol reference is entered in the ledger account folio (F) columns to cross-reference postings from the voucher register—VR8, for example, represents page 8 from the voucher register.

The check register columns are totaled at the end of the month. The total of the Vouchers Payable Debit column should equal the totals of the two credit columns, Purchases Discounts and Cash. Postings are made at the end of the month to the three general ledger accounts. The symbol CkR and the page number is used in the ledgers to cross-reference postings from the check register.

Elimination of the Accounts Payable Subsidiary Ledger

When the voucher system is used, the accounts payable subsidiary ledger can be eliminated. Each numbered voucher is entered on a separate line in the voucher register and may be considered as a credit to a creditor's account. When the liability is settled and a notation is made in the Paid column, it is equivalent to a debit to that same creditor's account. The file of unpaid vouchers replaces the accounts payable subsidiary ledger. When all posting is up to date, the total of the unpaid vouchers in the file must agree with the total of the Vouchers Payable controlling account.

Advantages and Limitations of the Voucher System

In a properly functioning voucher system, all invoices must be verified and approved for payment. As a result, responsibility is fixed and the possibility of error or fraud is reduced. The recording of all vouchers in a single journal (the voucher register) provides for prompt recognition of liabilities and their proper accounting classification as assets, expenses, or other costs. Economy in recording is effected by elimination of the accounts payable subsidiary ledger and by grouping a supplier's invoices under a single voucher. The maintenance of a chronological unpaid voucher file facilitates the payment of invoices without loss of discounts and also enables management to determine its future cash needs for the settlement of liabilities. The vendor's file of paid vouchers provides a ready reference source for data and underlying documents for audit of disbursements.

On the other hand, the voucher system has certain limitations. The difficulties in handling special transactions and the need for the preparation of separate vouchers involve extra clerical and accounting work. If the accounts payable subsidiary ledger is eliminated, the result is a loss of valuable reference data. This problem may be overcome, however, by maintaining a file, arranged in alphabetical order by name of vendor, of copies of all vouchers. In addition, a card file could be kept that would provide a cross-reference for any purpose desired.

Glossary

Adjusted cash balance The true cash balance resulting from reconciling the difference between the balance reported by the bank and the amount shown on the depositor's books.

Bank reconciliation A statement which shows the specific items that account for the differences between the balance reported by the bank and the amount shown on the depositor's books.

Cash over and short An income statement item that measures the amount of the discrepancy in the daily physical count of cash and the cash register readings or shortages or overages in the petty cash fund.

Certified check (CC) A depositor's check, payment of which is guaranteed by a bank by endorsement on the face of the check, the bank having previously deducted the amount of the check from the depositor's balance.

Check An order written by a depositor directing a bank to pay a specified amount of money to the order of the payee.

Check register A book of original entry for all cash disbursements except petty cash.

Cost of service (CS) A monthly service charge which may be imposed by the bank to cover its costs of handling an account.

Credit memo (CM) A form explaining an addition to the bank balance not caused by a deposit.

Debit memo (DM) A form explaining a deduction from the depositor's account.

Deposits in transit Deposits made too late in the month to be credited by the bank on the current statement.

Electronic fund credit/debit An entry made to a depositor's account from a computerized system to transfer funds between depositors' accounts.

Imprest petty cash fund A petty cash fund system in which the balance of the petty cash account remains unchanged because a specified amount is advanced to a custodian in trust.

List (L) A code on the bank statement to indicate that a tape is enclosed with the bank statement listing two or more amounts.

NSF check A customer's check that has been deposited but did not clear on presentation for payment because of "not sufficient funds"—the customer's bank balance was less than the amount of the check.

Outstanding checks Checks sent to payees but not yet presented to the depositor's bank for payment.

Overdraft (OD) The amount by which withdrawals exceed the depositor's available balance.

Petty cash fund A separate cash fund when payment by check is impractical for relatively minor items.

Petty cash voucher A signed receipt that shows the purpose of a petty cash expenditure, the date, and the amount.

Purchase order A formal written authorization to a vendor to provide certain goods or services and to bill the buyer for them at the specified price. The purchase order becomes a contract when it is accepted by the vendor.

Return check fee (RF) A fee imposed by the bank on a depositor who has written an NSF check without prior arrangements for an overdraft.

Service charge See *Cost of service.*

Voucher A serially numbered form that is the written authorization for each expenditure. It is prepared from the documents that serve as evidence of the liability.

Voucher register A columnar journal for recording and summarizing all liabilities approved for payment.

Voucher system A method of accumulating, verifying, recording, and disbursing all the expenditures of a business. It covers all payments except those from the petty cash fund.

Questions

Q9–1 What specific items qualify to be included in the term cash? What is a basic rule to determine whether or not an item is part of cash?

Q9–2 The extent of an auditor's examination of a client's accounts and records is influenced to a large extent by the auditor's evaluation of the adequacy of the existing internal controls. Why is this so? Do you believe this to be an acceptable practice?

Q9–3 Why is it important to involve two or more persons in the handling and recording of cash receipts?

Q9–4 How can the owner of a small business with just one bookkeeper maintain adequate control over the cash handling and cash reporting process?

Q9–5 Why is it advantageous to deposit total cash receipts intact and to make all disbursements by check?

Q9–6 (a) What is a petty cash fund? (b) How does it operate? (c) Why should the petty cash fund always be replenished at the end of each accounting period?

Q9–7 Explain the matching relationships between the cash records of the bank and those of the depositor.

Q9–8 Explain the following terms: certified check, total of listed checks, cost of service, NSF, overdraft, debit memo, credit memo.

Q9–9 Explain the effect, if any, on the bank statement balance of each of the following bank reconciliation items:
a. Outstanding checks total $323.
b. The bank recorded a $650 deposit as $560.
c. The cost of service for the month was $7.
d. Deposits in transit total $800.
e. A note payable of $500 made to the bank by the depositor became due.

Q9–10 (a) How often should bank reconciliations be prepared? (b) What are the steps to be followed when preparing the bank reconciliation? (c) Which items must be entered on the books? (d) What do you think is the most important function of a bank reconciliation?

Q9–11 What is the primary purpose of a voucher system? How does a properly functioning voucher system achieve that purpose?

Q9–12 (a) What is a voucher? (b) What is a voucher register? (c) What are the advantages of the voucher system? (d) What are the disadvantages?

Q9–13 (a) What is a check register? (b) What column headings are needed for the check register?

Q9–14 What procedures should be followed to control unpaid vouchers?

Q9–15 Do you believe that basic internal control concepts apply to assets other than cash (for example, supplies, inventory, or receivables)? If so, should there be a separate internal control system for each, or one company-wide internal control system?

Exercises

E9–1 *Establishing a petty cash fund*

On May 1, 1985, the Aiken Company established a petty cash fund in the amount of $1,250. Prepare a general journal entry for establishment of the fund.

E9–2 *Replenishment of petty cash fund*

Newberry, Inc., has an imprest petty cash fund of $1,000. On October 31, 1985, the fund consisted of cash and other items as follows:

Currency and coins		$ 98.10
Petty cash vouchers for:		
Transportation in	$316.70	
Telephone	24.30	
Postage expense	418.42	
Stationery	137.58	897.00
Total		$995.10

Assuming that the petty cash fund was replenished, make the necessary entry at October 31, 1985, in general journal form.

E9–3 *Cash over and short*

Saluda Company has a change fund of $50 in the cash register to start each day. At the end of the day on September 4, 1985, the cash register tape showed cash sales of $968.72. The total amount of cash and checks in the register was $1,017.10. Is there a cash shortage or overage? Compute it and prepare a general journal entry to record cash sales for the day.

E9–4 *Handling items on the bank reconciliation*

From the following information pertaining to the banking activities of the Cardinal Company, indicate which of the following items should be (a) added to the balance per bank statement, (b) deducted from the balance per bank statement, (c) added to the balance per books, or (d) deducted from the balance per books:

1. Bank service charges (cost of service).
2. Deposits in transit.
3. Outstanding checks.
4. Credit for a customer note collected by the bank.
5. A customer's check returned marked NSF.
6. Check for $68 entered in the cash payments journal as $86.
7. Check for $86 entered in the cash payments journal as $68.
8. Deposit of Forest Company credited in error to the Cardinal Company.
9. A check made out by the Avery Company charged in error to the Cardinal Company's account.
10. Interest earned on an interest checking account.

E9–5 *Simple bank reconciliation*

Westwego Company's Cash account shows a balance of $20,818.37 as of January 31, 1985. The balance on the bank statement on that date is $23,334.17. Checks for $750.00, $533.46, and $126.54 are outstanding. The bank statement shows a charge for $75, with a cancelled check enclosed, that belongs to another company. The statement shows a credit of $1,200 for maturity value of a note receivable that was left with the bank for collection; no collection fee is charged by the bank. A customer's NSF check for $19.20 was returned with a debit memo. What is the true cash balance as of January 31?

E9–6 *Recording reconciliation adjustments*

Following is a bank reconciliation for Greenstein Company:

GREENSTEIN COMPANY
Bank Reconciliation
October 31, 1985

Cash balance per ledger, October 31		$644.37	Cash balance per bank, October 31	$1,082.20
Add: Error in check number 407 for office rent. .	$ 5.00		Add: Deposit in transit . .	210.50
Note collected by bank	100.00		Subtotal	$1,292.70
Interest on account . .	3.39	108.39	Deduct: Outstanding checks	618.54
Subtotal		$752.76		
Deduct: NSF customer check	$ 75.60			
Cost of service . .	3.00	78.60		
Adjusted cash balance, October 31		$674.16	Adjusted cash balance, October 31	$ 674.16

In general journal form, make all entries required by this reconciliation.

E9–7 *Finding reconciliation errors*

Bonnie Marshall has just completed a bank reconciliation and finds it does not balance. The adjusted cash balance per ledger is $1,490.60; the adjusted cash balance per bank is $1,245.60. She has added to the Per Books section a deposit of $145.00 that was made on the 31st of last month but appeared on this month's statement. She has also deducted from the bank balance *all* outstanding checks regardless of date. Two of them for a total of $100.00 were also outstanding last month. A $100.00 certified check is included in the outstanding checks. Show the changes that must be made to correct her bank reconciliation.

E9–8 *Challenging bank reconciliation and journal entries*

The accountant for the Estes Drive Hotel has the following data for the bank reconciliation of February 28, 1985:

Balance per bank statement	$8,719.63
Balance per Cash account	8,721.60
NSF check from overnight guest returned by bank	57.50
Deposit made on February 28 not credited by bank	1,625.70
Check number 790 for $618 entered in the books as $681	63.00
Outstanding checks total	2,122.73
Debit memo for note payable of $500 plus interest that bank collected for holder of note	522.50
Credit memo to cancel January service charge	18.00

Prepare a bank reconciliation and the entries (in general journal form) to adjust the accounts.

E9–9 *Simple voucher and check register transactions*

M and W Stores uses a voucher system. During June 1985, the following selected transactions were completed:

1985		
Jun.	3	Purchased merchandise from the Debbie Company, $2,000; terms 2/10, n/30. Prepared voucher no. 675 approving payment to be made on June 13.
	6	Purchased merchandise from the Mollie Company, $3,200; terms, 2/10, n/30. Prepared voucher no. 676 authorizing payment on June 15.
	13	Paid the Debbie Company the total amount due; check no. 0207.
	15	Paid the Mollie Company the amount due; check no. 0208.
	17	Prepared voucher no. 677 for a $675 purchase of office equipment, to be paid in 30 days.
	19	Purchased merchandise from the Judy Company, $1,800; terms, 1/10, n/60. Decided not to take discount and prepared voucher no. 678 to be paid August 19.
	28	Prepared voucher no. 679 for June rent, $950.
	28	Paid June rent; check no. 0209.

Enter the above transactions in a voucher register and a check register using the gross price procedure.

E9–10 *Vouchers and payments—net price procedure*

New Bern Company uses a voucher system and records all vouchers at the net amount. The following transactions occurred during October and November 1985:

1985		
Oct.	3	Issued a voucher payable to the Gray Company for $2,400 of merchandise; terms 2/10, n/30.
	7	Issued a voucher payable to Greene, Inc., for $3,000 of merchandise; terms, 1/10, n/30.
	12	Issued a check to the Gray Company in payment of the October 3 voucher.
Nov.	7	Issued a voucher payable to Greene, Inc., for the discount not taken on the transaction of October 7.
	8	Issued a check payable to Greene, Inc., for the amount due.

Record the transactions in the voucher register and check register (assign voucher and check numbers).

E9–11 *Voucher cancellation*

Purewater Company prepared voucher no. 381 for a $5,000 purchase of merchandise on September 4, 1985. Terms were 2/10, n/30. On September 13, voucher no. 381 was cancelled and replaced with voucher no. 398 for $4,000, to be paid that date taking the discount, and voucher no. 399 for $1,000, to be paid on October 4. Record all transactions using the gross price method including both payments. Provide check numbers.

E9–12 *Partial payment—discount allowed*

On July 1, 1985, Stepson Company received $8,000 of merchandise with an invoice offering terms of 2/10, n/30. Unsure of the method of settlement of the bill, management did not authorize a voucher and did not record the purchase on that date. On July 10, learning that the supplier would allow discounts on partial payments, management authorized voucher no. 584 for which check no. 1670 was written for $6,321. Record that voucher (using the gross price procedure) and the payment on July 10.

A Problems

P9–1A *Petty cash fund*

Lihue Company established a petty cash fund of $1,500 by issuing a check to the custodian on November 1, 1985. On November 30, management desired to prepare financial statements for internal use and replenished the fund in order to record the expenditures. The content of the fund on November 30 was as follows:

Currency and coins		$ 518.65
Receipted petty cash vouchers for:		
Repairs to office equipment	$132.75	
Transportation in for merchandise	362.30	
Sales promotion at Aloha Fair	256.70	
Postage paid on outgoing mail	118.80	
Emergency payments for interisland sales travel	111.65	982.20
Total		$1,500.85

On December 31, the fund was again replenished. On that date, the contents were:

Currency and coins		$ 618.75
Receipted petty cash vouchers for:		
Repairs to office equipment	$162.80	
Transportation in for merchandise	375.82	
Christmas sales promotion	132.40	
Postage paid on outgoing mail	208.70	879.72
Total		$1,498.47

After two months of experience with the fund, management has decided to reduce the fund to about 30 days requirements; a reduction to $1,000 was ordered on December 31.

Required:

1. A general journal entry to establish the fund.

2. A general journal entry to replenish the fund on November 30.

3. A general journal entry to replenish and reduce the fund on December 31.

P9–2A *Bank reconciliation—routine items*

The Cash account of the Winnebago Company showed a balance of $7,410.60 on May 31, 1985. The bank statement showed a balance of $7,173.00. Other differences between the firm's Cash account and the bank's records are as follows:

1. A deposit of $630.00 made on May 31 was not included on the bank statement.
2. The following items were included with the bank statement:
   a. A debit memo for $60.00 with a customer's NSF check that the firm had included in its deposit of May 30.
   b. A debit memo for $30.00 for safe deposit box rental.
   c. A cancelled check for $690.00 drawn by another company charged against Winnebago by mistake.
3. Check number 607 was made out correctly for $61.74 in payment for office supplies but was entered in the cash payments journal as $62.34; it was returned with the statement.
4. Outstanding checks on May 31 totaled $1,171.80.

Required:

1. Prepare a bank reconciliation as of May 31, 1985.

2. Prepare entries in general journal form as required by the reconciliation.

P9–3A *Bank reconciliation—tracing items to statements*

Nussbaum Company had a Cash account balance of $9,934.31 on April 12, 1985. A special bank statement requested by the auditors for that date showed a balance of $12,011.77. At the end of March there were no deposits in transit. There were three checks outstanding on March 31 as follows:

Number	Amount
620	$ 12.00
621	462.40
622	397.60

Deposits made and checks written in the first 12 days of April were as follows:

Deposits		Checks	
Date	Amount	Number	Amount
Apr. 1	$346.25	623	$ 115.80
2	438.75	624	99.20
3	98.75	625	1,110.00
4	96.25	626	143.50
5	986.50	627	682.21
8	483.50	628	49.90
9	421.30	629	20.00
10	359.50	630	760.00
11	251.27	631	62.23
12	248.73	632	198.50

On the bank statement of April 12, the deposit of neither April 11 nor April 12 had yet been credited. Cancelled checks of the Nussbaum Company returned with the bank statement were in the amounts of $12.00, $462.40, $397.60, $115.80, $99.20, $1,110.00, $62.23, and $198.50. Also returned with the bank statement were the following:

a. A credit memo for $1,030.00 representing a customer note receivable for $1,000 plus interest collected by the bank for Nussbaum.
b. A debit memo for $2.75 for the note collection fee.
c. A $90.00 customer check marked NSF.
d. A $15.40 cancelled check made out by another company and charged to Nussbaum's account.

Required:

1. Prepare a bank reconciliation as of April 12, 1985.

2. Prepare the entries needed to adjust the books (use general journal form).

P9–4A *Voucher register and check register*

Fox Inc. used a voucher system in July 1985 and prepared its vouchers at gross amounts. The following transactions were completed during July:

1985

Jul. 3 Established a petty cash fund of $500 by the issuance of voucher no. 362; issued check no. 357 in payment of this voucher.

3 Purchased a one-year insurance policy from Liberty Insurance Company for $720. Issued voucher no. 363, and check no. 358 in payment of the voucher.

4 Issued voucher no. 364 payable to Kay Realty for $600 for the July rent; issued check no. 359 in payment of the voucher.

5 Issued voucher no. 365 payable to R. Kelly, Inc., for $1,200 of merchandise, terms 2/10, n/30.

10 Issued voucher no. 366 payable to L. Scotch Company for $3,600 of merchandise, terms n/10.

11 Issued voucher no. 367 payable to Danvers Supply Company for $200 of office supplies; issued check no. 360 in payment of the voucher.

17 Issued voucher no. 368 payable to J. Waitt Company for $1,800 of merchandise, terms 2/10, n/30.

18 Recorded the following payroll data in the general journal:

Gross salaries:	Sales	$ 750	
	Office	450	
	Executive	1,000	$2,200
Deductions:	FICA tax	$ 154	
	Federal income tax	378	
	U.S. bonds	75	
	Employee loan	20	
	Community fund	10	637
Net amount due			$1,563

Issued voucher no. 369 payable to Payroll for the net amount due to employees. Issued check no. 361 in payment of the voucher.

20 The L. Scotch Company agreed to an extension of time on its invoice due today, as follows: $1,800 payment due in 20 days, and another $1,800 payment due in 30 days. Cancelled voucher no. 366 and issued vouchers no. 370 and 371.

24 Purchased two electric typewriters from Atlas Office Company for $1,500. Issued voucher no. 372 for $500, and check no. 362, in partial payment. Issued voucher no. 373 for $1,000 for the balance, payable in 30 days.

25 Issued voucher no. 374 payable to the S. Furry Company for $800 of merchandise, terms 1/10, n/60.

26 Issued check no. 363 in payment of voucher no. 370.

27 Issued voucher no. 375 to the *Salem Sun* for $75 for advertising. Issued check no. 364 in payment of the voucher.

Required:

1. Prepare a voucher register, a check register, and a two-column general journal similar to the illustrations in the text, and record the July transactions.

2. Open a Vouchers Payable account and post all entries affecting that account.

3. Prove the end-of-month balance of the Vouchers Payable account by preparing a schedule of unpaid vouchers.

P9–5A
Internal control system (based on an actual occurrence)

An employee of the Edith Conklin Company, who takes the daily bank deposit to the bank each evening, stole the deposit of June 3. It contained $685.50 in cash and 10 checks totaling $492.75. Since he could not cash the checks, he held them until June 19 and inserted them in that deposit, extracting $492.75 of the cash. Because he was a long-standing employee, Conklin had made out deposit tickets in duplicate and let him take both the original and duplicate copy to the bank. It was his usual practice to place the duplicate copy in a file of deposit slips upon return from the bank each evening.

Required:

1. How is Ms. Conklin likely to discover the theft? What valid evidence will she have?

2. What action can she take to lessen future chances of this type of loss?

P9–6A
Thought-provoking problem: imprest change fund

On January 1, 1985, the proprietor of Yokoyama's began a new system of providing change for the restaurant's single cash register. He instructed the accountant to give a check for $100.00 to the cashier which she could convert to currency and coins to use for making change. Since she had the only key to the locked register, the cashier could leave the change fund in the cash register overnight.

On January 2, 1985, the cashier cashed the check and began to use the new change fund. At the end of the day when she and the proprietor balanced the register, they found the following:

a. The cash register tape and the food service checks had the same total: $1,824.70.

b. The cash register contained these items:

Currency and coins	$1,352.65
Traveler's checks	360.00
Bank credit card sales invoices	62.35
Personal checks	151.70
Total	$1,926.70

Required:

1. In general journal form, prepare entries to:

a. Establish the change fund.

b. Record the results of operations on January 2.

2. What are the internal control implications of formalizing the change fund by journal entry?

B Problems

P9–1B
Petty cash fund

Kona Company established a petty cash fund of $1,800 by issuing a check to the custodian on March 1, 1985. On March 31, management desired to prepare financial statements for internal use and replenished the fund in order to record the expenditures. The content of the fund on March 31 was as follows:

Currency and coins		$ 803.15
Receipted petty cash vouchers for:		
Repairs to office equipment	$121.15	
Transportation in on merchandise	408.90	
Sales promotion at Aloha Fair	262.30	
Postage paid on outgoing mail	102.50	
Emergency payment for interisland sales travel	100.15	995.00
Total		$1,798.15

On April 30, the fund was again replenished. On that date, the contents were:

Currency and coins		$ 825.60
Receipted petty cash vouchers for:		
Repairs to office equipment	$156.85	
Transportation in on merchandise	362.70	
Easter sales promotion	171.80	
Postage paid on outgoing mail	285.35	976.70
Total		$1,802.30

After two months of experience with the fund, management has decided to reduce the fund to about 30 days requirements; a reduction to $1,000 was ordered on April 30.

Required:

1. A general journal entry to establish the fund.

2. A general journal entry to replenish the fund on March 31.

3. A general journal entry to replenish and reduce the fund on April 30.

P9–2B *Bank reconciliation—routine items*

The Cash account of the Oshkosh Company showed a balance of $3,705.30 on September 30, 1985. The bank statement showed a balance of $3,586.50. Other differences between the firm's Cash account and the bank's records are as follows:

1. A deposit of $315.00 made on September 30 was not included on bank statement.
2. The following items were included with the bank statement:
   a. A debit memo for $30.00 with a customer's NSF check that had been included in the deposit of September 27.
   b. A debit memo for $15.00 for safe deposit box rental.
   c. A cancelled check for $345.00 drawn by another company and charged against Oshkosh by mistake.
3. Check no. 515 was made out correctly for $30.87 in payment for office supplies but was entered in the cash payments journal as $31.17.
4. Outstanding checks on September 30 totaled $585.90.

Required:

1. Prepare a bank reconciliation as of September 30, 1985.

2. Prepare entries in general journal form as required by the reconciliation.

P9–3B *Bank reconciliation—tracing items to statement*

Shapiro Company had a Cash account balance of $19,868.62 on October 11, 1985. A special bank statement requested by the auditors for that date showed a balance of $24,023.54. At the end of September there were no deposits in transit. There were three checks outstanding on September 30 as follows:

Number	Amount
862	$ 24.00
863	924.80
864	795.20

Deposits made and checks written in the first 11 days of October were as follows:

Deposits		Checks	
Date	**Amount**	**Number**	**Amount**
Oct. 1	$ 692.50	865	$ 231.60
2	877.50	866	198.40
3	197.50	867	2,220.00
4	192.50	868	287.00
7	1,973.00	869	1,364.42
8	967.00	870	99.80
9	842.60	871	40.00
10	719.00	872	1,520.00
11	1,000.00	873	124.60
		874	397.00

On the bank statement of October 11, the deposit of October 11 had not been credited. Cancelled checks of the Shapiro Company returned with the bank statement were in the amounts of $24.00, $924.80, $795.20, $231.60, $198.40, $2,220.00, $124.60, and $397.00. Also returned with the bank statement were the following:

a. A credit memo for $2,060.00 representing a customer note receivable for $2,000 plus interest collected by the bank for Shapiro.
b. A debit memo for $5.50 for the note collection fee.
c. A $180.00 customer check marked NSF.
d. A $30.80 cancelled check made out by another company and charged to Shapiro's account.

Required:

1. Prepare a bank reconciliation as of October 11, 1985.

2. Prepare the entries needed to adjust the books (use general journal form).

P9–4B *Voucher register and check register*

Triad Company used a voucher system in May 1985 and prepared its vouchers at gross amounts. The following transactions were completed during May.

1985		
May	3	Established a petty cash fund of $850 by issuance of voucher no. 472; issued check no. 467 in payment of this voucher.
	3	Purchased a one-year insurance policy from Downs Insurance Agency for $500. Issued voucher no. 473, and check no. 468 in payment of the voucher.
	4	Issued voucher no. 474 payable to Glynn Realty for $735 for the May rent; issued check no. 469 in payment of the voucher.
	6	Issued voucher no. 475 payable to J. Powell, Inc., for $3,210 of merchandise, terms 2/10, n/30.
	10	Issued voucher no. 476 payable to B. Childs Company for $4,150 of merchandise, terms 2/10, n/30.
	11	Issued voucher no. 477 payable to Burlington Office Supply Company for $300 of office supplies; issued check no. 470 in payment of the voucher.
	17	Issued voucher no. 478 payable to K. Wald Company for $3,100 of merchandise, terms 1/10, n/30.

17 Recorded the following payroll data in the general journal:

Gross salaries:	Sales	$1,500	
	Office	900	
	Executive	2,000	$4,400
Deductions:	FICA tax	$ 308	
	Federal income tax	850	
	U.S. bonds	150	
	Employee loan	50	
	Community fund	75	1,433
Net amount due			$2,967

Issued voucher no. 479 payable to Payroll for the net amount due to employees. Issued check no. 471 in payment of the voucher.

20 The B. Childs Company agreed to an extension of time on its invoice due today, as follows: $2,150 payment due in 20 days and another $2,000 payment due in 30 days. Cancelled voucher no. 476 and issued vouchers no. 480 and 481.

24 Purchased copying equipment from Dover Supply Company for $3,000. Issued voucher no. 482 for $1,500, and check no. 472 in partial payment. Issued voucher no. 483 for $1,500 for the balance, payable in 30 days.

25 Issued voucher no. 484 payable to the G. Floray Company for $1,620 of merchandise, terms 2/10, n/60.

27 Issued check no. 473 in payment of voucher no. 480.

28 Issued voucher no. 485 to the *Norwood Times* for $150 for advertising. Issued check no. 474 in payment of the voucher.

Required:

1. Prepare a voucher register, a check register, and a two-column general journal similar to the illustrations in the text, and record the May transactions.

2. Open a Vouchers Payable account and post all entries affecting that account.

3. Prove the end-of-month balance of the Vouchers Payable account by preparing a schedule of unpaid vouchers.

P9–5B
Internal control system (based on an actual occurrence)

At the Capital City public swimming pool, lockers are rented from the locker room attendant for $0.75 per visit. Several popular brands of candy bars are kept at the locker room entrance for sale to the pool patrons. All cash collected is placed in a metal cash box that is locked in the locker room when the pool is closed. When the locker room attendant is absent, she turns the box over to one of the lifeguards to collect cash and make change for locker rentals or candy sales. An assistant city recreation supervisor stops by every few days to deliver more candy and to take out cash for deposit to the city's bank account. There are no signatures for receipt of candy or for cash taken out for deposit.

One day in August, the city recreation supervisor noticed a full box of candy on the back seat of a lifeguard's car. Becoming suspicious, she compared total swimming pool operations with the same period to date last year. Although the number of swimmers had increased by about 20 percent, cash receipts were several hundred dollars less than for the same period last year. Obviously, someone was stealing candy or cash (or both), but who?

Required:

1. Point out the internal control weaknesses in the present system.

2. Suggest some steps that the city recreation supervisor might take to correct this situation. She cannot hire additional employees.

P9–6B *Thought-provoking problem: imprest change fund*

On January 1, 1985, the proprietor of Midori's began a new sytem of providing change for the restaurant's single cash register. He instructed the accountant to give a check for $100.00 to the cashier which she could convert to currency and coins to use for making change. Since she had the only key to the cash register, the cashier could leave the change fund in the register overnight.

On January 2, 1985, the cashier cashed the check and began to use the new change fund. At the end of the day when she and the proprietor balanced the register, they found the following:

a. The cash register tapes and food service checks had the same total; $2,562.70.

b. The cash register contained these items:

Currency and coins	$1,726.42
Traveler's checks	550.00
Bank credit card sales invoices	162.50
Personal checks	225.18
Total	$2,664.10

Required:

1. In general journal form, prepare entries to:

a. Establish the change fund.

b. Record the results of operations on January 2.

2. What are the internal control implications of formalizing the change fund by journal entry?

Part Three

Income Measurement

10 Short-Term Financing

Introduction

When interest rates are extremely high, interest is a large element of the cost of doing business. For instance, in the quarter that ended September 30, 1982, Republic Airlines had a net operating margin (referred to in its report as operating profit) of more than $18 million. However, the bottom line was a net loss of more than $5 million. The major deduction from net operating margin was interest expense of almost $25 million. It is imperative, therefore, that financial managers not only know how to calculate interest amounts, but also be able to apply this knowledge in managing both short-term and long-term debt. The area of short-term financing addressed in this chapter encompasses borrowing of money from banks (by issuing notes) and purchase of merchandise, supplies, and equipment on both open charge account and by the issuance of notes payable. This chapter starts with a discussion of simple interest—method of calculation and determination of an annual percentage rate. Then the accounting for the negotiable instruments (transferable to another party by endorsement) used in these short-term financing examples is considered. Next the mirror-image issue of accounting for short-term notes receivable is discussed as a means of introducing another method of obtaining short-term funds, that is, the discounting of customers' notes receivable.

Learning Goals

To understand the arithmetic of notes, determination of maturity dates, computation of number of days at interest, and computation of simple interest and bank discount.

To know the meaning of simple interest and of annual percentage rate (effective interest rate).

To know the characteristics of promissory notes, the method of transferring notes, and the meaning of various forms of endorsements.

To record transactions dealing with issuance of notes payable.

To record notes receivable transactions.

To calculate the proceeds of notes discounted at banks and to record the discounting of these notes.

To record end-of-period adjustments for items related to notes receivable and payable.

Simple Interest

Definition and Calculation of Simple Interest

Interest is the price of credit. Simply stated, interest is the rental charge made for the use of money. Because it is similar to the rental cost of equipment used during operations, interest to the borrower is an expense; to the lender it is a revenue.

Simple interest is computed on the original principal (face value) of a note or a time draft.[1] Interest amounts that may have accrued on the principal in past periods are *not* added to the amount on which interest is calculated.

Assume that Joan Rockness gives Thomas Blocher a 16 percent, 90-day note that has a principal amount of $10,000. The *simple interest rate* specified on a note is an annual fraction of the *principal,* or face amount of the instrument. A note—like a check—is a *negotiable instrument.* **Negotiable** means it can be transferred to another entity by endorsement on the back of the instrument. Thus, in Joan Rockness's note, the rental charge, for the use of $10,000 for one year is $1,600 = ($10,000 × 0.16). Since the *term of the note* (the length of time the note is to exist), however, is less than one year, the interest must be computed by multiplying the interest amount for one year by a fraction. The numerator is the term of the note in days and the denominator, the number of days in a year. As stated in Chapter 4, the formula is:

$$\text{Interest} = \text{Principal} \times \text{Rate} \times \text{Time}.$$

This is usually stated as I = PRT. In Rockness's note, the interest amount for the 90-day period is typically calculated in this manner:[2]

$$I = \$10{,}000 \times 0.16 \times \frac{90}{360} = \$400.$$

Number of Days at Interest

The number of days at interest to be used in both the numerator and denominator of the foregoing interest equation may be determined in one of several ways. These methods of computing the *time at interest* include the following typical methods, among others:

[1] A time draft is a written order to pay in the future a sum of money to order or bearer; when it is accepted, it becomes a negotiable instrument similar to a note.

[2] This type of calculation is referred to as ordinary interest at exact time.

1. *Accurate interest.* The exact number of days covered by the term of a note at interest is counted; the denominator or base is 365 days. This practice is followed by Federal Reserve Banks and certain other banks.

2. *Ordinary interest at exact time.* The actual number of days of the note term is counted and used as the numerator, but a 360-day business year is used as the denominator. This method is a common commercial practice.

3. *Ordinary interest at 30-day month time.* Each month is assumed to have 30 days in the numerator, and the 360-day business year is used as the denominator. This method is used for bonds (see Chapter 18).

In this book, *ordinary interest at exact time* is used for simple interest calculations on notes. In the foregoing illustration, for example, the exact stated time of 90 days is used for the numerator, and the 360-day business year is used as the denominator. It should be understood, however, that the difference between accurate interest and ordinary interest at exact time is 1/73, that is:

$$\frac{365 - 360}{365} = \frac{1}{73}.$$

Annual Percentage Rate (APR) or Annual Effective Interest

Because of various attempts by some lenders to disguise the **annual effective interest rate** (that is, by stating the interest rate for a month or describing it as a carrying charge), the federal *Truth in Lending Law,* enacted in 1969, requires grantors of credit to disclose the annual effective interest cost of borrowed funds.[3] Today, bankers and other grantors of credit commonly use the abbreviation APR, which stands for annual percentage rate. The terms *annual effective interest* and *APR* are used interchangeably in this book. Determining the effective interest rate or APR can be very simple or quite complex, requiring the use of compound interest techniques. Two simple cases are illustrated here; others are introduced later.

First, a loan that carries a 1½ percent monthly rate (as many monthly charge accounts have) would have an APR of 18 percent = (12 × 1½%). Instead of calculating the APR precisely, it may be necessary in some cases to approximate the annual effective interest rate. This is particularly true when individuals are not given the APR and are faced with the selection of a single method from among several short-term financing methods.

When merchandise is bought on the installment basis, for instance, payments are made over several months. If the effective interest rate is not stated, it is particularly important to approximate the APR. Such an approximation involves making the simplifying assumption that each payment constitutes an equal reduction in the principal amount owed; thus the average out-

[3]The law permits the grantor of credit to round the effective interest rate to the nearest 1/4 of one percent. This permissible practical application is not followed in this book; rather, the rounding is usually to the nearest 1/100 of one percent.

standing debt for the interest period is one-half the original principal. The interest for the period then can readily be compared with the average outstanding principal. For most comparative purposes, it is necessary to "annualize" any interest rate that is determined.

To illustrate this approximation, assume that merchandise costing $1,000 is purchased; this amount is to be paid in 24 equal monthly installments of $50 each (which includes interest). The calculation is as follows:

1. Average outstanding principal = $1,000 ÷ 2 = $500.

2. Annual absolute interest cost:
Total interest for two years = ($50 × 24) − $1,000 = $200.
Interest for one year = $200 ÷ 2 = $100.

3. Rough approximation of APR is:
$100 ÷ $500 = 20 percent per year, or 1⅔ percent each month.

Armed with this knowledge of simple interest, let us apply it to short-term financing methods.

The Short-Term Financing Climate

Business firms often find it more economical to use some means of short-term financing than to pay cash for various purchases; for example, many purchase merchandise, supplies, and equipment on 30-day or 60-day open charge accounts. (An open charge account is an extension of credit without a formal written promise to pay. It often includes a cash discount to encourage early payment—see Chapter 6.) The current financial climate is a factor in the decision to use a specific method of financing.

When various financing methods—both long-term and short-term—are available to a company, the financial manager must consider (1) the cost of the interest of each method, (2) whether the financing method will continue to be available to the firm, and (3) the possible effect that short-term financing will have on long-term borrowing; or the reverse, the effect that committing the organization for 10 to 20 years will have on short-term borrowing. In regard to short-term financing, the financial manager should choose the method that will produce consistently the desired short-term funds at the lowest possible cost. The rate of interest that an organization must pay depends on its ability to pledge assets as security, its record of financial integrity, and its prospects for the future.

Description of Promissory Notes

The promissory note was discussed briefly in Chapter 1 and other preceding chapters. Details about this credit form are now needed.

A **negotiable promissory note** may be defined as an unconditional written promise to pay a specified sum of money to the order of a designated person or to bearer at a fixed or determinable future time or on demand.

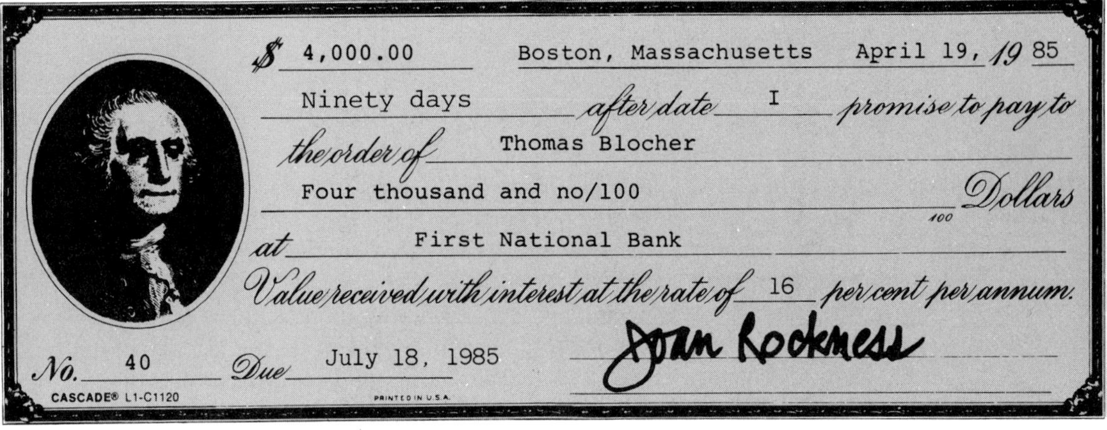

$ 4,000.00 Boston, Massachusetts April 19, 1985

Ninety days after date I promise to pay to the order of Thomas Blocher

Four thousand and no/100 Dollars

at First National Bank

Value received with interest at the rate of 16 per cent per annum.

No. 40 Due July 18, 1985 Joan Rockness

CASCADE® L1-C1120 PRINTED IN U.S.A.

Figure 10–1 **A Promissory Note**

The term **negotiable** indicates that it can be legally transferred by its owner to another person or institution, provided that the actions described in the following paragraphs are taken.

A typical note is illustrated in Figure 10–1. Joan Rockness, the *maker,* gives Thomas Blocher, the designated *payee,* a 16 percent note for $4,000 dated April 19, 1985. The outstanding characteristics of a note are that it:

- ☐ Must be in writing and be signed by the maker.
- ☐ Must contain an unconditional promise to pay a certain sum in money.
- ☐ May be payable to the order of a designated payee or to bearer (that is, anyone who holds the note).
- ☐ Must be payable either on demand or at a specified time in the future.
- ☐ May or may not be interest bearing.

The ownership of a negotiable promissory note is transferred simply by delivery if it is payable to the bearer; otherwise, it is transferred by endorsement and delivery.

A **blank endorsement** consists of a signature of the owner, or payee, on the back of the instrument. A **full endorsement** consists of a notation on the back of the document, "Pay to the order of (name of person or company)," accompanied by the signature of the owner, in this case, Thomas Blocher. If the endorser—the one who is transferring the document—wishes to pass title to the instrument and at the same time be relieved of any further liability, he or she gives a **qualified endorsement** by placing both signature and the phrase "without recourse" on the back of the note.

From the viewpoint of the maker, Joan Rockness, the note illustrated in Figure 10–1 is a liability and is recorded by crediting Notes Payable. From the viewpoint of the payee, Thomas Blocher, the same note is an asset and is recorded by debiting Notes Receivable. At the maturity date, July 18, 1985, Thomas Blocher or his agent, the First National Bank, will expect to receive

$4,160 in cash for the note and interest, and Joan Rockness will expect to pay $4,160 in cash.

Maturity Dates of Notes

The term of a note may be expressed in years, months, or days. A note expressed in years or months, matures on the corresponding date in the maturity year or month. For example, a two-year note dated April 3, 1985, is due on April 3, 1987, and a two-month note dated April 3, 1985, is due on June 3, 1985. Occasionally, when time is expressed in months, there may be no corresponding date in the maturity month, in which case the last day of the month of maturity is used. A three-month note dated March 31 is due on June 30, and a one-month note dated January 29, 30, or 31 is due on the last day of February. If the term of the note is expressed in days, the maturity date is found by counting forward the specified number of days *after* the date of the note, excluding the date of the note but including the maturity date. The note of Joan Rockness in Figure 10–1 has an issuance date of April 19; the due date of July 18 is determined as follows:

Total days in April	30
Deduct: Date of note in April	19
Number of days note runs in April (excluding April 19)	11
Add: Total days in May and June	61
Total number of days note has run through May 31	72
Add: Due date in July (90 days minus 72 days)	18
Term of note	90

For short-term credit instruments, simple interest (interest on the original principal only) is computed by using the ordinary interest at exact time approach. Thus, a three-month note dated April 19 is due 91 days later, on July 19. The interest amount by the ordinary interest at exact time method is computed for 91 days. This usual commercial practice is used here for short-term interest calculations. Accounting procedures for notes are described next beginning with notes payable.

Notes Payable

Recording Procedures Involving Notes Payable

All obligations backed up by promissory notes **(notes payable)** issued to others may be recorded in a single Notes Payable account in the general ledger, disclosing supplementary details including name of payee, interest rate, and terms of the note, as shown on page 347:

Notes Payable Acct. No. 205

Date		Explanation	F	Debit	Credit	Balance
1985						
Nov.	15	B. B. Barker, 16%, 60 days	J62		2,000	2,000
	24	B. T. Arnold, 15%, 30 days	J65		450	2,450
Dec.	3	J. L. Jones, 14%, 90 days	J70		800	3,250
	10	F. T. Merrick, 16%, 60 days	J74		1,000	4,250
	18	P. O. Paulson, 16%, 90 days	J76		950	5,200
	24	B. T. Arnold (paid)	CP40	450		4,750

Issuance of Notes for Property, Plant, and Equipment

The following examples illustrate the recording of notes payable in the acquisition of property, plant, and equipment.

Assume that on July 10, 1985, the Ace Company buys from the Triangle Machine Company a bookkeeping machine at a cost of $4,000; the creditor agrees to take a 90-day, 16 percent note for the purchase price. This transaction is recorded as follows:

1985					
Jul.	10	Office Equipment		4,000	
		Notes Payable			4,000
		To record the purchase of a bookkeeping machine and the issuance of a 16%, 90-day note to the Triangle Machine Company.			

On October 8, 1985, the payment of the note and interest to the Triangle Machine Company is recorded as follows:[4]

1985					
Oct.	8	Notes Payable		4,000	
		Interest Expense		160	
		Cash			4,160
		To record payment of a 16%, 90-day note and interest to the Triangle Machine Company.			

A special example of the issuance of a note for property, plant, and equipment is shown in the Appendix to Part Three.

Issuance of Notes for Merchandise

Especially when interest rates are high, a business must use notes if payment of merchandise purchased is delayed. These transactions may be recorded as were those in the preceding section. However, since the volume of business done with a particular supplier or customer must be known for managerial

[4]To simplify illustrations, the general journal form of entry is used, even though most companies would actually use special journals.

purposes, such as applying for any available discounts based upon quantity purchased, the subsidiary ledger account should show the total history of all transactions with a particular firm. To supply this information, the accountant should record all merchandise purchases involving notes through the Accounts Payable account and the individual creditors' accounts in the accounts payable subsidiary ledger. For example, assume that on October 11, 1985, the Ace Company purchases merchandise costing $3,600 from the Boone Company and issues a 16 percent, 45-day note to the creditor. The note and interest are paid on November 25, 1985. These transactions are recorded as follows:

1985					
Oct.	11	Purchases		3,600	
		Accounts Payable			3,600
		To record merchandise purchased:			
		Boone Company $3,600			
	11	Accounts Payable		3,600	
		Notes Payable			3,600
		To record the issuance of a 16%, 45-day note:			
		Boone Company $3,600			
Nov.	25	Notes Payable		3,600	
		Interest Expense		72	
		Cash			3,672
		To record payment of a note and interest to the Boone Company.			

Issuance of Notes in Settlement of Open Accounts

A firm may issue a note to an open-account creditor as a means of further postponing payment, or a creditor may require a debtor to give a note if the account is past due. The entry for the issuance of a note in settlement of an open account payable is similar to the second entry above, dated October 11.

Issuance of Notes to Borrow from Banks

A business faced with the possibility of losing cash discounts may find it advantageous to borrow money from a bank to pay the open accounts within the discount periods. A 2/10, n/30 cash discount, for example, represents an annual cost saving of 36 percent, as was illustrated in Chapter 6. It is a sound financial decision to borrow money at the interest rate of 16 percent, for example, to prevent the loss of a 36 percent cost saving.

Banks and other grantors of credit handle notes in two ways:

1. Money may be borrowed on a note *bearing interest on face value* signed by the borrower, in which case the borrower receives the face value of the note and pays the face value plus the accumulated interest on the maturity date.

2. Money may be advanced on a note issued for maturity value which includes interest, referred to by bankers as a note discounted to maturity. In this book, this device is called a *note payable discounted on face value.* This kind of note is sometimes erroneously called a noninterest-bearing note. This seems to be a misleading description since interest, or *discount,* is deducted in advance, and the borrower receives only the discounted value. At the maturity date, the borrower pays the face value of the note, which includes the interest. The element of interest is present in either case; the difference is primarily one of form.

The amount of the discount on a note is the difference between its value on the date of discount and its value at maturity. **Maturity value,** the amount that will be paid at maturity, is the principal plus total interest for the life of the note. Since discount and interest are similar in that each represents the charge for the use of money, the Interest Expense account is used in this text to record the *incurred* portion of expense for each of these items.

Bank discount

Bank discount *may be defined as a deduction made from a gross future sum (the discount is computed on maturity value) to arrive at the current present value of that sum.*

Issuance of Note Bearing Interest on Face Value On March 1, 1985, the Ace Company borrowed $12,000 from the First National Bank, issuing a 16 percent, 60-day note, and on April 30 paid the bank for the note and interest. The issuance and payment of the note are recorded in the Ace Company's books as follows:

1985					
Mar.	1	Cash		12,000	
		Notes Payable			12,000
		To record a 16%, 60-day note issued to the First National Bank.			
Apr.	30	Notes Payable		12,000	
		Interest Expense		320	
		Cash			12,320
		To record payment of a 16%, 60-day note issued to the First National Bank.			

Issuance of Note Payable Discounted on Face Value Also on May 1, 1985, the Ace Company borrowed money from the City National Bank, discounting on face value its own $12,000, 60-day note at the discount rate of 16 percent. The amount of cash received in this case is $11,680, or $12,000 less a discount of $320. The amount of bank discount is computed by applying the discount rate to the maturity value (the face value for this type of note) for the discount period of 60 days. The following entry is made in the Ace Company's books to record the initial borrowing:

1985					
May	1	Cash		11,680	
		Discount on Notes Payable		320	
		Notes Payable			12,000
		To record a note issued to City National Bank discounted on face value at 16% for 60 days.			

The $320 is debited to Discount on Notes Payable because the note is written for the maturity value.[5] The interest element is deducted when the borrowing takes place. Since this is a form of discounting, the account is properly called Discount on Notes Payable. It should *not* be called Prepaid Interest, because the interest is not paid until the note matures. At that time, the net amount borrowed of $11,680 plus interest of $320 is paid as is now illustrated.

At the maturity date, June 30, 1985, a journal entry could be made recognizing that the interest element of $320 has now become an incurred expense in the following manner:

1985					
Jun.	30	Interest Expense		320	
		Discount on Notes Payable			320
		To recognize the incurrence of interest expense.			

The foregoing entry is an adjusting entry and *could be postponed* to the end of the period and made when regular adjusting entries are made. It is made here to reinforce the nature of the expense item. After this entry is made, the only remaining entry is the one to record the payment of the principal amount of the note. It is:

1985					
Jun.	30	Notes Payable		12,000	
		Cash			12,000
		To record payment of a discounted note to the City National Bank.			

[5]If the maturity date of the note falls within the current accounting period and thus all of the discount wll be an expense by the time the books are closed, an acceptable alternative to the May 1, 1985, entry would be:

1985					
May	1	Cash		11,680	
		Interest Expense		320	
		Notes Payable			12,000
		To record a note issued to City National Bank discounted on face value at 16% for 60 days.			

If the Ace Company had issued the note on December 16, 1985, and the books were closed on December 31, 1985, an adjusting entry would have to be made transferring 15/60, or 1/4, of the discount amount to interest expense. Then at maturity in 1986 the remaining part of the discount could be recognized as an expense at the time the principal amount of the note is paid. (Alternatively, the remaining 45/60, or 3/4, of the discount could be transferred to Interest Expense as a regular adjusting entry at the end of the year.)

Discount on notes payable should be shown in the balance sheet as a contra account to (subtracted from) notes payable under current liabilities. Thus, on the date of issuance of the note, the carrying value indicates the net amount of funds received from creditors on the note. Later, as adjustments are made to the Discount on Notes Payable account, the difference between the Notes Payable account and the balance of the Discount on Notes Payable account shows the net amount borrowed plus accrued interest on that amount.

Effective Interest Calculation In both the March 1 and May 1 bank loans, the amount paid at maturity was $320 more than the amount received from the bank by the borrower. However, the borrower had the use of $12,000, or the full face value of the note bearing interest on face value (March 1 bank loan), whereas only $11,680 was available from the discounted note. The *annual effective interest rate* (i in the following equation) on a discounted note may be computed by the following formula:

$$i = \frac{D}{P} \times \frac{12}{T}$$

where D = The amount of the discount.
P = The net proceeds.
12 = Months in the year.
T = The term of the note in months.

The annual effective interest rate in the example thus is not 16 percent; rather it is 16.44% percent, calculated as follows:

$$i = \frac{\$320}{\$11{,}680} \times \frac{12}{2} = 0.16438356 \text{ or } 16.44\%.$$ [6]

As indicated previously, the accountant should carefully determine the annual effective interest rate or APR of a loan, since this is relevant to making any short-term financial decision.

---

[6]Under the ***Truth in Lending Law,*** this rate would probably be stated as 16.5 percent since the law permits the credit grantor to round the APR to the nearest quarter of a percent.

End-of-Period Adjusting Entries for Interest on Notes Payable

Since interest is incurred daily throughout the life of a note payable, it is necessary to make adjusting entries for the interest expense on those notes payable that are written in one accounting period and mature in a later accounting period. Two kinds of adjustments are considered: (1) the accrual of interest on a note payable bearing interest on its face, and (2) the expense apportionment on a discounted note payable.

Assume that the Adjusto Company has the following accounts in its general ledger as of December 31, 1985:

Notes Payable — Acct. No. 205

Date		Explanation	F	Debit	Credit	Balance
1985						
Dec.	1	Hamm Co., 16%, 90 days	J17		15,000	15,000
	16	Bank of Rodin, 120 days discounted at 16% . . .	CR12		18,000	33,000

Discount on Notes Payable — Acct. No. 205A

Date		Explanation	F	Debit	Credit	Balance
1985						
Dec.	16		CR12	960		960

At December 31, 1985, the following two adjusting entries were made:

Date		Account / Explanation	F	Debit	Credit
1985					
Dec.	31	Interest Expense		200	
		Accrued Interest Payable			200
		To record accrued interest on the note issued to the Hamm Co.; interest for 30 days at 16% on \$15,000 is \$200.			
	31	Interest Expense		120	
		Discount on Notes Payable			120
		To record the transfer of \$120 interest from the Discount on Notes Payable account to the Interest Expense account on the note discounted at the Bank of Rodin: \$18,000 × 0.16 × 15/360.			

Comments on these entries follow:

1. The amount of the accrued interest on a note issued to the Hamm Company is computed at 16 percent for 30 days—the number of days after December 1, including December 31. It is recorded in an account entitled Accrued Interest Payable. Of course, no interest for the time period after December 31, 1985, should be recorded as an expense of 1985.

2. The second adjusting entry transfers interest from the Discount on Notes Payable account to the Interest Expense account. There are two methods by which the interest expense of $120 for 1985 can be determined: (a) the amount of the discount may be multiplied by a fraction consisting of the age of the note as of the adjustment date divided by the term (in the example, 15/120 × $960 = $120); or (b) an ordinary interest computation may be made (interest at 16 percent on $18,000 for 15 days is $120).

On March 1, 1986, when the Adjusto Company pays the Hamm Company for the note and interest, the following journal entry (under the nonreversing approach) is made:

1986					
Mar.	1	Notes Payable		15,000	
		Accrued Interest Payable		200	
		Interest Expense		400	
		Cash			15,600
		To record payment of a 16%, 90-day note and interest to the Hamm Co.			

The $15,600 credit to Cash includes the payment of two liabilities already on the books—Notes Payable and Accrued Interest Payable. The interest expense of $400 = (16% × 60/360 × $15,000) is entirely applicable to 1986.

Two journal entries could be made on April 15, 1986, when the payment of $18,000 is made to the Bank of Rodin as indicated in general journal form below:

1986					
Apr.	15	Interest Expense[7]		840	
		Discount on Notes Payable			840
		To transfer the remainder of the discount amount to Interest Expense.			
	15	Notes Payable		18,000	
		Cash			18,000
		To record payment of the note to the Bank of Rodin.			

The first of the foregoing two entries (although an adjusting entry) is made as of April 15, 1986, to reinforce the fact that the remaining amount of the discount has changed—as time passed—to an expense. The debit to Notes Payable represents the payment of the full amount due at maturity. Discussed next is the topic Notes Receivable, which will use many of the same principles developed in this section.

[7]In practice this entry would be postponed and made at the end of the period. The accountant would establish a routine to confirm that all adjusting entries are being made. In so doing, it would be preferable to make them as of one date.

Notes Receivable

Many firms accept promissory notes from customers; these are recorded in an account entitled **Notes Receivable.** They may then discount these notes at (same as selling to) financial institutions as a means of obtaining short-term funds. The accounting for notes receivable is similar to that for notes payable. Hence, a pattern similar to that used in the foregoing section to describe notes payable is followed in the discussion of notes receivable.

Recording Procedures Involving Notes Receivable

Many businesses require promissory notes in sales of merchandise on credit. These businesses include firms selling high-priced durable goods such as furniture, farm machinery, and automobiles. Notes receivable are also received by a financial institution when it lends money.

It is perhaps even more important to keep good accounting records for notes receivable than it is for notes payable. After all, the payee of a note payable will send a statement to the maker that a note is due, so there is little danger that the maker will overlook the due date. The holder of notes receivable must have the records arranged so that he or she can notify the debtor that the note is due. This requires that notes receivable be filed according to maturity dates in a properly safeguarded tickler file. A **tickler file** reveals the due date of notes in an obvious manner—by dates or color coding or some other visual display indicating the due date.

All notes receivable are usually recorded in a single general ledger account. The tickler file of notes receivable takes the place of a subsidiary notes receivable ledger. The Notes Receivable account of the Travis Armour Company is shown here.

Notes Receivable — Acct. No. 111

Date		Explanation	F	Debit	Credit	Balance
1985						
Nov.	1	C. Anson, 45 days, 16%	J51	775		775
Dec.	16	C. Anson, paid	CR20		775	0
	20	B. Barker, 90 days, 17%	J60	425		425
	20	L. Watts, 60 days, 16%	J60	500		925

Each debit posting indicates that an asset, Notes Receivable, has been acquired from a customer. The credit entry indicates that a particular note has been settled by payment. Credits will also be recorded if a note has been dishonored (not paid) or renewed (matured and replaced by a new note). In addition to the dollar amounts in the money columns, the Explanation column gives the maker's name, the term of the note, the interest rate, and any other relevant information.

If the information is not provided in the Explanation column of the Notes Receivable account, then it must be provided in some supplementary records for use in later accounting, such as adjustments. For example, if the volume of transactions warrants it, a special notes receivable register could be created. Debit and credit money columns could be inserted, along with memorandum columns for supplementary information. This register could serve as both a journal and a subsidiary record of notes receivable.

Receipt of a Note for a Sale

Assume that on March 3, 1985, the Potter Company sells merchandise to John Rawson and receives a 16 percent, 90-day note for $1,300. The following entries are made:

1985					
Mar.	3	Accounts Receivable		1,300	
		Sales			1,300
		To record sale of merchandise:			
		John Rawson $1,300			
	3	Notes Receivable		1,300	
		Accounts Receivable			1,300
		To record the receipt of a 16%, 90-day note:			
		John Rawson $1,300			

The first entry is made so that the customer's account in the accounts receivable subsidiary ledger will contain a complete record of all credit sales transactions. This information is useful to management in making decisions about collection efforts and further extension of credit.

On June 1, 1985, when the Potter Company receives payment in full from John Rawson, the following entry is made:

1985					
Jun.	1	Cash		1,352	
		Notes Receivable			1,300
		Interest Earned			52
		To record receipt of payment from John Rawson for note and interest due today.			

The Interest Earned account is a revenue account. Its balance is closed to the Income Summary account at the end of the accounting period.

Receipt of a Note in Settlement of an Open Account

Because of the interest cost of money to replace inventories, it is normal to require customers to give notes if open accounts are not paid on time. The entry for such notes is in the same form as the second journal entry on March 3 in the Potter Company illustration in the previous section.

Dishonor of a Note Receivable by the Maker

If a note cannot be collected at maturity, it is said to be a **dishonored note,** or the maker is said to have **defaulted** on the note. If the maturity date of a note passes without the note being collected, an entry should be made transferring the face value of the note plus any uncollected accrued interest to the Accounts Receivable account.

Assume that on June 1, 1985, Ronald Raymond issued a 16 percent, 90-day note for $4,000 to the Potter Company. At the maturity date, August 30, 1985, Raymond fails to pay the amount of the note and interest, at which time the following entry is made on the books of the Potter Company:

1985					
Aug.	30	Accounts Receivable		4,160	
		Notes Receivable			4,000
		Interest Earned			160
		To record the dishonor of a 16%, 90-day note: Ronald Raymond $4,160			

Two questions arise in connection with this entry: (1) Why should $160 be recognized as revenue and credited to the Interest Earned account? (2) Why should the item be allowed to remain as a valid account receivable?

Under the accrual concept, the interest has been earned. It represents a valid claim against the maker of the note; if the face of the note is collectible, then so is the interest. This leads to the answer to the second question. The fact that a note is not collected at its maturity is not a definite indication that it will never be collected. In the absence of evidence to the contrary most business firms assume that notes will ultimately be collected. If the amounts involved are material, all possible steps, including legal action, will certainly be taken to collect both accounts and notes receivable, and only after such steps have failed will an account be considered to be written off as a loss (see Chapter 11 for the accounting for these losses).

End-of-Period Adjusting Entries for Interest on Notes Receivable

The adjusting entries for interest on notes receivable parallel the adjusting entries for interest on notes payable. The primary purpose is accurate measurement of the revenue, Interest Earned, and the asset, Accrued Interest Receivable. To illustrate the adjusting entries and the effect they have on the accounting for notes and interest in the next accounting period, assume that the Emerson Company has the following account in its general ledger as of December 31, 1985:

Notes Receivable — Acct. No. 111

Date		Explanation	F	Debit	Credit	Balance
1985						
Nov.	1	Linda Wilson, 16%, 150 days	J71	3,660		3,660

At December 31, 1985, the accountant for the Emerson Company makes the following adjusting entry:

1985 Dec.	31	Accrued Interest Receivable . . . . Interest Earned . . . . To record the accrued interest on the Linda Wilson note at 16% for 60 days.		97.60	 97.60

The accrued interest receivable on the note from Linda Wilson is computed at 16 percent for 60 days, the number of days after November 1 including December 31. No interest for the period after December 31, 1985, should be recorded as revenue in the year 1985.

The following entry is made on March 31, 1986, when the note is collected, assuming that the adjusting entry was not reversed:

1986 Mar.	31	Cash . . . . Notes Receivable . . . . Accrued Interest Receivable . . . . . . Interest Earned . . . . To record collection of a 16%, 150-day note and interest from Linda Wilson.		3,904.00	 3,660.00 97.60 146.40

The debit of $3,904 to Cash represents the collection of two receivables already on the books, Notes Receivable and Accrued Interest Receivable. It also includes a revenue, Interest Earned, of $146.40, which was earned in and is entirely applicable to the year 1986.

Discounting Customers' Notes Receivable

For a business that receives a large number of notes from customers and may need to obtain cash to continue operations, it may be economically advantageous to obtain this cash by *discounting its notes receivable* at a bank rather than holding them to maturity. The bank purchases the notes for cash less a discount. If the credit rating of the firm is good, most banks will usually discount customers' notes receivable. The firm that has discounted the note—having previously endorsed it—must make payment to the bank if the maker fails to pay.

Contingent liability

***A potential obligation on the part of the endorser such as the one described above requiring the endorser to pay a dishonored note is referred to as a* contingent liability.**

Determining the Cash Proceeds

As far as the bank is concerned, it is making a loan to the discounter based on the maturity value of the note including any interest because that is the amount the bank will collect from the maker at the maturity date. The discount the bank deducts is based on a stipulated rate applied to maturity value for the remaining period the note has to run. The discount subtracted from the maturity value yields a balance representing **cash proceeds.** To compute the proceeds of a discounted note:

1. Determine the maturity value (the principal plus the total interest to maturity).
2. Find the discount period (the number of days the note still has to run after the date of the discount).
3. Compute the discount on the maturity value at the stipulated bank discount rate for the discount period.
4. Deduct the discount from the maturity value to find the cash proceeds.

This approach may be stated as:

$$P = MV - (MV \times d \times RL)$$

where P = The cash proceeds.
MV = The maturity value.
d = The rate of discount.
RL = The remaining life of the note.

Assume that on April 19, 1985, the Fuller Company receives from Edward Grande a 16 percent, 60-day note for $6,000 in settlement of a past-due open account. This transaction is recorded as follows:

1985					
Apr.	19	Notes Receivable		6,000.00	
		Accounts Receivable			6,000.00
		To record receipt of a 16%, 60-day note in settlement of a past-due open account:			
		Edward Grande $6,000			

On May 1, 1985, the Fuller Company, needing short-term funds, decides to discount Grande's note at the bank's rate of 15 percent. Calculation of the proceeds follows:

1. Maturity value of note:			
Face value		$6,000	
Total interest to maturity		160	$6,160.00
2. Due date	June 18		
3. Period of discount:			
May 1–May 31 (not counting May 1)	30 days		
June 1–June 18 (including June 18)	18 days		
	48 days		
4. Discount at 15% for 48 days on the maturity value:			
$6,160 × 0.15 × 48/360			123.20
Net cash proceeds			$6,036.80

Recording the Proceeds

The entry on the Fuller Company's books is:

1985					
May	1	Cash		6,036.80	
		Notes Receivable Discounted			6,000.00
		Interest Earned			36.80
		To record the discounting of Edward Grande's 16%, 60-day note at the bank at 15%.			

The **Notes Receivable Discounted** account is used to indicate that the Fuller Company, having endorsed the note before turning it over to the bank, is now obligated to pay the bank if Grande fails to do so. That is, the Fuller Company must pay the $6,000 contingent liability plus the $160 interest at 16 percent for 60 days, plus any **protest fee** (charge made by the bank for notifying the last endorser that the maker has failed to pay the amount of the note and interest). The obligation assumed by the Fuller Company is contingent on Grande's failure to pay and the account is therefore referred to as a **contingent liability account.** The Notes Receivable Discounted account brings the existence of the contingent liability to the attention of the reader of the balance sheet.

Full disclosure

In preparing financial statements,* full disclosure *of all essential facts such as contingent liabilities is of paramount importance.

Grande does not need to be informed that the note has been discounted, and no entry is required on his books. His obligation to pay the maturity value of the note on its presentation by the legal owner remains unchanged.

Presentation on the Balance Sheet

Assume that on May 31 the Notes Receivable account shows a balance of $17,500 (including the $6,000 note discounted on May 1). The balance sheet prepared on that date may disclose the existence of the contingent liability by a footnote or supplementary note to the balance sheet, as follows:

FULLER COMPANY
Partial Balance Sheet
May 31, 1985

Assets

Current assets:	
Notes receivable (see Note 6)	$11,500

Note 6: The company is contingently liable for notes receivable discounted in the amount of $6,000.

Disclosure of the contingent liability can also be made by offsetting notes receivable discounted against notes receivable in the balance sheet in the following manner:

FULLER COMPANY
Partial Balance Sheet
May 31, 1985

Assets

Current assets:		
Notes receivable	$17,500	
Deduct: Notes receivable discounted	6,000	
Net notes receivable		$11,500

Elimination of Contingent Liability

On the maturity date, an entry is made to eliminate the contingent liability as follows:

1985					
Jun.	18	Notes Receivable Discounted		6,000	
		Notes Receivable			6,000
		To eliminate the contingent liability on Grande's note, which was discounted on May 1, 1985.			

As of this date, the contingent liability is eliminated because payment has been made by the maker of the note, or the contingent liability becomes a real liability as described below.

Payment of a Discounted Note

The bank normally does not notify the discounter of payment by the maker. Therefore, if notification of dishonor is not received from the bank, it is assumed that the maker has paid the note at the maturity date, and the discounter is released from the contingent liability. Since an entry recording the elimination of the contingent liability was made on the maturity date, no further accounting is required.

Nonpayment of a Discounted Note

If Edward Grande dishonors the note at the maturity date, the bank must follow a certain formal procedure involving the preparation of notarized protest documents to establish the legal basis for the collection of the full amount from the Fuller Company. Since this procedure usually requires a few days and technically a negotiable instrument ceases to exist on the maturity date (whether it is paid or not), the entry to eliminate the contingent liability as of the maturity date should be made as described above.

On June 21, 1985, assume that the bank advises that Grande has defaulted and charges a protest fee of $8. The following entries are made on the Fuller Company's books when the company pays the bank the face value of the note, the interest, and the protest fee:

1985				
Jun.	21	Accounts Receivable	6,168	
		Cash		6,168
		To record payment of Edward Grande's note, which was discounted and is now dishonored:		
		Protest fee . . . . $ 8		
		Interest 160		
		Face value 6,000		
		Total debited in subsidiary ledger to:		
		Edward Grande $6,168		

Observe that *Accounts Receivable,* instead of Notes Receivable Discounted, is debited in the entry recording the cash payment. The Notes Receivable Discounted account was debited when the contingent liability was removed on June 18, 1985.

The fact that a note is dishonored does not mean that it will be definitely uncollectible or that it should be written off as a loss. Grande, in this case, may pay at a later date, either voluntarily or on a court order. The account remains open in the general ledger and the accounts receivable subsidiary ledger until it is settled or definitely determined to be uncollectible and written off.

Glossary

Annual effective interest rate The correct interest rate computed on only the remaining balance of an unpaid debt for the specific time period, usually stated as an annual fraction.

Bank discount An amount subtracted from a maturity value to determine net cash proceeds as of the present time.

Blank endorsement The signature of the owner on the back of a negotiable instrument; the endorsement guarantees the validity of the instrument and warrants its payment in case of dishonor by the maker at maturity.

Cash proceeds The amount of cash that is received when a firm discounts a note at a bank.

Contingent liability An amount that may become a liability in the future *if* certain events occur.

Contingent liability account An account in which a contingent liability is recorded. See *Contingent liability.*

Defaulted Having failed to pay the amount owed on a negotiable instrument at its maturity. See *Dishonored note.*

Discount on Notes Payable A contra to the Notes Payable account representing the interest that was deducted from the face amount of the note; the discount on the notes payable amount is allocated to the applicable periods to which the interest expense belongs.

Dishonored note A note that has not been paid by the maker at the maturity date.

Full disclosure A concept requiring that all essential facts about an item (or activity) be shown in applicable financial statements. An example is the disclosure of contingent liabilities.

Full endorsement An endorsement consisting of a notation on the back of a negotiable instrument of "Pay to the order of (name of person or company)" accompanied by the signature of the owner; full endorsement requires subsequent endorsement of the named endorsee before the instrument can be transferred further.

Interest The price of credit; a rental charge for the use of money.

Maturity date The date on which a negotiable instrument is due and payable.

Maturity value The amount payable (or receivable) on a negotiable instrument at its maturity date; it includes face value plus any stated interest.

Negotiable A characteristic of a document that permits it to be transferred for value received by endorsement to another person.

Note bearing interest on face value A note with a specified interest rate with interest to be paid at maturity in addition to the face value of the note.

Note payable discounted at face value A note payable issued for its maturity value that includes interest; the interest is deducted as bank discount from face value at the time the note is issued.

Notes payable Amount payable to creditors supported by formal written promises to pay.

Notes receivable Claims against individuals or companies supported by formal written promises to pay; a note receivable may be either a trade note or a nontrade note.

Notes Receivable Discounted An account that discloses the contingent liability for customers' notes which have been discounted.

Promissory note An unconditional written promise to pay a specified sum of money to the order of a designated person, or to bearer, at a fixed or determinable future time or on demand.

Protest fee A fee charged by a bank or financial institution for a note which is dishonored (not paid) at maturity.

Qualified endorsement An endorsement accompanied by the phrase "without recourse" that tends to relieve the endorser of any further liability.

Simple interest Interest on the original principal only.

Tickler file A file that reveals the due date of notes in an obvious manner—by dates or color coding or some other visual display indicating the due date. Other, similar coding could be designed to reveal other needed information.

Questions

Q10–1 Define interest. How is interest similar to rent?

Q10–2 What is the meaning of APR? Why is APR significant?

Q10–3 What is a negotiable promissory note? What does the term "negotiable" indicate?

Q10–4 Discuss the managerial factors that a company must consider in determining what method of short-term financing should be used.

Q10–5 Describe briefly how a person can calculate the effective interest rate (APR) on a note discounted at the bank. Give an example.

Q10–6 Is it better for a company to borrow money on a note discounted at a bank at 16 percent or on a note bearing interest on the face at 16 percent? Explain.

Q10–7 Under what conditions would a company issue notes? Give four examples where notes are issued very frequently.

Q10–8 Explain the following terms and procedures:

a. Discounting a note
b. Bank discount rate
c. Contingent liability
d. Proceeds
e. Maturity value
f. A dishonored note.

Q10–9 The following account balances appear in the general ledger of the Hardison Company:

Notes Receivable	
87,500	

Notes Payable	
	50,000

Notes Receivable Discounted	
	37,500

a. What is the amount of customers' notes outstanding?
b. What amount of customers' notes are in the Hardison Company's possession?
c. What amount of customers' notes have been discounted?
d. What is the Hardison Company's contingent liability on discounted notes?
e. How would these accounts be shown in the balance sheet?

Q10–10 Explain full disclosure. Why is full disclosure important?

Q10–11 Why should the Notes Receivable Discounted account and the Notes Receivable account be eliminated at maturity date regardless of whether a discounted note is paid or not?

Q10–12 (a) What is a contingent liability? (b) Can there be more than one person contingently liable on a particular note? Explain. (c) What amounts must a person who is contingently liable on an interest-bearing note pay if the maker dishonors the note on its due date?

Exercises

E10–1 *Determining maturity value of notes*

Information regarding five notes is given below:

Date of Note	Term of Note	Interest Rate	Principal
March 1, 1985	150 days	16%	$3,000
April 5, 1985	60	15	4,000
August 24, 1985	45	17	5,000
September 13, 1985	120	18	2,500
November 3, 1985	90	14	4,860

Determine the maturity date and maturity value of each note.

E10–2 *Calculating and recording accrued interest*

Information regarding four notes receivable held by the Cowen Company follows:

Date of Note	Term of Note	Interest Rate	Principal
November 1, 1985	150 days	16%	$3,000
November 16, 1985	90	17	3,600
December 1, 1985	45	15	3,300
December 16, 1985	60	16	4,800

Assume that the books are closed on December 31, 1985. Compute the total amount of simple interest that should be debited to the Accrued Interest Receivable account.

E10–3 *Recording notes payable transactions with interest on face value*

The following were among the transactions of the Elfland Company for 1985 and 1986:

1985	
Jan. 2	Purchased $6,000 of merchandise from the Emmerson Company and issued a 16 percent, 45-day note.
Feb. 16	Paid note and interest due the Emmerson Company.
Mar. 15	Issued a 15 percent, 90-day note to the Franks Company in settlement of an open account of $9,000.
Jun. 13	Paid the Franks Company $4,000 on principal and all the interest for the preceding 90 days; issued a new 16 percent, 60-day note for the balance of the principal.
Aug. 12	Paid the remaining amount due the Franks Company.
Dec. 1	Issued a 17 percent, 90-day note to the Zelda Company in settlement of an open account of $12,000.

1986	
Mar. 1	Paid the amount due the Zelda Company.

Journalize the transactions, including any necessary adjusting entries on December 31, 1985.

E10–4 *Recording notes payable discounted*

The following were among the transactions of the Stephen Company for 1985 and 1986:

1985	
Aug. 3	Issued its own 90-day note, made out to the Bank of Winthrop in the maturity amount of $12,000, and discounted it at a rate of 16 percent.
Nov. 1	Paid the Bank of Winthrop the amount due.
Dec. 1	Issued its own 90-day note, made out to the Bank of Jamestown in the maturity amount of $15,000, and discounted it at a rate of 15 percent.

1986	
Mar. 1	Paid the amount due the Bank of Jamestown.

Journalize the transactions, including all necessary adjusting entries. Assume books are closed each December 31.

E10–5 *Recording notes receivable transactions*

The following were among the transactions of the Haw River Corporation for 1985 and 1986:

1985	
Apr. 19	Sold merchandise for $3,000 to René Burstaw and received a 16 percent, 60-day note.
Jun. 18	Collected the amount due from Burstaw.
21	Received a 17 percent, 120-day note from Roger Camero in settlement of an open account for $4,500.
Oct. 19	Roger Camero dishonored his note.
Nov. 15	Received a 15 percent, 90-day note from Lilly Dulane in settlement of an open account of $3,600.

1986	
Feb. 13	Collected the note and interest from Dulane.

Journalize the transactions, including any necessary adjusting entries on December 31, 1985.

E10–6 *Discounting a customer's note receivable: paid by customer*

Burlington Company completed the following transactions in 1985 and 1986:

1985

Aug. 1 Sold $1,200 of merchandise on account to the Owens Company.
Oct. 8 Received a 90-day, 16 percent note in full settlement of the Owens account.
Dec. 5 Discounted the above note at 15 percent at the Bank of Graham.

1986

Jan. 6 The October 8 note was paid at maturity.

Journalize the transactions on the books of Burlington Company and Owens Company, including any necessary adjusting entries on December 31, 1985.

E10–7 *Discounting a customer's note receivable: dishonored by customer*

On September 5, 1985, the Dunstan Company sold $5,400 of merchandise on account to Berne Company and received a 16 percent, 90-day note. This note was discounted at 15 percent on October 20, 1985, at the Foxhall Bank. At maturity date, the note was dishonored by Berne Company, and the Dunstan Company paid the maturity value plus a $10 protest fee. Journalize the transactions on the books of the Dunstan Company.

E10–8 *Recording note transaction: maker and payee*

Robert Johns received from William Nelson a 16 percent, 120-day note for $6,000 dated March 3, 1985, in settlement of an open account. Thirty days later, Johns discounted Nelson's note with Faison Bank at 17 percent. Nelson paid the note at maturity. Journalize the transactions on the books of Johns and Nelson.

E10–9 *Describing transactions from account data*

Six transactions related to a sale to a customer are recorded in the following T accounts. Describe each transaction.

Cash

(c)	912	(d)	944
(f)	989		

Accounts Receivable

(a)	900	(b)	900
(d)	944	(f)	944

Notes Receivable

(b)	900	(e)	900

Notes Receivable Discounted

(e)	900	(c)	900

Sales

		(a)	900

Interest Earned

		(c)	12
		(f)	45

E10–10 *Calculating effective interest rates*

What is the annual percentage rate for the following credit situations (calculate and discuss each):

a. Merchandise purchased on 1/10, n/60 basis and discount is forgone for payment at the end of 60 days.
b. Money is borrowed on the basis of a 1¼ percent interest rate each month.
c. Merchandise is purchased on installment basis and interest at 1½ percent is charged for unpaid balance at beginning of each month.
d. Money is borrowed from the bank for a year at a 16 percent annual rate, but the bank required that 20 percent of the amount borrowed remain in the bank on deposit in an account that does not earn any interest.

A Problems

P10–1A *Calculating and recording accrued interest*

Information regarding six notes issued by the Plumblee Company is given below:

Date of Note	Term of Note	Interest Rate	Principal
March 1, 1985	1 year	15%	$ 6,600
July 1, 1985	240 days	16	900
November 1, 1985	150 days	17	12,000
November 16, 1985	120 days	14	7,200
December 1, 1985	90 days	18	4,800
December 16, 1985	60 days	13	18,000

Required: Assume that the books of the Plumblee Company are closed each December 31. Compute the total amount of accrued interest payable and make the necessary adjusting entry as of December 31, 1985.

P10–2A *Recording notes payable transactions*

The Riggsbee Company completed the following transactions during 1985 and 1986 (the fiscal year ends December 31):

1985

Jan.	2	Purchased $2,400 of merchandise from the Dawson Company, issuing a 15 percent, 60-day note.
Mar.	3	Paid the Dawson Company the amount due for the note and interest.
	3	Issued a 16 percent, 45-day note for $4,800 to Macy, Inc., in settlement of an open account.
Apr.	17	Paid Macy, Inc., $3,800 on the March 3 note plus all the interest due; issued a new 15 percent, 30-day note for the balance of the principal.
May	17	Paid Macy, Inc., for the April 17 note.
Jun.	1	Discounted at 16 percent its own $7,200, 30-day note made out to the Raytown Bank for the maturity value.
Jul.	1	Paid the Raytown Bank the amount due.
Dec.	1	Issued to the Saul Company a 14 percent, 90-day note for $6,000 in settlement of an open account.
	16	Discounted at 16 percent its own $18,000, 60-day note, made out to the First National Bank for the maturity value.

1986

Feb.	14	Paid the First National Bank the amount due.
Mar.	1	Paid the amount due to Saul Company for the note issued on December 1, 1985.

Required: Journalize the transactions, including all necessary adjusting entries. Assume books are closed each December 31.

P10–3A *Recording various note transactions*

During 1985, the Douglas Company completed the following transactions, among others:

1985

Jan.	3	Purchased merchandise for $6,000 from the Glass Company, giving a 16 percent, 30-day note, payable at the First State Bank.
	4	Sold $3,000 of merchandise on account to Harry Epps.
	6	Sold $1,500 of merchandise on account to Gladys Cox.
	8	Purchased on account merchandise for $1,800 from Corkson Company.
	10	Gave Corkson Company a 15 percent, 30-day note in settlement of the open account (January 8 purchase), payable at the Brooklawn Bank.
	12	Gladys Cox gave a 17 percent, 20-day note, payable at the First State Bank, in full settlement of her account.

	15	Harry Epps gave a 16 percent, 30-day note, payable at the Chawson Bank, in full settlement of the $3,000 purchase on January 4.
	16	Sold $6,000 of merchandise on account to Andrew Peters.
	24	Received from Andrew Peters a 16 percent, 20-day note, payable at the Bragtown Bank, in settlement of the $6,000 purchase on January 16.
	24	Sold $9,000 of merchandise to Ennery Company and received a 17 percent, 30-day note, payable at the Roxboro Bank.
Feb.	1	Gladys Cox's note of January 12 was dishonored.
	2	Paid the Glass Company for the note due today.
	9	Paid the Corkson Company for the note due today.
	13	Received a check from Andrew Peters for $4,000 plus interest and accepted a new 16 percent, 90-day note, payable at the Bragtown Bank, for the balance of the note of January 24.
	14	Received payment from Harry Epps in settlement of his note due today.
	23	Received a check from Ennery Company for $5,000 plus interest and accepted a new 17 percent, 30-day note, payable at the Roxboro Bank, for the balance of the note of January 24.
	28	Discounted at 15 percent at the Yelverton Bank Ennery Company's note of February 23.
Mar.	25	Received notice that Ennery Company had dishonored its note of February 23. Paid the bank the maturity value of the note plus a $9 protest fee.

Required: Record the transactions in general journal form.

P10–4A *Determining cost of credit*

The Glenview Company negotiated a 90-day loan (reference l) with the Fairfield Bank. The loan was paid on its due date (reference m). Glenview Company arranged for another 90-day loan (reference x) with the Wilson Bank, which was also paid when due (reference y).

Cash				Notes Payable to Bank				Interest Expense			
(l)	9,000	(m)	9,360	(m)	9,000	(l)	9,000	(m)	360		
(x)	8,640	(y)	9,000	(y)	9,000	(x)	9,000	(x)	360		

Required:

1. Describe the type of negotiable instrument used by (a) the Fairfield Bank, and (b) the Wilson Bank.

2. Which loan is more favorable to the Glenview Company? Why?

P10–5A *Determining approximate APR*

The Greensboro Appliance Company sells standard washing machines for $720 in cash or on terms of $75 down and $120 a month for six months. In order to meet competition, Greensboro is considering changing its credit terms to a $75 down payment and $60 a month for 12 months.

Required: Compute the approximate effective annual interest rate (APR) under (a) the present plan, and (b) the proposed plan. Carry your computations to four decimal places. Assume that each installment includes a uniform monthly reduction in the carrying charge. Which credit terms would (c) the buyer prefer? (d) The seller prefer?

P10–6A *Thought-provoking problem: selecting best source of short-term credit*

The following two sources of credit were available to Boston Company:

a. The Barton Bank agreed to accept on a discount basis the Boston Company's one-year note made out for the maturity value of $20,000 discounted at a 16 percent rate.

b. The Bank of Timberlake agreed to loan cash of $19,400 on a note with interest at 12 percent for one year added to the $19,400, making the principal of the note $21,728. The note is to be paid off in monthly installments of $1,810.67 over 12 months.

Required: Which method of credit should Boston Company choose and why? Support your reasons with appropriate calculations.

B Problems

P10–1B *Calculating and recording accrued interest*

Information regarding six notes received by the Henderson Company is given below:

Date of Note	Term of Note	Interest Rate	Principal
March 15, 1985	330 days	15%	$ 4,400
August 1, 1985	1 year	14	1,720
November 1, 1985	150 days	16	7,200
November 16, 1985	120 days	17	3,100
December 1, 1985	90 days	16	4,800
December 16, 1985	45 days	18	12,200

Required: Assume that the books of the Henderson Company are closed each December 31. Compute the total amount of accrued interest receivable and make the necessary adjusting entry as of December 31, 1985.

P10–2B *Recording notes payable transactions*

The Dunbar Company completed the following transactions during 1985 and 1986 (the fiscal year ends December 31):

1985

Jan. 2	Purchased $4,400 of merchandise from the Brooks Company, issuing a 16 percent, 60-day note.
Mar. 3	Paid the Brooks Company the amount due for the note and interest.
3	Issued a 15 percent, 45-day note for $4,400 to Dimray, Inc., in settlement of an open account.
Apr. 17	Paid Dimray, Inc., $2,500 on the March 3 note plus all the interest due; issued a new 15 percent, 30-day note for the balance of the principal.
May 17	Paid Dimray, Inc., for the April 17 note.
Jun. 1	Discounted at 17 percent its own $4,200, 30-day note, made out to the Moriah Bank for the maturity value.
Jul. 1	Paid the Moriah Bank the amount due.
Dec. 1	Issued to the Smith Company an 18 percent, 90-day note for $6,500 in settlement of an open account.
16	Discounted at 15 percent its own $4,150, 60-day note, made out to the Second National Bank for the maturity value.

1986

Feb. 14	Paid the Second National Bank the amount due.
Mar. 1	Paid the amount due to Smith Company for the note issued on December 1, 1985.

Required: Journalize the transactions, including all necessary adjusting entries. Assume books are closed each December 31.

P10–3B *Recording various note transactions*

During 1985, the Barton Company completed the following transactions, among others:

1985

Jan. 3	Purchased merchandise for $8,000 from the Pinner Company, giving a 16 percent, 30-day note, payable at the Westtown Bank.
4	Sold $4,500 of merchandise on account to James David.
6	Sold $3,000 of merchandise on account to Dorothy Council.

	8	Purchased on account merchandise $4,600 from Colt Company.
	10	Gave Colt Company a 17 percent, 30-day note in settlement of open account (January 8 purchase), payable at the Village Westbank.
	12	Dorothy Council gave a 16 percent, 20-day note, payable at the Westtown Bank, in full settlement of her account.
	15	James David gave a 17 percent, 30-day note, payable at the Planters Bank, in settlement of the $4,500 purchase on January 4.
	16	Sold $3,600 of merchandise on account to William Turner.
	24	Received from William Turner a 16 percent, 20-day note, payable at the Planters Bank, in settlement of the $3,600 purchase on January 16.
	24	Sold $5,400 of merchandise to Jones Company and received a 16 percent, 30-day note, payable at the Boulevard Bank.
Feb.	1	Dorothy Council's note of January 12 was dishonored.
	2	Paid the Pinner Company for the note due today.
	9	Paid the Colt Company for the note due today.
	13	Received a check from William Turner for $1,600 plus interest and accepted a new 16 percent, 90-day note, payable at the Planters Bank, for the balance of the note of January 24.
	14	Received payment from James David in settlement of his note due today.
	23	Received a check from Jones Company for $2,400 plus interest and accepted a new 17 percent, 30-day note, payable at the Boulevard Bank, for the balance of the note of January 24.
	28	Discounted at 17 percent at the Towson Bank Jones Company's note of February 23.
Mar.	25	Received notice that Jones Company had dishonored its note of February 23. Paid the bank the maturity value of the note plus a $10 protest fee.

Required: Record the transactions in general journal form.

P10–4B *Determining cost of credit*

The Hillville Company negotiated a 90-day loan (reference h) with the Village East Bank. The loan was paid on its due date (reference i). Hillville Company arranged for another 90-day loan (reference j) with the Second Street Bank, which was also paid when due (reference k).

Cash				Notes Payable to Banks				Interest Expense			
(h)	6,000	(i)	6,240	(i)	6,000	(h)	6,000	(i)	240		
(j)	5,760	(k)	6,000	(k)	6,000	(j)	6,000	(j)	240		

Required:

1. Describe the type of negotiable instrument used by (a) the Village East Bank; (b) the Second Street Bank.

2. Which loan is more favorable to the Hillville Company? Why?

P10–5B *Determining approximate APR*

The Neighborhood Appliance Company sells standard washing machines for $450 in cash or on terms of $40 down and $75 a month for six months. In order to meet the competition, Neighborhood is considering changing its credit terms to a $40 down payment and $37.50 a month for 12 months.

Required: Compute the approximate effective annual interest rate (APR) under (a) the present plan, and (b) the proposed plan. Carry your computations to four decimal places. Assume that each installment includes a uniform monthly reduction in the carrying charge. Which credit terms would (c) the buyer prefer? (d) The seller prefer?

P10–6B *Thought-provoking problem: short-term borrowing decisions*

Because of a severe cash crunch, the Illinois Company finds itself needing sources of short-term funds. After investigating all possibilities, the controller lists these alternatives:

1. To forgo discounts on the purchases of merchandise and pay the full invoice price at the latest possible date. These discounts are generally on a 2/10, n/30 basis.
2. To borrow money from the local bank at 18 percent; but the local bank requires that a minimum balance of 10 percent of the amount borrowed by maintained in the company's checking account throughout the period of the loan.
3. To borrow money from the Brady Finance Company and pay a monthly fee of 2½ percent of the unpaid balance at the beginning of each month.
4. To borrow money for a year from Judson Funds Company on a contract basis, agreeing to pay 15 percent of the original amount and to add this interest to the amount borrowed, then to repay the loan and interest in equal monthly installments.

Required: Assuming that two or more of these sources will be needed to provide adequate short-term funds, indicate the order of the desirability of the sources, from most desirable to least desirable, by calculating an approximation of the annual effective simple interest rates for each alternative.

11 Accounts Receivable and Bad Debts

Introduction

Buying and selling on an open charge account is a standard practice in the United States. For example, at the American Telephone and Telegraph Company, net receivables from customers and agents consistently make up about two-thirds of the current assets. Another popular form of credit sales results from the widespread use of credit cards. Because of the amount of the credit transactions involving all types of goods and services, there is a need for careful internal control and analysis of receivables by management.

This chapter stresses the basic accounting for sources and classification of receivables, accounting for bad debts expense, aging of accounts receivable, comparison of the direct write-off method with the estimating method, credit card sales, and internal control of accounts receivable.

Learning Goals

To identify the sources and classification of receivables.

To understand the nature of bad debts expense and determine bad debts expense by the balance sheet and income statement approaches.

To record the bad debts adjustment, write-off, and recovery.

To describe the uses of the aging schedule of accounts receivable.

To distinguish between the direct write-off and the estimating method of accounting for bad debts expense.

To explain the balance sheet classification of an opposite balance in accounts receivable or accounts payable.

To understand the recording of credit card sales.

To recognize the importance of the internal control of accounts receivable.

Sources and Classification of Receivables

As stated previously, a receivable represents a claim against individuals or companies for cash or other assets. There are two broad categories of receivables:

1. Those arising out of a trade or a sale of goods or services, referred to as **trade receivables.**

2. All the other receivables arising out of a variety of claims of a source other than trade, referred to as **nontrade receivables.**

Trade Receivables

Trade receivables are of three classes: accounts receivable, notes receivable, and credit card receivables. *Accounts receivable* are claims against customers for sales made on account with the credit terms determined in advance. For individuals, these are usually 30-day charge accounts with a finance charge assessed on balances more than 30 days old. Generally these are shown in a ledger account entitled Accounts Receivable.

Notes receivable are claims supported by written formal promises to pay; that is, promissory notes from customers. Both categories represent the same legal claims against customers. One major advantage to a firm of holding a note receivable is that it is a written acknowledgment that the debt exists. The note also is a negotiable instrument and permits the firm to discount it for cash or use it as collateral for a loan from a bank. Notes can arise from either a trade or a nontrade situation. For a note to be a trade receivable, it must arise from a sale of goods or services. The accounting for notes was discussed in Chapter 10.

Credit card receivables are claims arising from sales made by the acceptance of credit cards where the resulting invoices are not accepted by banks for deposits. These are trade receivables but require a special type of accounting discussed later in this chapter.

Nontrade Receivables

Other types of receivables arise from nontrade sources, giving rise to a wide variety of nontrade receivable accounts. *Accounts Receivable, Employees* arises from loans made to employees or from sales to employees—usually at a discount—to be deducted from the next paycheck. *Accrued Interest Receivable* represents the accrual of interest on notes receivable or other interest-bearing instruments. *Investment in Bonds* represents claims against companies for money loaned to them for interest-yielding bonds. *Refundable Deposits* are made by companies as good-faith indications for such business events as contract bids with government agencies or others. *Notes Receivable, Officers and Employees* results from loans made by the company to officers and employees.

Classification of Receivables

Receivables that are due and collectible within a year (or one operating cycle if it is longer than a year) should be shown in the current assets section of the balance sheet. The terms *accounts receivable, receivables from credit card companies,* and *notes receivable,* if unqualified, should be understood to represent trade receivables collectible within one year or one operating cycle if it is longer than a year. Receivables that are not due or are not collectible within a year (or after an operating cycle that is longer than a year) should be shown under long-term investments. Accounting issues involved in open charge trade accounts receivable are discussed first in the next sections.

Bad Debts Expense

The cost of the goods sold and all other expenses incurred during the period should be related to or should be deducted from the revenue of that period.

Matching standard

***A basic principle in accounting, the* matching standard, *is that in any accounting period the earned revenue and the actual expense incurred in realizing that revenue should be* assigned to that period and used in calculating net income.**

The balance in the Accounts Receivable account normally represents uncollected amounts included in revenue. Accordingly, losses that may arise through failure to collect any of the receivables should be recognized as an expense of doing business **(bad debts expense)** during the period when the sales were made. Thus, accounts receivable originating from sales made for credit in 1985 and determined to be uncollectible in 1986 represent a bad debts expense of the year 1985. Bad debts expense may be occasioned by a careful enough credit investigation not being made at the time of a sale.

It also follows that, in the balance sheet, accounts receivable should be shown at the amount expected to be realized through actual cash collections from customers **(net realizable value).** Only in this way will the amount satisfy the definition of an asset. If accounts receivable were shown at their gross amount without any accompanying adjustment for the estimated uncollectible portion, the total assets and the total owner's equity would be overstated to the extent of the failure to recognize an expense that arises out of the uncollectible sale of goods on account. Accordingly, the Financial Accounting Standards Board has indicated that losses from uncollectible accounts shall be accrued and recognized as an expense even though the specific receivables that will become uncollectible are not known.[1]

Recording the Bad Debts Adjustment

Bad debts expense is estimated in an end-of-period adjusting entry. Assume that on December 31, 1985, after its first year of operations, the credit department of the Gadson Company, having analyzed 1985 sales and past-due accounts, determines that out of the current year's sales, $650 will be uncollectible. This amount represents a bad debts expense to be shown in the general and administrative expenses section of the income statement as a de-

[1]*Statement of Financial Accounting Standards No. 5,* "Accounting for Contingencies" (Stamford, Conn.: FASB, March 1975), paragraph 22.

duction from revenue. The expense pertains to accounts receivable resulting from sales of the current period; therefore, in accordance with the principle of periodic matching of expenses and revenue, the estimated amount of bad debts expense should be charged against current revenue. The adjusting general journal entry recorded on December 31, 1985, and the posting of the entry to the general ledger are:

Page 65

1985 Dec.	31	Bad Debts Expense . . . . Allowance for Doubtful Accounts . . . To record estimated future losses on uncollectible accounts receivable.	609 121A	650	 650

Expense

Bad Debts Expense — Acct. No. 609

Date		Explanation	F	Debit	Credit	Balance
1985 Dec.	31		J65	650		650

Contra asset

Allowance for Doubtful Accounts — Acct. No. 121A

Date		Explanation	F	Debit	Credit	Balance
1985 Dec.	31		J65		650	650

This method is called the allowance method. The Bad Debts Expense account is closed into Income Summary and represents an operating expense on the income statement. **Allowance for Doubtful Accounts** is a contra asset or a valuation account to Accounts Receivable. A **valuation account** is subtracted from another account to arrive at the book value or carrying value. As a contra to Accounts Receivable, the Allowance for Doubtful Accounts will cause accounts receivable to be shown on the balance sheet at their estimated collectible or net realizable value. In this first year, there was no previous balance before adjustment in Allowance for Doubtful Accounts and no account receivable was written off during the year 1985. These complications are discussed in more detail later in the chapter.

Since the amount of $650 is an estimate not related to specific customers' accounts, the credit must be made to the contra or valuation account. If the credit were to be made directly to Accounts Receivable without corresponding credits to subsidiary accounts, the equality of the controlling account and the subsidiary accounts would no longer exist. Using the Allowance for Doubtful Accounts account permits a reduction in the asset carrying value without destroying this essential equality between the controlling account and subsidiary ledger. Its effect on the balance sheet as a deduction from the related asset account is as follows:

GADSON COMPANY
Partial Balance Sheet
December 31, 1985

Assets

Current assets:		
Cash		$1,210
Accounts receivable	$6,945	
Deduct: Allowance for doubtful accounts	650	6,295
Notes receivable		1,000

The amount of $6,295 represents the net cash expected to be received when the accounts receivable are collected.

Writing Off Uncollectible Accounts

As actual accounts receivable are determined to be uncollectible during subsequent accounting periods, Allowance for Doubtful Accounts is debited instead of Bad Debts Expense, with offsetting credits to the Accounts Receivable account in the general ledger and to the specific customers' accounts in the accounts receivable subsidiary ledger. This contra account is debited because the expense already has been recognized by the bad debts adjusting entry. A debit to Bad Debts Expense at the time of write-off would cause the expense associated with the uncollectible item to be recorded twice: in 1985 when the expense was estimated and again when written off.

Assume that on January 15, 1986, the Gadson Company decides that a claim of $80 against Thomas Lee for a sale made on September 1, 1985, is uncollectible. The entry to record the write-off of this account is:

1986 Jan.	15	Allowance for Doubtful Accounts	80	
		Accounts Receivable		80
		To write off an uncollectible account: Thomas Lee . . . $80		

Estimating the Amount of Bad Debts Expense

Management must make a careful estimate, based on judgment and past experience, of the amount of its uncollectible accounts. Accurate records must be kept and overdue accounts must be carefully analyzed. Two alternative approaches are commonly used in estimating bad debts expense. They are referred to as (1) the **income statement approach,** based on the dollar volume of sales, and (2) the **balance sheet approach,** based on the amount of receivables.

The Income Statement Approach The income statement approach answers the question: How much bad debts expense is associated with this year's sales? Thus, in associating the bad debts expense directly with dollar volume of sales, the estimate is based on a percentage of an income statement item. Typically, it is based on a percentage of sales less sales returns and allowances. The percentage is determined from information derived from the company's past experience. Even though it is not usually done, it may be desirable to establish the percentage on the basis of credit sales only, excluding cash sales, particularly if the ratio of cash sales to total sales changes substantially from year to year. The method is simple to apply and furnishes an equitable basis for distributing bad debts expense. Since the computation used in this method yields the amount of the bad debts expense for the year directly, any existing balance in the Allowance for Doubtful Accounts is ignored. Thus, a small error in the same direction over the years could accumulate to a large amount in the Allowance for Doubtful Accounts, since its balance is ignored in the adjustment process.

To illustrate the adjustment by this approach, assume that an examination of the accounts of a given company for the preceding five years shows that approximately ½ of 1 percent of credit sales have proven to be uncollectible. Assume further that credit sales for a particular year are $200,000 and that there is a credit balance of $105 in Allowance for Doubtful Accounts before adjustments are made. The bad debts expense for the year is $1,000 = (0.005 × $200,000). In recording the adjustment, the $105 balance in the Allowance for Doubtful Accounts is ignored because it represents a carryover of potential losses from sales of prior years. Also, the $1,000 amount is the estimate of bad debts expense for the year and hence the amount of the adjustment. The adjusting journal entry to record the expense is:

Page 64

1985 Dec.	31	Bad Debts Expense	609	1,000	
		Allowance for Doubtful Accounts . . .	121A		1,000
		To record the bad debts expense for the year based on credit sales.			

Once the foregoing information is posted, the Allowance for Doubtful Accounts and Bad Debts Expense would appear as indicated below:

Allowance for Doubtful Accounts — Acct. No. 121A

Date		Explanation	F	Debit	Credit	Balance
1985 Dec.	31	Credit balance	✓			105
	31		J64		1,000	1,105

Bad Debts Expense Acct. No. 609

Date		Explanation	F	Debit	Credit	Balance
1985 Dec.	31		J64	1,000		1,000

After the adjusting entry is posted to the Allowance for Doubtful Accounts, its balance is $1,105. Notice that this amount is different from the $1,000 amount of Bad Debts Expense for the year. This does not represent an error, since the two accounts measure different things:

1. The Allowance for Doubtful Accounts measures the estimated uncollectible accounts receivable regardless of what year's sales gave rise to the receivables.

2. Bad Debts Expense measures the uncollectible portion of the current year's sales on account.

The Balance Sheet Approach The balance sheet approach requires an adjustment of the existing balance of Allowance for Doubtful Accounts to an amount that, when deducted from accounts receivable on the balance sheet, will show accounts receivable at their net realizable value. This approach seeks an answer to the question: How large a valuation allowance is needed to disclose our receivables at the net cash to be realized from those items? Thus the amount of the balance sheet item, accounts receivable, rather than the income statement item, sales, is used as the base for the adjustment.

The amount of bad debts expense is determined indirectly. The necessary balance of Allowance for Doubtful Accounts is determined by either of two procedures: (1) **aging** the accounts receivable (that is, analyzing them by the amount of time they have remained unpaid), or (2) the balance of Allowance for Doubtful Accounts is an amount equal to an estimated blanket percentage of current accounts receivable. The expense adjustment is the amount needed to produce the desired balance.

Aging the Accounts Receivable to Obtain Allowance for Doubtful Accounts Aging the accounts receivable involves consideration of the date on which payment was due, the number of days that have elapsed since the due date, and any other available data of a financial nature that give some clue to collectibility of the accounts. A columnar work sheet like the one shown in Figure 11–1 is often used to facilitate the analysis. It is sometimes referred to as an **aging schedule.** Computerized accounting systems produce an aging schedule as a standard procedure.

All accounts in the accounts receivable subsidiary ledger and their corresponding balances are listed in the Customer's Name and Total Balance columns. Each balance in the Total Balance column is then extended to the appropriate columns, after being analyzed into age classifications.

JOHN ROGERS COMPANY
Analysis of Accounts Receivable by Age
December 31, 1985

Customer's Name	Total Balance	Not Yet Due	Items Past Due 1–30 Days	31–60 Days	61–90 Days	Over 90 Days
Walter G. Arnold	$ 880	$ 800	$ 80			
Allan Conlon	1,800	1,000	500	$ 300		
Charles Peacock	50				$ 50	
Richard C. Smith	320	100	200	20		
Jerome Werther	960				900	$ 60
Others	51,990	27,220	15,460	5,280	730	3,300
Totals	$56,000	$29,120	$16,240	$5,600	$1,680	$3,360
Percent of total	100	52	29	10	3	6

Figure 11–1 **Analysis of Accounts Receivable by Age**

The aging method yields a more satisfactory Allowance for Doubtful Accounts than does any other method because the estimate is based on a study of individual customer accounts rather than on a blanket percentage of a single general ledger account balance. The bad debts expense, however, of a given year could be greatly distorted by the use of this method. For instance, if recoveries of accounts receivable previously written off or the write-off in the current year of accounts receivable arising from prior years' sales are credited or debited to the Allowance for Doubtful Accounts without any designation of which of these items affect prior years' net income, the bad debts expense of the current year will be distorted.

The analysis of accounts receivable aids management not only in the accounting for uncollectible accounts but also in making credit decisions. In interpreting this information for credit decisions, management should also compare the current analysis of accounts receivable by age with those of earlier periods, especially the age-group percentages. Currently, 52 percent of the total accounts receivable are not yet due, 29 percent are past due from 1 to 30 days, and so on. When compared with earlier years, percentage increases in the lower age classifications with offsetting decreases in the older classes are favorable.

The analysis in Figure 11–1 is also used to determine the proper balance to be established in Allowance for Doubtful Accounts. To make this determination, companies may apply a sliding scale of percents based on previous experience to the total amount shown in each column. The computation to determine expected uncollectible items for the John Rogers Company is as follows:

	Amount	Estimated Percent Uncollectible	Allowance for Doubtful Accounts
Not yet due	$29,120	3	$ 873.60
Past due			
1–30 days	16,240	4	649.60
31–60 days	5,600	10	560.00
61–90 days	1,680	20	336.00
Over 90 days	3,360	50	1,680.00
Total accounts receivable	$56,000		
Total balance needed in allowance . . .			$4,099.20

On the basis of this summary, $4,099.20 of the outstanding accounts receivable on December 31 will become uncollectible. Consequently, an Allowance for Doubtful Accounts with a balance of $4,099.20 is required. Before the adjusting entry is made, the existing balance in the account must be considered to measure the balance that is needed in the Allowance for Doubtful Accounts. The John Rogers Company has a present credit balance in Allowance for Doubtful Accounts of $150 remaining from earlier periods. The adjusting entry amount will be for $3,949.20 = ($4,099.20 − $150); when this amount is transferred to the allowance account, it will bring that account up to $4,099.20, the estimated probable uncollectible amount. The adjusting journal entry is:

1985					
Dec.	31	Bad Debts Expense		3,949.20	
		Allowance for Doubtful Accounts . . .			3,949.20
		To increase the asset valuation account by the estimated expense.			

Assume, however, that because of writing off some of the Accounts Receivable arising from 1985 sales in 1985 before an adjusting entry is made that the Allowance for Doubtful Accounts had a debit balance of $300 before adjustment rather than a credit balance of $150. The adjusting entry and thus the bad debts expense recognized in 1985 would then be $4,399.20 = ($4,099.20 + $300). After this entry is posted, the allowance account contains the desired credit balance of $4,099.20.

Use of Blanket Percentage to Obtain Allowance for Doubtful Accounts

Unless the subsidiary ledger is processed by computer, an analysis of accounts receivable by age is time consuming. If there is a reliable pattern, the Allowance for Doubtful Accounts may be based on a single blanket percentage of accounts receivable, computed as follows for the Garu Company:

End of Year	Balance of Accounts Receivable	Total Losses from Uncollectible Accounts
1982	$20,000	$ 800
1983	24,000	480
1984	22,000	700
Totals	$66,000	$1,980

The average loss of the past three years has been 3 percent = ($1,980 ÷ $66,000). Assume that at the end of 1985 total accounts receivable are $30,000 and a credit balance of $150 is in the allowance account. Estimated uncollectible accounts at 3 percent of accounts receivable are $900 = ($30,000 × 0.03). The following adjusting entry on the books of the Garu Company at the end of 1985 increases the Allowance for Doubtful Accounts to the desired amount of $900.

1985					
Dec.	31	Bad Debts Expense		750	
		Allowance for Doubtful Accounts			750
		To increase the asset valuation account by the estimated expense.			

A portion of the information for the following partial balance sheet is taken from the preceding data.

GARU COMPANY
Partial Balance Sheet
December 31, 1985

Assets

Current assets:		
Cash		$ 3,200
Accounts receivable	$30,000	
Deduct: Allowance for doubtful accounts	900	29,100
Notes receivable		18,000

Promissory notes receivable arising from the sale of merchandise may also prove to be uncollectible. As was learned in Chapter 10, the amount due from the customer on a dishonored note is removed from Notes Receivable and transferred to Accounts Receivable, where it will remain until it is either collected or determined to be uncollectible and written off in the usual manner. When notes receivable specifically arise from the sale of merchandise, the current allowance for estimated bad debts losses should be adequate to cover outstanding notes receivable and accounts receivable. The following partial balance sheet presentation shows that the allowance covers notes receivable and accounts receivable jointly:

GARU COMPANY
Partial Balance Sheet
December 31, 1985

Assets

Current assets:		
Cash		$ 3,200
Accounts receivable	$30,000	
Notes receivable	18,000	
Total	$48,000	
Deduct: Allowance for doubtful accounts and notes	900	47,100

Writing Off Uncollectible Accounts

When it is decided that a specific customer's account is definitely uncollectible, the amount due should be written off. Assuming that on February 15, 1986, the Garu Company definitely determined that the account of a customer, Joseph Nykerk, is uncollectible, the entry to record the write-off is:

1986					
Feb.	15	Allowance for Doubtful Accounts		75	
		Accounts Receivable			75
		To write off uncollectible account:			
		Joseph Nykerk . . . $75			

This entry has no effect on the net realizable value of the receivables; it only adjusts the balance of two accounts. The entry does not affect expenses, because no expense was incurred on February 15, 1986. The expense was recorded by the adjusting entry of December 31, 1985. Assume that immediately before this entry was made, the books of the Garu Company showed the following account balances:

Accounts Receivable	$30,000
Allowance for Doubtful Accounts (credit)	900

When the entry to write off Nykerk's account is posted, the result is:

	Balances before Write-Off	Write-Off	Balances after Write-Off
Accounts receivable	$30,000	$75	$29,925
Deduct: Allowance for doubtful accounts	900	75	825
Estimated realizable value	$29,100		$29,100

This calculation points up the fact that since the expense was recorded in the period when the sale was made, the subsequent write-off does not change net realizable value of assets, and since there was no net change in assets, there would likewise be no change in liabilities or owner's equity.

Recovery of Bad Debts

An account that is written off as uncollectible may later be recovered in part or in full. In that event, the entry that was made to write off the account is reversed to the extent of the amount recovered or expected to be recovered. Assuming that Joseph Nykerk settles with his creditors for 50 cents on the dollar and that a check for $37.50 is received, the required journal entries are:

1986					
Nov.	15	Accounts Receivable		37.50	
		Allowance for Doubtful Accounts . . .			37.50
		To restore the collectible portion of the account previously written off: Joseph Nykerk $37.50			
	15	Cash		37.50	
		Accounts Receivable			37.50
		To record payment received: Joseph Nykerk $37.50			

The debit and the credit to Accounts Receivable cancel each other, but they are necessary if a complete record of all transactions with the customer is to be maintained. Such a record may be of considerable aid if further extension of credit to Joseph Nykerk is considered at some future date.

Direct Write-Offs in Period of Discovery

If the amount of bad debts expense cannot be reasonably estimated, a company must use the direct write-off method for recognition of bad debts expense. This method postpones recording the expense until the specific receivable is definitely determined to be uncollectible. In this case, an Allowance for Doubtful Accounts is *not* used, and no end-of-period adjusting entry for estimated expense is made. The February 15, 1986, entry on the books of the Garu Company to remove Joseph Nykerk's account in full under the direct write-off method is:

1986					
Feb.	15	Bad Debts Expense		75	
		Accounts Receivable			75
		To write off uncollectible account: Joseph Nykerk $75			

The expense is recognized in the *period of write-off* rather than in the period when the sale is made. The direct write-off method, as well as the allowance method previously illustrated, is acceptable for federal income tax reporting purposes. However, it does not assign to each accounting period the expenses arising out of sales made in that period and therefore violates the principle of matching expenses and revenue in each accounting period. Thus the error in matching causes the net income shown in the income statement to be in error. It also causes the net receivables as shown in the balance sheet to be overstated.

Assume again that on November 15, 1986, Nykerk makes a settlement of 50 cents on the dollar and issues a check for $37.50. The required journal entries are:

1986					
Nov.	15	Accounts Receivable		37.50	
		Bad Debts Recovered			37.50
		To restore the collectible portion of the account previously written off: Joseph Nykerk $37.50			
	15	Cash		37.50	
		Accounts Receivable			37.50
		To record payment received: Joseph Nykerk $37.50			

Bad Debts Recovered is a revenue account; its balance should be reported in the other revenue section of the income statement.

Comparison of the Two Recording Procedures

The two methods of recording bad debts expense are compared in Figure 11–2, assuming the following data:

Allowance for doubtful accounts (credit balance, January 1)	$ 4,200
All sales on account	510,000
Cash collections on account	495,000
Sales returns and allowances	4,000
Accounts receivable written off as uncollectible	3,950
Bad debts recovered	250

The basis for estimating bad debt expenses is 1 percent × (Sales − Sales returns and allowances).

Valuation Accounts for Returns and Allowances and Cash Discounts

The net realizable amount of receivables on the balance sheet indicates the amount of collections available to the firm after allowing for bad debts expense. For example, accounts receivable of $30,000 and a corresponding allowance for doubtful accounts of $2,000 should result in a company's collecting approximately $28,000. In reality, other deductions may be made that will decrease this amount. Typical deductions are sales returns, sales allowances, cash discounts granted to customers for prompt payments, and collection ex-

Transactions (Jan. 1–Dec. 31, 1985)	Estimating Bad Debts Expense			Direct Write-Off		
All sales on account	Accounts Receivable Sales	510,000	 510,000	Accounts Receivable Sales	510,000	 510,000
Cash received on account	Cash Accounts Receivable	495,000	 495,000	Cash Accounts Receivable	495,000	 495,000
Sales returns and allowances	Sales Returns and Allowances Accounts Receivable	4,000	 4,000	Sales Returns and Allowances Accounts Receivable	4,000	 4,000
Accounts receivable determined to be uncollectible	Allowance for Doubtful Accounts Accounts Receivable	3,950	 3,950	Bad Debts Expense Accounts Receivable	3,950	 3,950
Bad debts recovered	Accounts Receivable Allowance for Doubtful Accounts	250	 250	Accounts Receivable Bad Debts Recovered	250	 250
	Cash Accounts Receivable	250	 250	Cash Accounts Receivable	250	 250
Adjusting entry, December 31, 1985: ($510,000 − $4,000 = $506,000; $506,000 × 0.01 = $5,060)	Bad Debts Expense Allowance for Doubtful Accounts	5,060	 5,060	(No entry is made.)		
Closing entry, December 31, 1985	Sales Sales Returns and Allowances Bad Debts Expense Income Summary	510,000	 4,000 5,060 500,940	Sales Bad Debts Recovered Bad Debts Expense Sales Returns and Allowances Income Summary	510,000 250	 3,950 4,000 502,300

Figure 11–2 **Two Methods of Accounting for Bad Debts Expense**

penses. Theoretically, all these additional deductions should have corresponding valuation accounts, so that accounts receivable will be stated in the balance sheet at an amount closer to the net amount that will be collected. However, such valuation accounts as *Allowance for Sales Returns* and *Allowance for Sales Discounts* are rarely used because the items carried over from one year and recognized during the next year are usually immaterial and counterbalance each other. Moreover, these adjustments are not recognizable for income tax purposes.

Credit Card Sales

At least four kinds of credit cards have become extremely popular during the last two decades: (1) those issued by banks (referred to as bank credit cards) such as VISA and MasterCard, (2) those issued by other financial institutions (referred to as nonbank credit cards) such as the green American Express card, (3) those issued by oil companies, such as Gulf Oil and Exxon, and

(4) those issued by department stores and certain airlines such as the Wings card issued by Eastern Airlines.

The first three of the issuing institutions usually charge the retailer a fee ranging from 3 to 7 percent for accepting and collecting the credit card receivable. This credit card fee represents an expense that is a combination of cash discount, bad debts expense, collection fee, and certain accounting expense for recording a receivable and later recording the collection in two or more installments.

Credit cards issued by oil companies are similar to nonbank credit cards such as the green American Express. They are classified separately because of the restriction on their use. Exxon cards are typically accepted (with some exceptions) only by Exxon service stations, while the American Express card is accepted by many different merchandizing and service entities. Credit cards issued by department stores such as Sears, Roebuck & Company are basically a means of identifying their own customers. When these cards are presented and a credit sale is made, the issuing store will debit Accounts Receivable, credit Sales, and do its own billing.[2] Only two types of credit card sales require additional explanations of their accounting: sales made on bank credit cards and sales made on nonbank credit cards.

The signed **credit card sales slips** received by a company upon making sales with bank credit cards are accepted for deposit by banks and hence are treated as cash items. To illustrate, assume that a typical day's bank credit card sales of a company amounted to $10,000 with a 5 percent credit card fee. These sales would be recorded as follows:

1985					
Apr.	3	Cash		9,500	
		Credit Card Fees Expense		500	
		Sales			10,000
		To record bank credit card sales.			

Sales slips recording sales on certain nonbank financial and other institutions are not accepted by banks for deposit. Rather, they must be sent to the issuing institution where a check will be written for the gross sales *less* the credit card fee. For these credit card sales, the company making the sale should record a special trade receivable for the net amount to be received from the credit card issuer since the credit card fee is a known amount. This receivable can be entitled Accounts Receivable, Credit Cards. It should not be merged with the other trade receivables that require a measurement of bad debts expense, discussed earlier in this chapter. A typical day's credit card sales of $3,000 with a 6 percent card fee may be recorded as follows:

---

[2]Many of these receivables result in installment-type receivables. Often these stores place a finance charge of 1½ percent per month on any unpaid balance at the beginning of each month, which is an annual rate of 18 percent (some state laws allow higher rates). A variation of the accounting for installment selling is discussed in the Appendix to Part Three.

1985					
Apr.	4	Accounts Receivable, Credit Cards . . .		2,820	
		Credit Card Fees Expense		180	
		Sales			3,000
		To record sales made and billed this date to credit card companies.			

Opposite Balances in Accounts Receivable and Accounts Payable

In the accounts receivable subsidiary ledger, the customers' accounts normally have debit balances. Sometimes an overpayment, a sales return or allowance after a customer has paid an account, or an advance payment may convert the balance into a credit. Assume that there is a net debit balance of $29,600 in an accounts receivable subsidiary ledger consisting of 100 accounts, as follows:

98 accounts with a debit balance	$30,000
2 accounts with a credit balance	400
Net debit balance of 100 accounts receivable	$29,600

The debit amount of $30,000 and the credit amount of $400 would appear on the balance sheet as follows:

Current assets:		Current liabilities:	
Accounts receivable	$30,000	Credit balances in customer accounts	$400

The controlling account balance of $29,600 should not be used in the balance sheet because it would conceal the current liability of $400, which should be shown with the caption **"credit balances in customer accounts."** Similarly, if the accounts payable subsidiary ledger contains creditors' accounts with debit balances, the balance sheet should show the total credit balances and the total debit balances of accounts payable. For example, a net balance in the Accounts Payable controlling account of $88,600 (with certain subsidiary ledger accounts having debit balances that total $1,400) would appear in the balance sheet as follows:

Current assets:		Current liabilities:	
Debit balances in creditor accounts	$1,400	Accounts payable	$90,000

Internal Control: Accounts Receivable

As in the case of cash, adequate safeguards must be established for accounts receivable. For adequate internal control of receivables, there should be a separation of duties so that the work of one employee can be checked and verified by the work of another employee. For example, it is important that persons who maintain the accounts receivable records should not have access to cash. Recording of returns and allowances, discounts, and bad debts write-offs should be authorized by an officer and separated from the cash receipt and cash disbursement functions. Statements of account should be checked and mailed to customers by someone other than the accounts receivable bookkeeper. An independent check should be established to see that the statements sent to customers are in agreement with the accounts receivable records. Delinquent accounts should be reviewed periodically by a responsible official. Adequate control over receivables begins with the approved sales order and continues through the remaining stages in the credit sales process: approval of credit terms, recording of shipment, customer billing, recording of the receivable and its collection, and approval of subsequent adjustments.

Glossary

Accounts Receivable, Credit Cards A special trade receivable account representing claims arising from sales made on credit cards whose sales slips are not accepted for deposit by banks.

Aging A method of classifying individual receivables by age groups, according to time elapsed from due date.

Aging schedule A columnar work sheet showing the individual receivables by age groups, according to time elapsed from due date. The individual age groups are also totaled, and a percentage analysis is computed to aid in determining the allowance for doubtful accounts.

Allowance for Doubtful Accounts A valuation account contra to accounts receivable showing the amount of estimated uncollectible accounts as of a given date.

Bad Debts Expense An expense account showing the estimated uncollectible credit sales made in a given time period (for one year if the accounting period is a year) or actual write-offs if the direct write-off method is used.

Bad Debts Recovered A revenue account that is credited for the recovery of an account receivable previously written off under the direct write-off method.

Balance sheet approach A method of estimating the adjusted amount that is needed in the Allowance for Doubtful Accounts; the estimate is based on the balance sheet item, accounts receivable.

Credit balances in customer accounts A liability item representing the amounts due customers because of overpayment or a sales return made after payment had been made.

Credit card sales slip A signed voucher prepared from a sale on a credit card. The item substantiates the sale and serves as an invoice.

Income statement approach A method of estimating the bad debts expense for a given period; the estimate is based on an income statement item, sales.

Matching standard A basic standard in accounting which requires that incurred expenses of a given period be offset against earned revenue of that same period to determine net income.

Net realizable value The estimated collectible amount of accounts receivable.

Nontrade receivable A receivable arising from a source other than sales of merchandise or sales of ordinary services.

Trade receivable Claim against a customer arising from sale of merchandise or sale of ordinary services.

Valuation account A contra account—one that is related to and offsets, in whole or in part, one or more other accounts. A contra asset account should be deducted from the asset to which it is related to determine a carrying or book value.

Questions

Q11–1 List five different categories of receivables and state the probable balance sheet classification of each.

Q11–2 How does the matching standard affect the valuation of trade receivables?

Q11–3 (a) What is the function of the Allowance for Doubtful Accounts account? (b) What methods may be used to estimate its amount? (c) How is this account shown on the balance sheet?

Q11–4 What is the difference between the income statement approach and the balance sheet approach in estimating bad debts expense? What are the advantages and disadvantages of each?

Q11–5 A company attempting to state its accounts receivable at net realizable value may have to establish accounts other than the Allowance for Doubtful Accounts. What are three other possible valuation accounts for Accounts Receivable? When would such accounts be useful?

Q11–6 What kind of account (asset, liability, expense, and so on) is Allowance for Doubtful Accounts? Is its normal balance a debit or a credit? What action is taken if its normal balance becomes negative?

Q11–7 The Rockwood Company, which had Accounts Receivable of $75,822 and an Allowance for Doubtful Accounts of $3,814 on January 1, 1985, wrote off a past due account of Mark Slater in 1985 for $680.
a. What effect will the write-off have on the total current assets of the company? Why?
b. What effect will the write-off have on 1985 net income? Why?

Q11–8 A company systematically adjusts its Allowance for Doubtful Accounts at the end of each year by adding a fixed percent of the year's sales minus sales returns and allowances. After five years, the credit balance of the Allowance for Doubtful Accounts has become disproportionately large in relationship to the balance in Accounts Receivable. What are two possible explanations for the large balance?

Q11–9 When a company adjusts its allowance for doubtful accounts to a percentage of accounts receivable, the balance of the allowance account will tend to be partially self-correcting, provided that there is only a small error in the percentage rate that is being applied. The bad debts expense for certain years, on the other hand, may contain a sizeable error. What are the reasons for this situation?

Q11–10 Credit card sales on other than bank credit cards basically result in two different types of accounting. Why?

Q11–11 How does the valuation of receivables arising from nonbank credit card sales differ from the valuation of other trade receivables?

Q11–12 (a) What are some reasons for credit balances occurring in individual accounts receivable accounts? (b) How are such balances presented in the balance sheet?

Q11–13 Discuss the internal control procedures applicable to accounts receivable.

Q11–14 At what point in the time sequence of selling and collecting does the bad debts expense occur? Discuss.

Q11–15 The Jamison Company had a debit balance in its Allowance for Doubtful Accounts account before adjustments. Does this mean an error has been made? Discuss.

Exercises

E11–1 *Balance sheet classification of receivables*

The Abelson Company had the following items in its adjusted trial balance as of December 31, 1985:

Account Title	Debits	Credits
Accounts Receivable	$60,000	
Accounts Receivable, Credit Cards	10,000	
Notes Receivable	52,000	
Allowance for Doubtful Accounts		$1,250
Accrued Interest on Mortgage Notes Receivable[a]	1,750	
Notes Receivable, Officers[b]	18,500	

[a]The mortgage notes receivable mature on October 1, 1995. The interest, however, is paid each April 1 and October 1.

[b]These three-year-old notes are demand notes but they are expected to remain outstanding indefinitely.

1. Prepare a partial balance sheet showing how you recommend that the foregoing should be reported using generally accepted accounting principles.

2. Explain why you classified each item as you did.

E11–2 *Balance sheet disclosure of receivables*

The East Town Company maintains a controlling account entitled Receivables, the balance of which was $75,936 on December 31, 1985. The subsidiary ledger and other information reveal the following:

a. 470 trade accounts (debit balances)	$57,200
b. 8 trade accounts (credit balances)	864
c. 9 trade notes	12,400
d. 4 loans to the president and vice-presidents (due June 30, 1990)	7,200
e. Allowance for doubtful accounts	4,800

Show how this information should be reported on the balance sheet.

E11–3 *Calculating credit sales from receivable information*

On December 31, 1985, after adjusting entries had been made, Allowance for Doubtful Accounts had a credit balance of $17,680. During 1985, accounts receivable of $13,720 were written off and accounts receivable totaling $1,680, which were previously written off as uncollectible, were recovered. On January 1, 1985, Allowance for Doubtful Accounts had a credit balance of $14,840. The bad debts expense was estimated to be 2 percent of credit sales. Calculate the credit sales for 1985.

E11–4 *Journalizing accounts written off and bad debts expense*

The Stallion Company, which uses an Allowance for Doubtful Accounts, had the following transactions involving worthless accounts in 1985 and 1986:

1985	
Dec. 31	Recorded bad debts expense of $12,600.

1986	
Apr. 23	Wrote off Fran Noody's account of $6,300 as uncollectible.
Jun. 12	Wrote off Marsh Toms's account of $1,320 as uncollectible.
Aug. 1	Recovered $1,320 from Marsh Toms.

Journalize the transactions.

E11–5 *Recording bad debts expense by use of allowance method*

The Youngsville Company had sales on credit of $965,000 during 1985 with accounts receivable of $97,800 and a credit balance of $300 in Allowance for Doubtful Accounts at the end of the year. Record the bad debts expense for the year, using each of the following methods for the estimate:

a. Allowance for doubtful accounts is to be increased to 4 percent of accounts receivable.

b. Bad debts expense is estimated to be 0.48 percent of sales on credit.

c. Allowance for doubtful accounts is to be increased to $6,058, as indicated by an aging schedule.

E11–6 *Recording bad debts expense, write-off, and balance sheet presentation*

The trial balance of the Levin Company included the following accounts on June 30, 1985, the end of the company's fiscal year:

Accounts Receivable	$ 95,800
Allowance for Doubtful Accounts (credit)	450
Sales	624,500

Uncollectible accounts are estimated at 4.8 percent of accounts receivable.

a. Make the adjusting entry to record the bad debts expense.

b. Show the presentation of accounts receivable and allowance for doubtful accounts in the June 30, 1985, balance sheet.

c. Give the entry to write off the account of an insolvent customer, Samuel Davids, for $1,310 on July 3, 1985.

E11–7 *Computing cash received from customers*

The Cash account page in the general ledger of the Xanadu Company has been temporarily misplaced. The following account data are available:

	December 31 1986	December 31 1985	Year 1986
Accounts Receivable, Trade	$68,400	$57,200	
Allowance for Doubtful Accounts	5,015	3,945	
Sales			$585,000
Sales Discounts			9,750

During 1986, accounts receivable of $3,850 were written off as uncollectible, and one account of $700, written off in 1984, was collected and recorded in the following manner:

Accounts Receivable	700	
Allowance for Doubtful Accounts		700
Cash	700	
Accounts Receivable		700

Compute the cash received from customers during 1986.

E11–8 *Aging accounts receivable and recording bad debts expense*

The accounts receivable subsidiary ledger of the Greer Distributing Company shows the following data on December 31, 1985 (the general ledger showed a $250 debit balance in Allowance for Doubtful Accounts before adjustments):

Name of Customer	Invoice Date	Amount
Atlantic Sand Company	May 2, 1985	$ 1,250
Pacific Company	August 15, 1985	675
Queen's Fruit Company	December 8, 1985	390
	October 2, 1985	780
Temptation Seedling Company	March 3, 1985	575
Udah Company	November 11, 1985	855
Yount Fruittrees Company	November 20, 1985	325
	September 4, 1985	492
	July 10, 1985	965
Others	December 5, 1985	40,850

Terms of sale are n/30.

1. Prepare an analysis of accounts receivable by age.

2. Compute the estimated uncollectibles based on the following rates:

	Estimated Percent Uncollectible
Accounts not due	1.2
Accounts past due:	
1–30 days	1.6
31–60 days	2.4
61–90 days	8.3
91–120 days	10.6
121–365 days	30.2

3. Record the bad debts expense.

E11–9 *Interpreting various receivable accounting*

The JR Company uses a cash receipts journal, a cash payments journal, a single-column purchases journal, a single-column sales journal, and a two-column general journal. The Accounts Receivable account in the general ledger at June 30, 1985, is given below (posting references have been omitted):

Accounts Receivable

1985						
Jun.	1	Debit balance	✓			47,000
	5				3,000	44,000
	10				250	43,750
	25			3,030		46,780
	28				3,030	43,750
	30			54,400		98,150
	30				39,500	58,650

During the month, the general journal was used to record transactions with only two customers. The subsidiary ledger accounts of these customers are shown below:

William Asserman

1985						
Jun.	1	Credit balance	✓			(600)
	6		S2	1,400		800
	10		J4		250	550

Tenneson Rhu

1985						
Jun.	1	Debit balance	✓			3,000
	5	(20-day note)	J4		3,000	0
	25		CP6	3,030		3,030
	28		J4		3,030	0

1. Explain the $600 credit balance on June 1 in William Asserman's account.

2. What would the posting references (without page numbers) for the June 30 entries in the Accounts Receivable controlling account be?

3. What should be the total of the schedule of accounts receivable on June 30?

4. Explain the transaction that resulted in the debit of $3,030 on June 25 in Tenneson Rhu's account.

5. State in narrative form the transactions that resulted in each of the following credits to the Accounts Receivable controlling account: June 5, $3,000; June 10, $250; June 28, $3,030.

E11–10
Applying direct write-off method

The Humphrey Company uses the direct write-off method of accounting for bad debts expense. The company had the following transactions involving worthless accounts in 1985:

1985

Apr. 18 Wrote off Thomas Emmerson's account of $930 as uncollectible. The merchandise had been sold in 1984.
Jul. 25 Wrote off Darrell Damson's account of $850 as uncollectible.
Nov. 28 Recovered $650 from Thomas Emmerson.

Journalize the transactions in general journal form.

E11–11
Accounting for credit card sales

The Davidson Corporation makes sales on account only to customers who charged purchases on credit cards from the Supercard Company (a bank credit card) and the Marksman Card Company (a nonbank credit card). These two credit card companies charge a fee of 4½ and 5½ percent, respectively, for paying for these sales and collecting from the credit customers. On December 12, 1985, customers of the Davidson Corporation charged merchandise to these credit cards that totaled the following:

Supercard Company	$21,200
Marksman Card Company	11,400

Journalize these sales on the books of the Davidson Corporation.

A Problems

P11–1A
Journalizing accounts written off and bad debts expense

The Napha Company, which uses an Allowance for Doubtful Accounts account, had the following transactions involving worthless accounts in 1985 and 1986:

1985

Dec. 31 Recorded bad debts expense of $4,750.

1986

Apr. 16 Wrote off Jones Toomes's account of $1,220 as uncollectible.
Jun. 10 Wrote off Sally Rand's account of $1,220 as uncollectible.
Oct. 29 Recovered $1,220 from Sally Rand.
Nov. 4 Wrote off James Goodson's $600 account as uncollectible.
Nov. 18 Wrote off Bryce Tilson's $880 account as uncollectible.
Dec. 2 Recovered $488 from James Goodson.

Required: Journalize the transactions in general journal form.

P11–2A *Recording various accounts receivable transactions*

The Allowance for Doubtful Accounts of the Yammerhead Company showed a credit balance of $1,900 on December 31, 1984, before adjustments were made. The bad debts expense for 1984 is estimated at 2 percent of the sales on credit of $950,000 for the year. The following transactions occurred during the next two years:

1985

May 12	Wrote off May Weston's $4,780 account as uncollectible.
Sep. 28	Wrote off Jane Eastman's account of $4,780 as uncollectible.
Oct. 29	Received a check for $900 in final settlement of May Weston's account written off in May. She had been adjudged bankrupt by the courts.
Dec. 31	An analysis of accounts receivable by age indicated that accounts doubtful of collection totaled $19,600. (Note that the method of estimating bad debts expense has been changed.)

1986

Aug. 21	Wrote off D. A. Dawson's $7,900 account as uncollectible.
Dec. 31	Estimated that uncollectible accounts receivable totaled $15,950.

Required:

1. Record in general journal form transactions and events, including adjusting entries, for December 31, 1984, 1985, and 1986.

2. Post to a ledger account for Allowance for Doubtful Accounts.

P11–3A *Recording various accounts receivable transactions*

During November and early December 1985, the Fox Company had the following sales and receivable transactions (all sales were made on account and except on credit cards carried terms of 2/10, n/30):

1985

Nov. 1	Sold merchandise to Bat Eason for $2,660 on invoice no. 1001.
2	Sold merchandise to C. Faison for $9,400 on invoice no. 1002.
7	Credited C. Faison for returned merchandise with an invoice price of $1,400.
9	Received a check from Bat Eason for the amount due on invoice no. 1001.
10	Sold merchandise to the Moriah Company for $3,200 on invoice no. 1003.
13	Received $862.40 in cash from the Moriah Company in partial payment of invoice no. 1003. Discounts are allowed on partial payments.
14	Received a check for the amount due from C. Faison.
15	Sold merchandise to the Dick Bracey Company for $18,000 on invoice no. 1004.
23	Received a check from the Dick Bracey Company for the amount due on invoice no. 1004.
30	Sold merchandise to the Annie Leigh Company for $12,600 on invoice no. 1005.
30	Sold merchandise to the Three F Company for $15,000 on invoice no. 1006.
30	Summary bank credit card sales for November were $12,800; nonbank credit card sales for November were $14,200 (these are normally recorded daily). A fee of 6 percent is charged for each of these sales.
30	Estimated the bad debts expense for November to be 3.6 percent of credit sales less sales returns and allowances (excluding credit card accounts receivable).
Dec. 8	Received a notice that the Moriah Company had been adjudged bankrupt. The balance of its account was therefore regarded as uncollectible.

Required:

1. Journalize the transactions in general journal form.

2. Post all entries *(excluding credit card sales)* to the Accounts Receivable controlling and subsidiary accounts. Post credit card receivables to appropriate accounts.

3. Prepare a schedule of accounts receivable after the December 8, 1985, transaction is recorded.

P11–4A

Aging accounts receivable and recording bad debts expense

The accounts receivable ledger of the Fresh Vegetable Distributing Company shows the following data on December 31, 1985 (the general ledger showed a $450 credit balance in Allowance for Doubtful Accounts before adjustments):

Name of Customer	Invoice Date	Amount
Buxton Vegetable Company	May 2, 1985	$ 1,280
Carson Brothers	August 15, 1985	600
Damson Picks, Inc.	October 20, 1985	2,150
	December 8, 1985	1,950
Eater Tomato Company	March 3, 1985	1,720
Funder Potato Company	November 11, 1985	380
Pacific Produce Company	November 20, 1985	240
	September 4, 1985	965
	July 10, 1985	720
Others	December 5, 1985	23,200

Terms of sale are n/30.

Required:

1. Prepare an analysis of accounts receivable by age.

2. Compute the estimated uncollectible accounts receivable based on the following fixed percentages:

	Estimated Percent Uncollectible
Accounts not due	1.1
Accounts past due:	
1–30 days	2.2
31–60 days	4.1
61–90 days	5.2
91–120 days	10.3
121–365 days	35.4

3. Record the bad debts expense.

P11–5A

Comparing direct write-off method with estimated method

On December 31, 1985, Lawson Tauson's trial balance showed the following:

Accounts Receivable	$39,500
Allowance for Doubtful Accounts (credit)	185

After making an analysis of the accounts receivable, Tauson estimated the accounts doubtful of collection at $1,400. During the year 1986, the following transactions occurred:

a. Sales on account were $165,200.

b. Accounts written off as uncollectible totaled $1,825.

c. Collections from customers on account were $155,450. This includes a receipt of $112 that had been written off during the year as uncollectible.

On December 31, 1986, the accounts doubtful of collection were estimated at $1,925.

Required:

1. Set up ledger accounts for Accounts Receivable and Allowance for Doubtful Accounts; record the balances as of December 31, 1985, in these accounts, and then make the entries for 1985 and 1986 directly into these accounts.

2. Compute the bad debts expense deduction for the income statement for the year 1986, using (a) the direct write-off method and (b) the Allowance for Doubtful Accounts method.

P11–6A
Thought-provoking problem: determining the rationale for bad debts recognition methods

Assume that you are the new accountant for the Village Industries, Inc.. The president approaches you and says, "I've been reading about the direct method of writing off our uncollectible accounts receivable. It seems to me that this is the best way to account for the bad debts expense. When it is known that someone is not going to pay you, it appears that then is the time to recognize the expense for the uncollectible item." The corporation has been using the allowance method.

Required: Frame a reply that you might make to the president. Use generally accepted accounting principles. In your reply, set up examples to show clearly the logic in your opening statement.

B Problems

P11–1B
Journalizing accounts written off and bad debts expense

The Brooks Company, which uses an Allowance for Doubtful Accounts, had the following transactions involving worthless accounts in 1985 and 1986:

1985	
Dec. 31	Recorded bad debts expense of $8,950.
1986	
Feb. 2	Wrote off Rand Randelson's account of $2,160 as uncollectible.
Mar. 16	Wrote off Mary Taylor's account of $1,960 as uncollectible.
Jul. 5	Recovered $1,960 from Mary Taylor.
Aug. 16	Wrote off Janice Gunter's $900 account as uncollectible.
Sep. 26	Wrote off Benjamin Burley's $1,810 account as uncollectible.
Nov. 13	Recovered $500 from Janice Gunter.

Required: Journalize the transactions in general journal form.

P11–2B
Recording various accounts receivable transactions

The Allowance for Doubtful Accounts of the Buckeroo Company showed a credit balance of $950 on December 31, 1984, before adjustments were made. The bad debts expense for 1984 is estimated at 3 percent of the sales on credit of $410,500 for the year. The following transactions occurred during the next two years:

1985	
May 1	Wrote off Earl Thomas's $1,905 account as uncollectible.
Oct. 15	Wrote off Calvin Jones's account of $3,750 as uncollectible.
Nov. 30	Received a check for $500 in final settlement of Earl Thomas's account written off in May. He had been adjudged bankrupt by the courts.
Dec. 31	An analysis of accounts receivable by age indicated that accounts doubtful of collection totaled $9,450. (Note that the method of estimating bad debts expense has been changed.)
1986	
Aug. 21	Wrote off Melvin Murrell's $3,980 account as uncollectible.
Dec. 31	Estimated that uncollectible accounts receivable totaled $7,650.

Required:

1. Record in general journal form transactions and events, including adjusting entry, for December 31, 1984, 1985, and 1986.

2. Post to a ledger account for Allowance for Doubtful Accounts.

P11–3B *Recording various accounts receivable transactions*

During October and early November 1985, the Hill Sales Company had the following sales and receivables transactions (all sales were made on account and except on credit cards carried terms of 2/10, n/30):

1985		
Oct.	1	Sold merchandise to A. Ainsleeg for $915 on invoice no. 1001.
	2	Sold merchandise to C. Carter for $4,350 on invoice no. 1002.
	7	Credited C. Carter for returned merchandise with an invoice price of $750.
	9	Received a check from A. Ainsleeg for the amount due on invoice no. 1001.
	10	Sold merchandise to the Piedmont Company for $1,250 on invoice no. 1003.
	13	Received $431.20 in cash from the Piedmont Company in partial payment of invoice no. 1003. Discounts are allowed on partial payments.
	14	Received a check for the amount due from C. Carter.
	15	Sold merchandise to the Coastal Plains Company for $8,500 on invoice no. 1004.
	23	Received a check from the Coastal Plains Company for the amount due on invoice 1004.
	30	Sold merchandise to the Albermele Company for $6,410 on invoice no. 1005.
	30	Sold merchandise to the Pamlico Company for $6,000 on invoice no. 1006.
	30	Summary bank credit card sales for October were $8,000; nonbank credit card sales for October were $6,500 (these are normally recorded daily). A fee of 5.5 percent is charged for these sales.
	31	Estimated the bad debts expense for October to be 3.8 percent of credit sales less sales returns and allowances (excluding credit card accounts receivable).
Nov.	8	Received a notice that the Piedmont Company had been adjudged bankrupt. The balance of its account was therefore regarded as uncollectible.

Required:

1. Journalize the transactions in general journal form.

2. Post all entries *(excluding credit card sales)* to the Accounts Receivable controlling and subsidiary accounts. Post credit card sales to appropriate accounts.

3. Prepare a schedule of accounts receivable after the November 8, 1985, transaction is recorded.

P11–4B *Aging accounts receivable and recording bad debts expense*

The accounts receivable subsidiary ledger of the Berry Distributing Company shows the following data on December 31, 1985 (the general ledger showed a $250 credit balance in Allowance for Doubtful Accounts before adjustments):

Name of Customer	Invoice Date	Amount
Conley Strawberry Company	February 1, 1985	$ 1,450
Higgins Blueberry Company	March 12, 1985	860
Isaacs's Berry Farm	September 10, 1985	640
	December 31, 1985	1,425
Jacob's Raspberry Palace	July 15, 1985	2,215
Kaul Berry Place	October 16, 1985	560
Lawson's Berry Supreme	January 16, 1985	1,190
	April 7, 1985	1,425
	November 8, 1985	250
Others	December 5, 1985	12,680

Terms of sale are n/30.

Required:

1. Prepare an analysis of accounts receivable by age.

2. Compute the estimated uncollectible accounts receivable based on the following fixed percentages:

	Estimated Percent Uncollectible
Accounts not due	2.1
Accounts past due:	
1–30 days	5.2
31–60 days	6.0
61–90 days	17.5
91–120 days	26.0
121–365 days	38.5

3. Record the bad debts expense.

P11–5B
Comparing direct write-off method with estimated method

On December 31, 1984, Ransom Stott's trial balance showed the following:

Accounts Receivable	$146,500
Allowance for Doubtful Accounts (credit)	650

After making an analysis of the accounts receivable, Stott estimates the accounts doubtful of collection at $6,250. During the year 1985, the following transactions occurred:

a. Sales on account were $643,710.

b. Accounts written off as uncollectible totaled $6,720.

c. Collections from customers on account were $620,200. This includes a receipt of $350 that had been written off during the year as uncollectible.

On December 31, 1985, the accounts doubtful of collection were estimated at $6,950.

Required:

1. Set up ledger accounts for Accounts Receivable and Allowance for Doubtful Accounts; record the balance as of December 31, 1984, in these accounts, and then make the entries for 1984 and 1985 directly into these accounts.

2. Compute the bad debts expense deduction for the income statement for the year 1985, using (a) the direct write-off method, and (b) the Allowance for Doubtful Accounts method.

P11–6B
Thought-provoking problem: determining reason for balance in Allowance before adjustment

The Orange Company has been in operation for 20 years. It has used the allowance method of accounting for bad debts expense with the percentage used being applied to sales less sales returns and allowances. At the present time, December 31, 1985, the Allowance for Doubtful Accounts has a credit balance of $20,000 before adjustment. A comptroller's study indicates that this is overstated by 400 percent.

Required: Assume that the comptroller asks you for possible reasons for this overstatement. Write a report giving your reasons. Support each reason with basic accounting logic and, where appropriate, set up examples to prove your statement of reason. What corrective action would you propose?

12 Inventories and Cost of Goods Sold

Introduction

In a nonmanufacturing business, **inventory** is generally understood to mean goods owned by the business for sale to customers. Other acceptable terms are merchandise inventory or simply merchandise. Up to this point in the text, the valuation of the merchandise inventory has been specified. In Chapter 12, the journal entries for a periodic inventory system and a perpetual inventory system are compared. Then, the basis for placing a valuation on inventory is explained. This discussion leads to the development of a figure necessary in the income statement, cost of goods sold. Cost of goods sold is a significant charge against sales in determination of net income. For Dow Chemical Company in 1981, it was more than 84 percent of net sales. Therefore, the determination of an inventory valuation and subsequent calculation of cost of goods sold is vital to income measurement.

Learning Goals

To distinguish between periodic and perpetual inventory systems.

To make journal entries recording transactions under each system.

To be able to use FIFO, LIFO, and average costing assumptions under both the periodic and the perpetual systems.

To record transactions on inventory record cards.

To compute cost of goods sold under the periodic and perpetual systems.

To explain the effect of various cost flow assumptions on financial statements.

To apply the lower-of-cost-or-market concept to the inventory valuation.

To use both the gross margin method and the retail method of estimating inventory values.

Basis of Inventory Valuation: Cost

Inventories are originally recorded at cost. The AICPA has defined **cost of an inventory item** to include all expenditures "incurred in bringing an article to its existing condition and location."[1] Cost consists of the invoice price of the merchandise (less purchases discounts) plus transportation in, insurance while in transit, and any other expenditures made by the buyer to get the merchandise to the place of business.

The determination of total cost valuation of an inventory is relatively simple when each stock item acquired can be marked and identified permanently with its specific cost. This procedure, the **specific identification method,** is possible in certain businesses—for example, with automobiles on a dealer's lot. In most businesses—say with gasoline in a service station—specific identification is not feasible. When it is not feasible, one of three cost-flow assumptions is used to assign costs. Being *assumptions* regarding flow of costs through the business, they do *not* necessarily represent the actual flow of the goods.

1. **First-in, first-out (FIFO).** FIFO is an assumption that the cost of the oldest goods on hand is the cost of the asset given up each time a sale is made.
2. **Last-in, first-out (LIFO).** LIFO is an opposite assumption that the cost of the newest goods on hand is the cost of the asset given up each time a sale is made.
3. **Average.** The cost of any items sold can be assumed to be a weighted average of the cost prices of that item.

Each of these three cost-flow assumptions is developed in more detail in later sections of the chapter.

The method used to determine cost should be the one that "most clearly reflects periodic income."[2] Regardless of the method used, the cost standard set by AICPA (also referred to as **historical cost**) restricts the proper uses of the word **valuation** in inventory accounting to the statement of items at cost or at modifications of cost.[3]

Two Inventory Systems

Two systems of accounting for inventory and determination of cost of goods sold are in use. The *periodic inventory system,* which depends on end-of-period determination of inventory valuation, was explained in Chapter 6. A second system, in which a continuous record of quantities (and sometimes valuation) of items on hand is maintained, is called the *perpetual inventory system.* Journal entries for the perpetual system are compared in this chapter to those for a periodic system. The method of assigning a cost valuation to items under both systems is also explained and illustrated.

---

[1] *Accounting Research Bulletin No. 43,* "Restatement and Revision of Accounting Research Bulletins" (New York: AICPA, 1953), Chapter 4, statement 3.

[2] Ibid., statement 4.

[3] *FASB Statement No. 33,* which requires reporting of current cost value of inventory, is discussed and illustrated in Chapter 14.

Under the periodic system cost of goods sold is determined by an end-of-period computation; thus no general ledger account is created for it. Under the perpetual system, however, Cost of Goods Sold becomes a general ledger account that is used to record the cost of the items sold at the time of the sale. Similar in nature to an expense account, it should be numbered in the chart of accounts as if it were an expense. Under the *periodic* system, entries to the Merchandise Inventory account are made only at the end of the accounting period to close out the old inventory and establish the new inventory as the current asset valuation both for income statement (computing the cost of goods sold) and balance sheet purposes. Under the *perpetual* system, the Merchandise Inventory account is constantly updated by journal entries to record receipts, cost of goods sold, and returns to vendors of merchandise. To compare the entries to record transactions under the two systems, assume the following data for Saint Josephs Company for April 1985:

1985		
Apr. 1	Total inventory on hand at cost	$100,000
4	Sales on account (cost $6,000)	10,000
5	Purchases on account from Ojata Company	2,000
6	Transportation charges paid on purchase of April 5	80
8	Return to Ojata Company of an incorrect item. Since it was Ojata's error, the company agreed to allow credit for the invoice price of $200 plus $8 of transportation cost that applied to this item	208

The entries to record the above transactions are shown in general journal form in Figure 12–1. As this comparison shows, the periodic system's

Figure 12–1 Entries for Periodic and Perpetual Inventory Systems Compared

Date	Periodic System			Perpetual System		
1983						
Apr. 4	Accounts Receivable	10,000		Accounts Receivable	10,000	
	Sales		10,000	Sales		10,000
	(Note: The cost of goods sold is not determined at this time but is determined at the end of the period.)			Cost of Goods Sold	6,000	
				Merchandise Inventory		6,000
5	Purchases	2,000		Merchandise Inventory	2,000	
	Accounts Payable		2,000	Accounts Payable		2,000
6	Transportation In	80		Merchandise Inventory	80	
	Cash		80	Cash		80
8	Accounts Payable	208		Accounts Payable	208	
	Transportation In		8	Merchandise Inventory		208
	Purchases Returns and Allowances		200			

Purchases, Purchases Returns and Allowances, and Transportation In accounts are replaced, in the perpetual system, by debits and credits direct to the Merchandise Inventory account. A second major difference is in the closing process. Under the periodic inventory system, all merchandising accounts are closed to Income Summary (see Chapter 6). Cost of goods sold is automatically a part of the determination of net income because the beginning and ending inventory amounts are a part of the closing process. Under the perpetual system, the only closing entry required is as follows (amount and end-of-fiscal-year dates are assumed):

1985					
Dec.	31	Income Summary		497,620	
		Cost of Goods Sold			497,620
		To close the Cost of Goods Sold account.			

Since the Merchandise Inventory account has been kept up to date with continuous entries under the perpetual system, it does not enter into the closing process. However, it is necessary to adjust the account if the physical inventory count (equally important for internal control under either system) finds items out of agreement with stock record quantities. The real-life example at the end of this chapter contains such an adjustment.

Assigning Inventory Cost

To illustrate both systems of assigning cost to inventories, the following information about a single inventory item, a stapler (stock number 802A), is given:

1985		
Apr.	1	Inventory on hand consisted of 40 units (or staplers) that were purchased in March at $2.20 each.
	5	Purchased 120 staplers at $2.60 each.
	12	Sold 110 staplers.
	16	Purchased 70 staplers at $2.80 each.
	28	Sold 60 staplers.

The number on hand on April 30, 1985, determined by physical count, is 60 staplers. This on-hand amount is verified on page 403. Presented with the calculation is a rearrangement of cost information to be used in later illustrations.

		Units	Unit Cost	Total Cost	Specific Identification of April 30 Inventory
Inventory, April 1		40	$2.20	$ 88	10
Purchases:					
April 5		120	2.60	312	30
April 16		70	2.80	196	20
Total units available for sale		230		$596	60
Sales:					
April 12	110				
April 28	60				
Total sales		170			
Inventory, April 30		60			

Periodic Inventory

With the **periodic inventory system,** the value of the inventory for the balance sheet and for computing the cost of goods sold is determined at the end of each annual accounting period by a complete physical count and costing of all inventory items. Acquired goods not on hand are assumed to have been sold. This causes losses due to theft, breakage, or other causes to be automatically included in the cost of goods sold as a deduction from revenue.

Specific Identification Costing

As previously mentioned, the specific identification method requires that inventory items be marked with a specific identity and cost. For example, using the foregoing data, the specific identification cost of the 60 items in stock on April 30 is:

Lot	Units	Unit Cost	Total Cost
April 1	10	$2.20	$ 22
5	30	2.60	78
16	20	2.80	56
	60		$156

This method cannot be used for inventory items whose specific identity is lost. Even in those situations in which identity is possible, use of this method is costly. Its use is restricted to special inventory situations such as automobiles on a dealer's lot. Therefore, cost flow assumptions are usually substituted for this method and are the only ones discussed in the remainder of this chapter.

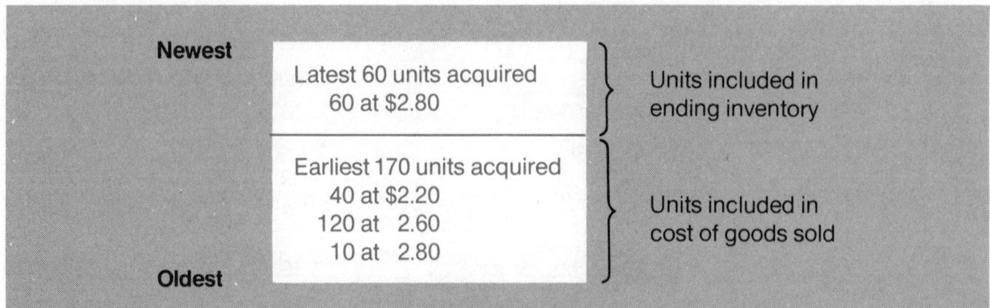

Figure12–2 Cost Lots for FIFO Costing Assumption

First-In, First-Out (FIFO) Costing

The periodic FIFO method of determining the cost of goods on hand and the cost of goods sold is based on the *assumption* that the cost flow follows the idea that units are sold in the order in which they were acquired; that is, the oldest units on hand are sold first, the units acquired next are sold next, and so on. *This assumption relates only to the method of accounting and not to the actual physical movement of the goods. It may or may not approximate the actual physical flow.* The unsold units on hand at the date of the inventory are assumed to be the units acquired most recently. Consequently, for income measurement, earlier costs are matched with revenue and the most current costs are used for balance sheet valuation.

The cost groupings for the FIFO assumption are presented in Figure 12–2. Under the periodic FIFO assumption, the 60 staplers on hand April 30, 1985, are part of the lot purchased on April 16. Since the last purchase made was large enough to make up the entire ending inventory, all 60 units are valued at $2.80. Therefore the cost assigned to the inventory is:

60 units at $2.80	$168

The assumption that oldest goods are sold first leads to the following method of computing cost of goods sold:

Date of Sale	Units Sold	Sales Made from	Units	Unit Cost	Total Cost
Apr. 12	110	Beginning inventory	40	$2.20	$ 88
		Purchase of April 5	70	2.60	182
Apr. 28	60	Purchase of April 5	50	2.60	130
		Purchase of April 16	10	2.80	28
			170		$428

Last-In, First-Out (LIFO) Costing

Periodic LIFO costing *assumes* that the cost of goods sold should be based on prices paid for the most recently acquired units and *the inventory consists of the oldest units on hand.*

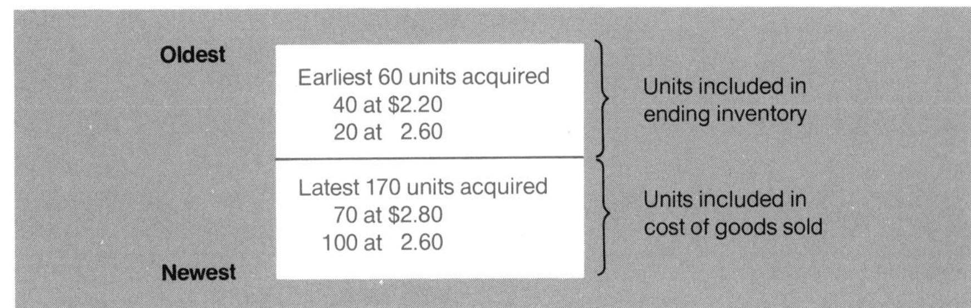

Figure 12–3 Cost Lots for LIFO Costing Assumption

The cost groupings for the LIFO assumption are presented in Figure 12–3. Since the oldest cost lot, beginning inventory, is not large enough to make up the entire ending inventory, sufficient units from the first April purchase have to be included. The cost assigned to inventory is:

Ending inventory (60 units):	
From beginning inventory, 40 units at $2.20	$ 88
From purchase of April 5, 20 units at $2.60	52
Cost assigned to April 30 inventory	$140

The assumption that newest goods are the first sold leads to the following method of computing cost of goods sold.[4]

Date of Sale	Units Sold	Sales Made from	Units	Unit Cost	Total Cost
Apr. 28	60	Purchase of April 16	60	$2.80	$168
Apr. 12	110	Purchase of April 16	10	2.80	28
		Purchase of April 5	100	2.60	260
			170		$456

Weighted Average Costing

Under **weighted average costing** the ending inventory is priced at the end of each accounting period at a unit cost computed by dividing the total cost of all goods available for sale by the total physical units available for sale. Similarly, all quantities sold are stated at a uniform cost—the computed weighted average unit cost for the period (typically one month). The assignment of costs to goods sold during the month must be delayed until the end of the month so that the weighted average cost computation can be made.

The weighted average cost for the period, the inventory valuation, and the cost of goods sold are computed as follows:

[4]Note that the sale of April 12 could not actually contain units from a purchase of April 16, but periodic LIFO causes us to make the *assumption* that it did.

Date			Units	Unit Cost	Total
1985					
Apr.	1	Beginning inventory	40	$2.20	$ 88
	5	Purchase	120	2.60	312
	16	Purchase	70	2.80	196
		Total available for sale	230		$596

$$\text{Weighted average unit cost} = \frac{\text{Cost of goods available for sale}}{\text{Units available for sale}} = \frac{\$596}{230} = \$2.5913.$$

Units on hand, April 30	60
Inventory valuation = (60 × $2.5913)	$155.48
Units sold	170
Cost of goods sold = (170 × $2.5913)	$440.52

Perpetual Inventory

The **perpetual inventory system** provides for a continuous book inventory of items on hand. An inventory record card (often called a **stock record card**) or a record in a computer file is kept for each inventory item. When units are purchased or sold, the inventory record for the item must be adjusted to show the updated quantity on hand.

The maintenance of continuous inventory records does not eliminate the need for a complete annual physical inventory. Companies that use the perpetual inventory system should take physical counts of portions of the inventory during the course of the year to test whether the records are in agreement with quantities actually on hand, or they should take a single end-of-year count. Only by physical count will shrinkage such as evaporation losses, theft, or duplicate shipments be discovered.

Perpetual inventory records are costly to maintain, especially when the inventory includes numerous items of small value. A company may want to maintain continuous records for only certain classifications of its inventory. A hardware supply company, for example, may find it better to use the perpetual inventory system only for items with a high unit selling price and the periodic inventory system for all other items. Perpetual inventory concepts are always appropriate when the specific identification method is used.

First-In, First-Out (FIFO) Costing

A perpetual inventory card using the FIFO costing method is illustrated in Figure 12–4. As each shipment of goods is received, its quantity, unit cost, and total cost are recorded as a separate batch or lot. When goods are sold, the oldest goods on hand are assumed to make up the sale. The balance on

Item: Stapler, Stock Number 802A, Location L–7

Date		Ref.	Purchased (or Received)			Sold (or Issued)			Balance		
			Quantity	Unit Cost	Total Cost	Quantity	Unit Cost	Total Cost	Quantity	Unit Cost	Total Cost
1985											
Apr.	1	Balance							40	2.20	88.00
	5	P.O.[a]673	120	2.60	312.00				{ 40	2.20	88.00
									120	2.60	312.00
	12	S.T.[b]401				{ 40	2.20	88.00			
						70	2.60	182.00	50	2.60	130.00
	16	P.O. 690	70	2.80	196.00				{ 50	2.60	130.00
									70	2.80	196.00
	28	S.T. 409				{ 50	2.60	130.00			
						10	2.80	28.00	60	2.80	168.00

[a]Purchase order: the document placing the order with the supplier.

[b]Shipping ticket: the internal document reporting a sale.

Figure 12–4 **Perpetual Inventory Card (FIFO)**

hand, unit cost, and total cost *for each batch from which units are assumed to remain* are recorded in the Balance columns.

Utilizing the FIFO cost flow assumption, the cost of the 110 units sold on April 12 is assumed to consist of the 40 units on hand on April 1 and 70 units from the April 5 purchase. The cost of the 60 units sold on April 28 is assumed to consist of the remaining 50 units from the April 5 purchase and 10 units from the April 16 purchase. When a sale or the balance on hand consists of units from more than one batch (see sale of April 12 in Figure 12–4) brackets are used to indicate that the sets of figures should be combined. Since the 60 units on hand on April 30 are all assumed to be from the batch purchased on April 16, no brackets are required for the balance. The cost of goods sold is the sum of the Total Cost column in the Sold (or Issued) section of the card. For this stapler the cost of goods sold is:

Sale of April 12 ($88 + $182)	$270
Sale of April 28 ($130 + $28)	158
Cost of goods sold	$428

Last-In, First-Out (LIFO) Costing

When LIFO is used with a perpetual system each sale is listed at the unit cost of the latest acquisitions. For instance, in Figure 12–5 the 110 units sold on April 12 are assumed to have come from the units received on April 5. The balance on hand, unit cost, and total cost for each batch from which units are assumed to be on hand are recorded in the Balance columns.

Item: Stapler, Stock Number 802A, Location L–7											
		Purchased (or Received)			Sold (or Issued)			Balance			
Date		Ref.	Quantity	Unit Cost	Total Cost	Quantity	Unit Cost	Total Cost	Quantity	Unit Cost	Total Cost
1985											
Apr.	1	Balance							40	2.20	88.00
	5	P.O. 673	120	2.60	312.00				40	2.20	88.00
									120	2.60	312.00
	12	S.T. 401				110	2.60	286.00	40	2.20	88.00
									10	2.60	26.00
	16	P.O. 690	70	2.80	196.00				70	2.80	196.00
	28	S.T. 409				60	2.80	168.00	40	2.20	88.00
									10	2.60	26.00
									10	2.80	28.00

Figure 12–5 **Perpetual Inventory Card (LIFO)**

The inventory on April 30 is assumed to consist of:

40 units at $2.20	$ 88
10 units at 2.60	26
10 units at 2.80	28
60 units	$142

The cost of goods sold is obtained by adding the Total Cost column of the Sold (or Issued) section of the inventory card: $286 + $168 = $454

Moving Average Costing

In the moving average costing method (illustrated in Figure 12–6), units are priced at the average cost—that is, the total cost of units on hand divided by quantity on hand. This average unit cost is used for sales until additional units are purchased at a different cost. Then a new average unit cost must be computed. For example, the receipt of 120 units on April 5 required computation (a) in Figure 12–6. Also, the purchase of April 16 required that a new unit cost again be computed (illustrated in computation (b) in Figure 12–6).

This method is called **moving average costing** because a new average unit cost must be computed and used after each receipt of goods at a unit cost that is different from the current one. It is not necessary to compute a new unit cost after each sale because sales do *not* change the unit cost of the balance.

Item: Stapler, Stock Number 802A, Location L–7

Date		Ref.	Purchased (or Received)			Sold (or Issued)			Balance			
			Quantity	Unit Cost	Total Cost	Quantity	Unit Cost	Total Cost	Quantity	Unit Cost	Total Cost	
1985												
Apr.	1	Balance							40	2.20	88.00	
	5	P.O. 673	120	2.60	312.00				160	2.50	400.00	(a)
	12	S.T. 401				110	2.50	275.00	50	2.50	125.00	
	16	P.O. 690	70	2.80	196.00				120	2.675	321.00	(b)
	28	S.T. 409				60	2.675	160.50	60	2.675	160.50	

(a)

40 at $2.20	=	$ 88
120 at 2.60	=	312
160	. . . . . .	$400

Average = $2.50 = ($400 ÷ 160)

(b)

50 at $2.50	=	$125
70 at 2.80	=	196
120	. . . . . .	$321

Average = $2.675 = ($321 ÷ 120)

Figure 12–6 **Perpetual Inventory Card (Moving Average)**

As in the other perpetual methods, the cost of goods sold is the sum of the amounts in the Total Cost column of the Sold (or Issued) section; under the moving average method, it is $435.50 = ($275.00 + $160.50). However, it is not necessary to separate batches, and brackets are not required. Receipts and issues (sales) are added to or deducted from the balance.

Two Systems Compared and Analyzed

The amount of the ending inventory as well as the amount of the cost of goods sold is identical under the periodic and the perpetual inventory systems when FIFO costing is used. This is because in each instance the goods on hand are assumed to consist of the most recently acquired units.

Under LIFO costing, however, the valuations of the cost of goods sold and ending inventory may differ under the two systems. Costs at the beginning of the period are assumed to be in the ending valuation with the periodic inventory system, whereas they may have been dropped from the running balance as sales or issues are recorded with the perpetual system. When the inventory is given a valuation only at the end of the period (as is the case in the periodic system), *the dates of sales are ignored.* Although the LIFO procedure may be used appropriately with either periodic or perpetual inventories, it is important that the system selected should be followed consistently. The following tabulation illustrates the different results of LIFO costing with the perpetual and the periodic inventory systems:

	LIFO	
	Periodic Inventory	Perpetual Inventory
Inventory, April 1	$ 88[a]	$ 88[a]
Purchases	508	508
Total goods available for sale	$596	$596
Inventory, April 30	140	142
Cost of goods sold	$456	$454

[a]These LIFO inventory amounts are the same for this illustration but are not likely to be the same in the future (see April 30 inventory).

Similarly, the weighted average (periodic system) and the moving average (perpetual system) yield different results. With the same example used to illustrate both, the results were:

	Weighted Average Periodic Inventory	Moving Average Perpetual Inventory
Inventory, April 1	$ 88.00	$ 88.00
Purchases	508.00	508.00
Total goods available for sale	$596.00	$596.00
Inventory, April 30	155.48	160.50
Cost of goods sold	$440.52	$435.50

Regardless of whether the periodic or perpetual system is used, the method used to determine inventory valuation can have a direct effect on the financial statements. In a period of rising or falling prices—especially if the inventory turnover is rapid—the difference in inventory valuation can be significant. In the example used in this chapter the price of a stapler rose from $2.20 to $2.80 in the month of April. To illustrate the comparative effect of rising prices on the financial statements under perpetual FIFO, moving average, and LIFO costing, the basic data for the preceding discussions are used again. Two additional assumptions are made: (1) the selling price of each unit is $5.50, and (2) the operating expenses for the month are $200.

The computations of income in this simple illustration are for a single inventory item. The effect of the different methods on net income would be proportionately increased with increasing volume and number of items. The effect of the three methods of allocating inventory cost and cost of goods sold under the stated assumptions is highlighted in Figure 12–7.

During a period of rising prices, FIFO costing results in the highest ending inventory valuation, gross margin on sales, and net income, while having the

	Perpetual Inventory		
	FIFO	Moving Average	LIFO
Sales (170 units × $5.50)	$935.00	$935.00	$935.00
Cost of goods sold	428.00	435.50	454.00
Gross margin on sales	$507.00	$499.50	$481.00
Deduct operating expenses	200.00	200.00	200.00
Net income	$307.00	$299.50	$281.00
Ending inventory	$168.00	$160.50	$142.00

Figure 12–7 Summary Tabulation

lowest cost of goods sold.[5] Given the same rising market conditions, the LIFO inventory method gives the opposite results: lowest ending inventory valuation, gross margin on sales, and net income, while having the highest cost of goods sold. During a period of falling prices, FIFO results in the lowest ending inventory valuation, gross margin on sales, and net income and the highest cost of goods sold; LIFO gives the opposite results.

LIFO's purpose is to match revenue with cost of last purchases rather than with earliest cost, as is done under FIFO costing. Also, during a prolonged period of generally rising prices, lower year-to-year earnings are reported under LIFO, resulting in lower income tax for the owner of a proprietorship or a lower taxable income for a corporation. However, during inflationary periods LIFO costing results in a significant understatement of current assets, which limits the significance and usefulness of the balance sheet.

Figure 12–7 shows that the amounts for the income statement items listed under moving average costing fall between the corresponding amounts for FIFO and LIFO costing. The same position would be maintained in a falling market. Moving average costing reduces the effect of widely fluctuating prices.

Ending inventory appears in the balance sheet as a current asset. Consequently, this statement as well as the income statement is affected by the method of inventory valuation used. Because inventory is often the largest single item in the current assets section, the method of assigning cost may have a significant effect on the results of statement analysis.

Lower of Cost or Market (LCM)

The various methods of inventory valuation discussed thus far in this chapter are means of arriving at the cost of the inventory. However, a long-standing convention in accounting holds that inventories may be valued at the **lower**

[5] This leads to a condition that accountants call *phantom profits* because units sold must be replaced at a cost greater than cost of goods sold. Hence, more cash is used than the income statement showed as a potential inflow from operations.

Item	Quantity	Unit Cost	Unit Market Price	Total Cost	Total Market	1 Basis for LCM: Item	2 Basis for LCM: Major Category	3 Basis for LCM: Total Inventory
Category X:								
Item A	100	$10	$9.00	$1,000	$ 900	$ 900		
Item B	200	4	6.00	800	1,200	800		
Subtotal				$1,800	$2,100		$1,800	
Category Y:								
Item C	400	1	1.25	$ 400	$ 500	400		
Item D	600	6	5.00	3,600	3,000	3,000		
Item E	250	3	2.50	750	625	625		
Subtotal				$4,750	$4,125		4,125	
Totals				$6,550	$6,225			$6,225
Inventory at lower of cost or market						$5,725	$5,925	$6,225

Figure 12–8 **Application of LCM**

of cost or market (LCM).[6] The term **market** broadly means the cost of replacing the goods as of the balance sheet date; this is also referred to as **replacement cost.** Cost is first determined by any of the methods already discussed in this chapter.

The process of valuing the inventory at LCM occurs at the end of the accounting period, when financial statements are prepared. It may be applied (1) to each item individually, (2) to each major inventory category, or (3) to the entire inventory. On the basis of the inventory tabulations in Figure 12–8 (FIFO costing is assumed), the valuation under each procedure is as follows:

1 If each item is valued individually, the inventory is reported as $5,725. This basis for LCM always produces the smallest possible inventory valuation.

2 If the inventory is valued by major categories, it is reported as $5,925. This basis for LCM produces an inventory valuation that is equal to or greater than in 1 and equal to or smaller than 3.

3 If the inventory is valued in total, it is reported as $6,225. This basis for LCM always produces the greatest possible LCM inventory valuation.

[6] *Accounting Research Bulletin No. 43,* Chapter 4, Statement 5 authorizes the use of LCM. Statement 6 of that chapter places an upper and lower limit on the *market value* used here. The rules for applying the limits to the term *market* are covered thoroughly in most intermediate accounting textbooks.

Estimation of Inventory

Gross Margin Method

Taking a physical inventory or maintaining perpetual inventory records is often costly and time consuming. For some purposes an estimate is needed. To prepare monthly financial statements, check the accuracy of a physical inventory, or estimate inventory valuation when an accurate valuation cannot be made (as in the case of a fire loss) the **gross margin method** of estimating inventory valuation may be used. This method consists of deducting the estimated cost of goods sold from the total cost of goods available for sale.

Assume that during the previous three years the Lander Company has averaged a gross margin rate on sales of 30 percent. Since gross margin as a percent of sales is 30 percent, cost of goods sold as a percent of sales must be 70 percent = (100% − 30%). For the current year, the following data are available from the records of the company:

Inventory, January 1, 1985	$ 20,000
Purchases during 1985	110,000
Sales during 1985	160,000

Under the gross margin method, the estimated inventory on December 31, 1985, would be computed as follows:[7]

a. Sales × Cost percent = Cost of goods sold:
$160,000 × 0.70 = $112,000.
b. Beginning inventory + Net cost of purchases − Cost of goods sold = Ending inventory:
$20,000 + $110,000 − $112,000 = $18,000

On the basis of the foregoing computation, the partial income statement is as follows:

LANDER COMPANY
Partial Income Statement
For the Year Ended December 31, 1985

Exhibit A

Sales		$160,000
Cost of goods sold:		
Inventory, January 1, 1985 (given)	$ 20,000	
Purchases (given)	110,000	
Total goods available for sale	$130,000	
Estimated inventory, December 31, 1985 (item b)	18,000	
Cost of goods sold (item a)		112,000
Gross margin (sales − cost of goods sold)		$ 48,000

[7]In both the gross margin method and the retail method (discussed next), transportation in should be added to purchases; discounts and returns and allowances should be deducted.

This method is based on the assumption that the rate of gross margin on sales is substantially the same in every period. It is accurate, therefore, only to the extent that the assumed gross margin rate is accurate. A careful study should be made of possible differences between the past data from which the assumed rate is derived and the corresponding current data. Appropriate adjustments should be made for significant differences. A recent change in the mix of products sold may add items with different **markons** (addition to cost to establish selling price). In such a case, the gross margin rate of the most recent year could be a more accurate estimate of the current rate than an average of several prior years.

Retail Method

Another method of estimating the ending inventory at cost when its retail valuation is known is the retail inventory method. Its value is twofold: (1) it serves as a means of computing the ending inventory without a physical count, and (2) it provides a method of centrally controlling inventories that consist of a variety of items dispersed over several departments or several branch stores.

Goods are charged to the departments or branches at their selling price, records of both cost and selling price of goods purchased are kept centrally, and records of sales are kept in the usual manner. From these records, the inventory valuation may be prepared at any time. Under the **retail inventory method** the estimated inventory at retail is derived by deducting the sales during the period from the total goods available for sale priced at retail. This amount is then converted to cost by applying the cost percent (the ratio of the cost of goods available for sale to the retail price of those goods).

Simple Example—No Changes in Price Consider the following set of data:

	Cost	Retail
Inventory at beginning of period	$ 20,000	$ 30,000
Purchases during period	180,000	270,000
Total goods available for sale	$200,000	$300,000
Cost percent (ratio of cost to retail) $\frac{\$200,000}{\$300,000} = 66.667\%$		
Sales during period		258,000
Inventory at retail		$ 42,000
Estimated inventory at cost (66.667% of $42,000)	$ 28,000	

Other methods are used to reduce the inventory at retail to inventory at cost. These are discussed in intermediate accounting textbooks.

Evaluation of Estimating Procedures

Both gross margin and retail inventory methods are based on a calculation of the cost-of-goods-sold rate. The gross margin method uses past experience as a basis; the retail inventory method uses current experience. The gross margin method may be less reliable because past experience may be different from current experience.

Both methods are useful because they enable the accountant to prepare frequent financial statements without the cost of a physical count each period or of maintaining perpetual inventory records. However, they do not eliminate the need for a careful physical count at least once a year. The physical count will disclose losses due to thefts or shrinkage and serves as the basis for an adjustment to the inventory records and the Merchandise Inventory account. Such an adjustment is illustrated in the real-life example at the end of this chapter.

Consistency in the Application of Inventory Valuation Procedures

Different procedures may be used to place a valuation on various classes of the inventory. It is most important, therefore, that the selected method should be followed consistently from year to year in each class. Inconsistency in inventory pricing, cost allocations, and financial statement presentation would make year-to-year comparisons of operating results and financial position meaningless. Since such comparisons often serve as the basis for managerial decisions and decisions of external users of accounting information, the importance of consistency becomes evident.

Consistency

Whatever the method of inventory valuation chosen, a company should follow it* consistently *from year to year.

The principle of consistency does not preclude required changes properly made and fully disclosed. A change from FIFO to LIFO inventory costing, for example, requires an explanation accompanying the financial statements of the year of change, giving the nature of the change and its cumulative effect.[8]

Internal Control over Inventory

Control of inventory through separation of duties is equally applicable to merchandise as control of cash is to a business's overall financial health. Internal controls must be established to protect against loss, theft, and misappropriation of inventory. The system for receiving, storing, issuing, and paying for merchandise must provide for records and supporting documents and

[8] *Opinions of the Accounting Principles Board No. 20,* "Accounting Changes" (New York: AICPA, July 1971), paragraph 19.

for the assignment of individual responsibility and accountability to safeguard the assets.

Absence of control over inventories can seriously damage a business. An excessive inventory is expensive to carry. Studies indicate that the costs of carrying an inventory—taxes, insurance, warehousing, handling, and inventory taking—may be as high as 25 percent of the original purchase price. This is exclusive of lost potential earnings (interest) on funds tied up in inventories. On the other hand, sufficient items and quantities must be stocked to provide customers with good service.

Maintaining a proper balance to avoid both shortages and excesses of inventory requires organization and planning. Control plans must provide for day-to-day comparisons of projected inventory acquisitions with current sales volume. A reduction in sales volume will result in excess inventories unless adjustments are made. The real-life example that follows illustrates one aspect of inventory control.

A Real-Life Example

The Shaw Paint Company used its perpetual inventory records to determine the inventory at the end of each month in 1985. These records enabled the accountant to prepare monthly financial statements for management. At the end of 1985, a physical count costed by moving average unit prices was recorded on inventory sheets. The last page and the latest account page are as follows:

SHAW PAINT COMPANY
Physical Inventory Sheet — Sheet No. 37

Stock Number	Description	Quantity	Unit Price	Amount
16×207	Enamel, Inside, Almond	210	$6.80	$ 1,428.00
17×503	Enamel, Outside, Yellow	108	6.50	702.00
	Enamel, Outside, Green	27	6.25	$ 168.75
17×519	Grand total			$27,602.83

Merchandise Inventory — Acct. No. 132

Date		Explanation	F	Debit	Credit	Balance
1985						
Dec.	29	Debit balance	✓			27,601.18
	31		P16	400.00		28,001.18

After the physical count had been completed on December 31, 1985, the inventory supervisor had recounts made on all items in which she suspected there could be errors. All inventory tickets are now considered to be correct and have been listed on 37 inventory sheets. Each item has been priced and extended.

The general ledger account Merchandise Inventory shows a balance ($28,001.18) that does not agree with the value of the physical count ($27,602.83). Since the priced count sheets are the best evidence of the correct valuation, an entry to adjust the account will be made as follows:

1985					
Dec.	31	Loss from Inventory Shrinkage		398.35	
		Merchandise Inventory			398.35
		To adjust account for merchandise evaporated, lost, stolen, or otherwise missing.			

The accounting task is not yet completed. Affected individual stock record cards must be changed to reflect the correct physical count.

Glossary

Consistency The concept that uniformity—with full disclosure for any departures—from year to year, especially in inventory pricing, cost allocation, and financial statement presentation, is essential to make comparisons meaningful.

Cost of an inventory item The expenditures incurred in bringing an inventory item to its existing condition and location.

Cost of goods sold The portion of total cost of merchandise allocated to items sold during the period.

FIFO (first-in, first-out) inventory costing A method of determining the cost of goods on hand and the cost of goods sold based on the assumption that the cost flows of the units sold are in the order in which they were acquired.

Gross margin method A method of estimating inventory value by deducting the cost of goods sold from the total cost of goods available for sale. The cost of goods sold is the result of the average gross margin percent for prior periods applied to sales for the current period.

Historical cost See *Cost of an inventory item.*

Inventory Goods owned by the business for sale to customers.

LIFO (last-in, first-out) inventory costing A costing method based on the assumption that the cost of goods sold should be calculated on prices paid for the most recently acquired units and that the units on hand consist of the oldest units acquired.

Lower of cost or market (LCM) An inventory valuation method by which units are valued at the lower of either original acquisition cost or replacement cost (market).

Market In LCM, the cost of replacing an item at the balance sheet date.

Markon The addition to cost price to establish a selling (or retail) price.

Moving average costing A perpetual inventory costing method by which the cost of each purchase is added to the cost of units on hand, and the total cost is divided by the total quantity on hand to find the new average unit price each time new merchandise is received at a different price.

Periodic inventory system An inventory system by which the valuation of the inventory for balance sheet presentation is determined at the end of each annual period by a complete physical count and pricing of all inventory items. Cost of goods sold must be computed.

Perpetual inventory system An inventory system of record keeping that provides for a continuous book inventory of items on hand.

Replacement cost The current cost of replacing inventory items using the usual sources of supply and in quantities usually bought.

Retail inventory method A method of estimating inventory value in which the ratio of the cost of goods to the selling price is used to convert the inventory valued at retail to cost.

Specific identification method An inventory costing method by which the unit cost is identified specifically with the related supporting acquisition document of the purchase lot from which the inventory item comes.

Stock record card Card on which a perpetual record is kept for an item of inventory.

Valuation (of inventory) The statement of inventory items in accounting records at cost or modifications of cost.

Weighted average costing A costing method by which the ending inventory and the cost of goods sold are priced at the end of each accounting period at a unit cost computed by dividing the total cost of goods available for sale by the physical units available for sale.

Questions

Q12–1 What specific elements are included in the cost of an item of inventory? For each item you name, explain why it is an inventory cost instead of an expense.

Q12–2 How do the perpetual and the periodic inventory systems differ? Does the perpetual inventory system eliminate the need for a physical inventory count? Explain.

Q12–3 (a) What is the relationship between the actual physical flow of goods in and out of inventory and the method used for inventory valuation? (b) What inventory valuation method should a company use if, as new shipments of inventory items are received, they are commingled with identical items on hand in storage bins?

Q12–4 How would overstatements or understatements of inventory affect net income in the period when the error is made? In the following year?

Q12–5 What effect do the different methods of inventory valuation have on the financial statements?

Q12–6 Explain the effect on the balance sheet valuation and on the income determination of the use of LIFO as compared with FIFO (a) if prices have risen during the year, and (b) if prices have fallen during the year.

Q12–7 Why is it important that the selected method of inventory valuation be applied consistently from year to year? Does strict compliance with the principle of consistency preclude a change from FIFO to LIFO?

Q12–8 Define the term market as used in LCM inventory valuation. What are reasons that a business would price inventory at LCM?

Q12–9 Compare the gross margin method with the retail inventory method.

Q12–10 An audit of the records of the Bates Company showed that the ending inventory on December 31, 1984, was overstated by $7,600. What was the effect of the error on the income statements for 1984 and 1985? What was the overall effect for the two-year period, assuming no further errors were made in inventories?

Exercises

E12–1
Elements of inventory cost

The records of Aku Company show the following data as of December 31, 1985:

a. Cost of merchandise on hand, based on a physical count $70,000
b. Merchandise sold to a customer and debited to Accounts Receivable, but held pending receipt of shipping instructions (included in item a) 4,800
c. Merchandise shipped out on December 30; invoice mailed and debited to Accounts Receivable (not included in item a) 5,200
d. Unrecorded bill for transportation in on some goods included in item a 600
e. Cost of spoiled merchandise (to be given away); included in item a 200

What is the cost of inventory on December 31, 1985, for balance sheet purposes?

E12–2
Income statement using specific identification

In October 1985, the Gaston Company began buying and selling a recently patented stamping machine. Transactions for the month follow:

1985	
Oct. 3	Purchased machine no. 1 at $11,800.
7	Purchased machine no. 2 at $12,600.
14	Sold machine no. 2 at $25,200.
21	Purchased machine no. 3 at $14,400.
28	Sold machine no. 1 at $25,200.

Prepare an income statement for the month of October through gross margin on sales, using the specific identification method of inventory costing.

E12–3
Computing inventory valuation and cost of goods sold assuming FIFO

The beginning inventory, purchases, and sales of an item by Bellvue Company for the month of July 1985, were as follows:

1985	
Jul. 1	Inventory on hand consisted of 100 units at $4.00 each.
10	Sold 50 units.
15	Purchased 40 units at $4.20 each.
17	Purchased 60 units at $4.30 each.
20	Sold 30 units.
27	Purchased 50 units at $4.50 each.
29	Sold 40 units.

Compute the July 31 inventory valuation and July cost of goods sold using periodic FIFO.

E12–4
Computing inventory valuation and cost of goods sold assuming LIFO

The Dutchess Company sells a single item. Using periodic LIFO, compute the March 31, 1985, inventory valuation and March cost of goods sold from the following:

1985	
Mar. 1	Inventory on hand consisted of 150 units at $3.75 each.
4	Sold 75 units.
14	Purchased 60 units at $4.00 each.
16	Purchased 90 units at $4.20 each.
21	Sold 45 units.
28	Sold 70 units.

E12–5 *Recording on perpetual cards using FIFO and LIFO*

The Alaska Machine Company buys and sells dryers. Purchases and sales during June 1985 are shown below.

Date	Purchases	Sales
1985		
Jun. 3	80 units at $300	
11		150 units
14	70 units at 310	
18	90 units at 315	
20		60 units
25	95 units at 325	
28		170 units

The inventory on June 1 consisted of 100 units at $280 each. Enter the beginning inventory on a perpetual inventory card and record the transactions using the FIFO assumption. Repeat the process, changing the assumption to LIFO.

E12–6 *Weighted average assumption to compute inventory valuation and cost of goods sold*

The following data are from purchase invoices and sales tickets for a notebook at the Gettysburg College bookstore during February 1985:

Purchases			Sales	
Date	Quantity	Cost	Date	Quantity
Feb. 4	400	$1.40	Feb. 8	240
13	200	1.50	11	120
25	200	1.60	19	200
			22	100

The balance on February 1 was 200 notebooks at a cost of $1.30 each. Using the weighted average assumption (periodic system), compute (a) inventory valuation on February 28, and (b) cost of notebooks sold in February.

E12–7 *Recording on perpetual inventory card using moving average*

Record on a perpetual inventory card the activity of the following item stocked and sold by Bay Path Store during November 1985. Use the moving average cost flow assumption.

1985	
Nov. 1	Balance on hand is 150 units at a cost of $3.00 each.
8	Sold 100 units.
11	Purchased 150 units at a total cost of $490.
22	Sold 160 units.
28	Purchased 100 units at $3.27 each.

E12–8 *Estimating inventory by gross margin method*

p. 413

The entire stock of the York Shop was destroyed by fire on June 22, 1985. The books of the company (kept in a fireproof vault) showed the value of goods on hand on June 1 to be $80,000. Transactions for the period June 1 through June 22 resulted in the following amounts:

Sales	$197,560
Sales returns	4,210
Purchases	159,600
Purchases returns	3,630
Transportation in	2,950

The rate of gross margin on net sales for the previous three years averaged 35 percent. Determine the cost of the inventory destroyed by the fire.

E12–9
Retail method

Iowa Traders estimates its merchandise inventory when preparing monthly financial statements. The following information was available on April 30:

	Cost	Retail
Merchandise inventory, April 1	$ 156,000	$ 253,500
Purchases during April (net)	1,267,500	2,145,000
Transportation in during April	15,600	
Sales during April (net)		1,248,000

Compute the estimated inventory on April 30, using the retail inventory method.

E12–10
Possible LCM valuations

Schotzberger Company had the following items in stock on May 31, 1985:

Item	Quantity	Unit Cost	Unit Market Price
Class A:			
Item M	50	$5.00	$4.00
Item N	100	2.50	3.00
Item O	200	7.00	6.50
Class B:			
Item X	200	1.00	1.25
Item Y	400	3.00	2.50
Item Z	800	1.25	1.50

Compute all inventory valuations that could be used in financial statements for lower of cost or market.

E12–11
Correction of inventory errors

The Merchandise Inventory account of Onondoga Traders has a debit balance of $268,152.50 on December 31, 1985. The final tally of inventory sheets shows that the total cost valuation per physical count and pricing is $267,225.25. Prepare a general journal entry to cause the proper balance to be reported in the December 31 balance sheet.

A Problems

P12–1A
Journal entries for a perpetual inventory system

Ann Folea Company maintains perpetual inventory records. All purchases are received F.O.B. destination, and returns are made at the supplier's expense. Following are summary data from the records for January 1985, the first month of operations:

Total purchases (on account)	$396,350
Total returns of defective merchandise for credit	6,420
Operating expenses (paid in cash)	141,672
Total sales (on account)	472,240
Cost of goods sold per stock records	283,344

Required:

1. Prepare summary general journal entries dated January 31 to record purchases, purchase returns, sales, and operating expenses.

2. Journalize all closing entries, including the transfer of net income to Folea's capital account.

P12–2A *Computing inventory and cost of goods sold—periodic inventory system*

The inventory of the Boko Company on January 1 and December 31, 1985, consisted of 42,500 and 12,500 units, respectively, of Commodity X-1. The beginning inventory was priced at $1,700. The following purchases were made during the year:

Date	Quantity	Cost
1985		
Jan. 3	25,000	$1,125.00
Apr. 16	42,500	1,905.00
Jul. 5	60,000	2,850.00
Oct. 3	15,000	750.00
Dec. 16	40,000	2,200.00

Required: Under the periodic inventory system, determine: (1) the ending inventory and (2) cost of goods sold, using (a) the FIFO cost flow assumption, (b) the LIFO cost flow assumption, and (c) the weighted average cost flow assumption.

P12–3A *Recording transactions on a perpetual inventory card*

Maple, Inc., uses a perpetual inventory system. During May 1985, the following activity was experienced with a wrench, stock number W-100:

1985		
May	1	Balance on hand is 200 units at $8.00 each.
	6	Sold 160 units.
	10	Received 160 units at $8.75 each.
	24	Sold 180 units.
	30	Received 80 units at $9.25 each.

Required: Record the beginning balance and the May activity on perpetual inventory cards, and determine: (1) the ending inventory valuation and (2) the cost of goods sold, using (a) the FIFO cost flow assumption, (b) the LIFO cost flow assumption, and (c) the moving average cost flow assumption.

P12–4A *Three LCM valuations and effect on gross margin*

Melba Assemblers has determined the following to be applicable to the inventory of August 31, 1985, the end of the accounting year:

		Unit	
Item	**Quantity**	**Cost**	**Market**
Frames:			
Type F–1	100	$14.75	$15.50
Type F–12	200	26.00	22.50
Type F–15	60	21.50	21.00
Spring (sets):			
Type S–1	500	7.40	8.50
Type S–12	1,000	10.50	11.25
Type S–15	300	8.60	6.00

Required:

1. Compute the ending inventory at the lower of cost or market, applied (a) to each item, (b) to each category, and (c) to the entire inventory.

2. What is the effect of each application of LCM on the gross margin in the current year? In the following year?

P12–5A *Estimating ending inventories—both methods*

Data for two companies are provided as follows:

Company A

Inventory, September 1	$ 281,600
Net purchases during September	847,140
Net sales during September	1,470,280

Average gross margin rate for the past three years has been 40 percent of sales.

Company B

Sales	$203,625
Transportation in	2,700
Purchases at cost	128,250
Purchases at retail	202,500
Inventory—June 1 (cost)	47,250
Inventory—June 1 (retail)	67,500

Required:

1. Estimate the September 30 inventory of Company A using the gross margin method.

2. Estimate the June 30 inventory of Company B using the retail method.

P12–6A *Thought-provoking problem: effect of cost flow assumptions on financial statements*

On July 1, 1985, Nora Policastro established Policastro Company with an investment of $80,000 in cash. Purchases and sales of an item during the month are shown below.

1985		
Jul.	1	Purchased 2,880 units at $19.20.
	10	Sold 1,680 units at $32.
	13	Purchased 2,400 units at $20.40.
	17	Sold 2,640 units at $32.
	22	Purchased 3,600 units at $21.20.
	29	Sold 2,160 units at $32.

Operating expenses were $22,400. Cash settlements on all transactions were completed by the end of the month.

Required:

1. Prepare perpetual inventory schedules, using (a) FIFO, (b) LIFO, and (c) moving average cost flow assumptions.

2. Prepare income statements and balance sheets based on each of the foregoing methods of inventory valuation.

3. Explain why the different methods yield different results. Which method is correct?

4. What factors should Policastro consider in her choice of method of inventory valuation?

5. Which method would you recommend? Explain.

6. FIFO reflects price increases of goods on hand in net income, but these are not real profits because, as the inventory is depleted, replacement costs will be higher. Do you agree? Explain.

B Problems

P12–1B *Journal entries for a perpetual inventory system*

San Juan Company maintains perpetual inventory records. All purchases are received F.O.B. destination, and returns are made at the supplier's expense. Following are summary data from the records for July 1985, the first month of operations:

Total purchases (on account)	$590,200
Total returns of defective merchandise for credit	10,150
Operating expenses (paid in cash)	140,150
Total sales (on account)	705,300
Cost of goods sold per stock records	419,800

Required:

1. Prepare summary general journal entries dated July 31 to record purchases, purchase returns, sales, and operating expenses.

2. Journalize all closing entries, including the transfer of net income to Carlos Pedras's capital account.

P12–2B *Computing inventory and cost of goods sold—periodic inventory system*

The inventory of Ohio Industries on January 1 and December 31, 1985, consisted of 10,625 and 15,625 units, respectively, of stock number L300. The beginning inventory was priced at a cost of $8,500. The following purchases were made during the year:

Date	Quantity	Cost
1985		
Feb. 7	6,250	$ 5,625.00
Apr. 4	10,625	10,362.50
Jun. 8	15,000	14,700.00
Sep. 19	3,750	3,750.00
Nov. 1	10,000	10,500.00

Required: Under the periodic inventory system determine: (1) the ending inventory, and (2) cost of goods sold, using (a) the FIFO cost flow assumption, (b) the LIFO cost flow assumption, and (c) the weighted average cost flow assumption.

P12–3B *Recording transactions on a perpetual card*

Mingo Company uses a perpetual inventory system. During August 1985, the following activity was experienced with a fruit crate, stock number 102–XA:

1985		
Aug.	1	Balance on hand is 300 units at $5.50.
	5	Sold 240 units.
	12	Received 240 units at $6.00.
	23	Sold 270 units.
	30	Received 120 units at $6.25.

Required: Record the beginning balance and the August activity on perpetual inventory cards, and determine: (1) the ending inventory valuation, and (2) the cost of goods sold, using (a) the FIFO cost flow assumption, (b) the LIFO cost flow assumption, and (c) the moving average cost flow assumption.

P12–4B *Three LCM valuations and effect on gross margin*

Blue Mountain Repair Shop has determined the following to be applicable to the inventory of December 31, 1985, the end of the accounting year:

		Unit	
Item	**Quantity**	**Cost**	**Market**
Boxes:			
Size A	300	$2.85	$3.10
Size B	600	5.20	4.50
Size C	180	4.30	4.20

Item	Quantity	Unit Cost	Unit Market
Corner seals:			
Size A	1,200	1.45	1.70
Size B	2,400	2.10	2.30
Size C	720	1.72	1.20

Required:

1. Compute the ending inventory at the lower of cost or market applied (a) to each item, (b) to each category, and (c) to the entire inventory.

2. What is the effect of each application of LCM on the gross margin in the current year? In the following year?

P12–5B *Estimating ending inventories—both methods*

Data for two companies are provided as follows:

Company A

Inventory, January 1	$120,600
Net purchases during January	363,060
Net sales during January	630,120

Average gross margin rate for the past three years has been 40 percent of sales.

Company B

Sales	$407,250
Transportation in	5,400
Purchases at cost	256,500
Purchases at retail	405,000
Inventory—July 1 (cost)	94,500
Inventory—July 1 (retail)	135,000

Required:

1. Estimate the January 31 inventory of Company A using the gross margin method.

2. Estimate the July 31 inventory of Company B using the retail method.

P12–6B *Thought-provoking problem: effect of inventory errors*

At Boiling Springs Company, where a periodic inventory system is used, the December 31, 1985, inventory was undervalued by $120,000 because of a failure to include some merchandise that had been received and debited to the Purchases account. As a result, additional orders were placed at the beginning of 1986 resulting in a duplication of items on hand that was not corrected until return of the merchandise three months later for credit. The company's short-term borrowing rate to finance the unnecessary purchase was 12 percent per year. Boiling Springs Company paid transportation costs of $620 for the return.

Required:

1. What was the effect of the error on the net income for 1985?

2. What was the effect of the error on 1986 net income? Support your answer with assumptions and computations.

3. What was the ultimate effect of the error on the owner's capital account?

13 Property, Plant, and Equipment; Intangible Assets

Introduction

Industry often requires large expenditures for three groups of long-term assets that are used in the operations of a business:

1. **Tangible plant assets,** such as land, building, machinery, equipment, and trucks.
2. Natural resources or **wasting assets,** such as those found in mining, oil and gas, forestry, and other extractive industries.
3. **Intangible assets,** such as patents, trademarks, and goodwill.

This chapter deals with the determination of and accounting for the costs of these long-lived assets, their allocation as expense (if applicable) to appropriate accounting periods, and their disposal or retirement.

Learning Goals

To know which cost elements are included in the original cost of property, plant, and equipment items.

To understand the nature of depreciation, depletion, and amortization.

To know the acceptable methods of computing depreciation and to make the necessary accounting entries.

To differentiate between capital and revenue expenditures.

To account for disposal of plant assets including trade-in transactions.

To record depletion of natural resources and to understand the accounting for depletion costs as part of cost of goods sold or as inventory.

To identify, define, and account for intangible plant assets.

To be familiar with financial statement disclosure requirements for plant assets.

Definition of Terms

The term **property, plant, and equipment** includes all tangible assets including natural resources of a relatively permanent nature, acquired for use in the regular operation of the business, but not for resale, whose use or consumption will cover more than one accounting period. Long-term intangible assets are those that have no form or substance but contribute to the operation of a business. These groups of assets are now considered in more detail.

Tangible Plant Assets

Some of the tangible plant assets have been discussed in preceding chapters. Now they are considered in more depth, including a determination of their costs and valuation, allocation of their cost to expense, and their disposal.

Valuation of Tangible Plant Assets

A tangible plant asset is initially recorded in the records at cost, which includes the purchase price (less any cash discount) plus *all other expenditures required to secure title and to get the asset ready for operating use.* The cost of a building includes permit fees, excavation and grading, architectural and engineering fees, and remodeling costs. In October 1979, the FASB issued *Statement No. 34,* "Capitalization of Interest Cost." As amended in 1982 by *FASB Statements No. 58 and 62,* it requires that certain interest paid or accrued during the period of construction, if material, be **capitalized** (that is, debited to the constructed plant asset). The cost of machinery includes transportation, installation, and all other costs incurred in preparing the machinery for operations.

Assume that a company purchases a machine for $5,000 at terms of 2/10, n/60, with freight to be paid by the buyer. Installation of the machine requires specialized electrical wiring and the construction of a cement foundation. All these expenditures are debited to the asset account. The total asset cost includes the following:

Purchase price	$5,000
Deduct 2 percent cash discount	100
Net purchase price	$4,900
Transportation	125
Cost of wiring	75
Construction of a special foundation	110
Total asset cost	$5,210

Using a net price approach and assuming that cash is paid immediately, the entry to record this purchase is:

1985 Jun.	1	Machinery . . . . Cash . . . . Purchased a machine.		4,900	 4,900

The entry for the freight payment on June 11 is:

1985 Jun.	11	Machinery . . . . Cash . . . . Paid freight on delivery of machine.		125	 125

The entry to record the payment for installation of the machine on June 13 is:

1985 Jun.	13	Machinery . . . . Cash . . . . Paid for installation of machine.		185	 185

When these entries are posted, the Machinery account shows a total cost for the machine of $5,210. If the discount of $100 is not taken, it should still be deducted from the purchase price of $5,000 and debited to Discounts Lost—Nonmerchandise Items. Some accountants prefer to debit the costs to a Construction in Progress account as they occur; then, the Machinery account is debited with a credit to clear the Construction in Progress account when the machine is ready for use. A tangible plant asset acquired in some manner other than cash or credit purchase—for example, by gift or in exchange for capital stock—is valued on the basis of the amount of cash that would be required for its acquisition **(fair market value).** When a used plant asset is acquired, all expenditures incurred in getting the asset ready for use—paint, replacement parts, and so on—are debited to the asset account.

The cost of land includes brokers' fees, legal fees, transfer taxes, and costs incurred in preparing the land for use, such as grading, clearing, and the removal of unwanted existing structures less amounts received for scrap and salvage. Land is shown separately on the balance sheet because it is not subject to depreciation. However, improvements to land—lighting, parking areas, fencing—which deteriorate through usage are subject to depreciation and should be classified in a separate account, Land Improvements.

Subsidiary Records

Within the accounts, there is grouping into similar asset categories. Typewriters, calculators, copying machines, and similar items are usually debited to an account called Office Equipment. Machinery, Buildings, Store Equipment, Delivery Equipment, and many other accounts each contain groups of similar assets. It is usually necessary for management to have specific information

EQUIPMENT RECORD

NAME OF ASSET	Package Sealer	ASSET NO.	1252	CLASS NO.	14	ACCT. NO.	163

Made by Northern Motors

Purchased From Mebane Company

Purchase Guarantee

Manufacturer's Serial No. 1BS50216

H. P. Generated or Required

Location: Packing Department

Year	Type	Model	Size
1985	A	Medium	

Estimated Life Years	Depreciation Rate % or $	Per	Estimated Residual Value $
10 Yrs.	10%	Year	$100

Insurance Carried: Under general equipment policy

Appraised by Gail Alston — When Appraised 1/12/85 — Appraised Value $ 580 — Appraisal Report Reference GA 2012

ACCUMULATED DEPRECIATION			NET ASSET VALUE	DATE	DESCRIPTION	POSTING REF.	COST		
YEAR	ANNUAL AMT.	TO DATE					DEBIT	CREDIT	BALANCE
1985	48	48	532	12/31		163	580		580

Figure 13–1 **Equipment Record**

about each long-lived asset for purposes of computing depreciation, making disposal and replacement decisions, and sometimes maintaining a repairs and maintenance history. To serve this need, a plant ledger contains an equipment record for each item. For a large company, such records are most efficiently maintained by computer. A smaller company may have a card file with a record similar to that shown in Figure 13–1 for each item.

Depreciation of Tangible Plant Assets

Depreciation is an allocation of cost. It recognizes that depreciable assets used in the business have a predictable and limited service life, over which asset costs should be allocated for the purpose of income measurement. The emphasis is on the systematic periodic debit to expense rather than the resulting balance sheet valuation. Recording depreciation was introduced along with adjusting entries in Chapter 4. Depreciation theory and practice are treated in more detail in the following sections.

A number of factors limit the serviceability of tangible plant assets, chiefly wear and tear through ordinary use, accidental damage, inadequacy, level of repairs or maintenance, and obsolescence. Although the serviceable life of the asset cannot be definitely known at the time of its acquisition, its cost cannot be considered as an expense chargeable entirely either to the period of acquisition or to the period of disposal. It is better to estimate the useful life of the asset for purposes of making periodic debits to expense than to omit the charge on the grounds that there is no definitely known period of service life.

Purpose of depreciation

Since most tangible plant assets have a limited useful life, their costs are properly allocable as expenses to the accounting periods in which the assets are used. The* purpose of depreciation *is to recognize the expiration of asset cost through use. Its primary purpose is cost allocation.

Estimated Useful Life (EUL)

It is often difficult to predict the useful service life of an asset. The estimate is important because the amount of cost assigned as expense of each period (depreciation for a period) is deducted from current revenue, thereby affecting net income for the period. Past experience, standard operating policies, and equipment replacement policies may be used in estimating the period during which the asset can or will be used by the business. A machine may be able to withstand wear and tear for 20 years, but it may be used for only 10 years because it has become too slow or too small for current requirements; or it may have become obsolete. The estimated useful service life over which the cost is allocated is called the **estimated useful life (EUL)** of the asset.

Estimated Salvage Value

The amount that is expected to be recovered when the asset is ultimately scrapped, sold, or traded in is called **salvage value** (or residual value). The salvage value is deducted from the cost to determine the **depreciable cost,** the total amount of depreciation to be recorded over the estimated useful life. If an expenditure will be required in dismantling or removing the asset, the estimated gross salvage value is reduced by the anticipated removal cost. It is frequently assumed that the salvage value will be offset by the removal cost, in which case the depreciable cost is the total cost of the asset. Also, total cost may be depreciated when the salvage value is known to be negligible.

A company may trade in any assets that have a market value. For example, some businesses trade in cars, trucks, and office equipment for new models after a period of use. In such instances, the expected market value at the date of trade-in should be deducted in arriving at the depreciable amount. Experience will enable the company to arrive at a salvage value estimate.

Method of Computing Depreciation

A number of methods are used to calculate periodic depreciation charges; each may give a significantly different result. The method selected in any specific instance should be based on a careful evaluation of all the factors involved, including estimated useful life, intensity of use, rapidity of changes in the technology of the industry and equipment, and revenue-generating potential. The objective is to debit expense of each period in proportion to the benefits over the asset's useful life. Depending upon the method used, the amounts apportioned to each period may be irregular, follow a regularly increasing or decreasing pattern, or be the same.

The depreciation methods described in the following sections include (1) the straight line method, (2) production methods, including the working hours and the production unit methods, and (3) accelerated methods, including the double-declining balance and the sum-of-the-years'-digits methods. The method selected for computing depreciation is crucial because the amount of the expense affects the net income for current and future periods and the carrying value of the asset in the balance sheet.

Straight Line Method Under the **straight line method,** depreciation is considered a function of time, and a uniform portion of the cost is allocated to each accounting period. It is popular because it is simple to use. It assumes, however, uniform levels of operating efficiency, repair and maintenance, and revenue contributions for each period of the asset's EUL.

A formula for the straight line method may be expressed as follows:

$$\frac{\text{Cost} - \text{Salvage value}}{\text{Number of accounting periods in estimated useful life of asset}} = \text{Depreciation expense for each accounting period.}$$

Assume that a machine costing \$20,000, with an estimated service life of five years and an estimated net salvage value of \$3,500, is purchased on January 3, 1985. The annual depreciation expense is:

$$\frac{\$20{,}000 - \$3{,}500}{5 \text{ years}} = \$3{,}300 \text{ per year.}$$

Straight line depreciation can also be computed by use of a *straight line rate,* calculated by dividing 100 percent by the number of years in EUL (alternatively calculated as $1/n$, where n = EUL). In the foregoing situation:

$$\frac{100\%}{5 \text{ years}} = 20\% \text{ per year, or } \frac{1}{n} = \frac{1}{5} = 0.20 = 20\%.$$

Production Methods Production methods relate depreciation to usage or to results rather than time, recognizing either working hours or units of output. Each hour or unit is charged an equal amount regardless of decline in service effectiveness, decline in revenue generated, or level of repair and maintenance requirements.

The **working hours method** requires an estimate of useful life in service hours instead of years. The depreciation expense for an accounting period is determined as follows:

$$\frac{\text{Cost} - \text{Salvage value}}{\text{Total estimated working hours}} = \text{Depreciation expense per hour, and}$$

$$\begin{bmatrix}\text{Depreciation}\\ \text{expense}\\ \text{per hour}\end{bmatrix} \times \begin{bmatrix}\text{Working hours}\\ \text{for the}\\ \text{period}\end{bmatrix} = \begin{bmatrix}\text{Depreciation}\\ \text{expense for}\\ \text{the period}\end{bmatrix}.$$

Assume, for example, that a machine costing $20,000 with a salvage value of $3,500 is expected to be operated 150,000 hours. If it is operated 10,000 hours during an accounting period, the computation for the period would be:

$$\frac{\$20{,}000 - \$3{,}500}{150{,}000 \text{ hours}} = \$0.11 \text{ per hour, and}$$

$$\$0.11 \times 10{,}000 \text{ hours} = \$1{,}100 \text{ depreciation expense for the period.}$$

Under the **production unit method,** depreciation is computed on units of output, and therefore an estimate of total units of output is required. Assume, for example, that the machine costing $20,000 with a salvage value of $3,500 has an estimated productive life of 10,000 units. If 1,500 units were processed during the current period, the debit to depreciation expense for the period would be:

$$\frac{\$20{,}000 - \$3{,}500}{10{,}000 \text{ units}} = \$1.65 \text{ per unit produced, and}$$

$$\$1.65 \times 1{,}500 \text{ units} = \$2{,}475 \text{ depreciation expense for the period.}$$

The production methods allocate cost in proportion to the use that is made of the asset, the assumption being that there is a correlation between units of use and revenue generated.

Accelerated Methods The use of **accelerated methods** results in larger depreciation expense during the early years of asset life, with gradually decreasing depreciation expense in later years. Two commonly used forms are (1) the declining balance method, and (2) the sum-of-the-years'-digits method.

Declining Balance Method Under a *declining balance method,* a uniform depreciation rate is applied in each period to the remaining **carrying value** (cost less accumulated depreciation).[1] One form that uses twice the straight line rate is termed **double-declining balance (DDB).** *Salvage value is not deducted under the declining balance method,* although the asset cannot be depreciated below salvage value.

[1] *Carrying value* is also known as *book value,* which is discussed later in this chapter.

In a period in which the use of DDB reduces the carrying value to an amount less than salvage value, the use of DDB should be discontinued. For that period and future periods of the EUL, the remaining depreciation may be computed by the straight line method.[2] On the other hand, a balance greater than salvage value may remain at the end of the EUL. Such a balance (less salvage value) may be depreciated under the straight line method over a period determined at that time, by an adjustment in the amount of depreciation for the final period, or by the fixed percentage of the carrying value until it is retired from use.

Assume the data used previously (a machine is purchased on January 3, 1985, at a cost of $20,000, salvage value estimated at $3,500, and EUL of five years). Use of DDB results in a 40 percent depreciation rate—twice the straight line rate of 20 percent—which is applied annually to remaining carrying value.

DDB—Case 1. Since the DDB rate is applied to carrying value, the salvage value is not deducted from cost in computing depreciation. The annual amounts are as follows:

Year	Computation	Annual Depreciation	Accumulated Depreciation	Carrying Value
1985	40% of $20,000	$8,000	$ 8,000	$12,000
1986	40% of 12,000	4,800	12,800	7,200
1987	40% of 7,200	2,880	15,680	4,320
1988	$4,320 − $3,500[a]	820	16,500	3,500
1989	None	None	16,500	3,500

[a]40% of $4,320 is $1,728, which would reduce the carrying value below estimated salvage value. Accordingly, only $820 is recorded in 1988.

Because depreciation was stopped after the fourth year of its useful life, no further depreciation expense is recorded for this asset even though it is kept in service. When the asset is disposed of, the $3,500 carrying value will be used to determine any loss or gain on disposal (discussed later in this chapter). A typical method is to change to straight line in the year that carrying value would fall below salvage value; it is illustrated next.

DDB—Case 2. In the fourth year of EUL, the carrying value would fall below salvage value if DDB is continued. Many companies plan to switch to straight line at this point, as follows:

---

[2]If planned at the time the depreciation method is adoped, a change to straight line at this point is not required to be reported as a change in accounting principle under *APB Opinion No. 20.*

Year	Computation	Annual Depreciation	Accumulated Depreciation	Carrying Value
1985	40% of $20,000	$8,000	$ 8,000	$12,000
1986	40% of 12,000	4,800	12,800	7,200
1987	40% of 7,200	2,880	15,680	4,320[a]
1988	½ of $820[b]	410	16,090	3,910
1989	½ of $820	410	16,500	3,500

[a]40% of $4,320 is $1,728, which would reduce carrying value below salvage value if recorded in 1988. Hence, the change to straight line.

[b]Carrying value of $4,320 minus salvage value of $3,500 equals $820, the amount to be depreciated by straight line over the last two years.

In the change to straight line in 1988, only the difference between end-1987 carrying value and estimated salvage value is to be depreciated over the remaining EUL.

Sum-of-the-Years-Digits Method Under the **sum-of-the-years'-digits method (SYD),** depreciation for any year is determined by multiplying the cost less salvage value by a fraction. The denominator is the sum of the numbers of years of estimated useful life of the asset and the numerator is the number of the specific period applied in reverse order, or the number of years remaining, including the current year. The following steps may be followed in sequence in making the calculations:

1. Calculate the sum of the series of digits represented by the life of the asset, starting with n (the EUL) and going down to 1:

$$5 + 4 + 3 + 2 + 1 = 15.$$

2. The denominator is: The sum of the years' digits from Step 1.

3. The numerators are the years in the EUL used in reverse order.

4. The annual depreciation expense is: (Cost of asset − Salvage) × Fraction for that year.

On the basis of the same facts as before (cost of $20,000 and salvage value of $3,500), the annual depreciation is computed as follows:

Year	Years' Digits	Fraction Times Depreciable Cost	Annual Depreciation
1985	5	5/15 × $16,500	$ 5,500
1986	4	4/15 × $16,500	4,400
1987	3	3/15 × $16,500	3,300
1988	2	2/15 × $16,500	2,200
1989	1	1/15 × $16,500	1,100
Total depreciation for 5 years			$16,500

For long-lived assets, the sum of the years' digits (S) can be found by using a formula based on arithmetical progression:

$$S = \frac{n(n + 1)}{2} = \frac{n}{2}(n + 1) = n\left(\frac{n + 1}{2}\right)$$

where n = EUL.

For example,

$$S = \frac{5(5 + 1)}{2} = \frac{5}{2}(5 + 1) = 5\left(\frac{5 + 1}{2}\right) = 15.$$

Comparison of Methods

For a machine purchased for $20,000 on January 3, 1985, with a salvage value of $3,500 and an EUL of five years, a comparison of methods shows the following depreciation expense under each method:

Year	Straight Line Only	Pure Double-Declining Balance[a]	DDB with a Switch to Straight Line	Sum-of-the Years'-Digits
1985	$ 3,300	$ 8,000	$ 8,000	$ 5,500
1986	3,300	4,800	4,800	4,400
1987	3,300	2,880	2,880	3,300
1988	3,300	820	410	2,200
1989	3,300	0	410	1,100
Totals	$16,500	$16,500	$16,500	$16,500

[a]Without a switch to straight line.

Double-declining balance results in the highest depreciation in the first year because of the higher rate (40 percent) and higher base ($20,000 as compared with $16,500). The total for both the DDB methods for the five-year period is the same as straight line and SYD because of the change in the fourth year to avoid depreciating the asset below salvage value. If the use of DDB leaves an undepreciated carrying value at the end of the EUL that is greater than estimated salvage value and the machine is kept in service, a changeover to straight line for the remainder of the revised EUL is in order at this point. If the item is disposed of at the end of the EUL, there is simply a greater book value to be considered in calculating a gain or loss.

Depreciation for Partial Accounting Periods

A consistent method should be followed for recording depreciation on assets acquired or retired during an accounting period. Since depreciation is an estimate, exact methods such as counting the number of days of use are not commonly used. One commonly used method that is both simple and relevant is to consider that a tangible plant asset is purchased as of the beginning of the month of acquisition if it is purchased on or before the fifteenth of the month, or as of the first day of the following month if it is purchased on or after the sixteenth of the month. The minimum measurable unit of time for the depreciation expense charge should be one month.

Computation of depreciation for a partial year presents no special problems when the straight line method or a production method is used. For accelerated methods, however, a special problem does arise. In both sum-of-the-years'-digits and declining balance methods, the amount of depreciation is associated with the *asset-life year*. When the asset-life year is not the same as the accounting year, depreciation is recorded based on a combination of fractions of asset-life years. To illustrate, assume that on January 3, 1985, Peggy Barber bought the $20,000 machine that has been used in the previous illustrations. Assume, however, that Barber's accounting year ends on June 30. Referring to the foregoing tables, her depreciation expense in the fiscal year ended June 30, 1985, would be:

Under DDB: 1/2 × $8,000 = $4,000.
Under SYD: 1/2 × $5,500 = $2,750.

However, for the fiscal year ended June 30, 1986, Barber should record:

Under DDB: (1/2 × $8,000) + (1/2 × $4,800) = $6,400.
Under SYD: (1/2 × $5,500) + (1/2 × $4,400) = $4,950.

These figures differ because in the fiscal (or accounting) year ended June 30, 1985, Barber has received the benefits of only one-half the first asset-life year of the machine, whereas in the fiscal year ended June 30, 1986, she is receiving the benefits of the second half of the machine's first asset-life year plus the first half of the machine's second asset-life year.[3]

Accelerated Cost Recovery System (ACRS)

To encourage increased capital investment by business, the *Economic Recovery Tax Act of 1981* revised federal income tax laws relating to depreciation. For tax purposes, businesses are entitled to "cost recovery deductions" at varying rates instead of depreciation deductions for tangible property placed in service after 1980. The methods authorized are called the **Accelerated Cost Recovery System (ACRS).** Depreciable personal property falls into four cost recovery classes: three-years; five-years; ten-years; and fifteen-years. Automobiles, light-duty trucks, and certain special tools fall into the three-year class, while most machinery and equipment fall into the five-year class. Certain heavy equipment such as railroad tank cars falls into the ten-year

[3]Under DDB, this process can be simplified by using only one-half year for 1985 in the amortization table. Thus 1985 depreciation is ½ × 40% × $20,000 = $4,000. The 1986 year begins with a carrying value of $16,000 = $20,000 − $4,000; depreciation for 1986 is 40% × $16,000 = $6,400. In future years, the annual DDB rate can be applied to carrying value. There is no parallel simplification for SYD.

class; permanent buildings usually fall into the fifteen-year class. Within each class, statutory percentages of cost can be deducted annually adding up to 100 percent of cost recovery in the class time period.

Assume that the $20,000 machine used in previous examples was placed in service on December 31, 1983. It falls into the five-year property category. At the rates then in effect as stipulated by the Internal Revenue Service, cost recovery tax deductions would be:

1984	15%	=	$ 3,000
1985	22	=	4,400
1986	21	=	4,200
1987	21	=	4,200
1988	21	=	4,200
Total	100%	=	$20,000

The ACRS amounts are for federal income tax purposes only; conventional methods are still used for financial reporting. Although income tax is not levied directly on the net income of a single proprietorship, the owner must include income from the business in his or her personal income tax return. This topic is covered in Appendix A.

Guidelines for Depreciation Methods

The user should select the depreciation method that is most practical and meaningful. Since the amount of the depreciation deduction has a direct effect on net income and since the alternative methods of calculating depreciation result in different amounts, the method chosen may significantly affect a business owner's income tax liability. Any tax savings become available for investment in new property, plant, and equipment or for any other use the owner chooses. *Minimization of income taxes by choice of depreciation method is a good management practice.* It is acceptable practice to use one depreciation method for income tax reporting and a different method for financial reporting.

The straight line method is simple to apply and is satisfactory under conditions of fairly uniform usage. The production methods allocate depreciation in proportion to usage or output. This is important if usage is the dominant cause of loss in usefulness of the asset. The accelerated methods are based on the idea that the service rendered by a tangible plant asset is greatest in the early years of use. Hence, depreciation charged under these methods results in a more accurate matching of expense and revenue. They also take into account the fact that as an asset gets older, it requires more maintenance. The increasing maintenance expenses in later years are offset by the diminishing depreciation expense, thus equalizing, to some extent, the total expense of the asset and thereby achieving a better matching of expense with revenue.

Recording and Financial Reporting

The basic entries to record depreciation expense and reporting of depreciation on the balance sheet were covered in Chapters 4 and 5. They are repeated here briefly for review. Only the straight line amounts are used—recording and reporting for all methods is the same except for dollar amounts. Using the above example, the entry to record 1985 depreciation expense is:

1985 Dec.	31	Depreciation Expense—Machinery		3,300	
		Accumulated Depreciation—Machinery			3,300
		To record depreciation for the year.			

On the balance sheet for December 31, 1985, the figures would be reported as follows:

Assets

Property, plant, and equipment:		
Machinery	$20,000	
Deduct: Accumulated depreciation	3,300	$16,700

As additional depreciation expense is recorded in subsequent periods and the accumulated depreciation increases in subsequent periods, the carrying value continues to decrease. In general, the carrying value will equal the estimated salvage value at the end of EUL.

Up to this point, all debits have been made to an expense account when depreciation is recorded. The debit to an expense account is correct when the depreciation represents an expired cost of the accounting period. In some cases, however—for example, manufacturing—depreciation represents an inventoriable cost rather than an expense. This concept is discussed later with depletion of natural resources and reinforced when patent amortization is illustrated.

Capital and Revenue Expenditures

Capital expenditures are significant payments benefiting two or more periods. They may be (1) initial costs of acquiring tangible plant assets (as previously illustrated), and (2) costs subsequent to the original purchase of these assets (asset alterations, additions or improvements to existing assets, or extraordinary repairs). They prolong the useful life of the asset or make it more valuable or adaptable. Expenditures that improve or enlarge existing assets *should be capitalized by a debit to the asset account.*

Expenditures for extraordinary repairs made to equipment during its life are also classified as capital expenditures if they extend the useful life or capacity of the asset or otherwise make it more serviceable (for example, overhaul of an aircraft engine). Accountants view an extraordinary repair as restoring the effects of previous wear, that is, as a recovery of previous asset services. They record the capitalization by debiting Accumulated Depreciation, thereby canceling past depreciation charges.

Assume that the $20,000 machine used in previous illustrations received a complete overhaul at the end of 1988. The overhaul, at a cost of $2,500, added two years to the original EUL of five years. The general journal entry to record the overhaul is:

1988 Dec.	30	Accumulated Depreciation—Machinery . . . Cash . . . . To record the overhaul of a machine.		2,500	 2,500

When any capital expenditure—an enlargement or extraordinary repair—is made on an asset already in service, the carrying value is changed, and a new depreciation schedule is needed. The method for doing this is explained in the next section.

Revenue expenditures benefit a current period and are made for the purpose of maintaining the asset in satisfactory operating condition. A routine repair or the replacement of a minor part that has worn out is an expense of the current accounting period. These expenditures do not increase the serviceability of the asset beyond the original estimate but rather represent normal maintenance costs.

Careful distinction between capital and revenue expenditures is one of the fundamental problems of accounting. It is essential for the matching of expenses and revenue and, therefore, for the proper measurement of net income. A capital expenditure recorded as a revenue expenditure (for example, a purchase of office equipment debited to Office Expense) causes an understatement of net income in that year. If the error is not corrected, net income for the following years will be overstated by the amount of depreciation expense that would otherwise have been recognized. Conversely, a revenue expenditure recorded as a capital expenditure (for example, an office expense debited to Office Equipment) overstates net income for that year. If the error is not corrected, net income for the following years will be understated by the depreciation charge on the overstated portion of the Office Equipment account.

Capital versus revenue expenditures

The term* expenditure *refers to a payment or a promise to make a future payment for benefits received—that is, for assets or services. Expenditures made on tangible plant assets during the period of ownership may be classified as either capital expenditures or revenue expenditures. A* capital expenditure *results in an increase in the book value of an asset account; a* revenue expenditure *results in an addition to an expense account.

Changing of Depreciation Expense

The periodic depreciation expense may require revision as the result of (1) an additional capital expenditure made on an original asset, or (2) errors in the original EUL or estimated salvage value. In either case, the new depreciable cost is typically allocated over the remaining life of the property on which the expenditure was made. Assume, for example, that an additional wing costing $80,000 is added to a five-year-old factory building. The original cost of the building was $330,000, the estimated salvage value was $30,000, and the estimated useful life was 25 years. The straight line method of depreciation has been used. The calculation of the revised annual depreciation charge is:

Original cost	$330,000
Deduct: Accumulated depreciation ($300,000 ÷ 25 = $12,000 per year × 5 years)	60,000
Book value	$270,000
Additional cost	80,000
New book value	$350,000
Deduct: Estimated salvage value	30,000
New depreciable cost	$320,000
New annual depreciation charge, based on a remaining useful life of 20 years ($320,000 ÷ 20)	$ 16,000

If the improvement prolongs the life of the asset or increases salvage value, the calculations must be altered to show the effect of such changes. For example, if after the addition of the wing the remaining useful life was estimated to be 24 years and the estimated salvage value was $38,000, the revised annual depreciation charge would be determined as follows:

New book value (from above)	$350,000
Deduct: Estimated salvage value	38,000
New depreciable cost	$312,000
New annual depreciation charge, based on a remaining useful life of 24 years ($312,000 ÷ 24)	$13,000

If at any time it is determined that an error has been made in EUL, a new depreciation schedule is prepared. From that point on, the new depreciation amount will be recorded.[4] It will be calculated in the manner just illustrated.

At some point, however, it is necessary to dispose of most items of tangible plant property. Accounting for such disposal of tangible plant property is explained in the next section.

[4] *Opinions of the Accounting Principles Board, No. 20,* "Accounting Changes" (New York: AICPA, July 1971) defines such a change as a change in accounting estimates and requires footnote disclosure in the financial statements. See Note 3 in "A Real Life Example" at the end of this chapter.

Disposal of Tangible Plant Assets

A tangible plant asset may be disposed of by sale, by being traded in as part of the purchase price of a replacement, or by being discarded. The accounting treatment of sales and discards is similar; that of trade-ins is somewhat different.

Sale or Discard of Tangible Plant Assets

When an asset is sold or discarded, the entry for the transaction must remove the appropriate amounts from the asset and the accumulated depreciation accounts. Assume, for example, that a company acquired a truck with a five-year EUL on January 3, 1985, at a cost of $18,000. It has no salvage value. Depreciation is recorded on a straight line basis at the rate of $3,600 annually. Three situations, together with the methods of accounting for the disposal of the truck, are illustrated.

Example 1: Sale of asset at a price equal to book value. The truck is sold on October 1, 1989, for $900. The first entry records the depreciation for the current year up to the date of sale:

1989 Oct.	1	Depreciation Expense—Trucks . . . . . . Accumulated Depreciation—Trucks . . To record depreciation on trucks for the 9-month period 1/1/89 to 10/1/89.		2,700	 2,700

The Accumulated Depreciation account now has a credit balance of $17,100 accumulated as follows:

Accumulated Depreciation—Trucks

Date		Explanation	F	Debit	Credit	Balance
1985 Dec.	31		J18		3,600	3,600
1986 Dec.	31		J37		3,600	7,200
1987 Dec.	31		J60		3,600	10,800
1988 Dec.	31		J79		3,600	14,400
1989 Oct.	1		J90		2,700	17,100

The book value of the truck is $900 computed as follows:

Cost at acquisition	$18,000
Deduct: Accumulated depreciation	17,100
Book value	$ 900

As shown above, the **book value** of an asset—as distinguished from market value and replacement value—is its cost at acquisition reduced by the portion of the accumulated depreciation account applicable to that asset. Other terms commonly used are *carrying value* and *undepreciated cost.* The entry to record the sale is:

1989 Oct.	1	Cash		900	
		Accumulated Depreciation—Trucks		17,100	
		Trucks			18,000
		To record sale of truck.			

Its purpose is to record the receipt of cash, eliminate the accumulated charges from the Accumulated Depreciation account, and reduce the asset account by the original cost of the truck.

Example 2: Sale of asset at a price above book value. The truck is sold on October 1, 1989, for $1,200. The entry to record the depreciation for the current year up to the date of sale is the same as in Example 1. The following entry is made to record the sale:

1989 Oct.	1	Cash			1,200	
		Accumulated Depreciation—Trucks			17,100	
		Trucks				18,000
		Gain on Disposal of Plant Assets				300
		To record sale of truck at a gain computed as follows:				
		Cost of truck	$18,000			
		Deduct: Accumulated depreciation	17,100			
		Book value of truck	$ 900			
		Amount received	1,200			
		Gain on disposal	$ 300			

Gains and losses on disposal of tangible plant assets result from differences between the book value of an asset and the proceeds from its disposal. A gain results when the proceeds are greater than the book value, a loss when they are less. Gain on disposal of plant assets is shown in the income statement under other revenue.

Example 3: Sale of asset at a price below book value. The truck is sold on October 1, 1989, for $400 in cash. Again, the entry to record the depreciation applicable to the year of sale is the same as in Example 1. The entry to record the sale is:

1989					
Oct.	1	Cash		400	
		Accumulated Depreciation—Trucks		17,100	
		Loss on Disposal of Plant Assets		500	
		Trucks			18,000
		To record sale of truck at a loss computed as follows:			
		Cost of truck	$18,000		
		Deduct: Accumulated depreciation	17,100		
		Book value of truck	$ 900		
		Amount received	400		
		Loss on disposal	$ 500		

Loss on disposal of plant assets is shown in the income statement under other expenses. In the three previous examples, some cash was received at the time of disposal. If the truck has been simply discarded (same as sold for $0) the loss would equal book value.

Trade-in of Tangible Plant Assets—General

When a plant asset is traded in connection with the purchase of a new asset, two situations are possible. Most frequently, the trade-in is on the purchase of a similar plant asset that continues the same stream of earnings function as the old one. Sometimes, however, the trade-in is on a dissimilar asset that discontinues the old stream of earnings function and starts a new and different one. The accounting issue in trade-ins involves recognizing gains and losses on the transactions. In trade-in transactions for dissimilar items, all gains and losses are recognized. Trade-in situations for dissimilar assets are considered first because the authors believe that the accounting procedures involved are easier to understand.

Trade-in of Tangible Plant Assets—Dissimilar Items

If the new property does not perform essentially the same function as the old property, the transaction is a trade-in for a dissimilar item; the earnings generated by the used asset have ended. The new asset will generate new and different earnings. In such cases, the new asset should be recorded at fair market value.[5]

If the trade-in allowance is not arbitrarily excessive (as a partial offset to an unrealistic list price of the new asset), it may be considered the fair market value and therefore the proper selling price of the old asset. The new asset is recorded at its purchase price. If the trade-in allowance *is* excessive, the list price is ignored and the fair market value of the asset traded in is used to compute the cost of the new asset.

---

[5]*Opinions of the Accounting Principles Board, No. 29,* "Accounting for Nonmonetary Transactions" (New York: AICPA, May 1973), paragraph 18.

In the following discussion, *it will be assumed that the fair market value of the old asset is equal to the trade-in allowance.* After the accumulated depreciation up to the date of the trade-in is recorded, the book value of the old asset is compared with its trade-in allowance. A gain is recognized if the trade-in allowance is greater than the book value, a loss if it is less. When the book value and the trade-in allowance are equal, however, there is no recognized gain or loss.

Example 1: Trade-in allowance the same as book value. A lathe that cost $5,000 with accumulated depreciation of $4,500 up to date of the trade-in is exchanged for land listed at $4,000; the trade-in allowance is $500. Cash given was $3,500. The new asset is recorded at its cash market price—the cash payment plus the fair market value of the old asset. The transaction is recorded as follows:

1989					
Sep.	1	Land		4,000	
		Accumulated Depreciation—Equipment		4,500	
		Cash			3,500
		Equipment			5,000
		To record trade-in of old lathe for land.			

The cash payment of $3,500 is calculated as follows:

Selling price—new asset	$4,000
Trade-in allowance—old asset	500
Cash payment	$3,500

There is no gain or loss in this example because the trade-in allowance is the same as the book value.

Example 2: Trade-in allowance less than book value. The old asset in Example 1 is traded in for an allowance of $400.

1989					
Sep.	1	Land		4,000	
		Accumulated Depreciation—Equipment		4,500	
		Loss on Disposal of Plant Assets		100	
		Cash			3,600
		Equipment			5,000
		To record trade-in of equipment at a loss, computed as follows:			
		Cost of old asset	$5,000		
		Accumulated depreciation to date of trade-in	4,500		
		Book value	$ 500		
		Trade-in allowance	400		
		Loss on trade-in	$ 100		

A loss is recorded because the book value of $500 is greater than the fair market value of $400. Furthermore, the new, dissimilar asset received cannot be recorded at more than its fair market value of $4,000.

Example 3: Trade-in allowance greater than book value. The old asset in Example 1 is exchanged for a new one listed at $4,000; the trade-in allowance is $800.

Date		Account		Debit	Credit
1989					
Sep.	1	Land		4,000	
		Accumulated Depreciation—Equipment		4,500	
		Cash			3,200
		Equipment			5,000
		Gain on Disposal of Plant Assets			300
		To record trade-in of old lathe for land at a gain computed as follows:			
		Cost of old asset			
		Cost of old asset	$5,000		
		Accumulated depreciation to date of trade-in	4,500		
		Book value	$ 500		
		Trade-in allowance	800		
		Gain on trade-in	$ 300		

A gain is recorded because the fair market value of $800 is greater than the book value of $500.

Trade-in of Tangible Plant Assets—Similar Items

In many cases, a tangible plant item is traded in on a similar asset—one that has essentially the same function as the old asset. The Accounting Principles Board viewed the new similar asset as being used to continue the same stream of earnings as the old one.[6] The board recognized that such an exchange may include a monetary consideration (sometimes called **boot**) and believed that the entity *paying* the monetary consideration should not recognize any gain on a trade-in for a similar asset but should record the asset received at the amount of the *monetary consideration paid plus the book value of the nonmonetary asset surrendered*[7] (emphasis added). The board's opinion further states that when a loss is indicated in exchanges of nonmonetary assets, the "entire indicated loss on the transaction should be recognized."[8]

At a Loss To examine first the loss situation, refer back to Example 2 in the preceding section. If the new asset received had been a similar asset—a newer model of a lathe in the same shop—the trade-in for a similar asset at a loss would have been recorded by the type of entry used to record the ex-

[6] *APB Opinion No. 29,* paragraph 21.

[7] Ibid., paragraph 22. A gain is not appropriate because the same stream of earnings is being continued.

[8] Ibid. If the loss were not recorded, it would be necessary to record the new asset at more than its fair market value. This would be inconsistent with generally accepted accounting principles.

change in Example 2. The loss on disposal of $100 would have been recognized. In other words, accounting for the trade-in for a similar asset at a loss is the same as the trade for a dissimilar asset at a loss.

At a Gain In a gain situation, however, the recording differs. In this book, it is assumed that the entity trading in the old asset is the one *paying* the monetary consideration (or boot); it will not recognize a gain.[9] To illustrate, refer back to Example 3. Assume that the old lathe is being traded in on a new lathe for the same shop. The entry to record the trade-in on a similar asset at a gain would be:

1989					
Sep.	1	Equipment (new lathe)		3,700	
		Accumulated Depreciation—Equipment (old lathe)		4,500	
		Cash			3,200
		Equipment (old lathe)			5,000
		To record trade-in of old lathe for new lathe. The valuation of the new lathe is computed as follows:			
		Book value of old lathe . . . $ 500			
		Cash paid . . . 3,200			
		Total given up for new lathe . . . $3,700			

The cost recorded for the new lathe is equal to the book value of the old lathe plus the cash paid. This is the same as the list price of the new lathe ($4,000) less the gain which is not recognized ($300). Federal tax laws do not allow the recognition of gains or losses on the trade-in of similar assets in computing taxes.

Natural Resources or Wasting Assets

Another property, plant, and equipment class of items, natural resources or wasting assets, includes oil wells or timber tracts. They are recorded in the asset account at cost. As the resouce is extracted, its asset value is reduced. The primary accounting task is to measure the exhaustion or expiration of a natural resource—called its **depletion.** Periodic depletion is determined in a manner similar to the production unit method of depreciation. It is recorded on the books by a debit to the Depletion Cost account or an inventory account and a credit to the Accumulated Depletion account. In the balance sheet, accumulated depletion is classified as a contra account to be deducted from the cost of the resource.

[9] *APB Opinion No. 29* addresses another kind of trade-in of a similar tangible plant asset—one where both a new asset and boot are received. In this kind of trade-in transaction, the book value of the old asset is allocated between the sales portion (cash received) and the traded portion in relation to the relative values of the two assets received: the cash amount and the fair market value of the new asset. A gain or loss equal to the difference between the book value assigned and the cash received will be recognized on the sales portion. A gain will not be recognized on the traded portion, but a loss will be recognized.

Depletion of Wasting Assets

The periodic depletion charge is usually calculated on an output basis similar to the production unit method of recording depreciation. The cost of the wasting asset is divided by the estimated available units of output to arrive at a per-unit depletion charge. The number of units removed during the accounting period multiplied by the per-unit depletion charge represents depletion for that period. For example, if the asset is a mineral measured in tons:

$$\frac{\text{Cost} - \text{Salvage value}}{\text{Estimated tons to be mined}} = \text{Depletion cost per ton.}$$

Assume that a mine costs $180,000 and contains an estimated 400,000 tons of ore. It is estimated that the net salvage value will be $20,000. The per unit depletion charge is:

$$\frac{\$180{,}000 - \$20{,}000}{400{,}000} = \$0.40 \text{ per ton.}$$

There is a basic difference between operations dealing with the depletion of natural resources and the depreciation of a long-lived tangible plant item. The depletion of natural resources is a process that provides an inventory of goods that can be sold. Normally, a merchandising firm buys its inventory, whereas a production firm—for example, a mining company—incurs certain costs to produce an inventory. All costs directly involved in production of inventory (including depletion costs) are referred to as **inventoriable costs.** They are not closed out as expenses of a period but become a part of the cost valuation of inventory. As such, they are carried as assets until they appear in the income statement as cost of goods sold. Continuing with our previous mining example, if 10,000 tons are mined during an accounting period and 8,000 tons sold, the cost of goods sold is calculated as follows:

Cost of goods sold:	
Depletion (10,000 tons × $0.40)	$ 4,000
Other costs of production (assumed to be $1 per ton)	10,000
Total cost of production ($14,000 ÷ 10,000 tons = $1.40 per ton)	$14,000
Deduct: Ending inventory (2,000 tons × $1.40 per ton)	2,800
Cost of goods sold (8,000 tons × $1.40)	$11,200

The journal entries to record these events depend on whether a perpetual or a periodic inventory system is used. In either case, the inventory valuation of $2,800 would be shown as a current asset in the balance sheet, and the cost of goods sold ($11,200) would appear in the income statement. The mine would appear as a property, plant, and equipment asset in the balance sheet at cost minus accumulated depletion ($180,000 − $4,000 = $176,000). A related but separate class of long-life assets, intangible assets, is discussed in the next section.

Intangible Assets

Intangible assets are long-lived nonmaterial rights that are of future value to a business. Some intangibles, whether purchased or self-developed, such as patents, copyrights, franchises, and leaseholds, can be readily identified and their cost measured. Others, such as goodwill, are not specifically identifiable or measurable.

The process of estimating and recording the periodic charges to operations due to the expiration of an intangible asset is called **amortization.** It is similar to computing and recording depreciation on a property, plant, and equipment item by the straight line method. The amount to be amortized annually is computed by dividing the asset cost by the legal life or the EUL, whichever is shorter. The entry is usually *a debit to an amortization expense account* and *a credit directly to the asset account.* The straight line method is generally used unless another systematic method is clearly more appropriate, that is, will better match revenues and expenses.

Difficulties and uncertainties arise from the uniqueness of intangibles. The EUL may be limited by law (copyright), by contract (franchise), or by the economic factors of demand and competition (patents). Other intangibles (goodwill, trademarks) have an indefinite, almost unlimited, life. Furthermore, some cannot be separately identified because they relate to the total entity (goodwill). Finally, some intangibles are purchased, while others are developed within the firm.

The AICPA Accounting Principles Board has concluded that a company should record as assets the costs of intangible assets acquired from others, including goodwill acquired in a business combination. The board also concluded that the cost of each type of intangible asset should be amortized by systematic charges to income over the period estimated to be benefited. The period of amortization should not, however, exceed 40 years.[10]

Patents

The United States Patent Office grants **patents**—exclusive rights to the owners to produce and sell their inventions or discoveries—for a period of 17 years. All the costs involved in acquiring a patent from others are included in the intangible asset account Patents. The cost of a patent should be capitalized and amortized over the economic useful life of the asset or 17 years, whichever is shorter. The Patents account is usually credited directly (intangibles usually do not have contra accounts) for the amortized portion; the account debited is Patent Amortization Cost (another form of inventoriable cost in manufacturing—see Chapter 23).

[10] *Opinions of the Accounting Principles Board, No. 17,* "Intangible Assets" (New York: AICPA, August 1970), paragraphs 24, 26, 28, and 29.

1985					
Dec.	31	Patent Amortization Cost[a]		1,000	
		Patents			1,000
		To record amortization of patents for 1985.			

[a]If the patent is used in a nonmanufacturing function such as sales, the debit is to an expense account.

In the past, patents that resulted from a company's own research and development expenditures were capitalized as intangible assets and amortized as described above. Under current accounting standards, however, the costs of research and development performed in an entity are usually debited to expense in the period in which they are incurred. The elements of such cost that should be recorded as expenses instead of intangible assets have been carefully defined by the Financial Accounting Standards Board.[11]

Other Intangible Assets

Other types of intangible assets have already been mentioned. Periodic amortization of such assets is computed by the straight line method and recorded in the same form as for patents except that the debit is to an expense account. Some of the intangibles commonly found in business are described in this section.

Goodwill is a general term combining a variety of intangible factors relating to the ability of a firm to realize above-normal net income returns on an investment. Goodwill can be recorded only in connection with purchase of all or part of a business, in which case it is that intangible asset represented by the amount of purchase price that cannot be identified with any other asset.

The amount to be paid for goodwill is usually a result of a bargaining process between the buyer and the seller.[12]

A **copyright,** granted by the federal government, is an exclusive right to publish a literary or an artistic work. It is granted for the life of the creator plus 50 years and gives the owner, or heirs, the exclusive rights to reproduce and sell the work. The copyright is recorded at cost and is subject to amortization either over its estimated legal life or its useful economic life.

---

[11]*Statement of Financial Accounting Standards No. 2,* "Accounting for Research and Development Costs" (Stamford, Conn.: FASB, June 1975), paragraph 11.

[12]*APB Opinion No. 17,* paragraph 29. In the bargaining process, there are many ways to arrive at the value of goodwill. One popular method is to capitalize excess earnings. A company with annual excess earnings of $15,000 on an expected rate of return of 12 percent would have goodwill of $125,000. It is computed as follows:

X = Assets producing excess earnings (goodwill), and
$0.12X = \$15,000$, so $X = \$15,000 \div 0.12 = \$125,000$.

A **franchise** is a monopolistic right granted by a government or an entity in the private sector to render a service or to produce a good. A right to operate a bus line or a railroad or the exclusive use of a television transmitting channel is a valuable asset to the owner. Franchises are also used in industry when a manufacturer grants a dealer the exclusive privilege to sell the manufacturer's product within a defined geographical area; examples are McDonald's, Dunkin' Donuts, and Holiday Inns. The cost of obtaining the franchise is amortized over its life or 40 years, whichever is shorter.

Leases are rights to the use of land, buildings, equipment, or other property that belongs to others.

Title to improvements made to leased property by a lessee reverts to the lessor upon termination of the lease. Accordingly, the lessee should record the cost of such improvements in an intangible asset account, *Leasehold Improvements.* Leasehold improvements should be amortized over their estimated useful lives or the remaining term of the lease, whichever is the shorter period.

Financial Statement Disclosure: A Real Life Example

Property, plant, and equipment items are reported on the balance sheet at cost less accumulated depreciation, depletion, or amortization. Additional disclosures in the notes to the statements usually include specific asset categories, estimated useful lives, and the method or methods of depreciation applied. The illustration on page 452 shows how a high-technology manufacturer of systems and equipment for the telecommunications industry provided such information. During periods of inflation the historical cost (and depreciation based thereon) of long-lived assets tends to become unrealistic in terms of current value. *FASB Statement No. 33* requires that annual reports for fiscal years ended after December 25, 1979, present price-level adjusted historical and current cost amounts of property, plant, and equipment.

Porta Systems Corp. and Subsidiaries

Consolidated Balance Sheet

December 31, 1981 and 1980

Assets	1981	1980
Plant and equipment—at cost (Notes 1 and 3)	**3,214,075**	2,680,352
Less accumulated depreciation and amortization	**1,435,451**	1,157,650
	1,778,624	1,522,702

Note 3: Plant and Equipment

The classification of plant and equipment, together with their estimated useful lives, is as follows:

	1981	1980	Estimated Useful Lives
Machinery and equipment	$1,028,689	$ 899,934	5-8 years
Furniture and fixtures	314,556	300,769	5-10 years
Transportation equipment	184,969	137,787	4 years
Tools and molds	1,190,306	907,537	8 years
Leasehold improvements	495,555	434,325	Term of lease
Total	3,214,075	2,680,352	
Less accumulated depreciation and amortization	1,435,451	1,157,650	
	$1,778,624	$1,522,702	

Effective January 1, 1980, the Company changed the estimated useful life of tools and molds from three to eight years. The effect of this change in 1980 was to increase net income by approximately $40,000 and earnings per share by approximately $.02.

Source: 1981 *Annual Report* of Porta Systems Corporation.

Glossary

Accelerated cost recovery system (ACRS) A method of tax deductions to recover cost of depreciable personal property.

Accelerated methods Depreciation methods that result in larger depreciation expense during the early years of asset life, with gradually decreasing expense in later years.

Amortization Often used as a general term to cover write-down of assets; it is most commonly used to describe periodic allocation of costs of intangible assets to expense.

Book value The net amount at which an asset is carried on the books or reported in the financial statements; it is the asset's cost at acquisition reduced by the amount of accumulated depreciation on the asset. Also called *carrying value* and *undepreciated cost.*

Boot The monetary consideration paid in an exchange of property.

Capital assets See *Property, plant, and equipment.*

Capital expenditures Payments or promises to make future payments for assets that will benefit more than one accounting period. They are carried forward as assets.

Capitalize To increase the property, plant, and equipment book value for expenditures which increase the EUL or the valuation of a property, plant, and equipment asset.

Carrying value See *Book value.*

Copyright An exclusive right granted by the federal government to reproduce and sell a literary or an artistic work.

Depletion The process of estimating and recording periodic charges to operations because of the exhaustion of a natural resource.

Depreciable cost The net cost of an asset to be recorded as expense over the EUL.

Double-declining balance method (DDB) An accelerated depreciation method in which a constant rate—twice that of the straight line rate—is applied to carrying value to compute annual charges.

Estimated useful life (EUL) An estimate, made at the time of acquisition, of the term of usefulness of an asset (may be in years, working hours, or units of output).

Fair market value Value determined by informed buyers and sellers based usually on current invoice or quoted prices.

Fixed assets See *Property, plant, and equipment.*

Franchise A monopolistic right granted by a government or other entity to produce goods or render services.

Goodwill A general term embodying a variety of intangible factors relating to the reputation of a firm and its ability to generate above-normal earnings.

Intangible assets Nonphysical assets whose ownership is expected to yield benefits.

Inventoriable costs All costs directly involved in the production of inventory (including depletion costs).

Lease The right to use, over a fixed period of time, property belonging to others.

Operational assets See *Property, plant, and equipment.*

Patent The exclusive right to exploit a method or a product over a legal life of 17 years.

Plant assets See *Property, plant, and equipment.*

Production methods Depreciation methods whose charges are based on usage or results (mileage, units of output) rather than time.

Production unit method A method of depreciation based on a fixed rate per unit of output determined by estimating the total units of output.

Property, plant, and equipment Assets whose use will provide benefits over more than one accounting period; these include tangible assets (land, buildings, machinery) and wasting assets (oil, gas, minerals).

Revenue expenditures Expenditures that benefit the current period only and are debited to expense.

Salvage value The amount of asset cost that is expected to be recovered when the asset is ultimately scrapped, sold, or traded in; also called *residual value.*

Straight line method A depreciation method that allocates a uniform portion of the depreciable asset cost to each accounting period over the estimated useful life of the asset.

Sum-of-the-years'-digits method (SYD) See *Accelerated methods.*

Tangible plant asset An asset with physical form such as buildings, machinery, or equipment.

Wasting assets Natural resources whose asset value to the firm is diminished through consumption or sale.

Working hours method A method of depreciation based on a fixed rate per hour of use, determined by estimating the number of hours the asset will be used during its useful life.

Questions

Q13–1 Define the term *property, plant, and equipment.* What groups of assets are included by this term? Give examples of each.

Q13–2 (a) List some expenditures other than the purchase price that make up the cost of tangible plant assets. (b) Why are cash discounts excluded from the cost of tangible plant assets?

Q13–3 (a) What distinguishes a capital expenditure from a revenue expenditure? (b) What is the effect on the financial statements if this distinction is not properly drawn?

Q13–4 Student A maintains that if a tangible plant asset has a fair market value greater than its cost after one year of use, no depreciation need be recorded for the year. Student B insists that the fair market value is irrelevant in this context. Indicate which position you support and give your reasons.

Q13–5 What are some factors that must be considered when the depreciation method to be used is chosen?

Q13–6 Since the total amount to be depreciated cannot exceed the cost of the asset, does it make any difference which method is used in calculating the periodic depreciation charges? Explain.

Q13–7 Does the recording of depreciation have any relation to the accounting standard of matching revenue and expenses? Explain

Q13–8 Describe the conditions that might lead to the use of each of the following methods of depreciation: (a) straight line, (b) production, (c) accelerated.

Q13–9 What procedures should be followed in computing depreciation on assets held for part of a month?

Q13–10 What is the relationship, if any, between the amount of annual depreciation expense on tangible plant assets and the amount of money available for new plant assets?

Q13–11 What accounting problems result (a) from the trade-in of a tangible plant asset? (b) From the sale of a plant asset?

Q13–12 (a) Distinguish among the terms *depreciation, depletion,* and *amortization.* (b) How is the periodic depletion charge determined?

Q13–13 Is depletion an operating expense? How does depletion cost reduce the net income?

Q13–14 (a) What are intangible assets? (b) What factors must be considered when the acquisition of intangibles is (i) recorded? (ii) Amortized? (c) Is a contra account used for accumulated amortization?

Q13–15 Why should intangibles such as goodwill or organization costs be carried on the books as assets and amortized, since they appear to have no separable market value?

Exercises

E13–1 *Accounts to be debited for capital and revenue expenditures*

For each of the following items, indicate the account to be debited:

a. Expenditure for installing machinery.

b. Expenditure for trial run of new machinery.

c. Expenditure for insurance on machinery after operations begin.

d. Payment of delinquent taxes on land (taxes were delinquent at the date of purchase of the land).

e. Expenditure for extensive plumbing repairs to make a newly purchased building usable.

f. Sales tax paid on new machinery just purchased.

g. Payment for the right to operate a Holiday Inn.

h. Expenditure for a major overhaul that restores a piece of machinery to its original condition and extends its useful life.

i. Expenditure for an addition to a building leased for 20 years.

j. Amount paid for a purchased business in excess of the appraised value of the net assets.

k. Ordinary repair to machinery.

l. Expenditure for leaflet to advertise new services available because of new machinery.

m. Interest on money borrowed to construct a new building.

E13–2 *Amount of debit to asset account*

The Napa Company made the following expenditures on the acquisition of a new machine:

Invoice cost ($19,000) less 2% cash discount	$18,620
Transportation charges	570
Installation charges	1,250
Remodeling to adapt to Napa's needs	2,425
Material and labor used during test runs	285

What is the amount of the debits to the Machinery account?

E13–3 *Recording an acquisition*

The Gila Company purchased office equipment for $1,500 subject to terms of 2/10, n/30. Record the payment of the invoice within the discount period.

E13–4 *Construction of own plant*

The Osaka Company solicited bids for a new wing for its factory building. The lowest bid received was $300,000. The company decided to do the work with its own staff, and the wing was completed for a total cost of $278,000, which was paid in cash. Record the expenditure in one summary entry.

E13–5 *Recording depreciation—all methods (full year)*

On January 2, 1985, Catawba Airlines bought a new aircraft for $3,000,000. At the end of its EUL, it is expected to have a salvage value of $280,000. Catawba estimates that the aircraft will be used in operations in their company for 16 years. Record, in general journal form, the depreciation adjustment at December 31, 1985, under each of the following assumptions:

a. The straight line method is used.

b. The double-declining balance method is used.

c. The sum-of-the-years'-digits method is used.

p. 432 **d.** The working hours method is used. It is estimated that the new aircraft has a useful life of 80,000 flying hours. It was flown 2,200 hours in 1985.

E13–6
Partial year depreciation—three methods (partial year and full year)

Jersey Company began business on July 1, 1985, with three new machines. Data for the machines are as follows:

Machine	Cost	Estimated Salvage Value	EUL (Years)
A	$ 93,000	$15,000	12
B	126,000	16,000	10
C	68,000	12,000	8

Compute the depreciation expense for calendar years 1985 and 1986 by each of the following methods: (a) straight line, (b) sum-of-the-years'-digits, and (c) double-declining balance.

E13–7
Overhaul and new rate

The Fish House acquired a new freezer on October 1, 1985, at an installed cost of $50,000. The freezer had an estimated useful life of eight years and a salvage value of $5,000. Two years later the freezer was completely overhauled at a cost of $10,000. These improvements were expected to increase the total useful life from eight years to twelve years. Salvage value remains at $5,000. Prepare, in general journal form, all entries pertaining to this freezer except closing entries from acquisition through December 31, 1987. The straight line method of depreciation is used.

E13–8
Sale of a used asset

On July 1, 1985, Defiance Corporation sold for $26,500 cash a piece of drilling machinery that had been in use since January 3, 1976. The original cost of the machine was $134,000; straight line depreciation of $12,000 has been recorded annually through December 31, 1984. In general journal form, record the sale.

E13–9
Trade-in on a similar and dissimilar item

On April 2, 1985, Movers, Inc., purchased a new forklift truck for $12,000 cash. It was estimated to have a useful life of five years and a salvage value of $2,000. At the end of 1985, it was concluded that the truck was the wrong model and it was traded in for a similar truck that had a cash price (and fair market value) of $20,000.

1. Record the purchase on April 2, 1985, and the depreciation adjustment on December 31, 1985 (straight line depreciation).

2. Record the trade-in on the following assumptions:
a. A fair value trade-in allowance of $11,500 was given by the dealer; the balance was paid in cash.
b. A fair value trade-in allowance of $9,000 was given by the dealer; the balance was paid in cash.

3. Using the assumptions in requirement 2 above, record the trade-in on a parcel of land that had a fair market price of $20,000.

E13–10
Computing depletion cost

Western Mines purchased a piece of land and the mineral rights for $1,200,000. Company engineers estimate that the property contains 500,000 tons of ore and that the land can be sold for $150,000 when mining operations are completed. In the first year, 120,000 tons of ore were mined. Compute depletion cost for the first year.

E13–11
Amortization of franchise

Radio station WSOE received a franchise to transmit on channel 89.0 for a period of seven years. The accounting, legal, clerical, and consultant fees in obtaining this franchise amounted to $21,000. These costs were recorded as an intangible asset, Franchise, on May 1, 1985. Make adjusting entries to record amortization of the franchise in the fiscal years ending December 31, 1985 and 1986.

E13–12
Amortization of patent

On July 1, 1985, Bay Producers purchased a patent for a new process at a cost of $33,600. It is estimated that the patent will give the firm an advantage over its competitors for the next seven years. In general journal form, record the amortization adjustments for the years ended December 31, 1985, and December 31, 1986.

A Problems

P13–1A *Depreciation for several years—three methods*

The Solar Products Company has plant assets as follows:

	Building	Production Equipment	Cleaning Equipment
Date acquired	January 2, 1980	January 2, 1984	January 2, 1984
Cost	$164,000	$600,000	$391,000
Estimated salvage value	14,000	100,000	31,000
EUL in years	30	10	8
Method of depreciation	SL	DDB	SYD

Required:

1. Compute the balance in the Accumulated Depreciation account for each category of plant assets at the beginning of calendar year 1985.

2. Prepare the adjusting entries for depreciation as of December 31, 1985.

P13–2A *Overhaul and new depreciation rate*

Hyper Motor Freight purchased a delivery truck for $48,000 cash on July 2, 1983. On July 5, 1983, the company paid an additional $3,000 to have a hydraulic lift installed on the truck. Estimating a useful life of six years and a salvage value of $6,000, the company is depreciating this truck on the straight line method. On January 4, 1986, the truck was overhauled at a cost of $16,100; it is estimated that this overhaul will extend the EUL for an additional two years, with the salvage value remaining at $6,000.

Required: In general journal form, prepare entries to record:

1. The purchase on July 2, 1983.

2. The installation of the lift on July 5, 1983.

3. Depreciation for the calendar years 1983, 1984, 1985.

4. The overhaul and the depreciation for 1986.

P13–3A *Entries over the life of a plant asset—SYD*

Auburn Corporation purchased a computer system in 1985. Significant events concerning this system were as follows:

1985

Jun. 5	Received equipment at an invoice price of $80,000, terms 2/10, n/30; recorded liability at net amount.
15	Paid for the equipment in cash.
19	Paid $8,600 for installation costs.
28	Paid $5,000 for testing and debugging.
Jul. 1	The computer was placed in full operation. It was estimated that the computer system had an EUL of seven years with a salvage value of $8,000. It is to be depreciated by the sum-of-the-years'-digits method.
Aug. 22	Paid $612 for minor repairs
Dec. 31	Recorded depreciation for 1985.

1986

Jul. 8	Paid $1,100 for minor repairs.
Dec. 31	Recorded depreciation for 1986.

1987

Jul. 3	Having decided that the system was not required, management sold it for $65,000 cash.

Required: In general journal form, record the above events using a Construction in Progress account until July 1.

P13–4A *Trade-in for similar and dissimilar items*

Tulsa Company purchased a drill press on July 1, 1985, at a cost of $65,000. It was estimated to have a useful life of eight years and a salvage value of $5,000. Tulsa uses the double-declining balance method of depreciation. After the depreciation was recorded on December 31, 1985, it was decided that this was not the correct model, so it was traded in on a similar model priced at a fair market value of $92,000 on January 2, 1986.

Required: Record the trade-in under the following independent assumptions:

1. A fair value trade-in allowance of $60,000 is received from the dealer; the balance is paid in cash.

2. A fair value trade-in allowance of $52,000 is received from the dealer; the balance is paid in cash.

3. Same as the problem and requirement 1 except that the drill press was traded on a tract of land with a fair market price of $92,000.

P13–5A *Depletion and inventoriable costs*

On October 1, 1985, Concordia Oil, Inc., purchased a tract of land and the oil rights to it for $8,000,000. Company engineers estimate that 500,000 barrels of oil will be extracted from this deposit over a period of about two years. It is further estimated that dismantling the drilling rig will cost $100,000, and resale of the land will bring in $300,000. Drilling operations were begun in October, and by December 31, 1985, the well had produced 120,000 barrels of oil; 100,000 barrels of this production were sold in 1985, and 20,000 barrels remained in inventory on December 31, 1985. Labor, materials, depreciation, and other costs in addition to depletion incurred in production operations amounted to $2,580,000. Oil sold in 1985 brought a selling price of $45 per barrel.

Required: For this well, compute:

1. Depletion cost in 1985.

2. Cost of oil sold in 1985.

3. Gross margin on 1985 sales.

4. The valuation to be placed on the December 31, 1985, inventory.

P13–6A *Thought-provoking problem: trade or overhaul?*

Cardinal Drive Company purchased a drying machine at a net cost of $78,000 on January 2, 1980. At the time of purchase, it was expected to dry 600,000 pounds of product and be sold for scrap at an estimated $6,000. By December 31, 1985, the machine had been used to dry 530,000 pounds of product and repair costs were beginning to increase rapidly. A contractor has offered to overhaul the machine at a cost of $29,400 and will guarantee to add 200,000 pounds of product drying capacity to the original estimate. The salvage value would remain at $6,000. Another option is to trade in the drying machine on a new $102,000 machine receiving a fair-market value trade-in allowance of $15,600. The new machine is estimated to be capable of drying 600,000 pounds of product and will have no salvage value at the end of its EUL.

Required:

1. Show general journal entries to record each option (overhaul vs. trade-in).

2. Show journal entries for depreciation in 1986 under each option assuming that 76,000 pounds were dried in 1986.

3. If the company desires to have the lowest possible depreciation expense per pound in 1986, which option will be chosen?

B Problems

P13–1B *Depreciation for several years—three methods*

Newberry Energy, Inc., has plant assets as follows:

	Building	Production Equipment	Cleaning Equipment
Date acquired	January 2, 1981	January 2, 1984	January 2, 1984
Cost	$105,000	$800,000	$275,000
Estimated salvage value	15,000	150,000	15,800
EUL in years	20	10	8
Method of depreciation	SL	DDB	SYD

Required:

1. Compute the balance in the Accumulated Depreciation account for each category of plant assets at the beginning of calendar year 1985.

2. Prepare the adjusting entries for depreciation as of December 31, 1985.

P13–2B *Overhaul and new depreciation rate*

Ferris Truckers purchased a delivery truck for $96,000 cash on July 2, 1983. On July 5, 1983, the company paid an additional $6,000 to have a hydraulic lift installed on the truck. Estimating a useful life of six years and a salvage value of $12,000, the company is depreciating this truck on the straight line method. On January 4, 1986, the truck was overhauled at a cost of $32,200; it is estimated that this overhaul will extend the EUL for an additional two years, with the salvage value remaining at $12,000.

Required: In general journal form, prepare entries to record:

1. The purchase on July 2, 1983.

2. The installation of the lift on July 5, 1983.

3. Depreciation for the calendar years 1983, 1984, 1985.

4. The overhaul and the depreciation for 1986.

P13–3B *Entries over the life of a plant item—straight line*

Augusta Airlines purchased a food warmer for in-flight meals in 1985. Significant events concerning this piece of equipment were as follows:

1985	
Apr. 4	Received equipment at an invoice price of $72,000, terms 2/10, n/30; recorded liability at net amount.
14	Paid for the equipment in cash.
20	Paid $3,600 for installation costs.
28	Paid $840 for testing and other start-up costs.
30	The equipment was placed in full operation. It was estimated that the food warmer would have an EUL of 10 years and no salvage value. It is to be depreciated by the straight line method.
Jul. 16	Paid $210 for minor repairs.
Dec. 31	Recorded depreciation for 1985.

1986	
Apr. 18	Paid $560 for minor repairs.
Dec. 31	Recorded depreciation for 1986.

1987	
Jun. 30	Having decided to have meals delivered to planes by a caterer, management sold the food warmer for $52,500 cash.

Required: In general journal form, record the above events using a Construction in Progress account until April 30.

P13–4B *Trade-in for similar and dissimilar items*

El Paso Company purchased a drill press on July 1, 1985, at a cost of $130,000. It was estimated to have a useful life of eight years and a salvage value of $10,000. The company uses the double-declining balance method of depreciation. After the depreciation was recorded on December 31, 1985, it was decided that this was not the correct model, so it was traded in on a similar model priced at a fair market value of $175,000 on January 2, 1986.

Required: Record the trade-in under the following independent assumptions:

1. A fair value trade-in allowance of $117,000 is received from the dealer; the balance is paid in cash.

2. A fair value trade-in allowance of $87,500 is received from the dealer; the balance is paid in cash.

3. Same as the problem and requirement 1 except that the drill press was traded on a sales building with a fair market price of $175,000.

P13–5B *Depletion and inventoriable costs*

On October 1, 1985, Towson Oil purchased a tract of land and the oil rights to it for $16,000,000. Company engineers estimate that 1,000,000 barrels of oil will be extracted from this deposit over a period of about two years. It is further estimated that dismantling the drilling rig will cost $250,000, and resale of the land will bring in $500,000. Drilling operations were begun in October, and by December 31, 1985, the well had produced 200,000 barrels of oil; 150,000 barrels of this production were sold in 1985, and 50,000 barrels remained in inventory on December 31, 1985. Labor, materials, depreciation, and other costs in addition to depletion incurred in production operations amounted to $3,000,000. Oil sold in 1985 for $35 per barrel.

Required: For this well, compute:

1. Depletion cost in 1985.

2. Cost of oil sold in 1985.

3. Gross margin on 1985 sales.

4. The valuation to be placed on the December 31, 1985, inventory.

P13–6B *Thought-provoking problem: effect of depreciation on income tax*

On January 2, 1985, Susan Kanahoe purchased a 10-passenger van for use in her local tourist business for $30,000. It has a salvage value of $9,000 at the end of its six-year EUL. All of the net income from the tourist business must be reported as an element of her personal income on Kanahoe's federal and state income tax returns. In 1985, Kanahoe expects to be taxed at a rate of 25% of her total income. She expects this tax rate to increase to 30% in 1986, and to level off at 36% in 1987. She can use straight line, DDB, or SYD to compute depreciation.

Required:

1. Compute the effect on net income after tax of use of each of the three methods in 1985, 1986, and 1987.

2. Once a method is chosen, she must continue to use it for this van. Which method should she choose?

Appendix to Part Three:[1]
Compound Interest and Application

Introduction

Managers must understand how both simple interest and compound interest are calculated because the concepts are used in so many decisions. Simple interest was discussed in Chapter 10; this appendix stresses compound interest, important in solving complex management problems involving the time value of future sums of money and in measuring the value of assets and liabilities. This information is used in Chapters 18, 19, and 28 and referred to in other chapters to help explain certain valuation issues. Specifically, compound interest concepts are used in: (1) accounting for installment receivables and payables, (2) accounting for notes used for purchase of equipment, (3) computing the issue price of bonds, and (4) equating the time value of future cash flows in decisions involving budgeting of capital expenditures.

Learning Goals

To be able to distinguish between simple interest and compound interest.

To know how to determine and to use the future compound amount of a single sum.

To know how to determine and to use the present value of a single sum due in the future.

To know how to determine and to use the future compound amount of an ordinary annuity.

---

[1]The exact point in a beginning principles course where this appendix might be taught is up to the instructor. It may be omitted entirely; if it is, the instructor should note that certain exercises and problems in Chapters 18, 19, and 28 require a knowledge of present value concepts. It may be taught as sequenced, or after Chapters 9, 12, or 17. The interest rates used in this chapter and throughout the book range from 14 to 20 percent. These rates were those typically in effect in 1982 and are not meant to be representative of what interest rates may be in 1985, the year used most often in this book.

To know how to determine and to use the present value of an ordinary annuity.

To understand basic applications of compound interest techniques.

A Comparison of Simple Interest and Compound Interest

A better understanding of compound interest may be gained by comparing it with simple interest. As indicated in Chapter 10, simple interest is interest computed on the original principal (face value) of a note or time draft.[2] To illustrate, assume that Joan Rockness gives Thomas Chope a 16 percent note that has a principal amount of $10,000. The simple interest calculations for two different terms follows:

1. If the note has a term of one year, the simple interest would be:

$$0.16 \times \frac{360}{360} \times \$10{,}000 = \$1{,}600.$$

2. If the note has a term of 90 days, the simple interest would be:

$$0.16 \times \frac{90}{360} \times \$10{,}000 = \$400.$$

Compound interest, on the other hand, is interest that accrues on unpaid interest of the past periods as well as on the principal. In other words, **compound interest** is interest earned on a principal sum that is increased at the end of each period by the interest for that period. To contrast the difference between simple interest, compare the simple *annual* interest of $1,600 on the Rockness note with compound interest. Suppose the 16 percent interest were to be compounded quarterly for one year. The total compound interest would then be $1,698.59, as shown in Figure AIII–1.

Period	Future Accumulated Amount at Beginning of Quarter (Principal)	×	Rate	×	Time	=	Compound Interest	Future Accumulated Amount at End of Quarter
1st quarter	$10,000.00		0.16		¼		$ 400.00	$10,400.00
2nd quarter	10,400.00		0.16		¼		416.00	10,816.00
3rd quarter	10,816.00		0.16		¼		432.64	11,248.64
4th quarter	11,248.64		0.16		¼		449.95	11,698.59
Compound interest on $10,000 at 16 percent compounded quarterly for one year							$1,698.59	

Figure AIII–1 Compound Interest Computation

[2]A **time draft** is a written order to pay in the future a sum of money to order of the payee or the bearer; when it is accepted, it becomes a negotiable instrument similar to a note.

In Figure AIII–1, note that the future accumulated amount at the *end* of each quarter becomes the principal sum for *purposes of computing* the interest for the next period.

Compound Interest Techniques

For the purpose of computing the information needed in helping to solve many modern business problems, the accounting student should be familiar with the following four basic types of compound interest computations.

1. Future amount of a single given sum at compound interest.
2. Present value of a single given sum due in the future.
3. Future amount of an ordinary annuity.
4. Present value of an ordinary annuity.

The following discussion of these basic types attempts to present them in as clear and straightforward a manner as possible. To help the reader discover how these computations are related to each other, the approach stated below is used to develop a logical thought pattern that is necessary for an understanding of the first compound interest technique, that of the future amount of a single sum at compound interest.

1. The idea or concept is graphically illustrated.
2. The computation is accomplished by a laborious, successive, longhand calculation.
3. The computation is accomplished by the use of formulas.
4. The method of constructing and using tables is discussed.
5. Finally, the use of the tables to solve various compound interest problems quickly is illustrated.

Although these steps are only used with the future amount of a single sum at compound interest presentation, the reader could develop a similar approach with each of the other three methods.

Future Amount of a Single Sum at Compound Interest

The Idea

The first of these compound interest techniques, the **future amount of a single given sum** at compound interest, is the original sum plus the compound interest which has been earned and added on up to a specific future date. It is also referred to as the future value of a single sum or sometimes simply as the amount of a single investment at compound interest. For example, suppose that a single amount of $10,000 is invested in a fund on January 1, 1986. What will be the future amount in the fund on December 31, 1989, if interest at 16 percent is *compounded annually?* The problem can be shown graphically as follows:

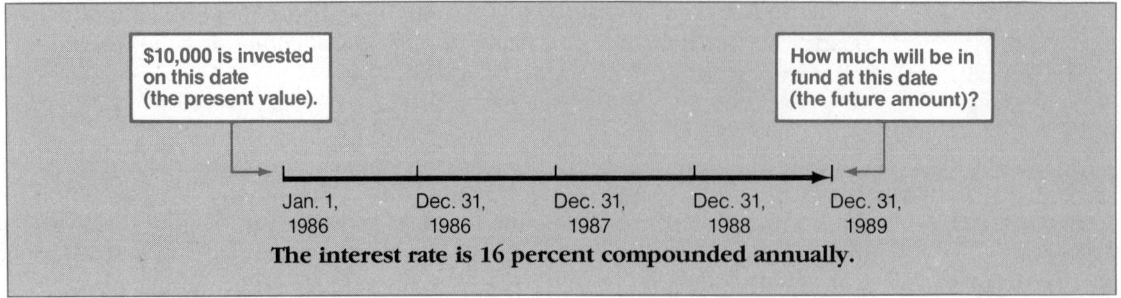

The Arithmetic Approach

With very few exceptions, compound interest calculations can be made by applying longhand arithmetic in a laborious, successive manner. To illustrate, the future amount of $10,000 for four years at 16 percent compounded annually is calculated in Figure AIII–2.

The single sum of $10,000 invested on January 1, 1986, has by December 31, 1989, grown to $18,106.39, known as the *future compound amount, future value,* or in this book simply as the **future amount.** The total interest for the four years ($8,106.39) is referred to as **compound interest.**

Another slight variation of a longhand arithmetic approach is to determine what $1 invested at January 1, 1986, would amount to by December 31, 1989, if interest at 16 percent is compounded annually. Then multiply this amount by the principal sum to find the future amount. In solving this problem, an individual *must not round* the intermediate figures to the nearest cent or else the final results will contain a significant rounding error. For example, $1 would amount to $1.810639 in four years. Given this fact, the future amount of an investment of 10,000 individual dollars for four years can be calculated by multiplying the 10,000 dollars by $1.810639. Thus:

$$10{,}000 \times \$1.810639 = \$18{,}106.39.$$

This particular variation leads to the table approach that is used later.

Figure AIII–2 Calculation of Future Amount of a Single Sum at Compound Interest

(1) Year	(2) Future Amount at Beginning of Year	(3) Annual Amount of Compound Interest (Col. 2 × 0.16)	(4) Future Accumulated Amount at End of Year (Col. 2 + Col. 3)
1986	$10,000.00	$1,600.00	$11,600.00
1987	11,600.00	1,856.00	13,456.00
1988	13,456.00	2,152.96	15,608.96
1989	15,608.96	2,497.43	18,106.39

The Formula Approach

Each amount in Column 4 of Figure AIII–2 is 116 percent of the corresponding amount in Column 2. The final future amount is:

$$\$10{,}000 \times 1.16 \times 1.16 \times 1.16 \times 1.16 = \$18{,}106.39.$$

This means that 116 percent, or 1.16, has been used as a multiplier four times; thus 1.16 has been raised to the fourth power. The future amount is, therefore, $10,000 multiplied by 1.16 to the fourth power, as shown below:

$$\text{Future amount} = \$10{,}000\ (1.16)^4 = \$18{,}106.39.$$

From the foregoing, we can state a formula for the future amount of a single sum at compound interest as follows:

$$a = p\,(1 + i)^n$$

where a = Future amount at compound interest i for n periods.
p = Principal sum (present value).
n = Number of time periods.
i = Interest rate for each of the stated time periods.

It is important to observe that the interest rate i must be *the* rate of interest applicable for each time period that interest is compounded. For example, a nominal *annual* rate of interest of 16 percent means that i is equal to:

- ☐ 16 percent if interest is compounded annually.
- ☐ 8 percent if interest is compounded semiannually.
- ☐ 4 percent if interest is compounded quarterly.
- ☐ 1⅓ percent if interest is compounded monthly.

Mathematicians, to obtain the future value calculation of $1 or 1 of any monetary unit, have derived a formula for the future amount of 1 as follows:

$$a_{n,i} = 1\,(1 + i)^n.$$

Because 1 multiplied by another number or factor is that number or that factor, the foregoing formula is usually presented without the principal amount of 1 being stated:

$$a_{n,i} = (1 + i)^n$$

where $a_{n,i}$ = Future amount of 1 ($1 or 1 of any other monetary unit) at interest rate i for n periods.
n = Number of time periods.
i = Interest rate per time period.

In this description of compound interest, the 1 usually appears in front of the formula to remind the reader that that is the given sum for which the future amount is to be determined. Using the foregoing formula for the future amount of a given sum of 1, we can restate the formula for the future compound amount of *any* single sum of compound interest as follows:

$$a = p(a_{n,i}).$$

Our example of the future amount of $10,000 invested at 16 percent with interest compounded annually can now be calculated in two steps by using the foregoing two formulas:

Step 1: $a_{n=4,\, i=16\%} = 1(1.16)^4 = 1.810639.$

Step 2: $a = \$10{,}000(1.810639) = \$18{,}106.39.$

Recall that this approach is exactly the same as the variation that was used in the successive, arithmetic method described above.

The Table Approach

As a means of further developing shortcuts to the solution of the compound interest problem, tables for the future amount of 1 have been constructed. These tables are nothing more than a precalculation of the future amount of $1(1 + i)^n$ for varying amounts of i and n. For example, suppose that tables of the future amount of 1 at 9 and 16 percent for time periods 1, 2, 3, 4, and 40 are needed. The information for these could be calculated as follows:

$a_{n=1,\, i=9\%} = 1(1.09)^1 = 1.090000.$ $a_{n=1,\, i=16\%} = 1(1.16)^1 = 1.160000.$
$a_{n=2,\, i=9\%} = 1(1.09)^2 = 1.188100.$ $a_{n=2,\, i=16\%} = 1(1.16)^2 = 1.345600.$
$a_{n=3,\, i=9\%} = 1(1.09)^3 = 1.295029.$ $a_{n=3,\, i=16\%} = 1(1.16)^3 = 1.560896.$
$a_{n=4,\, i=9\%} = 1(1.09)^4 = 1.411582.$ $a_{n=4,\, i=16\%} = 1(1.16)^4 = 1.810639.$
$a_{n=40,\, i=9\%} = 1(1.09)^{40} = 31.409420.$ $a_{n=40,\, i=16\%} = 1(1.16)^{40} = 378.721158.$

The foregoing information could then be accumulated in a partial table as indicated in Figure AIII–3. In this kind of table, the amounts are shown without dollar signs. Again, they could be the future amount of 1 of any monetary unit. More complete tables are given in Appendix C.

Since the table factors in Figure AIII–3 and Table 1 of the Compound Interest Tables (Appendix C), are reflections of the formula $1(1 + i)^n$, the table

Periods (n)	9%	16%
1	1.090000	1.160000
2	1.188100	1.345600
3	1.295029	1.560896
4	1.411582	1.810639
40	31.409420	378.721158

Figure AIII–3 Future Amount of 1 $= 1\,(1 + i)^n$

approach for *a,* the future amount of a single sum, can be expressed in this manner:

$$a = p(\text{Table factor for } a_{n,i}).$$

If tables for $a_{n,i}$ are available, it thus becomes a simple matter to calculate what an investment of $10,000 will accumulate to in four years at 16 percent compounded annually. First, look up the table factor for $a_{n=4,\ i=16\%}$ (that is, the table factor for the future amount of 1 for four time periods at 16 percent), which is 1.810639 (from Figure AIII–3). Then multiply the $10,000 times this factor, as follows:

$$a = \$10{,}000(1.810639) = \$18{,}106.39.$$

Example

An Extended Future Amount of a Single Investment Problem

Assume that on December 31, 1985, Benjamin Boykin plans to invest in a savings account $20,000 at 14 percent interest compounded semiannually. He would like to know how much he will have in the savings account on July 1, 1991, when he plans to retire. The problem can be graphically portrayed as follows:

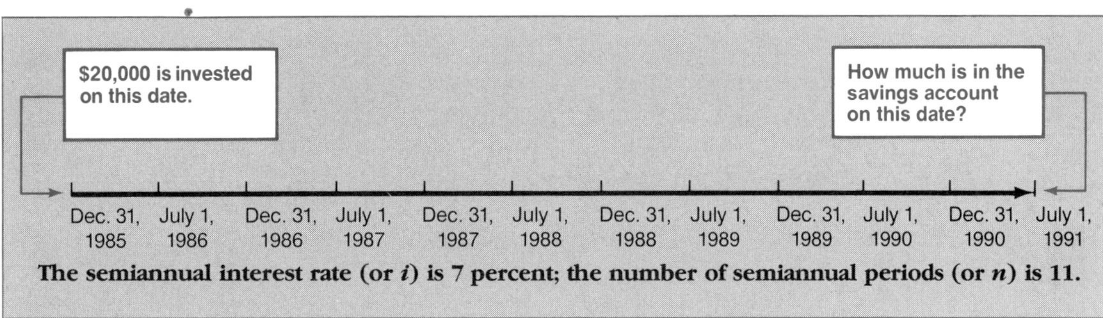

The semiannual interest rate (or *i*) is 7 percent; the number of semiannual periods (or *n*) is 11.

Solution First observe that the starting date in this example is December 31, 1985 (in the preceding example, it was January 1, 1986). One day is not considered material in a compound interest calculation involving several periods. Technically, the time at interest used with the compound interest calculation is 30-day month time. To solve the problem by the use of tables, look up the future-amount-of-1 table factor for 11 semiannual periods at 7 percent, which is a precalculation of $1(1.07)^{11}$, in Table 1, Compound Interest Tables. This value is 2.104852. To obtain the answer, multiply the $20,000 by the 2.104852 table factor as shown below:

$$a = \$20{,}000(2.104852) = \$42{,}097.04.$$

Present Value of Single Given Sum

The Idea

If $10,000 is worth $18,106.39 when it is left at 16 percent compound interest each year for four years, then it follows that cash of $18,106.39 four years from now should be worth $10,000 at the present time, **time period zero,** with an interest rate of 16 percent compounded annually; that is, $10,000 is the present value of $18,106.39 discounted backward in time for four years at 16 percent. Thus, the present value is the amount that must be invested at time period zero to produce the known future value. The difference between these two amounts is referred to as the **compound discount.**

In the discussion which follows, this amount is confirmed by calculating the present value of $18,106.39 discounted for four years at 16 percent compounded annually. This problem can be shown graphically as follows:

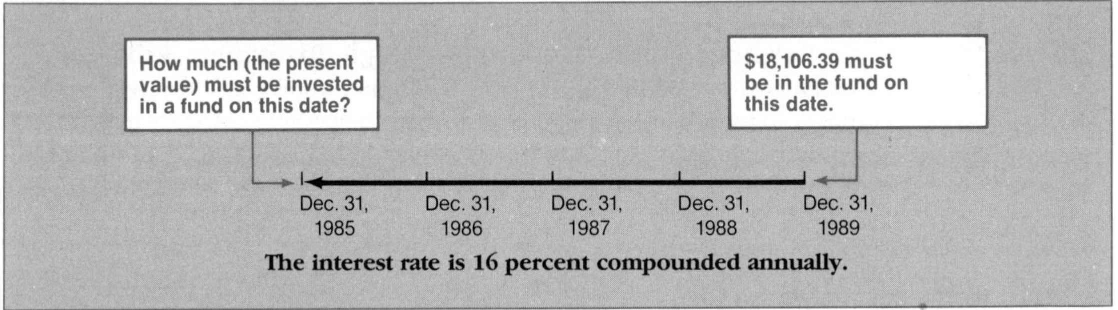

The Table Approach

Since the shortcut table approach is emphasized in this book, this concept will be rapidly developed with this and the next two techniques. Using the approach illustrated with the future amount of a single sum and the general formula for the present value of a single given sum of

$$p = a\left[\frac{1}{(1+i)^n}\right],$$

mathematicians have developed tables for different interest rates *(i)* and for different numbers of time periods *(n)* for the present value of a single sum of 1 (*p* value of 1). The formula for these table values ($p_{n,i}$) is:[3]

$$p_{n,i} = 1\left[\frac{1}{(1+i)^n}\right].$$

Table factors for selected interest rates for time periods of 1–40 have been precalculated and are given in compound interest Table 2. Turn to this table and note that the table factors are carried out to only six decimal places.

[3]Since 1 multiplied by another mathematical number is that number, this formula usually drops the 1 and is expressed as:

$$p_{n,i} = \frac{1}{(1+i)^n}.$$

Rounding errors would thus creep into a calculation where the present value of large numbers is determined. These figures, however, will serve reasonably well as a means of understanding the concept of present value.

Since Table C–2 reflects the precalculation of $1\left[\frac{1}{(1+i)^n}\right]$, the generalized table approach can be stated in this manner:

$$p = a(\text{Table factor for } p_{n,i}).$$

To calculate the present value of $18,106.39 discounted at 16 percent for four years, first look up the $p_{n=4,i=16\%}$ value in the present-value-of-1 table; it is 0.552291. Then the $18,106.39 needed future amount must be multiplied by the table factor for $p_{n=4,i=16\%}$ to determine the present value amount of $10,000, as shown below:

$$p = \$18{,}106.39 \times 0.552291 = \$10{,}000 \text{ (rounded)}.$$

Example: An Extended Illustration of the Calculation of the Present Value of a Single Sum

Assume that Elton Parker desires to have $50,000 in a given fund on December 31, 1990. How much must he invest on December 31, 1985, to produce $50,000 five years later if the investment earns 16 percent compounded semiannually? (Note that in financial jargon when it is said that an interest rate of 16 percent is to be compounded semiannually, it is meant that the semiannual rate is to be 8 percent.) Again, the problem can be shown graphically as follows:

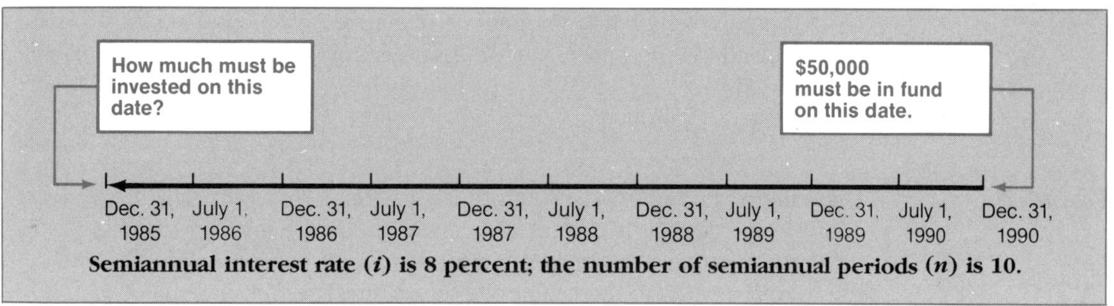

Solution To solve the problem by the use of present value tables, look up the present value of 1 for ten periods at 8 percent in Table C–2. This table factor for $p_{n=10,i=8\%}$ is 0.463193. Then multiply the $50,000 by this table discount factor. Thus:

$$p = \$50{,}000\ (0.463193) = \$23{,}159.65.$$

On December 31, 1985, Parker would have to invest $23,159.65 at 16 percent interest compounded semiannually to accumulate $50,000 by December 31, 1990.

Interrelationship of Future Amount of 1 and Present Value of 1

If present-value-of-1 tables are *not* available and future-amount-of-1 tables *are* available, it is easy to determine the applicable present-value-of-1 amounts by simply dividing the future amount figures into 1.

It should also be observed that $a_{n,i}$ should grow larger for increasing rates of interest and for increasing numbers of periods. In a reverse manner, the $p_{n,i}$ should become smaller as 1 is discounted by using increasing rates of interest and for increasing numbers of periods. A knowledge of this fact should help an individual to test intuitively the answer to future amount and present value problems. For instance, an individual must instantly realize that all future-amount-of-1 table factors must be greater than 1 and that all present-value-of-1 table factors must be less than 1. Assume that you look up the $a_{n=4, i=16\%}$ value and write down 0.552291; you should realize that this is wrong and that you are looking at the values in the wrong table, because the amount is less than 1. Upon rechecking the tables, you would find that you had looked up the value in the present-value-of-1 tables instead of the future-amount-of-1 tables.

Future Amount of an Ordinary Annuity

Introduction

An **annuity** is a series of equal payments (deposits, receipts, or withdrawals), often referred to as **rents,** made at regular intervals with interest compounded at a certain rate. The regular intervals between payments may be any time period: a year, a month, six months, or three months. In the simple case, the calculation of the future amount of an ordinary annuity, (1) the periodic rents must be equal in amount, (2) the time periods between rents must be of the same length, (3) the interest rate for each time period must be constant, and (4) the interest rate must be compounded at the end of each time period.

The Idea

If the future amount of a series of deposits (rents) is determined *immediately* after the last deposit in the series is made, the future amount calculation is referred to as that of an **ordinary annuity.** For the first example, assume that the requirement is to determine the future amount of four rents of $10,000 each with interest compounded annually at 16 percent, assuming that the first deposit is made on December 31, 1985, and the last deposit on December 31, 1988. This information is graphically presented as follows:[4]

[4]The time graphs presented from this point in the appendix deal with annuities and use asterisks rather than vertical lines. The lines in earlier graphs represented time periods, whereas the asterisks here represent *rents.*

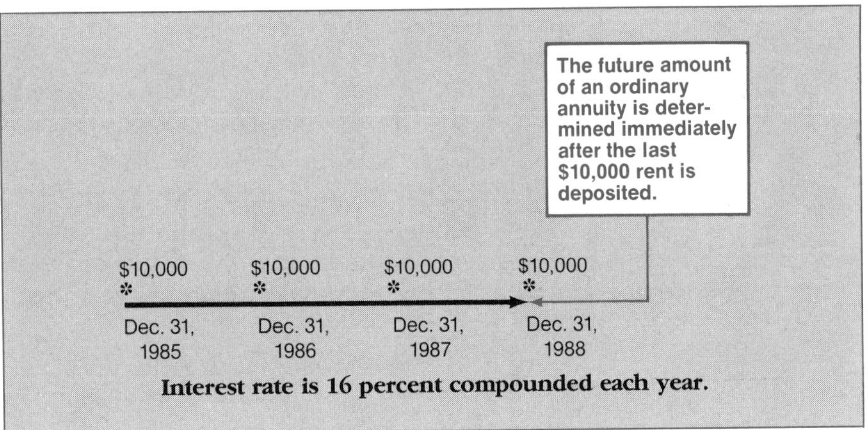

The Table Approach

As with the two preceding compound interest techniques, mathematicians start with the general formula for the future amount of an ordinary annuity of

$$A_o = R\left[\frac{(1 + i)^n - 1}{i}\right]$$

where A_o = The future amount of an ordinary annuity of a series of rents of *any* amount.

R = The value of each rent.

n = The number of rents (*not time periods;* remember that for an ordinary annuity there is always one more rent than there are time periods).

i = The interest rate per time period.

Then they develop tables for different interest rates and for different numbers of rents of 1 each. The formula for these table values ($A_{o n,i}$) is:[5]

$$A_{o n,i} = 1\left[\frac{(1 + i)^n - 1}{i}\right].$$

Table factors for selected interest rates and for rents of 1 each for 1–40 rents have been precalculated and are presented in Table 3, Compound Interest Tables. Turn to this table and note the following from these precalculations:

1. The numbers in the first column (n) represent the number of rents, not the number of time periods.

[5]This formula for the future amount of an ordinary annuity of rents of 1 each is usually stated as:

$$A_{o n,i} = \left[\frac{(1 + i)^n - 1}{i}\right].$$

2. The future amount values are always equal to or greater than the number of rents of 1; for example, the future value of three rents of 1 unit each at 14 percent is 3.439600. This figure comprises two elements: (a) the three rents of 1 each *without* any interest, and (b) the compound interest on the rents with the exception of the compound interest on the last rent in the series, which in the case of an ordinary annuity does *not* earn any interest.

Since compound interest Table 3 reveals the precalculation of

$1\left[\frac{(1+i)^n - 1}{i}\right]$, a generalized table approach can be stated as follows:

$$A_o = R\,(\text{Table factor for } A_{o_{n,i}}).$$

It thus becomes a simple matter to calculate the future amount of an ordinary annuity of four rents of \$10,000 each at 16 percent compounded annually. First. turn to Table C–3, Appendix C, and look up the table factor for $A_{o_{n=4,i=16\%}}$. That table factor is 5.066496. Second, multiply the \$10,000 by this table factor as follows:

$$A_o = \$10{,}000\ (5.066496) = \$50{,}664.96.$$

Two typical kinds of future-amount-of-an-annuity problems are: (1) given a known amount of each rent and known compound interest rate, calculate the future amount at compound interest—this is the example that has just been illustrated, and (2) given a known future amount of an ordinary annuity and known compound interest rate, calculate the amount or value of each rent. This second kind is now illustrated.

Example: Determining the Value of Rents when Future Amount Is Known

At the beginning of 1985, the Lasley Company issued a 10-year note with a principal amount of \$1,000,000 due on December 31, 1994. The company desires to accumulate a fund to retire this note at maturity. It wants to make annual deposits to the fund beginning with December 31, 1985. How much must the company deposit each year, assuming that the fund will earn 20 percent interest compounded annually?

The facts of the problem can be seen from the following diagram:

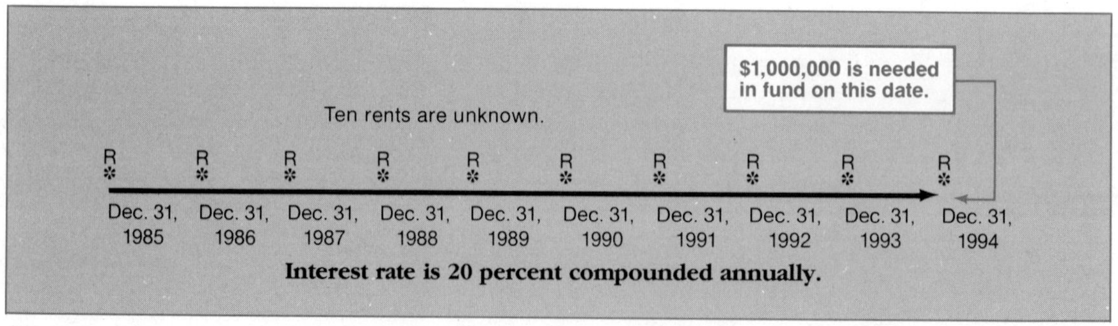

Solution The future amount, the number of rents, and the compound interest rate are known; the value of each of the ten rents is the unknown factor. Expressing the formula for A_o as

$$R(\text{Table factor for } A_{On,i}) = A_o,$$

then we could divide both sides of the equation by table factor for $A_{On,i}$ and derive this formula:

$$R = \frac{A_o}{\text{Table factor for } A_{On,i}}$$

Substituting the known amounts and the appropriate table values in this formula gives

$$R = \frac{\$1{,}000{,}000}{25.958682} = \$38{,}522.76.$$

Present Value of an Ordinary Annuity

Introduction

The **present value of an annuity** is the present value of a series of withdrawals or payments (rents) discounted at compound interest. In other words, it is the amount that must be invested now and, if left at compound interest, will provide for a withdrawal of a series of equal rents at regular intervals, the last withdrawal to be made on the final date. Over time, the present value balance is increased periodically for interest and decreased periodically for the withdrawal of each rent. Thus the last withdrawal (rent) in the series exhausts the balance on deposit.

The present value of an annuity concept is frequently used in the measuring and reporting of (1) notes payable and notes receivable when the interest rate differs from the current market rate, (2) the carrying value of investment in bonds and the bonds payable liability, (3) the receivable or debt under installment contracts, and (4) the desirability of capital investment projects.

The Idea

If the present value of the series of rents is determined one period *before* the withdrawal of the first rent, the series of rents is known as the **present value of an ordinary annuity.** For the illustrative problem, assume that the following is to be determined: the present value on January 1, 1985, of four withdrawals of $10,000 discounted at 16 percent, with the first withdrawal being made on December 31, 1985, one year after the determination of the present value.

This information is graphically presented below:

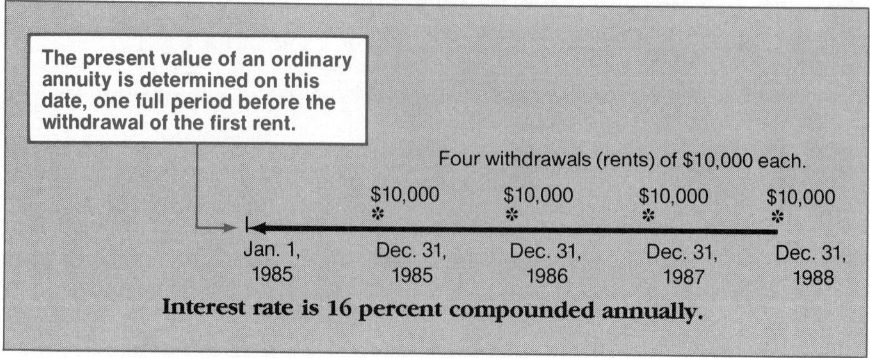

The Table Approach

Again, mathematicians start with the general formula for the present value of an ordinary annuity of

$$P_o = R\left[\frac{1 - \frac{1}{(1+i)^n}}{i}\right]$$

where P_o = The present value of an ordinary annuity of a series of rents of *any* amount.

R = The value of each rent.

n = The number of rents.

i = The interest rate per period.

They then develop tables for different interest rates and for different numbers of rents of 1 each. The formula for these table values($P_{on,i}$) is[6]:

$$P_{\text{On},i} = 1\left[\frac{1 - \frac{1}{(1+i)^n}}{i}\right].$$

Table factors for selected interest rates and for rents of 1 each for 1–40 rents have been precalculated and are presented in Table 4, Compound Interest Tables. Turn to this table and observe that:

[6]This formula for the present value of an ordinary annuity of rents of 1 each is usually stated at:

$$P_{On,i} = \left[\frac{1 - \frac{1}{(1+i)^n}}{i}\right].$$

1. The numbers in the first column (n) represent the number of rents of 1 each.

2. The present value amounts are *always smaller* than the number of rents of 1; for example, the present value of three rents of 1 at 14 percent is 2.321632. A user of compound interest tables should realize this fact and use this knowledge to test quickly whether the correct tables are being selected. If $P_{On=4,i=16\%}$ is looked up and the table value is 5.066496, then the user should realize that the wrong table value has been obtained. Upon investigating, the user would see that the future-amount-of-an-ordinary-annuity table value had been picked up rather than the present-value-of-an-ordinary-annuity table value.

Since Table C–4 reveals the precalculation of $P_{On,i}$ values, it is possible to express a generalized table approach as follows:

$$P_o = R \text{ (Table factor for } P_{On,i}).$$

Thus, to calculate the present value on January 1, 1985, of four rents of \$10,000 discounted at 16 percent, with the first rent being withdrawn on December 31, 1985, first look up the $P_{On=4,i=16\%}$ value in the table for present value of an ordinary annuity of 1. This value is 2.798181. Then multiply this factor by \$10,000 to determine the present value figure of \$27,981.81, as shown below:

$$P_o = \$10{,}000\ (2.798181) = \$27{,}981.81.$$

This calculated amount, \$27,981.81, can be proven to be true by reference to the schedule below.

Period	Amount on Deposit at Beginning of Period	Interest Earned	Withdrawal	Amount on Deposit at End of Period
1	\$27,981.81	\$4,477.09	\$10,000.00	\$22,458.90
2	22,458.90	3,593.42	10,000.00	16,052.32
3	16,052.32	2,568.37	10,000.00	8,620.69
4	8,620.69	1,379.31	10,000.00	0

Two typical kinds of present-value-of-an-ordinary-annuity problems can be solved by the use of these table factors: (1) for known amount of each rent and known compound interest rate, calculate the present value of the ordinary annuity—this is the example already illustrated, and (2) for known present value of an ordinary annuity and known compound interest rate, calculate the amount of each rent. The latter problem is now illustrated.

Example: Determining the Value of Period Rents When the Present Value Is Known

On January 1, 1985, Jan Owens borrows $100,000 to finance a plant expansion project. She plans to pay this amount back with interest at 14 percent on the beginning of the year balance over a 10-year period, with the first annual payment being due on December 31, 1985. What is the amount of each of the installment payments, provided that each is to be of an equal amount and to include both interest and a partial retirement of the principal of the debt?

The facts of the problem can be seen from the following diagram:

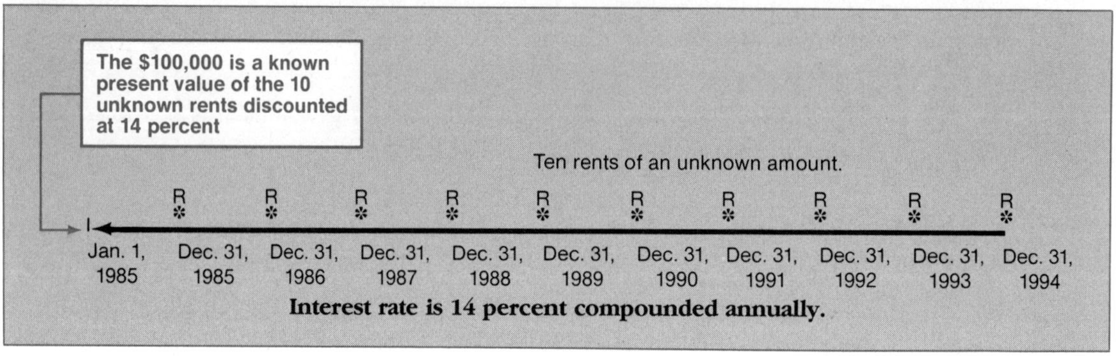

Solution The present value amount and the compound interest rate are known; the value of each of the ten rents is the unknown factor. We can use this formula for P_o:

$$R\ (\text{Table factor for } P_{On,i}) = P_o.$$

Then, dividing both sides of the equation by table factor for $P_{On,i}$

$$R = \frac{P_o}{\text{Table factor for } P_{On,i}}.$$

It is possible to solve for the amount of each payment (the R value) by looking up the $P_{On=10,i=14\%}$ value in Table C–4, Appendix C, and dividing this factor into the $100,000 present value figure, as shown below:

$$R = \frac{\$100{,}000}{5.216116} = \$19{,}171.35.$$

It should be remembered that each of these payments of $19,171.35 constitutes: (1) a payment of annual interest, and (2) a retirement of debt principal. For example, the interest for 1985 is $14,000 = (14 percent × $100,000); thus the amount of the payment on principal is $5,171.35 = ($19,171.35 − $14,000). For the year 1986, the interest is $13,276.01 = 14 percent × [($100,000 − $5,171.35)], and the retirement of principal is $5,895.34 = ($19,171.35 − $13,276.01). The *last* payment of $19,171.35, which will be made on December 31, 1994, should be sufficient to retire the remaining principal and to pay the interest for the tenth year.

Applications of Compound Interest Techniques

Compound interest techniques are used to measure the carrying value of many assets and liabilities and to equate the time value of future sums of cash involved in decisions for budgeting capital expenditures. Although some of these techniques are discussed in other chapters, two applications are examined in this appendix. These are: (1) accounting for installment payments, and (2) accounting for nontrade, noninterest-bearing notes.

Use of Compound Interest in Installment Payments

A popular form of short-term debt is the obligation that requires installment payments. Often this kind of obligation provides that it be liquidated by a series of equal payments that are to include both principal and accrued interest. The principal amount of the debt represents the present value of an annuity. The equal payments are calculated by dividing the principal sum owed by the present value of an annuity of $1. To illustrate, assume a debt of $1,000 incurred as of August 1, 1985, is to be paid off by 12 equal *monthly* installments including both principal and interest. Interest at the nominal annual rate of 18 percent, or monthly rate of 1½ percent, accrues on the unpaid balance, and the first payment is to be made on August 31, 1985. The monthly payments are determined by dividing $1,000 by 10.907505, the present value of an annuity of 12 rents of $1 each at 1½ percent. The equal payments, then, are $91.68.

Under the assumption that the obligation is represented by the issuance of an installment note payable, entries that would be made on August 1, August 31, and September 30, 1985, appear in Figure AIII–4. Similar entries would be made in subsequent periods.

The first monthly payment of $91.68 is divided between interest and principal by this calculation:

Interest: 1½% × $1,000 = $15.
Principal: $91.68 − $15.00 = $76.68.

The second monthly payment is divided between interest and principal in this manner:

Interest: 1½% × ($1,000.00 − $76.68) = $13.85.
Principal: $91.68 − $13.85 = $77.83.

Many department stores make sales that in fact result in installment collections. Originally the store does not know whether the sale will be paid within 30 days with no finance charge being assessed or whether payment will be postponed and paid over several months. These stores have a policy of requiring monthly payments based on a certain percent of the outstanding receivable. They then charge simple interest, usually at 1½ percent per month, on the balance of the receivable at the beginning of the month. The accounting procedures are similar to those illustrated in Figure AIII–4.

Transaction	Books of Party Issuing Note			Books of Party Receiving Note		
August 1, 1985. Note for $1,000 is issued for cash.	Cash	1,000.00		Notes Receivable[a]	1,000.00	
	Notes Payable[a]		1,000.00	Cash		1,000.00
August 31, 1985. Monthly payment is made.	Notes Payable	76.68		Cash	91.68	
	Interest Expense	15.00		Notes Receivable		76.68
	Cash		91.68	Interest Earned		15.00
September 30, 1985. Monthly payment is made.	Notes Payable	77.83		Cash	91.68	
	Interest Expense	13.85		Notes Receivable		77.83
	Cash		91.68	Interest Earned		13.85

[a]If the item arises out of a transaction involving the sale of merchandise, it should first be recorded in open Accounts Payable and Accounts Receivable accounts.

Figure AIII–4 **Accounting for Installment Purchases and Sales**

Accounting for Nontrade Notes Made Out for Maturity Value

As indicated in Chapter 10, short-term trade notes payable and receivable are recorded at face amount and are usually shown on the balance sheet at this figure. This is not the case, however, for nontrade notes (that is, notes issued for other than the purchase of merchandise) that bear no interest on the face amount or have an interest rate that is lower than the prevailing interest rate. In its *Opinion No. 21,* the Accounting Principles Board requires that these notes be discounted to their present value using the current market borrowing rate of interest for the firm.[7]

To illustrate, assume that on January 2, 1985, the Goldberg Company buys from the Office Products Company a minicomputer at a cost of $4,640; the creditor agrees to take a one-year note for the purchase price that does not bear any interest on the face. If the market rate of interest is 16 percent, $4,640 to be paid on December 31, 1985, is worth less than that same amount on January 2, 1985. Using the provisions of *APB Opinion No. 21,* the $4,640 must be discounted at 16 percent for one year in order to determine the implied present value of the note and thus the fair market value of the minicomputer.

In Table 2 of the Compound Interest Tables, the table factor for $p_{n=1,i=16\%}$ is given as 0.862069. Then the present value of the $4,640 discounted at 16 percent for one year is $4,000, calculated as follows:

$$\$4,640 \times 0.862069 = \$4,000.$$

The journal entry on Goldberg's books to record the purchase of the equipment is:

[7]*APB Opinion No. 21,* "Interest on Receivables and Payables" (New York: AICPA, 1971), paragraph 12.

1985					
Jan.	2	Office Equipment		4,000	
		Discount on Notes Payable		640	
		Notes Payable			4,640
		To record the purchase of a minicomputer and the issuance of a one-year note that does not bear any interest on the face amount.			

If the note matures on December 31, 1985, and if Goldberg closes its books on this date, two entries are required: (1) an entry for the payment of the note, and (2) another entry to record the recognition of the implied interest expense present in the transaction. These are shown as follows:

1985					
Dec.	31	Notes Payable		4,640	
		Cash			4,640
		To record payment of note to Office Products Company.			
	31	Interest Expense		640	
		Discount on Notes Payable			640
		To record implied interest expense on the Office Products note.			

If the maturity date of a nontrade note with no or with an unrealistic interest rate extends over several periods, *APB Opinion No. 21* requires that the unamortized portion of the discount on notes payable be written off over the life of the note. The recommended procedure recognizes the periodic interest in such a way as to result in a constant rate of interest. To measure the interest amount, the going rate is applied to the present value of the note at the *beginning* of each period. This approach, referred to as the *interest method,* is discussed more fully in Chapter 18.[8]

Glossary

Annuity A series of equal payments—deposits, receipts, or withdrawals—made at regular intervals with interest compounded at a certain rate.

Compound discount The difference between the future amount of a sum of money and the present value of the sum.

Compound interest Interest computed not only on the principal but also on any interest that has been earned in the past but not yet paid. This term also refers to the difference between the future compound amount and the original principal.

Effective interest The annual effective (as opposed to nominal) rate of interest applicable to outstanding principal.

Future amount of an ordinary annuity The future amount of a series of equal rents at equal intervals plus interest compounded at a certain rate, with the future amount being determined immediately after the last rent in the series is made.

[8] Ibid., paragraph 15.

Future amount of a single sum at compound interest This is also called future compound amount or amount of a single sum; the amount of a single investment plus compound interest for a given number of periods thereon.

Future compound amount See *Future amount of a single sum at compound interest.*

Interest Price of credit.

Interest rate The fraction applicable to principal or face amount or to the amount at the beginning of the interest period. It is typically stated as an annual percent of the outstanding principal.

Ordinary annuity A series of equal rents made at regular intervals with interest compounded at a certain rate and with the calculation of the present value or the future amount being determined as described by these two terms elsewhere in this glossary.

Present value In general, a future sum discounted back to the present time by the use of an interest factor. Present value is used in connection with two approaches: (1) the present value of a single sum due in the future, and (2) the present value of an annuity.

Present value of an annuity The present worth of a series of equal withdrawals or rents discounted at a given rate of interest.

Present value of an ordinary annuity Present value at time period zero (one period before withdrawal of the first rent) of a series of equal rents made at equal intervals of time in the future.

Present value of a sum due in the future Present value at time period zero of a single future investment.

Principal of a note The face amount of a note to which interest is applicable.

Rent The amount of each of a series of equal annuity deposits made or withdrawn.

Simple interest Interest on the original principal only.

Term of a note The length of time between date of the note and the maturity date of the note.

Time period zero The date at which the present value is determined.

Time value of money The concept that money earns interest over time periods; the term is used to include the future amount of a given sum or annuity or their present value.

Questions

QAIII–1 Some people consider that interest is a form of rent. Do you agree? Why or why not?

QAIII–2 Distinguish between simple interest and compound interest.

QAIII–3 Distinguish between the future amount of 1 and the present value of 1.

QAIII–4 Distinguish between the present value of 1 and the present value of an ordinary annuity of 1.

QAIII–5 Distinguish between the future amount of 1 and the future amount of an ordinary annuity of 1.

QAIII–6 What are i and n for two years in each of the following:

1. 20 percent compounded semiannually?

2. 16 percent compounded quarterly?

3. 18 percent compounded monthly?

QAIII–7 What are some uses of compound interest concepts in the business world? Since managers—not accountants—make decisions, why is it necessary for the accountant to understand compound interest?

QAIII–8 How are the table factors in the future-amount-of-a-single-sum table computed? Illustrate by preparing a partial table for three periods at 14 percent.

QAIII–9 If a student looks up a table factor for the present value of a single sum and writes down 1.810639, what should common sense tell him or her? Explain.

Exercises

EAIII–1 *Compound interest concepts*

Choose the correct response to complete the sentences below by indicating either a, b, or c to mean:
a. greater than (>)
b. less than (<)
c. equal to (=)

1. The present value of an amount on date zero should be (a, b, c) the amount desired on future date X.

2. The future value of an amount should be (a, b, c) the amount invested on date zero.

3. The table factor for the future amount of a single sum should be (a, b, c) 1.

4. The table factor for the present value of a single sum should be (a, b, c) 1.

EAIII–2 *Future amount of a single investment*

Using the future-amount-of-a-single-sum tables, solve the following problems:

1. What is the future amount on January 1, 1990, of $9,000 invested on January 1, 1985, to earn interest at 12 percent compounded annually?

2. What is the future amount on January 1, 1988, of $7,250 invested on July 1, 1985, to earn interest at 10 percent compounded semiannually?

3. What is the future amount on January 1, 1991, of $6,000 invested on January 1, 1985, to earn interest at 16 percent compounded quarterly?

EAIII–3 *Present value of a single sum*

Using the present-value-of-a-single-sum tables, solve the following problems:

1. What is the present value on January 1, 1985, of $20,550 due to be paid on January 1, 1990, discounted at 14 percent compounded annually?

2. What is the present value on January 1, 1985, of $4,000 due to be paid on July 1, 1987, discounted at 10 percent compounded quarterly?

3. What is the present value on July 1, 1985, of $10,000 due to be paid on July 1, 1995, discounted at 20 percent compounded annually?

EAIII–4 *Future amount of an annuity*

What is the future amount on April 1, 1990, of 20 equal quarterly rents of $400 beginning on July 1, 1985, compounded quarterly at a 16 percent annual rate?

EAIII–5 *Present value of an annuity*

What is the present value on January 1, 1985, of five equal annual rents of $2,000 beginning on January 1, 1986, compounded annually at 16 percent? Of $500 compounded semiannually at an annual rate of 18 percent?

EAIII–6 *Future amount issue*

Ben West deposited $20,000 in a special investment that provides for interest at the annual rate of 18 percent compounded monthly if the investment is maintained for three years. Using the future amount tables, calculate the balance of the savings account at the end of the three-year period.

EAIII–7 *Future amount of an annuity—determining amount of rents*

Five equal annual contributions are to be made to a fund, the first to be made on December 31, 1985. Using the future amount tables, determine the equal contributions that, if invested at 16 percent compounded annually, will produce a fund of $50,000 that is desired on December 31, 1989.

EAIII–8
Calculating equal installments for repayment of a loan

Charlene Murphy borrows $9,000 that is to be repaid in 18 equal monthly installments with interest at the rate of 2½ percent a month. Using the tables, calculate the equal installments.

EAIII–9
Future amount calculation

On September 1, 1985, Jo Jackson puts her hotel bill of $210 on a charge account. The stipulated annual interest rate is 18 percent compounded monthly. How much will she owe in three months? Six months? One year?

EAIII–10
Using future amount of 1 tables to calculate needed present value factors

While taking a test, Jane Tottingham, a student, realizes that she has failed to bring her present-value-of-a-single-sum tables, although she does have her future-value-of-a-single-sum tables. She needs to answer the following: How much needs to be invested now in order to have $6,000 at the end of three years at 2½ percent monthly interest?

1. Can the student use the future-amount-of-a-single-sum tables to solve this problem? Explain.

2. If the future-amount-of-a-single-sum table factor for 2½ percent for 36 months is 2.432535, how much needs to be invested now in order to have $5,000 at the end of three years?

EAIII–11
Future amount of an annuity calculation

Theo Owens is depositing his Christmas bonus in a special fund. Owens receives an $8,000 bonus each year. Assume that he will continue to receive this amount and that he deposits these bonuses each December 31 in a fund that will earn 14 percent compounded annually. Also assume that the first deposit was made on December 31, 1985.

Required: What amount will be in the fund after the deposit on December 31, 1989?

EAIII–12
Determining rents involved in an annuity

Joseph Cotten desires to accumulate $16,000 in his investment account by December 31, 1994. His investment account earns 16 percent compounded annually. Cotton will begin making equal annual deposits on December 31, 1985, and will continue to make deposits through December 31, 1994.

Required: What is the amount of each equal annual payment?

A Problems

PAIII–1A
Thought-provoking problem: determining which gift to accept

As a graduation present, your family offers you a choice among the following:
a. $10,000 cash.
b. $2,200 each year for five years.
c. $12,000 at the end of five years.

Required:

1. Which present should you choose? Determine by assuming an annual discount factor of 14 percent and then ranking the choices in order of preference (based on the highest present value).

2. If the discount factor were 7 percent, would your choice be different? Again rank the choices in order of your preference (based on the highest present value).

3. If your answer to requirement 2 is different from requirement 1, explain why.

B Problems

PAIII–1B
Thought-provoking problem: determining which gift to accept

Assume that you have a wealthy uncle. He has discussed three methods of sharing his estate with you. These alternatives are listed below:

1. A gift of $40,000 in cash made at the present time.

2. A gift of $45,000 to be made ten years from now when some bonds that the uncle owns matures.

3. A bequest in the uncle's will leaving you $50,000 in cash. Assume that the uncle is likely to live 12 more years.

Required: If the time value of money is 16 percent compounded annually, what method would be the most beneficial for you to accept? Discuss why. If the first offer turns out to be impossible, what method would be the next most beneficial? Why? Which method is the least beneficial? Why?

Part Four

Organizational Forms and Reporting Issues

14 Financial Reporting: Concepts and Price-Level Issues

Introduction

The first three parts of this book have introduced many of the basic rules in accounting. The reason for these accounting rules relates to the basic goal of financial statements, which is to provide economic information that is useful for decision making. Users of accounting information will be more effective decision makers if they understand the accounting standards that underlie the preparation of the financial statements.

This chapter summarizes the purpose of financial statements, and provides a brief description of some of the authoritative bodies which are directly or indirectly influential in setting accounting standards. It also discusses the concepts underlying accounting standards and some basic standards called generally accepted accounting principles (GAAP). The chapter concludes by discussing two issues facing accounting today: income disclosure and price-level accounting.

Learning Goals

To understand the purpose of financial statements.

To recognize the major sources of guidance for accounting methods.

To understand the commonly used, generally accepted accounting standards.

To recognize the disclosure of extraordinary items on the income statement.

To understand both the advantages and shortcomings of historical cost financial reporting.

To understand the purpose and effect of the financial reporting alternatives to historical cost accounting.

To distinguish between nominal dollar accounting, constant dollar accounting, and current cost accounting.

Financial Reporting Concepts and Authoritative Bodies

Purpose of Financial Reports

Financial reports, whether to management or in an annual report to stockholders, a prospectus for investors, or a report to grantors of credit, should furnish enough information to permit an intelligent decision concerning some aspect of the entity.

Basic purpose of financial statements

In short, the* basic purpose of financial statements *is to transmit to interested groups, both external and internal, information that is useful in making economic decisions.

The purpose of financial statements was stated rather well in 1936 by a group of forward-thinking accountants:

> Financial statements are prepared for the purpose of presenting a periodical review or report on progress by the management and deal with the status of the investment in the business and the results achieved during the period under review. They reflect a combination of recorded facts, accounting conventions, and personal judgments; and the judgments and conventions applied affect them materially. The soundness of the judgments necessarily depends on the competence and integrity of those who make them and on their adherence to generally accepted accounting principles and conventions.[1]

Recorded facts in the above statement refers to the data in financial statements that can be accurately measured when recorded in the accounting records. The amounts of cash and accounts receivable, and the cost of property, plant, and equipment, for example, represent recorded facts. *Accounting conventions* are basic accounting concepts accepted by common agreement. They are concerned with the problems of asset valuation, allocation of costs between asset and expense classifications in the accounting period, and the proper measurement of income.

Basic financial reporting concepts

Accounting statements are prepared on the assumption that each enterprise is a separate entity, that all business transactions can be expressed in dollars, that the enterprise will continue in business indefinitely, and that reports will be prepared at regular intervals.

Importance of personal judgment

Accounting is ultimately an art, not an exact science, and financial statements must therefore reflect the opinion and judgment of the accountant and of management.

For example, the estimated useful life and the method of depreciation to be used in the valuation of property, plant, and equipment, the method of inventory valuation, and the valuation of intangibles (patents, goodwill, and so on)

[1] "Examination of Financial Statements by Independent Public Accountants," *Bulletin of American Institute of Certified Public Accountants* (January 1936), p. 1.

are some areas that require opinion and judgment. Given the current institutional framework, equally competent accountants with the same set of facts may arrive at different results. Thus, the element of personal judgment and preference affects the financial statements. Because these can make a material difference in reported income and balance sheet items, authoritative bodies have developed guidelines or accounting standards for more comparable financial reporting. An **accounting standard** (or principle), discussed later in the chapter, is a fundamental guideline that serves to determine whether or not an accounting alternative constitutes an acceptable practice. The next section describes some of the authoritative bodies.

Authoritative Bodies

Although reference is made to several sources of accounting standards throughout this book, the focus in this chapter is on three major authoritative bodies: (1) the American Institute of Certified Public Accountants; (2) the Financial Accounting Foundation; and its two units—the Financial Accounting Standards Board and the Government Accounting Standards Board and (3) the Securities and Exchange Commission. The first two are private sector organizations; the last is a federal government agency. Several other bodies have some impact on accounting standards.

American Institute of Certified Public Accountants (AICPA)

The American Institute of Certified Public Accountants (AICPA)—formerly named the American Institute of Accountants (AIA)—was created in 1936 by the merger of the two national accounting organizations then in existence. Its formation created a basic authoritative body for the certified public accountants in the United States. Members possess the CPA certificate, which is issued by the states. Each certificate holder has passed a two-and-one-half day examination in accounting theory, accounting practice, business law, and auditing.

According to the Institute's *Code of Ethics,* all members must require that financial statements they certify as *fair* conform to pronouncements on standards made by an authoritative body.[2] The probable loss of confidence by the public in a company that does not receive a favorable audit report is a strong incentive for the firm's accountants to adhere to authoritative standards.

The AICPA played a very active role in the development of guidance for accountants during the period 1937 to 1973. The Committee on Accounting Procedure, the first AICPA committee, began issuing a series of *Accounting Research Bulletins (ARBs)* in 1938. These bulletins set forth the opinions of the committee on specific controversial methods of accounting procedure. In the early years the AICPA also had a committee on terminology, which issued

---

[2]Rule 103, *AICPA Code of Ethics* (New York: American Institute of Certified Public Accountants, 1981).

a series of *Accounting Terminology Bulletins (ATBs).* These bulletins were issued in the interest of standardizing descriptive terms used in accounting.

On September 1, 1959, these two committees were replaced by the Accounting Principles Board (APB). The APB left both of the prior series in effect and published a new set of pronouncements beginning in 1959 entitled *Opinions of the Accounting Principles Board (APB Opinions).* Each *APB Opinion* provides guidance in a specific area—for example, accounting for the cost of pension plans.

In mid-1973, the Financial Accounting Standards Board (discussed in the next section) assumed responsibility for issuance of financial accounting standards. The AICPA, having yielded the determination of accounting standards to the FASB, remains today as the primary source of *auditing standards* for CPAs. Because its members are the professionals whose certifications attest to the fairness of the financial statements of most businesses, the AICPA is still a powerful influence on public and private accounting.

Financial Accounting Foundation

In 1972, the accounting profession decided to create a standard-setting body which was independent of the AICPA. The Financial Accounting Foundation (FAF) was formed along with two related entities, the Financial Accounting Standards Board (FASB) and the Financial Accounting Standards Advisory Council (FASAC). In 1982, a change was made to incorporate standard setting for accounting by governmental units. This created a parallel set of entities for governmental accounting: the Government Accounting Standards Board (GASB) and the Government Accounting Standards Advisory Council (GASAC).

The FAF is an independent organization whose function is to appoint the members of the FASB, FASAC, GASB, and GASAC, to raise funds for the operation of the FASB and GASB, and to provide general oversight of the standard-setting process. The 14-member board of trustees of the foundation is elected by a panel made up of one member from each of the sponsoring institutions. This method of selection brings to the FAF educators, public accountants, investors and investment advisors, corporate executives, management accountants, government accountants, and investment bankers and brokers.

Figure 14–1 is a diagram of the financial accounting standard-setting structure as it now exists.[3]

Financial Accounting Standards Board The Financial Accounting Standards Board began to issue standards in 1973. It is now the independent nongovernmental body in the United States charged with the responsibility of developing and issuing standards of financial accounting affecting the private

[3]The structure described was in effect at the time of the writing of this text. Changes may have occurred since this writing.

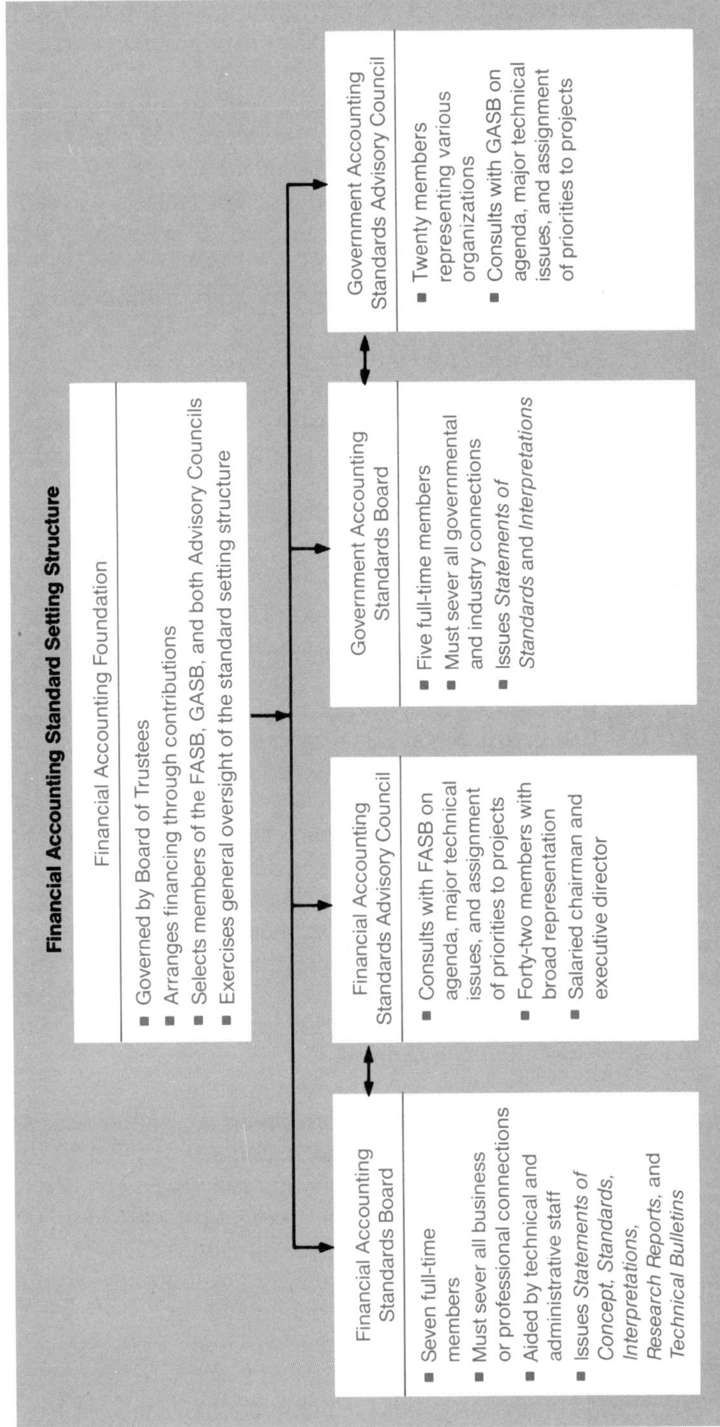

Figure 14–1 Financial Accounting Standard-Setting Structure

sector. Since all of the board's funding is derived from the FAF, it is free from financial or political pressure in the establishment of standards for financial reporting.

When the FASB assumed responsibilty for issuing accounting guidelines, it left the series of *APB Opinions* and other AICPA pronouncements in effect. As it issued *Statements of Financial Accounting Standards (SFAS)*—referred to as *FASB Statements*—some earlier issuances were replaced or modified. By early 1983, the FASB had issued 70 *Statements of Standards* and 36 *Interpretations.* Thus, accountants must look to a mixture of *ARB*s, *ATB*s, *APB Opinions,* and *FASB Statements* for authoritative guidance. The *FASB Statements* over time will probably become the primary nongovernmental source of authority for accounting in the United States.

Government Accounting Standards Board In 1982, after a two-year period of study, a change in the accounting standard-setting structure was made to create a structure for accounting by governmental units which would parallel the structure for the private sector. This established the Government Accounting Standards Board and the Government Accounting Standards Advisory Council.

The GASB is composed of five members whose responsibility is the establishment of accounting standards to be followed by state and municipal governments and agencies. The new advisory council is composed of 20 representatives from government and governmental accounting organizations, plus a municipal bond underwriter and a bond-rating agency.

Securities and Exchange Commission

The Securities and Exchange Commission was created by the Securities Exchange Act of 1934. The SEC has the legal authority to prescribe accounting methods for firms whose shares of stock and bonds are sold to the investing public on the stock exchanges. The law requires that such companies make reports to the SEC, giving detailed information about their operations. The SEC has broad powers as to the amount and type of information to be included in these annual and quarterly reports and the methods to be used to develop the information.

Since its creation in 1934, the SEC has concentrated on protection of investors. It has given high priority to the public disclosure of financial information in a fair and accurate manner. In its first 40 years, the SEC issued relatively few detailed accounting rules, preferring to leave this task to the accounting profession. In recent years, the SEC has exercised its legal power to prescribe accounting practices more actively. The SEC, however, has not recommended government regulation of the accounting profession, but it has continued to act in the public interest.

In 1980, the SEC began a program to integrate and simplify the disclosure requirements. This Integrated Disclosure System has focused on identifying the information that is important to security holders, and determining the circumstances under which the information should be disseminated and the form it should take. The goal is to reduce the burdens on issuers while providing users with meaningful, nonduplicated information.

American Accounting Association (AAA)

Beginning in 1916 as an association of accounting educators, the American Accounting Association (AAA) is oriented toward accounting research and matters of academic interest. As early as the 1930s, the AAA was working to develop standards to guide accountants. In the June 1936 issue of its quarterly journal, *The Accounting Review,* its executive committee published "A Tentative Statement of Accounting Principles Underlying Corporate Financial Statements."

Another example of the leadership of the AAA is its 1966 publication, *A Statement of Basic Accounting Theory.* The AAA continues to exert influence on accounting practices through standing committees, such as the Committee on Financial Accounting Standards, and representation on the FAF and committees of the FASB.

National Association of Accountants (NAA)

The National Association of Cost Accountants was formed in 1919. As its interests broadened to include all aspects of managerial accounting (oriented toward internal users of information), its name was changed to the National Association of Accountants (NAA). In addition to its research and publication activities, NAA is sponsor of the Institute of Management Accounting, which prepares and administers the national examination for the **Certificate in Management Accounting (CMA).**

Other Bodies

There is no single source of authority for accounting rules. While the groups just discussed exert the strongest influence on accounting practice, several others are part of the total group of authoritative bodies in accounting. The Institute of Internal Auditors sponsors the Certified Internal Auditor (CIA) examination. The Financial Executives Institute publishes a monthly journal and has sponsored studies on accounting problems. Another federal government body which completed its work in 1980, the Cost Accounting Standards Board, published several statements on cost accounting for reimbursement under government contracts.

As more and more standards were issued by the various authoritative bodies, concern was expressed that these standards were not based on a structure of fundamental concepts, the topic discussed next.

The Conceptual Framework of Accounting

The FASB has recognized the need for a conceptual framework, or underlying body of theory, of financial accounting and reporting. This Conceptual Framework Project has led to several *Statements of Financial Accounting Concepts.*

In 1978, the FASB issued the first *Concepts Statement,* "Objectives of Financial Reporting by Business Enterprises." This statement established three broad objectives of financial reporting:

1. To provide information that is useful to investors, creditors, and other users.

2. To provide information to help investors, creditors, and others to assess the amounts, timing, and uncertainty of cash flows.

3. To provide information about economic resources, claims to them, and the effects of transactions, events, and circumstances that may change resources and claims to them.

In 1980, the Board issued three more *Concepts Statements. FASB Concept No. 2* listed qualitative characteristics of accounting information, such as relevance, verifiability, timeliness, completeness, and consistency. The FASB made it clear that usefulness was at the head of any list of qualities of financial reporting. *Concept No. 3* recognized that financial statements are descriptions in words of resources, claims to resources, and events that change them. The elements of financial statements are described as building blocks from which statements are constructed. *FASB Concept No. 4* dealt with the objectives of financial reporting by nonbusiness organizations.

In 1981, an exposure draft was issued for a proposed *Statement of Concept* on reporting income, cash flows, and financial position of business enterprises. This exposure draft brings together what had previously been thought of as three separate but related aspects of the conceptual framework—objectives, qualitative characteristics, and elements of financial statements.

The framework presented in the concepts statements forms a basis to set and judge the accounting principles developed by the profession. The next section of the chapter discusses some of the major standards called generally accepted accounting principles.

Generally Accepted Accounting Principles

Over the years the accounting profession has developed a set of standards which are called **generally accepted accounting principles (GAAP)** from their widespread usage. Some of the basic generally accepted accounting principles are presented in this section.

Entity

The **entity** concept dictates that a separate set of records must be kept for each business enterprise of an owner. Owners will be required to make decisions regarding the operation of each of the businesses in which they have an interest. Therefore, the financial reports concerning a business must report only the resources of that business, claims to those resources, and changes in those resources. The accountant must guard against intermingling the transactions of the several businesses which may be owned by a single owner or the personal transactions of the owner with any one of the businesses. This concept is stressed in the first four chapters of the text which follow the accounting for the several business entities owned by Lucy Genova and the financial statements for each of these separate entities.

Going Concern

It is assumed that an entity is a **going concern**—that is, that it will continue in operation indefinitely—unless there is evidence to the contrary. Because of the going concern assumption, the accountant records prepaid insurance at the value of its unexpired fraction of cost and not at its cash surrender value. Long-term debts are reported at their face value and not at the amount it is estimated that creditors would receive if the company were to go out of business. This concept also supports reporting of plant items at historical cost.

Consistency

In some instances, acceptable alternative methods can be used in accounting records. Once a choice has been made, the principle of **consistency** requires that the same procedure be followed in all future entries so that statements covering different time periods will be comparable. This principle does not mean that a change to a better procedure cannot be made. If there is sufficient reason to change an accounting method, the accountant may do so as long as adequate disclosure is made.

Conservatism

Where acceptable alternatives exist, the one normally chosen is that which produces the least favorable immediate result. The principle of **conservatism** aims to avoid favorable exaggeration in accounting reports. Reporting inventories at lower of cost or market is an example of this standard.

Periodicity

Financial statements are prepared at regular specified time periods during the lifetime of a firm. The principle of **periodicity** holds that items of expense and revenue can be allocated to such time periods so that expenses and revenues can be properly matched for income determination. It is for this reason that adjusting entries are made. The accrual concept is essential to this standard. Items of expense and revenue should be recognized at the time of the occurrence of the economic events that produced them without regard to the timing of the related collection or payment of cash.

Objective Evidence

To the greatest extent possible, the amounts used in recording events are based upon **objective evidence** rather than subjective judgment. Sales invoices, receiver's reports, and other source documents provide such evidence. It should follow that two separate accountants, independently recording transactions from such documents would arrive at the same result. This does not mean that certain items are not to be estimated. For example, in calculating depreciation expense, it is necessary to estimate useful life and salvage value. When such estimates are necessary, however, they should be based upon past experience or upon some other logical base that is used consistently from year to year.

Materiality

An item small enough that it would not influence a decision based upon the statement in which it is used is immaterial. The accounting treatment thereof need not follow prescribed accounting standards. (For example, the inventory value of unused stationery in the typing pool or paper clips in the office would not be counted as part of the supplies inventory at the end of a period since it would not have a material effect on income or assets.) **Materiality** depends upon the size and the nature of the item relative to the size of the business. In a very small business, an inventory error of $300 may definitely be large enough to influence the decision of the user of the financial statement in which it is made. On the other hand, an error of $300 in valuation of inventories of a multimillion-dollar company would be unlikely to be considered material.

Full Disclosure

Financial statements should report all significant financial and economic information relating to an entity. If the accounting system does not automatically capture some specific item of significance, it should be included in a footnote to the accounting statements. As indicated earlier in this chapter, the SEC has placed primary emphasis on **full disclosure.**

Historical Cost

The **historical cost** principle states that actual incurred cost—arrived at through agreement by two independent entities—is the appropriate amount to be used to record the value of a newly acquired asset. There is little argument that historical cost is the only objective value at which an asset can be recorded at the time of its purchase. There are reasons, discussed later in the chapter, to believe that the historical cost of some assets becomes less useful as the asset grows older.

Stable Dollar

The **stable dollar concept** assumes that the dollar is sufficiently free from changes in purchasing power to be used as the basic unit of measure in accounting without adjustment for price-level changes. Many accountants challenge the general use of this principle on the grounds that it simply is not true.

Revenue Realization

Under the assumptions of accrual accounting, revenue is said to be realized when it is "earned." But, when is revenue earned? Is it earned when we do something to the product which adds value? Is it earned when the product changes hands? Or is it earned when the cash is collected?

With certain exceptions, generally accepted accounting principles require that revenue be realized at the *point of sale* (the method used in this text). For a business that deals with a product, the point of sale is commonly defined to be the delivery of the merchandise. For a service business, the point in time that the service is rendered is normally agreed to be the point of sale. Thus, revenue is earned in the accounting period in which the sale is construed to have taken place. Two other revenue realization methods are acceptable under specific circumstances: the collection method and the percentage of completion method.

Under the **collection method,** the realization of revenue is deferred until the cash is collected. This may be applied using either the cost recovery basis or the installment basis. With the **cost recovery basis,** all collections are first construed to be a recovery of the cost of the product sold. After the total cost is recovered, then the gross margin on the product is recognized. This method is appropriate when there is a high probability that total payment will never be received. It is considered to be a very conservative method.

Under the **installment basis,** each dollar collected is considered to be a proportionate return of the cost of the merchandise and a realization of the gross margin. For example, assume that a television set which cost $300 was sold for $400. Each dollar collected by the company would be construed to be a return of $0.75 = ($300 ÷ $400) of the cost of the set and a $0.25 = [($400 − $300) ÷ $400] realization of the gross margin from the sale. If in a given month the customer made a $100 installment payment, the company would consider $25.00 in gross margin realized. The installment basis should be used when the company has no reasonable basis for estimating the extent of uncollectability of the receivable.

The other alternative to point of sale, the **percentage of completion method,** is appropriate for large construction projects requiring more than one accounting period to complete, such as a high-rise office building. Under these circumstances, use of the point of sale method of revenue realization could significantly distort income reporting, since several periods might go by with no expense or revenue shown. Then in the period that the project was completed, a large amount of expense or revenue would be recorded. This distortion can be counteracted by realizing a portion of the gross margin from the project during each period in which the work on the project was done. The gross margin is allocated to each accounting period based upon the proportion of the project estimated to be complete. This estimated percentage of completion is the ratio of the current year's actual costs to the total estimated costs. In the final period, the remaining actual gross margin is recognized.

For example, assume that a construction company entered into a contract to build a high-rise condominium building at a price of $4 million. Also, assume that it was estimated that the total cost of the building would be $3 million, giving a gross margin of $1 million on the project. If the actual incurred costs year by year were as shown in the schedule on page 498, the gross margin recognized by the company would have been as shown in the schedule.

Year	Actual Incurred Cost	Percentage of Completion	X	Total Gross Margin	Gross Margin Recognized
1	$900,000	900,000/3,000,000		$1,000,000	$300,000
2	$1,200,000	1,200,000/3,000,000		$1,000,000	$400,000
3	$1,000,000				$200,000[a]
	$3,100,000				$900,000

[a]Balance of gross margin: ($4,000,000 − $3,100,000) − ($300,000 + $400,000) = $200,000.

If at the end of an accounting period a loss on the project becomes apparent, the loss should be recognized in that period.

Matching Expense and Revenue

The **matching** principle states that the expenses incurred in the generation of revenues should be matched against those revenues in the determination of income. As explained in Chapter 4, income is properly measured only when the expenses which were incurred to produce revenues are recorded in the same period as the revenues. This requires the accrual of expenses incurred or revenues earned because of the passage of time, for example, interest on a note. It also requires adjustment of deferrals to assign expenses associated with the sale of a product or the performance of a service to the period that revenues are recorded. Examples are recording of advertising expense in the period the advertisement to produce the sale appeared, or the proper determination of ending inventory to calculate accurately the cost of goods sold. Proper matching of revenue and expense is achieved through adherence to accrual accounting methods.

Other Concepts

Many other concepts and assumptions might be included in the list. As research and study continue, certain standards will be revised and new ones will be issued. Accounting systems are designed to meet changing user needs. These needs continue to increase in scope and complexity as changes occur in the environment in which users make economic decisions. It is the ongoing task of the authoritative bodies to develop and publish new and revised accounting standards that will keep pace with these changes. The next section discusses two of the issues which have recently been addressed by the authoritative bodies.

Reporting Issues

Standard-setting bodies are continually faced with reporting issues in accounting which require clarification through research and pronouncement. This section discusses two such issues which have been addressed by the FASB—extraordinary items and price-level changes.

Extraordinary Items

As stated earlier, one purpose of financial reporting is to permit the user to make accurate projections about future changes in the resources of a business. In order to do this, the user must be able to identify those activities which can be expected to continue and those which were unique to the period under study. Many different treatments for these latter types of items had developed in accounting.

APB Opinion No. 9, modified later by *Opinion No. 30,* was issued in an effort to resolve a long-standing controversy regarding the reporting of **extraordinary items** (items unrelated to the regular operations of the firm; those that are unusual in nature *and* that occur infrequently). Some held the view that all items affecting net income—for example, losses from fires or natural hazards and other nonrecurring extraordinary gains or losses—should be reported in the income statement. Others argued that only operating revenue and expenses should be included in measurements of net income and that the inclusion of extraordinary items would distort net income. *APB Opinion No. 9* attempted to resolve the two views by stating that "net income should reflect all items of profit and loss recognized during the period with the sole exception of prior period adjustments."[4] Extraordinary items, described carefully in terms of nature and amount, should be "segregated from the results of ordinary operations and shown separately in the income statement."[5] *Opinion No. 30* was issued to further define and restrict the classification of items as extraordinary. The board stated that "extraordinary items are events and transactions that are distinguished by their *unusual nature* and by the *infrequency of their occurrence.*"[6]

In its *Statement No. 4,* the FASB calls for the classification of any material gain or loss resulting from the extinguishment of debt—the difference between the book value and the redemption price of bonds reacquired by the issuer in the open market—as an extraordinary item.[7] Other extraordinary items include losses from major casualties such as riots and expropriation of property by foreign governments.

Assume that in 1985, Lusby Company had property, plant, and equipment located in a foreign country expropriated by the government of that country. These assets had a cost of $2,500,000 and accumulated depreciation of $1,000,000 at the time of the expropriation. The loss of $1,500,000 = ($2,500,000 − $1,000,000) should be shown separately from the income or loss from normal recurring operations. This is typically done by including a section at the bottom of the income statement to show this extraordinary loss. By segregating this extraordinary item in a separate section of the in-

---

[4]*Opinions of the Accounting Principles Board No. 9,* "Reporting the Results of Operations" (New York: AICPA, December 31, 1966), paragraph 2.

[5]Ibid., paragraph 17.

[6]*Opinions of the Accounting Principles Board No. 30,* "Reporting the Results of Operations" (New York: AICPA, June 1973), paragraph 20. Emphasis supplied.

[7]*Statement of Financial Accounting Standards No. 4,* "Reporting Gains and Losses from Extinguishment of Debt" (Stamford, Conn.: FASB, 1975).

come statement, the user can easily identify the income from recurring operations which is more valid for projecting future operations of the business. (A more complete discussion of sections of the income statement is found in Chapter 21.)

Price-Level Changes

Financial reporting relies on historical cost as the primary basis for asset valuation. Because of inflation, great concern has been expressed by many in the financial community as to the information value of traditional historical cost financial statements. On the average in 1981, it took $150 to buy the same amount of goods and services that $100 would buy in 1977, a 50 percent increase in just five years. In the decade ending in 1980, income reported by the 500 companies making up the Standard & Poor's Composite Index nearly tripled. Had this income been adjusted for the effects of changes in the purchasing power of the dollar, there would have been no increase, but instead a small decline. This section discusses alternative methods of accounting for changing prices.

Historical Cost Reporting

After several years of recording transactions at historical cost, the accounting records will contain amounts representing many different levels of purchasing power. For example, if a company purchased a milling machine in 1975 for $10,000, it would have been recorded at $10,000. If the company purchased a second identical milling machine in 1980, they would record it at the amount paid, say $15,000. Under the stable dollar assumption, each of the recorded costs would be assumed to represent dollars of equal purchasing power and would be added together to arrive at a plant asset total. Also, since each of the dollars are assumed to represent equal purchasing power, the second machine is assumed to have 50 percent more revenue-generating capability, because it has a 50 percent higher cost. This assumption is made even though it is an identical machine. If straight line depreciation were being used, this would translate into 50 percent more depreciation expense each year for the same productive capabilities.

Thus, in periods of changing price levels, the financial statements do not necessarily present an accurate financial picture. As the general level of prices of goods and services rises, the ability of each dollar to purchase goods and services declines—a change known as **inflation.** This means that when older assets, purchased at a lower price level, are used in generating revenues, the expense is recorded at an amount less than it would be if the assets had been acquired recently. In order for a company to continue in business, it must replace assets as they are consumed. In a period of inflation, therefore, each replacement of assets costs more than the previous one. The opposite is true during a period of **deflation** (a downward change in the price level.)

To overcome problems such as these, which stem from historical cost financial reporting in a period of changing prices, and to avoid mixing dollars of different values, several alternative reporting methods have been suggested.

Alternative Methods to Historical Cost

Since 1965, considerable research and discussion has centered on reporting methods which would report the effects of inflation. In September 1979, the Financial Accounting Standards Board published *Statement of Financial Accounting Standards No. 33,* which calls for two supplemental income computations. One deals with the effects of general inflation; the other deals with the effects of changes in the specific prices of resources used by the enterprise. The board believes both types of information are likely to be useful.[8] The FASB thus provided for three accounting bases to be used in financial statement reporting in the annual report to stockholders for certain large companies.[9]

1. Historical cost, still the generally accepted accounting principle, required for the audited financial statements.
2. Historical cost adjusted for general price-level changes.
3. Current cost based on price-level changes of specific items.

The latter two items are in an unaudited section of the financial statements.

General Price-Level Adjusted Accounting The purpose of using price-level adjusted cost figures in accounting is to restate historical costs in terms of dollars of common purchasing power (constant dollar accounting). The restated dollars then show the number of dollars now required to match the amount of general purchasing power invested when an item was acquired **(general price-level adjusted cost).** An expenditure of $10,000 for a tract of land, for example, represents a commitment of $10,000 of current purchasing power. The subsequent reporting of that item in financial statements should be in terms of dollars of purchasing power as of the respective statement date. If, a year later, prices in general have increased by 10 percent, the land should be reported at an amount 10 percent higher than the historical cost, or $11,000. Thus, the land will be stated in dollars of uniform size, or in common dollars—that is, the land will be stated in dollars with a purchasing power size prevailing at the statement date. The cost in the accounting records remains at $10,000, but it has been restated in more units (dollars) of lesser purchasing power for purposes of financial statement presentation.

The $1,000 increase is a recognition of the change in the value of the measuring unit, the dollar. This recognizes the fact that there has been a 10 per-

---

[8] *Statement of Financial Accounting Standards No. 33,* "Financial Reporting and Changing Prices" (Stamford, Conn.: Financial Accounting Standards Board, September, 1979), p. iii.

[9] The disclosure requirements apply to public companies that have inventories and property, plant, and equipment (before deducting accumulated depreciation and amortization) greater than $125 million or total assets net of accumulated depreciation and amortization of $1 billion or more.

cent increase in the general level of prices, so that $11,000 is now required to buy the goods and services that could have been bought for $10,000 a year before. The $1,000 increase is not a gain. It simply means that recorded assets and paid-in capital will have been increased by an amount sufficient to maintain the general purchasing power of the paid-in capital at its original amount.

The actual number of dollars needed to replace the *specific* tract of land may be greater or less than $11,000, depending on the current prevailing market conditions for that specific asset. If the tract of land has a current market value of $15,000, it will still be restated at $11,000 under general price-level accounting. The additional $4,000 = ($15,000 − $11,000) is due to a specific price change and is not recognized in statements adjusted for general price-level changes. It is recognized, however, in statements showing current cost or current value, the topic discussed in the next section.

Current Cost Accounting The alternative to general price-level accounting is current cost accounting. Statements based on current cost (or current value) accounting measure the changes in price levels of *specific* items used in the business. They measure changes in specific purchasing power of the dollar and are influenced by factors not common to all goods and services.

The difference between general price-level accounting and current cost accounting is significant. General price-level accounting adjusts historical cost to a common purchasing power measuring unit. **Current cost accounting,** on the other hand, revalues assets at what it would cost to replace them at the current time, assuming that they could be replaced in kind. If these assets cannot be replaced in kind, the current cost is measured by the cost to provide an equivalent productive capacity.

Measurements in current cost deal with the problem of changes in the prices of *specific* lines of goods and services, whereas measurements in historical cost/constant dollars measure the impact of *general* price-level changes on the cost of goods and services. The income measurement emphasis in current cost accounting is on the matching of revenue with the current cost of expenses to produce current revenue.

> **Current-value accounting may be particularly important to society in two areas. The first is that of providing warning signals about capital erosion at the levels of both the company and the economy. Primarily because of a lack of information about the real values of companies' resources, the public and policy-making officials are inadequately informed about the real profits available for reinvestment. Current-value [current cost] accounting can serve this need for information by informing society and policy makers about the need for additional capital as a consequence of capital erosion during inflation. The consequences of a lack of knowledge about current values may include excessive dividend distributions, a threat to the viability of our private enterprise system, and a deterioration of the ability of companies to raise new capital in the capital markets.**[10]

[10]George M. Soon, *Research Study on Current-Value Accounting Measurements and Utility* (New York: Touche Ross Foundation, 1978), p. 4.

Basic Concepts in General Price-Level Accounting

Several basic concepts related to general price-level accounting need to be discussed before proceeding with an illustration of price-level accounting.

Use of Index Numbers to Adjust Costs The financial reporting process should measure and report purchasing power. Therefore, the items being compared must be expressed in terms of a *comparable purchasing power yardstick,* or *price index.* A **price index** is a statistical average of prices expressed as a percentage of a base period.

The **Consumer Price Index for All Urban Consumers (CPI–U)** suggested by the FASB uses the *average* of 1967 prices as the base. Accordingly, the index for 1967 is 100. A year later the price index would be 100 plus the percent average prices have increased over 1967. CPI–U is measured monthly by the U.S. Department of Labor; at the end of each year, an average-for-the-year index is also determined. Since the index for the last month of each year is available (end-of-year index) historical dollar amounts may be adjusted by either set of index numbers (average-for-the-year or end-of-year).

A general formula to convert historical costs of items into constant dollars of a uniform purchasing power is as follows:

$$\text{Cost measured in current year's constant dollars} = \text{Historical Cost} \times \frac{\text{Index on date converted TO}}{\text{Index on date converted FROM}}$$

If the index number used in the numerator of this formula is an end-of-year index number, the amounts are said to be stated in **end-of-year constant dollars.** An alternative method is to use average-for-the-year index numbers in the numerator of the formula. In this case, the amounts are restated in **average-for-the-year constant dollars.** *FASB Statement No. 33* allows the use of either method, but most of its examples are shown using average-for-the-year constant dollars.

Monetary vs. Nonmonetary Items **Monetary items** are those items in which the dollar exchanged or to be exchanged is fixed, typically by contractual agreement. Monetary items include cash, notes and accounts receivable, notes and accounts payable, and bonds and mortgages payable. These items are fixed in terms of the total number of dollars that will be collected on the assets and the number of dollars that must be paid to creditors on the liabilities, regardless of changes in the price level.

This monetary position is significant in adjusting for the effects of inflation. Since cash or claims to cash will buy fewer goods during periods of rising prices, holding or acquiring these will cause the firm to lose purchasing power. Conversely, in periods of falling prices, they are worth more and will buy more and produce a gain. In a similar manner, the burden of paying off debt during periods of rising prices is eased by payment in current, cheaper dollars. Therefore, the firm experiences a gain by holding or incurring debt during rising prices. The opposite is true if prices are falling. These gains and losses are called **purchasing power gains and losses.** Observe that:

1. During a period of rising prices
   a. A purchasing power loss arises from holding monetary assets.
   b. A purchasing power gain arises from holding monetary liabilities.
2. Conversely, during a period of declining prices
   a. A purchasing power gain arises from holding monetary assets.
   b. A purchasing power loss arises from holding monetary liabilities.

A different effect is experienced from holding the other balance sheet items called **nonmonetary items.** Examples of nonmonetary items are merchandise inventory; land; property, plant, and equipment; and common stockholder's equity. Since they are not claims to specific amounts of cash, the purchasing power represented by their dollar amounts is not fixed contractually. Their balance in the historical cost accounting records is not stated in terms of current dollars. Rather, as price levels change, the purchasing power of their dollar amounts fluctuates. Therefore, nonmonetary items must be converted or restated by applying the general formula shown in the previous section.

FASB Requirements

In 1979, the FASB issued a comprehensive statement requiring the reporting of the effects of price-level changes in annual reports to stockholders. *FASB Statement No. 33* requires large qualifying companies—and encourages smaller companies—to present in their published annual reports the following as a supplement to the conventional historical cost financial statements:

1. Income adjusted for the effects of general inflation and the effects of changes in specific prices of resources used by the business.
2. The purchasing power gain or loss on net monetary items.
3. The current cost amounts of inventory and property, plant, and equipment.
4. Increases or decreases in current cost amounts of inventory and property, plant, and equipment, net of inflation.
5. A five year summary of selected financial data, with inventory and property, plant, and equipment adjusted for the effects of changing prices.

The statement requires the business to "measure the effects of changing prices on inventory, property, plant, and equipment, cost of goods sold and depreciation, depletion, and amortization expense. No adjustments are required to other revenues, expenses, gains, and losses."[11]

Statement of Income Adjusted for Changing Prices

In view of the importance of *FASB Statement No. 33,* a basic illustration of a statement of income adjusted for price changes is presented. *FASB Statement No. 33* permits a minimum disclosure in lieu of statements completely adjusted for price-level changes. Figure 14–2 is adapted from *FASB Statement*

[11] ***FASB Statement No. 33***, p. ii.

No. 33 as an illustration of the format that may be used to present the required information.[12] (The appendix to this chapter shows the manner in which General Motors presented the information.) The identification of the columns (A, B, C) and lines (1 through 12) have been added for cross-referencing with the explanations which follow.

Schedule B
Statement of Income Adjusted for Changing Prices
For the Year Ended December 31, 1985
(In Thousands of Dollars)

Line No.	Column A As Reported in the Primary Statements	Column B Adjusted for General Inflation	Column C Adjusted for Changes in Specific Prices (Current Costs)
1. Net sales and other operating revenues	$253,000	$253,000	$253,000
2. Cost of goods sold	$197,000	$204,384	$205,408
3. Depreciation and amortization expense	10,000	14,130	19,500
4. Other operating expense	20,835	20,835	20,835
5. Interest expense	7,165	7,165	7,165
6. Provision for income taxes	9,000	9,000	9,000
7. Total deductions from net sales	$244,000	$255,514	$261,908
8. Income (loss)	$ 9,000	$ (2,514)	$ (8,908)
9. Gain from decline in purchasing power of net amounts owed		$ 7,729	$ 7,729
10. Increase in specific prices (current cost) of inventories and property, plant, and equipment held during the year[a]			$ 24,608
11. Effect of increase in general price level			18,959
12. Excess of increase in specific prices over increase in the general price level			$ 5,649

[a]On December 31, 1985, current cost of inventory was $55,700, and current cost of property, plant, and equipment, net of accumulated depreciation, was $85,100.

Figure 14–2 **Statement of Income Adjusted for Changing Prices**

Explanations In order to get a better understanding of the accounting for changes in price levels, a brief discussion of the amounts in each of the columns is presented.

Historical Costs The amounts in Column A are based on historical cost valuations in accordance with generally accepted accounting principles, the same basis used throughout the text. The dollar amounts shown are the ac-

[12]Ibid., paragraph 70.

tual costs incurred in the transactions which generated the revenues and created the expenses. These amounts are often referred to as *nominal dollars.*

General Price Level Adjusted The amounts in Column B are the historical costs from Column A adjusted for changes in the general purchasing power of the dollar. Notice that only two of the amounts have required adjustment—all of the other amounts, by their nature, were already stated in average-for-the-year dollars. For example, other operating expenses (line 4) have not been restated. Since they were incurred uniformly throughout 1985, they are already stated in average dollars for 1985 without any adjustment. Cost of goods sold (line 2) and depreciation and amortization expense (line 3) required adjustment because their amounts included expired costs from assets acquired prior to the current year.

Cost of goods sold required adjustment because it included beginning inventory (last year's ending inventory). Beginning inventory would have been restated by multiplying the historical cost number by a ratio of the average-for-the-year index to the index when the inventory was acquired. Purchases and ending inventory would not have required restatement since they were purchased this year and are, therefore, already in current year's dollars.

Depreciation and amortization expense was restated by multiplying the expense amounts from the various assets by a ratio of the current average-for-the-year index to the index when the individual assets were acquired. These individually restated depreciation expense amounts would then be summed to get the expense shown on the statement. This removes some of the misleading effects of combining and comparing dollars of varying purchasing power.

Current Costs While the amounts in Column B measure the impact of general price-level changes, the amounts in Column C measure the change in the prices of specific goods and services that the company uses. The specific prices of the resources used by a firm may not change by the same amount (or in the same direction) as the average prices of all goods and services in the economy (that is, as does the general price level). The amounts in this column represent the current costs (as opposed to the actual incurred costs) of the goods and services used or sold.

Notice again that only two numbers have been restated—cost of goods sold (line 2) and depreciation and amortization expense (line 3). This is for basically the same reason as discussed for Column B. All of the other numbers by their nature are already stated in current costs and, therefore, do not require further restatement.

Restatement in Column C is not done by the use of price-level indexes but by determining the current (replacement) costs of the assets which expired producing the expense. For example, in the case of cost of goods sold, beginning inventory was not adjusted with indexes, but it was restated in terms of the current cost of the same inventory items. And with depreciation and amortization expense, the calculation of depreciation expense for each asset was redone using the current (or replacement) cost of the asset instead of the traditional historical cost.

The differences between Columns A and B and between Columns A and C measure the ability or inability of a firm to maintain business growth. Funds must be generated by operations to provide for increasing costs due to inflation and for the replacement of inventory and property, plant, and equipment. The income from continuing operations of $9,000 shown in Column A (historical cost) is restated into a loss of $2,514 in Column B (constant dollars) or a loss of $8,908 in Column C (current cost). These numbers reveal a significant erosion in the real value of the funds needed for dividend distributions and for reinvestment for future growth. A decline in the company's attractiveness to investors may be expected to follow.

Other Amounts The presentation also shows a gain from the decline in purchasing power of net amounts owed (line 9). Since the company in the example was in a net monetary liability position, that is, they had more monetary liabilities than monetary assets, they will experience a purchasing power gain during a period of inflation.

Lines 10, 11, and 12 show the effects of changes in price levels on selected balance sheet items. As required by *FASB Statement No. 33* the effects of inflation or deflation on ending inventory and net property, plant, and equipment must also be shown. The schedule shows the increase in current cost of these asset items (line 10), the portion of that amount due to general price-level changes (line 11), and the difference between the two (line 12).

Status of Accounting for Inflation

The FASB intended that *Statement No. 33* be reviewed at the end of a five-year experimentation period. At the time this book was being written, corporations had two years of experience with the requirements of *FASB Statement No. 33* and had begun to form some opinions regarding the required reporting of the effects of changing prices. One of the major public accounting firms, Arthur Young & Company, surveyed 300 corporations regarding their experiences and opinions on inflation reporting.

The survey respondents, who were preparers of financial statements, reported the following viewpoints:

- They generally favored the current cost method over the historical cost/constant dollar method, even though they believed it to be less precise.
- They expressed mixed views as to whether the restated information was worth the cost of preparing it.
- Most do not believe the information to be cost effective; that is, the benefit from use of the information is less than the cost to produce it.
- The preparers do not believe the data are being used by financial analysts.

EFFECTS OF INFLATION ON FINANCIAL DATA

Inflation remains the nemesis of the orderly conduct of business. Its adverse ramifications are dramatized when the effects of inflation are taken into account in the evaluation of comparative financial results.

The accompanying Schedules display the basic historical cost financial data adjusted for general inflation (constant dollar) and also for changes in specific prices (current cost) for use in such evaluation. The Schedules are intended to help readers of financial data assess results in the following specific areas:

a. The erosion of general purchasing power,
b. Enterprise performance,
c. The erosion of operating capability, and
d. Future cash flows.

In reviewing these Schedules, the following comments may be of assistance in understanding the reasons for the different "income" amounts and the uses of the data.

Financial statements—historical cost method

The objective of financial statements, and the primary purpose of accounting, is to furnish, to the fullest extent practicable, objective, quantifiable summaries of the results of financial transactions to those who need or wish to judge management's ability to manage. The data are prepared by management and audited by the independent public accountants.

The present accounting system in general use in the United States and the financial statements prepared by major companies from that system were never intended to be measures of relative economic value, but instead are basically a history of transactions which have occurred and by which current and potential investors and creditors can evaluate their expectations. There are many subjective, analytical, and economic factors which must be taken into consideration when evaluating a company. Those factors cannot be quantified objectively. Just as the financial statements cannot present in reasonable, objective, quantifiable form all of the data necessary to evaluate a business, they also should not be expected to furnish all the data needed to evaluate the effect of inflation on a company.

Data adjusted for general inflation—constant dollar method

Financial reporting is, of necessity, stated in dollars. It is generally recognized that the purchasing power of a dollar has deteriorated in recent years, and the costs of raw materials and other items as well as wage rates have increased and can be expected to increase further in the future. It is not as generally recognized, however, that profit dollars also are subject to the same degree of reduction in purchasing power. Far too much attention is given to the absolute level of profits rather than the relationship of profits to other factors in the business and to the general price level. For example, as shown in Schedule A, adjusting the annual amount of sales and net income (loss) to a constant 1967 dollar base, using the U.S. Bureau of Labor Statistics' Consumer Price Index for Urban Consumers (CPI-U), demonstrates that constant dollar profits have not increased in recent years in line with the changes in sales volume. This is reflected in the general decline in the net income (loss) as a percent of sales over that period as well as the decrease in the dividends paid in terms of constant dollars of purchasing power.

The constant dollar income statement contains only two basic adjustments. Most importantly, the provision for depreciation is recalculated. Historical dollar accounting understates the economic cost of plant and equipment consumed in production because the depreciation charge is based on the original dollar cost of assets acquired over a period of years. Constant dollar depreciation restates such expense based on asset values adjusted to reflect increases in the CPI-U subsequent to acquisition or construction of the related plant and equipment. In addition to recalculating depreciation expense, cost of goods sold is adjusted to reflect changes in the CPI-U for the portion of inventories not stated on the last-in, first-out (LIFO) basis in the conventional financial statements. Other items of income and expense are not adjusted because they generally reflect transactions that took place in 1981 and, therefore, were recorded in average 1981 dollars.

Data adjusted for changes in specific prices—current cost method

Another manner in which to analyze the effect of inflation on financial data (and thus the business) is by adjusting the historical cost data to the current costs for the major balance sheet items which have been accumulated through the accounting system over a period of years and which thus reflect different prices for the same commodities and services.

The purpose of this type of restatement is to furnish estimates of the effect of price increases for replacement of inventories and property on the potential future net income of the business and thus assess the probability of future cash flows. Although these data may be useful for this purpose, they do not reflect specific plans for the replacement of property. A more meaningful estimate of the effect of such costs on future earnings is the estimated level of future capital expenditures which is set forth on page 16 in the Financial Review: Management's Discussion and Analysis.

Summary

In the accompanying Schedules, the effects of the application of the preceding methods on the last five years' and the current year's operations are summarized. Under both the constant dollar and the current cost methods, the net income of General Motors is lower (or the net loss is higher) than that determined under the historical cost method. This means that business, as well as individuals, is affected by inflation and that the purchasing power of business dollars also has declined. In addition, the costs of maintaining the productive capacity, as reflected in the current cost data (and estimate of future capital expenditures), have increased, and thus management must seek ways to cope with the impact of inflation through accounting methods such as the LIFO method of inventory valuation, which matches current costs with current revenues, and through accelerated methods of depreciation.

Another significant adjustment is the restatement of stockholders' equity—the investment base. The adjustment for general inflation puts all the expenditures for these items on a consistent purchasing power basis—the average 1967 dollar. This adjustment decreases the historical stockholders' equity, as represented by net assets in Schedule A, of about $17.7 billion at December 31, 1981 to a constant dollar basis of $10.2 billion. In other words, the $17.7 billion represented in the financial statements has only $10.2 billion of purchasing power expressed in 1967 dollars. The net assets adjusted for specific prices, as shown in Schedule A, amounted to $10.4 billion at December 31, 1981. This is $0.2 billion higher than that shown on a constant dollar basis due to the fact that the CPI-U index is accelerating more rapidly than the indices of specific prices applicable to General Motors.

Finally, it must be emphasized that there is a continuing need for national monetary and fiscal policies designed to control inflation and to provide adequate capital for future business growth which, in turn, will mean increased productivity and employment.

28

SCHEDULE A **Comparison of Selected Data Adjusted for Effects of Changing Prices**

(Dollars in Millions Except Per Share Amounts)

Historical cost data adjusted for general inflation (constant dollar) and changes in specific prices (current cost). (A)

	1981	1980	1979	1978	1977
Net Sales—as reported	$62,698.5	$57,728.5	$66,311.2	$63,221.1	$54,961.3
—in constant 1967 dollars	23,017.1	23,390.8	30,501.9	32,354.7	30,281.7
Net Income (Loss)—as reported	$ 333.4	($ 762.5)	$ 2,892.7	$ 3,508.0	$ 3,337.5
—in constant 1967 dollars	(305.8)(B)	(1,023.8)	817.0	1,384.5	1,580.9
—in current cost 1967 dollars	(252.8)(B)	(829.5)	829.5		
Earnings (Loss) per share of common stock—as reported	$1.07	($2.65)	$10.04	$12.24	$11.62
—in constant 1967 dollars	(1.04)(B)	(3.52)	2.83	4.83	5.50
—in current cost 1967 dollars	(0.86)(B)	(2.86)	2.87		
Dividends per share of common stock—as reported	$2.40	$2.95	$5.30	$6.00	$6.80
—in constant 1967 dollars	0.88	1.20	2.44	3.07	3.75
Net income (loss) as a percent of sales—as reported	0.5%	(1.3%)	4.4%	5.5%	6.1%
—in constant 1967 dollars	(1.3)	(4.4)	2.7	4.3	5.2
—in current cost 1967 dollars	(1.1)	(3.5)	2.7		
Net income (loss) as a percent of stockholders' equity—as reported	1.9%	(4.3%)	15.1%	20.0%	21.2%
—in constant 1967 dollars	(3.0)	(9.4)	6.7	11.2	13.1
—in current cost 1967 dollars	(2.4)	(7.3)	6.4		
Net assets at year-end—as reported	$17,721.1	$17,814.6	$19,179.3	$17,569.9	$15,766.9
—in constant 1967 dollars	10,247.2	10,887.6	12,163.4	12,351.3	12,041.4
—in current cost 1967 dollars	10,450.9	11,377.2	12,982.7		
Unrealized gain from decline in purchasing power of dollars of net amounts owed	$ 241.3	$ 182.3	$ 83.8		
Excess of increase in general price level over increase in specific prices of inventory and property	$ 619.0	$ 689.2	$ 221.8		
Market price per common share at year-end—unadjusted	$38.50	$45.00	$50.00	$53.75	$62.88
—in constant 1967 dollars	14.13	18.23	23.00	27.51	34.64
Average Consumer Price Index	272.4	246.8	217.4	195.4	181.5

(A) Adjusted data have been determined by applying the Consumer Price Index—Urban to the data with 1967 (CPI-100) as the base year. Depreciation has been determined on a straight-line basis for this calculation.

(B) These amounts will differ from those shown for constant dollar and current cost in Schedule B because a different base year (1981) has been used in Schedule B in order to illustrate the effect of changing prices in an alternative form.

SCHEDULE B **Schedule of Income Adjusted for Changing Prices**

For The Year Ended December 31, 1981

(Dollars in Millions Except Per Share Amounts)

	As Reported in the Financial Statements (Historical Cost)	Adjusted for General Inflation (1981 Constant Dollar)	Adjusted for Changes in Specific Prices (1981 Current Cost)
Net Sales	$62,698.5	$62,698.5	$62,698.5
Cost of sales	55,185.2	55,766.5	55,413.5
Depreciation and amortization expense	4,406.2	4,991.6	5,200.1
Other operating and nonoperating items—net	2,896.8	2,896.8	2,896.8
United States and other income taxes (credit)	(123.1)	(123.1)	(123.1)
Total costs and expenses	62,365.1	63,531.8	63,387.3
Net Income (Loss)	$ 333.4	($ 833.3)(A)	($ 688.8)(A)
Earnings (Loss) per share of common stock	$1.07	($2.83)(A)	($2.35)(A)
Unrealized gain from decline in purchasing power of dollars of net amounts owed		$ 657.3	$ 657.3
Excess of increase in general price level over increase in specific prices of inventory and property			$ 1,686.2 (B)

(A) These amounts will differ from those shown for constant dollar and current cost in Schedule A because a different base year (1967) has been used in Schedule A in order to illustrate the effect of changing prices in an alternative form.

(B) At December 31, 1981, current cost of inventory was $9,299.8 million and current cost of property (including special tools), net of accumulated depreciation and amortization, was $28,710.8 million. The current cost of property owned and the related depreciation and amortization expense were calculated by applying (1) selected producer price indices to historical book values of machinery and equipment and (2) the Marshall Valuation Service index to buildings, and the use of assessed values for land.

29

Source: Courtesy of General Motors Corporation, *1981 Annual Report.*

☐ They do not plan to adopt *FASB Statement No. 33* data for internal management purposes.[13]

The majority of the respondents expressed the opinion that at the end of the five-year experimentation period (1984), the FASB should select between the two methods of presentation, historical cost/constant dollar and current cost. The respondents also believed that inflation information should continue to be presented on a supplementary basis and not as part of the main financial statements.[14]

Most users of the adjusted information believe that as people become more accustomed to using the information and that as preparers settle on a uniform method the inflation-adjusted information will increase in usefulness.

Appendix 14.1
Illustration of Price-Level Information in an Annual Report

FASB Statement No. 33 requires that the management of certain large corporations shall provide price-level information and explanations of its significance on the operating success of the business.[1] The statement applies to companies with more than $1 billion in assets or more than $125 million in inventory and gross property, plant, and equipment.

Shown on page 508 is an example of this reporting from the 1981 annual report of General Motors Corporation. As required by *FASB Statement No. 33*, the company has provided a discussion and explanation of the information disclosed.

Glossary

Accounting standard A fundamental guideline to determine an acceptable accounting practice.

Average-for-the-year constant dollars Financial statement amounts restated to average-for-the-year purchasing power equivalents.

Certificate in Management Accounting (CMA) A certificate issued to those persons who pass a national examination and meet stipulated experience requirements.

Certified public accountant (CPA) An accountant who has passed a national examination and has been licensed by his or her state of residence to practice public accounting.

Collection method The revenue realization method which defers the recognition of revenue until the cash is collected.

---

[13] *Financial Reporting and Changing Prices: A Survey of Preparer's Views and Practices* (New York: Arthur Young & Company, 1981), p. 3.

[14] Ibid.

[1] *FASB Statement No. 33,* paragraph 37.

Common dollars Amounts in financial statements (either historical cost or current cost) restated into units of constant purchasing power.

Conservatism Choosing the acceptable alternative that produces the least favorable immediate result.

Consistency Following an adopted accounting method in future periods in the same way.

Constant dollar accounting A method of reporting assets, liabilities, revenues, and expenses in dollars having the same purchasing power.

Consumer Price Index for All Urban Consumers (CPI–U) The index used to compute information on a constant dollar basis, published monthly by the Bureau of Labor Statistics of the U.S. Department of Labor.

Cost recovery basis The revenue realization method which considers the first dollars received to be recovery of the cost of the product sold.

Current cost accounting A method of measuring and reporting assets and expenses associated with the use or sale of assets at current cost on the balance sheet date or on the date of use or sale.

Deflation A downward change in the general price level resulting in an increase in the purchasing power of the dollar.

End-of-year constant dollars Financial statement amounts restated to end-of-year purchasing power equivalents.

Entity Concept that makes the focus of accounting records a specific organization.

Extraordinary items An item of gain or loss that is unrelated to the regular operations of the firm, and is unusual in nature and infrequent in occurrence.

Full disclosure The concept that financial statements should report all significant information about an entity.

GAAP See *Generally accepted accounting principles.*

General price-level adjusted cost The number of general purchasing power dollars currently required for the amount of purchasing power invested when the item was acquired.

Generally accepted accounting principles (GAAP) A body of guidelines that are followed because of broad acceptance by the accounting profession.

Going concern The idea that a business will continue to operate indefinitely.

Historical cost The principle that an asset should be recorded at the actual cost required to attain it.

Historical cost/constant dollar A method of accounting based on historical cost measurements with results reported in dollars having the same general purchasing power.

Index numbers (price) Statistical averages of prices expressed as percentages of a base period.

Inflation An upward change in the general price level resulting in a decrease in the purchasing power of the monetary unit.

Installment basis The revenue realization method which considers each dollar collected to be a proportionate return of the cost of the merchandise and the gross margin.

Matching Expenses incurred in the generation of revenues should be matched against those revenues in the determination of income.

Materiality The concept that accounting treatment of an item need follow generally accepted accounting principles only if it is significant enough to affect a decision of a user of the financial report on which it would appear.

Monetary items Assets and liabilities with a dollar value that would not be expected to change with changes in price levels (cash, accounts and notes receivable, accounts and notes payable, bonds payable).

Net monetary assets The excess of monetary assets over monetary liabilities.

Net monetary liabilities The excess of monetary liabilities over monetary assets.

Nonmonetary items Assets with a dollar value that would be expected to change with changes in price levels (inventories, property, plant, and equipment, intangible assets).

Objective evidence Evidence that can be verified; amounts recorded should be based on such evidence.

Percentage of completion method The revenue realization method, appropriate for large construction projects, which recognizes revenue in proportion to the percentage of estimated total costs which have been incurred.

Periodicity The idea that expenses and revenues can be identified to and matched in a period that is shorter than the life of the business.

Price index See *Index numbers.*

Purchasing power gains and losses Gains and losses arising out of holding monetary items during periods of inflation and deflation; the difference between the monetary items based on historical cost and the same items adjusted for changes in price levels.

Replacement cost The current cost of replacing one specific asset with another asset of equivalent capacity.

Revenue realization The assumption that revenue is recognized in the period it is earned. Acceptable methods are: point of sale, collection, installment, and percentage of completion.

Stable dollar assumption The assumption that the purchasing power of the dollar remains relatively constant and that financial statements may be prepared in terms of historical cost without restatement for the changes in purchasing power resulting from inflation or deflation.

Questions

Q14–1 What is the AICPA? What has been the role of the AICPA in standard setting? What is its current role?

Q14–2 What is the SEC? What is its basic purpose and authority? What is the legal basis for its authority?

Q14–3 What is the major purpose of the FASB? How does it affect the work of accountants?

Q14–4 Do you agree with the statement, "The FASB is a standard-setting body independent of and free from the influence of the accounting profession"? Why?

Q14–5 What is an extraordinary item? Why should extraordinary items be reported separately on the income statement?

Q14–6 Identify three alternatives for revenue recognition. Explain each.

Q14–7 What is an accounting concept? What is the purpose of the FASB's Conceptual Framework Project?

Q14–8 The term *generally accepted accounting principles* is frequently used in the accounting profession. What does it mean?

Q14–9 What are the major reasons to consider changing price levels in financial reports?

Q14–10 What is inflation? Deflation? What are their effects on financial statements?

Q14–11 What is meant by a price index? What is the major index used for adjusting financial statements and what does it measure?

Q14–12 What is the equation for restating historical cost items into (a) end-of-year constant dollars? (b) Average-for-the-year constant dollars?

Q14–13 What is the difference between a monetary item and a nonmonetary item?

Q14–14 Define the term *purchasing power gain or loss.* Under what circumstances could either occur?

Q14–15 Give three illustrations of distortions or inaccuracies in conventional financial statements resulting from changes in the purchasing power of the dollar.

Q14–16 Zuber Company constructed a plant in 1975 at a cost of $2 million and a second, similar plant in 1985 at a cost of $5 million. What will be that gross plant cost in conventional financial statements? Is this a fair report? Why?

Q14–17 On January 1, 1980, a company borrowed $200,000 which was payable on December 31, 1999. Ignoring interest, what is the relative position December 31, 1985, of (a) the company that borrowed the sum? (b) The lender?

Exercises

Note: Because the actual CPI-U index numbers are more difficult to use in calculations, assumed even-number indexes are used in the exercises.

E14–1 *Accounting standards*

What accounting standard is involved in each of the following cases? In each case explain the reason.

(a) The accountant does not count the paper clips in office desk drawers as part of the inventory of office supplies.

(b) At the end of each accounting period, an adjustment to the Prepaid Insurance account is made to recognize the amount of insurance applicable to that period.

(c) In the preparation of financial statements the accountant follows the same procedures used in previous periods.

(d) The accountant, to the extent possible, uses source documents in recording transactions.

E14–2 *Installment basis*

On January 19, 1985, Central Appliance sells a refrigerator which cost them $210 for $350. Following is a partial list of the payments received from the customer during 1985.

Date	Amount
January	$50.00
February	60.00
March	90.00

Calculate the dollar amount of cost to be shown as recovered and the gross margin recognized each month by the installment basis.

E14–3 *Percentage of Completion Basis*

On February 10, 1985, Ellis Construction Company signed a contract to build an office building at a total price of $2 million. They had estimated that the total cost of the building would be $1,400,000. During 1985, they incurred $840,000 in actual construction costs, and during 1986, they completed the building and incurred an additional $660,000. Calculate the gross margin that Ellis would recognize in each year under the percentage of completion basis.

E14–4 *Adjusting sales*

Newport Inc. reports the following data:

	1985	1984
Sales	$600,000	$500,000
January 1 price index	175	150
Average for the year price index	190	160
December 31 price index	210	175

Assuming no seasonal fluctuation in sales, what conclusions may be drawn about the two years' sales?

E14–5
Real growth in sales

The sales manager and the financial vice-president of the Byon Company disagree on the significance of the company's sales increases during the last 3 years. Gross sales were as follows:

1984	$3,000,000
1985	4,250,000
1986	5,000,000

Relevant average price indexes were, respectively, 100, 150, and 180. The sales manager is satisfied with the level of "growth" in sales during the three-year period. The financial vice-president argues that there has been a decline in sales. Who is correct? Why?

E14–6
Income adjusted for current cost

The Yam Company reported a net income for 1985 of $500,000. The owner observed that although physical levels of inventory had been nearly the same, the income statement showed merchandise inventory with an increase of $20,000. She also noted that the balance sheet reported property, plant, and equipment at $2,000,000 whereas it would require $5,000,000 to replace it. Depreciation expense was 10 percent of property, plant, and equipment. The owner questioned the accuracy of reported income. Comment.

E14–7
Monetary vs. nonmonetary assets

You have been asked by a fellow student for advice concerning the investment of some excess cash. He says that he has two alternatives. One is to buy a high grade corporate bond with a purchase price of $4,000 and a maturity value in five years of $5,000; no specific interest is paid. The other is to buy a small parcel of land for $4,000 in a growing neighborhood. Assuming that you expect the rate of inflation to be 10 percent per year, compare the impact of inflation on these two items as it affects the decision.

E14–8
Asset adjustment with index

The Luff Sales Company purchased a piece of equipment on January 2, 1980, for $250,000. The estimated useful life of the equipment was eight years with no salvage value. The company uses the straight line method, and price indexes were as follows:

January 1, 1980	160
December 31, 1985	220

1. Calculate the depreciation expense for 1985 using (a) historical cost, and (b) historical cost/constant dollar.

2. Comment on the usefulness of each amount.

A Problems

Note: As this chapter does not lend itself to computational type problems, only two thought-provoking problems are given.

P14–1A
Thought-provoking problem: is a withdrawal in order?

Assume that you are the chief accountant for Successful Supply Company. The company reported income for 1985 of $350,000. The president, who is also the owner and founder of the business, has asked your advice regarding his withdrawal of $300,000 for 1985, saying that the retention of $50,000 in the business should be sufficient for the planned growth he has in mind.

The business was founded in 1970 when substantially all of the property, plant, and equipment was purchased. Since that time the average rate of inflation has been 10 percent per year. During the past year it dropped to 8 percent and is expected to stay there for the near future.

Required: Prepare a memo to Mr. Success, the president, in which you either support his position or attempt to convince him of any error he may have made in his reasoning. Include any computation that you believe necessary, and create figures for the computations.

B Problems

P14–1B
Thought-provoking problem: effect of extraordinary items

The 1982 *Annual Report* of the Tyler Corporation showed the following information (rounded to the nearest $1,000):

	1982	1981	1980
Income before extraordinary items	$10,195	$27,357	$23,836
Extraordinary items	0	4,688	(10,192)
Net income	$10,195	$32,045	$13,644

The 1981 *Annual Report* noted that the company wrote off the entire cost of route permits associated with its trucking operations in 1980 as an extraordinary charge in accordance with *FASB Statement No. 44.* Under 1981 tax legislation, a tax deduction was allowed and recorded in 1981 as an extraordinary credit.

Required: How meaningful would the final net income figure have been without knowledge of the extraordinary items? Would the lack of knowledge that an extraordinary item was included in the net income figure have been misleading in decision making? How?

15 Partnership Accounting

Introduction

Many entities—especially those that deal in professional services—are partnerships. Certified public accountants, lawyers, doctors, architects, and producers of Broadway shows often use the partnership as their form of business organization. This chapter starts with an explanation of the distinctive features of the partnership and some of its advantages and disadvantages. Then it compares the equity accounts for the three basic forms of business organization: single proprietorship, partnership, and corporation.

The accounting treatment for operating transactions—incurring expenses and earning revenue—is the same for all forms of business. It is the accounting treatment for the formation of the business, withdrawal of funds, and the closing process that differs. After discussing the formation of a partnership, this chapter then discusses the division of partnership profits and losses and the preparation of financial statements. Changes in the capital structure are discussed next, including admission of a new partner, death or retirement of an existing partner, and the liquidation of a partnership.

Learning Goals

To understand the characteristics of a partnership.

To compare the accounts for owners' equity of a single proprietorship, a partnership, and a corporation.

To review accounting methods for recording transactions affecting partners' equity.

To compute the division of partnership profits and losses using different methods.

To be able to record the admission of a partner, the retirement of an existing partner, and the liquidation of a partnership.

To prepare a statement of partnership liquidation.

The Partnership Form of Business Organization

Before comparing the equity accounts of a single proprietorship, a corporation, and a partnership, a more intense look at the partnership form of business organization is now taken. "A **partnership** is an association of two or more persons to carry on as co-owners a business for profit" (emphasis added).[1] The association described in this definition may be based upon an oral or a written agreement. Although many partnerships have only two partners, some have many. For example, some of the nationally-known certified public accounting firms have a hundred or more partners. Of the three basic forms of business in the United States, the partnership is the least used.

Characteristics

Unlike a single proprietorship, the name of a partnership is likely to give a clue to the type of business organization. It is obvious that the firm of Ahern, Allen, and Arnold has more than one owner, and one would suspect that it is a partnership. Other characteristics of a partnership tend to be similar to those of a single proprietorship. For example, the personal assets of partners are available to satisfy partnership creditor claims (a characteristic called **unlimited liability** described in the Legal Liability section below).

Size One measure of size is the amount of capital invested. Because additional owners serve as sources of capital, partnerships tend to be somewhat larger than single proprietorships. However, their original capital investment must come from the personal wealth and borrowing power of the partners. Since many partnerships have only two or three partners, this form of business is not generally found among the larger firms in the United States.

Ease of Formation Like single proprietorships, partnerships are relatively easy to form. Although it is desirable that a written agreement form the basis of the association, partnerships may be formed on the basis of a verbal agreement. With a few exceptions, the states have enacted the provisions of the Uniform Partnership Act into law. The act contains no special provisions for the formation of a partnership but does contain provisions that regulate the relations of partners with each other and with persons outside the partnership. The written agreement should specify the terms and conditions on all matters that might otherwise lead to controversy. It should contain provisions for the distribution of earnings, investment or withdrawal of funds, the admission of a new partner, the death or withdrawal of a partner, and so on.

Legal Liability All partners are usually liable jointly and individually for the debts of the partnership. In certain states where the law allows it, a limited partnership may be created, and in this form of partnership, under certain circumstances, the liability of some partners may be limited to the amount of their investment. Such a partner, known as a **limited partner,** has restrictions placed upon the business activities in which he or she can en-

[1]*Uniform Partnership Act,* Part II, Section 6.

gage. There must be at least one **general partner** in each limited partnership. In the common form of partnership, all partners are general partners. These partners are subject to unlimited liability. Like single proprietors, their assets outside the business entity may be made available to satisfy partnership creditor claims.

Mutual Agency Another characteristic of a partnership related to the liability of partners is that of **mutual agency;** that is, every partner is an agent of the partnership when performing acts to carry on the business. Thus the act of a single partner is binding on the partnership and on each of the other partners, even though the act may be negligent or wrongful.[2]

Mutual agency

In a partnership, the acts of each partner are binding on all other partners.

Raising of Capital The initial capital of a partnership must be raised from the personal wealth (or borrowing) of the partners. While the additional persons involved would normally provide more capital than a single proprietorship, the partnership form of business does not provide for any special or unique method of bringing additional assets into the business. All property brought into the partnership is **partnership property.** Each partner is a co-owner with the other partners of the partnership's property.

Taxation of Income A partnership must file an income tax return, but it is for information only. The various forms of revenue, expenses, and other tax deductible items are identified with each individual partner on the partnership return. On the partnership federal income tax return, Form 1065, Schedule K shows each partner's share of the taxable items; each partner is then required to include those items in his or her personal income tax return (see Appendix A).

Advantages and Disadvantages

Partnerships, while restricted in amounts of original capital by the personal wealth and borrowing power of the partners, can raise larger amounts of money than single proprietorships. They also tend to have a better credit rating, because each general partner is personally liable for debts of the business.

Partnerships are easy to form. They have a definite legal status under the Uniform Partnership Act. Their relationships with the public—for example, rules pertaining to conveyance of real property—are provided for in specific sections of the act. The act contains provisions that may have been omitted from the partnership agreement. If, for example, there was no agreement

[2]Ibid., Part III, Section 13.

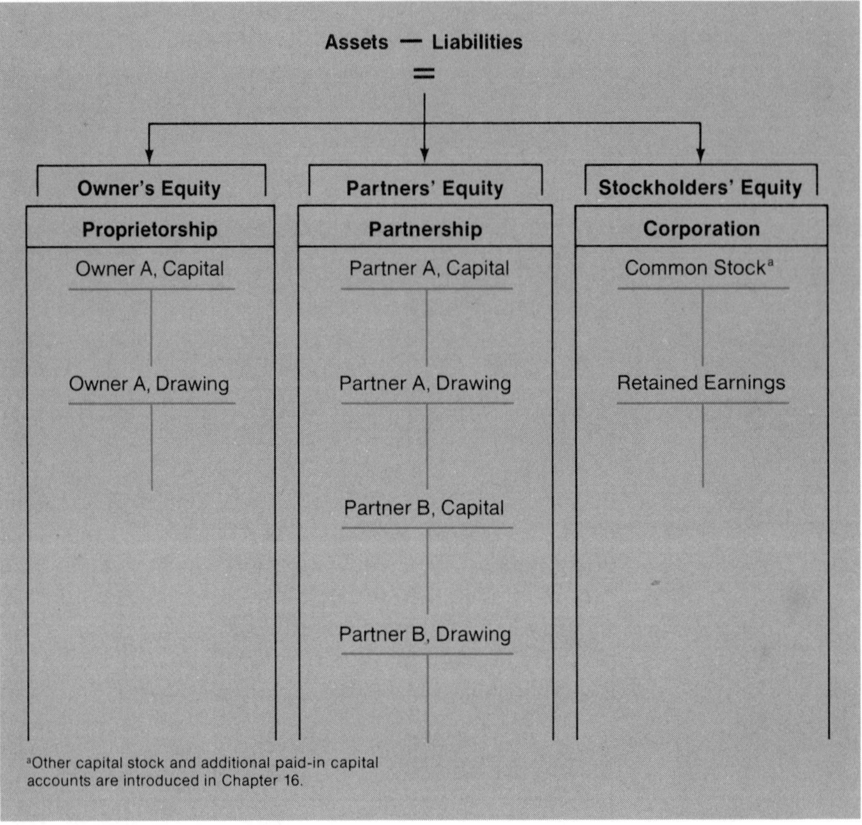

Figure 15–1 **Accounts for Recording Equity of Owners**

made as to distribution of partnership profits or losses, the act provides that they shall be shared equally.

By bringing more than one person into the operation of a business, there is greater opportunity to provide a variety of management skills. One partner may have expert knowledge in finance, another in marketing, and so on. Multiple management, however, has its disadvantages. Already mentioned is the mutual agency concept whereby the act of one partner is binding upon the others. Another disadvantage is the need to secure agreement among existing partners upon the admission of a new partner. Thus, transfer of ownership may be difficult to accomplish.

Partnerships suffer from the same lack of continuity that affects single proprietorships. Upon the death or retirement of a partner, the business form is dissolved. Dissolution should be distinguished from liquidation, in which all assets are sold and the business ceases operations. **Dissolution** means that the former partnership simply has ceased to exist; it includes liquidation but also includes other changes in ownership structure.

Overview of the Owner's Equity Accounts for the Three Basic Forms of Business Organization

Preliminary to a discussion of the accounting for a partnership, an overview of the owner's equity accounts for the three basic forms of business organization is presented. Figure 15–1 gives a pictorial view of the owner's equity accounts for a single proprietorship, partnership, and corporation.

The accounting for the equity of partners is very similar to that for the equity of a single proprietor except that a larger number of owner's accounts are involved. A corporation may be formed by receiving a charter from the state, creating a legal entity. Because state laws may restrict capital changes, a corporation must have special types of capital accounts. The accounting for a simple corporate capital structure uses as a minimum a Common Stock account and a Retained Earnings account. The detailed accounting for a corporation is discussed in Chapters 16 and 17.

Formation of a Partnership

The partnership form of business organization presents no new problems in accounting for assets, liabilities, expense, and revenue. With the exception of transactions with owners, these transactions are recorded in the same manner for all forms of business organization. The primary difference between a single proprietorship and a partnership is that the equity accounts of the partnership must show the equities of each of the individual partners of the partnership.

Each partner's share of ownership is recorded in a separate equity account, and its balance is in turn reported on the balance sheet. On formation of a partnership, the contribution of each partner is recorded in that equity account.

Example 1: Equal Investment of Cash

To illustrate, assume that on July 1, 1985, Susan Walsh and John Snow form a partnership, each investing $8,000 in cash. The journal entry to record the initial investment by the partners is shown below:

1985					
Jul.	1	Cash		16,000	
		Susan Walsh, Capital			8,000
		John Snow, Capital			8,000
		To record the investments of the partners in the Walsh and Snow Company.			

Example 2: Investment of Cash and Noncash Assets

It is not necessary that the original contributions be limited to cash. Assume that Walsh contributed land worth $3,000, a building worth $20,000, and merchandise costing $6,200, and that the partnership assumed her mortgage payable of $10,000 and $200 in interest accrued on the mortgage. Snow invested $15,000 in cash. The opening entry is shown on page 520.

1985					
Jul.	1	Cash		15,000	
		Merchandise Inventory (or Purchases)		6,200	
		Land		3,000	
		Building		20,000	
		Mortgage Payable			10,000
		Accrued Mortgage Interest Payable			200
		Susan Walsh, Capital			19,000
		John Snow, Capital			15,000
		To record the investments of the partners in the Walsh and Snow Company.			

Withdrawals by Partners

Withdrawals of assets by a partner in anticipation that profits have been earned are usually at a specified periodic amount as provided for in the partnership agreement. Such withdrawals are accounted for in the same manner as in a proprietorship; the amounts are debited to the respective **partner's drawing** account and the asset withdrawn is credited. To illustrate, assume that Susan Walsh and John Snow agree that each shall withdraw $1,000 per month in anticipation of profits. The entry for their first monthly withdrawal on July 31, 1985, is as follows:

1985					
Jul.	31	Susan Walsh, Drawing		1,000	
		John Snow, Drawing		1,000	
		Cash			2,000
		To record withdrawals in anticipation of profits earned.			

If Walsh and Snow withdraw $1,000 each month for the next five months, their drawing accounts at December 31, 1985, will have a balance of $6,000 each.

Because withdrawals in anticipation of income are routine and fixed by agreement, it follows that any withdrawals of assets by a partner in excess of the agreed amount are permanent reductions to capital. These should be recorded as debits to the partners' capital accounts. For example, suppose that on December 29, 1985, John Snow asks to be allowed to withdraw $5,000 to pay a personal debt and Susan Walsh consents. This is a capital reduction and it should be recorded as follows:

1985					
Dec.	29	John Snow, Capital		5,000	
		Cash			5,000
		To record a capital withdrawal by Snow.			

At the end of the accounting period, the drawing accounts are usually closed to the capital accounts because there is no legal distinction between capital invested and capital earned. The closing of the two drawing accounts with a balance of $6,000 each for the Walsh and Snow Company is illustrated below; this journal entry would normally follow the closing of the Income Summary account to the capital accounts (described in the next section).

1985					
Dec.	31	Susan Walsh, Capital		6,000	
		John Snow, Capital		6,000	
		Susan Walsh, Drawing			6,000
		John Snow, Drawing			6,000
		To close the drawing accounts to the capital accounts.			

Division of Partnership Profits and Losses

As stated previously, revenue and expense transactions are recorded in the same way regardless of the form of business organization. The operational issue peculiar to a partnership is the manner in which profits and losses are divided among its partners. That issue is addressed now. Assume that Kay Carter and Ann Foley are partners in the public accounting firm of Carter and Foley. The partners' equity section of the balance sheet at December 31, 1984, appears as follows:

CARTER AND FOLEY **Exhibit C**
Balance Sheet
December 31, 1984

Liabilities and Partners' Equity

Partners' equity:		
Kay Carter, capital	$62,500	
Ann Foley, capital	47,500	$110,000

Example 1: Division of Earnings in an Arbitrary Ratio

Profits and losses of a partnership can be divided in any manner on which the partners agree. If the partners desire to do so, they may adopt a loss-sharing ratio that is different from the method of sharing profits. The method chosen should be contained in the partnership agreement. If no articles or other evidence of agreement exist, however, the law assumes that profits and losses are both to be divided equally, even when the factors of investment, ability, or time are unequal. First assume that Carter and Foley share profits and losses equally. The journal entry to close a net income of $67,000 in 1985 would be:

1985				
Dec.	31	Income Summary	67,000	
		Kay Carter, Capital		33,500
		Ann Foley, Capital		33,500
		To transfer net income to capital accounts.		

Example 2: Division of Earnings Based on Interest and Agreed Ratio

The partners may agree to consider the differences in capital investments by allowing interest on capital balances and by distributing the remainder in an **agreed ratio. Interest allowance,** *as it is used here, is not an expense but rather a mechanism for dividing a portion of earnings in the ratio of contributed capitals,* with the remainder divided in some other ratio.[3] If 20 percent interest is allowed on beginning-of-year capital balances of Carter and Foley, and it is agreed to divide the remainder in a 2:1 ratio, the division of $67,000 net income is as follows:

	Carter	Foley	Total
Interest on beginning-of-year capital:			
20% of $62,500	$12,500		
20% of $47,500		$ 9,500	
Total interest allowances			$22,000
Remainder (⅔ and ⅓)	30,000	15,000	45,000
Net income division	$42,500	$24,500	$67,000

The journal entry to record this allocation of net income is:

1985				
Dec.	31	Income Summary	67,000	
		Kay Carter, Capital		42,500
		Ann Foley, Capital		24,500
		To allocate the net income for the year, divided 2:1 after 20% interest allowance on beginning-of-year capital balances.		

Example 3: Division of Earnings Based on Salaries, Interest, and Agreed Ratio

A part of the net income may be divided to recognize differences in capital balances, another part to recognize differences in the value of services rendered, and the remainder in an agreed ratio. Although entitled "salary allowances," as used here, these are not an expense. As with interest on capital balances, they are a mechanism for dividing a portion of the earnings. Assume that Carter and Foley agree to allow interest of 20 percent on begin-

[3]A partner may make a loan or advance to the partnership in addition to the capital that he or she has agreed to contribute. This is a different situation, and section 18(c) of the *Uniform Partnership Act* provides that the partner will be paid interest on these loans.

ning-of-year capital balances, salary allowances of $10,000 and $8,000, respectively, with the remainder to be divided 2:1. Computation is as follows:

	Carter	Foley	Total
Salary allowances	$10,000	$ 8,000	$18,000
Interest on beginning-of-year capital:			
20% of $62,500	12,500		
20% of $47,500		9,500	
Total interest allowances			22,000
Remainder (⅔ and ⅓)	18,000	9,000	27,000
Net income division	$40,500	$26,500	$67,000

The journal entry to record the allocation is:

1985					
Dec.	31	Income Summary		67,000	
		Kay Carter, Capital			40,500
		Ann Foley, Capital			26,500
		To allocate the net income for the year divided 2:1 after allowing for salaries and interest on capital balances.			

Example 4: Division of Earnings Based on Salaries, Interest, and Agreed Ratio with Net Income Less than Salaries and Interest

If there is an agreement for a salary allowance and interest allowance, the salary and interest allocations must be made, even though the net income is less than the total of such allocations. The negative remainder is divided in the same ratio used for dividing an excess of net income over total salaries and interest. To illustrate, assume the same facts as in the previous example, except that the net income for the year is $22,000. The computation is:

		Carter	Foley	Total
Salary allowances		$10,000	$ 8,000	$18,000
Interest on beginning-of-year capital:				
20% of $62,500		12,500		
20% of $47,500			9,500	
Total interest allowances				22,000
Total allowances		$22,500	$17,500	$40,000
Excess of allowances over net income:				
Total allowances	$40,000			
Net income	22,000			
Negative remainder (⅔ and ⅓)		(12,000)[a]	(6,000)[a]	(18,000)[a]
Net income division		$10,500	$11,500	$22,000

[a]Negative figures.

The reader should note carefully that a negative remainder does not necessarily indicate that a net loss has occurred. It simply reduces the share of profits allocated to each partner by the salary and interest allowances. The journal entry to record the allocation is:

1985					
Dec.	31	Income Summary		22,000	
		Kay Carter, Capital			10,500
		Ann Foley, Capital			11,500
		To allocate the net income for the year.			

Partnership Financial Statements

The changes in partners' equity accounts during the year are shown in a statement of partners' equity. Its form is similar to the statement of owner's equity for a single proprietorship. It is a supporting statement for the total partners' equities reported in the balance sheet. Assume the facts in Example 4 above. Also, assume that Carter and Foley each withdrew $12,000 in anticipation of income earned (Kay Carter, Drawing had a debit balance of $12,000 and Ann Foley, Drawing had a debit balance of $12,000), and that Carter made an additional investment of $10,000 and Foley, $8,000. The statement of partners' equity would reveal this information as shown in Figure 15–2.

The statement of partners' equity provides an explanation of the changes in partners' capital balances over a period of time. The basic format reconciles the old balance to the new balance in the same manner as a statement of owner's equity for a proprietorship. Note, however, in Figure 15–2, a separate column is provided for each partner. Thus, Ann Foley can trace the change in her capital from $47,500 on December 31, 1984, to its new total of $55,000 on December 31, 1985.

CARTER AND FOLEY — **Exhibit B**
Statement of Partners' Equity
For the Year Ended December 31, 1985

	Carter	Foley	Total
Partners' capital balances, December 31, 1984 . . .	$62,500	$47,500	$110,000
Add: Additional investments	10,000	8,000	18,000
Net income	10,500	11,500	22,000
Subtotals	$83,000	$67,000	$150,000
Deduct: Withdrawals	12,000	12,000	24,000
Partners' capital balances, December 31, 1985 . . .	$71,000	$55,000	$126,000

Figure 15–2 Statement of Partners' Equity

On December 31, 1985, the balance sheet would disclose the new equity balances as follows:

CARTER AND FOLEY
Balance Sheet
December 31, 1985

Exhibit C

Liabilities and Partners' Equity

Partners' equity:		
Kay Carter, capital	$71,000	
Ann Foley, capital	55,000	$126,000

The financial statements of a partnership are similar to those of a single proprietorship. The allocations of net income to the partners may be shown below the net income line of the income statement or, if they are too numerous, in a supplementary statement. The balance sheet shows the individual capital balances as of the end of the period and their total; or, if they are too numerous, the individual balances are shown in the supplementary statement of partners' equity.

Changes in Capital Structure

Once the partnership has been formed, changes in the capital structure are likely to follow in the future. Such changes result from (1) the admission of a new partner, (2) the death or retirement of an existing partner, or (3) the liquidation of the partnership. The accounting for these changes is discussed in the sections that follow.

Admission of a New Partner

The admission of a new partner technically dissolves the old partnership, although in the absence of complete liquidation or winding up of the business, it continues as before. In this sense, a dissolution means the legal end to a specific business. If the business continues, it is in fact a new business organization. A new partner may either (1) *purchase* an interest from one or more of the other partners or (2) be admitted as a partner by making an *investment* in the partnership. Both of these approaches are now illustrated.

Purchase of an Interest If the new partner buys an interest from one of the original partners, partnership assets are unchanged because the transfer of assets is direct between the persons involved. The only required entry on the partnership books is a transfer of the agreed share from the old partner's capital account to a capital account opened for the new partner. Assume that

Arthur Allen and Brian Barnes are partners sharing profits equally with the following capital structure:

Partners' equity:		
Arthur Allen, capital	$30,000	
Brian Barnes, capital	42,000	
Total partners' equity		$72,000

Then assume that on March 2, 1985, Allen, with Barnes's consent, sells one-half of his interest to Charles Cahn for $18,000. The minimum required journal entry to record Cahn's admission is:[4]

Date		Account		Debit	Credit
1985					
Mar.	2	Arthur Allen, Capital		15,000	
		Charles Cahn, Capital			15,000
		To record Charles Cahn's admission to partnership.			

The amount paid by Cahn to Allen has no effect on this entry, since there is no change in partnership assets or total capital. The cash was exchanged between the partners personally and the $3,000 gain is a personal profit to Allen which occurs outside the entity.

Investment to Acquire an Interest Cahn may be admitted by making an investment of cash or other assets directly to the firm, thereby increasing partnership assets and total capital. The amount credited to the incoming partner's capital account may be measured by the value of the investment. For Examples 1, 2, and 3, again assume that Allen and Barnes are partners, sharing gains and losses equally, with capital account balances of $30,000 and $42,000. Some conditions under which Charles Cahn, a new partner, may be admitted and the resulting journal entries are illustrated in the paragraphs that follow.

Example 1: Book Value Method Cahn invests an amount of cash sufficient to acquire a one-third interest on the basis of present book value of $72,000. Since Cahn is acquiring a one-third interest, after his investment the old partners' capital interest of $72,000 will be two-thirds of the new book value after admission. The total partners' equity after admission of Cahn will be $108,000 = ($72,000 ÷ 2/3). Cahn must invest $36,000 = (1/3 × $108,000). The journal entry to record Cahn's admission is:

[4]This transaction could be recorded by a recognition of an implied increase in assets called goodwill.

1985 Mar.	2	Cash
		  Charles Cahn, Capital
		    To record Charles Cahn's admission to partnership.
				36,000	
					36,000

Example 2: Goodwill Methods Admission of a new partner is often the occasion for recognizing **goodwill**—an intangible asset attributable to either the new partner or the old partnership.

Goodwill

Goodwill *is an intangible asset that represents an expectation of a greater than normal level of earnings of a business in its industry.*

If the old partnership has been successful, the new partner may agree, as a condition, that part of the investment he or she makes be considered a recognition of goodwill in the former partnership. Such goodwill would be attributable to the old partners. On the other hand, if the old partners need additional resources—funds, skills, or both—that the new partner will contribute, they may agree to credit the new partner with an amount greater than his or her investment in the form of goodwill. In other words, the new partner is investing a combination of cash plus goodwill. Under these circumstances, it is assumed that all other assets are valued approximately at current fair market value.

Goodwill to old partners. Cahn is admitted to a one-third interest on an invesment of $40,000 with the total capital to be $120,000. Cahn insists that his capital account be credited for the amount of his investment. The old partners agree. Since net assets (equal to partners' equity) before recognition of goodwill equal $112,000 after Cahn's $40,000 investment is added to present capital of $72,000, then goodwill is $8,000, calculated as follows:

Agreed total capital after Cahn's admission		$120,000
Present capital ($30,000 + $42,000)	$72,000	
Cahn's investment	40,000	
Net assets before recognition of goodwill		112,000
Goodwill		$ 8,000

The journal entry to record the goodwill and Cahn's admission is:

1985 Mar.	2	Cash
		Goodwill
		  Arthur Allen, Capital
		  Brian Barnes, Capital
		  Charles Cahn, Capital
		    To record Charles Cahn's admission to partnership.
				40,000
				8,000
					
					4,000
					4,000
					40,000

Since a dissolution occurs, it is considered acceptable to revalue assets to current fair market value. In this case, goodwill is recognized and credited to the old partners in their profit-and-loss-sharing ratios. On the other hand, if it is determined that the increase of $8,000 is attributable to a specific asset (or assets), then the specific asset account (or accounts) should be debited rather than the Goodwill account.

Goodwill to a new partner. In some instances, the partners may agree that a new partner, because of the possession of some special characteristic, is bringing goodwill to the business. Assume that Cahn is to be admitted to a one-third interest with an investment of $30,000, total capital to be $108,000. If there is no revaluation of existing partnership assets, the additional asset is recognized as goodwill, and it is to be attributed to Cahn, computed as follows:

Agreed total capital after Cahn's admission		$108,000
Present capital	$72,000	
Cahn's investment	30,000	102,000
Goodwill		$ 6,000

The journal entry to record this admission of Cahn is:

1985 Mar.	2	Cash		30,000	
		Goodwill		6,000	
		Charles Cahn, Capital			36,000
		To record Charles Cahn's admission to partnership; $36,000 = (⅓ × $108,000).			

In this instance, Cahn is viewed as investing two assets: (1) cash of $30,000 and (2) goodwill of $6,000. There are other variations of the goodwill method.

Sometimes a new partner may be willing to invest more or allowed to invest less than the share of ownership received. When this occurs with no valid basis to record goodwill (or the partners are unwilling to recognize goodwill), the investment must be recorded under a bonus method.

Example 3: Bonus Methods *Bonus to old partners.* Assume Cahn is admitted to a one-third interest by investing $48,000, total capital to be $120,000, of which Cahn is to be credited with $40,000. Since net assets equal $120,000, there is no goodwill. However, Cahn invests $48,000 but is credited with only $40,000 = (1/3 × $120,000). The difference of $8,000 is a bonus contributed by Cahn to Allen and Barnes. This bonus is credited to the old partners in their profit-and-loss-sharing ratio. The journal entry to record the admission of Cahn with the bonus going to the old partners is:

1985 Mar.	2	Cash		48,000	
		Arthur Allen, Capital			4,000
		Brian Barnes, Capital			4,000
		Charles Cahn, Capital			40,000
		To record Charles Cahn's admission to partnership.			

Bonus to new partner. In some cases, the bonus may be credited to the new partner. Suppose that Cahn invests \$30,000 for a one-third interest, total capital to be \$102,000. His interest is \$34,000 = (1/3 × \$102,000); thus, there is a bonus to him of \$4,000 = (\$34,000 − \$30,000). The journal entry to record this admission is:

1985 Mar.	2	Cash		30,000	
		Arthur Allen, Capital		2,000	
		Brian Barnes, Capital		2,000	
		Charles Cahn, Capital			34,000
		To record Charles Cahn's admission to partnership.			

Since total capital equals \$102,000 after Cahn's investment is added, there is no goodwill. However, since Cahn invests \$30,000 but is credited with \$34,000, the old partners are providing a special inducement by crediting Cahn with \$4,000 more than his actual investment. To give this extra credit to Cahn, the old partners must accept a reduction in their capital accounts for the amount of the bonus in their profit-and-loss-sharing ratio.

Retirement or Death of an Existing Partner

The next change in partners' ownership discussed is that caused by death or withdrawal of a partner. The partnership agreement usually contains provisions for determining a deceased partner's current equity and the manner and form of settlement with his or her estate. The partnership agreement should also provide for procedures to be followed when a partner withdraws from the partnership. In both cases, the agreement will *generally* provide for the adjustment of assets to their current fair market value.[5] Resulting increases or decreases are always distributed to the partners' capital accounts in their profit-and-loss-sharing ratios, after which the withdrawing partner receives cash or other assets equal to the adjusted balance in his or her capital account. The entry is a debit to the capital account and a credit to cash or other assets.

---

[5]A bonus method or a goodwill method similar to those illustrated in the admission of a partner could be used. They are not illustrated in this book since they are considered to be beyond its scope.

Voluntary Withdrawal of a Partner When a partner retires voluntarily, the partnership agreement or the negotiation for settlement with the retiring partner usually provides for (1) the recognition of profits or losses to the date of retirement and (2) the revaluation of partnership assets. Assume, for example, that Kirsten Rhodes, Megan Wills, and Fred Thomas are equal partners and that Thomas is retiring voluntarily as of May 1, 1985. Thomas's capital account, after having been credited with his share of the earnings through April 30, 1985, is $25,000. The partnership agreement provides for a complete appraisal of all partnership assets prior to the withdrawal of a partner. The professional appraiser's report recommends that Land and Building be revalued upward by $8,000 and $16,000, respectively. The journal entry to record the revaluation of these assets is:

1985					
May	1	Land		8,000	
		Building		16,000	
		Kirsten Rhodes, Capital			8,000
		Megan Wills, Capital			8,000
		Fred Thomas, Capital			8,000
		To increase the Land and Building accounts based on appraiser's revaluation report.			

After the foregoing entry, Fred Thomas's Capital account would show a balance of $33,000 = ($25,000 + $8,000). The journal entry to record Thomas's withdrawal, assuming payment is in partnership cash, is:

1985					
May	1	Fred Thomas, Capital		33,000	
		Cash			33,000
		To record the voluntary retirement of Fred Thomas.			

Death of a Partner Upon the death of a partner, similar revaluations of assets must be recognized. Then the books should be closed to bring the deceased partner's capital balance up-to-date. The capital account is then replaced by a liability account to his or her estate. Assume the same facts as in the foregoing example, except that Fred Thomas died on May 1, 1985. The journal entry for the revaluation of assets is the same. After the revaluation journal entry is posted, the following journal entry is made:

1985					
May	1	Fred Thomas, Capital		33,000	
		Liability to the Estate of Fred Thomas			33,000
		To record liability to the estate of deceased partner, Fred Thomas, and to close the capital account.			

The Liability to the Estate of Fred Thomas account may be liquidated by payment of cash, or payment may be postponed and interest at an agreed upon rate to be paid on the principal amount.[6]

Liquidation of a Partnership

A partnership may be terminated by selling the assets, paying the creditors, and distributing the remaining cash to the partners. This total process is called **liquidation** of a partnership; conversion of assets into cash is called **realization.** When a partnership is liquidated, gains and losses resulting from the sale of assets must first be distributed to the capital accounts in profit-and-loss-sharing ratios before cash can be distributed to the partners. If, after all gains and losses are distributed, a partner's capital account shows a debit balance, that partner must pay in the deficiency from personal resources. If that partner has no personal resources, the deficiency must be absorbed by the other partners. This deficiency absorption is on the basis of the solvent partners' profit-and-loss-sharing ratios *to each other*. Two illustrations are now presented: (1) where assets are sold at a gain, and (2) where assets are sold at a loss.

Example 1: Sale of Assets at a Gain To illustrate, assume that partners Ellen Dole, Ron Epps, and George Frank, whose balance sheet is shown below, decide to sell their noncash assets, pay their creditors, and distribute the remaining cash to themselves. The profits and losses are shared equally among the partners.

DOLE, EPPS, AND FRANK — **Exhibit C**
Balance Sheet
May 31, 1985

Assets	
Cash	$ 50,000
Other assets	250,000
Total assets	$300,000
Liabilities and Partners' Equities	
Liabilities	$100,000
Ellen Dole, capital	100,000
Ron Epps, capital	60,000
George Frank, capital	40,000
Total liabilities and partners' equities	$300,000

Assume that on June 8, the noncash assets are sold for $280,000; on June 15, the creditors are paid in full; and on June 20, the cash remaining is distrib-

[6] This liability does have priority over other unsecured claims according to the *Uniform Partnership Act,* Section 42.

uted to the partners in final liquidation. The following summary shows the liquidation sequence:

DOLE, EPPS, AND FRANK
Statement of Liquidation
For the Month of June 1985

	Cash	Other Assets	Liabilities	Capital Dole	Capital Epps	Capital Frank
Balances before realization	$ 50,000	$250,000	$100,000	$100,000	$60,000	$40,000
1 Sale of assets at a gain	280,000	(250,000)[a]		10,000	10,000	10,000
Balances	$330,000		$100,000	$110,000	$70,000	$50,000
2 Payment of creditors	(100,000)[a]		(100,000)[a]			
Balances	$230,000			$110,000	$70,000	$50,000
3 Cash distribution to partners	(230,000)[a]			(110,000)[a]	(70,000)[a]	(50,000)[a]

[a]Negative figure.

Explanation of the numbered line items above is as follows:

1 Other assets of $250,000 are sold for $280,000 cash. The gain of $30,000 is credited to each partner's capital account in the appropriate profit-and-loss-sharing ratio.

2 The liabilities of $100,000 are paid.

3 The available cash of $230,000 is distributed to the partners according to the capital balances, thereby reducing each partner's capital account to a zero balance.

The journal entries to record these transactions are:

Date		Account		Debit	Credit
1985		1			
Jun.	8	Cash		280,000	
		Other Assets			250,000
		Ellen Dole, Capital			10,000
		Ron Epps, Capital			10,000
		George Frank, Capital			10,000
		To record the sale of other assets and to allocate the gain to the partners' capital accounts in their profit-and-loss-sharing ratio.			
		2			
	15	Liabilities		100,000	
		Cash			100,000
		To record payment to creditors.			
		3			
	20	Ellen Dole, Capital		110,000	
		Ron Epps, Capital		70,000	
		George Frank, Capital		50,000	
		Cash			230,000
		To record the distribution to the partners and to close the capital accounts.			

Example 2: Sale of Assets at a Loss Sale of assets at a loss in the process of liquidation may result in a capital deficiency in a partner's capital account. For example, if the assets in the foregoing illustration are sold for $100,000, Frank's one-third share of the resulting loss of $150,000 = ($250,000 − $100,000) is $50,000, or $10,000 more than the balance in his capital account. If he is financially able to do so, Frank is legally obligated to invest personal assets to cover this capital deficiency. If any payments are made to Dole and Epps before it is determined whether Frank can invest enough personal assets to cover his capital deficiency, however, they should be made in such a way that will leave credit balances in Dole's and Epps's accounts that will exactly absorb each partner's share of Frank's $10,000 capital deficiency should he be unable to cover it. This calculation can be made in the following manner:

	Dole	Epps	Frank
Capital balances immediately before cash is to be distributed	$50,000	$10,000	$(10,000)[a]
Possible loss to Dole and Epps if Frank is unable to cover capital deficiency	(5,000)[a]	(5,000)[a]	10,000
Safe cash payments to partners	$45,000	$ 5,000	$ 0

[a]Negative figure.

If Frank is not able to pay in his capital deficiency, Dole and Epps would have to bear this as an additional loss divided in the relationship they previously held to each other; hence, it would be split between Dole and Epps equally (now 1:1).

The complete liquidation including the safe cash payments to Dole and Epps is shown in the summary statement of liquidation that follows:

DOLE, EPPS, AND FRANK
Statement of Liquidation
For the Month of June 1985

	Cash	Other Assets	Liabilities	Capital Dole	Capital Epps	Capital Frank
Balances before realization	$ 50,000	$250,000	$100,000	$100,000	$60,000	$ 40,000
1 Sale of assets at a loss	100,000	(250,000)[a]		(50,000)[a]	(50,000)[a]	(50,000)[a]
Balances	$150,000		$100,000	$50,000	$10,000	$(10,000)[a]
2 Payments to creditors	(100,000)[a]		(100,000)[a]			
Balances	$ 50,000			$ 50,000	$10,000	$(10,000)[a]
3 Cash distribution to partners	(50,000)[a]			(45,000)[a]	(5,000)[a]	
4 Balances				$ 5,000	$ 5,000	$(10,000)[a]

[a]Negative figure.

Explanation of the numbered line items is as follows:

[1] Other assets are sold for $100,000 cash. The loss of $150,000 = ($250,000 − $100,000) is debited to each partner's capital account in the appropriate profit-and-loss-sharing ratio.

[2] The liabilities are paid.

[3] The available cash of $50,000 is distributed to Dole and Epps in amounts so as to leave credit balances of $5,000 in each of their capital accounts to offset the $10,000 debit balance in Frank's account.

[4] The balances in the capital accounts are left open to show that Dole and Epps have a claim against Frank.

Subsequent Accounting for a Partner's Capital Deficiency As indicated in the foregoing discussion: (1) Frank may have sufficient personal assets to pay in his capital deficiency or (2) he may be personally insolvent and not have enough personal assets to contribute to the partnership to make good the capital deficiency. In the first case, Frank would make an additional cash investment of $10,000 in the partnership: Cash would be debited and George Frank, Capital would be credited. Assuming $50,000 in cash has already been distributed, this additional $10,000 in cash would then be distributed to Dole and Epps.

In the second case, upon determining that Frank is unable to contribute $10,000 to cover the capital deficiency, the debit balance in his capital account will be written off to Dole and Epps. After the cash payment of $50,000 is made to Dole and Epps, it is still necessary to reduce all partnership accounts to zero. The journal entries to record the liquidation for the second case are as follows:

Date		Account		Debit	Credit
1985		[1]			
Jun.	8	Cash		100,000	
		Ellen Dole, Capital		50,000	
		Ron Epps, Capital		50,000	
		George Frank, Capital		50,000	
		Other Assets			250,000
		To record the sale of other assets and to allocate the loss to the partners' capital accounts in their profit-and-loss-sharing ratio.			
		[2]			
	15	Liabilities		100,000	
		Cash			100,000
		To record payment to creditors.			
		[3]			
	20	Ellen Dole, Capital		45,000	
		Ron Epps, Capital		5,000	
		Cash			50,000
		To record the cash distribution to the partners.			
		[4]			
	20	Ellen Dole, Capital		5,000	
		Ron Epps, Capital		5,000	
		George Frank, Capital			10,000
		To absorb the uncollectible capital deficiency of Frank by Dole and Epps.			

Of course, Dole and Epps continue to have a legal claim against Frank for the unpaid deficiency that was in Frank's capital account.

Glossary

Agreed ratio The fixed proportions agreed upon in advance by the partners for the division of their partnership's earnings.

Dissolution The cessation of a partnership; the legal end of life of a business.

General partner A partner who has unlimited liability for the debts of a partnership.

Goodwill An intangible asset that represents an expected greater than normal level of earnings of a business in its industry.

Interest allowance A mechanism for dividing a portion of the earnings of a partnership by allowing interest on capital balances at a specified interest rate.

Limited partner A partner who has no personal responsibility for the debts of the partnership beyond the amount of his or her investment.

Liquidation The process of terminating a business by selling the assets, paying the creditors, and distributing the remaining cash to the owner(s).

Mutual agency A characteristic of partnerships whereby the act of a single partner is binding on the partnership and on each of the partners.

Partner's drawing The account representing the reduction in the equity of a partner resulting from cash or other assets withdrawn from the business in anticipation of income earned.

Partnership An association of two or more persons to carry on, as co-owners, a business for profit.

Partnership property All assets brought into a partnership; they belong to all partners as co-owners.

Realization The conversion of the noncash assets of a business to cash.

Unlimited liability A characteristic of single proprietorships and partnerships; an owner has personal liability for the debts of the business.

Questions

Q15–1 How is the accounting for a partnership similar to that of a single proprietorship? How is it different?

Q15–2 In what ways is the accounting the same for the three basic forms of business organization?

Q15–3 Differentiate between the following: general and limited partners; partnership realization and liquidation; single proprietorships and partnerships; goodwill account and drawing account.

Q15–4 What is meant by agreed ratio? Mutual agency? Unlimited liability?

Q15–5 Can a partnership exist without any general partners? Explain.

Q15–6 Jones and Smith form a partnership to manufacture microelectronic equipment. Without consulting Jones, Smith buys equipment costing $700,000 to be used in operations. Is this acquisition binding on Jones even though he was not consulted about its purchase? Give your reason.

Q15–7 Does each state have a different set of laws to regulate partnerships? Explain.

Q15–8 B. Wrenn and C. Robin formed a partnership. Wrenn invested $20,000 in cash. Robin invested land and a building with cash market value of $40,000. Five years later they agree to terminate the partnership, and Robin demands the return to her of the land and building. Is she justified in the demand? Explain.

Q15–9 T. Beal and K. Skerry are partners with capital account balances of $40,000 each. They share profits one-third and two-thirds, respectively. (a) Is this an equitable arrangement? (b) Assume that 10 percent interest on beginning balances is agreed upon, with any remainder to be distributed equally to Beal and to Skerry. How will profits of $17,000 be distributed? (c) Should an account be debited for the interest on the capital balances? Explain.

Q15–10 Can a partnership business continue after the death or retirement of one of the partners? Explain.

Q15–11 Does the dissolution of a partnership terminate the business? Explain.

Q15–12 What procedure is followed for dividing the negative remainder when the division of earnings is based on salaries, interest, and agreed ratio and the net income is less than the salaries and interest total?

Q15–13 What is the effect on partnership assets when a new partner (a) purchases an interest from one or more of the other partners? (b) Is admitted as a partner by making an investment in the partnership?

Exercises

E15–1
Recording investment by partners and preparing a balance sheet

Burt Barnes and Raymond Strong formed a partnership on May 12, 1985. Barnes contributed $38,000 in cash, land worth $16,000, a building appraised at $131,000, and a truck valued at $10,000. The land and building are encumbered by a mortgage of $30,000, which is assumed by the partnership; interest of $680 has accrued on this mortgage to May 12, 1985. Strong contributed $42,000 in cash.

1. Make the general journal entries on the books of the new partnership to record its formation.

2. Prepare a beginning balance sheet for the partnership, which will do business under the name of B and S Company.

E15–2
Recording investment of cash and noncash assets by partners

Samuel David and Elijah Hills are television repairers. They desire to form a partnership to open up a television sales outlet and repair shop. Their attorney prepares a partnership agreement requiring the assets of their respective businesses (operated as single proprietorships) be recorded at current fair market value. These assets that will be invested in the new partnership along with the liabilities to be assumed and their fair market value are as follows:

	David	Hills	Total
Cash	$ 18,000	$ 16,000	$ 34,000
Repair supplies	1,000	900	1,900
Equipment	34,500	29,200	63,700
Accounts payable	(14,000)[a]	(12,000)[a]	(26,000)[a]

[a]Credit balance.

Prepare the journal entry to record the original investments on the David and Hills partnership books.

E15–3
Recording transactions by partners

The following selected transactions occurred in the partnership of Whang and Ding:

1985

Jan. 1 Chi Whang and Pok Ding formed a partnership effective on this date, making the following investments: Whang invested $31,000 in cash. Ding contributed his equity in a building and lot. The partners agreed that the building was worth $49,500 and the land $6,000. There was a mortgage on the land and building with a face value of $12,000 and an interest rate of 14 percent. The interest was last paid on October 1, 1984. The partnership assumed all liabilities relating to the mortgage.

Mar. 2 Whang withdrew $1,200 cash in anticipation of income to be earned.

Apr. 1 Ding withdrew from the business merchandise that cost $800 and had a selling price of $1,200. The firm uses the periodic inventory system, and Purchases must be credited.

Oct. 3 Whang was allowed to withdraw $12,000 in cash to pay a personal debt. The amount exceeds any anticipated income to be earned.

Record the transactions in the general journal.

E15–4
Distribution of income—statements and entries

Jean Ormand, Betsy Peters, and Catherine Queens formed a partnership on May 1, 1984, with investments of $35,000, $27,000, and $30,000, respectively. During the next 12 months, Ormand and Peters made additional investments of $12,000 each. Queens invested an additional $15,000. No withdrawals were made by the partners during this first year of operations. Net income for the period was $60,000. The partnership agreement did not specify the method of dividing profits and losses. Prepare (a) a statement of partners' equity for the year ended April 30, 1985, and (b) an entry to close the Income Summary account.

E15–5
Preparing statement of partners' equity

Robert Hickson and Mary Sipps formed a partnership during their senior year in college to providing tutoring service to new students. After graduation they continued the business, hiring other students to help with much of the actual tutoring. Their account balances in alphabetical sequence on December 31, 1985, are as follows:

Accounts Receivable	$ 2,500
Cash	6,000
Mary Sipps, Capital	4,000
Mary Sipps, Drawing	12,000
Robert Hickson, Capital	15,550
Robert Hickson, Drawing	12,000
Salaries Expense	22,500
Supplies on Hand	3,250
Supplies Expense	5,040
Tutoring Fees Earned	43,740

1. Prepare the December 31, 1985, closing entries. Profits and losses are divided equally.

2. Prepare a statement of partners' equity using three money columns headed Hickson, Sipps, and Total.

3. Explain why the equity of each partner declined in a profitable year.

E15–6
Recording investment by partners and evaluating investment decision

L. Lloyd and M. Minton formed a partnership on September 1, 1985. Lloyd contributed $20,000 in cash, land worth $10,000, a building appraised at $60,000 (the land and the building are encumbered by a mortgage of $10,000, which is assumed by the partnership), and a truck valued at $8,000. Minton contributed $20,000 in cash.

1. Make the general journal entries to record the formation of the partnership.

2. Why may Lloyd be willing to enter into a partnership in which he contributes 4.4 times as much as his partner?

E15–7
Admitting a new partner by purchase of interest from an existing partner

J. Jacobs, K. Kroom, and L. Leuter are partners with capital balances of $40,000, $30,000, and $60,000, respectively. Leuter, with the consent of Jacobs and Kroom, sells one-third of his interest to M. Melson for $25,000. Prepare a journal entry to record the admission of Melson.

E15–8
Admitting a new partner

Jean Toony and Barbara Bone are equal partners with capital balances of $60,000 and $40,000, respectively. On May 15, 1985, Cindy Carter is admitted to the partnership with a one-third interest in net earnings and net assets. Record Carter's admission based on the following independent assumptions:

a. Carter invests $50,000; total capital to be $150,000.
b. Carter invests $62,000; total capital to be $162,000.
c. Carter invests $60,000; total capital to be $180,000.

E15–9
Liquidating a partnership

A. Ainsley, B. Baker, and C. Cart are equal partners with preliquidation capital balances of $200,000, $160,000, and $180,000, respectively. After the assets are sold and the creditors paid, $450,000 in cash is available for distribution to the partners. How should the cash be distributed?

E15–10
Liquidating a partnership with deficiency

D. Dawson, E. Eason, and F. Foster are partners with preliquidation capital balances of $37,500, $37,500, and $15,000, respectively. They share profits in the ratio of 2:2:1. After the assets are sold and the creditors paid, cash of $9,000 is available for distribution to the partners. How should the $9,000 be divided?

E15–11
Recording withdrawal of a partner

George Goodman, Lindy Hobson, and Samuel Isaacs share profits and losses in the ratio of 2:2:1, respectively. Their partnership agreement provides that upon the death, withdrawal, or voluntary retirement of a partner, partnership assets shall be revalued and the partners' capital accounts adjusted accordingly. George Goodman retires on July 1, 1985. The appraiser's report states that the inventory account is understated by $10,000 and the equipment account is understated by $8,000. Goodman's capital account shows a balance of $25,000 as of June 30, 1985, prior to the revaluation of the assets. Record, in general journal form, all entries related to Goodman's withdrawal, assuming settlement is in cash.

E15–12
Recording withdrawal by death of a partner

Assume the same facts as in E15–11, except that Goodman died in an automobile accident on July 1, 1985. Make all necessary general journal entries prior to the final cash settlement with the estate of Goodman.

A Problems

P15–1A
Recording investments of partners under different situations

Anson Strong and Winston Turner form a partnership.

Required: Journalize their investments on the new partnership books in the general journal on the basis of each of the following independent assumptions:

1. Each partner invests $12,000 in cash.

2. Strong invests $14,000 in cash, and Turner invests $15,000 in cash.

3. Strong invests $5,000 in cash, land worth $18,000, a building worth $40,000, and merchandise worth $6,000. Turner invests $46,000 in cash.

4. Strong invests $7,000 in cash, land worth $9,000, and a building worth $50,000. The partnership agrees to assume a mortgage payable of $18,000 on the land and building. Turner invests $6,500 in cash, store equipment worth $12,000, and merchandise worth $6,200.

P15–2A *Preparing financial statements for a partnership*

The accountant for Walters and Winston, business information systems consultants, prepared the following adjusted trial balances as of December 31, 1985:

WALTERS AND WINSTON, CONSULTANTS
Adjusted Trial Balance
December 31, 1985

Account Title	Debits	Credits
Cash	$ 9,700	
Accounts Receivable	25,200	
Supplies	7,600	
Prepaid Insurance	5,500	
Land	20,000	
Building	140,000	
Accumulated Depreciation—Building		$ 20,000
Office Equipment	24,000	
Accumulated Depreciation—Office Equipment		7,000
Accounts Payable		9,000
Accrued Salaries Payable		1,000
Mortgage Payable		40,000
Fallon Walters, Capital		40,000
Fallon Walters, Drawing	24,000	
Thomas Winston, Capital		50,000
Thomas Winston, Drawing	30,000	
Professional Fees		170,000
Supplies Expense	6,000	
Depreciation Expense—Office Equipment	2,400	
Depreciation Expense—Building	8,000	
Utilities Expense	2,400	
General Expense	3,000	
Property Tax Expense	2,000	
Interest Expense	3,200	
Salaries Expense	24,000	
Totals	$337,000	$337,000

Required:

1. Prepare an income statement for the year, showing at the bottom of the statement the allocation of net income to each partner. The partners have agreed to divide profits and losses as follows: (a) 20 percent interest on capital balances at the beginning of the year, (b) salaries of $16,000 and $14,000, respectively, and (c) the remainder divided in the ratio of 3:2. Each partner made an additional investment of $4,000 on July 1, 1985.

2. Prepare a statement of partners' equity for the year.

3. Prepare a balance sheet as of December 31, 1985.

P15–3A *Distributing profits and losses*

Sarah Gleem and Sandy Hooter formed a partnership on January 1, 1985, with investments of $45,000 and $72,000, respectively. On July 1, 1985, Gleem invested an additional $15,000.

Required: Make the appropriate journal entries to record the distribution of profits and losses on the basis of each of the following independent assumptions:

1. Net income is $24,000, and profits and losses are shared equally.

2. Net loss is $9,000; the partnership agreement provides that profits are to be distributed 60 percent to Gleem and 40 percent to Hooter; the method of distributing losses was not specified.

3. Net income is $24,000, to be distributed as follows: salaries of $12,000 to Gleem and $18,000 to Hooter; interest of 12 percent on ending capital balances before the addition of net income; remainder to be distributed equally.

P15–4A *Admitting a new partner by various assumptions*

Assume that Sharon Senter and James Ramsey are equal partners, each with a capital balance of $62,500.

Required: Record the admission of June Baker under each of the following independent assumptions:

1. Senter sells her interest to Baker for $64,000.

2. Baker invests $62,500 for a one-fourth interest, total capital to be $187,500.

3. Baker invests $62,500 for a one-fourth interest, total capital to be $250,000.

4. Baker invests $62,500 for a one-third interest, total capital to be $187,500.

5. Baker invests $40,000 for a one-third interest, total capital to be $187,500.

6. Baker invests $74,000 for a one-half interest, total capital to be $199,000.

P15–5A *Preparing a statement of liquidation*

Newton Fisher, John Medlin, and Roy Twain, whose balance sheet information on March 31, 1985, is shown below, have decided to liquidate their partnership.

Cash	$ 35,000
Accounts receivable	25,000
Inventories	100,000
Machinery	125,000
Accounts payable	20,000
Newton Fisher, capital	80,000
John Medlin, capital	130,000
Roy Twain, capital	55,000

Proceeds from the sale of noncash assets were as follows:

Accounts receivable	$15,000
Inventories	45,000
Machinery	25,000

Required: Prepare a statement in good form showing the final distribution of the remaining cash following the sale of the assets and the payment of creditors. Profits and losses are shared equally.

P15–6A *Recording the withdrawal of a partner under different conditions*

Fred Eidson, Earl Hunter, and Gordon Summer are partners with capital balances of $30,000, $50,000, and $60,000, respectively. They share profits and losses in the ratio of 2:2:1.

Required: Record, in general journal form, Eidson's withdrawal from the partnership under each of the following independent assumptions:

1. Eidson sells his interest to his brother-in-law, Burton Sams, for $35,000.

2. Eidson retires voluntarily. His capital account is increased by $10,000, his share of the increase following revaluation of the building owned by the partnership. Eidson is paid from partnership cash.

3. Eidson dies following a long illness. An appraiser reports that the partnership assets are fairly valued and require no revaluation; furthermore, the partners do not wish to record any goodwill on the partnership books, yet they settle with Eidson's estate for $36,000, payment being made from partnership cash. Use a bonus approach.

P15–7A
Thought-provoking problem: division of profits

On January 2, 1985, Amram Boheme and Thomas Martin formed a partnership. Boheme invested $70,000 in cash, Martin, $30,000. They wrote a simple partnership agreement, but forgot to mention the division of profits and losses. During 1985, the partners withdrew $24,000 in cash each. At the end of 1985, the Income Summary account showed a net credit balance of $36,000 after all expenses and revenues had been closed. The operating income was $100,000 but there was a loss of $64,000 brought about by a bad decision made by Martin in ordering the wrong kind of property, plant, and equipment. After referring back to the partnership agreement, Boheme argues that his account should be credited with $70,000, particularly since Martin cost the partnership $64,000 in net income because of his unwise decision. Martin disagrees; he says the division should be an equal split.

Required:

1. With which partner do you agree? Why? Does the loss caused by the action of one partner affect the division of net income?

2. Prepare journal entries to record the withdrawals, the proper division of net income, and the closing of the drawing accounts.

B Problems

P15–1B
Recording investments of partners under different situations

Sante Barnard and Leman Trotts form a partnership.

Required: Journalize their investments on the new partnership books in the general journal on the basis of each of the following independent assumptions:

1. Each partner invests $9,200 in cash.

2. Barnard invests $10,800 in cash, and Trotts invests $12,600 in cash.

3. Barnard invests $5,500 in cash, land worth $14,000, a building worth $32,000, and merchandise worth $6,000. Trotts invests $40,500.

4. Barnard invests $5,800 in cash, land worth $9,500, and a building worth $30,500. The partnership agrees to assume a mortgage payable of $10,500 on the land and building. Trotts invests $6,500 in cash, store equipment worth $11,000, and merchandise worth $4,800.

P15–2B
Preparing financial statements for a partnership

The accountants for Barbara and Merton, business information systems consultants, prepared the following adjusted trial balance as of December 31, 1985:

BARBARA AND MERTON, CONSULTANTS
Adjusted Trial Balance
December 31, 1985

Account Title	Debits	Credits
Cash	$ 22,125	
Accounts Receivable	32,500	
Supplies	9,500	
Prepaid Insurance	6,875	
Land	25,000	
Building	175,000	
Accumulated Depreciation—Building		$ 25,000
Office Equipment	30,000	
Accumulated Depreciation—Office Equipment		8,750
Accounts Payable		11,250
Accrued Salaries Payable		1,250
Mortgage Payable		50,000
Melissa Barbara, Capital		68,000
Melissa Barbara, Drawing	37,500	
Arnold Merton, Capital		55,500
Arnold Merton, Drawing	30,000	
Professional Fees		212,500
Supplies Expense	7,500	
Depreciation Expense—Office Equipment	3,000	
Depreciation Expense—Building	10,000	
Utilities Expense	3,000	
General Expense	3,750	
Property Tax Expense	2,500	
Interest Expense	4,000	
Salaries Expense	30,000	
Totals	$432,250	$432,250

Required:

1. Prepare an income statement for the year, showing the allocation of net income to each partner. The partners have agreed to divide profits and losses as follows: (a) 15 percent on capital balances at the beginning of the year, (b) salaries of $45,000 and $30,000, respectively, and (c) the remainder divided in the ratio of 3:2. Each partner made an additional investment of $6,000 on July 1, 1985.

2. Prepare a statement of partners' equity for the year.

3. Prepare a balance sheet as of December 31, 1985.

P15–3B *Distributing profits and losses*

Oscar Glenn and Robert Greer formed a partnership on January 1, 1985, with investments of $40,000 and $58,000, respectively. On July 1, 1985, Glenn invested an additional $14,000.

Required: Make the appropriate general journal entries to record the distribution of profits and losses on the basis of each of the following independent assumptions:

1. Net income is $20,000, and profits and losses are shared equally.

2. Net loss is $4,000; the partnership agreement provides that profits are to be distributed 60 percent to Glenn and 40 percent to Greer; the method of distributing losses was not specified.

3. Net income is $60,000, to be distributed as follows: salaries of $10,000 to Glenn and $15,000 to Greer; interest of 15 percent on ending capital balances before the addition of net income; the remainder to be distributed equally.

P15–4B *Admitting a new partner by various assumptions*

Assume that Faye Hamner and Addie Dell are equal partners, each with a capital balance of $30,000.

Required: Record the admission of Rob Hinton under each of the following independent assumptions:

1. Hamner sells her interest to Hinton for $32,500.

2. Hinton invests $30,000 for a one-fourth interest, total capital to be $90,000.

3. Hinton invests $30,000 for a one-fourth interest, total capital to be $120,000.

4. Hinton invests $30,000 for a one-third interest, total capital to be $90,000.

5. Hinton invests $20,000 for a one-third interest, total capital to be $90,000.

6. Hinton invests $32,000 for a one-half interest, total capital to be $92,000.

P15–5B *Preparing a statement of liquidation*

Mary Hazele, Sara Riggsbee, and Parks Rogers, whose balance sheet information on March 31, 1985, is shown below, have decided to liquidate their partnership.

Cash	$ 38,000
Accounts Receivable	50,000
Inventories	200,000
Machinery	250,000
Accounts payable	40,000
Mary Hazele, capital	249,000
Sara Riggsbee, capital	100,000
Parks Rogers, capital	149,000

Proceeds from the sale of noncash assets were as follows:

Accounts receivable	$33,000
Inventories	90,000
Machinery	50,000

Required: Prepare a statement in good form showing the final distribution of the remaining cash following the sale of the assets and the payment of creditors.

P15–6B *Recording the withdrawal of a partner under different conditions*

William Slayton, Ben Potter, and Raye Boling are partners with capital balances of $32,000, $52,000, and $62,000, respectively. They share profits and losses in the ratio of 2:2:1.

Required: Record, in general journal form, Slayton's withdrawal from the partnership under each of the following independent assumptions.

1. Slayton sells his interest to his brother-in-law, Joseph Soames, for $36,000.

2. Slayton retires voluntarily. His capital account is increased by $12,000, his share of the increase in the valuation of the building owned by the partnership. Slayton is paid from partnership cash.

3. Slayton dies following a long illness. An appraiser reports that the partnership assets are fairly valued and require no revaluation; furthermore, the partners do not wish to record any goodwill on the partnership books. On this basis, they settle with Slayton's estate for $38,000, payment being made from partnership cash. Use a bonus approach.

P15–7B *Thought-provoking problem: liquidation of a partnership*

On July 1, 1984, Laura Greene and Clara Mann formed a partnership. Greene invested land and building with values of $20,000 and $80,000, respectively; Mann invested cash of $40,000. Their attorney prepared a partnership agreement providing for an equal division of profits and losses. The two partners signed the agreement and prepared to take steps to order merchandise, supplies, and fixtures. Before they had a chance to place any orders, a fire destroyed the uninsured building completely. They had planned to wait and take out a comprehensive insurance policy after they had stocked their store. With this misfortune, they agreed to terminate the partnership. Greene said, "I claim the land and all the cash as my share of the liquidation." Mann replied, "Oh! No! I get back my cash of $40,000 and you get back your land."

Required:

1. Which partner is legally correct? Why?

2. Prepare a journal entry or entries to record the investment by Greene and Mann.

3. Prepare a journal entry or entries to record the fire loss and the liquidation of the partnership.

16 Corporations: Paid-In Capital

Introduction

The distinctive features of the accounting for owner's or owners' equity of single proprietorships and partnerships have already been discussed. The accounting for corporations is considered in this and the next chapter. The corporate form of business produces the vast majority of the revenue of all companies in the United States. Almost everyone is familiar with corporate giants such as American Telephone and Telegraph Company, General Motors, R. J. Reynolds Industries, and Burlington Industries. Most people, however, do not realize that even the corner grocery store is very likely to be incorporated today to limit the liability of its owners—a topic discussed in the next section.

Because so many organizations are organized as corporations, we should take a look at this point at the formation of a corporation, sources of corporate capital, the different classes of stock, the terms used to measure capital stock, and the recording of the issuance of capital stock.

Learning Goals

To understand the essential reasons for a group to use the corporate form of business organization.

To be aware of how corporations acquire funds.

To know the sources of paid-in capital of corporations.

To recognize and differentiate among classes of capital stock and their various value classifications.

To record the issuance of both common and preferred stock.

To account for stock subscriptions.

To understand the classifications of paid-in capital other than capital stock.

The Corporation as a Form of Business Organization

A **corporation** is a legal entity as well as an accounting entity. This means that, in the eyes of the law, a corporation is an artificial being. Hence, it has the powers and rights of and may act as a single individual. Acting through appropriately designated officials, a corporation may enter into contracts, sue or be sued in court, and carry on other activities of an individual in the business world. For this and other reasons, its income is subject to direct federal and state income taxes.

Deciding to Incorporate

When a group of people form a business, they must decide what type of business organization they should choose—corporation or partnership. The business group must consider a number of different issues.

Some Disadvantages of Incorporating The decision to incorporate depends upon balancing a number of disadvantages against advantages.

Difficulties of Incorporation Of the three types of business, the corporate form is the most difficult to establish. State laws require a group to apply to the state for a charter. In most states, at least three incorporators must be involved in applying to the secretary of state (or another designated state official) for a **charter.** This legal document is the copy of the articles of incorporation prepared by the incorporators, which is returned by the secretary of state with a certificate of incorporation. Routine and restricting provisions usually specified in a corporate charter are (1) the name of the corporation; (2) the type of business in which it is authorized to engage; (3) the duration of existence (usually perpetual unless specified otherwise); (4) the location of its principal office or place of business; and (5) the classes (or types) of shares of capital stock and the number of shares of each type that the corporation will be authorized to issue.

Costs of Incorporation A special incorporation fee is typically charged by the state in which the corporation is formed. Because of the legal complexities involved in starting a corporation, the incorporators usually hire an attorney. Another initial cost of incorporation is the design and printing of stock certificates. (All of these initial costs are recorded on the books of the new corporation after its incorporation as an intangible asset with the account title, **Organization Costs.**)

Taxation of Corporations Many feel that a disadvantage of most corporations is "double taxation" of their income.[1] First, as mentioned earlier, a corporation usually is taxed directly on its own corporate income. Then, except for an exclusion of the first $100 per individual, stockholders (also known as

[1]The Internal Revenue Code permits the taxation of income of certain closely-held corporations as partnerships; the net income is taxed to the stockholders whether it is distributed or not. "Double taxation" is not present in these cases.

shareholders) must again pay federal income tax on any portion of those earnings paid to them as dividends. Some states do not allow the $100 dividend exclusion in calculating state income tax.

Some Advantages of Incorporation If the decision is to incorporate, the advantages must outweigh the disadvantages.

Limited Liability For instance, since the corporation is a separate and distinct legal entity, it alone is liable to creditors; stockholders or shareholders are not personally liable for debts the corporation is unable to pay. If a corporation gets into serious financial difficulties, its shares of stock may become worthless. Even so, the personal assets of the owners who hold those shares are not legally available for satisfaction of corporate debts. This feature is called **limited liability.**

Other Significant Advantages of Incorporation Some additional advantages are the *ease of transferring ownership rights,* the *continuity of life,* and the *variety of ways to raise funds.* A stockholder has the right to sell his or her stock any time. A transfer of stock does not affect the life of the corporation or its operations. The life of the corporation is typically stated in the charter as being "perpetual," that is, forever. Even if the corporation's life is stated as being a specified number of years, the charter often may be renewed and that period extended. With the other advantages mentioned above and since the shares of ownership can be subdivided into minute parts, it is possible for a corporation to raise large amounts of capital from many different stockholders. Therefore the owners' equity of most corporations exceeds that of the other forms of business organization. If a decision is made to form a corporation, certain steps must then be taken to prepare it for operations.

Preparing the Corporation for Operations

Many corporations start off as small family or closely held corporations (with only a small group of stockholders), hoping to expand as business grows. Once this group receives the charter and certificate of incorporation, the capital stock (of one or more classes, discussed below) is issued. If the business is successful and does expand, it may then offer its stock to the general public.

The stockholders of a corporation elect directors to represent them in setting policies. In a new corporation, directors are likely to be stockholders of that corporation. These directors appoint officers—president, one or more vice presidents, secretary, treasurer, and other designated officers—to operate the new business as a corporation in conformity with the articles of incorporation. As a corporation expands and offers stock to the general public (referred to as "going public"), it often seeks individuals other than stockholders to be elected to its board of directors. These nonstockholder directors are called *outside directors.* These directors serve a "watchdog" purpose. They are often asked to serve on committees such as the audit committee that sets policies related to the audit process and the hiring of an independent auditing firm.

Now that the formation of the corporation has been briefly considered, the accounting issues peculiar to a corporation must be discussed. These issues primarily involve the accounting for the stockholders' equity. The stockholders' equity in a corporation comes from a number of sources. It is of the utmost importance that these sources be clearly identified and stated and that the terminology used to designate them be precise and meaningful. In the next section the various sources of stockholders' equity are indicated, followed by a description of the different classes of capital stock and the meaning and significance of terms used to measure capital stock.

Paid-in Capital

Sources of Capital

Operating transactions—revenue and expenses—are recorded in the same manner for all forms of business organization. Since the primary difference in the accounting for a corporation is in stockholders' equity, the chart of accounts for this business form must distinguish between investments by stockholders and the earnings retained (reinvested). This distinction is essential because most state laws normally allow only earnings to be distributed to the stockholders. Both for the protection of corporate creditors and for the continued operation of the business, amounts exceeding cumulative retained earnings usually cannot be legally distributed to the stockholders. Hence, separate accounts designating the several sources of stockholders' equity should be kept and clearly set forth in the stockholders' equity section of the corporate balance sheet. The various sources of paid-in capital are outlined in Figure 16–1. This chapter emphasizes the accounts used to record the capital paid in by stockholders. Retained earnings are dealt with more fully in Chapter 17.

Capital Stock

The charter granted by the state of incorporation authorizes the newly formed corporation to issue a designated number of shares of capital stock of one or more classes. The corporation usually secures authorization to issue sufficient shares of each class to allow enough sales in the present to acquire the investment desired and to hold back a substantial number of shares to issue for expansion of the business in the future. The total number of shares of any given class issued cannot exceed the number authorized.[2] Capital stock usually has an arbitrary dollar amount assigned per share called *par value*. Discussed in detail later, this amount is separated in the accounting records from all other invested capital.

[2]The owners of shares of stock are called stockholders or shareholders; the two terms mean the same thing.

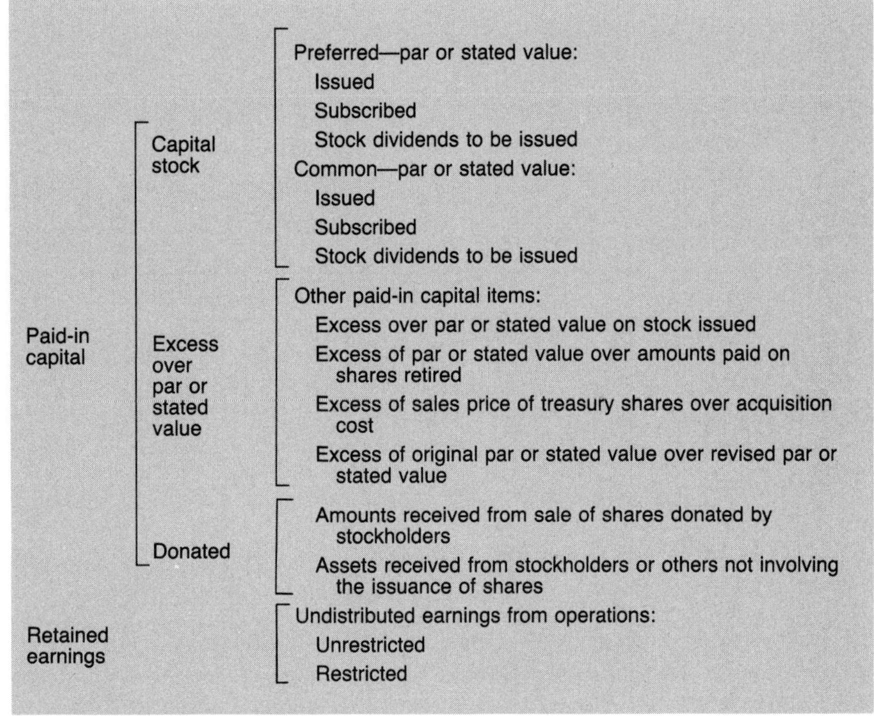

Figure 16–1 Sources of Stockholders' Equity

Detail with respect to the number of shares authorized is customarily included as part of the description in the stockholders' equity section of the balance sheet. The balance sheet presentation after the issuance of common stock may be as shown below:

Stockholders' equity:	
Paid-in capital:	
Common stock, $10 par value; authorized 10,000 shares, issued 5,000 shares	$50,000

Classes of Capital Stock **Capital stock** is usually issued in two classes—common and preferred. To help secure sales of additional capital stock, certain large corporations announce that stock is available for sale. The ad shown in Figure 16–2 (often referred to as a *tombstone ad* since the SEC restricts advertising) serves as an announcement that 1,800,000 common shares (plus certain warrants or options to buy other stock) are available for sale. This type of promotion is used to solicit interest in the future sale of capital stock. Stock certificates for both classes are serially numbered. Then these stock certificates (a common stock certificate of Dan River Inc. is shown in Figure 16–3) representing ownership in a corporation are issued to individuals or organizations who have obtained their shares of capital stock in ex-

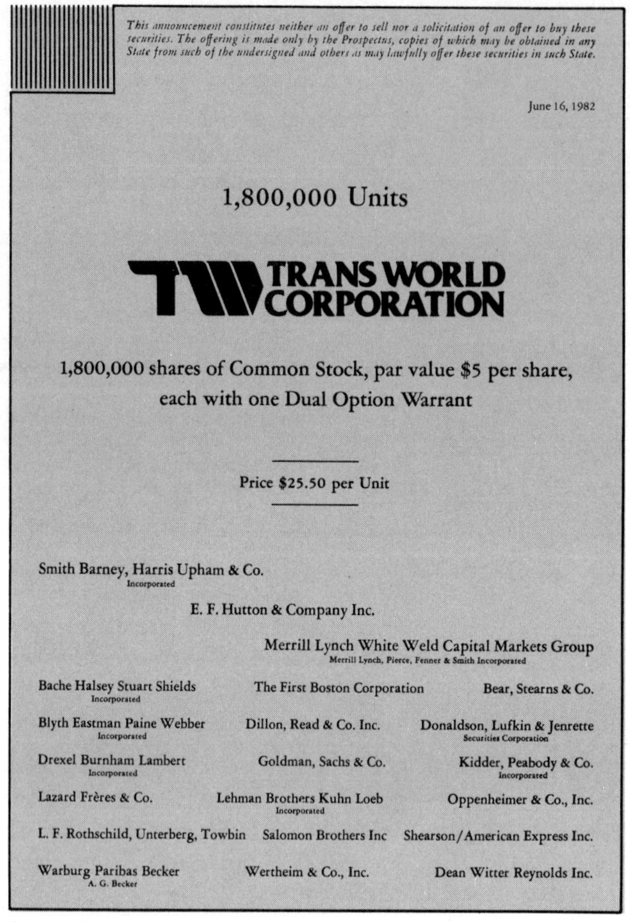

Figure 16–2 Announcement of Stock for Sale

Source: Reprinted by permission of Trans World Corporation.

change for funds invested in the company or for services rendered, or who have acquired shares from previous investors.

Preferred Stock **Preferred stock** represents a type of ownership with certain preferences. These preferences usually fall into two groups: (1) preference as to earnings—the dividend preference, and (2) preference as to assets in case of liquidation. The dividend preference may take several different forms depending upon how the preferred **stock indenture** (contract between the corporation and its preferred stockholders) is written. Preferred stock carries a stated dividend rate or amount of annual dividends per share. Most preferred stock is **cumulative;** that is, undeclared dividends accumulate. Accumulated undeclared preferred dividends are called an **arrearage.** Both the arrearage and the current dividend on preferred stock must be declared and paid by the corporation before any dividend payment is made on com-

Source: Reprinted with permission of Dan River Inc.

Figure 16–3 **A Stock Certificate**

mon stock.[3] Some preferred shares are issued with a stated rate or amount but without this dividend preference. These are called **noncumulative** preferred shares. On this type, if the dividend is not declared in a given period, it is lost to the stockholders.

The recording of dividends is discussed in detail in Chapter 17. However, to illustrate the meaning of cumulative preferred stock, the simplified example below shows the division of the *annual* amount available for dividends for both preferred and common shares.

Example—preferred stock is cumulative. To illustrate this preferred stock characteristic, assume that a corporation has outstanding 15 percent, cumulative preferred stock with a par value totaling $100,000 and common stock with a total par value of $200,000. There is a one year preferred dividend arrearage of $15,000 = (15% × $100,000). The board of directors decided

[3]A few types of preferred stock may be *participating* (in part or in full). This preference allows the preferred shareholders to share in the earnings (declared as dividends) in some manner beyond the stated dividend rate or amount. Since fully participating or partially participating preferred stock is a rarity, it is considered to be beyond the scope of this book.

that the *annual* amount available for dividends is $72,000. The calculation of the distribution of this annual amount between the two classes of shareholders is as follows:

Annual amount available for dividends	$72,000
To preferred shareholders:	
In arrears	$15,000
Current year's preference dividend (15% × $100,000)	15,000
Total to preferred shareholders	$30,000
To common shareholders:	
The remainder (being residual owners)	$42,000
Total that could be distributed	$72,000

The second type of preference applies to a corporation that is being liquidated. If, for example, a corporation is liquidated and all the creditors are paid in full, then the preferred shareholders who have a preference as to assets in liquidation must be paid before any liquidating payments are made to common shareholders. The manner of the preference application depends on the wording in the stock indenture. The preference may be for the par value of the preferred stock, the par value and accumulated unpaid dividends, or some other stipulated amount. If the preferred stock is not *preferred as to assets,* then the assets are usually distributed to all classes of shareholders on an equal basis proportionate to the respective par values.

Preferred stockholders, on the other hand, are often restricted to a specific dividend rate and do not, therefore, benefit from earnings above that rate. By the inclusion of a provision in the stock indenture, a preferred stockholder is usually denied the right to vote.

One of the reasons for issuing preferred stock is to provide the firm with long-term funds without increasing long-term liabilities or increasing the common stockholders' equity. Another reason is the ability to endow this class of stock with certain features that make it more salable. Thus, the corporation should be able to raise additional funds.

Common Stock If a corporation issues only *one* class of stock, then all shares are treated alike and called common stock. If there is more than one class, the class that does not have preferences and that shares only in the residual earnings or assets distribution is known as common stock. **Common stock,** therefore, represents the residual and proportionate ownership that *does* have voting privileges. In other words, common stock represents the part of ownership received in exchange for investment by voting shareholders. Their voting privilege is on the basis of one vote for each share of common stock held. These shareholders are often called residual owners because their dividends cannot be declared until the dividend rights of preferred shareholders are satisfied. They are the real controlling owners.

To repeat, because they hold the residual ownership stock, the common stockholders elect the members of the board of directors, who appoint the officers of the corporation. The officers execute the policies approved by the board of directors. In effect, the board of directors represents the stockholders in monitoring the activities of corporate management. The accounting for the issuance of both classes of capital stock is illustrated after certain key terms are defined and discussed.

Key Terms

Certain key terms are used to define and measure elements of stockholders' equity. These terms are *authorized capital stock, issued capital stock, treasury stock, outstanding capital stock, par value, no-par value, stated value, market value,* and *legal capital.*

The capital stock of one or more classes in terms of shares or par value granted by the charter is referred to as **authorized capital stock. Issued capital stock** refers to the number of shares of capital stock issued to stockholders and still considered to be part of legal capital (defined later). **Treasury stock** refers to the corporation's own capital stock issued and fully paid for, later reacquired by the corporation, but not normally canceled (discussed in Chapter 17).

Capital stock is outstanding when it remains in the hands of stockholders. **Outstanding capital stock** is the issued capital stock minus treasury stock. As explained in Chapter 17, treasury stock is still considered to be issued stock unless it is formally declared to be canceled by a resolution passed by the board of directors to cause the stock to be changed back to an unissued status.

Par value refers to a specific dollar amount per share, as set forth in the charter of the issuing corporation. It is printed on the stock certificate and generally *represents the minimum amount that must be paid to the issuing corporation* by the original purchaser of the stock. The par value of the common stock of Dan River Inc. is $5 (see Figure 16–3). Par value may be any amount set forth in the corporation's charter and is rarely an indication of what the stock is actually worth. Used as the basis for crediting the appropriate capital stock account on the corporate books, it is often established at a relatively low value with little or no economic significance.

Par value

Par value is the face amount of a share of stock as set forth in the charter of the issuing corporation; it is the amount credited to the appropriate capital stock account by the corporation to record the issue.

Because of the various difficulties involved with par value stock, such as a lack of understanding of its meaning at time of issuance and improper valuation of noncash assets received upon issuance, some companies issue stock without any par value written on the stock certificate. This kind of stock is referred to as **no-par value** capital stock. The entire proceeds from the issuance of no-par value stock (*without a stated value*—discussed below) is credited to the appropriate capital stock account. For capital stock without par value, the corporate directors may assign a value, the **stated value,** to each share. This amount, like par value, is the amount that is credited to the appropriate no-par capital stock account.

Stated value

For a stock without par value, the corporate directors may assign a value, the* stated value, *to each share.

Once assigned, a stated value is accounted for as if it were par value. However, it can be changed by the directors without approval of the chartering state; par value cannot.

The market value of stock is not determined by its par or stated value. The term **market value** indicates the actual price in dollars that a share of stock will bring at the time it is offered for sale. Market prices often change daily and can be determined for many stocks by reference to the stock market quotations in daily newspapers or to a financial magazine or financial service publication. Market value reflects economic and political factors and the feelings, hopes, and expectations of investors about the future growth and earning ability of a corporation.

Market value

***The actual price in dollars a share of stock will bring at the time it is offered for sale is called the* market value.**

The term **legal capital** (sometimes referred to as *stated capital*), contained in the laws of a number of states, places certain restrictions on the return of investment to the stockholders in order to protect creditors. The restriction limits the amount of assets that can be withdrawn by stockholders either as dividends or by other means so that sufficient funds should be left to satisfy creditors' claims. The creditors of a corporation do not have access to the personal resources of the stockholders; their only protection is in the corporate assets.

Legal capital

Legal capital *is the amount of capital that a statute requires must be left in the corporation for the protection of creditors because of the limited liability of stockholders. Consequently, creditors are assured that in the event of corporate losses the investors as a group will absorb the losses up to the amount of this capital.*

State laws vary considerably as to the method of determining and applying such restriction provisions. The accountant may require the assistance of an attorney on questions involving legal capital. In most states, legal capital is determined as follows:

1. On par value stock—the par value of all outstanding shares.
2. On no-par, stated value stock—the stated value of all outstanding shares.
3. On no-par, no stated value stock—the total proceeds from the issuance of all outstanding shares.

When, as is often the case, the par value is low in relation to the issue price, the legal capital will be much less than the total paid in by shareholders. In such a situation, legal capital is not a significant constraint on amounts to be distributed to stockholders, and the security of the creditors depends rather on the firm's operating and financial policies and resources.

Recording Capital Stock Transactions

Great care needs to be taken to record stock transactions in strict compliance with the corporate laws of the state of incorporation, keeping in mind the interests of stockholders and creditors and the statutory requirements regarding legal capital. Enough accounts should be created, especially those arising from invested capital, so that the stockholders' equity section shows in adequate detail the sources of corporate capital.

Two groups of illustrations are presented below: first, for a corporation that has only par value common stock authorized; then, for a corporation that has both common and preferred stock authorized.

Illustration Group A

On February 2, 1985, the Kheel Corporation, which is organized as a marine supply business, received its charter authorizing the issuance of 50,000 shares of common stock carrying a $10 par value.

Memorandum Entry to Record Charter Data The initial entry on a corporate set of books may be a simple memorandum narrative statement made in the general journal and the capital stock accounts. It notes certain basic data taken from the corporate charter, including the name of the corporation, the date of incorporation, the nature of the business, and the number and classes of shares authorized to be issued.

Example A–1, Common Stock Issued at Par for Cash On February 2, 1985, Kheel Corporation issued 10,000 shares of common stock at par value for cash. This transaction is recorded as follows (explanations to all of these journal entries are omitted):

1985					
Feb.	2	Cash		100,000	
		Common Stock			100,000

The Common Stock account represents a part of stockholders' equity. After stock has been issued to an investor, that individual may sell those shares to new owners. Such resales are not recorded in the accounting records. These transfers are private transactions between the buyers and sellers, but they are reported to the corporation for record-keeping purposes.[4] This information is needed by the corporation for determining the individual shareholder's dividend payment and the number of votes allowed at stockholders' meetings.

Example A–2, Common Stock Issued at Par for Cash and Noncash Assets On February 11, 1985, Kheel Corporation issued 9,000 shares for $40,000 in cash plus land and buildings having a fair cash value of $10,000 and $40,000, respectively. This transaction is recorded as follows:

[4]Most corporations use the services of agents—usually banks (referred to as *registrars*)—to maintain a current list of names and addresses of stockholders and to issue new certificates (for this latter function, the agent is referred to as a *transfer agent*).

1985					
Feb.	11	Cash		40,000	
		Land		10,000	
		Buildings		40,000	
		Common Stock			90,000

A key issue related to this transaction is that the accountant must make sure that the land and buildings are properly valued at current fair cash value. An error often made in the past was that the noncash assets were sometimes valued at the par amount of the common stock issued without any effort to determine a fair cash value.

Example A–3, Common Stock Issued for Organizing Services On March 4, 1985, the Kheel Corporation issued 1,000 shares of common stock to the organizers of the corporation in payment for their services billed at $10,000. This transaction is recorded as shown:

1985					
Mar.	4	Organization Costs		10,000	
		Common Stock			10,000

Organization costs are shown in the Kheel Corporation's balance sheet as an intangible asset.

After the above transactions, the stockholders' equity section of the Kheel Corporation balance sheet shows the following:

Stockholders' equity:
Paid-in capital:
Common stock, $10 par value; authorized 50,000 shares,
issued 20,000 shares $200,000

The asset and liability sections of the balance sheet are essentially the same regardless of the form of business organization. The only difference would be the inclusion of certain assets and liabilities that are peculiar to a particular organizational form. For example, in the foregoing A examples, one new asset account is present—Organization Costs. This account would be shown under the intangible assets section of the corporate balance sheet.

Example A–4, Common Stock Issued at a Premium for Cash On November 4, 1985, the Kheel Corporation issued 10,000 shares of common stock at $10.80 per share. The market price has changed since it depends on many factors such as the condition and reputation of the corporation and the availability of funds for investments. The entry to record this transaction is:

1985					
Nov.	4	Cash		108,000	
		Common Stock			100,000
		Paid-in Capital—Excess over Par Value, Common			8,000

The $8,000 **paid-in capital—excess over par value** is recorded in a separate paid-in capital account in order to establish the legal capital amount only in the Common Stock account. An alternative account title for this Paid-in Capital account is **Premium on Common Stock.** Both Common Stock and Paid-in Capital—Excess over Par Value, Common are paid-in capital investment items (see Figure 16–1); both are shown in the balance sheet under a stockholders' equity subsection, paid-in capital.

Immediately following the issuance of the 10,000 shares for $108,000, the stockholders' equity section of the balance sheet now appears as:[5]

Stockholders' equity:		
Paid-in capital:		
Common stock, $10 par value; authorized 50,000 shares, issued 30,000 shares	$300,000	
Paid-in capital—excess over par value, common	8,000	
Total paid-in capital		$308,000

Example A–5, Common Stock Subscribed The descriptions of stock issuance transactions in the previous examples were based on the assumption that the full payment for the stock was received and the stock certificates issued at once. Small or closely held corporations and often new banks sometimes sell and issue stock under a **stock subscription** plan. Pledges to buy the stock are taken first, and payment is made later in a lump sum or in installments. The stock certificates are *not* issued until completion of the payment.

On November 2, 1986, the Kheel Corporation received subscriptions for 10,000 shares of $10 par value common stock at $10.50 a share. Full payment was received on December 2, 1986, and the stock certificates were issued. The entries to record these transactions are:

1986					
Nov.	2	Subscriptions Receivable—Common		105,000	
		Common Stock Subscribed			100,000
		Paid-in Capital—Excess over Par Value, Common			5,000
Dec.	2	Cash		105,000	
		Subscriptions Receivable—Common			105,000
	2	Common Stock Subscribed		100,000	
		Common Stock			100,000

The Subscriptions Receivable—Common account is a current asset and shows the amount due on stock that has been subscribed but has not been fully paid for. The tentative nature of the ownership is indicated by the Common

[5]This method of disclosure of paid-in capital items is referred to as the "source of capital approach." Another variation, called the legal capital approach, is illustrated at the end of Chapter 17.

Stock Subscribed account, a temporary stockholders' equity account showing the par or stated value of subscribed stock (see Figure 16–1). Thus if a balance sheet were to be prepared between November 2 and December 2, the common stock subscribed item would be shown in the paid-in capital subsection of the stockholders' equity section immediately below the issued common stock. The excess of the issue price over par is typically credited to the permanent real account, Paid-in Capital—Excess over Par Value, Common, when the subscription is received.

Capital Stock Issued at a Discount

In most states, par value stock cannot be issued at a discount. If the state law permits the issuance at less than par value, the amount of the discount (recorded in the Discount on Capital Stock account) becomes a contingent liability to the investor. This contingent liability is passed to future holders of the shares. Since issuance at a discount is extremely rare, it is not illustrated here.

Illustration Group B

On March 1, 1985, the Village Corporation, which is authorized to operate a television cable company, received its charter authorizing the issuance of 100,000 no-par value common shares and 30,000, $10 par value, 15 percent preferred shares (15 percent is the annual dividend rate based on par value). Again, the initial entry may be a simple memorandum narrative statement made in the journal and capital stock accounts setting forth the basic data contained in the corporate charter. The following three examples illustrate the accounting in this more complex illustration.

Example B–1, Preferred Stock Issued at a Premium On March 5, 1985, the Village Corporation issued 10,000 shares of preferred stock at $11 per share for cash. The entry to record the issuance is:[6]

1985					
Mar.	5	Cash		110,000	
		Preferred Stock			100,000
		Paid-in Capital—Excess over Par Value, Preferred			10,000

The accounting for the issuance of par value preferred stock is the same as that for common stock, except that the names of the two accounts credited contain the description *preferred.* Both of these items are paid-in capital.

[6]Technically, a corporation would issue common stock before it would issue preferred stock. In the first two B group illustrations, preferred and common are issued on the same day. The issuance of the preferred stock is discussed first to show the similarity to the accounting for par value common stock.

Example B–2, No-par Common Stock Issued for Cash On March 5, 1985, the Village Corporation issued for cash 10,000 shares of its no-par common stock at $6 per share.

Assumption 1. As stated previously, no-par stock may be "pure" no-par, that is, it has no stated value (the entire proceeds in this case become the legal capital), or the board of directors may be authorized to set a stated value per share for the no-par stock. In the latter case, the stock is handled like par value stock. Assume here that the no-par stock has no stated value. Then the entry to record the issuance is:

1985					
Mar.	5	Cash		60,000	
		Common Stock			60,000

Assumption 2. The board of directors of the Village Corporation had set a stated value of $5 for each share of no-par common stock. The entry then would be:

1985					
Mar.	5	Cash		60,000	
		Common Stock			50,000
		Paid-in Capital—Excess over Stated Value, Common			10,000

The stated value amount typically becomes the legal capital and hence is the amount that is credited to Common Stock. Both of the foregoing credit items are shown in the paid-in capital section of stockholders' equity.

Example B–3, No-par Common Stock Subscribed On April 1, 1985, the Village Corporation received subscriptions for 10,000 shares of no-par common stock at $6.50 per share. Full payment was received on May 1, 1985, and the stock certificates were issued.

Assumption 1. If the no-par common stock has no stated value, these transactions are recorded as follows:

1985					
Apr.	1	Subscriptions Receivable—Common . . .		65,000	
		Common Stock Subscribed			65,000
May	1	Cash		65,000	
		Subscriptions Receivable—Common. .			65,000
	1	Common Stock Subscribed		65,000	
		Common Stock			65,000

Assumption 2. If the no-par common stock has a stated value of $5 per share, the transactions are recorded as follows:

Date		Account			Debit	Credit
1985						
Apr.	1	Subscriptions Receivable—Common			65,000	
		Common Stock Subscribed				50,000
		Paid-in Capital—Excess over Stated Value, Common				15,000
May	1	Cash			65,000	
		Subscriptions Receivable—Common				65,000
	1	Common Stock Subscribed			50,000	
		Common Stock				50,000

Donations

Cities, towns, and sometimes local organizations may donate land, buildings, and other facilities to entice a corporation to establish itself in the area. Sometimes donations of assets are made by the stockholders of a company in financial difficulty to enable it to raise funds. A gift or donation to a corporation increases the assets and the stockholders' equity and is credited to **Paid-in Capital—Donations.** A contribution of land and buildings by a town to a newly established firm is recorded by the receiving corporation at the fair market value of the assets contributed. To illustrate, assume that on October 4, 1985, Orange Village donated land (valued at $30,000) and buildings (valued at $70,000) to the Village Corporation for it to locate in Orange Village. The entry on the Village Corporation books is:

Date		Account			Debit	Credit
1985						
Oct.	4	Land			30,000	
		Buildings			70,000	
		Paid-in Capital—Donations				100,000
		To record, at fair market value, the land and buildings contributed by the town of Orange Village.				

Disclosure of Paid-in Capital on the Balance Sheet

Now that the key elements of paid-in capital have been discussed, the way they are disclosed on the balance sheet are illustrated. Once the journal entries involving the issuance of capital stock of the Village Corporation (used in Illustration Group B with the Assumption 2 for the no-par common stock) are posted, as of October 5, 1985, the paid-in capital items will be:

Preferred stock ($10 par value; authorized 30,000 shares, issued 10,000 shares)	$100,000
Paid-in capital—excess over par value, preferred	10,000
Common stock (no-par value with a stated value of $5 per share; authorized 100,000 shares, issued 20,000 shares)	100,000
Paid-in capital—excess over stated value, common	25,000
Paid-in capital—donations	100,000

Should a balance sheet be prepared on October 5, 1985, the paid-in capital would be disclosed by the Village Corporation as follows:

VILLAGE CORPORATION
Partial Balance Sheet
October 5, 1985

Exhibit C

Stockholders' equity:		
Paid-in capital:		
15% Preferred stock, $10 par value; authorized 30,000 shares, issued 10,000 shares	$100,000	
Paid-in capital—excess over par value, preferred	10,000	
Total capital paid in by preferred stockholders		$110,000
Common stock, no-par value, stated value established at $5 per share; authorized 100,000 shares, issued 20,000 shares	$100,000	
Paid-in capital—excess over stated value, common	25,000	
Total capital paid in by common stockholders		125,000
Other paid-in capital:		
Paid-in capital—donation of land and building by Orange Village		100,000
Total paid-in capital		$335,000

This method of disclosing the paid-in capital sources is referred to as the *source of capital approach.* Another variation (the legal capital approach) of disclosure of paid-in capital is discussed in Chapter 17, where a complete stockholders' equity section of a balance sheet is illustrated.

Glossary

Arrearage Accumulated undeclared preferred dividends.

Authorized capital stock Shares of capital stock granted by the charter.

Capital stock Shares representing fractional elements of ownership of a corporation; usually of two classes, preferred and common.

Charter The legal document issued by a state which includes the articles of incorporation and certificate of incorporation.

Common stock The residual class of ownership if more than one class of stock is issued; if only one class, then all shares are treated alike, and that stock is called common stock.

Corporation A form of business which is a legal entity as well as an accounting entity.

Cumulative preferred stock The class of preferred stock on which undeclared dividends are accumulated and must be paid together with the current dividends before any dividend payment can be made on common stock.

Directors Elected representatives of the stockholders who establish policies for the corporation.

Indenture to capital stock The corporate contractual agreement setting forth the rights and privileges of the holders of the capital stock.

Issued capital stock The capital stock issued and not reacquired and canceled by the corporation.

Legal capital The minimum amount of capital that state law requires to be left in the corporation for the protection of creditors and which cannot be withdrawn by the stockholders.

Limited liability A legal concept which does not allow the creditors of a corporation to hold the stockholders personally liable for the debts of the corporation.

Market value The amount that a share of stock will bring the seller if the stock is offered for sale.

Noncumulative preferred stock A class of preferred stock on which a dividend not declared (passed) in any one year is lost.

No-par value stock Stock without an indicated par value.

Organization Costs An intangible asset account that is debited for the initial cost of forming a corporation. These costs include incorporation fees, legal costs, and other similar costs.

Outstanding capital stock Capital stock still in the hands of the shareholders and not in the treasury of the corporation; it is issued capital stock minus any treasury stock of a given class.

Paid-in capital—donations A gift or donation to a corporation which increases the assets and the stockholders' equity.

Paid-in capital—excess over par value That part of capital paid in by stockholders that is not credited to the capital stock accounts and is usually not a part of legal capital.

Paid-in capital—excess over stated value See *Paid-in capital—excess over par value.*

Par value The nominal or face value printed on a stock certificate, representing the minimum amount to be paid to the issuing corporation by the original purchaser.

Preferred stock A class of capital stock having various preferences, two of which are preference as to dividends and preference as to assets in liquidation.

Premium on capital stock Another term for *paid-in capital—excess over par value.*

Stated value A value assigned to each share of no-par value stock by the directors of the corporation.

Stock subscription A pledge to buy capital stock with payment to be made later in a single lump sum or in installments.

Treasury stock A corporation's own capital stock issued and fully paid for, and later reacquired by the corporation.

Questions

Q16–1 What factors should a business group consider in determining whether to incorporate or not?

Q16–2 Differentiate between the following terms: common stock and preferred stock; par value and stated value; market value and no-par value.

Q16–3 What is the meaning of the following: limited liability, excess over par value, excess over stated value, paid-in capital, stock subscription?

Q16–4 What are at least four unique characteristics of the corporate form of business organization?

Q16–5 What is the legal responsibility of the owner of a majority of the stock of a corporation to pay its debts if the corporation gets into financial difficulties?

Q16–6 What is the meaning of *legal entity?* How does it differ from *accounting entity?*

Q16–7 Does a corporation earn revenue by selling its stock at a figure in excess of par value?

Q16–8 What is the meaning of no-par value? What are some reasons for a firm to seek authorization to issue no-par stock?

Q16–9 What are the balance sheet classifications of: (a) Subscriptions Receivable, (b) Common Stock Subscribed, (c) Organization Costs, and (d) Paid-in Capital—Excess over Par Value, Common?

Q16–10 Emery Air Freight Corporation at the end of 1981 had issued 15,840,613 shares of its authorized 20,000,000 shares of $0.20 par value common stock. Why do you think the par value was set so low?

Q16–11 In which form of business organization is ownership most readily transferable? Explain why.

Q16–12 Distinguish between "authorized and unissued stock" and "issued and outstanding stock."

Q16–13 Student A says that if she were buying stock, she would purchase only stock having a par value. Student B prefers no-par stock. Discuss.

Q16–14 What is legal capital? How is it determined? How does it differ from paid-in capital?

Q16–15 Student A says that Subscriptions Receivable is a current asset account. Student B argues that the account belongs in the stockholders' equity section. Discuss.

Exercises

E16–1
Recording common stock transactions

The Slavon Corporation was authorized to issue 10,000 shares of common stock. Record in general journal form the issue of 6,000 shares for cash at $7.25 a share on January 7, 1985, assuming:

1. That the shares have a $5 par value.

2. That the shares have no par and no stated value.

3. That the shares have no par value but have a stated value of $3.

E16–2
Recording par value common stock

The Lopez Corporation, organized on August 31, 1985, was authorized to issue 150,000 shares of $5 par value common stock.

1985	
Sep. 2	Issued 1,000 shares to an attorney for services valued at $5,000 in organizing the corporation.
25	Issued for cash 30,000 shares at $8 a share.
Nov. 11	Issued for cash 20,000 shares at $8.50 a share.

Record the transactions in general journal form.

E16–3
Issuing common stock for cash and noncash items

The County Computer Corporation is authorized to issue 500,000 shares of $5 par value common stock. The following transactions occurred in sequence:

1. Issued for cash 6,000 shares at par value.
2. Issued 2,000 shares to the promoters for services valued at $10,000 in organizing the corporation.
3. Issued 2,000 shares to attorneys for services valued at $10,000 in organizing the corporation and securing the corporate charter.
4. Issued 36,000 shares in exchange for a factory building and land valued at $170,400 and $24,000, respectively.
5. Issued for cash 30,000 shares at $5.50 a share.
6. Issued for cash 60,000 shares at $6 a share.

Record the transactions in general journal form using transaction numbers instead of dates.

E16–4 *Recording common and preferred stock subscriptions*

The World Finance Corporation received its charter on September 2, 1985, authorizing the issuance of 10,000 shares of $50 par value, 16 percent preferred stock and 100,000 shares of no-par common stock. No stated value was assigned to the no-par common stock. The following transactions took place in September and October:

1985	
Sep. 4	Issued 10,000 shares of the common stock at $12 per share for cash.
6	Issued 2,000 shares of the preferred stock at par for cash.
16	Received subscriptions for 1,000 preferred shares at $52 per share; no down payment was received.
20	Received subscriptions for 5,000 common shares at $12.50 per share; no down payment was received.
Oct. 15	Collected amount due from preferred subscribers and issued the 1,000 preferred shares.
21	Collected amount due from common subscribers and issued the 5,000 common shares.

Record the foregoing transactions in general journal form.

E16–5 *Preparing paid-in capital section of balance sheet*

On December 31, 1985, the ledger of the Rex Electronics Company included, among others, the following accounts:

Notes Receivable	$ 24,000
Merchandise Inventory	85,000
Temporary Investments—U.S. Treasury Certificates	18,000
Common Stock ($10 par value)	400,000
Subscriptions Receivable—Common Stock	40,000
Preferred Stock ($100 par value)	300,000
Goodwill	30,000
Common Stock Subscribed	175,000
Organization Costs	20,000
Paid-in Capital—Excess over Par Value, Preferred Stock	12,000
Building	225,000
Paid-in Capital—Excess over Par Value, Common Stock	45,000
Notes Receivable Discounted	7,000
Cash	90,000

Prepare the paid-in capital portion of the stockholders' equity section of the balance sheet as of December 31, 1985.

E16–6 *Issuing common stock for non-cash assets*

The Monroe Corporation acquired the equipment of the Rowan Company in exchange for 44,000 shares of Monroe $25 par value common stock. On the books of Monroe Corporation, record the acquisition in general journal form assuming that if the assets had been acquired for cash, the purchase price would have been (a) $1,150,000; (b) $1,100,000.

E16–7 *Recording donated assets*

The Hill Corporation entered into an agreement with the town of Carrboro to build a plant there. The town donated land and buildings valued at $30,000 and $150,000, respectively, on September 9, 1985. Record the transaction in general journal form.

E16–8 *Recording common stock transactions and donation of assets*

The Tri-County Sales Corporation received its charter on August 7, 1985, authorizing the issuance of 100,000 shares of $10 par value common stock. The following transactions took place during August:

1985

Aug.	7	Issued 10,000 shares of common stock at $15 per share for cash.
	15	The County of Cork donated land worth $60,000 to the new corporation for locating on its border.
	20	Issued 1,000 shares to incorporators as reimbursement for their expenses of $16,000 to form the corporation.

Record the foregoing transactions in general journal form.

E16–9
Various common and preferred stock issues

The Ruplkin Corporation was authorized to issue 40,000 shares of no-par value common stock and 10,000 shares of $20 par value preferred stock. Organizers of the corporation received 3,000 shares of the no-par common stock for services valued at $15,000. A total of 3,000 shares of the preferred stock was issued for cash at $22 a share, and 3,000 shares of common stock were issued for cash at $6 a share. A total of 5,000 shares of preferred stock was subscribed at $23 a share. Subscriptions to 2,500 preferred shares of stock were paid in full; these shares were issued. The subscribers to the other preferred shares made no payments.

1. Record the transactions in ledger accounts. Designate the transactions as a, b, c, etc.—then use these letters instead of dates.

2. Prepare a balance sheet (assume a date of July 10, 1985).

E16–10
Calculating the cash collections from stock transactions

The Malchman Corporation was authorized to issue 80,000 shares of no-par value common stock with a $20 stated value and 20,000 shares of 15 percent preferred stock, $100 par value. At the end of the first year of operations, the Malchman Corporation's trial balance included the following account balances:

Preferred Stock	$1,420,000
Common Stock	880,000
Subscriptions Receivable—Common	212,000
Subscriptions Receivable—Preferred	550,000
Preferred Stock Subscribed	660,000
Common Stock Subscribed	330,000
Paid-in Capital—Excess over Par Value, Common	154,000

How much cash has been collected from the stock transactions?

A Problems

P16–1A
Recording stockholders' common stock transactions and preparing a paid-in capital portion of the balance sheet

Thurman Industries, Inc., was organized on January 2, 1985, with authority to issue 200,000 shares of $10 par value common stock. The following transactions occurred during the year:

1985

Jan.	4	Issued for cash 1,000 shares at par value.
Mar.	18	Issued for cash 2,500 shares at $12 per share.
Apr.	1	Issued 20,000 shares for land and building with a fair market value of $280,000. One-eighth of the total valuation was allocable to the land.
	10	Paid $5,000 in cash for legal fees incurred in organizing the corporation.
Jul.	5	Purchased equipment for $60,000 in cash.
Dec.	16	Issued 10,000 shares for cash at $15.50 a share.

Required:

1. Record the transactions in general journal form.

2. Prepare the paid-in capital portion of the stockholders' equity section of the balance sheet as of December 31, 1985.

P16–2A *Recording capital stock transactions and preparing a paid-in capital portion of balance sheet*

The following selected transactions occurred at the newly formed Jordan Corporation:

1985

Jul. 1 Received a charter authorizing the issuance of 10,000 shares of $50 par value preferred stock and 100,000 shares of $5 par value common stock.
5 Issued for cash 25,000 shares of common stock at $10 per share.
5 Issued 500 shares of common stock to an incorporator for a patent that he had perfected valued at $5,000.
8 Received subscriptions from four investors for 250 shares each of preferred stock at $52.50 per share.
8 Received 60 percent down payments on the subscriptions from all four subscribers.
19 Received payment in full from three of the preferred subscribers and issued the stock.
29 Received payment in full from the fourth preferred subscriber and issued the stock.
Aug. 9 Purchased the following assets, shown at their fair market value, from Sanford Jones, who had been operating a single proprietorship in a similar business:

Land	$10,000
Building	40,000
Equipment	25,000

The Jordan Corporation would assume an outstanding $20,000 mortgage note payable on the building in addition to $500 representing two months' accrued interest. Jones agreed to accept common stock at $10 per share as payment for his net equity in the assets.
30 Issued common stock at $11 per share for equipment valued at $33,000.

Required:

1. Journalize the transactions in general journal form.

2. Post the transactions to appropriate ledger accounts.

3. Prepare the paid-in capital portion of the stockholders' equity section of the Jordan Corporation balance sheet as of August 31, 1985.

P16–3A *Recording various capital stock transactions and preparing a paid-in capital portion of balance sheet*

The paid-in capital portion of the stockholders' equity section of the Islands Import Company on July 1, 1985, was as follows:

Stockholders' equity:	
Paid-in capital:	
Preferred stock, $50 par value	$250,000
Paid-in capital—excess over par value, preferred stock	40,000
Common stock, $10 par value	300,000
Paid-in capital—excess over par value, common stock	25,000
Paid-in capital from warehouse donated by stockholder	50,000
Total paid-in capital	$665,000

The following transactions occurred during the next three months:

1985

Jul. 1 Issued for cash 1,000 shares of preferred stock at $52 a share.
1 Issued for cash 5,000 shares of common stock at $26 a share.
19 Issued for cash 8,000 shares of common stock at $27 a share.
Aug. 1 Issued for cash 12,000 shares of preferred stock at $52 a share.
2 Issued 100 shares of preferred stock in payment for a patent valued at $5,100.
Sep. 16 Issued 2,000 shares of common stock in exchange for land and a building appraised at $23,000 and $33,000, respectively.

Required:

1. Open ledger accounts for the stockholders' equity items; enter the balances from the partial stockholders' equity section.

2. Journalize the foregoing transactions.

3. Post the journal entries to the stockholders' equity accounts only.

4. Prepare the paid-in capital portion of the stockholders' equity section of the balance sheet as of September 30, 1985.

P16–4A *Preparing a stockholders' equity section of balance sheet*

On December 31, 1985, the ledger of the Cobb Corporation included the following accounts:

Land	$ 40,000
Notes Receivable	40,000
Merchandise Inventory	160,000
Temporary Investments—U.S. Treasury Notes	34,000
Common Stock, $10 par value	600,000
Retained Earnings	200,000
Subscriptions Receivable—Common Stock	80,000
Preferred Stock, $25 par value	300,000
Patents	10,000
Common Stock Subscribed	225,000
Organization Costs	10,000
Paid-in Capital—Excess over Par Value, Common Stock	20,000
Building	300,000
Paid-in Capital—Excess over Par Value, Preferred Stock	60,000
Paid-in Capital—Donation of Land by Town of Exeter	40,000

Required: Select the proper items and prepare the stockholders' equity section of the Cobb Corporation balance sheet as of December 31, 1985.

P16–5A *Recording capital stock transactions with specified subscribers*

The following selected transactions occurred at the newly formed Magnet Corporation:

1985

Mar. 1 Received a charter authorizing the issuance of 20,000 shares of $10 par value preferred stock and 1,000,000 shares of $1 par value common stock.

2 Received subscriptions for preferred stock at $12 per share from the following subscribers:

Samuel Tuten	2,000 shares
James Hassell	4,000

2 Received subscriptions for common stock at $3 per share from the following subscribers:

Earl Deal	4,000 shares
Eugene Motsinger	6,000
Randolph Owens	3,800
Thomas Peters	8,000

29 Tuten and Hassell paid 50 percent of their subscriptions.

29 Deal paid 100 percent of his subscription; Motsinger, Owens, and Peters paid 40 percent. The stock subscribed by Deal was issued.

Apr. 30 Tuten and Hassell paid the remaining amount owed on their stock subscriptions; their subscribed stock was issued.

30 Motsinger and Owens paid the remaining amount owed on their stock subscriptions; their subscribed stock was issued.

30 Peters informed the officials of the corporation that he would be unable to pay the balance of his subscription contract. Both parties agreed that 3,200 common shares would be issued to Peters and that the remaining account balances would be reversed and that the balance of the subscriptions would be cancelled.

Required:

1. Prepare journal entries to record the foregoing transactions.

2. Prepare a paid-in capital portion of the balance sheet of Magnet Corporation.

P16–6A *Thought-provoking problem: decision on form of organization*

William Triton, a professor of chemistry in a local university, had a hobby of working with engines of automobiles. He invented an automobile engine that he felt would yield about 200 miles to a gallon of gasoline for a small vehicle. He spent six months making a three-wheel automobile into which he inserted his specially built engine. Triton named the automobile the Triton Tricar. Upon testing the vehicle, he found that it in fact did produce slightly over 200 miles to a gallon of gasoline. Triton applied for a patent on his invention and received it. He was undecided whether to sell the patent to one of the "Big Three" automobile makers or whether to go into business for himself. He had about $100,000 he could make available as capital. He considered that he would need $400,000 more to start a limited production of the Triton Tricar. To see whether he might be able to go into business, Triton approached two other professor friends, a professor of marketing and a professor of engineering. They became excited about the potential of the Triton Tricar. These two agreed to put up $300,000 and to help in the management of the new business. Triton said that he would transfer the patent and invest his $100,000 in the business. More capital, at least $100,000, was necessary to organize, to launch an area marketing campaign, and to equip a factory to start production of the Triton Tricar.

The three promoters decided to seek additional capital from borrowing and to hire a professional staff to build and market the Triton Tricar, but they did not agree as to the form of organization for the new business.

Required:

1. Would you recommend that these three people form a partnership or a corporation for this business?

2. Write a report to these three justifying your recommendation. If you recommend a partnership, include in your report techniques for raising capital. If you recommend incorporation, include in your report a discussion of (a) types of stock to be issued, (b) par value, (c) number of shares, and (d) initial issue price.

B Problem

P16–1B *Recording common stock transactions and preparing a paid-in capital portion of balance sheet*

Rushmoor Industries, Inc., was organized on January 2, 1985, with authority to issue 300,000 shares of $5 par value common stock. The following transactions occurred during the year:

1985	
Jan. 10	Issued for cash 4,000 shares at $5.50 per share.
Feb. 18	Issued for cash 2,500 shares at $7 per share.
Mar. 1	Issued 40,000 shares for land and a building with a fair market value of $320,000. One-eighth of the total valuation was allocable to the land.
11	Issued 600 shares for reimbursement of $4,950 for legal fees incurred in organizing the corporation.
Jul. 5	Purchased equipment for $60,000 in cash.
Dec. 16	Issued 15,000 shares for cash at $8.50 a share.

Required:

1. Record the transactions in general journal form.

2. Prepare the paid-in capital portion of the stockholders' equity section of the balance sheet.

P16–2B

Recording capital stock transactions and preparing a paid-in capital portion of balance sheet

The following selected transactions occurred at the newly formed Franko Corporation:

1985

Aug. 1 Received a charter authorizing the issuance of 8,000 shares of $25 par value preferred stock and 100,000 shares of $5 par value common stock.

5 Issued for cash 30,000 shares of common stock at $8 per share.

5 Issued 800 shares of common stock to an incorporator for a patent that he had perfected valued at $6,400.

6 Received subscriptions from four investors for 300 shares each of preferred stock at $30 per share.

6 Received 50 percent down payments on the subscriptions from all four subscribers.

20 Received payment in full from three of the preferred subscribers and issued the stock.

29 Received payment in full from the fourth preferred subscriber and issued the stock.

Sep. 10 Purchased the following assets, shown at their fair market value, from Daisy Fox, who had been operating a single proprietorship in the same business:

Land	$ 8,100
Building	45,000
Equipment	30,000

The Franko Corporation would assume an outstanding $25,000, 12 percent mortgage note payable on the building in addition to two months' accrued interest. Fox agreed to accept common stock at $8 a share as payment for her net equity in the assets.

30 Issued common stock at $8 a share for equipment valued at $40,000.

Required:

1. Journalize the transactions in general journal form.

2. Post the transactions to appropriate ledger accounts.

3. Prepare the stockholders' equity section of the Franko Corporation's balance sheet as of September 30, 1985.

P16–3B

Recording various stock transactions and preparing a paid-in capital portion of balance sheet

The paid-in capital portion of the stockholders' equity section of the Texarca Import Company on August 1, 1985, was as follows:

Stockholders' equity:	
Paid-in capital:	
Preferred stock, $30 par value	$126,000
Paid-in capital—excess over par value, preferred stock	19,000
Common stock, $10 par value	150,000
Paid-in capital—excess over par value, common stock	12,500
Paid-in capital from warehouse donated by stockholder	25,000
Total paid-in capital	$332,500

The following transactions occurred during the next three months:

1985

Aug. 1 Issued for cash 2,000 shares of preferred stock at $32 a share.

12 Issued for cash 7,500 shares of common stock at $14 a share.

20 Issued for cash 10,000 shares of common stock at $16 a share.

Sep. 2 Issued for cash 6,000 shares of preferred stock at $33 a share.

2 Issued 200 shares of preferred stock in payment for a patent valued at $6,600.

Oct. 15 Issued 3,500 shares of common stock in exchange for land and a building appraised at $18,000 and $41,500, respectively.

Required:

1. Open ledger accounts for the stockholders' equity items; enter the balances from the partial stockholders' equity section.

2. Journalize the foregoing transactions.

3. Post the journal entries to the stockholders' equity accounts only.

4. Prepare the paid-in capital portion of the stockholders' equity section of the balance sheet as of October 31, 1985.

P16–4B *Preparing a stockholders' equity section of a balance sheet*

On December 31, 1985, the ledger of the Charles River Corporation included the following accounts (in scrambled order):

Accounts Receivable	$ 35,000
Merchandise Inventory	115,000
Temporary Investments—U.S. Treasury Notes	80,000
Land	42,500
Common Stock, $5 par value	800,000
Retained Earnings	165,000
Subscriptions Receivable, Common Stock	75,000
Preferred Stock, $50 par value	250,000
Franchises	25,000
Common Stock Subscribed	200,000
Organization Costs	20,000
Paid-in Capital—Excess over Par Value, Common Stock	85,000
Paid-in Capital—Excess over Par Value, Preferred Stock	90,000
Paid-in Capital—Donation of Land by City of Squares	42,500

Required: Select the proper items and prepare the stockholders' equity section of the Charles River Corporation's balance sheet as of December 31, 1985.

P16–5B *Recording capital stock transactions with specified subscribers*

The following selected transactions occurred at the newly formed Oakley Corporation:

1985

Oct. 1 Received a charter authorizing the issuance of 30,000 shares of $5 par value preferred stock and 750,000 shares of $2 par value common stock.

2 Received subscriptions for preferred stock at $8 per share from the following subscribers:

Henry Holton	5,000 shares
Philip Bolton	6,000
Sampson Dullard	4,000

2 Received subscriptions for common stock at $4 per share from the following subscribers:

Burl Davis	100,000 shares
Johnson Taylor	150,000

30 Holton, Bolton, and Dullard paid 60 percent of their subscriptions.

31 Davis paid 100 percent of his subscription; and Taylor paid 30 percent. The stock subscribed by Davis was issued.

Nov. 29 Holton and Bolton paid the remaining amount due on their stock subscriptions; their subscribed stock was issued.

29 Dullard informed the officials of the corporation that he was unable to pay the balance of his subscription contract. Both parties agreed that 2,400 = (60% × 4,000) preferred shares would be issued to Dullard, and that the remaining account balances would be reversed and the balance of the subscriptions; would be cancelled.

29 Taylor paid the remaining amount due on his stock; his subscribed stock was issued.

Required:

1. Prepare journal entries to record the foregoing transactions.
2. Prepare a paid-in capital portion of the balance sheet of Oakley Corporation.

P16–6B

Thought-provoking problem: decision involving par and no-par value stock

The 1985 annual report of Alton Company includes the following note to its financial statements:

During the year the stockholders and the secretary of state approved a change in the authorized capital stock of the company from 15,000 shares, $100 par value preferred stock to 500,000 shares, no-par value preferred, and from 2,000,000 shares, $1 par value common stock to 3,000,000 shares, $1 par value common stock.

Required:

1. What was the effect of these changes on the company's financial statements?
2. What was the purpose of the changes?
3. What other alternative could you suggest to accomplish this purpose?

17 Corporations: Retained Earnings, Dividends, Treasury Stock, and Other Equity Issues

Introduction

This chapter completes the discussion of corporate equity. It opens with a discussion of the sources and management of retained earnings, which constitute a significant percentage of total stockholders' equity for many companies. In Consolidated Freightways, Inc., for example, retained earnings at the end of a recent year represented 84.5 percent = ($395,720,000 ÷ $468,148,000) of stockholders' equity. Next follows a discussion of dividends, treasury stock, and other equity issues. Included are: (1) the meanings and computation of book value, (2) the meaning and simple computation of earnings per share, and (3) a complete stockholders' equity section of the balance sheet under two different variations.

Learning Goals

To understand the nature of retained earnings.

To make entries restricting retained earnings for various purposes.

To record transactions involving asset dividends, particularly cash dividends.

To record transactions involving both large and small stock dividends.

To understand and account for stock splits.

To record treasury stock transactions.

To compute book value of a share of stock.

To understand the importance of earnings per share.

Retained Earnings

Undistributed earnings arising from profitable operations are known as **retained earnings.** Retained earnings are total net income of past years minus total net losses and dividends declared during those years. These are sources of stockholders' equity other than paid-in capital. Such terms as *earned surplus, retained income, accumulated earnings,* and *earnings retained for use in the business* are alternative terms for earnings that have not been distributed to the stockholders as dividends. If cumulative losses and dividend distributions exceed earnings, the Retained Earnings account will have a debit balance and will be shown in the balance sheet as a deduction in the stockholders' equity section as a **deficit.**

The primary factors that affect retained earnings are discussed below. They include:

1. Net income or net loss.
2. Restrictions of retained earnings.
3. Prior period adjustments.
4. Dividends.

In addition, a parallel item to stock dividends, the stock split, is discussed in this section.

Net Income and Net Loss

It is important to note how the results of operations are recorded in the accounts of a corporation.

Example 1—Net Income

For the first example, suppose that all the 1985 revenues and expenses of Spirit Corporation have been closed to Income Summary. This account shows a credit balance of $106,500, which represents a net income for 1985. The entry to close this net income to Retained Earnings is:

1985					
Dec.	31	Income Summary		106,500	
		Retained Earnings			106,500
		To close net income to Retained Earnings.			

The credit to Retained Earnings would increase it by $106,500.

Example 2—Net Loss

For the next example, suppose that all the 1985 revenues and expenses of Truro Corporation have been closed to Income Summary. This account now shows a debit balance of $72,400, which represents a net loss for 1985. The entry to close this net loss to Retained Earnings is:

1985					
Dec.	31	Retained Earnings		72,400	
		Income Summary			72,400
		To close net loss to Retained Earnings.			

The debit to Retained Earnings would decrease it by $72,400. This action does not necessarily mean that now there will be a deficit. If a credit balance larger than $72,400 existed in Retained Earnings prior to the foregoing closing entry, there would still be a positive (credit) balance in the account. If a credit balance smaller than $72,400 existed in Retained Earnings prior to the foregoing closing entry, there would be a negative balance in the Retained Earnings account and a deficit on the balance sheet. Stockholders of a corporation cannot withdraw amounts in excess of retained earnings. This concept is explored further in the next section.

Retained Earnings—Restricted or Appropriated

The creation of special **restricted retained earnings** accounts (sometimes called *appropriated*) indicates that a portion of the earnings of the corporation is not available for dividends. This does not mean that a special cash fund has been set up, nor does the restriction provide cash funds. It is an accounting device by which a corporation, following a resolution of the board of directors, intentionally reduces the amount of earnings available for dividend distributions, thus indicating its intention to conserve corporate assets for other purposes. The restriction does not in any way alter the total retained earnings or the total stockholders' equity but merely earmarks a portion of the earnings in an account specifically designated to indicate its purpose. The same information can be communicated in the balance sheet by a footnote or by a parenthetical notation.

Each restricted account, although separated from the parent Retained Earnings account, is nevertheless a part of retained earnings and is so classified in the stockholders' equity section of the balance sheet. When the special account has served its purpose and the requirement for which it was set up no longer exists, the amount in the restricted account is transferred back into the Retained Earnings (unappropriated) account.

Restrictions may be either voluntary or involuntary and typically are made for three broad purposes:

1. To show management's intended use of earnings (voluntary).
2. To show compliance with legal and contractual arrangements (involuntary).
3. To provide a buffer against possible future losses (voluntary).

A restriction for plant expansion, for example, may be set up by voluntary action of the board of directors showing management's intention to retain cash or other assets for use in connection with a projected plant expansion program rather than to distribute them in the form of dividends. When cash dividends are paid, the assets of the corporation are depleted. To the degree, then, that dividend declarations are restricted, assets are retained for other business purposes, such as plant expansion.

To illustrate this first purpose of restrictions, assume that a company during 1985 plans to erect an additional building and equip it at an estimated cost of $250,000. Aware of the need to conserve current assets to meet the requirements of the expansion program, the board of directors on May 2, 1985, passes a resolution to restrict $250,000 of retained earnings to indicate that this amount is not available for dividends. The journal entry to record the restriction is:

1985					
May	2	Retained Earnings		250,000	
		Retained Earnings—Restricted for Plant Expansion			250,000
		To restrict retained earnings to conserve funds for plant expansion project.			

After the construction is completed and after debits have been made to one or more asset accounts, the restriction is removed by the following entry:

1985					
Dec.	1	Retained Earnings—Restricted for Plant Expansion		250,000	
		Retained Earnings			250,000
		To remove restriction upon completion of plant expansion project.			

The second broad purpose of restricting retained earnings is the involuntary restriction resulting from a state statute (covered later in this chapter) or by a contract. When a corporation enters into an agreement for a long-term loan, the terms of the loan contract may require periodic restrictions of retained earnings, accumulating over the term of the loan to an amount equal to the loan. The purpose of the restriction is to reduce the amount of cash earnings that are allowed to be distributed to the stockholders as dividends. The aim is to improve the corporation's ability to make periodic interest payments and any other payments required under the terms of the loan. The journal entry to record this type of restriction is a debit to Retained Earnings and a credit to Retained Earnings—Restricted for Long-Term Loan Retirement. This entry is reversed whenever its intended purpose has been accomplished and continuance of the restriction is no longer necessary.

The third purpose for the restriction of retained earnings represents another voluntary restriction. For example, suppose that a company is anticipating several losses in the next accounting period; it may desire to blunt demands for dividends by reducing retained earnings and creating an account entitled Retained Earnings—Restricted for Contingencies. The accounting is similar to that for the expansion program except for the names of the accounts. Any losses that materialize, however, must be debited to appropriately named loss accounts because they must be disclosed on the income statement.

If the restrictions on retained earnings are recorded on the books, they are shown in the stockholders' equity section of the balance sheet as an element of retained earnings. In other words, retained earnings would be broken down into two subsections: restricted and unrestricted (or free).

Prior Period Adjustments

A company may make an error in the financial statements of one accounting period that is not discovered until a subsequent period. The correction of this error, if material, should be treated as a prior period adjustment of retained earnings.[1] That is, the correction should be disclosed as an adjustment of the opening balance of retained earnings. For a very simple illustration, assume that the Whacker Corporation recorded depreciation of machinery in 1984 of $18,000; the correct amount was $81,000. This means that the depreciation expense for 1984 was understated by $63,000 = ($81,000 − $18,000), and thus net income for 1984 was overstated by $63,000. The Retained Earnings account will likewise be overstated by $63,000. The error was discovered on March 10, 1985, after the books had been closed for 1984. Ignoring the effect on income taxes, the entry to record this correction is:

1985					
Mar.	10	Retained Earnings		63,000	
		Accumulated Depreciation—Machinery			63,000
		To correct the error in depreciation of machinery in 1984.			

The foregoing prior period adjustments should be recorded net of any tax effect; this additional complexity is considered in Chapter 21.

Dividends

Another action of the board of directors resulting in a decrease in retained earnings is the declaration of a dividend. **Dividend** refers to the distribution of cash, stock, or other corporate property to the stockholders. A dividend must be declared formally by the board of directors, a record of which should be entered in the minutes of meetings of the board of directors. The entry should indicate declaration date, date of record, and payment date. For a cash dividend distribution to be made, there must be accumulated and unrestricted retained earnings and assets available for distribution. If there are no accumulated earnings, the dividend becomes a reduction in paid-in capital, which may be illegal. There must also be sufficient cash or other readily distributable type of assets. Only the board of directors has the authority to determine whether a dividend is to be paid, to which classes of stock it is to be paid, and the time, manner, and form of payment. This applies to both

[1]FASB *Statement of Financial Accounting Standards No. 16* (Stamford, Conn.: FASB, 1977), paragraphs 10–12.

classes of stockholders, preferred and common. Once formal action has been taken by the board the declaration immediately becomes a current liability of the corporation. It is customary, particularly for larger corporations with numerous stockholders, to make a public announcement of the dividend declaration in newspapers or magazines.

Cash Dividends

Declaration of a Dividend The dividend may be stated as a percent of par or as a specified amount per share. Following is a typical dividend notice:

National Ore Company
60 Rockefeller Plaza, New York, N.Y.
Dividend No. 310

The board of Directors has today declared a regular quarterly dividend at the rate of forty-seven and one-half cents (47½¢) per share on the Common Stock of this Company, payable January 15, 1986, to stockholders of record at the close of business December 31, 1985.

J. V. Couches
Secretary

December 14, 1985

The holder of 100 shares of common stock of National Ore Company will be mailed a check for $47.50 on January 15, 1986. An investor who buys the stock in time to be recorded as its owner by December 31, 1985, the record date, will receive the dividend. An investor who buys stock of this company too late to be recorded as owner by the record date is said to buy the stock **ex-dividend**—that is, without the right to receive the latest declared dividend. Stock traded on the stock exchanges is quoted ex-dividend typically three days prior to the record date to allow time for the recording and delivery of the securities. During the interval between December 31, 1985, and January 15, 1986, the list of eligible stockholders is prepared and all other tasks incident to the mailing of the dividend checks are performed. Usually these functions are carried out by independent transfer agents—banks or trust companies that also handle the recording and issuance of stock and transfer of stock.

Because of dividend priorities, it is a good idea to have a separate Dividends account for each class of stock. These Dividends accounts are debited each time a dividend is declared. Assume that the Elmer Corporation had 10,000 shares of common stock outstanding and declared its regular quarterly dividend of 30 cents a share on January 7, 1985, payable on January 28, 1985, to stockholders of record on January 20, 1985. Ignoring any required income tax withholdings[2] the declaration and payment of this quarterly dividend would be recorded as follows:

1985					
Jan.	7	Dividends—Common Stock		3,000	
		Dividends Payable— Common Stock			3,000
		To record the declaration of a 30-cents-a-share cash dividend on 10,000 shares of common stock outstanding.			
	28	Dividends Payable—Common Stock . . .		3,000	
		Cash			3,000
		To record payment of the dividend declared on January 7.			

Note that no journal entry is needed nor made on January 20, 1985, the date of record. Should a balance sheet be prepared between January 7 and January 28, the Dividends Payable—Common Stock account would be classified as a current liability. At the end of the year, if four quarterly dividends of the same amount are declared, the Dividends—Common Stock account would contain a debit balance of $12,000. Since they are temporary accounts that serve the purpose of reducing stockholders' equity, all Dividends accounts are closed into the permanent stockholders' equity account, Retained Earnings, at the end of the year. For the Elmer Corporation, such an entry would be:

1985					
Dec.	31	Retained Earnings		12,000	
		Dividends—Common Stock			12,000
		To close the Dividends account.			

Although some prefer to debit Retained Earnings to record a dividend declaration, the use of Dividends accounts segregates dividends declared during the year; it also keeps Retained Earnings clear of debits that would require analysis at the end of the year when the statement of retained earnings is prepared. The Dividends accounts, representing a reduction in the stockholders' equity, are then shown on the statement of retained earnings as deduc-

[2]The *Tax Equity and Fiscal Responsibility Act of 1982* requires that corporations paying dividends to individuals, partnerships, estates, and trusts withhold from the dividends under certain conditions income taxes at a rate of 10 percent. Withholding for income tax purposes is not required of corporations paying dividends to other investor corporations. At the time of this writing, intensive efforts are being made to effect the repeal of this provision of the act. The dividends withholding is not illustrated in this book.

tions from the total of the beginning balance of retained earnings plus net income and other increases to retained earnings. Dividends Payable, on either common or preferred stock, is a current liability.

Cash Dividends on Preferred Stock As mentioned previously, preferred stock has certain dividend preferences. The right of a preferred stockholder to a dividend, however, must await a formal declaration by the board of directors. On declaration, a stated amount per share is paid to the preferred stockholders before any dividend distribution is made to holders of common stock.

As indicated in Chapter 16, if the preferred stock is **cumulative,** undeclared dividends are accumulated, and the accumulated past dividends plus the current dividend on preferred must be paid before any dividend payment is made on common stock. These dividends not declared in past periods on cumulative preferred stock are referred to as a **dividend arrearage** (or **dividends in arrears**). If the preferred stock is *noncumulative,* a dividend not formally declared by the board of directors in any period is lost.

Preferred dividends are typically declared either quarterly or semiannually. To illustrate, assume that on July 1, 1985, the Columbia Corporation has outstanding 1,000 shares of 15 percent, cumulative preferred stock with a par value of $100. Normally preferred dividends are declared semiannually by Columbia Corporation, but no dividends on the preferred stock were declared during 1984. This means that $15,000 = (15% × $100,000) of dividends are in arrears as of July 1, 1985. The preferred dividend to be declared on this date is $22,500, calculated as follows:

Preferred dividends in arrears: 15% × $100,000	$15,000
Current semiannual preferred dividends: ½ × $15,000	7,500
Total preferred dividend declared	$22,500

The journal entry to record the declaration of this dividend is:

1985 Jul.	1	Dividends—Preferred Stock		22,500	
		Dividends Payable— Preferred Stock			22,500
		To record the declaration of the preferred dividend, which includes the current semiannual dividend plus the dividends in arrears for 1984.			

The payment of the foregoing liability results in a debit to Dividends Payable—Preferred Stock and a credit to Cash.

Stock Dividends

Stock dividend refers to the issuance by a corporation to its existing stockholders of additional shares of its authorized stock without investment of any kind by them. There are various occasions for the declaration of a stock dividend, such as:

- A large unappropriated retained earnings balance.
- A desire by the directors to reduce the market price of the stock.
- A desire to increase the permanent capitalization of the company by converting a portion of the retained earnings into capital stock.
- A need to conserve available cash.

While a cash dividend decreases both the assets and the stockholders' equity of a corporation, a stock dividend simply transfers a certain amount of retained earnings to paid-in capital accounts and has no effect on either total assets or *total* stockholders' equity. The change is within the stockholders' equity section (retained earnings decrease and paid-in capital increases).

Impact of Stock Dividend Consider that the Peet Corporation, with \$500,000 common stock, \$10 par value, issued and outstanding, and retained earnings of \$80,000, declares a 10 percent stock dividend. A distribution of 5,000 new shares = [(\$500,000 ÷ \$10) × 10%] is to be divided among existing stockholders in proportion to the number of shares each holds. For a stock dividend of this size, the amount of retained earnings transferred to paid-in capital is measured by the market price of the stock (discussed in the next section). The effect of the declaration on stockholders' equity is shown below. To simplify this illustration, assume that the market value of the stock is equal to its par value.

	Stockholders' Equity			Outstanding Shares	
	Immediately before Declaration	Immediately after Declaration	Immediately after Stock Issuance	Before Stock Issuance	After Stock Issuance
Stockholders' equity:					
Common stock, \$10 par value	\$500,000	\$500,000	\$550,000		
Stock dividends to be issued		50,000			
Retained earnings	80,000	30,000	30,000		
Total stockholders' equity	\$580,000	\$580,000	\$580,000	50,000	55,000

After the declaration of the stock dividend, but before the stock is formally issued, the par value of the 5,000 shares to be issued is carried in an account called Stock Dividends to Be Issued. As the foregoing illustrates, this account is part of the stockholders' equity. It is not a liability because its reduction will result in an increase in common stock, not in a reduction of a current asset. The account should therefore be shown following common stock in the stockholders' equity section of the balance sheet.

Because a stock dividend has no effect on the total stockholders' equity, the relative interest of each stockholder is unchanged. For example, Mary Pele, a stockholder with 1,000 shares before the stock dividend, will have 1,100 shares after the fact. Her proportionate holdings remain unchanged at two percent of the total stock outstanding. Hence, all her rights and privileges compared to other stockholders are unaltered, as shown below:

	Before Declaration and Issuance	After Declaration and Issuance
1. Total stockholders' equity	$580,000	$580,000
2. Number of shares outstanding	50,000	55,000
3. Stockholders' equity per share (Line 1 ÷ Line 2)	$11.60	$10.54½
4. Shares owned by Mary Pele	1,000	1,100
5. Pele's equity (Line 3 × Line 4)	$ 11,600	$ 11,600

A stock dividend is significant to the stockholder, even if it does not alter the recipient's equity in the company. If the stock dividend does not cause a significant decline in the price of stock, the stockholder's gain is equal to the market value of the new shares received. If, in addition, the corporation does not reduce the amount of its cash dividends per share, the stockholder gains the dividends on the additional shares in the future. The expectation of greater dividends as well as the availability of more shares for possible ultimate profitable resale creates a favorable reception for a stock dividend. A corporation could, however, continue to pay the same total dividend by simply adjusting the amount per share. In this case, the aggregate market price of the stock would change very little, and the stockholders would gain very little.

A stock dividend provides certain advantages to the corporation. Its earnings are capitalized (that is, retained earnings are transferred to paid-in capital accounts). There is no reduction in assets (other than for the cost of issuing the new stock). The corporation may use its earnings for expansion or other purposes. A large stock dividend (say, from 25 percent to 100 percent) allows the corporation to create conditions that reduce the market price of its shares to attract more buyers. Issuance of substantially more shares representing the same total equity will cause the price per share to decrease.

When there are two classes of stockholders, the stock dividend normally applies only to the common stockholders. Payment, however, may be in either preferred or common stock. Various court rulings are not consistent about the rights of preferred stockholders to participate in a stock dividend, although preferred stockholders generally have no such rights.

Recording Small Stock Dividends The AICPA has recommended that for **small stock dividends**—those involving less than 20 to 25 percent of the number of shares previously outstanding—the corporation should transfer from retained earnings to capital stock and other paid-in capital accounts "an amount equal to the fair value of the additional shares issued."[3]

Assume that the market value of the stock dividend shares issued by the Peet Corporation in the previous example was $60,000 = (5,000 shares × $12 a share) and that the board of directors, in authorizing the stock dividend, directed that it be recorded at market value. The entries to record the declaration and stock issuance are:

1985 May	1	Stock Dividends—Common (or Retained Earnings)		60,000	
		Stock Dividends to Be Issued—Common			50,000
		Paid-in Capital—Excess over Par Value on Stock Dividends . . .			10,000
		To record declaration of stock dividend.			
	15	Stock Dividends to Be Issued—Common		50,000	
		Common Stock			50,000
		To record issuance of stock dividend.			

Should a balance sheet be prepared between May 1 and May 15, the Stock Dividends to Be Issued—Common account would be disclosed in the stockholders' equity section of the balance sheet as a part of paid-in capital by the common shareholders. If the Stock Dividends account is used, it should be closed to Retained Earnings at the end of the year along with other Dividends accounts.

The rationale with respect to small stock dividends is that the market value of the shares previously held remains substantially unchanged. "Many recipients of stock dividends look upon them as distributions of corporate earnings and usually in an amount equivalent to the fair value of the additional shares issued."[4] Therefore, the accounting should show that the amount of retained earnings available for future dividend distribution has been reduced by the market value of the stock dividend.

Recording Large Stock Dividends For **large stock dividends**—those involving the issuance of more than 25 percent of the number of shares previously outstanding—the AICPA recommends that "there is no need to capitalize retained earnings other than to the extent occasioned by legal requirements."[5]

For large stock dividends the amount of retained earnings capitalized (transferred to paid-in capital) is represented by the par or stated value (the

[3]*Accounting Research Bulletin No. 43,* "Restatement and Revision of Accounting Research Bulletins" (New York: AICPA, 1953), Chapter 7, Section B, paragraphs 10 and 13. The question of whether to use 20 or 25 percent depends upon whether the market price is influenced if a rate higher than 20 percent is used.

[4]Ibid.

[5]Ibid., paragraph 11.

legal capital amount) of the shares issued.[6] To illustrate, assume that the Hart Corporation has sufficient retained earnings and declares a stock dividend of 20,000 shares, or 50 percent of the 40,000 shares of $10 par value common stock previously outstanding. The entry to record the declaration is shown below:

1985 May	1	Stock Dividends—Common (or Retained Earnings)		200,000	
		Stock Dividends to Be Issued—Common			200,000
		To record the declaration of 20,000 shares of additional common stock as a stock dividend.			

Recall that the par amount that is credited to Stock Dividends to Be Issued—Common is the amount that will be later transferred to Common Stock. The rationale with respect to accounting for large stock dividends is that the effect is to reduce materially the per share market value, and the transaction is "a split-up effected in the form of a dividend."[7] There is, therefore, no need to capitalize retained earnings beyond the legal requirements, as seen in the next section when stock split-ups are discussed.

Stock Split (or Stock Split-Up)

A corporation may wish to reduce the par value of its stock, or it may desire to reduce the price at which the stock is being issued to make it more salable. This is accomplished by a **stock split,** whereby the shares outstanding are increased and the par or stated value per share is reduced. The total capitalized value of the outstanding shares remains the same. There is no change in retained earnings. The Common Stock account is noted to show the new par or stated value per share and the subsidiary **stockholders' ledger** (the record of the shares owned by each stockholder) is revised by the registrar to show the new distribution of shares.

Assume, for example, that a corporation has outstanding 500,000 shares of $10 par value common stock. The current market price of the stock is $175 a share. The corporation, wishing to create a condition that will result in a reduction of the high market price to obtain a broader market for a forthcoming additional stock issue, reduces the par value from $10 to $5 and increases the number of shares from 500,000 to 1,000,000.[8] This "two-for-one split-up" should result in a decrease of the former market price by almost one-half. The split in shares may be accomplished by calling in all the old shares and issuing certificates for new shares on a two-for-one basis or by issuing an ad-

---

[7]*Accounting Research Bulletin No. 43,* Chapter 7, Section B, paragraph 11.

[8]To be able to take this action, this corporation must have at least 500,000 authorized but unissued shares or must obtain an amendment to the charter.

ditional share for each old share owned. This action is recorded either by a memorandum notation in the journal and Common Stock account or by the following journal entry:

1985 Dec.	1	Common Stock ($10 par value) . . . . . Common Stock ($5 par value) . . . . . To record a 2-for-1 split-up, increasing the number of outstanding shares from 500,000 to 1,000,000 and reducing par value from $10 to $5.		5,000,000	5,000,000

The market price of the shares should now be reduced sufficiently to enhance the marketability of the new issue. A split-up of no-par stated value stock would be recorded in a similar manner.

Both stock dividends and stock splits change the number of shares outstanding without changing either total stockholders' equity or the pro rata share of ownership of each stockholder. A stock dividend, unlike a stock split, requires a transfer from retained earnings to paid-in capital and increases the Common Stock account by the par or stated value of the dividend shares. A stock split, unlike a stock dividend, changes the par or stated value of the common stock without changing the dollar balances of any accounts.

Treasury Stock and Other Corporate Capital Concepts

Treasury Stock

A corporation may repurchase some of its own stock, preferred or common, or receive it as a donation or settlement of a debt. Such stock is known as **treasury stock.** Provided that the amount received when the stock was first issued was equal to or greater than par or stated value, the treasury stock may be reissued at a price below par or stated value. There will be no contingent liability to the corporation's creditors by the purchaser of this stock for the amount of this type of discount. Treasury stock does not fall into the category of new issues; it is the corporation's own stock that has been issued and later reacquired. While in the treasury, it has issued but not outstanding status and therefore does not have voting or dividend rights.

A corporation may purchase some of its own stock to bolster a sagging market or to distribute to its employees in place of other compensation. Sometimes the stock is purchased because it is available at a favorable price. Returning assets (the cash) to stockholders by acquisition of treasury stock reduces both the assets and the stockholders' equity. The Treasury Stock account, therefore, is disclosed in the stockholders' equity section as a deduction from total paid-in capital and retained earnings. Since the acquisition of treasury stock results in a distribution of corporate assets to stockholders, some states have enacted restrictive provisions pertaining to this kind of acquisition to protect the corporate creditors. Some require a restriction of retained earnings equal to the cost of the treasury stock as a means of preserving the legal capital.

Recording the Purchase of Treasury Stock

The most commonly used method for recording the purchase of treasury stock is cost; this is the only one used in this book.[9] The Treasury Stock account is debited for the cost of the shares acquired. To illustrate the cost method, assume that on August 5, 1985, the Ell Corporation reacquired 200 shares of its own $5 par value common stock at $5.50 a share. The entry to record this reacquisition is as shown below:

1985 Aug.	5	Treasury Stock—Common . . . . Cash . . . . Purchased 200 shares of own common stock at $5.50 a share.		1,100	 1,100

The purchase of the 200 shares of stock reduces cash by $1,100 and stockholders' equity by $1,100. It also reduces the number of shares outstanding, but does not legally reduce the amount of *issued* stock. State law or company policy may require the restriction of retained earnings in an amount equal to the cost of treasury stock held. The journal entry is a debit to Retained Earnings and a credit to Retained Earnings—Restricted for Treasury Stock Purchases. Such a restriction should be increased as more treasury stock is acquired and reduced by the cost of shares reissued.

Recording Reissuance of Treasury Stock

Above Cost The reissuance of treasury stock is recorded by a credit to Treasury Stock for the *cost of the shares.* The difference between the cost and the issue price of treasury stock when it is issued above cost is credited to Paid-in Capital from Treasury Stock Transactions. To illustrate, assume that on October 2, 1985, the Ell Corporation reissued 50 shares for $6.50 a share. The entry for reissuance is:

1985 Oct.	5	Cash . . . . Treasury Stock—Common . . . . Paid-in Capital from Treasury Stock Transactions, Common . . . . Reissued 50 shares of treasury stock at $6.50 a share.		325	 275 50

[9]Another method recommended by some accounting theorists is called the par value method—the Treasury Stock account is debited for par value and other stockholders' equity accounts are debited for the excess of cost over par. Later, when the stock is reissued, it is accounted for in a manner similar to the original issue of capital stock.

Below Cost The entry to record the issuance of treasury stock below cost depends on the existence of capital accounts that are not considered to be part of the legal capital. To illustrate, assume that on November 4, 1985, the Ell Corporation resissued another 50 shares of treasury stock (which cost $275) for $225. The difference of $50 is debited to Paid-in Capital from Treasury Stock Transactions, as follows:

1985					
Nov.	4	Cash		225	
		Paid-in Capital from Treasury Stock Transactions, Common		50	
		Treasury Stock—Common			275
		Reissued 50 shares of treasury stock at $4.50 each.			

If the excess of the cost of the treasury shares over the reissue price exceeds the amount in Paid-in Capital from Treasury Stock Transactions, the excess may be debited to any other paid-in capital account arising from the same class of stock that is not classified as legal capital. In the absence of such accounts, the difference between the cost and the selling price of the treasury stock is debited to Retained Earnings. To illustrate, assume that on November 29, 1985, the Ell Corporation reissued the remaining 100 shares at $5 per share. Assuming that the paid-in capital—excess over par value, common does not constitute legal capital, the entry to record the transaction is:

1985					
Nov.	29	Cash		500	
		Paid-in Capital—Excess over Par Value, Common		50	
		Treasury Stock			550
		Reissued the remaining 100 shares of treasury stock at $5 per share.			

If there had not been any paid-in capital in excess over par value, the debit would have been to Retained Earnings.

Recording Treasury Stock Donations

One or more shareholders may donate a portion of their shares to the corporation for reissuance to raise cash. Shares acquired by donation do not affect the total dollar amounts on the balance sheet, as there is no change in the assets, liabilities, or stockholders' equity. On acquisition, a memorandum is made in the journal and Treasury Stock account indicating the date and the number of shares donated. No dollar value is assigned at this point because treasury stock is recorded at cost. The cost of a donation is zero. When the shares are reissued, the proceeds are credited to Paid-in Capital—Donations.

Book Value of Common Stock

Book value per common share represents the net assets for each common share outstanding. The book value of a share of common stock (or the stockholders' equity per share), assuming there is only one class of stock outstanding, is computed as follows:

When Only One Class of Stock Is Outstanding

	Amount
1. Total stockholders' equity	$750,000
2. Number of common shares outstanding	60,000
3. Book value per share (Line 1 ÷ Line 2)	$12.50

As shown by this calculation, the book value of a share of stock of any class is derived by dividing the total stockholders' equity applicable to that class by the number of shares of stock of that class issued and outstanding. The stockholders' equity applicable to a given class of stock depends upon respective owners' claims against the assets in liquidation, *not upon the amounts invested by each class* of shareholders. The book value per share is the amount each stockholder would receive for each share held in the event of liquidation after the assets are sold without gain or loss; that is, at book value. Since the valuations on the books—especially for inventories and property, plant, and equipment—do not necessarily reflect asset market values, the book value of a share of stock may be of limited significance as an indicator of the resale value. Even so, many speculators study book value of companies with certain assets that have a reasonably determinable value to make a decision as to whether or not to buy stock in these particular companies.

When More than One Class of Stock Is Outstanding

When more than one class of stock is outstanding, it becomes necessary to determine the liquidation claims of each class against the assets of the corporation. The stockholders' equity is divided between the two classes on the basis of the preferences accorded to the preferred stock in liquidation. Assume that a corporation has the following capital structure:

Preferred stock, 12%, $100 par value, cumulative; issued 1,000 shares	$100,000
Common stock, $10 par value; issued 10,000 shares	100,000
Paid-in capital—excess over par value, common stock	5,000
Retained earnings—restricted for plant addition	10,000
Retained earnings	45,000
Total stockholders' equity	$260,000

Dividends are in arrears for two years. The indenture usually provides that preferred shareholders have a claim on the assets in liquidation of an amount equal to par value plus any dividends in arrears.

Using the foregoing typical assumption, the book value of a share of preferred stock at the end of the year is $124, computed as follows:

1. Preferred stock ($100 par value × 1,000 shares)	$100,000
2. Dividends in arrears (2 years × $12,000)	24,000
3. Total equity of preferred stockholders	$124,000
4. Number of preferred shares outstanding	1,000
5. Book value per preferred share (Line 3 ÷ Line 4)	$124

The book value of a share of common stock is $13.60, computed as shown:

1. Total stockholders' equity	$260,000
2. Deduct: Equity of preferred stockholders	124,000
3. Total equity of common stockholders	$136,000
4. Number of common shares outstanding	10,000
5. Book value per common share (Line 3 ÷ Line 4)	$13.60

Earnings per Share (EPS)

Earnings per common share (EPS) has long been of primary interest to investors, financial analysts, and readers of financial publications. Although this figure is not a satisfactory substitute for a thorough financial analysis, investors consider it a key indicator in investment decision making. Earnings per common share or net loss per share must be shown on the face of the income statements of large corporations for several elements of net income, among which are (1) income before extraordinary items, and (2) net income.[10] Earnings per share is calculated and is meaningful only for common shares.

Under *APB Opinion No. 15* the earnings per share computations and presentation vary with the company's capital structure, whether simple or complex.[11] When the capital structure consists of one class of common stock only, earnings per share are calculated by dividing the net income for the period by the *weighted average* number of shares of common stock outstanding during the period. For corporations with a capital structure containing common stock and other convertible securities, two types of earnings per share amounts may be necessary. The first type, **primary earnings per share,** is calculated by dividing the applicable net income for the period by the weighted average number of common shares outstanding plus **common stock equivalents** (securities which the holder is entitled to convert to common stock that meet a set of complex criteria in *APB Opinion No. 15*). The second type, **fully diluted earnings per share,** is calculated by dividing the applicable net income for the period by the weighted average number of common shares outstanding + common stock equivalents + any other securities with conversion privileges that could decrease earnings per share.

[10]As explained and illustrated in Chapter 21, *APB Opinion No. 30* specifies that EPS data must be disclosed on the face of the income statement for other elements of net income.

[11]*APB Opinion No. 15,* "Earnings per Share" (New York: AICPA, 1969).

Calculation of primary EPS:		
Actual net income	$100,000	
Deduct: Dividends on preferred stock, 1,000 shares at $12 a share	12,000	
Adjusted net income	$ 88,000	(A)
Adjusted shares outstanding:		
Actual weighted average shares outstanding	10,000	
Additional shares classified as common stock equivalents (the preferred shares are not specified as common stock equivalents)	None	
Adjusted shares outstanding	10,000	(B)
Primary EPS (A ÷ B)	$8.80	
Calculation of fully diluted EPS:		
Net income applicable to all classes ($88,000 + $12,000)	$100,000	(C)
Adjusted shares outstanding:		
Actual weighted average shares outstanding	10,000	
Additional shares issuable to preferred shareholders (although not common stock equivalents, they are securities with potential to decrease EPS)	2,000	
Adjusted shares outstanding	12,000	(D)
Fully diluted EPS (C ÷ D)	$8.33	

Figure 17–1
Calculation of EPS

To illustrate, assume that a company with net income for the year of $100,000 has a weighted average of 10,000 common shares outstanding. Also, 1,000 shares of 12 percent convertible preferred stock, $100 par convertible into two common shares for each share of preferred are outstanding. The preferred shares do not meet the specified conditions to qualify as common stock equivalents. The EPS calculation is shown in Figure 17–1.

APB Opinion No. 15, which details the procedures for the computation of earnings per share under a variety of conditions, has converted the figure from an historically oriented one to an hypothetical one based on the "as if" assumption of certain securities having been converted into common stock. The many complex problems that may be involved in determining common stock equivalents are beyond the scope of this text and therefore are not illustrated here.

Taxation of Income

Because the corporation is treated as a legal entity separate and distinct from its stockholders, it is taxed as a business entity. The tax is based on corporate net income before taxes and is recorded by an entry such as:[12]

[12]Such an entry is usually made quarterly when the corporation issues interim financial statements. *APB Opinion No. 28,* "Interim Financial Reporting" (New York: AICPA, May 1973) in paragraph 19 requires that a company use its best estimate of its effective tax rate in computing this quarterly expense.

1985 Mar.	31	Income Tax Expense . . . . Income Taxes Payable . . . . To record estimated taxes due on year-to-date income.		72,180.50	72,180.50[a]

[a]Amounts are assumed.

The income tax expense is deducted in the income statement from income before taxes to arrive at net income after taxes; at the end of the year, the account balance is closed into Income Summary as are other expense items. The following closing entry would be made to close the total income tax expense for the year:

1985 Dec.	31	Income Summary . . . . Income Tax Expense . . . . To close the Income Tax Expense account to Income Summary.		292,180.00	292,180.00[a]

[a]Amounts are assumed.

Income Taxes Payable is classified as a current liability in the balance sheet.

Stockholders' Equity Illustrated

There are two methods of disclosing the various paid-in capital items in stockholders' equity, the source of capital approach, and the legal capital approach. All the simple illustrations in Chapters 16 and 17 up to this point and Figure 17–2 use the source of capital approach. When the **source of capital approach** is used, the paid-in capital items are arranged under subsections showing the class of stockholders who paid in or made the respective investments. With the **legal capital approach,** (Figure 17–3) the paid-in capital items are arranged to reveal the legal capital subtotal; the remaining stockholders' equity items are shown in appropriately titled subsections. When this latter method is used, the stockholders' equity section usually discloses the par or stated amount of both preferred and common stock in a subsection to establish the legal capital amount; then all other paid-in capital items are shown under a subsection often called additional paid-in capital. The retained earnings subsection is shown in the same manner under both approaches.

To illustrate, the source of capital approach for the Bern Corporation is shown in Figure 17–2 using the data described below. The legal capital approach illustrated in Figure 17–3 for the Bern Corporation uses the same data. The data are numbered to permit the reader to trace the information to its method of disclosure in both figures.

BERN CORPORATION
Partial Balance Sheet
December 31, 1985

Exhibit C

Stockholders' equity:			
Paid-in capital:			
1 Preferred stock, 14% cumulative, $100 par value; authorized 2,500 shares, issued 2,000 shares	$200,000		
1 Paid-in capital—excess over par value, preferred stock	10,000		
Total paid in by preferred stockholders		$210,000	
2 Common stock, no-par value, $40 stated value; authorized 7,000 shares, issued 5,000 shares of which 500 shares are held in treasury	$200,000		
2 Paid-in capital—excess over stated value, common	50,000		
2 Paid-in capital—excess from reduction of stated value of 5,000 shares of common stock from $50 to $40 per share	50,000		
3 Paid-in capital from treasury stock transactions, common	2,500		
Total paid in by common stockholders		302,500	
6 Other paid-in capital:			
Donation of land by town of Stowe		50,000	
Total paid-in capital		$562,500	
5 Retained earnings:			
Restricted:			
4 For treasury stock acquisitions	$ 27,500		
For anticipated plant expansion	45,000		
Total restricted	$ 72,500		
Unrestricted	127,500		
Total retained earnings		200,000	
Total paid-in capital and retained earnings		$762,500	
4 Deduct: Cost of treasury stock—common		27,500	
Total stockholders' equity			$735,000

Figure 17–2 Partial Balance Sheet—Stockholders' Equity, Source of Capital Approach

1 The Bern Corporation has issued 2,000 shares of $100 par value, 14 percent, preferred stock at an average price of $105 per share. The total par value of these shares (2,000 × $100 = $200,000) is labeled preferred stock. This amount represents part of the legal capital. The excess ($5 × 2,000) over the par value of the preferred stock is reported separately as paid-in capital—excess over par value, preferred stock.

2 The Bern Corporation also issued 5,000 shares of no-par, stated value common stock at $60 per share. The stated value of the shares—originally $50 per share but reduced to $40 per share on December 31—multiplied by the number of shares issued ($40 × 5,000) is shown as common stock. The excess of the issue price ($60) over the original stated value ($50), multiplied

BERN CORPORATION
Partial Balance Sheet
December 31, 1985

Exhibit C

Stockholders' equity:			
Capital stock:			
[1] Preferred stock, 14% cumulative, $100 par value; authorized 2,500 shares, issued 2,000 shares	$200,000		
[2] Common stock, no-par value, $40 stated value; authorized 7,000 shares, issued 5,000 shares of which 500 shares are held in treasury	200,000		
Total capital stock		$400,000	
Additional paid-in capital:			
[1] Paid-in capital—excess over par value, preferred stock	$ 10,000		
[2] Paid-in capital—excess over stated value, common stock	50,000		
[2] Paid-in capital—excess from reduction of stated value of 5,000 shares of common stock from $50 to $40 per share	50,000		
[3] Paid-in capital from treasury stock transactions, common	2,500		
[6] Paid-in capital—donation of land by town of Stowe	50,000		
Total additional paid-in capital		162,500	
Total capital stock and additional paid-in capital		$562,500	
[5] Retained earnings:			
Restricted:			
[4] For treasury stock acquisitions	$ 27,500		
For anticipated plant expansion	45,000		
Total restricted	$ 72,500		
Unrestricted	127,500		
Total retained earnings		200,000	
Total paid-in capital and retained earnings		$762,500	
[4] Deduct: Cost of treasury stock—common		27,500	
Total stockholders' equity			$735,000

Figure 17–3 Partial Balance Sheet—Stockholders' Equity, Legal Capital Approach

by the number of shares issued ($10 × 5,000), not being part of the stated capital, is shown separately as paid-in capital—excess over stated value, common stock. The excess of the original stated value ($50) over the revised stated value ($40) multiplied by the number of shares issued ($10 × 5,000) is also entered separately.[13] As with all other excess paid-in capital, it is clearly labeled to show its source.

[13]This is not a stock split-up. The directors have reduced the stated value by $10 without increasing the number of shares outstanding. Accordingly, $10 per share is removed (by journal entry) from the Common Stock account and moved to a Paid-in Capital—Excess from Reduction of Stated Value, Common.

3 On July 10, the Bern Corporation acquired 1,000 shares of its own common stock for $55 per share. On August 3, it sold 500 shares for $60 per share. The paid-in capital—excess of the reissue price over the cost is shown as paid-in capital from treasury stock transactions, common.

4 The July 10 acquisition of 1,000 shares of its own common stock and reissuance of 500 shares on August 3 leaves 500 shares in the Bern Corporation treasury on December 31, 1985. The laws of the state of incorporation limit the payment of dividends to the extent of the amount in the unrestricted Retained Earnings account. Since both the purchase of treasury stock and the declaration of a cash dividend reduce corporate assets and stockholders' equity, the limitation applies equally to dividend payments and to treasury stock acquisitions. A company with unrestricted retained earnings of $25,000, for example, may either reacquire treasury stock or declare cash dividends or do both, provided the total disbursement is not over $25,000. Such a restriction improves the protection of the corporate creditors. The treasury stock balance of $27,500 ($55,000 from the transaction of July 10 less $27,500 from the transaction of August 3) appears twice in the stockholders' equity section: (1) as a restriction of retained earnings, and (2) as a reduction to the stockholders' equity resulting from a distribution of $27,500 in cash to the stockholders from whom the stock was acquired.

5 The retained earnings total represents undistributed earnings from current and prior years. Of that amount, $72,500 was restricted for specific purposes; the remainder, $127,500, is unrestricted.

6 A building site with an estimated cash market value of $50,000 was donated by the town of Stowe as an inducement to the Bern Corporation to establish itself there. This gift increased assets and paid-in capital.

Using the same numbered data, the stockholders' equity section is recast according to the legal capital approach in Figure 17–3.

The legal capital approach in Figure 17–3 differs from the source of capital approach in Figure 17–2 as follows:

- The total par value and stated value of the preferred stock and common stock are shown in one subsection, entitled capital stock.
- The paid-in capital from all sources except that represented by the par value of preferred stock and the stated value of common stock is shown in a separate subsection, entitled additional paid-in capital.

Note that the retained earnings subsection is the same under both approaches.

These two variations do not pose any great theoretical arguments. The authors favor the source of capital approach from a managerial viewpoint because the subsections reveal where the capital has come from. However, because the claims against the assets in liquidation are not the same as the capital sources, this approach may mislead an untrained reader. The legal capital approach also does not disclose the claims against the assets in liquidation, but it does not create a cloud about the issue either, and is used in practice more often than the source of capital approach.

Glossary

Book value per share The amount that a shareholder would receive on a per share basis in the theoretical event that assets were sold at no gain or loss; the portion of the stockholders' equity assigned to a class of stock divided by the number of shares of that class of stock issued and outstanding.

Common stock equivalents Securities which the holder is entitled to convert to common stock according to the terms under which they were issued, and which have a high probability that they will be converted.

Cumulative preferred stock The class of preferred stock on which undeclared dividends are accumulated and must be paid together with the current dividends before any dividend payment can be made on common stock.

Deficit The negative retained earnings caption used in the balance sheet to indicate that the retained earnings balance is negative.

Dividend A distribution of some portion of net income in the form of cash, stock, or other corporate property by a corporation to stockholders.

Dividend arrearage The amount of dividends on cumulative preferred stock not declared or in arrears for any dividend period or periods.

Donated capital Increases in paid-in capital resulting from gifts of assets made to the corporation.

Ex-dividend Stock purchased *without* the right to receive the latest declared but unpaid dividend.

Fully diluted earnings per share The earnings per share amount calculated by dividing the applicable net income for the period by the common stock outstanding, plus common stock equivalents, plus other securities with conversion privileges that could decrease earnings per share.

Indenture to capital stock The corporate contractual agreement setting forth the rights and privileges of the buyers of the capital stock.

Large stock dividend See *Stock dividend.*

Legal capital approach An approach used to prepare a stockholders' equity section with the various subsections arranged to reveal the legal capital, all other paid-in capital, and retained earnings.

Liquidating dividend A pro rata distribution of assets by a company being liquidated or a distribution whose effect is to return paid-in capital to the investors.

Primary earnings per share The earnings per share amount calculated by dividing the applicable net income for the period by the common stock plus common stock equivalents.

Restricted retained earnings The portion of retained earnings not available for dividends.

Retained earnings Cumulative earnings minus cumulative dividends.

Small stock dividend See *Stock dividend.*

Source of capital approach An approach used to prepare a stockholders' equity section with the various subsections arranged to reveal the broad sources of capital.

Stock dividend The issuance by a corporation of additional shares of its authorized stock without additional investment by the stockholders. A stock dividend may be classified as *large* (involving the issuance of more than 25 percent of the number of shares previously outstanding) or *small* (involving the issuance of less than 25 percent of the number of shares previously outstanding).

Stockholders' ledger A subsidiary ledger to the capital stock controlling accounts in the general ledger. Only those whose names appear in the stockholders' ledger are recognized as share owners.

Stock split An increase in the number of shares of stock outstanding without a change in the *total* par or *total* stated value of the outstanding shares (usually the par or stated value will be decreased).

Transfer agents Banks or trust companies which record the sale and transfer of stock and prepare cash dividend checks.

Treasury stock A company's own stock previously issued and outstanding but reacquired either by purchase or gift or in settlement of a debt.

Questions

Q17–1 Since it represents earnings retained for use in the business, is the Retained Earnings account an asset? Explain.

Q17–2 What is the meaning of the following terms: (a) retained earnings? (b) Restricted retained earnings? (c) Deficit?

Q17–3 Differentiate between the following pairs of terms: (a) authorized and unissued stock; (b) issued and outstanding stock; (c) cumulative and noncumulative stock; (d) restricted and unrestricted retained earnings; (e) stock dividend and stock split.

Q17–4 How does legal capital differ from retained earnings? From total stockholders' equity?

Q17–5 The following quotation is adapted from the notes to the financial statements of a large company: "Retained earnings of $28,500,000 are restricted from payment of cash dividends on common stock because of a promissory note agreement. Further restrictions of $1,700,000 are made to cover the cost of the company's own common stock reacquired." What is the significance of this note (a) to a short-term creditor? (b) To a long-term creditor? (c) To a stockholder?

Q17–6 Why should the state of incorporation regulate the amount that may be distributed to stockholders in the form of dividends?

Q17–7 (a) What is a stock dividend? (b) What conditions prompt its declaration?

Q17–8 How does a stock dividend affect (a) the total stockholders' equity? (b) The total assets? (c) The book value per share? (d) The taxable income of the recipient? (e) The market price per share?

Q17–9 (a) What is treasury stock? (b) Why do corporations buy back their own shares? (c) How does the reacquisition of a company's own shares affect its net assets?

Q17–10 (a) Why do some states place certain restrictions on treasury stock acquisitions? (b) How is the purchase of treasury stock recorded? (c) How is the issuance of treasury stock recorded? (d) How does the issuance of treasury stock affect the income statement?

Q17–11 (a) What are the major subdivisions of the stockholders' equity section of the balance sheet under the source of capital approach? (b) What are the major subdivisions under the legal capital approach? (c) What are the main arguments for each of these approaches?

Q17–12 Student A argued that she would rather buy 100 shares of $50 par value treasury common stock for $49 per share. Student B said that he would rather buy 100 shares of unissued common stock of the same company at a discount and pay $49. With which student do you agree? Why?

Exercises

E17–1
Recording restrictions on retained earnings

On July 1, 1985, the Expando Corporation decided to launch a plant expansion program. The board of directors voted to restrict retained earnings in the amount of $1,000,000. During the remainder of 1985, the company spent $1,002,560 on the construction of a plant building. At the end of the year, the board voted to release the restriction on the retained earnings. Prepare the journal entries to record the restriction of retained earnings, the expenditure for new building, and the release of the restriction.

E17–2
Recording cash dividends

The Davido Corporation has 100,000 shares of common stock outstanding. On June 4, 1985, the board of directors declared a $0.25-per-share dividend payable on July 10, 1985, to stockholders of record on June 24, 1985. Prepare the necessary journal entries on each of the foregoing dates.

E17–3
Recording a small stock dividend

The Phyllis Corporation had the following stockholders' equity on August 2, 1985:

Common stock, $5 par value; authorized 500,000 shares; issued and outstanding 225,000 shares	$1,125,000
Retained earnings, unrestricted	1,010,000
Total stockholders' equity	$2,135,000

On August 2, 1985, the board of directors declared a 10 percent stock dividend to be issued on September 5, 1985, to stockholders of record on August 26, 1985. The market price of the common stock at date of declaration of the dividend was $17.50 per share.

1. Prepare the necessary journal entries on each of the foregoing dates.

2. What is the total stockholders' equity after the foregoing entries are made?

E17–4
Effect of transactions on retained earnings

Indicate the effect—increase, decrease, no effect—of each of the following transactions on *total* retained earnings of the Fitch Company:

a. The board of directors declared a 5 percent stock dividend to be issued one month from the current date.
b. Issued the stock dividend declared in transaction a.
c. Wrote off accounts receivable against the allowance for doubtful accounts.
d. Paid accounts payable.
e. Collected accounts receivable.
f. Issued $50 par value common stock at $60 a share.
g. Restricted retained earnings for contingencies.
h. Issued $50 par value preferred stock at $58 a share.
i. Purchased machinery on open account.
j. Issued long-term notes and received cash in return.

E17–5
Recording stock and cash dividends and treasury stock

The stockholders' equity section of the Virginia Company's balance sheet shows the following:

Common stock, no-par value; issued 10,500 shares	$165,000
Retained earnings	125,000
Total	$290,000

Record each of the following events, occurring in sequence (using letters instead of dates in the journal):

a. The declaration of a 15 percent stock dividend; the market price of the stock is $18 per share.
b. The issuance of the dividend.
c. The acquisition of 200 shares of the company's own stock for $18 a share.
d. The reissuance of the 200 reacquired shares for $20 a share.

e. The declaration of a $1-per-share cash dividend.
f. The payment of the dividend.

E17–6 *Recapitalization transactions*

The Dunlap Company's balance sheet shows the following:

Common stock, par value $5, 150,000 shares	$750,000
Retained earnings	250,000

Give the monetary effect—increase, decrease, or no effect—on the foregoing items of each of the following independent situations:

a. All the stock is called in, and 450,000 shares of no-par value stock are issued in exchange, the entire proceeds constituting legal capital.
b. The old shares are replaced by 300,000 shares of no-par value, $2.50 stated value common stock.
c. Each stockholder receives a stock dividend of one additional share for every three shares now held.

E17–7 *Calculating dividends*

The Marina Corporation had the following stockholders' equity during 1985:

16% preferred stock, $100 par value	$200,000
Common stock, $10 par value	400,000
Total	$600,000

Assume that the Marina Corporation has $120,000 available for dividends during 1985 and that the preferred stock is cumulative and dividends are in arrears for the entire year of 1984. Calculate the amount that would be payable to preferred shareholders and to common shareholders if $120,000 is declared.

E17–8 *Recording treasury stock transactions*

The capital stock of the Citmon Corporation consists of $2 par value common stock. Record the following events, occurring in sequence (using letters instead of dates in the journal):

a. The issuance of 10,000 shares at $10 a share.
b. The reacquisition of 400 shares at $9 a share (restriction of retained earnings is not required).
c. The reissuance of the treasury stock at $13 a share.
d. A two-for-one stock split with a reduction of par value from $2 to $1.

E17–9 *Calculating earnings per share*

The net income after taxes of the Erno Corporation for 1985 was $212,205. The weighted average number of shares of common stock was 110,000; common stock equivalents amounted to 40,500 shares. There is no preferred stock. Calculate the primary earnings per share for 1985.

E17–10 *Recording treasury stock transactions*

On July 8, 1985, the Acme Corporation had the following stockholders' equity:

Common stock, $2 par value, authorized; issued and outstanding, 40,000 shares	$ 80,000
Paid-in capital—excess over par value, common stock (not a part of legal capital)	175,000
Retained earnings	610,500

The following selected transactions took place during July and August 1985:

1985		
Jul.	9	Reacquired 500 shares of own common stock at $22 per share. State law requires the restriction of retained earnings for the cost of the treasury shares.
	12	Reissued 100 treasury shares for $23 per share.
	18	Reissued 100 treasury shares for $21.50 per share.
Aug.	15	Reissued the remaining 300 shares to employees for $18 per share.

Prepare journal entries to record the foregoing transactions.

E17–11 *Calculating book value per share*

The condensed balance sheet of the K. Edwards Corporation as of December 31, 1985, contained the following items:

Total assets	$720,000
Liabilities	$200,000
Preferred stock, 12 percent, $50 par value; cumulative	100,000
Common stock, no-par value; stated value $5	300,000
Paid-in capital—excess over par value, preferred stock	10,000
Paid-in capital—excess over stated value, common stock	15,000
Retained earnings—restricted for plant expansion	45,000
Retained earnings	50,000
Total liabilities and stockholders' equity	$720,000

The liquidating value of the preferred stock is equal to the par value plus any dividends in arrears.

1. Determine the book value per share of common stock, assuming that there are no dividend arrearages.

2. Calculate the book value per share of common stock, assuming that dividends on the preferred stock are in arrears for the years 1984 and 1985.

E17–12 *Preparing stockholders' equity section*

The following account balances were taken from the ledger of the Sanderson Company as of December 31, 1985:

Paid-in Capital—Excess over Par Value, Preferred	$ 65,000
Paid-in Capital—Donated by Town of Pamet	144,000
Paid-in Capital from Treasury Stock Transactions—Common	12,000
Preferred Stock (12% cumulative, $100 par value; issued 9,600 shares)	960,000
Retained Earnings—Restricted for Plant Additions	192,000
Retained Earnings—Restricted for Contingencies	24,000
Paid-in Capital—Excess of Original Stated Value over Revised Stated Value of Common Stock	180,000
Common Stock ($5 stated value; issued 48,000 shares)	240,000
Retained Earnings	408,200
Treasury Stock—Common (600 shares)	18,000
Paid-in Capital—Excess over Stated Value, Common Stock	96,000
Estimated Income Taxes Payable	115,000
Organization Costs	24,000

Prepare the stockholders' equity section of the balance sheet as of December 31, 1985, using the source of capital approach.

E17–13 *Determining various stockholders' equity amouts*

Refer to E17–12. Compute (a) the amount contributed by the preferred stockholders, (b) the amount contributed by the common stockholders, (c) the book value per share of preferred stock, assuming that the current year's preferred dividends are in arrears, and (d) the book value per share of common stock.The liquidation value of the preferred is equal to par value plus any dividends in arrears.

E17–14 *Recording quarterly dividends*

National Agribusiness Company has 400,000 shares of $25 par value, 12 percent, cumulative preferred stock outstanding. It also has 45,000,000 shares of $1.20 par value common stock outstanding. The following actions occurred in 1985:

1985

Jan. 4 At its monthly meeting, the board of directors reviewed the tentative 1984 financial statements and approved the following:

a. The declaration of a total dividend of $8,400,000 as a fourth quarter 1984 dividend on both preferred and common stock payable on February 6 to stockholders of record on January 23, 1985.

b. The acceptance of an offer by a stockholder to sell back to the corporation 1,000,000 shares of common stock at $22 a share on January 9.

9 The acquisition of 1,000,000 shares of common stock was carried out for cash.

Apr. 4 The directors reviewed interim statements for the first quarter of 1985 and approved a first quarter total dividend of $8,220,000 on both preferred and common stock payable on May 10 to stockholders of record on April 25.

No dividends were in arrears and no other stock transactions occurred during the period. Dividends on both common and preferred are declared quarterly. All dividends declared were paid when due. In general journal form, record all events stemming from the directors' actions.

A Problems

P17–1A *Journalizing various stockholders' equity transactions*

The Lindwood Corporation was organized on January 3, 1985, with authority to issue 30,000 shares of no-par value common stock and 7,500 shares of 12 percent cumulative preferred stock, $50 par value. During 1985 and 1986, the following selected transactions occurred, in this sequence:

a. Issued 8,000 shares of common stock for cash at $12 a share. A stated value of $10 a share is set by the board of directors for the common stock.
b. Issued 1,000 shares of preferred stock at $60 a share.
c. Issued 150 shares of common stock, in lieu of a $1,800 fee, to the corporation's attorneys for their services in drafting the articles of incorporation and a set of bylaws.
d. Acquired 325 shares of common stock for $4,225 from the estate of a deceased stockholder.
e. Reissued the 325 shares of the treasury stock at $14 a share.
f. The 1985 end-of-year credit balance in the Income Summary account of $256,000 was closed. (Make the closing entry.)
g. Declared a 12 percent annual dividend on preferred stock and a $0.30-per-share cash dividend plus a 50 percent stock dividend on common stock. The dividends are distributable on February 10, 1986, to stockholders of record on January 31, 1985.
h. In 1986, the board authorized the restriction of retained earnings of $50,000 for plant expansion.

Required: Prepare the journal entries to record the transactions using letters in the place of dates.

P17–2A *Journalizing various stockholders' equity transactions and preparing a stockholders' equity section*

The stockholders' equity section of the Shaw Corporation's balance sheet as of December 31, 1984, was as follows:

Stockholders' equity:	
Capital stock:	
Preferred stock, 15 percent, $50 par value; authorized and issued 6,000 shares	$ 300,000
Common stock, $4 par value; authorized and issued 150,000 shares	600,000
Paid-in capital—excess over par value, common stock	85,000
Retained earnings	600,000
Total stockholders' equity	$1,585,000

Selected transactions for the year 1985 occurred in the following sequence:

a. Declared a total annual cash dividend of $140,000 for 1985. (The preferred stock is cumulative; there are no dividends in arrears.)
b. Paid the dividend declared in transaction a.
c. Purchased 1,200 shares of its own preferred stock for $75 a share. (A restriction of retained earnings is not required.)
d. Established a restriction on retained earnings of $75,000 for contingencies.

e. Reissued 500 shares of treasury stock for $80 a share.
f. Earnings from operations for the year after income taxes were $230,000. (Make the closing entry.) Also close the dividends accounts.
g. Reissued 400 shares of treasury stock for $90 a share.
h. A major stockholder donated to the corporation a warehouse valued at $50,000.

Required:

1. Prepare general journal entries to record the transaction using letters in place of dates.

2. Enter the December 31, 1984, balances in ledger accounts. Post the journal entries to these and other newly created *stockholders' equity accounts* only.

3. Prepare the stockholders' equity section of the balance sheet as of December 31, 1985. Use the source of capital approach.

4. Why do you think the major stockholder donated a warehouse to the corporation?

P17–3A
Journalizing various stockholders' equity transactions and preparing a stockholders' equity section

On January 6, 1984, the Havilock Corporation was authorized to issue 50,000 shares of $10 par value common stock and 4,000 shares of 15 percent cumulative preferred stock, $100 par value. The following selected transactions occurred between January 6, 1984, and December 31, 1985, in the sequence indicated:

a. Issued 8,000 shares of common stock at $18 a share and 2,500 shares of preferred stock at $103 a share.
b. Purchased the assets of the Bonger Company at their fair cash value; the assets consisted of land worth $20,000, buildings worth $110,000, and machinery worth $141,500. Issued 15,000 shares of common stock in payment.
c. The Income Summary account had a credit balance of $200,000 at the end of 1984 after all revenues and expenses had been closed to it. (Make closing entry.)
d. Purchased 1,000 shares of its own common stock at $19 a share. (The laws of the state of incorporation require a restriction of retained earnings equal to the cost of treasury stock.)
e. Established a restriction on retained earnings for contingencies of $50,000.
f. Reissued 400 shares of treasury stock for $20 a share.
g. The Income Summary account had a credit balance of $175,000 at the end of 1985 after all revenues and expenses had been closed to it. (Make closing entry.)
h. Declared an $0.80-per-share dividend on the common stock and a $7.50-per-share dividend on the preferred stock. (Assume that no preferred dividends are in arrears.)

Required:

1. Journalize the transactions, including any additional closing entries, and post to the stockholders' equity accounts using letters instead of dates.

2. Prepare the stockholders' equity section of the balance sheet as of December 31, 1985. Use the legal capital approach.

P17–4A
Book value issues

The condensed balance sheet data of the Cookerville Corporation as of December 31, 1985, were as follows:

Total assets	$825,000
Liabilities	$250,000
Preferred stock, 12 percent, $50 par value; cumulative	100,000
Common stock, no-par value; stated value $5	300,000
Paid-in capital—excess over par value, preferred stock	10,000
Paid-in capital—excess over stated value, common stock	15,000
Retained earnings—restricted for plant expansion	50,000
Retained earnings	100,000
Total liabilities and stockholders' equity	$825,000

Required:

1. Determine the book value per share of common stock, assuming that there are no dividend arrearages. The liquidation value of the preferred stock is equal to the par value plus any dividends in arrears.

2. Calculate the book value per share of common stock, assuming that dividends on the preferred stock are in arrears for the years 1983, 1984, and 1985.

3. What is the significance of the book value per share?

4. What is the interrelationship between book value per share and market value per share?

P17–5A *Calculating earnings per share*

Assume the following information for the Simplex Corporation:

Weighted average shares of common stock outstanding	100,000
12% Convertible preferred shares, Class A, $50 par value (not a common stock equivalent, but convertible to common shares on a 1 preferred share for 2 common shares basis)	20,000
6% Convertible preferred shares, Class B, $100 par value (a common stock equivalent convertible to common shares on a 1 preferred share for 3 common shares basis)	30,000
Net income for 1985	$650,800

Assume that both class A and B were outstanding during the entire year of 1985.

Required: Calculate (1) the primary earnings per share, and (2) the fully diluted earnings per share.

P17–6A *Thought-provoking problem: issues related to restrictions on retained earnings and dividends*

The 1985 annual report of Elkin Corporation states in a note to its financial statements: "The terms of certain note agreements restrict the payment of cash dividends on common stock. The amount of retained earnings not so restricted on December 31, 1985, was approximately $128,000."

Required:

1. Of what usefulness is the statement regarding the amount of restricted retained earnings? The amount not restricted?

2. The cash dividend distributions during 1985 were $14,908; net income for the year was $94,010. Do the stockholders have the right to dividends up to $94,010?

3. Total shareholders' equity at December 31, 1985, was $860,703. Does this indicate what the shareholders would receive in the event of liquidation? Of sale? Explain.

B Problems

P17–1B *Journalizing various stockholders' equity transactions*

The Pope Corporation was organized on April 1, 1985, with authority to issue 50,000 shares of no-par value common stock and 15,000 shares of 14 percent cumulative preferred stock, $25 par value. During 1985 and 1986, the following transactions occurred, in this sequence:

a. Issued 16,500 shares of common stock for cash at $15 a share. A stated value of $12 is set by the board of directors for the common stock.

b. Issued 1,500 shares of preferred stock at $28 a share.

c. Issued 200 shares of common stock in lieu of a $3,000 fee to the corporation's attorneys for their services in drafting the articles of incorporation and a set of bylaws.

d. Acquired 600 shares of common stock for $9,600 from the estate of a deceased stockholder.

e. Reissued the 600 shares of the treasury stock at $17 a share.

f. The 1985 end-of-year credit balance in the Income Summary account of $216,800 was closed. (Make the closing entry.)
g. Declared a 14 percent annual dividend on preferred stock and a $0.35-per-share cash dividend plus a 40 percent stock dividend on common stock. The dividends are distributable on February 12, 1986, to stockholders of record on January 31, 1986.
h. The board authorized the restriction of retained earnings of $60,000 for plant expansion.

Required: Prepare the journal entries to record the transactions using letters in the place of dates.

P17–2B *Journalizing various stockholders' equity transactions and preparing a stockholders' equity section*

The stockholders' equity section of the Nebraska-Lincoln Corporation's balance sheet as of December 31, 1984, was as follows:

Stockholders' equity:	
Capital stock:	
Preferred stock, 12 percent, $25 par value; authorized and issued 12,500 shares	$ 312,500
Common stock, $10 par value; authorized and issued 70,000 shares	700,000
Paid-in capital—excess over par value, common stock	190,000
Retained earnings	375,000
Total stockholders' equity	$1,577,500

Selected transactions for the year 1985 occurred in the following sequence:
a. Declared a total annual cash dividend of $150,000 for 1985. (The preferred stock is cumulative; there are no dividends in arrears.)
b. Paid the dividend in transaction a.
c. Purchased 4,000 shares of its own preferred stock for $20 a share. (A restriction of retained earnings is not required.)
d. Established a restriction on retained earnings of $50,000 for contingencies.
e. Reissued 1,500 shares of treasury stock for $25 a share.
f. Earnings from operations for the year after income taxes were $280,000. (Make the closing entry.) Also close the dividends accounts.
g. Reissued 1,000 shares of treasury stock for $26 a share.
h. A major stockholder donated to the corporation a warehouse valued at $125,000.

Required:

1. Prepare general journal entries to record the transactions using letters in place of dates.

2. Enter the December 31, 1984, balances in ledger accounts. Post the journal entries to these and other newly created *stockholders' equity accounts* only.

3. Prepare the stockholders' equity section of the balance sheet as of December 31, 1985. Use the legal capital approach.

4. Why do you think the major stockholder donated a warehouse to the corporation?

P17–3B *Journalizing various stockholders' equity transactions and preparing a stockholders' equity section*

On April 1, 1984, the Bethel Corporation was authorized to issue 150,000 shares of $5 par value common stock and 7,500 shares of 12 percent cumulative preferred stock, $50 par value. The following selected transactions occurred between April 1, 1984, and December 31, 1985, in the sequence indicated:
a. Issued 20,000 shares of common stock at $8 a share and 3,000 shares of preferred stock at $55 a share.
b. Purchased the assets of the Lemon Company at their fair cash value; the assets consisted of land worth $40,000, buildings worth $160,000, and machinery worth $295,000. Issued 60,000 shares of common stock in payment.
c. The Income Summary account had a credit balance of $250,000 at the end of 1984 after all revenues and expenses had been closed to it. (Make closing entry.)

d. Purchased 2,000 shares of its own common stock at $8.50 a share. (The laws of the state of incorporation require a restriction of retained earnings equal to the cost of treasury stock.)
e. Established a restriction on retained earnings for contingencies of $75,000.
f. Reissued 450 shares of treasury stock for $9 a share.
g. The Income Summary account had a credit balance of $210,000 at the end of 1985 after all revenues and expenses had been closed to it. (Make closing entry.)
h. Declared a $0.90-per-share dividend on the common stock and a $3-per-share dividend on the preferred stock. (Assume that no preferred dividends are in arrears.)

Required:

1. Journalize the transactions, including any additional closing entries, and post to the stockholders' equity accounts only, using letters instead of dates.

2. Prepare the stockholders' equity section of the balance sheet as of December 31, 1985. Use the source of capital approach.

P17–4B *Book value issues*

The condensed balance sheet data of the Princeville Corporation as of December 31, 1985, were as follows:

Total assets	$745,000
Liabilities	$179,000
Preferred stock, 15 percent, $25 par value; cumulative	100,000
Common stock, no-par value; stated value $6	312,000
Paid-in capital—excess over par value, preferred stock	15,000
Paid-in capital—excess over stated value, common stock	24,000
Retained earnings—restricted for plant expansion	75,000
Retained earnings	40,000
Total liabilities and stockholders' equity	$745,000

Required:

1. Determine the book value per share of common stock, assuming that there are no dividend arrearages. The liquidation value of the preferred stock is equal to the par value plus any dividends in arrears.

2. Determine the book value per share of common stock, assuming that dividends on the preferred stock are in arrears for the years 1983, 1984, and 1985.

3. What is the significance of the book value per share?

4. What is the interrelationship between book value per share and market value per share?

P17–5B *Calculating earnings per share*

Assume the following data for the Secondo Corporation:

Weighted average shares of common stock outstanding	130,000
14% Convertible preferred shares, preference 1 stock, $25 par value (not a common stock equivalent, but convertible to common shares on a 1 preferred share for 2.5 common shares basis)	28,000
5% Convertible preferred shares, preference 2 stock, $100 par value (a common stock equivalent convertible to common shares on a 1 preferred share for 4 common shares basis)	50,000
Net income for 1985	$1,264,000

Assume that both types of preferred stock were outstanding during the entire year of 1985.

Required: Calculate (1) the primary earnings per share, and (2) the fully diluted earnings per share.

P17–6B

Thought-provoking problem: stock dividends, restricting retained earnings, and other issues

The following is an adaptation of a footnote that appeared in a recent annual report of a United States corporation:

Shareholders' equity:
The Board of Directors on June 3, 1985, declared a 100 percent common stock distribution on common shares, payable July 15, 1985. The per share amounts in the consolidated statement of income have been adjusted retroactively to reflect this July 1985 stock distribution.

The $3.00 preferred is convertible into 3.6 common shares and has liquidating preferences of $100 per share, redeemable beginning in 1992 at $103 per share, and is entitled to one vote per share. The company has been advised by counsel that there are no restrictions on income retained in the business as a result of the excess of liquidating preference over stated value of the preferred stocks.

In January 1986, the company increased the number of authorized shares of common stock from 7,000,000 to 45,000,000 shares. Of the common shares authorized but unissued at December 31, 1986, a total of 15,949,307 were reserved for conversion of preferred stocks and convertible subordinated debentures [bonds] and for exercise of stock options and warrants.

Required:

1. What was achieved by the 100 percent common stock distribution (a) from the corporation's viewpoint? (b) From the stockholders' viewpoint?

2. How did the stock distribution affect the balance sheet?

3. What is the purpose of the conversion privilege attaching to the preferred shares?

4. What is the significance of the advice by counsel regarding retained earnings restrictions?

5. Give some reasons for the large increase in the number of authorized shares of common stock.

18 Bonds Payable and Other Long-Term Liabilities

Introduction

Doing business on credit is a way of life in the United States. It is not unusual for over half of the assets of a business to be financed by creditor sources. For example, on December 31, 1981, 56.7% = ($654,067,000 ÷ $1,154,158,000) of the assets of the Overseas Shipholding Group, Inc. came from all creditor sources. Because of the heavy reliance on debt, the accounting for the acquisition of both short-term and long-term creditor funds is extremely important. The short-term creditor source has already been discussed in Chapter 10 and other chapters. For a more complete understanding of borrowing from creditors, this chapter discusses bonds payable in depth and introduces certain other long-term liabilities.

Learning Goals

To understand the nature and classification of bonds payable.

To understand the reason for issuing bonds instead of capital stock.

To record transactions for (a) bond issuance, (b) bond retirement and refunding, and (c) conversion of bonds into capital stock.

To understand the nature of and reasons for amortization of premium and discount on bonds payable by both the straight line and the interest methods.

To record an early retirement of bonds payable.

To make the accounting entries for bond sinking funds.

To understand the nature of and account for mortgage notes payable and long-term unsecured notes payable.

Long-Term Liabilities: Definitions and Types

Obligations that have maturity dates beyond the next year or operating cycle are classified on the balance sheet as **long-term liabilities** or long-term debt. The maturity dates of some long-term debt items cover 20 to 30 or more years. Often these obligations are paid off from the proceeds derived from the issuance of other long-term debt instruments. This rollover of the long-term debt makes it similar to certain types of capital stock. This is because no net resources (other than interest payments) are paid out in the process of continuing the liability item for an indefinite period into the future.

Typical long-term liabilities are bonds payable, mortgages payable, and unsecured long-term notes payable.

Bonds Payable

One of the means by which businesses and governments borrow funds that will not be repaid for many years is the issuance of bonds. A **bond,** or **bond certificate,** is a written promise under the corporate seal to pay a specific sum of money on a specified or determinable future date to the order of a person named in the certificate or to the order of the bearer. An example of a bond is the 4 percent, County of Brunswick, Series A School Bond, due June 1, 2000. Figure 18–1 shows a specimen of a $5,000 bond of this series. These bonds were issued in 1978, when the interest on this kind of bond was extremely low. The interest rate on state and local government bonds is usually lower than that of commercial bonds because the interest revenue is not taxable by either the federal or issuing state governments. Figure 18–2 shows four specimen coupons attached to these bonds. At the time this is being written, interest rates on commercial bonds are ranging from approximately 12 percent to 16 percent.

Bonds for publicly-held large corporations are promoted by a notice as for common stock in a financial publication that the securities will be available for sale. This type of promotional piece, a *tombstone ad,* was used by the Philip Morris Credit Corporation to announce the sale of zero coupon guaranteed notes due in 1994 (see Figure 18–3).

Bonds are usually issued in denominations of $100, $500, $1,000, or $5,000 each. This variation enables the issuing company to obtain funds from many different investors or groups of investors. Denominations smaller than $100 have been used by the U.S. government in the past. On the other hand, municipal bonds issued in $5,000 denominations are also common. For instance, the denomination of the bond shown in Figure 18–1 is $5,000.

Bonds may be issued directly to buyers by the borrowing corporation or marketed through agents such as banks, brokers, or other underwriting syndicates (groups of firms that sell securities for issuing corporations for a fee). These agents, in turn, sell the bonds through their own channels and charge a fee to the issuing company for the sale; or they may in fact buy the whole issue and resell them at a profit. **Bondholders** are creditors of the corporation. Except for currently maturing amounts, the Bonds Payable account is a

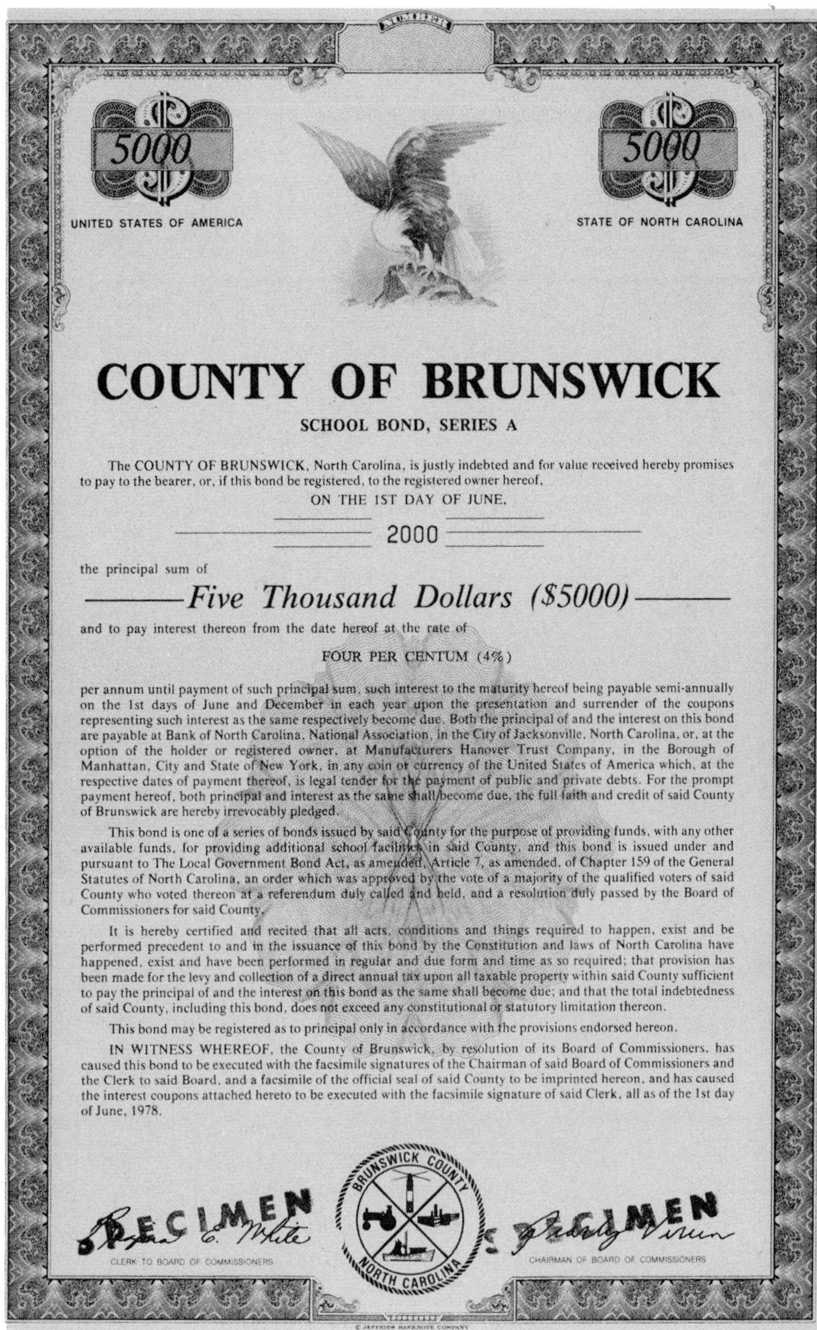

NUMBER

5000 | 5000

UNITED STATES OF AMERICA | STATE OF NORTH CAROLINA

COUNTY OF BRUNSWICK

SCHOOL BOND, SERIES A

The COUNTY OF BRUNSWICK, North Carolina, is justly indebted and for value received hereby promises to pay to the bearer, or, if this bond be registered, to the registered owner hereof,

ON THE 1ST DAY OF JUNE,

2000

the principal sum of

Five Thousand Dollars ($5000)

and to pay interest thereon from the date hereof at the rate of

FOUR PER CENTUM (4%)

per annum until payment of such principal sum, such interest to the maturity hereof being payable semi-annually on the 1st days of June and December in each year upon the presentation and surrender of the coupons representing such interest as the same respectively become due. Both the principal of and the interest on this bond are payable at Bank of North Carolina, National Association, in the City of Jacksonville, North Carolina, or, at the option of the holder or registered owner, at Manufacturers Hanover Trust Company, in the Borough of Manhattan, City and State of New York, in any coin or currency of the United States of America which, at the respective dates of payment thereof, is legal tender for the payment of public and private debts. For the prompt payment hereof, both principal and interest as the same shall become due, the full faith and credit of said County of Brunswick are hereby irrevocably pledged.

This bond is one of a series of bonds issued by said County for the purpose of providing funds, with any other available funds, for providing additional school facilities in said County, and this bond is issued under and pursuant to The Local Government Bond Act, as amended, Article 7, as amended, of Chapter 159 of the General Statutes of North Carolina, an order which was approved by the vote of a majority of the qualified voters of said County who voted thereon at a referendum duly called and held, and a resolution duly passed by the Board of Commissioners for said County.

It is hereby certified and recited that all acts, conditions and things required to happen, exist and be performed precedent to and in the issuance of this bond by the Constitution and laws of North Carolina have happened, exist and have been performed in regular and due form and time as so required; that provision has been made for the levy and collection of a direct annual tax upon all taxable property within said County sufficient to pay the principal of and the interest on this bond as the same shall become due; and that the total indebtedness of said County, including this bond, does not exceed any constitutional or statutory limitation thereon.

This bond may be registered as to principal only in accordance with the provisions endorsed hereon.

IN WITNESS WHEREOF, the County of Brunswick, by resolution of its Board of Commissioners, has caused this bond to be executed with the facsimile signatures of the Chairman of said Board of Commissioners and the Clerk to said Board, and a facsimile of the official seal of said County to be imprinted hereon, and has caused the interest coupons attached hereto to be executed with the facsimile signature of said Clerk, all as of the 1st day of June, 1978.

SPECIMEN | BRUNSWICK COUNTY NORTH CAROLINA | SPECIMEN

CLERK TO BOARD OF COMMISSIONERS | CHAIRMAN OF BOARD OF COMMISSIONERS

Source: Courtesy of Local Government Commission, State of North Carolina.

Figure 18–1 **Specimen of a Bond**

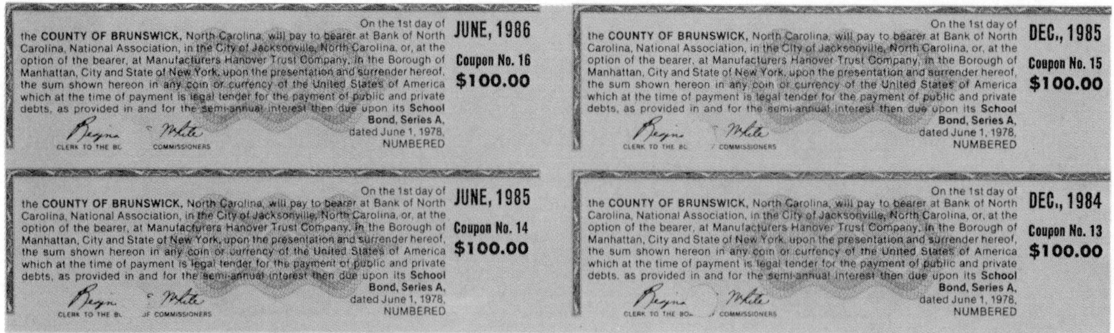

On the 1st day of JUNE, 1986 the **COUNTY OF BRUNSWICK**, North Carolina, will pay to bearer at Bank of North Carolina, National Association, in the City of Jacksonville, North Carolina, or, at the option of the bearer, at Manufacturers Hanover Trust Company, in the Borough of Manhattan, City and State of New York, upon the presentation and surrender hereof, the sum shown hereon in any coin or currency of the United States of America which at the time of payment is legal tender for the payment of public and private debts, as provided in and for the semi-annual interest then due upon its **School Bond, Series A**, dated June 1, 1978, NUMBERED

Coupon No. 16 $100.00

CLERK TO THE BC COMMISSIONERS

On the 1st day of DEC., 1985 the **COUNTY OF BRUNSWICK**, North Carolina, will pay to bearer at Bank of North Carolina, National Association, in the City of Jacksonville, North Carolina, or, at the option of the bearer, at Manufacturers Hanover Trust Company, in the Borough of Manhattan, City and State of New York, upon the presentation and surrender hereof, the sum shown hereon in any coin or currency of the United States of America which at the time of payment is legal tender for the payment of public and private debts, as provided in and for the semi-annual interest then due upon its **School Bond, Series A**, dated June 1, 1978, NUMBERED

Coupon No. 15 $100.00

CLERK TO THE BC COMMISSIONERS

On the 1st day of JUNE, 1985 the **COUNTY OF BRUNSWICK**, North Carolina, will pay to bearer at Bank of North Carolina, National Association, in the City of Jacksonville, North Carolina, or, at the option of the bearer, at Manufacturers Hanover Trust Company, in the Borough of Manhattan, City and State of New York, upon the presentation and surrender hereof, the sum shown hereon in any coin or currency of the United States of America which at the time of payment is legal tender for the payment of public and private debts, as provided in and for the semi-annual interest then due upon its **School Bond, Series A**, dated June 1, 1978, NUMBERED

Coupon No. 14 $100.00

CLERK TO THE B. OF COMMISSIONERS

On the 1st day of DEC., 1984 the **COUNTY OF BRUNSWICK**, North Carolina, will pay to bearer at Bank of North Carolina, National Association, in the City of Jacksonville, North Carolina, or, at the option of the bearer, at Manufacturers Hanover Trust Company, in the Borough of Manhattan, City and State of New York, upon the presentation and surrender hereof, the sum shown hereon in any coin or currency of the United States of America which at the time of payment is legal tender for the payment of public and private debts, as provided in and for the semi-annual interest then due upon its **School Bond, Series A**, dated June 1, 1978, NUMBERED

Coupon No. 13 $100.00

CLERK TO THE BO. COMMISSIONERS

Source: Courtesy of Local Government Commission, State of North Carolina.

Figure 18–2 **Specimen of Four Coupons**

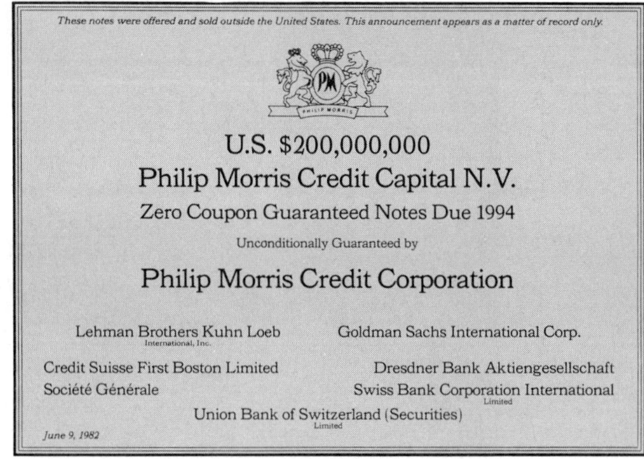

Source: Reprinted with permission of Philip Morris Credit Corportation.

Figure 18–3 **Tombstone Ad Announcing Sale of Zero Coupon Guaranteed Notes Due 1994**

long-term liability. Bonds contain provisions for interest to be paid at regularly stated intervals. Interest is usually paid semiannually on industrial bonds.

A bond, like a promissory note, represents a corporate debt to the borrower, which must be satisfied from the assets of the corporation in preference to stockholders' equity claims. Bonds, however, may be bought and sold by investors as common and preferred stocks are. The contract or covenant between the corporation and its bondholders is called a **bond indenture.**

Classification of Bonds

A corporation may issue several kinds of bonds that are tailored to meet the particular financial needs of the issuing corporation or to attract a wider variety of investors. Bonds may be registered to an individual or unregistered (bearer). They may be secured by assets or unsecured.

Registered Bonds

Registered bonds are issued in the name of the bondholder. They require proper endorsement on the bond certificate to effect a transfer from one owner to another. The debtor corporation or its transfer agent (usually a bank or trust company appointed by the corporation, which acting for the issuer physically makes the transfer of securities bought and records ownership of the securities) maintains complete ownership records. Bonds may be registered as to both principal and interest, in which case interest checks are issued only to bondholders of record. It is possible, however, to register the principal only. One way to do this is to issue coupon bonds. The owner of **coupon bonds** detaches interest coupons from the bond certificate and deposits them at the stated interest dates at the owner's bank or at a designated bank (see Figure 18–2).

The Tax Equity and Fiscal Responsibility Act of 1982 contained a provision requiring that under certain conditions payers of interest must withhold income taxes at a rate of 10 percent on payment of interest to individuals, partnerships, estates, and trusts. Payments of interest to corporations, however, are exempt from this withholding requirement. This act was modified by Congress in 1983, to eliminate this 10% withholding. The act, however, would require that a 20% withholding be instituted for those who are identified as "tax cheats." The effect of these tax laws and other related regulations may serve to restrict the use of coupon bonds by commercial-type corporations.

Bearer Bonds

Bearer bonds may be issued by certain entities without being registered in the name of the buyer; title to them is held by the bearer. These bonds must be coupon bonds. This method is least burdensome to the issuing corporation (most likely a state or municipal unit) because it does not have to maintain a list of people to whom semiannual interest checks must be mailed. It does, however, pay interest in that the interest coupon serves the purpose of a check (because the bondholder can deposit it at most banks). The owner must take particular care against loss or theft of the certificates or unauthorized removal of the coupons attached to the bonds.

Secured Bonds

A **secured bond** is one that pledges some part of the corporate assets as security for the bond. The asset pledged may consist of land and buildings (for *real estate mortgage* bonds), machinery (for *chattel mortgage* bonds), negotiable securities (for *collateral trust* bonds), or other corporate assets. Several loans may use the same assets for collateral; this gives rise to *first mortgage* bonds and *second mortgage* bonds. The numbers indicate the order to be followed in satisfying the bondholders' claims if the corporation fails to meet its obligations under the bond indenture. In the event of **default** (failure to pay the bonds by the issuer) the pledged property may be sold and the proceeds used to pay creditors. Second and third mortgage bonds necessarily carry a higher interest rate than first mortgage bonds because of the order of priority of payment in the event of a default. Thus they are not as marketable as first mortgage bonds and are more costly to the borrowing company. It is, therefore, desirable for the borrower to raise the required funds through a single, large first mortgage bond issue.

Unsecured Bonds

Holders of unsecured bonds rank as general, or ordinary, creditors of the corporation and rely upon the corporation's general credit. These **unsecured bonds** are commonly referred to as **debenture bonds,** or often simply as *debentures.* Sometimes debenture bonds are issued with a provision that interest payments will depend on earnings; these are called **income bonds.**

Other Bonds

Bonds may have other special features; for instance, the bonds may mature serially **(serial bonds);** specified portions of the outstanding bonds will mature in installments and be paid at stated intervals. Sometimes the issuing corporation retains an option to call in the bonds before maturity **(callable bonds);** in other cases the bondholder may be given an option to exchange the bonds for capital stock **(convertible bonds).** The bond indenture may require the issuing corporation to make deposits to a **sinking fund** (a fund created to retire bonds), often in the name of a trustee for the bondholders, at regular intervals. This ensures the availability of adequate funds for the redemption of the bonds at maturity.

Bonds Compared to Capital Stock

A better knowledge of bonds may be gained by referring to Figure 18–4, in which bonds are compared to capital stock.

Bonds	Capital Stock
Bondholders are creditors.	Stockholders are owners.
Bonds Payable is a long-term liability account.	Capital Stock is a stockholders' equity account.
Bondholders, along with other creditors, have primary claims on assets in liquidation.	Stockholders have residual claims on assets in liquidation.
Interest is typically a fixed charge; it must be paid or the creditors can institute bankruptcy proceedings against the debtor corporation.	Dividends are not fixed charges; even preferred dividends are at best only *contingent charges;* these are paid if income is sufficient and if declared by the corporate board of directors.
Interest is an expense.	Dividends are not expenses; they are distributions of net income.
Interest is deductible in arriving at both taxable and business income.	Dividends are not deductible in arriving at taxable and business income. (See Appendix A.)
Bonds do not carry voting rights.	All stock carries voting rights unless they are expressly denied by contract, as is usually the case with preferred stock.

Figure 18–4 Comparison of Bonds to Capital Stock

Reasons for Issuing Bonds instead of Capital Stock

It is important for an accountant to understand the variety of factors that cause managers to issue bonds rather than capital stock. One factor influencing this decision is that management, by issuing bonds, has access to an important market source of funds it would not have through a stock issue. Many banks and other financial institutions are restricted by law in the amount of stock they can buy. They then look for an alternative investment—often in bonds.

A second factor, **leverage,** involves **trading on the bondholder's equity.** Leverage can be described simply: If funds borrowed at 14 percent can be used in the business enterprise to earn 23 percent after taxes, additional earnings of 9 percent (23 percent − 14 percent) accrue to the common stockholders, who have invested no additional money for this return. However, the opposite effect is always possible: the borrowed funds may earn less than the cost of borrowing. This is an instance of unfavorable leverage.

A third reason why corporations decide to issue bonds instead of capital stock is the income tax on corporate net income. Because a corporation pays part of its net income in federal and state income taxes, it naturally considers the issuance of bonds as a means of effecting tax savings.

To illustrate how leverage and heavy income taxes affect the choice of alternative methods of fund raising, assume that the Levirite Corporation, which has $10 par value common stock outstanding in the amount of $1,000,000, needs $500,000 to purchase additional plant assets. Three plans are under consideration: Plan 1 is to issue additional common stock at $10 par value; Plan 2 is to issue 14½ percent cumulative preferred stock at $100 par value; Plan 3 is to issue 13 percent bonds at face. Figure 18–5 shows the calculations which would be helpful in making the decision. All three plans assume that the securities will be issued at face or par value, that annual earnings of

	Plan 1 (Common Stock)	Plan 2 (Preferred Stock)	Plan 3 (Bonds)
Common stock outstanding	$1,000,000.00	$1,000,000.00	$1,000,000.00
Additional funds needed	500,000.00	500,000.00	500,000.00
Total	$1,500,000.00	1,500,000.00	$1,500,000.00
Net income before bond interest and income taxes	$ 350,000.00	$ 350,000.00	$ 350,000.00
Deduct: Bond interest expense	0	0	65,000.00
Net income after bond interest expense	$ 350,000.00	$ 350,000.00	$ 285,000.00
Deduct: Income taxes (assumed rate of 40%)	140,000.00	140,000.00	114,000.00
Net income after income taxes	$ 210,000.00	$ 210,000.00	$ 171,000.00
Deduct: Dividends on preferred stock	0	72,500.00	0
Available for common stock dividends or reinvestment in Levirite Corporation	$ 210,000.00	$ 137,500.00	$ 171,000.00
Projected earnings per share on common stock (150,000 shares outstanding under Plan 1; 100,000 shares under Plans 2 and 3)	$ 1.40	$ 1.37½	$ 1.71

Figure 18–5 **Three Plans for Obtaining Long-Term Funds**

$350,000 before bond interest expense is deducted will be maintained, and that an income tax rate of 40 percent will prevail.

Assuming that projected earnings per share on common stock is the best basis for making the decision, Plan 3 is desirable for the common stockholders, particularly if the net income before income taxes exceeds $350,000, because the bond interest rate is fixed. If the annual net income falls below $350,000, one of the other plans may become more advantageous. Since the securities market and corporate net earnings remain uncertain, there is no exact mathematical formula to solve this financial problem. The decision requires sound judgment based on past experience and projected future needs.

A fourth reason for management to issue bonds instead of common stock is that bonds, and to a lesser extent preferred stock, aid in offsetting losses due to shrinkage in the purchasing power of the funds invested in assets. Bonds, for example, carry fixed contract maturity values in terms of the monetary unit at the maturity date. If the value of the dollar decreases before the bonds are paid, a gain resulting from the use of the more valuable money received at the time of borrowing accrues to the owners of the business.

A fifth factor is control. The issuance of additional common stock may result in a loss of management control because the ownership of the corporation is distributed over a larger number of stockholders. Bondholders, on the other hand, are creditors and do not participate in managerial decisions, except in the rare instances when this is a specific provision of the bond indenture.

Other reasons may influence the decision of management to issue bonds, but these five factors indicate the scope of the problem.

The Bond Issue

Authorizing the Bond Issue

Even after management decides that bonds should be issued, it is faced with months of preliminary work before the bonds can actually be floated, or sold. For example, the exact amount to be borrowed, the **nominal** or **contract interest rate** (the rate on the bond certificate that applies to the face value), the maturity date, and the assets, if any, to be pledged must be determined. The provisions of the bond indenture must be chosen with extreme care. For instance, should the bonds be callable, and should they be convertible into some other form of security? Careful long-range financial planning helps to reduce the cost of securing the long-term funds. For example, if there is any chance that the company will need additional funds in the near future, management—by pledging the company's total mortgageable assets—should not close the door on the possibility of marketing additional bonds. Management probably should seek authority for a bond issue large enough to meet all foreseeable needs.

The financial vice-president or the controller, working with other corporate officers, is responsible for answers to these and other questions. This officer prepares a written report for the board of directors, summarizing the proposed features of the bond financing and stating why the funds are needed, how they are to be used, and the means of ultimately retiring the bond issue. Various alternative methods of raising funds, such as those shown in the example of the Levirite Corporation, are presented to point up the financial advantage of issuing the bonds.

The board of directors studies this written report and other factors before passing a resolution recommending to the stockholders that bonds be issued. Next, the proposal is presented to the stockholders for their approval. Approval by the stockholders is required because the bondholders will have a preferred position. As creditors, they have a prior claim to the assets of the corporation in the event of liquidation.

Accounting for Authorization; Rating of Bonds

No formal journal entry is required to record the authorization of the bond issue by the stockholders, but a memorandum should be made in the Bonds Payable account indicating the total amount authorized. This information is needed when the balance sheet is prepared since a firm should disclose the total authorization as well as the amount issued.

The issue price, usually stated as a percentage of the face value, is affected primarily by the prevailing market interest rate on bonds of the same grade. Bonds are graded by independent investment advisory services; the grade depends on the financial condition of the issuing corporation. The two major investment advisory services in the United States are Moody's and Standard & Poor's. Standard & Poor's highest grade is AAA; the next, AA; and in descending order: A, BBB, and so on, down to a grade that is simply referred to as "unrated."

Example A: Bonds Issued at Face Value To show the essential similarity between the accounting for notes payable (see Chapter 10) and for bonds payable, Example A is a simple situation in which a corporation issues bonds at **face value** (sometimes called *issuance at par*) on an interest date. Suppose that the Amerson Corporation needs funds and that the best alternative is to issue bonds. The stockholders approve a bond issue of $200,000. Ten-year, 16 percent, first mortgage bonds are to be issued.[1] The interest will be paid semiannually on April 1 and October 1. Amerson Corporation closes its books each December 31. Assume that the corporation issues to banks and insurance companies all of the authorized bonds on April 1, 1985, at 100 or face value (*100* means 100 percent of face). The entries to record the issue,

[1]When this book was written the interest rate for borrowing money on all types of credit instruments was very erratic, ranging from 9.9 to 20 percent. The rates used in the illustrations should not be construed as typical 1985 rates.

to pay the first interest payment, and to make the adjusting entry on December 31 follow along with the entry for the first 1986 payment:[2]

Date		Account		Debit	Credit
1985					
Apr.	1	Cash		200,000	
		First Mortgage Bonds Payable			200,000
		To record the issuance of 16 percent bonds due April 1, 1995.			
Oct.	1	Bond Interest Expense		16,000	
		Cash			16,000
		To record the payment of interest on the first mortgage bonds.			
Dec.	31	Bond Interest Expense		8,000	
		Accrued Bond Interest Payable			8,000
		To record the accrual of bond interest for three months.			
1986					
Apr.	1	Bond Interest Expense		8,000	
		Accrued Bond Interest Payable		8,000	
		Cash			16,000
		To record payment of semiannual interest.			

Comments on these entries follow:

1. The First Mortgage Bonds Payable account is a long-term liability since it will not be repaid for 10 years. On the balance sheet, the particular real property that is pledged as security should be disclosed in a footnote.

2. The entries to record the Bond Interest Expense are very similar to those recording Interest Expense on notes payable discussed in Chapter 10.

3. The adjusting entry for accrued bond interest is similar to the recording of accrued interest on notes payable. Accrued bond interest payable is a current liability since it must be liquidated in three months—on April 1, 1986.

4. In computing bond interest to be paid or accrued in this book, each year is assumed to be divided into 12 equal months (30-day month time).

Why Bonds Sell at a Premium or Discount

If the average market interest rate on bonds of a comparable grade is higher than the contract interest rate on the bonds being issued, investors will offer less than the face value of the bonds in order to make up the difference between the rates. The difference **(discount)** between the issue price and the maturity values plus receipts of the semiannual interest will give the investors

[2]Transactions involving cash are normally recorded in the cash receipts and cash payments journals. They are shown here recorded in general journal form for ease of illustration and teachability.

a return on their investments approximating the return on similar amounts invested at the prevailing market interest rate. The effective rate is called the yield or yield rate. If the stated interest rate is higher than the current market rate, investors will tend to offer a **premium** (an amount greater than the face value) because they know that this premium will be returned to them to the extent that the periodic interest payments exceed the amount that they would receive on other investments made at the current market rate.

Two examples are presented to emphasize the reasons for bonds selling at a premium or a discount. First, assume that the Higho Company has an AAA financial rating and is planning to issue debenture bonds. Assume also that all AAA debenture bonds on the market have an effective average market interest rate of 16 percent. If the Higho Company issues debenture bonds with a 16 percent contract interest rate, it will receive the face value of the bonds. If, however, the Higho Company issues bonds with a 17 percent contract rate, it will receive an amount in excess of the face value; that is, the bonds will sell at a *premium.* On the other hand, even with its excellent credit rating, if the Higho Company issues bonds with a 15 percent contract rate, it will receive an amount less than face value; that is, the bonds will sell at a *discount.*

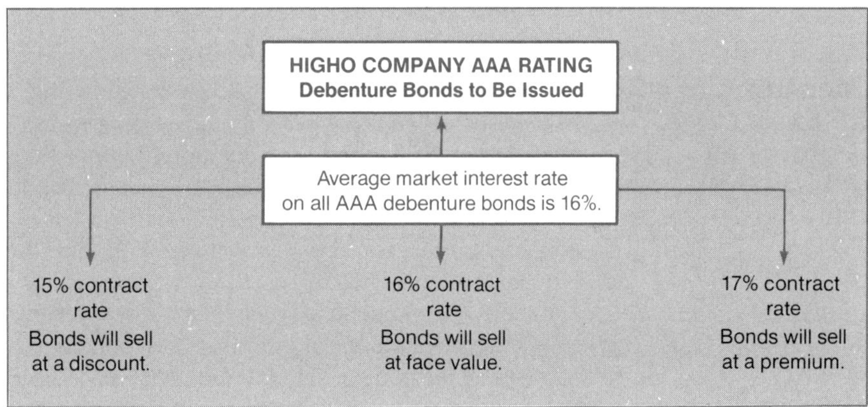

The second example shows that the single basic determinant of the issue price of the company's bonds is the fact that the contract interest rate is different from the going average effective rate on a particular grade of bond. Assume that the Lorat Company, with a BB financial rating, intends to issue first mortage bonds. Further assume that the average effective market interest rate on BB first mortgage bonds is 17 percent. If the Lorat Company issues its bonds with a 17 percent contract interest rate, it will receive the face value of the bonds. Even with its relatively poor credit rating, if it issues bonds with an 18 percent contract interest rate, the Lorat Company will receive an amount in excess of the face value; but if it issues bonds with a 16 percent contract interest rate, it will receive an amount less than the face value.

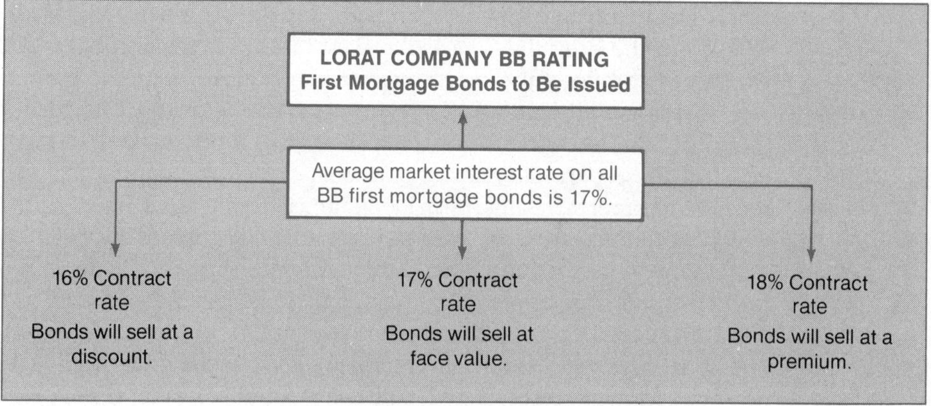

The premium and the discount arise as a result of differences in the average market rate of interest on a comparable grade of bond and the particular contract rate on these bonds. A knowledge of this fact suggests the approach to the accounting for the amortization of the premium and discount elements given in the illustrations which follow.

Calculation of the Exact Price of Bonds to Yield a Given Rate

The exact price that an investor must pay for the bonds to yield a given rate can be determined by a compound interest computation or by reference to a *bond yield table.* To illustrate the compound interest computation, assume that 20-year (40 semiannual periods), 16½ percent bonds with a face of $100,000 are issued at a price to yield 16 percent (or 8 percent every six months); the interest is to be paid semiannually. The calculation of the issue price involves the determination of the *present value* at the issue date of two separate items (see Appendix to Part Three for a review of present value concepts): (1) the face amount of the bonds discounted at the yield rate, and (2) the interest payments discounted at the yield rate. This calculation is shown below.

Present value of the face amount of $100,000 (a single sum) for 40 periods at yield rate of 8% ($100,000 × 0.046031)	$ 4,603.10
Add: Present value of 40 interest payments of $8,250 = (½ × 16½% × $100,000) (an ordinary annuity) each at yield rate of 8% ($8,250 × 11.924613)	98,378.06
Total price to yield 16% annually	$102,981.16

The foregoing bonds would be said to sell at approximately 103 percent of face. The price derived in the calculation shows that a premium is expected since the effective interest rate of 16 percent is below the contract or face interest rate of 16½ percent.

Methods of Amortization of Premium and Discount

In developing the accounting for the issuance of bonds, two methods of **amortization of the premium and discount on bonds payable** (the writing off of these items to bond interest expense) are presented: (1) the *straight line method,* and (2) the *interest method.* Theoretically, bond interest expense should be measured by the amount of the effective interest; that is, the yield rate multiplied by the **carrying value** of the bonds (face plus unamortized premium, or face minus unamortized discount) at the beginning of each interest period. This method results in the use of the **interest method of amortization.** The Accounting Principles Board states in its *Opinion 21* that the interest method is the correct one to be used for the amortization of discount or premium on notes receivable and payable; but it implies that it is equally applicable to discount or premium on bonds payable. The APB states that

> . . . the difference between the present value and the face amount should be treated as discount or premium and amortized as interest expense or income [revenue] over the life of the note in such a way as to result in a constant rate of interest when applied to the amount outstanding at the beginning of any period. This is the "interest" method. . . . However, other methods of amortization may be used if the results obtained are not materially different from those which result from the interest method.[3]

Practitioners have interpreted the last provision in the foregoing statement as permitting the use of the **straight line method** (recognition of equal interest expense each period over the life of the bonds) in those cases where the results obtained are not materially different from those resulting from the use of the interest method. In many cases, the difference is not material, and thus the simpler straight line method is still extremely popular.

Three examples follow showing the accounting for the issuance of bonds at a price other than face amount. They are first treated using the simpler straight line method of amortization (B set). The interest method of amortization is then used with the same three examples in the C set of illustrations.

B Set of Examples Using Straight Line Amortization

Example B–1: Bonds Issued at a Premium on an Interest Date

Problem Data Assume that on July 1, 1985, the Bonkers Corporation is authorized to issue 16½ percent first mortgage bonds with a face value of $100,000 and a maturity date of June 30, 2005. Interest is paid semiannually on June 30 and December 31. Books are closed each December 31. All the bonds are issued on July 1, 1985, for $102,981.16 (see previous calculation) to yield 16 percent.

Journal Entry to Record the Issue The issuance of these bonds to banks and insurance companies is recorded as follows:

---

[3] *Opinions of the Accounting Principles Board, No. 21,* "Interest on Receivables and Payables" (New York: AICPA, August 1971), paragraph 15.

Date		Account		Debit	Credit
1985 Jul.	1	Cash		102,981.16	
		First Mortgage Bonds Payable			100,000.00
		Premium on Bonds Payable			2,981.16
		To record the issuance of 16½ percent first mortgage bonds due June 30, 2005.			

Statement Disclosure A balance sheet prepared on July 1, 1985, would show bonds payable and premium on bonds payable as follows:

Long-term liabilities:		
16½% first mortgage bonds payable, due June 30, 2005	$100,000.00	
Add: Premium on bonds payable	2,981.16	
Total long-term liabilities		$102,981.16

The assets pledged as security for the bonds payable would be disclosed in the following footnote:

> Land and buildings costing $300,000 (market value $350,000) are pledged as security for the bonds payable.

This method of disclosure of the premium on bonds payable is consistent with the concept that the right-hand side of the balance sheet describes the sources of business funds. The footnote discloses important information that may influence the decision of an investor to buy or not to buy the company's bonds.

Recording Bond Interest Expense and Amortization of Premium As the premium account is reduced by periodic amortization, it becomes smaller on each subsequent statement. Again, this procedure is consistent with the concept that when bonds are issued at a premium each interest payment contains, in effect, a payment of the interest expense on the debt and also a partial return of the premium element borrowed. If part of the $2,981.16 premium is repaid, a balance sheet prepared at a later date would naturally show a smaller carrying value.

The amount received from the issuance of the bonds is $2,981.16 greater than the amount that must be repaid at maturity. This amount is not a gain, for by definition a gain or revenue cannot result directly from the borrowing process. The premium arose because the contract rate of interest on the bonds issued was higher than the prevailing market rate on similar grade bonds. Therefore, it is sound accounting practice to allocate part of the premium on bonds payable to each interest period as a reduction of the periodic bond interest expense. In summary, under the straight line amortization method, equal bond interest expense is recognized each period. This equal expense is the total cash paid for bond interest expense over the life of a bond issue, adjusted—and reduced—by equal periodic amortization of the premium on bonds payable.

The bond interest expense of the Bonkers Corporation is recorded on December 31, 1985, as follows:

1985					
Dec.	31	Bond Interest Expense		8,175.47	
		Premium on Bonds Payable		74.53	
		Cash			8,250.00
		To record the semiannual bond interest payment and amortization; the amount of amortization is $2,981.16 ÷ 40 semiannual periods = $74.53.			

If the $2,981.16 premium on the bonds payable represents a reduction in interest over the entire 20-year life of the bonds, it is evident that by the straight line amortization method the reduction in interest for the six months ended December 31, 1985, is $2,981.16 divided by 40 semiannual periods, or $74.53.

This compound entry emphasizes that the $8,250 constitutes the payment of measured bond interest expense of $8,175.47 and a partial return of the premium element borrowed, the $74.53 amortized. (For the problems in this text, premiums or discounts on bonds payable should be amortized each time the bond interest expense is recorded to emphasize that this amortization is an adjustment of the bond interest.) Even though the compound entry is acceptable under the straight line method, two separate entries may be made: (1) an entry to record the payment or accrual of the bond interest, and (2) a separate entry to record the semiannual amortization of the premium.[4]

[4]These two entries as of December 31, 1985, for the Bonkers Corporation could be:
In the cash payments journal:

1985					
Dec.	31	Bond Interest Expense		8,250.00	
		Cash			8,250.00
		To record cash payment for semiannual interest.			

In the general journal:

1985					
Dec.	31	Premium on Bonds Payable		74.53	
		Bond Interest Expense			74.53
		To record amortization of premium for six months.			

Assuming the use of straight line amortization of the premium on bonds payable, the proof of the $8,175.47 semiannual bond interest figure can be calculated by another means, as follows:

Cash payments to be made:	
Face value of bonds at maturity	$100,000.00
Total interest (16½% × 20 years × $100,000)	330,000.00
Total cash payments	$430,000.00
Cash receipts:	
Bonds with face value of $100,000 issued for	102,981.16
Net interest expense for 20 years	$327,018.84
Net semiannual interest expense: $\frac{\$327,018.84}{40 \text{ semiannual periods}}$	$ 8,175.47

Retirement of Bonds at Maturity Assume that the 16½ percent first mortgage bonds payable are repaid *(retired)* on June 30, 2005. After the June 30, 2005, semiannual interest payment entry is made, the Premium on Bonds Payable account has a zero balance. The second entry records the retirement of the bonds at maturity.

2005					
Jun.	30	Bond Interest Expense		8,175.51	
		Premium on Bonds Payable		74.49[a]	
		Cash			8,250.00
		To record the last semiannual interest payment on the 16½ percent bonds payable and the last semiannual amortization of bond premium.			
	30	First Mortgage Bonds Payable		100,000.00	
		Cash			100,000.00
		To record the retirement of the 16½% bonds payable at maturity.			

[a]The last amortization debit will be $0.04 less than all the others [$2,981.16 − (39 × $74.53)] due to rounding.

Example B–2: Bonds Issued at a Discount on an Interest Date

Problem Data Assume that on July 1, 1985, the Davidson Company is authorized to issue 16 percent debenture bonds with a face value of $200,000 and a maturity date of June 30, 1995. Interest is paid semiannually on June 30 and December 31. Books are closed each December 31. All the bonds are issued on July 1, 1985, for $181,742.91. This is a price that will yield 18 percent. The bonds sell at a discount because the **yield rate** (the prevailing market rate on similar grades of debenture bonds) is higher than the nominal (or contract) rate of interest on the bonds issued.

Journal Entry to Record the Issue The issuance of the bonds to banks and insurance companies is recorded as follows:

1985					
Jul.	1	Cash		181,742.91	
		Discount on Bonds Payable		18,257.09	
		Debenture Bonds Payable			200,000.00
		To record the issuance of 16 percent debenture bonds due June 30, 1995.			

Statement Disclosure A balance sheet prepared on July 1, 1985, would disclose bonds payable and discount on bonds payable as follows:

Long-term liabilities:		
16% Debenture bonds payable, due June 30, 1995	$200,000.00	
Deduct: Discount on bonds payable	18,257.09	
Total long-term liabilities		$181,742.91

Note the similarity of this method of disclosure to that of a premium on bonds payable.

Recording Bond Interest Expense and Amortization of Discount The following compound entry records the first semiannual interest payment by the Davidson Company and semiannual amortization of the Discount on Bonds Payable account by the straight line method.

1985					
Dec.	31	Bond Interest Expense		16,912.85	
		Cash			16,000.00
		Discount on Bonds Payable			912.85
		To record semiannual bond interest payment and amortization; the amount of amortization is $18,257.09 ÷ 20 semiannual periods = $912.85.			

This entry indicates that the measured absolute semiannual interest expense is $16,912.85, not $16,000. Assuming the straight line method of amortization, the measured interest is equal to the cash interest payment plus a pro rata share of the discount—in effect, a part of the total interest cost over the entire life of the bonds. This accounting procedure, therefore, recognizes the reason for the discount on the bonds—that the contract rate of interest was lower than the prevailing market interest rate on similar grades of securities. The proof of this semiannual bond interest expense can be seen by the following calculation:

Cash payments to be made:	
Face value of bonds at maturity	$200,000.00
Total interest (16% × 10 years × $200,000)	320,000.00
Total cash payments	$520,000.00
Cash receipts:	
Bonds with face value of $200,000 issued for	181,742.91
Net interest expense for 10 years	$338,257.09
Net semiannual interest expense: $\frac{\$338,257.09}{20 \text{ semiannual periods}}$	$ 16,912.85

Retirement of Bonds at Maturity On June 30, 1995, the 16 percent debenture bonds payable are retired. After the June 30, 1995, semiannual interest payment entry is made, the Discount on Bonds Payable account has a zero balance. The second entry records the retirement of the bonds at maturity.

Date		Account		Debit	Credit
1995					
Jun.	30	Bond Interest Expense		16,912.94	
		Cash			16,000.00
		Discount on Bonds Payable			912.94[a]
		To record the last semiannual interest payment and final amortization of bond discount on the 16 percent bonds payable.			
	30	Debenture Bonds Payable		200,000.00	
		Cash			200,000.00
		To record the retirement of 16 percent bonds payable at maturity.			

[a]The last amortization credit will be $0.09 more than all the others [($18,257.09 − (19 × $912.85)] due to rounding.

Example B–3: Bonds Issued at a Discount Requiring Interest to Be Accrued at End of Year

Problem Data Assume the same facts as stated in Example B–2 except that the Davidson Company issued the 16 percent bonds to banks and insurance companies on March 31, 1985, rather than on July 1, 1985, and that the interest dates are September 30 and March 31.

Journal Entry to Record the Issue Not all the steps in the preceding examples need to be repeated. The journal entry to record the issue is:

Date		Account		Debit	Credit
1985					
Mar.	31	Cash		181,742.91	
		Discount on Bonds Payable		18,257.09	
		Debenture Bonds Payable			200,000.00
		To record the issuance of 16 percent debenture bonds due March 31, 1995.			

Recording Bond Interest Expense and Amortization of Discount The entries from September 30, 1985, to March 31, 1986, with the accompanying calculation of straight line amortization included as a part of the explanation to the journal entries, are shown below:

1985					
Sep.	30	Bond Interest Expense		16,912.85	
		Cash			16,000.00
		Discount on Bonds Payable			912.85
		To record semiannual bond interest and amortization; the amount of amortization is $912.85.[a]			
Dec.	31	Bond Interest Expense		8,456.43	
		Accrued Bond Interest Payable			8,000.00
		Discount on Bonds Payable			456.43
		To record the accrual of bond interest and the amortization for three months; the amount of amortization is $456.43.[b]			
1986					
Mar.	31	Bond Interest Expense		8,456.42	
		Accrued Bond Interest Payable		8,000.00	
		Cash			16,000.00
		Discount on Bonds Payable			456.42
		To record payment of semiannual interest and recognition of interest expense for three months in 1986; the amount of amortization is $456.42.			

[a]Calculation: $\frac{6}{120} \times \$18,257.09 = \$912.85$. The fraction used in this calculation is stated in months as a means of establishing an approach that will be useful when interest is recorded for a partial period, such as the accrual at the end of year.

[b]Calculation: $\frac{3}{120} \times \$18,257.09 = \$456.43$.

Another method of calculating the amount of amortization for the period October 1–December 31, 1985, is to take 3/6 or 1/2 of the semiannual amortization of $912.85 = $456.43.

Examples Using the Interest Method of Amortization

The same three examples are now used with the interest method of amortization. Many of the accounting issues are identical regardless of whether the straight line method or the interest method of amortization is used.

Example C–1: Bond Issued at a Premium on an Interest Date

Problem Data On July 1, 1985, the Bonkers Corporation is authorized to issue 16½ percent first mortgage bonds with a face value of $100,000 and a maturity date of June 30, 2005. Interest dates are June 30 and December 31. Books are closed each December 31. These bonds are issued on July 1, 1985, for $102,981.16, a price to yield 16 percent.

Journal Entry to Record Issue The issuance of the bonds is recorded as follows:

Date		Account		Debit	Credit
1985					
Jul.	1	Cash		102,981.16	
		First Mortgage Bonds Payable			100,000.00
		Premium on Bonds Payable			2,981.16
		To record the issuance of 16½ percent first mortgage bonds due June 30, 2005.			

Recording Bond Interest Expense and Amortization of Premium

The interest method of amortization, sometimes referred to as the effective yield method, measures the interest expense on the basis of the effective yield rate multiplied by the carrying value of the bonds at the beginning of each interest period. The amount of amortization is *residually determined;* it is the difference between the effective interest computed as described above and the nominal interest, calculated by multiplying the nominal interest rate by the face value of the bonds.

The effective interest calculation at 16 percent (8 percent each six months) and the attendant amortization by the interest method for December 31, 1985, and June 30, 1986, appear below (calculations are shown in the journal entries):

Date		Account		Debit	Credit
1985					
Dec.	31	Bond Interest Expense (8% × $102,981.16)		8,238.49	
		Premium on Bonds Payable ($8,250.00 − $8,238.49)		11.51	
		Cash (Nominal rate of 8¼% × $100,000)			8,250.00
		To record payment of interest and amortization of premium on a 16 percent annual yield basis.			
1986					
Jun.	30	Bond Interest Expense [8% × ($102,981.16 − $11.51)]		8,237.57	
		Premium on Bonds Payable ($8,250.00 − $8,237.57)		12.43	
		Cash			8,250.00
		To record payment of interest and amortization of premium on a 16 percent annual yield basis.			

Comparison of Straight Line and Interest Methods An important fact is that the *total amount over the life of the bond* recognized as bond interest expense by the interest method is exactly the same as that recognized by the straight line method. The two methods differ in the amount of bond interest expense recognized in each period. The interest method will produce a *constant rate* of expense on the carrying value of the bonds payable (face plus unamortized premium). Compare this with the results achieved with the straight line method. The diagrams shown in Figure 18–6 reveal this difference.

When the straight line method is used, both the amount of the measured bond interest expense and the amount of premium amortization are uniform over time. If the bond interest expense is divided by the carrying value of the bonds each year, the resulting interest rate would be increasing, a phenomenon contrary in theory to what actually exists. When the interest method is

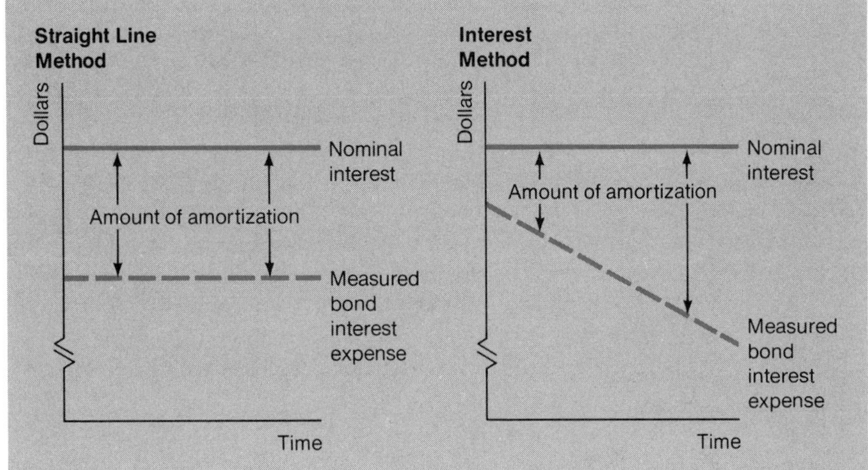

Figure 18–6 Comparison of Measured Interest by the Straight Line and Interest Methods for Bonds Issued at a Premium

used, the absolute amount of measured bond interest expense decreases over time with the amount of amortization increasing over time. Under this latter method, the interest rate calculated on the carrying value of the bonds will remain constant since as the bond interest expense declines so does the carrying value. In Figure 18–6, the total amount of amortization is the same under both methods. This is also true for the total amount of bond interest expense.

The diagram in Figure 18–6 shows a panoramic view of the entire life of the bond issue. Recall that the total bond interest expense over the entire life of the bond issue is the same under each of the two amortization methods. The difference is in the amount of bond interest expense that is recognized for each period of that life. The difference during the *first year* (the first twelve months) in the results of the two amortization methods is shown in Figure 18–7.

Although the absolute difference between the bond interest expense and the first year's amortization is $125.12, the percentage in the resulting expense is less than one percent (0.8 percent), a difference that would not be material in this particular case. The large percentage difference between the first year's amortization of the premium is irrelvant to the materiality decision

	Method		Difference	
	Interest	Straight Line	Absolute	Percent
Bond interest expense (first 12 months)	$16,476.06	$16,350.94	$125.12	0.8%
Amortization of premium (first 12 months)	23.94	149.06	125.12	522.6%

Figure 18–7 **Comparison of Interest (Example C–1) and Straight Line (Example B–1) Methods for First Year (16½ Percent, 20-Year Bonds Issued to Yield 16 Percent)**

since *APB Opinion No. 21* refers only to the difference arising from the measured bond interest expense— ". . . the results obtained."[5] It is presented here to show the total difference between the two methods during the first year.

Example C–2: Bonds Issued at a Discount on an Interest Date

Problem Data On July 1, 1985, the Davidson Company is authorized to issue 16 percent debenture bonds with a face value of $200,000 and a maturity date of June 30, 1995. Interest dates are June 30 and December 31. Books are closed each December 31. On July 1, 1985, all the bonds are issued for $181,742.91, a price yielding 18 percent (or 9 percent each six months).

Journal Entry to Record the Issue The issuance of these bonds is recorded as follows:

Date		Account		Debit	Credit
1985 Jul.	1	Cash		181,742.91	
		Discount on Bonds Payable		18,257.09	
		Debenture Bonds Payable			200,000.00
		To record the issuance of 16 percent debenture bonds due June 30, 1995.			

Recording Bond Interest Expense and Amortization of Discount The procedure used in applying the interest method in a discount case is exactly the same as it is with a premium case. The effective interest is measured by multiplying the effective semiannual interest rate (9 percent in the Davidson Company case) by the carrying value of the bonds at the beginning of the interest period. The amount of the periodic amortization is always residually determined and is the difference between the measured effective bond interest expense and the nominal interest amount. The effective interest calculation and the attendant amortization for the Davidson Company bonds by the interest method for December 31, 1985, and June 30, 1986, follow:

Date		Account		Debit	Credit
1985 Dec.	31	Bond Interest Expense (9% × $181,742.91)		16,356.86	
		Cash (8% × $200,000)			16,000.00
		Discount on Bonds Payable ($16,356.86 − $16,000)			356.86
		To record payment of interest and amortization of discount on an 18 percent annual yield basis.			
1986 Jun.	30	Bond Interest Expense [9% × ($181,742.91 + $356.86)]		16,388.98	
		Cash (8% × $200,000)			16,000.00
		Discount on Bonds Payable			388.98
		To record payment of interest and amortization of discount on an 18 percent annual yield basis.			

[5] *APB Opinion No. 21,* "Interest on Receivables and Payables" (New York: AICPA, August 1971), paragraph 15.

The recording of interest expense and the accompanying amortization by the interest method for the remaining interest period follows a pattern similar to that of the first two illustrated above.

Comparison of Straight Line and Interest Methods The difference between the results obtained from the use of the two amortization methods when amortizing a discount is shown in Figure 18–8. When the straight line method is used both the amount of the measured bond interest expense and the amount of discount amortization are uniform (equal) over time. Yet the interest rate calculated on the carrying value of the bonds will decrease over time because in subsequent years' calculation of this rate a constant numerator will be divided by an increasing denominator (face of bonds less the remaining unamortized discount). Under the interest method, on the other hand, the absolute amount of the measured bond interest expense increases over time, with the amount of the discount amortization also increasing over time. The interest rate on the carrying value is constant over the life of the bonds. The method of calculating the price to be paid for the bonds guarantees this uniform rate to occur. Again, it should be noted that total bond interest expense and total amortization are not affected by the method of amortization used.

The diagram in Figure 18–8 shows a panoramic view of the entire life of the bond issue. As indicated with the premium case, the total bond interest expense over the entire life of the bond issue is the same under each of the two amortization methods. The difference is in the amount of bond interest expense that is recognized for each period of that life. The difference during the first year (first twelve months) in the results of the two amortization methods is shown in Figure 18–9.

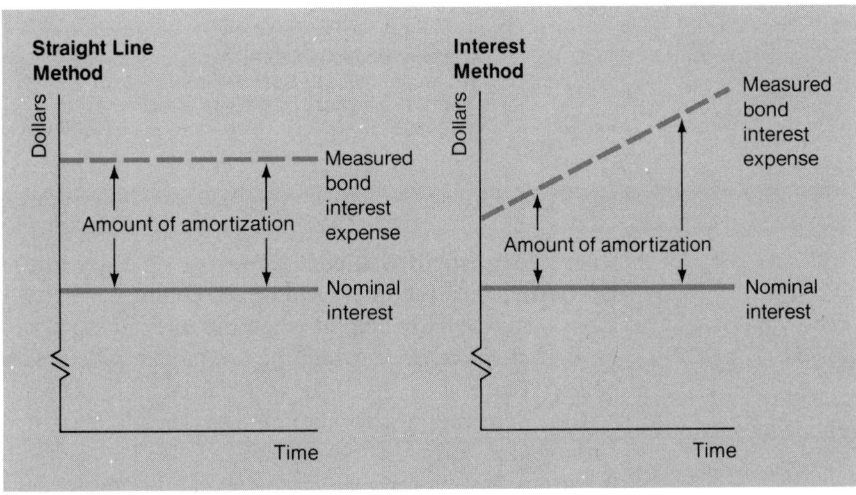

Figure 18–8 **Comparison of Measured Interest by the Straight Line and Interest Methods for Bonds Issued at a Discount**

	Method		Difference	
	Interest	Straight Line	Absolute	Percent
Bond interest expense (first 12 months)	$32,745.84	$33,825.70	$1,079.86	3.3%
Amortization of discount (first 12 months)	745.84	1,825.70	1,079.86	144.8%

Figure 18–9 **Comparison of Interest (Example C–2) and Straight Line (Example B–2) Methods for First Year (16 Percent, 10-Year Bonds Issued to Yield 18 Percent)**

Although the absolute difference between the bond interest expense and the first year's amortization is $1,079.86, the percentage in the resulting expense is only 3.3 percent, a difference that would probably not be deemed material in this particular case. The large percentage difference between the first year's amortization of the discount is irrelevant to the materiality guideline set forth by *APB Opinion No. 21.*

Example C–3: Bonds Issued at a Discount Requiring Interest to Be Accrued at End of Year

Problem Data For this illustration, assume the same facts as stated in Example C–2 except that the Davidson Company issued the 16 percent bonds on March 31, 1985, rather than on July 1, 1985, and the interest dates are September 30 and March 31.

Journal Entry to Record the Issue The journal entry to record the issue is:

1985					
Mar.	31	Cash		181,742.91	
		Discount on Bonds Payable		18,257.09	
		Debenture Bonds Payable			200,000.00
		To record the issuance of 16 percent debenture bonds due March 31, 1995.			

Recording Bond Interest Expense and Amortization of Discount A tool often used in accounting for bonds is an amortization table. It is particularly helpful when the interest method of amortization is used, perhaps more so when the accountant must deal with partial interest period data. Figure 18–10 shows a partial amortization table for Example C–3. The amortization table summarizes periodic bond interest expense and amortization and aids in the making of the regular interest period entries. It is extremely useful in making the accrued bond interest expense adjusting entry.

(1) 6 Months' Interest Period Ending	(2) Carrying Value at Beginning (Face − Discount)	(3) 6 Months' Interest Expense (9% × Col. 2)	(4) 6 Months' Interest Payment (8% × Face)	(5) 6 Months' Discount Amortization (Col. 3 − Col. 4)	(6) Carrying Value at End (Col. 2 + Col. 5)
September 30, 1985	$181,742.91	$16,356.86	$16,000	$356.86	$182,099.77
March 31, 1986	182,099.77	16,388.98	16,000	388.98	182,488.75
September 30, 1986	182,488.75	16,423.99	16,000	423.99	182,912.74

Figure 18–10 **Partial Amortization Table by Interest Method**

The September 30, 1985, entry for the first interest payment is the same as that made for December 31, 1985, under Example C–2:

Date		Account		Debit	Credit
1985 Sep.	30	Bond Interest Expense (see Col. 3, Figure 18–10)		16,356.86	
		Cash			16,000.00
		Discount on Bonds Payable (see Col. 5, Figure 18–10)			356.86
		To record the payment of interest and amortization of discount on an 18 percent annual yield basis.			

The adjusting entry for December 31, 1985, is:

Date		Account		Debit	Credit
1985 Dec.	31	Bond Interest Expense (½ × $16,388.98[a])		8,194.49	
		Accrued Bond Interest Payable			8,000.00
		Discount on Bonds Payable (½ × $388.98[b])			194.49
		To record the accrual of interest and the amortization of discount by the interest method.			

[a]Figure taken from Column 3, Figure 18–10.
[b]Figure taken from Column 5, Figure 18–10.

The entry for payment of interest on March 31, 1986, is:

Date		Account		Debit	Credit
1986 Mar.	31	Bond Interest Expense (½ × $16,388.98[a])		8,194.49	
		Accrued Bond Interest Payable		8,000.00	
		Cash			16,000.00
		Discount on Bonds Payable (½ × $388.98[b])			194.49
		To record the payment of semiannual interest and the amortization of discount for three months by the interest method.			

[a]Figure taken from Column 3, Figure 18–10.
[b]Figure taken from Column 5, Figure 18–10.

Note that the effective interest is only computed on a precise present value basis each six months. The interest for a shorter period is simply the pro rata portion (one-half in the foregoing case) of the six months' measured interest.

The Issuance of Bonds between Interest Dates

The preceding examples emphasized the basic accounting procedures, the reasons for amortizing bond premiums and discounts, and the amortization procedure by both the straight line and interest methods. A more complex problem involving the issuance of bonds between interest dates is presented below. In this illustration and other complex problems, only the straight line amortization method is used. The general principle, however, is the same regardless of which amortization method is used.

Bonds may be authorized by the stockholders but not issued for several months or even years because market conditions are not favorable. Some of the bonds may be issued and the rest held until a specific need for the additional funds arises. Often, the time needed for clerical work delays the issuance past an interest date.

The interest on bonds issued between interest dates will have accrued from the last interest date to the date of issuance. Since the bonds carry an inherent promise to pay not only the face value at maturity but six months' interest at each interest date, it is customary in these cases for the investor to pay the issue price of the bonds plus an amount equal to the accrued interest. In turn, the first interest payment to the bondholder will be for one full interest period—six months' interest—thereby returning to the bondholder the accrued interest paid plus the interest earned from the date of purchase to the current interest date. This practice allows corporations to avoid the expense of computing and paying interest for fractional periods.

Example D: Bonds Are Issued between Interest Dates Using Straight Line Amortization

Problem Data Assume that on October 1, 1983, the Greensboro Company is authorized to issue 18 percent debenture bonds with a face value of $1,000,000 and a maturity date of October 1, 1993. The semiannual interest dates are April 1 and October 1. The bonds are held until *June 1, 1985,* when bonds with a face value of only $400,000 are issued to financial corporations at 105 plus accrued interest. The amount of cash that the Greensboro Company receives is $432,000: $420,000 for the bonds plus $12,000 for accrued interest. Note that the promise to pay six months' interest is not retroactive beyond April 1, 1985, the last interest date preceding the date of issuance. Note also that the contract or face interest rate and face value are used

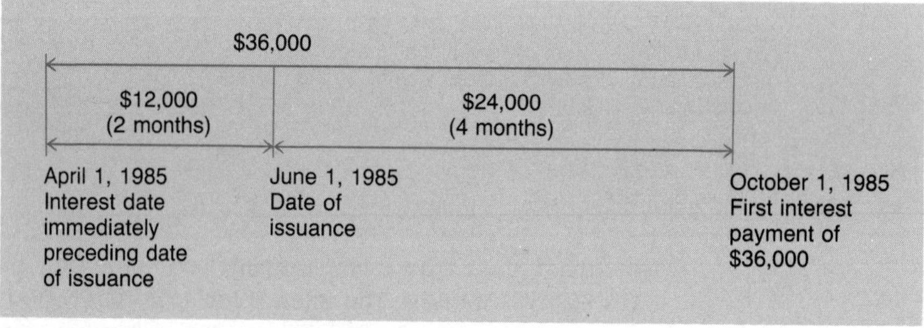

Figure 18–11 Accumulation of Interest

for calculating the accrued interest. On October 1, 1985, the purchaser of the bonds receives an interest payment of $36,000, although the interest on $400,000 at 18 percent from June 1 to October 1 is only $24,000. The payment includes a return of the $12,000 that the investor paid for accrued interest on June 1, as illustrated in Figure 18–11.

Journal Entry to Record the Issue The Greensboro Company records the bond issuance as shown below:

1985					
Jun.	1	Cash		432,000	
		Debenture Bonds Payable			400,000
		Premium on Bonds Payable			20,000
		Accrued Bond Interest Payable			12,000
		To record the issuance of bonds at 105 plus accrued interest.			

The accrued interest is credited to a current liability account since it must be repaid on the next interest date.

Recording Bond Interest Expense and Amortization of Premium In a complex example such as the Greensboro Company one, it is simpler to make two entries to record interest and amortization: (1) to record the cash payment for interest (this would actually be made in the cash payments journal), and (2) to record the amortization of the premium (this would be made in the general journal). These entries for the Greensboro Company, in general journal form, are shown below:

1985					
Oct.	1	Bond Interest Expense		24,000	
		Accrued Bond Interest Payable		12,000	
		Cash			36,000
		To record the payment of semiannual interest at 18 percent on bonds payable.			
	1	Premium on Bonds Payable		800	
		Bond Interest Expense			800
		To record the amortization of the bond premium for 4 months [($20,000 ÷ 100 mos.) × 4 = $800].			

The entry for the interest payment reflects the amounts shown in Figure 18–11; that is, the semiannual cash payment includes a return of $12,000 for the accrued interest that was sold to the investor plus $24,000 for interest actually earned by the investor for the four months' use of the money. Note that the **amortization period** is the period from the date of issuance to the maturity date only. The date of authorization and even the preceding interest date are not relevant to the start of the amortization. For the bonds of the Greensboro Company, the amortization period begins on June 1, 1985, and ends on October 1, 1993, a total of 100 months. The amount of bond premium to be amortized each month by the straight line method is $200 = ($20,000 ÷ 100 months); the amount for four months is $800 = ($200 × 4).

Assuming that the Greensboro Company closes its books on a calendar year basis, the following adjusting entries are made on December 31, 1985:

1985					
Dec.	31	Bond Interest Expense		18,000	
		Accrued Bond Interest Payable			18,000
		To record the accrual of bond interest for three months, computed as follows: $400,000 × 0.18 × 3/12 = $18,000.			
	31	Premium on Bonds Payable		600	
		Bond Interest Expense			600
		To record the amortization of bond premium for three months by the straight line method: 3 × $200 = $600.			

The effect of the end-of-year adjustment is that the Bond Interest Expense account reflects the correct interest expense for 1985 ($40,600) incurred for the seven months during which the bonds were outstanding (June 1 to December 31).

On April 1, 1986, the next regular interest date, the following entries are made to record the payment of interest and the amortization of the bond premium:

1986					
Apr.	1	Bond Interest Expense		18,000	
		Accrued Bond Interest Payable		18,000	
		Cash			36,000
		To record the payment of semiannual bond interest.			
	1	Premium on Bonds Payable		600	
		Bond Interest Expense			600
		To record the amortization of bond premium for three months (3 × $200 = $600).			

Note that only three months' amortization of the bond premium is recorded; the other three months' was applicable to a 1985 expense and was so recorded in the December 31, 1985, adjusting entry.

If the interest method had been used by the Greensboro Company, its accountant would measure the bond interest expense for the additional three months at the end of the fiscal year by multiplying the yield rate by the carrying value of the bonds as of October 1, 1985. The accountant then would multiply the results by 3/6 (1/2), the fraction of the semiannual period falling in 1985. The remaining procedure would be consistent with that previously described for the interest method.

Retirement of Bonds Payable

The borrowing company may retire its outstanding bonds at the maturity date by paying the contract face value in cash. Even if the bonds were originally issued at a premium or a discount, the entry to record the retirement *at maturity* is a debit to Bonds Payable and a credit to Cash for the face value. Serial bonds are retired in serial installments. Assume, for example, a $500,000, 10-year serial bond issue at face amount with $50,000 to be retired at the end of each year. The annual retirement of principal entry (ignoring any interest payments) is again a debit to Bonds Payable and a credit to Cash for $50,000.[6] The timing of the retirement of serial bonds is a matter of contractual provision. The foregoing example is a *regular serial bond* issue. Another popular variation involves the issuing corporation to provide for annual retirement dates to begin at a fixed number of years after date of issues—these are *deferred serial bonds.*

Other methods of bond **retirement** discussed below include the retirement of all or part of a bond issue by call (the exercise of the issuer's right to redeem) or purchase on the open market before the bonds are actually due; the conversion of bonds payable into capital stock; and the retirement of bonds with sinking fund assets and the attendant problem of accumulating the sinking fund. Another form of retirement is described according to the source of the funds used for the retirement. New bonds with favorable features are issued with the proceeds used to retire old bonds. Since no new accounting principles are introduced by this device, called *refunding,* it is not illustrated here.

Retirement of Bonds before Maturity

Recall or Purchase A corporation that has issued bonds may find itself with more cash than it expects to need for operations, thus permitting it to retire all or part of its outstanding bonded indebtedness prior to maturity date. Management may decide to retire the bonds immediately if the cash is available, if there appears to be no better use now or in the future for the excess cash, and if it wishes to decrease the fixed charges for the bond interest. Bonds may be retired early in different ways—the bonds may contain a *call provision,* or they may be purchased on the open market in the way any other investor would purchase them. For bonds to be *callable,* the indenture must contain a provision permitting the issuing corporation to redeem the bonds by paying a specified price, usually slightly above face value.

[6]The accounting for interest on serial bonds issued at a premium or discount is complex and beyond the scope of this book.

Retirement of bonds at a price less than the carrying value (face plus unamortized premium or face minus unamortized discount) adjusted to the date of retirement results in a gain; a loss is incurred if the purchase price exceeds the adjusted carrying value. Material gains and losses on the early retirement of bonds payable are classified in the income statement as extraordinary items (discussed in Chapter 14) and are shown in the income statement in a separate section.

To illustrate the early retirement of bonds payable, suppose that the Greensboro Company (see Example D for information) found itself with excess cash on October 1, 1986. Management decided to retire all of the debenture bonds which had been issued on June 1, 1985. These bonds were retired at 104½ on the October 1, 1986, interest date. The liability accounts as of this date follow:

Debenture Bonds Payable — Acct. No. 251

Date		Explanation	F	Debit	Credit	Balance
1985						
Jun.	1		CR62		400,000	400,000

Premium on Bonds Payable — Acct. No. 252

Date		Explanation	F	Debit	Credit	Balance
1985						
Jun.	1		CR62		20,000	20,000
Oct.	1		J75[a]	800		19,200
Dec.	31		J79	600		18,600
1986						
Apr.	1		J91	600		18,000
Oct.	1		J98	1,200		16,800

[a]Note that the last four entries to this account are posted from the general journal. If two entries are made for the interest and amortization, this is correct. If a compound entry were made, it would have to be made in the cash payments journal.

The carrying value of the liability (face plus unamortized premium) is \$416,800. Thus if the Greensboro Company pays \$418,000 = (1.045 × \$400,000) for the bonds, there is a loss on retirement of \$1,200 = (\$418,000 − \$416,800). This information is recorded in the journal as follows:

Date		Account	F	Debit	Credit
1986					
Oct.	1	Debenture Bonds Payable		400,000	
		Premium on Bonds Payable		16,800	
		Loss on Retirement of Bonds Payable		1,200	
		Cash			418,000
		To record the retirement of the debenture bonds at 104½.			

Once the foregoing is posted, the two liability accounts will be reduced to zero. The loss on retirement of bonds payable, if material, is shown as an extraordinary loss in the extraordinary items section of the income statement.

Conversion of Bonds into Common Stock

To make bonds more attractive to investors and thus increase their marketability, the bond agreement may give investors the option of exchanging bonds on a given interest date, or dates, for a certain number of shares of stock, usually common, of the issuing company. These securities, referred to as convertible bonds, have the advantage of offering the investor an initial fixed return on investment combined with an opportunity to share in profitable operations of the issuing company by later conversion of the bonds to stock. The terms and conditions for conversion are designated in the bond indenture. Conversion is at the option of the bondholder, so that if earnings are unfavorable he or she does not need to exercise the conversion privilege and may retain the fixed return and greater security of the bonds. The conversion of bonds into stock changes the legal and accounting status of the security holder from creditor to owner. When conversion occurs, the most often used accounting procedure is to transfer the *carrying value of the convertible bonds payable* to *paid-in capital accounts,* which probably will include both Common Stock and Paid-In Capital—Excess over Par Value, Common.

Bond Sinking Fund

The borrowing corporation may agree in the bond indenture to accumulate cash in a **bond sinking fund** to retire the bonds at maturity. Periodic cash payments are made to a sinking fund trustee, usually a bank or a trust company. These payments are ordinarily invested in revenue-producing securities. When the bonds mature, the sinking fund trustee sells the securities, and the proceeds are used to pay the bondholders. In some instances, the corporation itself may act as trustee, thereby retaining control over the activities of the sinking fund.

To illustrate the operation of a simple sinking fund managed by a trustee, assume that on the authorization date, January 1, 1985, the Rimson Corporation issues 10-year sinking fund bonds with a face value of $600,000. The bond indenture provides that at the end of each year a deposit of $60,000—reduced by any net earnings of the fund from its investments—be made to the trustee. The entry to record the initial deposit with the trustee is shown below:

Date		Account		Debit	Credit
1985					
Dec.	31	Bond Sinking Fund		60,000	
		Cash			60,000
		To record the initial sinking fund deposit with the trustee.			

The Bond Sinking Fund account is a controlling account. The trustee must invest all the available cash in the fund in revenue-producing securities. As a practical matter, it would not always be possible for the trustee to invest odd amounts of cash or to purchase securities immediately on the receipt of cash. Hence, the fund is composed of a number of individual items, such as cash, securities, and accrued interest receivable. Rimson Corporation does not need to maintain a separate general ledger account for each asset contained in the bond sinking fund because the trustee will keep detailed records.

If, at the end of the second year, the trustee reports net earnings of $4,800 from investments in bonds, the following entries record the second deposit:

1986					
Dec.	31	Bond Sinking Fund		4,800	
		Bond Interest Earned			4,800
		To record net earnings of the bond sinking fund per report of the trustee.			
	31	Bond Sinking Fund		55,200	
		Cash			55,200
		To record the second sinking fund deposit with the trustee; the amount is $60,000 less the earnings of $4,800, or $55,200.			

The following entry is made to record the retirement of the bonds at maturity by the payment of assets in the bond sinking fund (observe that the trustee would have to convert any investments to cash before the sinking fund bonds could be retired):

1995					
Jan.	1	Sinking Fund Bonds Payable		600,000	
		Bond Sinking Fund			600,000
		To record the retirement of the bonds at maturity date with the sinking fund.			

The bond sinking fund item is classified in the assets section as a long-term investment on each balance sheet except the one prepared at the end of the year preceding the date of the retirement of the bonds. On this statement, the bond sinking fund should be shown as a current asset, and sinking fund bonds payable should be disclosed as a current liability.

Restriction of Retained Earnings for Bond Redemption

In addition to the requirement for sinking fund deposits, the bond indenture may require a restriction of retained earnings up to the amount in the sinking fund. The bondholders thus are provided with twofold protection: the sinking fund ensures the availability of adequate cash for the redemption of the bonds, and the restriction of retained earnings for bond redemption reduces the amount available for distribution as dividends to the stockholders. This restriction tends to improve the company's cash position and its ability to meet its regular needs as well as its requirements for bond interest and bond sinking fund payments. An improved cash position also is advantageous in enabling the company to meet its regular operational cash requirements and to maintain a favorable credit standing.

To illustrate, assume that the bond indenture of Rimson Corporation provides for a restriction of retained earnings. The entry at the end of each year is:

1985– 1995 Dec.	31	Retained earnings . . . . Retained Earnings—Restricted for Bond Redemption . . . . To record the restriction of retained earnings equal to the annual increase in the bond sinking fund.		60,000	 60,000

Retained earnings—restricted for bond redemption is shown in the stockholders' equity section of the balance sheet under retained earnings. The provisions of the bond indenture may require (1) the creation of the bond sinking fund only, (2) a restriction on retained earnings until the bonds are redeemed only, or (3) both a bond sinking fund and a restriction on retained earnings. When the bonds are redeemed at maturity, the contractual restriction on retained earnings is removed. The journal entry to record the removal of the restriction is:

1995 Jan.	 1	 Retained Earnings—Restricted for Bond Redemption . . . . Retained Earnings . . . . To remove the restriction on retained earnings on retirement of the bonds.		 600,000	 600,000

The unrestricted balance of Retained Earnings now has been increased by an amount equal to the maturity value of the bonds. Bear in mind, however, that the reversal of the restriction on retained earnings does not create any assets that would be available for distribution to the stockholders. Assets may have been permanently committed to the enlargement of the business in the form of plant expansion. Thus, the earnings of the corporation may have been reinvested rather than being paid out as cash dividends.

Long-Term Notes Payable

Another long-term liability is mortgage notes payable, sometimes called mortgages payable, arising from the purchase on credit of land and buildings in which the purchaser gives to the seller a long-term note with a mortgage attached. A **mortgage note payable** involves the issuance of a long-term note with an assignment of an interest in property to the seller as collateral in case the purchaser defaults on the payment of the long-term obligation.

Money may be borrowed on a long-term basis by the issuance of a **long-term unsecured note payable.** Firms or individuals with a good credit rating are able to borrow significant amounts for longer periods of time and to issue to the credit grantor an unsecured long-term note. The credit grantor will require that annual financial statements be filed with it—usually a balance sheet and income statement.

If interest is payable semiannually, the accounting for the issuance of both items is essentially the same as the accounting for bonds payable issued at face value. The typical transaction would involve a debit to Cash and a credit to Long-Term Unsecured Notes Payable. The accounting for interest payment is exactly the same as for bonds issued at face value.

A special long-term debt disclosure issue is considered next—that of short-term debt expected to be refinanced.

Current Liabilities (Short-Term Debt) Expected to Be Refinanced

In its *Statement No. 6,* the FASB has taken the position that if a company (1) intends to refinance certain current liabilities on a long-term basis and (2) has or can demonstrate the ability to refinance them, it should show these liabilities on its balance sheet as long-term liabilities. The terms *refinancing* and *ability to refinance* require further explanation. *Refinancing* means that the company intends to substitute long-term debt such as bonds payable or ownership securities such as common stock for the short-term debt. *Ability to refinance* on a long-term basis must be demonstrated by one of two acts:

1. Actually having issued bonds or equity securities after the balance sheet date but before the statement is issued.
2. Having signed an agreement that will enable the company to refinance the short-term debt on a long-term basis when it becomes due.

This treatment causes the *working capital* amount (current assets minus current liabilities) to be more realistic. Thus, the statement is more useful to a user.

Glossary

Amortization of premium or discount on bonds payable The periodic writing off of the premium or discount on bonds payable as a decrease or an increase to interest expense, accomplished by either the straight line method or the interest method.

Amortization period The period for which the premium or discount should be amortized; it spans the period from the date of issuance of the bonds to the maturity date.

Bearer bond A bond issued without the owner's name being registered; the title to this kind of bond is deemed to be vested in the holder of the bond.

Bond A written promise under the corporate seal to pay a specified sum of money on a specified or determinable future date to the order of a person named in the bond certificate or to the order of bearer.

Bond certificate Evidence that a loan has been made to a corporation; it contains the written promise under the corporate seal to pay a specific sum of money on a specified or determinable future date to the order of a person named in the certificate or to the order of bearer.

Bondholder A creditor who has lent money to a corporation or government and has received a bond certificate as evidence of the loan.

Bond indenture A contract between the corporation issuing bonds and the bondholders, containing all privileges, restrictions, covenants, and other provisions of the contract.

Bond sinking fund A special fund in which assets are segregated for the purpose of retiring bonds, usually at maturity.

Callable bond A bond on which the issuing corporation retains an option to retire before maturity at a specified price on specific dates.

Carrying value of bonds payable The face or principal amount of the bonds payable plus the unamortized premium (or face minus the unamortized discount) on bonds payable.

Contract interest rate The rate of interest that is written in a bond indenture; it is the rate based on face or principal amount that will be paid on the stated periodic interest dates; this rate is also called the nominal interest rate.

Convertible bond A bond that contains a provision entitling the bondholder to exchange the bond at predetermined amounts for capital stock at the bondholder's option.

Coupon bond A bond that has the periodic interest coupons attached to the bond certificates.

Debenture bonds Often referred to as debentures; they are unsecured bonds carrying no pledge of collateral; also see *Unsecured bonds.*

Default The failure by the issuer to pay interest and principal on bonds.

Discount on bonds payable The amount by which the face value of bonds exceeds the price received for the bonds on issuance; it arises because the nominal (contract) rate of interest is lower than the going market rate of interest on similar grade bonds.

Face value The principal or par amount of bonds that will be repaid on the maturity date.

Income bond A bond with a provision that interest payments will depend upon earnings.

Interest method of amortization A method of amortization of premium or discount on bonds payable in which periodic amortization is the difference between the effective interest expense determined by multiplying the effective yield rate by the bond carrying value at the beginning of the interest period and the nominal interest calculated on the face of the bonds.

Leverage The practice of trading on the bondholders' equity, that is, of borrowing money at a given rate of interest and utilizing the borrowed funds in the business to earn a higher rate of return than the borrowing rate.

Long-term liabilities Obligations that are due to be paid after the coming year or operating cycle.

Long-term unsecured notes payable Long-term notes issued to grantors of credit without a pledge of collateral; they are long-term liabilities.

Mortgage notes payable Long-term notes issued with a pledge of specified property, plant, and equipment for the loan granted.

Nominal interest rate See *Contract interest rate.*

Premium on bonds payable The excess of the price received for bonds payable above face value; it arises because the nominal (contract) rate of interest is higher than the going market rate of interest on similar grade bonds.

Registered bond A bond whose owner's name is recorded by the issuing corporation; for this bond to be transferred to another individual, it must be endorsed and a request must be filed to have the owner's name changed on the records of the issuing corporation.

Retirement The payment of the principal amount at maturity or at an earlier date.

Secured bond A bond for which the issuing corporation pledges some part of the firm's assets as security.

Serial bonds Bonds that mature in periodic installments and will be paid at stated intervals of time.

Sinking fund A fund created to retire bonds.

Straight line method A method of amortizing bond premium or discount in equal amounts for each period over the term of the bonds in such a manner that equal interest expense will be recognized during each period.

Trading on the bondholders' equity See *Leverage.*

Unsecured bonds Bonds for which there is no pledge of assets for security; also called debenture bonds or often simply debentures.

Yield rate The rate of interest that, when applied on a discount basis to principal and interest, will yield a present value equal to the selling price of the bonds.

Questions

Q18–1 Distinguish between nominal and effective interest rates on bonds.

Q18–2 On January 1, 1985, the Columbia Sales Company issued 10-year, 16 percent bonds having a face value of $1,000,000. The proceeds to the company were $950,000; that is, on January 1, 1985, the bonds had a market price of 95 percent of face value. Explain the nature of the $50,000 difference between the face value and the market value of the bonds on January 1, 1985.

Q18–3 In light of the definition and criteria of liabilities set forth by the FASB, justify the classification of bonds payable and accrued interest payable as liabilities.

Q18–4 What is the difference (a) between a stock certificate and a bond? (b) Between a bond and a promissory note?

Q18–5 Identify the following terms: (a) registered bonds, (b) bearer bonds, (c) secured bonds, (d) unsecured bonds, (e) serial bonds, (f) convertible bonds, (g) coupon bonds, (h) income bonds.

Q18–6 A corporation needs cash for the acquisition of property, plant, and equipment. It is considering three alternative sources: additional common stock, 14 percent preferred stock, and 13 percent bonds. (a) What are some of the factors involved in this decision? (b) Will the decision affect the present common stockholders? Discuss.

Q18–7 (a) What are the general requirements for the approval of a bond issue? (b) Should the stockholders approve a bond issue? Why or why not?

Q18–8 (a) Why does the buyer of a bond purchased between interest dates pay the seller for accrued interest on the bond? (b) Is the accrued interest included in the stated purchase price of the bond?

Q18–9 List three ways that bonds can be retired.

Q18–10 Does the total amount of premium or discount amortized over the life of a bond differ if the interest method is used instead of the straight line method? What is the difference between the two methods?

Q18–11 The APB in *Opinion 21* stated that the interest method should be used in amortizing premium and discount on long-term debt instruments. From a theoretical point of view, state why this method is superior to the straight line method.

Q18–12 What is the significance of collateral? How is an asset which is pledged as collateral disclosed in the financial statements?

Q18–13 Why are bonds not always issued at the prevailing interest rate, thereby eliminating bond discount or bond premium?

Q18–14 (a) What is the difference to the issuing corporation between common stock issued at a premium and bonds issued at a premium? (b) Does revenue result from either?

Q18–15 When should short-term debt be excluded from current liabilities? Explain.

Exercises

E18–1 *Premium and discount concepts*

Fill in the proper response: (1) premium or (2) discount.

a. If the market rate of interest exceeds a bond's stated interest rate, the bonds will sell at a ________.
b. If a bond's stated interest rate exceeds the market rate of interest, the bonds will sell at a ________.
c. In computing the carrying value of a bond, unamortized ______ is subtracted from the face value of the bond.
d. In computing the carrying value of a bond, unamortized ______ is added to the face value of the bond.
e. If a bond sells at a ______, an amount in excess of the face value of the bond is received on the date of issuance.
f. If a bond sells at a ______, an amount less than the face value of the bond is received on the date of issuance.

E18–2 *Issuance of bonds payable at face and recording interest*

On the date of authorization, January 1, 1985, the McSwain Corporation issued 20-year, 15 percent bonds to financial corporations with a face value of $800,000 at 100. Interest is payable each January 1 and July 1.

1. Record the issuance of the bonds.

2. Record the first interest payment.

3. Record the accrued interest expense on December 31, 1985.

4. Record the payment of semiannual interest on January 1, 1986.

5. Record the last interest payment and the retirement of the bonds on January 1, 2005.

E18–3 *Carrying value issues*

Compute the carrying value as of October 1, 1985, of each of the following:

a. Ten-year bonds payable issued at 105 on October 1, 1985; face value $300,000, stated interest rate of 16 percent payable on April 1 and October 1 of each year.
b. Twenty-year bonds payable issued at 90 on October 1, 1985; face value $500,000, stated interest rate of 14 percent payable on April 1 and October 1 of each year.
c. Ten-year, 15 percent bonds with a face value of $600,000 issued at 102 on April 1, 1985. Interest is payable each April 1 and October 1. Assume straight line amortization.
d. Twenty-year, 14 percent bonds with a face value of $400,000 issued at 98 on April 1, 1985. Interest is payable each April 1 and October 1. Assume straight line amortization.
e. Ten-year, 13½ percent bonds with a face value of $700,000 issued at 97 on April 1, 1985. Interest is payable each April 1 and October 1. Assume amortization by the interest method and a yield rate of 14 percent.
f. Ten-year, 14 percent bonds with a face value of $200,000 issued at 105½ on April 1, 1985. Interest is payable each April 1 and October 1. Assume amortization by the interest method and a yield rate of 13 percent.

E18–4
Issuance of bonds—straight line amortization method

On the date of authorization, January 1, 1985, the Oxford Corporation issued 10-year, 16 percent bonds to financial corporations with a face value of $1,000,000 at 104. Interest is payable each January 1 and July 1.

1. Record the issuance of the bonds.

2. Record the first interest payment and amortization of the premium by the straight line method.

3. Record the accrued interest expense and amortization of the premium on December 31, 1985.

4. Open a Bond Interest Expense account and post the transactions.

5. Prepare a schedule proving the interest cost for 1985 by the straight line amortization method.

E18–5
Issuance of bonds—interest method of amortization

On the date of authorization, July 1, 1985, the Peters Investment Company issued 10-year, 14 percent bonds to financial corporations with a face value of $2,000,000, for $1,803,637.06, which is a price to yield 16 percent. Interest is payable June 30 and December 31.

1. Record the issuance of the bonds on July 1, 1985.

2. Record the December 31, 1985, and June 30, 1986, interest payments with accompanying amortization, using the interest method of amortization.

3. Briefly compare the reasons for using the interest method as compared to the straight line method of amortization.

E18–6
Issuance of bonds—interest method of amortization

On the date of authorization, July 1, 1985, the Owens Corporation issued 20-year, 14½ percent bonds to financial corporations with a face value of $600,000, for $619,997.56, which is a price to yield 14 percent. Interest is payable each January 1 and July 1.

1. Record the issuance of the bonds.

2. Record the accrued interest expense and amortization of the discount on December 31, 1985, by the interest method.

3. Record the interest payment on July 1, 1986, and amortization of the discount by the interest method.

E18–7
Issuance of bonds between interest dates

On October 1, 1985, the Elizabeth Corporation issued 16 percent bonds to financial corporations with a face value of $400,000 for $411,960 plus accrued interest. The bonds mature on June 1, 1993, and interest is paid each June 1 and December 1. The straight line amortization of premium is recorded each time bond interest expense is recorded. Prepare all the entries relating to the bond issue during 1985.

E18–8
Issuance of bonds—interest method of amortization (requires familiarity with compound interest techniques)

Dobblestein Corporation issued the following during 1985:

a. Issued on May 1, 1985, 15 percent, 20-year debenture bonds to financial corporations with a face of $300,000 at a price to yield 16 percent. Interest is paid each May 1 and November 1.

b. Issued on May 1, 1985, 14 percent, 10-year debenture bonds to banks with a face of $800,000 at a price to yield 12 percent. Interest is paid each May 1 and November 1.

c. Issued on November 1, 1985, 14 percent, 10-year debenture bonds to insurance companies with a face of $800,000 at a price to yield 16 percent. Interest is paid each May 1 and November 1.

d. Issued on November 1, 1985, 14 percent, 10-year debenture bonds to financial corporations with a face of $500,000 at a price to yield 13 percent. Interest is paid each May 1 and November 1.

Prepare journal entries related to the above bond issuances for the period from May 1, 1985, through November 1, 1985, assuming that amortization by the interest method is recorded.

E18–9
Convertible bonds

On July 1, 1983, Holmes Corporation issued $200,000 of 10-year, 15 percent convertible bonds to the Tew Corporation at 102. Each $10,000 bond is convertible into 1,000 shares of Holmes Corporation, $5 par value common stock. It is now July 1, 1985, and Tew Corporation is considering converting its bonds into common stock.

1. Why would a bondholder opt to convert bonds into common stock?

2. Assume that Tew Corporation does convert its bonds into common stock on July 1, 1985. Make the appropriate entry on the Holmes Corporation books, assuming straight line amortization of the premium.

3. Since amounts supplied by creditors and stockholders are both on the same side of the accounting equation, will the conversion of the bonds into stock by the Tew Corporation change the position of Tew's investment in the Holmes Corporation's balance sheet? Explain.

E18–10
Sinking fund

On January 1, 1985, the Beta Corporation issued 10-year sinking fund bonds to banks with a face value of $500,000. The bond indenture provides that at the end of each year, a deposit of $50,000—reduced by any net earnings of the fund from its investments—be made to the trustee. Interest is earned each year in the amount of 10 percent on the fund balance as of the beginning of the year. Beta must also restrict retained earnings for the amount of money in the sinking fund.

Required:

1. Prepare the necessary journal entries on the books of Beta Corporation for the sinking fund and the accompanying restriction on retained earnings for December 31, 1985, through December 31, 1988.

2. Prepare the necessary journal entries on January 1, 1995.

E18–11
Issuance of bonds—straight line amortization method

On the date of authorization, January 1, 1985, the Helen Company issued 10-year, 18 percent bonds to an insurance company. Interest is paid semiannually on January 1 and July 1. On July 1, 1985, the accountant for the Helen Company prepared the following journal entry to record the payment of bond interest and the straight line amortization of the discount:

1985 Jul.	1	Bond Interest Expense		23,000	
		Cash			22,500
		Discount on Bonds Payable			500
		To record the bond interest expense for the preceding six months.			

From this information, reconstruct the journal entry that was made to record the issuance of the bonds. Show all your calculations.

E18–12
Issuance and early retirement of bonds

On October 1, 1985, the Alpha Psi Corporation issued 10-year, 16 percent bonds to banks with a face of $200,000 at 100. Interest dates are April 1 and October 1. The maturity date is October 1, 1995. Apha Psi Corporation closes its books annually on December 31. On April 1, 1987, the Alpha Psi Corporation, having accumulated some excess cash, purchased its own bonds on the open market at 101½. Prepare all entries (including adjusting entries but excluding closing entries) related to these bonds from October 1, 1985, to April 1, 1987.

A Problems

P18–1A *Issuance of bonds—straight line amortization method*

On April 1, 1985, the stockholders of the Tronton Corporation authorized the issuance of 20-year, 16 percent first mortgage bonds with a face value of $800,000. The bonds mature on April 1, 2005, and interest is payable each April 1 and October 1.

Required: Make journal entries to record the following transactions:

1985	
Jun. 1	Issued all the bonds to financial corporations at 104 plus accrued interest.
Oct. 1	Paid the semiannual interest. (Assume that premium on bonds payable is amortized by the straight line method each time bond interest expense is recorded.)
Dec. 31	Accrued the bond interest.
31	Closed the Bond Interest Expense account.

1986	
Apr. 1	Paid the semiannual interest.
Oct. 1	Paid the semiannual interest.
Dec. 31	Accrued the bond interest.
31	Closed the Bond Interest Expense account.

P18–2A *Issuance of bonds—interest method of amortization*

On July 1, 1985, the Timberly Corporation issued 10-year, 14 percent bonds to a bank with a face value of $800,000 at $844,074.03, which is a price to yield 13 percent. Interest is payable June 30 and December 31.

Required:

1. Prepare journal entries to record the following transactions, assuming that the interest method of amortization is used:

1985	
Jul. 1	Issued all the bonds for cash.
Dec. 31	Paid the semiannual interest and recorded the proper amortization.

1986	
Jun. 30	Paid the semiannual interest and recorded the proper amortization.
Dec. 31	Paid the semiannual interest and recorded the proper amortization.

2. Calculate and state what would be the carrying value of the bonds payable after each of the foregoing interest payments.

P18–3A *Issuance of bonds—straight line amortization method*

On March 1, 1985, the authorization date, the Tyrrell Company issued 10-year, 15 percent debenture bonds to an insurance company with a face value of $600,000 at 96. Interest is payable each March 1 and September 1. The company closes its books on December 31. The following selected transactions and adjustments were made:

1985	
Mar. 1	Issued all the bonds for cash.
Sep. 1	Paid the semiannual interest.
Dec. 31	Accrued the bond interest.

1986	
Mar. 1	Paid the semiannual interest.
Sep. 1	Paid the semiannual interest.
Dec. 31	Accrued the bond interest.
1990	
Mar. 1	Paid the semiannual interest.
Sep. 1	Paid the semiannual interest.
Dec. 31	Accrued the bond interest.
1995	
Mar. 1	Paid the semiannual interest.
1	Paid the bonds outstanding at maturity.

Required: Record the foregoing transactions. (Assume that the discount is amortized by the straight line method each time the bond interest expense is recorded.)

P18–4A *Various bond issue situations*

The stockholders of the Ames Corporation authorized a 10-year, $500,000 bond issue with a stated interest rate of 15 percent on April 1, 1985. The maturity date is March 31, 1995. Interest is payable on March 31 and September 30.

Required: Consider the following independent cases:

1. Due to unfavorable market conditions, the bonds are not issued to financial institutions until December 1, 1986, at 103 plus accrued interest. Prepare the journal entries required on December 1, 1986, and December 31, 1986 (year-end). Assume straight line amortization.

2. The Ames Corporation issues the bonds to the Elon Investment Company on April 1, 1985, at 99. The underwriter then sells the bonds at 100. Prepare the journal entry required on April 1, 1985, on Ames's books.

3. The bonds are issued to a bank at 105 on April 1, 1985. On April 1, 1990, the corporation purchases the bonds on the open market at 102. Prepare the journal entry to record the purchase and retirement of the bonds after the March 31, 1990, interest payment has been made and recorded. Assume straight line amortization.

P18–5A *Reconstructing original issue data*

The Reliant Company issued 16 percent bonds to an investment corporation on September 1, 1985, at a certain price plus accrued interest. The bonds mature on June 1, 1995. Interest is paid each June 1 and December 1. The accountant for the company recorded the first semiannual bond interest payment as follows:

1985 Dec.	1	Bond Interest Expense		1,660	
		Accrued Bond Interest Payable		1,600	
		Discount on Bonds Payable			60
		Cash			3,200
		To record the payment of semiannual bond interest and the straight line amortization of the discount for three months.			

Required:

1. Compute the following: (a) face value of bonds issued, and (b) original issue price and discount.

2. Reconstruct the journal entry to record the issuance of the bonds on September 1, 1985.

3. Does the fact that the Reliant Company bonds sell at a discount mean that they have a relatively low rating (such as a B rating)? Discuss.

P18–6A
Thought-provoking problem: deciding on method of acquiring long-term funds

The Fenton Corporation, with 200,000 shares of $10 par value common stock outstanding, needs an additional $2,000,000 for plant expansion. Three plans for raising the funds have been proposed to the board of directors: (a) the issuance of additional common stock at $10 par value; (b) the issuance of 14 percent preferred stock; and (c) the issuance of 20-year, 13½ percent bonds. It is estimated that the corporation will earn $1,600,000 annually before bond interest and will pay income taxes of 42 percent.

Required:

1. Determine the earnings per share of common stock under each plan. Assume that the securities will be issued at *par* or *face* value.

2. Using earnings per share as a basis for your decision, which plan should the Fenton Corporation employ?

3. Discuss factors other than earnings per share that might influence your decision.

B Problems

P18–1B
Issuance of bonds—straight line amortization method

On April 1, 1985, the stockholders of the David Corporation authorized the issuance of 20-year, 16 percent first mortgage bonds with a face value of $900,000. The bonds mature on April 1, 2005, and interest is payable each April 1 and October 1.

Required: Make journal entries to record the following transactions:

1985	
Jun. 1	Issued all the bonds to a bank at 102 plus accrued interest.
Oct. 1	Paid the semiannual interest. (Assume that premium on bonds payable is amortized by the straight line method each time bond interest expense is recorded.)
Dec. 31	Accrued the bond interest.
31	Closed the Bond Interest Expense account.

1986	
Apr. 1	Paid the semiannual interest.
Oct. 1	Paid the semiannual interest.
Dec. 31	Accrued the bond interest.
31	Closed the Bond Interest Expense account.

P18–2B
Issuance of bonds—interest method of amortization

On July 1, 1985, Crumm Corporation issued 10-year, 15 percent bonds to an investment company with a face value of $500,000 for $526,485.04, which is a price to yield 14 percent. Interest is payable June 30 and December 31.

Required:

1. Prepare journal entries to record the following transactions, assuming that the interest method of amortization is used:

1985	
Jul. 1	Issued all the bonds for cash.
Dec. 31	Paid the semiannual interest and recorded the proper amortization.

1986	
Jun. 30	Paid the semiannual interest and recorded the proper amortization.
Dec. 31	Paid the semiannual interest and recorded the proper amortization.

2. Calculate and state what would be the carrying value of the bonds payable after each of the foregoing interest payments.

P18–3B
Issuance of bonds—straight line amortization method

On March 1, 1985, the authorization date, the Clunny Company issued 10-year, 14 percent debenture bonds to a bank with a face value of $400,000 at 98. Interest is payable each March 1 and September 1. The company closes its books on December 31. The following selected transactions and adjustments were made:

1985	
Mar. 1	Issued all the bonds for cash.
Sep. 1	Paid the semiannual interest.
Dec. 31	Accrued the bond interest.
1986	
Mar. 1	Paid the semiannual interest.
Sep. 1	Paid the semiannual interest.
Dec. 31	Accrued the bond interest.
1990	
Mar. 1	Paid the semiannual interest.
Sep. 1	Paid the semiannual interest.
Dec. 31	Accrued the bond interest.
1995	
Mar. 1	Paid the semiannual interest.
1	Paid the bonds outstanding at maturity.

Required: Record the foregoing transactions. (Assume that the discount is amortized by the straight line method each time the bond interest expense is recorded.)

P18–4B
Various bond issue situations

The stockholders of the Nisson Corporation authorized a 10-year, $750,000 bond issue with a stated interest rate of 15 percent on April 1, 1985. The maturity date is March 31, 1995. Interest is payable on March 31 and September 30.

Required: Consider the following independent cases:

1. Due to unfavorable market conditions, the bonds are not issued to banks until December 1, 1986, at 103 plus accrued interest. Prepare the journal entries required on December 1, 1986, and December 31, 1986 (year-end). Assume straight line amortization.

2. The Nisson Corporation issues the bonds to the Salmonid Investment Company on April 1, 1985, at 99. The underwriter then sells the bonds at 100. Prepare the journal entry required on April 1, 1985, on Nisson's books.

3. The bonds are issued to an insurance company at 105 on April 1, 1985. On April 1, 1990, the corporation purchases the bonds on the open market at 101. Prepare the journal entry to record the purchase and retirement of the bonds after the March 31, 1990, interest payment has been made and recorded. Assume straight line amortization.

P18–5B
Reconstructing original issue data

The Sanctum Company issued 16 percent bonds to a bank on September 1, 1985, at a certain price plus accrued interest. The bonds mature on June 1, 1995. Interest is paid each June 1 and December 1. The accountant for the company recorded the first semiannual bond interest payment as follows:

1985				
Dec.	1	Bond Interest Expense	6,610	
		Accrued Bond Interest Payable	6,400	
		Discount on Bonds Payable		210
		Cash		12,800
		To record the payment of semiannual bond interest and the straight line amortization of the discount for three months.		

Required:

1. Compute the following: (a) face value of bonds issued, and (b) original issue price and discount.

2. Reconstruct the journal entry to record the issuance of the bonds on September 1, 1985.

3. Does the fact that Sanctum Company's bonds sell at a discount mean that they have a relatively low rating such as a BB? Discuss.

P18–6B *Thought-provoking problem: determining various bonds payable issues*

The board of directors of the Howard Corporation has approved management's recommendation to expand the production facilities. The firm currently manufactures only heavy machinery, but plans are being developed for diversifying the corporation's activities through the production of smaller and more versatile equipment.

The directors have concluded that, whereas a number of factors should influence their choice of the method of financing to be used in obtaining investment funds of $2,000,000 needed, *prime attention should be devoted to observing the expected income effect on the corporate equity of the common stockholders as measured by earnings per share.* They are considering the following methods of providing funds:

a. They can issue 50,000 shares of $35 par value common stock at a net price of $40 a share.
b. They can issue 20,000 shares of $100 par value, 16 percent, cumulative preferred stock at a net price of $100 a share.
c. They can issue 20-year, 15 percent bonds with a $1,980,000 face value at a premium to produce $2,000,000.
d. They can issue 20-year, 14½ percent bonds with a $2,040,000 face value at a discount to produce $2,000,000.

The corporation's current liability and stockholders' equity structure is:

Current liabilities	$ 180,000
14% bonds payable, due in 10 years	300,000
$12% preferred stock, cumulative, $100 par value; authorized 100,000 shares, issued 10,000 shares	1,000,000
Common stock, $35 par value; authorized 200,000 shares, issued 40,000 shares	1,400,000
Paid-in capital—excess over par value, common	150,000
Retained earnings	600,000

Management expects that the new investment of $2,000,000 will yield a return of 22 percent before interest and income taxes, which will be computed at a 45 percent rate. The corporation is currently realizing a return of 20 percent on all long-term capital before interest and income taxes.

Required:

1. Compare the expected effect of each proposed financial method on the corporate equity of the common stockholders. Use straight line amortization.

2. Applying the single expressed criterion established by the directors, what method of financing should be employed? Why?

3. Discuss other factors that must influence a decision of this type.

19 Temporary and Long-Term Investments

Introduction

Most companies have various kinds of investments listed among their assets in either a current or noncurrent asset section. In 1981, General Motors Corporation, for example, had these long-term investments disclosed in noncurrent categories of its end-of-year consolidated balance sheet:

Equity in net assets of nonconsolidated subsidiaries and associates .	$3,379,400,000
Other investments and miscellaneous assets—at cost (less allowances)	1,783,500,000
Common stock held for the incentive program	71,500,000
Total investments	$5,234,400,000

These investments made up 13.4 percent = ($5,234,400,000 ÷ $38,991,200,000) of the total assets of General Motors Corporation. Obviously, this amount represents a material portion of the total assets. While all of these General Motors Corporation investments are noncurrent, companies buy securities (stocks and bonds) both as temporary (current assets) and as long-term investments. These investments, their differences, similarities, and valuation are the subjects of this chapter.

Learning Goals

To differentiate between long-term and temporary investments.

To understand and record temporary investments.

To be acquainted with the process of valuation of investments.

To understand and record transactions using the cost and equity methods of accounting for long-term investments in stock.

To record the amortization of premium and discount on long-term investments in bonds by both the straight line and the interest methods.

To compute the cost of bond investments to yield a given rate of interest.

To determine and record appropriate end-of-period adjustments for accrued interest on bond investments.

To understand the nature of other long-term investment items.

Temporary Investments

Nature of Temporary Investments

A firm should invest any seasonal excess of cash as it becomes available in order to maximize income by putting idle, nonrevenue-producing funds to work when they are not needed in the operations of the business. If it is expected that the funds will be needed in the near future, a **temporary investment** can be made; that is, they can be temporarily invested in readily salable securities which management intends to hold for a relatively short period of time and then sell when funds are needed. In order to be readily salable, the securities should be listed on a stock exchange or have another accepted medium through which they could be and normally are sold. They should be high-grade bonds, other debt instruments, or **blue-chip stocks** listed on a stock exchange by a financially strong corporation. The primary emphasis with temporary investments is the preservation of the amount originally invested while earning income during the holding period.

Because of the low risk involved, this kind of security usually yields a slightly lower rate of return than other securities, a common characteristic of readily salable, high-grade securities. Such temporary investments are classified as current assets because the intent of management is to convert them back into cash as soon as a seasonal shortage of cash is experienced. The accounting examples that follow illustrate the recording of the purchase of bonds and the receipt of interest and the purchase of stock and the receipt of dividends.

Bonds as Temporary Investments

Assume that on July 1, 1985, Bylinski Corporation purchased as a temporary investment 14 percent, AAA bonds of the Shields Company with a face value of $30,000 at 102 (that is, 102 percent of face). Interest is paid on January 1 and July 1. The brokerage fee and other costs incidental to the purchase are $60. This information is recorded as follows:

1985					
July	1	Temporary Investments in Bonds— Bonds of Shields Company		30,660	
		Cash			30,660
		To record the purchase of bonds of the Shields Company as temporary investments.			

Recording assets at cost

As are all assets, Temporary Investments in Bonds are recorded at full cost. **Cost** ***includes the bond price plus the brokerage fee as well as other incidental costs.***

The following points deserve emphasis:

1. In accordance with the generally accepted principle of recording all assets at historical cost, bonds purchased as temporary investments are recorded in one account at full cost. Cost includes the bond price including the addition of the premium or the deduction of the discount, the brokerage fee, and other incidental costs. Thus, no separate premium or discount account is used. With assets, this is the traditional approach.

2. The account title, Temporary Investments in Bonds—Bonds of Shields Company, includes the general ledger control account Temporary Investments in Bonds and the name of the individual bond for posting to a subsidiary record, referred to as an **investment register.** All temporary investments are assumed to be marketable securities, and the account used to record them is sometimes called Marketable Securities.

Assuming that books are closed on December 31, 1985, the accountant for the Bylinski Corporation should accrue the semiannual bond interest in a revenue account, **Bond Interest Earned,** and an accrued receivable asset account called **Accrued Bond Interest Receivable,** as follows:

1985 Dec.	31	Accrued Bond Interest Receivable . . . . Bond Interest Earned . . . . To accrue the semiannual interest on the Shields Company bonds.		2,100	 2,100

Note that in the foregoing entry the premium element of the temporary investments is not amortized. This procedure is generally acceptable because the length of time that the bonds will be held is not known. It is expected that they will not be held until maturity date. Also, since the bonds will be held for a short time, any amortization results, if applied, would likely be immaterial. Note that the revenue amount in this entry is credited to Bond Interest Earned. This revenue item would be shown as other revenue on the income statement.

The receipt of semiannual interest on January 1, 1986, is recorded as follows:[1]

1986 Jan.	1	Cash . . . . Accrued Bond Interest Receivable . . To record receipt of semiannual bond interest on the Shields Company bonds.		2,100	 2,100

[1]This cash receipt transaction is normally recorded in the cash receipts journal. It is shown here recorded in general journal form for ease of illustration and teachability.

To complete the cycle, assume that on February 1, 1986, Bylinski Corporation found that it needed cash and decided to sell the bonds of the Shields Company. They were sold at 101¾ (net of brokerage fees and other costs) plus accrued interest; the transaction is recorded as follows:

1986					
Feb.	1	Cash		30,875	
		Realized Loss on Disposal of Temporary Investments		135	
		Bond Interest Earned			350
		Temporary Investments in Bonds—Bonds of Shields Company			30,660
		To record sale of temporary investment securities.			

1. The computation of the income statement item **realized loss on disposal of temporary investments** (the loss occasioned by the actual sale) is:

Original full cost of bonds	$30,660
Deduct: Selling price of bonds ($30,000 × 101¾%)	30,525
Realized loss on disposal of temporary investments	$ 135

2. The cash received comes from two sources: (a) the sale of the bonds, $30,525, and (b) the sale of the accrued interest, $350. Interest accrues as time passes. The Bylinski Corporation has held the bonds for one more month, thus earning interest for that period.

3. The Temporary Investments in Bonds account must be credited with the same amount for which it was originally debited, that is, the cost.

Realized loss on disposal of temporary investments is shown in the income statement under the caption "other expense." Management must consider this loss, along with the bond interest earned, in evaluating the success of its decision to invest in the bonds of the Shields Company.

Stocks as Temporary Investments

To illustrate the recording of a purchase of stock as a temporary investment, assume that on April 1, 1985, Bowen Corporation purchases 200 shares of Edwin Corporation preferred stock at 105, which for stocks means $105 per share. (In this example, for the purpose of initial recording, the par value is irrevelant to the accounting; it could be $100 per share or some other value.) This stock is listed on the New York Stock Exchange and is readily marketable at any time. Brokerage fees are $108. The entry to record the purchase is:

1985					
Apr.	1	Temporary Investments in Stocks— Preferred Stock of Edwin Corporation		21,108	
		Cash			21,108
		To record the purchase of 200 shares of Edwin Corporation preferred stock at $105 a share.			

The amount of the debit to the asset is the full cost, including brokerage fees.

Assume that on July 1, 1985, a quarterly dividend of $1.50 per share is received on the 200 shares of the Edwin Corporation stock. The entry to record the cash and the revenue earned is:

1985 Jul.	1	Cash . . . . Dividends Earned . . . . To record the receipt of a quarterly dividend from the Edwin Corporation.		300	 300

Dividends earned is a revenue item and is classified under other revenue on the income statement.

To meet a seasonal cash shortage, on September 15, 1985, the preferred stock of Edwin Corporation is sold for 106½ (net of brokerage fees and other costs). The sale is recorded as follows:

1985 Sep.	15	Cash . . . . Temporary Investments in Stocks—Preferred Stock of Edwin Corporation . . . . Realized Gain on Disposal of Temporary Investments . . . . To record sale of preferred stock of Edwin Corporation at $106.50 a share.		21,300	 21,108 192

The income statement item **realized gain on disposal of temporary investments** is determined as follows:

Selling price of preferred stock (200 × $106.50)	$21,300
Deduct: Original full cost	21,108
Realized gain on disposal of temporary investments	$ 192

Realized gain on disposal of temporary investments is shown on the income statement under other revenue. Management must consider this amount, along with dividends earned, in evaluating the success of its decision to buy the preferred stock as a temporary investment.

Valuation of Temporary Investments

Ideally, all current assets should be shown at current market price on the balance sheet since this statement should reflect the financial position as of a given time. Certain companies, such as insurance companies, disclose their temporary investments at current market price. Most, however, following generally accepted accounting principles (GAAP), value these securities at either *cost* or **lower of cost or market (LCM).** These two methods of valuation are discussed in the following section and in an appendix to this chapter.

At Cost Current GAAP permit temporary investments in bonds or other debt instruments of other entities to be valued at *either* cost or lower of cost of market. Cost is certainly the simplest of all valuation methods to apply to these securities since they are initially recorded at cost. If they are valued at cost, the current market value, obtainable from the financial page of any daily newspaper, should also be disclosed in the balance sheet by a parenthetical notation, such as the following, to enable the reader to evaluate the item for purposes of financial position analysis:

Assets		
Current assets:		
Cash		$ 562,000
Temporary investments in bonds; shown at cost (current market price, $175,000)		158,000
Accounts receivable	$200,000	
Deduct: Allowance for doubtful accounts	8,000	192,000
Merchandise inventory		300,000
Prepaid insurance		2,000
Total current assets		$1,214,000

Note that even though the current market value is disclosed parenthetically, the securities are *still* valued at cost; that is, only the original cost is added into the figures that are totaled. The cost method of valuation is consistent with the fundamental principle of matching expired actual costs with revenues as well as being consistent with income tax requirements.

At Lower of Cost or Market Because of a substantial decline in the value of many ownership securities (common and some preferred stocks) during the middle 1970s, the Financial Accounting Standards Board concluded in 1975 that temporary investments in ownership securities should be valued at the lower of total market or total cost of all such security items.[2] This pronouncement makes the LCM method the current acceptable standard for valuation of these securities. Although it is somewhat complex, the authors still feel that students should be acquainted with the basic accounting for this method of valuation. Hence an illustration and more detailed discussion are presented in Appendix 19.1.

Long-Term Investments in Stocks and Bonds

Stocks and bonds, two major items in which firms make investments to be held for a long period of time (called **long-term investments**), are emphasized in this discussion. Other long-term investments include such items as: long-term accounts receivable and notes receivable, land held for future use, cash surrender value of life insurance on key officers, and special funds such

[2]*Statement of Financial Accounting Standards No. 12,* "Accounting for Certain Marketable Securities" (Stamford, Conn.: Financial Accounting Standards Board, December 1975), paragraph 7.

as sinking funds to retire bonded indebtedness or plant replacement funds to buy property, plant, and equipment items. Some firms make long-term investments in office or apartment buildings. These long-term investments are classified on the balance sheet in a noncurrent caption entitled "long-term investments."

Although a company may buy stock in another company specifically for the dividend revenue, it may also do so in order to influence that company. Buying a substantial percentage of the stock of another company (referred to as the **investee company**) allows expansion and diversification of operations as well as a better competitive position. Unless there are indications to the contrary, ownership by an **investor** company of from 20 percent to 50 percent of voting stock in an investee suggests the ability to exercise significant influence, but not control. Emphasized in this chapter is the purchase by the investor company of less than 50 percent of the stock of an investee company. Discussion of majority control of such a company is deferred to Chapter 22.

Accounting for Investments in Stocks

There are a number of issues involved in the accounting for investments in stocks. In this chapter, the following are discussed: (1) the cost method of recording and valuation, (2) the equity method of accounting for investment in an investee, and (3) the lower of cost or market method of valuation (Appendix 19.1).

The Cost Method of Recording and Valuation

Long-term investments in stocks as well as temporary investments should be initially recorded at full cost, including brokerage fees. Under the cost method of accounting for long-term investments, the investor recognizes dividends as revenue. The APB recognizes that the cost method is appropriate when the investor cannot exert *significant influence* over the policies of an investee. It has stated that ownership of less than 20 percent of the voting stock is presumptive evidence that an investor cannot exercise significant influence over an investee company.[3] If cash is paid for the purchase of stock, there is no problem in establishing the amount of the cost. Where payment is not in cash, problems of valuation may arise. A sound accounting rule is to record the investment asset at the most objective measurement of the *cash equivalent* cost of the securities.

Recording Purchase of Stocks To illustrate the accounting for investment in stocks, assume that the Phyllis Corporation makes two purchases of stock of David Corporation. First, on July 1, 1985, it purchases 10,000 shares of $10 par value common stock at $10.50 per share with a broker's fee of

[3] *APB Opinion No. 18,* "The Equity Method of Accounting for Investments in Common Stock" (New York: AICPA, March 1971), paragraph 17.

$440 (total cost, $105,440). Then, on July 15, 1985, it buys 20,000 shares of this stock at $10.60 per share with a broker's fee of $880 (total cost, $212,880). These two entries are made to record the investments:

1985					
Jul.	1	Investment in Stocks—Common Stock of David Corporation		105,440	
		Cash			105,440
		To record the purchase of 10,000 shares of $10 par value common stock of David Corporation; the cost is computed as follows: (10,000 shares × $10.50 = $105,000) + $440 = $105,440.			
	15	Investment in Stocks—Common Stock of David Corporation		212,880	
		Cash			212,880
		To record the purchase of 20,000 shares of $10 par value common stock of David Corporation; the cost is computed as follows: (20,000 shares × $10.60 = $212,000) + $880 = $212,880.			

Observe that the asset account, Investment in Stocks, is debited for the *cost,* not the par value, of the stock. The account title shows the general ledger controlling account, Investment in Stocks, and the subsidiary account, Common Stock of David Corporation. The information about the specific stock is transferred to a subsidiary record. In this case, assume that 30,000 shares is less than 20 percent of the common stock of David Corporation; Phyllis cannot exert significant influence over David's operating policies.

Receipt of Cash Dividend To illustrate the accounting for receipt of declared dividends, assume that the board of directors of David Corporation declared a quarterly dividend of $0.06 per share at the end of October. As a general rule, for convenience, a cash dividend is not recorded until it is actually received. If Phyllis Corporation receives the dividend check from David Corporation on November 20, 1985, it records this information as follows:

1985					
Nov.	20	Cash		1,800	
		Dividends Earned			1,800
		To record the receipt of a $0.06 per share dividend from the David Corporation.			

A necessary exception to the foregoing cash basis rule is the case of a dividend declared in one year and payable in another year.

Recognizing declared dividends

Sound accrual accounting theory dictates that the dividend revenue be recognized in the year in which the dividend is **declared,** ***if paid in a different year.***

To record a dividend declared in one year and payable in the next, the accountant should debit Dividends Receivable (a current asset) and credit Dividends Earned (a revenue item) as an adjusting entry at the end of the year of declaration. Then, when the dividend is received, the accountant should debit Cash and credit Dividends Receivable.

Another exception arises when stock is purchased *after a dividend has been declared* but before the ex-dividend date. In all cases of stock purchases, the *one* price (unlike the price of bonds) that an investor company pays includes *all* rights purchased, including the right to receive the declared dividend. Obviously, the dividend is from earnings accumulated before the investment was made. Thus the price paid for the stock under these circumstances should be divided between the investment in stock and the dividends receivable that are in fact purchased. The investment purchase entry would, therefore, include debits to Investment in Stocks and Dividends Receivable and a credit to Cash. Later, when the dividend is received by the investor company, it will debit Cash and credit Dividends Receivable, not Dividends Earned.

Receipt of Stock Dividend or Stock Split Instead of cash dividends, a corporation may issue additional shares of stock to stockholders as a *stock dividend,* or a *stock split*—see Chapter 17. The additional shares received by an investing company are not revenue to it. Only a memorandum entry is necessary to record the increase in the number of shares owned. Under the cost method, the unit cost is decreased, however, because of the larger number of shares held after the stock dividend is issued. For example, assume that David Corporation declared a 100 percent stock dividend (a two-for-one split would be treated in the same way). Using a specific identification approach, the receipt of the additional 30,000 shares on December 12, 1985, by Phyllis Corporation is typically noted in the journal as follows (observe that the stock of David Corporation was bought in two lots: the first 10,000 shares have a cost of $105,440; the second 20,000, of $212,880):

1985 Dec.	12	Memorandum Entry—Today there were received 30,000 additional shares of stock of David Corporation, representing a 100 percent stock dividend. The cost per share of the stock is recomputed as follows:			

Lot	Old Number of Shares	New Total Number of Shares
1	10,000	20,000
2	20,000	40,000
	Total Cost	**New Cost per Share**
1	$105,440	$5.272
2	212,880	5.322

Should there be a future disposal of the David Corporation stock, the realized gain or loss per share is determined by comparing the selling price with the applicable adjusted cost of the particular shares sold. If stock is sold from Lot 1, the cost per share is $5.272; if from Lot 2, $5.322. Instead of a specific identification assignment of cost, a FIFO approach is considered to be an acceptable alternative to the specific identification approach. Generally accepted accounting theory also permits the use of a weighted average approach. The new unit cost by this approach would be $5.305⅓ = [($105,440 + $212,880) ÷ 60,000 shares now held].

Financial Statement Disclosure The Dividends Earned account balance is disclosed in the income statement under other revenue, whereas the Investment in Stocks account is reported in the balance sheet under long-term investments, a noncurrent caption appearing between current assets and property, plant, and equipment. If the investment in stocks is considered to be a permanent, *nonmarketable* item and if the percentage of ownership is less than 20 percent, then cost is the generally accepted amount of balance sheet valuation. As with temporary investments, long-term investments are *initially* recorded at cost; therefore, there would be no immediate valuation problems. These items would be disclosed on the balance sheet at the figures that appear in the ledger accounts. If the long-term investments are in marketable equity securities, they are required by *FASB Statement No. 12* to be valued at lower of cost or market. This procedure is illustrated in Appendix 19.1.

The Equity Method of Accounting for an Investment

In the illustrations thus far, investments in stock of other corporations have been recorded at cost, and revenue from these investments has been recognized only as dividends were declared. When a corporation's investment in a domestic or foreign investee is large enough *to presume* ability to exercise significant influence over it (evidenced by ownership of 20 percent or more of the voting stock), the equity method should be used to account for the investment.[4]

When the **equity method** is used, the initial purchase of stock is also recorded at cost. After the initial acquisition, however, as shown by the example presented below, the investment account of the investor company is debited or credited to give recognition to income or losses and dividend declarations of the investee company. In other words, the investment account is increased or decreased to reflect changes in the stockholders' equity of the investee company.

Example: Stock of Investee Corporation Is Purchased at Book Value The following transactions of the Parento and Sunno Corporations are used to illustrate the equity method:

[4] *APB Opinion No. 18,* "The Equity Method of Accounting for Investments in Common Stock" (New York: AICPA, March 1971), paragraph 17.

1985	
Jan. 2	Parento Corporation purchased 40 percent of the stock of the Sunno Corporation at book value for $400,000.
Aug. 8	Sunno Corporation declared and paid a total dividend of $20,000.
Dec. 31	Sunno Corporation earned a net income of $80,000 for 1985.
1986	
Dec. 31	Sunno Corporation suffered a net loss of $3,000 in 1986.

Transactions affecting the Parento Corporation are recorded by the equity method, as follows:

Date		Account	F	Debit	Credit
1985 Jan.	2	Investment in Stocks—Common Stock of Sunno Corporation		400,000	
		Cash			400,000
		To record purchase of 40 percent of the stock of Sunno Corporation.			
Aug.	8	Cash		8,000	
		Investment in Stocks—Common Stock of Sunno Corporation . . .			8,000
		To record receipt of dividend from the Sunno Corporation.			
Dec.	31	Investment in Stocks—Common Stock of Sunno Corporation		32,000	
		Investor's Share of Investee Income			32,000
		To record investor's share of reported net income.			
1986 Dec.	31	Investor's Share of Investee Loss		1,200	
		Investment in Stocks—Common Stock of Sunno Corporation . . .			1,200
		To record investor's share of reported net loss.			

When the foregoing information is posted, the Investment in Stocks account will appear as presented below (the posting references have been replaced by explanations):

Investment in Stocks Acct. No. 152

Date		Explanation	F	Debit	Credit	Balance
1985 Jan.	2	Initial cost of 40 percent of stock of Sunno		400,000		400,000
Aug.	8	Receipt of dividend (40 percent of total)			8,000	392,000
Dec.	31	Share of Sunno's net income for 1985		32,000		424,000
1986 Dec.	31	Share of Sunno's net loss for 1986			1,200	422,800

Using the equity method, an investor corporation recognizes an economic reality: income and losses of the investee are essentially part of the investor corporation's own income and losses since it can influence the investee's operating policies. The **Investor's Share of Investee Income** and **Investor's Share of Investee Loss** accounts are used in this book to indicate the investor's share of net income or net loss of an investee under the equity method of accounting. They are closed to Income Summary and shown on Parento's income statement under other revenues and other expenses. Since the investor's share of the investee's net income is included in revenue by the entry made at the end of the year, the receipt of dividends is considered a return of a portion of previously recorded investor's investment—not revenue.

In the foregoing illustration, it is assumed that the Parento Corporation purchased the stock of Sunno Corporation at book value. If the stock had been purchased at a figure above or below book value, additional entries *amortizing* the excess or deficiency would be required under some circumstances. These are beyond the scope of this book.

In addition to investing in stocks of various companies, an investor often makes long-term investments in bonds. The accounting for this kind of investment is now considered.

Long-Term Investments in Bonds

A number of institutional investors are prohibited by law from buying common stock; others are restricted in the amount of common stock they may buy. Organizations such as banks, insurance companies, some trusts, and pension funds may acquire bonds as investments. Industrial companies also frequently buy bonds, either for the interest revenue to be received or for reasons of business connection.

Accounting by the purchaser of long-term bonds is somewhat the opposite of accounting by the issuer of bonds and notes. The decision to buy a given kind or grade of bond will depend upon: (1) the security desired (collateral required); (2) the amount of risk that is acceptable (with higher net interest rates as risk increases)—that is, the degree of safety of both principal and interest desired; and (3) other factors.

If, on the issue date, the stated interest applicable to the face value of the bonds issued—also called the **contract** or **nominal interest rate**—is the same as the prevailing market interest rate for the particular grade of bonds, the investor can buy these bonds at face value. On the other hand, if there is a difference between the contract bond interest rate and the prevailing market rate for the particular grade of bonds, the investor will pay a price for the bonds which is above or below face value; that is, the investor will buy the bonds at a *premium* or a *discount.*

The accounting for long-term investments in bonds is similar to that for bonds payable. It is discussed here in this manner:

- ☐ Example A: Bonds purchased at face value on an interest date.
- ☐ Examples using straight line amortization.
  - B–1. Bonds purchased at a premium on an interest date.
  - B–2. Bonds purchased at a discount on an interest date.
- ☐ Examples using the interest method of amortization.
  - C–1. Bonds purchased at a premium on an interest date (same data as B–1).

C–2. Bonds purchased at a discount on an interest date (same data as B–2).

□ Example D: Bonds purchased between interest dates.

This sequence is followed For example A and the B examples:

1. An entry is made to record the purchase of bonds.
2. Any peculiarity of financial statement presentation is discussed.
3. The accounting procedure for the receipt of interest is described.

Once the accounting pattern is established, some of these steps will not be shown for the C and D examples, while other comments for them may be required.

Example A: Bonds Purchased at Face Value on an Interest Date

Assume that on July 1, 1985, the Global Finance Corporation purchased Windham Corporation 15 percent debenture bonds with a face value of $200,000 and a maturity date of June 30, 2005. Interest is paid each June 30 and December 31. Books are closed each December 31. All of the bonds are purchased at 100, or at face value. (In this and the next examples, assume that all costs—for bonds, brokerage fees, and any transfer taxes—are included in the stated price of the bonds. This is standard practice.)

Recording the Purchase The following entry is made to record the purchase of these bonds as long-term investments:

1985					
Jul.	1	Investment in Bonds—Windham Corporation Debenture Bonds		200,000	
		Cash			200,000
		To record the purchase of Windham Corporation debenture bonds, 15 percent; maturity date, June 30, 2005.			

The debit entry shows the controlling account, Investment in Bonds, and the subsidiary ledger information (the specific bond issue which is purchased). The particular subsidiary ledger could be in the form of an investment register or a formal separate ledger, as is maintained for Accounts Receivable.

Statement Disclosure A balance sheet prepared after this transaction would report the bond investment as follows:

Assets	
Long-term investments:	
Investment in bonds, valued at cost	$200,000

The long-term investments caption appears on the balance sheet between current assets and property, plant, and equipment. Long-term investments in bonds are shown on the balance sheet at cost or at cost adjusted for amortization of any premium or discount (the valuation procedure discussed in the next two illustrations).

Receipt of Interest The Global Finance Corporation records the receipt of the first semiannual interest payment on December 31, 1985, as follows (the purchase of the bonds and the receipt of interest are normally recorded in the cash payments and cash receipts journals):

1985					
Dec.	31	Cash		15,000	
		Bond Interest Earned			15,000
		To record the receipt of the semiannual interest on the Windham Corporation bonds.			

A similar entry is made each June 30 and December 31 until the bonds are retired and the principal amount is paid to the Global Finance Corporation. It is possible for total interest received from all sources to be credited to a single Interest Earned (revenue) account. In the present case, however, the interest received on bonds is considered to be material enough to suggest a separate general ledger revenue account called Bond Interest Earned.

Collection of Last Interest and Principal at Maturity On June 30, 2005, when the principal amount of the bonds is paid to the Global Finance Corporation, the accountant makes the following entry to record the receipt of the *last* interest amount and the principal amount of the bonds:

2005					
Jun.	30	Cash		215,000	
		Investment in Bonds—Windham Corporation Debenture Bonds			200,000
		Bond Interest Earned			15,000
		To record receipt of the final interest payment and the principal amount of the Windham bonds.			

Methods of Amortization

The concept of accounting for the investment in bonds is the opposite of that for the issuance of bonds. This similarity extends to the *amortization of the premium and discount elements of the long-term investment in bonds* involving the write-off of these elements to the revenue account Bond Interest Earned. As with the issuance of bonds, there are two methods of amortization of the premium and discount elements of the long-term investments: (1) the interest method, which is preferred, and (2) the straight line method, which may be used if its results are not materially different from those produced by the interest method. It appears that often the straight line method does produce acceptable results, so it is still very popular.

B Set of Examples Using the Straight Line Method of Amortization

Problem Data Assume that on July 1, 1985, the Douglass Corporation purchased 15 percent, first mortgage AAA bonds of the Rice Corporation for $318,613.52, a price to yield 14 percent (7 percent each six months). The bonds were authorized on July 1, 1985, and have a face value of $300,000 with a maturity date of June 30, 2000. Interest is paid semiannually on June 30 and December 31. Books are closed each December 31.

Example B–1: Bonds Purchased at a Premium on an Interest Date

Recording the Purchase The purchase of the bonds is recorded in the following manner, assuming that all costs incidental to the purchase are included in the price:

1985 Jul.	1	Investment in Bonds—Rice Corporation First Mortgage Bonds		318,613.52	
		Cash			318,613.52
		To record the purchase of Rice Corporation 15 percent bonds that mature on June 30, 2000.			

As indicated in the discussion of temporary investments in bonds, observe that theory and tradition require that the asset account be debited for the *full* cost of the bonds. On the books of the investor, no separate premium or discount account is set up when bonds are purchased at a premium or discount.

Statement Disclosure A balance sheet prepared on July 1, 1985, would show the investment in bonds under long-term investments as follows:

Assets	
Long-term investments:	
Investment in bonds, valued at cost	$318,613.52

Interest Receipts and Straight Line Amortization of Premium Element The amount paid for the Rice Corporation bonds is $18,613.52 more than will be received when the bonds are collected at maturity. This amount is *not* a loss to the investor. As indicated in Chapter 18, it arose because the contract rate of interest on the bonds was higher than the prevailing average market rate on similar grade bonds. It therefore appears to be logical and is sound accounting practice to allocate part of the premium element to each period as a reduction of the periodic bond interest earned. In summary, by the straight line method equal bond interest revenue is recognized each interest period. This equal revenue is the total cash received for interest over the life of the bond issue adjusted (decreased) by equal amortization of the premium element.

Using straight line amortization, the Douglass Corporation would record the receipt of the first interest payment as follows:

1985					
Dec.	31	Cash		22,500.00	
		Bond Interest Earned			21,879.55
		Investment in Bonds—Rice Corporation First Mortgage Bonds .			620.45
		To record the receipt of semiannual bond interest and the amortization of the premium element: $18,613.52 ÷ 30 semiannual periods = $620.45.			

An entry similar to the foregoing would be made each June 30 and December 31 until the bonds were redeemed. Note that, since no separate premium account was set up, amortization of the premium element is credited directly to the Investment in Bonds account. If the $18,613.52 premium element represents a reduction in bond interest revenue over the entire 15-year life of the bonds, it is evident that by the straight line amortization method the reduction in bond interest revenue for the six months ended December 31, 1985, is $18,613.52 divided by 30 semiannual periods, or $620.45.

This compound entry shows that the $22,500 interest receipt is composed of receipt of net interest of only $21,879.55 and a partial recovery of the excess over par amount which was paid for the bonds. (It is suggested that, for the problems in this book, the premium and discount elements of the Investment in Bonds account be amortized each time the bond interest revenue is recorded to emphasize that this amortization is an adjustment of the bond interest earned.) Even though the compound entry is acceptable for the straight line method, two separate entries may and in practice probably will be made: (1) an entry to record the receipt of the semiannual interest, which *will be* made in the cash receipts journal, and (2) a separate entry to record the semiannual amortization of the premium element, which may be made in the general journal, often at the end of the year as an adjusting entry. (These two separate entries are illustrated with the more complex examples where bonds are purchased between interest dates and the straight line method is used: see Example D.)

The validity of the $21,879.55 semiannual bond interest revenue figure can be checked and proved by the following calculation:

Total cash receipts for the 15 years:	
Collection of face value at maturity	$300,000.00
Total interest at contract rate:	
15% × $300,000 × 15 years	675,000.00
Total cash collections	$975,000.00
Total cash payment to purchase bonds:	
Bonds with face of $300,000 purchased for	318,613.52
Net bond interest revenue for 15 years	$656,386.48
If Douglass Corporation recognizes the earning of this revenue equally over the 30 semiannual periods (the straight line approach), then the bond interest earned for a six-month period is:	
$656,386.48 ÷ 30 semiannual periods	$ 21,879.55

Example B–2: Bonds Purchased at a Discount on an Interest Date

Problem Data Assume that on July 1, 1985, the date of authorization, the Britton Corporation purchased Carson Company's 15 percent debenture bonds with a face of $400,000 and a maturity date of June 30, 1995. Britton paid $380,363.61 for these bonds, a price that will yield 16 percent. Interest dates are June 30 and December 31. Books are closed each December 31. The discount is caused by the difference in the existing average market rate on similar grades of debenture bonds and the contract rate of interest on the Carson bonds being purchased. The Carson Company's debenture bonds have a contract interest rate lower than the prevailing market rate on similar grade securities.

Recording the Purchase The purchase of these bonds may be recorded as follows:

1985					
Jul.	1	Investment in Bonds—Carson Company Debenture Bonds		380,363.61	
		Cash			380,363.61
		To record the purchase of 15 percent debenture bonds due June 30, 1995, at a price to yield 16 percent.			

Statement Disclosure A balance sheet prepared on July 1, 1985, would disclose the investment in bonds as follows:

Assets	
Long-term investments:	
Investment in bonds, valued at cost	$380,363.61

Note the similarity of disclosure with that of the premium case. After the first amortization entry is made, the Investment in Bonds account will be valued at cost plus the adjustment for amortization.

Interest Receipts and the Straight Line Amortization of Discount Element The following compound entry records the receipt of the first semiannual interest from the Carson Company and the semiannual amortization of the discount element of the Investment in Bonds account:

1985					
Dec.	31	Cash		30,000.00	
		Investment in Bonds—Carson Company			
		Debenture Bonds		981.82	
		Bond Interest Earned			30,981.82
		To record the receipt of semiannual bond interest and the amortization of the discount element: $19,636.39[a] ÷ 20 semiannual periods = $981.82.			

[a]The discount element is the difference between the face value of $400,000 and the purchase price of $380,363.61.

The amount of the amortization of the discount is debited, which increases the Investment in Bonds account. This entry indicates that the measured amount of the semiannual bond interest earned is $30,981.82, despite the fact that the company received only $30,000 in cash. With the use of straight line amortization, the net effective interest earned is equal to the semiannual cash collection plus an equal share of the discount element that will be received at the maturity date of the bonds. This accounting procedure, therefore, recognizes the reason for the discount on the bonds—the contract rate of interest on the Carson bonds was lower than the existing average market interest rate on similar grades of debenture bonds. The amount of the net semiannual bond interest revenue by the straight line method can be proved by a calculation parallel to the one used in Example B–1. The excess of total cash to be collected ($1,000,000) over cash invested ($380,363.61) of $619,636.39 divided by 20 semiannual periods equals $30,981.82.

Examples Using the Interest Method of Amortization

To compare the results achieved by the straight line amortization method with those achieved by the interest method (which is preferred), the two examples in the B illustrations are repeated using the interest method of amortization.

Example C–1: Bonds Purchased at Premium on an Interest Date

Problem Data On July 1, 1985, assume that the Douglass Corporation purchased 15 percent, first mortgage AAA bonds of the Rice Corporation for $318,613.52, which is a price to yield 14 percent (7 percent each six months). The bonds were authorized on July 1, 1985, and have a face value of $300,000 with a maturity date of June 30, 2000. Interest is paid semiannually on June 30 and December 31. Books are closed each December 31.

Recording the Purchase The entry to record the bond purchase is the same as that for Example B–1, and is not repeated here.

Interest Receipts and Interest Method of Amortization of Premium Element Under the interest method, the primary objective is to measure the amount of the bond interest earned (the yield amount) by multiplying the known actual *effective interest rate* by the carrying value of the investment at the beginning of each interest period. The amount of the amortization of the premium element is thus residually determined as simply being the difference between the measured bond interest earned amount and the cash interest received (or the accrued interest receivable recognized).

The effective interest calculation and the accompanying amortization by the interest method for December 31, 1985, and June 30, 1986, appear below. The calculations are shown with the account titles to reinforce the measurement of the amounts involved and their attachment to applicable account titles:

1985 Dec.	31	Cash		22,500.00	
		Bond Interest Earned (7% × $318,613.52)			22,302.95
		Investment in Bonds—Rice Corporation First Mortgage Bonds ($22,500 − $22,302.95)			197.05
		To record the receipt of the semiannual bond interest and the amortization of the premium element by the interest method.			
1986 Jun.	30	Cash		22,500.00	
		Bond Interest Earned [7% × ($318.613.52 − $197.05)]			22,289.15
		Investment in Bonds—Rice Corporation Bonds ($22,500 − $22,289.15)			210.85
		To record the receipt of the semiannual bond interest and the amortization of the premium element by the interest method.			

Comparison of Results of Straight Line and Interest Methods for the First Year A broad, panoramic comparison of the results achieved by the interest method as compared to the results by the straight line method for the bond interest earned on long-term investment in bonds is the same as that for bond interest expense on bonds payable. Turn to Figure 18–6 in Chapter 18 for a diagrammatic comparison. As with the bond interest expense, the total bond interest earned over the entire life of the bond issue is the same under each of the two amortization methods. There is a difference, however, in the amount of bond interest earned that is recognized for each period of that life. This difference during the first twelve months in the results of the two amortization methods is shown in Figure 19–1.

Annual Amount	Method: Interest	Method: Straight Line	Difference: Absolute	Difference: Percent
Bond interest earned (first twelve months)	$44,592.10	$43,759.10	$833.00	1.9
Amortization of premium element (first twelve months)	407.90	1,240.90	833.00	204.2

Figure 19–1 **Comparison of Straight Line and Interest Methods for First Year (15 Percent, 15-Year Bonds Issued to Yield 14 Percent)**

Although the absolute difference between the bond interest earned for the first twelve months under the two methods is $833, the percentage difference in the resulting revenue is only 1.9 percent, a difference that would probably not be deemed material in this particular case. The large percentage difference between the first year's amortization of the premium element under the two methods is irrelevant to the materiality decision since *APB Opinion No. 21* refers only to the difference arising from the measured interest revenue—" . . . the results obtained."[5] It is presented here to show the total difference between the two methods during the first year.

Example C–2: Bonds Purchased at a Discount on an Interest Date

Problem Data On July 1, 1985, the date of authorization, assume that the Britton Corporation purchases Carson Company's 15 percent debenture bonds with a face of $400,000 for $380,363.61, which is a price that will yield 16 percent. The maturity date is June 30, 1995, and the interest dates are June 30 and December 31. Books are closed each December 31.

Recording the Purchase The entry to record the purchase is the same as that for Example B–2 and is not repeated here.

Accounting for Interest Receipts and Interest Method of Amortization of Discount Element The measured amount of the bond interest earned for bonds purchased at a discount by the interest method is calculated the same as with a premium case: the effective interest rate is multiplied by the carrying value of the investment account at the beginning of the interest period. The discount amortization (sometimes called *discount accumulation* since the investment balance is being built up) is the difference between the measured bond interest earned amount and the cash interest received (or the accrued interest receivable recognized).

The effective interest calculation and the accompanying amortization by the interest method for December 31, 1985, and June 30, 1986, are presented below. The calculations are shown with the account titles to reinforce the

[5]*APB Opinion No. 21,* "Interest on Receivables and Payables" (New York: AICPA, August 1971), paragraph 15.

measurement of the amounts involved and their attachment to applicable account titles:

1985					
Dec.	31	Cash		30,000.00	
		Investment in Bonds—Carson Company Debenture Bonds ($30,429.09 − $30,000)		429.09	
		Bond Interest Earned (8% × $380,363.61)			30,429.09
		To record the receipt of semiannual bond interest and the amortization of the discount element by the interest method.			
1986					
Jun.	30	Cash		30,000.00	
		Investment in Bonds—Carson Company Debenture Bonds ($30,463.42 − $30,000)		463.42	
		Bond Interest Earned [8% × ($380,363.61 + $429.09)]			30,463.42
		To record the receipt of semiannual bond interest and the amortization of the discount element by the interest method.			

Comparison of Results of Straight Line and Interest Methods for the First Year The absolute difference between the bond interest earned for the first year under the two amortization methods is $1,071.13 = ($61,963.64 − $60,892.51). The determinant of materiality is the percentage difference of the impact on the revenue account Bond Interest Earned. In this case, the percentage difference between resulting revenue is 1.8 percent, which is probably not material. If the difference were material, only the interest method would be considered as generally acceptable. Also, recall that the difference between the two methods is in the timing of the recognition of the revenue in each year of the life of the bond investment; the total revenue realized during the entire life of the bonds is the same under both methods.

Example D: Bonds Purchased between Interest Dates

The preceding sets of examples emphasize basic accounting procedures, reasons for amortizing the premium and discount elements on the Investment in Bonds account, and the amortization procedure by both the straight line and interest methods. A more complex problem involving the purchase of bonds between interest dates, with the required end-of-period adjustments, is presented next. In this illustration and in other complex problems, only straight line amortization is used. The general principle, however, is the same regardless of which method is used.

Problem Data Bonds may be authorized by the stockholders but not issued for several months or even years because market conditions are not favorable. The interest on bonds issued between interest dates will have accrued from the last interest date to the date of issuance. Since the bonds carry a promise to pay not only the face value at maturity but six months' interest at each interest date, it is customary in these cases for the investor to

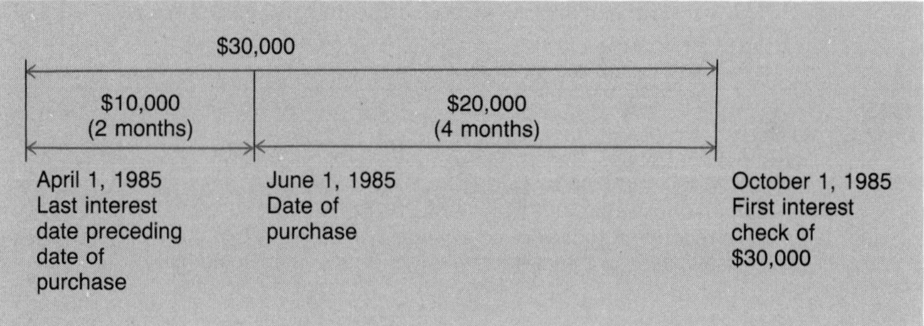

Figure 19–2 Accumulation of Interest on Bonds Purchased between Interest Dates

pay the issue price of the bonds plus any acquisition fees plus an amount equal to the accrued interest since the last interest date. In turn, the first interest payment (as promised in writing by the bond indenture) will be for one full interest period—six months—thereby returning to the purchaser the accrued interest that was paid plus the interest earned from the date of purchase to the current interest date.

Assume that on June 1, 1985, Dawson Corporation purchased Eason Company 15 percent debenture bonds with a face value of $400,000 and a maturity date of October 1, 1993. The bonds were authorized on October 1, 1983, but not issued until June 1, 1985. The interest is paid semiannually on April 1 and October 1. Dawson Corporation paid 105 plus accrued interest. The Dawson Corporation paid $430,000 in cash for these bonds: $420,000 for the bonds (including all costs), plus $10,000 for the accrued interest purchased. The promise to pay six months' interest is retroactive only to April 1, 1985, the interest date immediately preceding the date of purchase. On October 1, 1985, the Dawson Corporation receives an interest check in the amount of $30,000, although the interest on $400,000 at 15 percent from June 1 to October 1, the period Dawson held the bonds, is only $20,000. The semiannual interest check includes a return of the $10,000 the Dawson Corporation paid for the accrued bond interest receivable purchased on June 1, as illustrated in Figure 19–2.

Recording the Purchase The Dawson Corporation records the purchase of the bonds as follows:

1985					
Jun.	1	Investment in Bonds—Eason Company Debenture Bonds		420,000	
		Accrued Bond Interest Receivable		10,000	
		Cash			430,000
		To record the purchase of Eason Company debenture bonds at 105 plus accrued interest.			

The accrued bond interest receivable is debited to a current asset account since it will be collected on the next interest date.

Interest Receipt and Straight Line Amortization The entries to record the collection of the semiannual interest and the amortization of the premium element of the bond investment are shown below:

1985					
Oct.	1	Cash		30,000	
		Accrued Bond Interest Receivable			10,000
		Bond Interest Earned			20,000
		To record the collection of semiannual interest on 15 percent bonds of the Eason Company.			
	1	Bond Interest Earned		800	
		Investment in Bonds—Eason Company Debenture Bonds			800
		To record the amortization of the premium element for four months: $20,000 × 4/100 = $800.			

Instead of merging the foregoing information in one compound entry, two recording entries are made—it is easier to handle the more complex information one step at a time. The entry for the interest collection reflects the amounts shown in Figure 19–2; that is, the semiannual interest check includes a collection of $10,000 for accrued bond interest receivable purchased plus $20,000 for interest actually earned by the investor for the four months' use of its money. As indicated in Chapter 18, recall that the **amortization period** of a premium or discount element is only the period from the date of purchase to the maturity date. Neither the date of authorization nor the preceding interest date is relevant to the start of the amortization period. For the investment in Eason Company bonds, the amortization period begins on the *date of purchase,* June 1, 1985, and ends at the *maturity date,* October 1, 1993, a total of 100 months. The amount of the premium element to be amortized *each month* by the straight line method is $200 = ($20,000 ÷ 100 months); the amount for four months is $800 = (4 × $200) or, as stated in the foregoing journal entry, $800 = ($20,000 × 4/100).

End-of-Period Adjustments Assuming that the Dawson Corporation closes its books on a calendar year basis, the following entries are made on December 31, 1985:

1985					
Dec.	31	Accrued Bond Interest Receivable		15,000	
		Bond Interest Earned			15,000
		To record the accrual of bond interest earned for three months.			
	31	Bond Interest Earned		600	
		Investment in Bonds—Eason Company Debenture Bonds			600
		To record the amortization of premium element on bond investment for three months: 3/100 × $20,000 = $600.			

After the end-of-year adjustment is made, the Bond Interest Earned account reflects the correct interest revenue ($33,600) earned during the seven months when the bonds were held by the investor (June 1 to December 31). The Bond Interest Earned account is closed to Income Summary. Accrued bond interest receivable is shown as a current asset on the balance sheet and remains on the books until the next regular interest date.

Interest Collection in the Following Year On April 1, 1986, the next regular interest date, the following entries are made to record the collection of interest and amortization of the premium element of the bond investment:

Date		Account	Ref	Debit	Credit
1986 Apr.	1	Cash		30,000	
		Bond Interest Earned			15,000
		Accrued Bond Interest Receivable			15,000
		To record the collection of semiannual interest on the Eason Company bonds.			
	1	Bond Interest Earned		600	
		Investment in Bonds—Eason Company Debenture Bonds			600
		To record the amortization of premium element for three months: 3/100 × $20,000 = $600.			

Only three months' amortization of the premium element of the bond investment is recorded because only three months' bond interest revenue is earned and recorded on April 1, 1986.

In this chapter, only the basic topics involving long-term investments in bonds have been presented. Other complex bond investment topics, such as sales and conversion of one type into another type, are covered in intermediate and advanced accounting books.

Other Long-Term Investment Items

Other long-term investment items are briefly discussed below.

Long-Term Accounts Receivable

For accounts receivable to be classified as long-term investments, they should be nontrade items resulting, say, from loans to officers or to other employees. Observe that trade installment accounts receivable of three years' length would still be classified as *current assets* since the operating cycle would now be three years, not one year.

Long-Term Notes

Often either secured or unsecured notes may be acquired for long-term purposes. Much of the accounting for investments in bonds would apply to the accounting for investments in long-term notes.

Land Held for Future Plant Expansion

Only land actually used in operations should be classified as property, plant, and equipment. Land purchased for a future plant building site should be classified as a long-term investment.

Cash Surrender Value of Life Insurance

Many companies will insure the lives of their key officers and take out life insurance policies which, after a certain period of time, have a cash value that can be obtained upon the cancellation of the policies. This cash value, referred to as the **cash surrender value of life insurance,** reduces the effective life insurance expense and should be set up as a long-term investment by the company which has taken out the policies.

Long-Term Funds

Companies create long-term funds for various purposes—for example, to retire a long-term debt (sinking fund) or to buy property, plant, and equipment (property, plant, and equipment acquisition fund). Long-term funds are established through segregation of cash, which is then invested. These investments should be accounted for as other investments are, except that the investment account should have as a part of its title the name of the particular fund—for example, Property, Plant, and Equipment Acquisition Fund—Investments in Bonds or Sinking Fund—Investment in Bonds.

Appendix 19.1

Valuation of Investments in Marketable Equity Securities at Lower of Cost or Market

Introduction

Because of the substantial decline in market value of equity or ownership securities during 1973 and 1974, the Financial Accounting Standards Board concluded that both temporary and long-term investments in marketable equity securities should be shown on the balance sheet at lower of cost or market (LCM) value applied on a basis of comparing the total cost of all marketable equity securities with the market value of all marketable equity securities, the aggregate LCM method.[1] In its *Statement No. 12,* the FASB has defined **equity securities** as including ownership shares or the right to acquire or dispose of ownership shares in a company at fixed or determinable prices. The term does not include certain preferred stock that by its terms either must be redeemed by the issuing company or is redeemable at the option of the investor, nor does it include treasury stock or convertible bonds. In other words, equity securities include primarily all common stock and certain preferred

[1]*Statement of Financial Accounting Standards No. 12,* "Accounting for Certain Marketable Securities" (Stamford, Conn.: Financial Accounting Standards Board, December 1975), paragraph 7.

stocks that contain only basic ownership characteristics. If these securities are readily marketable and if management intends to sell them when cash is needed, they are called temporary investments in **marketable equity securities.**

FASB Statement No. 12 applies to *all* marketable equity securities, whether they are purchased as temporary investments or for long-term investments. The discussion in this appendix emphasizes the valuation of temporary investments. The LCM valuation of long-term investments is considered briefly at the end of this appendix.

Learning Goals

To be acquainted with the valuation process of temporary and long-term investments in marketable equity securities at lower of cost or market.

To record unrealized losses and gains in valuation of marketable equity securities.

To be acquainted with the method of disclosure of the unrealized losses and gains arising out of the valuation process.

LCM Valuation of Temporary Investments in Marketable Equity Securities

FASB Statement No. 12 requires that all temporary investments in marketable equity securities be valued at LCM, but temporary investments in *other types of securities,* such as bonds, may also be valued at LCM. In the discussion which follows, it will be assumed that the temporary investments involve only equity securities—common stock, for the most part.

When temporary investments are sold, the *realized gain or loss* is determined by comparing the selling price with the original cost, regardless of the method of valuation used. When valuation is by the LCM method, an *unrealized loss* or *gain* may be recorded—one that is recognized before the sale of the securities. Unrealized losses and gains arise from change in the asset valuation account **Allowance to Reduce Temporary Investments in Equity Securities to Market.** (This account reveals the amount by which the total cost of the temporary investments exceeds the total market value.) Both realized and unrealized gains and losses on temporary investments are included in the determination of net income of the period in which they occur.

Example

To illustrate the method recommended by the FASB, suppose that the Brummet Company purchased the following three readily marketable common stocks as a temporary investment during 1985:

Common Stock	Cost
A	$10,000
B	5,000
C	7,000

Suppose further that the Brummet Company held all these securities through 1986, and then on January 15, 1987, sold Common Stock A for $9,500. The accounting for the valuation at December 31, 1985, and December 31, 1986, and the sale on January 15, 1987, is presented in the following paragraphs. Value information concerning the portfolio as of December 31, 1985, is presented below:

Common Stock	Cost When Purchased	Market Value as of December 31, 1985
A	$10,000	$12,000
B	5,000	3,000
C	7,000	2,000
Total	$22,000	$17,000

The difference between the *total cost* of $22,000 and the *total market* of $17,000 is a $5,000 loss, an *unrealized* one since no sale has been made (this is the aggregate LCM method required by *FASB Statement No. 12).* The recommended title of the loss account is **Unrealized Loss on Temporary Investment in Equity Securities,** and, as stated previously, the loss should be shown on the 1985 income statement even though it is called an unrealized one.

The adjusting entry necessary to give recognition to the valuation as of December 31, 1985, is:

					Debit	Credit
1985						
Dec.	31	Unrealized Loss on Temporary Investment in Equity Securities			5,000	
		Allowance to Reduce Temporary Investments in Equity Securities to Market				5,000
		To give recognition to lower of cost or market method of valuation of temporary investments.				

The Allowance to Reduce Temporary Investments in Equity Securities to Market is a valuation offset to Temporary Investments on the balance sheet. This allowance and the accompanying temporary investments are shown on the balance sheet on December 31, 1985, as indicated below:

Assets

Current assets:		
Temporary investments in equity securities (at cost)	$22,000	
Deduct: Allowance to reduce temporary investments in equity securities to market	5,000	
Temporary investments in equity securities at lower of cost or market		$17,000

Brummet Company will have to go through the same valuation process again on December 31, 1986. Assume that the price of Common Stock A goes down in 1986 and the price of the other securities goes up. This value information follows:

Common Stock	Cost When Purchased in 1985	Market Value as of December 31, 1985	Market Value as of December 31, 1986
A	$10,000	$12,000	$ 9,000
B	5,000	3,000	6,000
C	7,000	2,000	5,000
Total	$22,000	$17,000	$20,000

There is still an *unrealized loss* of $2,000 between the original total cost and the total market value as of December 31, 1986, but, since there was an unrealized loss recognized during 1985, there has been a *net recovery* of $3,000 of that amount during 1986. Thus, the Allowance to Reduce Temporary Investments in Equity Securities to Market must be decreased, and an *unrealized gain* must be recorded in an income statement account entitled **Unrealized Gain on Temporary Investments in Equity Securities** by the following adjusting entry at December 31, 1986:

1986 Dec.	31	Allowance to Reduce Temporary Investments in Equity Securities to Market		3,000	
		Unrealized Gain on Temporary Investment in Equity Securities			3,000
		To give recognition to lower of cost or market method of valuation of temporary investments.			

This unrealized gain is recognized only to the extent that it represents a recovery of an unrealized loss recognized in past years. If the total market value should increase above the total original cost, no unrealized gain would be recognized for any increase above original cost. The gain is referred to as unrealized since no sale has been made, but it is still closed to the Income Summary and shown on the income statement under other income.

The balance sheet of December 31, 1986, shows an LCM valuation of $20,000 for temporary investments. To illustrate the accounting for a subsequent sale of a security, consider the sale of Common Stock A as of January 15, 1987, for $9,500. Remember that only the original cost of the common stock of $10,000 and the selling price of $9,500 now need to be considered to determine the realized loss or gain. Thus the sales transaction is recorded as follows:

1987					
Jan.	15	Cash		9,500	
		Realized Loss on Sale of Temporary Investments		500	
		Temporary Investments in Equity Securities— Common Stock A			10,000
		To record sale of equity security A.			

To repeat, the realized loss on sale of temporary investments is calculated in the typical manner by comparing only the original cost with the selling price, thus:

Cost of Common Stock A, when purchased	$10,000
Deduct: Sellling price as of January 15, 1987	9,500
Realized loss on sale of temporary investments	$ 500

The loss, shown in the income statement under other expenses, is *realized* since the sale has now taken place.

In the adjusting entry of December 31, 1987, any change in the Allowance to Reduce Temporary Investments in Equity Securities to Market would be recorded as an unrealized loss or gain. However, the amount of the unrealized gain which is recognized *must not and cannot reduce the valuation allowance below zero.*

Valuation of Long-Term Investments in Marketable Equity Securities at Lower of Cost or Market

As indicated before, *FASB Statement No. 12* also requires that long-term investments in marketable equity securities be valued at the lower of total cost (of all such securities) and total market. The procedure for valuation of these noncurrent equity securities is exactly the same as that described for temporary investments.

A major difference arises in the disclosure area: the **unrealized loss on noncurrent investments in marketable equity securities** is not shown in the income statement and thus is not absorbed into current net income. Rather, it is disclosed as a negative item directly *in the stockholders' equity section* of the balance sheet. For example, suppose the trial balance of the Dorothy Corporation contained the following items:

DOROTHY CORPORATION
Partial Trial Balance
December 31, 1985

	Debits	Credits
Investment in Noncurrent Marketable Equity Securities	$210,000	
Allowance to Reduce Noncurrent Marketable Equity Investments to Market		$8,000
Unrealized Loss on Investment in Noncurrent Marketable Equity Securities	8,000	

These data are shown on the Dorothy Corporation balance sheet on December 31, 1985, as follows:

DOROTHY CORPORATION
Partial Balance Sheet
December 31, 1985

Assets

Long-term investments:	
Investment in noncurrent marketable equity securities, at cost	$210,000
Deduct: Allowance to reduce noncurrent marketable equity investments to market	8,000
Investment in noncurrent marketable equity securities, at lower of cost or market	$202,000
Stockholders' equity:	
Unrealized loss on investment in noncurrent marketable equity securities[a]	($ 8,000)

[a]This item appears in the stockholders' equity section in an unlabeled section between the paid-in capital group and the retained earnings group.

A number of other complex issues discussed in *Statement No. 12* are beyond the scope of this book.

Glossary

Accrued Bond Interest Receivable A current asset account which shows the amount of interest that has accumulated at the end of an accounting period but is not yet due to be received.

Allowance to Reduce Noncurrent Marketable Equity Investments to Market A valuation offset to Investment in Noncurrent Marketable Equity Securities reflecting the excess of total cost of the securities over the total market value of the noncurrent investment.

Allowance to Reduce Temporary Investments in Equity Securities to Market A valuation offset to Temporary Investments in Equity Securities reflecting the excess of total cost of the securities over the total market value of the temporary investments.

Amortization period The period over which the premium or discount elements are written off; it starts with date of purchase and ends with the maturity date.

Blue-chip stocks High-grade stocks that are listed on one of the stock exchanges.

Bond Interest Earned A revenue account which shows the net interest earned on bonds—the gross amount received adjusted for amortization of premium or discount element of bond investment.

Cash surrender value of life insurance The cash value that can be received if an insurance policy is canceled.

Contract interest rate The interest rate that is stated on the bonds themselves; sometimes called *nominal rate.*

Cost method of accounting for investment in stocks An accounting method whereby stock is recorded at cost and dividends received are recorded as revenue—no other income or loss from the investee is recognized.

Dividends Earned A revenue account representing the amount received as dividends declared on investments in stock.

Equity method of accounting for investment in stocks An accounting method which adjusts the cost of the investments by the investor's share of the net income or net loss of the investee and treats receipts of dividends as a return of the investment in stock.

Equity securities Ownership shares in common stock and certain preferred stock with basic ownership characteristics.

Investee company A corporation whose stock is partially or fully owned by another corporation, the investor company.

Investment register A subsidiary record containing the specific name and number of individual securities owned.

Investor company A corporation owning stock in another corporation.

Investor's Share of Investee Income As used in this book, a revenue account used to record the investor's share of investee's net income under the equity method.

Investor's Share of Investee Loss As used in this book, an expense or loss account used to record the investor's share of investee's net loss under the equity method.

Long-term investments Investments in stocks, bonds, other securities, and certain other kinds of property that management intends to hold for a long period.

Lower of cost or market (LCM) A method of valuation of investments in marketable equity securities in the lower of cost or market is chosen as the value to be presented on the balance sheet.

Marketable equity securities Equity securities that can readily be resold, usually on a stock exchange.

Nominal interest rate See *Contract interest rate.*

Realized gain on disposal of temporary investments The excess of actual selling price at the time of sale over the original cost of the temporary investments.

Realized loss on disposal of temporary investments The excess of original cost of temporary investments over the actual selling price at the time of sale.

Temporary investments Investments in high-grade, blue-chip securities that management intends to hold for a relatively short period; these are always classified as current assets on the balance sheet.

Unrealized gain on temporary investments in equity securities An income statement gain item that is considered to be unrealized since the securities have not yet been sold; it arises when securities recover some previously lost market value.

Unrealized loss on investment in noncurrent marketable equity securities A stockholders' equity item that is considered to be unrealized since it is recognized on securities that have not yet been sold; it arises when the market value of the noncurrent marketable securities is lower than cost.

Unrealized loss on temporary investments in equity securities An income statement loss item that is considered to be unrealized since the securities have not yet been sold; it arises out of the lower of cost or market valuation process when the market value is lower than cost.

Questions

Q19–1 Discuss the following statement: Generally speaking, the accounting for investment in bonds is the mirror image of the accounting for the issuance of bonds. In your discussion, state the differences and similarities in the accounting for each. Be specific in regard to the account titles used and the accounting for temporary and long-term investments.

Q19–2 What are temporary investments? How are they classified on the balance sheet?

Q19–3 List four types of investments that may qualify as temporary investments.

Q19–4 Name and discuss the methods of valuation of temporary investments.

Q19–5 Discuss the accounting involved in the lower of cost or market method of valuation of temporary investments in marketable securities. Give journal entries to illustrate your discussion.

Q19–6 Why do firms acquire stock as a long-term investment?

Q19–7 Do dividends legally accrue? Can a firm buy dividends receivable? Explain.

Q19–8 What is a stock split-up? Discuss the accounting for a stock split-up from the point of view of the investor. Would there be any difference in the accounting for a stock dividend and for a stock split-up on the investor's books? Explain.

Q19–9 Name the various groups of investors who typically buy bonds as a long-term investment.

Q19–10 Why is the interest method theoretically preferable to the straight line method of amortization?

Q19–11 Does the straight line amortization method in the first year of an investment in bonds always produce a larger bond interest earned amount than does the interest method? Discuss.

Q19–12 State the balance sheet classifications of these accounts: (a) Bond Sinking Fund, (b) Accrued Bond Interest Receivable, (c) Accrued Bond Interest Payable, (d) Cash Surrender Value of Life Insurance, and (e) Long-Term Secured Notes Receivable.

Q19–13 When are investments accounted for by the equity method? How is the receipt of dividends treated under this method?

Q19–14 Where would the "Unrealized loss on investment in equity marketable securities" caption appear on the financial statements if it relates to short-term investments? To long-term investments?

Q19–15 By valuing investments in short-term equity securities and long-term marketable securities at lower of cost or market, the financial statements deviate from the historical cost measurement principle. Why, then, does the Financial Accounting Standards Board require valuation at lower of cost or market?

Exercises

E19–1
Differentiating between temporary and long-term investments

On July 1, 1985, the De Angelis Corporation purchased 13½ percent, AAA, first mortgage bonds of the Taylor Company with a face value of $180,000 at 102½ plus $136 brokerage fees. Interest is payable on July 1 and January 1.

1. If these bonds were purchased as a *temporary investment,* what account title(s) would be debited and for what amount(s)?

2. If these bonds were purchased as a *long-term investment,* what account title(s) would be debited and for what amount(s)?

3. Explain briefly the difference in accounting for the purchase of the bonds and the subsequent treatment of the investment as a temporary investment as compared to a long-term investment.

E19–2
Various transactions in temporary investments

The Wayne Corporation had the following transactions in *temporary* investments during 1985:

1985	
Mar. 1	Purchased 14 percent, AAA bonds of Raymond Company with a face value of $300,000 at 102 plus accrued interest. Interest is paid on January 1 and July 1. Brokerage fees and other costs incident to the purchase were $360. The bonds have a maturity date of July 1, 2005.

Apr. 10 Purchased 900 shares of $100 par value, 15 percent preferred stock of Arnold Company at $105 a share. Dividends are paid semiannually on January 1 and July 1. Brokerage fees and other costs incident to the purchase were $250.
Jul. 1 Received the semiannual interest from the Raymond Company.
5 Received the semiannual dividends from the Arnold Company.
Aug. 1 Sold the bonds of Raymond Company at 102½ plus accrued interest.

Journalize the transactions on the books of Wayne Corporation.

E19–3
Valuation of temporary investments (Appendix)

The Faison Company had the following *temporary* investments in equity securities for the period 1985 to 1986:

		Market Price at December 31	
	Cost	**1985**	**1986**
Common stock of Norris Company	$70,000	$67,600	
Preferred stock of Raymond Company	40,000	40,300	$40,800

On February 1, 1986, immediately after receiving and recording the semiannual dividend, the Faison Company sold the common stock of Norris Company for $67,000. Assuming the use of a valuation offset account, record the necessary adjusting entry under the lower of cost or market method as of December 31, 1985, and December 31, 1986, and the sale on February 1, 1986.

E19–4
Recording temporary investments with dividends attached

The Cork Corporation had the following transactions in temporary investment in stocks during 1985:

1985

Jan. 5 Purchased 60,000 shares of $10 par value common stock of Birmingham Company at $10.60 per share. The Birmingham Company had declared a $0.10 per share dividend on January 2, 1985, payable on January 20, 1985, to stockholders of record January 10, 1985.
20 Received the cash dividend from the Birmingham Company.
Mar 10 Purchased 40,000 shares of $10 par value common stock of Birmingham Company at $11.00 per share.
Jul. 20 Received a $0.12 per share cash dividend from the Birmingham Company.
Dec. 16 The Birmingham Company declared a $0.15 per share cash dividend, payable January 20, 1986, to stockholders of record on December 31, 1985.

Journalize the transactions on the books of Cork Corporation, assuming that all the Birmingham stock was still owned on December 31, 1985.

E19–5
Long-term investment in bonds—straight line amortization of premium

On January 1, 1985, the Cannes Corporation purchased as a *long-term* investment 15 percent bonds of Blough Corporation with a face value of $400,000 at 102. The bonds have a maturity date of January 1, 1995. Interest is payable each January 1 and July 1. Record (a) the purchase of the bonds by the Cannes Corporation, and (b) all the necessary remaining entries for 1985. Use the straight line method of amortization.

E19–6
Long-term investment in bonds—straight line amortization of discount

Assume that the Cannes Corporation (see E19–5) purchased the Blough Corporation bonds at 99 instead of 102. Prepare all the required entries for 1985. Use the straight line method of amortization.

E19–7 *Accounting for long-term investment in stocks*

On December 31, 1984, the Hackney Corporation made a *long-term* investment in the Sparrow Company by acquiring stock at book value. During 1985, the Sparrow Company paid dividends of $24,000 and had net income of $84,000. During 1986, it paid dividends of $12,000 and had a net loss of $20,000.

1. Assuming that Hackney Corporation purchased 12 percent of Sparrow Company's stock, journalize all transactions for 1985 and 1986 that should appear on Hackney Corporation's books. Use the year date only; in the date column use a, b, etc.

2. Assuming that Hackney Corporation purchased 30 percent of Sparrow Company's stock, journalize all transactions for 1985 and 1986 that should appear on Hackney Corporation's books. Use the year date only; in the date column use a, b, etc.

E19–8 *Accounting for long-term investment in stock*

The Gary Corporation acquired 4,000 of the 16,000 total shares of the Littlefield Company on January 1, 1985, for $480,000, the book value of the stock. During 1985, Littlefield paid total dividends of $40,000 ($10,000 on July 11 and $30,000 on November 14) and had net income of $80,000. Journalize the transactions on Gary Corporation's books, including any necessary end-of-year adjusting entries on December 31, 1985.

E19–9 *Reconstructing original issue data*

On May 1, 1985, the Lennox Corporation purchased as a *long-term* investment 16 percent bonds of Steeler Company. Interest is paid semiannually on May 1 and November 1. The bonds mature on May 1, 1997. On November 1, 1985, the accountant for the Lennox Company prepared the following entry to record the receipt of bond interest and the amortization of the premium:

1985 Nov.	1	Cash		24,000	
		Investment in Bonds—Steeler Company Bonds			750
		Bond Interest Earned			23,250
		To record the receipt of bond interest from the Steeler Company and to amortize the premium for six months by the straight line method.			

From this information, reconstruct the journal entry that was made to record the purchase of the bonds. Show all your calculations.

E19–10 *Long-term investment in bonds—interest method of amortization*

On July 1, 1985, the Benson Corporation purchased as a *long-term* investment 15 percent, 10-year bonds of McDaniel Company with a face value of $300,000 for $315,891.02, which is a price to yield 14 percent (7 percent each six months). Interest is paid June 30 and December 31. Maturity date of the bonds is June 30, 1995. Record the purchase of the bonds on the books of the Benson Corporation; record the receipt of interest on December 31, 1985, and June 30, 1986, and the amortization of the premium element, using the interest method.

E19–11 *Long-term investment in bonds purchased between the interest dates—straight line amortization*

Janzen Corporation acquired as a *long-term* investment on March 1, 1985, Truman Company bonds for $260,730 plus accrued interest. The date of authorization is January 1, 1985. The bonds of the Truman Company have a face value of $300,000 with an interest rate of 12 percent. The maturity date is January 1, 2005. Interest is payable each January 1 and July 1.

1. For 1985, record the acquisition of the bonds; receipt of the interest on July 1, including amortization of the discount by the straight line method; and any necessary adjusting entries on December 31, 1985 (year-end).

2. For 1986, record receipt of the semiannual interest payments, including amortization of the discount by the straight line method.

E19–12
Long-term investment in bonds—interest method of amortization

On February 1, 1985, the date of authorization, Watagua Corporation acquired as a *long-term* investment 10-year, 16 percent bonds of Lincoln Company for $737,639.05, which is a price to yield 12 percent. Interest is payable each February 1 and August 1. The face amount of the bonds is $600,000.

1. For 1985, prepare journal entries to record the acquisition of the bonds; receipt of interest on August 1, including amortization of the premium by the interest method; and any necessary adjusting entries on December 31 (year-end).

2. For 1986, prepare journal entries to record the receipt of semiannual interest, including amortization of the premium by the interest method.

E19–13
Valuation of noncurrent marketable equity securities at LCM (Appendix)

The Edwards Corporation had the following *long-term* investments in noncurrent marketable equity securities for the period 1985 to 1986:

		Market Price at December 31	
	Cost	**1985**	**1986**
Common stock of Todd Corporation	$300,000	$299,120	$297,000
Common stock of Hutch Corporation	251,000	250,000	250,200
Common stock of Hank Corporation	312,000	310,000	310,800

Record the necessary adjusting entries for December 31, 1985, and 1986, for valuation of these long-term investments in noncurrent marketable equity securities.

A Problems

P19–1A
Recording temporary investments

The Jaimson Corporation had the following selected transactions involving *temporary* investments during 1985:

1985		
Jan.	1	Purchased 14 percent, AAA bonds of Kelly Company with a face value of $300,000 at 101 plus accrued interest. Interest is paid each March 1 and September 1. Brokerage fees and other costs incidental to the purchase were $300. The bonds have a maturity date of September 1, 1995.
Mar.	1	Received semiannual interest on the bonds of Kelly Company.
	15	Purchased 4,000 shares of $10 par value, 15 percent preferred stock of Brown Company at $12 a share. Dividends are paid semiannually on February 25 and August 25. Brokerage fees and other costs incidental to the purchase were $205.
Aug.	15	Sold 600 shares of preferred stock of Brown Company at $13 a share. On August 10, the board of directors of the Brown Company declared the regular semiannual dividend on this stock, payable on August 25 to stockholders of record on August 20.
	25	Received the dividend on the remaining preferred stock of Brown Company.
Sep.	1	Received semiannual interest on the bonds of Kelly Company.
Oct.	1	Sold the bonds of Kelly Company at 102 plus accrued interest.

Required: Journalize the transactions on the books of Jaimson Corporation.

P19–2A *Valuation of temporary investments (Appendix)*

The Faber Corporation had the following *temporary* investments in marketable equity securities for the period January 1, 1985, to February 15, 1987:

	Cost	Market Price at December 31 1985	Market Price at December 31 1986
Common stock of Kolb Company	$62,500	$63,000	$64,000
Common stock of Scott Company	56,250	55,250	
Common stock of Ford Company	77,500	76,250	79,200

The following transactions involving the investments occurred in 1986 and 1987:

1986

Jan. 15 Sold the common stock of Scott Company for $55,500.

1987

Feb. 15 Sold the common stock of Ford Company for $79,100.

Required:

1. Assuming the use of a valuation offset account, record the necessary adjusting entries for December 31, 1985 and 1986, under the lower of cost or market method.

2. Show how the temporary investments valuation, losses, and gains should be disclosed on the end-of-period financial statements as of December 31, 1985.

3. Record the sales of the temporary investments in 1986 and 1987.

P19–3A *Recording transactions of long-term investments in stock—cost method*

The Wright Corporation had the following transactions involving *long-term* investment in stocks in 1985:

1985

Jan. 4 Purchased 2,000 shares of $50 par value common stock of Enchanto Company at 58.

Feb. 10 Purchased 3,000 shares of $50 par value common stock of Enchanto Company at 62.

Mar. 2 Received a cash dividend of $1.20 per share on the stock of Enchanto Company.

3 Purchased 2,000 shares of $50 par value common stock of Enchanto Company at 64.

Sep. 10 The Enchanto Company declared a 100 percent stock dividend. The Wright Company received 7,000 additional shares of $50 par value common stock from the Enchanto Company.

Nov. 1 Sold 2,500 shares of lot number 1 of the common stock of Enchanto Company at 40. Assign cost on a specific identification basis.

Dec. 31 The Enchanto Company declared a $0.72 a share cash dividend payable January 16, 1986, to stockholders of record on December 31, 1985.

Required:

1. Journalize the transactions on the books of the Wright Corporation using the *cost* method.

2. Show how the long-term investment in stock should be shown on the balance sheet of the Wright Corporation as of December 31, 1985.

3. What does the use of the cost method imply about the securities?

P19–4A
Issues involving long-term investments in stock

The Hilton Corporation purchased 12,000 of the total 48,000 outstanding shares of Marko Corporation common stock on January 1, 1985, at the book value price of $40 per share. The following summary of results of operations for Marko Corporation is available:

	Operations of Marko		
	Total Net Income (Net Loss)	**Total Cash Dividend**	**Transactions of Hilton**
1985	$16,000	$4,000	
1986	20,000	8,000	
1987	4,000	2,000	Sold 2,000 shares at $44 per share on December 31, 1987
1988	(8,000)	2,000	
1989	8,000	1,000	Received 10 percent stock dividend

Required:

1. Which method of accounting should Hilton Corporation use for the investment in Marko Corporation stock? Why?

2. What would be the balance in the investment account at the end of each year, 1985 through 1989?

P19–5A
Long-term investment in bonds—both methods of amortization of premium

On June 30, 1985, the Gnee Corporation purchased as a *long-term* investment 15 percent bonds of the Rouddy Corporation for $395,705.37, which is a price to yield 13 percent. Interest is payable each June 30 and December 31. The bonds mature on June 30, 2000. The face amount of the bonds purchased is $350,000.

Required: Prepare all entries for 1985 and 1986 on the books of the Gnee Corporation except closing entries using the:

1. Straight line method of amortization.

2. Interest method of amortization.

P19–6A
Long-term investment in bonds—interest method of amortization of discount

On February 1, 1985, the date of authorization, Starship Corporation acquired as a *long-term* investment 20-year, 13 percent bonds of CSN Company for $746,673.16, which is a price to yield 14 percent. Interest is payable each February 1 and August 1. The face amount of the bonds is $800,000.

Required: Prepare all entries for 1985, 1986, and 1987, including adjusting entries at December 31 of each year on the books of Starship Corporation. Do not prepare closing entries. Starship Corporation uses the interest method of amortization.

P19–7A
Thought-provoking problem: convert or accept redemption?

The Goodwin Corporation owns as a temporary investment 10,000 shares of Newco Corporation $50 par value, 10 percent preferred stock on January 1, 1985. The Newco stock is callable at $50 per share and convertible at the rate of 1.1 shares of common per share of preferred. Newco has announced its intention of exercising the call privilege simultaneously with payment of the quarterly dividend on January 8, 1985. Newco common is currently selling for $55 per share. Newco's common dividends per share for the past three years have been $1.28, $1.70, and $1.95 respectively.

Required: As an accounting consultant to Goodwin Corporation, prepare a recommendation as to whether to convert to Newco common before January 8 or to wait and accept the redemption. Show calculations to support your conclusion. If you need additional information, what would it be?

B Problems

P19–1B
Recording temporary investments

The Roark Corporation had the following selected transactions involving *temporary* investments during 1985:

1985		
Jan.	1	Purchased 13 percent, AAA bonds of Cannister Company with a face value of $400,000 at 101 plus accrued interest. Interest is paid each March 1 and September 1. Brokerage fees and other costs incidental to the purchase were $380. The bonds have a maturity date of September 1, 1995.
Mar.	1	Received semiannual interest on the bonds of Cannister Company.
	15	Purchased 800 shares of $40 par value, 12 percent preferred stock of Roxboro Company at $50 a share. Dividends are paid semiannually on February 25 and August 25. Brokerage fees and other costs incidental to the purchase were $178.
Aug.	15	Sold 200 shares of preferred stock of Roxboro Company at $55 a share. On August 10, the board of directors of the Roxboro Company declared the regular semiannual dividend on this stock, payable on August 25 to stockholders of record on August 20.
	25	Received the dividend on the remaining preferred stock of Roxboro Company.
Sep.	1	Received semiannual interest on the bonds of Cannister Company.
Oct.	1	Sold the bonds of Cannister Company at 102 plus accrued interest.

Required: Journalize the transactions on the books of Roark Corporation.

P19–2B
Valuation of temporary investments

The Tamy Corporation had the following *temporary* investments in marketable equity securities for the period January 1, 1985, to February 15, 1987:

		Market Price at December 31	
	Cost	**1985**	**1986**
Common stock of Albert Company	$53,000	$53,600	$53,360
Common stock of Eddie Company	45,500	44,300	
Common stock of Wayne Company	71,000	69,500	69,440

The following transactions involving the investments occurred in 1986 and 1987:

1986	
Jan. 15	Sold the common stock of Eddie Company for $44,600.

1987	
Feb. 15	Sold the common stock of Wayne Company for $71,350.

Required:

1. Assuming the use of a valuation offset account, record the necessary adjusting entries for December 31, 1985, and 1986, under the lower of cost or market method.

2. Show how the temporary investments valuation, losses, and gains should be disclosed on the end-of-period financial statements as of December 31, 1985.

3. Record the sales of the temporary investments in 1986 and 1987.

P19–3B
Recording transactions of long-term investments at cost

The Morrisville Corporation had the following transactions involving *long-term* investments in stocks in 1985:

1985	
Jan. 4	Purchased 400 shares of $25 par value common stock of Raleigh Company at 28.
Feb. 10	Purchased 600 shares of $25 par value common stock of Raleigh Company at 30.
Mar. 12	Received a cash dividend of $0.60 per share on the stock of Raleigh Company.
14	Purchased 1,000 shares of $25 par value common stock of Raleigh Company at 32.
Sep. 10	The Raleigh Company declared a 100 percent stock dividend. The Morrisville Company received 2,000 additional shares of $25 par value common stock from the Raleigh Company.
Nov. 1	Sold 600 shares of lot number 1 of the common stock of Raleigh Company at 20. Assign cost on a specific identification basis.
Dec. 31	The Raleigh Company declared a $0.30 a share cash dividend payable January 16, 1986, to stockholders of record on December 31, 1985.

Required:

1. Journalize the transactions on the books of Morrisville Corporation using the cost method.

2. Show how the long-term investment in stock should be shown on the balance sheet of the Morrisville Corporation as of December 31, 1985.

3. What does the use of the cost method imply about the securities?

P19–4B
Issues involving long-term investments in stock

The Elm Corporation purchased 3,000 of the total 10,000 outstanding shares of Hickory Corporation common stock on January 1, 1985, at the book value price of $10 per share. The following summary of results of operations for Hickory Corporation is available:

	Operations of Hickory		
	Total Net Income (Net Loss)	**Total Cash Dividend**	**Transactions of Elm**
1985	$4,000	$1,000	
1986	5,000	2,000	
1987	1,000	500	Sold 500 shares at $11 per share on December 31, 1987
1988	(2,000)	500	
1989	2,000	250	Received 10 percent stock dividend

Required:

1. Which method of accounting should Elm Corporation use for the investment in Hickory Corporation stock? Why?

2. What amount would be reflected in the investment account at the end of each year, 1985 through 1989?

P19–5B
Long-term investment in bonds—both methods of amortization

On March 31, 1985, the Changeor Corporation purchased as a *long-term* investment 14 percent bonds of the Nelson Corporation for $925,200.34, which is a price to yield 12 percent. Interest is payable March 31 and September 30. The bonds mature on March 31, 1995. The face amount of the bonds purchased is $830,000. Changeor Corporation has a fiscal year that ends on March 31 of each year.

Required: Prepare all entries from March 31, 1985, to March 31, 1987, except closing entries, on the books of the Changeor Corporation using the:

1. Straight line method of amortization.

2. Interest method of amortization.

P19–6B
Long-term investment in bonds—interest method of amortization

As a *long-term* investment, Snuffy Corporation purchased on March 1, 1985, $300,000, 15 percent bonds of Barny Corporation for $285,272.78, which is a price to yield 16 percent. The bonds mature in 10 years, and interest is payable each March 1 and September 1.

Required: Prepare all entries for 1985, 1986, and 1987, including adjusting entries at December 31 of each year on the books of Snuffy Corporation. Do not prepare closing entries. Snuffy Corporation uses the interest method of amortization.

P19–7B
Thought-provoking problem: decision about what investment to make

The Ringling Corporation has excess funds that it desires to invest at the present time (January 1, 1985). It narrows down the investment opportunities to two securities:

1. 13½ percent, 10-year AAA first mortgage bonds of the Disco Corporation currently selling at 97.4.

2. 15½ percent, 10-year AAA first mortgage bonds of the Excello Corporation currently selling at 108.

Assume that the average price of all AAA first mortgage bonds is approximately 14 percent.

Required: Assume that you are asked as a consultant to advise the Ringling Corporation which investment appears to be the better choice; what would be your advice and why?

20 Statement of Changes in Financial Position

Introduction

In the preceding chapters, only three of the four basic financial statements have been emphasized. Recall that the major objective of a business enterprise is to earn net income. To do so, it must engage in operations that provide a product or service that is exchanged for revenue. Resources for these operations are provided by the earnings process, by financing activities (such as borrowing of money and issuance of common stock), and by investing activities (such as acquisition of plant items). The balance sheet shows the status of these resources as of a specific moment in time. The liabilities and stockholders' equity section reveals the net effect of certain financing activities; the assets section shows the net results of investment activity. The income statement discloses the results of operations and thus the progress of the enterprise toward earning net income. The statement of retained earnings reconciles the beginning balance of retained earnings to the ending balance, showing primarily the net income earned and dividends declared. None of these statements indicates the *cause of the changes in financial position* resulting from operating, financing, and investing activities that the company engaged in during the year. It is important to statement readers to know details of the resources provided, such as those from (1) operations, (2) the issuance of bonds, and (3) the issuance of common stock; and the resources used in (1) the purchase of property, plant, and equipment, (2) the purchase of long-term investments, and (3) other similar investing activities. These activities change financial position. A fourth major accounting statement is prepared to disclose the causes of changes in resources of a firm. It is the **statement of changes in financial position.** This chapter starts with a description of this statement and its broad objectives and content, considering both working capital and cash concepts. The single concept of working capital is explored to develop the analytical background steps for the statement of changes in financial position. Then, two different approaches are presented that may be used to collect information for the statement based on a working capital concept. Last, the statement is considered as it relates to a cash basis.

Learning Goals

To understand the meaning of the statement of changes in financial position.

To understand the various definitions of funds.

To recognize the effect on working capital of increases or decreases in noncurrent items.

To prepare a schedule of changes in working capital components that becomes a part of the statement of changes in financial position.

To compute the amount of working capital provided by (or used in) operations.

To use a simple work sheet to develop sources and uses of funds based on the all financial resources on a working capital basis concept of funds.

To prepare a statement of changes in financial position based on the all financial resources on a cash basis concept of funds.

Statement of Changes in Financial Position: Broad Objectives and Content

Broad Objectives

According to *APB Opinion No. 19,* the statement of changes in financial position has two broad objectives:

1. To summarize the financing and investing activities of the entity, including the extent to which the enterprise has generated funds from operations during the period.

2. To complete the disclosure of changes in financial position during the period.[1]

Figure 20–1 shows how this statement fits in with other financial statements to accomplish these objectives.

The information shown on the statement of changes in financial position is useful to a variety of users of financial statements in making economic decisions regarding the enterprise. For example, when *budgets* (financial plans) for items such as capital equipment are prepared, the accountant looks to past statements of changes in financial position as a reference point. Also, the statement of changes in financial position is the only document, for example,

[1]*Opinions of the Accounting Principles Board No. 19,* "Reporting Changes in Financial Position" (New York: AICPA, March 1971), paragraph 4.

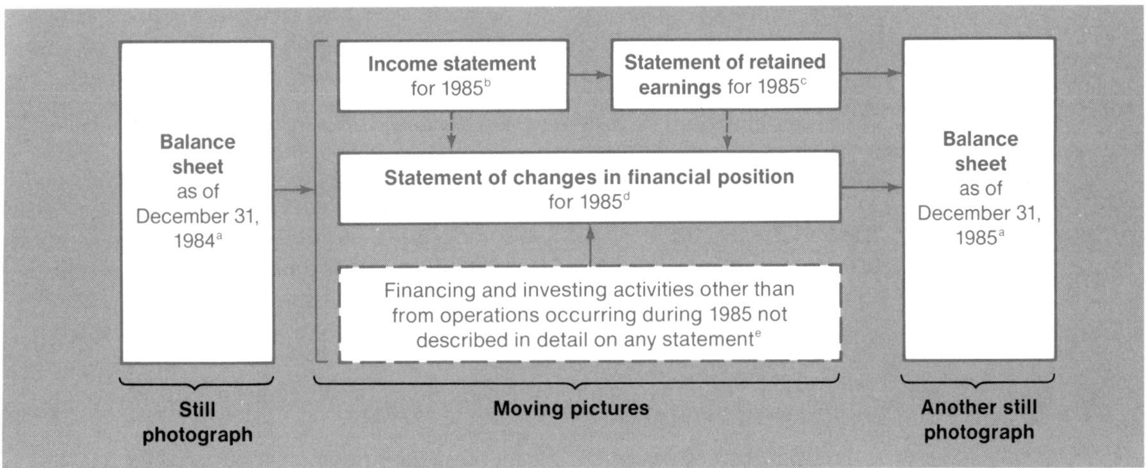

[a]The balance sheets show the financial position as at the close of business on any given date (in this case, December 31, 1984 and 1985).

[b]The income statement shows the results of operations for a given period. It does not disclose all the sources and uses of financial resources for the period. It includes those items used in measuring net income.

[c]The statement of retained earnings reconciles the beginning balance of retained earnings with the ending balance. Net income is shown in this statement as an item increasing retained earnings. The end-of-period retained earnings balance is shown in the end-of-period balance sheet (in this case, December 31, 1985).

[d]The statement of changes in financial position uses the information shown in both of the other period statements, but it is the only statement that collects and systematically discloses in one statement the causes of changes in financial position.

[e]The actual incurrence of most financing and investing activities is not shown on any of the statements studied up to now.

Figure 20–1 **Relationship of Financial Statements**

to show why dividends may not be declared when net income has been earned. It shows inflows and outflows of funds and the change in working capital or cash position that may make it unwise to declare a dividend. Before proceeding to a specific study of the statement, its evolution and content is presented in the next section.

Evolution and Content of the Statement

Prior to 1971, some annual reports presented various **statements of sources and uses of funds** (the typical name used for the present statement of changes in financial position). These older statements disclosed the operating, financing, and investing activities of a firm during a given period of time, but they defined **funds** in several different ways: working capital, cash only, cash and securities, current assets, or all financial resources. The most often used definition of funds has been **working capital,** which is total current assets minus total current liabilities; mathematically, CA − CL = WC.

Now however, a cash basis or cash and near cash (temporary investments) basis for the statement of changes in financial position is receiving emphasis. Deloitte Haskins & Sells in its January 8, 1982, *The Week in Review,* states:

> **The Financial Executives Institute (FEI) has issued an alert which urges its members to consider a format for their statement of changes in financial position that emphasizes cash flow instead of working capital.[2]**

This recommendation, as well as some studies currently under way by other CPA firms and by the FASB, suggests that the cash concept of funds may be emphasized in the future. Another concept of funds developed in the late 1960s and early 1970s is that of **all financial resources.** This concept encompasses all important aspects of a company's "financing and investing activities regardless of whether cash or other elements of working capital are directly affected."[3]

In 1971, *APB Opinion No. 19* recommended that a variation of the concept of "all financial resources" be used. It also recommended (1) that the statements be titled *statement of changes in financial position* and (2) that it be a basic financial statement for each period for which an income statement is presented.[4] This latter requirement elevates the statement of changes in financial position to a major statement status.

APB Opinion No. 19 requires a business to disclose in this statement the **sources of financial resources** and **uses of financial resources** –the inflows and outflows—of all these resources of the business. The *Opinion* specifically permits flexibility in form, content, and terminology but requires that information about sources and uses of funds be presented on either (1) all financial resources on a working capital basis, or (2) all financial resources on a cash basis. The first variation will show sources and uses of *working capital* plus other sources and uses of financial resources not affecting working capital (such as the issuance of bonds payable in exchange for land, the issuance of common stock to acquire property, plant, and equipment items, and the conversion of bonds into common stock). The other variation will show the sources and uses of *cash,* plus other noncash sources and uses of financial resources.

Since both bases specified by *APB Opinion No. 19* require that the sources and uses not affecting working capital or cash be included, the two variations of the all financial resources approaches hereafter are referred to as (1) statement of changes in financial position—working capital basis or (2) statement of changes in financial position—cash basis. Both are illustrated in this chapter.

The next issue is a more specific look at each of the two bases. The working capital basis is covered first.

---

[2]*The Week in Review* (New York: Deloitte Haskins & Sells, January 8, 1982), p. 1.

[3]*Opinions of the Accounting Principles Board No. 19,* "Reporting Changes in Financial Position" (New York: AICPA, March 1971), paragraph 8.

[4]Ibid.

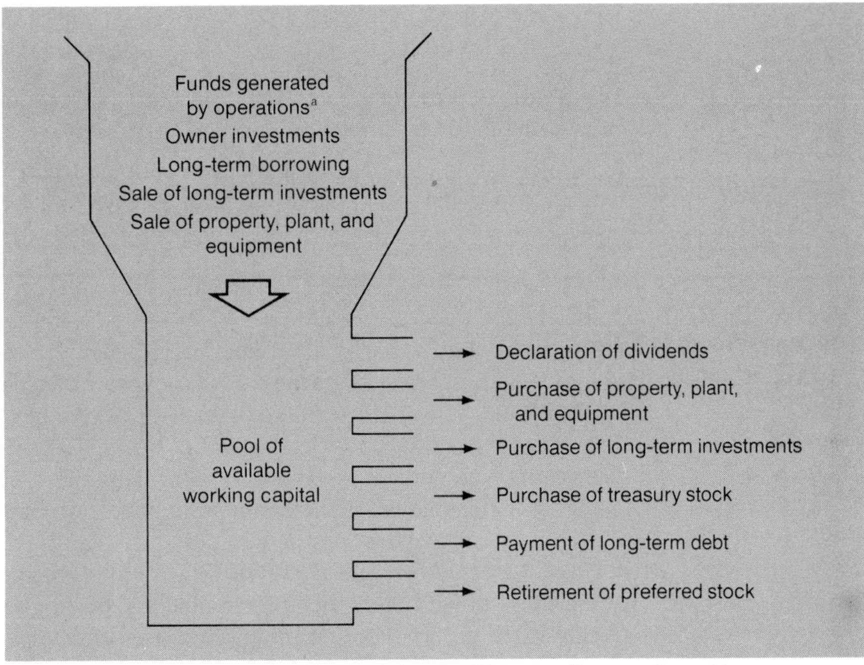

[a]This is a net item, the excess of working capital received from operations over the working capital used in operations.

Figure 20–2 Working Capital Inflows and Outflows

All Financial Resources on a Working Capital Basis

Sources and Uses of Working Capital

The chief sources of working capital are operations, additional investments by owners, long-term borrowing, and the sale of noncurrent assets. The chief uses of working capital are purchases of noncurrent assets, payment of long-term debt, reduction of stockholders' equity by declaration of dividends, and purchases of treasury stock. The statement of changes in financial position—working capital basis starts with an emphasis of the interrelationship of the sources (inflows) and uses (outflows) of working capital. A chart of working capital inflows and outflows based on an analogy between the flow of working capital through a business and the flow of water through a container is shown in Figure 20–2.

Causes of Changes in Working Capital

An *increase* in working capital (source of working capital) must result when there is:

1. An increase in total current assets without a corresponding increase in total current liabilities (example: issuance of bonds or common stock).

2. A decrease in total current liabilities without a corresponding decrease in total current assets (example: issuance of bonds payable directly to a short-term creditor to settle a note payable).

A *decrease* in working capital (use of working capital) must result when there is:

1. A decrease in total current assets without a corresponding decrease in total current liabilities (example: purchase of machinery).

2. An increase in total current liabilities without a corresponding increase in total current assets (example: declaration of dividend to be paid at a later date).

Approaches to Determination of Sources and Uses of Working Capital

To determine the sources and uses of working capital for a specific period, say a year or a quarter, the accountant could analyze every transaction occurring during the period that affects a current asset or a current liability—the **current accounts**—to determine the causes of changes in working capital. This method requires considerable effort, but many transactions cause changes in both current assets and current liabilities and hence *do not* change working capital—for example, the collection of accounts receivable.

A shorter approach would be to analyze in total the transactions occurring during the period that affect **noncurrent accounts**—long-term investments; property, plant, and equipment; intangible assets; long-term liabilities; and stockholders' equity—to determine the causes of change in working capital. Every change in working capital must result in a change in one or more of the noncurrent accounts. The application of this approach requires a knowledge of how business transactions affect balance sheet elements—the topic considered next.

Analysis of Business Transactions and Their Effect on Balance Sheet Elements

Since the transactions that enter into the inflow and outflow of financial resources vary greatly, it is helpful to classify transactions in distinctive categories indicating their effect on balance sheet elements. Figure 20–3 shows a number of ways that transactions may be classified by their effect on specific balance sheet elements, identified by letter. From this diagram it is possible to determine the effects of the illustrated transactions on the sources and uses of working capital.

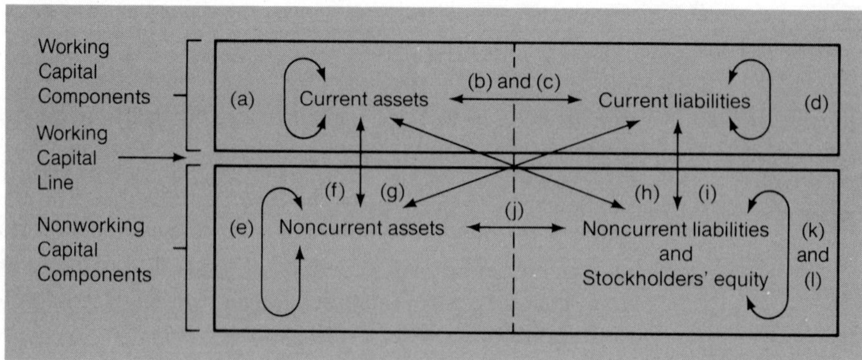

Figure 20–3 Kinds of Business Transactions That Affect and Do Not Affect Working Capital

The analysis of the transactions in Figure 20–3 is essential to understanding the method used to collect the information that appears on the statement of changes in financial position. Each example of the transactions shown in this figure is analyzed as follows:

(a) Collected an account receivable (increased a current asset, cash, and decreased a current asset, accounts receivable, thus not changing the total working capital amount).

(b) Purchased merchandise on account (increased a current asset, merchandise inventory, and increased a current liability, accounts payable; this transaction did not change total working capital).

(c) Payment of accounts payable (decreased a current liability, accounts payable, and also decreased a current asset, cash, thus not changing the total working capital amount).

(d) Issued a note payable to settle an open accounts payable (increased a current liability, notes payable, and decreased a current liability, accounts payable, thus not changing the total working capital amount).

(e) Exchanged land for machinery, incurring no gain or loss (increased a noncurrent asset, machinery, and decreased a noncurrent asset, land; this transaction did not change working capital, but it is an example of a special financing transaction that is discussed later as both a source and a use of financial resources).

(f) Purchased land and paid cash (increased a noncurrent asset, land, and decreased a current asset, cash; this transaction is a use or decrease in working capital).

(g) Purchased machinery on open charge account (increased a noncurrent asset, machinery, and increased a current liability, accounts payable; this transaction resulted in a use or decrease in working capital).

(h) Liquidated bonds payable before they became a current liability (decreased a current asset, cash, and decreased a noncurrent liability, bonds payable; this transaction is another example of a use or decrease in working capital).

(i) Declared a dividend payable in the near future (increased a current liability, dividends payable, and decreased a noncurrent item, retained earnings; this transaction resulted in a use or decrease in working capital).

(j) Issued common stock at par for land (increased a noncurrent asset, land, and increased a stockholders' equity item, common stock, thus not changing working capital; this is another example of a special financing transaction that is discussed later as both a source and a use of total financial resources).

(k) Converted bonds into common stock with no premium (increased a noncurrent stockholders' equity item, common stock, and decreased a noncurrent liability item, convertible bonds payable; this transaction did not change total working capital. This is another example of a special financing transaction that is discussed later as both a source and a use of financial resources).

(1) Declared and issued a stock dividend on common stock (this increases noncurrent stockholders' equity items, common stock and, possibly, paid-in capital—excess over par value on stock dividends, and decreases a noncurrent stockholders' equity item, retained earnings; this transaction did not change total working capital. According to *APB Opinion No. 19,* this transaction is considered an internal change in capital structure and *not* a source and use of financial resources).

Reviewing the transactions illustrated in Figure 20–3, two important observations can be made:

1. A transaction that causes a change in working capital must cross the working capital line shown in the figure; in other words, one account in the transaction was above the line, and the other account was below the line.
2. Every source and use of working capital affects the nonworking capital components thus showing pictorially the validity of using the noncurrent accounts method of determining the sources and uses of total resources. Even those special examples of financing and investing that do not affect working capital but that must be shown as both a source and use of financial resources can be determined by an analysis of the noncurrent accounts, since only these are affected by the special types of transactions.

Working Capital Provided by Operations

In Chapter 3, it was suggested that for cross-referencing purposes the income statement be marked Exhibit A; the statement of retained earnings, Exhibit B; and the balance sheet, Exhibit C. The statement of changes in financial position will now be marked Exhibit D.

Direct Method of Calculating Working Capital Provided by Operations

An important primary source of working capital is the regular operating activities of the business. The determination of working capital from this source is complicated by the fact that the change in working capital may be greater than, or less than, the net income shown in the income statement. To illustrate what the FASB refers to as the direct method of calculating the working capital provided by operations, assume that the CHL Company's income statement for its first year of operation, which ended December 31, 1985, is as shown in Figure 20–4. Figure 20–5 presents an analysis of this statement in terms of the change in working capital resulting from operations. It shows the excess of inflows of working capital over the outflows to be $3,600. Note that the depreciation expense is properly shown on the income statement as reducing net income. Yet in the second column (Figure 20–5) it is shown as not reducing working capital in the year depreciation is recorded, because the recording of the depreciation expense results in a credit to Accumulated Depreciation (that decreases noncurrent assets) and does not decrease current assets or increase current liabilities.

CHL COMPANY
Income Statement
For the Year Ended December 31, 1985

Exhibit A

Sales		$250,200
Cost of goods sold		165,000
Gross margin on sales		$ 85,200
Operating expenses:		
Depreciation—machinery	$ 2,100	
Other	81,600	
Total operating expenses		83,700
Net income		$ 1,500

Figure 20–4 Income Statement of CHL Company for 1985

CHL COMPANY
Income Statement
For the Year Ended December 31, 1985
(Converted from Accrual Basis to a Working Capital Basis)

	Income Statement Increase or (Decrease)	Working Capital Increase or (Decrease)	Explanation of Effect on Working Capital
Sales	$250,200	$250,200	Increase in cash or accounts receivable
Cost of goods sold	(165,000)	(165,000)	Decrease in inventories
Gross margin on sales	$ 85,200	$ 85,200	Gross inflows of working capital
Deduct: Operating expenses:			
Depreciation—machinery	$(2,100)	$ 0	Decrease in net income and the carrying value of machinery; but no change to working capital
Other	(81,600)	(81,600)	Decrease in cash or increase in accounts payable
Total operating expenses	$ (83,700)		
Total outflow of working capital		$ (81,600)	Gross outflows of working capital
Net income	$ 1,500		
Working capital provided by operations		$ 3,600	Gross inflows in excess of outflows

Figure 20–5 **Working Capital Basis Income Statement for CHL Company for 1985**

Indirect Method of Calculating Working Capital Provided by Operations

Another method, most often used in practice, to calculate working capital provided by operations is the indirect method. This method requires a backward-type calculative adjustment to net income to compute working capital provided by operations. The calculation involves the use of **nonworking capital charges to operations** and **nonworking capital credits to operations** —defined more specifically below. These two groups of items properly change net income but do not change working capital. For the simple example of the CHL Company (data shown in Figure 20–5), the working capital from operations is determined as shown in Figure 20–6.

Working capital provided by operations:	
Net income	$1,500
Add: Nonworking capital charges to operations:	
Depreciation expense—machinery	2,100
Subtotal	$3,600
Deduct: Nonworking capital credits to operations[a]	0
Working capital provided by operations	$3,600

[a]Although there are no nonworking capital credits to operations in this case, it is shown with a zero value to establish a generalized approach.

Figure 20–6 Indirect Calculation of Working Capital Provided by Operations for CHL Company

Had the CHL Company suffered a net loss in 1985, the calculation of working capital provided by operations would start the same as described in Figure 20–6, except that the first item would be a negative figure, net loss. For example, if a net loss of $300 had occurred in 1985, this negative item would have been added to $2,100 to get $1,800 working capital provided by operations.

APB Opinion No. 19 specifies that when the indirect method of calculation is used, it must start with net income before extraordinary items. Since *APB Opinion No. 30,* however, more strictly qualifies **extraordinary items** (see Chapter 14) as being both *unusual* and *infrequent,* it seems that the final net income figure will typically be the net income before extraordinary items. Hence, the illustrations used in this chapter make the assumption that there are no extraordinary items; therefore the starting figure for them is net income.

The indirect method of converting net income to working capital provided by operations is the method in general use. An expanded version of the indirect calculation of working capital provided by operations is as follows:

Working capital provided by operations:	
Net income	$XX
Add: Nonworking capital charges to operations [expenses, losses, adjuncts (additions) to expenses or contra items (offsets) to revenue, which do not affect working capital]	XX
Subtotal	$XX
Deduct: Nonworking capital credits to operations (revenues, gains, adjuncts to revenue or contra items to expense, which do not affect working capital)	XX
Working capital provided by operations	$XX

Figure 20–7 illustrates the calculation of working capital provided by operations. All of the additions and deductions included in the computation are reflected in the income statement. They represent costs and expenses or gains and losses that enter into the determination of net income but do not affect working capital in the current period. The expenditures or receipts related to those items were made or received in a prior period, or will be made or received in a future period. The recognition of depreciation, for ex-

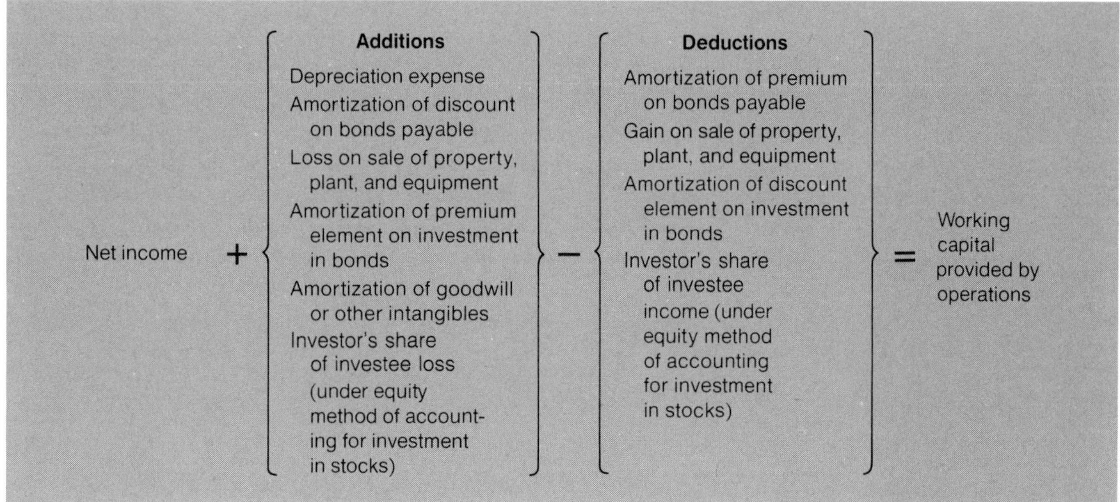

Figure 20–7 **Generalized Approach to Computing Working Capital Provided by Operations**

ample, while essential to income measurement, does not change the amount of working capital.

Preparation of Statements by Two Approaches: Simple Analytical and Work Sheet Methods

Different approaches can be used to obtain the information that appears on the statement of changes in financial position—working capital basis. In very simple cases, an accountant may determine the sources and uses of financial resources by analyzing the changes that occur in the noncurrent accounts determined from the **comparative balance sheets** (two balance sheets prepared as of the end of two succeeding periods). This is done by the use of a series of computations and schedules, referred to in this book as the **simple analytical approach.** In more complex cases, a work sheet approach may be used. Both approaches are illustrated below.

Example 1: The Simple Analytical Approach

Recall that the statement of changes in financial position includes all financial resources on either a working capital basis or a cash basis. Example 1, however, includes only sources and uses of working capital, omitting those special sources and uses of financial resources that do not affect working capital. These are illustrated in Example 2.

Example 1 is simple and can be illustrated without the use of a work sheet; that is, it can be solved by the use of the simple analytical approach.

This illustration considers the CHL Company, which received its charter on December 31, 1984, and during the early part of 1985 issued stock, received necessary licenses, and then started revenue operations. Its comparative bal-

CHL COMPANY
Comparative Balance Sheet Accounts
December 31, 1985 and 1984

Exhibit C

	December 31 1985	December 31 1984	Change Increase or (Decrease)
Debit Accounts			
Cash	$25,600	$0	$25,600
Accounts Receivable (net)	10,400	0	10,400
Merchandise Inventory	8,750	0	8,750
Prepaid Insurance	910	0	910
Machinery	21,000	0	21,000
Totals	$66,660	$0	$66,660
Credit Accounts			
Accumulated Depreciation—Machinery	$ 2,100	$0	$ 2,100
Accounts Payable	4,710	0	4,710
Notes Payable—Banks	5,000	0	5,000
Accrued Payables	850	0	850
Common Stock, $10 par	53,500	0	53,500
Retained Earnings	500	0	500
Totals	$66,660	$0	$66,660

Additional information:
Net income for 1985, $1,500 (see Figure 20–4)
Dividends declared and paid during 1985, $1,000

Figure 20–8 **Comparative Balance Sheet Accounts of CHL Company**

ance sheets and a note as to the amount of net income earned and dividends declared during 1985 are shown in Figure 20–8.

Step 1: Preparing the Schedule of Changes in Working Capital Components (Part B)

Regardless of what approach is used, the first step in preparing the statement of changes in financial position—working capital basis is to determine the net change in working capital and the change in its components. For the CHL Company, these are shown in Figure 20–9. Labeled "Part B," the schedule of changes in working capital components becomes an integral part of the final formal statement of changes in financial position (shown in Figure 20–10). This schedule shows what working capital items changed but not what caused the items to change.

Step 2: Analysis of Changes in Noncurrent Accounts

The next simple analytical step is the analysis of changes in all noncurrent accounts to determine the sources and uses of financial resources—working capital in this example. Throughout this analysis, the abbreviation *EB* is used to mean *ending balance*, and *BB, beginning balance.*

Working Capital Provided by Operations The amount of working capital provided by operations is usually determined first. The change in the noncurrent account, Retained Earnings, of $500 = ($500 *EB* − $0 *BB*) is accounted for by the net income for 1985 of $1,500 and the declaration of dividends of $1,000. The net income increased retained earnings and dividends decreased them, leaving a balance of $500. The change in Accumulated De-

Part B—Schedule of Changes in Working Capital Components

	December 31		Changes in Working Capital	
	1985	1984[a]	Increase	Decrease
Current assets:				
Cash	$25,600	$0	$25,600	
Accounts receivable (net)	10,400	0	10,400	
Merchandise inventory	8,750	0	8,750	
Prepaid insurance	910	0	910	
Total current assets	$45,660	$0		
Current liabilities:				
Accounts payable	$ 4,710	$0		$ 4,710
Notes payable—banks (short-term)	5,000	0		5,000
Accrued payables	850	0		850
Total current liabilities	$10,560	$0		
Working capital	$35,100	$0		
Totals			$45,660	$10,560
Net increase in working capital				35,100
Totals			$45,660	$45,660

[a]Obviously there is no balance sheet on December 31, 1984, but one is shown with all items having zero balances so as to establish a basic format.

Figure 20–9 Schedule of Changes in Working Capital Components of CHL Company

preciation of $2,100 = ($2,100 *EB* − $0 *BB*) is caused by the normal depreciation for 1985 (see income statement in Figure 20–4). With this information, the working capital provided by operations can be calculated by the indirect method as follows (the calculation shown in Figure 20–6):

Working capital provided by operations:	
Net income	$1,500
Add: Nonworking capital charges to operations:	
Depreciation expense	2,100
Working capital provided by operations	$3,600

Other Sources and Uses of Working Capital As indicated in the foregoing section, the declaration of dividends of $1,000 reduced retained earnings. This transaction represents a use of working capital in the amount of $1,000. Two other noncurrent items changed: Machinery has increased and Common Stock has increased. Machinery increased by $21,000 = ($21,000 *EB* − $0 *BB*). In the absence of proof to the contrary, it must be assumed that this change was brought about by the purchase of machinery using working capital of $21,000. Common stock increased by $53,500. Since this is a new company, the stock was presumably issued for working capital, probably in the form of cash.

It is always necessary to test to see if the excess of sources of working capital over uses of working capital equals the net increase in working capital as shown in Part B—the schedule of changes in working capital components. This test should explain the cause of the change in working capital of

$35,100, that is, the excess of $57,100 sources over $22,000 uses. Once this test is applied, the solution is virtually complete; all that remains is the preparation of the formal statement of changes in financial position, as illustrated in Step 3.

Step 3: Preparing the Statement of Changes in Financial Position—Working Capital Basis

The information derived from the analysis of the noncurrent accounts (Step 2) is combined with Part B from Figure 20–9 to form a statement of changes in financial position—working capital basis. This statement is shown in Figure 20–10. *APB Opinion No. 19* requires that working capital provided (or used) by operations be shown first on the statement.

CHL COMPANY **Exhibit D**
Statement of Changes in Financial Position—Working Capital Basis
For the Year Ended December 31, 1985

Part A—Sources and Uses of Financial Resources

Financial resources were provided by:		
Operations:		
Net income	$ 1,500	
Add: Nonworking capital charges against operations:		
Depreciation of machinery	2,100	
Working capital provided by operations	$ 3,600	
Issuance of common stock	53,500	
Total financial resources provided		$57,100
Financial resources were used for:		
Purchase of machinery	$21,000	
Declaration of dividends	1,000	
Total financial resources used		22,000
Net increase in working capital		$35,100

Part B—Schedule of Changes in Working Capital Components

	December 31		Changes in Working Capital	
	1985	1984	Increase	Decrease
Current assets:				
Cash	$25,600	$0	$25,600	
Accounts receivable (net)	10,400	0	10,400	
Merchandise inventory	8,750	0	8,750	
Prepaid insurance	910	0	910	
Total current assets	$45,660	$0		
Current liabilities:				
Accounts payable	$ 4,710	$0		$ 4,710
Notes payable—banks (short-term)	5,000	0		5,000
Accrued payables	850	0		850
Total current liabilities	$10,560	$0		
Working capital	$35,100	$0		
Totals			$45,660	$10,560
Net increase in working capital				35,100
Totals			$45,660	$45,660

Figure 20–10 Formal Statement of Changes in Financial Position

Example 2: The Work Sheet Approach

The preceding example contained no unusual financial activities that are required to be shown in the statement of changes in financial position. Example 2 includes both the sources and uses of working capital and other sources and uses of financial resources, using the work sheet approach. *APB Opinion No. 19* makes it clear that the all financial resources concept on a working capital basis requires the inclusion of the following:

1. Sources and uses of working capital.
2. Sources and uses of other financial resources not affecting working capital, such as:
   a. Issuance of bonds payable or other long-term debt instruments in exchange for property, plant, and equipment items.
   b. Issuance of capital stock in exchange for property, plant, and equipment items.
   c. Conversion of bonds payable into common stock.
   d. Conversion of preferred stock into common stock.[5]

Each item listed in 2 above would be shown *both* as a source and as a use of financial resources. For example, in the issuance of bonds payable for land, the issuance of bonds payable would be listed as a source and the acquisition of land as a use. It is viewed as essentially being two transactions: the issuance of bonds for cash and the use of the cash received to buy land.

Not all changes in balance sheet items are to be listed as sources and uses of financial resources. *APB Opinion No. 19* excludes (1) stock dividends and stock splits and (2) restrictions on retained earnings. These items are considered to be primarily changes in accounts that do not alter the basic nature of financial resources.

For Example 2, assume that business picked up rapidly during the latter part of 1985; during 1986 the CHL Company planned an expansion campaign and engaged in financing and investing transactions, some of which affected working capital. Where more complex transactions are involved, a work sheet may be helpful in collecting and analyzing the information to appear on the statement of changes in financial position. To illustrate the more complex example, assume that CHL Company has information for 1985 and 1986 as shown in Figures 20–11 and 20–12. These data are accumulated from the comparative balance sheets, the income statement and statement of retained earnings for the period, and the journals and ledger accounts.

Step 1: Preparing the Schedule of Changes in Working Capital Components

As with the preceding example, the first step is to prepare the schedule of changes in working capital accounts, Part B to the statement of changes in financial position. This is presented first in Figure 20–13, and is incorporated in the formal statement (Figure 20–15).

[5]*Opinions of the Accounting Principles Board No. 19,* "Reporting Changes in Financial Position" (New York: AICPA, March 1971), paragraph 14.

CHL COMPANY
Comparative Balance Sheet Accounts
December 31, 1986 and 1985

Exhibit C

	December 31 1986	December 31 1985[a]	Change Increase or (Decrease)
Debit Accounts			
Cash	$197,560	$25,600	$171,960
Accounts Receivable (net)	30,250	10,400	19,850
Merchandise Inventory	89,850	8,750	81,100
Prepaid Insurance	3,750	910	2,840
Land	200,000	0	200,000
Machinery	196,000	21,000	175,000
Totals	$717,410	$66,660	$650,750
Credit Accounts			
Accumulated Depreciation—Machinery	$ 14,200	$ 2,100	$ 12,100
Accounts Payable	16,710	4,710	12,000
Notes Payable—Banks (short-term)	0	5,000	(5,000)
Dividends Payable	40,000	0	40,000
Accrued Payables	1,500	850	650
15% Bonds Payable	300,000	0	300,000
Premium on 15% Bonds Payable	9,000	0	9,000
Convertible Preferred Stock	100,000	0	100,000
Common Stock, $10 Par	153,500	53,500	100,000
Paid-In Capital—Excess over Par, Common	2,000	0	2,000
Retained Earnings	30,500	500	30,000
Retained Earnings—Restricted for Plant Expansion	50,000	0	50,000
Totals	$717,410	$66,660	$650,750

[a]These figures are from Figure 20–8.

Figure 20–11 Comparative Balance Sheet Accounts for CHL Company

a. Net income for 1986 was $120,000.
b. A dividend of $40,000 was declared on December 15, 1986, payable on January 12, 1987.
c. During 1986, machinery was purchased for $175,000.
d. The annual depreciation expense on machinery was $12,100.
e. On January 1, 1986, the company issued at 105 for cash 15 percent bonds with a face value of $200,000. The maturity date of the bonds is January 1, 1996.
f. On December 31, 1986, the company issued directly to Jefferson Realty Company 15 percent bonds with a face value of $100,000 at 100 for land valued at $100,000.
g. On December 31, 1986, convertible preferred stock was issued at par to Jefferson Realty Company for an adjoining parcel of land valued at $100,000.
h. An additional 10,000 shares of common stock was issued for cash at $10.20 per share.
i. On December 31, 1986, the board of directors voted to restrict retained earnings in the amount of $50,000 for plant expansion.
j. The annual amortization of premium on 15 percent bonds payable was $1,000.

Figure 20–12 Additional Information Relating to CHL Company

	December 31		Changes in Working Capital	
	1986	1985	Increase	Decrease
Current assets:				
Cash	$197,560	$25,600	$171,960	
Accounts receivable (net)	30,250	10,400	19,850	
Merchandise inventory	89,850	8,750	81,100	
Prepaid insurance	3,750	910	2,840	
Total current assets	$321,410	$45,660		
Current liabilities:				
Accounts payable	$ 16,710	$ 4,710		$ 12,000
Notes payable—banks (short-term)	0	5,000	5,000	
Dividends payable	40,000	0		40,000
Accrued payables	1,500	850		650
Total current liabilities	$ 58,210	$10,560		
Working capital	$263,200	$35,100		
Totals			$280,750	$ 52,650
Net increase in working capital				228,100
Totals			$280,750	$280,750

Figure 20–13 Schedule of Changes in Working Capital Components of CHL Company

Step 2: Preparing the Work Sheet for the Statement of Changes in Financial Position

A work sheet showing the analysis of changes in noncurrent accounts may be prepared. This work sheet shows the beginning and ending working capital (summarized into amounts) and the account balances of all noncurrent accounts. Space is provided—two columns' width—between these beginning and ending balances to permit the necessary analysis of the transactions producing the change in the noncurrent accounts. The work sheet ready to begin analysis entries is shown in Figure 20–14, on page 708.

The analytical work sheet entries involve a reconstruction in summary form of all the transactions that occurred during the period that changed these accounts. Those summary transactions that increase financial resources or decrease financial resources are noted in the work sheet on the bottom part under sections entitled "Sources of financial resources" and "Uses of financial resources." In the work sheet for this more complex example, note that there are some financial activities that do not affect working capital but do affect the sources and uses of financial resources. As required by *APB Opinion No. 19,* these activities must be determined. The completed work sheet is shown in Figure 20–15. The explanations to the work sheet reconstruction entries are keyed to the letters (a), (b), (c), etc. from Figure 20–12.

CHL COMPANY
Work Sheet for Statement of Changes in Financial Position
For the Year Ended December 31, 1986

	Balances December 31, 1985	Analysis of Transactions for Current Year		Balances December 31, 1986
		Debit	Credit	
Debit Accounts				
Working Capital	35,100			263,200
Land	0			200,000
Machinery	21,000			196,000
Totals	56,100			659,200
Credit Accounts				
Accumulated Depreciation—Machinery	2,100			14,200
15% Bonds Payable	0			300,000
Premium on 15% Bonds Payable	0			9,000
Convertible Preferred Stock	0			100,000
Common Stock, $10 Par	53,500			153,500
Paid-in Capital—Excess over Par, Common	0			2,000
Retained Earnings	500			30,500
Retained Earnings—Restricted for Plant Expansion	0			50,000
Totals	56,100			659,200
		Sources	**Uses**	**Remarks**
Sources of financial resources:				
Operations:				
Uses of financial resources:				

Figure 20–14 Work Sheet Ready for Analysis of Changes in Noncurrent Accounts

Explanation of Work Sheet Entries—CHL Company The work sheet reconstruction entries for this more complex example are explained in more depth.

(a) The Retained Earnings account has increased by a net change of $30,000 = ($30,500 *EB* − $500 *BB*). Entries (a), (b), and (i)—net income increased retained earnings, dividends and the restriction on retained earnings decreased retained earnings—explain this change. To record the impact of net income on financial resources, a debit is made to Sources of financial resources: Operations, $120,000; and a credit to Retained Earnings, $120,000.

(b) Dividends were declared payable in 1987. Financial resources are used in 1986 since working capital is *reduced* in 1986 by the creation of a current liability. The work sheet entry is a debit to Retained Earnings, $40,000; and a credit to Uses of financial resources: Declaration of dividends, $40,000.

(c) The Machinery account has increased by $175,000 = ($196,000 *EB* − $21,000 *BB*). This change was caused by the purchase of machinery. This transaction represents a use of financial resources of $175,000—the acquisition of machinery. The work sheet entry is a *debit* to Machinery, $175,000; and a *credit* to Uses of financial resources: Purchase of machinery, $175,000. This transaction explains the cause of the change in Machinery, $175,000 and a check mark (√) is placed by the ending balance.

(d) The Accumulated Depreciation—Machinery account has increased by $12,100 = ($14,200 *EB* − $2,100 *BB*). The depreciation expense on machinery is $12,100 (see Figure 20–12), which explains the change in the account. The work sheet entry for this transaction is a debit to Sources of financial resources: Operations (add-back for depreciation of machinery), $12,100; and a credit to Accumulated Depreciation—Machinery, $12,100.

(e) Two noncurrent accounts were affected by transactions involving 15 percent bonds payable: (1) the 15% Bonds Payable account was increased by a total amount of $300,000 = ($300,000 *EB* − $0 *BB*); and (2) Premium on 15% Bonds Payable, by $9,000 = ($9,000 *EB* − $0 *BB*). These bonds were issued at two different times at different prices. One lot (e) was issued at 105, thus providing financial resources of $210,000. The work sheet reconstruction entry for the first issuance is a debit to Sources of financial resources: Issuance of bonds payable at 105, $210,000; and credits to 15% Bonds Payable, $200,000 and Premium on 15% Bonds Payable, $10,000. This transaction does not fully explain either of the noncurrent accounts. Entries (f) and (j) are required before the two account changes are explained.

(f) Bonds payable were issued at face value directly to realtor for land, $100,000. This transaction does not affect working capital but represents *both* a source and a use of financial resources under the all financial resources concept of funds. Two separate work sheet entries are needed in the analysis in this transaction: (1) a debit to Sources of financial resources: Issuance of bonds payable at 100, $100,000; and a credit to 15% Bonds Payable, $100,000;

CHL COMPANY
Work Sheet for Statement of Changes in Financial Position
For the Year Ended December 31, 1986

	Balances December 31, 1985	Analysis of Transactions for Current Year		Balances December 31, 1986
		Debit	Credit	
Debit Accounts				
Working Capital	35,100	(z) 228,100		263,200 √[c]
Land[a]	0	(f) 100,000		200,000 √
		(g) 100,000		
Machinery	21,000	(c) 175,000		196,000 √
Totals	56,100			659,200
Credit Accounts				
Accumulated Depreciation—Machinery	2,100		(d) 12,100	14,200 √
15% Bonds Payable[a]	0		(e) 200,000	300,000 √
			(f) 100,000	
Premium on 15% Bonds Payable	0	(j) 1,000	(e) 10,000	9,000 √
Convertible Preferred Stock	0		(g) 100,000	100,000 √
Common Stock, $10 Par	53,500		(h) 100,000	153,500 √
Paid-in Capital—Excess over Par, Common	0		(h) 2,000	2,000 √
Retained Earnings[a]	500	(b) 40,000	(a) 120,000	30,500 √
		(i) 50,000		
Retained Earnings—Restricted for Plant Expansion	0		(i) 50,000	50,000 √
Totals	56,100	694,100	694,100	659,200
		Sources	**Uses**	**Remarks**
Sources of financial resources:				
Operations:				
Net income		(a) 120,000		From operations, 131,100
Add: Depreciation expense—machinery		(d) 12,100		
Deduct: Amortization of premium on 15% bonds payable			(j) 1,000	
Issuance of bonds payable at 105		(e) 210,000		
Issuance of bonds payable at 100		(f) 100,000		
Issuance of preferred stock		(g) 100,000		
Issuance of common stock		(h) 102,000		
Uses of financial resources:				
Declaration of dividends			(b) 40,000	
Purchase of machinery			(c) 175,000	
Purchase of land			(f) 100,000	
			(g) 100,000	
Total sources and uses of financial resources[b]		644,100	416,000	
Increase in working capital			(z) 228,100	
Totals		644,100	644,100	

[a]Where more than one debit or credit to an item can be anticipated, an extra line should be left blank.

[b]The total sources and uses of financial resources are really $643,100 and $415,000, respectively, when the deduct item, amortization of premium on 15% bonds payable, is deducted from the sum of other operational items. From a work sheet check and balance point of view, it is better to add the debits and credits under the Sources and Uses columns.

[c]A check mark (√) can be used to show that a line representing an account has been "explained." A line (account) is explained when the debits and credits in the Analysis columns reconcile the difference between beginning and ending balances.

Figure 20–15 **Work Sheet After Analysis of Changes in Noncurrent Accounts**

(2) a debit to Land, $100,000; and a credit to Uses of financial resources: Purchase of land, $100,000. This transaction now fully explains the remaining change in the 15% Bonds Payable amount.

(g) This reconstruction is similar to (f). Convertible preferred stock was issued at par directly for land, $100,000. This transaction [like (f)] does not affect working capital; but it represents *both* a source and a use of financial resources under the all financial resources concept of funds. Two separate work sheet entries are needed in the analysis in this transaction: (1) a debit to Sources of financial resources: Issuance of preferred stock, $100,000; and a credit to Convertible Preferred Stock, $100,000; and (2) a debit to Land, $100,000; and a credit to Uses of financial resources: Purchase of land, $100,000. This transaction explains the change in Convertible Preferred Stock of $100,000. It also completes the explanation of the change in the Land account: (f) explains $100,000 and (g) explains the remaining $100,000.

(h) An additional 10,000 shares of common stock were issued at $10.20 per share. This transaction provided working capital of $102,000. The work sheet entry to explain two noncurrent accounts, Common Stock and Paid-in Capital—Excess over Par, Common, is a debit to Sources of financial resources: Issuance of common stock, $102,000; and two credits—(1) Common Stock, $10 Par (for par amount), $100,000 and (2) Paid-in Capital—Excess over Par, Common, $2,000. The change in both of the accounts credited is now explained.

(i) The board of directors voted to restrict retained earnings for expansion in the amount of $50,000. This transaction is deemed simply to be a book-type entry to show management's intended use of earnings; hence, the APB indicated that it need not be shown on the statement of changes in financial position. A work sheet entry is *required,* however, to explain the change in Retained Earnings—Restricted for Plant Expansion and to complete the explanation of the change in Retained Earnings. Thus, to keep from drawing a wrong conclusion about what produced this change, it is necessary to make a work sheet entry debiting Retained Earnings for $50,000 and crediting Retained Earnings—Restricted for Plant Expansion for $50,000.

(j) The Premium on 15% Bonds Payable account needs a debit of $1,000 to show that the total change has been explained. The amortization of premium on bonds payable for 1986 was $1,000; this amortization explains what produced the remaining net change in the Premium on 15% Bonds Payable amount. This amortization reduced the Bond Interest Expense account, *thus causing an increase in net income without producing an increase in working capital.* To provide for a subtraction from the working capital provided by operations, a work sheet reconstruction entry must be made debiting Premium on 15% Bonds Payable for $1,000 and crediting Sources of financial resources: Operations (deduct for the nonworking capital credit item, amortization of premium on 15 percent bonds payable) for $1,000. This entry completes the explanation of the changes in all the noncurrent accounts.

(z) The net increase in working capital is $228,100 = ($263,200 *EB* – $35,100 *BB*). The details of this change are shown in Schedule B (see Figure 20–13). An entry, lettered (z) to distinguish it from the regular transaction analysis entries, is made on the work sheet debiting Working Capital and crediting Increase in working capital (shown in the uses section) for $228,100 to provide a balancing figure. If the analysis is accurate and complete, the sum of the sources will equal the sum of the uses plus the increase in working capital. Or, if there had been a decrease in working capital, the sum of the sources plus the net decrease in working capital should equal the sum of the uses. The fact, however, that the Sources and Uses columns are in balance provides only a limited proof of accuracy, a proof that debits equal credits in all the analytical entries. Many errors could still exist within these equal debits and credits, for example, counterbalancing errors, amounts debited or credited to wrong accounts, and various omissions. In like manner, if the work is accurate and complete, all changes in accounts in the upper half of the work sheet will be explained and total debits will equal total credits in the Analysis columns.

Since the work sheet indicated total sources of $644,100 equal the total uses of $416,000 plus the increase in working capital of $228,100, it can be presumed that the work sheet is correct up to this point. Next, the work sheet is completed by determining the net source of working capital from operations by adding to net income the nonworking capital addbacks and subtracting any nonworking capital deductions. The working capital provided by operations can then be summarized and shown as noted in the Remarks column. After the work sheet is completed, the formal statement of changes in financial position—working capital basis is prepared.

Step 3: Preparing the Statement of Changes in Financial Position—Working Capital Basis

Now that the work sheet has been completed, Part A of the formal statement of changes in financial position on the working capital basis can be prepared directly from the Sources and Uses section of the work sheet. The debits represent sources of financial resources; the credits, uses of financial resources. Supporting figures for working capital received from operations must be taken from the add-back and deduct items shown under the Sources of Financial Resources: Operations title. The completed statement showing both Parts A and B is shown in Figure 20–16.

All Financial Resources—Cash Basis

As indicated previously, *APB Opinion No. 19* permits the presentation of the all financial resources statement of changes in financial position on either a cash or a working capital basis. Also with the current emphasis on **liquidity** (the nearness of assets and liabilities to cash), the cash basis format may be

CHL COMPANY **Exhibit D**
Statement of Changes in Financial Position—Working Capital Basis
For the Year Ended Decmeber 31, 1986

Part A—Sources and Uses of Financial Resources

Financial resources were provided by:		
Operations:		
Net income	$120,000	
Add: Nonworking capital charges to operations:		
Depreciation of machinery	12,100	
Subtotal	$132,100	
Deduct: Nonworking capital credits to operations:		
Amortization of premium on 15% bonds payable	1,000	
Working capital provided by operations	$131,100	
Issuance of 15% bonds payable at 105	210,000	
Issuance of 15% bonds payable at 100	100,000	
Issuance of convertible preferred stock at par	100,000	
Issuance of common stock	102,000	
Total financial resources provided		$643,100
Financial resources were used for:		
Declaration of dividends	$ 40,000	
Purchase of machinery	175,000	
Purchase of land (by issuance of bonds and convertible preferred stock)	200,000	
Total financial resources used		415,000
Net increase in working capital		$228,100

Part B—Schedule of Changes in Working Capital Components

	December 31		Changes in Working Capital	
	1986	1985	Increase	Decrease
Current assets:				
Cash	$197,560	$25,600	$171,960	
Accounts receivable (net)	30,250	10,400	19,850	
Merchandise inventory	89,850	8,750	81,100	
Prepaid insurance	3,750	910	2,840	
Total current assets	$321,410	$45,660		
Current liabilities:				
Accounts payable	$ 16,710	$ 4,710		$ 12,000
Notes payable—banks (short-term)	0	5,000	5,000	
Dividends payable	40,000	0		40,000
Accrued payables	1,500	850		650
Total current liabilities	$ 58,210	$10,560		
Working capital	$263,200	$35,100		
Totals			$280,750	$ 52,650
Net increase in working capital				228,100
Totals			$280,750	$280,750

Figure 20–16
Formal Statement of Changes in Financial Position for CHL Company

the trend in the future. The all financial resources statement prepared on a cash basis approach requires the inclusion of the following:

1. Sources and uses of cash, including the calculation of cash provided by (or used in) operations.
2. Sources and uses of other financial resources not affecting cash, such as:
   a. Issuance of bonds payable or other long-term debt instruments in exchange for property, plant, and equipment items.
   b. Issuance of common stock in exchange for property, plant, and equipment items.
   c. Conversion of bonds payable into common stock.
   d. Conversion of preferred stock into common stock.
   e. The exchange of temporary investments for repurchase of treasury stock.

The *Opinion* specifically excludes the declaration of stock dividends and the restriction of retained earnings from being shown in the statement of changes in financial position on a cash basis. As with the working capital basis, these exclusions are required because they are essentially book-type changes. Hence they do not represent financing and investing activities.

Objectives of Cash Basis Statement of Changes in Financial Position

Besides the trend toward the cash basis format for external reporting purposes, the cash basis statement often will be more important to an internal user than the working capital basis statement. For example, for many short-run financial purposes, a statement based on cash is useful to management for analysis in budgeting and forecasting cash requirements. When interest rates are extremely high, the administration of cash and the attention accorded the concept of liquidity are of paramount importance.

Generalized Approach to Cash Basis Statement

The logic of the analysis for a cash basis statement of changes in financial position is the same as that for a working capital basis statement: both consider the relationships of the items in the financial statements. The cause of the changes in cash—sources and uses—are determined by analyzing the changes in *all* accounts other than Cash. Figures from the income statement are used to determine the changes in cash as a result of operations, and figures from the balance sheet together with supplementary data reveal the remaining causes for change.

As with working capital provided by operations, determination of the cash generated by operations presents a major problem, which is complicated by the fact that the revenue and expense figures used for income measurement are different from cash receipts and cash disbursements. The time lag in the settlement of accounts with customers and creditors and the prepayment of certain expenses, for example, necessitate the conversion of accrual basis revenue and expense amounts to their cash equivalents.

If the work sheet method were to be used to accumulate information for the statement of changes in financial position—cash basis, as indicated above, it would be necessary to create a work sheet item for each account for which a periodic change is recorded. Transactions causing changes in cash would then be reconstructed in summary form by analyzing the changes in all accounts other than Cash and by reference to supplementary information. Since the procedural approach is similar to the preceding illustrations, a work sheet for the cash basis is not illustrated here. Rather, in the illustration that follows, the *simple analytical approach* is used to determine the information that appears on the statement of changes in financial position—cash basis.

Example of Cash Basis Statement

Information related to the Athens Corporation is shown in Figure 20–17. The simple analytical method of determining the sources and uses of cash for the Athens Corporation is then used, based on this information.

Cash Provided by Operations

The first step in preparing a statement of changes in financial position on a cash basis is to determine the amount of cash provided by (or used in) operations. As indicated in the foregoing section, this calculation focuses on the operating (income statement) transactions affecting cash. As with determining working capital provided by operations, there are two general approaches: (1) the direct approach where the income statement is in effect converted to a cash basis statement, or (2) the indirect approach where the net cash provided by operations is determined by adding the noncash charges against operations to net income and subtracting from the resulting total the noncash credits to operations. As with working capital, the shorter indirect method is preferred in practice and is the only one illustrated here.

Indirect Method of Calculating Cash Provided by (or Used in) Operations A short-cut method of calculating the net cash provided by (or used in) operations can be developed by the same techniques for working capital. This indirect method starts with net income to which is added the *noncash charges against operations.* (This term includes expenses, losses, adjunct to expenses, contra to revenues, and changes in current items that decrease net income but *do not decrease cash.*) From the total of net income and noncash charges is subtracted the *noncash credits to operations.* (This term includes revenues, gains, adjunct to revenues, contra to expenses, and changes in current items that *increase net income but not cash.*) The difference is net cash provided by (or used in) operations. Figure 20–18 shows that the net cash provided by operations is $217,000.

Comparative Balance Sheet Accounts:

	December 31 1985	December 31 1984	Change Increase or (Decrease)
Debit Accounts			
Cash	$ 78,000	$ 61,000	$ 17,000
Accounts Receivable (net)	270,000	240,000	30,000
Merchandise Inventory	300,000	193,000	107,000
Long-Term Investments	36,000	30,000	6,000
Land	60,000	60,000	0
Buildings (net)[a]	480,000	510,000	(30,000)
Machinery (net)[a]	600,000	370,000	230,000
Totals	$1,824,000	$1,464,000	$360,000
Credit Accounts			
Accounts Payable	$ 225,000	$ 195,000	$ 30,000
Accrued Payables	9,000	12,000	(3,000)
14% Bonds Payable	210,000	174,000	36,000
Common Stock, $10 Par Value	900,000	750,000	150,000
Retained Earnings	480,000	333,000	147,000
Totals	$1,824,000	$1,464,000	$360,000

[a]These assets are shown net of the accumulated depreciation; but the depreciation for the year will have to be considered in determining the cause of change.

Abbreviated Income Statement Accounts for 1985:

	Debits	Credits
Sales		$2,430,000
Cost of Goods Sold	$1,440,000	
Depreciation Expense—Machinery	60,000	
Depreciation Expense—Building	30,000	
Other Operationg Expenses (requiring cash)	663,000	

Additional Data:

a. From the above operating data, net income is determined to be $237,000.
b. Dividends declared and paid during 1985, $90,000.
c. The change in the machinery account is caused by two transactions:
(1) depreciation and (2) purchases of machinery for cash.
d. Long-term investments were from purchases for cash.
e. The decrease in buildings (net) was from depreciation expense.
f. Common stock was issued at par value for cash.

Figure 20–17 Information Required for Statement of Changes in Financial Position—Cash Basis Approach for Athens Corporation

Increases in most of the current liabilities and decreases in most of the current assets other than cash are noncash charges to operations; that is, they result in decreases in net income without decreasing cash. In a similar but opposing way, decreases in most of the current liabilities and increases in most of the current assets are treated as noncash credits to operations since they result in increases in net income without increasing cash. Exceptions to this generalization are those current items not affecting operations, such as temporary investments (these changes are treated separately). Depreciation expense and other noncash charges and noncash credits are similar to the

Net income		$237,000
Add: Noncash charges against operations:		
Depreciation expense—machinery		60,000
Depreciation expense—building		30,000
Increases in accounts payable		30,000
Subtotal		$357,000
Deduct: Noncash credits to operations:		
Increase in accounts receivable	$ 30,000	
Increase in merchandise inventory	107,000	
Decrease in accrued payables	3,000	140,000
Net cash provided by operations		$217,000

Figure 20–18 Indirect Method of Calculating Cash Provided by (or Used in) Operations

nonworking capital charges and credits to operations. Again, both the direct and indirect methods will produce the same answer. The indirect method is used more often than the direct method because it highlights the differences between net income and the net cash provided by operations. These differences (application of the exception principle) help a manager in making certain decisions affecting the distribution of net income.

Completing the Cash Basis Statement of Changes in Financial Position The sources and uses of cash other than that resulting from operations can be determined by examining the changes that have occurred in the noncurrent accounts and certain nonoperating current accounts along with any additional information that is given. First, using the additional data (Figure 20–17), item b describes a specific use of cash, the payment of dividends of $90,000. Note that retained earnings increased by $147,000 = ($480,000 *EB* − $333,000 *BB*). Net income of $237,000 used in calculating net cash provided by operations increased retained earnings; the dividends declared decreased retained earnings by $90,000. The *net increase* is $147,000 = ($237,000 − $90,000); thus the change in retained earnings is explained.

The net increase in machinery (item c) is the result of a purchase of machinery and depreciation. Since there is a decrease caused by depreciation, the increase caused by the purchase of $290,000 is calculated as follows:

End-of-year balance	$600,000
Beginning-of-year balance	370,000
Net increase	$230,000
Add: Depreciation expense	60,000
Machinery purchased during 1985	$290,000

The increase in long-term investments results from purchases of securities (item d). This increase of $6,000 = ($36,000 *EB* − $30,000 *BB*) is a use of cash.

The decrease in buildings (net) is caused by depreciation (item e). This amount was used in calculating the net cash provided by operations; hence nothing more is required to be done. The net decrease in the noncurrent account, Buildings, is explained.

Item f explicitly states that cash is provided by the issuance of common stock at par. This amount is $150,000 = ($900,000 *EB* − $750,000 *BB*).

The changes in all accounts have now been explained except the change in the 14% Bonds Payable account. This account increased by $36,000 = ($210,000 *EB* − $174,000 *BB*). An assumption must be made as to what produced this increase. A logical one is that additional bonds of $36,000 must have been issued for cash, hence this transaction results in a source of cash. The excess of the total sources of cash over the total uses of cash must produce a figure that equals the net increases in cash of $17,000 = ($78,000 *EB* − $61,000 *BB*). The foregoing analysis is summarized in a statement of changes in financial position prepared on a cash basis, shown in Figure 20–19.

ATHENS CORPORATION
Statement of Changes in Financial Position—Cash Basis
For the Year Ended December 31, 1985

Exhibit D

Part A—Sources and Uses of Financial Resources

Financial resources were provided by:[a]			
Operations:[b]			
Net income		$237,000	
Add: Noncash charges against operations:			
Depreciation expense—machinery		60,000	
Depreciation expense—building		30,000	
Increase in accounts payable		30,000	
Subtotal		$357,000	
Deduct: Noncash credits to operations:			
Increase in accounts receivable	$ 30,000		
Increase in merchandise inventory	107,000		
Decrease in accrued payables	3,000	140,000	
Net cash provided by operations		$217,000	
Issuance of common stock at par		150,000	
Issuance of 14% bonds payable at par		36,000	
Total sources of financial resources			$403,000
Financial resources were used for:			
Payment of dividends		$ 90,000	
Purchase of long-term investments		6,000	
Purchase of machinery		290,000	
Total uses of financial resources			386,000
Net increase in cash			$ 17,000

Part B—Schedule of Changes in Cash

Cash, December 31, 1985	$78,000
Cash, December 31, 1984	61,000
Net increase in cash	$17,000

[a] In this example, these are all cash and the item could be called Cash was provided by.

[b] See Figure 20–18.

Figure 20–19 Statement of Changes in Financial Position—Cash Basis for Athens Corporation

The work sheet method could be easily adapted to provide the data for the foregoing statement. Work sheet account items could be opened for all accounts, and various subsections could be created at the bottom of the work sheet for the sources of cash including the sources from operations and for the uses of cash. Then it would be necessary to reconstruct in summary form those transactions affecting the changes in the noncash accounts. Also, to repeat, in addition to the sources and uses of cash (as illustrated in the Athens Corporation case), *APB Opinion No. 19* requires that the financing and investing activities other than those affecting cash (such as the issuance of bonds directly for land) be included in the statement of changes in financial position prepared on a cash basis. The topic of statement of changes in financial position is a current one; the FASB has this topic on its agenda at the time of this writing and had issued both a Discussion Memorandum and a related exposure draft on it.

Glossary

All financial resources A concept of funds that includes the disclosure of not only the sources and uses of working capital or cash but also other financial and investment information that does not affect working capital or cash.

Comparative balance sheets The balance sheet as of a given date compared with one or more immediately preceding balance sheets.

Current account Any current asset or current liability account.

Extraordinary items Gains and losses that are both infrequent and unusual; they are shown on the income statement in a separate section at the bottom.

Financial Resources Summary A work sheet item used to record on the debit side the sources of all financial resources and on the credit side the uses of all financial resources.

Funds In the context of the statement of changes in financial position, *funds* may mean cash, working capital, cash and temporary investments in marketable securities, current assets, or all financial resources, depending upon the needs of the user.

Liquidity The nearness to cash of assets and liabilities.

Noncurrent account Any account on the balance sheet *other than* current assets and current liabilities—specifically, any one of the long-term investments, property, plant, and equipment, intangibles, long-term liabilities, or stockholders' equity accounts.

Nonworking capital charges to operations Losses, expenses, adjunct to losses or contra to revenue that decrease net income but do not affect working capital.

Nonworking capital credits to operations Gains, revenues, adjunct to revenues or contra to expenses that increase net income but do not affect working capital.

Schedule of changes in working capital components A schedule of comparative balances in current assets and current liabilities that shows how each account balance change affected working capital; it is usually shown as part of the statement of changes in financial position.

Simple analytical approach for statement of changes in financial position The analysis of noncurrent account changes by the use of a series of computations and schedules to obtain the information for this statement.

Sources of financial resources Inflows of working capital and other financial resources.

Sources of funds See *Sources of financial resources.*

Statement of changes in financial position A statement showing sources and uses of funds prepared on either (1) an all financial resources—working capital basis or (2) an all financial resources—cash basis.

Statement of sources and uses of funds A title formerly used for the statement of changes in financial position.

Uses of financial resources Outflows of working capital and other financial resources.

Uses of funds See *Uses of financial resources.*

Work sheet for statement of changes in financial position A device that provides an orderly means for determining the sources and uses of financial resources.

Working capital Current assets less current liabilities, or amount of current assets not required to liquidate current liabilities.

Questions

Q20–1 What is meant by the term *funds?* Discuss three popular concepts of funds.

Q20–2 In *APB Opinion No. 19,* what concepts of funds are recommended for typical presentation in annual reports?

Q20–3 Student A argues that net income is the same as the amount of working capital provided by operations. Student B says the amount of working capital provided by operations may be more or less than the net income amount. Which student is right? State why.

Q20–4 Why does an analysis of changes in noncurrent accounts reveal the net change in the current accounts?

Q20–5 What is the purpose of the statement of changes in financial position?

Q20–6 How may working capital provided by operations be determined?

Q20–7 What are the major elements that increase working capital from operations? The major elements that decrease working capital in operations?

Q20–8 Certain transactions changing noncurrent balance sheet amounts do not appear in the statement of changes in financial position. Why? Give two examples.

Q20–9 How may the statement of changes in financial position—all financial resources on a working capital basis be used to advantage by management? By investors? By others?

Q20–10 How may the statement of changes in financial position—all financial resources on a cash basis be used to advantage by management? By investors? By others?

Q20–11 What are some of the sources of information for the preparation of the statement of changes in financial position—working capital basis?

Q20–12 What is the effect of a cash dividend declaration on working capital? Of the payment of a dividend?

Q20–13 When interest rates are extremely high, is the statement of changes in financial position more useful on a working capital basis or on a cash basis? Why?

Q20–14 Describe how an accountant would use the simple analytical approach to determine the sources and uses of cash to appear on the statement of changes in financial position prepared on a cash basis.

Q20–15 What is the effect on working capital of a change from straight line to an accelerated method of depreciation? Ignore income taxes.

Q20–16 In arriving at working capital provided by operations, certain items are added to net income and other items are deducted. Illustrate and explain.

Q20–17 Payment on a noncurrent note payable affects working capital, whereas payment on a current note payable does not. Why? If the exchange of stock for land does not affect working capital, why is it included on the statement of changes in financial position?

Q20–18 A distinguished professor has stated, "A statement of changes in financial position is like a motion picture, explaining the difference between two photographs, the balance sheet as of the end of the current year and the balance sheet as of the end of the preceding year." Do you agree with this analogy? Justify your response.

Exercises

E20–1
Determining effect on working capital

For each of the following transactions, state whether (a) it was a source of working capital (strictly interpreted), (b) it was a use of working capital, or (c) it had no effect on working capital.

1. Purchased U.S. Treasury bills maturing in 6 months.
2. Declared and issued a stock dividend to common stockholders.
3. Restricted retained earnings for anticipated contingencies.
4. Issued common stock in exchange for land.
5. Acquired machinery for $75,000; paid $30,000 in cash and issued a long-term note for the balance.
6. Reacquired some outstanding preferred stock for retirement.
7. Issued additional common stock at a premium for cash.
8. Issued bonds directly to preferred shareholders to retire preferred stock.
9. Purchased treasury stock for cash.

E20–2
Financing sources and uses not affecting working capital

Refer to E20–1 and state which of the transactions are a source or use of total financial resources yet are *not* a source or use of working capital.

E20–3
Explaining decrease in working capital

Comparative financial statements of the Burris Corporation showed the following balances:

	December 31	
	1985	1984
Cash	$ 75,000	$ 78,000
Other current assets	165,000	172,500
Property, plant, and equipment (net)	210,000	165,000
Current liabilities	165,000	172,500
Stockholders' equity	285,000	243,000

There were no disposals of property, plant, and equipment during the year. Dividend payments totaled $15,000; depreciation expense was $16,500. Prepare a schedule explaining the cause of the decrease in working capital in spite of reported net income of $57,000.

E20–4
Partial statement of changes in financial position—working capital basis

The property, plant, and equipment section of the Johns Company's comparative balance sheet shows the following amounts:

	December 31	
	1985	1984
Property, plant, and equipment:		
Machinery	$412,500	$375,000
Deduct: Accumulated depreciation	187,500	180,000
Total property, plant, and equipment	$225,000	$195,000

Acquisitions of new machinery during the year totaled $107,500. The income statement shows depreciation expense of $50,000 for the year and a loss from machinery disposals of $18,000.

1. Determine the original cost and accumulated depreciation of machinery sold during the year and the proceeds of the sale.

2. Prepare a partial statement of changes in financial position—working capital basis.

E20–5
Working capital provided by or used in operations

For each of the following cases, compute the working capital generated by operations:

	a	b	c	d	e
Net income (loss) per income statement	$45,000	$(46,000)	$165,000	$140,000	$(58,000)
Depreciation of property, plant, and equipment	5,000	6,000	13,000	8,000	4,000
Gain (loss) on sale of long-term investments			(4,000)	6,000	(1,500)
Periodic amortization of discount on bonds payable			3,000	1,500	750
Periodic amortization of patents				1,500	900

E20–6
Explaining reason for change in noncurrent accounts

Analyze the following changes in noncurrent accounts to determine the possible cause of each change; describe each cause of change.

a. Abandoned fully depreciated equipment costing $62,000. No other dispositions of equipment. Equipment account increased $8,000.
b. The Accumulated Depreciation—Equipment account decreased $4,000 (consider in conjunction with a).
c. The Patents account decreased $2,000 (10-year life).
d. The Mortgage Payable account decreased $20,000.
e. The Retained Earnings balance on January 1, $76,000. Dividends declared and paid during year, $6,000. No other dividends declared or paid. Balance of Retained Earnings on December 31 (year-end), $74,000.
f. Investments costing $14,000 were sold for $26,000; balance of the Investments account increased $8,000. There were no additional dispositions of investments.
g. One hundred shares of $10 par value common stock were issued. No other stock transactions occurred. What was the dollar amount of the increase to this account if the stock was issued for $14 per share? What other account would be affected if the stock were issued at $14 per share?

E20–7
Statement of changes in financial position—working capital basis by the simple analytical approach

During the year 1985, the changes in the accounts of the Wiggins Company were as follows:

	Increases	Decreases
Cash		$10,000
Accounts Receivable	$ 9,000	
Merchandise Inventory	30,000	
Long-Term Investments	9,000	
Property, Plant, and Equipment	87,000	
Accumulated Depreciation	6,000	
Accounts Payable	11,250	
Taxes Payable		750
Mortgage Payable		9,000
Common Stock	74,000	
Retained Earnings	43,500	

Additional information:

a. Net income per statement, $57,975.
b. Dividends declared, $14,475.
c. There were no disposals of property, plant, or equipment during the year.

Prepare a statement of changes in financial position—working capital basis concept for the year 1985. Use the simple analytical approach.

E20–8 *Statement of changes in financial position—working capital basis by the work sheet method*

The following information regarding the changes in financial position is indicated for the year 1985 for The Sandra Company:

THE SANDRA COMPANY
Comparative Balance Sheet Accounts
December 31, 1985 and 1984

	December 31 1985	December 31 1984	Change Increase or (Decrease)
Debit Accounts			
Cash	$206,875	$165,625	$ 41,250
Accounts Receivable (net)	33,750	30,000	3,750
Merchandise Inventory	222,375	150,000	72,375
Prepaid Insurance	2,250	1,875	375
Land	37,500	0	37,500
Machinery	168,750	150,000	18,750
Totals	$671,500	$497,500	$174,000
Credit Accounts			
Accumulated Depreciation—Machinery	$ 11,250	$ 7,500	$ 3,750
Accounts Payable	9,375	7,500	1,875
Dividends Payable	18,750	3,750	15,000
14% Bonds Payable	112,500	0	112,500
Premium on 14% Bonds Payable	3,375	0	3,375
Convertible Preferred Stock	0	66,250	(66,250)
Common Stock, $10 Par Value	347,500	300,000	47,500
Paid-in-Capital—Excess over Par, Common	18,750	0	18,750
Retained Earnings	150,000	112,500	37,500
Totals	$671,500	$497,500	$174,000

Additional information:

a. Net income for 1985 was $56,250.
b. A dividend of $18,750 was declared on December 16, 1985, payable on January 14, 1986.
c. On December 27, 1985, the company sold a machine that cost $37,500 and had an accumulated depreciation of $3,750 for $30,000 cash. The loss of $3,750 was an ordinary loss.
d. The company purchased new machinery for $56,250.
e. The annual depreciation expense on machinery was $7,500.
f. On January 1, 1985, the company issued 14 percent bonds with a face value of $75,000 at 105 for cash. The maturity date of the bonds is January 1, 1995.
g. On December 31, 1985, the company issued directly to Cates Realty Company 14 percent bonds with a face value of $37,500 at 100 for land valued at $37,500.
h. The convertible preferred stock was converted during 1985 into 4,750 shares of $10 par value common stock.
i. The annual amortization of premium on 14 percent bonds payable was $375.

1. Prepare a separate Part B (schedule of changes in working capital components).

2. Prepare Part A of a statement of changes in financial position—working capital basis concept for 1985. Use the work sheet method.

E20–9 *Calculating cash received from customers*

The accounts receivable of a business totaled $36,000 at the beginning of the year and $30,000 at the end of the year. Accounts receivable written off as uncollectible during the year amounted to $2,800, and cash discounts allowed to customers amounted to

$1,100. The sales for the year were $80,000. What were the cash receipts during the year from sales of the current and prior periods?

E20–10 *Calculating cash paid to suppliers of merchandise*

The purchases of merchandise of a business amounted to $150,000 during 1985. Accounts payable at the beginning and end of the year were $43,000 and $39,600, respectively; notes payable given to trade creditors in settlement of open accounts were $9,000 at the beginning of the year and $9,800 at year-end. Returns and allowances on purchases were $1,020. What were the cash payments during 1985 for purchases of 1985 and prior periods?

E20–11 *Calculating cash generated by operations*

The financial statement information of Propst Company is given below:

PROPST COMPANY
Income Statement
For the Year Ended December 31, 1985

Exhibit A

Net sales		$98,500
Cost of goods sold		70,950
Gross margin on sales		$27,550
Expenses:		
Salaries expense	$13,800	
Depreciation expense	2,250	
Rent expense	3,600	
Supplies expense	1,500	21,150
Net income		$ 6,400

PROPST COMPANY
Comparative Balance Sheet Accounts
December 31, 1985 and 1984

	December 31	
	1985	**1984**
Debit Accounts		
Cash	$25,075	$17,040
Accounts Receivable	9,165	10,830
Merchandise Inventory	12,150	12,150
Supplies on Hand	450	1,050
Equipment	22,680	18,000
Totals	$69,520	$59,070
Credit Accounts		
Accounts Payable	$ 5,850	$ 4,650
Accrued Rent Payable	600	300
Accrued Salaries Payable	450	150
Accumulated Depreciation	9,450	7,200
Common Stock	37,500	37,500
Retained Earnings	15,670	9,270
Totals	$69,520	$59,070

Prepare a schedule of net cash generated by operations for 1985.

E20–12 The data of Ralston Company follow:

Statement of changes in financial position—cash basis by the simple analytical method

RALSTON COMPANY
Comparative Balance Sheet Accounts
December 31, 1985 and 1984

	December 31	
	1985	**1984**
Debit Accounts		
Cash	$ 164,000	$ 51,000
Accounts Receivable (net)	270,000	288,000
Merchandise Inventory	300,000	240,000
Land	60,000	45,000
Buildings (net)	480,000	300,000
Machinery (net)	600,000	450,000
Totals	$1,874,000	$1,374,000
Credit Accounts		
Accounts Payable	$ 225,000	$ 195,000
Accrued Payables	9,000	12,000
Mortgage Payable	210,000	174,000
Common Stock, $1 par value	950,000	750,000
Retained Earnings	480,000	243,000
Totals	$1,874,000	$1,374,000

RALSTON COMPANY **Exhibit A**
Income Statement
For the Year Ended December 31, 1985

Sales		$2,430,000
Cost of goods sold		1,440,000
Gross margin on sales		$ 990,000
Operating expenses:		
Depreciation—machinery	$ 60,000	
Depreciation—buildings	30,000	
Other operating expenses	663,000	753,000
Net income		$ 237,000

Additional data:

a. No dividends were declared during the year.

b. The increase in machinery, buildings, and land were from purchases for cash.

c. 200,000 additional shares of common stock were issued for cash at par value.

Prepare a statement of changes in financial position—cash basis for 1985, using the simple analytical approach.

A Problems

P20–1A *Statement of changes in financial position—working capital basis by the simple analytical approach*

The comparative balance sheet accounts of Wilfong Company, as of December 31, 1985 and 1984, disclosed the following:

WILFONG COMPANY
Comparative Balance Sheet Accounts
December 31, 1985 and 1984

	December 31	
	1985	**1984**
Debit Accounts		
Cash	$ 82,000	$ 194,500
Accounts Receivable (net)	88,200	74,700
Merchandise Inventory	127,500	97,500
Long-Term Investments	102,000	90,000
Machinery	525,000	450,000
Buildings	405,000	337,500
Land	75,000	75,000
Patents	27,000	30,000
Totals	$1,431,700	$1,349,200
Credit Accounts		
Accumulated Depreciation—Machinery	$ 60,000	$ 45,000
Accumulated Depreciation—Buildings	52,500	30,000
Accounts Payable—Trade	82,500	75,000
Notes Payable—Trade	12,000	15,000
Mortgage Payable	75,000	190,000
Common Stock	825,000	750,000
Retained Earnings	324,700	244,200
Totals	$1,431,700	$1,349,200

Additional data:

a. Net income for the year was $80,500.
b. There were no sales or disposals of property, plant, and equipment during the year.

Required: Prepare a statement of changes in financial position—working capital basis concept for 1985. Use the simple analytical approach.

P20–2A *Statement of changes in financial position—working capital basis by the work sheet approach*

Following is the comparative postclosing trial balance of the Werley Company:

WERLEY COMPANY
Comparative Postclosing Trial Balance
December 31, 1985 and 1984

	December 31	
	1985	**1984**
Debit Accounts		
Cash	$ 152,500	$ 125,000
Temporary Investments	0	165,000
Accounts Receivable (net)	102,500	110,000
Merchandise Inventory	380,000	302,500
Prepaid Expenses	6,000	3,750
Property, Plant, and Equipment	750,000	450,000
Patents	96,000	102,000
Totals	$1,487,000	$1,258,250

Credit Accounts

Accumulated Depreciation—Property, Plant, and Equipment	$ 202,500	$ 150,000
Accounts Payable	150,000	90,000
Common Stock	800,000	800,000
Retained Earnings	334,500	218,250
Totals	$1,487,000	$1,258,250

Additional data:

a. Net income for the period was $187,500.
b. Dividends declared were $71,250.
c. The temporary investments were sold at a gain (included in Item a) of $22,500.
d. Equipment with an original cost of $30,000 and accumulated depreciation of $15,000 was sold at an ordinary loss (included in Item a) of $3,000.
e. Patents are being amortized over their legal life of 17 years.

Required: Prepare a statement of changes in financial position—working capital basis concept for 1985. Use the work sheet approach.

P20–3A *Statement of changes in financial position—working capital basis by the work sheet method*

Data of Westerhoff, Inc., are given below.

WESTERHOFF, INC.
Comparative Balance Sheet Accounts
December 31, 1985 and 1984

	December 31	
	1985	**1984**
Debit Accounts		
Cash	$ 95,000	$ 72,500
Accounts Receivable	136,000	121,000
Merchandise Inventory	60,000	48,000
Investments (Long-Term)	45,000	75,000
Machinery	60,000	37,500
Buildings	135,000	112,500
Land	15,000	15,000
Totals	$546,000	$481,500
Credit Accounts		
Allowance for Doubtful Accounts	$ 5,500	$ 4,000
Accumulated Depreciation—Machinery	11,250	4,500
Accumulated Depreciation—Buildings	27,000	18,000
Accounts Payable	65,000	54,500
Accrued Payables	6,750	5,250
Mortgage Payable	52,500	60,000
Common Stock, $2 par value	300,000	300,000
Retained Earnings	78,000	35,250
Totals	$546,000	$481,500

Additional data:

a. Net income for the year was $90,000.
b. Dividends declared during the year were $47,250.
c. Investments that cost $30,000 were sold during the year for $37,500. The gain is an ordinary one and is included in Item a.
d. Machinery that cost $7,500, on which $1,500 in depreciation had accumulated, was sold for $9,000. The gain is ordinary and is included in Item a.

Required: Prepare a statement of changes in financial position—working capital basis for 1985. Use the work sheet approach.

P20–4A *Statement of changes in financial position—working capital basis by work sheet method*

You are given the following information from the books of the Murrell Corporation:

MURRELL CORPORATION
Balance Sheet Accounts
December 31, 1985 and 1984

	December 31		Change
	1985	1984	Increase or (Decrease)
Debit Accounts			
Cash	$ 29,800	$ 28,400	$ 1,400
Accounts Receivable	81,400	53,600	27,800
Merchandise Inventory	33,000	42,000	(9,000)
Machinery	123,600	131,100	(7,500)
Sinking Fund Cash[a]	25,000	0	25,000
Totals	$292,800	$255,100	$37,700
Credit Accounts			
Allowance for Doubtful Accounts	$ 4,200	$ 3,750	$ 450
Accumulated Depreciation—Machinery	34,300	37,300	(3,000)
Accounts Payable	31,500	26,300	5,200
Dividends Payable	3,000	0	3,000
Bonds Payable	30,000	0	30,000
Premium on Bonds Payable	1,425	0	1,425
Common Stock	150,000	150,000	0
Retained Earnings	13,375	37,750	(24,375)
Retained Earnings—Restricted for Sinking Fund[b]	25,000	0	25,000
Totals	$292,800	$255,100	$37,700

[a]The original entry to create the sinking fund was a debit to Sinking Fund Cash and a credit to Cash.

[b]The original entry to restrict retained earnings for the sinking fund was a debit to Retained Earnings and a credit to Retained Earnings—Restricted for Sinking Fund.

MURRELL CORPORATION **Exhibit B**
Statement of Retained Earnings
For the Year Ended December 31, 1985

Retained earnings, December 31, 1984		$37,750
Add: Net income for year ended December 31, 1985		11,125
Subtotal		$48,875
Deduct: Dividends declared and paid in cash	$ 7,500	
Dividend declared in 1985, payable January 15, 1986	3,000	
Restriction for sinking fund	25,000	35,500
Retained earnings, December 31, 1985		$13,375

MURRELL CORPORATION **Exhibit A**
Income Statement
For the Year Ended December 31, 1985

Sales		$138,175
Cost of goods sold		97,500
Gross margin on sales		$ 40,675
Operating expenses:		
Salaries expense	$22,050	
Bad debts expense	450	
Depreciation of machinery	5,250	
Taxes expense	600	
Insurance expense	450	28,800
Net income from operations		$ 11,875
Other ordinary expenses:		
Bond interest expense	$ 1,575	
Deduct: Amortization of bond premium	75	
Net bond interest expense	$ 1,500	
Other ordinary revenue:		
Gain on sale of machinery	750	750
Net income to retained earnings		$ 11,125

Additional data:

a. Bonds payable in the amount of $30,000 were issued on April 30, 1985, at 105.

b. Machinery that cost $10,500 and had accumulated depreciation of $8,250 was sold for $3,000 in cash.

Required: Prepare a statement of changes in financial position—working capital basis for 1985. Submit all supporting computations. Use the work sheet approach.

P20–5A *Statement of changes in financial position—cash basis by the simple analytical method*

The data of the Bello Company follow:

BELLO COMPANY
Comparative Balance Sheet Accounts
December 31, 1985 and 1984

	December 31	
	1985	**1984**
Debit Accounts		
Cash	$ 49,000	$ 65,500
Accounts Receivable (net)	145,000	154,000
Merchandise Inventory	160,000	130,000
Investments (Long-Term)	18,000	15,000
Land	30,000	22,500
Buildings (net)	240,000	150,000
Machinery (net)	300,000	225,000
Totals	$942,000	$762,000
Credit Accounts		
Accounts Payable	$132,500	$117,500
Accrued Payables	14,500	16,000
Mortgage Payable	105,000	87,000
Common Stock, $1 Par Value	450,000	375,000
Retained Earnings	240,000	166,500
Totals	$942,000	$762,000

BELLO COMPANY **Exhibit A**
Income Statement
For the Year Ended December 31, 1986

Sales		$1,215,000
Cost of goods sold		720,000
Gross margin on sales		$ 495,000
Operating expenses:		
Depreciation—machinery	$ 30,000	
Depreciation—buildings	15,000	
Other operating expenses	331,500	376,500
Net income		$ 118,500

Additional data:

a. Dividends paid during the year were $45,000.
b. The increase in long-term investments, machinery, buildings, and land were from cash purchases.
c. Issued 75,000 shares of common stock at par value for cash.

Required: Prepare a statement of changes in financial position—cash basis for 1985, using the simple analytical approach.

P20–6A *Thought-provoking problem: justifying decision not to declare a cash dividend*

The following information is presented in the annual report of the Woodbury Corporation.

WOODBURY CORPORATION **Exhibit A**
Income Statement
For the Year Ended December 31, 1985

Sales		$3,550,000
Cost of goods sold		2,110,000
Gross margin on sales		$1,440,000
Operating expenses:		
Depreciation—property, plant, and equipment	$ 55,000	
Other expenses	110,000	165,000
Net income before taxes		$1,275,000
Income taxes @ 48%		612,000
Net income		$ 663,000

WOODBURY CORPORATION **Exhibit D**
Statement of Changes in Financial Position—Working Capital Basis
For the Year Ended December 31, 1985

Part A—Sources and Uses of Financial Resources

Financial resources were provided by:		
Operations:		
Net income		$663,000
Add: Nonworking capital charges to operations:		
Depreciation of property, plant, and equipment		55,000
Working capital provided by operations		$718,000
Financial resources were used for:		
Purchase of equipment	$450,000	
Early retirement of bonds payable in current year	300,000	
Total working capital used		750,000
Net increase (decrease) in working capital		$ (32,000)

Part B—Schedule of Changes in Working Capital Components

	December 31		Changes in Working Capital	
	1985	1984	Increase	Decrease
Current assets:				
Cash	$ 30,000	$ 35,000		$ 5,000
Accounts receivable (net)	65,000	50,000	$15,000	
Merchandise inventory	100,000	95,000	5,000	
Prepaid insurance	2,000	3,000		1,000
Total current assets	$197,000	$183,000		
Current liabilities:				
Accounts payable	$110,000	$ 85,000		25,000
Bank loans payable (short-term)	48,000	30,000		18,000
Accrued payables	8,000	5,000		3,000
Total current liabilities	$166,000	$120,000		
Working capital	$ 31,000	$ 63,000		
Totals			$20,000	$52,000
Net decrease in working capital			32,000	
Totals			$52,000	$52,000

Walter Davis and his wife own 10,000 shares of stock in Woodbury Corporation and would like to know why no dividends were declared in 1985, even though net income for the year was $663,000.

Required: Using the information given above, justify to Mr. and Mrs. Walter Davis the corporation's decision not to declare a dividend.

B Problems

P20–1B

Statement of changes in financial position—working capital basis by the simple analytical approach

The comparative balance sheet accounts of the Post Company, as of December 31, 1985 and 1984, disclosed the following:

POST COMPANY
Comparative Balance Sheet Accounts
December 31, 1985 and 1984

	December 31	
	1985	1984
Debit Accounts		
Cash	$ 144,500	$ 189,500
Accounts Receivable (net)	176,900	149,900
Merchandise Inventory	256,000	196,000
Long-Term Investments	204,000	180,000
Machinery	1,050,000	900,000
Buildings	810,000	675,000
Land	150,000	150,000
Patents	54,000	60,000
Totals	$2,845,400	$2,500,400

Credit Accounts		
Accumulated Depreciation—Machinery	$ 120,000	$ 90,000
Accumulated Depreciation—Buildings	105,000	60,000
Accounts Payable—Trade	167,000	152,000
Notes Payable—Trade	24,000	30,000
Mortgage Payable	150,000	180,000
Common Stock	1,650,000	1,500,000
Retained Earnings	629,400	488,400
Totals	$2,845,400	$2,500,400

Additional information:

a. Net income for the year was $141,000.

b. There were no sales or disposals of property, plant, and equipment during the year.

Required: Prepare a statement of changes in financial position—working capital basis concept for 1985. Use the simple analytical approach.

P20–2B *Statement of changes in financial position—working capital basis by the work sheet method*

Following is the comparative postclosing trial balance of the Davis Company:

DAVIS COMPANY
Comparative Postclosing Trial Balance
December 31, 1985 and 1984

	December 31	
	1985	**1984**
Debit Accounts		
Cash	$ 26,500	$ 37,750
Temporary Investments	0	82,500
Accounts Receivable (net)	71,500	60,250
Merchandise Inventory	195,000	146,250
Prepaid Expenses	3,000	1,875
Property, Plant, and Equipment	375,000	225,000
Patents	48,000	51,000
Totals	$719,000	$604,625
Credit Accounts		
Accumulated Depreciation—Property, Plant, and Equipment	$101,250	$ 75,000
Accounts Payable	75,500	45,500
Common Stock	375,000	375,000
Retained Earnings	167,250	109,125
Totals	$719,000	$604,625

Additional data:

a. Net income for the period was $93,750.

b. Dividends declared were $35,625.

c. The temporary investments were sold at a gain (included in Item a) of $11,250.

d. Equipment with an original cost of $15,000 and accumulated depreciation of $7,500 was sold at an ordinary loss (included in Item a) of $1,500.

e. Patents are being amortized over their legal life of 17 years.

Required: Prepare a statement of changes in financial position—working capital basis concept for 1985. Use the work sheet approach.

P20 – 3B Data of Efland Corporation are given below.

Statement of changes in financial position—working capital basis by the work sheet method

EFLAND CORPORATION
Comparative Balance Sheet Accounts
December 31, 1985 and 1984

	December 31	
	1985	**1984**
Debit Accounts		
Cash	$ 45,500	$ 34,250
Accounts Receivable	68,000	60,500
Merchandise Inventory	31,000	25,000
Investments (Long-Term)	22,500	37,500
Machinery	30,000	18,750
Buildings	67,500	56,250
Land	7,500	7,500
Totals	$272,000	$239,750
Credit Accounts		
Allowance for Doubtful Accounts	$ 2,250	$ 1,500
Accumulated Depreciation—Machinery	5,625	2,250
Accumulated Depreciation—Buildings	13,500	9,000
Accounts Payable	31,000	25,750
Accrued Payables	4,375	3,625
Mortgage Payable	26,250	30,000
Common Stock, $1 Par Value	150,000	150,000
Retained Earnings	39,000	17,625
Totals	$272,000	$239,750

Additional data:

a. Net income for the year was $45,000.
b. Dividends declared during the year were $23,625.
c. Investments that cost $15,000 were sold during the year for $18,750. The gain is an ordinary one and is included in Item a.
d. Machinery that cost $3,750, on which $750 in depreciation had accumulated, was sold for $4,500. The gain is ordinary and is included in Item a.

Required: Prepare a statement of changes in financial position—working capital basis concept for 1985. Use the work sheet approach.

P20–4B *Statement of changes in financial position—working capital basis by the work sheet method*

You are given the following information from the books of the Hunt Corporation:

HUNT CORPORATION
Balance Sheet Accounts
December 31, 1985 and 1984

	December 31		Change
	1985	**1984**	**Increase or (Decrease)**
Debit Accounts			
Cash	$ 40,600	$ 47,800	$ (7,200)
Accounts Receivable	142,800	97,200	45,600
Merchandise Inventory	66,000	104,000	(38,000)
Machinery	247,200	262,200	(15,000)
Sinking Fund Cash[a]	50,000	0	50,000
Totals	$546,600	$511,200	$35,400
Credit Accounts			
Allowance for Doubtful Accounts	$ 8,400	$ 7,500	$ 900
Accumulated Depreciation—Machinery	48,600	54,600	(6,000)
Accounts Payable	64,000	73,600	(9,600)
Dividends Payable	6,000	0	6,000
Bonds Payable	60,000	0	60,000
Premium on Bonds Payable	2,850	0	2,850
Common Stock	300,000	300,000	0
Retained Earnings	6,750	75,500	(68,750)
Retained Earnings—Restricted for Sinking Fund[b]	50,000	0	50,000
Totals	$546,600	$511,200	$35,400

[a]The original entry to create the sinking fund was a debit to Sinking Fund Cash and a credit to Cash.

[b]The original entry to restrict retained earnings for the sinking fund was a debit to Retained Earnings and a credit to Retained Earnings—Restricted for Sinking Fund.

HUNT CORPORATION **Exhibit B**
Statement of Retained Earnings
For the Year Ended December 31, 1985

Retained earnings, December 31, 1984		$75,500
Add: Net income for year ended December 31, 1985		2,250
Subtotal		$77,750
Deduct: Dividends declared and paid in cash	$15,000	
Dividend declared in 1985, payable January 15, 1986	6,000	
Restriction for sinking fund	50,000	71,000
Retained earnings, December 31, 1985		$ 6,750

HUNT CORPORATION — **Exhibit A**
Income Statement
For the Year Ended December 31, 1985

Sales		$256,350
Cost of goods sold		195,000
Gross margin on sales		$ 61,350
Operating expenses:		
Salaries expense	$44,100	
Bad debts expense	900	
Depreciation of machinery	10,500	
Taxes expense	1,200	
Insurance expense	900	57,600
Net income from operations		$ 3,750
Other ordinary expenses:		
Bond interest expense	$ 3,150	
Deduct: Amortization of bond premium	150	
Net bond interest expense	$ 3,000	
Other ordinary revenue:		
Gain on sale of machinery	1,500	1,500
Net income to retained earnings		$ 2,250

Additional data:

a. Bonds payable in the amount of $60,000 were issued on April 30, 1985, at 105.
b. Machinery that cost $21,000 and had accumulated depreciation of $16,500 was sold for $6,000 in cash.

Required: Prepare a statement of changes in financial position—working capital basis concept for 1985. Submit all supporting computations. Use the work sheet approach.

P20–5B *Statement of changes in financial position—cash basis by the simple analytical method*

The data of Kathey Company follow:

KATHEY COMPANY
Comparative Balance Sheet Accounts
December 31, 1985 and 1984

	December 31	
	1985	**1984**
Debit Accounts		
Cash	$ 78,500	$ 111,500
Accounts Receivable (net)	270,500	288,500
Merchandise Inventory	301,000	241,000
Investments (Long-Term)	36,000	30,000
Land	60,000	45,000
Buildings (net)	480,000	300,000
Machinery (net)	600,000	450,000
Totals	$1,826,000	$1,466,000
Credit Accounts		
Accounts Payable	$ 226,000	$ 196,000
Accrued Payables	10,000	13,000
Mortgage Payable	210,000	174,000
Common Stock, $1 Par Value	900,000	750,000
Retained Earnings	480,000	333,000
Totals	$1,826,000	$1,466,000

KATHEY COMPANY **Exhibit A**
Income Statement
For the Year Ended December 31, 1985

Sales		$2,435,000
Cost of goods sold		1,445,000
Gross margin on sales		$ 990,000
Operating expenses:		
Depreciation—machinery	$ 60,000	
Depreciation—buildings	30,000	
Other operating expenses	663,000	753,000
Net income		$ 237,000

Additional data:

a. Dividends paid during the year were $90,000.
b. The increase in long-term investments, machinery, buildings, and land was from cash purchases.
c. There were 150,000 shares of common stock issued at par value for cash.

Required: Prepare a statement of changes in financial position for 1985, using the all financial resources—cash basis concept. Use the simple analytical approach.

P20 – 6B *Thought-provoking problem: various funds issues*

You have been assigned by the acquisitions committee of Control Group, Inc., to examine a potential acquisition, Retailers, Inc. This company is a merchandising firm that appears to be available because of the death of its founder and principal shareholder. Recent statements of Retailer, Inc., are shown below.

RETAILERS, INC.
Comparative Balance Sheets
As of January 31

	1985	1984	1983
Cash	$ 130,000	$ 120,000	$ 100,000
Accounts receivable	430,000	370,000	300,000
Merchandise inventory	400,000	400,000	200,000
Property, plant, and equipment	900,000	800,000	700,000
Deduct: Accumulated depreciation	(325,000)	(250,000)	(200,000)
Total assets	$1,535,000	$1,440,000	$1,100,000
Accounts payable	$ 300,000	$ 260,000	$ 220,000
8% Notes payable due 1/31/90	280,000	280,000	0
Common stock outstanding	690,000	690,000	690,000
Retained earnings	265,000	210,000	190,000
Total equity	$1,535,000	$1,440,000	$1,100,000

RETAILERS, INC.
Comparative Income Statements
For the Years Ended January 31, 1985 and 1984

	1985	1984
Sales	$2,943,000	$2,629,000
Operating expense:		
Cost of goods sold	$2,200,000	$2,000,000
Wages expense	350,000	300,000
Supplies expense	42,600	36,600
Depreciation expense	100,000	75,000
Interest expense	22,400	22,400
Loss on sale of property, plant, and equipment	75,000	105,000
Total deductions	$2,790,000	$2,539,000
Net income before taxes	$ 153,000	$ 90,000
Income taxes	68,000	40,000
Net income	$ 85,000	$ 50,000

RETAILERS, INC.
Statement of Changes in Financial Position
For the Years Ended January 31

	1985	1984
Financial resources were provided by:		
Net income	$ 85,000	$ 50,000
Add: Depreciation	100,000	75,000
Loss	75,000	105,000
Notes payable	0	280,000
Total	$260,000	$510,000
Financial resources were used for:		
Net plant assets purchased	$200,000	$230,000
Dividends paid	30,000	30,000
Total	$230,000	$260,000
Increase (decrease) in net working capital	$ 30,000	$250,000

Required:

1. Describe the cash flow for 1985 by redrawing the statement of changes in financial position to explain the changes in cash position instead of net working capital.

2. Does the amount shown for net plant assets purchased equal the funds spent for newly acquired assets? Explain your answer.

3. The statement of changes in financial position is required in published financial reports. What reasons are given to support the requirement that this statement be included in published financial reports?

21 Analysis and Interpretation of Financial Statements

Introduction

Throughout this book a major emphasis has been placed on accurate determination of net income. A single net income figure, however, fails to tell the whole story. For example, a recent annual report of the American Indian National Bank revealed that net income was 44 percent greater than operating income because of an extraordinary credit.

This chapter focuses on issues that are faced by large corporations engaged in a variety of national and international operations. Attention is first given to income statement disclosure and the statement of retained earnings. Techniques for analysis are then described and illustrated. Special emphasis is placed on interpretation of the results of such analysis.

Learning Goals

To understand how financial reports are used to make decisions about management, investment, or granting of credit by internal and external groups.

To understand the major guidelines for financial reporting and requirements for disclosure in financial statements.

To use comparative financial statements to draw conclusions about the organization's year-to-year changes.

To compute and interpret trend percentages.

To prepare and interpret common-size statements.

To compute and interpret commonly used ratios.

To develop the ability to use ratio analysis in evaluating solvency and profitability of an organization.

Broad Guidelines for Financial Reporting

Reporting to Management

If users of financial statements are to make intelligent decisions based on accounting data, they must understand this information. A major function of the accounting department of a corporation is to supply the necessary financial reports to management in meaningful form. The accounting department records the data, prepares the financial statements, and may also prepare ratio, trend, and percentage analyses. The results are used by corporate executives for the measurement of past performance in terms of costs and revenues, for the determination of the efficiency and effectiveness of the various departments (internal control), for the determination of future business policies, and for reporting to the stockholders.

The form of managerial reports depends on the decision that is to be made. They should be current, contain sufficient details regarding the particular problem to be solved, and present acceptable alternatives. A 1982 journal article presenting the results of interviews with four senior executives stated that: "At Motorola, the management team expects that the traditional accounting functions will be accomplished effectively, but it also expects controllers to provide a direct input into the managing of the business."[1]

There is a constantly increasing reliance by business executives on information systems. Large-scale production, wide geographical distribution, the increasing trend toward corporate business expansion and delegation of authority, complex income tax legislation, and government regulation of business are some of the factors requiring greater management reliance on corporate financial reports.

Reporting to Creditors and Investors

With the growth of corporations, the New York Stock Exchange became interested in information that was being furnished to stockholders. In 1898, for example, the exchange, in reviewing the application of a particular company for a listing of its stock, requested that the applicant present detailed statements to the stockholders prior to each annual meeting. This was the birth of the detailed annual corporate reports made available today to the stockholders and to other interested persons. In addition to a summary letter from the president or the chairperson of the board of directors, these reports contain a detailed set of audited financial statements with footnotes and other descriptive and analytical information about the present and future outlook of the corporation. A typical set of financial statements from an annual report is contained in Appendix B to this book.

A common practice for publicly-owned corporations (those whose stock is available to the general public) is to release unaudited quarterly reports,

[1]Dorothy L. Hines, Douglas A. Johnson, and William V. Lennox, "The Semiconductor Industry Controller: A Profile," *Management Accounting,* June 1982, pp. 30–36.

known as **interim reports,** for each three-month period up to the last quarter of the year. Interim reports typically contain income statements and balance sheets that relate to the quarter just ended and to the year-to-date. Both annual reports and interim reports contain comparative data for the year just ended and the previous year. It has become common practice in annual reports to show two years of data for the balance sheet and three years of data for the other statements. This is part of the SEC's *Integrated Disclosure System,* an extensive program begun in 1980 to harmonize disclosure requirements of the 1933 and 1934 Securities Acts. Other authoritative bodies have also developed some guidelines for more comparable financial reporting and disclosure in areas discussed in the sections that follow.

Guidelines for Income and Retained Earnings Disclosure

Since the form of the balance sheet has been discussed and illustrated in previous chapters, emphasis in this part is on the income statement and statement of retained earnings. A broad conceptual framework of the statement form and certain guidelines for reporting on operations are discussed.

Conceptual Framework for the Income Statement

The income statement is generally prepared in either single-step or multiple-step form. The **single-step income statement** shows all the revenue items and the amount of total revenues, followed by a listing of all expenses and losses, the total of which is deducted in a single step from total revenue to determine net income. This form of statement has the advantage of easy readability. There are no intermediate additions and deductions, with accompanying labeled subtotals, that may confuse the untrained reader. It is primarily for this reason that this form has been popular in annual reports to stockholders. However, certain intermediate figures that are important for management purposes, such as the gross margin on sales and the net income before income taxes, are not shown. Furthermore, only a skilled reader is able to determine operating income because operating items are intermingled with nonoperating items.

In the **multiple-step income statement,** net income is computed in stages with certain useful subtotals being developed in the process. A conceptual framework for the multiple-step income statement is shown in Figure 21–1. The numbered items that follow contain comments on some of the unusual steps.

Gross margin section	Sales		$XXX
	Cost of goods sold		XXX
	Gross margin on sales		$XXX
Operating expenses section	Selling expenses	$XXX	
	General and administrative expenses	XXX	
	Total operating expenses		XXX
	Net operating income		$ XX
Other revenues and expenses	Certain subordinate gains and losses, interest, and other recurring items		XX
	Net income from continuing operations before income tax		$ XX
Income tax expense	Federal and state income tax		XX
	Net income from continuing operations (per share $X)	1	$ XX
Discontinued operations	Net income (loss) from operations net of tax effect (per share $X)	$ XX	
	Gain (loss) on disposal net of tax effect (per share $X)	2 XX	XX
	Net income before extraordinary items		$ XX
Extraordinary items	Unusual and infrequent gains (losses) net of tax effect	3	XX
	Net income (per share $X)	4	$ XX

Figure 21–1 Conceptual Framework for Multiple-Step Income Statement

1 The amount of tax related to continuing operations should be shown as a separate amount. The income tax (or tax savings) related to other items should be shown with those items or they can be shown net of tax effect.

2 **Discontinued operations** refers to a segment of a business whose operations represent a separate major line of business or customer that has been sold or otherwise disposed of. Because the segment is a major separate line, statement comparability is improved if operating results from that segment are reported separately. Examples are Koppers Company, Inc.'s sale of its Canadian lumber operations in 1981 or National Distillers and Chemical Corporation's sale of its textile division in 1980. Any gain or loss from disposal of the business segment should be reported with the operating results as shown.

3 Extraordinary items (discussed in Chapter 14) must be a part of net income, but failure to disclose them separately could lead to incorrect assumptions about operating results.

4 There are alternate methods of disclosing earnings per share (EPS) amounts. A popular form is to show them in table form in the notes to finan-

cial statements. Regardless of the form, disclosure of EPS at various steps is important to statement users' decisions.

Intraperiod Tax Allocation

As indicated in Figure 21–1, certain significant income statement elements, such as results of discontinued operations or extraordinary items, are shown separately. One thing is common to all of them; they are reported net of income tax effects.

Each unusual item that affects the net income of a corporation also affects the total amount of income tax. Comparisons of year-to-year statements are more meaningful if the income tax expense from normal operations is reported separately. The applicable income tax expense (or saving) caused by the unusual occurrences should then be related to and shown with those items. This technique to make the statements more useful is called **intraperiod tax allocation.** It is used both on the income statement and the statement of retained earnings if adjustments are required. It is termed *intraperiod* as opposed to *interperiod* (see Appendix A) because the allocations are made within—not between—accounting periods.

Conceptual Framework for Statement of Retained Earnings

In some annual reports, the income statement is followed by a statement of retained earnings in the form used previously in this book. Others include the information on retained earnings in a statement of stockholders' equity. Such a statement shows beginning balances, changes, and ending balances of preferred stock, common stock, additional paid-in capital, and retained earnings. A third popular method of reporting retained earnings is to combine it with the income statement, as shown in Figure 21–2.

Figure 21–2 Conceptual Framework for Combined Statement of Income and Retained Earnings

Gross margin section	Sales	$XXX
	Cost of goods sold	XXX
	Gross margin on sales	$XXX
	Net income	$ XX
Retained earnings	Retained earnings at beginning of year	XXX
	Subtotal	$XXX
	Dividends declared	XX
	Retained earnings at the end of year	$XXX

When the statement of retained earnings is shown in a separate statement, the form follows the conceptual framework shown in Figure 21–3.

Beginning-of-period balance	Retained earnings at beginning of year as reported	1	$XXX
	Add (Deduct): Prior period adjustments net of tax effect . .	2	XX
	Retained earnings at beginning or year as adjusted		$XXX
Add items	Add: Net income	3	XX
	Subtotal		$XXX
Deduct items	Deduct: Dividends	4	XX
End-of-period balance	Retained earnings at end of year	5	$XXX

Figure 21–3 Conceptual Framework for Statement of Retained Earnings

Explanation of numbered items follows:

1 The first item shown on the statement of retained earnings is the retained earnings figure that was shown on the balance sheet at the end of the preceding period.

2 Prior period adjustments are corrections to beginning retained earnings for events that occurred in accounting periods before the current one. They are excluded from net income of the current period. The correction of an error in the financial statements of a prior period is a typical prior period adjustment. Provisions of certain other pronouncements also lead to adjustments to retained earnings. These are usually made to bring statements into compliance with a new FASB pronouncement. For example, *FASB Statement No. 43,* "Accounting for Compensated Absences," (see Chapter 8) was allowed to be applied retroactively. In 1981, Ingersoll-Rand Company revised its accounting practices to include accruals for compensated absences but did not restate prior period financial statements because the amounts were considered to be immaterial. The cumulative effect of the transition was reflected as a five-million-dollar adjustment to beginning retained earnings in 1981. The auditors concurred in this treatment.

3 This is the net income for the current year as reported in the income statement.

4 All dividends declared, whether or not paid in the current year, should be deducted.

5 The last item shown is the amount that should be reported in the balance sheet at the end of the current period.

Having discussed certain specific financial reporting issues, attention is now turned to analysis and interpretation issues.

Analysis and Interpretation of Financial Statements

Interpretation of Financial Data

The figures in financial statements have significance in the following respects:

1. In themselves, they are measures of absolute quantity. When an analyst sees that a company has $50,000 in cash, he or she understands that figure in terms of current purchasing power (see Chapter 14). However, the absolute amount does not tell whether it is adequate for the current needs of the particular company. Some other means of determining its significance is required.

2. When figures are compared with similar amounts for other years and other companies, a degree of significance is indicated. If $50,000 in cash was shown on the balance sheet at the end of the previous year, if that amount was sufficient at that time, and if no changes in needs are foreseen, then it can be assumed that a cash balance of $50,000 is adequate now (except for effects of inflation).

3. When financial data are considered in conjunction with related figures, they are also significant. When current assets are compared with current liabilities, for instance, the ability to pay short-term debts can be determined. This comparison is often accomplished by what is termed a ratio. More specifically, a **ratio** is one amount in direct relationship to another amount.

Four tools of financial statement analysis are available to the user of the data. Each is related to the ways in which financial data have significance. They are (in the order discussed in this chapter):

1. Comparative statements.
2. Percentage analyses (horizontal and vertical).
3. Ratio analyses.
4. Combinations of the above.

The goal of any analysis is the evaluation of financial data through comparisons and measurement by some consistent standard to determine performance. Standards for comparison include a company's past performance, the performance of companies in the same field, and industry comparisons.

In using each of these standards, the analyst should be aware of certain basic limitations. For example, if a company earned only $100 last year and earns $200 during the current year, it has improved 100 percent; yet it may not be a growth company. Comparisons with performance of other companies and industry standards have similar pitfalls. Even with these difficulties, the standards of comparison can be beneficial as a means of revealing improvements and declines and thus can be helpful in interpreting statement data.

It should be emphasized that financial statement analysis involves more than just numbers. It requires an understanding of the nature and limitations of accounting and some knowledge of the business and the people operating the business. Discussions with the people involved may yield valuable insights that are not apparent from the application of the financial analysis tools.

Comparative Financial Statements

A study of the balance sheet of a company and the results of its operations for a period is more meaningful if the analyst has available the balance sheets and the income statements for several periods. Trends can be better ascertained when three or more financial statements are compared. Statements in which two or more years of data are shown in single parallel columns for each year are called **comparative financial statements.** Typical current practice in corporate annual reports is to show two years of data for the balance sheet and three years of data for the other three audited statements.

Another requirement for effective financial reports is that they follow the standard of consistency.

Consistency

For effective analysis, the company statements being compared must be based on the consistent application of generally accepted accounting principles over the period covered by the comparison. If there is an absence of **consistency*****, it should be disclosed.***

If one company is to be compared with one or more other companies or with an entire industry, it must also first be carefully established that the data in the comparison are based on reasonably uniform and consistent accounting methods and principles.

The use of comparative information in annual corporate reports to stockholders is nearly universal. Other devices are also used to present the entire financial story as clearly and attractively as possible. Although there are no rules for uniformity in the kind of visual and statistical aids used, some of the more common are:

- Comparative statements with accompanying trend percentages.
- Common-size statements, which present individual figures as percentages of a base total or some other established norm.
- Pictorial statements using bar or line graphs to emphasize particular trends, ratios, or relationships.
- Pie charts showing the allocation of each company sales dollar.

Any of these methods of presentation can make an informative report. Some of these devices are illustrated in the following sections.

Percent of Change—Horizontal Analysis

Comparative Balance Sheets Comparative balance sheets of a company are given side by side. These statements can be made more meaningful if the dollar amount of increase or decrease and the percent of increase or decrease are also shown. This percentage analysis is one type of **horizontal analysis** because the comparisons are on a horizontal plane from left to

MORCO COMPANY
Comparative Balance Sheet
December 31, 1985 and 1984

Exhibit C

Assets	**December 31 1985**	**December 31 1984**	**Amount of Increase or (Decrease) during 1985**	**Percent of Increase or (Decrease) during 1985**
Current assets:				
Cash	$ 32,000	$ 16,000	$16,000	100.0
Accounts receivable (net)	34,000	26,000	8,000	30.8
Inventories	45,000	36,000	9,000	25.0
Total current assets	$111,000	$ 78,000	$33,000	42.3
Property, plant, and equipment:				
Land	$ 7,000	$ 7,000	$ 0	0.0
Building (net)	116,000	119,000	(3,000)	(2.5)
Store equipment (net)	23,000	25,000	(2,000)	(8.0)
Total property, plant, and equipment	$146,000	$151,000	$ (5,000)	(3.3)
Total assets	$257,000	$229,000	$28,000	12.2
Liabilities and Stockholders' Equity				
Current liabilities:				
Accounts payable	$ 26,550	$ 23,000	$ 3,550	15.4
Notes payable	19,000	20,000	(1,000)	(5.0)
Accrued payables	11,000	8,000	3,000	37.5
Total current liabilities	$ 56,550	$ 51,000	$ 5,550	10.9
Long-term liabilities:				
Mortgage payable	55,000	60,000	(5,000)	(8.3)
Total liabilities	$111,550	$111,000	$ 550	0.5
Stockholders' equity:				
Common stock	$109,000	$100,000	$ 9,000	9.0
Retained earnings	36,450	18,000	18,450	102.5
Total stockholders' equity	$145,450	$118,000	$27,450	23.3
Total liabilities and stockholders' equity	$257,000	$229,000	$28,000	12.2

Figure 21–4 **Comparative Balance Sheet—Horizontal Analysis**

right. In a two-year comparison, the earlier year is the base year. The percent of change is usually rounded to the nearest tenth of a percent.

This form of statement is illustrated in Figure 21–4—the comparative balance sheet of the Morco Company. In this illustration, the date December 31, 1984, is the base point and represents 100 percent. Accounts receivable increased by 30.8 percent = ($8,000 ÷ $26,000) during 1985; notes payable decreased by 5 percent = ($1,000 ÷ $20,000); and cash increased by $16,000, or 100 percent. The December 31, 1985, cash balance is twice the December 31, 1984, balance. Retained earnings as of December 31, 1985, is more than twice the amount shown on December 31, 1984. No additional property, plant, and equipment assets were acquired; the decreases reflect the annual depreciation deductions.

The change that occurred during 1985 for the Morco Company is apparently favorable. The statements show that current assets increased by 42.3

percent, whereas current liabilities increased by only 10.9 percent. The total stockholders' equity increased by 23.3 percent; this is reflected by an increase in all the current assets. The favorable position of retained earnings, accompanied by an increase in working capital, was accomplished without resort to borrowing, because mortgage payable and notes payable decreased during the period. Additional working capital was acquired by the issuance of stock.

Comparative Income Statements A single income statement is just one link in a continuous chain reporting the operating results of the business. Comparative income statements are required for an analysis of trends and for

MORCO COMPANY
Comparative Statement of Income and Retained Earnings
For the Years Ended December 31, 1985, 1984, and 1983

Exhibit A

	Years Ended December 31			Amount of Increase or (Decrease) during 1985	Percent of Increase or (Decrease) during 1985
	1985	1984	1983		
Sales (net)	$197,000	$151,000	$123,000	$46,000	30.5
Cost of goods sold	123,000	92,000	74,000	31,000	33.7
Gross margin on sales	$ 74,000	$ 59,000	$ 49,000	$15,000	25.4
Operating expenses:					
Selling expenses:					
Advertising expense	$ 1,200	$ 1,100	$ 900	$ 100	9.1
Sales salaries expense	18,300	17,900	17,100	400	2.2
Depreciation expense—store equipment	2,000	2,000	2,000	0	0.0
Total selling expenses	$ 21,500	$ 21,000	$ 20,000	$ 500	2.4
General and administrative expense:					
Insurance expense	$ 675	$ 650	$ 600	$ 25	3.8
General salaries expense	7,200	8,000	8,200	(800)	(10.0)
Depreciation expense—building	3,000	3,000	3,000	0	0.0
Miscellaneous general expense	425	350	320	75	21.4
Total general and administrative expenses	$ 11,300	$ 12,000	$ 12,120	$ (700)	(5.8)
Total operating expenses	$ 32,800	$ 33,000	$ 32,120	$ (200)	(0.6)
Net operating income	$ 41,200	$ 26,000	$ 16,880	$15,200	58.5
Other expenses:					
Interest expense	2,750	3,000	3,300	(250)	(8.3)
Net income before income taxes	$ 38,450	$ 23,000	$ 13,580	$15,450	67.2
Income taxes	7,700	4,600	2,700	3,100	67.4
Net income	$ 30,750	$ 18,400	$ 10,880	$12,350	67.1
Retained earnings, January 1	18,000	10,880	9,000	7,120	65.4
Subtotal	$ 48,750	$ 29,280	$ 19,880	$19,470	66.5
Dividends declared	12,300	11,280	9,000	1,020	9.0
Retained earnings, December 31	$ 36,450	$ 18,000	$ 10,880	$18,450	102.5
Earnings per share	$ 0.28	$ 0.18	$ 0.11	$ 0.10	55.6

Figure 21–5 **Comparative Statement of Income and Retained Earnings—Horizontal Analysis**

making decisions regarding possible future developments. An income statement showing the results of operations for a single year is inadequate for purposes of analyzing the significance of the changes that have occurred.

The comparative statement of income and retained earnings of the Morco Company is shown in Figure 21–5. The year 1984 is again used as the base year.[2] Gross margin on sales increased by 25.4 percent, net income before income taxes increased by 67.2 percent, and total operating expenses decreased by 0.6 percent. These favorable changes resulted primarily from an increase in sales.

There is a close relationship between the cost of goods sold, the volume of sales, and net income before income taxes. In periods of exceptionally high sales volume, net income before income taxes tends to rise (percent of increase, 67.2) at a faster rate than do sales (percent of increase, 30.5) because certain costs are fixed in amount and do not change. In periods of declining sales volume, earnings fall more sharply than sales because a significant part of the operating expenses are constant (or fixed)—not affected by the current sales volume. Such fluctuations in net income can be eliminated if unit sales prices are increased in periods of low sales volume and reduced in periods of high sales volume. Such a pricing policy, however, would be undesirable from the customers' viewpoint and impracticable from the company's viewpoint.

Percent increases or decreases are calculated *only when the base figure is positive.* When there is no figure for the base year or when base year amounts are negative, there is no extension into the Percent of Increase or (Decrease) column. When there is a positive amount in the base year and none in the following year, the percent of decrease is 100, shown as follows:

	1985	1984 (Base Year)	Amount of Increase or (Decrease) during 1985	Percent of Increase or (Decrease) during 1985
Notes receivable	$3,000	0	$3,000	[a]
Notes payable	0	$2,000	(2,000)	(100)
Net income (or loss)	4,000	(1,000)	5,000	[a]

[a]Cannot be computed.

Trend Percentages—Horizontal Analysis

Comparative financial statements for several years may be expressed in terms of trend percentages for horizontal analysis.

[2]Because of the availability of three years of data, other amounts and percents could be computed, for example, 1985 over 1983, and 1984 over 1983. A more meaningful way to get such a comparison is the trend percentage analysis, discussed later.

Trend percentages

***Management can more readily study changes in financial statements between periods by establishing a base year and expressing the other years in percentages of that year. The base year may be any typical year in the comparison—in this book, it is the earliest year. The percentages are known as* trend percentages.**

To illustrate, selected income statement items are presented in Figure 21–6. The amounts in Figure 21–6 are converted into trend percentages with 1982 as the base year in Figure 21–7.

Figure 21–6 Selected Comparative Income Statement Items for Four Years

	1985	1984	1983	1982
Sales (net)	$130,000	$120,000	$95,000	$100,000
Cost of goods sold	72,800	69,600	58,900	60,000
Gross margin on sales	$ 57,200	$ 50,400	$36,100	$ 40,000
Total selling expenses	12,000	11,000	9,700	10,000
Net income before income tax	10,400	8,400	3,800	5,000

Figure 21–7 Comparative Trend Percentages for Four Years[a]

	1985	1984	1983	1982
Sales (net)	130%	120%	95%	100%
Cost of goods sold	121	116	98	100
Gross margin on sales	143	126	90	100
Total selling expenses	120	110	97	100
Net income before income tax	208	168	76	100

[a]Normally rounded to nearest percent.

In Figure 21–7, 1982 is assumed to be the base year and becomes 100 percent. All the amounts in other years are expressed as trend percentages, or percentages of the figures for the base year. Each base year amount is divided into the same item for the other years. Trend percentages for sales, for example, are calculated as follows:

1983: $ 95,000 ÷ $100,000 = 95;
1984: $120,000 ÷ $100,000 = 120;
1985: $130,000 ÷ $100,000 = 130.

When the base amount is larger than the corresponding amount in another year, the trend percentage is less than 100 percent; conversely, when the base year amount is the lesser, the trend percentage is more than 100 percent.

The trend percentage statement is an analytical device for condensing the absolute dollar data of comparative statements. The device is especially valuable to management because comparability and brevity are achieved by substituting percentages for dollar amounts, which in themselves are difficult to compare. Trend percentages are generally computed for major items in the statements; minor amounts are omitted, the objective being to highlight significant changes. An evaluation of the trend percentages requires a careful analysis of the interrelated items. Sales, for example, may show increases over a four-year period leading up to a trend percentage of 150 percent for the fourth year. This is unfavorable if it is accompanied by trend percentages of 200 percent for cost of goods sold, 175 percent for selling expenses, and 95 percent for net income before income taxes. Other unfavorable trends include an upward trend in receivables and inventories accompanied by a downward trend in sales, and a downward trend in sales accompanied by an upward trend in property, plant, and equipment. Favorable trends would be an increase in sales accompanied by a decrease in cost of goods sold and selling expenses or an increase in current assets accompanied by a decrease in current liabilities.

Trend percentages show the degree of increase and decrease; they do not indicate the causes of the changes. They do, however, single out unfavorable developments for further analysis and investigation by management. A marked change may have been caused by inconsistency in the application of accounting principles, by fluctuating price levels, or by controllable internal factors (for example, an unnecessary increase in merchandise inventory or a decrease in operating efficiency).

Common-Size Statements—Vertical Analysis

Comparative statements with percent of increase or decrease and trend percentages provide for horizontal analysis. Similarly, common-size statements provide for **vertical analysis.** In this form, the comparisons are made vertically from top to bottom for an analysis of the component changes that occur from period to period with certain base totals within those periods.

Common-size statements

***Total assets, total liabilities and stockholders' equity, and net sales are each converted to a base of 100 percent. Each item within each of these three classifications is expressed as a percentage of the base; each asset, for example, is expressed as a percentage of total assets. Since these bases represent 100 percent in all the statements in the comparison, there is a common basis for analysis; therefore, the statements are referred to as* common-size statements.**

Comparisons can be made within the company, with other companies in the same industry, or with the entire industry. Thus, important relationships can be spotted even when comparisons are made with companies of unlike size; and significant differences may indicate that further investigation is required. The common-size statements supplemented by additional analytical financial data are effective tools for a historical financial study of a business or industry. The Morco Company's comparative common-size balance sheet and the comparative common-size income statement are shown in Figures 21–8 and 21–9.

Common-Size Balance Sheets

The method of converting dollar amounts into common-size percentages, using data from Figure 21–8, is shown below:

$$\frac{\text{Accounts receivable (December 31, 1985)}}{\text{Total assets (December 31, 1985)}} = \frac{\$34{,}000}{\$257{,}000} = 13.2\%.$$

Accounts receivable as of December 31, 1985, represent 13.2 percent of the total assets. For each dollar of total assets, there are 13.2 cents of accounts receivable.

$$\frac{\text{Accounts payable (December 31, 1984)}}{\text{Total liabilities and stockholders' equity (December 31, 1984)}} = \frac{\$23{,}000}{\$229{,}000} = 10\%.$$

Accounts payable as of December 31, 1984, represent 10 percent of total liabilities and stockholders' equity.

MORCO COMPANY
Comparative Common-Size Balance Sheet
December 31, 1985 and 1984

Exhibit C

	December 31		Common-Size Percentages December 31	
Assets	**1985**	**1984**	**1985**	**1984**
Current assets:				
Cash	$ 32,000	$ 16,000	12.5	7.0
Accounts receivable (net)	34,000	26,000	13.2	11.4
Inventories	45,000	36,000	17.5	15.7
Total current assets	$111,000	$ 78,000	43.2	34.1
Property, plant, and equipment:				
Land	$ 7,000	$ 7,000	2.8	3.0
Building (net)	116,000	119,000	45.1	52.0
Store equipment (net)	23,000	25,000	8.9	10.9
Total property, plant, and equipment	$146,000	$151,000	56.8	65.9
Total assets	$257,000	$229,000	100.0	100.0
Liabilities and Stockholders' Equity				
Current liabilities:				
Accounts payable	$ 26,550	$ 23,000	10.3	10.0
Notes payable	19,000	20,000	7.4	8.7
Accrued payables	11,000	8,000	4.3	3.5
Total current liabilities	$ 56,550	$ 51,000	22.0	22.2
Long-term liabilities:				
Mortgage payable	55,000	60,000	21.4	26.2
Total liabilities	$111,550	$111,000	43.4	48.4
Stockholders' equity:				
Common stock	$109,000	$100,000	42.4	43.7
Retained earnings	36,450	18,000	14.2	7.9
Total stockholders' equity	$145,450	$118,000	56.6	51.6
Total liabilities and stockholders' equity	$257,000	$229,000	100.0	100.0

Figure 21–8 Comparative Common-Size Balance Sheet—Vertical Analysis

Each current asset item has increased both in dollar amount and as a percentage of the total assets. Total current assets as of December 31, 1985, are 43.2 percent compared with 34.1 percent as of December 31, 1984. The comparative percentages for total current liabilities are 22 percent and 22.2 percent. Thus, the working capital position has been strengthened. Further analysis would disclose that increases in net income and proceeds from the sale of stock appear to have caused increases in each current asset item. The company did not invest in property, plant, and equipment; the decreases in net (book value) store equipment and building are due to deductions for annual depreciation charges.

The stockholders' equity percentage was increased, with corresponding decreases in the total liabilities percentage. On December 31, 1984, the total liabilities percentage was 48.4 percent. A year later, it had decreased to 43.4 percent. The overall financial position of the Morco Company has improved.

Common-Size Income Statement

The common-size income statement of the Morco Company is shown in Figure 21–9. Examples of the conversion of income statement dollar amounts into common-size percentages are shown below:

$$\frac{\text{Gross margin on sales (1985)}}{\text{Net sales (1985)}} = \frac{\$\ 74{,}000}{\$197{,}000} = 37.6\%.$$

Gross margin on sales for 1985 represents 37.6 percent of net sales; for each dollar of net sales there was a margin of 37.6 cents.

$$\frac{\text{Total operating expenses (1983)}}{\text{Net sales (1983)}} = \frac{\$\ 32{,}120}{\$123{,}000} = 26.1\%.$$

Total operating expenses for 1983 represent 26.1 percent of net sales. They have improved over the next two years, falling to 16.7 percent in 1985.

An example of use of these data would be a comparison of the cost of goods sold. The statement shows a higher percentage for 1985 (62.4, up from 60.2) and a corresponding decrease in the gross margin percentage. This relatively modest change may result from reductions of original sales prices or increases in inventory cost. Increases in amounts and percentages of inventories (balance sheet) accompanied by a decrease in gross margin (income statement) may indicate an overinvestment in inventories.

The change in total operating expenses is favorable. Sales increased by $46,000 = ($197,000 − $151,000), whereas dollar volume of total operating expenses remained approximately the same. The Morco Company has increased the efficiency of its operations by increasing the dollar sales without increasing its operating costs—a favorable development. This shows up as a decline in operating expenses from 26.1 percent to 16.7 percent of net sales. The amount of increase in income taxes is at best a partially uncontrollable factor.

MORCO COMPANY
Comparative Common-Size Income Statement
For the Years Ended December 31, 1985, 1984, and 1983

Exhibit A

	Years Ended December 31			Common-Size Percentages Years Ended December 31		
	1985	1984	1983	1985	1984	1983
Sales (net)	$197,000	$151,000	$123,000	100.0	100.0	100.0
Cost of goods sold	123,000	92,000	74,000	62.4	60.9	60.2
Gross margin on sales	$ 74,000	$ 59,000	$ 49,000	37.6	39.1	39.8
Operating expenses:						
Selling expenses:						
Advertising expense	$ 1,200	$ 1,100	$ 900	0.6	0.7	0.7
Sales salaries expense	18,300	17,900	17,100	9.3	11.9	13.9
Depreciation expense—store equipment	2,000	2,000	2,000	1.0	1.3	1.6
Total selling expenses	$ 21,500	$ 21,000	$ 20,000	10.9	13.9	16.2
General and administrative expenses:						
Insurance expense	$ 675	$ 650	$ 600	0.4	0.4	0.5
General salaries expense	7,200	8,000	8,200	3.7	5.3	6.7
Depreciation expense—building	3,000	3,000	3,000	1.5	2.0	2.4
Miscellaneous general expense	425	350	320	0.2	0.2	0.3
Total general and administrative expenses	$ 11,300	$ 12,000	$ 12,120	5.8	7.9	9.9
Total operating expenses	$ 32,800	$ 33,000	$ 32,120	16.7	21.8	26.1
Net operating income	$ 41,200	$ 26,000	$ 16,880	20.9	17.3	13.7
Other expenses:						
Interest expense	2,750	3,000	3,300	1.4	2.0	2.7
Net income before income taxes	$ 38,450	$ 23,000	$ 13,580	19.5	15.3	11.0
Income taxes	7,700	4,600	2,700	3.9	3.0	2.2
Net income	$ 30,750	$ 18,400	$ 10,880	15.6	12.3	8.8
Earnings per share	$ 0.28	$ 0.18	$ 0.11			

Figure 21–9 **Comparative Common-Size Income Statement—Vertical Analysis**

In addition to the analyses already illustrated, other vertical percentage relationships—such as sales returns and allowances to sales revenue, sales discounts to sales revenue, purchases returns and allowances to purchases, and purchases discounts to purchases—furnish information useful to management for controlling various activities, especially when they are compared from period to period.

Disposition of Each Sales Dollar

Annual reports often include graphic presentations of the disposition of each revenue dollar. They may take the form of a pie chart, bar graph, or simple statement. Such presentations are often more meaningful to the reader than are detailed income statements and are popular for their simplicity and effectiveness.

A **revenue-dollar statement** for Morco Company is shown below. Each sales dollar was allocated as follows:

	1985	1984	1983
Cost of goods sold	$0.624	$0.609	$0.602
Selling expenses	0.109	0.139	0.162
General and administrative expenses	0.058	0.079	0.099
Interest expenses	0.014	0.020	0.027
Income taxes	0.039	0.030	0.022
Net income	0.156	0.123	0.088
Total sales dollar	$1.000	$1.000	$1.000

The revenue-dollar allocations to each category are computed by applying the common-size percentages to one dollar. The disposition of each sales dollar from the foregoing statement for 1985 is shown in a pie chart in Figure 21–10. Another informative way to show the same type of information is shown in Chapter 1 (Figure 1–1).

To provide information that will be of maximum assistance in decision making, the financial data should be presented in a form and manner that make them understandable, meaningful, and useful. The absolute amounts contained in the balance sheet for the Morco Company are quite useful to management, but they tell only part of the story. For example, a total current asset amount of $111,000 indicates a certain purchasing power command over goods and services, but how adequate is this amount for the Morco Company? The data become more meaningful when they are compared with

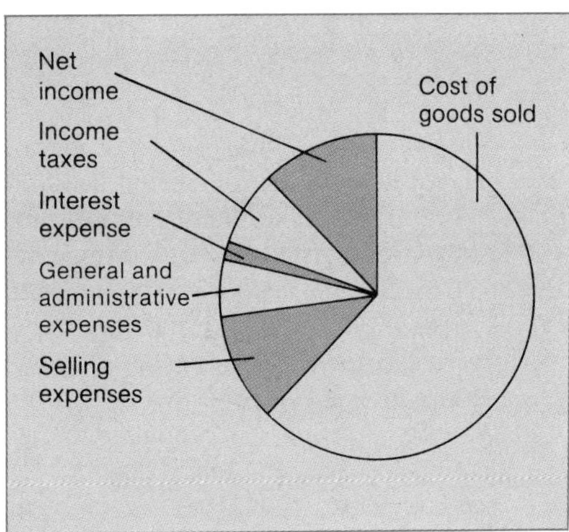

Figure 21–10
Pie Chart to Show Disposition of Sales Dollar

related information of current or past years. Another basis for evaluation is *ratio analysis.* It is discussed in the next section.

Ratio Analysis

A **ratio** is a comparison of two numbers; it shows the relative degree of an amount by expressing it as a fraction of another. **Ratio analysis,** therefore, shows the relative size of one dollar amount to another. A financial decision should not be based on any one ratio. The ratios are effective only when used in combination with related ratios and with other relevant financial information.

Three types of measurements based on the financial statements are central to certain financial management decisions. They are discussed below under the following headings: *short-run solvency measurements, long-run solvency measurements,* and *earning power measurements.*

Short-Run Solvency Measurements

Basic indicators of ability to pay short-term debts are the current ratio, the acid-test ratio, and other working capital ratios.

Current Ratio The relationship of current assets to current liabilities gives some indication of the firm's ability to pay its current debts as they mature. This relationship, called the **current ratio,** is computed by dividing the current assets by the current liabilities. The computation for the Morco Company is shown below:

	December 31	
	1985	1984
1. Total current assets	$111,000	$78,000
2. Total current liabilities	56,550	51,000
3. Current ratio (Line 1 ÷ Line 2)	1.96:1	1.53:1

At 1985 year-end, the Morco Company had approximately $1.96 of current assets for every dollar of current liabilities.

In the past, as a rule of thumb, a current ratio of 2:1 (read as 2 to 1) was considered satisfactory. Analysts generally agree, however, that no one ratio is sufficient; other factors to be considered include the nature of the business, the season of the year, the composition of the specific items in the current assets category, and the quality of the company's management. A higher current ratio is not necessarily better. It may reflect missed opportunities to invest the current assets profitably in the operations of the business.

Grantors of credit emphasize the relative convertibility of the current assets into cash. To illustrate, assume that Company A and Company B have the following current ratios:

	Company A	Company B
Current assets:		
Cash	$ 500	$10,000
Accounts receivable	700	14,000
Merchandise inventory	28,800	6,000
Total current assets	$30,000	$30,000
Current liabilities:		
Accounts payable	$15,000	$15,000
Current ratio	2:1	2:1

Although each company has a current ratio of 2 to 1, Company B is apparently in a far better position to meet its obligations. Company A first must sell its $28,800 merchandise inventory and then convert the resulting receivables into cash—or sell its inventory for cash as a single lot, probably for less than the stated value. Company B has $24,000 in cash and receivables and only $6,000 in merchandise inventory to be converted. Company A thus may have a favorable current ratio and still may be unable to pay its current liabilities because of an unfavorable distribution of the current assets.

Acid-Test Ratio A supplementary test of the ability of a business to meet its current obligations is the **acid-test ratio,** which is expressed as follows:

$$\text{Acid-test ratio} = \frac{\text{Quick current assets}}{\text{Current liabilities}}.$$

The analyst who is not satisfied with the current ratio as an indicator of liquidity may use the acid-test ratio, which excludes merchandise inventory and prepaid items and is therefore a more rigorous test of short-run solvency than is the current ratio. **Quick current assets** include only cash, readily marketable temporary investments, and receivables. If the quick current assets are larger than the current liabilities (that is, if the acid-test ratio is better than 1 to 1), there is evidence of a strong short-term credit position and indication that the company is able to meet its currently maturing obligations.

The acid-test ratio for the Morco Company is computed as follows:

	December 31	
	1985	1984
Quick current assets:		
Cash	$32,000	$16,000
Accounts receivable	34,000	26,000
1. Total quick current assets	$66,000	$42,000
2. Current liabilities	56,550	51,000
Acid-test ratio (Line 1 ÷ Line 2)	1.17:1	0.82:1

On December 31, 1985, the Morco Company had $1.17 in quick current assets for each dollar of current liabilities. This ratio means that the company does not have to rely on the liquidation of inventories as a source of funds for the payment of current liabilities as they did at 1984 year-end.

Other Working Capital Ratios Four other types of working capital ratios are working capital turnover, receivables turnover, and two kinds of inventory ratios.

Working Capital Turnover The relationships between working capital and sales (**working capital turnover**) tests the efficiency with which the working capital is used to produce sales. This is the first example that relates a balance sheet item to an income statement item. Since an income statement item covers an entire period, it can only be related to a balance sheet item *that also spans the entire period.* Hence, the ratio should show the relationship of the income statement item to an average of the balance sheet item. The computation is shown below:

	December 31	
	1985	**1984**
Working capital:		
Current assets	$111,000	$78,000
Current liabilities	56,550	51,000
Working capital	$ 54,450	$27,000
Average working capital ($54,450 + $27,000) ÷ 2[a]	$ 40,725	
Net sales for 1985	197,000	
Working capital turnover for 1985 ($197,000 ÷ $40,725)	4.84	

[a]When any balance sheet amount is related to an income statement amount, the balance sheet item should be the average for the year, since the income statement amount spans the entire year.

The Morco Company sold $4.84 worth of merchandise for each dollar of working capital. Another viewpoint is that each dollar invested in working capital was recovered, reinvested, and recovered again 4.84 times. The degree of financial strength indicated by this ratio is best determined by comparison with other businesses in the same line.

Receivables Turnover and Average Collection Period Two guides to the overall condition of the accounts receivable are the average collection period and the annual **receivables turnover.** If goods are sold on terms of 2/10, n/30, the amount of accounts receivable outstanding at any time should be less than the credit sales for the last 30 days because many of the sales will have been paid within the discount period. If allowance is made for slow-paying accounts, the receivables may represent 30 to 35 days' sales. If the receivables exceed this limitation, a careful analysis of all the accounts should be made.

Average collection periods vary with the industry and with the firm's credit policy. Wholesalers of shoes may average 45 days, while grocery wholesalers may average 15 days. For a standard of comparison, the preceding year's rate or the industry rate may be used. The increase in the turnover rate for the Morco Company indicates an improvement and reflects a decreasing relative amount of working capital tied up in receivables.

	1985	1984
1. Net credit sales	$197,000	$151,000
2. Days in year	365	365[a]
3. Net credit sales per day (Line 1 ÷ Line 2)	$540	$414
4. Average trade receivables (balance at beginning of year + balance at end of year) ÷ 2	$30,000	$28,000 (assumed)[b]
Average collection period (Line 4 ÷ Line 3)	56 days	68 days
Receivables turnover per year (Line 1 ÷ Line 4)	6.6 times	5.4 times

[a]Although a 360-day year has been used previously for such things as interest calculations, for ratio analysis in this chapter a 365-day year is used.

[b]It is necessary to make an assumption here because the January 1, 1984, trade receivables balance is not given.

If Line 1 covered sales for a period of less than one year, then Line 2 would be changed accordingly. Thus, if the sales were for a 3-month period, Line 2 would show 91 days (one-fourth of 365 days).

Turnover of Merchandise Inventory The quantity of goods to be kept on hand is a major business decision. It is considered good management to carry as little inventory as possible without losing sales and to turn it over as rapidly as possible. Good management must guard against excessive inventories, the consequences of which could be an abnormal drain on cash that could lead to financial difficulties. The greater the inventory, the greater is the amount of money tied up, the extra space required, the extra handling costs, as well as the increased possibility of loss through shrinkage, style changes, or other factors. Inadequate inventories, on the other hand, may result in higher costs due to buying in smaller quantities and the possible loss of business if the item the customer wants is out of stock. Good management therefore requires a careful evaluation of all these factors in establishing inventory levels.

One of the ratios used in inventory analysis is the **inventory turnover**—the relationship between inventory and the cost of goods sold. It is computed by dividing the cost of goods sold by the average inventory. The figure used may be the average of the beginning and ending inventories of the period or, preferably, the average of the end-of-month inventories to minimize the effect of seasonal fluctuations. Although high turnover is usually a sign of good management, the ratio varies widely from one industry to another. A wholesaler of automobile parts and accessories may average five inventory turnovers per year, while a wholesaler of perishables such as meat and poultry may average 35 or more. Also, a high-volume, low-margin business such as a fast-food chain would have to turn over its inventory more often than a business having a low-volume, high-margin policy, such as an art gallery.

The inventory turnover is computed as shown:

	1985	1984
1. Cost of goods sold	$123,000	$92,000
Average merchandise inventory:		
2. January 1	$ 36,000	$29,700[a]
3. December 31	45,000	36,000
4. Total	$ 81,000	$65,700
5. Average (Line 4 ÷ 2)	$ 40,500	$32,850
Inventory turnover (Line 1 ÷ Line 5)	3.0	2.8

[a]Assumed because actual information is not available.

The Morco Company sold and replaced its merchandise inventory three times during the year 1985; that is, the cost of merchandise sold was three times greater than the average cost of merchandise on hand. This is an improvement over 1984. The rate may be computed for major categories or for individual items in order to establish item-by-item control.

Ratio of Inventory to Working Capital The *ratio of inventory to working capital* is an indication of the amount of working capital represented by inventory. For the Morco Company in 1985, it is:

$$\frac{\text{Ending inventory}}{\text{Working capital}} = \frac{\$45{,}000}{\$54{,}450} = 82.6\%.$$

This 1985 ratio, being less than 100 percent, indicates that the current debt can be paid in full from quick current assets, assuming that all receivables can be collected. For the ratio to be less than 100 percent, the quick current assets must be greater than current liabilities. Note that the 1984 ratio was 133.3 percent = ($36,000 ÷ $27,000) when quick current assets were less than current liabilities. The 1985 ratio is an improvement over 1984.

Long-Run Solvency Measurements

Ratios for Investment in Property, Plant, and Equipment The investment by a company in property, plant, and equipment assets may vary considerably, depending on the nature of the business. Manufacturing concerns require a greater investment in machinery and equipment than do retail or wholesale firms. The relationship of the property, plant, and equipment to total assets and sales should be in proper proportion for the industry. If the amount invested in property, plant, and equipment is too high, fewer funds are available for working capital purposes. Depreciation charges will also be high, resulting in either higher prices or lower profits. Finally, the long-term liabilities will be greater, resulting in greater interest costs and the need for funds to pay off debts as they mature.

Three ratios used to determine the suitability of investment in property, plant, and equipment are discussed next.

The *ratio of property, plant, and equipment to long-term liabilities* is obtained by dividing the total book value of the property, plant, and equipment by the long-term liabilities. This comparison is important to the long-term creditors if any of the property, plant, and equipment has been mortgaged as security for loans. The smaller the ratio, the greater the dependence on long-term borrowing to finance property, plant, and equipment acquisitions.

The *ratio of property, plant, and equipment to stockholders' equity* is obtained by dividing the total book value of the property, plant, and equipment by the stockholders' equity. An investment in property, plant, and equipment that is equal to or less than stockholders' equity (a ratio equal to or less than 1.0) indicates that the entire amount of property, plant, and equipment could have been bought by the capital obtained from the owners.

The *ratio of net sales to property, plant, and equipment,* or property, plant, and equipment turnover, is found by dividing net sales by the average total book value of the property, plant, and equipment. A decreasing ratio over a time period shows a possible overinvestment in property, plant, and equipment. For example, an average investment in property, plant, and equipment that exceeds sales (ratio less than 1.0) indicates an overinvestment, which results in higher interest, taxes, maintenance expenses, and depreciation charges and lower working capital. A heavy investment in land, buildings, and machinery greatly restricts the mobility of a company if a change in plant location or type of product manufactured is desirable.

Number of Times Bond Interest Earned In addition to the effective interest rate computations discussed previously, another important ratio is used by investors in bonds. The number of times bond interest expense is earned is of special interest to bond investors as a measure of the safety of their investment; it is an indication of a firm's ability to meet its annual bond interest requirement. To illustrate, assume that Afco Corporation has bonds outstanding with a face value of $500,000 and that in 1985 it reports bond interest expense of $40,000, income taxes of $60,000, and net income (after income taxes) of $80,000. Since bond interest expense is deductible in determining taxable income, the following formula seems appropriate:

$$\text{Number of times bond interest expense is earned} = \frac{\text{Net income} + \text{Income tax expense} + \text{Annual bond interest expense}}{\text{Annual bond interest expense}}.$$

Substituting the amounts given for the Afco Corporation:

$$\text{Number of times bond interest earned} = \frac{\$80{,}000 + \$60{,}000 + \$40{,}000}{\$40{,}000} = 4.5 \text{ times.}$$

Although there are no established universal standards of safety, a ratio of 4.5 appears to be relatively safe for investors holding bonds of Afco Corporation.

The safety margin depends in part on the type of collateral used, the type of business in which the firm is engaged, and the liquidity of the firm. Investors in a privately owned public utility with mortgageable plant assets, for example, may feel secure with a ratio of 2.5 times, whereas investors in businesses without mortgageable assets may feel insecure with a ratio smaller than five times.

Number of Times Preferred Dividends Earned A similar investor-oriented ratio is the *number of times preferred dividends are earned.* This ratio is of particular interest to investors in preferred stock. To illustrate, assume that Afco Corporation has 10 percent preferred stock outstanding with a par value of $700,000. Since preferred dividends are *not* deductible in determining taxable income, the following formula is appropriate:

$$\text{Number of times preferred dividends are earned} = \frac{\text{Net income after taxes}}{\text{Annual preferred dividends}}.$$

Substituting the amounts given for Afco Corporation:

$$\text{Number of times preferred dividends are earned} = \$80{,}000 \div \$70{,}000 = 1.14 \text{ times.}$$

The adequacy of this ratio must be interpreted in a manner similar to that described for the number of times bond interest expense is earned; that is, the safety margin that is acceptable will depend in part on the type of business in which the firm is engaged, the liquidity of the firm, and other factors.

Equity Ratios A significant measure of the stability of a business is the percentage relationship of the equities of the creditors and the owners in the total assets. The equity ratios for the Morco Company at the end of 1985 are computed as follows:

a. Creditors' interest in assets:

$$\frac{\text{Total liabilities}}{\text{Total assets}} = \frac{\$111{,}550}{\$257{,}000} = 43.4\%.$$

b. Stockholders' interest in assets:

$$\frac{\text{Total stockholders' equity}}{\text{Total assets}} = \frac{\$145{,}450}{\$257{,}000} = 56.6\%.$$

The sum of these two ratios must always be 100 percent because they equal total claims against assets. These ratios are popularly known as debt/equity ratios. Many analysts consider them to be equal in importance to the current ratio as indicators of credit strength and sound management. There are no universally accepted percentage relationships to serve as guides for the equity ratios, but it is generally felt that when interest rates are high the larger the stockholders' equity ratio, the stronger the financial condition of the business. A company may, for example, borrow money on a long-term note for working capital purposes. The loan increases the current assets and creates a more favorable current ratio, but it also reduces the stockholders' equity ratio, signaling a possible overdependence on outside sources for financial needs.

The pursuit of a favorable stockholders' equity ratio has its disadvantages. The long-term debt may be reduced to a point where the company is forgoing the tax deduction for interest expense and the opportunity to use borrowed funds to generate a higher rate of return than the borrowing rate.

Earning Power Measurements

Per-Share Profitability Of considerable significance and usefulness to the investor are the ratios of earnings and dividends to the market value of the shares, because it is the cash represented by the market value of the shares that can be put to other uses. Three such ratios are:

$$\text{Earnings yield rate} = \frac{\text{Earnings per share}}{\text{Market value per share}}.$$

$$\text{Dividends yield rate} = \frac{\text{Dividends per share}}{\text{Market value per share}}.$$

$$\text{Price-earnings ratio} = \frac{\text{Market value per share}}{\text{Earnings per share}}.$$

Two of the above ratios use EPS which, in itself, is a form of ratio analysis (see Chapter 17). A careful analysis of the relationship and trend of these ratios indicates the profitability of the firm as related to the market value of its shares, its growth prospects, and its ability to pay dividends. In 1982, several large power companies such as Commonwealth Edison had dividend yield rates in the 10–12 percent range comparing favorably with short-term interest rates. Sometimes known as **times earnings,** the **price-earnings ratio (P/E)** is watched carefully by investors. This measure varies greatly; many blue-chip companies' stock sold for six to twelve times earnings in 1982.

Rate of Return on Total Investment The relationship of the earnings of a business to its total resources is an important indicator of the effectiveness of management in generating a return to suppliers of capital; it is also a method of predicting future earnings. The **rate of return on total investment** is:

$$(\text{Net income for year} + \text{Interest expense}) \div \text{Average total assets} = \begin{array}{l}\text{Rate of return on}\\ \text{total investment.}\end{array}$$

The Morco Company's 1985 computation is:

$$(\$30{,}750 + \$2{,}750) \div \frac{(\$257{,}000 + \$229{,}000)}{2} = 13.8\%.$$

This rate shows the degree of profitability measured against total investments by creditors and owners combined.

Rate of Return on Stockholders' Equity The relationship between earnings and the average stockholders' investment is a significant measure of the profitability of a business and is of particular interest to the corporate shareholders. The 1985 **rate of return on stockholders' equity** for Morco is:

$$\frac{\text{Net income}}{\text{Average stockholders' equity}} = \frac{\$30{,}750}{(\$145{,}450 + \$118{,}000) \div 2} = 23.3\%.$$

This rate is higher by 65.2 percent = [(23.3% − 14.1%) ÷ 14.1%] than the rate of return on total investments. This means that the return to stockholders is well above the fixed rates on the mortgage payable. The Morco Company is favorably "trading on the equity" of its creditors by using that portion of total equities as a cushion or base from which to borrow from outside sources at rates below those earned on stockholders' equity.

Other Influences on Profitability

The techniques and procedures for the analysis of financial statements are useful tools for gaining an insight into the financial affairs of a business. The analyst must also evaluate many other influences that, although not specifically reflected in the statements, may nevertheless influence the future of the company. The analyst should look for sudden changes in key management personnel; shifts in employee or customer loyalty; development of new competing products; and broad shifts in the social, political, or economic environment. Another factor that must be evaluated with care is the impact of changing price levels on the statements (this topic is covered in Chapter 14). Differences in financial statements may also be due to the wide variations that exist within the framework of generally accepted accounting principles and procedures—in, for example, the valuation of inventories, the selection of depreciation methods, the treatment of intangibles, and extraordinary and other nonoperating items.

Limitations of Ratio Analysis

A particular ratio may be satisfactory under one set of circumstances and entirely unsatisfactory under another set. Ratios are generalizations, and they reflect conditions that exist only at a particular time. The ratios change continually with the continuing operations of the business. Sole reliance on ratio analysis may at times give a misleading indication of financial condition. The ability to understand and interpret ratios correctly, however, reduces the area over which subjective judgment must be exercised and thus aids the analyst in making sound decisions.

The ratios and comparisons discussed in this chapter are valuable managerial aids, provided the user is aware of their limitations. For example, the current ratio of 1.96 to 1 for the Morco Company at the end of 1985 shows the relationship between two groups of items as of a given moment in time. The ratio may fluctuate considerably during the course of the year. The ratio may have little meaning unless it is related to the other ratios. Also, some ratios may be biased by advancing or deferring selected transactions, especially at or near the end of the reporting period.

Finally and most importantly, the ratios and other comparisons based on the conventional (historical cost) financial statements should be compared with the same ratios recalculated using the financial statement amounts adjusted for changing prices. In many instances, the latter set of measurements will produce more meaningful relationships.

Tabulation of Major Ratios

A tabulation of significant ratios arranged in an outline of their primary measurements is shown in Figure 21–11; it indicates the range of possibilities in the analysis of financial statements.

Ratio	Computation of Ratio	Indicates
Short-run solvency measurements		
1. Current ratio	$\dfrac{\text{Current assets}}{\text{Current liabilities}}$	The ability of a business to meet its current obligations
2. Acid-test ratio (quick ratio)	$\dfrac{\text{Quick current assets}}{\text{Current liabilities}}$	The ability of a business to quickly meet unexpected demands from assets readily convertible into cash
3. Average number of days' sales uncollected (collection period)	$\dfrac{\text{Average accounts receivable}}{\text{Net credit sales}} \times 365$ OR (1) Net credit sales ÷ 365 = Net credit sales per day (2) $\dfrac{\text{Average accounts receivable}}{\text{Net credit sales per day}}$	The rapidity with which the accounts receivable are collected; the average number of days elapsing from the time of sale to the time of payment
4. Merchandise inventory turnover	$\dfrac{\text{Cost of goods sold}}{\text{Average inventory}}$	The number of times the merchandise inventory was replenished during the period or the number of dollars in the cost of goods sold for each dollar of inventory
Long-run solvency measurements		
5. Property, plant, and equipment to long-term liabilities	$\dfrac{\text{Property, plant, and equipment (net)}}{\text{Long-term debt}}$	The adequacy of protection to long-term creditors
6. Property, plant, and equipment to stockholders' equity	$\dfrac{\text{Property, plant, and equipment (net)}}{\text{Stockholders' equity}}$	The extent to which owner sources are being used to finance property, plant, and equipment acquisitions
7. Sales to property, plant, and equipment (plant turnover)	$\dfrac{\text{Net sales}}{\text{Average property, plant, and equipment (net)}}$	Dollar of sales per dollar of investment in property, plant, and equipment assets
8. Number of times bond interest earned	$\dfrac{\text{Net income + Income taxes + Annual bond interest expense}}{\text{Annual bond interest expense}}$	The primary measure of the safety of an investment in bonds—the ability of a firm to meet its bond interest requirement
9. Number of times preferred dividends earned	$\dfrac{\text{Net income}}{\text{Annual preferred dividends}}$	The primary measure of the safety of an investment in preferred stock—the ability of a firm to meet its preferred dividend requirement

Figure 21–11 **Major Ratios**

Ratio	Computation of Ratio	Indicates
Long-run solvency measurements		
10. Creditors' equity ratio	$\frac{\text{Total liabilities}}{\text{Total assets}}$	The percent of creditor sources of total assets
11. Stockholders' equity ratio	$\frac{\text{Stockholders' equity}}{\text{Total assets}}$	The percent of owner sources of total assets
Earning power and growth potential measurements		
12. Earnings yield rate	$\frac{\text{Earnings per share}}{\text{Market price per share}}$	Earnings as related to market value of the shares
13. Dividends yield rate	$\frac{\text{Dividends per share}}{\text{Market price per share}}$	Dividend payout as related to market value of the shares
14. Earnings per share of common[a] stock for a corporation with a simple capital structure	$\frac{\text{Net income} - \text{Annual preferred dividend}}{\text{Average outstanding common shares}}$	The company's earning power as related to common stockholders' equity
15. Price-earnings ratio	$\frac{\text{Market price per share}}{\text{Earnings per share}}$	Market value per share as related to profitability of the firm
16. Rate of return on total investment	$\frac{\text{Net income} + \text{Interest expense}}{\text{Average total assets}}$	The profitability of the firm expressed as a rate of return on total investments by both owners and creditors
17. Rate of return on stockholders' equity	$\frac{\text{Net income}}{\text{Average stockholders' equity}}$	The profitability of the firm expressed as a rate of return on stockholders' equity

Other measurements

Financial structure measurements: These measurements can be determined from a common-size balance sheet that shows the composition of items on the balance sheet.

Asset utilization ratios: These are measures of asset turnover or the dollars of sales generated by each dollar of investment in total assets or in each individual asset.

Operating performance ratios: These are measures that show the relationship of each income statement item or groups of items to sales.

[a]See Chapter 17.

Figure 21–11 **(Continued)**

Glossary

Acid-test ratio The ratio of quick current assets to current liabilities; an indicator of the ability of a business to meet quickly unexpected demands for working capital from assets readily convertible into cash.

Base year The one year in a series of years with which all the other years in the series are compared.

Common-size statements Statements in which each element is shown as a percentage of some major total.

Comparative financial statements Current and past financial statements of a company with single-column, side-by-side data.

Consistency Adhering to a selected method of accounting (valuation bases, methods of amortization) period after period.

Current ratio The relationship of current assets to current liabilities; an indicator of the ability of a business to meet its current obligations.

Discontinued operations Operations with a separate class of customers or line of business that has been sold or otherwise disposed of.

Horizontal analysis Current and past balance sheets of a company presented side by side with the dollar amount of increase or decrease together with the percentage of proportionate increase or decrease. *Trend percentages* are another form of horizontal analysis.

Interim reports Publicly released quarterly unaudited financial statements of corporations.

Intraperiod income tax allocation Refers to the concept that income tax expense for a period should be separately identified with income from operations, extraordinary items, adjustment of prior period earnings, and other unusual events.

Merchandise inventory turnover The number of times the merchandise inventory is replenished during a period.

Multiple-step income statement A form of income statement that groups revenue and deductions so as to arrive at a series of intermediate subtotals culminating in net income after extraordinary items.

Price-earnings (P/E) ratio Market value per share as related to the profitability of the firm.

Prior period adjustments Transactions of a previous period that are handled as direct adjustments to retained earnings and are therefore excluded from net income of the current period.

Quick current assets Cash, temporary investments, and receivables.

Rate of return on stockholders' equity Net income expressed as a percent of stockholders' equity.

Rate of return on total investment Net income plus interest expense expressed as a percent of the average total assets.

Ratio The relationship of one amount to another.

Ratio analysis The analysis of the proportion of financial items from period to period by converting the dollar amounts to a percentage, a decimal, or a fraction.

Receivables turnover The number of times accounts receivable are generated and collected during a period.

Revenue-dollar statement The conversion of the ratio of each item in the income statement to a dollar amount, with net sales representing a base of one dollar.

Single-step income statement A form of income statement in which all revenues appear in one section and all deductions from revenue in another section, without any intermediate subtotals.

Statement of stockholders' equity A comprehensive statement that shows beginning balances, changes, and ending balances of preferred stock, common stock, additional paid-in capital, and retained earnings.

Times earnings See *Price-earnings (P/E) ratio.*

Trend percentages An analytical device for changing the absolute dollar data of comparative statements to percentages of a base year.

Turnover A form of analysis (for example, inventory turnover and receivables turnover) that describes an element of operating efficiency.

Vertical analysis Current and past financial statements of a company presented side by side with comparisons made of each component as a percent of certain base totals within those statements. See *Common-size statements.*

Working capital turnover The relationship between working capital and sales.

Questions

Q21–1 What is the difference in reporting to internal users and to external users? Be specific as to the goals of each type of reporting and how to achieve them.

Q21–2 Some people feel that a good financial report should be understood by a person who knows nothing about accounting. Do you agree? Why or why not?

Q21–3 What are some requirements by authoritative bodies that have attempted to make the reporting of income (loss) more useful? Explain how each requirement is helpful to a statement reader.

Q21–4 What is the difference between the items in each of the following sets: single-step and multiple-step income statement; horizontal and vertical analysis; common-size statements, comparative statements, and revenue-dollar statements; short-run and long-run solvency measurements; ratio analysis and turnover analysis.

Q21–5 What is meant by extraordinary items? Prior period adjustments? Discontinued operations?

Q21–6 (a) What are some limitations of financial statements? (b) List and discuss some factors contributing to the development of financial reporting to outside groups.

Q21–7 (a) Discuss the characteristics of a good managerial report. (b) Discuss the purposes of financial statements.

Q21–8 "The financial statement analyst should have available comparative statements that show changes in absolute amounts and percentage changes." Explain.

Q21–9 Trend percentages are of limited usefulness (a) because they do not indicate whether the change is favorable or unfavorable, (b) because the change may be in relation to a year that is not typical or normal, and (c) because they do not measure the effectiveness of management. Do you agree? Discuss.

Q21–10 What are the advantages and limitations to the analyst of the following:

a. Comparative statements.
b. Trend percentages.
c. Common-size percentages.

Q21–11 Explain how each of the following would be determined:

a. A company's earning power.
b. The extent to which owner sources have been used to finance property, plant, and equipment acquisitions.
c. The adequacy of protection to long-term creditors.
d. The rapidity with which the accounts receivable are collected.
e. The ability of a business to meet quickly the unexpected demands for working capital.

Q21–12 What ratios or other analytical devices will help in answering each of the following questions?

a. Is there an overinvestment in property, plant, and equipment?
b. Are the assets distributed satisfactorily?
c. Is there adequate protection for creditors?

d. How is the business being financed?
e. Are earnings adequate?
f. Is there a satisfactory relationship between creditor and owner financing?
g. Are costs and expenses too high?
h. Are sales adequate?

Exercises

E21–1 *Reporting of expenses, gains and losses, and discontinued operations*

Describe how and in what statement each of the following should be reported at the end of 1985:

a. Earthquake damages in Boston, Mass.
b. Interest expense.
c. A computer purchased for $10,000 in 1984 and debited to office expense.
d. Overtime pay of employees called in on Saturday to process a special order.
e. Net loss of electronics division of a textile company; the electronics division was sold in 1985.
f. A loss on sale of the electronics division.
g. Change of EUL of an asset from eight to twelve years.

E21–2 *Intraperiod tax allocation*

On December 20, 1985, the Sevierville Corporation lost a $28,000 uninsured building in an unexpected explosion. On December 31, 1985, the following data for the year were available:

Sales	$875,000
Cost of goods sold	525,000
Selling expenses	170,000
General and administrative expenses	80,000
Loss from explosion	28,000

Prepare a condensed income statement for 1985 assuming an income tax rate of 40 percent.

E21–3 *Computing percent of change*

The following data are presented for two companies as of December 31, 1985 and 1984 for the years then ended:

	Company A		Company B	
	1985	1984	1985	1984
Sales	$68,200	$52,800	$131,500	$142,000
Cost of goods sold	44,000	38,200	78,900	88,040
Operating expenses	11,000	8,800	26,300	25,560
Interest expense	3,200	8,000	9,200	6,300
Net income (loss)	10,000	(2,200)	17,100	22,100

Compute the percent of increase or decrease for each item (where possible).

E21–4 *Computing trend percentages*

Following are selected data for three years for the Havelock Company:

	1985	1984	1983
Net sales	$150,000	$138,000	$120,000
Cost of goods sold	96,768	89,208	75,600
Operating expenses	30,240	28,224	25,200
Net income	22,992	20,568	19,200
Current assets at end of year	20,444	22,596	21,520
Current liabilities at end of year	9,790	10,780	11,000
Property, plant, and equipment at end of year	60,264	54,432	48,600

Compute trend percentages for all items, rounding to the nearest tenth of a percent where necessary.

E21–5 *Computing common-size percentages—income statement*

Following are selected data for two years for Roca Company:

	1985	1984
Net sales	$152,000	$130,000
Cost of goods sold	94,240	92,950
Operating expenses	27,360	21,450
Interest expense	11,400	6,500
Extraordinary gains (losses)	(4,560)	(12,480)
Net income (loss)	14,440	(3,380)

Compute common-size percentages rounded to the nearest tenth of a percent

E21–6 *Computing common-size percentages—balance sheet*

Following are condensed comparative balance sheet data for the Denton Company:

	December 31	
	1985	1984
Current assets	$100,848	$ 91,324
Investments	42,402	21,804
Property, plant, and equipment (net)	238,750	202,872
Total assets	$382,000	$316,000
Current liabilities	$ 48,132	$ 33,812
Long-term liabilities	155,474	125,768
Common stock	145,924	113,760
Retained earnings	32,470	42,660
Total liabilities and stockholders' equity	$382,000	$316,000

Compute common-size percentages rounded to the nearest tenth of a percent.

E21–7 *Revenue-dollar statement*

The following revenue and expense data of Omaha Company for the year 1985 are given:

Sales	$336,000
Cost of goods sold	216,720
Selling expenses	34,272
General and administrative expenses	31,920
Interest expense	11,424
Income taxes	18,816
Net income	22,848

Prepare a revenue-dollar statement.

E21–8 *Short-run solvency measures*

Selected data for Platte River Company are given for December 31, 1985, 1984, and 1983, and for the years then ended (all assets and liabilities are shown):

	1985	1984	1983
Net sales	$628,000	$600,000	$540,000
Cost of goods sold	389,360	381,000	345,600
Net income	56,520	52,800	41,310
Cash	17,600	15,260	18,800
Temporary investments	12,800	16,200	10,500
Accounts receivable	52,400	50,500	44,600
Merchandise inventory	64,800	63,200	58,600
Property, plant, and equipment (net)	122,400	124,840	127,500
Current liabilities	78,000	83,000	92,100
Long-term liabilities	106,600	112,000	118,000

Compute the following:

a. Current ratio for December 31, 1985.

b. Acid-test ratio for December 31, 1985.

c. Receivables turnover and average collection period in 1985 and 1984.

d. Merchandise inventory turnover in 1985 and 1984.

E21–9 *Long-run solvency measures*

Using the data in E21–8, compute the following ratios or percentages:
a. Property, plant, and equipment to long-term liabilities for December 31, 1985.
b. Property, plant, and equipment to stockholders' equity for December 31, 1984.
c. Sales to property, plant, and equipment in 1985.
d. Creditors' equity ratio for December 31, 1985.
e. Stockholders' equity ratio for December 31, 1985.

E21–10 *Earning power measures*

Using the data in E21–8, compute the following:
a. Rate of return on total investment in 1985 and 1984.
b. Rate of return on stockholders' equity in 1985 and 1984.

E21–11 *Evaluation of comparative data*

The following data have been computed for Abono Terme Company:

ABONO TERME COMPANY
Comparative Trend Percentages
For the Years Ended October 31 or at October 31

	1985	1984	1983	1982
Sales (net)	125%	115%	109%	100%
Cost of goods sold	128	118	112	100
Gross margin on sales	120	112	105	100
Net income	116	103	101	100
Accounts receivable	136	121	120	100
Merchandise inventory	130	121	114	100

Point out the favorable and unfavorable trends and suggest some areas for management study.

E21–12 *Earnings and growth potential*

Po Valley, Inc. had the following experience in 1985 and 1984 (there is no preferred stock):

	1985	1984
Net income	$558,000	$336,000
Dividends on common stock	288,000	160,000
Market price per share	56	42
Average number of common shares outstanding	120,000	80,000

Compute the following for both years (rounded to nearest cent or tenth of a percent):
a. Earnings per share.
b. Price-earnings ratio.
c. Earnings yield rate.
d. Dividends yield rate.

A Problems

P21–1A *Income statement and statement of retained earnings—tax allocations given*

The following information is taken from the books of the Grand Forks Company on December 31, 1985 (50,000 shares of common stock are outstanding):

Retained earnings (credit), December 31, 1984	$ 42,500
Sales	375,000
Dividends declared	32,500
Selling and general and administrative expenses	140,000
Income tax expense	16,000
Cost of goods sold	195,000
Overstatement of depreciation in 1984 (net of tax of $2,800)	4,200
Extraordinary loss (net of income tax reduction of $5,000)	7,500
Net income from discontinued operations (net of tax of $7,200)	10,800
Gain on sale of electronics plant discontinued (net of tax of $10,000)	15,000

Required:

1. Prepare a multiple-step income statement and a statement of retained earnings.

2. Prepare a combined statement of income and retained earnings.

P21–2A *Horizontal analysis—percent of change and evaluation*

The condensed comparative statements of Arvila, Inc., are given:

ARVILA, INC.
Comparative Balance Sheet
December 31, 1985 and 1984

Exhibit C

	December 31	
	1985	**1984**
Current assets	$ 540,000	$ 465,000
Property, plant, and equipment	570,000	615,000
Total assets	$1,110,000	$1,080,000
Current liabilities	$ 207,000	$ 163,500
Long-term liabilities	210,000	225,000
Total liabilities	$ 417,000	$ 388,500
Common stock	$ 600,000	$ 600,000
Retained earnings	93,000	91,500
Total stockholders' equity	$ 693,000	$ 691,500
Total liabilities and stockholders' equity	$1,110,000	$1,080,000

ARVILA, INC.
Comparative Statement of Income and Retained Earnings
For the Years Ended December 31, 1985 and 1984

Exhibit A

	Years Ended December 31	
	1985	**1984**
Sales (net)	$1,485,000	$1,650,000
Cost of goods sold	1,128,000	1,230,000
Gross margin on sales	$ 357,000	$ 420,000
Operating expenses	246,000	285,000
Net income before income taxes	$ 111,000	$ 135,000
Income taxes	55,500	67,500
Net income	$ 55,500	$ 67,500
Retained earnings, January 1	91,500	90,000
Subtotal	$ 147,000	$ 157,500
Dividends paid	54,000	66,000
Retained earnings, December 31	$ 93,000	$ 91,500
Earnings per share	$ 1.39	$ 1.69

Required (rounding to the nearest tenth of a percent):

1. For the comparative statement of income and retained earnings, show the amount and percent of increase or decrease during 1985.

2. For the comparative balance sheet, show the amount and percent of increase or decrease during 1985.

3. Write a report indicating whether the financial condition and 1985 operating results are favorable or unfavorable, and state your reasons.

P21–3A *Horizontal analysis—trend percentages and debt/equity ratios*

Condensed comparative balance sheets for Fargo Company appear below:

FARGO COMPANY
Comparative Balance Sheet
October 31, 1985, 1984, and 1983
(in Thousands of Dollars)

Exhibit C

	October 31		
Assets	**1985**	**1984**	**1983**
Current assets	$ 13,600	$15,000	$20,000
Investments	6,000	8,000	10,000
Property, plant, and equipment (net of accumulated depreciation)	84,000	72,000	60,000
Total assets	$103,600	$95,000	$90,000
Liabilities and Stockholders' Equity			
Liabilities:			
Current liabilities	$ 10,400	$10,000	$ 8,000
Long-term liabilities (net of discount)	19,600	19,200	18,800
Stockholders' equity:			
Common stock ($5 par)	48,000	40,000	40,000
Paid-in capital in excess of par value, common	3,600	2,000	2,000
Retained earnings	22,000	23,800	21,200
Total liabilities and stockholders' equity	$103,600	$95,000	$90,000

Required: Compute the following, rounded to the nearest tenth of a percent:

1. Trend percentages for all items.

2. Creditors' equity ratio for October 31, 1985 and 1984.

3. Stockholders' equity ratio for October 31, 1985 and 1984.

P21–4A *Common-size statements with evaluation*

The comparative financial statements of Plonski Company are given below:

PLONSKI COMPANY
Comparative Balance Sheet
December 31, 1985 and 1984

Exhibit C

	December 31	
	1985	**1984**
Current assets	$160,000	$195,000
Property, plant, and equipment	420,000	325,000
Total assets	$580,000	$520,000
Current liabilities	$104,000	$230,000
Long-term liabilities	252,000	120,000
Total liabilities	$356,000	$350,000
Common stock	$196,000	$150,000
Retained earnings	28,000	20,000
Total stockholders' equity	$224,000	$170,000
Total liabilities and stockholders' equity	$580,000	$520,000

PLONSKI COMPANY **Exhibit A**
Comparative Income Statement
For the Years Ended December 31, 1985 and 1984

	Years Ended December 31	
	1985	**1984**
Sales (net)	$640,000	$570,000
Cost of goods sold	367,200	322,500
Gross margin on sales	$272,800	$247,500
Operating expenses:		
Selling expenses	$136,400	$110,000
General and administrative expenses	80,600	55,000
Total operating expenses	$217,000	$165,000
Net income	$ 55,800	$ 82,500

Required:

1. Prepare (with amounts rounded to the nearest tenth of a percent):
a. A comparative common-size balance sheet.
b. A comparative common-size income statement.
c. A comparative revenue-dollar statement.

2. Discuss the financial condition and operating results of the company, emphasizing favorable and unfavorable trends.

P21–5A
Calculation of ratios for a real-life company

R. J. Reynolds Industries, Inc., included the following information in millions of dollars in its 1981 *Annual Report:*

	1981	**1980**	**1979**
Net sales and operating revenues	$11,691.8	$10,354.1	$8,935.2
Cost of products sold	7,007.5	6,320.8	5,505.5
Interest expense	149.6	127.3	NR[a]
Net income	768.8	670.4	550.9
Preferred dividends	29.6	30.6	30.7
Common dividends	260.6	223.9	194.0
Income taxes	633.3	468.8	466.3
Current assets:			
Cash and short-term investments	60.7	188.3	NR[a]
Accounts and notes receivable (net)	1,157.4	1,019.6	NR[a]
Inventories	2,694.1	2,371.8	NR[a]
Prepaid expenses	74.7	61.8	NR[a]
Total current liabilities	1,971.2	1,809.8	NR[a]
Total assets	8,096.0	7,355.3	NR[a]
Common shareholders' equity	3,926.5	3,445.4	NR[a]
Average number of common shares outstanding	104,251,000	102,709,000	NA[b]

[a]Only two years reported for balance sheet items.
[b]Not applicable.

Required: Compute the following:

1. Current ratio for December 31, 1981 and 1980.

2. Acid-test ratio for December 31, 1981 and 1980.

3. Receivables turnover for 1981.

4. Inventory turnover for 1981.

5. Earnings per common share for 1981 and 1980.

6. Number of times preferred dividends earned in 1981 and 1980.

7. Number of times interest expense earned in 1981 and 1980.

8. Rate of return on stockholders' equity in 1981.

9. Rate of return on total investment in 1981.

P21–6A
Thought-provoking problem: analysis of results

In its 1981 *Annual Report,* Northwest Energy Company reported the following selected information:

	Year Ended December 31				
	1981	**1980**	**1979**	**1978**	**1977**
Net income per common share	$ 3.83	$ 3.23	$ 3.03	$ 3.01	$ 1.82
Dividends per common share	1.15	0.95	0.85	0.783	0.717
Year-end market price per share	20⅞	31⅞	20⅝	8⅞	12¾
Book value per common share	21.68	18.78	16.37	14.77	12.68

The late 1970s and early 1980s saw many uncertainties in the stock market.

Required:

1. Compute the price-earnings ratio, earnings yield rate, and dividends yield rate for each year.

2. Compute market price per share as a percent of book value for each year.

3. What could be some reasons for the fluctuations in market value in the face of steady increases in all other factors above? (Suggestion: You might look at some 1980–81 issues of the *Wall Street Journal* or *Business Week* for ideas.)

B Problems

P21–1B
Income statement and statement of retained earnings—tax allocations given

The following information is taken from the books of Cedar Falls Company on December 31, 1985 (50,000 shares of common stock are outstanding):

Retained earnings (credit), December 31, 1984	$ 85,000
Sales	750,000
Dividends declared	65,000
Selling and general and administrative expenses	280,000
Income tax expense	32,000
Cost of goods sold	390,000
Overstatement of depreciation in 1984 (net of tax of $5,600)	8,400
Extraordinary loss (net of tax reduction of $10,000)	15,000
Net income from discontinued operations (net of tax of $14,400)	21,600
Gain from sale of textile plant discontinued (net of tax of $20,000)	30,000

Required:

1. Prepare a multiple-step income statement and a statement of retained earnings.

2. Prepare a combined statement of income and retained earnings.

P21–2B *Horizontal analysis—percent of change*

The condensed comparative statements of Black Hawk Mines are given:

BLACK HAWK MINES
Comparative Balance Sheet
December 31, 1985 and 1984

Exhibit C

	December 31	
	1985	**1984**
Current assets	$270,000	$232,500
Property, plant, and equipment	285,000	307,500
Total assets	$555,000	$540,000
Current liabilities	$103,500	$ 81,750
Long-term liabilities	105,000	112,500
Total liabilities	$208,500	$194,250
Common stock	$300,000	$300,000
Retained earnings	46,500	45,750
Total stockholders' equity	$346,500	$345,750
Total liabilities and stockholders' equity	$555,000	$540,000

BLACK HAWK MINES
Comparative Statement of Income and Retained Earnings
For the Years Ended December 31, 1985 and 1984

Exhibit A

	Years Ended December 31	
	1985	**1984**
Sales (net)	$742,500	$825,000
Cost of goods sold	564,000	615,000
Gross margin on sales	$178,500	$210,000
Operating expenses	123,000	142,500
Net income before income taxes	$ 55,500	$ 67,500
Income taxes	27,750	33,750
Net income	$ 27,750	$ 33,750
Retained earnings, January 1	45,750	45,000
Subtotal	$ 73,500	$ 78,750
Dividends paid	27,000	33,000
Retained earnings, December 31	$ 46,500	$ 45,750
Earnings per share	$ 1.39	$ 1.69

Required: Rounding to the nearest tenth of a percent:

1. For the comparative statement of income and retained earnings, show the amount and percent of increase and decrease during 1985.

2. For the comparative balance sheet, show the amount and percent of increase or decrease during 1985.

3. Write a report stating whether the financial condition and operating results are favorable or unfavorable, and state your reasons.

P21–3B *Horizontal analysis—trend percentages and debt/equity ratios*

Condensed comparative balance sheets for Parkersburg Company appear below:

PARKERSBURG COMPANY
Comparative Balance Sheet
October 31, 1985, 1984, and 1983
(in Thousands of Dollars)

Exhibit C

	October 31		
Assets	**1985**	**1984**	**1983**
Current assets	$ 17,000	$ 18,750	$ 25,000
Investments	7,500	10,000	12,500
Property, plant, and equipment (net of accumulated depreciation)	105,000	90,000	75,000
Total assets	$129,500	$118,750	$112,500
Liabilities and Stockholders' Equity			
Liabilities:			
Current liabilities	$ 13,000	$ 12,500	$ 10,000
Long-term liabilities (net of discount)	24,500	24,000	23,500
Stockholders' equity:			
Common stock ($2 par)	60,000	50,000	50,000
Paid-in capital in excess of par value, common	4,500	2,500	2,500
Retained earnings	27,500	29,750	26,500
Total liabilities and stockholders' equity	$129,500	$118,750	$112,500

Required: Compute the following rounded to the nearest tenth of a percent:

1. Trend percentages for all items.
2. Creditors' equity ratio for October 31, 1985 and 1984.
3. Stockholders' equity ratio for October 31, 1985 and 1984.

P21–4B *Common-size statements with evaluation*

The comparative condensed financial statements of Voorhies, Inc., are given below:

VOORHIES, INC.
Comparative Balance Sheet
December 31, 1985 and 1984

Exhibit C

	December 31	
	1985	**1984**
Current assets	$240,000	$292,500
Property, plant, and equipment	630,000	487,500
Total assets	$870,000	$780,000
Current liabilities	$156,000	$345,000
Long-term liabilities	378,000	180,000
Total liabilities	$534,000	$525,000
Common stock	$294,000	$225,000
Retained earnings	42,000	30,000
Total stockholders' equity	$336,000	$255,000
Total liabilities and stockholders' equity	$870,000	$780,000

VOORHIES, INC. **Exhibit A**
Comparative Income Statement
For the Years Ended December 31, 1985 and 1984

	Years Ended December 31	
	1985	**1984**
Sales (net)	$960,000	$855,000
Cost of goods sold	550,800	483,750
Gross margin on sales	$409,200	$371,250
Operating expenses:		
Selling expenses	$204,600	$165,000
General and administrative expenses	120,900	82,500
Total operating expenses	$325,500	$247,500
Net income	$ 83,700	$123,750

Required: With amounts rounded to the nearest tenth of a percent:

1. Prepare:
a. A comparative common-size balance sheet.
b. A comparative common-size income statement.
c. A comparative revenue-dollar statement.

2. Discuss the financial condition and operating results of the company, emphasizing favorable and unfavorable trends.

P21–5B
Calulation of ratios for a real-life company

Ingersoll-Rand Company included the following information in millions of dollars in its 1981 *Annual Report:*

	1981	**1980**	**1979**
Net sales	$3,377.6	$2,971.0	$2,542.1
Cost of goods sold	2,413.7	2,091.4	1,764.1
Interest expense	105.6	81.5	63.7
Net income	193.3	160.3	149.3
Preferred dividends	6.3	6.8	6.9
Common dividends	65.3	63.0	59.9
Income taxes	123.8	113.5	112.7
Current assets:			
Cash	45.9	50.2	NR[a]
Accounts and notes receivable (net)	749.2	760.0	NR[a]
Inventories	1,035.2	942.2	NR[a]
Prepaid expenses	22.8	20.2	NR[a]
Total current liabilities	773.8	716.8	NR[a]
Total assets	2,678.1	2,526.8	NR[a]
Common stockholders' equity	1,277.6	1,170.3	NR[a]
Average number of common shares outstanding	19,264,000	18,985,000	NA[b]

[a]Only two years reported for balance sheet items.
[b]Not applicable.

Required: Compute the following:

1. Current ratio for December 31, 1981 and 1980.

2. Acid-test ratio for December 31, 1981 and 1980.

3. Receivables turnover for 1981.

4. Inventory turnover for 1981.

5. Earnings per common share for 1981 and 1980.
6. Number of times preferred dividends earned in 1981 and 1980.
7. Number of times interest expense earned in 1981 and 1980.
8. Rate of return on stockholders' equity in 1981.
9. Rate of return on total investment in 1981.

P21–6B *Thought-provoking problem: analysis of results*

The following are taken from *Business Week*, "1983 Investment Outlook Scoreboard" (December 27, 1982, pp. 97–116):

Company	Recent Share Price	1982 Dividend Rate	Estimated EPS[a] 1982	Estimated EPS[a] 1983
Allied Stores	$36	$1.80	$4.21	$5.05
American Express	69	2.20	5.96	6.74
AT&T	60	5.40	8.80	9.48
BankAmerica	22	1.52	3.10	3.66
CBS	63	2.80	5.60	7.00
Duke Power	21	2.28	3.36	3.54

[a]Estimated by Institutional Brokers Estimate System.

Required:

1. For each company compute:
   a. Earnings yield rate for 1982 and 1983.
   b. Dividends yield rate for 1982 and 1983.
   c. Price/earnings ratio for 1982.
2. Based on 1982 data, which stock would you purchase if you were seeking:
   a. Maximum dividend yield in 1982?
   b. Maximum earnings yield in 1982?
   c. Maximum percent of earnings increase in 1983?
3. Do you believe that dividends rate or EPS is more influential in determining market price of the shares? Why? Discuss these relationships and other factors that investors consider in their investment decisions.

22 Branch Accounting and Consolidated Statements

Introduction

As populations change and new areas are developed, businesses must adapt to those changes. New shopping centers create the opportunity for a business to expand its market by opening new branches. Because branch managers need information on which to base decisions, the accounting system can be decentralized into sets of branch and home office records. Large corporations grow as a result of their own operations; most, however, speed up the growth process by acquiring other companies. Typically, companies combine by:

- Purchase of part or all of the voting stock of another company where the purchased company *continues to exist* (an *acquisition*).
- Purchase of all the stock of another company where the purchased company *is eliminated* (a *merger*).
- Formation of a new corporation to purchase all the voting stock of two companies that are put together under a new name (a *consolidation*).

In this chapter, accounting for home offices and their branches is described. Then the concept of consolidated financial statements is described with only enough detail to understand the types of eliminations needed in the consolidation process.

Learning Goals

To understand the concept of reciprocal accounts.

To be able to make entries in a decentralized accounting system for a home office and its branches.

To know why corporations acquire and hold majority or total ownership of other corporations.

To recognize the nature and types of affiliations and intercompany transactions.

To understand some of the basic concepts of preparation of consolidated financial statements.

To understand the need for elimination of certain transactions in preparing consolidated statements.

Branch Accounting

As opportunities for larger markets arise, a company may open a branch to carry on operations in a location away from the home office. It is possible to have the branch report transactions (often on a daily basis) to the home office so that all operations of both the home office and branch are centralized in the single set of accounting records at the home office. However, as branch operations become more complex or as a company opens additional branches, centralized accounting records become more difficult to maintain. Individual branch records also create incentives and provide better information for local branch managers. To strengthen local control, accounting records are established at each branch to record *details* of branch transactions. At the end of each accounting period, the branch accounts are combined with home office accounts to produce operating results and financial statements for the company as a whole.

Purpose of Branch Accounting

Decentralized records located in a branch are useful for individual decision making by the manager of a branch and control of branch operations.

Involved in this accounting procedure is the use of *reciprocal accounts.* The basic concept of reciprocal accounts is explained in the next section.

Reciprocal Account Concept

Accounts in two sets of books—in this case, a home office and a branch—that represent common elements and would offset each other if the books were combined are called **reciprocal accounts.** For example, if the San Diego Company established a branch at Fullerton and desired to use decentralized records at the branch, there would be an investment-type account in the San Diego home office named *Fullerton Branch* with a debit balance representing the amount of the home office investment in the branch. At the Fullerton branch, an equity-type account with a credit balance named *Home Office* would reflect the San Diego Company's equity in that branch; the function of the Home Office account is identical to a proprietor's capital account. To illustrate, assume that the San Diego Company established the Fullerton Branch on July 31, 1985 by transfer of $40,000 in cash and $60,000 of merchandise to the branch. After the transfer is recorded on each set of books, the reciprocal accounts of the home office and branch appear as shown in

In the San Diego Home Office		At the Fullerton Branch	
Fullerton Branch		Home Office	
1985 Jul. 31 . . 100,000 (At the home office, this is the amount of investment in this branch.)			1985 Jul. 31 . . 100,000 (At the branch, this is the amount of home office equity.)

Figure 22–1
Reciprocal Account Relationship

Figure 22–1. Note that the two accounts duplicate or offset each other. Each of them represents $100,000 of assets (cash of $40,000 plus merchandise of $60,000) owned by the company. However, each is required to keep the respective ledgers in balance. At the San Diego home office, the Fullerton Branch account substitutes for $100,000 of assets that have been transferred to the branch. When the ledgers of the home office and branch are combined, these reciprocal accounts must be *eliminated* to avoid duplication since each of the reciprocal accounts is representing the same set of resources. The resources they represent are in their own accounts and are summed into a single set of financial records for the company.

The techniques for use of reciprocal accounts and their elimination are explained in the illustration that follows in the next section. The elimination of reciprocal accounts is accomplished on a work sheet in Figure 22–5.

Branch Accounting Illustrated

To illustrate branch accounting concepts at the simplest but most effective level, assume that the San Diego Company with its Fullerton branch example is continued. Both use the periodic inventory system. Assume transactions as follows:

1985		
Jul.	31	The branch was established at Fullerton with a transfer of $40,000 in cash and $60,000 in merchandise.
Aug.	1	Additional merchandise was purchased by the Fullerton branch for $10,000 cash.
	16	Selling expenses of $8,000 were paid by the Fullerton branch.
	16	General and administrative expenses of $4,200 were paid by the San Diego home office for the Fullerton branch.
	30	Total branch sales amounting to $98,500 were recorded on the books of the Fullerton branch; terms 2/10, n/30.
	30	Cash collections for August in amount $92,000 were recorded by the Fullerton branch; $75,000 was remitted to the San Diego home office.
	31	Books were closed for the month of August at the branch and home office; by physical count, branch merchandise inventory is $10,900.

The journal entries *up to closing* are shown in Figure 22–2. Comments on the numbered items in the journal entries are in the boxes that follow.

		On Books of San Diego Home Office				On Books of Fullerton Branch			
1985 Jul.	31	Fullerton Branch . . .		100,000		Cash		40,000	
		Cash			40,000	Shipments from Home Office [2] . .		60,000	
		Shipments to Fullerton Branch [1]			60,000	Home Office . .			100,000
Aug.	1	No entry required.				Purchases		10,000	
						Cash			10,000
	16	No entry required.				Selling Expense [3]		8,000	
						Cash			8,000
	16	Fullerton Branch [4] .		4,200		General and Administrative Expense [5]		4,200	
		Cash			4,200	Home Office . .			4,200
	30	No entry required.				Accounts Receivable		98,500	
						Sales			98,500
	30	No entry required.				Cash		92,000	
						Accounts Receivable . . .			92,000
	30	Cash		75,000		Home Office		75,000	
		Fullerton Branch .			75,000	Cash [6]			75,000

Figure 22–2 **Journal Entries up to Closing**

[1] On the books of the home office, the Shipments to Fullerton Branch account shows the cost valuation of merchandise shipped to that branch. In the closing entries of the home office, this account is closed to Income Summary so that the cost of goods sold amount for home office operations will not be overstated.

[2] In a periodic inventory system, the Shipments from Home Office account serves as a special form of Purchases account. It shows the manager the cost valuation of merchandise received from the home office in addition to that purchased by the branch.

[3] A branch has the usual number of selling expense accounts. To simplify this illustration, they are all shown in one summary account.

[4] The branch account is debited in this transaction because additional home office assets have been used to produce branch income (see Figure 22–1); it is an additional investment in the branch.

[5] A branch also has a number of general and administrative expense accounts. In this illustration, they are all shown in one summary account to shorten the example.

[6] As excess cash is remitted by the branch to the home office, the home office equity in the branch is reduced.

After the entries for transactions through August 30 are journalized (see Figure 22–2) *and posted,* a trial balance of the *branch* books is shown as follows:

FULLERTON BRANCH–SAN DIEGO COMPANY
Trial Balance
August 30, 1985

Account Title	Debits	Credits
Cash	$ 39,000	
Accounts Receivable	6,500	
Merchandise Inventory	0	
Home Office		$ 29,200
Sales		98,500
Shipments from Home Office	60,000	
Purchases	10,000	
Selling Expense	8,000	
General and Administrative Expense	4,200	
Totals	$127,700	$127,700

In order to verify the branch account balances, it is suggested that the reader prepare a set of T accounts, post the journal entries through August 30, and determine the balances in each account. The Merchandise Inventory account is shown in the trial balance to emphasize the fact that there usually would be a beginning inventory at the branch. The balance is zero in this case because it is the first month of branch operations.

Note also that under a periodic inventory system, receipts of merchandise from the home office are debited to an account called Shipments from Home Office. This account enables the branch manager to distinguish such receipts of merchandise from those purchased by the branch and debited to Purchases. Under a perpetual inventory system, both the July 31 and the August 1 transactions would have been debited to Merchandise Inventory (see Chapter 12).

The reader should note another very important fact about the journal entries: *Whenever a reciprocal account is involved, there must be an entry on both sets of books.* Otherwise, the entry is made only on the books of the unit involved.

The August 31 closing entries are shown in Figure 22–3. As with the transaction entries, an entry is required on both sets of books each time a reciprocal account is involved. For example, the branch Income Summary account is closed on August 31 to show the increase of $27,200 to the home office equity brought about by branch operations. The home office must make an entry at the same time to record the increase in its investment in the branch and the matching branch net income. As indicated in Figure 22–3, the last entry of August 31 is simply a part of the overall closing process at the home office; it is not necessary to show that process in detail here.

On Books of San Diego Home Office					On Books of Fullerton Branch		
1985 Aug.	31	No entry required.			Sales	98,500	
					Merchandise Inventory	10,900[b]	
					Income Summary . . .		109,400
	31	No entry required.			Income Summary . .	82,200	
					Shipments from Home Office . .		60,000
					Purchases		10,000
					Selling Expense . .		8,000
					General and Administrative Expense		4,200
	31	Fullerton Branch . . .	27,200		Income Summary . .	27,200	
		Branch Income . .		27,200	Home Office		27,200
	31	Branch Income	27,200		No entry required.		
		Income Summary .		27,200[a]			

[a]This last entry is part of the overall closing entries at the home office.
[b]Periodic inventory system is used; determined by physical count.

Figure 22–3 **Closing Entries**

The posting of all foregoing entries including closing would be reflected in the reciprocal accounts as shown in Figure 22–4. As can be seen, the balances of the two accounts are equal, thus reinforcing the concept of reciprocal accounts.

Preparation of Financial Statements After closing entries are journalized and posted at the branch, the branch postclosing trial balance contains only asset, liability, and equity accounts. It appears as shown in Figure 22–5. Again, the reader should take time to be sure that the source of the amounts is understood. Assets and liabilities (if any existed) would be the same as those in the preclosing branch trial balance. Details of the reciprocal account balances are shown in Figure 22–4. The temporary accounts have been closed; their net sum is represented by an increase in the Home Office account.

In the San Diego Home Office		At the Fullerton Branch	
Fullerton Branch		Home Office	
1985	1985	1985	1985
Jul. 31 . . . 100,000	Aug. 30 . . . 75,000	Aug. 30 . . . 75,000	Jul. 31 . . . 100,000
Aug. 16 . . . 4,200			Aug. 16 . . . 4,200
31 . . . 27,200			31 . . . 27,200
Balance 56,400			Balance 56,400

Figure 22–4 Reciprocal Accounts after Closing

SAN DIEGO COMPANY
Work Sheet to Combine Branch and Home Office Balance Sheet Accounts
August 31, 1985

Account Titles	Home Office	Fullerton Branch	Eliminations Debits	Eliminations Credits	Balance Sheet
Debit Accounts					
Cash	180,000	39,000			219,000
Accounts Receivable	82,000	6,500			88,500
Merchandise Inventory	62,500	10,900			73,400
Property, Plant, and Equipment	182,600	0			182,600
Fullerton Branch	56,400	0		(a) 56,400	0
Totals	563,500	56,400			563,500
Credit Accounts					
Liabilities	38,200	0			38,200
Home Office	0	56,400	(a) 56,400		0
Common Stock	300,000	0			300,000
Retained Earnings	225,300	0			225,300
Totals	563,500	56,400	56,400	56,400	563,500

Figure 22–5 **Work Sheet for Combined Balance Sheet**

Figure 22–5 shows a work sheet to prepare a combined balance sheet for the company, including its Fullerton Branch. The amounts in the Home Office trial balance column of the work sheet are assumed to shorten this illustration. It is also assumed that the home office books have been closed. A special pair of columns entitled *Eliminations* is provided in the work sheet to combine home office and branch accounts. Entry (a) in the Eliminations columns removes the duplication caused by the reciprocal account that appears in each ledger. In this simple illustration, only one elimination is needed. When combined with the trial balance figures by adding horizontally across the work sheet, the two amounts eliminate duplication. The result is that the summary of asset, liabilities, and stockholders' equity accounts represents the true combined resources of the company and its branches.

In this simple illustration, the income statement and other financial statements can be prepared without the use of a work sheet. In a more complex situation, a work sheet may be used for those statements also.

Reciprocal accounts are found in many other situations. For example, a manufacturing firm may find it provides more effective control to split off some accounts from the general ledger and place them in a factory ledger. In each of the two ledgers—the general ledger and the factory ledger—a reciprocal account carries a balance equal to the total of the split-off group located in the factory. At any time the ledgers may be combined by elimination of the reciprocal accounts and combining the others.

With the basic concept of reciprocal accounts in mind, the preparation of consolidated statements for corporations and the subsidiary companies that they own can be discussed. Before details of such consolidations can be considered, however, some basic ideas about corporations holding controlling interests in other businesses are discussed in the following sections.

Reasons for Business Acquisitions

As indicated in the introduction to this chapter, it is typical for large corporations to acquire ownership in other corporations. One reason for acquisition is the *opening of new markets for products.* In its *1981 Annual Report,* Dennison Manufacturing Company reported the acquisition of Mitchell Ross Company of Sydney, Australia ". . . which gives us a major position in the Australian stationery market. . ."[1] A related reason for acquisition is the development and establishment of *a fair market share in new products.* Amp, Incorporated, reported that: "Several years ago, we began developing membrane switches and keyboards. Then in May 1981, we acquired the membrane switch and keyboard business of Chomerics, Inc., which was the industry leader with 1980 sales of $11,000,000 in this rapidly growing product area."[2]

A third reason for acquisition is *to achieve growth.* In its *1981 Annual Report,* Knight-Ridder Newspapers, Inc., recounts the history of its growth as two groups—one that started with an Akron, Ohio newspaper in 1933 and another that began with a German-language newspaper in 1892—combined in 1974 to form the present group. By 1981, Knight-Ridder had grown to the point that it owned 59 subsidiaries and divisions incorporated in 19 states.[3] Included are such newspapers as *The Miami Herald, The Philadelphia Inquirer* and *The Philadelphia Daily News,* and *The Charlotte Observer and News.* Also owned in 1981 by Knight-Ridder were four major television stations. Total revenues have grown from $399 million in 1971 to $1.237 billion in 1981—a tripling in 10 years.[4]

Some companies acquire other companies *to complement existing operations.* Noble Affiliates, Inc., reported in 1981 on its contract drilling subsidiary, Noble Drilling Corporation; its own oil company, Samedon Oil Corporation; and its trucking subsidiary, B. F. Walker, Inc.[5] The trucking subsidiary generates substantial revenue from hauling oilfield equipment. In the opposite direction, some companies continue *to diversify into nonrelated fields.* In 1981, oil and natural gas production, pipeline transportation, and oil processing and sales made up about 49 percent of Tenneco Inc.'s total revenues, but there were also revenues from chemicals (13 percent), shipbuilding (6½ per-

[1]Dennison Manufacturing Company, *1981 Annual Report,* p. 1.

[2]Amp, Incorporated, *1981 Annual Report,* p. 3.

[3]Knight-Ridder Newspapers, Inc., *1981 Annual Report,* p. 53.

[4]Knight-Ridder, *Annual Report,* pp. 28–29.

[5]Noble Affiliates, Inc., *1981 Annual Report,* pp. 4, 9, 16.

cent), construction and farm equipment (21 percent), automotive (7 percent), and a remainder from fiber, food, land, and other lines.[6] A typical diversified company, National Distillers and Chemical Corporation, reported 1981 sales in petrochemicals (25 percent), natural gas liquids (5 percent), oleochemicals (12 percent), liquors and wines (35 percent), and metals (23 percent).[7]

The one overriding objective in business acquisitions is an attempt to *achieve and improve overall profitability,* especially as reflected in earnings per share. All other reasons support this one. One successful company probably summarizes the goals of many corporations as follows:

> United Technologies' diversification strategy has withstood the test of economic difficulties that have beset America and its trading partners in recent years. Many of our businesses are cyclical, but the cycles have tended to be staggered because of our involvement across a span of industries and our growing involvement in overseas markets. Despite adverse economic conditions, our sales and net income increased again in 1981, rising 11 percent and 16 percent respectively. Fully diluted earnings per share rose 8 percent.[8]

Against this background, it is appropriate to consider the nature of parent-subsidiary relationships in the next section.

Parent-Subsidiary Relationships

The equity method of accounting for long-term investments in stock of another corporation was described in Chapter 19. Ownership of 20 percent or more of the voting stock of another company leads to the presumption that the investor can exercise *significant influence* over the policies of the investee and should account for its investment by the equity method.[9] The term **investor company** is used here to describe the company acquiring some percent of ownership in another company. The term **investee company** describes the company whose voting stock is held by another company.

Exercise of Control

When an investor holds 50 percent or more of the voting stock of an investee, it is presumed to have the ability to *control* rather than just exert substantial influence.[10] At this point, the investor is known as a **parent company** and the investee as a **subsidiary company.** When the parent/subsidiary relationship exists or when several subsidiary companies have a common parent, the group is known as **affiliates** or **affiliated companies.** The share of own-

[6] Tenneco, Inc., *1981 Annual Report,* p. 47.

[7] National Distillers and Chemical Corporation, *1981 Annual Report,* p. 23.

[8] United Technologies Corporation, *1981 Annual Report,* p. 2. Fully diluted earnings per share (explained in Chapter 17) represents the most conservative possible EPS computation.

[9] *Opinions of the Accounting Principles Board No. 18,* "Equity Method for Investments in Common Stock" (AICPA: New York, March 1971), paragraph 17.

[10] *Ibid.,* paragraph 3c.

ership not held by the subsidiary is known as the **minority interest.** Usually, the minority share of ownership is scattered among many shareholders.

A subsidiary company that is totally owned by a parent company (holding 100 percent of voting stock) is often left as a legal entity operating under its own name. Such a subsidiary would have its own set of accounting records and prepare its own financial statements for management purposes, although they may not be released publicly. A parent company may choose such an arrangement because the liability of a subsidiary corporation to its creditors is limited to the extent of its own assets.

Some wholly-owned corporations operate in one state or foreign country. In such cases, it may be advantageous from the viewpoint of regulations as to legal capital (see Chapter 16) or state or foreign tax laws for the subsidiary to operate as a legal entity.

Federal income taxes are levied at a lower rate on the first $100,000 of taxable income of a corporation. When separate legal entities file separate income tax returns, each can take advantage of the lower rates. Certain federal laws provide incentives and aid to smaller businesses; in some cases, this may be a reason to retain separate corporate identity.

Although the legal status of entities owned by a parent company may not be changed, the economic status is changed. This aspect is discussed next.

Economic versus Legal Entity

Although a group of affiliated corporations may be separate *legal* entities, the nature of their affiliation is often such that they are in substance a single *economic* entity (see Figure 22–6). In these cases, the operating results and financial condition of the economic entity are more meaningful when reported in consolidated financial statements. **Consolidated financial statements** are reports in which the assets, liabilities, revenues, and expenses of subsidiary companies are combined with those of the parent company. The result is a set of statements that represents all the individual corporations as a single economic unit. Consolidated statements do not take the place of individual financial reports for the investee corporations. However, when individual financial statements are included in a set of consolidated statements, they are not published in annual reports—the consolidated statements being considered more meaningful.

Shown in Figure 22–6 is the simple situation where one parent company (Company P) owns one subsidiary company (Company S).[11] Company P exercises control over the operating policies of Company S. If S is 100% owned by P, all dividends it pays go to P. Although each will have independent transactions with other companies in the business environment, they also have many *controlled* transactions between themselves. There may be loans or sales to each other, for instance. When such events occur between two affiliates, they are called **intercompany transactions** (discussed later). For these

[11]Recall that in the typical situation, one parent company owns many subsidiaries.

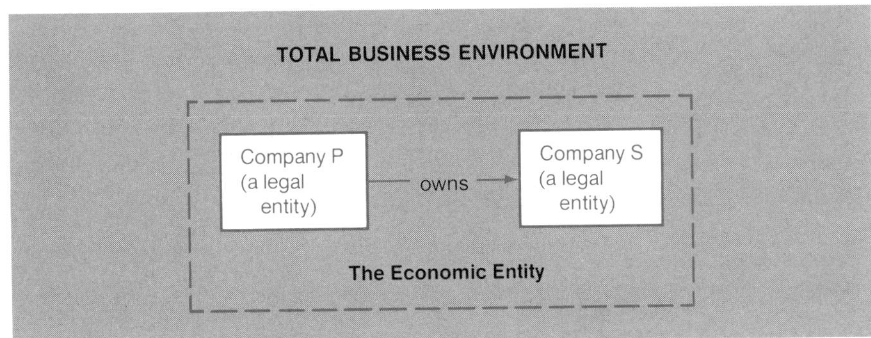

Figure 22–6 Concept of Economic Entity

reasons consolidated financial statements for the economic entity as a whole are more useful to the public than the individual statements of P and S.

The AICPA has indicated the existence of ". . . a presumption that consolidated statements are more meaningful than separate statements and that they are usually necessary for a fair presentation when one of the companies in the group directly or indirectly has a *controlling* financial interest in the other companies."[12] Such a presumption had a sound basis in the 1950s when most business combinations tended to enhance concentration in a single line of business. In today's business climate, where combinations have brought forth large diversified firms, a set of consolidated financial statements is probably less useful.

The usual definition of *controlling interest* for purposes of consolidation of financial statements is the ownership of more than 50 percent of the voting stock of the investee company.[13] The AICPA recognized certain exceptions to this general rule. Consolidated financial statements should not be prepared where:

1. Control is temporary.
2. The minority interest is so large that separate statements may be more meaningful and useful.
3. The presentation of separate statements for a subsidiary would be more informative to shareholders and creditors (for example, a subsidiary finance company owned by an industrial corporation.)
4. Control does not rest with the majority owners (as may be the case when the organization is in the hands of a trustee for reorganization or bankruptcy).[14]

In a later pronouncement, the AICPA stated that information about the accounting policies of a company is needed by financial statement users.

[12] *Accounting Research Bulletin No. 51,* "Consolidated Financial Statements" (New York: AICPA, August 1959), paragraph 1 (emphasis added).

[13] Ibid., paragraph 2.

[14] *ARB No. 51,* paragraphs 2 and 3.

Among significant accounting policies to be disclosed as an integral part of the statements is the *basis of consolidation.*[15] Recall from Chapter 19 that investments in other companies may be accounted for by the cost or equity method. This fact is recognized in the consolidation process. The consolidated statements are the same regardless of the method used to account for the investment.

In its 1982 *Annual Report,* the Ford Motor Company stated that the consolidated financial statements presented therein included ". . . the accounts of the Company and its majority-owned domestic and foreign subsidiaries except the finance, insurance, real estate, and dealership subsidiaries which are included on an equity basis."[16] Since the annual reports of practically all large corporations include consolidated financial statements, it is useful to consider some techniques of consolidation. Before this can be done, the nature of certain reciprocal accounts in the books of a parent and subsidiary must be understood. They are discussed in the next section.

Reciprocal Accounts in Different Companies

Accounts in the books of affiliates that have offsetting elements and would duplicate each other if combined are also reciprocal accounts. They can arise from the act of investment or from transactions that occur after an acquisition has been completed. Both circumstances are illustrated in the sections that follow. The similarity between reciprocal accounts in a home office and its branch and in a parent and its subsidiary is illustrated in Figure 22–7. In the

In a Home Office and Branch

In the San Diego Home Office		At the Fullerton Branch	
Fullerton Branch		**Home Office**	
1985 Jul. 31 . . . 100,000			1985 Jul. 31 . . . 100,000

In a Parent Company and Subsidiary

On the Books of Company P		On the Books of Company S	
Investment in Company S		**Common Stock**	
1985 Jan. 3. . . . 100,000			1985 Jan. 3. . . . 80,000
		Retained Earnings	
			1985 Jan. 3. . . . 20,000

Figure 22–7 Reciprocal Account Relationships

[15] *Opinions of the Accounting Principles Board No. 22,* "Disclosure of Accounting Policies" (New York: AICPA, April, 1972), paragraphs 8 and 13.

[16] P. 27.

branch and home office situation, the reciprocal accounts are in the decentralized accounts of a single company. In the parent-subsidiary situation, they are accounts in the books of two separate legal entities. Because of the purpose they serve, they are reciprocal in concept.

Example 1—Arising from Investment Assume that Company P purchased from stockholders 100 percent of the voting stock of Company S at its *book value* of $100,000 on January 3, 1985.[17] The entry on the books of Company P to record the acquisition is:

1985					
Jan.	3	Investment in Company S		100,000	
		Cash			100,000
		To record the purchase of 100 percent of common stock of S.			

There would be no entry on the books of Company S to record this purchase; its stock remains outstanding in the hands of a new stockholder. Note also that Company S does not receive the cash; it goes to its former stockholders who sold their stock to Company P.

Assume further that immediately after the purchase, the balance sheet amounts of the two companies were as follows:

	Company P	Company S
Cash	$ 50,000	$ 40,000
Investment in Company S	100,000	0
Property, plant, and equipment	150,000	65,000
Total assets	$300,000	$105,000
Liabilities	$ 75,000	$ 5,000
Common stock	175,000	80,000
Retained earnings	50,000	20,000
Total liabilities and stockholders' equity	$300,000	$105,000

From the above, it would appear that the combined assets of the two corporations are $405,000 = ($300,000 + $105,000). The combined liabilities and stockholders' equity would appear to be the same amount. Such an assumption, however, fails to consider the presence of reciprocal accounts in the books of the two affiliates. The Investment in Company S account in the assets of P represents equity in Company S. At the same time, the Common Stock and Retained Earnings accounts on the books of S represent ownership equity held by Company P. These sets of accounts are reciprocal accounts that must be eliminated by use of a work sheet before a consolidated balance

[17]At the introductory principles level, the investment at book value of acquired assets is the only example used. Accounting for investments at other than book value raises issues of fair market value of assets and liabilities that are beyond the scope of this book.

sheet *on the date of acquistion* can be prepared. Such a work sheet is shown in Figure 22–8. It is important to note that the elimination entry made in the work sheet would *never be journalized or posted* in the accounting records of either the parent or subsidiary company. It is a work sheet entry only to remove the reciprocal accounts (or reciprocal elements of accounts to be discussed later) before preparing a consolidated financial statement. Note in Figure 22–8 that the work sheet amounts are added horizontally, taking into consideration the amounts in the Eliminations columns. As can be seen from the work sheet, the combined assets of the economic entity are $305,000 (not $405,000). To have failed to eliminate reciprocal elements before combining all amounts would give an inflated picture of its total worth.

In recording corporate acquisitions, there are two types of accounting that apply. One is *purchase* accounting, which involves the recognition of the assets and liabilities of the subsidiary at their fair market value as of the date of acquisition in the consolidated statements. The other is *pooling of interests,* in which assets and liabilities are recognized at book value in the consolidated financial statements. Which method to use depends upon how the acquisition was made and the nature of ownership after the acquisition. Since the accounting issues discussed in the next section apply to both methods because of the assumption that cost of the subsidiary is at book value, a detailed discussion of purchase versus pooling of interests is not essential at this point.

Example 2—Arising after Acquisition Affiliated companies often have transactions with each other. Such transactions introduce both new reciprocal accounts and reciprocal elements into existing accounts. Some typical examples of such transactions are:

☐ Intercompany revenue and expense, for example, sales of merchandise that inflate both the Sales and Purchases accounts from the viewpoint of the economic entity.

☐ Intercompany receivables and payables that may arise from sales or loans to each other.

☐ Intercompany dividends—for example, any dividends paid by Company S would be received by its parent, Company P.

Because of transactions of this nature, it is not possible to convey an accurate picture of the financial position of an *economic entity* by simply combining the balance sheet accounts into a consolidated statement. Neither can the results of operations be correctly portrayed by combining accounts to produce a consolidated income statement and statement of retained earnings. To eliminate the "double counting" of reciprocal accounts or their elements, the accountant prepares a work sheet on which eliminations similar to those in Figure 22–8 are made. To illustrate the concept and techniques of consolidation after acquisition, Example 1 is modified slightly to include intercompany receivables and payables. Assume that Company P loaned $20,000 on a 15 per-

COMPANY P AND SUBSIDIARY S Work Sheet for Consolidated Statements January 3, 1985					
			Eliminations		Consolidated Balance Sheet
Account Titles	Company P	Company S	Debit	Credit	
Debit Accounts					
Cash	50,000	40,000			90,000
Investment in Company S	100,000	0		(a) 100,000	0
Property, Plant, and Equipment	150,000	65,000			215,000
Totals	300,000	105,000			305,000
Credit Accounts					
Liabilities	75,000	5,000			80,000
Common Stock	175,000	80,000	(a) 80,000		175,000
Retained Earnings	50,000	20,000	(a) 20,000		50,000
Totals	300,000	105,000	100,000	100,000	305,000

Figure 22–8 **Work Sheet for Consolidated Statements at Date of Acquisition**

cent 180-day note to its subsidiary on January 4, 1985. The entries to record the loan are below.

On the books of Company P:

1985					
Jan.	4	Notes Receivable from S		20,000	
		Cash			20,000
		To record 180-day loan to subsidiary at 15%.			

On the books of Company S:

1985					
Jan.	4	Cash		20,000	
		Notes Payable to P			20,000
		To record 180-day loan from parent at 15%.			

If consolidated statements are to be prepared as of January 4, the eliminations shown in Figure 22–9 would be needed. Since there have been no transactions with the outside business environment, the total assets of the economic entity are still $305,000. The elimination of $120,000 in reciprocal accounts shown in Figure 22–9 prevents the combining of amounts that are generated internally within the economic entity. Note that there is no need to make an elimination to reflect the transfer of cash. Although $20,000 has

COMPANY P AND SUBSIDIARY S[a]
Work Sheet for Consolidated Statements
January 4, 1985

Account Titles	Company P	Company S	Eliminations Debit	Eliminations Credit	Consolidated Balance Sheet
Debit Accounts					
Cash	30,000	60,000			90,000
Notes Receivable from S	20,000	0		(b) 20,000	0
Investment in Company S	100,000	0		(a) 100,000	0
Property, Plant, and Equipment	150,000	65,000			215,000
Totals	300,000	125,000			305,000
Credit Accounts					
Liabilities	75,000	5,000			80,000
Notes Payable to P	0	20,000	(b) 20,000		0
Common Stock	175,000	80,000	(a) 80,000		175,000
Retained Earnings	50,000	20,000	(a) 20,000		50,000
Totals	300,000	125,000	120,000	120,000	305,000

[a]This illustration makes the simplifying assumption that no revenue and expense transactions took place between P and S during January 1 to 4. The only intercompany transaction was the loaning of $20,000 on the note.

Figure 22–9 **Work Sheet for Consolidated Statements after Date of Acquisition—Balance Sheet Items**

moved from P to S, the combined amount of $90,000 is still an accurate measure of total cash in the economic entity. By the end of the accounting year, many other transactions would have taken place. Some of them would be intercompany transactions of the type described earlier. Because they affect the operating results as well as the balance sheet, one more illustration is given to show the elimination of such an item.

Example 3—Elimination of Income Statement Item In Example 2, an intercompany loan was made by the parent to the subsidiary. When this loan was repaid the parent would record interest earned and the subsidiary would record interest expense of $1,500 = ($20,000 × 0.15 × 180/360). To include these items in the consolidated income statement would inflate both the interest earned and the interest expense of the economic entity. Thus, they should be eliminated so that the consolidated income statement will reflect only revenue and expense transactions with outsiders. The elimination of this item is shown in Figure 22–10.

COMPANY P AND SUBSIDIARY S
Work Sheet for Consolidated Statements
December 31, 1985

Account Titles	Company P	Company S	Eliminations Debit	Eliminations Credit	Consolidated Trial Balance
Debit Accounts					
Cash	81,500	71,500			153,000
Investment in Company S	100,000[a]	0		(a) 100,000	0
Property, Plant, and Equipment	150,000	65,000			215,000
Purchases	300,000	200,000			500,000
Interest Expense	0	1,500		(b) 1,500	0
Cost of Goods Sold and Other Expenses	55,000	40,000			95,000
Totals	686,500	378,000			963,000
Credit Accounts					
Liabilities	60,000	18,000			78,000
Common Stock	175,000	80,000	(a) 80,000		175,000
Retained Earnings	50,000	20,000	(a) 20,000		50,000
Sales	400,000	260,000			660,000
Interest Earned	1,500	0	(b) 1,500		0
Totals	686,500	378,000	101,500	101,500	963,000

[a] In order to keep this illustration simple, it is assumed that the cost method was used to account for the investment. Accordingly, the Investment account balance remains unchanged and there is no Investor's Share of Investee Income (or Loss) account on P's books.

Figure 22–10 **Work Sheet for Year-End Consolidated Statements—Income Statement Items**

Other amounts except the Investment account—property, plant, and equipment—and the stockholders' equity in Figure 22–10 are assumed to have arisen from 1985 transactions, and represent the preclosing trial balances of Companies P and S. There were no intercompany sales between these two affiliates. If there had been, the amounts would be reflected in both the Sales and the Purchases accounts of the two companies and should be eliminated against each other. In Figure 22–10, elimination (a) (under the cost method) is necessary to avoid double counting the investment, as explained in Example 1. This problem still remains at the end of the year. Elimination (b) removes $1,500 of interest paid by Company S to Company P from the consolidated income statement because this transaction does not extend outside the scope of the economic entity.

statements. There would be columns added for the consolidated income statement, consolidated statement of retained earnings, and consolidated balance sheet. The formal consolidated financial statements would be prepared from the work sheet. Since this chapter is designed to introduce only the basic concepts, this extension is not illustrated here.

As noted earlier, some eliminations are quite complex and will not be illustrated here. Two points should be kept in mind about the techniques of consolidation:

1. The only events that change the status of the economic entity are transactions with outside business environment. In consolidated statements, therefore, the effects of intercompany transactions must be eliminated.

2. The elimination entries on the work sheet are for the purposes of preparing consolidated statements only. They are never reflected in the records of any of the affiliates or in any affiliate's financial statements.

Minority Interest

In the examples used up to this point, it has been assumed that the parent company owned 100 percent of the voting stock of subsidiary companies. Remember, however, that unless there are indications to the contrary, ownership of more than 50 percent of the voting stock of a subsidiary is sufficient to presume control and thus to present consolidated financial statements. The voting stock held by companies or persons other than the parent company (obviously less than 50 percent) determines the amount of minority interest in all subsidiaries not wholly-owned by the parent company. In a consolidated balance sheet, the minority interests represent neither liabilities nor stockholders' equity of the parent. The total amount represented by minority interest is usually presented as a single amount in the total liabilities and stockholders' equity side of a balance sheet *between* the liabilities and the stockholders' equity. For example, Ford Motor Company reported total liabilities and stockholders' equity of $21,961.7 billion at December 31, 1982. Of this total, $130.1 million was reported between the liabilities and the stockholders' equity as "Minority interests in net assets of consolidated subsidiaries."[18]

Importance of Acquisition Information

The reader of a set of consolidated financial statements should be alert to acquisitions because they affect the operating results. They are normally disclosed in the "Notes to Financial Statements"—often referred to as **footnote disclosure.** For example, Dow Chemical disclosed in Note G to its 1981 *Annual Report* that "Under the terms of an Agreement and Plan of Reorganization with Richarson-Merrill, Inc. (RMI), the Company acquired the ethical

[18]1982 *Annual Report,* p. 26.

pharmaceutical business of RMI in exchange for approximately 7.3 million shares of Dow common stock having a fair market value of $250 million."[19] The footnote goes on to explain details of the acquisition.

As indicated in Chapter 21, corporations are required to show the effects of discontinued operations—the opposite of acquisitions—in their income statements. No such requirement exists for acquisitions, yet they can have a significant effect on income and changes in assets and liabilities. The informed reader will look carefully at footnotes to financial statements to determine the effect of acquisitions of all types.

Appendix 22.1 International Accounting

Introduction

Many corporations today are multinational. For example, Ford Motor Company's 1982 *Annual Report* indicated that about 54 percent of its total revenues were generated in the United States. Sales in Europe were about 22 percent; in Canada, 10 percent; and in Latin America, 8 percent; with remaining sales in several other countries. Because the values of national currencies fluctuate constantly with respect to each other, international operations create special problems in accounting. The basic issues and related concepts of international accounting are explained in this appendix.

Learning Goals

To understand the nature of changes in relative values of national currencies.

To understand the concept of a functional currency.

To be able to compute and record exchange gains and losses.

Currency Fluctuations

When a seller in the United States makes a sale to a buyer in France, the seller expects to end up with dollars when the collection is made. In a similar manner, the buyer in France expects to pay in francs. If the buyer pays in francs, the seller must use those francs to purchase dollars—a transaction called **foreign currency exchange.** If the relative values of the dollar and the franc remain constant during the period from sale to collection and exchange, there would be no problem. However, currencies don't remain constant; in fact, they consistently fluctuate in value against each other. May 23, 1983 was considered to be a quiet trading Monday on the foreign exchange markets. Yet, the French franc was traded at a low of 13.38 cents per franc,

[19] P. 24.

recovering to 13.45 cents at the end of the trading day in New York. Other national currencies rise and fall in a similar manner daily as they are exchanged for each other. This relationship can be expressed in either currency. For example, assume that the franc gained strength against the dollar and rose to an exchange value of 15 cents. We could simply say that it required $0.15 to purchase one franc. A company in France would probably take the opposite view; that is, that the dollar is worth 6⅔ francs = ($1.00 ÷ $0.15) because it would have to exchange 6⅔ francs to obtain one dollar.

Financial Reporting Issues

Two basic financial reporting issues arise when international transactions involve dealings in more than one national currency. One of these basic issues is the problem of translating financial statement items from foreign currencies into the *reporting currency* used in combined statements. Such a problem arises when a company has a foreign branch or when a parent corporation has a foreign subsidiary. The other basic issue is the problem of foreign currency fluctuations which occur while a transaction is being completed. In both cases, the translation of foreign currencies may result in a gain or loss from currency exchange.

Translation for Combined Statements

In December 1981, the Financial Accounting Standards Board (FASB) issued revised guidelines for transactions in which the currency of one country must be exchanged for that of another.[1] In that issuance, the FASB introduced the concept of a functional currency. Basically, the **functional currency** is the currency that is being used to *measure* the assets, liabilities, revenues, or expenses. For example, a United States corporation may have a subsidiary, located in France, that makes sales both in France and Germany. A basic problem is determining whether those sales should be measured in French francs or German marks before being translated into dollars in preparation of a consolidated income statement. The FASB said that the functional currency should be ". . . the currency of the environment in which an entity primarily generates revenues and expends cash."[2] Based on a set of rather complex rules, an entity must decide which country's currency is the functional currency before the translation into dollars can be made. When the functional currency and the reporting currency are not the same, **foreign currency exchange gains and losses** result from translation into the reporting currency.[3] An example that illustrates the problems of translation of a foreign currency into dollars for recording international transactions is illustrated next.

[1]*Statement of Financial Accounting Standards No. 52,* "Foreign Currency Translation" (Stamford, Conn.: Financial Accounting Standards Board, December, 1981).

[2]*FASB Statement No. 52,* paragraph 5.

[3]For example, if demand in the United States for French goods or services increases significantly, there will be a greater dollar demand for French francs. As a result, the price of francs will increase, and it may be said that the franc has risen relative to the dollar.

Translation for Specific Transactions

Assume that Alabama Corporation is a United States company engaged in significant foreign operations. Its basic reporting currency is dollars; it closes the books annually each December 31. On December 16, 1985, it made a sale in France for 2,000,000 francs when the exchange rate was \$0.15 per franc. On Alabama Corporation's books, the sale would be recorded as follows:

1985					
Dec.	16	Accounts Receivable		300,000	
		Sales			300,000
		To record a sale for 2,000,000 francs at an exchange rate of \$0.15, n/30.			

Recall that the rate of \$0.15 translates into 6⅔ francs per dollar. The dollar translation on the date of sale is \$300,000 = (2,000,000 ÷ 6⅔). The franc is the functional currency in this case.

When Alabama Corporation closed its books on December 31, 1985, the exchange rate had risen to \$0.16⅔ per franc. The franc had gained in respect to the dollar. Since payment is to be measured in the *functional currency,* the 2,000,000 francs to be collected now have a dollar value of \$333,333.33 = (2,000,000 × \$0.16⅔). The exchange gain is recognized when the books are closed as follows:

1985					
Dec.	31	Accounts Receivable		33,333.33	
		Foreign Currency Exchange Gain			33,333.33
		To recognize gain from translation of asset receivable in foreign currency.			

The exchange gain is a part of net income of Alabama Corporation in 1985. It is reported in the other revenues section of the income statement.

Assume further that, on the date of collection, the dollar has gained. The new exchange rate is \$0.135 per franc. The journal entry for collection of the receivable is as follows:

1986					
Jan.	15	Cash		270,000.00	
		Foreign Currency Exchange Loss		63,333.33	
		Accounts Receivable			333,333.33
		To record collection of 2,000,000 francs at an exchange rate of \$0.135.			

The exchange loss is a part of 1986 net income. It is reported in the other expenses section of the income statement.

Recording these gains and losses is a major accounting problem in international operations. Other problems in accounting arise when international corporations take actions to protect themselves against the effect of translation gains and losses. They do this by buying and selling contracts for future acceptance of foreign currencies. This practice, known as *hedging,* raises complex accounting issues that are treated in more advanced accounting courses.

Glossary

Affiliates (or **affiliated companies**) Companies between which a parent/subsidiary relationship exists.

Consolidated financial statements Financial reports in which the assets, liabilities, revenues, and expenses of subsidiary companies are combined with those of the parent company.

Eliminations Removal of duplicate items in subsidiary and parent financial statements from the consolidated amount.

Footnote disclosure Information disclosed in notes to financial statements rather than in the bodies of the statements.

Foreign currency exchange A transaction in which one currency is used to purchase another.

Foreign currency exchange gains and losses Gains and losses from translation of a functional currency into a reporting currency.

Functional currency The currency that is being used to *measure* the assets, liabilities, revenues, and expenses.

Intercompany transactions Transactions that take place between affiliated companies.

Investee company A corporation whose stock is acquired by another corporation.

Investor company A corporation acquiring the stock of another corporation.

Minority interest The portion of subsidiary corporation ownership held by stockholders other than the parent company.

Parent company A company that owns a controlling interest (more than 50 percent) in voting stock of another company.

Reciprocal accounts Accounts in two locations that offset each other and would cause double counting if combined into a consolidated total.

Subsidiary company A company controlled by another corporation that holds a controlling interest (more than 50 percent) in its voting stock.

Questions

Q22–1 What advantage is gained from decentralizing the accounts of a branch into a separate set of records away from the home office? How does the home office ledger reflect the absence of those records?

Q22–2 What is the nature and purpose of reciprocal accounts in a single company? In different companies?

Q22–3 What are some reasons that a corporation would make a long-term investment in stock of another corporation? How do these reasons compare with reasons for *temporary* investments in stock of another company?

Q22–4 What is the difference between ability to "exert substantial influence" and ability to "control"? Why do you believe a company making an investment of 33⅓ percent of the stock of another company would not go ahead and buy at least 51 percent, since it is already past the 20 percent area?

Q22–5 In its 1982 *Annual Report,* Gearhart Industries, Inc., reported that it had issued 150,000 shares valued at $4,344,000 to acquire the outstanding minority interest of a consolidated subsidiary. Does this make Gearhart a parent company, or was it already one? Explain your answer.

Q22–6 Some corporations report that they are accounting for investments in other companies by the equity method. What does this tell you about the percent of ownership? Why do you think a company would benefit from having ownership in this proportion?

Q22–7 Is a parent company an investor company? Is an investor company always a parent company? Explain.

Q22–8 What is required for a group of companies to be called "affiliated"? Must each affiliate own a portion of each of the other affiliates? Explain.

Q22–9 What is the minority interest? Do the investors holding the minority interests have voting rights? Do they receive dividends? Explain.

Q22–10 What are consolidated financial statements? When is it appropriate to use them in reporting to stockholders and to the public?

Q22–11 What is an intercompany transaction? Give three examples. How do they fit into consolidated statements? Why?

Q22–12 Look at Appendix B to this book. What are some significant footnote disclosures that are not in the body of the statements? For each that you name, discuss how the information is useful to stockholders; potential investors; creditors.

Exercises

E22–1 *Establishment of a branch*

On April 1, 1985, Tampa Company opened a branch in Sarasota with the transfer of $20,000 in cash and $53,000 of merchandise. Record the establishment of the branch (1) on the home office books, and (2) on the books of the branch office. Both use a periodic inventory system.

E22–2 *Selected branch and home office entries*

In general journal form, record the following transactions on the books of Gala Department Store and its Holly Hill Mall Branch (both use a periodic inventory system):

1985		
Jul.	1	The main store transferred $8,650 of merchandise to the branch.
	1	Branch sales were $2,050 in cash and $4,725 on account. The main store had sales of $1,125 in cash and $5,750 on account.
	2	Monthly rent for the branch of $1,200 was paid by check from the home office.
	2	The branch deposited surplus cash of $2,500 to the account of Gala Department Store.
	3	The branch paid miscellaneous expenses of $225 from its own bank account.
	3	The branch purchased merchandise on account at a cost of $1,630.
	5	Store supplies that cost $370 were transferred from the main store to the branch.

E22–3 *Branch closing entries*

On September 30, 1985, the books of Gettysburg branch of the Pennsylvania Company showed the following selected account balances:

Account Title	Debits	Credits
Sales		$87,600
Shipments from Home Office	$42,100	
Purchases	20,400	
Rent Expense	975	
Sales Salaries Expense	3,100	
Supplies Expense	670	
Advertising Expense	880	
Inventory (August 31, 1985)	19,750	

By physical count, the valuation of the branch inventory on September 30 was determined to be $16,020. Record the closing entries for the branch making any necessary entries on the home office books.

E22–4 *Review of equity method*

On April 13, 1985, Valencia, Inc., purchased for cash 18,000 of the 45,000 outstanding shares of voting common stock of the Keys Corporation at $20 per share. On June 6, 1985, Valencia received a cash dividend from Keys of $0.30 per share, and on June 30, 1985 (the end of its fiscal year), Keys Corporation reported a net income of $60,000. Record these events in general journal form.

E22–5 *Exceptions to consolidated statements*

Pensacola Company (a machine manufacturer) owns 100 percent of the voting stock in three other corporations: (1) Gull Point Company, a producer of parts used in Pensacola's assembly operations; (2) Warrington Finance Company, which provides loans to purchasers of Pensacola's products; and (3) Santa Rosa Company, a company in the hands of a trustee during bankruptcy proceedings. Which of these affiliates should be combined in the consolidated financial statements? Give reasons if you decide that any should not.

E22–6 *Income tax effect of organization*

Milton Health Care, Inc., owns 100 percent of the stock in three companies. The affiliates had net incomes before income tax in 1985 as follows:

Milton Health Care, Inc.	$60,000
Bagdad Rest Home	24,000
Yellow River Bestcare, Inc.	75,600
Cottagehill Village, Inc.	54,650

Assume corporate federal income tax rates to be:

Taxable Income	**Rate**
$0 to $25,000	15%
$25,001 to $50,000	18
$50,001 to $75,000	30
$75,001 to $100,000	40
Over $100,000	46

Compute the income tax expense of the affiliated group filing tax returns as individual corporations. Then compute the income tax expense if all the corporate identities were merged into the parent company and filed a single tax return. Which do you recommend? (Assume that the income tax rates apply uniformly to individual companies and the consolidated group.)

E22–7 *Intercompany transactions—eliminations*

Parents Company owns 100 percent of the voting stock of Daughter, Inc. Included in the trial balances of the two companies at the end of the accounting year 1985 are the following:

a. A note payable to Downtown Bank on the books of Parents for $50,000.
b. A note payable to Parents from Daughter for $30,000.
c. Sales as follows:
   Parents: $60,000 (10 percent to Daughter).
   Daughter: $180,000 (75 percent to Parents).
d. Accounts receivable as follows:
   Parents: $50,000 (15 percent from Daughter).
   Daughter: $30,000 (90 percent from Parents).

What amounts (if any) should be eliminated when the financial statements are combined into consolidated statements?

E22–8
Intercompany transactions—inventory profits

Mile High Corporation sold 120 hang gliders to Grandfather Mountain Dealers, its 100 percent owned subsidiary, in 1985. The gliders cost $4,800 each and were sold to the dealer for $5,280 each. At the end of 1985, Grandfather Mountain Dealers had sold 107 of these gliders; the remaining 13 were still on hand in ending inventory. Compute the amount of Grandfather Mountain Dealers' inventory to be eliminated from the inventory amount in the consolidated balance sheet.

E22–9
Elimination of investment accounts

At the end of 1985, the following accounts were in the trial balances of Columbus Corporation and its wholly-owned subsidiary, Grandview Company:

Account Titles	Columbus Corporation	Grandview Company
Investment in Stocks—Common Stock of Grandview Company	$1,250,000	$ 0
Common Stock, $5 Par Value	500,000	400,000
Paid-in Capital—Excess over Par Value, Common	2,600,000	675,000
Retained Earnings	1,565,000	175,000

What is the amount of each account to be shown in the consolidated balance sheet?

E22–10
Preparing a partial balance sheet with minority interest

On December 31, 1981, American Telephone and Telegraph Company included the following items in millions of dollars in its *Annual Report:*

Current liabilities	$15,071.0
Long-term and intermediate-term debt	43,876.9
Common stock, $16⅔ par value, 900,000,000 shares authorized, 815,108,000 shares outstanding	13,585.1
Proceeds in excess of par value, common	14,929.1
Reinvested earnings	26,520.6
Convertible $4 cumulative preferred stock (includes proceeds in excess of stated value)	335.8
Ownership interest of others in consolidated subsidiaries	968.8

Using these selected items and the terminology used in the textbook, prepare a partial balance sheet.

E22–11
Work sheet for home office and branch

On June 30, 1985, the account balances of the Ceredo Company and its Kenova branch were as follows:

Account Title	Ceredo Home Office	Kenova Branch
Cash	$ 60,000	$25,600
Accounts Receivable	185,620	42,150
Merchandise Inventory	47,050	32,115
Property, Plant, and Equipment	196,000	0
Kenova Branch	71,115	0
Accounts Payable	72,800	28,750
Home Office	0	71,115
Common Stock	400,000	0
Retained Earnings	86,985	0

Enter the trial balance figures on a work sheet to combine the accounts, complete the work sheet, and prepare a combined balance sheet.

E22–12 *Work sheet for parent and subsidiary*

On December 31, 1985, the accounts of Antelope Corporation and its wholly-owned subsidiary, Eagle Corporation, showed the following balances:

Account Title	Antelope Corporation	Eagle Corporation
Cash	$100,000	$ 40,000
Accounts Receivable from Eagle	15,600	0
Accounts Receivable—Other	60,500	32,180
Investment in Eagle Corporation	163,930	0
Property, Plant, and Equipment	182,250	125,600
Accounts Payable to Antelope	0	15,600
Accounts Payable—Other	31,500	18,250
Common Stock	400,000	125,000
Retained Earnings	90,780	38,930

Enter the balances on a work sheet to prepare consolidated financial statements, complete the work sheet, and prepare a consolidated balance sheet.

E22–13 *Computing foreign exchange rates*

(Appendix) As of May 24, 1983, the following exchange rates were in effect:

	Cost in U.S. Dollars
German mark	$0.4009
Swiss franc	0.4811
French franc	0.1336
British pound	1.5683

Compute the number of units of each currency needed to obtain one U.S. dollar. Round out your answer to four decimal points.

E22–14 *Computing exchange gains or losses.*

(Appendix) On June 16, 1985, American Grain Company sold a shipment to German importers for 2,500,000 marks when the exchange rate in New York was $0.40 = 1 mark. The invoice carries terms of n/30 and is to be paid in marks. On June 30, when American Grain closed its books to prepare year-end consolidated statements, the mark closed on the foreign exchange market at $0.41 = 1 mark. On July 16, 1985, the bill was collected when the mark closed on the foreign exchange market at $0.395 = 1 mark. Prepare journal entries on American Grain Company's books to record the sale, closing of the books, and the collection.

A Problems

P22–1A *Branch and home office entries*

On May 1, 1985, Toledo Company opened a branch in Harbor View with the transfer of $30,000 in cash and $90,000 in merchandise to the new branch. Both the company and the branch use a periodic inventory system. The following additional transactions occurred in May:

1985		
May	1	The home office paid $1,500 of May rent for the branch by check.
	2	The branch purchased $12,000 of additional merchandise for cash.
	6	During its grand opening sale this date, the branch made sales as follows: cash, $6,870; on account, $3,245.
	7	Salaries expense paid by the branch in cash were as follows: sales salaries, $825; general and administrative salaries, $550 (ignore payroll taxes).

8 Office supplies that cost $300 and store supplies that cost $650 were transferred from the main store to the branch. The home office carries these supplies in asset accounts, but the branch debits expense each time they are received.

10 Cumulative branch sales since opening day were recorded as follows: cash, $32,100; on account, $20,670.

13 The branch transferred excess cash of $35,595 to the company's bank account.

15 An additional $30,000 of merchandise was transferred from the main store to the branch.

17 Cumulative sales for the week at the branch were recorded as follows: cash, $36,800; on account, $23,500.

17 After the transfer of $35,000 excess cash from the branch to the company's bank account, it was decided to close the branch books to review results of operations. By physical count, the branch inventory was determined to be $45,200.

Required:

1. In general journal form, record all transactions (including establishment of the branch) and closing entries on (1) the books of the branch, and (2) the home office books.

2. Open reciprocal accounts in the branch and home office ledgers and post appropriate journal entries to them.

P22–2A *Branch and home office individual and combined statements*

On April 30, 1985, the accounts at Saskatoon Company and its branch at Moose Jaw had the following balances:

Account Title	Saskatoon Home Office	Moose Jaw Branch
Cash	$ 32,100	$ 26,850
Accounts Receivable	186,310	60,130
Merchandise Inventory	79,185	52,140
Land	38,500	0
Building	146,300	0
Equipment	67,280	0
Moose Jaw Branch	96,115	0
Accounts Payable	60,870	15,085
Notes Payable	0	2,000
Bonds Payable	80,000	0
Common Stock	300,000	0
Retained Earnings	138,960	0
Saskatoon Home Office	0	96,115
Sales	790,000	295,250
Cost of Goods Sold	534,200	201,910
Selling Expenses	148,200	43,820
General and Administrative Expenses	41,640	23,600

Required (ignoring income tax):

1. Prepare an income statement for April and a balance sheet at April 30 that reflect home office operations only.

2. Prepare an income statement for April and a balance sheet at April 30 that reflect branch operations only.

3. Enter the balances on a work sheet, complete the work sheet, and prepare a combined income statement for April and a balance sheet at April 30, 1985.

P22–3A *Elimination of investment*

Gardner Corporation and its wholly-owned subsidiary, Webb Inc., have the following items in their trial balances on December 2, 1985, immediately after Gardner made the investment at book value:

Account Titles	Gardner Corporation	Webb Inc.
Investment in Stocks—Common Stock of Webb Inc.	$867,500	$ 0
Common Stock, $1 Par Value	500,000	0
Common Stock, $2 Par Value	0	300,000
Paid-in Capital—Excess over Par Value, Common	623,200	212,500
Retained Earnings	311,520	355,000

Required: Enter the balances on a work sheet for consolidated statements, make the necessary eliminations, and carry the consolidated amounts to the proper column.

P22–4A *Elimination of intercompany payables and receivables*

Austin Corporation and its wholly-owned subsidiary, Lufkin Inc., have the following items in their trial balances on June 30, 1985, the end of the fiscal year for both companies:

Account Titles	Austin Corporation	Lufkin Inc.
Accounts Receivable—General Customers	$275,000	$118,000
Accounts Receivable—Affiliate	42,500	15,650
Accounts Payable—General Creditors	186,750	92,670
Accounts Payable—Affiliate	15,650	42,500
Notes Receivable—Affiliate	75,000	0
Notes Payable to Banks	150,000	0
Notes Payable to Affiliate	0	75,000

Required: Enter the balances on a work sheet for consolidated statements, make the necessary eliminations, and carry the consolidated amounts to the proper column.

P22–5A *Minority interest on the balance sheet*

Ivaco Inc., whose stock is traded on the Toronto and Montreal Stock Exchanges, had the following items as part of the liabilities and shareholders' equity in its 1981 *Annual Report* (dollars are in thousands and items are listed here in alphabetical sequence):

	December 31, 1981 Amount
Accounts payable and accrued liabilities:	
Trade and other	$ 86,470
Directors	2,086
Bank indebtedness, partly secured	106,942
Capital stock	60,616
Current maturities of long-term liabilities	19,326
Current portion of deferred income taxes	8,882
Deferred income taxes	65,024
Long-term liabilities	207,319
Minority interest	3,970
Retained earnings	145,667
Total liabilities and shareholders' equity	706,302

Required:

1. Treating deferred income taxes as long-term liabilities except where otherwise indicated, prepare the liabilities and shareholders' equity section of the balance sheet.

2. Describe the nature of the minority interest and explain its placement in the balance sheet.

P22–6A

Thought-provoking problem: evaluation of branch performance

On December 31, 1985, after Houston Company had operated a branch at Baytown for a year, the trial balances of the two sets of books are as follows:

Account Title	Houston Company	Baytown Branch
Cash	$ 98,510	$ 32,160
Accounts Receivable	196,315	63,110
Merchandise Inventory	394,250	128,560
Property, Plant, and Equipment (net)	322,400	0
Baytown Branch	175,691	0
Accounts Payable	86,980	21,540
Bonds Payable	100,000	0
Common Stock	550,000	0
Retained Earnings	137,213	0
Houston Home Office	0	175,691
Sales	1,970,280	625,200
Cost of Goods Sold	1,280,682	487,656
Selling Expenses	199,300	62,640
General and Administrative Expenses	177,325	48,315

The chief accountant has expressed some concern over the rate of return on the investment in the branch at Baytown. The weighted average balance of the Baytown Branch account has been $180,000 during 1985. The branch manager has been given rather strict guidance with regard to inventory policies, but has complete freedom to establish branch selling prices.

Required: Evaluate the performance of the Baytown branch as compared to the performance of the home office during 1985 and make appropriate recommendations. Support your conclusions and recommendations with computations.

B Problems

P22–1B

Branch and home office entries

On October 1, 1985, San Marcos Company opened a branch in Kyle with the transfer of $24,000 in cash and $72,000 in merchandise to the new branch. Both the company and the branch use the periodic inventory system. The following additional transactions occurred in October:

1985

Oct. 1 The home office paid $1,200 of October rent for the branch by check.

2 The branch purchased $9,600 of additional merchandise for cash.

7 During its grand opening sale, the branch made sales as follows: cash, $5,496; on account, $2,596.

8 Salaries expense paid by the branch in cash were as follows: sales salaries, $660; general and administrative salaries, $440 (ignore payroll taxes).

9 Office supplies that cost $240 and store supplies that cost $520 were transferred from the main store to the branch. The home office carries these supplies in asset accounts, but the branch debits expense each time they are received.

11 Cumulative branch sales since opening day were recorded as follows: cash, $25,680; on account, $16,536.

14 The branch transferred excess cash of $28,476 to the company's bank account.

15 An additional $24,000 of merchandise was transferred from the main store to the branch.

18 Cumulative sales for the week at the branch were recorded as follows: cash, $29,440; on account, $18,800.

18 After the transfer of $28,000 excess cash from the branch to the company's bank account, it was decided to close the branch books to review the results of operations. By physical count, the branch inventory was determined to be $36,160.

Required:

1. In general journal form, record all transactions (including establishment of the branch) and closing entries on (1) the books of the branch, and (2) the home office books.

2. Open reciprocal accounts in the branch and home office ledgers and post appropriate journal entries to them.

P22–2B *Branch and home office individual and combined statements*

On June 30, 1985, the accounts at Las Cruces Company and its branch at Dona Ana had the following balances:

Account Title	Las Cruces Home Office	Dona Ana Branch
Cash	$ 38,520	$ 32,220
Accounts Receivable	223,572	72,156
Merchandise Inventory	95,022	62,568
Land	46,200	0
Building	175,560	0
Equipment	80,736	0
Dona Ana Branch	115,338	0
Accounts Payable	73,044	18,102
Notes Payable	0	2,400
Bonds Payable	96,000	0
Common Stock	360,000	0
Retained Earnings	166,752	0
Las Cruces Home Office	0	115,338
Sales	948,000	354,300
Cost of Goods Sold	641,040	242,292
Selling Expenses	177,840	52,584
General and Administrative Expenses	49,968	28,320

Required (ignoring income tax):

1. Prepare an income statement for June and a balance sheet at June 30 that reflect home office operations only.

2. Prepare an income statement for June and a balance sheet at June 30 that reflect branch operations only.

3. Enter the balances on a work sheet, complete the work sheet, and prepare a combined income statement for June and a balance sheet at June 30, 1985.

P22–3B *Elimination of investment*

Boiling Corporation and its wholly-owned subsidiary, Springs Inc., have the following items in their trial balances on December 1, 1985, immediately after Boiling made the investment at book value:

Account Titles	Boiling Corporation	Springs Inc.
Investment in Stocks—Common Stock of Springs Inc.	$433,750	$ 0
Common Stock, $1 Par Value	250,000	0
Common Stock, $2 Par Value	0	150,000
Paid-in Capital—Excess over Par Value, Common	311,600	106,250
Retained Earnings	155,760	177,500

Required: Enter the balances on a work sheet for consolidated statements, make the necessary eliminations, and carry the consolidated amounts to the proper column.

P22–4B
Elimination of intercompany payables and receivables

Loyola Corporation and its wholly-owned subsidiary, Bayou Inc., have the following items in their trial balances on June 30, 1985, the end of the fiscal year of both companies:

Account Titles	Loyola Corporation	Bayou Inc.
Accounts Receivable—General Customers	$137,500	$59,000
Accounts Receivable—Affiliate	21,250	7,825
Accounts Payable—General Creditors	93,375	46,335
Accounts Payable—Affiliate	7,825	21,250
Notes Receivable—Affiliate	37,500	0
Notes Payable to Bank	75,000	0
Notes Payable to Affiliate	0	37,500

Required: Enter the balances on a work sheet for consolidated statements, make the necessary eliminations, and carry the consolidated amounts to the proper column.

P22–5B
Minority interest on the balance sheet

Ivaco Inc., whose stock is traded on the Toronto and Montreal Stock Exchanges, had the following items as part of the liabilities and shareholders' equity in its 1981 *Annual Report* (dollars are in thousands and items are listed here in alphabetical sequence):

	December 31, 1980 Amount
Accounts payable and accrued liabilities:	
Trade and other	$ 85,926
Directors	3,414
Bank indebtedness, partly secured	33,463
Capital stock	61,162
Current maturities of long-term liabilities	12,791
Current portion of deferred income taxes	8,273
Deferred income taxes	52,071
Long-term liabilities	187,473
Minority interest	1,444
Retained earnings	126,663
Total liabilities and shareholders' equity	572,680

Required:

1. Treating deferred income taxes as long-term liabilities except where otherwise indicated, prepare the liabilities and shareholders' equity section of the balance sheet.

2. Describe the nature of the minority interest and explain its placement in the balance sheet.

P22–6B
Thought-provoking problem: reason for elimination

While preparing 1985 consolidated financial statements for Buffalo Corporation and its subsidiaries, two accountants discovered that the parent company had manufactured a machine at a cost of $200,000 and sold it to Lackawanna Inc. (a subsidiary being consolidated) at the usual company profit of 20 percent of cost. They were about to add it to other plant and equipment at Lackawanna's historical cost figure of $240,000, but this did not make sense to one of them. In the discussion that followed, Eydie Poling argued that the real cost to the economic entity was only $200,000 instead of $240,000, and that the $40,000 should be eliminated in preparing the consolidated balance sheet.

James Henry responded that to do so would not be consistent with the income statement because the $40,000 profit was included in Buffalo's net income. Then both wondered whether the consolidated statements should show depreciation expense and accumulated depreciation based on $200,000 or the $240,000 amount used by Lackawanna.

Required: Recognizing that the consolidated financial statements report on an economic entity, discuss the eliminations that would be made in this situation giving your reasons for each.

Part Five

Cost Accumulation and Control

23 Accounting for a Manufacturing Firm

Introduction

Up to this point in the text, only the accounting for service or trading businesses has been considered. A trading business buys goods in finished form and resells them in the same form. However, many businesses are manufacturers; they also need financial reports. This chapter begins the study of accounting for a manufacturing business, which buys materials and uses labor and other factory services to convert those materials into finished goods for sale. It concentrates on financial accounting in a manufacturing firm and the procedures to produce financial statements for a manufacturer. In Chapters 24 and 25, concepts and techniques that relate to determination of cost of products produced and cost accumulation for cost control and managerial decision purposes are explained.

Learning Goals

To understand that the cost of goods manufactured by a manufacturing firm represents the same concept as purchases by a merchandising firm.

To know the nature of the three types of inventories in a manufacturing concern.

To compute cost of materials used under a periodic inventory system.

To develop an understanding of manufacturing overhead and to identify specific overhead cost items.

To distinguish between inventoriable costs and period expenses.

To prepare schedules of cost of goods manufactured and cost of goods sold.

To add to knowledge of work sheet techniques by addition of the Manufacturing columns.

To understand the concepts of allocation of common costs between manufacturing costs and period expenses.

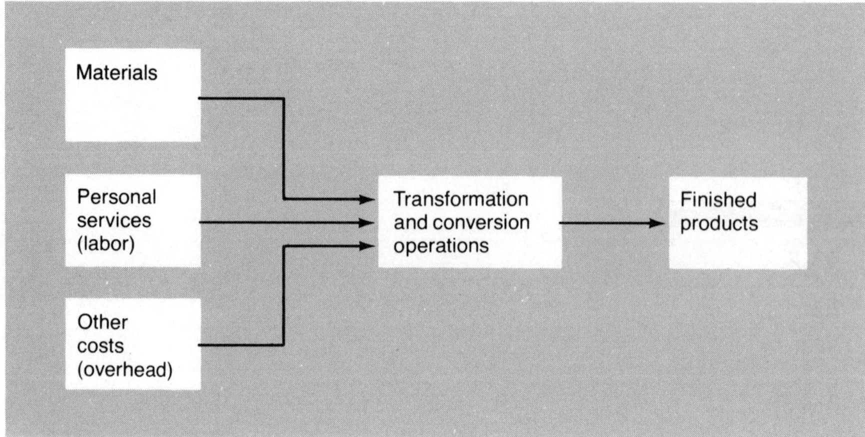

Figure 23–1
The Manufacturing Process

The Manufacturing Process

Manufacturing firms produce thousands of products, which are sold to merchandising firms for resale to individuals, government and other institutions, overseas customers, or are sold to other manufacturing firms. In the discussion that follows, the term **manufacturing firm** is used to designate a firm that makes and sells a product. The term *nonmanufacturing firm* includes merchandising firms, financial institutions, and others that do not make a product. The term *merchandising firm* describes a nonmanufacturing trading firm. Production techniques vary greatly, but all manufacturing firms use the same basic process. As shown in Figure 23–1, the manufacturing firm brings together materials, labor, and other manufacturing costs; through a process or series of operations, they are transformed into finished products for market. In a nonmanufacturing firm, costs become expenses **(period expenses)** of the period in which the benefit was received—the cost is said to have expired. In a manufacturing firm, some costs become a part of the product produced for resale, and are called **product costs.** Until the products are sold and their costs reflected in the income statement as cost of goods sold, these product costs continue to have asset status as product inventory. Not all such costs of a manufacturing firm are inventoriable costs. Manufacturing firms also have selling and general and administrative functions using materials, labor, and other costs. Expired costs in these functions are period expenses similar to those studied in the nonmanufacturing firm and are so treated in accounting.

Inventoriable costs

***Product costs are costs that become the cost of the asset, inventory. They are also known as* inventoriable costs.**

The concept of inventoriable costs was introduced in Chapter 6, where transportation in on goods became part of the cost of goods sold. It was expanded in Chapter 13, where the accounting for depletion of natural resources was described. The process of developing natural resources into products for resale is a form of manufacturing usually involving extraction of a basic material—say, coal—and its conversion into salable form. In the following sections, the inventoriable cost concepts are expanded.

Inventories

A merchandising firm has a single inventory account; it represents goods purchased for resale and is usually called *Merchandise Inventory*. A manufacturing firm has three major inventory accounts.

1. **Materials inventory** consists of the materials and parts used in making the company's product or products. Some of the items may be raw materials such as ore or crude petroleum products. Others may be finished products of a supplying manufacturer—say gaskets, cement, or sheet steel. They have the common characteristic that they are intended to be used in the manufacturing process. Some become part of the final product; others are used in support of the manufacturing process (see discussion in section headed "Materials Used").

2. **Work-in-process inventory** represents the sum to date of costs invested in those items that are partly completed in the manufacturing process. At the end of any period, a firm will have some items on the workbenches and assembly lines in the factory that are incomplete. They will probably be completed in the next accounting period, and the cost incurred to date in this period is carried on the end-of-period balance sheet as work-in-process inventory. The work-in-process inventory valuation is determined by identifying the cost of the materials and direct labor that are incorporated in the unfinished product. The amount of other manufacturing costs (overhead) included in work-in-process inventory is often estimated.

3. **Finished goods inventory** comprises the stock of products that have been completed and are ready for sale. The cost to manufacture those goods that are transferred to the finished goods inventory during an accounting period is usually shown in a supporting accounting schedule. This schedule is very important to management; it gives details of the *cost of goods manufactured.* As can be seen in Figure 23–2, *cost of goods manufactured represents to a manufacturing firm the same concept that net purchases represent to a trading firm.*

Figure 23–2 compares the cost of goods sold section of the income statements of two firms. The same dollar amounts have been used to make the point that the only real difference is the source of the input of goods into the stock of resale merchandise. In the merchandising firm, there is the problem (explained in Chapter 6) of accounting for the net cost of purchases. The parallel accounting problem in a manufacturing firm is the determination of cost of goods manufactured.

Merchandising Firm		**Manufacturing Firm**	
Merchandise inventory, January 1, 1985	$ 23,200	Finished goods inventory, January 1, 1985	$ 23,200
Add: Purchases (net)	229,845	Add: Cost of goods manufactured (Schedule A–1)	229,845
Cost of merchandise available for sale	$253,045	Cost of finished goods available for sale	$253,045
Deduct: Merchandise inventory, December 31, 1985	19,600	Deduct: Finished goods inventory, December 31, 1985	19,600
Cost of goods sold	$233,445	Cost of goods sold	$233,445

Figure 23–2 **Comparison of Cost of Goods Sold Sections**

Cost of Goods Manufactured

The three basic classifications of manufacturing costs are (1) materials used, (2) direct labor, and (3) manufacturing overhead. Each is described in detail in the sections that follow. First, however, to present a broad picture of how they contribute to the stock of goods for resale, a summary schedule of cost of goods manufactured is shown in Figure 23–3. The dollar amounts used in Figure 23–2, Figure 23–3, and all others in this chapter are from the records of the Cola Manufacturing Company. This example is carried throughout so that the interrelationship of the various cost elements can be understood more clearly.

Materials Used

All materials that can be identified as becoming a part of the finished product are known as **direct materials.** The cloth used in the manufacture of a suit, for example, is obviously a direct material. Some items may be incorporated into the finished product, but it may not be economical to measure and record them. An example would be the thread used to manufacture the same garment. Although it is part of the suit, tracing given amounts of thread to the product being manufactured would be too costly. Accordingly, such items are

COLA MANUFACTURING COMPANY **Schedule A–1**
Summary Schedule of Cost of Goods Manufactured
For the Year Ended December 31, 1985

Work-in-process inventory, January 1, 1985		$ 31,725
Add: Materials used	$ 92,350	
Direct labor	102,030	
Manufacturing overhead	50,740	245,120
Total		$276,845
Deduct: Work-in-process inventory, December 31, 1985		47,000
Cost of goods manufactured		$229,845

Figure 23–3 Summary Schedule of Cost of Goods Manufactured

Materials used:			
Materials inventory, January 1, 1985			$ 58,300
Add: Materials purchases		$91,000	
Deduct: Materials purchases returns and allowances	$2,800		
Materials purchases discounts	2,650	5,450	
Net cost of materials purchases			85,550
Cost of materials available for use			$143,850
Deduct: Materials inventory, December 31, 1985 . . .			51,500
Cost of materials used			$ 92,350

Figure 23–4 Computation of Materials Used

known as **indirect materials.** Another form of indirect materials is those items necessary to the production process but not used in the product—oil for the machinery or cleaning compound for the floor, for example. Indirect materials are accounted for as an element of other manufacturing costs called manufacturing overhead (discussed in more detail later in the chapter). This distinction becomes extremely important when a cost accounting system (discussed in following chapters) is used.

The cost of materials used in manufacturing a product may be determined by the periodic inventory method in a calculation parallel to the cost of goods sold in a trading business.[1] Figure 23–4 shows the computation of cost of materials used by the Cola Manufacturing Company in 1985. The calculation of materials used in Figure 23–4 makes use of the same concepts as those for calculation of cost of goods sold (explained in Chapter 6). The treatment of indirect materials is taken up in Chapters 24 and 25.

Direct Labor and Indirect Labor

The wages paid to factory employees performing operations directly on the product are referred to as **direct labor.** Other factory employees perform tasks in support of production operations but do not work directly in the construction, composition, or fabrication of the finished goods. Their salaries are classified as **indirect labor.** Wages and salaries of the supervisors, repair personnel, and stockroom storekeepers fall into this category. Indirect labor is an element of manufacturing overhead. It is the function of the timekeeping personnel to identify labor charges as direct or indirect when the payroll is prepared. In a general manufacturing accounting system, the gross pay of factory personnel is debited to either the Direct Labor or Indirect Labor account. These product costs like many others are first recorded in nominal

[1]Manufacturing businesses often find that a perpetual inventory system is more effective for materials control. In this chapter, periodic inventory systems are used to provide a review. The reader should note, however, that such a system causes both direct and indirect materials to be lumped together as "materials used." This is acceptable for financial reporting. However, for cost accounting study in Chapters 24 and 25, these are separated.

accounts. They are later closed into a summary account so that they become cost of goods available for sale.

During 1985, Cola Manufacturing Company incurred (including both paid and accrued) total wages and salaries of $266,230. This figure was made up of the following:

Direct labor (inventoriable cost)	$102,030
Indirect labor (inventoriable cost)	22,600
Sales salaries (expense)	55,100
Executive salaries (expense)	60,500
Office salaries (expense)	26,000
Total	$266,230

Two of the above items—direct labor and indirect labor—are *inventoriable costs.* The others are *period expenses.* The accounting entries to record these and other costs are shown later after other manufacturing concepts are explained.

Manufacturing Overhead

All factory costs incurred in the manufacturing process other than the cost of materials used and direct labor are classified as **manufacturing overhead.** Other terms used for this group of costs are **indirect manufacturing costs** and **manufacturing burden.** Selling expenses and general and administrative expenses are not considered manufacturing overhead. They reflect the costs of distribution of the product and of administration of the overall firm and are not part of the manufacturing function; they are period expenses. In accounting for a general manufacturing operation, nominal (temporary) accounts are carried in the general ledger for each of the elements of manufacturing overhead. Separate nominal accounts are carried for period expenses.

Two manufacturing overhead elements that have already been explained are indirect materials and indirect labor. Some other typical examples are:

Small tools used: This represents the cost of small hand tools that are lost or broken during the year. Because of the great variety of such tools, their low unit cost, and the difficulty of predicting an estimated useful life, it is not economical to carry small tools in a property, plant, and equipment account and depreciate them. It is much simpler to debit all acquisitions to an asset account, Small Tools. At the end of each accounting period, a physical count is made; the difference between the asset account balance and the value of tools on hand as shown by the physical count is the cost of small tools used —an element of manufacturing overhead.

Amortization of patents: Most patents are for manufacturing processes. The cost of patents is amortized over their economically useful life or their legal life, whichever is shorter. The periodic amortization charge is an element of manufacturing overhead.

Factory rent: The amount of rent charged for the buildings that house the factory is a part of manufacturing overhead. In some cases, the same building may contain *production* operations along with activities related to selling and administration. *If so, the total cost* (called **common cost**) *must be allocated among manufacturing overhead, selling expense, and general and administrative expense.* Procedures for allocation of costs and expenses are discussed later in this chapter.

Heat, light, and power: This manufacturing overhead item is either the cost of purchasing or of producing in one's own power plant the energy to operate production equipment and to provide heat and light to the factory. As with factory rent, it is sometimes necessary to allocate this common cost between manufacturing overhead and period expenses.

Factory insurance: Insurance that covers factory equipment or materials and work-in-process inventories is a cost of manufacturing. Insurance on the finished goods inventory is usually a selling expense. As in the case of rent, insurance may be a common cost to be allocated between manufacturing overhead and period expenses.

Depreciation—machinery and equipment: In a manufacturing firm, depreciation of all items of property, plant, and equipment that are used in production is a part of manufacturing cost and a part of manufacturing overhead. As discussed in previous chapters, depreciation charges in a *nonmanufacturing* business are all treated as expenses of the accounting period in which recorded. In either case, depreciation of delivery equipment continues to be a selling expense and depreciation of office equipment a general and administrative expense.

Others: Brief descriptions have been given only of manufacturing overhead items that had been previously mentioned or will be encountered in the Cola Manufacturing Company illustration. It is important to recognize that any *cost of manufacturing* a firm's product that is not direct materials or direct labor is classified as manufacturing overhead. Some other typical *factory costs* that are overhead items are:

- ☐ Overtime premium pay.
- ☐ Employer's FICA taxes.
- ☐ Unemployment compensation taxes.
- ☐ Vacation pay.
- ☐ Pension plan contributions.
- ☐ Repairs and maintenance.
- ☐ Hospitalization insurance.
- ☐ Group insurance.
- ☐ Property taxes on productive property.
- ☐ Factory supplies used.

Manufacturing overhead:	
Indirect labor	$22,600
Factory rent[a]	9,600
Heat, light, and power[a]	7,290
Factory insurance[a]	1,050
Depreciation—machinery and equipment	10,200
Total manufacturing overhead	$50,740

[a]Allocated share of common cost.

Figure 23–5 Computation of Manufacturing Overhead Cost

In Figure 23–3, the total manufacturing overhead cost for Cola Manufacturing Company was shown in a single amount, $50,740. Figure 23–5 provides information in detail by element of factory overhead cost incurred. This information and the materials used (Figure 23–4) can be combined with direct labor cost and work-in-process inventories to provide a more complete schedule of cost of goods manufactured in 1985. Such a schedule is included with the statements found in the later section "Financial Statements."

Cost of Goods Sold

The **cost of goods sold for a manufacturing firm** that uses the periodic inventory system is computed in a manner similar to that of a merchandising firm. The ending finished goods inventory is determined by physical count. The Cola Manufacturing Company's cost of goods sold was computed in summary form in Figure 23–2. After the work sheet has been illustrated, complete details of cost of goods manufactured and sold are shown in Figures 23–7 and 23–8.

Work Sheet for a Manufacturing Firm

Aside from the fact that there are three inventories instead of one, there is another important difference between the work sheets of a manufacturing firm and a merchandising firm. In the work sheet for a manufacturing firm, a pair of columns headed *Manufacturing* is added (see Figure 23–6). Into these columns are extended all the debit and credit balances representing elements that enter into the cost of manufacturing the product. These include materials inventory, direct labor, manufacturing overhead items, and the work-in-process inventory. The debits in this pair of columns should always be larger than the credits; the difference is **cost of goods manufactured.** This is the amount being added to finished goods inventory. The cost of goods manufactured is transferred to the Income Statement Debit column at the bottom of the work sheet as illustrated in Figure 23–6. Items in the Manufacturing columns become a part of the closing entries as shown at the end of this chapter.

COLA MANUFACTURING COMPANY
Work Sheet
For the Year Ended December 31, 1985[a]

Account Title	Trial Balance Dr.	Trial Balance Cr.	Adjustments Dr.	Adjustments Cr.	Manufacturing Dr.	Manufacturing Cr.	Income Statement Dr.	Income Statement Cr.	Balance Sheet Dr.	Balance Sheet Cr.
Cash	12,000								12,000	
Accounts Receivable	78,350								78,350	
Allowance for Doubtful Accounts		650		(a) 1,037						1,687
Materials Inventory	58,300				58,300	51,500			51,500	
Work-in-Process Inventory	31,725				31,725	47,000			47,000	
Finished Goods Inventory	23,200						23,200	19,600	19,600	
Prepaid Insurance	2,100			(b) 1,500					600	
Office Equipment	6,050								6,050	
Accumulated Depreciation—Office Equipment		2,000		(d) 605						2,605
Store Equipment	10,000								10,000	
Accumulated Depreciation—Store Equipment		4,000		(d) 1,000						5,000
Machinery and Equipment	51,000								51,000	
Accumulated Depreciation—Machinery and Equipment		10,000		(c) 10,200						20,200
Accounts Payable		29,200								29,200
Common Stock		180,000								180,000
Retained Earnings		12,855								12,855
Dividends	10,000								10,000	
Sales		420,000						420,000		
Sales Returns and Allowances	5,200						5,200			
Sales Discounts	2,400						2,400			
Materials Purchases	91,000				91,000					
Materials Purchases Returns and Allowances		2,800				2,800				
Materials Purchases Discounts		2,650				2,650				
Direct Labor	98,530		(e) 3,500		102,030					
Indirect Labor	21,200		(e) 1,400		22,600					
Rent	12,000				9,600		1,800S[b]			
							600G[c]			
Heat, Light, and Power	8,100				7,290		405S			
							405G			
Advertising Expense	6,500						6,500			
Sales Salaries Expense	50,000		(e) 5,100				55,100			
Executive Salaries Expense	60,500						60,500			
Office Salaries Expense	26,000						26,000			
Totals	664,155	664,155								
Bad Debts Expense			(a) 1,037				1,037			
Insurance			(b) 1,500		1,050		300S			
							150G			
Depreciation—Machinery and Equipment			(c) 10,200		10,200					
Depreciation Expense—Office Equipment			(d) 605				605			
Depreciation Expense—Store Equipment			(d) 1,000				1,000			
Accrued Wages and Salaries Payable				(e) 10,000						10,000
Income Tax Expense			(f) 7,368				7,368			
Income Taxes Payable				(f) 7,368						7,368
Totals			31,710	31,710	333,795	103,950				
Cost of goods manufactured						229,845	229,845			
Totals					333,795	333,795	422,415	439,600	286,100	268,915
Net income							17,185			17,185
Totals							439,600	439,600	286,100	286,100

[a]A manufacturing work sheet sometimes has 12 columns. The Adjusted Trial Balance columns have been omitted here because of space limitations. [b]S denotes selling expenses. [c]G denotes general and administrative expenses.

Figure 23–6 **Work Sheet for a Manufacturing Company**

Adjusting Entries on the Manufacturing Work Sheet

The entries in the Adjustments columns of the work sheet are based on the information that follows (the letters correspond to those used on the work sheet):

Entry a: The bad debts expense was estimated at ¼ of 1 percent of gross sales less sales returns and allowances. The amount of the adjustment was computed as follows:

Gross sales	$420,000
Deduct: Sales returns and allowances	5,200
Net sales	$414,800
Bad debts expense percent	×0.0025
Bad debts expense	$ 1,037

The debit records the estimated bad debts expense; the credit increases Allowance for Doubtful Accounts to $1,687 = ($650 + $1,037). This adjustment debits an expense account, not a manufacturing account. Accordingly, the expense is extended into the Income Statement columns.

Entry b: Insurance of $1,500 has expired. The debit records the cost of the expired insurance; the credit decreases the asset account. Note that a portion of the common cost of insurance is classified as manufacturing overhead. The remainder is a period expense. The procedure for allocating the $1,500 total is explained in the next section. Of the total, $1,050 is extended to Manufacturing; the remaining $450 is divided between selling expense (indicated by S) and general and administrative expense (indicated by G) in the Income Statement columns.

Entry c: The annual depreciation rate for factory machinery and equipment is 20 percent. Since all the equipment was acquired prior to 1985, a full year's depreciation is taken, based on the amount shown in the trial balance. The computation is as follows:

Cost of $51,000 × 0.20 = $10,200 for 1985.

The debit records the depreciation of the machinery and equipment as a manufacturing overhead item, not as an expense; the credit increases the Accumulated Depreciation—Machinery and Equipment account.

Entry d: The annual depreciation rate for both office equipment and store equipment is 10 percent. All the office and store equipment was acquired prior to 1985. Consequently a full year's depreciation expense is taken, based on the amount of each account shown in the trial balance. The computations are as follows:

Costs of $6,050 and $10,000 × 0.10 = $605 and $1,000 for 1985.

The debits record the depreciation expense for the office and store equipment; the credits increase the corresponding Accumulated Depreciation accounts.

Entry e: The accrued wages and salaries payable as of December 31, 1985, were as follows:

Direct labor (inventoriable cost)	$ 3,500
Indirect labor (inventoriable cost)	1,400
Sales salaries (expense)	5,100
Total	$10,000

The debits record all the wages and salaries incurred but not paid; the credit records the accrued liability. Here is an example of debits both to manufacturing accounts and to a period expense. Note carefully how these three labor cost items are extended across the work sheet.

Entry f: The estimated income tax liability is $7,368. The debit records the expense; the credit records the estimated income tax liability.

Allocation of Costs and Expenses on the Work Sheet

In the Trial Balance and Adjustments columns, certain accounts represent common costs incurred partly in the manufacturing processes and partly in the selling and general and administrative functions. Assume that a study was made late in 1984 to find an equitable method for allocating these items. As a result of this study, the following bases for allocation were decided on:

Rent	Square footage of building space used.
Heat, light, and power	Actual readings from meters in the factory, in the sales rooms, and in the general and administrative areas.
Insurance	Cost of comprehensive policies covering the buildings allocated on the basis of square footage; other insurance costs on basis of value of items insured.

The base chosen for allocation of common costs should be a readily measurable item that management believes reasonably indicates the amount of benefits to each organizational unit. The base is then changed to a percentage. Assume that Cola has 100,000 square feet, of which 80,000 is devoted to manufacturing, 15,000 to selling, and 5,000 to general and administrative work. The percent figures for allocation of rent are 80, 15, and 5 percent. Making additional assumptions for heat, light, and power and insurance, the following allocations were made:

		Allocation					
		Manufacturing		Selling		General	
Item	Total	%	Amount	%	Amount	%	Amount
Rent	$12,000	80	$9,600	15	$1,800	5	$600
Heat, light, and power	8,100	90	7,290	5	405	5	405
Insurance	1,500	70	1,050	20	300	10	150

As indicated earlier, in "The Manufacturing Process" section of the chapter, these allocations are necessary to separate common costs that serve more than one function. For example, the rent cost of $12,000 is now separated into $9,600 of inventoriable cost and $1,800 and $600 of period expenses.

On the line of the work sheet for each of the allocated items, the total of the Trial Balance and Adjustments columns is extended to the appropriate column. The Rent debit balance of $12,000, for example, is distributed as follows: $9,600 = ($12,000 × 0.80) is extended to the Manufacturing Debit column; $1,800 = ($12,000 × 0.15) and $600 = ($12,000 × 0.05) are extended to the Income Statement Debit column. Note that the $9,600 is classified as manufacturing overhead (Factory Rent), $600 as a general and administrative expense, and $1,800 as selling expense.

The expense figures are specifically identified as either selling or general and administrative expenses by the letter S or G. These letters may be further used for amounts extended as a lump sum in a single column to facilitate the precise classification of the accounts if the formal income statement is prepared directly from the work sheet.

Ending Inventories on the Manufacturing Work Sheet

The ending inventories on December 31, 1985, are as follows:

Materials	$51,500
Work in process	47,000
Finished goods	19,600

All three amounts are entered as debits in the Balance Sheet columns. The two that affect manufacturing cost—for materials and work-in-process inventories—are entered as *credits* in the Manufacturing columns. The finished goods inventory amount is a part of the cost of goods sold computation and is entered as a *credit* in the Income Statement columns.

Entering the three inventories as debits in the Balance Sheet columns establishes them as the new end-of-year current asset value of inventories. Entering these same amounts as credits serves to reduce the cost of goods manufactured and the cost of goods sold because they offset the debits (including beginning inventory figures) that are extended to the Manufacturing columns and the Income Statement columns.

Financial Statements

The Manufacturing columns of the work sheet contain all the amounts required for the preparation of the schedule of cost of goods manufactured; each amount is used once. Similarly, the Income Statement and Balance Sheet columns contain the figures needed for the preparation of the income statement, statement of retained earnings, and balance sheet. The financial statements and the schedule of cost of goods manufactured are illustrated in Figures 23–7, 23–8, 23–9, and 23–10.

COLA MANUFACTURING COMPANY
Schedule of Cost of Goods Manufactured
For the Year Ended December 31, 1985

Schedule A–1

Work-in-process inventory, January 1, 1985				$ 31,725
Materials used:				
Materials inventory, January 1, 1985			$ 58,300	
Materials purchases		$91,000		
Deduct: Materials purchases returns and allowances	$2,800			
Materials purchases discounts	2,650	5,450		
Net cost of materials purchases			85,550	
Cost of materials available for use			$143,850	
Deduct: Materials inventory, December 31, 1985			51,500	
Cost of materials used			$ 92,350	
Direct labor			102,030	
Manufacturing overhead:				
Indirect labor		$22,600		
Factory rent		9,600		
Heat, light, and power		7,290		
Factory insurance		1,050		
Depreciation—machinery and equipment		10,200		
Total manufacturing overhead			50,740	
Total manufacturing costs				245,120
Total				$276,845
Deduct: Work-in-process inventory, December 31, 1985				47,000
Cost of goods manufactured (to Exhibit A)				$229,845

Figure 23–7 **Schedule of Cost of Goods Manufactured**

As indicated in Chapter 20, a statement of changes in financial position must also be prepared. Because the format of this statement for a manufacturing firm is essentially the same as that indicated in Chatper 20, the statement is not repeated here.

Accounting Entries

During the Period

The accounting entries for daily transactions in a manufacturing firm follow the general pattern of those in a merchandising firm. There are some slight changes in account titles in the chart of accounts. For example, a Materials Purchases account is used with the periodic inventory system to record the acquisition of materials.[2] Assume that Cola Manufacturing Company had

[2]Although not included in this illustration, debits to the Materials Transportation In account also increase the cost of materials available.

COLA MANUFACTURING COMPANY
Income Statement
For the Year Ended December 31, 1985

Exhibit A

Sales			$420,000
Deduct: Sales returns and allowances		$ 5,200	
Sales discounts		2,400	7,600
Net sales revenue			$412,400
Cost of goods sold:			
Finished goods inventory, January 1, 1985		$ 23,200	
Add: Cost of goods manufactured (Schedule A–1)		229,845	
Cost of finished goods available for sale		$253,045	
Deduct: Finished goods inventory, December 31, 1985		19,600	
Cost of goods sold			233,445
Gross margin on sales			$178,955
Operating expenses:			
Selling expenses:			
Rent expense	$ 1,800		
Heat, light, and power expense	405		
Advertising expense	6,500		
Sales salaries expense	55,100		
Insurance expense	300		
Depreciation expense—store equipment	1,000		
Total selling expenses		$ 65,105	
General and administrative expenses:			
Rent expense	$ 600		
Heat, light, and power expense	405		
Executive salaries expense	60,500		
Office salaries expense	26,000		
Bad debts expense	1,037		
Insurance expense	150		
Depreciation expense—office equipment	605		
Total general and administrative expenses		89,297	
Total operating expenses			154,402
Net income before income taxes			$ 24,553
Income tax expense			7,368
Net income after income taxes (to Exhibit B)			$ 17,185

Earnings per share $0.95

Figure 23–8 **Income Statement**

COLA MANUFACTURING COMPANY
Statement of Retained Earnings
For the Year Ended December 31, 1985

Exhibit B

Retained earnings, January 1, 1985	$12,855
Add: Net income for the year (Exhibit A)	17,185
Subtotal	$30,040
Deduct: Dividends	10,000
Retained earnings, December 31, 1985 (to Exhibit C)	$20,040

Figure 23–9
Statement of Retained Earnings

COLA MANUFACTURING COMPANY Balance Sheet December 31, 1985			Exhibit C
Assets			
Current assets:			
Cash		$ 12,000	
Accounts receivable	$78,350		
Deduct: Allowance for doubtful accounts	1,687	76,663	
Materials inventory		51,500	
Work-in-process inventory		47,000	
Finished goods inventory		19,600	
Prepaid insurance		600	
Total current assets			$207,363
Property, plant, and equipment:			
Office equipment	$ 6,050		
Deduct: Accumulated depreciation	2,605	$ 3,445	
Store equipment	$10,000		
Deduct: Accumulated depreciation	5,000	5,000	
Machinery and equipment	$51,000		
Deduct: Accumulated depreciation	20,200	30,800	
Total property, plant, and equipment			39,245
Total assets			$246,608
Liabilities and Stockholders' Equity			
Current liabilities:			
Accounts payable		$ 29,200	
Accrued salaries and wages payable		10,000	
Income taxes payable		7,368	
Total current liabilities			$ 46,568
Stockholders' equity:			
Common stock, $10 par value		$180,000	
Retained earnings (Exhibit B)		20,040	
Total stockholders' equity			200,040
Total liabilities and stockholders' equity			$246,608

Figure 23–10 **Balance Sheet**

received a shipment of fasteners on June 17, 1985, at a cost of $2,100, terms 2/10, n/30. On June 18, the company returned fasteners with an invoice price of $100 found to be defective; the balance due was paid on June 27. The accounting entries under the gross price method would be as follows:

1985					
Jun.	17	Materials Purchases		2,100	
		Accounts Payable			2,100
		To record acquisition of fasteners.			
	18	Accounts Payable		100	
		Materials Purchases Returns and Allowances			100
		To record return of defective fasteners.			
	27	Accounts Payable		2,000	
		Materials Purchases Discounts			40
		Cash			1,960
		To record payment on account.			

Payroll procedures were discussed in Chapter 8. The computation of amounts earned, deductions, and employer's payroll taxes are the same in a manufacturing firm as in a nonmanufacturing firm. However, payroll and timekeeping records in a manufacturing firm must be designed to collect direct labor, indirect labor, sales salaries (or commissions), and general and administrative salaries in separate accounts. A typical entry to show the payroll for the semi-monthly period ended on June 30, 1985 for the Cola Manufacturing Company is as follows *(all taxes and deductions omitted)*:

1985					
Jun.	30	Direct Labor		3,900	
		Indirect Labor		870	
		Sales Salaries Expense		2,000	
		Executive Salaries Expense		2,300	
		Office Salaries Expense		1,000	
		Salaries and Wages Payable			10,070
		To record payroll for period ended this date.			

In the foregoing entry, observe that a deliberate effort is made to distinguish period expenses from costs that are later incorporated in inventories. The word *expense* is attached to period expenses; it is omitted from the inventoriable costs. Although taxes are omitted from this entry to avoid making the illustration unnecessarily complex, an important point should be made here. In a manufacturing firm, the employer's matching FICA tax and both federal and state unemployment compensation tax *on direct labor and indirect labor are debited to an overhead account* and *not* to period expense. The employer's payroll taxes on employees other than factory employees are debited to period expense accounts.

Overhead costs may be incurred in the form of periodic payments. For example, Cola Manufacturing Company's rent payment for December would be recorded as follows:

1985					
Dec.	2	Rent		1,000	
		Cash			1,000
		To record payment of December rent.			

Other overhead costs such as depreciation or expiration of insurance are included in the adjusting entries. Whether recorded as transactions during the period or adjustments at the end of the period, total manufacturing costs are brought together in the work sheet as illustrated in Figure 23–6.

The inclusion of the Manufacturing columns in the work sheet is important in ensuring the accuracy of the cost of goods manufactured computation and in assisting in preparation of Schedule A–1 (Figure 23–7). The work sheet also facilitates end-of-period adjusting and closing entries as described in the next section.

At the End of the Period

The adjusting entries for a manufacturing firm are the same as for other firms and can be taken directly from the work sheet (see Figure 23–6). Shown below are adjusting journal entries:

1985					
Dec.	31	Bad Debts Expense		1,037	
		Allowance for Doubtful Accounts			1,037
		Estimated expense of ¼ of 1 percent of net sales.			
	31	Insurance		1,500	
		Prepaid insurance			1,500
		To record amount expired during 1985.			
	31	Depreciation—Machinery and Equipment		10,200	
		Accumulated Depreciation—Machinery and Equipment			10,200
		To record 1985 depreciation.			
	31	Depreciation Expense—Office Equipment		605	
		Accumulated Depreciation—Office Equipment			605
		To record 1985 depreciation.			
	31	Depreciation Expense—Store Equipment		1,000	
		Accumulated Depreciation—Store Equipment			1,000
		To record 1985 depreciation.			
	31	Direct Labor		3,500	
		Indirect Labor		1,400	
		Sales Salaries Expense		5,100	
		Accrued Salaries and Wages Payable			10,000
		To record wages accrued on December 31, 1985.			
	31	Income Tax Expense		7,368	
		Income Taxes Payable			7,368
		To record estimated amount of 1985 tax.			

In the closing process for a manufacturing firm, a new general ledger account, **Manufacturing Summary,** is opened at the end of each accounting period. All account balances that enter into the computation of cost of goods manufactured are closed into this account. These balances are the same figures that are found in the Manufacturing columns of the work sheet. The final balance of the Manufacturing Summary account is the cost of goods manufactured. It is closed into the Income Summary account. The remaining closing entries are the same as for a merchandising business.

The closing journal entries for Cola Manufacturing Company are as follows:[3]

[3]Note the allocations of the common costs such as rent, with $9,600 of rent closed to Manufacturing Summary and $2,400 of rent closed to Income Summary.

Date		Account		Debit	Credit
1985					
Dec.	31	Manufacturing Summary		333,795	
		Materials Inventory			58,300
		Work-in-Process Inventory			31,725
		Materials Purchases			91,000
		Direct Labor			102,030
		Indirect Labor			22,600
		Rent			9,600
		Heat, Light, and Power			7,290
		Insurance			1,050
		Depreciation—Machinery and Equipment			10,200
		To close beginning manufacturing inventories and the debit-balance manufacturing accounts.			
	31	Materials Inventory		51,500	
		Work-in-Process Inventory		47,000	
		Materials Purchases Returns and Allowances		2,800	
		Materials Purchases Discounts		2,650	
		Manufacturing Summary			103,950
		To enter ending manufacturing inventories and to close the credit-balance manufacturing accounts.			
	31	Income Summary		229,845	
		Manufacturing Summary			229,845
		To close the Manufacturing Summary account.			
	31	Income Summary		192,570	
		Finished Goods Inventory			23,200
		Sales Returns and Allowances			5,200
		Sales Discounts			2,400
		Rent			2,400
		Heat, Light, and Power			810
		Advertising Expense			6,500
		Sales Salaries Expense			55,100
		Executive Salaries Expense			60,500
		Office Salaries Expense			26,000
		Bad Debts Expense			1,037
		Insurance			450
		Depreciation Expense—Office Equipment			605
		Depreciation Expense—Store Equipment			1,000
		Income Tax Expense			7,368
		To close beginning inventory of finished goods and the debit-balance income accounts.			
	31	Finished Goods Inventory		19,600	
		Sales		420,000	
		Income Summary			439,600
		To enter the ending finished goods inventory and to close the credit-balance revenue accounts.			
	31	Income Summary		17,185	
		Retained Earnings			17,185
		To close net income into Retained Earnings.			
	31	Retained Earnings		10,000	
		Dividends			10,000
		To close the Dividends account.			

The posting of closing entries and the preparation of a postclosing trial balance for a manufacturing firm do not differ from procedures illustrated for other businesses in earlier chapters. Upon completion of posting, all nominal (temporary) accounts have a zero balance.

As mentioned in the chapter introduction, these procedures using a periodic inventory system are adequate to provide financial statements for a general manufacturing firm. They do not, however, provide the information needed for effective managerial control. If a manufacturing firm is to continue doing business, it should establish a cost accounting system using a manufacturing budget and a perpetual inventory system. These topics are covered in Chapters 24 and 25.

Glossary

Allocation basis See *Manufacturing overhead allocation basis.*

Amortization of patents The amount of patent cost applicable to a given time period; it is an element of manufacturing overhead for a manufacturing firm.

Common cost A cost shared by two or more functions that must be allocated among them.

Cost allocation The process of apportioning costs among functions.

Cost of goods manufactured The cost of finished product units completed during a given period; it is calculated by adding the beginning work-in-process inventory to the three manufacturing cost elements and deducting the ending work-in-process inventory.

Direct labor The wages of employees performing operations directly on the product being manufactured.

Direct materials Materials that can be identified as becoming part of the finished product.

Finished goods inventory The inventory of finished products of a manufacturing firm.

Indirect labor The labor cost of those workers whose efforts are not directly identified with the conversion of specific material into specific finished products; for example, the factory janitor's salary is an indirect labor cost.

Indirect manufacturing costs See *Manufacturing overhead.*

Indirect materials Materials used in production that cannot be identified as becoming part of the finished product.

Inventoriable costs Transformed costs that become part of the finished goods inventory. Such costs do not appear as period expenses in the income statement. Ultimately, they become part of cost of goods sold.

Manufacturing burden See *Manufacturing overhead.*

Manufacturing firm A firm that makes finished products by applying direct labor costs and other manufacturing costs to convert basic materials into finished goods.

Manufacturing overhead All factory costs incurred in the manufacturing process other than the cost of direct materials used and direct labor; examples are indirect labor, small tools used, and factory insurance.

Manufacturing overhead allocation basis Method by which common costs incurred in several company functions, including the manufacturing function, are allocated to the respective functions. For example, rent may be allocated on the basis of square footage of building space used by each function.

Manufacturing Summary A summary account used in the closing process for a manufacturing firm; all items used in the calculation of cost of goods manufactured are closed to this account.

Materials inventory The inventory of material, at cost, held for consumption (as direct or indirect material) in fabricating the finished product of a manufacturing firm.

Materials used The cost of the materials used in manufacturing during a given period. Under the periodic inventory method, the amount is the sum of beginning materials inventory plus net cost of materials purchases minus ending materials inventory.

Period expenses Expired costs that are reported in the income statement as expenses of the current period.

Product costs Transformed costs that become inventories for later sale.

Work-in-process inventory The inventory of partly finished products in various stages of completion at any given time.

Questions

Q23–1 What is the difference between an inventoriable cost and a period expense? Give examples of each.

Q23–2 A manufacturing firm has three inventory accounts. Name each of these accounts, and describe briefly what the balance in each at the end of any accounting period represents.

Q23–3 Explain each of the following terms: (a) materials used, (b) direct labor, and (c) manufacturing overhead.

Q23–4 What are the criteria that differentiate between direct labor and indirect labor? Direct material and indirect material?

Q23–5 What is the difference between cost of goods manufactured and cost of goods sold?

Q23–6 What is the purpose and function of the Manufacturing columns in the work sheet?

Q23–7 During a given period, the cost of materials used by a manufacturing firm was $50,000. The materials inventory increased by $5,000 during the period. What was the cost of materials purchased?

Q23–8 The books of the Klein Corporation showed the following information:

Inventories	December 31 1985	1984
Finished goods	$24,000	$18,000
Work in process	17,250	10,500
Materials	15,900	19,050

How will each appropriate amount be shown in (a) the work sheet, (b) the schedule of cost of goods manufactured, (c) the income statement, and (d) the balance sheet?

Q23–9 What is a common cost? How are common cost allocations for various functions such as manufacturing, selling, or general and administrative determined?

Q23–10 Identify some of the problems involved in the measurement of the periodic inventories of work in process and finished goods.

Q23–11 Would the accounting system explained in Chapter 23 be acceptable for a major automobile manufacturer? Why or why not?

Q23–12 What financial statement is prepared from the information in the Manufacturing columns of the work sheet?

Exercises

E23–1 *Cost of materials used*

The following information is available from the records of the Eden Manufacturing Company:

Materials inventory, December 31, 1984	$ 45,900
Materials inventory, December 31, 1985	36,000
Materials purchases, 1985	720,000
Materials purchases returns and allowances, 1985	18,000
Materials purchases discounts, 1985	12,600

In schedule form, compute the cost of materials used in 1985.

E23–2 *Cost of goods sold*

The following information is available from the records of the Huntsville Company:

Finished goods inventory, December 31, 1984	$ 90,000
Cost of goods manufactured in 1985	1,080,000
Finished goods inventory, December 31, 1985	108,000
Work-in-process inventory, December 31, 1984	37,800
Work-in-process inventory, December 31, 1985	45,540

In schedule form, compute the cost of goods sold in 1985.

E23–3 *Cost of materials computations*

Compute the missing amounts in the following tabulation:

	Beginning Inventory of Materials	Materials Purchases	Transportation In on Materials	Materials Purchases Returns and Allowances	Materials Purchases Discounts	Net Cost of Materials Purchases	Cost of Materials Available for Use	Ending Inventory of Materials	Cost of Materials Used
1.	$2,250	$12,900	$2,025	$450	$?	$14,250	$?	$3,750	$?
2.	?	3,750	450	?	150	3,750	8,250	?	5,400
3.	5,250	?	1,050	300	600	?	29,850	7,500	?

E23–4 *Cost of goods sold computations*

Compute the missing amounts in the following tabulation:

	Net Sales	Beginning Inventory of Finished Goods	Cost of Goods Manufactured	Cost of Finished Goods Available for Sale	Ending Inventory of Finished Goods	Cost of Goods Sold	Gross Margin on Sales
1.	$61,500	$15,000	$?	$60,000	$?	$?	$23,250
2.	?	?	99,000	?	15,000	121,500	30,000
3.	90,000	?	60,000	90,000	?	74,250	?

E23–5 *Inventoriable cost or period expense*

Classify each of the following as (a) an inventoriable cost, or (b) a period expense.

a. Direct labor.
b. Indirect labor.
c. Advertising.
d. Depreciation of a delivery van.
e. Employer's FICA taxes on direct labor.
f. Small tools used.
g. Pension fund costs on indirect labor.
h. Pension fund costs on sales salaries.
i. Materials used in the accounting department.
j. Materials used to repair factory machinery.
k. Vacation pay of the direct labor employees.
l. Power cost for the general office.
m. Power cost for the production department.
n. Transportation in on materials.
o. Costs of purchasing materials.

E23–6 *Common cost allocations*

Cuny Company has its manufacturing and other functions in the same building. Both property taxes and depreciation of building are allocated to functions on the basis of square feet occupied. Occupancy data for 1985 were:

	Total	Manufacturing	Selling	General and Administrative
Square feet	600,000	540,000	24,000	36,000

Compute the allocation of the annual property tax of $15,000 and depreciation of $50,000.

E23–7 *Small tools used*

The following Small Tools account is from the books of the Alonzo Corporation:

Small Tools

Date		Explanation	F	Debit	Credit	Balance
1985						
Jan.	2	Debit balance	✓			26,000
Aug.	5	Purchase	J58	5,200		31,200

The inventory of small tools on hand on December 31, 1985, was priced at $16,875 based on physical count. Prepare the general journal entry to adjust the Small Tools account.

E23–8 *Cost of goods manufactured*

Make-Em Company had the following data in the accounting records on February 28, 1986, the end of its fiscal year:

Materials inventory, February 28, 1985	$ 30,500
Work-in-process inventory, February 28, 1985	40,270
Materials purchased in 1985–86	482,300
Materials purchases returns and allowances	3,250
Materials purchases discounts	8,560
Direct labor used	342,680
Indirect labor used	28,100
Depreciation—factory machinery	20,100
Amortization of patents	6,000
Small tools used	11,230

By physical count on February 28, 1986, the inventory of materials is determined to be $42,500. The accountant estimates that the valuation of work-in process inventory on February 28, 1986, is $45,600. Prepare a schedule of cost of goods manufactured.

E23–9 *Cost of goods manufactured and sold; gross margin*

The following information is from the books of Casco Bay Company:

	June 30, 1985	June 30, 1984	Year Ended June 30, 1985
Materials inventory	$ 30,000	$ 34,500	
Work-in-process inventory	44,700	43,050	
Finished goods inventory	140,250	145,600	
Materials purchases			$ 413,250
Transportation in—materials			20,550
Direct labor			465,000
Manufacturing overhead			395,200
Sales			1,750,000

Compute the cost of goods manufactured, the cost of goods sold, and the gross margin on sales.

E23–10 *Inventories on the work sheet*

Enter the following ending inventories into a work sheet and extend the beginning inventories to the proper columns:

Ending Inventory	Amount
Materials	$1,500
Work in process	4,650
Finished goods	7,500

ALFREDO COMPANY
Work Sheet
For the Year Ended December 31, 1985

	Trial Balance		Adjustments		Manufacturing		Income Statement		Balance Sheet	
Account Title	**Dr.**	**Cr.**	**Dr.**	**Cr.**	**Dr.**	**Cr.**	**Dr.**	**Cr.**	**Dr.**	**Cr.**
Cash	4,100									
Materials Inventory	900									
Work-in-Process Inventory	6,750									
Finished Goods Inventory	9,000									

E23–11 *Completion of work sheet*

Enter the following condensed *adjusted* trial balance of Elite Company on a work sheet and complete the work sheet for 1985.

Account Title	Debits	Credits
Cash	$ 300	
Accounts Receivable	210	
Materials Inventory	150	
Work-in-Process Inventory	120	
Finished Goods Inventory	180	
Machinery and Equipment	750	
Accumulated Depreciation—Machinery & Equipment		$ 150
Accounts Payable		360
Common Stock ($1 par value)		730
Retained Earnings		290
Sales		1,260
Materials Purchases	450	
Direct Labor	300	
Manufacturing Overhead	240	
Selling Expenses	60	
General and Administrative Expenses	30	
Totals	$2,790	$2,790

Ending inventories on December 31, 1985:

Materials	$215
Work in process	175
Finished goods	150

E23–12 *Purchase and return of materials*

Prepare general journal entries to record the following materials transactions at the World Company in August 1985:

1985		
Aug.	5	Purchased 5,000 kilograms of extending fluid in 5 kilogram cans at $9 per can, terms 2/10, n/30.
	6	Returned to vendor 1,000 kilograms that were of incorrect color.
	12	Paid amount due on this purchase, using check no. 8011.

E23–13 *Computing missing elements*

Empire Builders had a work-in-process inventory of $50,000 on January 31, 1985. It contained direct labor costing $18,000. Manufacturing overhead in the inventory was equal to 90 percent of direct labor. How much materials cost was in the inventory?

E23–14 *Effects of inventory changes*

Bloomington Company had the following costs in 1985:

Direct materials used	$275,000
Direct labor	428,000
Manufacturing overhead	321,000

The ending work-in-process inventory was $8,000 greater than the beginning work-in-process inventory. At the same time, the finished goods inventory at the end of 1985 was $13,500 less than at the beginning. Compute (a) cost of goods manufactured, and (b) cost of goods sold.

E23–15 *Journalizing closing entries*

Allegheny Corporation had the following accounts in its trial balance on December 31, 1985:

Materials Inventory	$ 16,200
Work-in-Process Inventory	34,600
Finished Goods Inventory	42,100
Sales	1,950,000
Materials Purchases	382,750
Materials Purchases Discounts	7,600
Direct Labor	482,130
Manufacturing Overhead	530,000
Selling Expense Control	121,670
General and Administrative Expense Control	62,300

Inventories on December 31, 1985 were:

Materials	$ 18,000
Work-in-process	31,200
Finished goods	37,750

Journalize the closing entries.

A Problems

P23–1A *Cost of goods manufactured and sold*

The following data are taken from the books of the Creditable Company for 1985:

Materials purchases	$ 55,000
Direct labor	110,000
Manufacturing overhead	110,000
Materials inventory change (amount of increase of ending inventory over beginning inventory)	16,500
Work-in-process inventory decrease	11,000
Finished goods inventory increase	5,500

Required: Determine (a) the cost of goods manufactured, and (b) the cost of goods sold.

P23–2A *Schedule of cost of goods manufactured*

Following are selected account balances from the trial balance of Altoona Producers on January 31, 1985:

Cash	$23,210
Materials Inventory, January 1, 1985	5,775
Work-in-Process Inventory, January 1, 1985	2,200
Prepaid Insurance	1,375
Small Tools	275
Accumulated Depreciation—Machinery	15,125
Accounts Payable	10,725
Materials Purchases	69,025
Transportation In—Materials	2,255
Materials Purchases Returns and Allowances	3,025
Direct Labor	41,250
Factory Rent	3,025
Heat, Light, and Power—Factory	3,740
Indirect Labor	2,860
Insurance (on machinery) Expired	1,375
Small Tools Used	825
Depreciation Cost—Machinery	4,125
Miscellaneous Factory Costs	660

Inventories on January 31, 1985:

Materials	$ 4,675
Work in process	2,530

Required: Prepare a schedule of cost of goods manufactured in January.

P23–3A *Manufacturing work sheet*

The condensed year-end trial balance of Towanda Manufacturers before adjustments on December 31, 1985, is as follows:

Account Title	Debits	Credits
Cash	$10,500	
Accounts Receivable	7,350	
Materials Inventory	5,250	
Work-in-Process Inventory	4,200	
Finished Goods Inventory	6,300	
Machinery	26,250	
Accumulated Depreciation—Machinery		$ 5,250
Accounts Payable		12,600
Common Stock ($1 par value)		26,250
Retained Earnings		9,450
Sales		44,100
Materials Purchases	15,750	
Direct Labor	10,500	
Manufacturing Overhead	8,400	
Selling Expenses	2,100	
General and Administrative Expenses	1,050	
Totals	$97,650	$97,650

Additional information:

a. Inventories, December 31, 1985:

Materials	$7,350
Work in process	6,300
Finished goods	5,250

b. Depreciation of machinery for 1985 2,625

c. Wages accrued and unpaid on December 31, 1985:

Direct labor	350
Sales salaries	84
Office salaries	42

Required:

1. Enter the trial balance on a work sheet.

2. Make work sheet entries indicated by the additional information and complete the work sheet.

P23–4A
Financial statements

The adjusted trial balance of Manoa Company for the year ended December 31, 1985, is shown below:

MANOA COMPANY
Adjusted Trial Balance
December 31, 1985

Account Title	Debits	Credits
Cash	$ 29,340	
Accounts Receivable	71,802	
Allowance for Doubtful Accounts		$ 2,160
Materials Inventory	53,280	
Work-in-Process Inventory	2,862	
Finished Goods Inventory	21,780	
Prepaid Insurance	768	
Machinery and Equipment	81,540	
Accumulated Depreciation—Machinery and Equipment		36,576
Office Equipment	14,418	
Accumulated Depreciation—Office Equipment		6,840
Accounts Payable		26,280
Income Taxes Payable		6,300
Accrued Wages and Salaries Payable		9,900
Common Stock, $2 Par Value		108,000
Retained Earnings		63,180
Sales		396,000
Sales Returns and Allowances	4,860	
Sales Discounts	2,280	
Materials Purchases	82,440	
Materials Purchases Returns and Allowances		2,478
Materials Purchases Discounts		2,700
Direct Labor	91,926	
Depreciation—Machinery and Equipment	9,360	
Indirect Labor	19,620	
Rent	12,960	
Heat, Light, and Power	8,280	
Insurance	3,120	
Advertising Expense	6,840	
Sales Salaries Expense	92,340	
Executive Salaries Expense	40,860	
Bad Debts Expense	1,980	
Depreciation Expense—Office Equipment	1,458	
Income Taxes Expenses	6,300	
Totals	$660,414	$660,414

Additional data:
December 31, 1985 inventories:

Materials	$48,792
Work in process	2,880
Finished goods	30,204

Allocation percentages:

Item	Manufacturing	Selling	General
Rent	70%	20%	10%
Heat, light, and power	80	10	10
Insurance	70	15	15

Required: Prepare:

1. A schedule of cost of goods manufactured for 1985.

2. An income statement.

3. A statement of retained earnings.

4. A balance sheet.

P23–5A *Schedule of cost of goods manufactured and partial closing*

Following are the Manufacturing columns of the work sheet of Anchorage Corporation for the year ended December 31, 1985:

	Manufacturing	
	Debits	**Credits**
Materials Inventory	85,500	82,650
Work-in-Process Inventory	57,000	71,250
Materials Purchases	199,500	
Direct Labor	99,750	
Indirect Labor	21,375	
Rent	9,120	
Heat, Light, and Power	6,840	
Depreciation—Machinery and Equipment	8,550	
Miscellaneous Factory Costs	7,125	
Totals	494,760	153,900
Cost of goods manufactured		340,860
Totals	494,760	494,760

Required:

1. Prepare a schedule of cost of goods manufactured for 1985.

2. Journalize the closing entries pertaining to the manufacturing function.

P23–6A *Thought-provoking problem: is a farmer a manufacturer?*

David Poling is a farmer who produces and sells Silver Queen corn. In 1985, his records—while rather informal—indicated the following:

Corn sold for cash	$146,500
Corn sold on credit	62,315
Wages (gross pay) of farm hands	68,180
Employer's FICA taxes	4,772
Employer's state and federal unemployment taxes	1,704
Seed purchased	21,500
Fertilizer purchased	36,050
Depreciation of farm machinery	7,000
Repairs to farm machinery	2,740

Because all produce is sold as fresh corn, there are no inventories carried over from year to year.

Required:

1. Prepare a schedule of the cost of corn produced. Is this similar to cost of goods manufactured? Explain.

2. Compute the gross margin on sales.

3. In what respects is a farmer's business similar to a manufacturer?

B Problems

P23–1B
Cost of goods manufactured and sold

The following data are taken from the accounting records of Forestbrook Company for the year 1985:

Materials purchases	$ 77,500
Direct labor	155,000
Manufacturing overhead	155,000
Materials inventory change (amount of increase of ending inventory over beginning inventory)	23,250
Work-in-process inventory decrease	15,500
Finished goods inventory increase	7,750

Required: Determine (a) the cost of goods manufactured, and (b) the cost of goods sold.

P23–2B
Schedule of cost of goods manufactured

Following are selected account balances from the trial balance of Glen Ulna Manufacturing Company on May 31, 1985:

Cash	$ 35,448
Materials Inventory, May 1, 1985	8,820
Work-in-Process Inventory, May 1, 1985	3,360
Prepaid Insurance	2,100
Small Tools	420
Accumulated Depreciation—Machinery	23,100
Accounts Payable	16,380
Materials Purchases	105,420
Transportation In—Materials	3,444
Materials Purchases Returns and Allowances	4,620
Direct Labor	63,000
Factory Rent	4,620
Heat, Light, and Power—Factory	5,712
Indirect Labor	4,368
Insurance (on machinery) Expired	2,100
Small Tools Used	1,260
Depreciation Cost—Machinery	6,300
Miscellaneous Factory Costs	1,008

Inventories on May 31 were:

Materials	$ 7,140
Work in process	3,864

Required: Prepare a schedule of cost of goods manufactured in May.

P23–3B *Manufacturing work sheet*

The condensed year-end trial balance of San Jacinto Company before adjustments on June 30, 1985, is as follows:

Account Title	Debits	Credits
Cash	$ 11,880	
Accounts Receivable	8,316	
Materials Inventory	5,940	
Work-in-Process Inventory	4,752	
Finished Goods Inventory	7,128	
Machinery	29,700	
Accumulated Depreciation—Machinery		$ 5,940
Accounts Payable		14,256
Common Stock ($5 par value)		29,700
Retained Earnings		10,692
Sales		49,896
Materials Purchases	17,820	
Direct Labor	11,880	
Manufacturing Overhead	9,504	
Selling Expenses	2,376	
General and Administrative Expenses	1,188	
Totals	$110,484	$110,484

Additional information:

a. Inventories, June 30, 1985:

Materials	$8,316
Work in process	7,128
Finished goods	5,940

b. Depreciation of machinery for 1985 . . . 2,970

c. Wages accrued and unpaid on June 30, 1985:

Direct labor	396
Sales salaries	96
Office salaries	48

Required:

1. Enter the trial balance on a work sheet.

2. Make work sheet entries indicated by the additional information and complete the work sheet.

P23–4B *Financial statements* The adjusted trial balance of the Brazonport Company for the year ended October 31, 1985, follows:

BRAZONPORT COMPANY
Adjusted Trial Balance
October 31, 1985

Account Title	Debits	Credits
Cash	$ 4,890	
Accounts Receivable	11,967	
Allowance for Doubtful Accounts		$ 360
Materials Inventory	8,880	
Work-in-Process Inventory	477	
Finished Goods Inventory	3,630	
Prepaid Insurance	128	
Machinery and Equipment	13,590	
Accumulated Depreciation—Machinery and Equipment		6,096
Office Equipment	2,403	
Accumulated Depreciation—Office Equipment		1,140
Accounts Payable		4,380
Income Taxes Payable		1,050
Accrued Wages and Salaries Payable		1,650
Common Stock, $2 Par Value		18,000
Retained Earnings		10,530
Sales		66,000
Sales Returns and Allowances	810	
Sales Discounts	375	
Materials Purchases	13,740	
Materials Purchases Returns and Allowances		413
Materials Purchases Discounts		450
Direct Labor	15,321	
Depreciation—Machinery and Equipment	1,560	
Indirect Labor	3,270	
Rent	2,160	
Heat, Light, and Power	1,380	
Insurance	525	
Advertising Expense	1,140	
Sales Salaries Expense	15,390	
Executive Salaries Expense	6,810	
Bad Debts Expense	330	
Depreciation Expense—Office Equipment	243	
Income Taxes Expense	1,050	
Totals	$110,069	$110,069

Additional data:

October 31, 1985 inventories:

Materials	$9,600
Work in process	1,020
Finished goods	8,000

Allocation percentages:

Item	Manufacturing	Selling	General
Rent	80%	10%	10%
Heat, light, and power	75	15	10
Insurance	60	20	20

Required: Prepare:

1. A schedule of cost of goods manufactured for 1985.
2. An income statement.
3. A statement of retained earnings.
4. A balance sheet.

P23–5B *Schedule of cost of goods manufactured and partial closing*

Following are the manufacturing columns of the work sheet of the Smaller Corporation for the year ended March 31, 1985:

	Manufacturing	
	Debits	**Credits**
Materials Inventory	15,000	14,500
Work-in-Process Inventory	10,000	12,500
Materials Purchases	35,000	
Direct Labor	17,500	
Indirect Labor	3,750	
Rent	1,600	
Heat, Light, and Power	1,200	
Depreciation—Machinery and Equipment	1,500	
Miscellaneous Factory Costs	1,250	
Totals	86,800	27,000
Cost of goods manufactured		59,800
Totals	86,800	86,800

Required:

1. Prepare a schedule of cost of goods manufactured for the year.
2. Journalize the closing entries pertaining to the manufacturing function.

P23–6B *Thought-provoking problem: change in inventory methods for materials*

Snooker Corporation had 50,000 shares of $1.00 par value common stock outstanding during 1985. In the same year, its earnings were subject to an income tax rate of 40 percent. Using the FIFO method of accounting for materials inventory as it has for years, the 1985 net income before income tax would be $325,000. The controller suggests that the company should change to the LIFO method to account for materials in 1985 to conform to the general practice in the industry. The December 31, 1985, materials inventory valuation under FIFO was $200,000; under LIFO the valuation would be $160,000. There were no finished goods inventories at the beginning or end of 1985.

Required:

1. What would be the effect of the change to LIFO on net income before taxes? Aftertax net income?
2. What would be the effect of the change to LIFO on aftertax earnings per share?
3. What would be the effect of the change to LIFO on income taxes paid?
4. Discuss the merits of the controller's proposal considering these points among others:
   a. Stockholder reaction to the change in earnings per share.
   b. Effect on the cash available for operations in 1986.
   c. Effect on the current ratio.

24 Job Order Cost Accounting

Introduction

As explained in Chapter 23, a company that makes the product it sells needs to use some additional accounts in its ledger to gather information for calculating the cost of goods manufactured. Probably the leading management strategy used by United States manufacturers to survive the economic decline of 1982 was cost control. For example, Ford Motor Company announced in 1983 that operating costs had been reduced by more than $3 billion over the past three years. The type of financial accounting for general manufacturing operations described in Chapter 23 is often not adequate to meet such needs of management. The additional records needed to provide this information are known as a *cost accounting system.* This chapter explains the nature and purpose of one type of cost accounting system, job order cost accounting, and also introduces the concept of the budget.

Learning Goals

To understand the general flow of costs in the manufacturing process.

To understand the flow of manufacturing overhead costs through the accounts.

To understand the concept of cost accounting systems.

To increase knowledge of the perpetual inventory concept.

To compute and use a predetermined overhead rate.

To understand the use of cost sheets as a subsidiary work-in-process inventory ledger.

To journalize the entries involved in using a job order cost accounting system.

Cost Accounting Systems

If the Cola Manufacturing Company described in Chapter 23 made only a single product, it would be simple to compute the unit cost of manufacturing that product. For a single-product manufacturing firm, the **unit cost** equals the cost of goods manufactured (which is the cost of the units that are completed) divided by the number of units produced. Assume that 200,000 units had been produced by the Cola Manufacturing Company in 1985. Then, using the cost of goods manufactured from Figure 23–7,

$$\frac{\$229,845}{200,000} = \$1.149225.^{1}$$

With the knowledge that manufacturing costs per unit were approximately $1.15, management can do a better job of decision making, for example in establishing selling prices.

Suppose that the company makes more than one product. Then, what is the cost *per unit* to make each of them? Or, what is the total cost for a single line of products? Neither of these questions can be answered with the information provided in a simple financial accounting system.

In many industries, since supply and demand are major controlling influences, there is little that a manufacturer can do to control selling prices. For example, most brands of fuel seem to sell at about the same price regardless of cost. Under such circumstances, a firm is successful not so much because of the prices it charges but through cost control. The firm that can deliver a comparable product at a lower cost is the one that will survive and grow. Cost control in a large firm requires knowledge of costs on an immediate basis in small segments of the manufacturing process and swift management action if costs begin to depart from planned or experienced levels. To further both of these aims—(1) cost control and (2) to the extent practicable, price setting—management needs the information provided by a **cost accounting system** (accounting records that gather cost information in detail).

General Flow of Costs in Cost Accounting

At the beginning of Chapter 23, the manufacturing process is described. The reader should refer to Figure 23–1 to review the flow of materials, labor, and overhead through the manufacturing process to finished goods inventory. When a manufacturer uses a cost accounting system, it is possible to have up-to-date knowledge of costs of these specific items as they are incurred and assigned to production. In general, manufacturing costs flow in a parallel manner. They are first recorded in accounts that describe their nature—Materials Inventory for materials purchased; Factory Payroll for labor paid; and Manufacturing Overhead Control for manufacturing overhead costs paid, recorded as depreciation, or otherwise incurred. Periodically an appropriate

[1] The accuracy of this unit cost depends on the ability to make reasonably accurate estimates of the beginning and ending work-in-process inventory valuations. This task requires the use of some of the techniques discussed in this chapter.

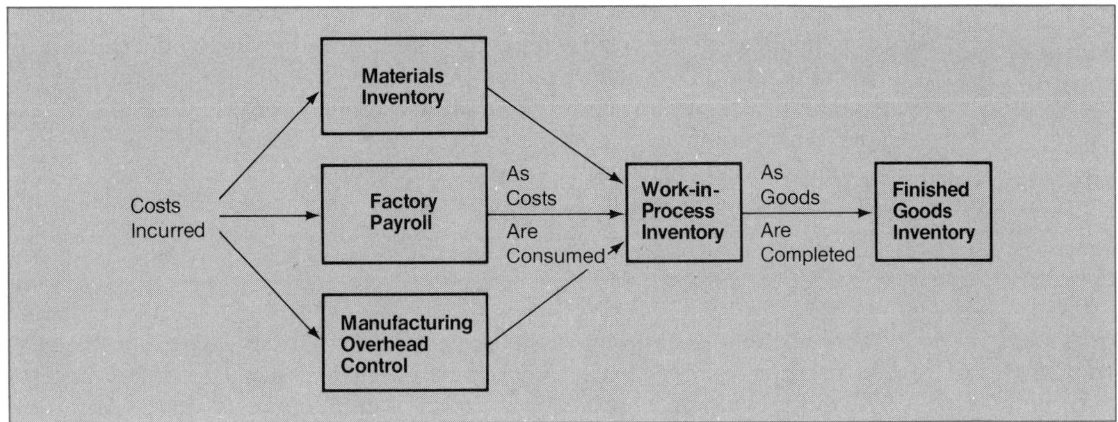

Figure 24–1 **General Manufacturing Cost Flow**

amount of these costs are assigned to Work-in-Process Inventory as they are consumed in the manufacturing process. Then as goods are completed, the costs of completed units of product are transferred to the Finished Goods Inventory account where they remain as current assets until the product is sold. This general cost flow is shown in Fig. 24–1.

Management decision making requires information about total costs and costs per unit of product as they flow through the Work-in-Process Inventory account. It is at this point that it is possible to exercise cost control. Cost accounting systems provide the data that a manager needs constantly. There are two basic types of cost accounting systems, the *job order cost system* and the *process cost system.* The nature of the production process in a business is the major factor to determine which is the appropriate system for that business. This chapter describes the job order cost system; the process cost system is described in Chapter 25. The major difference between the two systems is in the method of determining unit costs of product in the Work-in-Process Inventory account.

Inventories and Manufacturing Overhead

Before detailing the techniques used in a job order cost system, it is necessary to discuss two topics that are important to all cost accounting systems.

1. *Inventory method.* For a cost accounting system, the periodic inventory method *does not* provide materials cost and quantity information that is current enough to be useful. Therefore, a perpetual inventory system is needed for materials inventory accounting and is often used. The perpetual system was described in Chapter 12 and is discussed further in the following section.

2. *Recording of overhead costs.* Because overhead costs are subject to various uncontrollable influences—for example, heating costs are greater in winter than in summer—it is desirable to find a method that will match a propor-

tionate share of overhead costs with each unit of product. The method used is to debit actual overhead costs as they are incurred to an account called **Manufacturing Overhead Control.**[2] As work on the product progresses, overhead costs are transferred from Manufacturing Overhead Control (applied) to Work-in-Process Inventory by the use of a factory overhead rate determined at the beginning of the year. The method of establishing such a rate and the use of the overhead rate are explained after the inventory illustrations.

Perpetual Inventories— A Review

When the perpetual inventory system is used, a subsidiary ledger composed of a separate record for each item in the inventory is maintained. In Chapter 12, this record was illustrated in the form of inventory record cards. Many companies keep the inventory records on computer files, but the principles are the same. One use of a perpetual system is in control of materials inventory. Figure 24–2 illustrates the relationship between the Materials Inventory account in the general ledger and the subsidiary ledger composed of the inventory record cards. Assuming that the October 3 entry represents a pur-

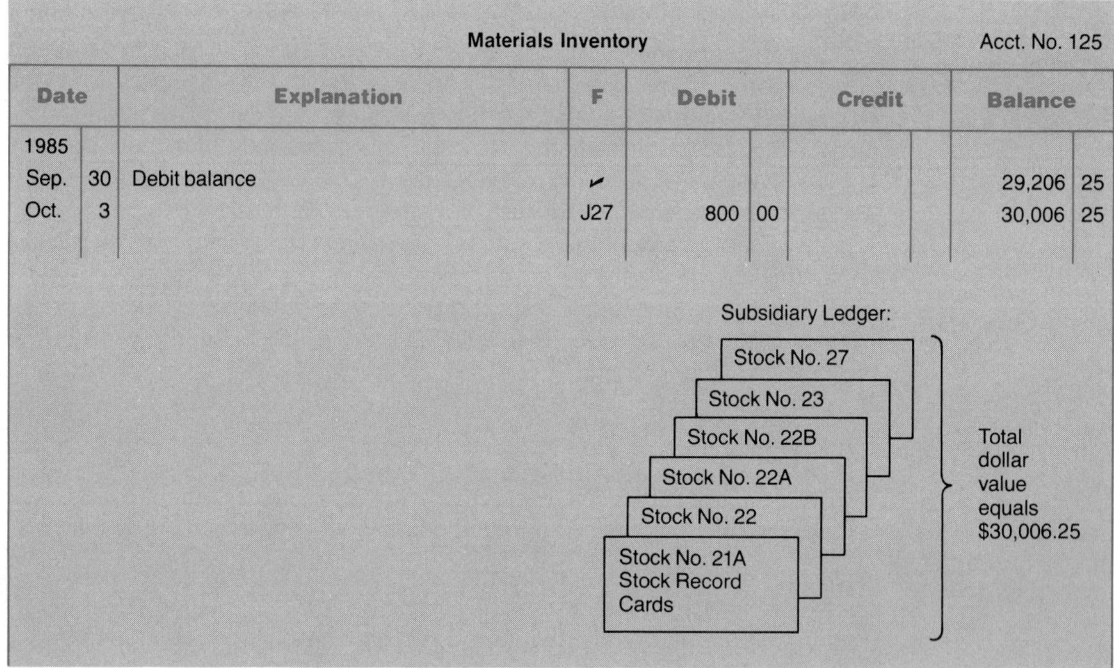

Materials Inventory Acct. No. 125

Date		Explanation	F	Debit	Credit	Balance
1985						
Sep.	30	Debit balance	✓			29,206 25
Oct.	3		J27	800 00		30,006 25

Figure 24–2 **Materials Inventory Account and Subsidiary Ledger**

[2]Specific items of cost are recorded in a subsidiary ledger leaving totals only in the controlling account.

chase of 400 units of stock number 22B at $2 each and that Whittier Company makes the entry in the general journal, it would appear as follows:

Page 27

1985 Oct.	3	Materials Inventory	125	800	
		Accounts Payable	216		800
		To record purchase of 400 units of stock number 22B.			

The cost of the receipt of 400 units is posted to the Materials Inventory account in the general ledger, as can be seen by the posting of October 3 in Figure 24–2. It is also posted to the stock record or materials inventory card (see Chapter 12) for stock number 22B, causing the total dollar amount in the subsidiary ledger to be equal to the general ledger controlling account when all posting is up-to-date. This is the same subsidiary ledger/controlling account relationship that exists with accounts receivable or payable.

The receipts into and issues out of the materials storeroom are posted daily to stock record cards (illustrated in Chapter 12). Receipts are posted from copies of *receiving reports* (illustrated in Figure 7–2). Issues are posted to the stock record cards daily from a source document called a **materials requisition.** A typical materials requisition is illustrated in Figure 24–3. If it is possible to identify the job on which issued materials are to be used, it is an issue of **direct materials.** Issues of material for general use (for example, lubricating oil for factory machinery) are called issues of **indirect materials.** In most manufacturing firms, materials requisitions are not journalized and posted to the general ledger account daily but are summarized, journalized, and posted at the end of a period—say monthly. Of course, the equality of total dollar value of the Materials Inventory account in the general ledger and the total dollar value of the stock record cards (as shown in Figure 24–2) is true only when all postings are up-to-date.

MATERIALS REQUISITION

No. 00326

Date 10-4-85 Issue to Dept 2 Charge to Job No. 62

Stock Number	Description	Qty.	Unit Cost	Amount
21A	Gaskets	50	1.00	50.00
22B	Couplings	100	2.00	200.00
	Total			250.00

Approved by J. Seibert Received by O. Haines

Figure 24–3 **Materials Requisition**

Similar procedures are used for the Finished Goods Inventory account. There is a set of inventory records (stock record cards) with a separate card for each item of product manufactured. Increases are posted to the stock record cards as manufacturing jobs are completed and transferred to the finished goods storeroom. Decreases are posted as sales are made. As finished goods are sold, journal entries are required to record these inventory decreases. The account debited in such entries is called **Cost of Goods Sold.** Its use is illustrated later in the "Journal Entries and Flow of Costs" section. When postings to both the general ledger and subsidiary ledger are up-to-date, the balance in the Finished Goods Inventory account is equal to the total dollar value of balances in the subsidiary ledger.

The second topic that is important to all cost accounting systems is recording of manufacturing overhead costs. This topic is discussed next.

The Manufacturing Overhead Budget and Rate

Direct material and direct labor costs incurred can easily be identified to specific jobs. Manufacturing overhead, however, cannot be economically traced to specific jobs. Some manufacturing overhead items—depreciation, insurance, rent, and property taxes, for example—are related to the passage of time and are not affected by production volume. Other manufacturing overhead costs—power, cutting oil, and small tools, for example—vary with the volume of production. If completed product costs are to be available to management when the job is completed, it becomes necessary to assign manufacturing overhead to work-in-process when the jobs are in production, *not at year-end.* Since the actual incurred overhead is not yet known, it is assigned on an estimated or predetermined basis. As manufacturing overhead cost is assigned to work-in-process inventory, it becomes **applied manufacturing overhead.** This cost flow is shown in Figure 24–4. The process of applying manufacturing overhead and the disposition of underapplied or overapplied cost are discussed in more detail later.

To facilitate this application of overhead on a predetermined basis, management must prepare an estimate of manufacturing overhead cost for the forthcoming year. This estimate (or financial plan), called a **budget,** provides management with the information necessary to apply overhead to a job before the amount of actual incurred overhead cost is known. It also provides management with a tool to control manufacturing overhead costs.

Predetermined overhead rate

The calculation of* predetermined overhead rate *is based (1) on budgeted manufacturing overhead cost for the planned future production, and (2) on an estimated volume factor that reflects planned future production.

Calculation of Overhead Rate A cause and effect relationship should exist between the volume factor selected and the amount of manufacturing

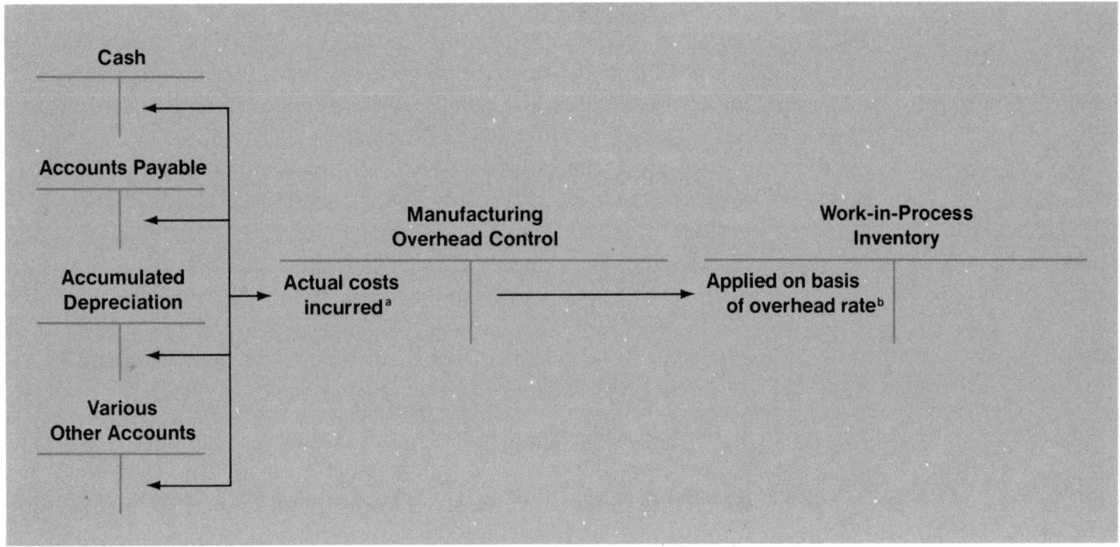

[a]If actual costs are greater than applied, an underapplied condition exists.

[b]If applied costs are greater than actual, an overapplied condition exists.

Figure 24–4 **Flow of Manufacturing Overhead Cost**

overhead cost. In highly automated operations, machine hours may be the best indicator of overhead cost used. Many companies find that manufacturing overhead usage is closely related to direct labor hours worked. These companies use direct labor hours as the volume factor to apply overhead. To illustrate, assume that the Whittier Company budget plans for manufacturing overhead costs of $800,000 and a production level of 200,000 direct labor hours during 1985. In this plant, there is a close relationship between direct labor hours and manufacturing overhead. The predetermined rate for 1985 is calculated as follows:

$$\frac{\text{Budgeted manufacturing overhead}}{\text{Planned direct labor hours}} = \frac{\$800{,}000}{200{,}000} = \$4 \text{ per direct labor hour.}$$

The $4 per hour rate is used to apply overhead cost to work-in-process inventory as diagrammed in Figure 24–4.

If actual direct labor hours during 1985 are 200,000, as estimated, the Whittier Company will have applied $800,000 = (200,000 hours × $4) in manufacturing overhead costs to the various job order cost sheets. If, as is likely, a difference exists between the actual costs and the applied amounts, there will be an end-of-period balance in the Manufacturing Overhead Control account. A debit balance indicates **underapplied** overhead (overhead applied is *less* than actual overhead) and a credit balance indicates **overapplied** overhead (overhead applied is *more* than actual overhead).

Other bases (activity level factors) for applying manufacturing overhead are (1) direct labor dollars, (2) machine hours, (3) units of production, and (4) material cost. The method of computation of a predetermined overhead rate using any of these bases is the same as for direct labor hours. Assume that the Whittier Company finds that the most appropriate base for determining the overhead rate is direct labor cost. Assuming planned direct labor cost of $1,600,000 for planned production in 1985, the computation of the predetermined overhead rate based on labor cost is as follows:

$$\frac{\text{Budgeted manufacturing overhead}}{\text{Budgeted labor cost}} = \frac{\$800{,}000}{\$1{,}600{,}000} = 50\% \text{ of labor cost.}$$

Thus for each dollar of direct labor cost incurred, 50¢ of manufacturing overhead cost will be applied to work-in-process inventory.

Selecting the Basis of Allocation An important management decision is the selection of the proper basis for allocating overhead. The basis that should be selected is one that charges the job with an amount of manufacturing overhead most nearly corresponding to the actual manufacturing overhead costs incurred on the job. A detailed analysis should be made of all cost and production factors involved prior to the selection of a base, and it should be continuously reconsidered.

The direct labor hours method is used widely because it recognizes the relationship between work effort and overhead cost: that is, an increase in direct labor hours on a job will normally result in a corresponding increase in the factory overhead costs caused by that job. If there is a relationship between direct labor cost and volume of activity, direct labor cost rather than hours may give a better basis for allocating a fair share of overhead. In like manner, machine hours, units of production, or material cost may be used if one of these more clearly indicates productive activity than the use of a rate based on labor. A knowledge of the reason for choosing different overhead allocation bases becomes particularly important when a firm has several departments where different bases might be required.

Against this background, the next section describes how materials, direct labor, and manufacturing overhead costs are recorded in the Work-in-Process Inventory account and its subsidiary records in a job order cost accounting system.

Job Order Cost Accounting

In some types of industry, it is useful to identify costs with a specific product unit, or *job*. A shipyard, for example, builds several ships (and repairs others) of various sizes and types at the same time. A bridge contractor may have several bridges (all different) under construction at the same time. In these instances, it is desirable to record the costs of each job separately, using a **job order cost accounting system.** A job order cost system is also effective in some instances in which a batch (or job lot) of identical products is made either for stock or for a special order. It is used whenever the focus of cost recording is on the batch of like products or a job. Because each item or batch of items is different from other product units, the system must identify specific costs with the item or lot.

Cost Sheets

In a job order cost accounting system, a subsidiary record to Work-in-Process Inventory called a **cost sheet** is maintained *for each job* that is in process. Figure 24–5 illustrates a typical cost sheet for the Whittier Company, showing materials, direct labor, and manufacturing overhead costs recorded separately. These costs are recorded daily on each cost sheet from copies of various internal documents. The following sections give a more detailed explanation of how each cost is recorded.

WHITTIER COMPANY

Cost Sheet

Quantity and Description: 2 Power Brake Assemblies Job No. 62

Date Started: Oct. 4, 1985 Date Completed: Oct. 10, 1985

For: Stock

Direct Materials			Direct Labor			
Date	Requisition Number	Amount	Date	Time Ticket Number	Hours	Amount
10/4	00326	$250	10/4	976	8	$ 80
10/6	00418	151	10/5	1021 & 1022	16	136
10/10	00672	450	10/6	1101 & 1102	12	131
			10/8	1135 & 1140	10	116
			10/10	1200	4	60
	Total	$851		Totals	50	$523

Summary

	Amount	Per Unit
Materials	$ 851.00	$425.50
Labor	523.00	261.50
Overhead (50 hours at $4.00)	200.00	100.00
	$1,574.00	$787.00

Figure 24–5 **Job Order Cost Sheet**

Materials Used Figure 24–3 showed requisition no. 00326, on which $250 of materials was issued to job number 62 on October 4, 1985. A copy of that requisition is used to record this issuance of materials on the cost sheet (see first entry in Figure 24–5). Figure 24–5 indicates that two other issuances of materials were made to job number 62 on requisitions 00418 and 00672.

Both of these issuances were also recorded on the cost sheet from copies of the requisitions. The total of direct materials used on job number 62 is $851. These requisitions are held until the end of the period and grouped with all the others for general journal entries that reflect the materials cost flows through the accounts as follows:

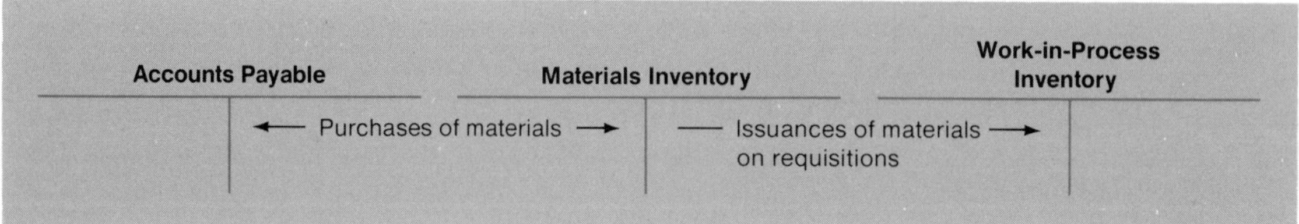

Direct Labor Usage In a job order cost accounting system, **direct labor** is production personnel cost that can be identified with a specific job. Labor costs that cannot be pinpointed to specific jobs (for example, stockroom personnel wages) are **indirect labor.** Direct labor costs are recorded on individual **time tickets** each time employees work on a job. Figure 24–6 illustrates time ticket no. 976, showing that John Seibert worked a full eight-hour day on job number 62 on October 4. From a copy of the time ticket, the cost of Seibert's time on October 4, $80 = (8 hours × $10), is entered on the cost sheet (Figure 24–5). The cost sheet indicates that at least two persons worked on job number 62 on October 5, because two time tickets for a total of 16 hours have been recorded. In addition, time tickets for October 6, 8, and 10 are charged to job number 62. The total direct labor cost for the job is $523. Along with other payroll records, the time tickets form the basis for end-of-period journal entries for the payroll. When the payroll for production workers is recorded, an account called **Factory Payroll** is debited for the gross pay. The proper withholding accounts (see Chapter 8) and Salaries and Wages Payable are credited. The Factory Payroll account serves a purpose similar to Manufacturing Overhead Control. It is a temporary clearing account

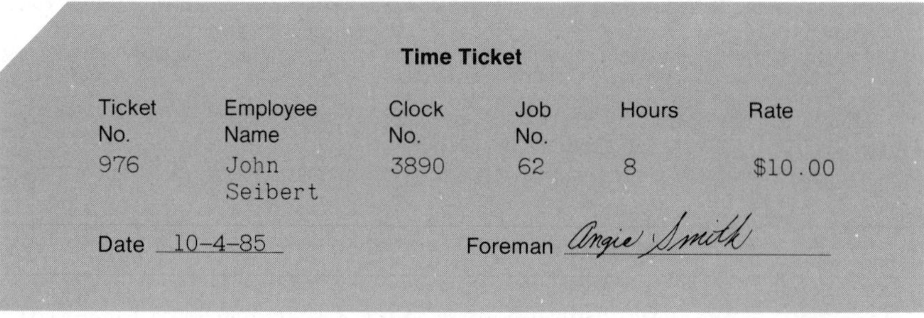

Time Ticket

Ticket No.	Employee Name	Clock No.	Job No.	Hours	Rate
976	John Seibert	3890	62	8	$10.00

Date 10-4-85 Foreman Angie Smith

Figure 24–6
Time Ticket

for labor costs until they are transferred to Work-in-Process Inventory or to Manufacturing Overhead Control. The sequence works as follows:

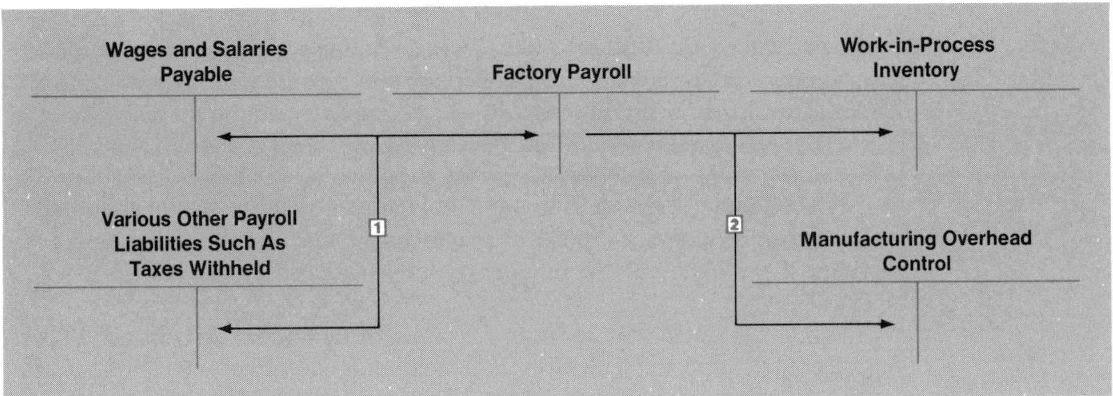

1 As the payroll is recorded, the Factory Payroll account is debited to store the factory labor costs until they are transferred out.

2 At least monthly, an entry is made to transfer the direct labor portion to Work-in-Process Inventory and the indirect labor portion to Manufacturing Overhead Control. This entry is called the **distribution** of payroll costs.

Note that the balance in the Factory Payroll account should be zero when this entry is complete and all labor costs have been assigned to the proper manufacturing cost account. Yet the Factory Payroll account serves a second useful purpose. It measures the gross factory wages, and that information is useful for cost control.

Manufacturing Overhead Applied Manufacturing overhead costs are usually allocated to all jobs by the use of a rate that was determined at the beginning of the year. In this firm, there is a close relationship between direct labor hours worked and the use of manufacturing overhead items. Therefore, direct labor hours was determined to be the best basis for assigning (allocation) of overhead costs to jobs. That rate in Whittier Company is $4 per direct labor hour. (The method of determining an overhead rate was explained earlier.) The cost sheet (Figure 24–5) shows that 50 direct labor hours were used on job number 62 before it was completed on October 10, 1985. Thus, the amount of overhead used on this job is $200 = (50 × $4). The recording of manufacturing overhead as a part of work-in-process inventory by the use of a predetermined rate is described by the word **applied.** An end-of-month journal entry (see Figure 24–4) to record the amount of overhead applied to production contains a debit to Work-in-Process Inventory and a credit to Manufacturing Overhead Control for $4 per direct labor hour times the number of direct labor hours worked on all jobs. After this journal entry is made, the total manufacturing overhead costs assigned to individual cost sheets are a part of the work-in-process inventory.

Summary of Cost Sheet Data When a job is completed, the total direct materials cost and total direct labor hours and cost are determined. Using a base for allocation (in this case, direct labor hours) and the predetermined overhead rate, the amount of manufacturing overhead is allocated and recorded on the cost sheet. Total cost of the two power brake assemblies produced under job order number 62 is the sum of three elements of cost: materials, labor, and overhead. The unit cost of $787 is determined by dividing the total cost by the number of units produced; in this case, $787 = ($1,574 ÷ 2).

While a job is in the production process, or *producing department,* its cost sheet is being posted daily with direct materials and direct labor charges. The total file of cost sheets representing all jobs in process at any time is a subsidiary ledger to the Work-in-Process Inventory account. At the end of an accounting period, the incomplete job cost sheets are footed, and the amount of overhead allocated to date is recorded on them. Their total cost is then equal to the general ledger account, Work-in-Process Inventory.

Journal Entries and Flow of Costs

The manufacturing costs in a cost accounting system flow through various accounts on their way to becoming part of the cost of goods sold. They are called **product costs** because they become part of the cost of the product made. Parts of this cost flow have been diagrammed as the individual costs were discussed.

These are now brought together in Figure 24–7. It can be seen that costs are first captured in the Materials Inventory, Factory Payroll, and Manufacturing Overhead Control accounts. As materials are used, labor is performed, and overhead is applied, the costs move into Work-in-Process Inventory. Upon completion of specific jobs, the costs that have been gathered in Work-in-Process Inventory are transferred to Finished Goods Inventory. Then as goods are sold, the costs move into the Cost of Goods Sold account, later to be closed into the Income Summary.

Although the emphasis here has been on product costs, selling expenses and general and administrative expenses (period expenses) do exist in manufacturing firms. Period expenses are accounted for in the same manner as in a nonmanufacturing firm.

Journal entries are, of course, required to record the flow of costs diagrammed in Figure 24–7. Although special journals can be used in a cost accounting system, the entries for the Whittier Company are made in general journal form. Some of these entries are accumulated during the period and at

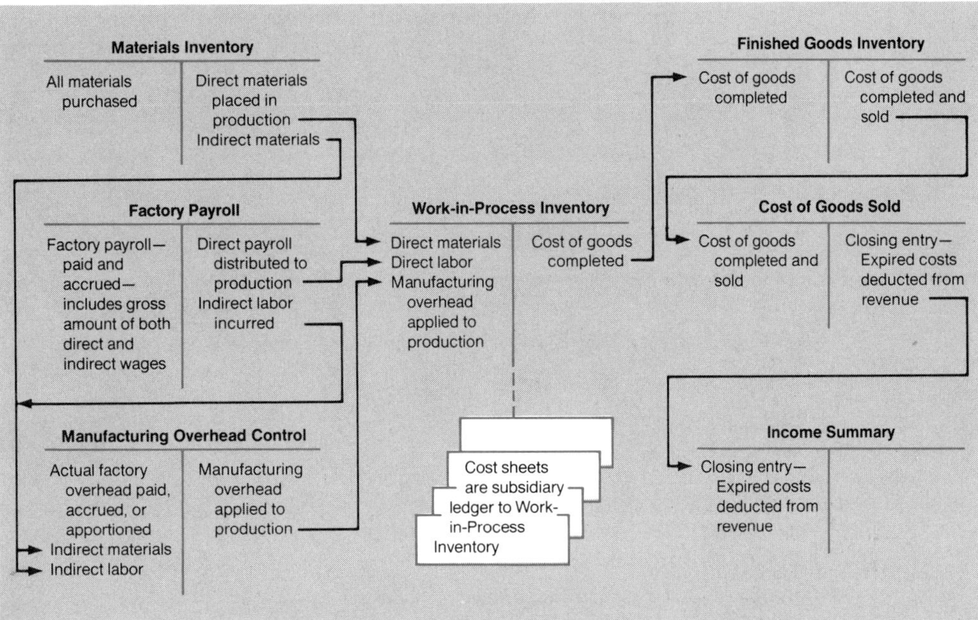

Figure 24–7 **Flow Chart for Job Order Cost System**

the end of a month are made in summary form.[3] The illustration for the Whittier Company is based on the following assumptions:

- ☐ No jobs were in process on October 1, 1985.
- ☐ Job nos. 62, 63, 64, and 65 were started in October.
- ☐ Job no. 62 (Figure 24–5) at a total cost of $1,574 and job no. 63 at a total cost of $2,100 were completed in October.
- ☐ Total costs in October for all jobs whether completed in this period or not were:

Direct materials	$3,150
Indirect materials	200
Direct labor	2,640
Indirect labor	160
Other manufacturing overhead costs incurred	640
Manufacturing overhead applied	980

- ☐ One power brake made in job number 62 was sold at a selling price of $1,200.

[3]Many companies with computerized accounting systems record these entries as each transaction occurs.

The journal entries to record the cost flows are shown in Figure 24–8.

Date		Accounts and Explanation		Debit	Credit
1985 Oct.	31	Work-in-Process Inventory		3,150	
		Manufacturing Overhead Control		200	
		Materials Inventory			3,350
		To record the issuance of direct and indirect materials to production.			
	31	Factory Payroll		2,800	
		Cash or Accrued Factory Wages Payable (and liabilities for all payroll deductions)			2,800
		To record the factory payroll for the period.			
	31	Work-in-Process Inventory		2,640	
		Manufacturing Overhead Control		160	
		Factory Payroll			2,800
		To record the distribution of all factory wages—direct wages to production and indirect wages to manufacturing overhead.			
	31	Manufacturing Overhead Control		640	
		Various accounts (Cash, Accumulated Depreciation, and so on)			640
		To record actual factory overhead paid, accrued, or apportioned.			
	31	Work-in-Process Inventory		980	
		Manufacturing Overhead Control			980
		To record the overhead applied to production by the use of a predetermined rate.			
	31	Finished Goods Inventory		3,674	
		Work-in-Process Inventory			3,674
		To record the cost of jobs 62 and 63 completed in the current period.			
	31	Cost of Goods Sold		787	
		Finished Goods Inventory			787
		To record the expired cost of goods sold during the period (the sale of one of the two power brakes = $1,574 ÷ 2).			
Dec.	31	Income Summary		787	
		Cost of Goods Sold			787
		To close the Cost of Goods Sold account at the end of the period.			

Figure 24–8 **Journal Entries for Cost Flows**

Two additional journal entries are needed to complete this illustration. These are not part of the cost accumulation system, but illustrate the matching of revenue with costs.

1985					
Oct.	31	Accounts Receivable		1,200	
		Sales			1,200
		To record the sale of one power brake.			
Dec.	31	Sales		1,200	
		Income Summary			1,200
		To close the Sales account into Income Summary at the end of the period.			

Underapplied and Overapplied Manufacturing Overhead

In the illustration for the Whittier Company, overhead incurred is $1,000 = (indirect materials of $200, indirect labor of $160, and miscellaneous cost of $640). Only $980 was applied to jobs leaving an underapplied balance of $20. Actual overhead costs tend to fluctuate because of seasonal and other factors. Therefore, underapplied and overapplied balances are carried forward from month to month. In the final month of the accounting year, such balances are closed—usually to Cost of Goods Sold.

Evaluation of the Job Order Cost System

In some industries, such as shipbuilding or automobile repairs, direct materials and direct labor can readily be traced to a specific unit of product. In these low-volume or high-unit-cost situations where the product is produced on a special made-to-order basis, job order systems are necessary. They provide data for planning, bidding on future contracts, and determining whether past operations have been successful. With knowledge of specific costs, management can control costs and set prices more effectively.

But job order systems are expensive to maintain. The need to trace carefully the time of individual direct labor personnel to a product requires extra effort. Separate materials requisitions must be made for each job number even though a number of jobs may be underway in the same department. Some companies use job order procedures for part of their operations and process cost accounting procedures for other parts. Chapter 25 covers process cost accounting procedures.

Glossary

Applied manufacturing overhead The amount of overhead cost allocated (debited) to Work-in-Process Inventory using a predetermined rate.

Budget A financial plan for future operations.

Cost accounting system An accounting system in which period-to-period cost information is developed for management.

Cost of Goods Sold An account used to accumulate the cost of goods that have been sold when a perpetual inventory system is used.

Cost sheet A record of costs of each job in a job order cost accounting system. The file of cost sheets is a subsidiary ledger to the Work-in-Process Inventory account.

Direct labor Costs of labor that can be identified directly with a job.

Direct materials Materials issued that can be identified with a specific job.

Distribution (of payroll cost) The transfer of direct labor costs to Work-in-Process Inventory and indirect labor costs to Manufacturing Overhead Control.

Factory Payroll An account used in cost accounting as a clearing account for factory labor costs. It is debited with the gross amount of factory labor. It is credited as direct labor is tranferred into Work-in-Process Inventory and indirect labor is transferred into Manufacturing Overhead Control.

Indirect labor Cost of factory labor that cannot be identified with a specific job.

Indirect materials Materials used in production operations that cannot be identified with a specific job.

Job order cost accounting system A cost accounting system that accumulates cost information by specific jobs. It is used in low-volume or high-unit-cost situations. It is needed when the product is custom-made.

Manufacturing Overhead Control The account that accumulates actual charges to manufacturing other than direct materials and direct labor.

Materials requisition A source document used to withdraw materials from the storeroom for use in the production departments.

Overapplied overhead The amount of manufacturing overhead applied in excess of actual overhead cost.

Predetermined overhead rate A rate based on budgeted overhead costs and planned production and used to apply (allocate) overhead charges to the Work-in-Process Inventory account.

Process The series of production operations.

Product cost An inventoriable cost, one incorporated in the inventories instead of being charged as an expense of the period.

Time ticket A record of hours and rate of pay per hour that is prepared each time a person works on a job.

Underapplied overhead The amount of actual manufacturing overhead cost not applied when the amount applied is less than actual cost.

Unit cost The cost to produce one unit. When a job order calls for more than one unit, the unit cost is found by dividing total cost by the number of units.

Questions

Q24–1 What factors should be taken into account in deciding when to use a job order cost accounting system?

Q24–2 What subsidiary records are controlled by (a) Work-in-Process Inventory, (b) Materials Inventory, and (c) Finished Goods Inventory?

Q24–3 What is the function of a job order cost sheet? How does it serve as a part of a subsidiary ledger?

Q24–4 What documents provide information for direct materials and direct labor costs on a job order cost sheet? How often are these costs recorded on the cost sheets?

Q24–5 Under a job order cost accounting system, does indirect labor ever become a part of work-in-process inventory? Explain.

Q24–6 What is a manufacturing overhead rate? Explain how it is computed, and describe some possible bases for establishing an overhead rate.

Q24–7 Since actual manufacturing overhead costs are known as they are incurred, why would a company use a predetermined overhead application rate?

Q24–8 What is a budget? Why is the manufacturing overhead budget necessary to computation of the overhead rate?

Q24–9 What is the meaning of the term *applied* when it is used in connection with manufacturing overhead cost?

Q24–10 Diagram the flow of materials, labor, and overhead costs from the time they are originally incurred until they become part of cost of goods sold. Use T accounts to do this.

Q24–11 When materials are issued to be used on a specified job, how is that information sent to the person who maintains the cost sheets? Describe the procedure.

Q24–12 Is the equality of the Work-in-Process Inventory controlling account and the subsidiary ledger maintained on a daily basis? Explain.

Exercises

E24–1 *When to use a job order system*

Indicate which of the following manufacturers would be likely to use a job order cost accounting system and explain why:

a. A textile company that produces canvas in large rolls of identical weight and color.
b. A manufacturer of razor blades.
c. A shipyard that builds and repairs both surface ships and submarines.
d. A soft drink bottling company.
e. A building contractor who erects houses to buyers' specifications.
f. An automobile repair shop.

E24–2 *Materials receipts—perpetual inventory*

Henri Company uses a perpetual inventory system. On October 18, 1985, six receiving reports were prepared in amounts of $260, $1,080, $382, $430, $215, and $612. Prepare a general journal entry to record the total receipts of materials for the day (all purchases on account with terms of n/30).

E24–3 *Materials issues—cost sheets and journal entry*

During the month of May 1985, the Cody Company had issues of materials for two jobs as follows:

Date	Job Number	Requisition Number	Amount
1985			
May 6	A401	128	$ 161.20
10	A402	129	96.80
13	A401	130	448.00
19	A401	131	173.60
23	A402	132	1,008.90
31	A402	133	137.20
Total			$2,025.70

Assuming that these were the only jobs worked on in May, record the issues in cost sheets and prepare a summary general journal entry to record the materials issues for the month.

E24–4 *Labor usage—cost sheets and journal entry*

The Cody Company (see E24–3) had the following labor time tickets for May 1985:

Date	Job Number	Time Ticket Number	Hours
1985			
May 6	A401	637	8
9	A401	638	4
10	A402	639	8
11	Indirect labor	640	8
17	A401	641–643	24
19	A401	644	8
23	A402	645–647	24
31	A402	648	8

All labor is paid at the rate of $12 per hour. Using the cost sheets prepared for E24–3, record the labor costs as appropriate. In a single end-of-month journal entry, transfer these labor costs from the Factory Payroll account in the manner indicated in Figure 24–7.

E24–5 *Computing overhead rate*

Polacek Corporation has prepared its manufacturing overhead budget for 1985 at a total estimated cost of $840,000. Production schedules indicate that usage of direct materials will be $1,120,000 and that 120,000 direct labor hours will be used at a cost of $1,400,000. Compute the manufacturing overhead rate for 1985 based on (a) direct labor hours, (b) direct labor cost, and (c) direct materials cost.

E24–6 *Cost sheet, computing sales price, and flow of costs*

The cost sheet shown below was taken from the files of Massasoit Company:

Description 10 H.D. Dryers   Job No. 820

Date Started 4-4-85   Date Completed 4-12-85

For Special Order

Direct Materials			Direct Labor			
Date	Requisition	Amount	Date	Time Ticket	Hours	Amount
4/4	028	$202.00	4/4	1036	8	$108.00
4/5	047	168.75	4/11	1213	8	110.00
4/7	049	10.25	4/12	1272	6	84.00

Summary

Direct Materials	$381.00
Direct Labor	302.00
Manufacturing Overhead	?
Total	$?

Overhead is applied at the rate of 150 percent of direct labor cost. The dryers were delivered to the finished goods storeroom on April 12, 1985, and to the customer for whom they were made on April 13, 1985. The company feels that it is necessary to add 10 percent of cost for selling and general and administrative expenses and 15 percent for profit.

1. Provide the missing figures on the cost sheet.

2. Prepare the general journal entry for transfer of the job to the finished goods storeroom.

3. Compute the contract price and prepare the general journal entries for delivery to the customer assuming terms of n/30.

E24–7 *Computing inventory balances*

The information shown below was taken from the job order cost sheets in the files of Illinois Company. All items completed prior to August 22, 1985, had been sold.

Job Order No.	Balance, September 1	Production Cost in September	Remarks
531	$2,500	$ 0	Completed 8/22
532	6,000	0	Completed 8/30
533	1,620	2,075	Completed 9/6
534	860	3,260	Completed 9/13
535	370	3,180	Completed 9/21
536	0	5,182	Incomplete 9/30
537	0	2,097	Incomplete 9/30

Jobs 531, 532, and 533 were sold to customers in September. Compute balances of:
a. Work-in-Process Inventory at September 1.
b. Finished Goods Inventory at September 1.
c. Cost of Goods sold in September.
d. Work-in-Process Inventory at September 30.
e. Finished Goods Inventory at September 30.

E24–8 *Determining overhead rate and labor cost*

The Work-in-Process Inventory account at the end of November 1985 is as follows:

Work-in-Process Inventory **Acct. No. 112**

Date		Explanation	F	Debit	Credit	Balance
1985						
Nov.	30	(Direct materials)	J60	60,000		60,000
	30	(Direct labor)	J60	84,000		144,000
	30	(Manufacturing overhead)	J61	42,000		186,000
	30	(To finished goods)	J62		174,000	12,000

Only job number 137 is in process after November 30, 1985. Direct materials charged to job number 137 total $3,000. Manufacturing overhead is applied to Work-in-Process Inventory on the basis of direct labor cost. Determine the amount charged to job number 137 for direct labor and the amount of manufacturing overhead applied to job number 137.

E24–9 *Determining overhead rate and recording job completion*

Following is the general ledger Work-in-Process Inventory account for a company for which posting is up-to-date in all ledgers:

Work-in-Process Inventory **Acct. No. 112**

Date		Explanation	F	Debit	Credit	Balance
1985						
May	30	(Materials)	J16	19,824.75		19,824.75
	30	(Labor)	J16	39,000.00		58,824.75
	30	(Manufacturing overhead)	J16	58,500.00		117,324.75

Manufacturing overhead is applied on the basis of *direct labor cost.*

1. Compute the manufacturing overhead rate.

2. Job no. 317 is completed on June 5, 1985 and transferred to the finished goods storeroom. Its total cost is $21,580. Prepare the journal entry to record the transfer.

E24–10 *Recording overhead incurred and applied*

Friedman Company applies overhead at the rate of $6 per direct labor hour. The following overhead costs were incurred in January 1985:

Indirect labor	$23,400
Depreciation of machinery	22,750
Various other costs paid by checks	13,000
Total	$59,150

A totoal of 9,750 direct labor hours was recorded in the cost sheets for work done in January. Prepare general journal entries to record as of January 31, 1985, the total overhead incurred and the overhead applied.

E24–11 *Disposition of overhead balance*

Following is the general ledger Manufacturing Overhead Control account for Pocatello Company at the end of December 1985:

Manufacturing Overhead Control **Acct. No. 520**

Date		Explanation	F	Debit	Credit	Balance
1985						
Nov.	30	Debit balance	√			1,920
Dec.	31	(Actual December costs)	J90	30,720		32,640
	31	(Applied)	J90		32,000	640

Pocatello Company's accountant carries monthly overapplied or underapplied balances until December 31, the end of the fiscal year. Prepare a general journal entry to close the Manufacturing Overhead Control account.

E24–12 *Journalizing completed work*

Althena Builders had job nos. 124 and 125 in process on May 31, 1985, with total costs of $2,100 and $3,200 respectively. In June, an additional $1,150 was recorded in the cost sheet for job no. 124 and an additional $975 for job no. 125. Both jobs were completed in June. Other jobs were started in June but not completed. Show the June 30 journal entry to record transfer of completed work.

E24–13 *Distributing payroll charges to production*

At the end of September 1985, the Factory Payroll account of Bluestone Company appeared as follows:

Factory Payroll **Acct. No. 802**

Date		Explanation	F	Debit	Credit	Balance
1985						
Sep.	16		J70	36,400		36,400
	30		J85	42,000		78,400

The payrolls were made up as follows:

	Direct Labor	Indirect Labor
Payroll of September 1–16	$34,000	$2,400
Payroll of September 17–30	38,550	3,450

Prepare a general journal entry to distribute the September payroll costs to production.

E24–14 *Locating cost sheet error*

Canesius Repair had four jobs in process on July 31, 1985, as follows:

Job Number	Materials	Labor	Overhead
A62	$1,624	$ 600	$ 900
A63	3,284	4,000	6,000
A65	430	1,400	1,800
A68	2,512	6,400	9,600
Totals	$7,850	$12,400	$18,300

The Work-in-Process Inventory account in the general ledger shows a debit balance of $38,850. This balance is correct. The accountant for the company believes that any error in recording must be in overhead applied. Locate the error in the cost sheets.

A Problems

P24–1A *Computing overhead rates*

Yuma Company's manufacturing overhead budget for 1985 is $4,500,000. Production plans call for 200,000 direct labor hours and a total direct labor cost of $3,000,000. Planned direct materials cost is $1,000,000.

Required: Compute the rate at which manufacturing overhead is to be applied to the Work-in-Process Inventory account if the base is:

1. Direct labor hours.

2. Direct labor cost.

3. Direct materials cost.

P24–2A *Recording on a cost sheet*

Sound Engineers uses a job order cost accounting system. For job no. 0862, the following information is available:

Direct Materials			Direct Labor			
Date	Requisition No.	Amount	Date	Time Ticket No.	Hours	Rate
5–2–85	136	$403.00	5–2–85	3260	6	$18
5–6–85	182	120.00	5–3–85	3310	8	19
5–7–85	205	236.50	5–6–85	3331	8	19
			5–7–85	3346	8	20

The manufacturing overhead rate is $12 per direct labor hour.

Required:

1. Record the above data in a cost sheet similar to the one pictured in Figure 24–5.

2. If job no. 0862 calls for production of ten stereo receivers, what is the unit cost?

P24–3A *Journal entries for material, labor, overhead, and job completion*

Digger Group uses a job order cost accounting system in accounting for construction of special design drilling equipment. During August 1985, the following summary transactions occurred:

a. Issued materials with a cost of $64,000 for use in jobs and $4,800 for general factory use.

b. Distributed a factory payroll (already recorded) with $80,000 direct labor and $6,400 indirect labor.

c. Applied manufacturing overhead at 150 percent of direct labor cost.

d. Completed jobs that cost $148,000.

Required: Prepare general journal entries to record the transactions using letters instead of dates.

P24–4A *Journal entries for a single contract*

Boise Construction Company completed construction of a special order snow removal machine on November 7, 1985. Total costs on the cost sheet at the time of completion were:

Direct materials	$54,400
Direct labor	30,600
Total	$85,000

Manufacturing overhead is applied at the rate of 80 percent of direct labor cost. The machine was delivered to the city maintenance department on November 11 at a contract price of $132,000.

Required: Prepare the following:

1. The general journal entry to apply manufacturing overhead.

2. The general journal entry to record the completion of the job.

3. The general journal entries to record delivery to the city.

4. Assuming that this was the only job completed and sold in 1985, the entry to close accounts affecting this machine into Income Summary.

P24–5A *Journal entries and cost sheets*

The following were among the transactions completed by the McGuire Company during December 1985. There was no work in process on December 1, 1985.

a. Purchased materials on account for $70,200.

b. Requisitioned materials for production as follows:

Job 90	$15,600
Job 91	13,650
Job 92	17,550
Job 93	9,750
Total	$56,550

c. Requisitioned materials for general factory use, $5,850.

d. Distributed factory payroll (already recorded). Direct labor was distributed as follows:

Job 90	$19,500
Job 91	17,550
Job 92	22,425
Job 93	14,625
Total	$74,100

Indirect labor was $7,800. There were no accrued wages at the beginning or end of month.

e. Recorded additional actual overhead costs for the month of $16,100, all paid by check.

f. Total direct labor hours worked on jobs were as follows:

Job 90	2,000
Job 91	1,800
Job 92	2,300
Job 93	1,500
Total	7,600 hours

Manufacturing overhead is applied to jobs at the rate of $3.90 per direct labor hour.

g. Completed jobs 90, 91, and 93 and transferred them to finished goods inventory.

h. Sold jobs 90 and 93 on account for $95,000.

Required:

1. Journalize the transactions in end-of-month summary entries.

2. Post to a Work-in-Process Inventory account.

3. Prepare a cost sheet for each job and post the required cost data to them using letters instead of dates.

4. Verify the ending work-in-process inventory.

P24–6A *Thought-provoking problem: need to determine costs?*

At the Regis Heating Repair Service, a gradual conversion resulted in about 90 to 95 percent of the repair work being done on methanol-fueled heaters. Five years ago when most of the repair work was done on oil-fueled heaters, a scale of prices charged for various types of jobs seemed to work well. In the past two years, Maria Regis has been seeing an increasing number of problems, such as:

a. Customers appearing to fall into two classes: (1) complaining that they had been overcharged, or (2) obviously relieved that they had received such a good price.
b. Customer dissatisfaction because of a long wait for a new type of part that had been allowed to run out of stock. (During the days of oil-fueled repair work, the supervisor had developed a sense of what was needed and kept a good stock of parts by making notes on a card carried in his pocket).
c. Although she has a capable work force of people with various levels of skills, many customers have been lost because of customer dissatisfaction with prices and parts delays.
d. She expected the 1985 net income to be about $120,000 because the shop had increased the number of jobs by 50 percent over 1984 when the net income was $80,000. Actual 1985 net income was $78,000—a decline from 1984.
e. She has asked the shop supervisor several times to suggest a better method to set prices on jobs. He simply has not had that much experience on methanol-fueled devices.

At this point, you are called in as a consultant. In discussing the problems with Ms. Regis, you learn that nobody in the shop has even a reasonable estimate of the cost of any of the jobs done in 1985. There was, however, a great variety of types of repairs.

Required: Prepare a report recommending a solution to the problems of this business. Be complete and specific as to (1) the types of records needed, and (2) the supporting procedures to develop information to be recorded.

B Problems

P24–1B *Computing overhead rates*

Tucson Company's manufacturing overhead budget for 1985 is $1,200,000. Production plans call for 200,000 direct labor hours and a direct labor cost of $2,400,000. Planned direct materials cost is $960,000.

Required: Compute the rate at which manufacturing overhead is to be applied to the Work-in-Process Inventory account if the base is:

1. Direct labor hours.

2. Direct labor cost.

3. Direct materials cost.

P24–2B *Recording on a cost sheet*

Nasus Custom Cabinet Makers uses a job order cost accounting system. For job no. 31X5, the following information is available:

Direct Materials			Direct Labor			
Date	Requisition No.	Amount	Date	Time Ticket No.	Hours	Rate
2–7–85	632	$605.30	2–7–85	8602	6	$17
2–8–85	700	181.50	2–8–85	8660	8	18
2–11–85	737	425.20	2–11–85	8706	8	18
			2–14–85	8777	8	17

The manufacturing overhead rate is $10 per direct labor hour.

Required:

1. Record the above data in a cost sheet similar to the one in Figure 24–5.

2. If job no. 31X5 calls for production of eight sectional cabinets, what is the unit cost?

P24–3B
Journal entries for materials, labor, overhead, and job completion

Elizabeth City Fabricators uses a job order cost accounting system for construction of special design electronic monitoring systems. During July 1985, the following summary transactions occurred:

a. Issued $141,000 of materials for use in jobs and $10,575 for general factory use.
b. Distributed a payroll (already recorded) with $176,250 direct labor and $14,100 indirect labor.
c. Applied manufacturing overhead at the rate of 120 percent of direct labor cost.
d. Completed jobs that cost $232,120.

Required: Prepare general journal entries to record the transactions using letters instead of dates.

P24–4B
Journal entries for a single contract

Capital Company completed the construction of a special order street cleaning machine on September 6, 1985. Total costs on the cost sheet at the time of completion were:

Direct materials	$12,800
Direct labor	63,450
Total	$76,250

Manufacturing overhead was applied at the rate of 90 percent of direct labor cost. The machine was delivered to the city maintenance department on September 9, 1985, at a contract price of $160,000.

Required: Prepare the following:

1. The general journal entry to apply manufacturing overhead.

2. The general journal entry to record completion of the job.

3. The general journal entries to record delivery to the city.

4. Assuming that this was the only job completed and sold in 1985, the entry to close accounts affecting this machine into Income Summary.

P24–5B
Journal entries and cost sheets

The following were among the transactions at Rock Hill Solar Works during August 1985. There was no work in process on August 1, 1985.

a. Purchased materials on account for $98,280.
b. Requisitioned materials for production as follows:

Job 283	$21,840
Job 284	19,110
Job 285	24,570
Job 286	13,650
Total	$79,170

c. Requisitioned materials for general factory use, $8,190.
d. Distributed factory payroll (already recorded). Direct labor was distributed as follows:

Job 283	$ 27,300
Job 284	24,570
Job 285	31,395
Job 286	20,475
Total	$103,740

Indirect labor was $10,920. There were no accrued wages at the beginning or end of the month.

e. Recorded additional actual overhead costs for the month of $23,750, all paid by check.

f. Total direct labor hours worked on jobs were as follows:

Job 283	2,600	
Job 284	2,340	
Job 285	2,990	
Job 286	1,950	
Total	9,880	hours

Manufacturing overhead is applied to jobs at the rate of $4.30 per direct labor hour.

g. Completed jobs 283, 284, and 286 and tranferred them to finished goods inventory.

h. Sold jobs 283 and 284 on account for $148,500.

Required:

1. Journalize the transactions in end-of-month summary entries.

2. Post to a Work-in-Process Inventory account.

3. Prepare a cost sheet for each job and post the required cost data to them, using letters instead of dates.

4. Verify the ending work-in-process inventory.

P24–6B *Thought-provoking problem: need to determine costs?*

Donna Stone invented a process that gives automobile, truck, and other vehicle tires a renewed life plus a special road-gripping characteristic for wet or icy road conditions. The process requires several types of materials and different labor skills depending on the type and age of the tire. There is an immediate demand for this service, but she is having two major problems:

a. She does not know how to set a price for each of the variety of jobs to be done.

b. Some material is on hand in plentiful supply (in fact, there appears to be too much of some items), while work is constantly delayed waiting for other materials.

It appears to Ms. Stone that she must charge a price that is 25 percent above manufacturing cost in order to cover expenses and make a fair profit. No one in the shop has any idea of the manufacturing cost of any job. At this point, you are called in as a consultant.

Required: Prepare a report recommending a solution to the problems of this business. Be complete and specific as to (1) the types of records that are needed, and (2) the supporting procedures to develop information to be recorded.

25 Process Cost Accounting

Introduction

Thus far, only job order cost accounting, where costs are identified with specific jobs, has been considered. In many companies, large quantities of identical units of product—for example, sheets of plywood—are produced in a continuous flow through successive departments. Georgia-Pacific Corporation, the world's largest producer of plywood, operated at a capacity of 4.4 billion square feet in a recent year. This chapter introduces the process cost accounting system used by companies in which the manufacturing process is continuous and the product is uniform.

Learning Goals

To apply the concept of cost accumulation by departments or cost centers.

To describe the flow of costs in a process cost accounting system.

To define the concept of equivalent units.

To compute equivalent units and unit costs for materials, labor, and overhead.

To understand a cost of production report.

To record the journal entries for the flow of costs in a process cost accounting system.

The Process System

Identical units of product are often manufactured by passing these units through a series of processes or operations. In each process, additional work is done to further the completion. The production of aspirin, for example, involves the making of a white crystalline compound of acetylsalicylic acid, which is then formed into the familiar white aspirin tablets. In the various processes used to produce aspirin tablets, it would be impossible to identify costs with a single tablet or even a batch of tablets. However, it is feasible to identify costs with the process. When the process is the focus of cost accumulation, we are using a **process cost accounting system.**

In a firm, a department may carry out a single process—for example, packaging of aspirin tablets. However, some departments may carry out more than one process; the Painting Department may have a priming process and a final-finish process in producing file cabinets. The lowest level process to which costs are identified or charged is called a **cost center.** In a process cost accounting system, the costs are identified with each cost center through which the product flows from its beginning until it is completed and sent to the finished goods storeroom. Once the total costs for a period are assigned to a cost center, an average unit cost is then calculated in each. Unit costs are accumulated as the product passes through all processes (cost centers) to determine the final cost of a unit of product.

Process Cost Accounting: The Basic Structure

Recall that the primary objectives of cost accounting are to develop cost control and product pricing information. In any process, there could be direct materials costs, but some processes consist only of further fabrication or assembly of materials that began production in a prior process; under these circumstances, there is no addition of new batches of materials. Unless a process is fully automated, direct labor cost is likely to be incurred. In all processes, some overhead cost should be assigned. Accordingly, there is a buildup of costs as pictured in Figure 25–1. It is assumed that materials are started in Process A, where direct labor is incurred and manufacturing overhead costs are applied.

The line going to Process B represents the accumulated costs of Process A that are being transferred into Process B as the product is being transferred for further work. In Process B, it is assumed that *no further materials* are added but that both direct labor and manufacturing overhead costs are added. The line from Process B to Process C represents the *total accumulated costs* of both Processes A and B that are being transferred into Process C for the final work to produce the finished goods. In this illustration, all three elements of cost are used in Process C. In a final process, the materials cost often includes packaging materials. The line from Process C to the T account represents the total accumulated costs of all the production processes as the units of product are transferred to finished goods inventory.

To record the cost accumulation as the product flows through the process, it is necessary to have a separate Work-in-Process Inventory account for each process. For example, the company whose flow is pictured in Figure 25–1 would have three such accounts, as follows: Work-in-Process Inventory—Process A, Work-in-Process Inventory—Process B, and Work-in-Process Inventory—Process C.

In a process cost accounting system, all requisitions for direct materials must be identified not with the product but with the process to which the

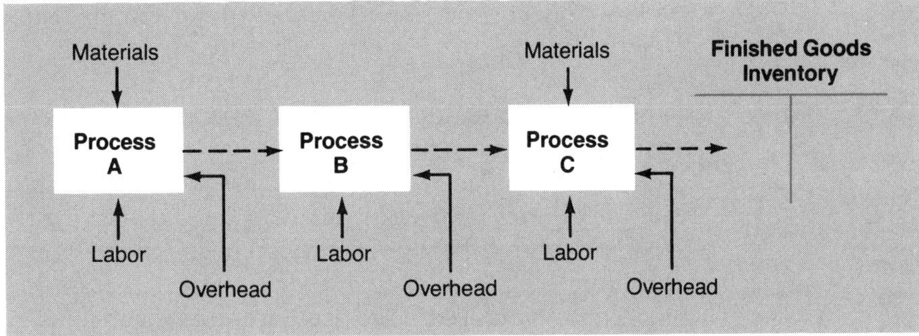

Figure 25–1 Process Cost Accumulation

materials are being issued. It may not be necessary to use time tickets to record direct labor, but the timekeeping system must provide a means of identifying direct labor costs with each process. Manufacturing overhead costs must also be identified with each process. An overhead rate is used in the same manner as in a job order system, except that overhead is applied to a process rather than to a job. There is usually a separate (and different) overhead rate computed for each process.

Finally, in considering the basic structure of process cost accounting, note that development of total costs in each process is not sufficient to exercise effective cost control. Since the amount of production varies from period to period, total labor costs for one month compared with total labor costs for another month are not very meaningful to management. A more useful comparison can be made by the use of unit costs. A **unit cost** is the cost per unit of product; it is computed separately for each cost element—materials, labor, and overhead, and in total for each cost center.

Equivalent Units of Work

If unit costs of production are to be developed for each process, they should be based on the actual amount of work done. The number of units of product transferred out of a process during a period—say the month of May—may *not* represent the actual amount of work done in May. If there was a beginning inventory on May 1 of work in process, work on some of the units transferred out was begun before May 1. Also, there may be an ending work-in-process inventory on May 31, consisting of units partly completed in May. To obtain an accurate measure of the actual work done in a process in a period, a figure known as equivalent units of work done must be computed. **Equivalent units of work** (often referred to as *equivalent units*) is the number of *whole units* of product that could have been produced if only *whole units* were made with the cost of production for the month of May. However, producers are not able to concentrate efforts only on whole units but must spread their efforts over many. Most processes have an ending inventory of partially-complete units in work in process at the end of a period—say a month. For example, assume that the ending inventory of a process contains a group of 100 units, each of which had 40 percent of the total work completed in that process. The *equivalent units* in that ending inventory would be the number of units that could have been completely produced had it been possible to concentrate efforts on starting and completing whole units only. In this case, it is 40 = (100 × 40 percent). Total equivalent units of work for the period is usually the sum of three kinds of work: (1) work required to complete the beginning inventory, (2) work on units started in the process during the period and completed during the period, and (3) work on units started during the period but still in the work-in-process inventory at the end.[1]

Since unit costs are averaged over equivalent units produced in each cost center, it is necessary to compute equivalent units in each process for each reporting period. The unit cost of any element of cost—say materials in Process A—is equal to total materials costs incurred in that process divided by the number of equivalent units of material in Process A. Note that equivalent units of work for materials may be different from those for labor or overhead in the same process.

Referring again to Figure 25–1, assume that all materials are added at the *beginning* of Process A. This means that any product units still in process at the end of a period will be 100 percent complete as to materials. These same units in ending inventory may be less than 100 percent complete as to labor and overhead. Assume that 1,000 product units are in the ending work-in-process inventory of Process A on May 31 and only 35 percent of the labor and overhead necessary to complete the units has been added as of May 31. The equivalent units represented by this ending inventory are:

	Equivalent Units
Materials (1,000 units × 100%)	1,000
Labor (1,000 units × 35%)	350
Overhead, if based on direct labor (1,000 units × 35%)	350

The computation of equivalent units is essential to the development of accurate unit costs and is illustrated in detail in the example of the Pompano Chemical Company that follows.

Process Cost Accounting Illustration

The Pompano Chemical Company produces a single product named Browardmint, which is processed in two departments, Cooking and Finishing. The flow of costs for this company is diagrammed in Figure 25–2. The product is begun in the Cooking Department, where materials, labor, and overhead costs are incurred. As units are completed in the Cooking Department, they are transferred to the Finishing Department for further processing. In a

[1]This description of the elements that make up equivalent units is for the FIFO cost-flow assumption. Another commonly used cost-flow assumption—weighted average—is not described in this chapter because its unit cost computation is more complex.

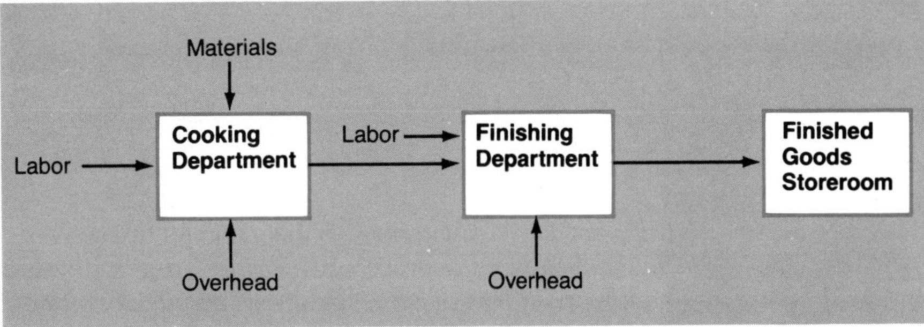

Figure 25–2 Flow of Costs in Pompano Chemical Company

second department, additional materials, labor, and overhead may be added, but for this example, as is indicated in the diagram in Figure 25–2, the manufacture of Browardmint does not require any additional materials in the Finishing Department.

On July 1, 1985, there is no beginning work-in-process inventory in the Cooking Department. During July, 50,000 units of Browardmint are started in the Cooking Department; of this amount, 40,000 units are completely processed and transferred to the Finishing Department. As of July 31, 10,000 units are still in the cooking process—these 10,000 units are 100 percent complete as to materials and 40 percent complete as to labor and overhead. The July costs in the Cooking Department are shown in the following ledger account with explanations to show the source:

Work in Process—Cooking Department

1985						
Jul.	1	Balance	✓			0
	31	Direct materials	J65	10,000		10,000
	31	Direct labor	J65	13,200		23,200
	31	Manufacturing overhead applied	J65	11,000		34,200

In the Finishing Department, there is a beginning (July 1) work-in-process inventory of 4,000 units. These units are 75 percent complete as to labor and overhead; no materials are added in the Finishing Department. During July, the 40,000 units completed in Cooking are received, and they form the units started by the Finishing Department. Of the 44,000 units of Browardmint that the Finishing Department worked on, 38,000 are finished and transferred to Finished Goods Inventory, leaving 6,000 units still in process in Finishing on July 31. These 6,000 units in the Finishing Department's ending work-in-process inventory are 33⅓ percent complete as to labor and overhead. Remember that any units present in the Finishing Department must have all of the Cooking Department's work (and associated cost) in them. This is known as **prior department cost.** The dollar amounts for the beginning inventory and the *costs incurred in* the Finishing Department for July (note that these latter costs do not include costs transferred in from Cooking) are:

July 1 work-in-process inventory	$ 5,300
July costs:	
Direct materials	0
Direct labor	14,800
Manufacturing overhead	13,320

The situation just described is diagrammed in Figure 25–3. The beginning and ending work-in-process inventories are not shown in the diagram but are an important part of computation of the unit costs in each department. In the Finishing Department, there is an additional cost element in July—those transferred in from Cooking. This cost element is introduced later in the illustration.

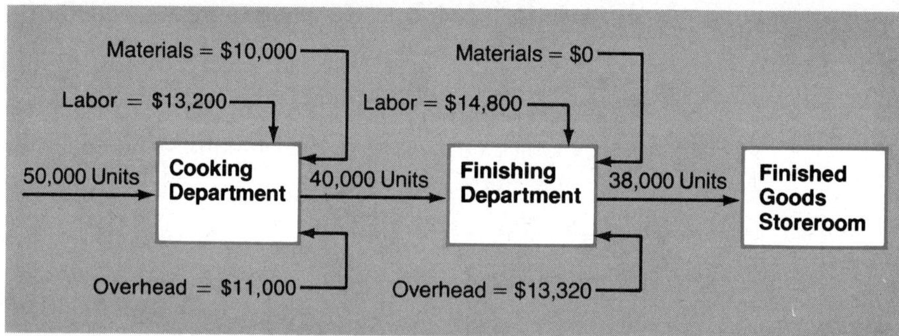

Figure 25–3 Pompano Chemical Company—July Production

Allocation of Costs in the Cooking Department

Quantity Schedule A **quantity schedule** is prepared for each department, showing the number of actual physical units of the product processed during a given period. Such a schedule for the Cooking Department is illustrated in Figure 25–4. The stage of completion for the July 31 work-in-process inventory is an estimate; the average goods in work in process *in this case* have 100 percent of the material cost and 40 percent of the labor (L) and overhead (O) costs.

	Units	
Quantity to be accounted for:		
Units in process at beginning of period	0	
Units started in process	50,000	
Total	50,000	
Quantity accounted for:		
Transferred to Finishing Department	40,000	
Units still in process at end of period	10,000	(all materials; 40% L and O)
Total	50,000	

Figure 25–4 Quantity Schedule, Cooking Department

Schedule of Equivalent Units To repeat, **equivalent units of work** *is the number of whole units that could have been completed if all the effort and costs for the period had been applied only to wholly finished units.* The changing of work-in-process units to the equivalent of whole units is necessary when computing unit costs. Also, there may be a different number of equivalent units for material and for labor and overhead. The schedule of equivalent production for the Cooking Department is illustrated in Figure 25–5. An explanation of the numbered items in Figure 25–5 follows the schedule:

		Materials		Labor and Overhead[a]	
1	Equivalent whole units to complete beginning work-in-process inventory	0		0	
2	Units started and finished this period	40,000		40,000	
3	Equivalent whole units contained in ending work-in-process inventory (stage of completion)	10,000	= (10,000 × 100%)	4,000	= (10,000 × 0.40)
4	Equivalent units	50,000		44,000	

[a]Labor and overhead are the same here because the overhead rate is based on direct labor hours.

Figure 25–5 **Schedule of Equivalent Production, Cooking Department**

1 In the Cooking Department, there is no beginning inventory to complete; hence zeros are entered in the Materials column and the Labor and Overhead column to show a generalized approach.

2 Units started and finished in this period (July) totaled 40,000, shown in both the Materials column and the Labor and Overhead column. **Units started and finished** are those units that were begun this period with no prior period work of this department in them and completely finished in the department in this period. The amount of such units is computed by subtracting the number of units in beginning work in process from units transferred out. Since all of the work was done on these units during this period, the equivalent units are equal to the actual units.

3 The ending work-in-process inventory consists of 10,000 units. Its stage of completion is such that all the materials have been added (10,000 is entered in the Materials column) and 40 percent of the labor and overhead has been done (4,000 is entered in the Labor and Overhead column). The assumption made in process costing is that the costs expended in completing 40 percent of the work on 10,000 units are the same as the cost of completing 4,000 units.

4 The total of the three kinds of work—(1) finishing the beginning inventory, (2) starting and completing additional whole units, and (3) partially

completing an ending inventory—is the equivalent units of work done in the Cooking Department in July.

Unit Cost Computation Each cost element in the Total Cost column is divided by the corresponding equivalent units produced to determine the unit costs as indicated in Figure 25–6.

	A	÷	B	=	C
Element	Total Cost		Equivalent Units		Unit Cost
Materials	$10,000		50,000		$0.20
Labor	13,200		44,000		0.30
Overhead	11,000		44,000		0.25
Totals	$34,200				$0.75

Figure 25–6 Unit Cost Computation, Cooking Department

Accumulated Cost Distribution The total accumulated cost of the Cooking Department ($34,200) is divided between the 40,000 units transferred to the next department and the ending inventory. The cost of 40,000 units transferred to the Finishing Department is computed as follows:

Cost in the beginning work-in-process inventory	$ 0
Cost to complete the beginning work-in-process inventory	0
Cost of units started and completed in July (40,000 × $0.75)	30,000
Total cost of goods transferred to next department	$30,000

The ending work-in-process inventory is valued as follows:

	A	×	B	=	C
Element	Equivalent Units (from Figure 25–5)		Unit Cost (from Figure 25–6)		Ending Work-in-Process Inventory
Materials	10,000		$0.20		$2,000
Direct labor	4,000		0.30		1,200
Manufacturing overhead	4,000		0.25		1,000
Work-in-process inventory—Cooking Department, July 31, 1985					$4,200

The section of the cost of production report (Figure 25–7) that displays the acumulated cost distribution is called the **cost schedule.**

Cost of Production Report in the Cooking Department

At the end of each month, the accountant prepares for each department a **cost of production report.** The parts of the cost of production report for Pompano Chemical Company's Cooking Department have been developed in this illustration. Figure 25–7 combines all of the elements just described to provide to management an overview of production activity for July 1985. An explanation of the numbered items accompanies Figure 25–7 so that the reader can determine the source of the amounts in the cost of production report.

POMPANO CHEMICAL COMPANY—COOKING DEPARTMENT
Cost of Production Report
For the Month Ended July 31, 1985

		Units	
1	Quantity schedule:		
	Quantity to be accounted for:		
	Units in process, July 1	0	
	Units started in process	50,000	50,000
	Quantity accounted for:		
	Transferred to next department	40,000	
	Units in process, July 31	10,000	50,000
		Total Costs	**Unit Costs**
	Cost schedule:		
	Work in process, July 1	$ 0	—
2	Costs added in July:		
	Materials	10,000	$0.20
	Labor	13,200	0.30
	Overhead	11,000	0.25
4	Total to be accounted for	$34,200	$0.75
3	Transferred to next department	$30,000	
	Work in process, July 31	4,200	
4	Total accounted for	$34,200	

5 Computation of unit costs[a]

$$\text{Materials} = \frac{\$10{,}000 \text{ July costs}}{50{,}000 \text{ equivalent units}} = \$0.20.$$

$$\text{Labor} = \frac{\$13{,}200 \text{ July costs}}{44{,}000 \text{ equivalent units}} = \$0.30.$$

$$\text{Overhead} = \frac{\$11{,}000 \text{ July costs}}{44{,}000 \text{ equivalent units}} = \$0.25.$$

[a]Computation of equivalent units (see Figure 25–5) is usually shown on this report. It is not represented here because of space limitations.

Figure 25–7 Cooking Department Cost of Production Report

1 The quantity schedule is stated in terms of whole units. It is a balanced schedule to show an accounting for all units which the department handled in July. It was described in Figure 25–4.

2 The costs added in July are the actual costs of materials and labor used and the total overhead applied in July. The inflow of these costs was diagrammed in Figure 25–3.

[3] Because there was no beginning inventory, all units of Browardmint transferred to the Finishing Department were started and finished in July. Therefore, their cost is \$30,000 = (40,000 units × \$0.75).

[4] The cost schedule is also a balanced schedule in that it shows an accounting for all production costs. The Cooking Department must account for \$34,200 in July. It is accounted for by two items: (1) the units transferred out at a cost of \$30,000, and (2) the ending inventory of \$4,200.

[5] The computation of equivalent units and unit costs was explained and illustrated in Figures 25–5 and 25–6.

The production cost report serves many managerial uses. These points are important:

1. It is a three-part report consisting of (a) a quantity schedule, (b) a cost schedule, and (c) computation of unit costs (and usually equivalent units).

2. Management studies the cost of production carefully each month, making comparisons of current unit costs with those of previous months. Rising unit costs of materials may indicate a machine out of adjustment, need for better training of workers, and so on.

3. For unit costs to be comparable from month to month, they must be based on the actual amount of work done, as indicated by equivalent units of work.

4. The report serves as the basis for an end-of-month journal entry transferring costs to the next department. This is the fourth entry in Figure 25–13.

Allocation of Costs in the Finishing Department

The Finishing Department works only on units completed in Cooking and transferred to Finishing. Recall from the basic data that it had a beginning inventory. Costs of that beginning inventory and the direct costs to the department have been given previously. They can now be combined with prior department costs in a ledger account to show total costs, as were done for Cooking. It would appear as follows:

Work-in-Process—Finishing Department

1985						
Jul.	1	Debit balance	✓			5,300
	31	Direct labor	J65	14,800		20,100
	31	Manufacturing overhead applied	J65	13,320		33,420
	31	Transfer from Cooking . .	J65	30,000		63,420

Quantity Schedule The quantity schedule for the Finishing Department is shown in Figure 25–8.

Schedule of Equivalent Units The 4,000 units in the beginning work-in-process inventory were three-fourths complete as to the elements of labor

	Units	
Quantity to be accounted for:		
Units in process at beginning of period	4,000	(¾ L and O[a])
Units received from Cooking Department	40,000[b]	
Total	44,000	
Quantity accounted for:		
Transferred to finished goods inventory	38,000	
Units still in process at end of period	6,000	(⅓ L and O)
Total	44,000	

[a]No materials are added in the Finishing Department; L = labor; O = overhead.
[b]Note that these are the same units transferred out of the Cooking Department.

Figure 25–8 Quantity Schedule, Finishing Department

and overhead on July 1. Therefore, these 4,000 units receive the last one-fourth of their labor and overhead during this cost period (July). Each should be equated with one-fourth of a unit of labor and of overhead. Consequently, 1,000 equivalent units = (4,000 units × ¼) are entered in the L and O column, as shown in Figure 25–9. The number of units started and finished during this period is determined as follows:

$$\begin{bmatrix}\text{Units transferred}\\ \text{to finished goods}\\ \text{inventory}\\ (38{,}000)\end{bmatrix} - \begin{bmatrix}\text{Units in beginning}\\ \text{work-in-process}\\ \text{inventory}\\ (4{,}000)\end{bmatrix} = \begin{bmatrix}\text{Units started}\\ \text{and finished}\\ \\ (34{,}000)\end{bmatrix}$$

Since these 34,000 units were started and completed this period, 100 percent of the labor and overhead were added in this period (July). All 34,000 units are recorded in the L and O column. Each unit in the ending work-in-process inventory of 6,000 units received one-third of its labor and overhead this month. The stage of completion of the ending work-in-process inventory expressed as an equivalent of whole units, is 2,000 = (6,000 units × ⅓). This quantity is recorded in the L and O column. The column's total (37,000 units) represents equivalent units for the month of July. An explanation of the numbered items is used to summarize the computation of equivalent units in the Finishing Department.

	Materials	L and O	
	1		
2 Equivalent whole units to complete beginning work-in-process inventory	0	1,000	= (4,000 units × ¼)
3 Units started and finished	0	34,000	
4 Equivalent whole units contained in ending work-in-process inventory (stage of completion)	0	2,000	= (6,000 units × ⅓)
5 Equivalent units	0	37,000	

Figure 25–9 Schedule of Equivalent Production, Finishing Department

1 No materials were added in this department. Thus the equivalent units for materials are zero.

2 The beginning (July 1) inventory in Finishing was three-fourths complete as to labor and overhead; the equivalent of 3,000 units of labor and overhead were done in June, leaving 1,000 = (4,000 units × ¼) to be done in July to complete the beginning inventory.

3 Only 4,000 of the 38,000 units transferred out came from the beginning inventory; therefore, there must have been an additional 34,000 units started and completed in July (100 percent of their work was done this period).

4 The ending (July 31) inventory in Finishing was one-third complete as to labor and overhead. This amounts to the equivalent of 2,000 units of work = (6,000 × ⅓) done in July to bring the ending inventory to this stage of completion.

5 Since no materials are added in the Finishing Department, the equivalent units of materials resources used is zero. The sum of equivalent units of labor and overhead resources used in this department is 37,000.

Unit Cost Computation Since no materials are added in the Finishing Department, the departmental unit cost is computed by dividing the cost of labor and overhead added in July by the equivalent production for July. This computation is shown in Figure 25–10.

Figure 25–10 Unit Cost Computation, Finishing Department

	A	÷	B	=	C
Element	**Total Cost**		**Equivalent Production**		**Unit Cost**
Labor	$14,800		37,000		$0.40
Overhead	13,320		37,000		0.36
Totals	$28,120				$0.76

Note that the unit cost of $0.76 is the unit cost for the Finishing Department only. The total unit cost is $1.51 = ($0.76 from the Finishing Department + $0.75 from the Cooking Department).

Accumulated Cost Distribution The total cost to be accounted for in the Finishing Department is shown as follows:

Work-in-process inventory (July 1) beginning	$ 5,300
Cost from the preceding department transferred to the Finishing Department during July:	
40,000 units (unit cost $0.75) from the Cooking Department report	30,000
Cost added to the foregoing units by the Finishing Department during July (labor and overhead only) See Figure 25–10	28,120
Total cost for which an accounting must be made	$63,420

The completed cost of the 4,000 units in the beginning work-in-process inventory:			
Cost of the July 1 work-in-process inventory from June		$5,300	
Added July cost to complete these 4,000 units:[a]			
Labor added 4,000 × ¼ × $0.40	$400		
Overhead added 4,000 × ¼ × $0.36	360	760	
Total cost of the 4,000 completed units (unit cost, $1.515 = $6,060 ÷ 4,000)			$ 6,060
The completed cost of the new production, the units started and finished during July:			
34,000 × $1.51[b]			51,340
Total cost of the 38,000 units completed			$57,400
The cost of the work-in-process inventory, July 31:			
Cost from the Cooking Department (6,000 × $0.75)		$4,500	
Labor added during July (6,000 × ⅓ × $0.40)		800	
Overhead added during July (6,000 × ⅓ × $0.36)		720	
The cost of the work-in-process inventory, July 31			6,020
Total accumulated cost distribution			$63,420

[a]No Cooking cost needs to be added here; all Cooking cost is in the beginning inventory cost of $5,300.
[b]Prior department cost of $0.75 + current department cost of $0.76 = $1.51.

Figure 25–11 **Cost Accounted For, Finishing Department**

This cost is accounted for by the amount assigned to the 38,000 units finished and transferred to the storeroom and the amount assigned to the July 31 work-in-process inventory. It is shown in detail in Figure 25–11. Under the FIFO cost-flow assumption, the beginning work-in-process inventory and the new July production (started and finished) are typically computed separately; that is, the beginning work-in-process inventory is assumed to be completed before the new production is started, completed, and costed. The cost of the completed 4,000 units which were in the July 1 (beginning) work-in-process inventory, the cost of the new production of 34,000 units which were started and finished during July, and the cost of the 6,000 units in the July 31 (ending) work-in-process inventory are shown in Figure 25–11. In a more concise form, this is usually a part of the cost of production report.

Note from Figure 25–11 that under the FIFO assumption the total cost of the first 4,000 units finished and transferred to finished goods is $6,060, or $1.515 per unit. The 34,000 new units that were started and completed in July have a cumulative cost of $1.51 = ($0.75 carried forward from the Cooking Department plus $0.76 added in Finishing). The $0.75 per unit cost carried from cooking to finishing is known in the Finishing Department as **prior department cost.** The overall weighted average unit cost in finished goods inventory is $1.5105 = ($57,400 ÷ 38,000).

Cost of Production Report in the Finishing Department

The schedule of equivalent production, the quantity schedule, the accumulated costs, and the distribution of these for the Finishing Department are combined into a cost of production report shown in Figure 25–12. Again, certain items are numbered for further explanation.

POMPANO CHEMICAL COMPANY—FINISHING DEPARTMENT
Cost of Production Report
For the Month Ended July 31, 1985

		Units	
1	Quantity schedule:		
	Quantity to be accounted for:		
	Units in process, July 1	4,000	
	Received from prior department	40,000	44,000
	Quantity accounted for:		
	Transferred to finished goods	38,000	
	Units in process, July 31	6,000	44,000
		Total Cost	**Unit Cost**
	Cost schedule:		
2	Work in process, July 1	$ 5,300	—
	Cost added in July:		
3	Prior department costs (from Cooking Department)	30,000	$0.75
	Labor (see Figure 25–10)	14,800	0.40
	Overhead (see Figure 25–10)	13,320	0.36
	Total to be accounted for	$63,420	$1.51
4	Transferred to finished goods[a]	$57,400	
	Work in process, July 31,[a]	6,020	
	Total accounted for	$63,420	

Computation of unit costs:

Prior department costs (see Figure 25–7) = $0.75

5

$$\text{Labor} = \frac{\$14{,}800 \text{ July costs}}{37{,}000 \text{ equivalent units}} = \$0.40.$$

$$\text{Overhead} = \frac{\$13{,}320 \text{ July costs}}{37{,}000 \text{ equivalent units}} = \$0.36.$$

[a]Shown in detail in Figure 25–11.

Figure 25–12 Finishing Department Cost of Production Report

1 The quantity schedule is in numbers of units handled in the department in July.

2 Because a beginning (July 1) inventory is present in the Finishing Department, its cost must be accounted for.

3 See Figure 25–7. The cost of 40,000 units received from the Cooking Department in July is a current cost to be accounted for in Finishing.

4 The 38,000 units finished in July are composed of 4,000 in Finishing's beginning inventory plus 34,000 of the units received in July from Cooking and processed completely into finished Browardmint. Note that the total cost transferred out is *not* equal to 38,000 units × $1.51 because of different June unit costs in the beginning inventory of 4,000 units.[2]

5 The equivalent units are computed in Figure 25–9.

[2]Any lost or spoiled units must be accounted for. Because this topic is beyond the scope of this book, it is assumed that no units of Browardmint were lost or spoiled.

Flow of Process Costs—Summary Journal Entries

Summary entries to record the flow of costs for the Pompano Chemical Company are shown in Figure 25–13 (assuming that the same units manufactured were sold). Some of these entries may be made throughout the month—issues of material, use of labor, or sales, for example. However, the entries for transfers between departments and to finished goods can only be made at the end of the month from cost of production reports.

When the finished goods are sold, the costs are transferred to Cost of Goods Sold (last entry), and the customers are billed for the sales. The entry to record the billing of customers would be a debit to Accounts Receivable and a credit to Sales at the selling price. Note that the accountant of the Pompano Chemical Company was able to assign all materials and labor costs to the applicable department; hence, there are no indirect materials or labor costs in manufacturing overhead.

Page 65

Date		Account	Ref.	Debit	Credit
1985 Jul.	31	Work-in-Process—Cooking Department		10,000	
		Materials Inventory			10,000
		To record issuance of direct materials in July.			
	31	Work-in-Process—Cooking Department		13,200	
		Work-in-Process—Finishing Department		14,800	
		Factory Payroll			28,000
		To record direct labor costs in July.			
	31	Work-in-Process—Cooking Department		11,000	
		Work-in-Process—Finishing Department		13,320	
		Manufacturing Overhead			24,320
		To record manufacturing overhead applied in July.			
	31	Work-in-Process—Finishing Department		30,000	
		Work-in-Process —Cooking Department			30,000
		To record transfer of 40,000 units to Finishing Department.			
	31	Finished Goods Inventory		57,400	
		Work-in-Process—Finishing Department			57,400
		To record transfer of 38,000 units of Browardmint to finished goods storeroom.			
	31	Cost of Goods Sold[a]		57,400	
		Finished Goods Inventory			57,400
		To record cost of sales of 38,000 units of Browardmint.			

[a]This and the other entries record only the cost flows. The sales entry at selling price (not cost) would precede the cost of goods sold entry.

Figure 25–13 **Summary Entries Recording Flow of Costs in Pompano Chemical Company**

To reinforce the concept that unit costs are accumulated as they move through the processes, the July Pompano Chemical Company's unit cost flow is diagrammed in Figure 25–14. Note that 40,000 units were completed in Cooking and sent to Finishing at a unit cost of $0.75. Added costs in Finishing were a combination of some June costs, brought forward in the beginning

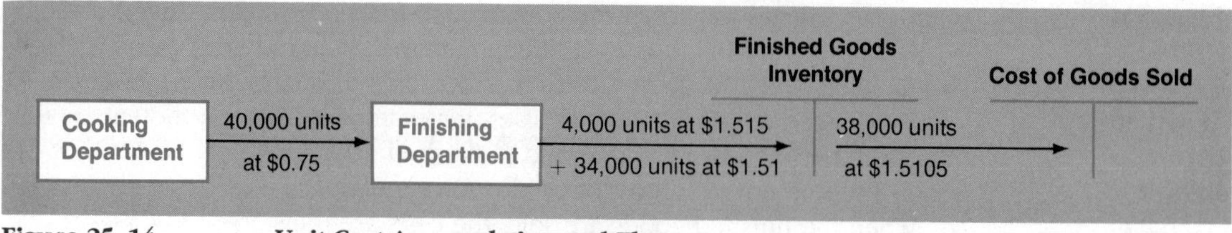

Figure 25–14 **Unit Cost Accumulation and Flow**

inventory, and the July costs, that averaged $0.76 per unit. With the Finishing costs added to the Cooking costs, the final product flowed to finished goods inventory at a weighted average unit cost of $1.5105. Since these units were all sold, these costs all flowed on to cost of goods sold.

Despite their value to managers in planning and control, job order and process cost accounting systems as described in Chapters 24 and 25 are limited to recording historical costs. Chapter 27 will take up a modification of these systems that allows the accountant to record what costs ought to be as well as what costs actually are. That system is called a **standard cost accounting system.** To provide a better basis for understanding standard cost concepts, Chapter 26 discusses budgets and responsibility accounting.

Glossary

Cost center An organizational unit for which costs are accumulated within a firm. The commonly used cost center in this chapter is a producing department.

Cost of production report A report combining the quantity schedule, equivalent units of production, the accumulated costs, the distribution of cost, and the calculation of unit costs for each department.

Cost schedule A segment of a cost of production report. It shows total and unit costs.

Equivalent units of work The number of whole units that could have been completed if all the effort and costs for the period had been applied only to wholly finished units.

Prior department costs Costs attaching to units of product received from a prior department. These are costs already invested in the product in one or more departments before it is received to be worked on in the present department.

Process cost accounting system A cost accounting system appropriate for production operations that make large quantities of an identical product in a continuous process. Costs are traced and identified with producing segments (departments or other cost centers) rather than to jobs.

Quantity schedule A schedule accounting for the number of units of product worked on in a given time period.

Standard cost accounting system A system that allows the accountant to record costs at the amounts they ought to be as well as the amounts they actually are.

Unit cost The cost per unit of product of the work done in a production department. It is computed by dividing equivalent units into current period costs for materials, labor, and overhead.

Units started and finished Those units begun this period with no prior work of this department in them and completely finished in the department in this period.

Questions

Q25–1 What type of industry is likely to use a process cost accounting system? Give some examples.

Q25–2 What are the major differences between a process cost accounting system and a job order cost accounting system? What are the major similarities?

Q25–3 What is a cost center? Could it be the same as a department? A process? Explain.

Q25–4 What is the function of a quantity schedule?

Q25–5 What are equivalent units of work? How are they concerned with percent of completion? Why is it necessary to compute equivalent units?

Q25–6 Distinguish between a quantity schedule and a schedule of equivalent units.

Q25–7 Do costs incurred in a prior department show on the cost schedule for the present department? Why or why not?

Q25–8 Student A says that it should be necessary to prepare a production cost report for only the last department that works on a product because it contains cumulative cost. Do you agree? Explain.

Q25–9 How would it help management to compare production cost reports for a department for consecutive months? What specific bits of information might be studied and why?

Q25–10 Is it necessary to prepare a time ticket in Department A each time an employee moves to a new task? Explain.

Q25–11 Does a process cost accounting system eliminate the need for materials requisitions? Explain.

Q25–12 Total costs to be accounted for in a cost of production report are accounted for in what two major ways?

Q25–13 Why are equivalent units sometimes different for materials and for labor in the same department for an accounting period?

Q25–14 What are prior department costs? Why should they be part of the cost of an ending inventory in a process? Would prior department costs ever be found in the first department to work on a product? Explain.

Q25–15 What do you consider to be the major difference between journal entries for a job order and a process cost accounting system? Explain.

Exercises

E25–1 *Diagramming quantity flows and cost inputs*

As a help in developing quantity and cost schedules in a process cost situation, it is useful to diagram the facts. Using a block diagram similar to Figure 25–3, picture the July activity in Rushmore Company. With no beginning inventory in Department A, Rushmore started 80,000 kilograms of product. Of these, 72,000 were completed and transferred to Department B. Department B—also with no beginning inventory—completed and transferred to the finished goods storeroom all but 5,000 kilograms of product. Costs in July were as follows:

Department	Materials	Labor	Overhead
A	$42,000	$ 8,000	$12,000
B	8,000	60,000	90,000

E25–2 *Quantity schedules—no beginning inventory*

Taos Company makes a product in two departments. On April 1, 1985, there was no beginning inventory in either department. The company started 18,000 product units in the Shaping Department in April; 16,200 of these were transferred to the Finishing Department. The remaining units were incomplete in Shaping. The Finishing Department completed 14,600 units and sent them to the finished goods storeroom in April. No units were lost in Finishing. Prepare in good form a quantity schedule for both departments.

E25–3
Quantity schedules with beginning inventory

King's Mountain Company makes a product called Teragram in two processes. In Process A, 1,250 gallons were on hand on June 1, 1985; on the same date, 4,000 gallons were on hand in Process B. During June, 38,400 additional gallons were started in Process A; 38,250 gallons were transferred from Process A to Process B in June. At the end of June, 2,250 gallons were incomplete in Process B; all others had been transferred to the finished goods storeroom. Prepare a quantity schedule for both departments.

E25–4
Computing equivalent units

Tupelo Company began February 1985 with 2,000 units in process in the Mixing Department. These units were 100 percent complete as to materials and 60 percent complete as to labor and overhead. During February, 10,000 additional units were started in Mixing. At the end of the month, 1,800 units were on hand in Mixing; they were 100 percent complete as to materials and 40 percent complete as to labor and overhead. Compute the equivalent units of work done in February.

E25–5
Total costs to be accounted for

The Cutting Department of Itasca Company had a balance of $3,600 in work in process on May 1, 1985. During May, the department requisitioned direct materials costing $48,000 and used 6,000 hours of direct labor at $12 per hour. Manufacturing overhead was applied at the rate of $6 per direct labor hour. What are the total costs to be accounted for in the Cutting Department?

E25–6
Computing unit costs

Durant Company's Assembly Department received 20,000 units of product from the Forming Department in October 1985 at a total transferred-in cost of $160,000. In the Assembly Department, materials costing $76,440 were requisitioned, and direct labor cost was $143,750. Manufacturing overhead of $46,000 was applied. Equivalent units for materials were 18,200; for labor and overhead they were 11,500. Compute unit costs for all elements including prior department cost.

E25–7
Assigning cost to ending inventory

Tulsa Company had an ending inventory on August 31, 1985, of 3,000 units that were 100 percent complete as to materials and 60 percent complete as to labor and overhead in the Blending Department. During August, 40,000 units had been received from the Mixing Department at a total cost of $90,000. Unit cost of materials was $1.60 in the Blending Department in August. Also in Blending, unit costs of labor and overhead were $1.40 and $1.20 respectively. Compute the cost assigned to the Blending Department's ending inventory of work-in-process.

E25–8
Equivalent units and unit costs

Fairfax Company manufactures a single product in several processes. The following data apply to the Canning Process for January 1985:

Units in beginning inventory	0
Units received from previous department	33,600
Units completed and sent to next department	30,000
Units in ending inventory	3,600
Costs for January:	
Transferred in	$30,240
Materials	47,040
Direct labor	38,160
Manufacturing overhead applied	57,240

Overhead is applied at a rate based on direct labor. The ending inventory is 100 percent complete as to materials and 50 percent complete as to labor and overhead. Compute (a) equivalent units, and (b) unit costs for January.

E25–9

Transferred-out costs—no beginning inventory

Cost information for Department B of Georgia Corporation for October 1985 is shown below (no beginning inventory):

Costs from Department A	$ 90,000
Materials	20,000
Direct labor	27,600
Manufacturing overhead applied	9,200
Total cost to be accounted for	$146,800
Units transferred from Department A	25,000
Units transferred to Department C	22,000
Units unfinished October 31	3,000
Total accounted for	25,000

The ending work in process is complete as to materials and one-third complete as to labor and overhead. Allocate the total cost to goods transferred to Department C and the ending work-in-process inventory. Show all computations.

E25–10

Transferred-out costs with beginning inventory

On September 1, 1985, Dakota Corporation had 4,000 units of product in the Blending Department that were 90 percent complete as to materials and 40 percent complete as to labor and overhead. During September 60,000 additional units were started; a total of 58,000 units were transferred to the next department. The 6,000 units left in process at the end of September were 75 percent complete as to materials and 30 percent complete as to labor and overhead. Cost data are:

Beginning work-in-process inventory cost from August	$ 18,000
Materials in September	135,470
Direct labor in September	203,700
Manufacturing overhead applied in September	174,600
Total cost to be accounted for	$531,770

Allocate the total cost between cost of goods transferred to the next department and cost of ending work-in-process inventory. Show all computations.

E25–11

All elements of cost of production report for two months

Dauphin Company began operations on January 1, 1985. It plans to manufacture a single standardized product called Enzo, which requires a single process. During January, it started and finished 12,000 units of Enzo. There was no January 31 work-in-process inventory. The company's costs for January were:

Materials	$117,000
Direct labor	153,000
Manufacturing overhead applied	183,600

During February, the company started and finished 13,500 units of Enzo; it had 600 units in process as of February 28, 1985, in the following stage of completion:

Materials	75%
Direct labor and manufacturing overhead	50%

Costs for February were:

Materials	$129,735
Direct labor	169,740
Manufacturing overhead applied	203,688

For each month, where applicable: (a) prepare a schedule of equivalent production; (b) compute the unit of cost of materials, direct labor, and manufacturing overhead; (c) compute the total cost to be accounted for; (d) compute the cost of completed units; and (e) compute the cost of the ending work-in-process inventory.

E25–12

Journal entries for cost flows

Oglala Corporation had the following costs in its Firing Department in October 1985:

Materials	$ 40,620
Direct labor	300,570
Manufacturing overhead applied	150,285

The cost of production report shows that product units with a total cost of $162,500 were received in Firing from the Shaping Department in October. Also, product units with a total cost of $602,500 were transferred from Firing to the Packing Department. Show general journal entries as of October 31, 1985, to record all the cost flows.

A Problems

P25–1A
Quantity schedule, equivalent units, unit costs, and cost to complete beginning inventory

Foothills Corporation produces a single product in one department. The following production data for November 1985 are available:

a. Beginning work-in-process inventory: 3,000 units, 75 percent complete as to materials and 40 percent complete as to direct labor and manufacturing overhead.
b. Finished and transferred to finished goods inventory: 90,000 units during the period.
c. Ending work-in-process inventory: 1,500 units, 60 percent complete as to materials and 20 percent complete as to direct labor and manufacturing overhead.

Cost data for November are:

Beginning work-in-process inventory	$ 9,075
Materials	97,515
Direct labor	204,930
Manufacturing overhead applied	196,020

Required:

1. Prepare a quantity schedule.

2. Compute equivalent units and unit costs.

3. Compute the cost of *completion* of the beginning inventory.

P25–2A
Costs transferred out and ending inventory

The following information is taken from the books of the Zugu Company for August 1985 Zugulite production. The beginning work-in-process consisted of 1,500 units, 70 percent complete as to materials and 40 percent complete as to direct labor and overhead. The August 1985 cost to manufacture was:

Materials	$12,075
Direct labor	15,800
Manufacturing overhead applied	19,750

Cost of the beginning work-in-process inventory was $4,275. There were 7,500 units of Zugulite finished during August. The ending work-in-process inventory was 2,000 units that were 80 percent complete as to materials and 50 percent complete at to labor and overhead.

Required: Compute the cost of units finished in August and the cost of the ending work-in-process inventory.

P25–3A
Cost of production report—no beginning inventory

Sweetwater Canyon Corporation had the following costs for June 1985 in Department 3 (there is no beginning inventory):

	Total Cost	Unit Cost
Production costs:		
Costs from preceding department in June	$270,000	$1.80
Costs added during June within department:		
Materials	$ 60,000	
Direct labor	82,800	
Manufacturing overhead applied	27,600	
Total costs added	$170,400	
Total costs	$440,400	

The quantity schedule is:	Units
Quantity to be accounted for:	
Units transferred from Department 2	150,000
Quantity accounted for:	
Units completed and transferred to storeroom	132,000
Units unfinished at end of month	18,000
Total	150,000

The work in process in Department 3 at the end of June is complete as to materials and one-third complete as to direct labor and manufacturing overhead.

Required: Prepare a cost of production report for Department 3 for June.

P25–4A *Cost of production report with beginning inventory*

Vermillion Company began January 1985 with 5,000 units of product in process in Department A. They were 100 percent completed as to materials and 50 percent completed as to labor and overhead. During January, 50,000 units were transferred to Department B. There were 3,000 units in process in Department A at the end of January that were 100 percent complete as to materials and 30 percent complete as to labor and overhead. Cost data are as follows:

Beginning work-in-process inventory	$13,100
Materials	57,600
Direct labor	72,600
Manufacturing overhead applied	70,180

Required: Prepare a cost of production report.

P25–5A *Cost of production report for two departments*

The Seattle Chemical Company manufactures a product in two processes: grinding and blending. All materials go into process at the beginning in the Grinding Department; materials, however, are added continuously in proportion to labor and overhead in the Blending Department. During September 1985, the company started 36,000 units in the Grinding Department; at the end of the month, 6,000 of them remained in the work-in-process inventory and were one-quarter complete. The others went to the Blending Department, where there were 9,000 units one-third complete at the start of the month, and 12,000 units three-quarters complete at the end. Beginning work-in-process inventory and manufacturing costs were as follows:

	Grinding	Blending
Work in process, August 31, 1985	$ 0	$54,720
Materials	79,200	33,000
Direct labor	44,100	52,800
Manufacturing overhead applied	31,500	42,900

Required: Prepare a cost of production report for each department.

P25–6A *Journal entries for flow of costs*

Without prejudice to the solution of P25–5A, add the following assumptions to that problem:

a. Cost of the units transferred from Grinding to Blending was $120,000.
b. Cost of units transferred from Blending to the finished goods storeroom was $155,250.
c. There was no beginning inventory of finished goods on September 1, 1985. During September, 18,000 product units were sold for $130,000 on account.

Required: Prepare journal entries dated September 30 to record all manufacturing and sales in September.

P25–7A
Thought-provoking problem: the learning curve

During World War II, it was noticed that as workers gained experience with a new product, productive efficiency increased. This concept known as the *learning curve* is used to control costs in production situations today. The Tuskegee Corporation began to build a new computer in several departments in January 1985. The Wiring Department handled 12,000 units in January and 12,000 units in February. There were no ending work-in-process units for either month. Manufacturing costs for the two months were as follows:

	January	February
Materials	$ 33,600	$33,000
Direct labor	108,000	64,800
Manufacturing overhead applied	75% of labor cost	

Required:

1. Compute unit costs for materials, labor, and manufacturing overhead for both months.

2. Do you believe that a learning curve effect is being experienced in the Wiring Department? Describe fully indications that it is or is not present.

B Problems

P25–1B
Quantity schedule, equivalent units, unit costs, and cost to complete beginning inventory

Mission Corporation produces a single product in one department. The following production data for October 1985 are available:

a. Beginning work-in-process inventory: 6,300 units, 80 percent complete as to materials and 45 percent complete as to direct labor and manufacturing overhead.
b. Finished and transferred to finished goods inventory: 189,000 units during the period.
c. Ending work-in-process inventory: 3,150 units, 90 percent complete as to materials and 70 percent complete as to direct labor and manufacturing overhead.

Cost data for October are:

Beginning work-in-process inventory	$ 13,986
Materials	224,154
Direct labor	282,555
Manufacturing overhead applied	244,881

Required:

1. Prepare a quantity schedule.

2. Compute equivalent units and unit costs.

3. Compute the cost of the *completion* of the beginning inventory.

P25–2B
Costs transferred out and ending inventory

The following information is taken from the books of Yokoyama Corporation for September 1985 Fujicake production. The beginning work-in-process inventory consisted of 3,000 units, 60 percent complete as to materials and 35 percent as to direct labor and overhead. The September 1985 cost to manufacture was:

Materials	$4,300
Direct labor	2,715
Manufacturing overhead applied	3,620

Cost of the beginning work-in-process inventory was $1,635. There were 9,500 units of Fujicake transferred out during September 1985. The ending work-in-process inventory was 1,000 units that were 90 percent complete as to materials and 60 percent complete as to labor and overhead.

Required: Compute the cost of units finished in September and the cost of the ending work-in-process inventory.

P25–3B *Cost of production report—no beginning inventory*

Mission Gorge Corporation had the following costs in the Painting Department for August 1985 (there is no beginning inventory):

	Total Cost	Unit Cost
Production costs:		
Costs from preceding department	$ 90,000	$1.20
Costs added during August within department:		
Materials	$131,250	
Direct labor	94,500	
Manufacturing overhead applied	144,000	
Total costs added	$369,750	
Total costs	$459,750	

The quantity schedule is;	
Quantity to be accounted for:	**Units**
Units from preceding department	75,000
Quantity accounted for:	
Units completed and transferred out	66,000
Units unfinished at end of month	9,000
Total	75,000

The work in process in the Painting Department at the end of August is complete as to materials and two-thirds complete as to direct labor and manufacturing overhead.

Required: Prepare a cost of production report for the Painting Department for August.

P25–4B *Cost of production report with beginning inventory*

Emerald Isle Corporation began May 1985 with 3,000 units of product in process in Department A. They were 100 percent complete as to materials and 40 percent complete as to labor and overhead. During May, 40,000 units were transferred to Department B. There were 2,000 units in process in Department A at the end of May that were 100 percent complete as to materials and 20 percent complete as to labor and overhead. Cost data are as follows:

Beginning work-in-process inventory	$ 9,030
Materials	56,550
Direct labor	82,320
Manufacturing overhead applied	70,560

Required: Prepare a cost of production report.

P25–5B *Cost of production report for two departments*

The New England Company makes a product in two processes. In both processes, all materials are added when the units of product are started in the processing. During May 1985 the company started 24,000 units in Process A; 18,000 units were completed and transferred to Process B. The remaining 6,000 were one-half complete in Process A. There were 3,000 units three-quarters complete in Process B at the beginning of the month; at the end of the month, 5,400 were on hand, two-thirds complete. Beginning work-in-process inventory and manufacturing costs were as follows:

	Process A	Process B
Beginning work-in-process inventory	$ 0	$10,650
Materials	144,000	18,000
Direct labor	67,200	27,120
Manufacturing overhead applied	92,400	30,510

Required: Prepare a cost of production report for each department.

P25–6B

Journal entries for flow of costs

Without prejudice to the solution of P25–5B, add the following assumptions:

a. Cost of the units transferred from Process A to Process B was $240,000.

b. Cost of units transferred from Process B to the finished goods storeroom was $280,020.

c. There was no beginning inventory of finished goods on May 1, 1985. During May, 12,000 product units were sold for $280,800 on account.

Required: Prepare journal entries dated May 31 to record all manufacturing and sales in May.

P25–7B

Thought-provoking problem: need for cost control action

Because its product is highly perishable, Diamond Head Company has no carryover of work in process from month to month. Accordingly, units completed are the same as equivalent units each month. Following are production and cost data for the second quarter of 1985:

	April	May	June
Units produced	21,200	24,150	23,800
Cost data:			
Materials	$47,700	$60,375	$63,070
Direct labor	67,840	74,865	72,590
Manufacturing overhead applied	80 percent of labor cost.		

Required:

1. Compute unit costs of materials, direct labor, and manufacturing overhead for each month.

2. Prepare a report to management analyzing manufacturing costs. Show favorable and unfavorable trends and suggest possible causes.

26 Forecasting and Budgeting: The Flexible Budget

Introduction

In the first chapter of this book, two functions of management—planning and controlling—were described as examples of internal uses of accounting information. This chapter is about planning and controlling. It contains a discussion of profit planning and an example of the budget formulation process. The concept of responsibility accounting is introduced, along with the use of flexible budgets. When many of today's major corporations were formed, their close competitors were usually located across town or at most in another state. Now they are worldwide. Budget planning is the key to survival in this environment. The budget techniques described in this chapter link the two previous cost accounting chapters (Chapters 24 and 25) to standard costs (Chapter 27).

Learning Goals

To differentiate between fixed and variable costs.

To know the basic concepts of budget preparation and profit planning.

To describe a typical business budget structure.

To formulate specific business budget schedules beginning with a sales forecast.

To know how to use specific business budget schedules to prepare a projected income statement.

To define the concept of a flexible budget.

To discuss the control function and the concepts of responsibility accounting.

Cost Behavior: The Nature of Costs

Fundamental to management decisions in budgeting and profit planning is a knowledge of the patterns of cost (cost behavior) for the various cost elements. Managers need to know how costs behave as volume changes. Costs can generally be classified as fixed or variable. A **fixed cost** remains the same *in total* regardless of changes in volume of production. In other words, as volume increases total fixed cost does *not* increase. This means that the fixed cost *per unit* decreases as volume increases because the same fixed cost is spread over more units. Total **variable cost** changes directly in proportion to changes in volume. This means that variable cost per unit remains constant. Thus, for every one-unit increase in volume, total variable cost will increase by a specific amount—the per-unit variable cost. Say volume in the second quarter is 120 percent of volume in the first quarter of the year. Building rent, depreciation, and property taxes should remain the same; they are fixed costs. However, direct labor or direct materials usage should increase by 20 percent because they are variable costs.

Some costs are neither fixed nor variable but tend to be *semivariable.* Within a limited volume range, however, all costs can be separated into fixed and variable components. This volume range over which cost behavior can be predicted is called the **relevant volume range** or **relevant range.**[1]

Figure 26–1 illustrates the types of cost classified as to their expected behavior. Explanations of the numbered items in Figure 26–1 follow the figure.

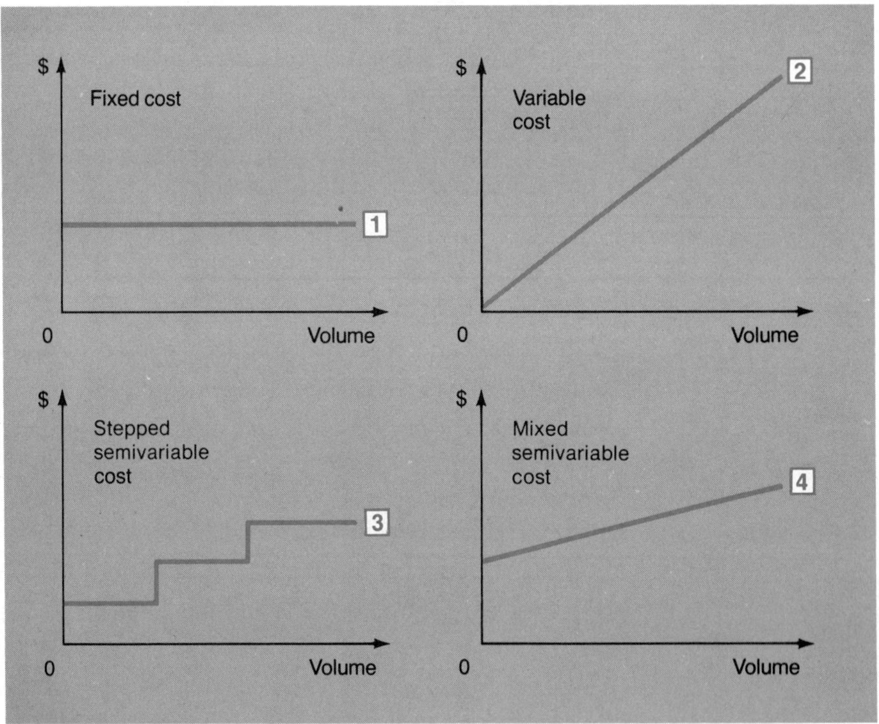

Figure 26–1 Patterns of Total Cost Behavior

[1]Obviously, cost behavior patterns are not stable over the entire range of production possibilities from zero to 100 percent of capacity. Somewhere between those extremes is a range—different for each firm—over which costs can be predicted to follow a pattern. It is this range that is relevant to production planning.

1 *Total* fixed cost does not change as volume changes. For example, property tax on a factory building remains the same regardless of the amount of production volume attained by the company using the building.

2 Total variable cost changes directly with changes in volume of activity. Direct materials and direct labor are typical examples of variable costs. Many overhead costs and period expenses are also variable.

3 Some costs are neither pure fixed nor pure variable costs. The costs of supervisory salaries may remain the same over a span of production volume, but when a certain level of volume is reached, it will become necessary to add an additional supervisor, and so on. Such a cost is known as a **stepped semivariable cost.**

4 A **mixed semivariable cost** is fixed at the beginning then changes directly with production thereafter. Building and equipment maintenance costs are examples. It is necessary to perform a certain amount of maintenance even if factory equipment is not being used at all. As volume (and the use of facilities) increases, maintenance costs become variable, that is, they increase in proportion to the activity that takes place.

In practice, it is useful to split semivariable costs into their fixed and variable components and deal only with fixed and variable costs—for example, fixed supervision costs and variable supervision costs. The techniques for separating such costs are covered in cost accounting courses and are beyond the scope of this book. In this book, it is assumed that such separation has been made and costs are classified as either fixed or variable.

An important feature of cost behavior must be thoroughly understood. Because fixed costs *do not change in total* as volume changes, the fixed costs per unit *do change.* Assume that a company has fixed cost of $10,000 per month. If only one unit is produced, the fixed cost per unit is $10,000. However, if production increases to 10 units, the fixed cost per unit is $1,000 = ($10,000 ÷ 10 units). Also, because variable costs *do change* in total directly with volume, their *per unit costs do not change.* If one unit costs $10, it is expected that 10 units will cost $100 = ($10 × 10). Unit variable costs remain the same regardless of volume change. Although it may appear to contradict the basic definitions of fixed costs and variable costs, it should become obvious in later illustrations that the behavior of total costs and unit costs is opposite. The types of costs and the way they can be expected to behave must be understood before a firm can engage in budgeting and forecasting.

The Budget: The Basic Planning Tool

Profit planning is carried out by the use of budgets. A **budget** is a financial plan for a future period. Budgets are usually prepared on a short-term basis; the most common time period used is one year. All individuals and groups perform budgeting to some degree. John Smith, before leaving school for a weekend at the beach, gives some thought to the expenses he will have and to how he plans to meet them. Families tend to budget on a month-to-month basis. Most do not prepare a formal written budget, but they do have knowledge of upcoming expenditures such as house payments, utility bills, food bills, and other items that tend to recur each month. They also have a fairly good idea of the amount of take-home pay that can be expected to meet expenses. Unfortunately, most families—and many businesses—never get beyond this informal stage. For a business, the failure to establish and use a formal budget structure often results in (1) lost sales due to underproduction, (2) excessive inventory costs due to overproduction, (3) excessive personnel turnover, and (4) general lack of control over the outcome of business operations in terms of profits. The result for many firms is a business failure that might have been avoided by **profit planning** (budgeting toward a planned profit percent).

The Budget Structure

The budget planning process must begin with a forecast of sales known as the **sales budget.** It is usually prepared in detail by product and by territory, using several techniques. One method is to ask salespersons to submit an estimate of the quantities they expect to sell in the next year. Another approach is to study sales from the customers' point of view by conducting a market survey in which customers are asked what they plan to buy. A third method in common use is to project trends by using historical data from the accounting records and adjust the trends by a factor which reflects the amount of price competition in the particular industry, the state of the economy, and the effect it is estimated these factors will have on sales of specific products in the coming year.

With the sales budget prepared, a company can then develop supporting budget schedules. Figure 26–2 pictures a typical budget structure for a manufacturing business. For a manufacturer, the *major supporting* schedule is the **production budget.** After production requirements are known, schedules can be developed for labor costs, materials costs, and manufacturing overhead costs. Each of these is a separate budget and, as shown in Figure 26–2, flows from information contained in the production budget.

From the sales budget (and studies of economic conditions), expenses can be forecasted and a **general and administrative expense budget** and a **selling expense budget** prepared. Along with the schedules of labor, materials, and overhead costs, these provide information on cash outflows. The sales budget provides information on expected cash inflows. Using these schedules, a *cash forecast* can be prepared. The cash forecast, like the other schedules, is broken into quarterly (or monthly) receipts and payments; it allows management to arrange in advance for any necessary borrowing of money or for temporary investment of excess cash.

At the right-hand side of Figure 26–2, the ultimate goal of the total budget process is indicated. With information from the individual schedules, it is possible to develop a *projected income statement* and a *projected balance sheet* for the budget period. If the indicated profit is not in line with management's target, it may be necessary to adjust some of the plans to intensify

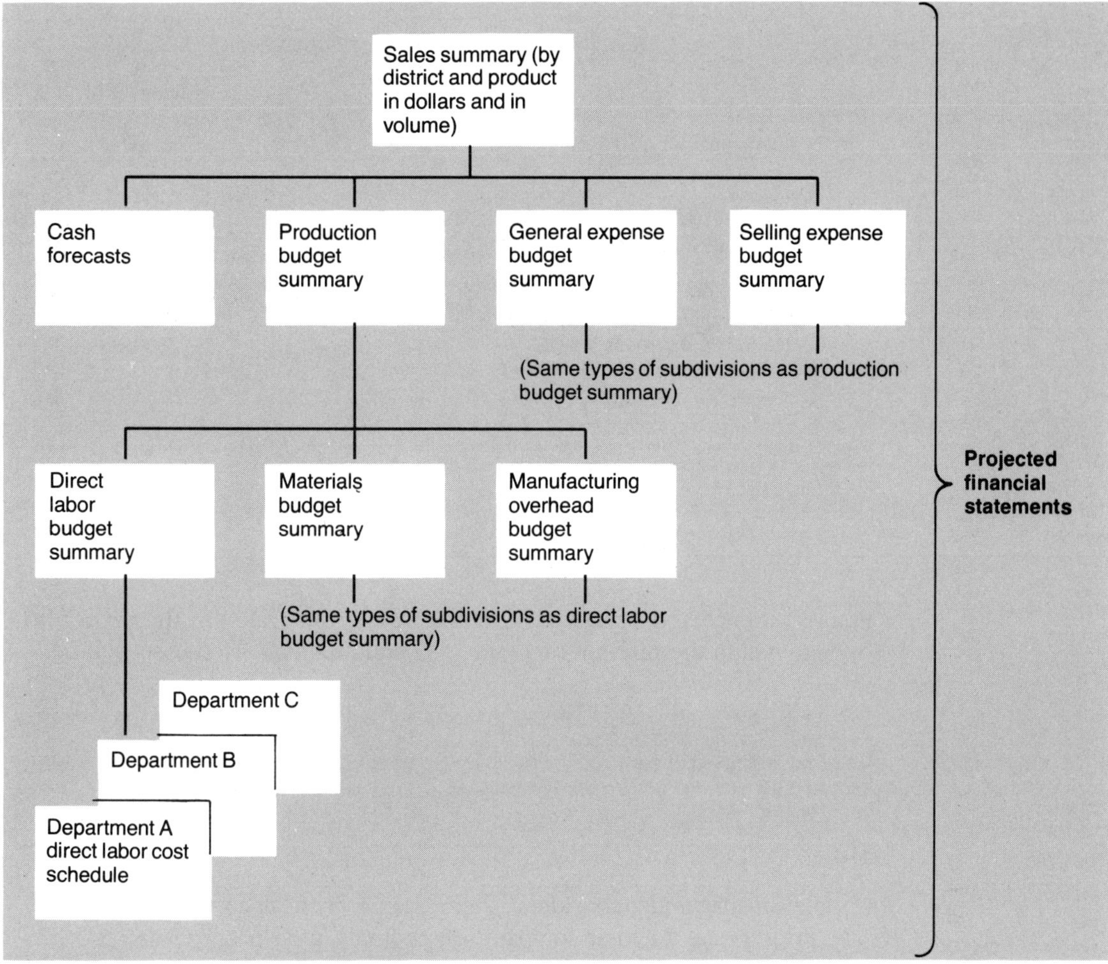

Figure 26–2 **Budget Structure**

sales efforts or reduce cost. When the indicated profit and balance sheet relationships are in line with management's target, it is then the task of supervisory personnel to exercise control over sales and costs to attain the profit goals that were set in the budget process.

The Budget Process: An Illustration

As an example of the development of projected financial statements, consider the case of Upstate Manufacturing Company, which produces two styles of plastic hats. Figure 26–3 provides cost information on the two styles. From past experience and special cost studies, the variable costs per unit of production (per hat) have been determined.

Requirements for Each Hat of Two Styles[a]

	Style I	Style II
Materials:		
2 feet @ $0.30	$0.60	
5 feet @ $0.30		$1.50
Direct labor:		
1/10 hour @ $8.00	0.80	
1/4 hour @ $8.00		2.00
Variable manufacturing overhead:		
100% of direct labor cost	0.80	2.00
Variable manufacturing costs per hat	$2.20	$5.50
Variable selling expenses per hat	0.20	0.20
Variable general and administrative expenses per hat	0.10	0.30
Total variable costs per hat	$2.50	$6.00

[a]These are unit variable costs; they are the same for each unit produced. The total variable costs, however, will vary with volume.

Figure 26–3 Variable Costs for Upstate Manufacturing Company

Past experience and Upstate's accounting records indicate that they expect to operate within the relevant range in 1985 and that *total* fixed costs will be:

Fixed manufacturing overhead	$ 50,000
Fixed selling expenses	45,000
Fixed general and administrative expenses	75,000
Total	$170,000

Upstate's management considers a before-taxes profit of about 12 percent of sales appropriate for their company. Accordingly, their profit planning will use 12 percent as a target figure.

Sales Budget

The sales force has prepared estimates of sales, and, after consideration of the economic outlook, management has approved the sales budget shown in Figure 26–4. Style I sells for $7.50, and Style II sells for $15.00. To make the illustration less complex, both styles are assumed to be sold in only one territory. In actual practice, a company would further divide its sales budgets by districts or territories.

Production Budget

In order to protect against loss of sales from being out of stock, Upstate policy requires that the inventory of finished goods at the end of each quarter be equal to 20 percent of the anticipated sales of the next quarter. From the sales budget and the application of this inventory policy, a production budget in units has been developed and is shown in Figure 26–5. Note that the required ending inventory of each quarter (the 20 percent of anticipated sales

UPSTATE MANUFACTURING COMPANY
Sales Budget
For the Year Ending December 31, 1985

	Product			
	Style I		Style II	
	Units	Amount	Units	Amount
First quarter	2,000	$15,000	3,000	$ 45,000
Second quarter	1,800	13,500	2,500	37,500
Third quarter	3,200	24,000	5,000	75,000
Fourth quarter	4,000	30,000	7,000	105,000
Total	11,000	$82,500	17,500	$262,500

Figure 26–4
Sales Summary

UPSTATE MANUFACTURING COMPANY
Production Budget (in units)
For the Year Ending December 31, 1985

	1st Quarter	2nd Quarter	3rd Quarter	4th Quarter
	Style I			
Required for sales	2,000	1,800	3,200	4,000
Required for ending inventory	360[a]	640	800	440[b]
Total required	2,360	2,440	4,000	4,440
Less: Beginning inventory	400[c]	360	640	800
Production requirements	1,960	2,080	3,360	3,640
	Style II			
Required for sales	3,000	2,500	5,000	7,000
Required for ending inventory	500	1,000	1,400	640[b]
Total required	3,500	3,500	6,400	7,640
Less: Beginning inventory	600[c]	500	1,000	1,400
Production requirements	2,900	3,000	5,400	6,240

[a]Next quarter sales times 20 percent = 1,800 × 0.20 = 360.
[b]Based on estimate of sales for first quarter of 1986.
[c]Estimated as 20 percent of sales in first quarter of 1985.

Figure 26–5
Production Summary

of the next quarter) becomes a beginning inventory of the next quarter, thus reducing production requirements in that period.

Labor, Materials, and Overhead Budgets

With the production requirements for each quarter of 1985 known, Upstate can now develop estimates of labor, materials, and overhead costs. These would normally be presented as separate schedules but are gathered together in one summary budget in Figure 26–6. The figure has also been made simpler by omission of beginning and ending inventories of raw materials. Although this is not realistic, it does allow us to assume that all materials used in a quarter are purchased in that same quarter. An actual materials purchases budget would recognize beginning and ending inventories to determine purchase requirements in the same way inventories were used in Figure 26–5. Explanation of numbered items in Figure 26–6 follows the figure.

UPSTATE MANUFACTURING COMPANY
Direct Labor, Materials, and Variable Manufacturing Overhead Budget
For the Year Ending December 31, 1985

		1st Quarter		2nd Quarter		3rd Quarter		4th Quarter	
		Units	Amount	Units	Amount	Units	Amount	Units	Amount
	Direct Labor:								
1	Style I @ $8	196	$ 1,568	208	$ 1,664	336	$ 2,688	364	$ 2,912
	Style II @ $8	725	5,800	750	6,000	1,350	10,800	1,560	12,480
	Total direct labor	921	$ 7,368	958	$ 7,664	1,686	$13,488	1,924	$15,392
	Materials in feet:								
2	Style I @ $0.30	3,920	$ 1,176	4,160	$ 1,248	6,720	$ 2,016	7,280	$ 2,184
	Style II @ $0.30	14,500	4,350	15,000	4,500	27,000	8,100	31,200	9,360
	Total materials	18,420	$ 5,526	19,160	$ 5,748	33,720	$10,116	38,480	$11,544
3	Variable manufacturing overhead		$ 7,368		$ 7,664		$13,488		$15,392
4	Total variable manufacturing cost		$20,262		$21,076		$37,092		$42,328

Figure 26–6 **Direct Labor, Materials, and Variable Manufacturing Overhead Summary**

1 The special cost studies (see Figure 26–3) showed that one-tenth labor hour was required to produce a Style I hat and one-fourth labor hour to produce a Style II. Planned first quarter production (see Figure 26–5) is 1,960 and 2,900 hats, respectively. Thus, 1,960 ÷ 10 = 196 labor hours for Style I and 2,900 ÷ 4 = 725 labor hours for Style II. Other quarters are computed in the same manner.

2 The special cost studies (see Figure 26–3) indicate that two feet of material are required per Style I and five feet per Style II hat. Referring again to first quarter production plans (Figure 26–5), 1,960 Style I hats × 2 feet per hat = 3,920 feet of material; in like manner, 2,900 Style II hats × 5 feet per hat = 14,500 feet of material. Other quarters are computed in the same manner.

3 Variable manufacturing costs were revealed by the cost studies to be 100 percent of direct labor cost. Or, from data in Figures 26–3 and 26–5:

Type Hat	1st Quarter Production	Unit Cost	Total Cost
Style I	1,960	$0.80	$1,568
Style II	2,900	2.00	5,800
Total			$7,368

[4] This is variable manufacturing cost only. Fixed manufacturing costs are expected to be an additional $50,000 in 1985.

Other Cost Budgets

Separate schedules would be made for variable selling expenses, variable general and administrative expenses, fixed manufacturing overhead costs, fixed selling expenses, and fixed general and administrative expenses. They would be presented in detail with the cost and description of each applicable item, such as indirect labor, indirect materials, advertising, or office salaries, being shown on a separate line of the budget. To keep this illustration simple, they are presented in summary form only in Figures 26–7 and 26–8.

Cash Forecast

Managers of a business must have adequate amounts of cash available to pay invoices during the discount period, meet payrolls, and pay other operating

UPSTATE MANUFACTURING COMPANY
Variable Nonmanufacturing Expense Budget
For the Year Ending December 31, 1985

	1st Quarter	2nd Quarter	3rd Quarter	4th Quarter
Variable selling expenses:				
Style I @ $0.20	$ 400	$ 360	$ 640	$ 800
Style II @ $0.20	600	500	1,000	1,400
Variable general and administrative expenses:				
Style I @ $0.10	200	180	320	400
Style II @ $0.30	900	750	1,500	2,100
Totals	$2,100	$1,790	$3,460	$4,700

Figure 26–7 Summary of Variable Nonmanufacturing Expenses

UPSTATE MANUFACTURING COMPANY
Fixed Costs Budget
For the Year Ending December 31, 1985

	Period[a]			
	1st Quarter	2nd Quarter	3rd Quarter	4th Quarter
Manufacturing overhead	$12,500	$12,500	$12,500	$12,500
Selling expenses	11,250	11,250	11,250	11,250
General and administrative expenses	18,750	18,750	18,750	18,750
Totals	$42,500	$42,500	$42,500	$42,500

[a]Costs are assumed to be incurred evenly over the year.

Figure 26–8 Summary of Fixed Costs

expenses. However, excessive cash balances should be avoided, especially during inflationary periods when cash suffers a purchasing power loss and very high rates of interest can be earned on investments. Accordingly, it is essential to plan ahead so that short-term borrowing or investment can be anticipated and done at the best available terms.

A **cash forecast** (also a budget) is a projection based on the budgeted items that will cause cash inflows and outflows. The forecast deals exclusively with estimates involving cash. Noncash items such as depreciation are not included. Assume that Upstate Manufacturing Company makes one-half of its sales for cash and collects the credit sales, the other half, on the following pattern:

- ☐ 60 percent in the month of sale.
- ☐ 35 percent in the month following sale.
- ☐ 5 percent in the second month following sale.

November 1984 credit sales were $20,000, and December credit sales were $18,000. Quarterly sales and expenses are incurred evenly over the quarter; expenses are paid in cash in the month in which they are incurred.[2]

It is helpful to prepare a schedule of collections from sales to support the cash forecast. Collections for the first quarter of 1985 would be as follows (based on the budgeted first quarter sales of $60,000):

UPSTATE MANUFACTURING COMPANY
Schedule of Collections from Sales[a]
For the Quarter Ending March 31, 1985

	January	February	March
From cash sales of month	$10,000	$10,000	$10,000
From November credit sales (5%)	1,000	0	0
From December credit sales (35% and 5%)	6,300	900	0
From January credit sales (60%, 35%, and 5%)	6,000	3,500	500
From February credit sales (60% and 35%)	0	6,000	3,500
From March credit sales (60%)	0	0	6,000
Total cash collections	$23,300	$20,400	$20,000

[a]Total sales each month are $20,000 = ($60,000 ÷ 3).

This schedule can now be incorporated into a cash forecast (Figure 26–9) for the first quarter of 1985. It is estimated that the January 1, 1985, cash balance will be $15,000 and that *expenses of each month will be one-third of the amount for the quarter.* Quarterly budgeted payments from Figures 26–6,

[2]To assume that all of Upstate's expenses are paid in cash allows a less complex illustration of the cash forecast, but the assumption is not realistic. Obviously, some noncash items such as depreciation are included in the fixed expenses.

UPSTATE MANUFACTURING COMPANY
Cash Forecast
For the Quarter Ending March 31, 1985

	January	February	March
Receipts:			
Beginning balance	$15,000	$16,679	$15,458
Collections (from schedule)	23,300	20,400	20,000
Total cash available	$38,300	$37,079	$35,458
Payments[a]:			
Materials, labor, and variable overhead (Figure 26–6)	$ 6,754	$ 6,754	$ 6,754
Other variable costs (Figure 26–7)	700	700	700
Fixed costs (Figure 26–8)	14,167	14,167	14,167
Total payments	$21,621	$21,621	$21,621
Ending balance	$16,679	$15,458	$13,837

[a]Incurred one-third each month.

Figure 26–9
Cash Forecast

26–7, and 26–8 are converted to monthly figures. For example, materials, labor, and variable overhead are $6,754 = ($20,262 ÷ 3) from the first quarter in Figure 26–6. Other monthly figures are estimated in a parallel manner. Other types of receipts that are not shown in this illustration could be collection of notes receivable, interest on bond investments, or dividends from investments in stock. Also, probably there would be other nonrecurring payments such as debt payments or income tax and property tax payments.

Cash forecasts are typically prepared for a three- or six-month period and revised each month by dropping out the current month and adding a new month to the forecast. From the data in Upstate Manufacturing Company's cash forecast, it appears that management should consider a temporary investment of cash in readily marketable securities. The cash balance being carried forward each month is equal to approximately three weeks' operating needs; this appears to be excessive. The ability to predict such a situation and act upon it in advance—referred to as financial flexibility—is the primary advantage of the cash forecast.

Projected Financial Statements

Using data from the budget structure, the projected income statement in Figure 26–10 has been prepared. The net income before taxes of $42,192 is 12.2 percent of sales, which is in line with management's profit-planning goal of 12 percent. The amounts in Figure 26–10 are explained in the numbered items that follow. Since there is not enough information available about Upstate Manufacturing Company to develop a projected balance sheet, it is not illustrated here.

UPSTATE MANUFACTURING COMPANY
Projected Income Statement
For the Year Ending December 31, 1985

1	Sales (Figure 26–4)		$345,000
	Cost of goods sold:		
2	Finished goods inventory, December 31, 1984	$ 5,600[a]	
3	Add: Cost of goods manufactured (Figures 26–6 and 26–8)	170,758[b]	
	Total available for sale	$176,358	
4	Finished goods inventory, December 31, 1985	5,600[a]	170,758
	Gross margin on sales		$174,242
5	Operating expenses (Figures 26–7 and 26–8)		132,050
	Net income		$ 42,192

[a]Fixed costs in inventory assumed.
[b]No beginning or ending work-in-process inventories.

Figure 26–10 Projected Income Statement

1 The sales budget (Figure 26–4) contains an estimate that 1985 sales of both styles will be $345,000 = ($82,500 + $262,500).

2 Variable costs in the beginning inventory are $4,180 = (400 × $2.20) + (600 × $5.50) from Figures 26–3 and 26–5. The remainder of cost in this inventory is an assumed amount of fixed cost.

3 Variable cost of manufacturing ($120,758) is the sum of the four quarterly totals in Figure 26–6. Fixed manufacturing cost shown in Figure 26–8 is $50,000 = ($12,500 × 4). The total cost is $170,758 = ($120,758 + $50,000).

4 Variable costs in the ending inventory are $4,488 = (440 × $2.20) + (640 × $5.50) from Figures 26–3 and 26–5. Again, the amount of fixed cost making up the remainder is assumed.

5 Figure 26–7 shows $12,050 of variable selling and general and administrative expenses for the year (the sum of four quarterly totals). Fixed selling and general and administrative expenses in Figure 26–8 are $11,250 and $18,750 per quarter for an annual total of $120,000. Total operating expenses are $132,050 = ($12,050 + $120,000).

Responsibility Accounting: Control through Budgeting

Although the Upstate Manufacturing Company illustration was not developed to that depth, Figure 26–2 shows that the labor, materials, overhead, general and administrative expense, and selling expense budgets should be developed for each department that is involved in such costs. The labor budget is a summary of three labor cost schedules—those for Departments A, B, and C. The supervisor of Department A is responsible for control of labor costs for that department and for all other Department A cost schedules. To measure the performance of departmental supervisors in carrying out this task, companies practice responsibility accounting.

Responsibility accounting

Responsibility accounting ***traces cost to specific segments of the organization (usually departments, divisions, or sections thereof) supervised by one person. Periodic comparisons of actual figures with budgeted (planned) figures can then provide a basis for the evaluation of performance of each organizational segment and for corrective action where needed (controlling).***

Responsibility accounting does not require a separate set of accounting records. However, the accounts described in Chapters 24 and 25 for developing product costs must be classified and subdivided *to the same organizational level as the budget.* When this is done, reports such as the one illustrated in Figure 26–11 can be prepared.

UPSTATE MANUFACTURING COMPANY
Department A—Manufacturing Overhead
For the Quarter Ended June 30, 1985

	Expenditures		
Budget Item	**Budget**	**Actual**	**Variance[a]**
Factory supplies	$ 300	$ 295	$ 5(F)
Light and power	400	410	10(U)
Indirect labor	350	500	150(U)
Fixed costs	1,000	975	25(F)
Totals	$2,050	$2,180	$130(U)

[a]F indicates a favorable variance; U indicates an unfavorable variance.

Figure 26–11 Budget Performance Report

Similar reports are issued for each department for each schedule in the budget structure. Managers at all levels are responsible for explaining the **variances** (deviations from planned results) and for taking action for correction when necessary. Note, for example, that indirect labor in Upstate's Department A has exceeded the budget by more than 40 percent. The weakness in the type of performance report shown in Figure 26–11 is that it makes no allowance for change in production volume. Thus, a factor that is beyond the control of the supervisor of Department A may be affecting this unfavorable report. This weakness can be overcome by the use of a flexible budget.

A Flexible Manufacturing Overhead Budget

A budget that gives recognition to varying levels of production and to the costs that change with these levels is called a **flexible budget.** It provides management with a basis for analyzing—and, therefore, controlling—the variances between budgeted and actual costs. This is accomplished by comparing actual expenditures with previously established budgeted amounts, *adjusted for varying levels of production.* A series of budgets is prepared, showing

UPSTATE MANUFACTURING COMPANY
Department A—Manufacturing Overhead
For the Quarter Ending June 30, 1985

	Production Volume			
Percent of plan	85%	90%	95%	100%
Units of product	425	450	475	500
Variable costs:				
Factory supplies	$ 255.00	$ 270.00	$ 285.00	$ 300.00
Light and power	340.00	360.00	380.00	400.00
Indirect labor	297.50	315.00	332.50	350.00
Total variable costs	$ 892.50	$ 945.00	$ 997.50	$1,050.00
Fixed costs:	1,000.00	1,000.00	1,000.00	1,000.00
Total budgeted costs	$1,892.50	$1,945.00	$1,997.50	$2,050.00

Figure 26–12 Department A Flexible Manufacturing Budget

estimated costs at various levels of production. Since it is not practical to set up budgets for every possible level of operation, adjustment may be necessary if, for example, the flexible budgets are at five-percent intervals and actual production falls at a point between the intervals. The preparation of a flexible budget involves an analysis of the degree and extent to which each item of cost is affected by changes in volume of production. The flexible budget, therefore, is essentially a series of fixed budgets.

If Upstate produces at a volume other than planned, the budget for Department A should be adjusted accordingly. Assuming that normal production at 100 percent is 500 units, Figure 26–12 shows a flexible manufacturing overhead budget for various possible levels of production. Note that the basic budget in Figure 26–11 is established as normal, or 100 percent of capacity, in Figure 26–12. The variable costs are each adjusted to the other levels; *fixed costs remain the same.* For example, factory supplies—a variable cost—is expected to be $285 = (95% of $300) in the budget at the 95 percent production level. Fixed costs, however, remain the same.

Assume that Upstate's *actual production* in the second quarter is 465 units of product; this is 93 percent of the plan. Figure 26–12 shows that Department A should incur manufacturing overhead costs somewhere between $1,945 and $1,997.50. The variable costs should be 93 percent of the original production plan, while the fixed costs should remain the same as originally budgeted. Accordingly, a new performance report can be prepared as shown in Figure 26–13. It is important to understand why and how the Adjusted Budget column in Figure 26–13 was developed. *Variable costs are adjusted to 93 percent of the original budget because Upstate's actual production was that percentage of normal.* Factory supplies were budgeted at $300; the expected cost, however, is $279 = ($300 × 0.93). The other two variable costs are adjusted in the same manner, but the *total fixed costs* (by definition) *should remain the same* as they were at 100 percent of volume. A comparison of Figures 26–11 and 26–13 shows that the flexible budget is a much more useful tool; this one shows clearly that the total variance is significantly

UPSTATE MANUFACTURING COMPANY
Department A—Manufacturing Overhead
For the Quarter Ended June 30, 1985

Budget Item	Expenditures: Adjusted Budget	Actual	Variance[a]
Variable costs:			
Factory supplies	$ 279.00	$ 295.00	$ 16.00(U)
Light and power	372.00	410.00	38.00(U)
Indirect labor	325.50	500.00	174.50(U)
Totals	$ 976.50	$1,205.00	
Fixed costs	1,000.00	975.00	25.00(F)
Totals	$1,976.50	$2,180.00	$203.50(U)

[a]F indicates a favorable variance; U indicates an unfavorable variance.

Figure 26–13 Budget Performance Report

greater after the volume reduction is taken into consideration. In Figure 26–11, actual expenditures are a little more than 6.3 percent = ($130 ÷ $2,050) in excess of the budget. That **unfavorable variance** (actual expenditures greater than the budget) is not a correct reflection of how well Department A has exercised its responsibility to control costs. The more realistic unfavorable variance of $203.50 is revealed when the budget is adjusted. It is actually 10.3 percent = ($203.50 ÷ $1,976.50); moreover, what appeared (in Figure 26–11) to be a favorable variance of $5 in the use of factory supplies is actually a $16 unfavorable variance when production volume is considered.

The supervisor of Department A needs to review carefully the causes of excess usage of variable items. There may be valid explanations for the differences; or the use of manpower and other resources may be inefficient. Reports such as the one in Figure 26–13 bring the exceptions to the attention of management; efforts can then be concentrated on them.

In this chapter, variances were developed by comparison of actual expenditures with budgeted expenditures. In Chapter 27, the idea is expanded to develop a *standard cost accounting system,* in which variances between actual expenditures and a predetermined amount that is standard for certain costs are revealed.

Appendix 26.1
Direct Costing: Cost-Volume-Profit Analysis

Introduction

Management decisions based on the traditional income statement are sometimes weakened by the fact that *fixed* and *variable* costs are not separated in that statement. A technique known as *direct costing* (also called *variable costing*) allows the accountant to overcome this weakness. In a direct costing income statement, a figure known as the contribution margin (excess of revenue over variable cost) is developed. The contribution margin helps in many ways in making better management decisions. One way is in the analysis of the relationships among cost, volume, and profits. These concepts are explained in this appendix.

Learning goals

To understand the concept of direct (or variable) costing as a management tool.

To differentiate between direct costing and full absorption costing in an income statement.

To understand the concept of a contribution margin.

To know the other concepts in analysis of cost, volume, and profits.

To be able to use cost, volume, and profit relationships in break-even analysis.

The Direct Costing Concept

In the manufacturing accounting chapters in this book (Chapters 23, 24, and 25) and in this chapter, both variable and fixed manufacturing costs have been assigned to work in process and have become part of the finished goods inventory cost. They both have been considered to be a part of product cost. Recall that all direct materials and direct labor costs are variable; manufacturing overhead costs, however, typically include both fixed and variable components. For example, depreciation of factory buildings and equipment, property taxes on factory items, salaries of supervisors, and other significant manufacturing overhead costs are fixed. When these fixed overhead costs are used with the variable overhead costs to compute the overhead rate, the result is that inventories of finished goods contain both variable and fixed costs. Although this is a proper procedure for financial reporting, it does not necessarily produce the best information for management decisions. Fixed costs are often not controllable at the departmental and sometimes not even at the plant level. A manager has a better opportunity to exercise control over the variable costs.

The manager who desires to plan and control costs can obtain useful information from a method of assigning costs to the product called **direct costing** (or **variable costing**). *Under this method, only variable manufacturing costs are assigned to the product as inventoriable costs.* All fixed costs are treated as period expenses and deducted from income in the period in which they are incurred. This procedure allows the income statement to be presented in a form to reveal the **contribution margin**—the excess of revenue over variable costs. To illustrate the basic concept of direct costing, assume the monthly budget for William Woods Company to be as shown in Figure A26–1.

	Costs: Fixed	Costs: Variable	Budgeted Net Income Calculation	Variable Cost[b] per Unit
Budgeted sales:				
20,000 units @ $30			$600,000	
Budgeted costs:				
Direct materials		$ 50,000		$ 2.50
Direct labor		70,000		3.50
Manufacturing overhead	$100,000	80,000		4.00
Selling expenses	60,000	30,000[a]		1.50
General and administrative expenses	50,000	10,000[a]		0.50
Totals	$210,000	$240,000	450,000	$12.00
Budgeted net income			$150,000	

[a]Note that operating expenses are divided into variable and fixed behavior patterns, as are manufacturing costs.

[b]Per-unit cost data = total variable cost ÷ 20,000 units.

Figure A26–1 **Monthly Budget Data**

In order to focus on the basic concepts, it will be assumed that this company never has a work-in-process inventory carryover from month to month, and income taxes are ignored. In April 1985 the company's actual experience was exactly the same as planned in the budget. Also for the month of April, there are no beginning or ending inventories of finished goods; in other words, they sold exactly the same number of units produced. The direct cost income statement is shown in Figure A26–2. Note these points about the direct cost income statement:

WILLIAM WOODS COMPANY
Direct Cost Income Statement
For the Month Ended April 30, 1985

Sales (20,000 × $30)		$600,000
Cost of goods sold:		
Finished goods inventory, April 1, 1985	$ 0	
Variable cost of goods manufactured (20,000 × $10)[a]	200,000	
Total available for sale	$200,000	
Finished goods inventory, April 30, 1985	0	200,000
Gross contribution margin		$400,000
Deduct: Variable operating expenses:		
Variable selling expenses (20,000 × $1.50)[b]	$ 30,000	
Variable general and administrative expenses (20,000 × $0.50)[b]	10,000	40,000
Contribution margin		$360,000
Deduct: Fixed costs and expenses:		
Fixed manufacturing overhead cost	$100,000	
Fixed selling expenses	60,000	
Fixed general and administrative expenses	50,000	210,000
Net income		$150,000

[a]Variable unit manufacturing costs = $10 = ($2.50 + $3.50 + $4.00) from Figure A26–1.
[b]See Figure A26–1 for unit cost data.

Figure A26–2
Direct Cost Income Statement

☐ Cost of goods manufactured includes variable costs only. The fixed manufacturing overhead cost of $100,000 is treated as a period expense.

☐ Gross contribution margin is $400,000. The *gross* contribution margin differs from the contribution margin in that the variable operating expenses have not yet been deducted.

☐ The contribution margin of $360,000 is shown as a separate figure for management's use in profit planning and control.

☐ In this example, because there are no beginning or ending inventories of finished goods, the final net income is the same as it would have been if traditional absorption costing had been used. The difference is that fixed manufacturing overhead cost is not a part of cost of goods sold but is charged against income as a period expense.

When the traditional method of assigning both variable and fixed costs to the product is used, the practice is known as **full absorption costing** (sometimes known simply as **absorption costing**). With beginning or ending finished goods inventories, the two methods can produce different net income figures, as illustrated in the next section.

Direct Costing Compared with Full Absorption Costing

Assume the following data for William Woods Company for the two months following the month of April just illustrated, with monthly budgeted data from Figure A26–1 applying also to May and June:

	May	June
Product units produced	20,000	20,000
Product units sold	17,000	23,000
Direct materials cost (20,000 × $2.50)	$ 50,000	$ 50,000
Direct labor cost (20,000 × $3.50)	70,000	70,000
Variable manufacturing overhead cost (20,000 × $4.00)	80,000	80,000
Fixed manufacturing overhead cost	100,000	100,000
Selling expenses:		
Variable ($1.50 per unit sold)	25,500	34,500
Fixed	60,000	60,000
General and administrative expenses:		
Variable ($0.50 per unit sold)	8,500	11,500
Fixed	50,000	50,000

Condensed direct costing income statements for the three month period (April through June) are shown in Figure A26–3. Compare the results in the direct costing income statements with full absorption costing shown in Figure A26–4.

Following are explanatory notes about Figures A26–3 and A26–4.

☐ Sales are computed at the selling price of $30 per product unit.

☐ Since 20,000 units were produced each month, the cost of goods manufactured is the same for all three months. Under full absorption costing, the

	April	May	June
Sales	$600,000	$510,000	$690,000
Cost of goods sold:			
Beginning inventory of finished goods	$ 0	$ 0	$ 30,000
Variable cost of goods manufactured	200,000	200,000	200,000
Total available for sale	$200,000	$200,000	$230,000
Ending inventory of finished goods	0	30,000	0
Cost of goods sold	$200,000	$170,000	$230,000
Gross contribution margin	$400,000	$340,000	$460,000
Deduct: Variable expenses	40,000	34,000	46,000
Contribution margin	$360,000	$306,000	$414,000
Deduct: Fixed manufacturing cost and fixed expenses	210,000	210,000	210,000
Net income	$150,000	$ 96,000	$204,000

Figure A26–3 Three Monthly Income Statements—Direct Costing

	April	May	June
Sales	$600,000	$510,000	$690,000
Cost of goods sold:			
Beginning inventory of finished goods	$ 0	$ 0	$ 45,000
Cost of goods manufactured	300,000	300,000	300,000
Total available for sale	$300,000	$300,000	$345,000
Ending inventory of finished goods	0	45,000	0
Cost of goods sold	$300,000	$255,000	$345,000
Gross margin on sales	$300,000	$255,000	$345,000
Operating expenses:			
Selling expenses	$ 90,000	$ 85,500	$ 94,500
General and administrative expenses	60,000	58,500	61,500
Total operating expenses	$150,000	$144,000	$156,000
Net income	$150,000	$111,000	$189,000

Figure A26–4 Three Monthly Income Statements—Full Absorption Costing

fixed manufacturing overhead of $100,000 is assigned to product costs rather than period expense; this is the reason for the difference between the $300,000 and $200,000 amounts.

☐ Only 17,000 of the 20,000 units produced in May were sold in May, leaving 3,000 units in ending inventory. Unit variable cost to manufacture is $10 = ($50,000 + $70,000 + $80,000) ÷ 20,000 units. Since only variable costs are included in inventory under direct costing, the May ending inventory in Figure A26–3 is $30,000 = ($10 × 3,000 units). Under full absorption costing (Figure A26–4), 3/20 = (3,000 units ÷ 20,000 units) of the *fixed* manufacturing overhead cost remains in ending inventory. Accordingly, the cost of ending inventory under full absorption costing includes $15,000 of fixed cost = (3/20 × $100,000) and $30,000 of variable cost for a total of $45,000.

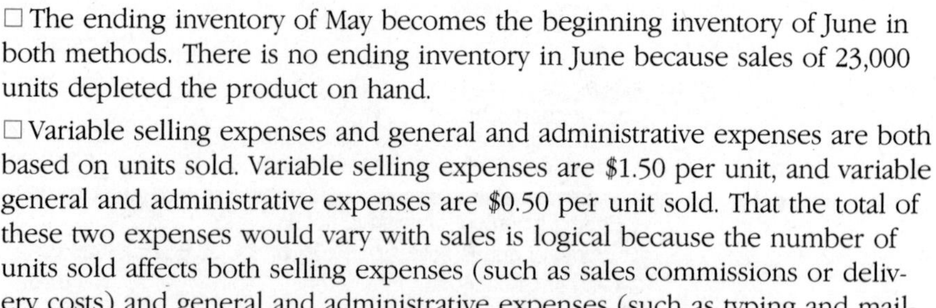

☐ The ending inventory of May becomes the beginning inventory of June in both methods. There is no ending inventory in June because sales of 23,000 units depleted the product on hand.

☐ Variable selling expenses and general and administrative expenses are both based on units sold. Variable selling expenses are $1.50 per unit, and variable general and administrative expenses are $0.50 per unit sold. That the total of these two expenses would vary with sales is logical because the number of units sold affects both selling expenses (such as sales commissions or delivery costs) and general and administrative expenses (such as typing and mailing invoices and processing collections).

Difference in Net Income under the Two Methods

A study of Figures A26–3 and A26–4 reveals the following comparison of net income under the two methods:

☐ In April, when the amount sold was the same as the amount produced, net income ($150,000) is the same under both methods.

☐ In May, when the amount sold was less than the amount produced, net income under full absorption costing ($111,000) is greater than net income under direct costing ($96,000). This difference of $15,000 = ($111,000 – $96,000) is the result of including fixed manufacturing costs in inventory under full absorption costing. These costs are carried forward to June and released into cost of goods sold in June when the units were sold. In May, 3/20 of the fixed manufacturing cost (3/20 × $100,000 = $15,000) was *held back in finished goods inventory* under full absorption costing. (Under direct costing all fixed manufacturing costs are debited to expense in the period incurred.) However, when the 3,000 beginning inventory units were sold in June, the fixed manufacturing cost in them ($15,000) was released as an increase to cost of goods sold under full absorption costing.

☐ In June, when the amount sold was greater than the amount produced, net income under full absorption costing ($189,000) is less than net income under direct costing ($204,000), because the $15,000 of fixed manufacturing costs in the beginning inventory that were released increased the cost of goods sold.[1]

Evaluation of Direct Costing

Direct costing is *not* acceptable under generally accepted accounting standards for financial reporting to external users, including readers of annual reports or the SEC. It is also not acceptable to the Internal Revenue Service for income tax reporting. However, this does not diminish its usefulness as a management planning tool. It develops for management a contribution margin figure that can be used in many ways. With the separation of fixed and

[1]While generally true of direct versus absorption costing, the foregoing pattern does not always hold under certain inventory cost flow assumptions.

variable costs, the accountant can also develop a unit contribution margin, which is equal to unit selling price minus unit variable cost. In the William Woods Company, it is $18 = [$30 − ($10 variable manufacturing cost + $1.50 variable selling expense + $0.50 variable general and administrative expense)]. The accountant can also develop a **variable cost percent** (variable cost as a percentage of sales) and a **contribution margin percent** (contribution margin as a percent of sales). An alternative to the term contribution margin percent is **profit-volume (P/V) ratio.** In the William Woods Company, for example:

	Variable Cost Percent	Contribution Margin Percent
On a unit basis	$\frac{\$12}{\$30} = 40\%$	$\frac{\$18}{\$30} = 60\%$
On a total basis for April	$\frac{\$240{,}000}{\$600{,}000} = 40\%$	$\frac{\$360{,}000}{\$600{,}000} = 60\%$

At this point, it is suggested that the reader verify these percent figures by calculating them for May and June using total sales, contribution margin, and total variable costs from Figures A26–3 and A26–4. These same data are now used to illustrate and explain management use of these concepts to examine and plan relationships of cost, volume, and profits.

Cost-Volume-Profit Analysis

Cost-volume-profit analysis allows managers to answer questions such as: How will actual or proposed changes in volume of sales, fixed cost, or variable cost affect profit? Is it a good idea to increase advertising expenditures to raise the volume of sales? Should existing plant facilities be enlarged? The beginning focus of this analysis is the break-even point. The **break-even point** is the volume of sales at which the business will neither earn income nor incur a loss—that is, net income is zero. It is the point at which total costs or expenses and total revenue are exactly equal. The break-even point can be expressed in terms of dollars of total sales, total units of a product sold, or percentage of capacity to produce and sell. In all cases, it is the level of business at which total revenues will recover the exact amount of total costs and, therefore, the business will break even. The next sections are concerned with the concept of break-even and extension into cost-volume-profit analysis and the computation of figures under each.

Break-Even Point

The break-even point can be computed in units simply by asking the question: How many times must the unit contribution margin be generated in order to cover fixed costs? Figure A26–1 shows that total fixed costs of $210,000 per month are expected to be incurred in the William Woods Company in 1985. (Recall that by definition fixed costs will remain the same even though production volume changes.) As has been previously noted, each unit manufactured and sold will contribute $18 toward fixed costs and profit. Accordingly, the fixed costs of $210,000 will be covered when 11,667 units are sold, as indicated by the following:

$$\frac{\$210{,}000}{\$18} = 11{,}666\tfrac{2}{3}.$$

Since the company cannot sell fractional units, the number of units to break even in any month is rounded up to 11,667. This number of units is the break-even volume. Proof of the break-even situation is shown by calculating net income as follows:

Sales (11,667 × $30)		$350,010
Total fixed costs	$210,000	
Total variable costs (11,667 × $12)	140,004	
Total costs		350,004
Profit		$ 6[a]

[a]At exactly 11,666 ⅔ units, the company would break even. The profit of $6 is ⅓ of the contribution margin on the 11,667th unit.

The break-even point in units has been converted to break-even dollar sales volume in the foregoing computation by multiplying the units at the break-even point by their selling price for a total of $350,010. To express the break-even point as a percent of capacity, the units to break even can be related to total budgeted capacity of 20,000 units, as follows:

$$\frac{11{,}667}{20{,}000} = 0.583 = 58.3 \text{ percent of capacity.}$$

The break-even volume as a percent of capacity is also equal to break-even sales volume as a percent of normal capacity sales volume. Thus:

$$\frac{\$350{,}000}{\$600{,}000} = 0.583 = 58.3 \text{ percent of capacity.}$$

Contribution margin percent is equal to the unit contribution margin divided by unit selling price. The dollar volume of sales to break even can be computed directly by using the contribution margin percent. The formula to do so is:

$$\frac{\text{Total fixed costs}}{\text{Contribution margin percent}} = \text{Break-even sales volume.}^{2}$$

[2]The contribution margin percent represents the proportion of each sales dollar available to pay fixed costs and—above the break-even point—to generate profit. At the break-even point, the fixed costs are exactly paid off by the contribution margin. Thus,

$$\text{Total fixed costs} = \text{Break-even sales volume} \times \text{Contribution margin percent.}$$

This equation can be rearranged to solve for the break-even sales volume resulting in the formula given.

For William Woods Company, this computation is:

$$\frac{\$210{,}000}{(\$18 \div \$30)} = \frac{\$210{,}000}{0.60} = \$350{,}000.$$

Break-even volume in units then is found by the alternative calculation of dividing this dollar sales volume by unit selling price, as follows:

$$\frac{\$350{,}000}{\$30} = 11{,}666\tfrac{2}{3} \text{ or } 11{,}667 \text{ units.}$$

The method used to compute the break-even point depends upon whether reliable data are available for unit sales and costs or whether total figures are the most reliable data. Either approach yields the same results.

The Break-Even Chart

One effective way of presenting the relationship of fixed and variable costs to sales at different volume levels is the break-even chart. Two variations of a break-even chart for William Woods Company are shown in Figures A26–5 and A26–6. On both charts, the vertical line (Y axis) measures dollars. Both cost dollars and sales dollars are measured on the Y axis. The horizontal base line (X axis) measures volume in units of product sales and percent of production capacity. On both charts, the volume (or output) is measured in two ways: (1) percent of capacity, and (2) units of product. It is assumed for purposes of illustration that total output can be sold and that costs include all costs of producing and selling the product. In both charts, there is a shaded

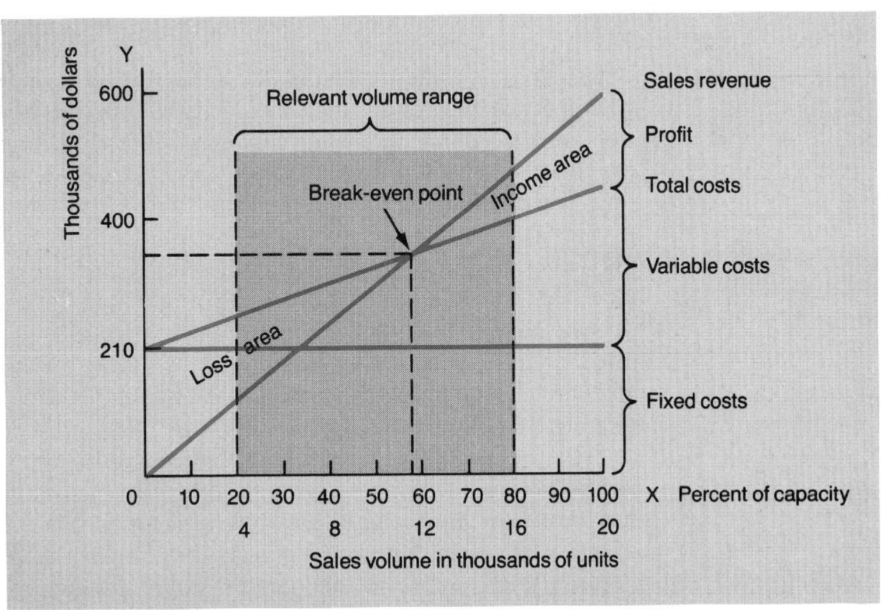

Figure A26–5
Typical Break-Even Chart

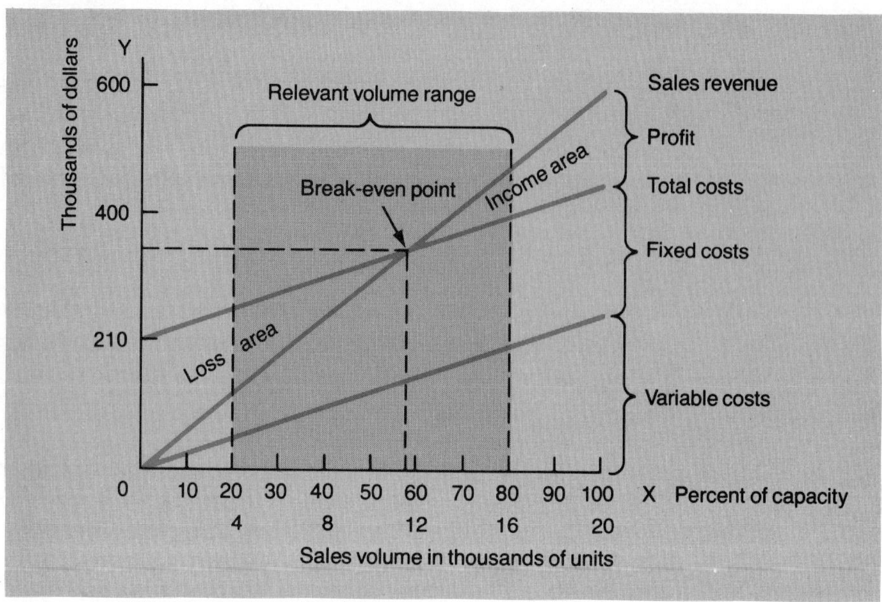

Figure A26–6 Inverted Break-Even Chart

area labeled relevant volume range. The **relevant volume range** is that range of production and sales over which the behavior of costs (fixed or variable) can be predicted with a reasonable degree of accuracy; therefore, it is the range over which information is relevant for decision making.

Figure A26–5 is the conventional form of break-even chart. The fixed costs, assumed to be unaffected by volume changes, are represented by a horizontal line that starts at $210,000 on the Y axis and runs parallel to the base line out to 100 percent capacity of 20,000 units. The variable costs represent the distance between the total costs line and the fixed costs line. Because variable costs increase directly in relation to volume, they cause the total costs line to slope upward, showing greater total costs as volume increases. This cost increase is caused entirely by increase in total variable costs; the fixed costs remain the same.

The sales are measured on a line rising upward from zero, or the origin. The intersection of the sales line and the total costs line is the point where total sales equal total costs—the break-even point. The distance between the sales line and the total costs line (measured vertically on the Y axis at any given volume) is income or loss. To the left of the break-even point, the amount is a loss; to the right, a profit. The loss area and income area are indicated on the chart.

In Figure A26–6, the fixed costs are shown above the variable costs. This form of inverted break-even chart shows the amount of unrecovered fixed costs (total costs line minus sales revenue line) with movement upward on the sales line toward the break-even point. Note that the contribution margin can be read from this inverted chart. It is the amount represented by the distance between the sales revenue line and the variable costs line. Both charts show (the heavily shaded area) the relevant volume range as a distance measured horizontally on the X axis. For William Woods Company, this area runs from 20 percent to 80 percent capacity, but there is no specific area that can be designated for all businesses.

Sales to Earn a Specified Profit

An extension of break-even analysis called cost-volume-profit analysis can be used to determine the amount of sales needed to earn a predetermined amount of profit. The amount of specified profit can be added to fixed costs in either form of this type of analysis to determine the amount of sales needed to earn that sum. Called the *planned profit formula* in this book, it may be expressed in either of the following ways:

$$(1) \quad \frac{\text{Total fixed cost} + \text{Desired profit}}{\text{Unit contribution margin}} = \text{Units to earn desired profit;}$$

or

$$(2) \quad \frac{\text{Total fixed cost} + \text{Desired profit}}{\text{Contribution margin percent}} = \text{Dollar sales to earn desired profit.}$$

Suppose the William Woods Company's president poses the question: How many units must be sold in a month to earn at least $100,000? The answer, using formula 1, is:

$$\frac{\$210{,}000 + \$100{,}000}{\$18} = 17{,}222.222.$$

Since fractional units cannot be sold, the company must sell at least 17,223 units to earn a profit of $100,000. The question may be posed as: What sales volume is required to earn at least $100,000 in a month? Using formula 2, the answer is:

$$\frac{\$210{,}000 + \$100{,}000}{0.60} = \$516{,}666.67.$$

Obviously, this amount involves the sale of fractional amounts since the product is priced at a whole-dollar amount of $30 per unit. It can easily be converted into units by dividing by $30: $516,666.67 ÷ $30 = 17,222.222 or 17,223 units. In whole units, the answer to either question is 17,223 units × $30 = $516,690.

Margin of Safety

The **margin of safety** is the dollar volume of sales above the break-even point, or the amount by which sales may decrease before losses are incurred. The margin of safety for William Woods Company is computed as follows:

Sales (as budgeted)	$600,000
Deduct: Break-even sales	350,000
Margin of safety	$250,000

A loss will not be incurred unless budgeted sales decrease by more than $250,000. The **percent of safety** is computed as follows:

$$\text{Percent of safety} = \frac{\text{Margin of safety}}{\text{Net sales}} = \frac{\$250{,}000}{\$600{,}000} = 0.41667 \text{ or } 41.67\%$$

Any decrease in sales up to 41.67 percent from the $600,000 volume can be absorbed before a loss is incurred.

There is a relationship between the contribution margin percent, the percent of safety, and profit earned as a percent of sales. It is:

$$\text{Contribution margin percent} \times \text{Percent of safety} = \text{Profit as a percent of sales.}$$

For William Woods Company at a sales level of $600,000:

$$0.60 \times 0.4167 = 0.25, \text{ or } 25\%.$$

Note that 25 percent of $600,000 is $150,000, the net income shown in Figure A26–2 where the company's actual results were the same as the budget.

Other Uses of Cost-Volume-Profit Techniques

As previously mentioned, cost-volume-profit techniques can be used to determine what can be expected to happen if certain changes are made. A company considering purchase of additional equipment can expect greater fixed costs (depreciation). The estimated new fixed cost figure can be used in the break-even formula to see what would happen to the break-even point or the volume necessary to earn a specified profit. With estimates of how the volume and variable costs would change upon the installation of the new equipment, a new break-even point, margin of safety, and profit percent can be computed before the purchase is made. A possible wage increase or materials cost increase will change the contribution margin percent allowing a computation of the effect on profits. For example, a 10 percent increase ($1.20 per unit) in variable costs at William Woods Company would result in a new variable cost of $13.20 and a new contribution margin of $16.80 = ($30.00 − $13.20). The contribution margin percent would become 56 percent = ($16.80 ÷ $30.00). The new break-even point would be $375,000 = ($210,000 ÷ 0.56). Both the margin of safety and percent of safety would be reduced. Direct costing with its relationship to cost-volume-profit analysis and the better data for decision making are important aids to management at all times.

Summary of Formulas Used in Appendix 26.1

For the convenience of the reader, a summary of formulas used in this appendix is as follows:

1. $$\frac{\text{Total fixed cost}}{\text{Unit contribution margin}} = \text{Break-even sales in units.}$$

2. $$\frac{\text{Unit (or total) variable costs}}{\text{Unit (or total) sales price}} = \text{Variable cost percent.}$$

3. $1 - \text{Variable cost percent} = \text{Contribution margin percent, or P/V ratio.}$

4. $$\frac{\text{Total fixed costs}}{\text{Contribution margin percent}} = \text{Break-even sales in dollars.}$$

5. $\text{Margin of safety} = \text{Budgeted sales} - \text{Break-even sales in dollars.}$

6. $$\frac{\text{Margin of safety}}{\text{Net sales}} = \text{Percent of safety.}$$

7. $\text{Contribution margin percent} \times \text{Percent of safety} = \text{Profit as a percent of sales.}$

Glossary

Absorption costing See *Full absorption costing.*

Break-even point The volume of sales at which the business will neither earn income nor incur a loss.

Budget A plan (broken down by organizational segments—sales, production, and so on) for a future period's operations. It is usually expressed in financial terms.

Cash forecast A subdivision of the budget structure, this schedule sets forth a prediction of monthly cash inflows and outflows.

Contribution margin Total sales revenue minus total variable cost; on a unit basis, it is selling price minus unit variable cost.

Contribution margin percent Contribution margin as a percentage of sales; also called the profit-volume (P/V) ratio.

Cost-volume-profit analysis Techniques that allow managers to estimate the effect of proposed changes in cost or volume.

Direct costing An accounting method in which only variable manufacturing costs are assigned to the product.

Fixed costs These costs can be defined in two different ways. In total, fixed costs remain the same as volume changes. On a per unit basis, fixed costs decline as volume increases.

Flexible budget A budget that gives recognition to varying levels of production and the costs that change with these levels. A series of fixed budgets for various levels of production.

Full absorption costing An accounting method in which both fixed and variable manufacturing costs are assigned to the product.

General and administrative expense budget A budget showing planned general and administrative expenses for the coming operating period.

Margin of safety The dollar volume of sales above the break-even point.

Mixed semivariable costs Costs that are fixed at the beginning and change with volume thereafter.

Percent of safety The margin of safety as a percent of net sales.

Performance report A report of actual versus planned performance. An example is a report showing factory overhead budget by line item, actual costs for the same items, and the variances.

Production budget A budget showing estimates of quantities of each item of product to be produced in the coming budget period.

Profit planning Budgeting of sales and costs with a specific profit percentage as a target. Adjustments are made to the budget to attain the planned profit.

Profit-volume (P/V) ratio See *Contribution margin percent.*

Relevant volume range The volume range over which cost behavior is somewhat stable and can be reasonably predicted.

Responsibility accounting Tracing of costs, expenses, and revenues identified with specific persons or segments of the organization supervised by one person. Periodic comparisons are made of actual versus planned performance in order to evaluate performance.

Sales budget A budget showing estimates of sales by product in the coming budget period. It is often broken down by districts or territories.

Selling expense budget A budget showing estimates of selling expenses for the coming budget period.

Stepped semivariable costs Costs that remain the same over a limited range of volume and then rise to a higher fixed level.

Unit contribution margin The difference between revenue and variable costs per unit.

Variable cost percent Variable cost as a percent of net sales.

Variable costing See *Direct costing.*

Variable costs These costs can be defined in two different ways. In total, variable costs change directly in proportion to changes in volume. On a per unit basis, variable costs remain the same regardless of changes in volume.

Variance The difference—favorable or unfavorable—between actual and planned performance.

Questions

Q26–1 What are some of the advantages of budgeting in a business organization?

Q26–2 Are budgets and profit planning related? How?

Q26–3 List eight different budget schedules and explain the purpose of each.

Q26–4 In a profit-making organization, which budget schedule is usually prepared first? Why?

Q26–5 Production planning must consider inventory quantities. Which inventories affect production schedules? How?

Q26–6 What are the reasons for making a cash forecast?

Q26–7 Should a not-for-profit organization such as a local community fund have a budget? Why or why not?

Q26–8 Does responsibility accounting require a separate accounting system? Explain.

Q26–9 On completion of the budgeting process, management finds that the projected profit is short of the planned profit target. What actions can be taken?

Q26–10 How does flexible budgeting make responsibility reporting more useful?

Q26–11 (Appendix) How does direct costing differ from full absorption costing? Is direct costing useful for financial reporting to external users? For internal reports to management? Explain.

Q26–12 (Appendix) What is a contribution margin? What is its significance in relation to fixed costs? To profit?

Q26–13 (Appendix) What is a break-even point? In what ways may it be expressed?

Q26–14 (Appendix) How is knowledge of the break-even point useful to management?

Exercises

E26–1 *Single-item sales budget*

Elco Electronics is preparing the sales budget for a new model citizens band radio—Model CB2X1—to be introduced in 1985. It has planned to accept orders for deliveries commencing October 1, 1985, to take advantage of year-end holiday sales opportunities. The sales department has learned that a competitor sold an average of 16,000 units per month in 1984 of a similar model, and it believes it can do as well. The economic forecast predicts a general increase in all sales of 5 percent in 1985 over 1984. In addition, November sales should be 3,500 units greater than average because of gifts. Prepare a monthly sales forecast in units and dollars for the fourth quarter of 1985 assuming a sales price of $60 per set.

E26–2 *Production budget*

Wichita Incorporated produces three products and forecasts sales for the quarter ended March 31, 1985, as follows:

Product	**Sales in Units**
Standard	129,600
Premium	108,000
Supreme	139,200

Management believes that ending inventories for each quarter must be equal to one-fifth of sales in that quarter just ended. Beginning inventories are:

Standard	20,000
Premium	12,000
Supreme	20,000

Prepare a production budget in units.

E26–3 *Territorial sales forecast*

World Company sold Product A at $300 and Product B at $250 in 1984. Total 1984 sales were:

	Units of Product	
	A	**B**
United States sales	13,000	19,500
European sales	6,500	10,400
Asian sales	11,700	3,900
Other international sales	10,400	10,400
Total	41,600	44,200

After studying data pertaining to operating costs, management has decided on a sales price increase of 10 percent for each model in 1985. With the new selling price, a sales decrease (in units) of 5 percent is expected in all sales territories except other international, where sales in newly developing countries are expected to cause an increase of 10 percent over 1984. Prepare a forecast of sales in units and in dollars by territory for 1985.

E26–4 *Unit variable cost*

Bellvue Sales Company had total manufacturing costs of $7,200,000 to produce 4,000,000 units of product in 1985. Fixed costs of $2,000,000 are included in the total. What was the variable cost per unit?

E26–5 *Manufacturing overhead budget; unit cost*

Environmental Systems expects to manufacture 39,000 clean air units in 1985, with a fixed manufacturing overhead cost of $780,000. Past variable overhead costs have been $30 per unit. What is the total manufacturing overhead budget for 1985? The expected overhead cost per unit in 1985? What will be the actual overhead cost per unit if demand in 1985 forces the company to make 52,000 units?

E26–6 *Direct labor budget*

Washington Lewis Company has found that it requires one-fifth labor hour to manufacture one liter of its product, Siwel. The 1985 production budget indicates that a total of 2,600,000 liters will be required. What is the direct labor budget in hours and dollars if Lewis has just negotiated a labor contract that calls for $13.50 per hour effective January 2, 1985?

E26–7 *Materials required for production*

Elizabethtown Equipment Company has a production budget that indicates a need to produce 80,000 desks and 200,000 filing cabinets in 1985. A desk requires 40 pounds of X-gauge steel, and a filing cabinet requires 20 pounds of Y-gauge steel. It is estimated that X-gauge steel can be bought for $450 per ton and Y-gauge for $400 per ton in 1985. What are the requirements in tons and dollar amount of each product?

E26–8 *Cash forecast*

Pensacola Company's accountant has gathered the following data for the first calendar quarter of 1985:

a. Estimated sales (collected 60 percent during month of sale and 40 percent in month following):

December 1984	$23,400
January 1985	23,400
February 1985	31,200
March 1985	45,500

b. Materials purchases (90 percent paid in month of purchase and 10 percent in month following):

December 1984	$15,600
January 1985	10,400
February 1985	19,500
March 1985	26,000

c. Wages paid in cash:

January 1985	$7,800
February 1985	7,800
March 1985	7,800

d. Other cash expenses:

January 1985	$5,850
February 1985	4,160
March 1985	6,500

e. Expected cash balance on January 1, 1985 . . . . . . $11,219

Prepare a cash forecast for the first three months of 1985.

E26–9 *Preparing a flexible budget*

Rehobeth Company prepares a flexible manufacturing overhead budget for volume levels of 75 percent, 80 percent, 90 percent, and 100 percent of capacity. In 1985, it is planned that 100,000 direct labor hours will be worked at 100 percent of capacity. At that volume level, expected costs are:

Fixed manufacturing costs	$ 520,000
Variable manufacturing costs	1,040,000

Prepare a flexible budget for Rehobeth showing fixed and variable costs and overhead rate per hour at each of the levels indicated above.

E26–10 *Computing a variance*

Island Frozen Foods' manufacturing overhead budget for 1985 included the following summary data:

Planned direct labor hours	80,000
Fixed manufacturing costs	$120,000
Variable manufacturing costs	960,000

The company actually worked 75,000 direct labor hours in 1985, incurring actual manufacturing cost of $1,050,000. Compute the total manufacturing overhead variance and show whether it is favorable or unfavorable.

E26–11
Projected income statement

Indiana Packers has prepared budgets for 1985 as follows:

Sales budget total	$110,400
Variable manufacturing costs	38,640
Other variable costs	3,850
Fixed costs and expenses	54,400

Assuming no beginning or ending inventories, prepare a projected income statement for 1985. The company believes that it should earn at least 12 percent before taxes. Does the 1985 budget meet this goal? Show computations. How much would the company earn if actual sales turned out to be $88,320?

E26–12
Direct costing income statement

(Appendix) Monroe Company, with no beginning inventory of finished goods, manufactured 50,000 units of product in September 1985. During September, 45,000 of these units were sold at $10 each. September manufacturing costs were:

Materials	$100,000
Direct labor	75,000
Manufacturing overhead	150,000

Two-thirds of the manufacturing overhead cost was variable; one-third was fixed. Selling expenses (one-half fixed) were $80,000; general and administrative expenses (two-thirds fixed) were $45,000. Prepare a direct costing income statement.

E26–13
Break-even point in units and dollars

(Appendix) Towson Corporation's sales budget for 1986 projected sales of 80,000 units of Secnarf at $10 per unit. Total variable costs in 1986 were expected to be $520,000; fixed costs are expected to be $140,000. Compute the following: (a) variable cost per unit, (b) unit contribution margin, (c) break-even point in units, and (d) break-even sales volume.

E26–14
Break-even sales volume; margin of safety

(Appendix) Kenosha Corporation has budgeted sales of $900,000 in 1986 with total variable costs expected to be $576,000 and total fixed costs expected to be $180,000. Compute the break-even sales volume and margin of safety.

E26–15
Contribution margin percent; percent of safety; profit percent

(Appendix) Grand Forks Company's product has a unit variable cost of $15 and a sales price of $20. Sales for 1985 amounted to $1,000,000 with a break-even point of $600,000. Compute (a) the contribution margin percent, (b) percent of safety, (c) total fixed costs, and (d) profit as a percent of sales.

A Problems

P26–1A
Quarterly sales forecast

Livingston Inc. produces three products. Sales information for 1984, taken from the accounting records, shows the following:

Product	Unit Selling Price	Total Sales
X	$15	$258,000
Y	12	216,000
Z	20	300,000

The general economic outlook is for a 10 percent increase in consumer purchases of products of this nature. In addition, the sales manager feels certain that the company can obtain in the first quarter of 1985 a one-time order for 9,000 units of product Z that will be in addition to expected sales of Z. Normal sales occur 20 percent, 25 percent, 25 percent, and 30 percent, respectively, in the four quarters.

Required: Prepare, in good form, a sales budget for 1985 that will contain both units and dollar amounts of forecast sales by quarters.

P26–2A *Production budget and supporting budgets*

Expected sales of the Texas Company for 1985 are as follows:

	Units of Product			
Product	**1st Quarter**	**2nd Quarter**	**3rd Quarter**	**4th Quarter**
A	36,000	39,600	32,400	54,000
B	28,800	19,800	25,200	32,400
C	19,800	27,000	21,600	23,400

It is company policy to have on hand at the end of each quarter an inventory of finished goods equal to 10 percent of planned sales for the next quarter. (In the first quarter of 1986, it is estimated that 27,000 of each product will be sold.) Cost studies have produced the following predicted factory costs for 1985 per unit of product:

	Product		
	A	**B**	**C**
Materials @ $0.60 per pound	$6.00	$3.00	$4.80
Direct labor @ $13.50 per hour	6.75	4.50	2.70
Variable manufacturing overhead	100% of direct labor		

Materials are produced by a nearby firm; it is never necessary for Texas Company to carry an inventory.

Required: Prepare the following with quarterly data:

1. A production budget by units of product.
2. A materials purchases budget.
3. A direct labor budget.
4. A schedule showing a summary of total variable manufacturing costs per quarter.

P26–3A *Cash forecast*

Williamsport Company makes all sales on credit. Their accounts receivable records show that 50 percent of their sales are paid for in the month of sale with a 2 percent cash discount taken; 48 percent are paid in the month following sale without discount; and 2 percent are written off as bad debts. Payments for purchases are made two-thirds in the month of purchase and one-third in the month following. No discounts are offered by their vendors. Payrolls and other expenses are paid as incurred. The following estimates apply to the year 1985:

	March	April	May	June
Sales	$85,000	$122,400	$102,000	$136,000
Payrolls	17,000	17,850	17,850	18,700
Purchases	40,800	45,900	51,000	61,200
Other expenses	13,600	34,000	17,000	17,000

Cash balance on hand April 1, 1985, is expected to be $8,160.

Required:

1. Prepare a cash forecast for the second quarter of 1985.

2. Will the company need to borrow funds? If so, in what month can they plan to make repayment?

P26–4A *Budget versus performance; variances*

The manufacturing overhead budget for the Blending Department of the Hernandez Company for 1985 is as follows:

HERNANDEZ COMPANY
Blending Department
Manufacturing Overhead Budget for the Year 1985
Based on Production of 50,000 Units

Variable costs:	
Indirect labor	$ 255,000
Indirect materials	127,500
Other items	510,000
Total variable costs	$ 892,500
Fixed costs:	
Superintendence	$ 85,000
Depreciation of building	42,500
Other fixed costs	255,000
Total fixed costs	$ 382,500
Total costs	$1,275,000

The company works 50 weeks each year, closing for two weeks for vacations. Fixed costs are expected to be incurred evenly throughout the year. In the second week of April 1985, the Blending Department produced 1,000 units and incurred costs as follows:

Indirect labor	$5,321.00
Indirect materials	2,533.00
Other variable items	10,042.95
Superintendence	1,700.00
Depreciation of building	850.00
Other fixed costs	5,100.00

Required:

1. Prepare a report for the week ended April 11, 1985, showing the adjusted Blending Department budgeted costs, actual costs, and variances.

2. Indicate which variances, if any, are the responsibility of the supervisor of the Blending Department.

P26–5A *Direct versus absorption costing*

(Appendix) Jubilee Corporation with no beginning inventory on September 1, 1985, manufactured 30,000 units in September and 28,000 units in October. September sales were 25,000 units and October sales were 33,000 units. Selling price is $15 per unit. Variable costs are:

	Per Unit
Materials	$2.50
Direct labor	3.00
Manufacturing overhead	2.50
Selling expense	0.50
General and administrative expense	1.00

Monthly fixed costs are:

	Total Costs
Manufacturing overhead	$84,000
Selling expense	12,000
General and administrative expense	18,000

Required:

1. Prepare income statements for September and October on (a) a direct costing basis, and (b) a full absorption cost basis.

2. Explain the reason for the difference in net income between the two statements for each month.

P26–6A
Cost-volume-profit analysis

(Appendix) Aiken Corporation is operating at full capacity. It has under consideration a plan to expand its plant facilities. Current and projected income statement data are as follows:

	Under Present Plant Facilities		Under Proposed Plant Facilities	
Sales		$675,000		$1,012,500
Variable costs	$270,000		$405,000	
Fixed costs	324,000	594,000	486,000	891,000
Net income		$ 81,000		$ 121,500

Required:

1. What is the present break-even point?

2. What is the break-even point under the proposed plan?

3. What amount of sales will be needed to realize the current net income of $81,000 under the proposed plan?

4. Under the proposed plan, are the percent of safety and profit as a percent of sales projected to be less than, equal to, or greater than the present plan? Show computations to support your answer.

P26–7A
Thought-provoking problem: evaluation of performance

Huntsville Products manufactures a line of containers using a process system through several departments. The budget for the Packing Department for August 1985 was based on packing 8,000 cases of containers. Summarized budgeted costs were:

Variable manufacturing costs	$43,200
Fixed manufacturing costs	48,000
Total	$91,200

Actual output of the Packing Department was 9,600 cases in August, with costs as follows:

Variable manufacturing costs	$50,918
Fixed manufacturing costs	48,000
Total	$98,918

Management thinks that the supervisor of the Packing Department has not performed very well because August costs are $7,718 in excess of the budget.

Required: Present computations to show whether the Packing Department has actually performed below or above the standard set by the budget.

B Problems

P26–1B *Quarterly sales forecast*

Mississippi Company produces three products. Sales information for 1984 taken from the accounting records shows the following:

Product	Unit Selling Price	Total Sales
M	$ 7.50	$232,500
N	6.00	198,000
O	10.00	280,000

The general economic outlook is for a 10 percent increase in consumer purchases of products of this nature. In addition, the sales manager is confident that the company can obtain in the first quarter of 1985 a one-time order for 3,000 units of product 0 that will be in addition to expected sales of product 0. Normal sales occur 15 percent, 25 percent, 30 percent, and 30 percent, respectively, in the four quarters of the year.

Required: Prepare, in good form, a sales budget for 1985 that will contain both units and dollar amounts of forecast sales by quarters.

P26–2B *Production budget and supporting budgets*

Expected sales of New York Company for 1985 are as follows:

	Units of Product			
Product	**1st Quarter**	**2nd Quarter**	**3rd Quarter**	**4th Quarter**
L	28,600	31,460	25,740	42,900
M	22,880	15,730	20,020	25,740
N	15,730	21,450	17,160	18,590

It is company policy to have on hand at the end of each quarter an inventory of finished goods equal to 20 percent of planned sales for the next quarter. (In the first quarter of 1986, it is estimated that 21,450 of each product will be sold.) Cost studies have produced the following predicted factory costs for 1985 per unit of product:

	Product		
	L	**M**	**N**
Materials @ $0.50 per pound	$8.00	$4.00	$5.50
Direct labor @ $10 per hour	5.00	2.50	2.00
Variable manufacturing overhead	100% of direct labor		

Materials are produced by a nearby firm; it is never necessary for New York Company to carry an inventory.

Required: Prepare the following with quarterly data:

1. A production budget by units of product.
2. A materials purchases budget.
3. A direct labor budget.
4. A schedule showing a summary of total variable manufacturing costs per quarter.

P26–3B *Cash forecast*

Akron, Inc., makes all sales on credit. Their accounts receivable records show that 50 percent of their sales are collected in the month of sale with a 2 percent cash discount taken; 48 percent are collected in the month following sale without discount; and the remaining 2 percent are written off as bad debts. Payments for purchases are made two-thirds in the month of purchase and one-third in the month following. No discounts are offered by their vendors. Payrolls and other expenses are paid as incurred. The following estimates apply to the year 1985:

	June	July	August	September
Sales	$63,000	$90,720	$75,600	$100,800
Payrolls	12,600	13,230	13,230	13,860
Purchases	30,240	34,020	37,800	45,360
Other expenses	10,080	25,200	12,600	12,600

Cash balance on hand on July 1, 1985, is expected to be $6,048.

Required:

1. Prepare a cash forecast for the third quarter of 1985.

2. Will the company need to borrow funds? If so, in what month can they plan to make repayment?

P26–4B *Budget versus performance; variances*

The manufacturing overhead budget for the Forming Department of the Concord Company for 1985 is as follows:

CONCORD COMPANY
Forming Department
Manufacturing Overhead Budget for the Year 1985
Based on Production of 60,000 Units

Variable costs:	
Indirect labor	$216,000
Indirect materials	135,000
Other items	270,000
Total variable costs	$621,000
Fixed costs:	
Superintendence	$ 56,250
Depreciation of machinery	28,125
Other items	168,750
Total fixed costs	$253,125
Total costs	$874,125

The company works 50 weeks each year, closing for two weeks for vacations. Fixed costs are expected to be incurred evenly throughout the year. In the second week of August 1985, the Forming Department produced 1,200 units and incurred costs as follows:

Indirect labor	$4,387.50
Indirect materials	2,682.00
Other variable items	5,418.00
Superintendence	1,125.00
Depreciation of machinery	562.50
Other fixed items	3,375.00

Required:

1. Prepare a report for the week ended August 15, 1985, showing adjusted budgeted costs, actual costs, and variances for the Forming Department.

2. Indicate which variances, if any, are the responsibility of the supervisor of the Forming Department.

P26–5B *Direct versus absorption costing*

(Appendix) Bloomington Company, with no beginning inventory on April 1, 1985, manufactured 27,000 units in April and 25,200 in May. April sales were 22,500 units and May sales were 29,700 units. Selling price is $15 per unit. Variable costs are:

	Per Unit
Materials	$2.50
Direct labor	3.00
Manufacturing overhead	2.50
Selling expense	0.50
General and administrative expense	1.00

Monthly fixed costs are:

	Total Costs
Manufacturing overhead	$75,600
Selling expense	10,800
General and administrative expense	16,200

Required:

1. Prepare income statements for April and May on (a) a direct costing basis, and (b) a full absorption costing basis.

2. Explain the reason for the difference in net income between the two statements each month.

P26–6B *Cost-volume-profit analysis*

(Appendix) Laramie Company is operating at full capacity. It has under consideration a plan for expansion of its plant facilities. Current and projected income statement data are as follows:

	Under Present Plant Facilities		Under Proposed Plant Facilities	
Sales		$640,000		$1,125,000
Variable costs	$192,000		$450,000	
Fixed costs	336,000	528,000	540,000	990,000
Net income		$112,000		$ 135,000

Required:

1. What is the present break-even point?

2. What is the break-even point under the new plan?

3. What amount of sales will be needed to realize the present net income of $112,000 under the proposed plan?

4. Under the proposed plan, are the percent of safety and the profit as a percent of sales projected to be less than, equal to, or greater than the present plan? Show computations to support your answer.

P26–7B *Thought-provoking problem: effect of fixed costs on profit*

Dutchess Company has fixed costs of $400,000 per year. Variable costs are $12 per unit sold at a selling price of $20 per unit. Following is a comparison of operating results of the past two years:

	1985	1984
Sales	$1,500,000	$1,200,000
Variable costs	$ 900,000	$ 720,000
Fixed costs	400,000	400,000
Total costs	$1,300,000	$1,120,000
Profit	$ 200,000	$ 80,000

One of the directors is unable to account for a 150 percent increase in profit with only a 25 percent increase in sales. The controller explains that with fixed costs present, an increase in sales should bring a greater increase in profit percent.

Required:

1. Compute the number of units sold in each year.

2. Compute the fixed cost per unit in each year.

3. Do you believe that the controller's explanation was correct? Explain in detail the reasons for your conclusion.

27 Standard Cost Accounting

Introduction

Process cost and job order cost accounting systems can be more useful to management if predetermined costs are accumulated and compared with actual costs. A *standard cost accounting system* is not a third type of cost accounting system but is the application of predetermined costs to either a process or job order system. This chapter illustrates standard costing with a process cost accounting system because standards are more often found in process situations. However, standard costing concepts can be equally useful in a job order situation. Standards for costs can also be a useful tool for cost control in nonmanufacturing functions. Illustrated in this chapter is the use of standards for the marketing function of a business. The same concepts can also be applied to banks, hospitals, and many other situations not connected with manufacturing.

Learning Goals

To understand the concept of standards.

To know how standards are developed.

To apply standard costs to a process cost accounting system.

To analyze variances from standard and to interpret those variances.

To apply standard cost concepts to other functions—for example, marketing.

The Concept of a Standard

A **standard** is a predetermined measurement of what the amount of input should be and what that input should cost per unit. A standard should be reasonable in that it should be attainable by skilled and motivated workers and also should enable the company to produce a product that is high enough in quality and low enough in cost to be competitive in the market. A certain plaster compound, for example, may be designed to be mixed one part plaster with four parts of water. To prepare one quart of plaster, then, the standard quantities would be 1/5 quart of plaster compound and 4/5 quart of water. It has been determined in advance that these physical quantities are the amounts that *ought to be used* per quart of plaster. The standard for the cost of these physical quantities must then be determined. In practice, five standards are usually predetermined for the product of a manufacturing firm, as follows:

1. *Materials quantity standard:* the amount of material that should be used per unit of product. In some cases, more than one type of material is used; if so a standard is set for each material.
2. *Materials price standard:* the cost per unit of material. When more than one type of material is used in a product, a standard unit price is set for each material to be used.
3. *Labor quantity standard:* the amount of labor—usually expressed in direct labor hours—that should be used per unit of product (in this book, called the *labor efficiency standard* because that is a term commonly used in business).
4. *Labor price standard:* the cost of direct labor per direct labor hour. The common name for this type of standard is *wage rate standard.*
5. *Overhead standard:* the amount of overhead cost that should be incurred per direct labor hour (or per unit of some other factor that represents volume of production).

The establishment of standards involves checking of prices from various material sources, labor negotiations to determine the proper wage rates for the local area, and engineering studies to determine the best mix of materials, level of training of the work force, and the amount of overhead to be incurred. Establishment of proper standards is extremely important because management will evaluate past performance and predict future performance on the basis of standards for specific jobs. Developing proper standards represents the work of highly specialized people, and it is not necessary to go into details of standard setting here.

Some firms may establish standards and use them for comparison with actual production (for pay purposes as well as other managerial reasons) without incorporating them in the accounts. Much more useful is a standard cost accounting system that incorporates the standards in the accounts and adds to the chart of accounts a series of **variance accounts** to record deviations from standard (this is done in this chapter).

Illustration of a Standard Cost Accounting System

Megware Specialty Company makes a high-quality coffee mug decorated with emblems of various colleges and universities and sold in campus shops throughout the country. The first step in production occurs in the Casting Department, where clay is formed into the shape of a mug and then transferred to the first kiln operation for heating to harden the mug. The casting process requires skilled labor. If too much clay is used in a mug, the materials cost is increased; if too little is used, cracks will appear in the mug in the next process, and it will be a complete loss. The casters must work quickly but carefully. If they try to work at an excessive speed, the product will have defects; it must be scrapped and a new casting begun. Although workers can salvage and reuse the clay from defective mugs at this point, the time spent casting them has been lost. On the other hand, working at too slow a pace increases labor cost per mug and hurts the company's competitive position in the market.

Because of the nature of the process, there is never a beginning or an ending inventory of work in process in the Casting Department. Accordingly, equivalent units of materials and of labor and overhead are always the same for all three elements and are equal to the number of mugs transferred to the next department. Careful engineering studies and experience have led to the establishment of materials and labor standards as follows:

- ☐ Clay, 2 ounces (or 1/8 pound) per mug.
- ☐ Labor, 2 minutes (or 1/30 hour) per mug.

The standard cost of clay, based on experience with purchases, is $0.40 per pound, and the standard wage rate for personnel trained in the casting operation is $12 per hour.

The overhead standard is determined by the departmental overhead rate. Normal production for the Casting Department is 600,000 mugs per month. Budgeted overhead cost is $72,000; *$54,000 of this total is variable cost and $18,000 is fixed cost.* At the normal level of production (600,000 mugs per month), it is expected that direct labor hours will be 20,000 = (600,000 × 1/30 hour). The standard departmental overhead rate is computed as follows:[1]

$$\frac{\text{Total overhead cost}}{\text{Direct labor hours}} = \frac{\$72{,}000}{20{,}000} = \$3.60 \text{ per direct labor hour.}$$

Summarizing the foregoing information yields the standard cost specifications (sometimes called a **standard cost card**) for a mug shown in Figure 27–1.

[1]The $3.60 rate is used to apply overhead to production. It should be noted, however, that the rate consists of a variable element and a fixed element computed as follows:

$$\frac{\text{Variable overhead cost}}{\text{Direct labor hours}} = \frac{\$54{,}000}{20{,}000} = \$2.70 \text{ variable element, and}$$

$$\frac{\text{Fixed overhead cost}}{\text{Direct labor hours}} = \frac{\$18{,}000}{20{,}000} = \$0.90 \text{ fixed element.}$$

Materials: 1/8 pound of clay at $0.40 per pound	$0.05
Direct labor: 1/30 hour at $12 per hour	0.40
Manufacturing overhead: 1/30 hour at $3.60 per direct labor hour	0.12
Standard cost per mug	$0.57

Figure 27–1 Standard Cost per Mug—Casting Department

The expected cost (the amount that cost ought to be) is $0.57 per mug in the Casting Department. Notice that this standard cost contains the five elements mentioned earlier: (1) materials quantity, (2) materials price, (3) labor quantity, (4) labor price, and (5) manufacturing overhead.

Production records and cost records indicate the *actual* performance in the Casting Department in May 1985, as shown in Figure 27–2. The actual and standard data in Figures 27–1 and 27–2 are used for computing variances from standard and for recording manufacturing costs in the following sections.

Mugs cast and transferred out		612,000
Materials purchased: 80,000 pounds at $0.39	$ 31,200	
Materials used: 76,800 pounds at $0.40	30,720	
Direct labor: 20,350 hours at $12.10	246,235	
Manufacturing overhead:		
Variable costs	55,100	
Fixed costs	18,000	

Figure 27–2 Casting Department Performance Data

Variances

A **variance** is the difference between actual and standard cost. Since it is practically impossible to produce exactly at standard, variances do occur in materials, labor, and overhead. If the actual cost is greater than the standard, an *unfavorable variance* exists (designated in this book by U). When actual cost is less than standard, a *favorable variance* arises (designated F). By computing variances and recording them in special variance accounts, the accountant provides information about the types and amount of deviation from standard. Managers responsible for various processes of the operation are then alerted and can take the necessary corrective action for these exceptions. In the next sections, variances are computed, and then the journal entries for the month are made.

Materials Two variances arise with respect to materials: the *materials purchase price variance* and the *materials quantity variance.* The **materials purchase price variance** is caused by purchasing materials at prices other than standard.[2] Figure 27–2 shows that Megware Specialty Company purchased 80,000 pounds of clay at 39 cents per pound. The materials price variance is:

Pounds purchased at standard price (80,000 × $0.40)	$32,000
Pounds purchased at actual price (80,000 × $0.39)	31,200
Materials purchase price variance	$ 800 (F)

An alternative method of computing this variance is to multiply the pounds purchased by the difference between actual price and standard price. Thus:

$$80{,}000 \text{ pounds} \times (\$0.40 - \$0.39) = 80{,}000 \times \$0.01 = \$800 \text{ (F)}.$$

The variance is favorable because the actual cost is less than standard. This fact may or may not indicate commendable performance in the Purchasing Department. It is commendable if the buyers are obtaining clay of the proper quality at a better price. However, if they are purchasing a lower-quality clay, there may be greater losses in production or an inferior product produced. Management is alerted and should investigate this variance (as well as all other significant variances) to determine whether any correction is necessary.

The **materials quantity variance** is caused by using more or less material than the standard quantity allowed for production achieved. Megware Specialty Company's Casting Department produced 612,000 mugs in May. Since the standard is 1/8 pound of clay per mug, the department should have used 76,500 = (612,000 × 1/8) pounds of materials. Figure 27–2 indicates that 76,800 pounds (300 pounds in excess of standard) were used. The computation of the variance is:

Standard usage for production achieved (76,500 lbs. × $0.40)	$30,600
Actual usage at standard price (76,800 × $0.40)	30,720
Materials quantity variance	$(120) (U)

An alternative computation is:

$$(76{,}800 \text{ lbs. used} - 76{,}500 \text{ lbs. standard}) \times \$0.40 = 300 \times \$0.40 = \$120 \text{ (U)}$$

Standard price is used because the price variance has already been removed by the price variance computation. Again, management is alerted that a condition exists that should be studied to see if corrective action is needed. The formulas used to compute materials variances are summarized in Figure 27–3.

---

[2]An acceptable alternative not used in this book is to delay recognition of materials price variances until issuance to production. The price variance recognized under that method is called a *materials price usage variance.*

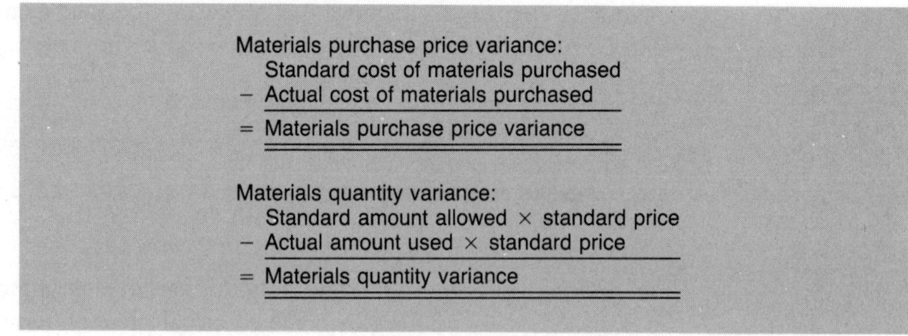
Materials purchase price variance:
Standard cost of materials purchased
− Actual cost of materials purchased
= Materials purchase price variance

Materials quantity variance:
Standard amount allowed × standard price
− Actual amount used × standard price
= Materials quantity variance

Figure 27–3 Formulas for Materials Variances

Similar formulas are used to compute the labor variances discussed in the next section.

Labor As indicated in Figure 27–1, casting a mug should require 1/30 direct labor hour at a wage rate of $12 per hour. The standard labor cost in May is $244,800 = (612,000 mugs × 1/30 × $12). Figure 27–2 indicates that actual cost was $246,235 = (20,350 hours × $12.10). This means that actual labor cost exceeded standard labor cost by $1,435. The cause of this excessive cost is explained by two variances. The two variances that arise with respect to labor are the *wage rate variance* and the *labor efficiency variance.* The **wage rate variance** (sometimes called the labor price variance) is caused by paying more or less than the standard rate for labor. A glance at Figure 27–2 indicates that it will be unfavorable because Megware Specialty Company paid an average rate of $12.10 per hour in this department, where the standard rate is $12. The variance calculation is based on actual hours of labor used. The computation is:

Actual hours used at standard rate (20,350 × $12)	$244,200
Actual hours used at actual rate (20,350 × $12.10)	246,235
Wage rate variance	$(2,035) (U)

This wage rate (price) variance arose because the price paid for labor in May was greater than standard. An alternative computation is

20,350 hours × ($12.10 − $12.00) = 20,350 × $0.10 = $2,035 (U).

The **labor efficiency variance** (sometimes called the labor quantity variance) is caused by using more or less labor than the standard allows for units produced. Production of 612,000 mugs should require 20,400 hours of labor (using the Figure 27–1 standard of 1/30 hour per mug: 612,000 × 1/30 = 20,400). Since only 20,350 hours were used in May, there obviously will be a favorable variance. The calculation uses the standard rate for labor. It is computed as follows:

Standard usage for production achieved (20,400 × $12)[a]	$244,800
Actual usage at standard rate (20,350 × $12)	244,200
Labor efficiency variance	$ 600 (F)

[a]Standard wage rate is used because the price variance was removed when the wage rate variance was computed.

An alternative computation is:

(20,400 standard hours − 20,350 actual hours) × $12 = 50 × $12 = $600 (F).

Note that the combination of the two labor variances—$2,035 (U) and $600 (F)—explains the $1,435 excess cost of labor. Because materials and labor variances are quite similar, the formulas in Figure 27–3 can be modified slightly to compute both labor variances. This is done in Figure 27–4.

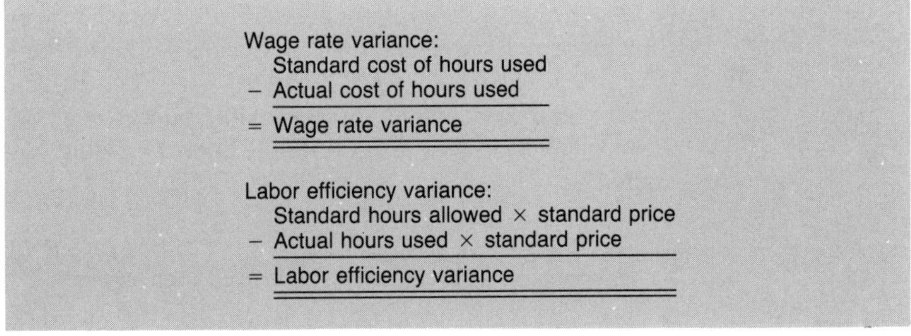

Figure 27–4
Formulas for Labor Variances

Manufacturing Overhead When a standard cost accounting system is used, *overhead is applied to production based on the standard for production achieved* and not on actual work. In the Casting Department of Megware Specialty Company, overhead is applied at the rate of $3.60 per direct labor hour (see Figure 27–1). Since the standard direct labor hours allowed for production achieved in May were 20,400 as calculated above, overhead applied to production was $73,440 = (20,400 standard hours × $3.60). The total overhead variance is:

Manufacturing overhead applied	$73,440
Actual overhead costs (Figure 27–2)	73,100
Overapplied manufacturing overhead	$ 340 (F)

This total variance is favorable because the actual costs are less than standard, but the total overhead variance does not tell the whole story. Even though there is only one overhead standard, there are many ways to analyze manufacturing overhead variances to determine their causes. In this book, a two-variance analysis is used; overapplied overhead is analyzed into a *controllable variance* and a *volume variance.* Such an analysis is possible through the use of flexible budget techniques explained in Chapter 26. To determine the amount that manufacturing overhead costs ought to be, the budget should be adjusted to reflect actual performance, in a manner similar to the adjustment in Figure 26–13. Megware's budget, however, should be adjusted to standard labor hours allowed for production attained—not actual hours used.

The departmental budget for May planned that 20,000 direct labor hours would be used. It also planned that $54,000 of the total budgeted $72,000 for manufacturing overhead cost would be variable. Therefore, the variable portion of the total rate is $54,000 ÷ 20,000 hours = $2.70. Since only the variable costs portion of the budget need be adjusted, *only the variable portion of the total overhead rate is multiplied by standard hours* allowed for production attained to see what variable costs ought to be. The fixed cost of $18,000 is expected to remain the same at any level of production in a flexible budget.

The **controllable variance** essentially is caused by incurring variable costs at a higher or lower rate than the standard allows. The simple assumption that actual fixed costs equal budgeted fixed costs is maintained throughout this book to concentrate on the flexible budget concept. This makes the controllable variance as used in this book a variable cost variance. It is computed as:

Budget adjusted to standard hours for production attained:		
Fixed costs	$18,000	
Variable costs (20,400 hours × $2.70)	55,080	$73,080
Deduct: Actual overhead costs incurred		73,100
Controllable variance		$(20) (U)

The controllable variance is generally considered to be the responsibility of the departmental supervisor who has the authority to control the level of variable costs within the department.[3]

The **volume variance** is caused by overapplying or underapplying fixed manufacturing overhead by producing at a level different from the production level used to establish the overhead rate. The Casting Department has produced at a level greater than anticipated by the budget and has overapplied fixed costs. The computation is:

Applied overhead (20,400 hours × $3.60)		$73,440
Budget adjusted to standard hours for production attained:		
Fixed costs	$18,000	
Variable costs (20,400 hours × $2.70)	55,080	73,080
Volume variance		$ 360 (F)

[3]If fixed costs are not the same as budgeted, this variance is a total spending variance. Some of the fixed costs may not be controllable at the department level.

Recall that 20,000 direct labor hours were budgeted, with total fixed overhead costs of $18,000. The fixed portion of the overhead rate is $0.90 = ($18,000 ÷ 20,000 hours). The overhead rate is divided into its variable and fixed portions as follows:

Variable portion ($54,000 ÷ 20,000 hours)	$2.70
Fixed portion ($18,000 ÷ 20,000 hours)	0.90
Total overhead rate	$3.60

In this case, the volume variance is a direct result of applying more fixed costs than were budgeted. It could be computed as follows:

(20,400 standard hours − 20,000 budgeted hours) × $0.90 = 400 × $0.90 = $360 (F).

Since overhead was applied to production based on standard hours allowed for production achieved, 400 excess hours were applied with no actual increase in incurred fixed costs. In other words, the Manufacturing Overhead Control account was credited with 400 hours times the fixed rate of $0.90 that were not actually incurred. The total overapplied overhead can now be explained as follows:

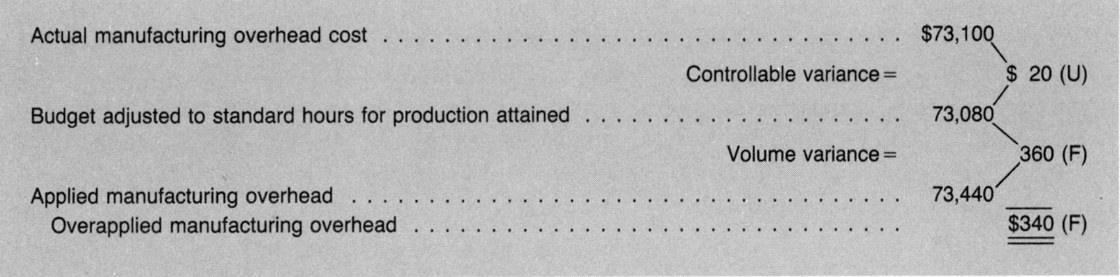

Actual manufacturing overhead cost		$73,100	
	Controllable variance =		$ 20 (U)
Budget adjusted to standard hours for production attained		73,080	
	Volume variance =		360 (F)
Applied manufacturing overhead		73,440	
Overapplied manufacturing overhead			$340 (F)

Standard Costs in the Accounts

There are alternative methods for recording costs under a standard cost system. The authors prefer the simple method, in which only standard costs are allowed to enter the Work-in-Process Inventory account. All variances are entered in variance accounts at the time of purchase (materials only) or when entries are made to charge materials, labor, and overhead to production. Unfavorable variances are recorded as *debits;* favorable variances are recorded as *credits.* Using the same company and data as for the earlier sections of the chapter, the end-of-month entries for Megware Specialty Company's Casting Department (the first manufacturing process) are broken into segments in the illustrations that follow so that each can be diagrammed.

Materials

Figure 27–5 shows the standard cost flows and the journal entries for materials purchased. The variance account is credited in this case because the variance is favorable. An unfavorable variance would result in a debit. Note that recognition of the price variance at this point causes materials to be carried in inventory at standard cost.

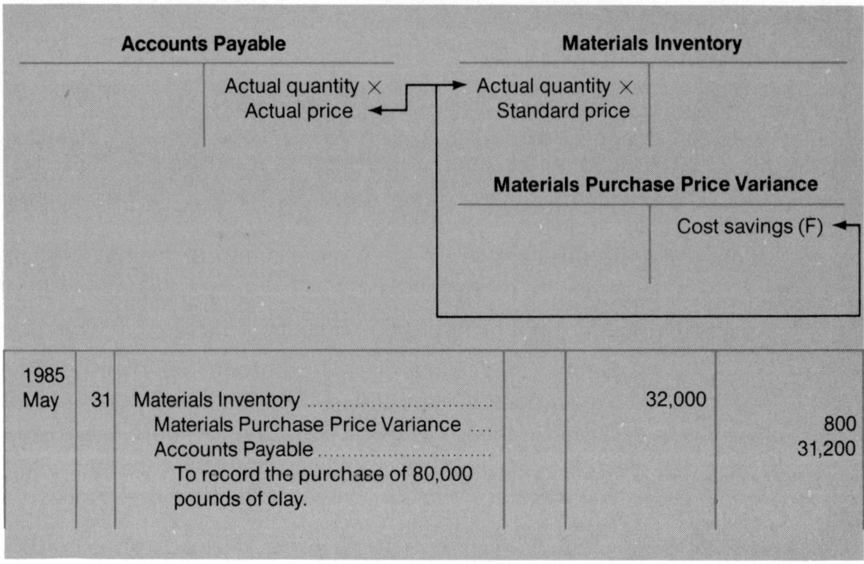

1985					
May	31	Materials Inventory		32,000	
		Materials Purchase Price Variance			800
		Accounts Payable			31,200
		To record the purchase of 80,000 pounds of clay.			

Figure 27–5 Purchase of Materials

The issuance of materials is shown in Figure 27–6. Production of 612,000 mugs should have required 76,500 pounds of clay = (612,000 × 1/8) at a standard cost of $0.40 per pound. The standard cost debited to Work-in-Process Inventory—Casting is $30,600 = (76,500 × $0.40). The excess quantity of 300 pounds used causes a debit of $120 = (300 × $0.40) to the variance account.

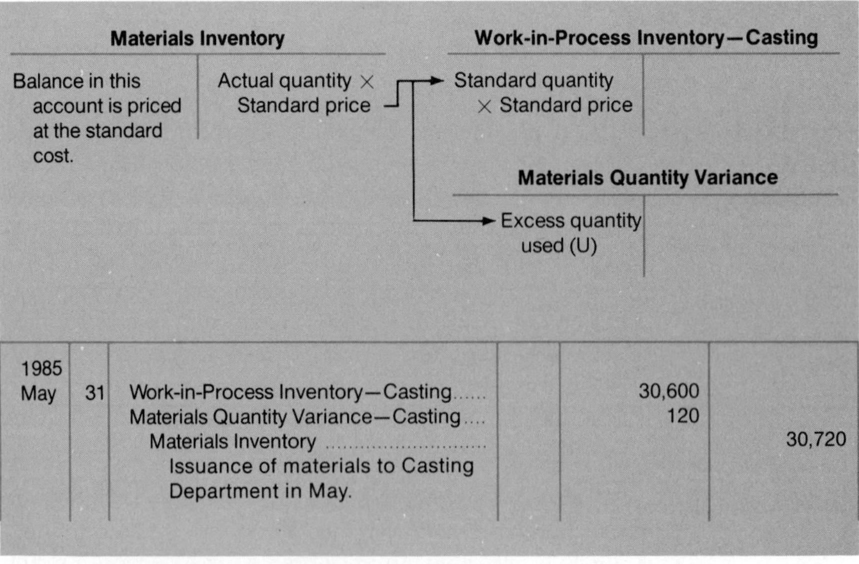

1985					
May	31	Work-in-Process Inventory—Casting		30,600	
		Materials Quantity Variance—Casting		120	
		Materials Inventory			30,720
		Issuance of materials to Casting Department in May.			

Figure 27–6 Issuance of Materials

In Figure 27–5, the Materials Inventory account was increased by the standard cost of actual materials purchased. In Figure 27–6, it was decreased by the standard cost of actual materials issued. This leaves the balance of materials in stock at standard cost. Note also that debiting Work-in-Process Inventory—Casting with standard cost of the standard quantity of materials allowed for production attained (Figure 27–6) will cause the work-in-process inventory to be carried at standard.

Labor

In order to focus on the standard cost and variances for labor, all indirect labor and personnel costs chargeable to selling expense or to general and administrative expense are ignored at this point. Also, all payroll deductions and payroll taxes are ignored for the same reason. Figure 27–2 indicates that 20,350 hours of direct labor were used in May, at an average cost of $12.10 per hour. The recording of this payroll is shown in Figure 27–7. As in previous entries, it is shown in diagram form followed by the journal entry. The total amount debited to the Factory Payroll account is then distributed to Work-in-Process Inventory—Casting and the variance accounts (see Figure 27–8, on page 946). The debit to Work-in-Process Inventory—Casting is for standard hours allowed for production attained times the standard rate. The amount is $244,800 = (20,400 × $12). This amount can also be computed from the standard labor cost per mug from Figure 27–1 as 612,000 × $0.40 = $244,800. The credit of $246,235 clears the actual cost of direct labor from the Factory Payroll account. Again, the variances explain the differences between standard and actual cost. The unfavorable variance is a debit; the favorable variance is a credit.

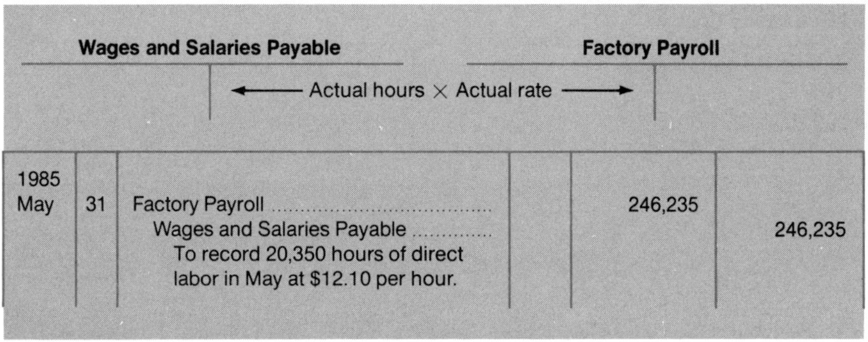

1985					
May	31	Factory Payroll		246,235	
		Wages and Salaries Payable			246,235
		To record 20,350 hours of direct labor in May at $12.10 per hour.			

Figure 27–7 Recording Direct Labor Payroll

Manufacturing Overhead

Various actual manufacturing overhead costs incurred in May totaled $73,100. Accounts that were actually credited for these costs include Cash, Accounts Payable, Accumulated Depreciation, and Factory Payroll (for indirect labor), as shown in Figure 27–9. In the journal entry, these are simply shown as various credits since the separate costs for each have not been specified.

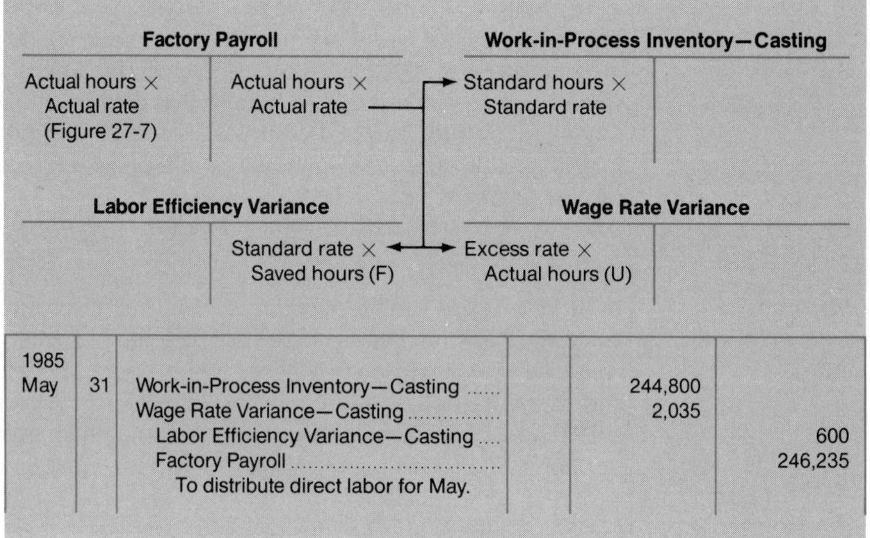

1985					
May	31	Work-in-Process Inventory—Casting		244,800	
		Wage Rate Variance—Casting		2,035	
		Labor Efficiency Variance—Casting			600
		Factory Payroll			246,235
		To distribute direct labor for May.			

Figure 27–8 Distribution of Direct Labor Cost

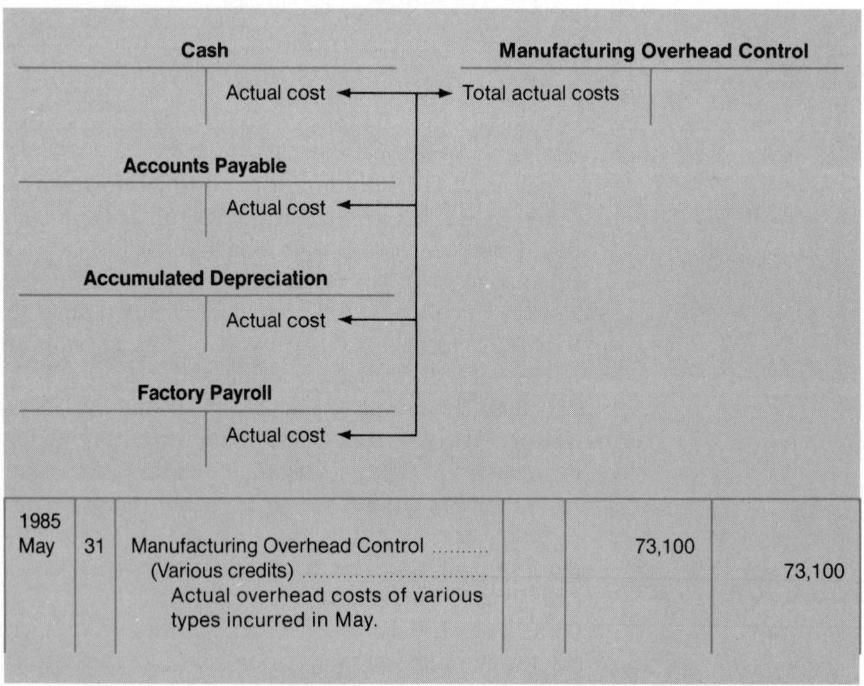

1985					
May	31	Manufacturing Overhead Control		73,100	
		(Various credits)			73,100
		Actual overhead costs of various types incurred in May.			

Figure 27–9 Overhead Costs Incurred

The journal entry to apply overhead to production also clears the Manufacturing Overhead Control account, as shown in Figure 27–10. Several comments should be made about the entry to apply overhead:

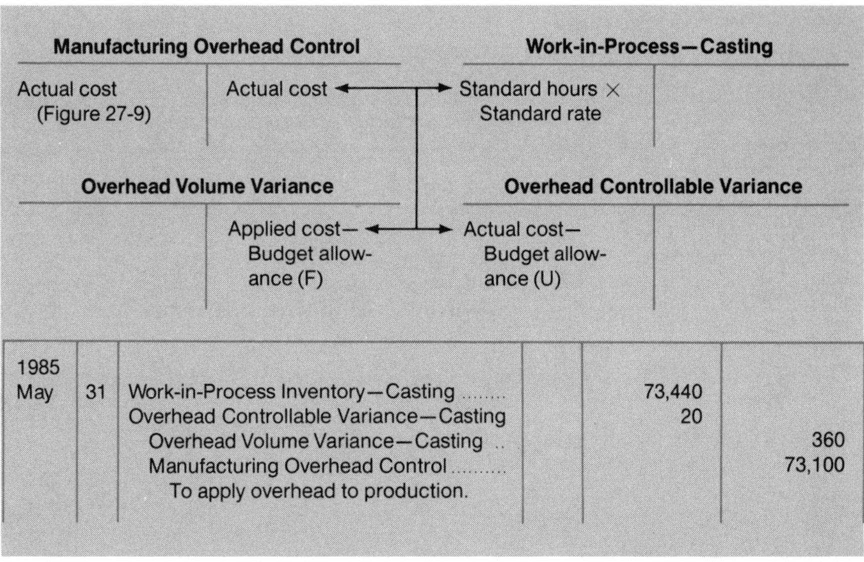

Figure 27–10 Application of Overhead

1. Figure 27–1 indicates that the standard overhead cost per mug is $0.12. The debit to Work-in-Process Inventory—Casting could also have been computed from this information as 612,000 mugs × $0.12 = $73,440.

2. The controllable variance is caused by excessive variable cost because actual fixed cost was the same as budgeted. To determine that amount, the budget allowance was adjusted to standard hours for production attained before comparison with actual costs to determine the variance.

3. The volume variance is a fixed cost variance. Megware Specialty Company established the departmental overhead rate of $3.60 per direct labor hour on the basis of a planned production of 600,000 mugs. The fixed element of that rate is $0.90 = ($18,000 fixed cost ÷ 20,000 planned direct labor hours). For every standard hour allowed by production attained, $0.90 will be applied to production. Megware attained standard hours in excess of budget of 400 = (20,400 − 20,000). These 400 hours × $0.90 = $360 of fixed cost overapplied.

Transfer to the Next Process

The transfer to the next process is recorded at standard cost, as shown in Figure 27–11. Since Figure 27–1 shows the standard cost per mug as $0.57, the amount transferred can be computed as 612,000 mugs × $0.57 = $348,840. Any work remaining in process in the Casting Department would show in the records at standard cost times stage of completion. In this in-

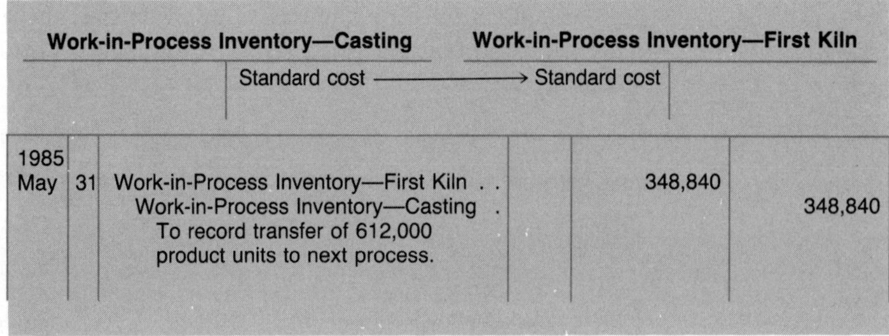

1985					
May	31	Work-in-Process Inventory—First Kiln . .		348,840	
		Work-in-Process Inventory—Casting .			348,840
		To record transfer of 612,000 product units to next process.			

Figure 27–11
Transfer to Next Process

stance, there is no ending inventory in the Casting Department. Therefore, all standard costs from Casting have been transferred to First Kiln, as follows:

Materials	$ 30,600
Direct labor	244,800
Manufacturing overhead	73,440
Total standard costs	$348,840

The journal entries for the First Kiln process and subsequent processes are similar to those for the Casting process.

In like manner, the cost of product units transferred to the Finished Goods Inventory account at the end of the last process is the total standard cost. Generally accepted accounting principles indicate that standard costs are acceptable for inventory pricing if they reasonably approximate actual costs.[4]

Evaluation and Disposition of Variances

The variance accounts serve to highlight periodically for management attention certain deviations from standard. In some cases, they may be indications that tasks are being done efficiently; in others, they may alert management to problems such as machinery out of adjustment, inadequately trained personnel, or poor quality of materials. Having served this management purpose, the variance accounts must be disposed of. If it is assumed that inventory and cost of goods sold should reflect actual historical cost, accounting theory suggests that they be apportioned among ending inventory of work in process, ending inventory of finished goods, and cost of goods sold. In practice, they are often closed directly to the Cost of Goods Sold account.

[4] *Accounting Research Bulletin No. 43,* "Restatement and Revision of Accounting Research Bulletins" (New York: AICPA, June 1953), paragraph 4, statement 4.

Standard cost techniques can be used to evaluate and control costs in functions of the business other than the production of a product. Even nonmanufacturing enterprises such as banks or hospitals use standards. An example is shown in the next section.

Marketing Expenses

A nonmanufacturing area in which standard cost techniques can be useful is the set of functions involved in selling the company's product—for example, advertising, sales, billing, and delivery. They involve both variable expenses (sales commissions, for example) and fixed expenses (such as depreciation of trucks). Budgets should be prepared for these functions with the variable and fixed expenses separately identified. With estimates of sales already included in the budget structure (see Chapter 26), it is possible to establish rates for various marketing functions and to analyze actual results, just as overhead costs in a production function were analyzed. Rates established for such functions are sometimes called **charging rates.**

To illustrate the use of charging rates, assume that Megware Specialty Company's sales budget indicates that 500,000 mugs will be sold in May 1985. The Delivery Department budget indicates that 800 direct labor hours will be used in this department in May and that total departmental expenses will be:[5]

Variable expenses	$10,000
Fixed expenses	3,000
Total delivery expenses	$13,000

The charging rate for the Delivery Department for May 1985 is $16.25 per direct labor hour = ($13,000 ÷ 800 direct labor hours). Assume actual data for May as shown in Figure 27–12. A comparison of total expenses with the budget appears to indicate a job well done since the department spent $30 less than was budgeted. However, an analysis of expenses similar to overhead cost analysis presents a different story.

Total mugs shipped		481,250 mugs
Direct labor hours worked in Delivery		780 hours
Departmental expenses:		
Variable expenses	$9,770	
Fixed expenses	3,000	
Total actual departmental expenses		$12,770

Figure 27–12 Delivery Department Data for May

[5]Direct labor hours may not be the best basis for computing a charging rate. Other bases that could be used are number of mugs shipped or number of pounds shipped.

The cost that should have been incurred (the standard cost) for the delivery of the mugs is equal to the standard hours allowed for production achieved (mugs delivered) times the charging rate. Since the budget called for 800 direct labor hours to deliver 500,000 mugs, the standard would call for the delivery of 625 mugs per direct labor hour = (500,000 ÷ 800). In this case, 481,250 mugs were actually shipped. Thus, the standard hours allowed for the delivery of mugs is 770 hours = (481,250 ÷ 625). From this, we can calculate the standard cost for the delivery of 481,250 mugs as $12,512.50 = (770 × $16.25). This amount compares unfavorably to the actual costs incurred by the Delivery Department as follows:

Total actual Delivery Department expenses	$12,770.00
Standard amount charged	12,512.50
Undercharged (or excessive) expenses	$ 257.50 (U)

The $257.50 in excess expenses can be broken down into the controllable and volume variances as was done with overhead. The controllable variance would be computed by subtracting the budget adjusted to standard expenses for production attained (mugs delivered) from the actual expenses in the department as shown below:

Actual expenses in department		$12,770
Budget adjusted to standard hours for production attained:		
Variable expenses (770 × $12.50)	$9,625	
Fixed expenses	3,000	12,625
Controllable variance		$ 145 (U)

Note carefully how the adjusted budget was computed. The original budget contained $10,000 of variable expenses for 800 direct labor hours. Therefore, the variable portion of the charging rate is $12.50 per direct labor hour = ($10,000 ÷ 800 hours). To adjust variable expenses in the budget to production attained, this variable portion is multiplied by the number of direct labor hours that *should have been used* (770) to deliver 481,250 mugs. When compared to the actual expense the adjusted budget shows an unfavorable controllable variance of $145. Because actual fixed costs are the same as budgeted, this variance is made up of variable expenses that supposedly could be controlled by the Delivery Department supervisor.

The remaining difference is beyond the control of the departmental supervisor. It is fixed expense incurred but not charged because only 481,250 mugs were available to ship instead of the intended 500,000. It can be computed as follows:

Budget adjusted to standard hours for production attained:		
Variable expenses (770 × $12.50)	$9,625.00	
Fixed expenses	3,000.00	$12,625.00
Amount charged (770 × $16.25)		12,512.50
Volume variance		$ 112.50 (U)

The variance is unfavorable because fixed expenses of $3,000 were incurred to provide the capacity to ship 500,000 mugs. This amounts to $0.006 per mug = (3,000 ÷ 500,000). Each mug up to 500,000 not shipped represents $0.006 of idle or unused fixed expenses. Since 18,750 mugs = (500,000 − 481,250) were not shipped as planned, a provided capacity costing $112.50 = (18,750 × $0.006) was unused. It is the task of the company management to fix responsibility for failure to deliver the number of mugs planned and to take corrective action.

Note that the sum of the two unfavorable variances ($145.00 + $112.50) equals the total undercharged expenses of $257.50. In this context, the word *charged* is similar in concept to the word *applied* in connection with recording manufacturing overhead cost. Accounts can be established to record the *charged-in* expenses and the variances. Most companies, however, develop the rates and compute the variances for control purposes but do not enter them in accounts. These expenses and variances are useful for cost control and other management decisions. The next chapter takes a closer look at the use of cost data for decision making.

Glossary

Charging rate A rate used in a nonmanufacturing department to compute amount of standard cost (expense) that ought to be incurred.

Favorable variance A variance in which actual cost is less than standard cost allowed, applied, or charged.

Labor efficiency variance The difference between actual and standard labor hours multiplied by the standard rate.

Materials purchase price variance The difference between the actual and standard unit prices of materials multiplied by the quantity purchased.

Materials quantity variance The difference between the actual and standard quantities of materials used multiplied by the standard price.

Overhead controllable variance The difference between the actual amount of total overhead cost and that called for by the budget adjusted to standard hours for production attained.

Overhead volume variance The difference between overhead applied and that called for by the budget adjusted to standard hours for production attained.

Standard A predetermined measure of what the quantity or cost of resources to produce a specified amount of product ought to be assuming good performance from typical workers.

Standard cost accounting system A cost accounting system devised to collect both actual and standard costs. The standard costs end up in the inventory accounts; any differences between standard and actual appear in variance accounts.

Standard cost card The specification that describes the standard materials, labor, and overhead cost for a product.

Standard costs Predetermined costs based upon the concept of a standard and upon engineering studies.

Unfavorable variance A variance in which actual cost is greater than standard cost allowed, applied, or charged.

Variance The difference—favorable or unfavorable—between actual and standard performance.

Variance accounts General ledger accounts that accumulate the amounts of deviations of actual cost from standard cost.

Wage rate variance The difference between the actual and standard rates of direct labor multiplied by the actual hours of direct labor.

Questions

Q27–1 What is a standard? What are the types of standards usually recognized in a manufacturing firm?

Q27–2 How are materials standards established? Labor standards? Manufacturing overhead standards?

Q27–3 Why would a company use a standard cost accounting system?

Q27–4 When a standard cost accounting system is used, are work-in-process inventories priced at standard costs or actual costs? Explain.

Q27–5 What is a variance? How are variances recognized in the accounts?

Q27–6 What are the two materials variances? Explain what each represents.

Q27–7 What are the two labor variances? Explain what each represents.

Q27–8 Are there variances in manufacturing overhead costs? Explain.

Q27–9 What is meant by *standard direct labor hours for production attained?*

Q27–10 If 270,000 units of product are transferred to finished goods, can they be priced without their actual costs being known? How, or why not?

Q27–11 Total manufacturing overhead is underapplied. Does this mean that both overhead variances are unfavorable? Explain.

Q27–12 What overhead variance is concerned only with fixed costs? Why?

Q27–13 Can the concept of standards be useful in controlling nonmanufacturing costs? How, or why not?

Q27–14 Compare a charging rate with a factory overhead rate. What are their similarities? Their differences?

Q27–15 An experienced accounting professor claims that it is as important to be able to explain the meaning of a variance "in words" as it is to compute it. Do you agree? Why or why not?

Exercises

In the exercises and problems whenever a variance is computed, show whether it is favorable or unfavorable.

E27–1 *Determining standard amount of materials*

Sardone Company manufactures a product in which metal tubing is used. Each unit of product requires six tubes that are each 10 inches long. The 10-inch tubes are obtained by cutting an eight-foot tube into 10 pieces. (This means that every 10th piece is only six inches long.) The metal tubing is available only in eight-foot lengths. How many eight-foot lengths of tubing would be considered standard for production of 300 units of product?

E27–2
Establishing a labor standard

Betty Loo is considered by the Queen Company's industrial engineers to be a typical production worker in the Packing Department. Her record for five consecutive eight-hour days is as follows:

	Units Packed
Monday	94
Tuesday	96
Wednesday	97
Thursday	95
Friday	98

Because she is considered typical, her packing rate is used to establish the standard. Compute the labor quantity in terms of direct labor hours to pack one unit.

E27–3
Computing debits to Work-in-Process Inventory

Golden State Company has set the following standards to produce one dozen stamped metal desk trays:

Materials: 18 linear feet at $0.90 per foot	$16.20
Direct labor: 10 minutes at $12 per hour	2.00
Manufacturing overhead: $6 per direct labor hour	1.00
Standard cost per dozen	$19.20

In April 1985, the total production is 21,600 trays. Actual costs were as follows:
Materials: 33,000 feet at $0.89 per foot.
Direct labor: 297 hours at $12.05 per hour.
Manufacturing overhead: $1,872.
What are the amounts to be debited to Work-in-Process Inventory for issuance of materials, distribution of labor costs, and manufacturing overhead applied?

E27–4
Computing overhead standard

Better Brands, Inc. expects to work a total of 600,000 direct labor hours in 1986 to produce its budgeted production of 2,400,000 units. Total labor cost is expected to be $4,800,000 and manufacturing overhead cost is expected to be $3,600,000. What is the standard overhead cost per direct labor hour? Per unit of product?

E27–5
Computing standard materials allowed

Zenk Company's Mixing Department material standards include one pint of hydraulic fluid for each dozen product units. In June 1985, the department produced the equivalent of 78,000 units. Compute the total amount of standard pints of hydraulic fluid for production attained.

E27–6
Computing standard hours allowed

Deep Mining Company has set a direct labor standard of six minutes per foot for its boring operation. In a month when 450,000 feet were bored, how many direct labor hours should have been used?

E27–7
Computing debit to Work-in-Process Inventory for overhead

In the Stamping Department of Goins Company, the direct labor standard allows two minutes per unit of product. The overhead standard rate is $2 per direct labor hour. In February 1985, 29,800 direct labor hours were used to stamp a total of 900,000 product units. Total overhead cost incurred in the department was $59,900. Compute the amount of the debit to Work-in-Process—Stamping when overhead is applied at the end of the month.

E27–8
Computing materials variances

Kobate Corporation's materials standards in its Blending Department include two pounds of rice meal at $0.40 per pound for each unit of product. In October 1985, the department blended 35,000 units of product. Materials purchased for and used in the department included 69,870 pounds of rice meal at a total cost of $28,646.70. Compute the dollar amounts of the materials purchase price variance and the materials quantity variance for rice meal.

E27–9 *Computing labor variances*

The Merchants Bancorp has set labor standards for posting of checks as follows:

Checks to be posted per direct labor hour	720
Wage rate per direct labor hour	$12

In April 1985, 800 direct labor hours were used at a total cost of $9,720 to post a total of 581,760 checks. Compute the dollar amounts of the wage rate and the labor efficiency variances.

E27–10 *Adjusting an overhead budget to production attained*

Platte Producers' manufacturing overhead budget for 1985 based on planned normal production of 2,000,000 units of product is the following:

Variable costs	$6,000,000
Fixed costs	1,000,000
Total overhead budget	$7,000,000

Actual production in 1985 was 2,100,000 units. Prepare an overhead budget adjusted to standard hours for production attained.

E27–11 *Computing overhead variances*

Ann Bullard Company has established a standard overhead rate of $0.20 per unit of product in the Screening Department. The overhead rate is composed of 80 percent variable cost and 20 percent fixed cost. In the month of October 1985, 420,000 units were screened. Actual manufacturing overhead costs were:

Variable costs	$68,000
Fixed costs	16,000
Total overhead costs	$84,000

Budgeted production was 400,000 units with a budgeted cost of $80,000. Although total costs were in excess of the budget, Bullard recognizes that production also was greater than budgeted. She wants to know whether the excess cost was justified. By computing the overhead controllable variance and the overhead volume variance, determine how actual costs compared with the amount that they ought to be.

E27–12 *Journal entries for purchase and issue of materials*

Bestmade Inc.'s materials standards per 100 units of product processed in the Finishing Department are two pints of polishing compound at $1.80 per pint and one jar of cleaner at $3.20 per jar. In June 1985, the department finished 1,200,000 units of product. Materials purchased for and used in the department were 24,800 pints of polishing compound at $1.78 per pint and 11,860 jars of cleaner at $3.22 per jar. Prepare summary journal entries dated June 30, 1985, to record the purchase and issuance of the materials.

E27–13 *Journal entries for use of direct labor*

Reno Company's direct labor standards in the Filling Department allow one hour per dozen units filled at a standard wage rate of $14 per hour. In August 1985, 86,400 units were filled using 7,160 direct labor hours at a total cost debited to the Factory Payroll account of $101,672 for direct labor. Prepare a summary general journal entry dated August 31, 1985 to distribute direct labor cost to production.

E27–14 *Standard cost concepts in a nonmanufacturing department*

Ames Associates planned to use 2,400 direct labor hours to produce 144,000 invoices in the Billing Department in September. Expected expenses for the department for the month were:

Variable expenses	$14,400
Fixed expenses	9,600
Total expenses expected	$24,000

In September 1985, 2,380 direct labor hours were used to produce 145,200 invoices. Actual expenses in the department were as follows:

Variable expenses	$14,994
Fixed expenses	9,600
Total actual expenses in September	$24,594

Compute a charging rate per direct labor hour and use it to analyze billing expenses for September into controllable and volume variances.

A Problems

P27–1A *Journalizing purchase and issue of materials with variances*

Iona Industries has a single production department. Following are materials standards for the manufacture of a unit of its product:

Material A: 3 pounds at $0.60	$1.80
Material B: ½ pound at $1.50	0.75
Total standard materials per unit	$2.55

Total production in June 1985 was 18,000 units of product. Materials purchased and used in production were:

Material A: 54,200 pounds at $0.58	$31,436
Material B: 8,970 pounds at $1.60	14,352
Total materials purchased and used	$45,788

Required:

1. Compute the materials purchase price variance and the materials quantity variance.

2. Prepare summary general journal entries as of June 30, 1985, to record the purchase on account and issuance of materials in June.

P27–2A *Journalizing use of direct labor with variances*

Akron Company has established in its Cutting Department the following direct labor standard for a model LG conference table:

½ hour at $12	$6

In August 1985, parts for 3,750 tables were cut using 1,850 direct labor hours at a total cost of $22,570.

Required:

1. Compute the wage rate variance and the labor efficiency variance.

2. Prepare a summary journal entry dated August 31 to record the distribution of direct labor from the Factory Payroll account.

P27–3A *Computation of all variances; journalizing*

Fayetteville Shipyard has established the following standards to build a Type A locker in its Metalworking Department:

Materials: 3 pounds of corrosion resistant steel at $3.50	$10.50
Labor: ¼ hour at $13	3.25
Overhead: $6 per direct labor hour	1.50
Total standard cost per locker	$15.25

The July 1985 production budget for this department planned that 6,000 Type A lockers would be built. The July overhead budget was as follows:

Variable costs	$4,800
Fixed costs	4,200
Total budgeted overhead costs	$9,000

In July, 6,100 lockers were built. Actual costs were:

Materials purchased and used: 18,600 pounds	$63,240
Direct labor: 1,500 hours	19,650
Variable overhead costs	4,920
Fixed overhead costs	4,200
Total actual costs	$92,010

Required:

1. Compute two variances each for materials, labor, and overhead.

2. Comment on possible causes of each of the variances.

3. Prepare summary general journal entries dated July 31 to record purchase on account and issuance of materials, distribution of direct labor from the Factory Payroll account, and application of manufacturing overhead.

P27–4A *Integrated problem: computing all variances and journalizing*

Tempe Corporation is a manufacturing company that produces a single product called Elpam. Standard costs to produce a unit of Elpam are materials, one pound at $8 per pound; direct labor, three hours at $12 per hour; and overhead, three hours at $2.50 per direct labor hour. Budgeted manufacturing overhead for June 1985 production was $90,000 of which 20 percent is fixed cost. It was planned that 12,000 units of Elpam would be produced; actual production in June was 10,300 units. Costs were incurred as follows:

Materials purchased and used: 11,000 pounds	$ 86,900
Direct labor: 31,000 hours	368,900
Manufacturing overhead (of which $18,000 is fixed)	80,250
Total actual costs	$536,050

Required:

1. Prepare a schedule analyzing the following variances as favorable or unfavorable (show all computations):

a. Total materials.
b. Materials purchase price.
c. Materials quantity.
d. Total labor.
e. Wage rate.
f. Labor efficiency.
g. Total manufacturing overhead.
h. Overhead controllable.
i. Overhead volume.

2. Prepare summary general journal entries dated June 30 to record the purchase of materials on account, issuance to production, distribution of direct labor from the Factory Payroll account, and the application of overhead.

P27–5A *Transfer and closing entries*

Ozarks Company had the following account balances as of December 31, 1985:

	Debits	Credits
Work-in-Process Inventory	$ 496,000	
Finished Goods Inventory	96,480	
Cost of Goods Sold	4,800,000	
Sales		$7,384,000
Materials Purchase Price Variance	1,680	
Materials Quantity Variance		1,000
Wage Rate Variance		1,680
Labor Efficiency Variance	1,008	
Overhead Controllable Variance	1,760	
Overhead Volume Variance	3,600	

The following additional information is available about unrecorded transactions:

a. Goods with a standard cost of $408,000 were transferred to finished goods in December.
b. Sales on account in December were $736,000; standard cost of those sales was $485,760.
c. The company closes variance accounts to Cost of Goods Sold at the end of each year.

Required: Prepare general journal entries to record:

1. The transfer of work completed in December to the finished goods storeroom.

2. The sales in December.

3. Closing of the variance accounts.

4. Closing of nominal accounts to Income Summary.

P27–6A

Thought-provoking problem: how well did a department perform?

Bronx Lehman Company's sales budget estimated that 1985 sales would be 1,000,000 units of product. Based on the idea that advertising expenses would be directly related to amount of sales, the manager of the Advertising Department prepared a budget that would use 5,000 direct labor hours at the following cost:

Variable expenses	$72,000
Fixed expenses	24,000
Total budgeted advertising expenses	$96,000

Actual sales in 1985 were 1,200,000 units of product. The Advertising Department used 6,120 direct labor hours and incurred the following expenses:

Variable expenses	$ 88,200
Fixed expenses	24,000
Total actual advertising expenses	$112,200

The company's controller is concerned that the Advertising Department may have an unjustified overexpenditure of its budget. The manager of the Advertising Department feels that her department's extra effort brought on the sales increase and that the over-expenditure is justified.

Required:

1. Compute a charging rate per direct labor hour for 1985 for the Advertising Department.

2. Analyze the department's 1985 performance by computing a controllable variance and a volume variance assuming that sales are directly related to advertising expenses.

3. Comment on whether the expenditures of the Advertising Department were reasonable. Use the variance computations and other data to support your comments.

B Problems

P27–1B

Journalizing purchase and issue of materials with variances

Fort Collins Company produces a product called Nasus in its single production department. Following are materials standards for one box of Nasus:

Material X: 6 pounds at $2.25	$13.50
Material Y: 1 pound at $1.30	1.30
Total standard materials per unit of Nasus	$14.80

Total production in September 1985 was 16,000 boxes of Nasus. Materials purchased and used in production were:

Material X: 97,500 pounds at $2.10	$204,750
Material Y: 15,475 pounds at $1.40	21,665
Total materials purchased and used	$226,415

Required:

1. Compute the materials purchase price variance and the materials quantity variance.

2. Prepare summary general journal entries as of September 30 to record the purchase on account and the issuance of materials to production in September.

P27–2B *Journalizing use of direct labor with variances*

Buies Creek Company has established in its Packing Department the following direct labor standards to pack one case of its product:

⅓ hour at $15	$5

In January 1985, 21,000 cases were packed using 6,970 direct labor hours at a total cost of $105,595.50.

Required:

1. Compute the wage rate variance and the labor efficiency variance.

2. Prepare a summary journal entry dated January 31 to record the distribution of direct labor from the Factory Payroll account.

P27–3B *Computation of all variances; journalizing*

Shaw Aircraft has established the following standards to produce one engine cowling:

Materials: 2 pounds of metal at $9	$18.00
Labor: ½ hour at $14.20	7.10
Overhead: $12 per direct labor hour	6.00
Total standard cost per cowling	$31.10

The February 1985 production budget for the Cowling Department planned that 15,000 cowlings would be built. The February manufacturing overhead budget was:

Variable costs	$60,000
Fixed costs	30,000
Total budgeted manufacturing overhead costs	$90,000

In February 1985, 14,500 cowlings were built. Actual costs were:

Materials purchased and used: 29,200 pounds	$261,340
Direct labor: 7,300 hours	102,930
Variable overhead costs	57,275
Fixed overhead costs	30,000
Total actual costs	$451,545

Required:

1. Compute two variances each for materials, labor, and overhead.

2. Comment on possible causes of each of the variances.

3. Prepare summary general journal entries dated February 28, 1985, to record purchase on account and issuance of materials, distribution of direct labor from the Factory Payroll account, and application of manufacturing overhead.

P27–4B *Integrated problem: computing all variances and journalizing*

Mankato Corporation is a manufacturing company that produces a single product called Senga. Standard costs to produce a unit of Senga are materials, two pounds at $8 per pound; direct labor, four hours at $12.50 per hour; and manufacturing overhead, four hours at $6 per hour. Budgeted manufacturing overhead for July 1985 production was $432,000, of which 25 percent is fixed cost. It was planned that 18,000 units of Senga would be produced. Actual production in July was 17,200 units. Costs were incurred as follows:

Materials purchased and used: 34,000 pounds	$ 272,000
Direct labor: 70,000 hours	910,000
Manufacturing overhead (of which $108,000 is fixed)	418,450
Total actual costs	$1,600,450

Required:

1. Prepare a schedule analyzing the following variances as favorable or unfavorable (show all computations):

a. Total materials.
b. Materials purchase price.
c. Materials quantity.
d. Total labor.
e. Wage rate.
f. Labor efficiency.
g. Total manufacturing overhead.
h. Overhead controllable.
i. Overhead volume.

2. Prepare summary general entries dated July 31 to record the purchase of materials on account, issuance to production, distribution of direct labor from the Factory Payroll account, and application of overhead.

P27–5B
Transfer and closing entries

Seneca Company had the following account balances as of June 30, 1985, the end of the fiscal year:

	Debits	Credits
Work-in-Process Inventory	$ 371,900	
Finished Goods Inventory	72,360	
Cost of Goods Sold	3,600,000	
Sales		$5,537,997
Materials Purchase Price Variance		1,260
Materials Quantity Variance	747	
Wage Rate Variance		1,278
Labor Efficiency Variance		756
Overhead Controllable Variance		1,314
Overhead Volume Variance	2,700	

The following additional information is available about unrecorded transactions:

a. Goods with a standard cost of $306,000 were transferred to finished goods in June.
b. Sales on account in June were $551,700; standard cost of these sales was $364,320.
c. The company closes variance accounts to Cost of Goods Sold at the end of the year.

Required: Prepare general journal entries to record:

1. The transfer of work completed in June to the finished goods storeroom.

2. The sales in June.

3. Closing of the variance accounts.

4. Closing of nominal accounts to Income Summary.

P27–6B
Thought-provoking problem: something is not right

Simon Fraser Company has the following standards for a unit of its product, Adnil:

Material A: 1 yard at $3.50	$ 3.50
Material B: 3 pounds at $1.75	5.25
Direct labor: 1/10 hour at $14.20	1.42
Manufacturing overhead: 1/10 hour at $6.50	0.65
Standard cost per unit of Adnil	$10.82

The normal monthly production of Adnil is 20,000 units. Monthly fixed overhead cost is budgeted at $6,000; monthly variable overhead cost is expected to be $7,000 if 20,000 units are produced.

In the second quarter of 1985, the following data were recorded:

	April	May	June
Units of Adnil produced	17,000	16,500	16,700
Material A used (yards)	19,500	18,900	19,150
Material B used (pounds)	61,200	59,400	60,120
Direct labor hours	2,100	2,050	2,065
Production costs:			
Material A	$ 67,665	$ 65,772	$ 66,259
Material B	104,040	102,168	102,204
Direct labor	27,720	27,060	27,258
Manufacturing overhead:			
Variable	5,950	5,775	6,012
Fixed	6,000	6,000	6,000
Total costs	$211,375	$206,775	$207,733

After studying reports for the quarter, the company president is shocked to find that sales and profits have fallen sharply. "Something is not right here," he said to the supervisor. "I just computed the unit cost of Adnil and it's running much higher than standard." The supervisor is sure that it must be a problem in the Purchasing Department. He said, "I've been able to save a dollar an hour on labor for the past three months, and my total overhead cost has been less than the $13,000 budget each month." "I still say that something is not right here, and I'm going to have the Accounting Department look into it," the president insisted.

Required: As the head of the Accounting Department, you respond to the president's request by first checking to verify that the elements making up the basic standard cost of $10.82 per unit of Adnil are valid. After finding them to be correct, you begin to study the data available. Using any analysis you think necessary, advise the president what you believe is going wrong. Support your conclusions with computations.

28 Using Cost Information for Management Decisions

Introduction

Throughout this book, examples of business decisions have been illustrated. Management is constantly faced with choices having to do with purchase or replacement of equipment, raising funds through the issue of stock or issuing bonds, sale of plants or divisions and acquisitions of all or part of other businesses, and many other major decisions. Such decisions are made only after a careful consideration of alternative courses of action. But possible courses of action can be evaluated only if the consequences of such choices can be predicted with reasonable accuracy. In this chapter, certain types of decisions based on cost analysis are discussed.[1] Then, techniques for evaluating long-term capital expenditures are explained. Because it is important to understand the nature of costs used in these analyses, a brief review of basic cost concepts is presented first.

Learning Goals

To explain the various concepts of costs.

To understand the application of knowledge of cost behavior to specific management decisions such as special order pricing, make or buy, or discontinuance of a department.

To describe how capital budgeting decisions affect each other and how they affect income.

To use specific techniques to evaluate capital expenditure proposals.

[1]For an explanation of cost-volume-profit analysis—another form of use of cost data for decision making—see Appendix 26.1.

Concepts of Cost: A Review

Seven basic cost concepts are used in this chapter:

Fixed costs are costs whose total amount is not affected by changes in production volume. For instance, rent on a factory building is a fixed cost because it does not change in total when productive volume increases or decreases. On a per unit basis, it changes.

Variable costs are those that are affected in total by changes in the volume of output. The cost of materials, for example, is a variable cost because it increases in direct proportion to the increase in number of units produced. On a per unit basis, however, it remains constant.

Semivariable costs are costs that include both a fixed and a variable component. Two types—stepped and mixed—are illustrated in Figure 26–1.

Differential cost is the difference in costs between two levels of output or two alternative courses of action. For example, this may be the additional cost to produce one more unit or to move from 90 percent to 95 percent capacity.

Opportunity costs are the benefits given up by forgoing one alternative for another acceptable alternative. For example, a company may make a large investment in property, plant, and equipment, thereby giving up an opportunity to invest the same money in bonds. The lost interest is an opportunity cost.

Out-of-pocket costs are costs that require direct expenditures such as wages. These are costs that may be saved if a specific project or plan is not carried out.

Sunk costs are costs that have already been incurred and which cannot be recovered if the project in which they are invested is dropped. An example is the book value of a machine that stamps the company's brand name on boxes and has no resale value. Sunk costs are usually not a factor in decisions concerning the future.

In the next section, some of these cost concepts are used to illustrate managerial decisions based on cost analysis.

Managerial Decisions Based on Cost Analysis

Pricing of Special Orders

A decision management often faces is whether or not to accept a special order involving the production of additional units beyond outstanding commitments. Preexisting cost patterns will not necessarily furnish the required data for such a decision. Each new situation requires a new cost analysis, and the concept of differential cost must be considered. If the price of the special order exceeds its *differential costs* and will not affect normal sales of the same product, the offer should be accepted.

To illustrate, assume the following unit cost data for the Lane Company, based on a budgeted annual production of 60,000 units, which is 75 percent of capacity; that is, total capacity is 80,000 units. For Lane Company to increase production from 60,000 to 60,001 units, an increase in cost (variable cost only; no increase in fixed cost) of $6 would be incurred:

Manufacturing costs:	
Direct materials	$2.00
Direct labor	2.50
Variable overhead costs	1.50
Total variable costs	$6.00
Fixed overhead costs ($180,000 ÷ 60,000 units)	3.00
Total unit cost	$9.00
Fixed selling and general and administrative expenses	$100,000.00

The Lane Company has been offered a long-term contract for 20,000 additional units annually at a unit price of $8.50. Since the purchaser is to attach its own label to the product, the Lane Company's normal sales price of $15 each will not be affected. Since no label is required, direct materials cost will be reduced by $0.05. Because fixed costs are not affected by the volume of production, fixed manufacturing overhead will remain at $180,000. The special offer price of $8.50 exceeds the unit differential cost (unit variable cost) of $5.95. The regular sales are not affected, and a gain of $51,000 is realized on the additional order as follows:

Added revenue (20,000 units × $8.50)	$170,000
Differential cost (20,000 units × $5.95)	119,000
Increased income	$ 51,000

The comparative budget data verify that this offer should be accepted as follows:

LANE COMPANY
Budgeted Comparative Income Statement
For the Year Ending December 31, 1985

	Present Production	Additional Order	Totals
Sales:			
60,000 units at $15	$900,000		
20,000 units at $8.50		$170,000	
Total sales			$1,070,000
Variable manufacturing costs:			
60,000 units at $6.00	360,000		
20,000 units at $5.95		119,000	
Total variable manufacturing costs			479,000
Contribution margin	$540,000	$ 51,000	$ 591,000
Fixed costs[a]	280,000	0	280,000
Net income	$260,000	$ 51,000	$ 311,000

[a]Includes fixed manufacturing overhead cost of $180,000 and selling and general and administrative expenses of $100,000.

It should be noted that the differential cost is not limited to variable costs. Also, note that the analysis is done using a contribution margin format. This highlights the importance of the fixed cost versus variable cost distinction. In the foregoing example, unused capacity was available with no alternative uses for that unused capacity. No additional fixed cost was required to use it. This makes the change in variable cost equal to the differential cost. If it had been necessary for the Lane Company to incur additional fixed cost—for example, $12,000 to prepare for the additional production run—the incremental cost would have both a variable and a fixed element. With such an assumption, the differential cost would have been $131,000: $119,000 in differential variable cost plus $12,000 in differential fixed cost. The decision still would be to accept the special order, since incremental revenue ($170,000) still would be greater than total incremental cost ($131,000).

Deciding Whether to Make or Buy

If adequate plant facilities and the ability to assure proper quality exist, management may have the option of making a particular part or buying it from an outside supplier. The **make or buy decision** depends upon a comparison of cost to make with cost to buy. In making such a comparison, *opportunity cost* may be a consideration.

Assume that the Nivals Company uses 10,000 fan blades per year that it manufactures at a unit cost of $20.40. The cost to make consists of the following:

Direct materials	$ 4.50
Direct labor	7.50
Variable overhead costs	3.60
Total variable costs	$15.60
Fixed overhead costs	4.80
Total unit cost	$20.40

Assumption 1: No Opportunity Cost The Nivals Company can purchase this part from a reliable supplier for $18.15. If the available plant facilities represent sunk costs that cannot be recovered by some other use of the facilities, then the firm should continue to make the part even though the total cost of $20.40 is greater than the quoted purchase price of $18.15. This is true because Nivals Company will eliminate only the variable cost per unit of $15.60 by buying the blades. The $4.80 in fixed costs will continue to be incurred. Thus, $15.60 becomes the differential cost to make, and $18.15 becomes the differential cost to buy. When compared, the differential cost to make is less than the differential cost to buy the part.

On a total cost basis, the comparison is as follows:

Variable cost to make (10,000 × $15.60)	$156,000
Opportunity cost to make	0
Subtotal	$156,000
Cost to buy (10,000 × $18.15)	181,500
Saving (loss) from buying	$ (25,500)

Assumption 2: With Opportunity Cost If, however, the Nivals Company can make an alternative use of these facilities, it may save money by purchasing the part. *Opportunity cost,* the amount of revenue forgone by not making the alternative use of the facilities, becomes relevant to the decision. Assume that the company could rent these facilities to Lani Pau if they stopped manufacture of the part and bought it instead. The amount of rent to be received becomes an opportunity cost. Consider these possible situations:

		Rent to Lani Pau for:	
	No Alternative Use	$20,000	$40,000
Variable cost to make (10,000 × $15.60)	$ 156,000	$156,000	$156,000
Opportunity cost to make	0	20,000	40,000
Subtotal	$ 156,000	$176,000	$196,000
Cost to buy	181,500	181,500	181,500
Saving (loss) from buying	$(25,500)[a]	$(5,500)[a]	$ 14,500

[a]Negative figure.

If there is no alternative use of the facilities or if the rent that could be earned is only $20,000, Nivals Company would save by making the part. However, if rent of $40,000 can be earned the cost to buy is less than the cost to make, and Nivals should purchase the part. Note that in none of the alternatives was the fixed cost considered. This is because the fixed cost is the same in each alternative and, therefore, not a differential cost.

Nivals Company's decision was whether to continue making a part or to buy it. The parallel problem—whether to make a part that is now being bought—involves essentially the same factors for consideration.

Abandonment of a Department, Territory, or Product

Deciding whether or not to abandon a supposedly unprofitable department, territory, or product involves a careful analysis of the effect of the abandonment on fixed and variable costs and the contribution margin.[2] If a department, territory, or product produces any contribution margin, it should not be abandoned unless the substituted new department, territory, or product will provide a greater contribution margin.

[2]See Appendix 26.1 for explanation of the contribution margin.

A departmental income statement of the Muskegon Clothing Company is shown in Figure 28–1. The accountant has been asked by management for the probable effect on total costs if the Children's Department is eliminated.

MUSKEGON CLOTHING COMPANY
Income Statement
For the Month Ended December 31, 1985

	Men's Department	Women's Department	Children's Department	Total All Departments
Sales (net)	$39,455.00	$64,000.00	$17,200.00	$120,655.00
Cost of goods sold	26,828.00	45,222.00	13,315.00	85,365.00
Gross margin on sales	$12,627.00	$18,778.00	$ 3,885.00	$ 35,290.00
Deduct: Operating expenses:				
Fixed expenses:				
Rent	$ 1,080.00	$ 1,800.00	$ 720.00	$ 3,600.00
Depreciation of store equipment	200.00	250.00	50.00	500.00
Executive salaries	1,301.50	2,598.00	650.50	4,550.00
Office salaries	579.00	1,156.50	289.50	2,025.00
Heat and light	225.00	375.00	150.00	750.00
Totals	$ 3,385.50	$ 6,179.50	$ 1,860.00	$ 11,425.00
Variable expenses:				
Advertising	$ 490.50	$ 795.00	$ 214.50	$ 1,500.00
Sales salaries	4,525.00	6,015.00	1,757.50	12,297.50
Sales commissions	375.00	550.00	120.00	1,045.00
Insurance	240.00	300.00	60.00	600.00
Bad debts expense	37.50	87.50	25.00	150.00
Miscellaneous general expense	200.00	250.00	50.00	500.00
Totals	$ 5,868.00	$ 7,997.50	$ 2,227.00	$ 16,092.50
Total operating expense	$ 9,253.50	$14,177.00	$ 4,087.00	$ 27,517.50
Net income or (loss)	$ 3,373.50	$ 4,601.00	$(202.00)	$ 7,772.50

Figure 28–1 **Departmental Income Statement**

MUSKEGON CLOTHING COMPANY
Summary Income Statement—Children's Department
For the Month Ended December 31, 1985

Sales	$17,200
Cost of goods sold[a]	13,315
Gross margin on sales	$ 3,885
Deduct: Variable expenses[b]	2,227
Contribution margin	$ 1,658
Deduct: Fixed expenses	1,860
Net income or (loss)	$ (202)

[a]This is a nonmanufacturing firm; its cost of goods sold is purchased and, therefore, variable.
[b]The firm must be able to eliminate these variable costs, or they become nondifferential for this particular decision

Figure 28–2 **Restatement of Children's Department Income**

To make this effect clear, the accountant has separated fixed costs and variable costs in the income statement. Management knows that closing the department will entirely eliminate its sales, cost of goods sold, and gross margin, but fixed costs now being allocated to it will continue and must be reallocated to other departments. To highlight the effectiveness of the Children's Department, the accountant prepared a summary income statement for it on a contribution margin basis (as shown in Figure 28–2).

Management can readily see that elimination of this department will result in a loss of contribution margin of $1,658. In spite of the net loss of $202 in the Children's Department, its December contribution margin absorbed $1,658 of fixed cost that would otherwise have to be absorbed by the remaining departments. The company's overall net income would be affected as follows:

Present operating income of all departments (Figure 28–1)	$7,772.50
Loss of contribution margin of Children's Department (Figure 28–2)	1,658.00
Operating income of remaining departments	$6,114.50

Note carefully, however, that the foregoing analysis assumes that there is no profitable alternative use for the space occupied by the Children's Department. Management must now explore possible uses of this space but will not accept one unless it generates a monthly contribution margin greater than $1,658 or provides other attractive offsetting benefits.

The foregoing example assumed that no fixed cost allocated to the Children's Department could be eliminated. If there had been fixed cost in the Children's Department that could be eliminated by closing it down, the contribution margin would be offset by that amount. Assume, for example, that there is a $450 fixed cost in Muskegon Clothing Company that is directly identified with the Children's Department. The contribution margin lost by closing the department would be reduced as follows:

Loss of contribution margin in Children's Department	$1,658
Deduct: Eliminated fixed cost	450
Net loss of income by closing Children's Department	$1,208

In this instance, closing the Children's Department would still reduce overall income, although by a lesser amount.

The following summary shows the effect on total net income of closing the Children's Department under each of the previous assumptions:

	With Children's Department (Figure 28–1)	Without Children's Department No Fixed Cost Eliminated	Without Children's Department Some Fixed Cost Eliminated
Sales (net)	$120,655.00	$103,455.00	$103,455.00
Cost of goods sold	85,365.00	72,050.00	72,050.00
Gross margin on sales	$ 35,290.00	$ 31,405.00	$ 31,405.00
Deduct: Variable expenses	16,092.50	13,865.50	13,865.50
Contribution margin	$ 19,197.50	$ 17,539.50	$ 17,539.50
Deduct: Fixed expenses	11,425.00	11,425.00	10,975.00
Net income	$ 7,772.50	$ 6,114.50	$ 6,564.50

To eliminate the Children's Department, under either of the foregoing assumptions, would reduce the company's total net income. Of total fixed cost of $1,680 allocated to the Children's Department, it would be necessary to eliminate more than $1,658 to increase overall net income. Even then, management would need to consider certain factors not measured in dollars. Some customers who buy both children's and adult clothing may be lost, em ployees may need to be relocated or laid off, and other undesirable consequences may bear upon the decision.

Budgeting Capital Expenditures

Capital budgeting refers to the allocation and commitment of funds to long-term capital investment projects. The amount of such investments or expenditures is usually large, and they are made with the expectation that benefits will be received over a number of years. Capital budgeting concerns itself with the development, selection, and evaluation of proposals for plant expansion and modernization, equipment replacement, product development, and so on. The nature of these investments and their effect on the long-range welfare of a company make it very important that they be analyzed and evaluated with the utmost care.

Types of Capital Expenditures

The types of capital expenditures can perhaps best be illustrated by questions involving capital investment decisions, such as the following:

Expansion Shall we buy additional equipment to supply the actual or anticipated increase in demand for our product? Shall we expand our facilities to produce new products? Shall we acquire the necessary facilities to make parts that we are now buying from outside sources?

Replacement Shall we replace present equipment with new and more efficient equipment? Shall we automate our production lines? Shall we buy machine A or machine B? Shall we lease the new equipment or shall we buy it?

Other Some investments are made on noneconomic grounds. Will more recreational facilities for use by employees—even though they may not directly reduce costs or increase revenue—improve employer-employee relations? Must an investment to eliminate sound nuisances or smoke hazards be made in compliance with Environmental Protection Agency requirements? Even if it is not mandatory, should the company choose to make such an investment in acknowledgement of corporate social responsibility?

Rate of Return

Business people make investments to earn a satisfactory return. The definition of a satisfactory rate of return depends on a number of economic factors. In the long run, it must be adequate to attract new capital. The selection of a **rate of return** which should be equaled or exceeded is central to the capital expenditures decision since it has a direct influence on the decision.[3]

Determining the Cash Flows

A capital investment generates flows of cash into and out of the business over a period. A comparison of several investment projects from which the best choice is to be made requires a comparison of the projects' expected cash flows. The concern is with future, not past, amounts and with amounts that will be different under alternative choices. A cost or a revenue amount that will be the same under all the alternatives from which a choice is to be made does not affect the decision. The *investment cost* is an immediate outflow. Aftertax *increases in revenue* or *reductions in costs* represent the equivalent of inflows. Management must use cost accounting and budget data to predict the amounts of inflows. After expected cash flows have been determined, a method is needed to compare projects and determine the order of desirability.

Evaluating Capital Expenditures

In the remaining section of this chapter, the following methods of measuring the desirability of investments are discussed:

- ☐ The payback method.
- ☐ The accounting rate of return.
- ☐ The excess present value method.
- ☐ The profitability index.

[3]Some companies establish a desired rate of return as the rate necessary for the firm to continue to attract sufficient capital. That concept, referred to as "cost of capital," is left for more advanced courses in finance.

Payback

Desirability of a project can be measured by a single criterion, payback. That is, how soon will the cash invested in the project be returned? **Payback** is a measure of the time required for the accumulated cash earnings from a project to equal the cash investment.

$$\frac{\text{Investment}}{\text{Annual net cash inflows}} = \text{Payback period.}$$

In theory, the shorter the payback time, the less the risk. The popularity of this measure is due to its simplicity and to its effectiveness as an initial screening measure, especially for high-risk property, plant, and equipment for which the useful life is difficult to estimate. It is also useful in evaluating projects of such obvious merit that refined analysis is not needed and in evaluating projects showing no financial merit. The factors it ignores are (1) the useful life, (2) the amount and pattern of cash flows beyond the payback point, (3) disposal values, (4) the time value of money, and (5) the profitability of the investment. To illustrate, assume the following figures:

Project	Net Investment	÷	Annual Net Cash Savings[a]	=	Payback Period
A	$10,000		$2,500		4 years
B	20,000		5,000		4

[a]Aftertax revenue increase or cost saving.

Since the net investment divided by the annual cash savings for each of these proposals yields a payback period of four years, they appear on this basis to be equally desirable. However, assume that Project A has a four-year life and Project B a five-year life. Since B provides a $5,000 inflow in its fifth year that is not considered in the payback computation, it is better than A. In spite of its weaknesses, the payback technique with its emphasis on quick recovery of investment is extremely appealing to management during periods of highly uncertain economic factors, for example, interest rates.

Accounting Rate of Return

To overcome a limitation of the payback method—the lack of a profitability measure—some companies use a second capital expenditure model, the **accounting rate of return.** Two variations of this model are commonly used: (1) rate of return on original investment, and (2) rate of return on average investment.

Rate of Return on Original Investment The formula for the first of these is:

$$\frac{\text{Annual aftertax cash inflows} - \text{Annual depreciation}}{\text{Original investment}} = \text{Rate of return on original investment.}$$

The numerator of this fraction attempts to measure an approximate income that will be produced by the use of this plant asset. To illustrate, assume the purchase of a machine for $30,000 that will provide aftertax cash savings of $6,000 per year for an estimated useful life (EUL) of 10 years (no salvage value). If the straight-line method of depreciation is used, the depreciation charge is $3,000 per year. Then

$$\frac{\$6{,}000 - \$3{,}000}{\$30{,}000} = 10 \text{ percent return on original investment.}$$

Rate of Return on Average Investment Some accountants compute the rate of return on average investment. In the above example, this rate would be

$$\frac{\$6{,}000 - \$3{,}000}{\$30{,}000 \div 2} = 20 \text{ percent return on average investment.}$$

When there is a salvage value, the average investment is cost plus ending book value (same as salvage value) divided by two. Whichever rate of return is used, the investment's profitability is emphasized. With this model, higher rates of return indicate more desirable investments. However, the accounting rate of return still shares a limitation of the payback method; it ignores the time value of money. To recognize the compound interest aspect (or time value of money), one of the discounted cash flow methods, such as the excess present value method, may be used.

Excess Present Value Method

As we have seen in the methods discussed above, evaluating the profitability of a proposed investment in capital equipment requires that the cost, a cash outflow, be compared with the net cash inflows generated by the project. The cash outflow takes place at the beginning of the project life and the inflows take place at various points over the project's life. Therefore, these flows are not directly comparable without taking into consideration the time value of money. A method which compares the present value of the cash outflows with the present value of the inflows is the **excess present value** method.[4]

Discounted Cash Flows A capital investment project has basically two different cash flows: a cash outflow associated with the purchase of the new asset, and a series of cash inflows over the life of the new project. The excess present value method discounts each of the cash flows back to the time when the investment is made and subtracts the present value of the outflows from the inflows. The discount rate which is used is the company's cost of obtaining capital, discussed earlier in the chapter.

[4]Because the concept of present value of a single amount and of an ordinary annuity are used in these evaluations, some readers may find it desirable to review both at this point.

Since the cash outflows associated with the investment normally take place at the time the asset is purchased (called time period 0), they are already stated at the proper present value. Thus, no discounting calculations are required. These outflows are the net cost of the investment (cost minus the cash received or trade-in allowed from any displaced equipment.)

The cash inflows are quite different. The benefits (inflows) from an investment in a piece of capital equipment can be viewed as consisting of two elements:

1. The periodic cash inflows, either increases in revenues or decreases in costs, generated by the project. Each of these cash inflows is assumed to take place at the end of its respective year and should be net of tax effect.
2. The salvage or recovery value of the new asset at the end of the EUL.

The periodic cash inflows from the project may be uniform, the same amount each year of the EUL, or they may vary from year to year. If they are uniform, they are the same as rents withdrawn from an ordinary annuity, and their present value may be calculated using the annuity tables. If they vary from year to year, the individual present values must be calculated using the present value of a single sum table. In either case, this discounting will produce the present value of the periodic cash inflows from the project.

The salvage value that a capital item may have at the end of its useful life also produces a cash inflow which must be discounted back to the present value. Since this is a cash flow which takes place at a single point in time, the present value of a single sum table would be used.

The **excess present value** of the project is then found by subtracting the present value of the outflows from the present value of the inflows. If this amount is positive, it means that the project will earn a rate of return greater than the discount rate used. Thus, the project is a desirable one on the basis of cost and revenue information. If the net present value is negative, the project would only be considered if other information suggests the need for the project even though it would not contribute to the profitability of the firm. This may be the case, for example, with some environmental control projects.

Excess Present Value Method Illustrated Assume that the East Company is planning to buy a new press for $25,000, with an EUL of ten years. Freight and installation costs will be $2,000. The press being replaced had an original cost of $20,000, a book value of $4,500, and can be sold for $4,500. The new press is not expected to change revenue, but is expected to reduce annual maintenance and labor costs (including fringe benefits) by $5,500 and to increase yearly power costs by $1,000 (all net of taxes). Insurance cost will be unchanged. The advisability of the replacement is being questioned. Money has a cost to the company of 14 percent per year compounded annually.

Step 1: Net Cash Investment. The first step is to determine the net amount of initial cash investment required. For East Company, this amounts to:

Purchase price of new press	$25,000
Freight and installation	2,000
Subtotal	$27,000
Deduct: Proceeds from sale of old press	4,500[a]
Net investment	$22,500

[a]To avoid a complexity, the income tax effect of gain or loss on sale is avoided in this illustration. In an actual situation, it must be considered in calculating net investment.

Except for a possible income tax effect of gain or loss on disposal, the book value of the old press is irrelevant because it represents a past (or sunk) cost, not a future cost. The selling price of the old machine is relevant because it represents a reduction of the cash outflow for the investment.

Step 2: Net cash inflows. The East Company proposal falls into the cost reduction category. The relevant cash inflows are the costs that will be different (saved) if the proposal is adopted. The expected change in annual operating cash flows will be as follows:

Cost decreases (maintenance and labor)	$5,500
Deduct: Cost increases (power)	1,000
Net annual savings	$4,500[a]

[a]Assumed to be aftertax savings.

This step involves a careful analysis of all operating costs to determine which will be increased and which decreased. Only those cost changes that will change cash flows should be considered.

Step 3: Estimated Useful Life and Resale Value. This step is necessary for any long-life asset. The question to be answered is: How long will the new press contribute to the earnings of the firm? The East Company has already estimated this to be 10 years. It is also estimated that the new press will have a resale value of $4,000 at the end of 10 years.

Step 4: Excess Present Value. The net annual saving is $4,500. By using compound interest tables, the East Company can determine the present value of this cash inflow for the next 10 years. With money worth 14 percent compounded annually, the present value of the cash inflows is as follows:

Present value of 10 annual rents of $4,500 at 14 percent per period = $4,500 × 5.216116	$23,472.52
Present value of resale value of new press at end of EUL = $4,000 × 0.269744	1,078.98
Present value of inflows	$24,551.50

The present value of the cash inflows (cash savings plus resale value of the new asset) is then compared with the present value of the cash outflows (net actual cash investment) as follows:

Present value of inflows	$24,551.50
Net cash investment (actual and already at present value)	22,500.00
Excess present value	$ 2,051.50

Since the present value of the cash inflows is in excess of the present outflows, this investment is earning a rate of return better than the 14 percent that East uses as the required rate of return. If the present value of cash inflows were less than the net investment, East Company should look for another use of its available funds or do nothing since it will cost more to acquire the money than can be earned by its use.

Profitability Index A greater excess present value may not always indicate a more desirable investment. A device or index that allows a company to rank several proposals in order of desirability is the **profitability index,** calculated as follows:

$$\frac{\text{Present value of inflows}}{\text{Net investment}} = \text{Profitability index.}$$

For the East Company, this is:

$$\frac{\$24{,}551.50}{\$22{,}500.00} = 1.091.$$

Any alternative investment with a profitability index greater than 1.091 would be ranked above this proposed new press in order of desirability. If the company had enough investment funds, management would consider all projects with an index greater than 1.0. Most firms have limited funds to invest and would choose only those with highest indexes up to the limit of funds available.

Limitations of the Present Value Method The primary objective of investment cost analysis is to find a way to compare and choose the best from several proposed capital expenditures. The concept of present value has theoretical validity and practicability in the capital budgeting process. It provides the basis for a systematic analysis of available alternative investment proposals. But sophistication and refinement of procedure cannot ensure a best choice if the data are wrong. The data used are projections of expectations—often long-range—involving revenue, cost, equipment life, human and material performance, and so on. Such a complexity of variables demands skillful managerial judgment. Finally, some factors cannot be quantified. An investment may have a direct or indirect effect on morale or on relations with the community, which, if not carefully judged, could cause harm. There is usually no single right answer. Sophisticated analytical procedures will not cancel the effects of poor judgment as to market potential, available resources, and environmental factors—economic, political, and social.

Summary of Methods

The discussions in this chapter have omitted many important quantitative decision-making techniques that require accounting data. Topics such as linear programming and use of probabilities and expected value have been left for more advanced courses in accounting. Figure 28–3 summarizes the formulas that have been explained.

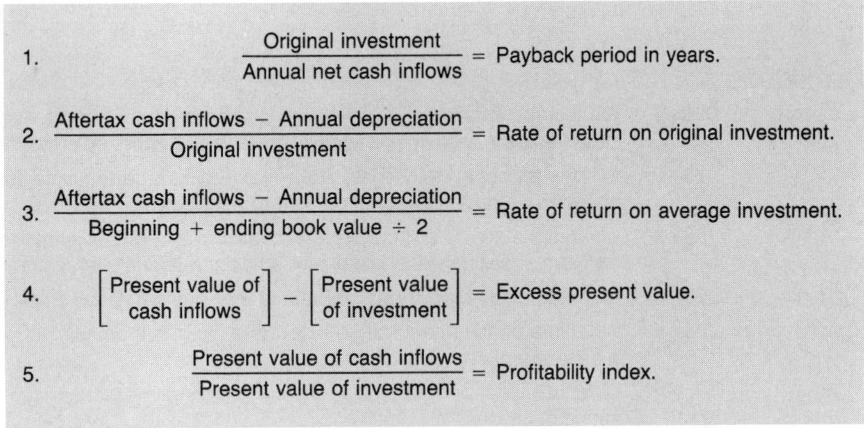

1. $$\frac{\text{Original investment}}{\text{Annual net cash inflows}} = \text{Payback period in years.}$$

2. $$\frac{\text{Aftertax cash inflows} - \text{Annual depreciation}}{\text{Original investment}} = \text{Rate of return on original investment.}$$

3. $$\frac{\text{Aftertax cash inflows} - \text{Annual depreciation}}{\text{Beginning} + \text{ending book value} \div 2} = \text{Rate of return on average investment.}$$

4. $$\begin{bmatrix}\text{Present value of} \\ \text{cash inflows}\end{bmatrix} - \begin{bmatrix}\text{Present value} \\ \text{of investment}\end{bmatrix} = \text{Excess present value.}$$

5. $$\frac{\text{Present value of cash inflows}}{\text{Present value of investment}} = \text{Profitability index.}$$

Figure 28–3 Formulas Used in This Chapter for Decision Making

Glossary

Accounting rate of return A method of evaluating capital investments; it equals (aftertax inflows − depreciation) ÷ cost of original (or average) investment.

Capital budgeting The allocation and commitment of funds to long-term capital investment projects.

Contribution margin Total sales revenue minus total variable cost; on a unit basis, it is selling price minus unit variable cost.

Differential cost The difference in cost between two levels of output. On a unit basis, it is this difference divided by the units produced by this additional level.

Excess present value The difference, at a common point of time, between the cost of an investment (its present value) and the present value of earnings expected from it.

Fixed costs Costs that, without a change in present productive capacity, are not affected by changes in volume of output.

Make-or-buy decision A decision whether to make a product within the firm or to buy it outside.

Opportunity costs The costs of forgoing one thing—investment, operation, materials, or process, for example—to get an acceptable alternative.

Out-of-pocket costs Costs that give rise to direct expenditures.

Payback A method of measuring the desirability of a project in terms of how soon the cash invested in a project will be recovered.

Present value method A means of converting cash inflows and outflows over time to their present value, using an estimated discounting rate, in order to compare capital expenditures.

Profitability index Ratio of the present value of inflows to net investment in a capital expenditures project.

Rate of return The rate that funds could earn if invested in the best available alternative project.

Semivariable costs Costs that include both a fixed and a variable component.

Sunk costs Already incurred costs that cannot be recovered by abandonment of a project.

Variable costs Costs that are affected in total by changes in the volume of output.

Questions

Q28–1 What is the difference between an out-of-pocket cost and a sunk cost? Could a cost be classified as out-of-pocket today and as a sunk cost next month? Explain.

Q28–2 What is an opportunity cost? How does it play a part in a decision to make or buy? To abandon an apparently unprofitable department?

Q28–3 What is the key to a decision to accept or reject a special order at a price lower than the normal selling price, assuming sufficient capacity is available to fulfill it?

Q28–4 Are fixed costs ever a part of the make or buy decision? Explain.

Q28–5 What is a contribution margin? How is it used in the decision to continue or close down a department showing a net loss?

Q28–6 What is capital budgeting? How are compound interest concepts useful in capital budgeting decisions?

Q28–7 Define *payback.* What are its advantages? Its disadvantages?

Q28–8 What is an accounting rate of return? How does it differ from the excess present value method?

Q28–9 What is excess present value? A profitability index? How reliable are they in helping to make a decision?

Q28–10 An experienced accountant claims that the excess present value method appears to be sound in theory but requires so many estimates that the simplicity of the payback method is more attractive. What are some of the estimates required under the excess present value method that are not required under payback? Do you think the need for these estimates makes payback a better method of evaluating capital budgeting projects?

Exercises

E28–1 *Computing total and unit contribution margin*

The Village Green Company produced and sold 1,500,000 packets of potato chips in 1985 at a sales price of $0.57 per packet. Summarized costs were:

Direct materials	$105,000
Direct labor	126,000
Variable manufacturing overhead	99,000
Fixed manufacturing overhead	24,000
Other fixed expenses	60,000

Compute (a) the total contribution margin, and (b) the unit contribution margin.

E28–2 *Contribution margin income statement*

Using the following summarized information for Melissa's Sales Outlet in 1985, prepare an income statement on a contribution margin basis:

Total sales	$832,000
Variable production costs	260,000
Fixed production costs	286,000
Variable selling and general and administrative expenses	104,000
Fixed selling and general and administrative expenses	78,000

There were no beginning or ending inventories.

E28–3 *Unit variable cost*

Tacoma Company's unit costs are:

Materials	$ 2.50
Direct labor	6.00
Manufacturing overhead (60 percent fixed)	6.00
Total unit cost	$14.50

What are Tacoma's unit variable costs? Show computations.

E28–4 *Accept or reject an order?*

Shreveport Company's cost of making an underwater fish detector are:

Direct materials	$32.15
Direct labor	18.70
Variable manufacturing overhead	10.50
Fixed manufacturing overhead (at the usual production level)	17.60
Total cost	$78.95

Shreveport has an opportunity to sell 10,000 units in Akureyri, Iceland for $60 each if it will leave its brand name off. Shreveport has never sold in Iceland, has the unused plant capacity to produce the additional 10,000 units, and there will be no selling or other expenses in connection with the sale. Should the offer be accepted? Show computations.

E28–5 *Continue to make or buy a part?*

West Lafayette Company makes a safety valve that is used in an air compressor it assembles. The Purchasing Department has found an equal quality valve available to be purchased at $26.50. West Lafayette uses 10,000 valves per year. Fixed costs of the facilities used to make the valve are $40,000 per year. Other costs to make this valve are:

Direct materials	$16.00
Direct labor	8.00
Variable manufacturing overhead	1.00
Total variable costs per valve	$25.00

The facilities presently used to make the valve could be rented for $32,000 per year. Should the company continue to make or should it change over to purchase of the valve? Show computations.

E28–6 *Computing payback period*

Dallas Company has a proposal to purchase a new machine for a cash price of $36,000. With this new machine, a cash saving of $10,800 per year can be generated. Compute the payback period to the nearest month.

E28–7 *Is payback alone sufficient?*

Nacogdoches Inc. has two proposals for a replacement item of equipment. The data gathered are as follows:

	Machine A	Machine B
Cost	$40,000	$36,000
Annual aftertax savings	$10,000	$ 9,000
Estimated useful life	6 years	5 years

Neither has a salvage value. Compute the payback period for each. Which should be chosen? Why?

E28–8 *Accounting rate of return*

Maple Company proposes to buy a new press for $90,000. It will provide annual aftertax cash savings of $25,500 for 12 years, after which it will be obsolete and have no salvage value. Compute the accounting rate of return on (a) the original investment, and (b) the average investment.

E28–9 *Computing cash flows*

Urbana Company is considering the purchase of a new machine that will cost $200,000. It will replace an existing machine with a book value of $45,000 that can be sold for $30,000. It is expected to increase the contribution margin of the company by $48,000 per year, but will require a $1,200 semiannual inspection and adjustment. Compute (a) the investment outflow, and (b) the annual cash inflows. Ignore income taxes and gain or loss on sale.

E28–10 *Excess present value method*

June Chee is considering a purchase of a new piece of equipment at a cost of $200,000. It will have an estimated useful life of 10 years and a salvage value of $30,000. Net annual cash inflows to be generated by the machine after taxes will be $48,000. Use the excess present value method to decide whether this capital investment should be made if Chee's required rate of return is 20 percent compounded annually.

E28–11 *Profitability index; net present values given*

Better Company is limited to an investment in one capital project per year. It can purchase at a cost of $120,000 a machine that will produce net cash inflows with a present value of $130,000. An alternative is to purchase a machine at a cost of $117,500 that will generate cash inflows with a net present value of $124,500. Compute the profitability index for each machine and recommend which one to buy.

E28–12 *Profitability index; net present values not given*

Two machines are under consideration for purchase by Niagra Company. Applicable data are as follows:

	Machine A	Machine B
Cost	$175,000	$198,000
Salvage value	26,250	28,500
Annual aftertax cash inflows	42,000	45,600
Estimated useful life	10 years	10 years

The company's required rate of return on new assets is 16 percent compounded annually. Compute a profitability index for each proposal and use it to rank them in order of desirability.

A Problems

P28–1A
Make or buy decision

The Storrs Company can produce a part at the following unit costs:

Direct materials	$12.96
Direct labor	17.28
Variable overhead costs	7.20
Subtotal	$37.44
Fixed manufacturing overhead costs	11.52
Total unit costs	$48.96

The company can purchase the part for $40.32. It makes and uses 1,000 per year.

Required: Should the part be purchased if fixed overhead costs of $11.52 are sunk costs? If Maggie Bell Herbin will pay $4,500 per year to rent those plant facilities now used to make the part?

P28–2A
Continue or eliminate a department?

The following condensed departmental income information is available for the Romney Department Store for 1985:

	Department A	Department B	Department C	Total
Net sales	$33,600	$28,800	$24,000	$86,400
Variable costs	17,280	25,920	11,520	54,720
Contribution margin	$16,320	$ 2,880	$12,480	$31,680
Fixed costs	9,600	7,680	6,540	23,820
Net income (loss)	$ 6,720	$ (4,800)	$ 5,940	$ 7,860

Required:

1. Should Department B be eliminated if the fixed costs cannot be eliminated? If $3,000 of the fixed costs can be eliminated? Show computations.

2. Assume that none of the fixed costs can be eliminated if Department B is abandoned and that the 1986 operational results for Departments A and C are the same as 1985. Prepare condensed income statements on a contribution margin basis for 1986 with Department B eliminated.

P28–3A
Accept or reject a special order?

Mission Valley Shop is operating at 65 percent of capacity producing 225,000 pairs of men's boots annually. Actual unit cost and selling price data for 1985 are as follows:

Direct materials	$19.50
Direct labor	11.70
Variable manufacturing overhead costs	5.85
Total variable costs	$37.05
Fixed manufacturing overhead costs ($3,510,000 ÷ 225,000)	15.60
Total unit cost	$52.65
Selling price	$99.45

The company has been offered a one-time contract to sell 80,000 pairs of men's boots to a Mexican importing firm at $44.85 per pair. This will not affect domestic sales. Fixed manufacturing overhead costs of $3,510,000 as well as total selling and general and administrative expenses of $3,120,000 will not be affected by the order.

Required: Prepare comparative statements for management indicating whether or not this contract should be accepted.

P28–4A
Capital investment; no salvage value

Hampshire, Inc. plans to invest $450,000 in improved metal fabrication equipment that is expected to save $112,500 after taxes annually for 10 years. Assume straight line depreciation with no salvage value.

Required:

1. Compute the payback period.

2. Compute the accounting rate of return on original investment.

3. Compute the accounting rate of return on average investment.

4. Compute excess present value if the value of money is 20 percent compounded annually.

5. Compute the profitability index.

P28–5A
Capital investment with salvage value

A machine that costs $104,000 will reduce present operating costs by $6,250 after taxes each quarter for the next 10 years. It will have a salvage value of $10,000. The cost of money is 16 percent per year compounded quarterly.

Required:

1. Compute the payback period.

2. Compute the accounting rate of return on original investment.

3. Compute the accounting rate of return on average investment.

4. Compute the excess present value.

5. Compute the profitability index.

P28–6A
Thought-provoking problem: effect of income taxes

In the examples in this chapter, aftertax cash flows were used. If the figures available are pretax amounts, they must be adjusted to reflect the effect of income tax. Cullowhee Corporation expects its income to be subject to federal and state taxes at the rate of 40 percent. A project to update the computer system will require new equipment at a cost of $320,000. Existing equipment can be sold at book value of $10,000. Pretax cash savings of $100,000 per year will be generated by the new equipment. The new equipment has an estimated useful life of 10 years, a salvage value of $20,000, and will be depreciated under the straight line method.

Required:

1. Compute the aftertax cash flows for this project.

2. Compute the payback period to the nearest month.

3. Compute the excess present value and the profitability index assuming that money is worth 16 percent compounded annually.

4. Comment on the desirability of this project.

B Problems

P28–1B
Make or buy decision

West Georgia Aviation can produce a part at the following unit costs:

Direct materials	$108
Direct labor	144
Variable manufacturing overhead costs	60
Subtotal	$312
Fixed manufacturing overhead costs	96
Total unit costs	$408

The company can purchase the part for $336. It makes and uses 1,000 per year.

Required: Should the part be purchased if fixed overhead costs of $96 are sunk costs? If Christine Carroll will pay $37,500 per year to rent the plant facilities now used to make the part?

P28–2B *Continue or abandon a territory?*

The following condensed departmental income information is available for Frostburg Sales Company for 1985:

	East Territory	West Territory	South Territory	Total
Net sales	$64,800	$56,160	$46,800	$167,760
Variable costs	33,696	50,544	22,464	106,704
Contribution margin	$31,104	$ 5,616	$24,336	$ 61,056
Fixed costs	18,720	14,976	12,753	46,449
Net income (loss)	$12,384	$ (9,360)	$11,583	$ 14,607

Required:

1. Should West Territory be abandoned if fixed costs cannot be eliminated? If $4,400 of fixed costs can be eliminated? Show computations.

2. Assume that none of the fixed costs can be eliminated if West Territory is abandoned and that the 1986 operational results for the other territories are the same as 1985. Prepare condensed income statements on a contribution margin basis for 1986 with West Territory abandoned.

P28–3B *Accept or reject a special order?*

Muncie Company is operating at 60 percent of capacity producing 112,500 sets of swimfins annually. Actual unit cost and selling price data for 1985 are as follows:

Direct materials	$ 6.00
Direct labor	3.60
Variable manufacturing overhead costs	1.80
Total variable costs	$11.40
Fixed manufacturing overhead costs ($540,000 ÷ 112,500)	4.80
Total unit cost	$16.20
Selling price	$30.60

The company has been offered a one-time contract to sell 40,000 sets of fins to a Japanese importing firm at $13.80 per set. This will not affect domestic sales. Fixed manufacturing overhead costs of $540,000 as well as total selling and general and administrative expenses of $480,000 will not be affected by the new order.

Required: Prepare comparative statements for management indicating whether or not this contract should be accepted.

P28–4B *Capital investment; no salvage value*

Hardy, Inc., plans to invest $600,000 in certain improved production equipment that is expected to save $150,000 after taxes annually for 10 years. Assume straight line depreciation with no salvage value.

Required:

1. Compute the payback period.

2. Compute the accounting rate of return on original investment.

3. Compute the accounting rate of return on average investment.

4. Compute excess present value if money is worth 16 percent compounded annually.

5. Compute the profitability index.

P28–5B *Capital investment with salvage value*

A machine that costs $92,500 will reduce present operating expenses by $6,412.50 after taxes each quarter for the next 10 years. It will have a salvage value of $2,500. Money is worth 16 percent per year compounded quarterly.

Required:

1. Compute the payback period.

2. Compute the accounting rate of return on original investment.

3. Compute the accounting rate of return on average investment.

4. Compute the excess present value.

5. Compute the profitability index.

P28–6B *Thought-provoking problem: how important are the estimates?*

Eau Claire Corporation had a proposal to invest $500,000 in a capital project that was estimated to have a useful life of 12 years and a salvage value of $25,000. The aftertax cash saving was expected to be $96,000 per year. The corporation earns 16 percent compounded annually on alternative uses of the $500,000, so this investment must provide a return of at least 16 percent. Because the payback period was slightly greater than five years, the president was somewhat concerned about the project, but the investment committee voted to proceed with it. Two years after the investment, company engineers decided that the estimated useful life should have been 10 years instead of 12 years. The estimated cash saving of $96,000 has been found to be accurate.

Required:

1. Compute the excess present value of the investment originally used by the investment committee.

2. Compute the revised excess present value based on the new estimated useful life of 10 years.

3. Has the two-year error in estimated useful life caused the company to make an undesirable investment? If the engineers changed the estimate of salvage value at the end of 10 years to $100,000, would you change your mind? Show computations to support your answer.

A Federal Income Taxes

Introduction

Since its origin in 1913, the federal income tax law has been frequently—often annually—altered by the Congress of the United States. In 1981, the *Economic Recovery Tax Act of 1981* (ERTA) was enacted into law. Then in 1982, the *Tax Equity and Fiscal Responsibility Act of 1982* (TEFRA) was passed. These acts amend the basic Internal Revenue Code. Other tax acts, no doubt, will be enacted into law and will change the basic income tax model. This appendix takes a broad overview approach based on the tax laws in existence at the time of this writing. This broad overview is included in this book to familiarize the reader with (1) the taxation of income for individuals and corporations, (2) the tax requirements of partnerships, and (3) some of the differences between business income and taxable income needed to introduce interperiod income tax allocation. In the computational illustrations in the following discussion, the currently projected tax laws for 1983 are used. When illustrations are presented on actual tax forms, 1982 forms (the latest ones available when this was written) are used.

Learning Goals

To gain an appreciation of the federal income tax task.

To differentiate between business income and taxable income.

To understand the broad tax requirements for partnerships.

To examine some basic differences between the corporate income tax and the individual income tax.

To understand the basic recording requirements for interperiod income tax allocation.

Classes of Taxpayers

Four separate kinds of entities are subject to the federal income tax: individuals, corporations, estates, and trusts. Two of these—estates and trusts—need a brief description. *Estates* are subject to income tax when an individual dies and leaves income-producing assets in an estate. Even if these assets are to be distributed to the heirs, they will remain in the estate for a certain period of time. A *trust,* created by a contract or will, transfers assets to a trustee to be managed for the specific purpose named in the trust document.

Each of these entities must submit a calculation of the income tax on a specific type of tax return to the Internal Revenue Service. This submission is referred to as the *filing* of the tax return. The entity filing the return is called the **filer.** In addition to filing of a return, each entity must pay a tax, if applicable, on its taxable income.[1] Single business proprietorships and partnerships are not taxed as separate business entities. Rather, the single proprietor reports business income on Schedule C of Form 1040, the U.S. Individual Income Tax Return. The partnership files a separate informational return, Form 1065, but each partner includes his or her share of partnership net income, together with the personal nonpartnership income, on Form 1040.

Tax Accounting Methods

The Internal Revenue Code, enacted and often amended by Congress, sets forth the law, and the Internal Revenue Service establishes regulations regarding the inclusion and exclusion of certain revenue and expense items and the use of certain methods and procedures in computing taxable income. The Internal Revenue Code, however, permits taxpayers to select certain options, among them the alternative of choosing the cash or accrual basis of computing net income under certain circumstances. The taxpayer should choose the method permissible under the law that will postpone and avoid taxes **(tax avoidance),** thereby conserving working capital and achieving the taxpayer's goal of the lowest long-run tax cost. On the other hand, the taxpayer should not illegally attempt to evade the payment of taxes **(tax evasion)** by not reporting income or by overreporting expenses.

Cash Basis

When the **cash basis** is used, income is recognized when cash is received and expenses are considered to be incurred when the cash payment is made. The cash basis usually is *not* a satisfactory method of measuring net business income. For tax purposes, however, it is well suited for individuals not engaged in business and also, to a lesser extent, for businesses that do not have inventories, payables, and receivables. In the latter case, the calculation of net income by the cash method may approximate that calculated on an accrual

[1]Some trusts, all of whose income goes to beneficiaries, file tax returns for information purposes only. The income received from these trusts should be reported by the individual beneficiaries on their individual tax returns. Under these circumstances, the trust would not pay any income taxes.

basis. An individual whose only income is salary is required to use the cash basis.

For income tax purposes, the cash basis is modified in two ways. First, the cost of long-lived assets, such as machinery or a truck, cannot be deducted in the year of purchase when cash is paid. The taxpayer must treat these items as assets and apportion their cost over their useful service lives. Second, revenue is recognized when it is constructively received, that is, when the revenue is in the control of the taxpayer. For example, interest credited to a savings account is deemed to be constructively received, even though the cash is not yet in the hands of the taxpayer.

Accrual Basis

Under the **accrual basis** of measuring income, revenue is recognized in the period when a sale is made or a service is rendered, regardless of when cash is received. Expenses are recognized in the period when services or goods are utilized in the production of revenue. The accrual basis is required of those businesses in which production, purchases, and sales of merchandise are significant factors. Under these circumstances, the Internal Revenue Code requirement that the accrual basis be used follows generally accepted accounting principles. The sales and cost-of-goods-sold figures are typically calculated by the accrual basis. Thus, since a significant difference could result from the use of the cash basis as compared with the accrual basis under the circumstances described above, the Internal Revenue Code specifies the use of the accrual basis as the generally accepted method. Any taxpayer (other than a person whose only income is salary) who maintains a set of accounting records may elect to use the accrual basis.

Individual Income Tax

The formula for computing the federal income tax (as reported on U.S. Individual Income Tax Return, Form 1040) is introduced in different steps. First, a broad general formula is presented to show the direction of the calculation. Then the formula is broken down into sections that reveal some variations in the tax formula approach of various taxpayers.

Figure A–1 shows a general formula that an individual taxpayer must use to determine the additional or net tax payable (remaining tax due) to the Internal Revenue Service or the tax refund expected because of an overpayment of taxes.

Determination of Gross Income

The various parts of this formula are now considered in more detail. Figure A–2 shows an expanded version of the first three items to determine gross income that is legally subject to the income tax.

Income Broadly Conceived A good starting point for determining income tax is to consider income in its broadest context. It would include all receipts or claims against entities for receipts arising out of an earning pro-

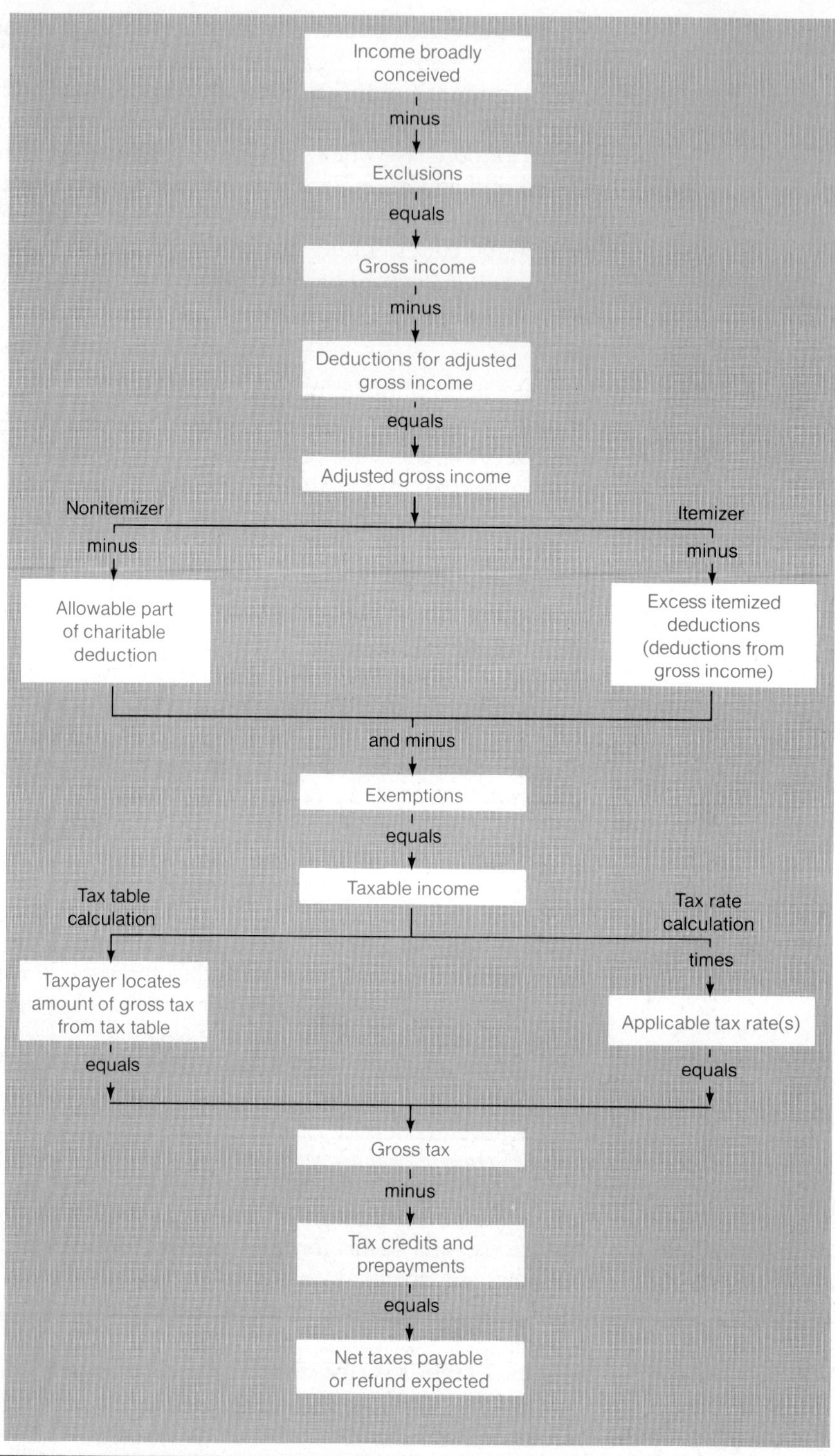

Figure A–1 General Individual Income Tax Formula

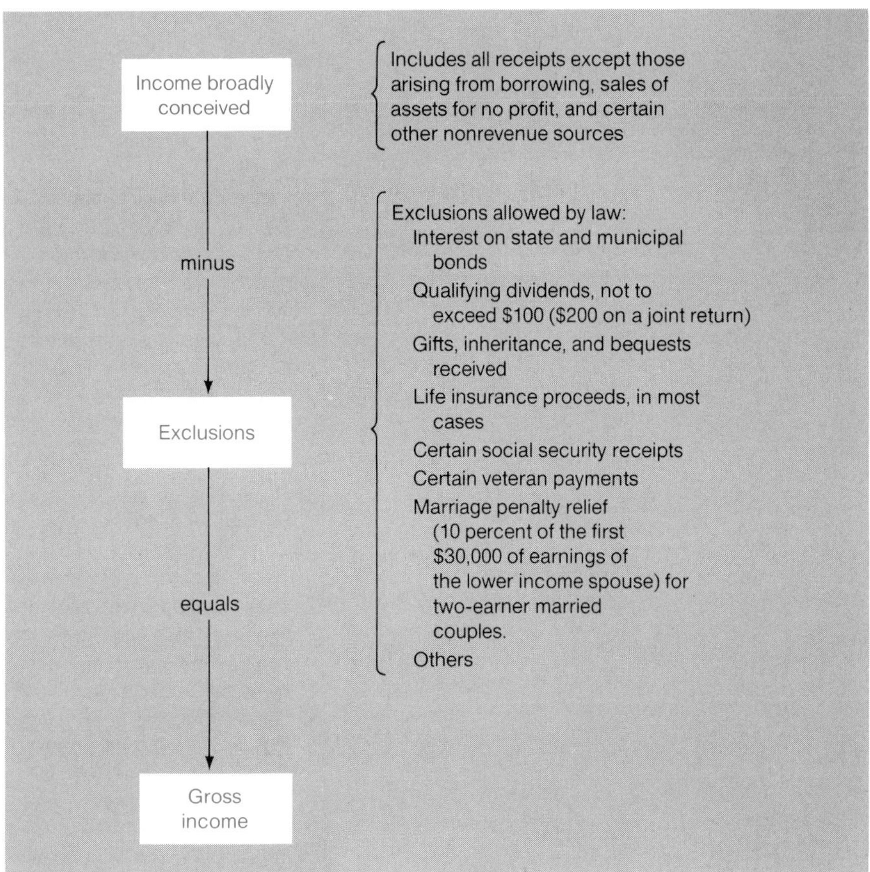

Figure A–2
Tax Formula for Determining Gross Income

cess. This excludes receipts from borrowing, the sales of assets for no profit or at a loss, the obtaining of current funds from savings sources, and other similar nonrevenue receipt sources. Some of the broadly-conceived income called exclusions, are not included in legal gross income that is subject to tax.

Exclusions Those items that do not qualify as gross income are referred to as **exclusions.** They are specifically excluded by law, Treasury regulations, or court decisions. Among others, these include the items shown in Figure A–2.

Determination of Adjusted Gross Income

Taxpayers may take different paths in the income tax calculation. The calculation is identical down through adjusted gross income. In Figure A–3, the determination of adjusted gross income subject to individual income tax is described.

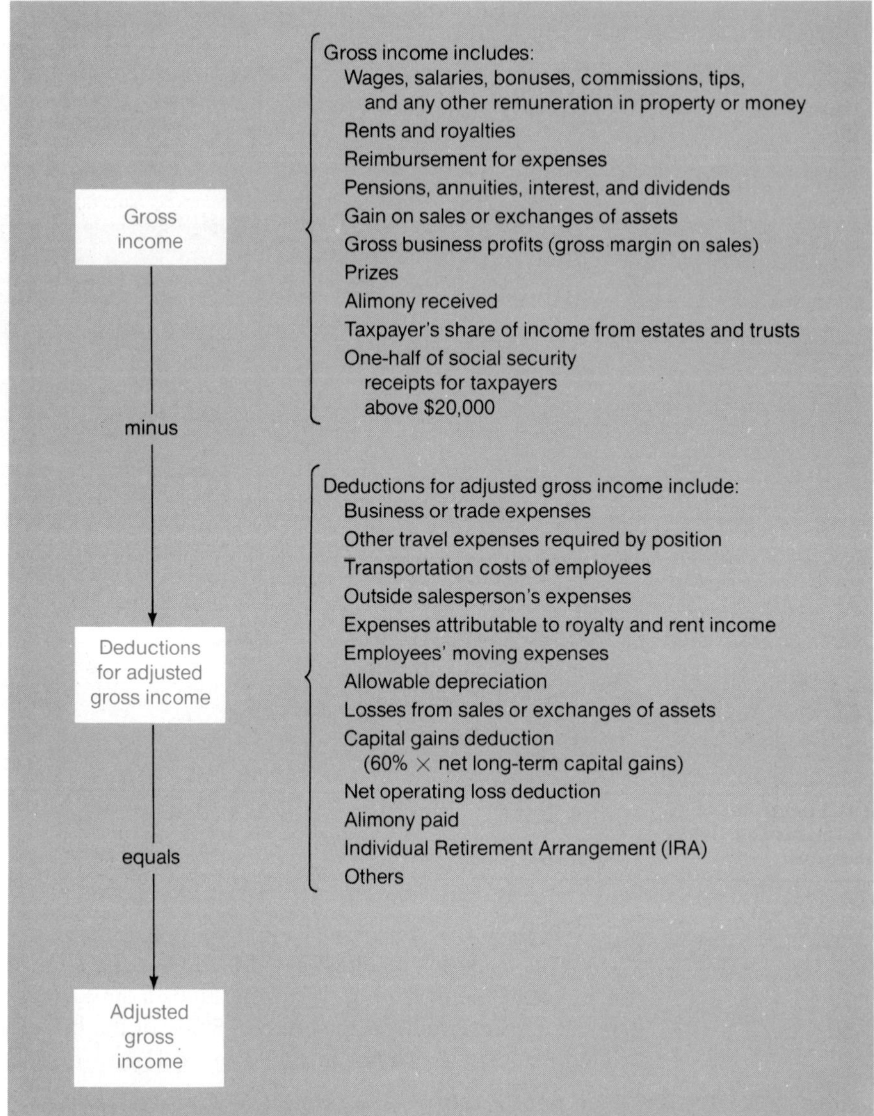

Figure A–3
Tax Formula for Adjusted Gross Income

Gross Income **Gross income** includes all regular income (revenue) not specifically excluded as such by law. Various items of income are specifically stated in the internal revenue code to clarify their status as elements of gross income (for example, wages, salaries, bonuses, commissions, tips, rents, royalties, and the other items shown in Figure A–3).

One additional item deserves brief comment. Gains from the sale of certain types of assets that are legally designated as capital assets (mainly stocks and bonds held as investments) are **capital gains.** A short-term capital gain results from the sale of a capital asset held for one year or less and is taxed as ordinary income. A long-term capital gain results from the sale of a capital asset held for more than a year. Long-term capital gains receive favorable tax treatment in that only 40 percent of the net long-term gain is subject to tax (60 percent of the gain is called a capital gains deduction).

Deductions for Adjusted Gross Income **Adjusted gross income** is the excess of gross income over deductions for adjusted gross income indicated in Figure A–3. In general, the deductions are self-explanatory. A brief word about a few is necessary. Business expenses must be ordinary recurring expired costs necessary to conduct a trade, business, or profession. In actual practice, business expenses are deducted from business revenue on a separate Schedule C to Form 1040 (which is simply an income statement—see Figure A–13). Only the net income from business is included in adjusted gross income. Employees such as salespersons and certified public accountants also may have deductible expenses that are computed on Form 2106 for deduction from gross income. Losses from sales or exchanges of capital assets qualify as **capital losses.** The allowable capital gains deduction is 60 percent of the net long-term capital gains.

A special type of deduction for adjusted gross income is contributions to an Individual Retirement Arrangement (IRA). Persons who do not participate in a retirement plan other than Social Security may pay a certain percentage of annual earnings into an individual retirement account (including bonds and annuities). This provision was liberalized by the *Economic Recovery Tax Act of 1981.* Even if already in a retirement plan, a taxpayer may set aside $2,000 per year ($2,250 if married to a nonworking spouse) in an IRA. Such amounts are deducted from the current year's tax return. Payments to an IRA provide for annuities that are paid to the taxpayers beginning as early as age 59½. All such annuity payments received by the taxpayer are part of taxable income; since they are normally received after retirement, he or she would expect to be in a lower tax bracket.

A Generalized Approach for the Determination of Income Tax

Figure A–4 shows an expanded version of that part of the tax formula from adjusted gross income to taxable income. The tax tables and tax rate schedules contain standard deductions called zero bracket amounts for certain personal deductions. However, if a filer (either a single taxpayer or married taxpayers filing a tax return) has enough allowable personal deductions, it is advantageous to itemize them (list and deduct them individually). A taxpayer who itemizes allowable personal deductions is an **itemizer taxpayer;** one who does not is a **nonitemizer taxpayer.** Under the *Economic Recovery Tax Act of 1981,* nonitemizer filers are allowed to deduct a limited amount of their charitable contributions from adjusted gross income—this is illustrated after the discussion of the itemized personal deduction for contributions.

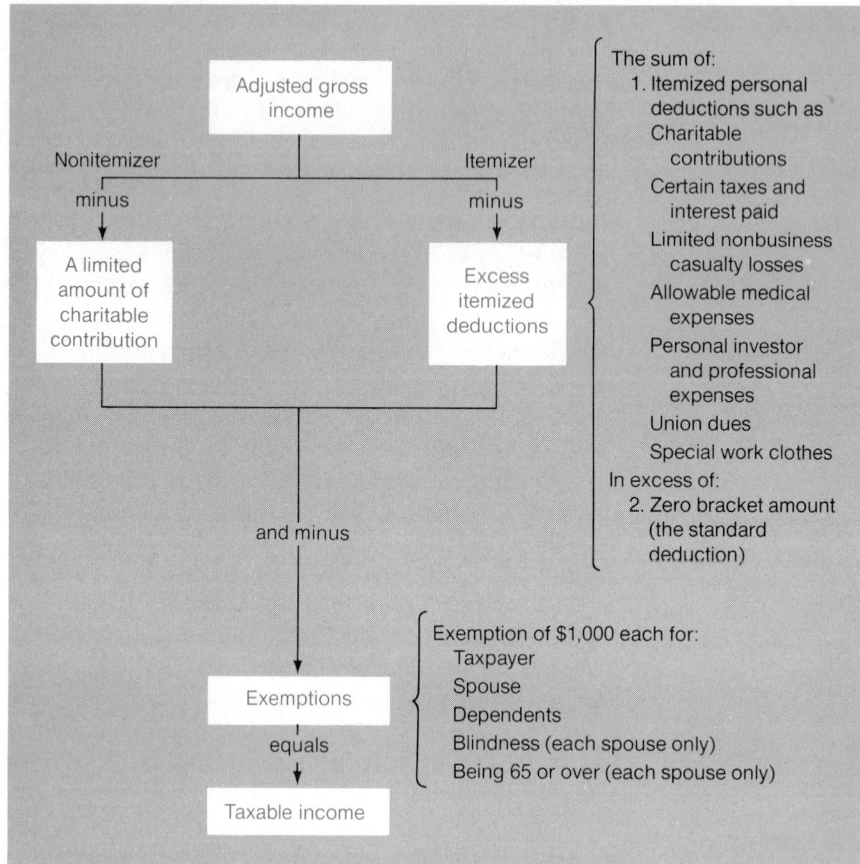

Figure A–4 Expanded Part of Tax Formula: Adjusted Gross Income to Taxable Income

Zero Bracket Amount

The Internal Revenue Code provides zero bracket amounts; for 1983, these are as follows:

Zero Bracket Amount (Flat Standard Deduction)	Applicable to Following Taxpayers
$3,400	Married persons filing joint returns and certain qualifying surviving spouses who are allowed to file joint returns
1,700	Married persons filing separate returns
2,300	Single persons and heads of households

The zero bracket amounts appear as the lowest tax brackets (at zero tax rate) in the tax rate schedules (see Figure A–9) and are incorporated in the tax table (see Figure A–5 for a page of the tax table using 1982 tax rates). They apply to both itemizer and nonitemizer taxpayers. Itemizer taxpayers whose itemized deductions exceed the zero bracket amount may deduct only their

excess itemized deductions, that is, the excess of the itemized allowable personal deductions over the zero bracket amount.

Personal Deductions

Some of the main allowable itemized personal deductions for itemized returns are shown in Figure A–4. Many of these have restrictions and limits that are examined in more detail.

For an *itemizer taxpayer,* allowable **contributions** to recognized charitable, religious, and educational organizations are limited to a percentage that may vary from 20 to 50 percent of adjusted gross income. An itemizer may deduct contributions up to 50 percent of adjusted gross income actually paid to religious, educational, Community Chest, and other charitable organizations that derive their funds from the general public. Deductions for contributions to certain other charities—particularly private foundations—may under certain conditions be limited to 20 percent of adjusted gross income.

The *Economic Recovery Act of 1981* liberalized the contribution deduction available to *nonitemizer taxpayers* by providing for a special deduction of a limited amount of their allowable charitable contributions. For 1983 and 1984, a deduction is allowed for 25 percent of allowable contributions, with a maximum deduction of $25 for 1983 and $75 for 1984. For 1985, 50 percent of all allowable contributions will be deductible; in 1986, 100 percent will be deductible. Note, however, that this law applies only to the years through 1986. Unless extended, this relief provision for nonitemizers will not apply to 1987 and future years.

To illustrate, suppose in 1983 a nonitemizer had only one contribution, $200 to a church. Then this taxpayer could deduct the lower of $50 = (25% × $200) or $25 (the maximum limit). The deduction would be $25.

Deductible Taxes Taxes that may be deducted in calculating the federal income tax fall into five general categories: state and local income taxes, real estate taxes, general sales taxes, personal property taxes (including intangible property tax), and a few other specialized taxes. Gasoline taxes and license plate fees are not allowable itemized personal deductions but may be deducted as business expenses if incurred in operating a business.

Nonbusiness Casualty Losses These may also be itemized on Schedule A to Form 1040. A portion of large casualty losses not compensated by insurance, such as damage done by storms or wrecks, is deductible. Starting in 1983, the amount allowable is determined in a two-step calculation:

(1) The gross loss for each casualty is the amount that exceeds $100.

(2) Then the gross casualty losses are aggregated, and the deductible portion is the amount that exceeds 10 percent of adjusted gross income.

To illustrate, assume that a taxpayer in 1983 with an adjusted gross of $20,000 has two casualty losses: (1) uninsured fire loss of $2,100, and (2) uninsured theft of $900. The deductible portion of the casualty loss is calculated as follows:

Deductible casualty losses:		
Gross casualty losses:		
Uninsured fire loss	$2,100	
Deduct	100	$2,000
Uninsured theft	$ 900	
Deduct	100	800
Gross casualty losses		$2,800
Deduct: 10% × $20,000		2,000
Deductible casualty losses		$ 800

Gross Medical and Dental Expenses These include doctor, hospital, and dental fees; in 1983 the amount paid for drugs and medicines in excess of one percent of adjusted gross income (included in the law to eliminate the ordinary cost of most nonprescription drugs); travel to receive medical treatment; and medical and hospital insurance. For 1984 and future years, the one percent limitation on drugs and medicines is eliminated, and the definition of drugs and medicines includes only prescription drugs and insulin.

Deductible Medical and Dental Expenses These consist of the allowable portion of medicines and drugs, medical and hospital insurance, and the amount of medical and dental expenses in excess of 5 percent of adjusted gross income, with no maximum limit (the 5 percent limit started in 1983).[2] The computation of itemized deductible medical expenses for a taxpayer filing a return in 1983 with an adjusted gross income of $20,000 is illustrated below.

Deductible medical and drug expenses:		
Gross medical and dental expenses:		
Insurance premium		$ 210
Medicines and drugs	$310	
Deduct: 1% of AGI[a] of $20,000	200	
Medicines and drugs includable in gross medical expenses		110
Other medical, dental, and hospital expenses		1,800
Gross medical and dental expenses		$2,120
Deduct: 5% of AGI of $20,000		1,000
Deductible medical and dental expenses		$1,120

[a]AGI = Adjusted gross income. This 1 percent limit would not apply to 1984 taxpayers.

[2]The limit for 1982 was 3 percent.

Miscellaneous Personal Deductions These include: (1) various *employee expenses* such as union dues, safety equipment, protective clothing, and dues to professional organizations, and (2) *expenses of producing income* such as tax return preparation fee, safe deposit box rental, and clerical help.

An itemizer taxpayer adds the allowable personal deductions on Schedule A to Form 1040; then subtracts the applicable zero bracket amount (the flat standard deduction built into the table and rate structure) to determine the amount deductible in calculating income before exemptions. A nonitemizer taxpayer deducts only the special allowable amount of charitable contributions to determine the income before exemptions.

Exemptions

A personal **exemption** of $1,000 is allowed for the taxpayer, for the spouse if a joint return is filed, and for each person who qualifies as a dependent of the taxpayer. Additional exemptions may be claimed if the taxpayer or spouse is blind and if either is 65 years or over.

Under the law, a **dependent** is a person who receives over one-half of his or her support from the taxpayer; who is closely related to the taxpayer or lives in the taxpayer's home; who has received less than $1,000 in gross income during the year (unless the dependent is a child of the taxpayer under 19 years old or a full-time student); and who has not filed a joint return.[3] The calculation of taxable income for both a nonitemizer and an itemizer is illustrated below.

Example 1: A Nonitemizer Taxpayer Edward Brummet, an unmarried taxpayer, age 41, has an adjusted gross income of $50,500 for 1983. His personal deductions total $2,000 for the year, which include a contribution to his church of $300. He therefore does not itemize the personal deductions because they are less than $2,300, the zero bracket amount for a single taxpayer. Brummet is allowed the special charitable contribution deduction of $25 in 1983 = (lower of 25% × $300 or $25). Assuming Brummet is eligible for only one exemption, his taxable income is $49,475, calculated as follows:

Adjusted gross income	$50,500
Deduct: Special charitable contribution deduction	25
Taxable income before exemption	$50,475
Deduct: Exemption; 1 × $1,000	1,000
Taxable income	$49,475

[3]Full-time students may claim an exemption for themselves on their own tax return. In addition, their parents may also claim them as an exemption if the parent has provided more than one-half the students' support.

Example 2: An Itemizer Taxpayer Nancy Strubhart, who is single, age 28, had an adjusted gross income of $70,000 for 1983. Her itemized deductions for the year totaled $6,000. She would compute her taxable income as follows:

Adjusted gross income		$70,000
Deduct: Excess itemized deductions:		
Total itemized deductions	$6,000	
Deduct: Zero bracket amount	2,300	3,700
Taxable income before exemptions		$66,300
Deduct: Exemption: 1 × $1,000		1,000
Taxable income		$65,300

Because the zero bracket amount is built into the tax rate schedule and table, a taxpayer must reduce the total amount of the itemized deductions by the amount of the applicable zero bracket amount and then subtract the remaining excess itemized deductions from the adjusted gross income. The exemptions are then deducted to determine taxable income. The zero bracket amount and the method of determining the amount of tax depends upon the filing status of the taxpayer, discussed next.

Filing Status of Taxpayers

The rates that are built into the tax table (see Figure A–5) or the tax rate schedules (see Figure A–9) depend upon the filing status of taxpayers. Different tax rates apply to (1) a single person who does not qualify as a head of household, (2) an individual who does qualify as head of household, (3) a married couple filing a joint return, and (4) married taxpayers filing separate returns. Federal income tax rates are *progressive;* that is, taxpayers with the lowest taxable incomes are taxed at the lowest rate, and those with larger incomes at progressively higher rates.

The separate tax schedule for married taxpayers filing a joint return is designed to eliminate tax inequity arising from differences in state laws. Some states have community property laws that permit married couples to divide gross income, and some do not. Marital status is determined as of December 31 of a given taxable year. For example, a couple that married on December 31, 1983, would qualify to file a joint return for 1983.

The special tax rates applicable to single heads of households provide partial compensation for the additional family burden. Persons who qualify as a **head of household** must be (1) unmarried (or separated) at the end of the taxable year, or (2) married at the end of the year to an individual who was a nonresident alien at any time during the taxable year. Heads of households must also have paid more than half the cost of maintaining a principal home for the entire year for certain specified dependents.

Figure A–5
Last Page of 1982 Tax Table

1982 Tax Table (Continued)

If line 37 (taxable income) is—		And you are—				If line 37 (taxable income) is—		And you are—				If line 37 (taxable income) is—		And you are—			
At least	But less than	Single	Married filing jointly *	Married filing separately	Head of a household	At least	But less than	Single	Married filing jointly *	Married filing separately	Head of a household	At least	But less than	Single	Married filing jointly *	Married filing separately	Head of a household
		Your tax is—						Your tax is—						Your tax is—			
41,000						**44,000**						**47,000**					
41,000	41,050	11,859	9,595	14,255	10,991	44,000	44,050	13,331	10,765	15,737	12,221	47,000	47,050	14,831	11,996	17,237	13,637
41,050	41,100	11,881	9,614	14,279	11,012	44,050	44,100	13,356	10,784	15,762	12,242	47,050	47,100	14,856	12,018	17,262	13,662
41,100	41,150	11,903	9,634	14,304	11,032	44,100	44,150	13,381	10,804	15,787	12,262	47,100	47,150	14,881	12,040	17,287	13,686
41,150	41,200	11,925	9,653	14,328	11,053	44,150	44,200	13,406	10,823	15,812	12,283	47,150	47,200	14,906	12,062	17,312	13,711
41,200	41,250	11,947	9,673	14,353	11,073	44,200	44,250	13,431	10,843	15,837	12,303	47,200	47,250	14,931	12,084	17,337	13,735
41,250	41,300	11,969	9,692	14,377	11,094	44,250	44,300	13,456	10,862	15,862	12,324	47,250	47,300	14,956	12,106	17,362	13,760
41,300	41,350	11,991	9,712	14,402	11,114	44,300	44,350	13,481	10,882	15,887	12,344	47,300	47,350	14,981	12,128	17,387	13,784
41,350	41,400	12,013	9,731	14,426	11,135	44,350	44,400	13,506	10,901	15,912	12,365	47,350	47,400	15,006	12,150	17,412	13,809
41,400	41,450	12,035	9,751	14,451	11,155	44,400	44,450	13,531	10,921	15,937	12,385	47,400	47,450	15,031	12,172	17,437	13,833
41,450	41,500	12,057	9,770	14,475	11,176	44,450	44,500	13,556	10,940	15,962	12,406	47,450	47,500	15,056	12,194	17,462	13,858
41,500	41,550	12,081	9,790	14,500	11,196	44,500	44,550	13,581	10,960	15,987	12,426	47,500	47,550	15,081	12,216	17,487	13,882
41,550	41,600	12,106	9,809	14,524	11,217	44,550	44,600	13,606	10,979	16,012	12,447	47,550	47,600	15,106	12,238	17,512	13,907
41,600	41,650	12,131	9,829	14,549	11,237	44,600	44,650	13,631	10,999	16,037	12,467	47,600	47,650	15,131	12,260	17,537	13,931
41,650	41,700	12,156	9,848	14,573	11,258	44,650	44,700	13,656	11,018	16,062	12,488	47,650	47,700	15,156	12,282	17,562	13,956
41,700	41,750	12,181	9,868	14,598	11,278	44,700	44,750	13,681	11,038	16,087	12,510	47,700	47,750	15,181	12,304	17,587	13,980
41,750	41,800	12,206	9,887	14,622	11,299	44,750	44,800	13,706	11,057	16,112	12,535	47,750	47,800	15,206	12,326	17,612	14,005
41,800	41,850	12,231	9,907	14,647	11,319	44,800	44,850	13,731	11,077	16,137	12,559	47,800	47,850	15,231	12,348	17,637	14,029
41,850	41,900	12,256	9,926	14,671	11,340	44,850	44,900	13,756	11,096	16,162	12,584	47,850	47,900	15,256	12,370	17,662	14,054
41,900	41,950	12,281	9,946	14,696	11,360	44,900	44,950	13,781	11,116	16,187	12,608	47,900	47,950	15,281	12,392	17,687	14,078
41,950	42,000	12,306	9,965	14,720	11,381	44,950	45,000	13,806	11,135	16,212	12,633	47,950	48,000	15,306	12,414	17,712	14,103
42,000						**45,000**						**48,000**					
42,000	42,050	12,331	9,985	14,745	11,401	45,000	45,050	13,831	11,155	16,237	12,657	48,000	48,050	15,331	12,436	17,737	14,127
42,050	42,100	12,356	10,004	14,769	11,422	45,050	45,100	13,856	11,174	16,262	12,682	48,050	48,100	15,356	12,458	17,762	14,152
42,100	42,150	12,381	10,024	14,794	11,442	45,100	45,150	13,881	11,194	16,287	12,706	48,100	48,150	15,381	12,480	17,787	14,176
42,150	42,200	12,406	10,043	14,818	11,463	45,150	45,200	13,906	11,213	16,312	12,731	48,150	48,200	15,406	12,502	17,812	14,201
42,200	42,250	12,431	10,063	14,843	11,483	45,200	45,250	13,931	11,233	16,337	12,755	48,200	48,250	15,431	12,524	17,837	14,225
42,250	42,300	12,456	10,082	14,867	11,504	45,250	45,300	13,956	11,252	16,362	12,780	48,250	48,300	15,456	12,546	17,862	14,250
42,300	42,350	12,481	10,102	14,892	11,524	45,300	45,350	13,981	11,272	16,387	12,804	48,300	48,350	15,481	12,568	17,887	14,274
42,350	42,400	12,506	10,121	14,916	11,545	45,350	45,400	14,006	11,291	16,412	12,829	48,350	48,400	15,506	12,590	17,912	14,299
42,400	42,450	12,531	10,141	14,941	11,565	45,400	45,450	14,031	11,311	16,437	12,853	48,400	48,450	15,531	12,612	17,937	14,323
42,450	42,500	12,556	10,160	14,965	11,586	45,450	45,500	14,056	11,330	16,462	12,878	48,450	48,500	15,556	12,634	17,962	14,348
42,500	42,550	12,581	10,180	14,990	11,606	45,500	45,550	14,081	11,350	16,487	12,902	48,500	48,550	15,581	12,656	17,987	14,372
42,550	42,600	12,606	10,199	15,014	11,627	45,550	45,600	14,106	11,369	16,512	12,927	48,550	48,600	15,606	12,678	18,012	14,397
42,600	42,650	12,631	10,219	15,039	11,647	45,600	45,650	14,131	11,389	16,537	12,951	48,600	48,650	15,631	12,700	18,037	14,421
42,650	42,700	12,656	10,238	15,063	11,668	45,650	45,700	14,156	11,408	16,562	12,976	48,650	48,700	15,656	12,722	18,062	14,446
42,700	42,750	12,681	10,258	15,088	11,688	45,700	45,750	14,181	11,428	16,587	13,000	48,700	48,750	15,681	12,744	18,087	14,470
42,750	42,800	12,706	10,277	15,112	11,709	45,750	45,800	14,206	11,447	16,612	13,025	48,750	48,800	15,706	12,766	18,112	14,495
42,800	42,850	12,731	10,297	15,137	11,729	45,800	45,850	14,231	11,468	16,637	13,049	48,800	48,850	15,731	12,788	18,137	14,519
42,850	42,900	12,756	10,316	15,162	11,750	45,850	45,900	14,256	11,490	16,662	13,074	48,850	48,900	15,756	12,810	18,162	14,544
42,900	42,950	12,781	10,336	15,187	11,770	45,900	45,950	14,281	11,512	16,687	13,098	48,900	48,950	15,781	12,832	18,187	14,568
42,950	43,000	12,806	10,355	15,212	11,791	45,950	46,000	14,306	11,534	16,712	13,123	48,950	49,000	15,806	12,854	18,212	14,593
43,000						**46,000**						**49,000**					
43,000	43,050	12,831	10,375	15,237	11,811	46,000	46,050	14,331	11,556	16,737	13,147	49,000	49,050	15,831	12,876	18,237	14,617
43,050	43,100	12,856	10,394	15,262	11,832	46,050	46,100	14,356	11,578	16,762	13,172	49,050	49,100	15,856	12,898	18,262	14,642
43,100	43,150	12,881	10,414	15,287	11,852	46,100	46,150	14,381	11,600	16,787	13,196	49,100	49,150	15,881	12,920	18,287	14,666
43,150	43,200	12,906	10,433	15,312	11,873	46,150	46,200	14,406	11,622	16,812	13,221	49,150	49,200	15,906	12,942	18,312	14,691
43,200	43,250	12,931	10,453	15,337	11,893	46,200	46,250	14,431	11,644	16,837	13,245	49,200	49,250	15,931	12,964	18,337	14,715
43,250	43,300	12,956	10,472	15,362	11,914	46,250	46,300	14,456	11,666	16,862	13,270	49,250	49,300	15,956	12,986	18,362	14,740
43,300	43,350	12,981	10,492	15,387	11,934	46,300	46,350	14,481	11,688	16,887	13,294	49,300	49,350	15,981	13,008	18,387	14,764
43,350	43,400	13,006	10,511	15,412	11,955	46,350	46,400	14,506	11,710	16,912	13,319	49,350	49,400	16,006	13,030	18,412	14,789
43,400	43,450	13,031	10,531	15,437	11,975	46,400	46,450	14,531	11,732	16,937	13,343	49,400	49,450	16,031	13,052	18,437	14,813
43,450	43,500	13,056	10,550	15,462	11,996	46,450	46,500	14,556	11,754	16,962	13,368	49,450	49,500	16,056	13,074	18,462	14,838
43,500	43,550	13,081	10,570	15,487	12,016	46,500	46,550	14,581	11,776	16,987	13,392	49,500	49,550	16,081	13,096	18,487	14,862
43,550	43,600	13,106	10,589	15,512	12,037	46,550	46,600	14,606	11,798	17,012	13,417	49,550	49,600	16,106	13,118	18,512	14,887
43,600	43,650	13,131	10,609	15,537	12,057	46,600	46,650	14,631	11,820	17,037	13,441	49,600	49,650	16,131	13,140	18,537	14,911
43,650	43,700	13,156	10,628	15,562	12,078	46,650	46,700	14,656	11,842	17,062	13,466	49,650	49,700	16,156	13,162	18,562	14,936
43,700	43,750	13,181	10,648	15,587	12,098	46,700	46,750	14,681	11,864	17,087	13,490	49,700	49,750	16,181	13,184	18,587	14,960
43,750	43,800	13,206	10,667	15,612	12,119	46,750	46,800	14,706	11,886	17,112	13,515	49,750	49,800	16,206	13,206	18,612	14,985
43,800	43,850	13,231	10,687	15,637	12,139	46,800	46,850	14,731	11,908	17,137	13,539	49,800	49,850	16,231	13,228	18,637	15,009
43,850	43,900	13,256	10,706	15,662	12,160	46,850	46,900	14,756	11,930	17,162	13,564	49,850	49,900	16,256	13,250	18,662	15,034
43,900	43,950	13,281	10,726	15,687	12,180	46,900	46,950	14,781	11,952	17,187	13,588	49,900	49,950	16,281	13,272	18,687	15,058
43,950	44,000	13,306	10,745	15,712	12,201	46,950	47,000	14,806	11,974	17,212	13,613	49,950	50,000	16,306	13,294	18,712	15,083

*This column must also be used by a qualifying widow(er).

50,000 or over—use tax rate schedules

Taxpayers Required to Use Tax Table

Filers with a taxable income of $50,000 or less must calculate their tax by the use of a tax table. This tax table, prepared by the Internal Revenue Service, incorporates the zero bracket amounts (the flat standard deduction) and the tax on taxable income of various brackets for each filing status. Figure A–5 shows the last page of the tax table for 1982 for taxable income of $41,000 to $50,000. The *Economic Recovery Tax Act of 1981* provides for a reduction of taxes in 1983 and 1984. The taxable amounts specified in Fgure A–5 should be slightly lower for 1983 and 1984 unless the law is changed. The tax table cannot be used by certain taxpayers—for example, an estate or trust, or those who use income averaging. The generalized approach for a taxpayer who must use the tax table is shown in Figure A–6.

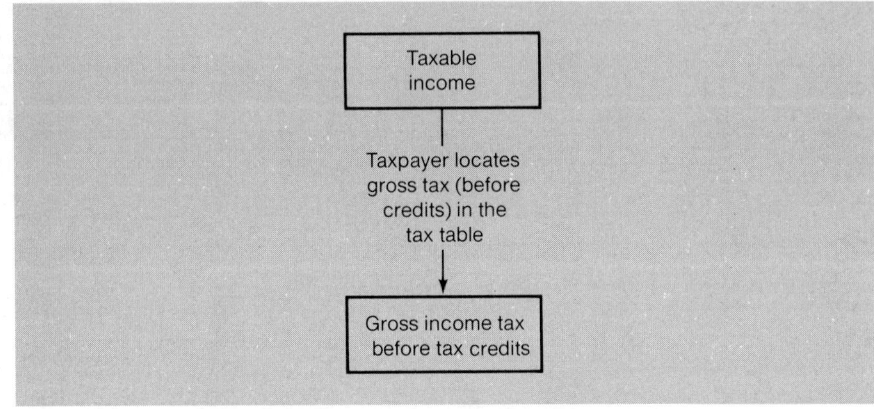

Figure A–6 Generalized Tax Table Approach

Figure A–7 illustrates the tax amounts as found in the tax table for 1982.

Figure A–7 Gross Income Tax before Tax Credits, Determined from Tax Table

Filing Status of Taxpayer	Amount of Taxable Income	Gross Income Tax
Single taxpayer	$41,510	$12,081
Married filing jointly	42,215	10,063
Married filing separately	41,020	14,255
Head of household	47,030	13,637

For a taxpayer who has only a salary and a few charitable contributions, the taxable income can be determined in two or three simple calculations. Then the gross tax before tax credits can be determined from the tax table in the column under the appropriate filing status.

Taxpayers Required to Use Tax Rate Schedules

As shown in Figure A–8, a slight variation in the tax calculation must be made if the taxable income of the filer is $50,000 or more. Separate tax rate schedules are provided for the four types of filers indicated in Figure A–8. Figure A–9 shows the projected rates applicable to these filers for the years 1983 and 1984. The tax rate in each of these schedules ranges from a low of 11

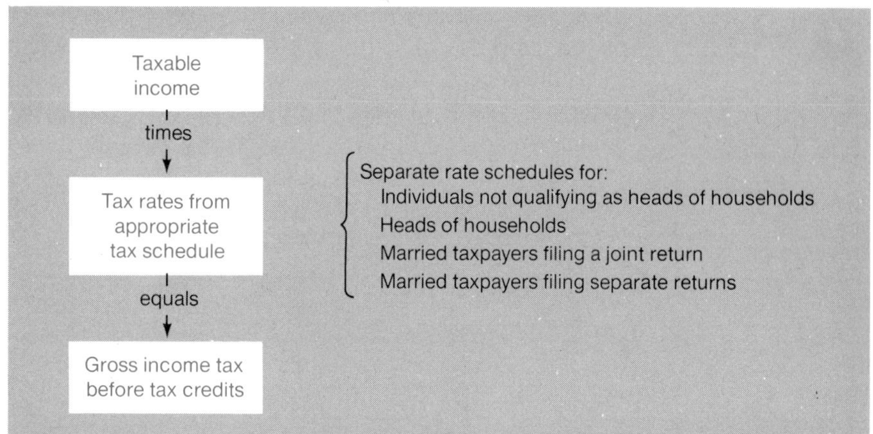

Figure A–8 Generalized Tax Rate Schedules Approach

Schedule 1
Tax Rate Schedules for Married Individuals Filing Joint Returns and Surviving Spouses

Taxable Income	1982 Tax	1982 % on Excess	1983 Tax	1983 % on Excess	1984 Tax	1984 % on Excess
$0–3,400	$ 0	0	$ 0	0	$ 0	0
Over $ 3,400	0	12	0	11	0	11
5,500	252	14	231	13	231	12
7,600	546	16	504	15	483	14
11,900	1,234	19	1,149	17	1,085	16
16,000	2,013	22	1,846	19	1,741	18
20,200	2,937	25	2,644	23	2,497	22
24,600	4,037	29	3,656	26	3,465	25
29,900	5,574	33	5,034	30	4,790	28
35,200	7,323	39	6,624	35	6,274	33
45,800	11,457	44	10,334	40	9,772	38
60,000	17,705	49	16,014	44	15,168	42
85,600	30,249	50	27,278	48	25,920	45
109,400	42,149	50	38,702	50	36,630	49
162,400	68,649	50	65,202	50	62,600	50
215,400	95,149	50	91,702	50	89,100	50

Schedule 2
Tax Rate Schedules for Married Individuals Filing Separate Returns

Taxable Income	1982 Tax	1982 % on Excess	1983 Tax	1983 % on Excess	1984 Tax	1984 % on Excess
$0–1,700	$ 0	0	$ 0	0	$ 0	0
Over $ 1,700	0	12	0	11	0	11
2,750	126	14	115	13	115	12
3,800	273	16	252	15	241	14
5,950	617	19	574	17	542	16
8,000	1,006	22	923	19	870	18
10,100	1,468	25	1,322	23	1,248	22
12,300	2,018	29	1,828	26	1,732	25
14,950	2,787	33	2,517	30	2,395	28
17,600	3,661	39	3,312	35	3,137	33
22,900	5,728	44	5,167	40	4,886	38
30,000	8,852	49	8,007	44	7,584	42
42,800	15,124	50	13,639	48	12,960	45
54,700	21,074	50	19,351	50	18,315	49
81,200	34,324	50	32,601	50	31,300	50
107,700	47,574	50	45,851	50	44,550	50

Schedule 3
Tax Rate Schedules for Single Individuals

Taxable Income	1982 Tax	1982 % on Excess	1983 Tax	1983 % on Excess	1984 Tax	1984 % on Excess
$0–2,300	$ 0	0	$ 0	0	$ 0	0
Over $ 2,300	0	12	0	11	0	11
3,400	132	14	121	13	121	12
4,400	272	16	251	15	241	14
6,500	608	17	566	15	535	15
8,500	948	19	866	17	835	16
10,800	1,385	22	1,257	19	1,203	18
12,900	1,847	23	1,656	21	1,581	20
15,000	2,330	27	2,097	24	2,001	23
18,200	3,194	31	2,865	28	2,737	26
23,500	4,837	35	4,349	32	4,115	30
28,800	6,692	40	6,045	36	5,705	34
34,100	8,812	44	7,953	40	7,507	38
41,500	12,068	50	10,913	45	10,319	42
55,300	18,968	50	17,123	50	16,115	48
81,800	32,218	50	30,373	50	28,835	50
108,300	45,468	50	43,623	50	42,085	50

Schedule 4
Tax Rate Schedules for Heads of Households

Taxable Income	1982 Tax	1982 % on Excess	1983 Tax	1983 % on Excess	1984 Tax	1984 % on Excess
$0–2,300	$ 0	0	$ 0	0	$ 0	0
Over $ 2,300	0	12	0	11	0	11
4,400	252	14	231	13	231	12
6,500	546	16	504	15	483	14
8,700	898	20	834	18	791	17
11,800	1,518	22	1,392	19	1,318	18
15,000	2,222	23	2,000	21	1,894	20
18,200	2,958	28	2,672	25	2,534	24
23,500	4,442	32	3,997	29	3,806	28
28,800	6,138	38	5,534	34	5,290	32
34,100	8,152	41	7,336	37	6,986	35
44,700	12,498	49	11,258	44	10,696	42
60,600	20,289	50	18,254	48	17,374	45
81,800	30,889	50	28,430	50	26,914	48
108,300	44,139	50	41,680	50	39,634	50
161,300	70,639	50	68,180	50	66,134	50

Figure A–9 Tax Rate Schedules for Four Types of Filers

percent to a high of 50 percent. The *Economic Recovery Tax Act of 1981* placed a top rate of 50 percent on taxable income regardless of source.

To illustrate how to use the tax rate schedules, assume that a single taxpayer has taxable income of $57,300 in 1983. The gross income tax before tax credits would be $18,123, calculated as follows:

Tax on first $55,300 (from rate schedule 3)	$17,123
Tax on next $2,000 at 50%	1,000
Gross income tax before tax credits	$18,123

Next, assume that Harold and Rose Brooks, a married couple, file a joint return for their taxable income of $88,600 in 1983. Their gross income tax before tax credits would be $28,718, calculated as follows:

Tax on first $85,600 (from rate schedule 1)	$27,278
Tax on next $3,000 at 48%	1,440
Gross income tax before tax credits	$28,718

Calculation of Remaining Income Tax Due or Refund Expected

After the gross income tax before tax credits is determined, additional steps must be taken to determine whether any remaining tax is due or whether a refund is expected. Figure A–10 shows in the income tax model the steps that individuals must take to complete the requirements for filing Form 1040 (and appropriate schedules to Form 1040). The next step is to determine whether a filer has any available income tax credits.

Tax Credits Certain special **tax credits** may be deducted from the gross income tax in computing the amount of the net tax liability currently outstanding. Tax credits are typically allowed for the items discussed below.[4]

Credit for the Elderly This credit was previously called retirement income credit. Elderly persons who are now receiving qualifying retirement pay and those who meet an earnings test and receive primarily rents, interest, and dividends are entitled to a tax credit. The amount of this tax credit has been changed frequently by Congress. It also depends upon the taxpayer's adjusted gross income and Social Security income.

[4]The credits against the income tax are changed frequently by Congress. The ones listed here are the ones applicable to 1983 income taxes.

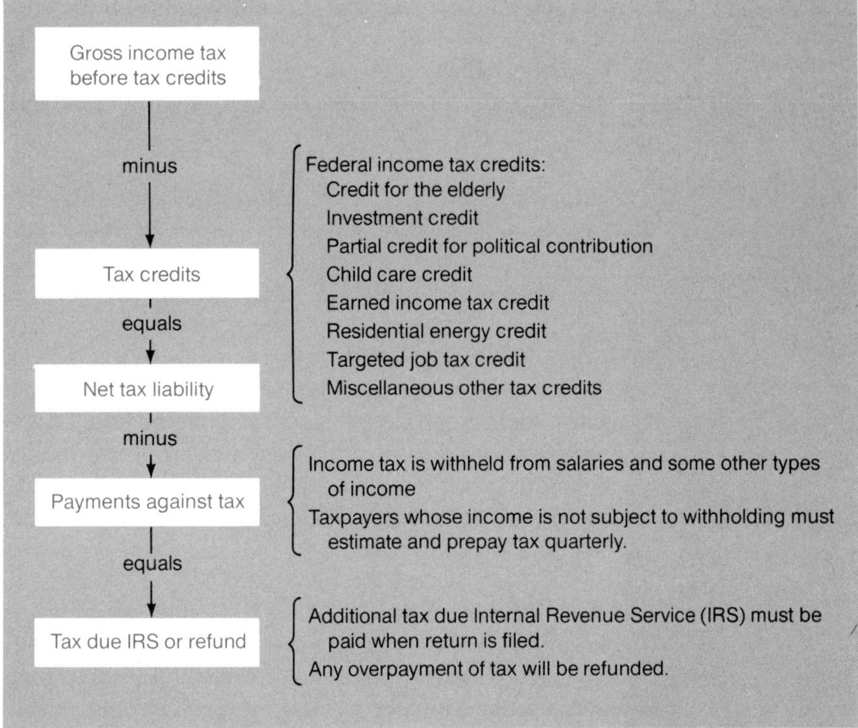

Figure A–10 Remaining Steps Necessary to Complete the Income Tax Model

Investment Credit In conjunction with the Accelerated Cost Recovery System (see Chapter 13), the law allows an investment credit for qualifying business equipment purchased in a given year. The credit is six percent of cost of property in the 3-year class and ten percent of property in other classes. It is granted to encourage businesses to keep their plants up-to-date.

Credit for Political Contributions A tax credit amounting to one-half a taxpayer's actual political contributions, subject to a maximum limitation, is allowed. A number of stipulations govern this tax credit.

Child and Dependent Care Credit Within certain limitations, taxpayers who pay someone to care for their child or dependent so that they can work or look for work may take a limited amount as a credit against their tax. The amount of this credit is determined by a formula specified by the Internal Revenue Service.

Earned Income Credit The earned income credit is applicable to low-income workers who have an *earned income*—wages, salaries, and earnings from self-employment. The credit is figured on the adjusted gross income (or earned income, if greater) of amounts up to $10,000. The maximum credit is 10 percent of a worker's first $5,000, or $500. The credit is reduced by 12½ percent of any amount of earned income in excess of $6,000. This credit includes a negative income tax element.

Residential Energy Credit Since the cost of fuels has increased in recent years, Congress has provided taxpayers with a tax credit for installing energy saving items in their principal residence. Taxpayers must follow a set of specific instructions to calculate the amount of this tax credit.

Targeted Job Tax Credit Amendments to the Internal Revenue Code allow corporations and individuals and partners running a business to take a credit against their gross income tax of a limited amount for wages paid to new employees hired from certain groups (primarily disadvantaged workers). A maximum credit for each new employee is stipulated. These acts also specify a bonus credit for hiring handicapped individuals referred through vocational rehabilitation programs.

Miscellaneous Tax Credits A few other tax credits are allowed. For example, credits are allowed for taxes paid to foreign countries on income that is also taxed by the United States, for alcohol used as fuel, and for certain other energy-saving activities.

Calculation of Net Tax Liability and Remaining Tax Due or Refund Expected

The tax credits are totaled and then subtracted from the gross income tax. The difference is the **net tax liability.** As shown in Figure A–10, the taxpayer must subtract any prepayments to determine if additional tax is due or if a refund is forthcoming. These prepayments take two forms: (1) income taxes withheld by employers from the salaries of all employees (see Chapter 8) and possibly from certain interest and dividend payments, and (2) income tax prepaid in quarterly installments by taxpayers who have income not subject to withholding and who estimate the tax for the year.

Taxpayers whose prepayments exceed the income tax liability claim a refund. Taxpayers who owe additional tax pay the tax due.

Other Tax Considerations

Three other tax issues deserve consideration: capital gains and losses, income averaging, and indexing of tax items.

Capital Gains and Losses

As indicated earlier, gains and losses on the sale of assets legally designated as **capital assets** (stocks, bonds, family residences, household furnishings, automobiles, coin or stamp collections, and certain other personal assets) are classified as **capital gains and losses.** *Short-term capital gains and losses* result from the sale of capital assets held for one year or less; *long-term capital gains and losses* from the sale of those held more than one year.

Short-term capital gains are included at 100 percent in adjusted gross income and are taxed as ordinary income items. Only 40 percent of net long-term gains is included in adjusted gross income. Therefore, the maximum tax rate that could apply to long-term capital gains is 20 percent = (40% × 50%, the top income tax rate). In computing deductible capital losses, the sum of 100 percent of short-term losses plus 50 percent of long-term losses may be deducted from other gross income up to a maximum of $3,000 ($1,500 if married and filing a separate return) or the taxable income, whichever is smaller. The unused portion of capital losses may be carried forward to future years.

Income Averaging for Individuals

Those taxpayers who have unusual fluctuations in income can use income averaging to ease the tax burden in peak income years. For example, suppose that an unmarried author who had been earning approximately $30,000 during the past four years wrote a best seller and received royalties of $100,000 in a given year. Without income averaging, this taxpayer could pay as much as 50 percent (the highest bracket rate) on part of the taxable income. A specific formula set forth in Schedule G of Form 1040 allows the taxpayer to calculate the income tax of the current year based on an average taxable income over a five-year period. *All* the income is taxable, but income averaging permits the unusual part of income to be taxed at lower rates.

Indexing of Tax Items Scheduled to Begin in 1985

Beginning in 1985, the *Economic Recovery Tax Act of 1981* provides for the following three tax formula items to be adjusted for inflation by applying to them the changes in the Consumer Price Index: (1) the individual income tax brackets, (2) the personal exemption, and (3) the zero bracket amount. This indexing should equalize the effect of inflation on the taxpayer's bracket, wherein the taxpayer is in a higher tax bracket without receiving any additional purchasing power.

Comprehensive Illustration Using Tax Forms

Many of the foregoing tax provisions are pulled together and illustrated now by the use of tax forms. Suppose that John and Jane Fallo are married and have two children—a son, John, Jr., age 4, and a daughter, Janet, age 6. Both John and Jane are under 65 and are not blind. They had the following income tax items for 1982:

Gross income:		
Salary of Jane Fallo from Orange High-Tech Company	$ 35,000	
Net income from Orange Recreation Supplier, a single proprietorship owned by John Fallo (full details itemized in next section)	177,050	
Interest received:		
From Hill City bonds	400	
From corporate industrial bonds	3,500	
Summary of business operations of Orange Recreation Supplier:		
Sales	$1,500,000	
Sales returns and allowances	6,000	
Cost of goods sold	854,000	
Depreciation using the Accelerated Cost Recovery System (ACRS)	12,000	
Advertising	5,900	
Bad debts expense	1,200	
Insurance	4,600	
Interest expense on business indebtedness	3,700	
Cost of pension and profit-sharing plans	7,500	
Rent on business property	5,900	
Supplies used	3,100	
Telephone expense	1,650	
Utilities expense	5,720	
Salaries and wages expense	411,680	
Personal items:		
Medical and dental expenses:		
Hospital insurance premiums	$ 380	
Prescription drugs and insulin	480	
All other medical and dental bills	2,600	$ 3,460
Taxes:		
State and local income tax	$ 13,140	
Real estate taxes (other than business)	2,400	
Sales taxes (personal)	710	
Personal property tax	965	$17,215
Interest expense:		
Home mortgage	$ 2,910	
Credit and charge cards	195	$ 3,105
Contributions to qualifying organizations		$20,000
Casualty or theft losses		$ 0
Miscellaneous deductions:		
Union dues	$ 310	
Tax return preparation fee	250	
Safe deposit box rent	18	$ 578
Withheld income taxes and prepayments on income taxes:		
Withheld from Jane Fallo's salary	$ 5,650	
Prepayments made by the Fallos on their estimated tax	68,000	$73,650
Income Tax Credits		$ 0
Individual contributions to IRAs		$ 4,000

The calculation of the remaining income tax due for John and Jane Fallo's joint return is shown on tax forms in Figures A–11, A–12, and A–13. Certain of the more obvious steps are not shown on the tax forms. Brief explanations are provided for certain steps.

Form **1040** Department of the Treasury—Internal Revenue Service **U.S. Individual Income Tax Return 1982** (0)

For the year January 1–December 31, 1982, or other tax year beginning , 1982, ending , 19 . OMB No. 1545-0074

Use IRS label. Otherwise, please print or type.

Your first name and initial (if joint return, also give spouse's name and initial) Last name: John and Jane Fallo — Your social security number: 123 78 4532

Present home address (Number and street, including apartment number, or rural route): 3102 Everyperson Street — Spouse's social security no.: 467 89 6543

City, town or post office, State and ZIP code: Chapel Hill, North Carolina 27514 — Your occupation ▶ Merchant — Spouse's occupation ▶ Administrative Asst.

Presidential Election Campaign ▶ Do you want $1 to go to this fund? . . . X Yes No — If joint return, does your spouse want $1 to go to this fund? . . . X Yes No — Note: Checking "Yes" will not increase your tax or reduce your refund.

For Privacy Act and Paperwork Reduction Act Notice, see Instructions.

Filing Status — Check only one box.

1 ☐ Single
2 ☒ Married filing joint return (even if only one had income)
3 ☐ Married filing separate return. Enter spouse's social security no. above and full name here ▶
4 ☐ Head of household (with qualifying person). (See page 6 of Instructions.) If the qualifying person is your unmarried child but not your dependent, enter child's name ▶
5 ☐ Qualifying widow(er) with dependent child (Year spouse died ▶ 19). (See page 6 of Instructions.)

Exemptions — Always check the box labeled Yourself. Check other boxes if they apply.

6a ☒ Yourself ☐ 65 or over ☐ Blind
b ☒ Spouse ☐ 65 or over ☐ Blind — Enter number of boxes checked on 6a and b ▶ 2
c First names of your dependent children who lived with you ▶ John, Jr. Janet — Enter number of children listed on 6c ▶ 2
d Other dependents: (1) Name (2) Relationship (3) Number of months lived in your home (4) Did dependent have income of $1,000 or more? (5) Did you provide more than one-half of dependent's support? — Enter number of other dependents ▶
e Total number of exemptions claimed . . . Add numbers entered in boxes above ▶ 4

Income — Please attach Copy B of your Forms W-2 here. If you do not have a W-2, see page 5 of Instructions. Please attach check or money order here.

Line	Description	Amount
7	Wages, salaries, tips, etc.	35,000 00
8	Interest income (attach Schedule B if over $400 or you have any All-Savers interest)	3,500 00
9a	Dividends (attach Schedule B if over $400) ______, 9b Exclusion ______	
9c	Subtract line 9b from line 9a	
10	Refunds of State and local income taxes (do not enter an amount unless you deducted those taxes in an earlier year—see page 9 of Instructions)	
11	Alimony received	
12	Business income or (loss) (attach Schedule C) ▶	177,050 00
13	Capital gain or (loss) (attach Schedule D)	
14	40% capital gain distributions not reported on line 13 (See page 9 of Instructions)	
15	Supplemental gains or (losses) (attach Form 4797)	
16	Fully taxable pensions, IRA distributions, and annuities not reported on line 17	
17a	Other pensions and annuities. Total received 17a	
17b	Taxable amount, if any, from worksheet on page 10 of Instructions	
18	Rents, royalties, partnerships, estates, trusts, etc. (attach Schedule E)	
19	Farm income or (loss) (attach Schedule F) ▶	
20a	Unemployment compensation (insurance). Total received 20a	
20b	Taxable amount, if any, from worksheet on page 10 of Instructions	
21	Other income (state nature and source—see page 10 of Instructions) ▶	
22	**Total income.** Add amounts in column for lines 7 through 21 ▶	215,550 00

Adjustments to Income (See Instructions on page 11)

Line	Description	Amount
23	Moving expense (attach Form 3903 or 3903F)	
24	Employee business expenses (attach Form 2106)	
25	Payments to an IRA. You **must** enter code from page 11 (2)	4,000 00
26	Payments to a Keogh (H.R. 10) retirement plan	
27	Penalty on early withdrawal of savings	
28	Alimony paid	
29	Deduction for a married couple when both work (attach Schedule W)	
30	Disability income exclusion (attach Form 2440)	
31	**Total adjustments.** Add lines 23 through 30 ▶	4,000 00

Adjusted Gross Income

Line	Description	Amount
32	**Adjusted gross income.** Subtract line 31 from line 22. If this line is less than $10,000, see "Earned Income Credit" (line 62) on page 15 of Instructions. If you want IRS to figure your tax, see page 3 of Instructions ▶	211,550 00

☆ U.S. GOVERNMENT PRINTING OFFICE: 1982—O—363-302 48-0627165

Figure A–11 U.S. Individual Income Return, Form 1040

Form 1040 (1982) Page **2**

Section	Line	Description			Line	Amount	
Tax Computation (See Instructions on page 12)	33	Amount from line 32 *(adjusted gross income)*			33	211,550	00
	34a	If you itemize, complete Schedule A (Form 1040) and enter the amount from Schedule A, line 30			34a	37,648	00
		Caution: If you have unearned income and can be claimed as a dependent on your parent's return, check here ▶ ☐ and see page 12 of the Instructions. Also see page 12 of the Instructions if: ● *You are married filing a separate return and your spouse itemizes deductions, OR* ● *You file Form 4563, OR* ● *You are a dual-status alien.*					
	34b	If you do not itemize, complete the worksheet on page 13. Then enter the allowable part of your charitable contributions here			34b		
	35	Subtract line 34a or 34b, whichever applies, from line 33			35	173,902	00
	36	Multiply $1,000 by the total number of exemptions claimed on Form 1040, line 6e			36	4,000	00
	37	Taxable Income. Subtract line 36 from line 35			37	169,902	00
	38	Tax. Enter tax here and check if from ☐ Tax Table, ☒ Tax Rate Schedule X, Y, or Z, or ☐ Schedule G			38	72,400	00
	39	Additional Taxes. (See page 13 of Instructions.) Enter here and check if from ☐ Form 4970, ☐ Form 4972, ☐ Form 5544, or ☐ section 72 penalty taxes			39		00
	40	**Total.** Add lines 38 and 39 ▶			40	72,400	00
Credits (See Instructions on page 13)	41	Credit for the elderly *(attach Schedules R&RP)*	41				
	42	Foreign tax credit *(attach Form 1116)*	42				
	43	Investment credit *(attach Form 3468)*	43				
	44	Partial credit for political contributions	44				
	45	Credit for child and dependent care expenses *(attach Form 2441)*	45				
	46	Jobs credit *(attach Form 5884)*	46				
	47	Residential energy credit *(attach Form 5695)*	47				
	48	Other credits—see page 14 ▶	48				
	49	**Total credits.** Add lines 41 through 48			49		00
	50	**Balance.** Subtract line 49 from line 40 and enter difference (but not less than zero) ▶			50	72,400	00
Other Taxes (Including Advance EIC Payments)	51	Self-employment tax *(attach Schedule SE)*			51	3,029	40
	52	Minimum tax *(attach Form 4625)*			52		
	53	Alternative minimum tax *(attach Form 6251)*			53		
	54	Tax from recapture of investment credit *(attach Form 4255)*			54		
	55	Social security (FICA) tax on tip income not reported to employer *(attach Form 4137)*			55		
	56	Uncollected employee FICA and RRTA tax on tips *(from Form W–2)*			56		
	57	Tax on an IRA *(attach Form 5329)*			57		
	58	Advance earned income credit (EIC) payments received *(from Form W–2)*			58		
06	59	**Total tax.** Add lines 50 through 58 ■			59	75,429	40
Payments Attach Forms W–2, W–2G, and W–2P to front.	60	Total Federal income tax withheld	60	5,650 00			
	61	1982 estimated tax payments and amount applied from 1981 return	61	68,000 00			
	62	Earned income credit. If line 33 is under $10,000, see page 15 of Instructions	62				
	63	Amount paid with Form 4868	63				
	64	Excess FICA and RRTA tax withheld (two or more employers)	64				
	65	Credit for Federal tax on special fuels and oils *(attach Form 4136)*	65				
	66	Regulated Investment Company credit *(attach Form 2439)*	66				
	67	**Total.** Add lines 60 through 66 ▶			67	73,650	00
Refund or Amount You Owe	68	If line 67 is larger than line 59, enter amount **OVERPAID** ▶			68		
	69	Amount of line 68 to be **REFUNDED TO YOU** ▶			69		
	70	Amount of line 68 to be applied to your 1983 estimated tax ▶	70	1,779 40			
	71	If line 59 is larger than line 67, enter **AMOUNT YOU OWE.** Attach check or money order for full amount payable to Internal Revenue Service. Write your social security number and "1982 Form 1040" on it. ▶ (Check ▶ ☐ if Form 2210 (2210F) is attached. See page 16 of Instructions.) ▶ $			71	1,779	40

Please Sign Here

Under penalties of perjury, I declare that I have examined this return, including accompanying schedules and statements, and to the best of my knowledge and belief, it is true, correct, and complete. Declaration of preparer (other than taxpayer) is based on all information of which preparer has any knowledge.

▶ *John Fallo* — Your signature | April 15, 1983 — Date | *Jane Fallo* — Spouse's signature (if filing jointly, BOTH must sign)

Paid Preparer's Use Only

Preparer's signature	Date	Check if self-employed	Preparer's social security no.
▶ *A. M. Parks*	April 15, 1983	▶ ☐	972 : 40 : 0001
Firm's name (or yours, if self-employed) and address ▶ A. M. Parks, CPA, 810 Third Street, Eastowne, NC 27514		E.I. No. ▶	
		ZIP code ▶	

Figure A–11 (Continued)

The top part of Figure A–11 includes name, address, filing status, and allowable exemptions for John and Jane Fallo and their children. The Income section shows the gross salary (not net pay) of Jane Fallo of $35,000, the taxable interest of $3,500, and the net income from Orange Recreation Supplier of $177,050. The interest on the state and local government bonds is not taxable. (Since total interest exceeds $400, the details of payors and other infor-

Schedules A&B (Form 1040) — Department of the Treasury Internal Revenue Service (0)

Schedule A—Itemized Deductions

(Schedule B is on back)

▶ Attach to Form 1040. ▶ See Instructions for Schedules A and B (Form 1040).

OMB No. 1545-0074 — 1982 — 07

Name(s) as shown on Form 1040: John and Jane Fallo — Your social security number: 123 78 4532

Section	Line		Amount		Total
Medical and Dental Expenses (Do not include expenses reimbursed or paid by others.) (See page 17 of Instructions.)	1 Medicines and drugs	1	480 00		
	2 Write 1% of Form 1040, line 33	2	2,115 50		
	3 Subtract line 2 from line 1. If line 2 is more than line 1, write zero	3		00	
	4 Total insurance premiums you paid for medical and dental care	4		380 00	
	5 Other medical and dental expenses:				
	a Doctors, dentists, nurses, hospitals, etc	5a		2,600 00	
	b Transportation	5b			
	c Other (list—include hearing aids, dentures, eyeglasses, etc.) ▶	5c			
	6 Add lines 3 through 5c	6		2,980 00	
	7 Multiply amount on Form 1040, line 33, by 3% (.03)	7		6,346 00	
	8 Subtract line 7 from line 6. If line 7 is more than line 6, write zero	8		00	
	9 Write one-half of amount on line 4, but not more than $150	9		150 00	
	10 COMPARE amounts on line 8 and line 9, and write the LARGER amount here ▶	10			150 00
Taxes (See page 18 of Instructions.)	11 State and local income	11		13,140 00	
	12 Real estate	12		2,400 00	
	13 a General sales (see sales tax tables)	13a		710 00	
	b General sales on motor vehicles	13b			
	14 Other (list—include personal property) ▶ Personal Property	14		965 00	
	15 Add lines 11 through 14. Write your answer here ▶	15			17,215 00
Interest Expense (See page 19 of Instructions.)	16 a Home mortgage interest paid to financial institutions	16a		2,910 00	
	b Home mortgage interest paid to individuals (show that person's name and address) ▶	16b			
	17 Credit cards and charge accounts	17		195 00	
	18 Other (list) ▶	18			
	19 Add lines 16a through 18. Write your answer here ▶	19			3,105 00
Contributions (See page 19 of Instructions.)	20 a Cash contributions. (If you gave $3,000 or more to any one organization, report those contributions on line 20b.)	20a		20,000 00	
	b Cash contributions totaling $3,000 or more to any one organization. (Show to whom you gave and how much you gave.) ▶	20b			
	21 Other than cash (see page 19 of Instructions for required statement)	21			
	22 Carryover from prior years	22			
	23 Add lines 20a through 22. Write your answer here ▶	23			20,000 00
Casualty and Theft Losses and Miscellaneous Deductions (See page 20 of Instructions.)	24 Total casualty or theft loss(es) (attach Form 4684)	24		00	
	25 a Union and professional dues	25a		310 00	
	b Tax return preparation fee	25b		250 00	
	26 Other (list) ▶ Safe deposit box rent	26		18 00	
	27 Add lines 24 through 26. Write your answer here ▶	27			578 00
Summary of Itemized Deductions (See page 20 of Instructions.)	28 Add lines 10, 15, 19, 23, and 27	28			41,048 00
	29 If you checked Form 1040, Filing Status box { 2 or 5, write $3,400; 1 or 4, write $2,300; 3, write $1,700 }	29			3,400 00
	30 Subtract line 29 from line 28. Write your answer here and on Form 1040, line 34a. (If line 29 is more than line 28, see the Instructions for line 30 on page 20.) ▶	30			37,648 00

For Paperwork Reduction Act Notice, see Form 1040 Instructions.

A

Figure A–12 Itemized Deductions, Schedule A, Form 1040

mation must be shown on Schedule B to Form 1040, not included in this illustration.)

The net income from Orange Recreation Supplier is calculated on Schedule C (Figure A–13). This schedule contains the information that appears on the income statement for the single proprietorship. Most items are self-

SCHEDULE C (Form 1040)
Department of the Treasury
Internal Revenue Service (0)

Profit or (Loss) From Business or Profession
(Sole Proprietorship)
Partnerships, Joint Ventures, etc., Must File Form 1065.
▶ Attach to Form 1040 or Form 1041. ▶ See Instructions for Schedule C (Form 1040).

OMB. No. 1545-0074
1982
08

Name of proprietor: John Fallo
Social security number of proprietor: 123 | 78 | 4532

A Main business activity (see Instructions) ▶ Retail sales ; product ▶ Recreation supplies
B Business name ▶ Orange Recreational Supplier
C Employer identification number: 3 | 8 | 4 | 6 | 7 | 4 | 4 | 2 | 1
D Business address (number and street) ▶ 2102 Second Street
City, State and ZIP Code ▶ Chapel Hill, North Carolina 27514
E Accounting method: (1) ☐ Cash (2) ☒ Accrual (3) ☐ Other (specify) ▶
F Method(s) used to value closing inventory:
(1) ☐ Cost (2) ☒ Lower of cost or market (3) ☐ Other (if other, attach explanation)

	Yes	No
G Was there any major change in determining quantities, costs, or valuations between opening and closing inventory? If "Yes," attach explanation.		X
H Did you deduct expenses for an office in your home?		X
I Did you operate this business at the end of 1982?	X	
J How many months in 1982 did you actively operate this business? ▶	12	

Part I Income

Line	Description				Amount
1 a	Gross receipts or sales	1a	1,500,000 00		
b	Returns and allowances	1b	6,000 00		
c	Balance (subtract line 1b from line 1a)			1c	1,494,000 00
2	Cost of goods sold and/or operations (Schedule C–1, line 8)			2	854,000 00
3	Gross profit (subtract line 2 from line 1c)			3	640,000 00
4 a	Windfall Profit Tax Credit or Refund received in 1982 (see Instructions)			4a	00
b	Other income			4b	00
5	Total income (add lines 3, 4a, and 4b) ▶			5	640,000 00

Part II Deductions

Line	Description	Amount	Line	Description	Amount
6	Advertising	5,900 00	25	Taxes (Do not include Windfall Profit Tax here. See line 29.)	
7	Bad debts from sales or services (Cash method taxpayers, see Instructions)	1,200 00	26	Travel and entertainment	
8	Bank service charges		27	Utilities and telephone	7,370 00
9	Car and truck expenses		28 a	Wages 411,680 00	
10	Commissions		b	Jobs credit 00	
11	Depletion		c	Subtract line 28b from 28a	411,680 00
12	Depreciation, including Section 179 expense deduction (from Form 4562)	12,000 00	29	Windfall Profit Tax withheld in 1982	
13	Dues and publications		30	Other expenses (specify):	
14	Employee benefit programs		a		
15	Freight (not included on Schedule C–1)		b		
16	Insurance	4,600 00	c		
17	Interest on business indebtedness	3,700 00	d		
18	Laundry and cleaning		e		
19	Legal and professional services		f		
20	Office supplies and postage		g		
21	Pension and profit-sharing plans	7,500 00	h		
22	Rent on business property	5,900 00	i		
23	Repairs		j		
24	Supplies (not included on Schedule C–1)	3,100 00	k		
			l		
			m		

Line	Description		Amount
31	Total deductions (add amounts in columns for lines 6 through 30m) ▶	31	462,950 00
32	Net profit or (loss) (subtract line 31 from line 5). If a profit, enter on Form 1040, line 12, and on Schedule SE, Part I, line 2 (or Form 1041, line 6). If a loss, go on to line 33	32	177,050 00

33 If you have a loss, do you have amounts for which you are not "at risk" in this business (see Instructions)? ☐ Yes ☐ No
If you checked "No," enter the loss on Form 1040, line 12, and on Schedule SE, Part I, line 2 (or Form 1041, line 6).
For Paperwork Reduction Act Notice, see Form 1040 Instructions.

Figure A–13 Profit or Loss from Business or Profession, Schedule C, Form 1040

explanatory. Depreciation using the ACRS system would have to be detailed on a separate schedule. On line 27, two expenses are combined. Schedule SE accompanying Schedule C is not shown; it would disclose the detailed calculation of the maximum self-employment tax (Social Security tax) for John Fallo of \$3,029.40 = (9.35% × \$32,400, the maximum).

Figure A–11 shows a summary of adjusted gross income, excess itemized deductions, self-employment tax, and the prepayments that are subtracted from the total of the taxes. The calculation of the gross income tax for 1982, before tax credits, is shown as follows:

Tax on first $162,400 (from Schedule 1, Figure A–9)	$68,649
Tax on next $7,502	3,751
Totals	72,400

Since the prepayments of $73,650 were less than the income tax and self-employment tax, the Fallos must pay $1,779.40 to the Internal Revenue Service to complete the payment of their 1982 federal income tax.

Figure A–12 lists the various categories of personal deductions. As stated previously, the *Tax Equity and Fiscal Responsibility Act of 1982* made several changes in the medical and dental expense deduction. For 1983 and future years, it increased the 3 percent limitation, shown on Figure A–12, to 5 percent, and eliminated the separate deduction for medical insurance (line 9, Figure A–12). The separate 1 percent limitation on drugs and medicines is eliminated after 1983, and the definition of drugs and medicines is limited to prescription drugs and insulin. The deductible medical and dental expenses for 1982 is $150 using the formula shown on Figure A–11 (c). The remaining personal deductions are self-explanatory.

Reporting Partnership Income

Partnerships are not taxed as separate entities. The relevant revenues and expenses of the partnership are reported on an informational return, Form 1065, and the individual partners report their respective shares of operating income, net long-term and short-term capital gains, dividends received, contributions, tax-exempt income, and any other items that require special treatment on their own individual income tax returns.

Corporate Income Taxes

The income of a business corporation is subject to a separate income tax. The owners, the stockholders, are *also partially taxed* on any income from dividends received from the corporation. Yet the corporation is not allowed to deduct any of these dividends paid to stockholders. The corporate tax rate schedule for 1983 is a simple five-step progressive structure:

Taxable Income	Tax Rate
First $0 to $25,000	15%
Next $25,000.01 to $50,000	18
Next $50,000.01 to $75,000	30
Next $75,000.01 to $100,000	40
Income in excess of $100,000	46

In general, the taxable income of a corporation is computed in the same manner as that of an individual. Among the exceptions is the fact that a corporation may not itemize certain personal deductions allowed to individuals. For example, a corporation is not entitled to personal exemptions, the zero bracket amount, or such personal deductions as medical expenses. Personal deductions and the concept of adjusted gross income are not applicable to the corporation.

The $100 dividend exclusion is not applicable to corporations. Normally, they may deduct from gross income 85 percent of dividends received from domestic corporations. Under certain conditions, when a consolidated return is filed for a parent and those companies that it owns, the consolidated group may, in effect, deduct 100 percent of dividends received by members of the group from each other, that is, of the intercompany dividend amount.

Capital losses of a corporation can be deducted *only* against capital gains. Capital losses may be carried back three years and forward five years and may be offset against any capital gains earned during those years, not counting the year of the loss. Net long-term capital gains are 100 percent includable in taxable income of corporations but are subject to a maximum flat alternative tax rate of 28 percent. In any one year, a corporation's contributions are deductible up to a maximum limit of 10 percent of net income figured without regard to the contribution deduction. Any contribution in excess of this limit may be carried over to the five succeeding years and deducted, provided the total contributions including the carried-over amounts are within the 10 percent limit of the appropriate years.

The Corporate Income Tax Return, Form 1120, must be filed 2½ months after the end of the taxable fiscal year. The major features of the corporate income tax are illustrated by the tax computation for the Perkins Corporation, shown in Figures A–14 and A–15. Corporations must prepay most of the in-

PERKINS CORPORATION
Income Statement—Per the Books
For the Year Ended December 31, 1983

Revenues		
Net sales		$500,000
Expenses		
Cost of goods sold	$250,000	
Operating expenses other than capital losses and charitable contributions	80,000	
Capital losses	500	
Charitable contributions	19,500	
Total expenses		350,000
Net income before income taxes		$150,000
Less federal income taxes (see Figure A–15)		50,130
Net income		$ 99,870

Figure A–14 Book Income Statement

PERKINS CORPORATION
Tax Computation—Taxable Year 1983

Revenues:		
Net sales		$500,000
Expenses:		
Cost of goods sold	$250,000	
Operating expenses other than capital losses and charitable contributions	80,000	
Capital losses (none allowed)	0	
Charitable contributions (the smaller of actual of $19,500 or 10% × $170,000[a] = $17,000)	17,000	347,000
Net final taxable income		$153,000
Tax computation:		
Tax on first $25,000 of taxable income at 15% (15% × $25,000)		$ 3,750
Tax on next $25,000 at 18% (18% × $25,000)		4,500
Tax on next $25,000 at 30% (30% × $25,000)		7,500
Tax on next $25,000 at 40% (40% × $25,000)		10,000
Tax on remaining taxable income at 46% (46% × $53,000)		24,380
		$ 50,130

[a]Since capital losses are not deductible, the net income on which the charitable contribution is based is $170,000 = [$500,000 − ($250,000 + $80,000)].

Figure A–15
Corporate Income Tax Computation

come tax during the year in which it is earned. Starting in 1983, at least 75 percent of the income tax must be prepaid.

Differences between Financial Accounting Income and Taxable Income

The causes of differences between financial accounting income and taxable income are now examined so that the related reporting issues can be considered. Taxable income must be computed in accordance with federal statutes and administrative regulations. Computation of business income for financial reporting purposes, however, should be based on generally accepted accounting standards. Using two methods of computation will lead to apparent discrepancies between the two net income figures. Any feature of the tax law that increases taxable income also increases the amount of tax; likewise, any feature of the law that decreases the amount of taxable income decreases the amount of tax. The four major differences between traditional business income and taxable income are as follows:

1. Some items not considered to be revenue by generally accepted accounting principles are taxed as revenue by the law.

2. Some items considered as business expenses are not deductible for tax purposes.

3. Some items generally considered to be business revenue are exempt from tax by law.

4. Some items not generally considered to be business expenses are deductible for tax purposes.

Taxable Nonbusiness Revenues

The most important taxable receipts that are not generally considered business revenues are certain unearned revenue items such as advance receipts of rent, interest, or royalties. The federal government levies the tax in the year of receipt, when the cash for payment is presumably available. Sound accrual accounting, on the other hand, recognizes these items as revenue in the year in which they are earned. An exception to the general rule stated is the unearned subscriptions revenue received by publishing companies. They are permitted to report taxable revenue on the basis of the accrual earning process as opposed to the time of the cash receipt.

Nondeductible Business Expenses

Several kinds of items would normally be considered business expenses but are not allowed for tax purposes. Five representative examples are listed below:

1. As indicated in the discussion of corporate income tax, charitable contributions in excess of 10 percent of net income, figured without regard to the contribution deduction, are not deductible even when they are made for a business purpose.
2. Interest on money borrowed to purchase tax-exempt securities is not deductible.
3. Premiums paid on life insurance policies carried by the corporation on the lives of its key personnel are not deductible if the corporation names itself as beneficiary—sound accounting requires that the amount of the premium in excess of increases in cash surrender value (the investment in the policies) should be considered an expense.
4. The federal income tax itself is not an expense for tax purposes.
5. Amortization of goodwill is not deductible.

Tax-Exempt Business Revenue

Several revenue items are exempt from taxation for various reasons, ranging from social desirability to administrative expediency. Three representative examples of items specifically exempted by the Internal Revenue Code are listed here:

1. Total interest received on state and municipal bonds and notes is specifically exempt from federal taxation.
2. A portion of net long-term capital gains, in effect, is exempt, since usually there is a maximum tax rate on such gains.
3. Life insurance proceeds received on the death of the insured are not taxed.

Deductions Allowed by Tax Law but Not Generally Considered Business Expenses

The tax law provides special relief provisions and investment incentives that are not generally deducted from business revenue to measure net income. Among these are the following:

1. The part of allowable accelerated depreciation (ACRS) that is in excess of sound depreciation expense.
2. The net operating loss deduction—a special feature of the tax law designed to give taxpayers who suffer a loss in a given year some relief from taxes paid in the three years immediately preceding or the five years following the year of the loss for most taxpayers.

Financial Reporting Problems—Interperiod Income Tax Allocation

The differences between taxable income and business income fall into two classes: (1) those that tend to result in a permanent difference between taxable and business income and (2) those that cancel each other out over a period of time (timing differences). Financial reporting problems caused by the latter class are magnified by the size of the current income tax. The controversy centers around the proper measurement of federal income tax expense. If the income tax is a business expense, the matching concept seems to dictate that income tax expense be computed on the basis of reported business book income that will be subject to the income tax (as opposed to the tax based on taxable income).

Because the above assumption seems to be valid for those companies that have material timing differences between taxable income and reported business book income, the Accounting Principles Board has concluded (in *Opinion No. 11*) that the income tax expense must be allocated among the relevant periods and that the deferred method of tax allocation should be followed.

Interperiod Income Tax Allocation: Two Illustrations

The income tax expense for the current year under the matching concept is based on book net income. When differences exist between book net income and taxable net income, the accepted practice is to allocate income taxes among the relevant periods. The practice is referred to as **interperiod income tax allocation.** This procedure is made necessary because of two types of timing differences that cancel each other out over time. One type of timing difference arises when revenue is recognized in one accounting period for book purposes but is not taxed until later periods or when an expense is recognized on the tax return but is not recognized in the accounting records until a later period. A second type of timing difference arises when revenue is recognized on the tax return before it is recognized in the books or when expenses are recognized for book accounting purposes before they are deducted on the tax return. The first difference will give rise to a postponed income tax liability, which will be paid at a later date. The second will create prepaid income tax items, whose expense will be postponed and allocated as income tax expense of future periods. Specific examples of the cause of these two timing differences were cited in the preceding section.

Two illustrations are given here to introduce the accounting procedures involved in the deferred method of interperiod income tax allocation. First, consider an example that would create a postponed or deferred income tax liability; the classic example is the difference between book depreciation and tax depreciation. Assume, for example, that the Calgary Corporation finds the straight line depreciation method appropriate for its books but uses the sum-of-the-years'-digits method for its tax return. Assume that the company acquired a major machine at a cost $300,000, with an estimated five-year life and no salvage value; also assume that the income tax rate is 50 percent. If the company earns $500,000 each year (before depreciation expense and income tax expense), the effect of these procedures on pretax book accounting income and taxable income is as follows:

Year	Accounting Income before Depreciation and Income Taxes	Accounting Depreciation (Straight Line)	Tax Return Depreciation (SYD)	Pretax Book Accounting Income	Taxable Income
1	$ 500,000	$ 60,000	$100,000	$ 440,000	$400,000
2	500,000	60,000	80,000	440,000	420,000
3	500,000	60,000	60,000	440,000	440,000
4	500,000	60,000	40,000	440,000	460,000
5	500,000	60,000	20,000	440,000	480,000
Totals	$2,500,000	$300,000	$300,000	$2,200,000	$2,200,000

Note that *total* pretax accounting income and taxable income are the same for the five-year period. The journal entries to record the income tax liability and the income tax expense at the assumed rate of 50 percent are presented below:

Year		Account		Debit	Credit
Year	1	Income Tax Expense		220,000	
		Income Taxes Payable			200,000
		Deferred Income Tax Liability			20,000
		To record tax expense on reported net income of $440,000 at assumed rate of 50 percent.			
Year	2	Income Tax Expense		220,000	
		Income Taxes Payable			210,000
		Deferred Income Tax Liability			10,000
		(The explanations for years 2 to 5 are omitted, since they are essentially the same as those for year 1.)			
Year	3	Income Tax Expense		220,000	
		Income Taxes Payable			220,000
Year	4	Income Tax Expense		220,000	
		Deferred Income Tax Liability		10,000	
		Income Taxes Payable			230,000
Year	5	Income Tax Expense		220,000	
		Deferred Income Tax Liability		20,000	
		Income Taxes Payable			240,000

Under the assumptions that the tax law has not changed and that the Deferred Income Tax Liability account refers only to the machinery purchased in Year 1, the five-year history of this account is shown below:

Deferred Income Tax Liability — Acct. No. 251

Date		Explanation	F	Debit	Credit	Balance
Year	1		J176		20,000	20,000
	2		J276		10,000	30,000
	4		J376	10,000		20,000
	5		J476	20,000		0

This example of a firm using one depreciation method for book purposes and another for tax purposes is only one of many available alternative practices that cause differences between tax accounting and book accounting, resulting in a temporary difference between taxable income and business income—a difference that is cancelled out over a period of time. Other cases must be considered carefully to see whether they warrant the allocation of the income tax between periods. Although it appears theoretically sound to make use of this practice in all relevant cases, the deciding factors, of course, are the size of the amounts involved and the complexity of the procedure in regard to a particular case. A company may use a depreciation method for tax purposes different from the theoretically appropriate book method because it allows interest-free use of the funds freed by postponement of the tax payments.

The next illustration involves a timing difference that creates a prepaid income tax item. Consider, for example, the advance receipt of a three-year rental revenue of $600,000 by the Guelph Company. Other book net income before taxes is $100,000 each year. The advanced receipt of rent is fully taxable in the year of receipt; for book purposes, however, $200,000 would be recognized in each of the three years. The book income and taxable income are summarized below:

Year	Book Accounting Income Other Than Rental Income	Additions to Book Accounting for Rental Revenue	Pretax Book Accounting Income	Taxable Income
1	$100,000	$200,000	$300,000	$700,000
2	100,000	200,000	300,000	100,000
3	100,000	200,000	300,000	100,000
Totals	$300,000	$600,000	$900,000	$900,000

Using interperiod income tax allocation procedures, the Guelph Company would determine the income tax expense for each period on the basis of accounting income and record the difference between the current income tax liability and income tax expense as prepaid income taxes. Journal entries to record income taxes at the assumed rate of 50 percent for the three years are shown below:

Year	1	Income Tax Expense (50% × $300,000)	150,000	
		Prepaid Income Taxes	200,000	
		Income Taxes Payable		350,000
Year	2	Income Tax Expense	150,000	
		Prepaid Income Taxes		100,000
		Income Taxes Payable		50,000
Year	3	Income Tax Expense	150,000	
		Prepaid Income Taxes		100,000
		Income Taxes Payable		50,000

The income tax expense of $150,000 would be shown on the income statement, but the statement should include a footnote disclosing the fact that the income tax liability is different each year. The deferred income tax liability and the prepaid income taxes items, however, should usually be split between current and long-term captions on the balance sheet based on the classification of assets or liabilities related to the timing differences. In some cases the timing differences are indirectly related to specific assets and liabilities; hence, under these circumstances, according to *FASB Statement No. 37,* the deferred income tax liability and prepaid income taxes items "shall be classified based on the expected reversal date of the specific timing difference. Such classification disregards any additional timing differences that may arise and is based on the criteria used for classifying other assets and liabilities."[5]

Some accountants oppose the recognition of interperiod income tax allocation. They state that the income tax is a distribution of income, not an expense, and that the matching concept is therefore not involved. They also argue that the timing differences are not temporary, especially when a firm continues to replace and to add plant items each year. Where the amounts are material and the differences are expected to be reversed, it is the authors' opinion that the interperiod income tax allocation is a theoretically sound procedure and should be recorded in the accounts of the corporation.

Glossary

Accrual basis An accounting basis which measures net income by offsetting incurred expenses (regardless of when paid) against earned income (regardless of when collected) for a given period.

Adjusted gross income Gross income less allowable deductions (including business-related and revenue-producing expenses).

[5]*Statement of Financial Accounting Standards No. 37.* "Balance Sheet Classification of Deferred Income Taxes" (Stamford, Conn.: Financial Accounting Standards Board, July 1980), paragraph 4.

Capital assets Stocks, bonds, and other assets that by law specifically are identified as capital assets.

Capital gains and losses Any excesses or deficiencies of cash receipts above or below the bases (usually cost) of capital assets sold; gains and losses on capital assets held for one year or less are short-term, whereas those on capital assets held for more than one year are long-term.

Cash basis An accounting basis which measures net income by offsetting paid expenses against collected revenue for a given period (modified versions of this basis are usually found in practice).

Dependent Under the law, a person who receives over one-half of his or her support from the taxpayer; is closely related to the taxpayer or lives in the taxpayer's home; has received less than $1,000 in gross income during the year (unless the dependent is a child of the taxpayer under 19 years old or a full-time student); and has not filed a joint return.

Excess itemized deductions The amount of the total itemized personal deductions in excess of the zero bracket amount.

Exclusions Items of income broadly conceived that are not required by law to be reported as gross income.

Exemptions Deductions allowed by law, valued at $1,000 each for taxpayer, spouse, dependents, and other allowable exemptions.

Filer An entity—individual, married couple filing a joint return, estate or trust, or head of household—filing the tax return.

Flat standard deductions See *Zero bracket amount.*

Gross income Income required by law to be reported on the tax return and subject to the income tax.

Gross income tax The amount of tax before tax credits are deducted.

Head of household A single individual who heads a household that contains dependent persons; special tax schedules are provided for heads of households to partially compensate them for the additional family burden they must carry.

Individual Retirement Arrangement (IRA) A plan under which a taxpayer pays into a personal retirement plan an annual amount that can be deducted from gross income. All returns from such plans are taxable when received by the taxpayer at age 59½ or later.

Interperiod income tax allocation The allocation of income tax expense among periods to compensate for a temporary timing difference between reported book income and taxable income.

Itemized personal deductions Personal items that are allowed by law to be deducted from adjusted gross income; these include contributions, allowable medical expenses, union dues, and others.

Itemizer taxpayer A taxpayer who elects to itemize personal deductions.

Net tax liability The amount of tax after the tax credits have been deducted; this amount must be paid to the Internal Revenue Service.

Nonitemizer taxpayer A taxpayer who elects not to itemize personal deductions.

Tax avoidance A legal method of postponing taxes or preventing a tax liability from coming into existence.

Tax credits Credits that are allowed to be subtracted from the income tax itself; examples are: credit for the elderly, investment credits, child care credit, and earned income credits.

Tax evasion Illegal tax reporting, failure to report taxes, or nonpayment of taxes.

Tax rate schedule Any of four tax schedules for single individuals, married taxpayers filing separate returns, married taxpayers and surviving spouses filing joint returns, and heads of households.

Tax table A table showing the amount of income tax for those taxpayers with a taxable income of a given amount specified by the Internal Revenue Service.

Taxable income Adjusted gross income less either the special charitable deduction or the sum of excess itemized deductions and personal exemptions.

Zero bracket amount This amount was formerly called the standard deduction; it is $2,300 for a single taxpayer and head of household; $3,400 for married taxpayers filing a joint return; and $1,700 for married taxpayers filing separate returns.

Questions

QA–1 (a) Distinguish between the cash and accrual bases of accounting. (b) What is a modified cash basis?

QA–2 (a) Define the term "gross income" from an individual income tax point of view. (b) List six items that must be reported as gross income. (c) List four items that are excludable from gross income.

QA–3 (a) What is the individual income tax zero bracket amount? (b) State the amount applicable for all kinds of individual taxpayers.

QA–4 Smith, a bachelor, earned $60,000 in taxable income in 1983. What amount of federal income tax would be saved if he were to marry on December 31, 1983, a woman who had no taxable income in 1983? (Use tax rate schedules.)

QA–5 (a) For tax purposes, what are capital assets? (b) Distinguish between short-term and long-term capital gains.

QA–6 John Allen, age 21, is attending the State University. During the summer of 1983, he worked as a construction laborer and earned $1,050. His parents contributed more than one-half toward his support in 1983. Can Allen's parents claim him as an exemption?

QA–7 Sandra Sawyer elected to use the cash basis for tax purposes. During 1983 she collected $12,000 from clients for services rendered in prior years and billed clients for $30,000 for services rendered in 1983. Her accounts receivable as of December 31, 1983, totaled $8,700, all arising out of services rendered in 1983. What is the amount of gross income she should report on her Form 1040 for 1983?

QA–8 John and Susan Adams own some shares of stock. During 1983, they received $700 in dividends. Dividends of $610 were received on stock owned by John Adams only. The remainder was received on stock owned by Susan Adams. What would be the dividends included in gross income on a joint return?

QA–9 List and briefly discuss the differences in computation of the individual income tax and the corporate income tax.

QA–10 Compare the income tax treatment of capital losses for the individual income taxpayer with that for the corporate taxpayer.

QA–11 In outline form, state four ways that traditional business income may differ from taxable income; give two specific illustrations for each way.

Class Demonstration Exercises and Problems

Note: The following exercises and problems are presented with this appendix. They may be used as class demonstration problems or assigned as outside work. All tax data except CDPA–2 are as of 1983. Tax law applicable to 1983 may be changed by Congress.

CDPA–1 *Calculation of adjusted gross income*

Roy and Abigail Butters had the following income and related information for 1983:

Salary to Roy Butters	$40,000
Dividends on stock owned by Roy Butters	2,000
Dividends on stock owned by Abigail Butters	1,000
On March 15, 1983, Abigail Butters sold some stock she had acquired on April 1, 1978 at a gain of	4,000

Required: Compute the adjusted gross income subject to tax on a joint return filed by Roy and Abigail Butters.

CDPA–2 *Tax calculation using tax table*

The Individual Tax Return (Form 1040) of Samuel L. Vaughn, who is single and has one exemption for himself, showed a taxable income of $48,500.

Required: Using the tax table (Figure A–5) in the text, calculate the amount of the gross income tax on this return.

CDPA–3 *Comprehensive individual income tax calculation*

Adam Carter, 66 years old, is married to Sara Carter, who is 56. They have two children: John, 16; and Susan, 20, who is attending a university. The Carters furnish over one-half the support for both their children, although Susan works as a salesclerk in the summer and earned $1,250 in 1983. Carter owns and operates a service station under the name of Carter Service Station. Mrs. Carter did not have any earned income in 1983. Relevant business and personal information for the family is shown:

Cash Receipts:

Gross revenue from Carter Service Station	$200,000
Interest on corporate industrial bonds	1,000
Interest on State of Virginia bonds	3,450
Dividends on stock jointly owned	4,200
Cash proceeds from insurance policy for fire damage on nonbusiness property that had an original cost of $1,800	1,800

Capital gains:

Sale of 200 shares of National Fruit Company common stock:

Date Acquired	Date Sold	Cost	Selling Price
3/4/80	5/2/83	$24,000	$28,000

Sale of 100 shares of United Fusbits Company common stock:

Date Acquired	Date Sold	Cost	Selling Price
4/2/83	8/10/83	$10,000	$10,600

Expenditures:

Cost of goods sold ($105,000) and operating expenses ($30,000) of Carter Service Station	$135,000
Contributions to church and university	2,000
Contribution to Community Chest	800
Interest paid on personal loans	600
Property taxes paid to town and county	800
State taxes paid:	
Sales tax	160
State income tax	5,200
Gasoline tax	100
Family medical expenses:	
Doctor and hospital fees	650
Drugs and medicine	118
Amount paid in 1983 on declared estimated tax for 1983	16,000

Required: In an orderly schedule form, compute the income tax liability remaining to be paid or tax refund due for 1983, assuming that a joint return is filed.

CDPA–4 *Comprehensive individual income tax calculation*

Parm Quarles is single and is 67 years old. He has the receipts and expenditures listed below.

Cash receipts:	
Salary received from University of Nugo	$62,500
Interest received on school district bonds	2,000
Expenditures:	
Contribution to church and university	6,000
Contribution to United Fund	200
Personal property taxes	1,000
Insurance on residence	200
Automobile license plates	24
State income taxes	4,560
State sales taxes	150
State gasoline tax	100
Medical expenses:	
Drugs and medicines	380
Doctor and hospital bills	1,050
Interest on personal loans	700
Withheld income tax as shown by W–2 Form	14,000

Required: Compute the remaining tax liability or the claim for refund for 1983 for Parm Quarles.

CDPA–5 *Calculation of corporation income tax*

The Heller Corporation reported the following information for 1983:

Sales	$1,890,000
Cost of goods sold	920,000
Operating expenses, other than capital losses and charitable contributions	380,000
Capital losses	18,000
Charitable contributions	31,000

Required: Compute the corporate income tax for 1983.

CDPA–6 *Interperiod income tax allocation issues*

The Intergrove Company began business on January 1, 1983. Anticipating a growth in its delivery business over the next few years, the company has developed plans for the purchase of delivery equipment as shown below:

Planned Acquisitions (beginning of year)	Cost of New Equipment	Salvage Value	Estimated Service Life (in years)
1983	$100,000	$10,000	5
1984	480,000	30,000	5
1985	690,000	60,000	5
1986	200,000	80,000	5
1987	150,000	30,000	5
1988	166,000	16,000	5

The head accountant of the company is studying the question of depreciation policies on the delivery equipment. The accountant feels that the company should adopt the sum-of-the-years'-digits method of depreciation for income tax purposes but still continue to use the straight line method for normal accounting and reporting purposes. If this policy is adopted, book net income would differ from taxable income; and this difference would require, in the head accountant's opinion, the use of interperiod income tax allocation procedures in the company's accounting records.

Required:

1. Prepare a schedule showing the difference between taxable income and book income that will result in each year of the six-year period if the head accountant adopts the policy described.

2. Determine the balance that would appear in the Deferred Income Tax Liability account at the close of 1988 if interperiod income tax allocation procedures were followed, and assuming that an income tax rate of 45 percent were applicable.

CDPA–7

Thought-provoking problem: reconciling difference between taxable income and accounting income

The Cannady Production Company, a textile manufacturer, has recently had a change in ownership and top management. Robert James, the new president, is a retired military officer and is noted for being an excellent organizer and administrator. James is gaining a reputation around the office for asking hard questions and for requiring complete and logical answers.

During one of the mornings that James is devoting to familiarizing himself with the workings of the accounting department, he reviews the latest federal corporate tax return and the latest income statement in the corporate annual report. He immediately notices that the taxable income of $136,495 on the tax return and the net income before income taxes of $219,400 on the income statement are not the same amount. On closer examination he observes that the following items are not the same on each report.

a. Depreciation expense is $92,510 on the income statement and $147,250 on the tax return.

b. Cost of goods sold is $929,180 on the income statement and $951,200 on the tax return.

c. Interest earned is $1,200 on the income statement and $880 on the tax return.

d. Gain on disposal of machinery is $5,790 on the income statement and does not appear on the tax return. (Hint: Gains on certain trade-ins are not taxable.)

e. Bad debt expense is $6,400 on the income statement and $6,350 on the tax return.

f. Amortization of organization costs is $100 on the income statement and is $185 on the tax return.

He also notes that the income tax expense on the income statement is not the same as the income tax on the tax report.

By this time he is confused and bewildered. He approaches you, an assistant accountant in the tax division, and questions the discrepancies. (He has a dual purpose in asking you questions. He wishes answers to his questions and wishes to evaluate your knowledge of tax accounting.)

Required:

1. Reconcile the two different income amounts. (Hint: A corporation may amortize organization costs over five years or more.)

2. Identify what might be a complete and logical reason for each of the six differences. (Remember that you wish to convince the new president of your competence.)

3. (a) Why does income tax expense on the income statement differ from the income tax on the tax report? (b) What is the basis for each calculation? (c) Which would you expect to be the larger? Why?

B

Consolidated Financial Statements Illustrated

Dennison Manufacturing Company, a Fortune 500 company, manufactures and distributes a wide range of products which can be found in just about every home, office, school, and industrial facility. These products range from labels, notebooks, and felt markers to highly sophisticated computerized identification control systems. They extend through four broad market areas: stationery products and systems, retail systems, technical papers, and industrial systems. Dennison holds leadership positions in important segments of all these major market areas.[1] Their 1982 financial statements are reproduced here.

Statement of Management Responsibility for Financial Statements

The management of Dennison Manufacturing Company has prepared and is responsible for the consolidated financial information contained in this report. The financial statements have been prepared in conformity with generally accepted accounting principles consistently applied and thus include amounts based on management's best estimates and judgments.

Management believes that the company's internal control systems provide reasonable assurance that assets are safeguarded against loss from unauthorized use or disposition, and that the financial records are reliable for preparing financial statements and maintaining accountability for assets. These systems are augmented by written policies, an organizational structure providing division of responsibilities, careful selection and training of qualified people, and a program of internal audits. Informed judgments are required by management to assess and balance the relative cost and expected benefit of the systems and controls.

The examination performed by Ernst & Whinney, our independent certified public accountants, includes a study and evaluation of the company's accounting systems, procedures and internal controls, and tests and other auditing procedures sufficient to provide reasonable assurance that the financial statements are neither materially misleading nor contain material errors.

The Board of Directors, through its Audit Committee consisting solely of outside directors of the company, is responsible for reviewing and monitoring the company's financial reporting and accounting practices. Ernst & Whinney and the internal auditors both have access to the Audit Committee, and meet with it regularly, with and without the presence of management.

N. S. Gifford
President

Report of Ernst & Whinney, Independent Auditors

To the Shareholders
Dennison Manufacturing Company
Framingham, Massachusetts

We have examined the consolidated balance sheets of Dennison Manufacturing Company and subsidiaries as of December 31, 1982 and 1981, and the related consolidated statements of earnings, earnings reinvested, and changes in financial position for each of the three years in the period ended December 31, 1982. Our examinations were made in accordance with generally accepted auditing standards and, accordingly, included such tests of the accounting records and such other auditing procedures as we considered necessary in the circumstances.

In our opinion, the financial statements referred to above present fairly the consolidated financial position of Dennison Manufacturing Company and subsidiaries at December 31, 1982 and 1981, and the consolidated results of their operations and changes in their financial position for each of the three years in the period ended December 31, 1982, in conformity with generally accepted accounting principles applied on a consistent basis.

Ernst & Whinney

Boston, Massachusetts
February 9, 1983

Source: Reprinted with permission of Dennison Manufacturing Company.

[1] Dennison Manufacturing Company, *Annual Report,* 1982, p. 1.

Consolidated Balance Sheet
Dennison Manufacturing Company and Subsidiaries

(Thousands of Dollars)

December 31	1982	1981
Assets		
Current Assets		
Cash and marketable securities	**$ 24,618**	$ 15,505
Trade accounts receivable, less allowance of $3,147 ($2,264 in 1981) for doubtful accounts	**94,147**	96,621
Inventories:		
Finished products	**35,039**	33,049
In process	**25,747**	23,703
Raw materials and supplies	**32,559**	35,011
	93,345	91,763
Prepaid expenses and other current assets	**3,110**	3,416
Total Current Assets	**215,220**	207,305
Other Assets		
Cost in excess of net assets acquired — Note B	**6,618**	7,110
Miscellaneous receivables and investments	**7,770**	6,812
Total Other Assets	**14,388**	13,922
Property, Plant and Equipment		
Land	**4,030**	3,764
Buildings and building equipment	**56,736**	49,611
Machinery and equipment	**190,501**	181,991
Construction in progress	**5,603**	7,600
	256,870	242,966
Less allowance for depreciation	**127,977**	123,664
Property, Plant and Equipment — Net	**128,893**	119,302
	$358,501	$340,529

The accompanying notes are an integral part of the consolidated financial statements.

December 31	1982	1981
Liabilities and Shareholders' Equity		
Current Liabilities		
Notes payable to banks	**$ 19,991**	$ 17,369
Accounts payable	**39,854**	39,906
Accrued compensation and amounts withheld	**18,339**	14,414
United States and foreign income taxes	**4,936**	4,876
Taxes, other than income taxes	**1,578**	1,462
Other accrued expenses	**6,816**	4,937
Current maturities of long-term debt	**2,241**	1,642
Total Current Liabilities	**93,755**	84,606
Long-Term Debt, less current maturities — Note C	**54,313**	52,442
Other Long-Term Liabilities	**6,687**	4,484
Deferred Income Taxes — Note L	**8,543**	7,830
Shareholders' Equity — Notes C, G, H and I		
Capital Stock:		
$1 Cumulative Convertible Preferred Stock, par value $10 per share, 395,000 shares authorized; issued and outstanding, 225,000 in 1982 and 1981	**2,250**	2,250
Common Stock, par value $1 per share, 30,000,000 shares authorized; issued and outstanding, 9,316,903 in 1982 and 9,300,691 in 1981	**9,317**	9,301
Capital in excess of par value	**32,654**	32,375
Earnings reinvested	**162,352**	155,763
Equity adjustment for foreign currency translation — Note F	**(6,386)**	(2,835)
	200,187	196,854
Less account receivable from Employee Stock Ownership Trust	**4,984**	5,687
Total Shareholders' Equity	**195,203**	191,167
	$358,501	$340,529

Statement of Consolidated Earnings
Dennison Manufacturing Company and Subsidiaries

Year Ended December 31	1982	1981	1980
	(Thousands of Dollars, Except Per-Share Amounts)		
Net Sales	**$577,281**	$569,701	$492,414
Operating Expenses — Notes E, I and K			
Cost of products sold	**383,412**	375,776	321,361
Selling, general and administrative	**148,089**	142,642	127,218
	531,501	518,418	448,579
Operating Earnings	**45,780**	51,283	43,835
Other Income (Expense), net — Note J	**(9,801)**	359	(2,253)
Earnings Before Income Taxes	**35,979**	51,642	41,582
Income Taxes — Note L	**15,342**	21,568	18,327
Net Earnings	**$ 20,637**	$ 30,074	$ 23,255
Net Earnings per Share	**$2.10**	$3.05	$2.42

Statement of Consolidated Earnings Reinvested
Dennison Manufacturing Company and Subsidiaries

Year Ended December 31	1982	1981	1980
Balance at Beginning of Year	**$155,763**	$138,240	$125,989
Net earnings for the year	**20,637**	30,074	23,255
	176,400	168,314	149,244
Less cash dividends paid:			
Preferred Stock ($2.88, $2.60 and $2.32 per share in 1982, 1981 and 1980, respectively)	**648**	566	452
Common Stock ($1.44, $1.30 and $1.16 per share in 1982, 1981 and 1980, respectively)	**13,400**	11,985	10,552
	14,048	12,551	11,004
Balance at End of Year	**$162,352**	$155,763	$138,240

The accompanying notes are an integral part of the consolidated financial statements.

Statement of Changes in Consolidated Financial Position
Dennison Manufacturing Company and Subsidiaries

Years Ended December 31	1982	1981	1980
	(Thousands of Dollars)		
Cash Provided by Operations:			
Net earnings	**$20,637**	$30,074	$23,255
Non-cash items included in net earnings:			
Depreciation	**18,353**	15,432	13,826
Deferred income taxes	**521**	655	985
Other	**298**	591	476
	39,809	46,752	38,542
Increase (decrease) in cash caused by certain working capital items:			
Trade accounts receivable	**2,474**	(16,812)	(5,404)
Inventories	**(1,582)**	(15,933)	(1,300)
Prepaid expenses and other current assets	**306**	(13)	2,031
Accounts payable	**(52)**	8,183	3,839
Other current liabilities	**5,980**	3,297	2,266
Effect of exchange rate changes	**(181)**	(477)	
Net Cash Flow from Operations	**46,754**	24,997	39,974
Financing Activities:			
Issuance of long-term debt	**2,500**	27,000	
Payment of long-term debt	**(1,104)**	(3,785)	(2,222)
Increase in current notes payable to banks	**2,622**	1,799	6,313
Payments from Employee Stock Ownership Trust	**703**	1,267	1,289
Common Stock issued in connection with acquisition of a business		2,278	
Proceeds from the exercise of stock options	**24**	487	217
Other — net	**592**	(427)	591
	5,337	28,619	6,188
Net Cash Provided from All Sources	**52,091**	53,616	46,162
Cash Used For:			
Purchase of property, plant and equipment, net	**23,206**	29,001	24,885
Net non-current assets of businesses acquired	**5,724**	6,690	
Acquisition of minority interests		2,840	
Cash dividends to shareholders	**14,048**	12,551	11,004
	42,978	51,082	35,889
Net Increase in Cash and Marketable Securities	**9,113**	2,534	10,273
Cash and Marketable Securities at Beginning of Year	**15,505**	12,971	2,698
Cash and Marketable Securities at End of Year	**$24,618**	$15,505	$12,971

The accompanying notes are an integral part of the consolidated financial statements.

Notes to Consolidated Financial Statements

Dennison Manufacturing Company and Subsidiaries

Note A — Summary of Significant Accounting Policies

Principles of Consolidation: The consolidated financial statements include the accounts of the company and its domestic and foreign subsidiaries. All significant intercompany accounts and transactions have been eliminated in consolidation. Certain reclassifications have been made in prior year statements to conform to the 1982 presentation.

Foreign Currency Translation: The company adopted the provisions of the Statement of Financial Accounting Standards No. 52, "Foreign Currency Translation" in 1981. Under the provisions of FASB No. 52 assets and liabilities of most foreign subsidiaries are translated at the exchange rate in effect at the balance sheet dates. Income statement accounts are translated at the average rate of exchange prevailing during each year. The resulting translation adjustments are excluded from net earnings and accumulated as a separate component of shareholders' equity. Transaction adjustments are included in net income. For 1980 and prior years, certain balance sheet accounts including inventory, property, plant and equipment, and other nonmonetary items were translated at historical exchange rates, and all translation adjustments were made directly to income. If the company had adopted the new standard in 1980, reported net earnings for that year would not have changed significantly and no significant translation adjustment would have been required at January 1, 1980. Net realized exchange losses in 1982 and 1981 and net exchange losses in 1980 are reflected in operations and are not material.

Marketable Securities: These assets are carried at cost which approximates market.

Inventories: Inventories are valued at the lower of cost or market. Of the total inventories at December 31, 1982 and 1981, $62,447,000 and $64,417,000, respectively, were determined on the last-in, first-out method (LIFO) and $30,898,000 and $27,346,000, respectively, on the first-in, first-out method (FIFO). If the entire inventory were valued on the basis of estimated replacement cost, inventories would have been $37,656,000 and $40,294,000 higher than reported at December 31, 1982 and 1981, respectively.

Intangible Assets: The excess cost over net assets of businesses acquired is, in general, being amortized over a forty-year period. Patents, copyrights, trademarks and other intangible assets are being amortized over their estimated useful lives.

Property, Plant and Equipment: These assets are carried at cost. Expenditures for maintenance, repairs and renewals are charged to expense as incurred, while major betterments are capitalized. The company provides for depreciation of property, plant and equipment principally by use of the double-declining method; however, the straight-line method is used for certain classes of assets. These methods have been applied in a manner that is intended to amortize the cost of the assets over their useful lives.

Research and Development Costs: Research and development costs are charged to earnings as incurred. The total expense for research and development was $15,684,000 in 1982, $12,827,000 in 1981 and $8,844,000 in 1980. Certain amounts have been reclassified in 1981 to conform to the 1982 presentation.

Income Taxes: The company provides for income taxes actually payable and for deferred taxes related to timing differences between financial and taxable income. Investment tax credits are reflected as a reduction in the provision for income taxes to the extent allowable (flow-through method). Deferred income taxes are not provided on undistributed earnings of foreign subsidiaries, which are considered to be reinvested indefinitely. United States taxes payable, on foreign earnings which may be remitted, will be largely offset by foreign tax credits.

Pension Plans: The company maintains various pension plans covering qualified employees. Under the actuarial cost methods used, pension expense includes current cost and amortization of prior service costs over thirty-year periods. Pension expense is accrued and funded annually.

Earnings Per Share: Computations of earnings per share are based on the weighted average of common shares outstanding and the dilutive effect of shares issuable upon the assumed exercise of stock options and Performance Convertible Debenture Units and the conversion of Preferred Stock. The number of shares used in the computation was 9,827,440 in 1982, 9,873,219 in 1981, and 9,645,133 in 1980. Fully diluted earnings per share are substantially the same as reported earnings per share.

Note B — Business Combinations

During 1982 the company acquired 75% of the H. Weiss-Buob Company of Wolfhalden, Switzerland, a supplier of stationery products. Also acquired was Metallised Films and Papers, Ltd., of Blaenavon, Wales (UK), a manufacturer of metallized products. These companies were acquired in purchase transactions for approximately $5,600,000. The excess of cost over net assets acquired was approximately $1,000,000.

During 1981 three companies, a 70% interest in a fourth company, and the minority interests in two companies were acquired in purchase transactions for approximately $15,400,000 in cash and stock. The excess of cost over net assets acquired was approximately $4,000,000.

The statements of consolidated earnings include the results of operations of companies acquired from their respective dates of acquisition. The effect on revenues and net earnings of the acquired companies in the years acquired and in the period prior to acquisition is not material.

Note C — Long-Term Debt

Long-term debt consisted of the following at December 31:

	1982	1981
13% Senior Notes due in annual principal installments of $2,300,000 beginning April 15, 1987	$23,000,000	$23,000,000
8¼% Sinking Fund Debentures	11,616,000	11,810,000
8¾% Senior Notes due in annual principal installments of $500,000 beginning January 15, 1983	5,000,000	5,000,000
9¾% Senior Notes due in annual principal installments of $833,000	2,501,000	3,334,000
Capital lease obligations	1,137,000	1,212,000
7⅜% to 12¾% Industrial Revenue Bonds, due 1985 through 2001	7,500,000	5,000,000
Other	5,800,000	4,728,000
	56,554,000	54,084,000
Less current maturities	2,241,000	1,642,000
	$54,313,000	$52,442,000

The 8¼% Sinking Fund Debentures were issued under an indenture which annually requires the company to redeem through a sinking fund not less than $1,000,000 nor more than $2,000,000 principal amount of Debentures through 1996. The indenture permits the company to make additional redemptions of Debentures at prices which decline each year from 103.71% effective June 1, 1982, to 100% after May 31, 1991.

Through December 31, 1982, the company had acquired $2,384,000 principal amount of Debentures for future sinking fund requirements.

The long-term debt agreements restrict the payment of cash dividends and purchases of capital stock. Under the most restrictive provisions of these agreements, consolidated net earnings reinvested of $37,243,000 were unrestricted at December 31, 1982.

The aggregate annual principal payments due for each of the next five years are as follows:
1983 – $2,241,000; 1984 – $2,296,000; 1985 – $2,637,000;
1986 – $2,116,000; 1987 – $4,859,000.

Note D — Credit Arrangements

Under line of credit arrangements for short-term debt with banks, the company may borrow up to $62,181,000 on such terms as the company and the banks may mutually agree upon. The majority of these arrangements do not have termination dates and can be withdrawn at the bank's option. At December 31, 1982, the unused portion of the credit lines was $47,262,000. In connection with these credit lines, the company maintains compensating cash balances which are not material.

Note E — Leases

The aggregate future minimum lease payments under capital leases (not material in amount) and noncancellable operating leases with initial or remaining terms of one year or more were as follows December 31, 1982:

1983	$5,172,000
1984	3,768,000
1985	2,645,000
1986	1,569,000
1987	780,000
After 1987	4,495,000
Total minimum future lease payments	$18,429,000

Rental expense for all operating leases was $8,433,000 in 1982, $7,844,000 in 1981 and $6,616,000 in 1980. Contingent rentals were not material.

Note F — Equity Adjustment for Foreign Currency Translation

Following is a reconciliation of the equity adjustment for foreign currency translation.

	1982	1981
Balance at beginning of year	$(2,835,000)	
Adjustment from restating asset and liability balances to adopt the current rate method of translation		$ (627,000)
Current year adjustment	(3,551,000)	(2,208,000)
Balance at end of year	$(6,386,000)	$(2,835,000)

Note G — Capital Stock and Capital in Excess of Par Value

The following table summarizes the changes in the company's capital stock and capital in excess of par value accounts for the three years ended December 31, 1982:

	Common Stock	$1 Cumulative Convertible Preferred Stock	Capital in Excess of Par Value
	(Thousands of Dollars)		
Balance at January 1, 1980	$9,090	$1,300	$28,281
Issuance of Common Shares upon exercise of options	18		199
Issuance of 65,000 Preferred Shares		650	849
Balance at December 31, 1980	9,108	1,950	29,329
Issuance of Common Shares upon exercise of options	39		448
Issuance of 30,000 Preferred Shares		300	474
Issuance of Common Shares in connection with acquisition	154		2,124
Balance at December 31, 1981	9,301	2,250	32,375
Issuance of Common Shares in connection with the Performance Convertible Debenture Unit Plan	14		257
Issuance of Common Shares upon exercise of options	2		22
Balance at December 31, 1982	$9,317	$2,250	$32,654

The Preferred Shares are entitled to preferential cumulative dividends at the greater of (a) $1 per share per year, or (b) twice the amount per share paid on Common Shares (adjusted for any stock splits), as and when declared by the Board of Directors. In the event of a distribution of the company's assets on dissolution, sale of its property, or liquidation, the Preferred Shares shall receive $25 per share ($5,625,000 in the aggregate) plus any unpaid accumulated dividends. The Preferred Shares may be converted by the holder into Common Shares at any time after the fifth anniversary of the issuance thereof.

The number of Common Shares into which each Preferred Share may be converted varies from one and one-half shares to two and one-half shares. The conversion ratio is determined by comparing the average market value of Common Shares at conversion with the average market value preceding issuance. The Preferred Shares are redeemable by the company at $25 per share at any time after the tenth anniversary of issuance, but any holder has the right to convert into Common Shares rather than sell. The Preferred Shares vote share for share with the Common Shares on most issues presented to shareholders for action. Under certain circumstances, including a proposal to merge the company into another business or to sell substantially all of its assets, approval is required by three-fourths of each outstanding class, voting separately.

At December 31, 1982, 1,003,404 Common Shares were reserved for issuance upon the exercise of options, conversion of Preferred Shares and conversions of Performance Convertible Debenture Units (Note H).

Note H — Stock Options and Incentive Plans

The company's 1973 Qualified Stock Option Plan expired on December 31, 1982. During 1982, 1981 and 1980, options for 1,750, 39,191, and 18,000 shares, respectively, were exercised at prices ranging from $10.11 to $13.57.

During the year, the company adopted the 1982 Incentive Stock Option Plan. This plan is intended to encourage ownership of stock by key employees, through issuance of Incentive Stock Options, as defined under the Internal Revenue Code. The plan provides for the granting of options for up to 250,000 shares at prices not less than the fair market value on the date of grant. No option may be exercised later than the fifth anniversary of the date on which it is granted. On April 30, 1982, the company granted 150,000 options under this plan at $17.00 per share, the fair market value on that date. An additional 1,000 options were granted on August 2, 1982, at $18.50 per share. Options granted are exercisable on a cumulative basis at a rate of 25% for each full year of service completed following the grant date. At December 31, 1982, after cancellation of 4,000 options, there were outstanding options to purchase an aggregate of 147,000 shares of Common Stock.

Under the company's Performance Convertible Debenture Unit Plan, awards are made by the Board of Directors to eligible executives in the form of units, which generally mature at the end of five years. At such time each participant must elect to receive either (a) Common Stock of the company, the number of shares of which are established at the award date, or (b) cash for each unit in an amount equal to the book value per share of the Common Stock at maturity date. During 1982, 14,462 shares of Common Stock were issued under this plan upon maturity of awarded units. At December 31, 1982, the total number of units outstanding may be converted into 190,904 shares of Common Stock at maturity.

Note I — Employee Stock Benefit Plans

The company has an Employee Stock Ownership Plan (ESOP) and a Stock Savings Plan (SSP) which enable most employees to acquire shares of the company's Common Stock. The cost of the ESOP is borne by the company through annual contributions to an Employee Stock Ownership Trust in amounts determined by the Board of Directors. Through December 31, 1982, the SSP provided for employee and company contributions up to a specified amount. Effective January 1, 1983, the SSP does not provide for employee contributions.

Shares of Common Stock acquired by the plans are to be allocated to each employee and held until the employee's retirement or death. Contributions to the plans amounted to $1,042,000 in 1982, $1,523,000 in 1981 and $1,484,000 in 1980.

At December 31, 1982 and 1981, indebtedness of the Employee Stock Ownership Trust to the company in the amount of $4,984,000 and $5,687,000, respectively, has been shown as a deduction from shareholders' equity in the consolidated balance sheet. At December 31, 1982, the Employee Stock Ownership Trust owned 761,484 shares of Common Stock, of which 652,979 shares have been allocated to employees, and 225,000 shares of Preferred Stock. Employees are entitled to vote allocated shares. The Trustees are entitled to vote unallocated Common Shares and all Preferred Shares.

Note J — Other Income (Expense), Net

Other income (expense), net, for the years ended December 31, consisted of the following.

	1982	1981	1980
Gains on exchange and sale of assets	**$ 1,875,000**		
Gain on sale of Ofrex shares		$4,956,000	
Research and development — Delphax Systems and Biological Technology Corporation	**(4,498,000)**	(2,895,000)	$ (33,000)
Interest expense	**(9,344,000)**	(7,544,000)	(5,828,000)
Interest and other income (expense), net	**2,166,000**	5,842,000	3,608,000
	$(9,801,000)	$ 359,000	$(2,253,000)

In a nonmonetary exchange of property during 1982, the company acquired a building and tract of land, resulting in a before-tax gain of approximately $1,426,000 and a net gain of $929,000 ($.09 per share).

Delphax Systems is a joint venture of the company and Canada Development Corporation formed for the purpose of developing a high-speed, non-impact printer. Biological Technology Corporation is a subsidiary developing diagnostic products. The company's equity share of all expenditures made by these development-stage companies is charged to research and development expense as incurred.

During the months of July and August, 1981, the company acquired 27% of the outstanding shares of Ofrex Group Limited, U.K. In August, 1981, the company sold those shares, which resulted in an after-tax gain of approximately $2,400,000 ($.24 per share).

Note K — Pension Plans

Total pension expense for 1982, 1981 and 1980 was $4,901,000, $5,173,000 and $4,434,000, respectively.

A comparison of accumulated plan benefits and plan net assets for the company's domestic defined benefit plans, as reported at the most recent actuarial report dates, is presented below:

	1982	1981
Actuarial present value of accumulated plan benefits		
Vested	**$46,223,000**	$42,182,000
Nonvested	**2,949,000**	2,025,000
	$49,172,000	$44,207,000
Net assets available for benefits	**$54,257,000**	$46,715,000

The weighted average assumed rate of return used in determining the actuarial present value of accumulated plan benefits was 8% and 7½% for 1982 and 1981, respectively. The effect of the change in the assumed rate of return was not material. For the company's foreign plans, the actuarially computed value of vested benefits as of December 31, 1982 and 1981, does not exceed the total of those plans' pension funds and net balance sheet accruals.

Note L — Income Taxes

The components of earnings before income taxes and income tax expense for the years ended December 31, 1982, 1981 and 1980 are as follows:

	1982	1981	1980
Earnings before income taxes			
United States	**$30,376,000**	$45,492,000	$35,444,000
Foreign	**5,603,000**	6,150,000	6,138,000
	$35,979,000	$51,642,000	$41,582,000
Currently payable income taxes:			
United States	**$10,350,000**	$16,143,000	$12,635,000
State	**2,191,000**	2,193,000	2,586,000
Foreign	**2,280,000**	2,577,000	2,121,000
	$14,821,000	$20,913,000	$17,342,000
Deferred income taxes:			
United States	**$ 358,000**	$ 997,000	$ 593,000
Foreign	**163,000**	(342,000)	392,000
	$15,342,000	$21,568,000	$18,327,000

Deferred income taxes are due primarily to an excess of tax depreciation over that charged against earnings for financial accounting purposes. This amount is reduced by various charges including deferred compensation.

The difference between the U.S. federal income tax rate of 46% and the company's effective income tax rate is as follows.

December 31	**1982**	1981	1980
Federal income tax rate	**46.0%**	46.0%	46.0%
State taxes, net of reduction of federal tax	**3.3**	2.3	3.4
Investment tax credit	**(6.7)**	(5.3)	(4.6)
Other, net		(1.2)	(0.7)
Effective income tax rate	**42.6%**	41.8%	44.1%

Federal income taxes have been reduced by investment tax credits of $2,398,000 in 1982, $2,753,000 in 1981, and $1,929,000 in 1980.

Note M — Business Segments

Financial information about the company's business segments for the three years ended December 31, 1982, is as follows:

(in thousands of dollars)	Retail Systems	Stationery Products and Systems	Technical Papers	Industrial Systems	Corporate	Eliminations	Consolidated
Net Sales to Unaffiliated Customers:							
1982	**$64,228**	**$254,950**	**$ 92,588**	**$165,515**			**$577,281**
1981	66,350	242,005	91,282	170,064			569,701
1980	57,024	217,196	67,799	150,395			492,414
Intersegment Net Sales:							
1982	**$ 932**	**$ 2,169**	**$ 13,822**	**$ 11,760**		**$(28,683)**	
1981	1,922	3,152	13,200	11,076		(29,350)	
1980	1,668	2,399	12,765	11,090		(27,922)	
Total Net Sales:							
1982	**$65,160**	**$257,119**	**$106,410**	**$177,275**		**$(28,683)**	**$577,281**
1981	68,272	245,157	104,482	181,140		(29,350)	569,701
1980	58,692	219,595	80,564	161,485		(27,922)	492,414
Segment Income (Loss) from Operations:							
1982	**$ 5,654**	**$ 30,885**	**$ 1,653**	**$ 16,021**	**$(8,433)**		**$ 45,780**
1981	9,805	29,652	3,554	15,980	(7,708)		51,283
1980	8,149	27,596	(1,970)	16,783	(6,723)		43,835
Identifiable Assets:							
1982	**$37,392**	**$147,859**	**$ 48,919**	**$ 98,163**	**$26,020**	**$ 148**	**$358,501**
1981	37,812	142,659	49,002	89,156	21,646	254	340,529
1980	28,229	112,907	39,908	76,811	18,667	6,850	283,372
Capital Expenditures:							
1982	**$ 3,714**	**$ 7,540**	**$ 3,573**	**$ 11,781**	**$ 246**		**$ 26,854**
1981	3,610	9,309	5,027	12,415	361		30,722
1980	3,854	8,203	3,235	10,087	562		25,941
Depreciation Expense:							
1982	**$ 2,721**	**$ 4,978**	**$ 3,416**	**$ 6,781**	**$ 457**		**$ 18,353**
1981	1,989	4,522	2,991	5,384	546		15,432
1980	1,669	3,790	2,722	4,853	792		13,826

The major products of each of the above business segments are described on pages 4 through 13 of the Annual Report. Corporate Assets are principally cash and marketable securities. The corporate charge to operations includes general and administrative corporate expenses. Certain amounts previously reflected as general corporate expenses in 1980 and 1981 have been allocated to the company's business segments to provide consistent treatment with 1982.

The following table summarizes Dennison's operations in different geographic areas for the three years ended December 31, 1982:

(in thousands of dollars)	United States	Foreign (a)	Corporate	Eliminations	Consolidated
Net Sales to Unaffiliated Customers:					
1982	**$480,522**	**$96,759**			**$577,281**
1981	492,986	76,715			569,701
1980	419,920	72,494			492,414
Income (Loss) from Operations:					
1982	**$ 44,994**	**$ 9,219**	**$(8,433)**		**$ 45,780**
1981	50,115	8,876	(7,708)		51,283
1980	41,346	9,212	(6,723)		43,835
Identifiable Assets:					
1982	**$288,681**	**$69,672**		**$ 148**	**$358,501**
1981	275,358	64,917		254	340,529
1980	232,368	44,154		6,850	283,372

(a)No single geographic area accounts for more than 10% of consolidated amounts.

Intersegment and interarea sales and transfer prices are subject to negotiation annually between the buying and selling operating units. The prices are generally at cost plus a percentage markup.

Export sales and interarea sales are less than 10% of total consolidated sales.

Note N — Supplemental Information on the Effects of Changing Prices (Unaudited)

The following financial information has been prepared in accordance with the methods outlined by Financial Accounting Standard No. 33 — Financial Reporting and Changing Prices. In 1982 Financial Accounting Standard No. 70 — Changing Prices: Foreign Currency Translation, was issued, amending FASB No. 33 to accommodate the change in the method of translating foreign currency financial statements required by FASB No. 52. Under the provisions of FASB No. 70, a company measuring a significant part of its operations in foreign currencies is no longer required to disclose historical cost information in units of constant purchasing power. The supplemental current cost information has been prepared on a basis consistent with the method used in the primary statements to account for foreign currency translation. Accordingly, 1982 and 1981 current cost information has been calculated excluding the effects of exchange rate changes. Adjustments to the current cost information to reflect the effects of general inflation are based on the U.S. CPI-U for both domestic and foreign operations.

The purpose of Statement No. 33 is to provide, on an experimental basis, certain measurements of the effects of changes in prices on a company's operations. It should be noted, however, that the development of current cost information involves the use of assumptions and estimates, and, therefore, the resulting measurements should be viewed in that context and not as precise indicators of the effects of changes in prices.

The objective of the current cost method is to reflect the effects of changes in specific prices (current cost) of the resources actually used in a company's operations. Current replacement costs have been used for these items. That is, specific prices that would have to be paid currently have been used as replacement costs. For the most part, the replacement data represents replacement in-place and in-kind. No consideration has been given to the replacement of assets of a different type, to improve operating cost efficiencies of replacement assets. The replacement costs used, while reasonable, are necessarily subjective.

The gain in purchasing power of net amounts owed is derived from the concept that monetary assets and monetary liabilities decrease in value with inflation. The gain is calculated by measuring the increase in purchasing power for the year attributable to general inflation, having taken into account net balances of monetary liabilities at the beginning and end of the year and transactions for the year.

Statement of Income from Operations Adjusted for Changing Prices for the Year Ended 1982

(in thousands of dollars, except per-share amounts)	As Reported in the Primary Statements	Specific Prices (Current Cost)
Net Sales	$577,281	$577,281
Cost of products sold	369,120	370,097
Selling, general and administrative	144,028	144,028
Depreciation expense	18,353	24,853
Other income (expense)	(9,801)	(9,801)
Earnings before income taxes	35,979	28,502
Income taxes	15,342	15,342
Net earnings	$ 20,637	$ 13,160
Effective income tax rate	43%	54%
Other Information:		
Increase in specific prices (current costs) of inventories and property, plant and equipment held during the year (a)		$ 10,268
Less effect of increase in general price level		13,014
Increase in general price level over increase in specific prices		$ 2,746

(a) At December 31, 1982, current cost of inventory was $131,001,000, and current cost of property, plant and equipment, net of accumulated depreciation was $211,539,000.

Note N — Supplemental Information on the Effects of Changing Prices (Unaudited) — Continued

Five-Year Comparison of Selected Supplementary Financial Data Adjusted for Effects of Changing Prices

Net sales for the five-year period from 1978 to 1982, expressed in average 1982 dollars, show a decrease of 1.2 percent as compared with a 9.0 percent annual compounded growth rate calculated on a historical dollar basis.

Actual dividends per Common Share grew at a 17.3 percent compounded rate through 1982. This increase is adjusted to 6.5 percent when calculated on the basis of restating dividends for the five years into average 1982 dollars. Similarly, the market price per Common Share over the five-year period, in terms of average 1982 dollars, grew at an annual rate of 2.4 percent compared to an annual rate of increase of 12.2 percent in historical dollars.

Information relative to the change in specific prices of property and inventory excludes the effect of exchange rate changes in 1982 and 1981, in amounts approximating $4,500,000 and $3,200,000, respectively.

Five Year Comparison of Selected Supplementary Financial Data Adjusted for Effects of General Inflation

(In Average 1982 Dollars — in thousands)

Years Ended December 31	1982	1981	1980	1979	1978
Net Sales:					
Historical	**$577,281**	$569,701	$492,414	$449,594	$408,897
Adjusted for General Inflation	**577,281**	604,628	576,811	597,873	604,975
Current Cost Information:					
Net Earnings	**13,160**	23,051	14,218	20,060	
Net Earnings per Common Share	**1.34**	2.33	1.47	2.16	
Net Assets at Year-End	**$309,967**	$327,816	$311,238	$302,138	
Other Information:					
Gain from decline in purchasing power of net amounts owed	**$ 1,270**	$ 1,528	$ 1,369	$ 1,446	
Excess of increase in specific prices over the increase in the general price level		4,168	9,268	6,390	
Increase in general price level over increase in specific prices	**2,746**				
Dividends per Common Share	**1.44**	1.38	1.36	1.33	
Market Price per Common Share at Year-End	**23.48**	22.85	19.44	22.64	21.37
Average Consumer Price Index	**289.1**	272.4	246.8	217.4	195.4

C Compound Interest Tables

Table C–1 Future Amount of a Single Sum of 1

n	1½%	2½%	4%	4½%	5%	5½%	6%	6½%
1	1.015000	1.025000	1.040000	1.045000	1.050000	1.055000	1.060000	1.065000
2	1.030225	1.050625	1.081600	1.092025	1.102500	1.113025	1.123600	1.134225
3	1.045678	1.076891	1.124864	1.141166	1.157625	1.174241	1.191016	1.207950
4	1.061364	1.103813	1.169859	1.192519	1.215506	1.238825	1.262477	1.286466
5	1.077284	1.131408	1.216653	1.246182	1.276282	1.306960	1.338226	1.370087
6	1.093443	1.159693	1.265319	1.302260	1.340096	1.378843	1.418519	1.459142
7	1.109845	1.188686	1.315932	1.360862	1.407100	1.454679	1.503630	1.553987
8	1.126493	1.218403	1.368569	1.422101	1.477455	1.534687	1.593848	1.654996
9	1.143390	1.248863	1.423312	1.486095	1.551328	1.619094	1.689479	1.762570
10	1.160541	1.280085	1.480244	1.552969	1.628895	1.708144	1.790848	1.877137
11	1.177949	1.312087	1.539454	1.622853	1.710339	1.802092	1.898299	1.999151
12	1.195618	1.344889	1.601032	1.695881	1.795856	1.901207	2.012196	2.129096
13	1.213552	1.378511	1.665074	1.772196	1.885649	2.005774	2.132928	2.267487
14	1.231756	1.412974	1.731676	1.851945	1.979932	2.116091	2.260904	2.414874
15	1.250232	1.448298	1.800944	1.935282	2.078928	2.232476	2.396558	2.571841
16	1.268986	1.484506	1.872981	2.022370	2.182875	2.355263	2.540352	2.739011
17	1.288020	1.521618	1.947900	2.113377	2.292018	2.484802	2.692773	2.917046
18	1.307341	1.559659	2.025817	2.208479	2.406619	2.621466	2.854339	3.106654
19	1.326951	1.598650	2.106849	2.307860	2.526950	2.765647	3.025600	3.308587
20	1.346855	1.638616	2.191123	2.411714	2.653298	2.917757	3.207135	3.523645
21	1.367058	1.679582	2.278768	2.520241	2.785963	3.078234	3.399564	3.752682
22	1.387564	1.721571	2.369919	2.633652	2.925261	3.247537	3.603537	3.996606
23	1.408377	1.764611	2.464716	2.752166	3.071524	3.426152	3.819750	4.256386
24	1.429503	1.808726	2.563304	2.876014	3.225100	3.614590	4.048935	4.533051
25	1.450945	1.853944	2.665836	3.005434	3.386355	3.813392	4.291871	4.827699
26	1.472710	1.900293	2.772470	3.140679	3.555673	4.023129	4.549383	5.141500
27	1.494800	1.947800	2.883369	3.282010	3.733456	4.244401	4.822346	5.475697
28	1.517222	1.996495	2.998703	3.429700	3.920129	4.477843	5.111687	5.831617
29	1.539981	2.046407	3.118651	3.584036	4.116136	4.724124	5.418388	6.210672
30	1.563080	2.097568	3.243398	3.745318	4.321942	4.983951	5.743491	6.614366
31	1.586526	2.150007	3.373133	3.913857	4.538039	5.258069	6.088101	7.044300
32	1.610324	2.203757	3.508059	4.089981	4.764941	5.547262	6.453387	7.502179
33	1.634479	2.258851	3.648381	4.274030	5.003189	5.852362	6.840590	7.989821
34	1.658996	2.315322	3.794316	4.466362	5.253348	6.174242	7.251025	8.509159
35	1.683881	2.373205	3.946089	4.667348	5.516015	6.513825	7.686087	9.062255
36	1.709140	2.432535	4.103933	4.877378	5.791816	6.872085	8.147252	9.651301
37	1.734777	2.493349	4.268090	5.096860	6.081407	7.250050	8.636087	10.278636
38	1.760798	2.555682	4.438813	5.326219	6.385477	7.648803	9.154252	10.946747
39	1.787210	2.619574	4.616366	5.565899	6.704751	8.069487	9.703507	11.658286
40	1.814018	2.685064	4.801021	5.816365	7.039989	8.513309	10.285718	12.416075

Table C—1 Future Amount of a Single Sum of 1 *(continued)*

n	7%	8%	9%	10%	12%	14%	16%	20%
1	1.070000	1.080000	1.090000	1.100000	1.120000	1.140000	1.160000	1.200000
2	1.144900	1.166400	1.188100	1.210000	1.254400	1.299600	1.345600	1.440000
3	1.225043	1.259712	1.295029	1.331000	1.404928	1.481544	1.560896	1.728000
4	1.310796	1.360489	1.411582	1.464100	1.573519	1.688960	1.810639	2.073600
5	1.402552	1.469328	1.538624	1.610510	1.762342	1.925415	2.100342	2.488320
6	1.500730	1.586874	1.677100	1.771561	1.973823	2.194973	2.436396	2.985984
7	1.605781	1.713824	1.828039	1.948717	2.210681	2.502269	2.826220	3.583181
8	1.718186	1.850930	1.992563	2.143589	2.475963	2.852586	3.278415	4.299817
9	1.838459	1.999005	2.171893	2.357948	2.773079	3.251949	3.802961	5.159780
10	1.967151	2.158925	2.367364	2.593742	3.105848	3.707221	4.411435	6.191736
11	2.104852	2.331639	2.580426	2.853117	3.478550	4.226232	5.117265	7.430084
12	2.252192	2.518170	2.812665	3.138428	3.895976	4.817905	5.936027	8.916100
13	2.409845	2.719624	3.065805	3.452271	4.363493	5.492411	6.885791	10.699321
14	2.578534	2.937194	3.341727	3.797498	4.887112	6.261349	7.987518	12.839185
15	2.759032	3.172169	3.642482	4.177248	5.473566	7.137938	9.265521	15.407022
16	2.952164	3.425943	3.970306	4.594973	6.130394	8.137249	10.748004	18.488426
17	3.158815	3.700018	4.327633	5.054470	6.866041	9.276464	12.467685	22.186111
18	3.379932	3.996019	4.717120	5.559917	7.689966	10.575169	14.462514	26.623333
19	3.616528	4.315701	5.141661	6.115909	8.612762	12.055693	16.776517	31.948000
20	3.869684	4.660957	5.604411	6.727500	9.646293	13.743490	19.460759	38.337600
21	4.140562	5.033834	6.108808	7.400250	10.803848	15.667578	22.574481	46.005120
22	4.430402	5.436540	6.658600	8.140275	12.100310	17.861039	26.186398	55.206144
23	4.740530	5.871464	7.257874	8.954302	13.552347	20.361585	30.376222	66.247373
24	5.072367	6.341181	7.911083	9.849733	15.178629	23.212207	35.236417	79.496847
25	5.427433	6.848475	8.623081	10.834706	17.000064	26.461916	40.874244	95.396217
26	5.807353	7.396353	9.399158	11.918177	19.040072	30.166584	47.414123	114.475460
27	6.213868	7.988061	10.245082	13.109994	21.324881	34.389906	55.000382	137.370552
28	6.648838	8.627106	11.167140	14.420994	23.883866	39.204493	63.800444	164.844662
29	7.114257	9.317275	12.172182	15.863093	26.749930	44.693122	74.008515	197.813595
30	7.612255	10.062657	13.267678	17.449402	29.959922	50.950159	85.849877	237.376314
31	8.145113	10.867669	14.461770	19.194342	33.555113	58.083181	99.585857	284.851577
32	8.715271	11.737083	15.763329	21.113777	37.581726	66.214826	115.519594	341.821892
33	9.325340	12.676050	17.182028	23.225154	42.091533	75.484902	134.002729	410.186270
34	9.978114	13.690134	18.728411	25.547670	47.142517	86.052788	155.443166	492.223524
35	10.676581	14.785344	20.413968	28.102437	52.799620	98.100178	180.314073	590.668229
36	11.423942	15.968172	22.251225	30.912681	59.135574	111.834203	209.164324	708.801875
37	12.223618	17.245626	24.253835	34.003949	66.231843	127.490992	242.630616	850.562250
38	13.079271	18.625276	26.436680	37.404343	74.179664	145.339731	281.451515	1020.674700
39	13.994820	20.115298	28.815982	41.144778	83.081224	165.687293	326.483757	1224.809640
40	14.974458	21.724521	31.409420	45.259256	93.050970	188.883514	378.721158	1469.771568

Table C–2 Present Value of a Single Sum of 1

n	1½%	2½%	4%	4½%	5%	5½%	6%	6½%
1	0.985222	0.975610	0.961538	0.956938	0.952381	0.947867	0.943396	0.938967
2	0.970662	0.951814	0.924556	0.915730	0.907029	0.898452	0.889996	0.881659
3	0.956317	0.928599	0.888996	0.876297	0.863838	0.851614	0.839619	0.827849
4	0.942184	0.905951	0.854804	0.838561	0.822702	0.807217	0.792094	0.777323
5	0.928260	0.883854	0.821927	0.802451	0.783526	0.765134	0.747258	0.729881
6	0.914542	0.862297	0.790315	0.767896	0.746215	0.725246	0.704961	0.685334
7	0.901027	0.841265	0.759918	0.734828	0.710681	0.687437	0.665057	0.643506
8	0.887711	0.820747	0.730690	0.703185	0.676839	0.651599	0.627412	0.604231
9	0.874592	0.800728	0.702587	0.672904	0.644609	0.617629	0.591898	0.567353
10	0.861667	0.781198	0.675564	0.643928	0.613913	0.585431	0.558395	0.532726
11	0.848933	0.762145	0.649581	0.616199	0.584679	0.554911	0.526788	0.500212
12	0.836387	0.743556	0.624597	0.589664	0.556837	0.525982	0.496969	0.469683
13	0.824027	0.725420	0.600574	0.564272	0.530321	0.498561	0.468839	0.441017
14	0.811849	0.707727	0.577475	0.539973	0.505068	0.472569	0.442301	0.414100
15	0.799852	0.690466	0.555265	0.516720	0.481017	0.447933	0.417265	0.388827
16	0.788031	0.673625	0.533908	0.494469	0.458112	0.424581	0.393646	0.365095
17	0.776385	0.657195	0.513373	0.473176	0.436297	0.402447	0.371364	0.342813
18	0.764912	0.641166	0.493628	0.452800	0.415521	0.381466	0.350344	0.321890
19	0.753607	0.625528	0.474642	0.433302	0.395734	0.361579	0.330513	0.302244
20	0.742470	0.610271	0.456387	0.414643	0.376889	0.342729	0.311805	0.283797
21	0.731498	0.595386	0.438834	0.396787	0.358942	0.324862	0.294155	0.266476
22	0.720688	0.580865	0.421955	0.379701	0.341850	0.307926	0.277505	0.250212
23	0.710037	0.566697	0.405726	0.363350	0.325571	0.291873	0.261797	0.234941
24	0.699544	0.552875	0.390121	0.347703	0.310068	0.276657	0.246979	0.220602
25	0.689206	0.539391	0.375117	0.332731	0.295303	0.262234	0.232999	0.207138
26	0.679021	0.526235	0.360689	0.318402	0.281241	0.248563	0.219810	0.194496
27	0.668986	0.513400	0.346817	0.304691	0.267848	0.235605	0.207368	0.182625
28	0.659099	0.500878	0.333477	0.291571	0.255094	0.223322	0.195630	0.171479
29	0.649359	0.488661	0.320651	0.279015	0.242946	0.211679	0.184557	0.161013
30	0.639762	0.476743	0.308319	0.267000	0.231377	0.200644	0.174110	0.151186
31	0.630308	0.465115	0.296460	0.255502	0.220359	0.190184	0.164255	0.141959
32	0.620993	0.453771	0.285058	0.244500	0.209866	0.180269	0.154957	0.133295
33	0.611816	0.442703	0.274094	0.233971	0.199873	0.170871	0.146186	0.125159
34	0.602774	0.431905	0.263552	0.223896	0.190355	0.161963	0.137912	0.117520
35	0.593866	0.421371	0.253415	0.214254	0.181290	0.153520	0.130105	0.110348
36	0.585090	0.411094	0.243669	0.205028	0.172657	0.145516	0.122741	0.103613
37	0.576443	0.401067	0.234297	0.196199	0.164436	0.137930	0.115793	0.097289
38	0.567924	0.391285	0.225285	0.187750	0.156605	0.130739	0.109239	0.091351
39	0.559531	0.381741	0.216621	0.179665	0.149148	0.123924	0.103056	0.085776
40	0.551262	0.372431	0.208289	0.171929	0.142046	0.117463	0.097222	0.080541

Table C—2 Present Value of a Single Sum of 1 *(continued)*

n	7%	8%	9%	10%	12%	14%	16%	20%
1	0.934579	0.925926	0.917431	0.909091	0.892857	0.877193	0.862069	0.833333
2	0.873439	0.857339	0.841680	0.826446	0.797194	0.769468	0.743163	0.694444
3	0.816298	0.793832	0.772183	0.751315	0.711780	0.674972	0.640658	0.578704
4	0.762895	0.735030	0.708425	0.683013	0.635518	0.592080	0.552291	0.482253
5	0.712986	0.680583	0.649931	0.620921	0.567427	0.519369	0.476113	0.401878
6	0.666342	0.630170	0.596267	0.564474	0.506631	0.455587	0.410442	0.334898
7	0.622750	0.583490	0.547034	0.513158	0.452349	0.399637	0.353830	0.279082
8	0.582009	0.540269	0.501866	0.466507	0.403883	0.350559	0.305025	0.232568
9	0.543934	0.500249	0.460428	0.424098	0.360610	0.307508	0.262953	0.193807
10	0.508349	0.463193	0.422411	0.385543	0.321973	0.269744	0.226684	0.161506
11	0.475093	0.428883	0.387533	0.350494	0.287476	0.236617	0.195417	0.134588
12	0.444012	0.397114	0.355535	0.318631	0.256675	0.207559	0.168463	0.112157
13	0.414964	0.367698	0.326179	0.289664	0.229174	0.182069	0.145227	0.093464
14	0.387817	0.340461	0.299246	0.263331	0.204620	0.159710	0.125195	0.077887
15	0.362446	0.315242	0.274538	0.239392	0.182696	0.140096	0.107927	0.064905
16	0.338735	0.291890	0.251870	0.217629	0.163122	0.122892	0.093041	0.054088
17	0.316574	0.270269	0.231073	0.197845	0.145644	0.107800	0.080207	0.045073
18	0.295864	0.250249	0.211994	0.179859	0.130040	0.094561	0.069144	0.037561
19	0.276508	0.231712	0.194490	0.163508	0.116107	0.082948	0.059607	0.031301
20	0.258419	0.214548	0.178431	0.148644	0.103667	0.072762	0.051385	0.026084
21	0.241513	0.198656	0.163698	0.135131	0.092560	0.063826	0.044298	0.021737
22	0.225713	0.183941	0.150182	0.122846	0.082643	0.055988	0.038188	0.018114
23	0.210947	0.170315	0.137781	0.111678	0.073788	0.049112	0.032920	0.015095
24	0.197147	0.157699	0.126405	0.101526	0.065882	0.043081	0.028380	0.012579
25	0.184249	0.146018	0.115968	0.092296	0.058823	0.037790	0.024465	0.010483
26	0.172195	0.135202	0.106393	0.083905	0.052521	0.033149	0.021091	0.008735
27	0.160930	0.125187	0.097608	0.076278	0.046894	0.029078	0.018182	0.007280
28	0.150402	0.115914	0.089548	0.069343	0.041869	0.025507	0.015674	0.006066
29	0.140563	0.107328	0.082155	0.063039	0.037383	0.022375	0.013512	0.005055
30	0.131367	0.099377	0.075371	0.057309	0.033378	0.019627	0.011648	0.004213
31	0.122773	0.092016	0.069148	0.052099	0.029802	0.017217	0.010042	0.003511
32	0.114741	0.085200	0.063438	0.047362	0.026609	0.015102	0.008657	0.002926
33	0.107235	0.078889	0.058200	0.043057	0.023758	0.013248	0.007463	0.002438
34	0.100219	0.073045	0.053395	0.039143	0.021212	0.011621	0.006433	0.002032
35	0.093663	0.067635	0.048986	0.035584	0.018940	0.010194	0.005546	0.001693
36	0.087535	0.062625	0.044941	0.032349	0.016910	0.008942	0.004781	0.001411
37	0.081809	0.057986	0.041231	0.029408	0.015098	0.007844	0.004121	0.001176
38	0.076457	0.053690	0.037826	0.026735	0.013481	0.006880	0.003553	0.000980
39	0.071455	0.049713	0.034703	0.024304	0.012036	0.006035	0.003063	0.000816
40	0.066780	0.046031	0.031838	0.022095	0.010747	0.005294	0.002640	0.000680

Table C–3 Future Amount of an Ordinary Annuity of 1

n	1½%	2½%	4%	4½%	5%	5½%	6%	6½%
1	1.000000	1.000000	1.000000	1.000000	1.000000	1.000000	1.000000	1.000000
2	2.015000	2.025000	2.040000	2.045000	2.050000	2.055000	2.060000	2.065000
3	3.045225	3.075625	3.121600	3.137025	3.152500	3.168025	3.183600	3.199225
4	4.090903	4.152516	4.246464	4.278191	4.310125	4.342266	4.374616	4.407175
5	5.152267	5.256329	5.416323	5.470710	5.525631	5.581091	5.637093	5.693641
6	6.229551	6.387737	6.632975	6.716892	6.801913	6.888051	6.975319	7.063728
7	7.322994	7.547430	7.898294	8.019152	8.142008	8.266894	8.393838	8.522870
8	8.432839	8.736116	9.214226	9.380014	9.549109	9.721573	9.897468	10.076856
9	9.559332	9.954519	10.582795	10.802114	11.026564	11.256260	11.491316	11.731852
10	10.702722	11.203382	12.006107	12.288209	12.577893	12.875354	13.180795	13.494423
11	11.863262	12.483466	13.486351	13.841179	14.206787	14.583498	14.971643	15.371560
12	13.041211	13.795553	15.025805	15.464032	15.917127	16.385591	16.869941	17.370711
13	14.236830	15.140442	16.626838	17.159913	17.712983	18.286798	18.882138	19.499808
14	15.450382	16.518953	18.291911	18.932109	19.598632	20.292572	21.015066	21.767295
15	16.682138	17.931927	20.023588	20.784054	21.578564	22.408663	23.275970	24.182169
16	17.932370	19.380225	21.824531	22.719337	23.657492	24.641140	25.672528	26.754010
17	19.201355	20.864730	23.697512	24.741707	25.840366	26.996403	28.212880	29.493021
18	20.489376	22.386349	25.645413	26.855084	28.132385	29.481205	30.905653	32.410067
19	21.796716	23.946007	27.671229	29.063562	30.539004	32.102671	33.759992	35.516722
20	23.123667	25.544658	29.778079	31.371423	33.065954	34.868318	36.785591	38.825309
21	24.470522	27.183274	31.969202	33.783137	35.719252	37.786076	39.992727	42.348954
22	25.837580	28.862856	34.247970	36.303378	38.505214	40.864310	43.392290	46.101636
23	27.225144	30.584427	36.617889	38.937030	41.430475	44.111847	46.995828	50.098242
24	28.633521	32.349038	39.082604	41.689196	44.501999	47.537998	50.815577	54.354628
25	30.063024	34.157764	41.645908	44.565210	47.727099	51.152588	54.864512	58.887679
26	31.513969	36.011708	44.311745	47.570645	51.113454	54.965981	59.156383	63.715378
27	32.986678	37.912001	47.084214	50.711324	54.669126	58.989109	63.705766	68.856877
28	34.481479	39.859801	49.967583	53.993333	58.402583	63.233510	68.528112	74.332574
29	35.998701	41.856296	52.966286	57.423033	62.322712	67.711354	73.639798	80.164192
30	37.538681	43.902703	56.084938	61.007070	66.438848	72.435478	79.058186	86.374864
31	39.101762	46.000271	59.328335	64.752388	70.760790	77.419429	84.801677	92.989230
32	40.688288	48.150278	62.701469	68.666245	75.298829	82.677498	90.889778	100.033530
33	42.298612	50.354034	66.209527	72.756226	80.063771	88.224760	97.343165	107.535710
34	43.933092	52.612885	69.857909	77.030256	85.066959	94.077122	104.183755	115.525531
35	45.592088	54.928207	73.652225	81.496618	90.320307	100.251364	111.434780	124.034690
36	47.275969	57.301413	77.598314	86.163966	95.836323	106.765189	119.120867	133.096945
37	48.985109	59.733948	81.702246	91.041344	101.628139	113.637274	127.268119	142.748247
38	50.719885	62.227297	85.970336	96.138205	107.709546	120.887324	135.904206	153.026883
39	52.480634	64.782979	90.409150	101.464424	114.095023	128.536127	145.058458	163.973630
40	54.267894	67.402554	95.025516	107.030323	120.799774	136.605614	154.761966	175.631916

Table C—3 Future Amount of an Ordinary Annuity of 1 *(continued)*

n	7%	8%	9%	10%	12%	14%	16%	20%
1	1.000000	1.000000	1.000000	1.000000	1.000000	1.000000	1.000000	1.000000
2	2.070000	2.080000	2.090000	2.100000	2.120000	2.140000	2.160000	2.200000
3	3.214900	3.246400	3.278100	3.310000	3.374400	3.439600	3.505600	3.640000
4	4.439943	4.506112	4.573129	4.641000	4.779328	4.921144	5.066496	5.368000
5	5.750739	5.866601	5.984711	6.105100	6.352847	6.610104	6.877135	7.441600
6	7.153291	7.335929	7.523335	7.715610	8.115189	8.535519	8.977477	9.929920
7	8.654021	8.922803	9.200435	9.487171	10.089012	10.730491	11.413873	12.915904
8	10.259803	10.636628	11.028474	11.435888	12.299693	13.232760	14.240093	16.499085
9	11.977989	12.487558	13.021036	13.579477	14.775656	16.085347	17.518508	20.798902
10	13.816448	14.486562	15.192930	15.937425	17.548735	19.337295	21.321469	25.958682
11	15.783599	16.645487	17.560293	18.531167	20.654583	23.044516	25.732904	32.150419
12	17.888451	18.977126	20.140720	21.384284	24.133133	27.270749	30.850169	39.580502
13	20.140643	21.495297	22.953385	24.522712	28.029109	32.088654	36.786196	48.496603
14	22.550488	24.214920	26.019189	27.974983	32.392602	37.581065	43.671987	59.195923
15	25.129022	27.152114	29.360916	31.772482	37.279715	43.842414	51.659505	72.035108
16	27.888054	30.324283	33.003399	35.949730	42.753280	50.980352	60.925026	87.442129
17	30.840217	33.750226	36.973705	40.544703	48.883674	59.117601	71.673030	105.930555
18	33.999033	37.450244	41.301338	45.599173	55.749715	68.394066	84.140715	128.116666
19	37.378965	41.446263	46.018458	51.159090	63.439681	78.969235	98.603230	154.740000
20	40.995492	45.761964	51.160120	57.274999	72.052442	91.024928	115.379747	186.688000
21	44.865177	50.422921	56.764530	64.002499	81.698736	104.768418	134.840506	225.025600
22	49.005739	55.456755	62.873338	71.402749	92.502584	120.435996	157.414987	271.030719
23	53.436141	60.893296	69.531939	79.543024	104.602894	138.297035	183.601385	326.236863
24	58.176671	66.764759	76.789813	88.497327	118.155241	158.658620	213.977607	392.484236
25	63.249038	73.105940	84.700896	98.347059	133.333870	181.870827	249.214024	471.981083
26	68.676470	79.954415	93.323977	109.181765	150.333934	208.332743	290.088267	567.377300
27	74.483823	87.350768	102.723135	121.099942	169.374007	238.499327	337.502390	681.852760
28	80.697691	95.338830	112.968217	134.209936	190.698887	272.889233	392.502773	819.223312
29	87.346529	103.965936	124.135356	148.630930	214.582754	312.093725	456.303216	984.067974
30	94.460786	113.283211	136.307539	164.494023	241.332684	356.786847	530.311731	1181.881569
31	102.073041	123.345868	149.575217	181.943425	271.292606	407.737006	616.161608	1419.257883
32	110.218154	134.213537	164.036987	201.137767	304.847719	465.820186	715.747465	1704.109459
33	118.933425	145.950620	179.800315	222.251544	342.429446	532.035012	831.267059	2045.931351
34	128.258765	158.626670	196.982344	245.476699	384.520979	607.519914	965.269789	2456.117621
35	138.236878	172.316804	215.710755	271.024368	431.663496	693.572702	1120.712955	2948.341146
36	148.913460	187.102148	236.124723	299.126805	484.463116	791.672881	1301.027028	3539.009375
37	160.337402	203.070320	258.375948	330.039486	543.598690	903.507084	1510.191352	4247.811250
38	172.561020	220.315945	282.629783	364.043434	609.830533	1030.998076	1752.821968	5098.373500
39	185.640292	238.941221	309.066463	401.447778	684.010197	1176.337806	2034.273483	6119.048200
40	199.635112	259.056519	337.882445	442.592556	767.091420	1342.025099	2360.757241	7343.857840

Table C–4 Present Value of an Ordinary Annuity of 1

n	1½%	2½%	4%	4½%	5%	5½%	6%	6½%
1	0.985222	0.975610	0.961538	0.956938	0.952381	0.947867	0.943396	0.938967
2	1.955883	1.927424	1.886095	1.872668	1.859410	1.846320	1.833393	1.820626
3	2.912200	2.856024	2.775091	2.748964	2.723248	2.697933	2.673012	2.648476
4	3.854385	3.761974	3.629895	3.587526	3.545951	3.505150	3.465106	3.425799
5	4.782645	4.645828	4.451822	4.389977	4.329477	4.270284	4.212364	4.155679
6	5.697187	5.508125	5.242137	5.157872	5.075692	4.995530	4.917324	4.841014
7	6.598214	6.349391	6.002055	5.892701	5.786373	5.682967	5.582381	5.484520
8	7.485925	7.170137	6.732745	6.595886	6.463213	6.334566	6.209794	6.088751
9	8.360517	7.970866	7.435332	7.268790	7.107822	6.952195	6.801692	6.656104
10	9.222185	8.752064	8.110896	7.912718	7.721735	7.537626	7.360087	7.188830
11	10.071118	9.514209	8.760477	8.528917	8.306414	8.092536	7.886875	7.689042
12	10.907505	10.257765	9.385074	9.118581	8.863252	8.618518	8.383844	8.158725
13	11.731532	10.983185	9.985648	9.682852	9.393573	9.117079	8.852683	8.599742
14	12.543382	11.690912	10.563123	10.222825	9.898641	9.589648	9.294984	9.013842
15	13.343233	12.381378	11.118387	10.739546	10.379658	10.037581	9.712249	9.402669
16	14.131264	13.055003	11.652296	11.234015	10.837770	10.462162	10.105895	9.767764
17	14.907649	13.712198	12.165669	11.707191	11.274066	10.864609	10.477260	10.110577
18	15.672561	14.353364	12.659297	12.159992	11.689587	11.246074	10.827603	10.432466
19	16.426168	14.978891	13.133939	12.593294	12.085321	11.607654	11.158116	10.734710
20	17.168639	15.589162	13.590326	13.007936	12.462210	11.950382	11.469921	11.018507
21	17.900137	16.184549	14.029160	13.404724	12.821153	12.275244	11.764077	11.284983
22	18.620824	16.765413	14.451115	13.784425	13.163003	12.583170	12.041582	11.535196
23	19.330861	17.332110	14.856842	14.147775	13.488574	12.875042	12.303379	11.770137
24	20.030405	17.884986	15.246963	14.495478	13.798642	13.151699	12.550358	11.990739
25	20.719611	18.424376	15.622080	14.828209	14.093945	13.413933	12.783356	12.197877
26	21.398632	18.950611	15.982769	15.146611	14.375185	13.662495	13.003166	12.392373
27	22.067617	19.464011	16.329586	15.451303	14.643034	13.898100	13.210534	12.574998
28	22.726717	19.964889	16.663063	15.742874	14.898127	14.121422	13.406164	12.746477
29	23.376076	20.453550	16.983715	16.021889	15.141074	14.333101	13.590721	12.907490
30	24.015838	20.930293	17.292033	16.288869	15.372451	14.533745	13.764831	13.058676
31	24.646146	21.395407	17.588494	16.544391	15.592811	14.723929	13.929086	13.200635
32	25.267139	21.849178	17.873551	16.788891	15.802677	14.904198	14.084043	13.333929
33	25.878954	22.291881	18.147646	17.022862	16.002549	15.075069	14.230230	13.459088
34	26.481728	22.723786	18.411198	17.246758	16.192904	15.237033	14.368141	13.576609
35	27.075595	23.145157	18.664613	17.461012	16.374194	15.390552	14.498246	13.686957
36	27.660684	23.556251	18.908282	17.666041	16.546852	15.536068	14.620987	13.790570
37	28.237127	23.957318	19.142579	17.862240	16.711287	15.673999	14.736780	13.887859
38	28.805052	24.348603	19.367864	18.049990	16.867893	15.804738	14.846019	13.979210
39	29.364583	24.730344	19.584485	18.229656	17.017041	15.929662	14.949075	14.064986
40	29.915845	25.102775	19.792774	18.401584	17.159086	16.046125	15.046297	14.145527

Table C—4 Present Value of an Ordinary Annuity of 1 *(continued)*

n	7%	8%	9%	10%	12%	14%	16%	20%
1	0.934579	0.925926	0.917431	0.909091	0.892857	0.877193	0.862069	0.833333
2	1.808018	1.783265	1.759111	1.735537	1.690051	1.646661	1.605232	1.527778
3	2.624316	2.577097	2.531295	2.486852	2.401831	2.321632	2.245890	2.106481
4	3.387211	3.312127	3.239720	3.169865	3.037349	2.913712	2.798181	2.588735
5	4.100197	3.992710	3.889651	3.790787	3.604776	3.433081	3.274294	2.990612
6	4.766540	4.622880	4.485919	4.355261	4.111407	3.888668	3.684736	3.325510
7	5.389289	5.206370	5.032953	4.868419	4.563757	4.288305	4.038565	3.604592
8	5.971299	5.746639	5.534819	5.334926	4.967640	4.638864	4.343591	3.837160
9	6.515232	6.246888	5.995247	5.759024	5.328250	4.946372	4.606544	4.030967
10	7.023582	6.710081	6.417658	6.144567	5.650223	5.216116	4.833227	4.192472
11	7.498674	7.138964	6.805191	6.495061	5.937699	5.452733	5.028644	4.327060
12	7.942686	7.536078	7.160725	6.813692	6.194374	5.660292	5.197107	4.439217
13	8.357651	7.903776	7.486904	7.103356	6.423548	5.842362	5.342334	4.532681
14	8.745468	8.244237	7.786150	7.366687	6.628168	6.002072	5.467529	4.610567
15	9.107914	8.559479	8.060688	7.606080	6.810864	6.142168	5.575456	4.675473
16	9.446649	8.851369	8.312558	7.823709	6.973986	6.265060	5.668497	4.729561
17	9.763223	9.121638	8.543631	8.021553	7.119630	6.372859	5.748704	4.774634
18	10.059087	9.371887	8.755625	8.201412	7.249670	6.467420	5.817848	4.812195
19	10.335595	9.603599	8.950115	8.364920	7.365777	6.550369	5.877455	4.843496
20	10.594014	9.818147	9.128546	8.513564	7.469444	6.623131	5.928841	4.869580
21	10.835527	10.016803	9.292244	8.648694	7.562003	6.686957	5.973139	4.891316
22	11.061240	10.200744	9.442425	8.771540	7.644646	6.742944	6.011326	4.909430
23	11.272187	10.371059	9.580207	8.883218	7.718434	6.792056	6.044247	4.924525
24	11.469334	10.528758	9.706612	8.984744	7.784316	6.835137	6.072627	4.937104
25	11.653583	10.674776	9.822580	9.077040	7.843139	6.872927	6.097092	4.947587
26	11.825779	10.809978	9.928972	9.160945	7.895660	6.906077	6.118183	4.956323
27	11.986709	10.935165	10.026580	9.237223	7.942554	6.935155	6.136364	4.963602
28	12.137111	11.051078	10.116128	9.306567	7.984423	6.960662	6.152038	4.969668
29	12.277674	11.158406	10.198283	9.369606	8.021806	6.983037	6.165550	4.974724
30	12.409041	11.257783	10.273654	9.426914	8.055184	7.002664	6.177198	4.978936
31	12.531814	11.349799	10.342802	9.479013	8.084986	7.019881	6.187240	4.982447
32	12.646555	11.434999	10.406240	9.526376	8.111594	7.034983	6.195897	4.985372
33	12.753790	11.513888	10.464441	9.569432	8.135352	7.048231	6.203359	4.987810
34	12.854009	11.586934	10.517835	9.608575	8.156564	7.059852	6.209792	4.989842
35	12.947672	11.654568	10.566821	9.644159	8.175504	7.070045	6.215338	4.991535
36	13.035208	11.717193	10.611763	9.676508	8.192414	7.078987	6.220119	4.992946
37	13.117017	11.775179	10.652993	9.705917	8.207513	7.086831	6.224241	4.994122
38	13.193473	11.828869	10.690820	9.732651	8.220993	7.093711	6.227794	4.995101
39	13.264928	11.878582	10.725523	9.756956	8.233030	7.099747	6.230857	4.995918
40	13.331709	11.924613	10.757360	9.779051	8.243777	7.105041	6.233497	4.996598

Index

Check List of Key Figures for Exercises and Problems

Chapter 1

E1–1	Biomedical, 9.86%
E1–3	Total liabilities $366.1
E1–4	Long-term liabilities, $25,000
E1–6	Total current assets, $72,975
E1–7	Total assets, $1,143,000
E1–8	Trial balance totals, $127,010
E1–10	Cash balance, $67,270
E1–13	Trial balance totals, $106,380
P1–1A	Notes payable, $100,800
P1–2A	Total assets, $114,850
P1–3A	Trial balance totals, $113,900
P1–4A	Trial balance totals, $104,000
P1–5A	Trial balance totals, $170,000
P1–1B	Notes payable, $16,800
P1–2B	Total assets, $137,820
P1–3B	Trial balance totals, $136,680
P1–4B	Trial balance totals, $126,000
P1–5B	Trial balance totals, $73,000

Chapter 2

E2–1	Balance of Cash, $97,550
E2–3	Yes, Yes, Yes, Yes
E2–4	Balance of Cash after posting, $41,200
E2–6	Aug. 7, 31, 31 revenue transactions
E2–7	May 7, 22 expense transactions
E2–9	(3) Total accounts receivable per schedule, $70
E2–10	(1) $2,625
	(2) It cannot be determined
E2–11	Net income, $863
P2–1A	(3) Trial balance totals, $226,400
	(4) On balance sheet, cash $86,350
P2–2A	(2) Balance of Cash, $6,500
	(3) Total accounts payable per schedule, $6,800
P2–4A	(2) Net income, $40,000
P2–5A	(3) Trial balance totals, $277,755
P2–6A	(2) Balance, Accounts Receivable, $50; Balance, Accounts Payable, $103
P2–7A	(2) Accounts Receivable and Accounts Payable
P2–1B	(3) Trial balance totals, $82,850
	(4) On balance sheet, cash, $24,735
P2–2B	(2) Balance of cash, $135
	(3) Total accounts receivable per schedule, $150
P2–4B	(2) Net income, $43,890
P2–5B	(3) Trial balance totals, $238,695
P2–6B	(2) Balance, Accounts Receivable, $85; Balance, Accounts Payable, $65
P2–7B	(1) Current assets, $20,200
	(2) Current liabilities, $52,000

Chapter 3

E3–1	(2) Jackson Davido, Capital, December 31, 1985, $61,000
E3–2	(3) Accounts Receivable balance, $85
E3–3	(3) Accounts Payable balance, $240
E3–4	Net income, $41,908; Harold Brooks, Capital, December 31, 1984, $64,566; Total assets, $82,311;
E3–6	Net income closed to Joseph Sylvan, Capital, $39,300
E3–7	(a) $160,500
	(b) $9,600
	(c) 16,200
E3–8	Commissions earned, $127,920
E3–9	Net income closed to Richard Daye, Capital, $15,800
P3–1A	(3) Trial balance totals, $71,300
	(5) Net income, $3,500
	(7) Postclosing trial balance totals, $65,100
P3–2A	(3) Trial balance totals, $34,210
	(4) Net income, $4,925
	(6) Postclosing trial balance totals, $30,025
P3–3A	(2) Net income closed to capital account, $16,857
	(3) Postclosing trial balance totals, $129,828
P3–4A	(3) Trial balance totals, $35,850
	(5) Net loss, $880
	(7) Postclosing trial balance totals $33,520
P3–5A	(1) Net loss, $2,840
	(3) Cash balance, $11,940
P3–1B	(3) Trial balance, totals, $46,625
	(5) Net income, $825
	(7) Postclosing trial balance totals, $42,425
P3–2B	(3) Trial balance totals, $49,220
	(4) Net income, $6,650
	(6) Postclosing trial balance, $40,800
P3–3B	(2) Net income closed to capital account, $34,814
	(3) Postclosing trial balance totals, $201,456
P3–4B	(3) Trial balance totals, $38,560
	(5) Net loss, $210
	(7) Postclosing trial balance totals, $35,540
P3–5B	(1) Net loss, $9,180
	(3) Cash balance, $15,900

Chapter 4

E4–1	(a) Office supplies expense, $3,920
	(b) Cash paid for insurance, $1,315
E4–2	(b) Accumulated Depreciation—Vans balance at end of 1987, $7,200
E4–3	Wages Expense if period ends on Wednesday, $1,536
E4–4	(a) Debit to Insurance Expense, $165
	(d) Debit to Office Supplies Expense, $2,574
E4–5	(c) Debit to Office Supplies Expense, $1,442
E4–6	(1) Debit to Subscription Revenue, $30,000
	(2) No
E4–7	(e) Debit to Rental Expense, $8,160
E4–8	Debit to Accrued Interest Receivable, $16; Amount of accrued interest on notes payable, $30.22
E4–9	(d) Debit Rent Expense—Salesmen's Cars, $14,600
	(e) Debit to Wages Expense, $2,880
E4–10	Case I: Debit to Magazine Subscription Expense, $104; Case II: Debit to Prepaid Magazine Subscriptions, $52
E4–11	a, c, e, f
E4–12	(1) Credit to Rent Earned, $2,400
	(4) Credit to Unearned Rent, $1,200
P4–1A	(2) Debit to Insurance Expense, $900; Debit to Depreciation Expense, $3,750
P4–2A	(e) Debit to Insurance Expense, $1,200
	(g) Debit to Interest Expense, $1,620
	(k) Debit to Accrued Rent Receivable, $250
P4–3A	(c) Debit to Insurance Expense, $1,920
	(e) Debit to Accrued Interest Receivable, $745
	(f) Debit to Interest Expense, $1,530
P4–4A	(3) Credit to Income Summary to close revenue accounts, $214,870; Debit to Income Summary to close expense accounts, $63,530
P4–5A	(5) Preclosing trial balance totals, $15,624
	(7) Net income, $5,485.50
	(11) Postclosing trial balance totals, $12,898
P4–6A	(3) Net income under revised statements, $63,500
P4–1B	(2) Debit to Insurance Expense, $900; Debit to Depreciation Expense, $1,700
P4–2B	(e) Debit to Insurance Expense, $1,440
	(g) Debit to Interest Expense, $1,908
	(k) Debit to Accrued Rent Receivable, $400
P4–3B	(c) Debit to Insurance Expense, $2,955.75
	(e) Debit to Accrued Interest Receivable, $1,105.14
	(f) Debit to Interest Expense, $2,460.53
P4–4B	Credit to Income Summary to close revenue accounts, $121,770; Debit to Income Summary to close expense accounts, $135,435
P4–5B	(5) Preclosing trial balance, totals, $31,748
	(7) Net income, $10,941.28
	(11) Postclosing trial balance, $26,276.00
P4–6B	(3) Tyson Fulton, Capital balance, December 31, 1984 (beginning), $18,050

Chapter 5

E5–1	Net income, $33,902.50; Total assets, $77,717.50
E5–2	Net income, $20,000; Total assets, $99,900
E5–3	Dec. 31. Debit to Accrued Interest Receivable, $213.33; Credit to Accrued Interest Payable, $31.25
E5–4	(2b) Income statement, $9,000
	(2c) Balance sheet, $3,000
	(5b) Income statement, $2,400
	(5c) Balance sheet, $4,800
E5–5	(3) Net income, $682
	(4) Net loss, cash basis, ($1,570)
E5–6	Net income, $13,650
P5–1A	(2) Net income, $8,999
	(3) Total assets, $55,835
P5–2A	(2) Net income, $27,909
P5–3A	(6) Net income, $5,626.00
	(7) Total assets, $16,946.89
	(13) Postclosing trial balance totals, $16,958.00
P5–4A	(2) Net income, $12,357
	(3) Total assets, $236,560
P5–5A	(3) Credit to Income Summary, $642,510; Debit to Income Summary, $182,370
P5–6A	(1) Net income, $15,654
P5–1B	(2) Net income, $12,187
	(3) Total assets, $69,060
P5–2B	(2) Net income, $14,898.33
P5–3B	(6) Net income, $13,385.92
	(7) Total assets, $30,285.92
	(13) Postclosing trial balance totals, $30,305.50
P5–4B	(2) Net income, $15,082
	(3) Total assets, $283,072
P5–5B	Credit to Income Summary, $126,695; Debit to Income Summary, $145,000
P5–6B	(1) Net income, $7,050

Chapter 6

E6–1	Case 4 (a), $45,000
E6–2	Gross margin, $6,500
E6–3	Gross sales, $52,000
E6–6	Net income, $30,105
E6–7	Osaka sales, $50,100; Kobe purchases, $19,074; Hilo sales, $49,750
E6–9	Net cost of purchases: net procedure, $6,860; gross procedure, $7,000
E6–11	June 20 Accounts Receivable credit on Juan's books, $10,204.08
E6–12	Purchases debit, $8,208
P6–1A	Cash balance, $8,114.60
P6–2A	Cost of goods sold, $283,920
P6–3A	Net income, $19,110
P6–4A	Net income, $175,901; total assets, $1,115,021
P6–5A	Cost of goods sold: gross price method, $695; net price method, $691.25
P6–1B	Cash balance, $10,652.60
P6–2B	Cost of goods sold, $454,272
P6–3B	Net income, $25,772
P6–4B	Net income, $178,312; total assets, $1,023,518
P6–5B	Cost of goods sold: gross price method, $1,430: net price method, $1,421

Chapter 7

E7–1	Total journal entries, $500
E7–2	Total journal entries, $11,620
E7–3	Cash column total, $20,462
E7–4	Cash column total, $26,270
E7–9	Cash balance, $31,970
P7–1A	Account balances: Cash, $22,889; Accounts Receivable, $2,600
P7–2A	Account balances: Cash, $12,886; Accounts Payable, $2,750
P7–3A	Cash totals: CR, $66,141; CP, $29,772
P7–4A	Cash totals: CR, $8,000; CP, $82,300
P7–5A	Accounts Receivable balance, $2,160
P7–1B	Account balances: Cash, $27,759.80; Accounts Receivable, $4,420
P7–2B	Account balances: Cash, $21,189.60; Accounts Payable, $4,400
P7–3B	Cash totals: CR, $116,352.50; CP, $74,427.50
P7–4B	Cash totals: CR, $13,200; CP, $131,480
P7–5B	Accounts Receivable balance, $3,456

Chapter 8

E8–1	Gross pay, $588
E8–2	Jay Learned, $131
E8–3	Oscar LeHand, $35
E8–4	Betty Wolfe: (a) $0; (b) $2,520
E8–5	Jay Learned, state: (a) $8; (b) $400

E8–6 Payroll tax expense, $660
E8–7 Payroll tax expense, $67,500
E8–8 Total cost, $40,020
E8–9 FICA deductions, $66.47
E8–10 Liability: (a) credit, $2,800; (b) debit, $4,200
P8–1A Net pay, $1,585.05
P8–2A Net pay, $2,302.72
P8–3A Net pay, $1,406.35
P8–4A Net pay, $2,516.70; employer's tax, $220
P8–5A Liability: (1) credit, $26,000; (2) debit, $32,500
P8–1B Net pay, $1,688.19
P8–2B Net pay, $2,287.92
P8–3B Net pay, $1,344.20
P8–4B Net pay, $2,481.40; employer's tax, $212.05
P8–5B Liability: (1) credit, $18,000; (2) debit, $30,000

Chapter 9

E9–2 Cash shortage, $4.90
E9–3 Cash shortage, $1.62
E9–5 Adjusted balance, $21,999.17
E9–7 Corrected adjusted balance, $1,345.60
E9–8 Adjusted balance, $8,222.60
E9–9 Vouchers Payable totals: VR, $8,625; CkR, $6,150
E9–10 Vouchers Payable totals: VR, $5,352; CkR, $5,352
E9–12 Vouchers Payable amount, $6,450
P9–1A Cash Over and Short: (1) $0.85 credit; (2) $1.53 debit
P9–2A Adjusted balance, $7,321.20
P9–3A Adjusted balance, $10,871.56
P9–4A Vouchers Payable total: VR, $16,158; CkR, $5,958
P9–1B Cash Over and Short: (1) $1.85 debit; (2) $2.30 credit
P9–2B Adjusted balance, $3,660.60
P9–3B Adjusted balance, $21,743.12
P9–4B Vouchers Payable total: VR, $24,732; CkR, $9,152

Chapter 10

E10–1 (1) Maturity value, $3,200
(4) Maturity value, $2,650
E10–2 Total accrued interest, $229.75
E10–3 Dec. 31, 1985, debit to Interest Expense, $170
E10–4 Dec. 31, 1985, debit to Interest Expense, $187.50
E10–5 Dec. 31, 1985, debit to Accrued Interest Receivable, $69
E10–7 Cash proceeds upon discounting, $5,510.70
E10–8 Cash proceeds upon discounting, $6,051.40
E10–10 (a) 7.2%
(d) 20%
P10–1A Total accrued interest, $1,547.45
P10–2A Dec. 31, 1985, credit to Accrued Interest Payable, $70; and to Discount on Notes Payable, $120
P10–3A Feb. 28, 1985, cash proceeds, $4,014.41
P10–4A (1a) Interest-bearing note
(1b) Note made out for maturity value and discounted.
P10–5A APR under present plan, 41.67%;
APR under proposed plan, 20.83%
P10–1B Total accrued interest, $1,048.55
P10–2B Dec. 31, 1985 credit to Accrued Interest Payable, $97.50; and to Discount on Notes Payable, $25.94
P10–3B Feb. 28, 1985, cash proceeds, $3,006.58
P10–4B (1a) Interest-bearing note
(1b) Note made out for maturity value and discounted
P10–5B APR under present plan, 35.56%; APR under proposed plan, 17.78%

Chapter 11

E11–2 $57,200 would be a current asset
E11–3 Credit sales, $744,000
E11–4 Balance in allowance for Doubtful Accounts after Aug. 1, 1985 transaction, $6,300
E11–5 (a) Debit to Bad Debts Expense, $3,612
(b) Debit to Bad Debts Expense, $4,632
(c) Credit to Allowance for Doubtful Accounts, $5,758
E11–6 (a) Credit to Allowance for Doubtful Accounts $4,148.40
E11–7 Cash received, $560,900
E11–8 (3) Debit to Bad Debts Expense, $1,737.45
E11–9 (3) $58,650
E11–11 Total debit to Credit Card Fees Expense, $1,581
P11–1A Balance in Allowance for Doubtful Accounts after Dec. 2, 1986, transaction, $2,538
P11–2A (2) Balance in Allowance for Doubtful Accounts on Dec. 31, 1986, $15,950
P11–3A (3) Total accounts receivable per schedule, $27,600
P11–4A (3) Debit to Bad Debts Expense, $1,357.30
P11–5A (2a) Bad Debts Expense, $1,825
(2b) Bad Debts Expense, $2,198
P11–1B Balance in Allowance for Doubtful Accounts after Nov. 13, 1986, transaction, $4,580
P11–2B (2) Balance in Allowance for Doubtful Accounts on Dec. 31, 1986, $7,650
P11–3B (3) Total accounts receivable per schedule, $12,410
P11–4B (3) Debit to Bad Debts Expense, $2,953.71
P11–5B (2a) Bad Debts Expense, $6,720
(2b) Bad Debts Expense, $7,070

Chapter 12

E12–1 Inventory, $65,600
E12–2 Gross margin, $26,000
E12–3 Inventory, $567
E12–4 Cost of goods sold, $768
E12–5 Inventory: FIFO, $17,875; LIFO, $16,150
E12–6 Inventory, $489.60
E12–7 Inventory, $455
E12–8 Estimated inventory, $113,242.50
E12–9 Estimated inventory, $690,300
E12–10 Unit, $3,950; class, $4,200; total, $4,250
P12–1A Net income, $47,224
P12–2A Inventory: FIFO, $687,50; LIFO, $500; average, $585
P12–3A Cost of goods sold: FIFO, $2,825; LIFO, $2,840; average, $2,828
P12–4A Unit, $23,235; class $24,090; total $24,610
P12–5A Estimated inventory: (1) $246,572; (2) $43,807.50
P12–6A Net income: FIFO, $55,264; LIFO, $53,344; average, $54,658
P12–1B Net income, $145,350
P12–2B Inventory: FIFO, $16,087.50; LIFO, $13,000; average, $14,843.75
P12–3B Cost of goods sold: FIFO, $2,910; LIFO, $2,925; average, $2,913
P12–4B Unit, $11,955; class $12,404.40; total, $12,767.40
P12–5B Estimated inventory: (1) $105,588; (2) $87,615

Chapter 13

E13–2 Machinery, $23,150
E13–3 Office Equipment, $1,470
E13–4 Factory Building, $278,000
E13–5 (a) $170,000; (b) $375,000; (c) $320,000; (d) $74,800
E13–6 Total expense (SYD): 1985, $22,222.22; 1986, $42,166.66
E13–7 Revised annual rate, $4,375
E13–8 Gain on disposal, $6,500
E13–9 Gain or loss on disposal: (3a) gain, $1,000; (3b) loss, $1,500
E13–10 Depletion cost, $252,000
E13–11 1985, $2,000; 1986, $3,000
E13–12 1985, $2,400; 1986, $4,800
P13–1A Accumulated Depreciation balances: Building, $25,000; Production Equipment, $120,000; Cleaning Equipment, $80,000
P13–2A Revised annual rate, $7,700
P13–3A Gain on disposal, $12,000
P13–4A (1) new press debit, $88,875;
(2) loss on disposal, $4,875;
(3) gain on disposal, $3,125
P13–5A Depletion cost per ton, $15.60
P13–1B Accumulated Depreciation balances: Building, $18,000; Production Equipment, $160,000; Cleaning Equipment, $57,600
P13–2B Revised annual rate, $15,400
P13–3B Loss on disposal, $6,250
P13–4B (1) new press debit, $171,750;
(2) loss on disposal, $26,250;
(3) gain on disposal, $3,250
P13–5B Depletion cost per ton, $15.75

Appendix to Part Three

EAIII–6 $34,182.20
EAIII–7 $7,270.47
EAIII–8 $627.03
EAIII–9 After one year, $251.08
EAIII–10 (2) $2,055.47
EAIII–11 $52,880.83
EAIII–12 $750.42

Chapter 14

E14–2 Gross margin percentage 40%
March gross margin $36.00
E14–3 1986 gross margin recognized $140,000
E14–4 1984: $593,750
E14–5 1984: $5,400,000
E14–8 (1a) $31,250
(1b) $42,969

Chapter 15

E15–1 (2) Total partners' capital, $206,320
E15–3 Credit balance in Whang, Capital account on October 3, 1985, $19,000
E15–4 Balance of Jean Ormand, Capital, $67,000; total capital, $191,000
E15–5 Credit balance in Robert Hickson, Capital after closing, $11,650
E15–7 Credit to M. Melson, Capital, $20,000
E15–8 (b) Bonus to old partners, $8,000
(c) Goodwill to old partners, $20,000
E15–9 Cash to Aisley, $170,000
E15–10 Cash to Foster, $0
E15–11 Goodman would be paid $32,200
E15–12 Liability to Estate of Goodman, $32,200
P15–1A (4) Credit to Strong, Capital, $48,000
P15–2A (1) Net income, $119,000
(2) December 31, 1985 balance in Thomas Winston, Capital, $72,240
P15–3A (2) Gleem's share of net loss, $5,400
(3) Hooter's share of net income, $15,720
P15–4A (2) Bonus to old partners, $15,625
(3) Goodwill, $62,500
(5) Goodwill to new partner, $22,500
(6) Bonus to new partner, $25,500
P15–5A Cash distributed to Medlin, $75,000
P15–6A (2) Cash paid to Eidson, $40,000
(3) Bonus of $6,000 would be split $4 000 to Hunter and $2,000 to Summer
P15–1B (4) Credit to Sante Barnard, Capital, $35,300
P15–2B (1) Net income, $148,750
(2) December 31, 1985 balance in Melissa Barbara, Capital, $119,015
P15–3B (2) Robert Greer's share of net loss, $1,600
(3) Oscar Glenn's share of net income, $27,200
P15–4B (2) Bonus to old partners, $7,500
(3) Goodwill, $30,000
(5) Goodwill to new partner, $10,000
(6) Bonus to new partner, $14,000
P15–5B Cash distributed to Sara Riggsbee, $0
P15–6B (2) Cash paid to Slaton, $44,000
(3) Liability to Estate of Slayton, $38,000

Chapter 16

E16–1 (3) Credit to Paid-in Capital—Excess over Stated Value, Common, $25,500
E16–2 In Nov. 11, 1985, transaction, Credit to Paid-in Capital—excess over Par Value, Common, $70,000
E16–3 For transaction no. 4, credit to Paid-in Capital—Excess over Par Value, Common, $14,400
E16–4 For Sept. 16, 1985, credit to Paid-in Capital—Excess over Par Value, Preferred, $2,000
E16–5 Total paid-in capital, $932,000
E16–6 (a) Debit to Equipment, $1,150,000
E16–7 Credit Paid-in Capital—Donations, $180,000
E16–8 Aug. 20 transaction, debit to Organization Costs, $16,000
E16–9 Total stockholders' equity, $214,000
E16–10 Cash collected, $2,682,000
P16–1A (2) Total paid-in capital, $475,000
P16–2A (3) Total paid-in capital, $395,000
P16–3A (4) Total paid-in capital, $1,748,100
P16–4A Total stockholders' equity, $1,445,000
P16–5A (2) Total paid-in capital, $123,000
P16–1B (2) Total paid-in capital, $491,950
P16–2B (3) Total paid-in capital, $380,000
P16–3B (4) Total paid-in capital, $925,600
P16–4B Total stockholders' equity, $1,632,500
P16–5B (2) Total paid-in capital, $1,107,200

Chapter 17

E17–1 For the expenditure, the debit is to Buildings, $1,002,560
E17–2 On June 4, debit Dividends, $25,000
E17–3 (2) Total stockholders' equity, $2,135,000
E17–4 (a) Decrease
(b) No effect
E17–5 (e) Amount of dividend, $12,075
E17–6 No effect for a and b.
E17–7 Amount payable to preferred, $64,000

E17–9 Primary EPS, $1.41
E17–11 (1) Book value per common share, $7.00
(2) Book value per common share, $6.60
E17–12 Total stockholders' equity, $2,303,200
E17–13 (c) Book value per preferred share, $112
(d) Book value per common share, $25.91
E17–14 Jan. 4, a transaction, dividends payable to preferred, $300,000
P17–1A (g) Dividend payable to common stockholders, $2,445
P17–2A (3) Total stockholders' equity, $1,711,000
P17–3A (2) Total stockholders' equity, $1,000,330
P17–4A (1) Book value per share of common, $7.92
(2) Book value per share of common, $7.32
P17–5A (1) Primary EPS $2.79
(2) Fully diluted EPS, $2.83 (would not disclose because it is larger than primary EPS)
P17–1B (g) Dividend payable to common stockholders, $5,845
P17–2B (3) Total stockholders' equity, $1,816,000
P17–3B (2) Total stockholders' equity, $1,187,445
P17–4B (1) Book value per share of common, $8.96
(2) Book value per share of common, $8.10
P17–5B (1) Primary EPS, $3.53
(2) Fully diluted EPS, $3.16

Chapter 18
E18–1 (a) Discount
(b) Premium
E18–2 Bond Interest Expense for 1985 has a balance of $120,000
E18–3 (a) $315,000
(c) $611,400
(f) $210,715
E18–4 (4) Balance of Bond Interest Expense account, $156,000
E18–5 (2) On June 30, 1986, Discount on Bonds Payable is credited for $4,634.24
E18–6 (3) On July 1, 1986, Bond Interest Expense is debited for $43,392.82
E18–7 On Dec. 31, 1986, Premium on Bonds Payable is debited for $130.
E18–8 (a) Cash received, $282,113.09
(b) Cash received, $891,759.58
(c) Cash received, $721,454.63
(d) Cash received, $527,546.25
E18–9 (2) 20,000 shares of common stock are issued
E18–10 (2) On Jan. 1, 1995, Bond Sinking Fund is credited for $500,000
E18–11 Original proceeds of bond issue, $240,000
E18–12 Loss on retirement of bonds, $3,000
P18–1A At end of 1985, the Bond Interest Expense account had a balance of $73,725.49
P18–2A (2) Carrying value on Dec. 31, 1985, $842,938.84; Carrying value on June 30, 1986, $841,729.86
P18–3A The Bond Interest Expense balance at end-of-1985 is $77,000
P18–4A (1) Bond interest expense for 1986, $6,100
(2) Cash proceeds, $495,000
(3) Gain on retirement of bonds payable, $2,500
P18–5A (1b) Original issue price, $37,660
P18–1B At end of 1985, the Bond Interest Expense account had a balance of $83,470.59
P18–2B (2) Carrying value on Dec. 31, 1985, $525,838.99 Carrying value on June 30, 1985, $525,147.72
P18–3B The Bond Interest Expense balance at end of 1985 is $47,333.34
P18–4B (1) Bond interest expense for 1986, $9,150
(2) Cash proceeds, $742,500
(3) Gain on retirement of bonds payable, $11,250
P18–5B (1b) Original issue price, $151,810

Chapter 19
E19–1 Investments in Bonds—Taylor Company, $184,636
E19–2 Realized gain on disposal, $1,140
E19–3 The Dec. 31, 1986 debit to Allowance to Reduce Temporary Investments in Equity Securities to Market is $2,100
E19–4 Balance in Dividends Earned account at end of year, $27,000
E19–5 Dec. 31, 1985, balance in Bond Interest Earned, $59,200
E19–6 Dec. 31, 1986, balance in Bond Interest Earned, $60,400
E19–7 (1) Total dividends earned for two years, $4,320
(2) In 1985 a credit is made to Investor's Share of Investee Income for $25,200
E19–8 In 1985 a credit is made to Investor's Share of Investee Income for $20,000
E19–9 Cost of the original investment, $318,000
E19–10 The amortization of premium element for period ending June 30, 1986 is $414.76
E19–11 On Dec. 31, 1985, a debit is made to Investment in Bonds for $990
E19–12 (1) A credit made to Investment in Bonds on Dec. 31, 1985, for $3,305.13
E19–13 On Dec. 31, 1986, the Allowance to Reduce Noncurrent Marketable Equity Investments to market is credited for $1,120
P19–1A On Aug. 15, 1985, the realized gain is $119.25
P19–2A (1) On Dec. 31, 1986, Allowance to Reduce Temporary Investments in Equity Securities to Market is debited for $1,750
P19–3A On Dec. 31, 1985, the 11,500 remaining shares had a cost of $357,500
P19–4A Balance in Investment account at end of 1989, $404,791.67
P19–5A (1) Interest revenue for 1985 is $24,726.49
(2) Interest revenue for 1985 is $25,720.85
P19–6A Bond interest earned for 1985 is $95,838.64
P19–1B On Aug. 15, 1985, the realized gain is $475.50
P19–2B (1) On Dec. 31, 1986, Allowance to Reduce Temporary Investments in Equity Securities to Market is debited for $900
P19–3B On Dec. 31, 1985, the 3,400 remaining shares had a cost of $52,800
P19–4B Balance in Investment account at end of 1989, $26,437.50
P19–5B (1) Interest revenue for fiscal year ending March 31, 1986 is $106,679.96
(2) Interest revenue for fiscal year ending March 31, 1986 is $110,868.76
P19–6B Bond interest earned for 1985 is $38,053.53

Chapter 20
E20–2 4, part of 5, and 8
E20–3 Working capital provided by operations, $73,500
E20–4 (1) Original cost of machinery sold, $70,000; proceeds from sale, $9,500
E20–5 (c) source, $185,000
(e) Use, $50,850
E20–6 (a) New equipment purchased, $70,000
(e) Net income for year, $4,000
(g) Dollar amount increase to Common Stock, $1,000
E20–7 Total sources of financial resources, $137,975; total uses, $119,475
E20–8 Total sources of financial resources, $279,625; total uses, $178,750
E20–9 Cash received, $82,100
E20–10 Cash paid, $151,580
E20–11 Cash generated by operations, $12,715
E20–12 Sources of cash, $548,000; uses, $435,000
P20–1A Sources of financial resources, $196,000; uses, $269,500
P20–2A Sources of financial resources, $276,000; uses, $401,250
P20–3A Sources of financial resources, $143,250; uses, $107,250
P20–4A Sources of financial resources, $50,050; uses, $38,500
P20–5A Sources of cash, $249,000; uses, $265,500
P20–1B Sources of financial resources, $372,000; uses, $339,000
P20–2B Sources of financial resources, $138,000; uses, $200,625
P20–3B Sources of financial resources, $71,625; uses, $53,625
P20–4B Sources of financial resources, $80,100; uses, $77,000
P20–5B Sources of cash, $498,000; uses, $531,000

Chapter 21
E21–2 Net income, $43,200
E21–3 Sales Company A, $15,400, 29.2%
E21–4 Net sales 1985, 125%; 1984, 115%; 1983, 100%
E21–5 Net income (loss) 1985, 9.5%; 1984, (2.6)%
E21–6 Common stock 1985, 38.2%; 1984, 36.0%
E21–7 Net income, $0.068
E21–8 Receivables turnover 1985, 12.21; 1984, 12.62
E21–9 Creditor's equity, 68.37%; stockholder's equity, 31.63%
E21–10 On total investment in 1985, 20.93⅓%; 1984, 19.92%
E21–12 P/E ratio 1985, 12; 1984, 10
P21–1A Net income, $42,300; retained earnings, December 31, $56,500
P21–2A Sales change, $(165,000), percent (10.0)%; current assets change, $75,000, percent, 16.1%
P21–3A Current assets 1985, 68.0%; 1984, 75.0%; 1983, 100.0%; creditors' equity ratio 1985, 28.96%
P21–4A Current assets 1985, 27.6%; 1984, 37.5%; cost of goods sold 1985, 57.4%; 1984, 56.6%
P21–5A EPS 1981, $7.09; 1980, $6.23
P21–6A Dividends yield rate 1981, 5.5%; 1980, 3.0%; 1979, 4.1%
P21–1B Net income, $84,600; retained earnings, December 31, $113,000
P21–2B Sales change, $(82,500); percent (10.0)%
P21–3B Current liabilities 1985, 130%; 1984, 125%; 1983, 100%
P21–4B Total liabilities 1985, 61.4%; 1984, 67.3%; gross margin 1985, 42.6%; 1984, 43.4%
P21–5B Preferred dividends earned 1981, 30.68 times; 1980, 23.57 times
P21–6B Maximum earnings increase, CBS, 25.0%

Chapter 22
E22–2 Reciprocal accounts balance (not required), $7,720
E22–3 Branch net income, $15,745
E22–4 Investment account balance (not required), $378,600
E22–6 Tax reporting separately, $40,485; as a group, $78,305
E22–8 Intercompany profit in unsold gliders, $6,240
E22–9 Consolidated retained earnings, $1,565,000
E22–10 Total liabilities, $58,947.9
E22–11 Combined totals, $588,535
E22–12 Consolidated total assets, $540,530
E22–13 German marks per dollar, 2.4944
E22–14 June 30 gain, $25,000; July 16 loss, $37,500
P22–1A Branch net income, $32,560
P22–2A Combined net income, $91,880
P22–3A Elimination totals, $867,500
P22–4A Elimination totals, $133,150
P22–5A Total liabilities, $496,049
P22–6A Home office return on sales, 15.9%
P22–1B Branch net income, $26,048
P22–2B Combined net income, $110,256
P22–3B Elimination totals, $433,750
P22–4B Elimination totals, $66,575
P22–5B Total liabilities, $383,411
P22–6B $40,000 should be eliminated.

Chapter 23
E23–1 Materials used, $699,300
E23–2 Cost of goods sold, $1,062,000
E23–3 (1) Purchases discounts, $225; (2) ending inventory, $2,850; (3) materials used, $22,350
E23–4 (1) Ending inventory, $21,750; (2) net sales, $151,500
E23–6 Manufacturing share of depreciation, $45,000; property tax, $13,500
E23–7 Small tools used, $14,325
E23–8 Cost of goods manufactured, $861,270
E23–9 Cost of goods sold, $1,302,200
E23–11 Net income, $270
E23–13 Direct materials in work-in-process inventory, $15,800
E23–14 Cost of goods manufactured, $1,016,000
E23–15 Manufacturing Summary balance closed, $1,388,880
P23–1A Cost of goods sold, $264,000
P23–2A Cost of goods manufactured, $126,885
P23–3A Net income, $6,349
P23–4A Cost of goods manufactured, $220,518
P23–5A Cost of materials used, $202,350
P23–6A Cost of corn produced and sold, $141,946
P23–1B Cost of goods sold, $372,000
P23–2B Cost of goods manufactured, $193,788
P23–3B Net income, $7,182
P23–4B Cost of goods manufactured, $34,843
P23–5B Cost of materials used, $35,500
P23–6B (3) Income tax paid is $16,000 less under LIFO.

Chapter 24
E24–3 Job A401, $782.80
E24–4 Job A401, $528
E24–5 (a) $7 per direct labor hour
E24–6 Total job cost, $1,136

E24–7 (d) Work-in-process inventory, September 30, $7,279
E24–8 Manufacturing overhead applied, $3,000
E24–9 Manufacturing overhead rate, 150% of direct labor cost
E24–10 Manufacturing overhead applied, $58,500
E24–12 Debit to Finished Goods Inventory, $7,425
E24–13 Debit to Manufacturing Overhead Control, $5,850
E24–14 Incorrect rate used in A65
P24–1A (1) $22.50 per direct labor hour
P24–2A Total job cost, $1,691.50
P24–3A (c) Manufacturing overhead applied, $120,000
P24–4A Cost of goods sold, $109,480
P24–5A Completed jobs cost, $111,345
P24–1B (1) $6 per direct labor hour
P24–2B Total job cost, $2,038
P24–3B Manufacturing overhead applied, $211,500
P24–4B Cost of goods sold, $133,355
P24–5B Completed jobs cost, $156,572

Chapter 25
E25–2 Total accounted for in Shaping, 18,000; in Finishing, 16,200
E25–3 Total accounted for in A, 39,650; in B, 42,250
E25–4 Materials, 10,000; L and O, 9,720
E25–5 Total costs to be accounted for, $159,600
E25–6 Unit prior department cost, $8
E25–7 Ending inventory, $16,230
E25–8 Unit cost of materials, $1.40; direct labor, $1.20
E25–9 Transferred out, $132,000
E25–10 Transferred out, $509,720
E25–11 Overhead unit cost in January, $15.30; February, $14.76
P25–1A (3) Cost to complete beginning inventory, $8,925
P25–2A Units finished, $45,000
P25–3A Total unit cost, $3
P25–4A Total unit cost, $4.15
P25–5A Total cost transferred to Blending, $138,000; total unit Blending cost, $8.50
P25–1B (2) Unit cost of materials, $1,20; overhead, $1.30
P25–2B Units finished, $11,400
P25–3B Total unit cost, $6.2625
P25–4B Total unit cost, $5.35
P25–5B Total unit cost in A $13.60; transferred to finished goods, $240,000

Chapter 26
E26–1 November sales, 20,300 units, $1,218,000
E26–2 Total production of Standard, 135,520
E26–3 United States sales, Product A, 12,350 units, $4,075,500; Product B, 18,525 units, $5,094,375
E26–4 Unit variable cost, $1.30
E26–5 Cost per unit at 52,000 level, $45
E26–6 Direct labor, 520,000 hours
E26–7 X-gauge, 1,600 tons
E26–8 Cash balance, January 31, $10,049
E26–9 Rate per hour, 100%, $15.60; 90%, $16.18 (rounded)
E26–10 Overhead variance, $30,000 (U)
E26–11 Projected net income, 12.2%
E26–12 Net income, $27,500
E26–13 Break-even point, 40,000 units, $400,000
E26–14 Break-even sales, $500,000
E26–15 Percent of safety, 40%
P26–1A First quarter, Product X, 3,784 units, $56,760
P26–2A First quarter production, Product A, 36,360 units
P26–3A Cash balance, April 30, $12,886
P26–4A Total variance, $46.95 (U)
P26–5A Net income difference in September, $14,000
P26–6A Present break-even sales, $540,000
P26–7A Expected variable costs, $51,840
P26–1B First quarter, Product M, 5,115 units, $38,362.50
P26–2B First quarter production, Product L, 29,172 units
P26–3B Cash balance, July 31, $9,550.80
P26–4B Total variance, $67.50 (U)
P26–5B Net income difference in April, $12,600
P26–6B Present break-even sales, $480,000
P26–7B Units sold 1985, 75,000; 1984; 60,000

Chapter 27
E27–1 200 lengths
E27–2 1/12 hour per unit
E27–3 Materials, $29,160
E27–4 $6 per hour
E27–5 6,500 pints
E27–6 45,000 hours
E27–7 $60,000
E27–8 Purchase price variance, $698.70 (U)
E27–9 Labor efficiency variance, $96 (F)
E27–10 Adjusted budget, $7,300,000
E27–11 Controllable variance, $800 (U)
E27–12 Materials quantity variance, $992 (U)
E27–13 Wage rate variance, $1,432 (U)
E27–14 Volume variance, $80 (F)
P27–1A Purchase price variance, $187 (F); quantity variance, $75 (U)
P27–2A Wage rate variance, $370 (U); efficiency variance, $300 (F)
P27–3A Controllable variance, $40 (U); volume variance, $70 (F)
P27–4A Purchase price variance, $1,100 (F); materials quantity variance, $5,600 (U)
P27–5A Debit to close variances to Cost of Goods Sold, $5,368
P27–6A Controllable variance, $1,600 (U)
P27–1B Purchase price variance, $13,077.50 (F); quantity variance, $2,692.50 (U)
P27–2B Wage rate variance, $1,045.50 (U); efficiency variance, $450 (F)
P27–3B Controllable variance, $725 (F); volume variance, $1,000 (U)
P27–4B Purchase price variance, $0; materials quantity variance, $3,200 (F)
P27–5B Credit to close variances to Cost of Goods Sold, $1,161
P27–6B All materials purchase price variances favorable; all materials quantity variances unfavorable

Chapter 28
E28–1 Contribution margin, $525,000
E28–2 Contribution margin, $468,000
E28–3 $10.90
E28–4 Loss if accepted, $13,500
E28–5 Excess cost to make, $17,000
E28–6 3⅓ years
E28–7 Machine A will generate $15,000 greater savings
E28–8 20% on original investment
E28–9 Annual cash inflows, $45,600
E28–10 Excess present value, $6,083.84
E28–11 Indexes, 1.08⅓ and 1.0596
E28–12 Machine A, 1.1940 Machine B, 1.1457
P28–1A Saving (excess) to buy, $(2,880) if sunk; $1,620 if rented
P28–2A With $3,000 eliminated, $120 loss to retain B
P28–3A Accept; increase in net income, $624,000
P28–4A Excess present value, $21,653.10
P28–5A Profitability index, 1.2095
P28–6A Annual aftertax cash inflows, $72,000
P28–1B Saving (excess) to buy, $(24,000) if sunk; $13,500 if rented
P28–2B With $4,000 eliminated, $1,216 saving to retain West
P28–3B Accept; increase in net income, $96,000
P28–4B Excess present value, $124,984.05
P28–5B Profitability index, 1.3778
P28–6B Negative excess present value based on 10 years, $(30,343.11)

Appendix A
CDPA–1 Adjusted gross income, $44,400
CDPA–2 Gross income tax, $15,581
CDPA–3 Gross income tax, $16,471.60
CDPA–4 Gross income tax, $14,823.50
CDPA–5 Corporate income tax for 1983, $236,890
CDPA–6 (2) Balance in Deferred Income Tax Liability, $68,400